SERIES

(ex•ploring)

1. Investigating in a systematic way: examining. 2. Searching into or ranging over for the purpose of discovery.

Microsoft® SharePoint® 2010 Brief

Robert T. Grauer

Daniela Marghitu

PEARSON

Boston Columbus Indianapolis New York San Francisco Upper Saddle River
Amsterdam Cape Town Dubai London Madrid Milan Munich Paris Montreal Toronto
Delhi Mexico City São Paulo Sydney Hong Kong Seoul Singapore Taipei Tokyo

Editor in Chief: Michael Payne
Acquisitions Editor: Samantha McAfee
Product Development Manager: Laura Burgess
Editorial Project Manager: Anne Garcia
Development Editor: Laura Town
Editorial Assistant: Laura Karahalis
Director of Digital Development: Zara Wanlass
Executive Editor, Digital Learning & Assessment: Paul Gentile
Director, Media Development: Cathi Profitko
Senior Editorial Media Project Manager: Alana Coles
Production Media Project Manager: John Cassar
Director of Marketing: Patrice Jones
Marketing Coordinator: Susan Osterlitz
Marketing Assistant: Darshika Vyas
Senior Managing Editor: Cynthia Zonneveld
Associate Managing Editor: Camille Trentacoste
Senior Operations Specialist: Nick Sklitsis
Operations Specialist: Natacha Moore
Senior Art Director: Jonathan Boylan
Manager, Cover Visual Research & Permissions: Karen Sanatar
Cover Design: Jonathan Boylan
Cover Illustration/Photo: Courtesy of Shutterstock® Images
Composition: PreMediaGlobal
Full-Service Project Management: Andrea Stefanowicz, PreMediaGlobal
Typeface: Minion 10.5/12.5

Library of Congress Cataloging-in-Publication Data
Grauer, Robert T., 1945–
Microsoft SharePoint 2010 brief / Robert T. Grauer, Daniela Marghitu.
p. cm.—(Exploring series)
Includes index.
ISBN-13: 978-0-13-800737-9
ISBN-10: 0-13-800737-3
1. Intranets (Computer networks) 2. Microsoft SharePoint (Electronic resource) 3. Web servers. I. Marghitu, Daniela. II. Title.
TK5105.875.I6G723 2012
004.6'82—dc23

2011039850

10 9 8 7 6 5 4 3 2 1

ISBN-13: 978-0-13-800737-9
ISBN-10: 0-13-800737-3

ABOUT THE AUTHORS

Daniela Marghitu

Dr. Daniela Marghitu has been a faculty coordinator in the Computer Science and Software Engineering Department at Auburn University since 1996. She is the founder/director of the Auburn University Educational and Assistive Technology Laboratory. She has published three IT books for the Pearson Exploring Series, over forty peer-reviewed articles, and international conference papers, and she has given numerous presentations at national and international professional events. Dr. Daniela Marghitu has been involved for many years in efforts to increase the participation of students with disabilities and women in STEM, with a focus on computing careers. She is the CO-PI and Technology Director of the NSF/HDR Alabama Alliance for Students with Disabilities in STEM, and AccessComputing Alliance institutional partner. She is the founder/director of Auburn University Computer Literacy Academy for children (dealing with disabilities), Robo Camp, and other innovative K12 outreach STEM programs. She is the recipient of the 2011 AccessComputing Capacity Building and Auburn University ACCESS awards.

Dr. Robert T. Grauer, Creator of the Exploring Series

Bob Grauer is an Associate Professor in the Department of Computer Information Systems at the University of Miami, where he is a multiple winner of the Outstanding Teaching Award in the School of Business, most recently in 2009. He has written numerous COBOL texts and is the vision behind the Exploring Office series, with more than three million books in print. His work has been translated into three foreign languages and is used in all aspects of higher education at both national and international levels. Bob Grauer has consulted for several major corporations including IBM and American Express. He received his Ph.D. in operations research in 1972 from the Polytechnic Institute of Brooklyn.

DEDICATION

To my family—Stefania, Dan, Elena, and Dumitru.

Daniela Marghitu

CONTENTS

SHAREPOINT

CHAPTER ONE ➤ SharePoint Technologies 1

CHAPTER TWO ➤ Web Sites 81

CHAPTER THREE ➤ Web Pages 165

CHAPTER FOUR ➤ Microsoft Office 2010 277

APPENDIX A ➤ Internet and World Wide Web 417

APPENDIX B ➤ HTML, XHTML, XML, and CSS 440

APPENDIX C ➤ Accessibility and Compatibility 470

ACKNOWLEDGMENTS

The Exploring team would like to acknowledge and thank all the reviewers who helped us prepare for the Exploring Office 2010 revision by providing us with their invaluable comments, suggestions, and constructive criticism:

Alan S. Abrahams
Virginia Tech

Allen Alexander
Delaware Technical & Community College

Andrea Marchese
Maritime College, State University of New York

Andrew Blitz
Broward College, Edison State College

Angela Clark
University of South Alabama

Astrid Todd
Guilford Technical Community College

Audrey Gillant
Maritime College, State University of New York

Barbara Stover
Marion Technical College

Barbara Tollinger
Sinclair Community College

Ben Brahim Taha
Auburn University

Beverly Amer
Northern Arizona University

Beverly Fite
Amarillo College

Bonnie Homan
San Francisco State University

Brad West
Sinclair Community College

Brian Powell
West Virginia University

Carol Buser
Owens Community College

Carol Roberts
University of Maine

Cathy Poyner
Truman State University

Charles Hodgson
Delgado Community College

Cheryl Hinds
Norfolk State University

Cindy Herbert
Metropolitan Community College–Longview

Dana Hooper
University of Alabama

Dana Johnson
North Dakota State University

Daniela Marghitu
Auburn University

David Noel
University of Central Oklahoma

David Pulis
Maritime College, State University of New York

David Thornton
Jacksonville State University

Dawn Medlin
Appalachian State University

Debby Keen
University of Kentucky

Debra Chapman
University of South Alabama

Derrick Huang
Florida Atlantic University

Diana Baran
Henry Ford Community College

Diane Cassidy
The University of North Carolina at Charlotte

Diane Smith
Henry Ford Community College

Don Danner
San Francisco State University

Don Hoggan
Solano College

Elaine Crable
Xavier University

Erhan Uskup
Houston Community College–Northwest

Erika Nadas
Wilbur Wright College

Floyd Winters
Manatee Community College

Frank Lucente
Westmoreland County Community College

G. Jan Wilms
Union University

Gail Cope
Sinclair Community College

Gary DeLorenzo
California University of Pennsylvania

Gary Garrison
Belmont University

Gerald Braun
Xavier University

Gladys Swindler
Fort Hays State University

Heith Hennel
Valencia Community College

Irene Joos
La Roche College

Iwona Rusin
Baker College; Davenport University

J. Roberto Guzman
San Diego Mesa College

James Pepe
Bentley University

Jan Wilms
Union University

Janet Bringhurst
Utah State University

Jim Chaffee
The University of Iowa Tippie College of Business

Joanne Lazirko
University of Wisconsin–Milwaukee

Jodi Milliner
Kansas State University

John Hollenbeck
Blue Ridge Community College

John Seydel
Arkansas State University

Judith A. Scheeren
Westmoreland County Community College

Judith Brown
The University of Memphis

Karen Priestly
Northern Virginia Community College

Karen Ravan
Spartanburg Community College

Kathleen Brenan
Ashland University

Ken Busbee
Houston Community College

Kent Foster
Winthrop University

Kevin Anderson
Solano Community College

Kim Wright
The University of Alabama

Kristen Hockman
University of Missouri–Columbia

Kristi Smith
Allegany College of Maryland

Laura McManamon
University of Dayton

Leanne Chun
Leeward Community College

Lee McClain
Western Washington University

Linda D. Collins
Mesa Community College

Linda Johnsonius
Murray State University

Linda Lau
Longwood University

Linda Theus
Jackson State Community College

Lisa Miller
University of Central Oklahoma

Lister Horn
Pensacola Junior College

Lixin Tao
Pace University

Loraine Miller
Cayuga Community College

Lori Kielty
Central Florida Community College

Lorna Wells
Salt Lake Community College

Lucy Parakhovnik (Parker)
California State University, Northridge

Marcia Welch
Highline Community College

Margaret McManus
Northwest Florida State College

Margaret Warrick
Allan Hancock College

Marilyn Hibbert
Salt Lake Community College

Mark Choman
Luzerne County Community College

Mary Duncan
University of Missouri – St. Louis

Melissa Nemeth
Indiana University Purdue University Indianapolis

Melody Alexander
Ball State University

Michael Douglas
University of Arkansas at Little Rock

Michael Dunklebarger
Alamance Community College

Michael G. Skaff
College of the Sequoias

Michele Budnovitch
Pennsylvania College of Technology

Mike Jochen
East Stroudsburg University

Mike Scroggins
Missouri State University

Nanette Lareau
University of Arkansas Community College–Morrilton

Pam Uhlenkamp
Iowa Central Community College

Patrick Smith
Marshall Community and Technical College

Paula Ruby
Arkansas State University

Peggy Burrus
Red Rocks Community College

Peter Ross
SUNY Albany

Philip H Nielson
Salt Lake Community College

Ralph Hooper
University of Alabama

Ranette Halverson
Midwestern State University

Richard Cacace
Pensacola Junior College

Robert Dušek
Northern Virginia Community College

Robert Sindt
Johnson County Commu nity College

Rocky Belcher
Sinclair Community College

Roger Pick
University of Missouri at Kansas City

Ronnie Creel
Troy University

Rosalie Westerberg
Clover Park Technical College

Ruth Neal
Navarro College

Sandra Thomas
Troy University

Sophie Lee
California State University, Long Beach

Steven Schwarz
Raritan Valley Community College

Sue McCrory
Missouri State University

Susan Fuschetto
Cerritos College

Susan Medlin
UNC Charlotte

Suzan Spitzberg
Oakton Community College

Sven Aelterman
Troy University

Terri Holly
Indian River State College

Thomas Rienzo
Western Michigan University

Tina Johnson
Midwestern State University

Tommy Lu
Delaware Technical and Community College

Troy S. Cash
NorthWest Arkansas Community College

Vicki Robertson
Southwest Tennessee Community College

Weifeng Chen
California University of Pennsylvania

Wes Anthony
Houston Community College

William Ayen
University of Colorado at Colorado Springs

Wilma Andrews
Virginia Commonwealth University

Yvonne Galusha
University of Iowa

Special thanks to our development and technical team:

Janet Pickard

Jodie Silla

Kevin Stone

Barbara Stover

Laura Town

PREFACE

The Exploring Series and You

Exploring is Pearson's Office Application series which requires students like you to think "beyond the point and click." With Office 2010, Exploring has embraced today's student learning styles to support extended learning beyond the classroom.

The goal of Exploring is, as it has always been, to go further than teaching just the steps to accomplish a task—the series provides the theoretical foundation for you to understand when and why to apply a skill. As a result, you achieve a deeper understanding of each application and can apply this critical thinking beyond Office and the classroom.

You are plugged in constantly, and Exploring has evolved to meet you half-way to work within your changing learning styles. Pearson has paid attention to the habits of students today, how you get information, how you are motivated to do well in class, and what your future goals look like. We asked you and your peers for acceptance of new tools we designed to address these points, and you responded with a resounding "YES!"

Here Is What We Learned About You

You go to college now with a different set of skills than students did five years ago. The new edition of Exploring moves you beyond the basics of the software at a faster pace, without sacrificing coverage of the fundamental skills that you need to know. This ensures that you will be engaged from page 1 to the end of the book.

You and your peers have diverse learning styles. With this in mind, we broadened our definition of "student resources" to include Compass, an online skill database; movable Visual Reference cards; relevant Set-Up Videos filmed in a familiar, commercial style; and the most powerful online homework and assessment tool around, my**it**lab. Exploring will be accessible to all students, regardless of learning style.

You read, prepare, and study differently than students used to. You use textbooks like a tool—you want to easily identify what you need to know and learn it efficiently. We have added key features that make the content accessible to you and make the text easy to use.

You are goal-oriented. You want a good grade and you want to be successful in your future career. With this in mind, we used motivating case studies and Set-Up Videos to aid in the learning now and to show the relevance of the skills to your future careers.

Moving Beyond the Point and Click and Extending Your Learning Beyond the Classroom

All of these additions will keep you more engaged, helping you to achieve a higher level of understanding and to complete this course and go on to be successful in your career. In addition to the vision and experience of the series creator, Robert T. Grauer, we have assembled a tremendously talented team of Office Applications authors who have devoted themselves to teaching you the ins and outs of Microsoft Word, Excel, Access, and PowerPoint. Led in this edition by series editor Mary Anne Poatsy, the whole team is equally dedicated to the Exploring mission of **moving you beyond the point and click, and extending your learning beyond the classroom**.

Key Features of Exploring Office 2010

- **White Pages/Yellow Pages** clearly distinguish the theory (white pages) from the skills covered in the Hands-On Exercises (yellow pages) so students always know what they are supposed to be doing.
- **Objective Mapping** enables students to skip the skills and concepts they know and quickly find those they do not know by scanning the chapter opener pages for the page numbers of the material they need.
- **Pull Quotes** entice students into the theory by highlighting the most interesting points.
- **Case Study** presents a scenario for the chapter, creating a story that ties the Hands-On Exercises together.

FYI

- **FYI Icon** indicates that an exercise step includes a skill that is common to more than one application.
- **Key Terms** are defined in the margins to ensure student comprehension.
- **End-of-Chapter Exercises** offer instructors several options for assessment. Each chapter has approximately 12–15 exercises ranging from multiple choice questions to open-ended projects.

CREATIVE CASE

DISCOVER

- **Enhanced Mid-Level Exercises** include a **Creative Case**, which allows students some flexibility and creativity, not being bound by a definitive solution, as well as **Discover Steps**, which encourage students to use Help or to problem-solve to accomplish a task.

Instructor Resources

The Instructor's Resource Center, available at www.pearsonhighered.com includes the following:

- **Solution Files with Scorecards** assist with grading the Hands-On Exercises and end-of-chapter exercises.
- **Rubrics** for Mid-Level Creative Cases and Beyond the Classroom Cases in Microsoft® Word format enable instructors to customize the assignments for their classes.
- **PowerPoint® Presentations** with notes for each chapter are included for out-of-class study or review.
- **Lesson Plans** provide a detailed blueprint to achieve chapter learning objectives and outcomes.
- **Objectives List** maps chapter objectives to Hands-On Exercises and end-of-chapter exercises.
- **Multiple Choice Answer Key**
- **Complete Test Bank**

Student Resources

Prentice Hall's Companion Web Site

www.pearsonhighered.com/exploring offers expanded IT resources and downloadable supplements and it also instructs students how to access their own SharePoint collection required to complete the exercises in this book. Students can find the following self-study tools for each chapter:

- Online Study Guide
- Chapter Objectives
- Glossary
- Chapter Objectives Review
- Web Resources

SHAREPOINT

1 SHAREPOINT TECHNOLOGIES

Introduction to SharePoint 2010

CASE STUDY | Can Someone Help Me Understand What SharePoint Can Do for Me, Please?

Stephanie has recently graduated with a degree in journalism and was hired by an independent record label as junior publicist. She is very excited about this job and would like to apply the knowledge and skills she accumulated in school toward upgrading the company's portal.

Stephanie requested technical assistance, and you will fill this role. She will provide you with the portal content and will be an active team member. The company uses SharePoint Technologies 2010 to provide a presence on the Internet. Stephanie is familiar with the SharePoint technologies because she was briefly introduced to SharePoint Technologies 2007 while she was a student. She knows that SharePoint Technologies enable business organizations to organize information, manage documents, increase efficiency in business processes, and provide a robust collaboration environment. She is asking for your help in exploring the enhanced capabilities of SharePoint 2010 Technologies that can make the portal upgrade a success for her and the record label.

You will explore the SharePoint Foundation and SharePoint Designer 2010 capabilities, working with the Ribbon user interface, Foundation site templates, site layouts, and the Designer user interface. You will investigate master pages and SharePoint categories for pages. You will prepare a site for SharePoint pages.

OBJECTIVES AFTER YOU READ THIS CHAPTER, YOU WILL BE ABLE TO:

Introduction to SharePoint Technologies

In recent years there has been an ever-growing flood of digital information. The World Wide Web (WWW) has become the most popular way to publish, distribute, and share electronic information. The immense success of the Web is helping millions of people, from students to business professionals, share, research, and conduct business online. User-friendly Web-oriented technologies and Web authoring applications empower people to develop and manage their own personal or business Web sites. Microsoft SharePoint 2010, the fourth and most recent release of SharePoint technologies, is a comprehensive platform that is highly customizable while simplifying how people find and share information. Blog sites for social networking, team Web sites for collaboration, extranet sites for partners, and Internet sites for customers are all possibilities using the SharePoint user-friendly platform. Microsoft SharePoint 2010 includes SharePoint Foundation 2010 and SharePoint Server 2010. SharePoint Designer 2010 is a specialized desktop application for SharePoint Web site customization. Each part of the platform has a specific purpose:

- SharePoint Foundation 2010 is a collection of software applications that enable organizations, such as business or government, to collaborate, and store and manage documents within the organization.
- SharePoint Server 2010 provides the same services as the SharePoint Foundation while introducing additional services such as form and process integration automation and management, data integration, reporting, and analysis, application integration.
- SharePoint Designer 2010 provides a user-friendly, "what you see is what you get" (WYSIWYG) interface and tools to develop and customize SharePoint-based applications and workflow solutions with a minimum knowledge of any mark-up language, such as Hypertext Mark-up Language (HTML), or style sheet language, such as Cascading Style Sheets (CSS).

In addition, SharePoint 2010 is integrated with the Microsoft Office applications to provide ways to store, manage, and share information using those software applications. SharePoint 2010 works with the Web companions of Word, Excel, PowerPoint, and OneNote, so people can access Word documents, Excel spreadsheets, PowerPoint presentations, and notes without having Office programs installed on their computers.

This book provides a comprehensive hands-on introduction to SharePoint Foundation 2010 and SharePoint Designer 2010. However, since SharePoint Server 2010 was developed upon the SharePoint Foundation 2010, this book provides the fundamental concepts and skills needed for a SharePoint Server 2010 developer.

In this chapter, you will build upon knowledge covered in this textbook's Appendices and learn about SharePoint Technologies, SharePoint Foundation capabilities, and the relationship between SharePoint Foundation and SharePoint Server. After you have mastered these concepts, you will become familiar with the SharePoint Designer interface components and tools, and will be introduced to SharePoint master pages and SharePoint pages.

Exploring SharePoint 2010 Capabilities

Microsoft Office System is a collection of server platforms, desktop applications, and online services that all work together to improve productivity, make information sharing more effective, and facilitate business decision-making processes.

Microsoft Office System is a collection of server platforms, desktop applications, and online services that all work together to improve productivity, make information sharing more effective, and facilitate business decision-making processes. The Office System includes many of Microsoft's products such as SharePoint Server, SharePoint Foundation, Word, Excel, PowerPoint, Live Communications Server, and SQL Server. SharePoint enables organizations to create solutions to solve their business problems in an easily managed, cost-effective way.

SharePoint 2010 is the Microsoft central information sharing and business collaboration platform, integrating the Microsoft Office System and Internet.

SharePoint 2010 is the Microsoft central information sharing and business collaboration platform for organizations, integrating the Microsoft Office System and the Internet. SharePoint can be deployed both inside the organization (using intranets) and outside of the organization's firewall (using extranets and the Internet) so employees, customers, and business partners can work together.

SharePoint can be deployed both inside the organization (using intranets) and outside of the organization's firewall (using extranets and the Internet) so employees, customers, and business partners can work together.

The SharePoint capabilities, used to create solutions that bring together people, information, systems, and business processes, are summarized by Microsoft into the following six categories, as shown in Figure 1.1:

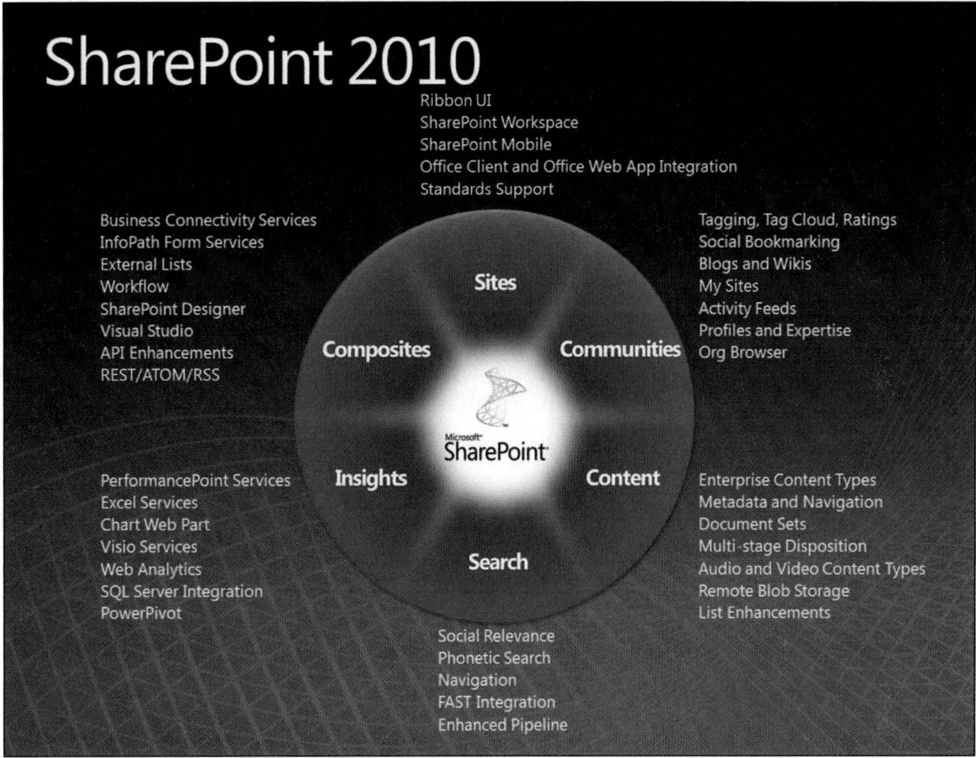

FIGURE 1.1 SharePoint Capabilities ➤

- Sites: SharePoint can be used to create Web sites which facilitate operations with co-workers, business partners, and customers.
- Communities: By creating virtual communities, people can use the collaboration tools SharePoint offers for working together regardless of their location.
- Content: SharePoint, when combined with Microsoft Office, enables people to manage documents with specific features that support document types, retention policies, and compliance measures.
- Search: SharePoint search tools can be used to locate information throughout the organization, tapping into the content, people, and data the organization has.
- Insights: Supported by applications such as Excel Services, Performance Point Services, Visio Services, and Power Pivot, SharePoint enables people to make decisions based on data visualization.
- Composites: SharePoint helps people make informed decisions by giving them access to data and information in databases, reports, and business applications.

SharePoint Foundation 2010 is the underlying technology for all SharePoint sites, enabling you to quickly create a wide range of sites where you can collaborate using Web pages, documents, lists, calendars, and data.

SharePoint 2010 is composed of two core products: SharePoint Foundation 2010 and SharePoint Server 2010. ***SharePoint Foundation 2010*** is the underlying technology for all SharePoint sites, enabling you to quickly create a wide range of sites where you can collaborate using Web pages, documents, lists, calendars, and data.

SharePoint Server 2010 builds on the SharePoint Foundation 2010 applications, providing additional services and enabling the organization to scale their Internet presence.

SharePoint Server 2010 builds on the SharePoint Foundation 2010 applications, providing additional services and enabling the organization to scale its Internet presence. It is recommended for large companies, deployments of information throughout the organization, and Internet portals. A ***SharePoint site*** is a collection of related Web pages, Web parts, lists, and document libraries that enable you to organize and manage documents and information, and to create workflows for the organization. ***Web Parts*** are reusable elements used to display information stored in lists and libraries.

SharePoint Foundation 2010 is the fourth generation in a basically free line of products, whereas SharePoint Server is the fourth generation in a line of expensive and more complex products.

SharePoint Foundation 2010 is the fourth generation in a basically free line of products, whereas SharePoint Server 2010, also in its fourth generation, is an expensive and more complex product. Combining SharePoint Foundation and SharePoint Server you can create solutions to solve common business problems:

A **SharePoint site** is a collection of related Web pages, Web Parts, lists, and document libraries that enables you to organize and manage documents and information, and to create workflows for the organization.

A **Web Part** is a reusable element used to display information stored in lists and libraries.

- Information can be consolidated into secure Web sites or workspaces to be accessed via an intranet or the Web.
- Libraries and lists enable the management of documents while providing security.
- Workflows bring required information into business processes to increase efficiency and accuracy.
- Records management capabilities enable you to regulate access to documents.
- Alerts provide notifications to users when information has been added or changed.
- Web Parts enable you to reorganize existing information to provide a better understanding of the information.
- Navigation and search capabilities provide the resources necessary to find relevant information in a timely manner.

Working with the SharePoint 2010 Ribbon User Interface

The **SharePoint 2010 Ribbon** is a fixed position toolbar that appears across the top of each page and displays many of the most commonly-used tools, controls, and commands.

A **tab** contains similar commands that can be performed on a page.

A **group** is a collection of commands related to a specific task.

A **menu** is a hierarchical, customizable, drop-down, or fly-out collection of commands related to a specific task.

SharePoint 2010 features the Microsoft Office Fluent User Interface (UI), including the Ribbon UI. The Ribbon UI provides you with a user-friendly interface for accessing the SharePoint Foundation commands and tools. The ***SharePoint 2010 Ribbon*** is a fixed position toolbar that appears across the top of each page and displays many of the most commonly-used tools, controls, and commands. The Ribbon has by three categories of components, as shown in Figure 1.2:

- ***Tabs*** contain similar commands that can be performed on a page. Shown in Figure 1.2 are Browse and Page tabs.
- ***Groups*** are collections of commands related to a specific task. For instance, the Edit group contains Edit and Check out functions, while the Share & Track group contains E-mail a Link and Alert Me functions.
- ***Menus*** are hierarchical, customizable, drop down, or fly-out collections of commands related to a specific task. The Site Actions menu arrow to display the menu is shown in Figure 1.2.

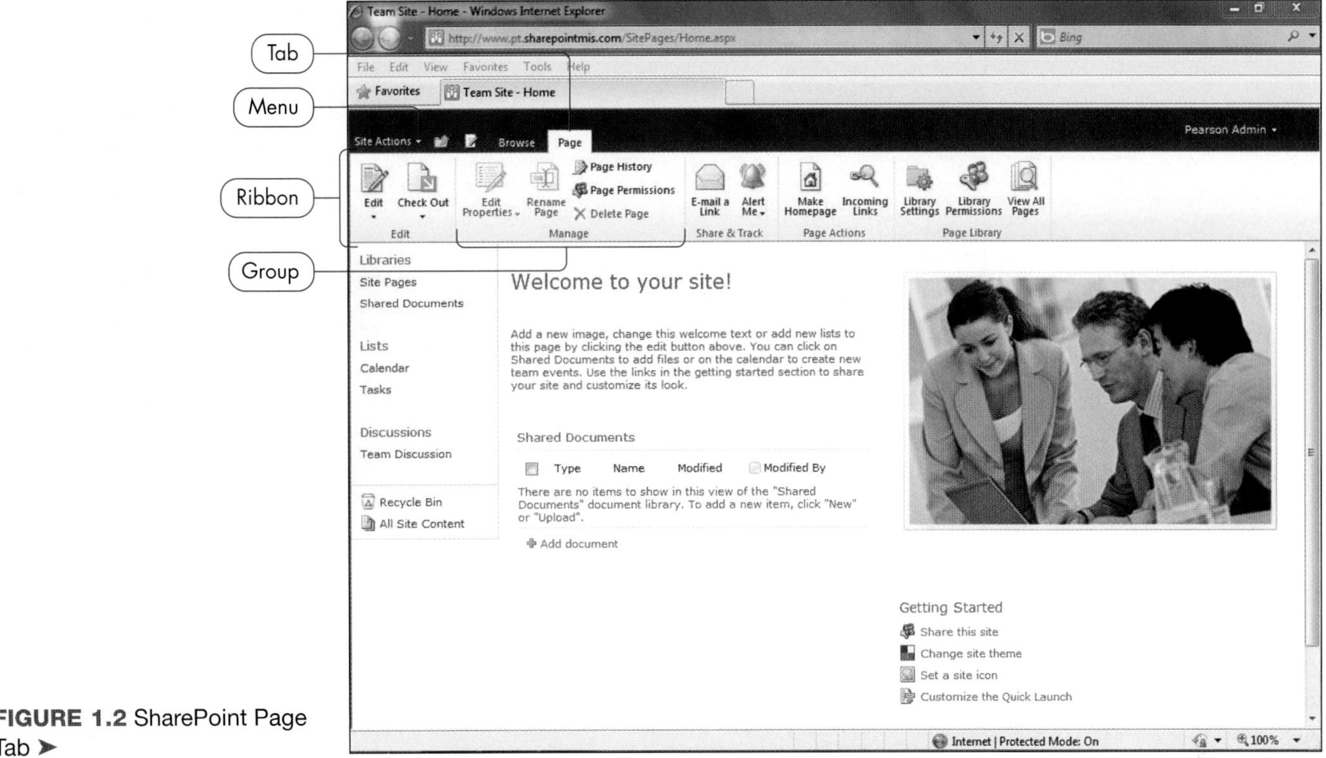

FIGURE 1.2 SharePoint Page Tab ➤

Functions are organized under the Ribbon tabs. By default, when viewing a site, the Browse Ribbon tab will be the active tab. This tab does not display any command options, as shown in Figure 1.3. The number and types of controls that appear on the Ribbon are context-related and depend in part on the type of page you are viewing, the level of control the SharePoint Administrator has granted to you, and the configuration of your site. For example, the Shared Documents page, shown in Figure 1.4, includes the Library Tools tab, meaning that you have permission to add documents to the library. As you select Ribbon tabs, available commands are presented. For example, if you select the Page tab while viewing the Team Site home page, the list of page management commands is presented, as shown in Figure 1.2. When you finish working with Ribbon commands, clicking the Browse tab will display the site page and navigation.

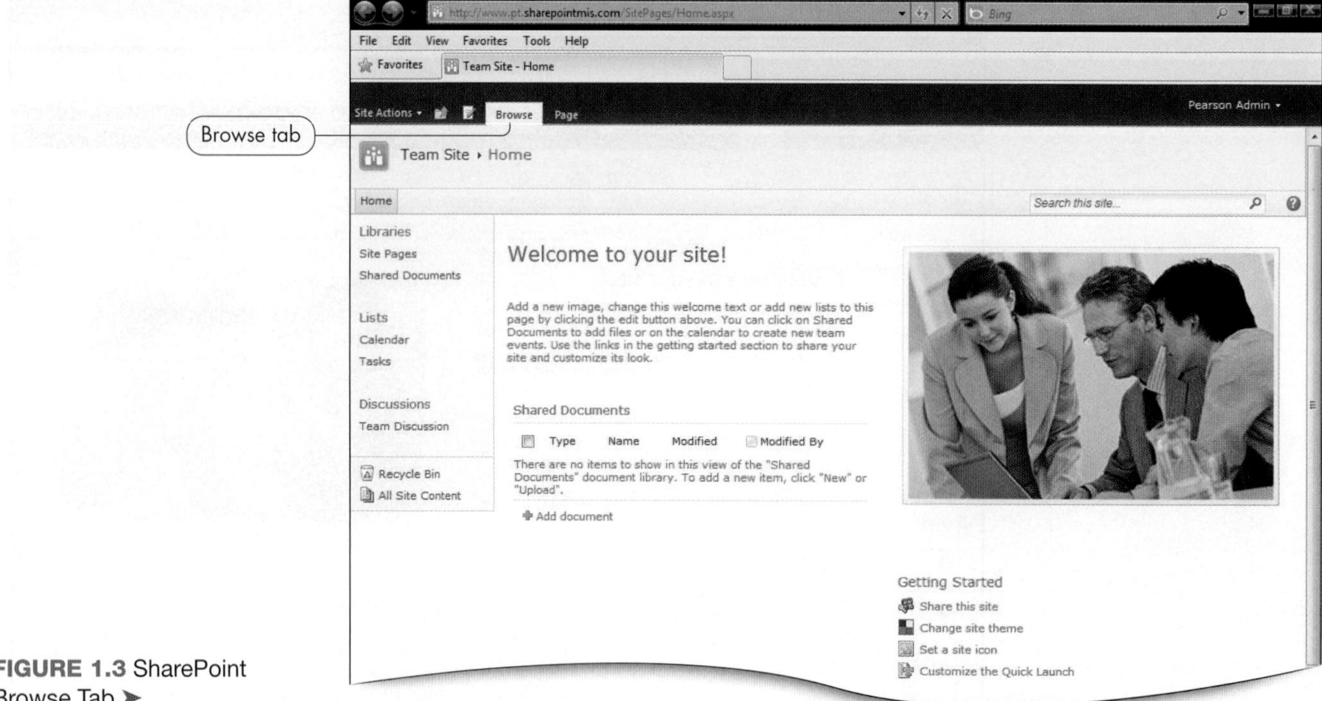

FIGURE 1.3 SharePoint Browse Tab ➤

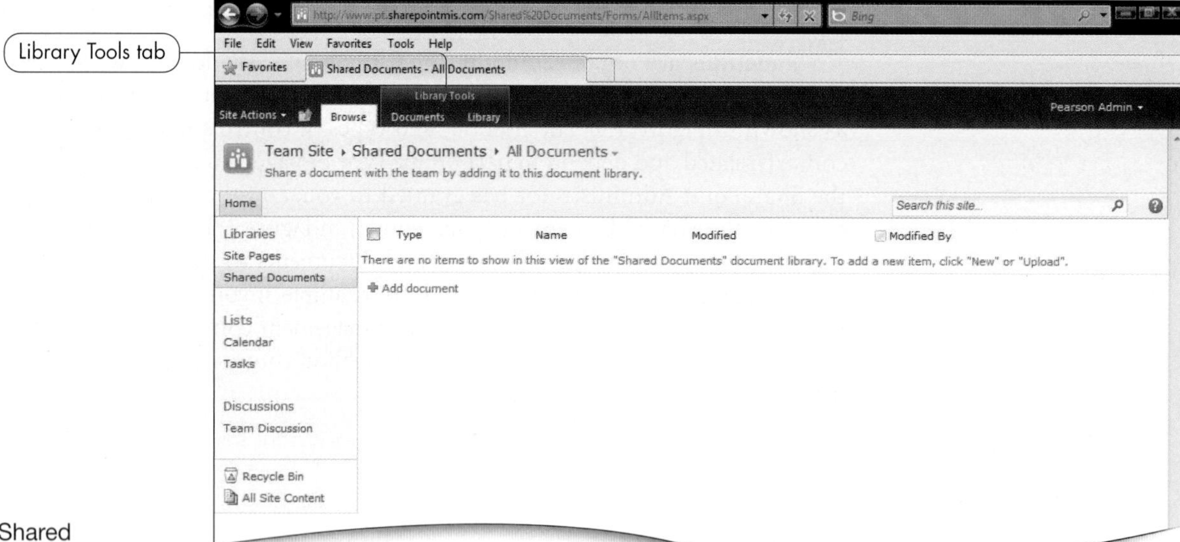

FIGURE 1.4 Shared Documents Page ➤

The **Site Actions menu** provides options for managing the site based on the features available within the site and your permissions within the site.

The ***Site Actions menu*** provides options for managing the site based on the features available within the site and your permissions within the site (you will learn about site permission levels later in this chapter). The Site Actions menu provides functions, such as create a new page or assign site permissions, that may not be available on the Ribbon. The Site Actions menu is available on every SharePoint page, as shown in Figure 1.5.

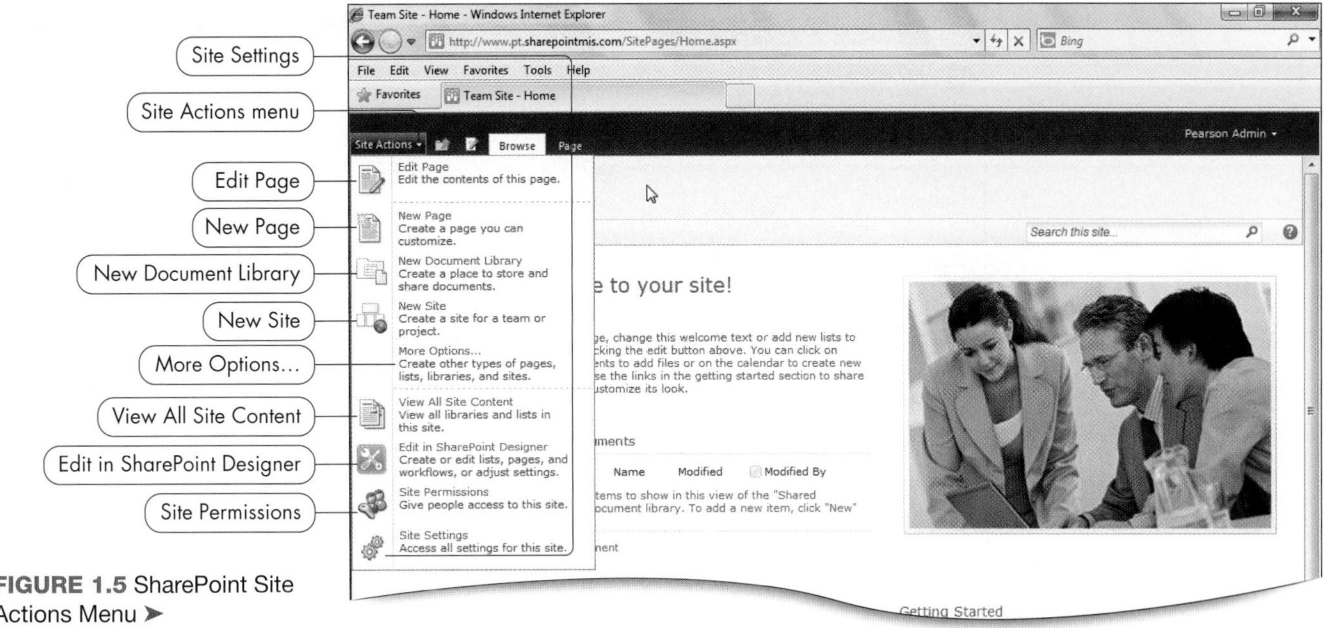

FIGURE 1.5 SharePoint Site Actions Menu ➤

The Site Settings page, available by clicking Site Settings on the Site Action menu, looks very similar to the Windows Control Panel. Each category, shown in Figure 1.6, has links to several specific settings or subcategories.

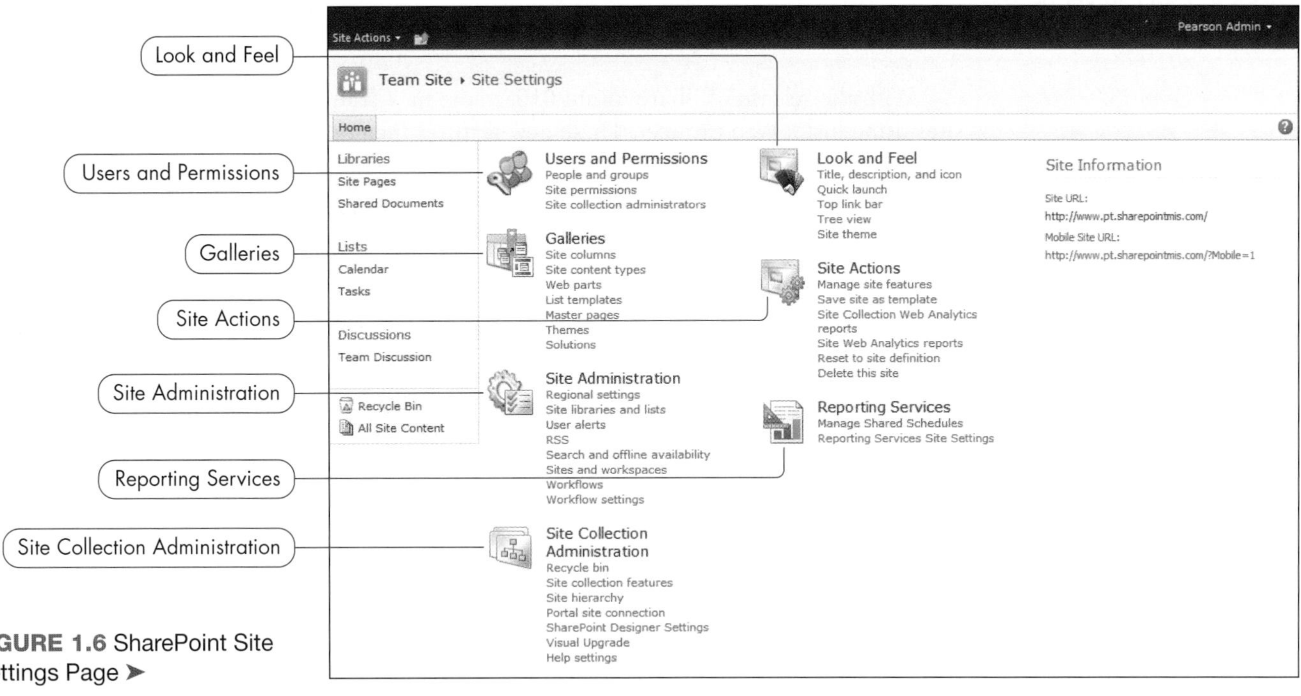

FIGURE 1.6 SharePoint Site Settings Page ➤

Many of the subcategories in the SharePoint 2010 Site Settings, such as Users and Permissions – People and groups, allow management of SharePoint lists. Other subcategories, such as Users and Permissions – Site collection administrators, provide dialog boxes with option settings.

The All Site Content page lists all libraries, lists, workspaces, discussion boards, and sites currently available to the current user based on permission levels, and the last date each document was modified, as shown in Figure 1.7. You can click the name of any listed item to view the detail page for that item.

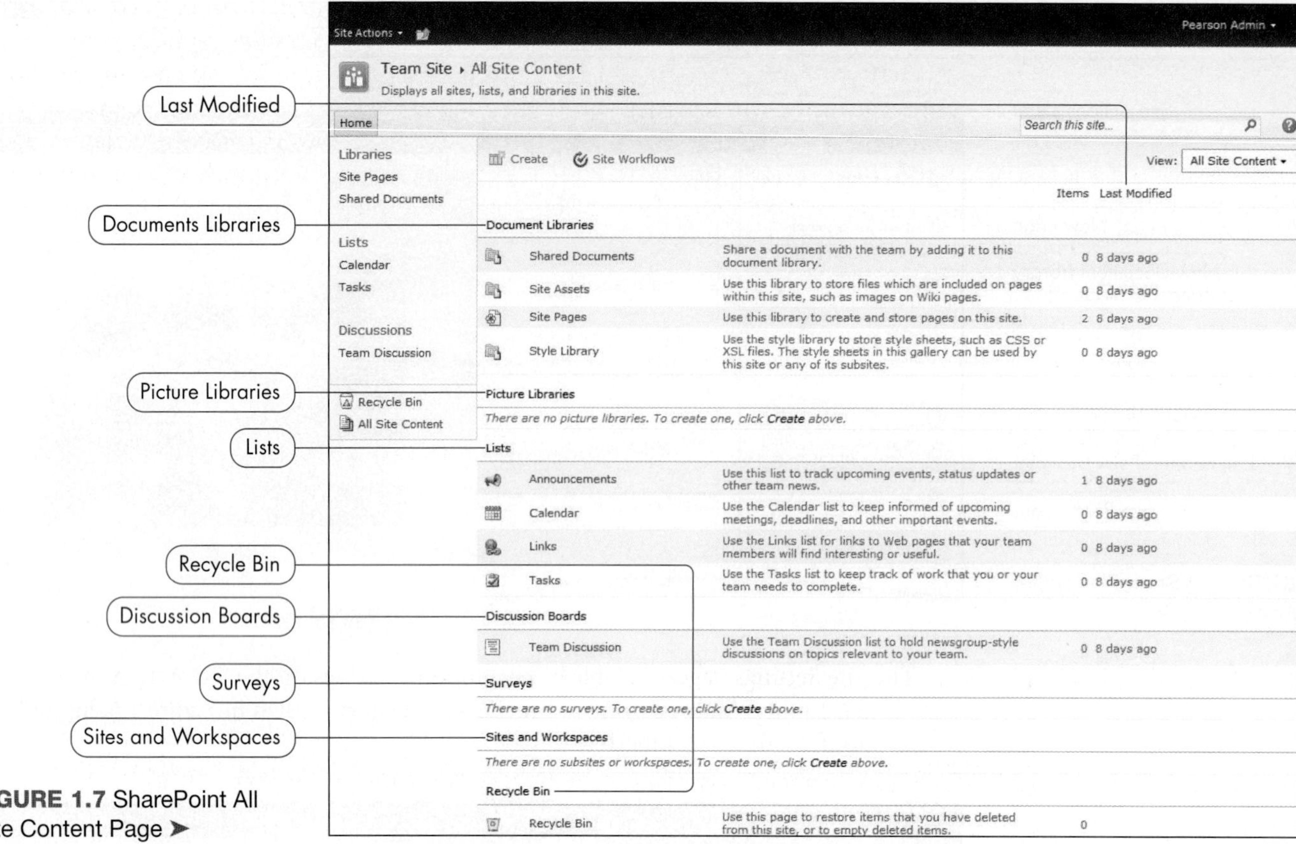

FIGURE 1.7 SharePoint All Site Content Page ➤

With the release of SharePoint 2010, many new features are available for configuring sites using just a Web browser. These new features include the ability to edit a page using a "what you see is what you get" (WYSIWYG) editor. This editor is available by clicking the Page tab on the Ribbon. Click Edit in the Edit group to display the WYSIWYG editor. The Editing Tools tab will be displayed on the Ribbon, as shown in Figure 1.8, with tools with which you may be familiar from working with other Office applications, to some that are more specific to working with Web pages. The Editing Tools tab is broken down into the Format Text and Insert tabs.

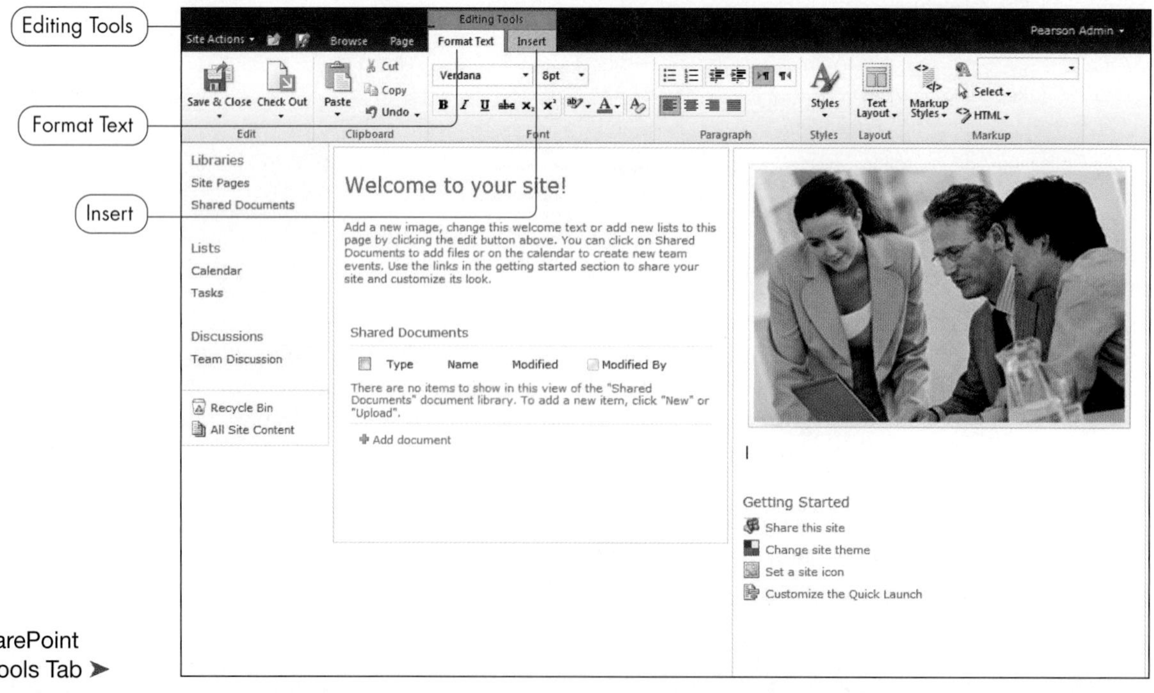

FIGURE 1.8 SharePoint Ribbon Editing Tools Tab ➤

The **Status bar**, below the Ribbon, gives the user instant information, in context, such as page status or version.

The **Notification area** appears on the right side of the window underneath the Ribbon, and displays transient messages which communicate the progress of an operation.

The ***Status bar***, below the Ribbon, gives the user instant information, in context, such as page status or version. The Status bar will display one of four pre-set background colors, depending on the importance of the status message. The ***Notification area*** appears on the right side of the window underneath the Ribbon, and displays transient messages which communicate the progress of an operation. By default, messages displayed in the Notification area will last five seconds. For example, if you click the Check Out command in the Edit Group, the Status bar and Notification area will look similar to the way they are displayed in Figure 1.9.

FIGURE 1.9 SharePoint Status Bar and Notification Area ➤

You will learn more about the contextual tabs, groups, and menus of the SharePoint 2010 Ribbon later in this chapter and in the following chapters.

The SharePoint Foundation

SharePoint Foundation provides many of the SharePoint platform capabilities and core collaboration features (see Figure 1.10).

The SharePoint capabilities, as discussed in the last section, bring together many of the Microsoft technologies. Microsoft SQL Server provides database services which enable you to access data and combine it in ways which give you information you and colleagues can use to make decisions. Web page hosting is provided by the combination of the .Net 3.51 Framework and Internet Information Services 7.0. ASP.NET 3.5 and above provide support for elements such as master pages, Web Parts pages, and Web Parts (which you will learn about later in this chapter).

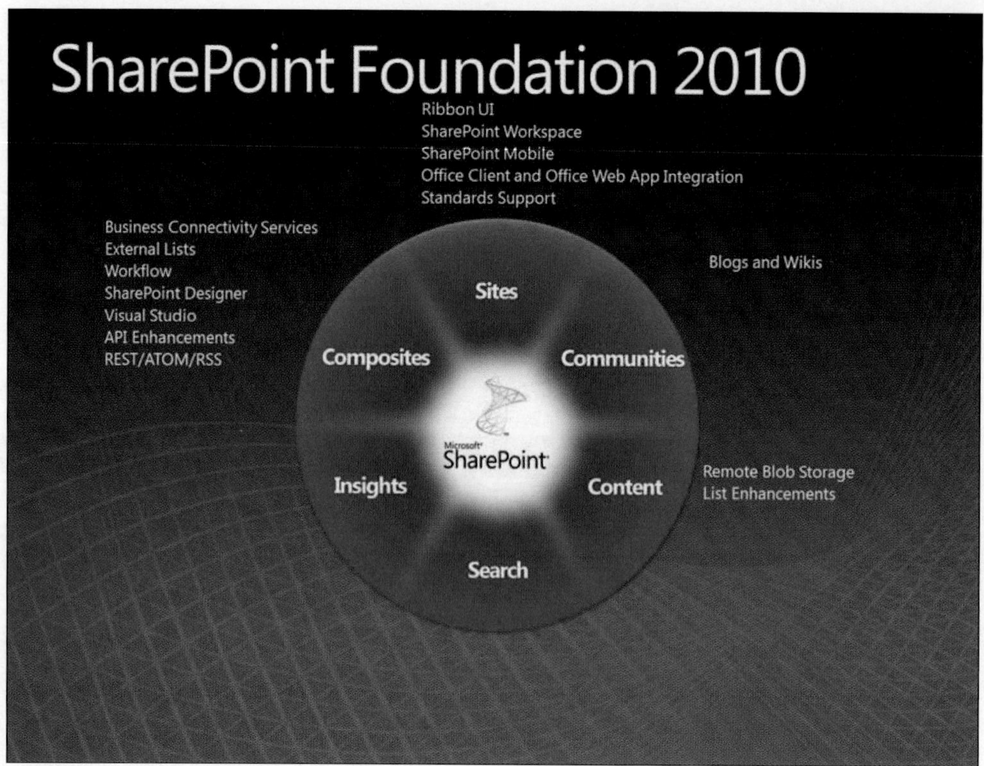

FIGURE 1.10 SharePoint Foundation 2010 Capabilities ➤

In this section, you will learn about the requirements of installing a SharePoint Foundation environment, and about the SharePoint categories of SharePoint sites and their site components. Then, you will learn about the SharePoint Foundation collections and permission levels.

SharePoint Designer 2010 is the Web and application design program for SharePoint 2010 used to create custom solutions without any prior programming knowledge.

Microsoft Visual Studio 2010 is a tool for basic development tasks, simplifying the creation, debugging, and deployment of applications on a variety of platforms including SharePoint.

You can use a Web browser, SharePoint Designer, and Microsoft Visual Studio 2010 for specific SharePoint Foundation tasks. ***SharePoint Designer 2010*** is the Web and application design program for SharePoint 2010 used to create custom solutions, such as Web pages, without any prior programming knowledge. It runs on SharePoint Foundation 2010 and Microsoft SharePoint Server 2010. ***Microsoft Visual Studio 2010*** is a tool for basic development tasks, simplifying the creation, debugging, and deployment of applications on a variety of platforms including SharePoint. The Microsoft Visual Studio environment enables you to visually design Web Pages, Web Parts, and Workflows, but does not provide you with any visual designers for core SharePoint elements such as custom lists, custom content types, custom site columns, and SharePoint content databases. Visual Studio cannot render a SharePoint site in browser view. You can edit a SharePoint site in SharePoint Designer, export it to a Web Solutions Packet (WSP) solution, and import it in Visual Studio for further development. Visual Studio enables SharePoint developers to create one or more projects using elements typical for a SharePoint WSP solution. Visual Studio captures, in the Visual Studio project, any actions taken in the process of developing a SharePoint solution as code and XML. The resulting SharePoint solution can be deployed to an existing site and retracted from the same site.

TIP SharePoint 2010 Versions Are 64-bit

The SharePoint 2010 products can be installed only on 64-bit hardware, running 64-bit operating systems, and are themselves 64-bit applications. They can still be used with 32- or 64-bit versions of Office and can still be accessed using 32- and 64-bit versions of SharePoint Designer 2010.

Preparing to Install a SharePoint Foundation 2010 Environment

Microsoft does not charge for SharePoint Foundation 2010. However, to install it, you need to pay full product and licensing costs for an appropriate operating system....

Microsoft does not charge for SharePoint Foundation 2010. However, to install it, you need to pay full product and licensing costs for an appropriate operating system (a version of 64-bit Windows Server 2008, or, for learning, testing and development only, a copy of 64-bit Windows 7). To implement a SharePoint Foundation 2010 environment, your infrastructure must support the following minimum requirements (http://sharepoint.microsoft.com):

- Windows Server® 2008 64-bit operating system with SP2 or later, or Windows Server 2008 R2 64-bit
- Microsoft SQL Server® 2005 64-bit with SP2, SQL Server 2005 Express 64-bit, SQL Server 2008 64-bit or SQL Server 2008 Express 64-bit
- Microsoft .NET Framework 3.5 with SP1 installed
- Level 1 Internet browser options for Windows:
  - Windows Internet Explorer® 7 32-bit
  - Windows Internet Explorer 8 32-bit
  - Firefox 3.x 32-bit
- Level 2 Internet browser options:
  - Windows Internet Explorer 7 64-bit
  - Windows Internet Explorer 8 64-bit
  - Firefox 3.x and Apple Safari 4.x on an Apple Mac OS X Snow Leopard
  - Firefox 3.x on UNIX/Linux 8.1

TIP Windows 7 and SharePoint Foundation 2010

The SharePoint Foundation 2010 environment can be installed on a 64-bit version of Windows 7 (any version, including Home Premium). The operating system can either be native or in a Virtual Machine (VM). The Microsoft recommendation is to install SharePoint Foundation 2010 in a VM system because then you can still run Windows 7 as your main operating system, with the VM system running "under" it. You can run both the Windows 7 environment and SharePoint Foundation 2010 in a VM on a computer with 4 GB of main memory or more.

Using SharePoint Foundation Site Templates

As you have read, SharePoint Foundation 2010 provides many functions that enable people to work together. Through virtual locations, groups of people can share information and collect the knowledge of the organization. Using templates, these virtual locations are easy to create and manage. Some examples of these templates are team sites, document workspaces, meeting workspaces, blogs, and group work sites. Keep in mind that SharePoint Foundation is a tool mostly used within an organization through an intranet.

A **template** provides a SharePoint developer with a beginning set of tools and a layout for a site or workspace.

SharePoint includes templates for creating sites and workspaces as previously listed. A ***template*** provides a SharePoint developer with a beginning set of tools and a layout for a site or workspace. The most commonly needed tools for the type of site or workspace are available on the various templates. You can quickly create a site without having to build site parts from scratch. Discussion boards, for instance, appear on templates for Group Work sites as built-in lists. You can customize the site that began with a template so that it meets the needs of your organization.

Get Started with SharePoint Sites

... sites are the foundation of all SharePoint installations and include a variety of components and services that can be used to solve business problems.

SharePoint sites are the foundation of all SharePoint installations and include a variety of components and services that can be used to solve business problems. SharePoint developers, from beginner to advanced, benefit from these features of SharePoint:

- Beginner through professional developers can easily create, customize, and publish a professional business site.
- The Office Ribbon user interface makes it easy to navigate and find the features.
- SharePoint Workspaces enable users to access content, edit it, and quickly sync the edits to the server.
- Using Windows Mobile devices, SharePoint Workspaces can be accessed, making content available to users while away from a desktop computer.
- Office Web Apps can be used to access, edit, and save Microsoft Word, Excel, PowerPoint, and OneNote documents in a browser without loss of formatting.
- SharePoint sites are supported by current browsers, including mobile browsers, enabling users to work together regardless of the type of browser they have.
- SharePoint enables interoperability of non-Microsoft software applications within the SharePoint environment.
- SharePoint has accessible (as described below) templates and tools which comply with the Web Content Accessibility Guidelines (WCAG 2.0).

The United Nations Convention on the Rights of Persons with Disabilities recognizes access to information and communications technologies, including the Web, as a basic human right. Accessible Web sites feature support for people with a range of disabilities including hearing, movement, sight, and cognitive ability. The SharePoint Designer 2010 Accessibility Report and Compatibility Report tools enable you to maximize the accessibility of Web pages. Refer to the appendices of this textbook to learn more about the Web design guidelines that are included in the World Wide Web Consortium's (W3C) Web Accessibility Initiative (WAI) and U.S. federal law, subsection 1194.22 of Section 508, concerning Web-based intranet and Internet information and applications. You will be also introduced to some of the most popular assistive and adaptive technologies.

Explore SharePoint Foundation Sites Categories

SharePoint Foundation was developed for the average user.

SharePoint Foundation was developed for the average user. It enables the user to easily create and customize a site. With little training or skills, a user can create sites, add lists and libraries, and apply formatting to customize the site to meet the demands of organizations.

A **home page** is the main page of a SharePoint site that provides a navigational structure for the site.

A **team site** facilitates collaboration.

A **document workspace** is used to create, update, and store documents.

A **group work site** provides a managed environment for team collaboration.

A **meeting workspace** facilitates the management of meetings.

A **blog site** is used to post information for comment and discussion.

A ***home page*** is the main page of a SharePoint site that provides a navigational structure for the site. In SharePoint 2010, the home page is named home.aspx and can be found in the Site Pages Library. SharePoint Foundation includes five site categories:

- ***Team sites*** facilitate team collaboration. This type of site provides tools for information sharing and management, and other team collaboration activities.
- ***Document workspaces*** are used to create, update, and store documents. Workspaces enable multiple people to work together on documents.
- ***Group work sites*** provide a managed environment for team collaboration. Through this type of site, team members can be tracked and scheduled into group events. Tools for team communication are available. Documents are shared by members through group work sites.
- ***Meeting workspaces*** facilitate the management of meetings. Meeting planning, information sharing, and material management tools are available in this kind of workspace. Action items can also be tracked using meeting workspaces.
- ***Blog sites*** are used to post information for comment and discussion. Discussions on specific topics are captured and managed on blog sites.

SharePoint Server 2010 provides additional categories of sites. You will be briefly introduced to these additional site types and their capabilities later in this chapter.

Explore SharePoint Foundation Sites Components

A variety of types of components are available in SharePoint Foundation to manage information, facilitate collaboration, and enable workflow. These components include the following:

A **list** is a collection of announcements, links, surveys, discussion boards, or tasks.

- ***Lists*** are collections of announcements, links, surveys, discussion boards, or tasks. Lists contain structured and tabular data. SharePoint Services has built-in default lists, and depending on the site that you initially create, some lists (such as Announcements, Events, and Links) appear by default when the site is created. You can customize these default lists and also create new lists. We will discuss lists in detail in Chapter 2.

A **library** is a collection of documents, pictures, or form libraries that can be shared with others.

- ***Libraries*** are collections of documents, pictures, or form libraries that can be shared with others. Libraries contain unstructured data such as image, video, and audio files. When you create a new SharePoint site, a generic document library called Shared Documents is created. Using SharePoint document libraries, you can filter and group documents as well as view metadata. You can create new custom libraries for a particular business category or subject. We will discuss libraries in more detail in Chapter 2.

TIP Unstructured Data and Metadata

Unstructured data is basically any information that does not reside in fixed locations, such as a database. Unstructured data can be textual or non-textual. Textual unstructured data is generated in media like e-mail messages, PowerPoint presentations, Word documents, and instant messages. Non-textual unstructured data is generated in media like JPEG images, MP3 audio files, and Flash video files. A common and useful description of metadata is "data about data contents." Metadata is describing the contents and context of data files. For example, the metadata included in Microsoft Office documents may specify authors of the document, deleted content, and drafting history. Web pages may include metadata specifying what language it is written in, what tools were used to create it, and where to go for more on the subject, allowing browsers to automatically improve the experience of users.

A **workflow** allows you to manage business processes and the associated content.

- ***Workflow*** allows you to manage business processes and the associated content. Workflow includes organization notifications, tracking, and transactions. The only built-in workflow offered in SharePoint Foundation 2010 is the Three-state workflow, which tracks a list item through the states of Active, Ready for Review, and Complete. However, you can use SharePoint Designer or Visual Studio to create and deploy custom workflows that manage business processes that require organizations to track a high volume of issues or items, such as customer support issues, sales leads, or project tasks.

A **Web Part zone** is a container for Web Parts.

- ***Web Part zones*** are containers for Web Parts. As you customize your site, you can personalize, remove, and/or add more Web Parts. We will discuss Web Parts and Web Part zones in more detail in Chapter 3.

The **Recycle Bin** holds, and enables you to restore, deleted elements, such as files, lists, and libraries.

- The ***Recycle Bin*** holds, and enables you to restore deleted elements for a SharePoint Site, such as files, lists and libraries.

By default, each template may have document libraries, form libraries, picture libraries, and Wiki libraries. Every template has list tools for announcements, calendars, contacts, discussion boards, issue tracking, links, surveys, and project tasks. Group Web sites have a Microsoft Input Method Editor (IME) and circulations available as default tools. Meeting workspaces feature unique list tools, such as agendas, decisions, objectives, text boxes, and things to bring, which enable the management of meetings. Pages, sites and workspaces, and Web parts pages are available in all of the templates but the Meeting Workspaces template.

TIP InfoPath 2010

InfoPath 2010 is included in the Office Professional Plus 2010 and enables users to easily create forms within a SharePoint site to gather information more quickly. InfoPath 2010 is designed for beginner through advanced users and developers.

Office Web Apps services include Web-based versions of Microsoft Word 2010, Excel 2010, PowerPoint 2010, and OneNote 2010.

Office Web Apps services include Web-based versions of Microsoft Word 2010, Excel 2010, PowerPoint 2010, and OneNote 2010. These are available on Windows Live at no cost to users. Office Web Apps can be hosted on SharePoint Foundation 2010 or the SharePoint Server 2010 either on-premise or online, as shown in Figures 1.1 and 1.10. Office Web Apps are licensed with Office 2010 and need to be installed and enabled on top of SharePoint 2010. These applications are focused on offering access to Word 2010, PowerPoint 2010, Excel 2010, and OneNote 2010 documents through any browser, across multiple platforms, and enabling creation and editing capabilities in standard formats. You will learn more about SharePoint and Microsoft Office in Chapter 4.

TIP Free Microsoft Windows Live Accounts

At the time this book is being developed, the Microsoft Windows Live Web site (live.com/) is offering free access to Office Web Apps.

A **Document Library** stores most file types and provides integration with Office products such as Word 2010, PowerPoint 2010, Excel 2010, and OneNote 2010.

The SharePoint ***Document Libraries*** store most file types and provide integration with Office products such as Word 2010, PowerPoint 2010, Excel 2010, and OneNote 2010. When a user clicks on an Office document in a Document Library it will launch the Office Web App viewer, if Office 2010 is not installed. When a user clicks New Document in a Document Library to create a new Office document, or double-clicks the name of an Office document included in a Document Library but does not have the respective desktop application, the Office Web App will be launched to author the document, as shown in Figure 1.11. Not all of the features available of the four Office products are also available in the Web-based version of the application. You can open a document anytime in your installed Office application.

Office Web Apps are supported by the following browsers:

- Internet Explorer 7 and later
- Firefox 3.5 and later on Windows Mac and Linux
- Safari 4 and later on Mac

Office Web Apps support mobile access using the following phones and browsers:

- IE on Windows Mobile 5/6/6.1/6.5
- Safari4 on iPhone 3G/S and iPod
- BlackBerry 4.x and newer versions
- Nokia S60
- NetFront 3.4, 3.5, and newer versions
- Opera Mobile 8.65 and newer versions
- Openwave 6.2, 7.0, and newer versions

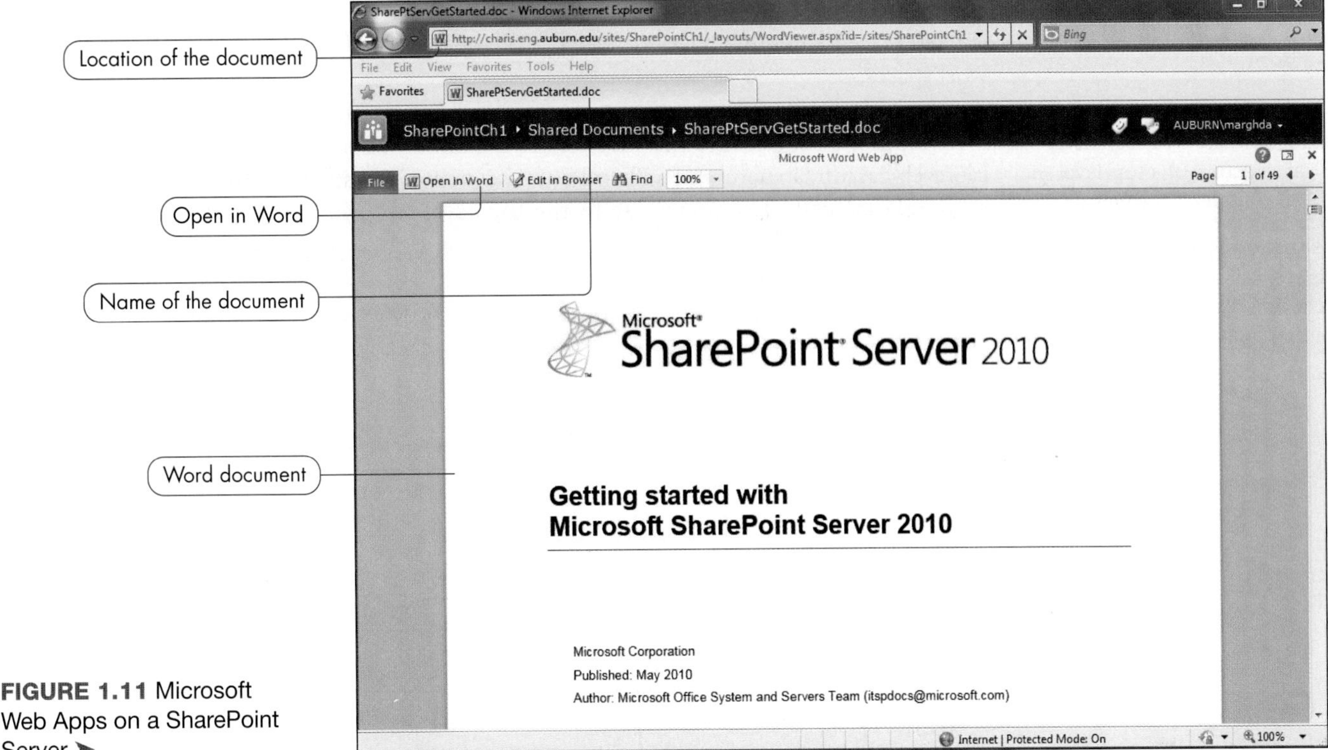

FIGURE 1.11 Microsoft Web Apps on a SharePoint Server ➤

> **TIP The SharePoint Foundation Recycle Bin**
>
> The SharePoint Recycle Bin is included in all SharePoint sites, and provides two-stage protection against accidental deletions. When you delete a document or other item from the Windows SharePoint Services site, it is deleted from the site and moved to the site's Recycle Bin, where it can be restored if needed. If you then delete this item from the site's Recycle Bin, it is moved to the site collection's Recycle Bin. From there, the document can be either restored to its original location or deleted. Deleting a site permanently removes the site and all of its content. Be aware that site deletions are not managed through the SharePoint Recycle Bin.

Using SharePoint Collections and Permission Levels

A SharePoint collection is formed by a mandatory top-level site and one or more optional subsites.

A **top-level site** is the topmost site (or parent site) within a site collection.

A SharePoint collection is formed by a mandatory top-level site and one or more optional subsites. A ***top-level site*** is the topmost site (or parent site) within a site collection. Usually the top-level site is a Team Site. A ***subsite*** (or child site) is a site that is created within a top-level site. As shown in Figure 1.12 the infrastructure of a SharePoint site looks very similar to the tree-like hierarchy of folders in a file system.

A ***site collection*** is the SharePoint Site tree-like hierarchical structure of the top-level site and all contained subsites, as shown in Figure 1.12. The Central Administration site,

A **subsite** (or child site) is a site that is created within a top-level site.

A **site collection** is the SharePoint Site tree-like hierarchical structure of a top-level site and all contained subsites.

A **site hierarchy** is the complete hierarchical infrastructure including subsites and all its components.

shown in Figure 1.29 on page 29, as an exception from this definition, is regarded as a site collection even though it has no subsites. A SharePoint Workspace cannot include subsites or workspaces.

A ***site hierarchy*** is the complete hierarchical infrastructure including subsites and its own components. Because the subsites are contained within the parent site, the complete hierarchical infrastructure of a SharePoint site includes its subsites. To view the hierarchy of a SharePoint collection, navigate to the top-level site, click Site Settings from the Site Actions menu on the site home page, and then click Site hierarchy in the Site Collection Administration section. The subsites are displayed in the Sites and Workspaces section of the All Site Content page, as shown in Figure 1.7. You can click any of the listed subsites to open it.

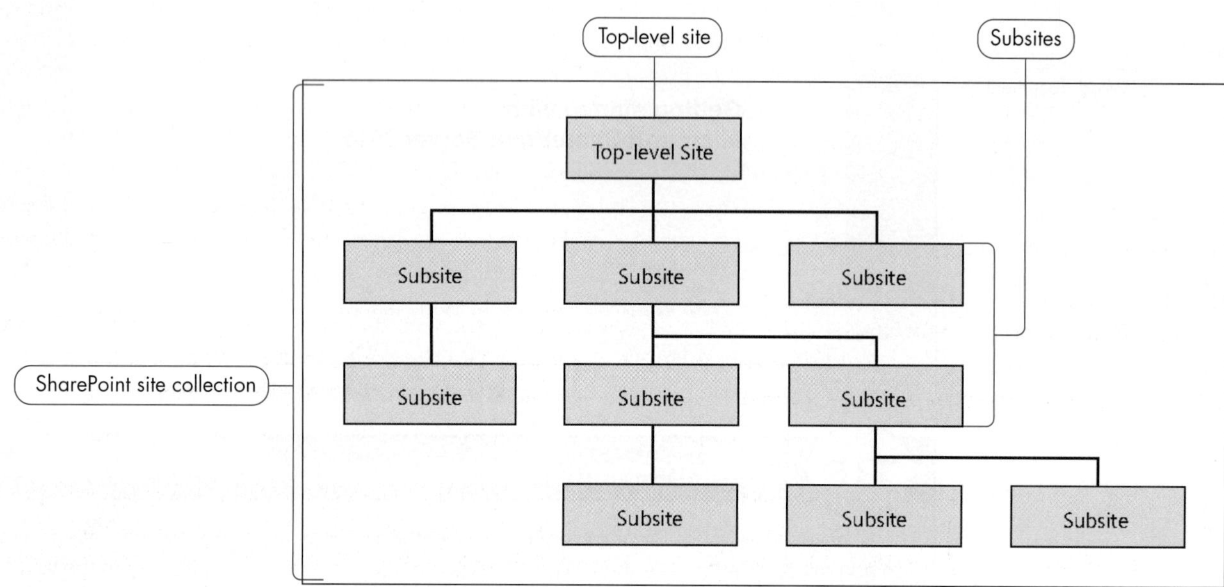

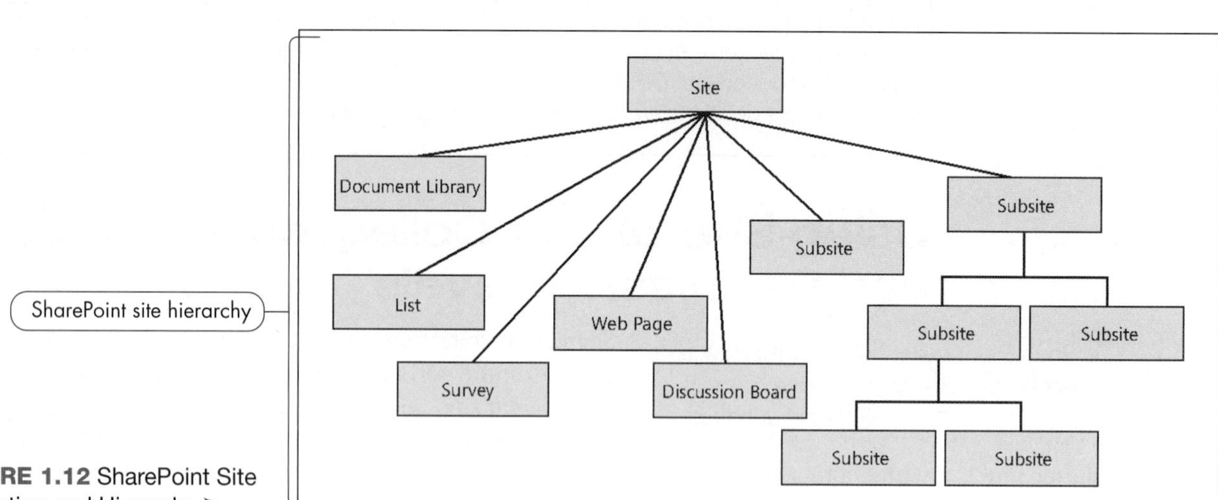

FIGURE 1.12 SharePoint Site Collection and Hierarchy ➤

Permission levels are rights within a site and can be assigned to individual users or groups giving every group member the same rights within the same level.

Access to SharePoint sites is controlled through a system that uses permission levels. ***Permission levels*** are rights within a site and can be assigned to individual users or groups giving every group member the same rights within the same level. When new users are added to a SharePoint site, they can be assigned to a SharePoint group, inheriting the same permission level to the site as the other group members, or they can be assigned permissions individually. Rights to sites, lists, and libraries can be granted to SharePoint groups throughout the site hierarchy.

Usually top-level sites are created for an entire team, and have many visitors (people who can only read the content), a few members (people who can create and update content), and one or two owners (people who add, customize, or delete items within a site). Owners of a site have broad rights and can create and delete additional subsites of the current site, add additional users to one or more of the site groups, or create their own new custom groups of permissions. As subsites are created at different levels of the tree-like infrastructure, the total number people with visitors permissions usually decreases, whereas the number of people designated as members increases. These permissions determine what specific actions users can perform on the site. The default permission levels available in SharePoint Foundation are:

- Full control which enables the user to access, edit, and delete all parts of the site. This permission level cannot be changed or deleted from SharePoint.
- Design permission, which can be added to the Contribute permission level, provides the ability to manage lists, libraries, and pages within a SharePoint site and approve content.
- Contribute, as an additional level added to the Read permission level, enables the user to create and edit items in existing lists and document libraries.
- Read provides read-only access to site resources.
- Limited Access enables access to selected resources within a site, such as a specific list, document library, folder, list item, or document. It cannot be changed or deleted from SharePoint, and cannot be manually set.

When a new top-level site is created, three default site group permission levels are created. These site groups and their default permission levels are shown in Table 1.1. The site groups can be customized to comply with the necessary security levels as specified by the organization.

TABLE 1.1 SharePoint Foundation Default Site Groups and Their Permission Levels

Site Group	Default Permission Level
***Site Name* Owners**	Full control
***Site Name* Members**	Contribute
***Site Name* Visitors**	Read

Because SharePoint groups can be used across sites, having the ability to see all sites where a group has been assigned permissions can be very valuable. From within one site, you can use the Site Settings page to explore the people and groups who have permissions within the site. Click People and Groups in the Users and Permissions section of the Site Settings page to display the People and Groups page, as shown in Figure 1.13. On the People and Groups page, click the arrow to the left of the Settings to display the View Site Collection Permissions window. The View Site Collection Permissions window, as shown in Figure 1.13, displays the sites, lists, and libraries where the group has been assigned permissions and the permission levels assigned. You can click any of the listed object names to go to the default page of an item.

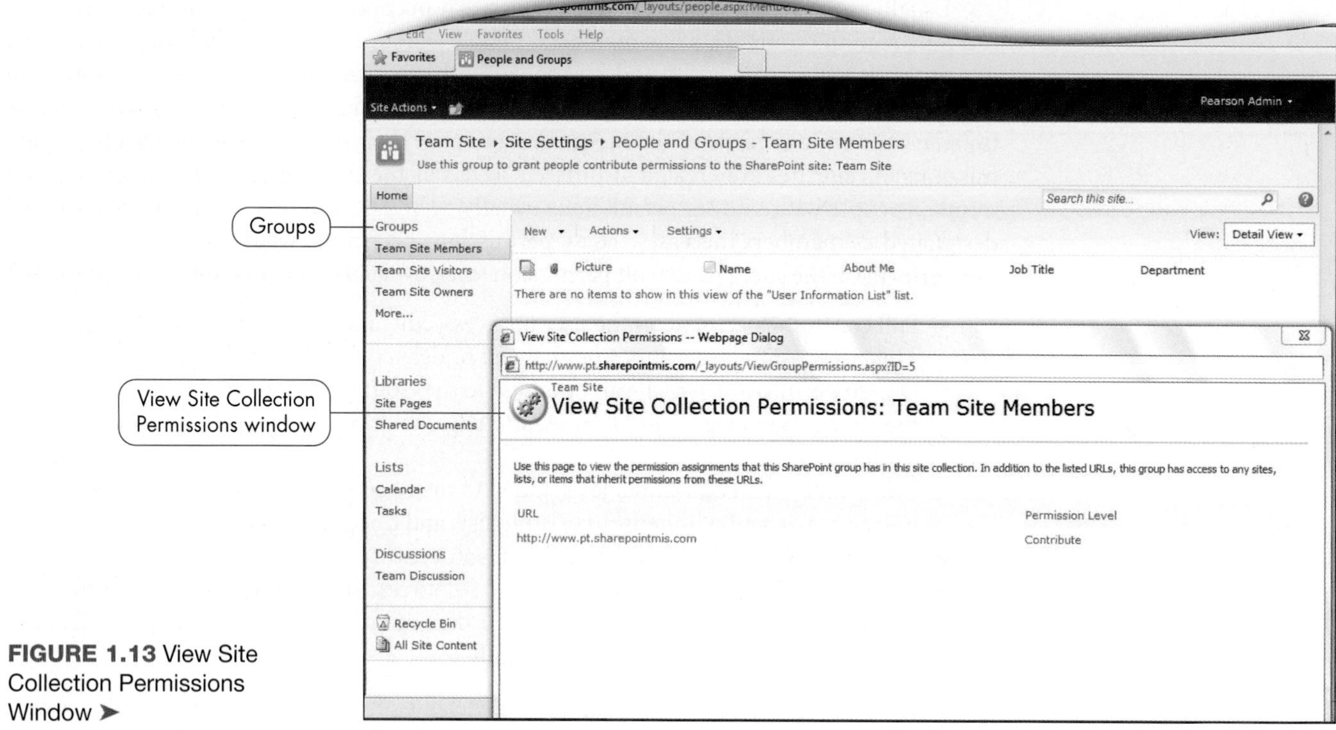

FIGURE 1.13 View Site Collection Permissions Window ➤

Working with Site Templates

As discussed earlier in this chapter, SharePoint enables you to create a site from a site template. The default templates are for team sites, document workspaces, group work sites, meeting spaces, and blog sites. The layout of the site is defined and a beginning set of components, such as a discussion board or document library, are provided by the template. Sites that are created based on a template can be saved as a new template for use in the development of future sites.

Sites that are created based on a template can be saved as a new template for use in the development of future sites.

Create a Site Template

The owner of a site can create templates from the site. As you save the template, it will be stored in the Solution Gallery of the same site collection you used to create the new template. For instance, if you create a new Team Site using the default Team Site template and modify it with your organization's logo, images, welcome text, and so on, you can save your customized template into the Team Site collection for use in creating other customized Team Sites. This saves you time and gives the sites within your organization a cohesive feel. You can also distribute this template to others as a file.

A **solution** is a site template that can be distributed to others.

A ***solution*** is a site template that can be distributed to others. It can contain just the framework for the site, or it can also contain site content. For instance, saving a template after applying a new layout or a new theme is an example of a solution. If you also add lists and libraries, Web Parts, or Wiki pages, that is content which can also be included as part of the solution. It is important to note that templates have a default size limit of 50 MB. Adding additional content to a template can cause it to exceed the size limit. The site collection administrator can increase the limit up to 2 GB. A ***solution file*** is a file that has a .wsp (Web Solution Packet) extension. The actual solution file is what you can transfer to someone else when they need to use your template. Solutions are stored in the Solution Gallery and must be activated on the server before they can be used to create new sites. To access the Solution Gallery, navigate to the top-level site, click Site Settings from the Site Actions menu on the site home page, and then click Solutions in the Galleries section of the Site Settings page.

A **solution file** is a file that has a .wsp (Web Solution Packet) extension.

TIP Making Site Templates Available

Templates remain within the site collection from which they were created. For example, if you create a template called My Organization, based on the Team Site template, the template you created is stored in the Team Site collection. To use the template in other top-level site collections, the technical administrator must register the template in those top-level sites or copy the template into the Solution Gallery.

To create a site template based on another site, open that site, and then from the Site Actions menu, select Site Settings page. After clicking Save Site as Template, as shown in Figure 1.14, you will provide a name for the file, a name and description for the template, and mark whether to include content within the site template.

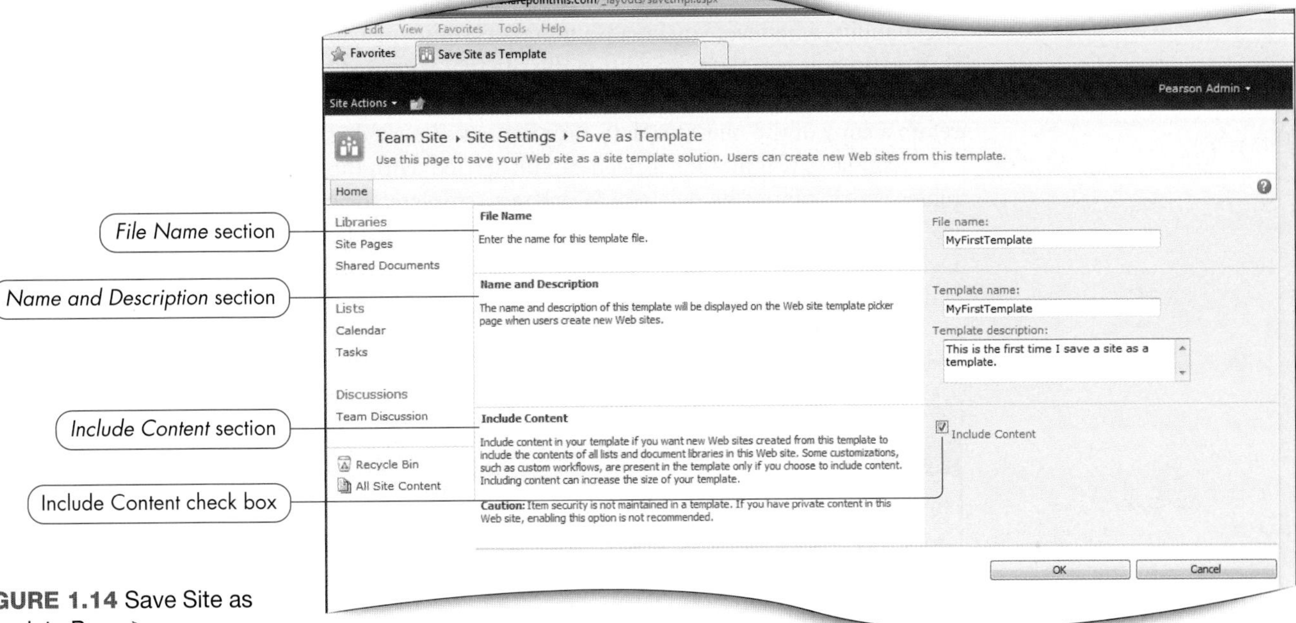

FIGURE 1.14 Save Site as Template Page ➤

The new site template is added to the Solution Gallery, as shown in Figure. 1.15. At this stage it is activated and users can begin to use the template to create new sites.

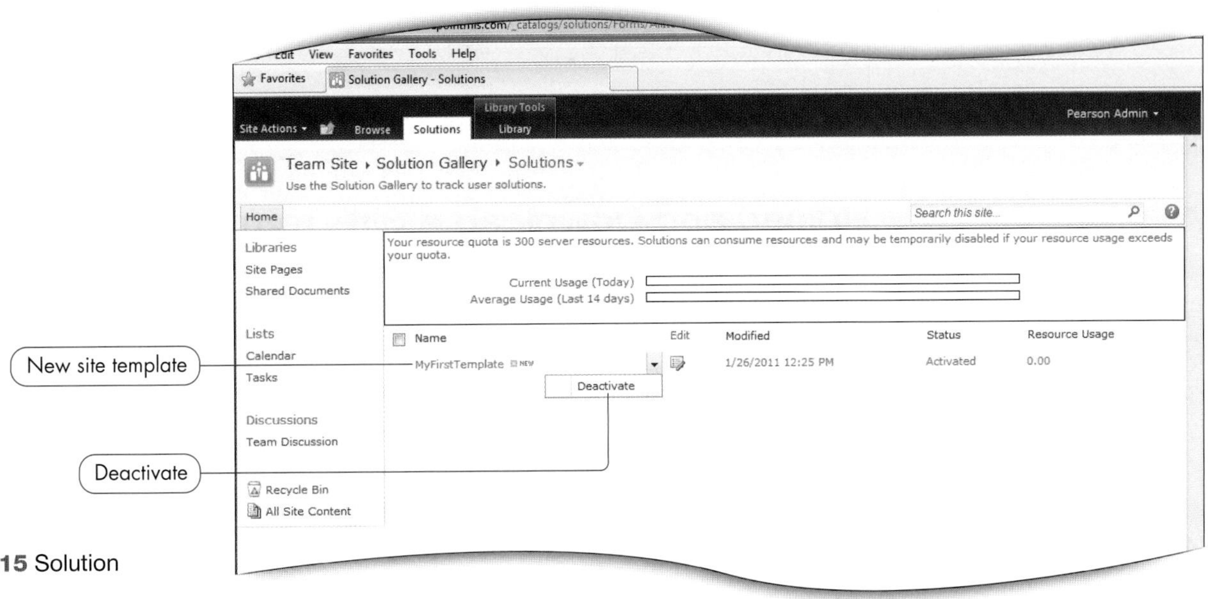

FIGURE 1.15 Solution Gallery ➤

Activate and Deactivate Site Templates

Site templates can be activated or deactivated. For example, you may be proposing a new site template for a department in your organization, but not yet have the authorization to make the template available to the department's users. In this case, you may store the template in the Solution Gallery in a deactivated state.

From the Solution Gallery, point to the site template you wish to activate or deactivate, and then click the down arrow to see the context menu. Select the appropriate action, as shown in Figure 1.15, to display the Solution Gallery Activate or Deactivate Solution dialog box. Select Activate Solution or Deactivate Solution on the View tab of the dialog box to complete the action. You can also activate or deactivate a solution in the Commands group of the Solutions tab, as shown in Figure 1.16. The Solution Gallery will continue to display the template solution, but the status will be changed.

Edit, Save, and Delete Site Templates

Inevitability, whenever you create a template, someone will suggest some changes to improve it. You can edit templates by editing the site that you used to create a template. You also have the option to use the template to create a new site which you then edit. In either case, to retain a copy of the new template, save it as previously discussed.

Templates you no longer need can be deleted, with the exception of the default site templates which cannot be deleted. To delete a template, locate it in the Solution Gallery page, point to the template name, click the down arrow to display the context menu, and then click Delete, as shown in Figure 1.16. Click OK on the Delete confirmation box and the template is deleted.

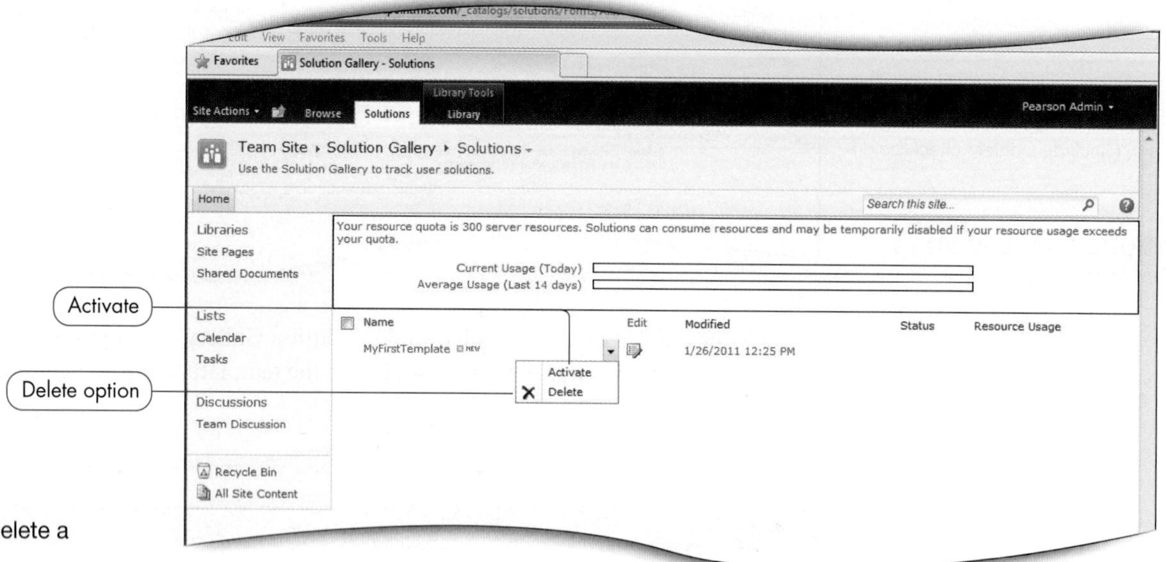

FIGURE 1.16 Delete a Template ➤

Upload and Download a Site Template

If you need to use a custom template for creating a site outside the site collection where the custom template was initially created, you will need to download the custom template from the Solution Gallery of the original site collection and upload it to the Solution Gallery of the new site collection.

With the .wsp file saved on your local computer or flash drive, you can upload the custom template to a new collection. From the root of the site collection, open the Solution Gallery page, and then click the Solutions tab. Click Upload Solution, as shown in Figure 1.17. In the Upload Document dialog box, browse for the file, and with it selected, click Open. Click OK to close the dialog box and upload the template into the Solution Gallery.

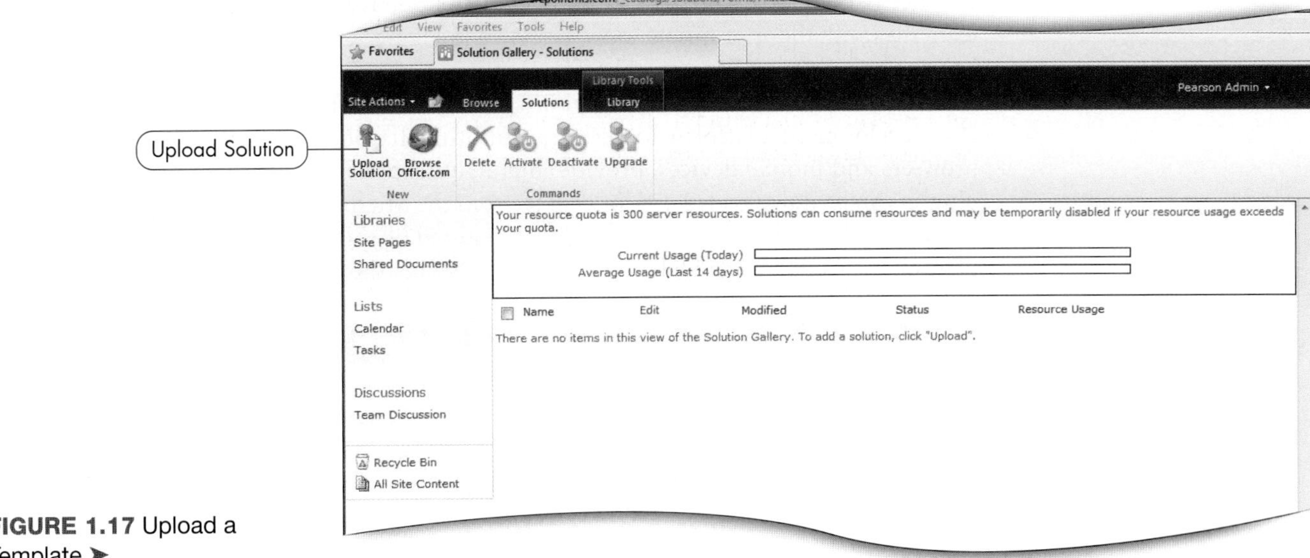

FIGURE 1.17 Upload a Template ➤

To download a custom template, navigate to the Solution Gallery of the top-level site, and then click the Solutions tab. Right-click the file name with the .wsp extension, and then click Save Target As, as shown in Figure 1.18. Navigate to the location where you store your files, and then click Save on the dialog box.

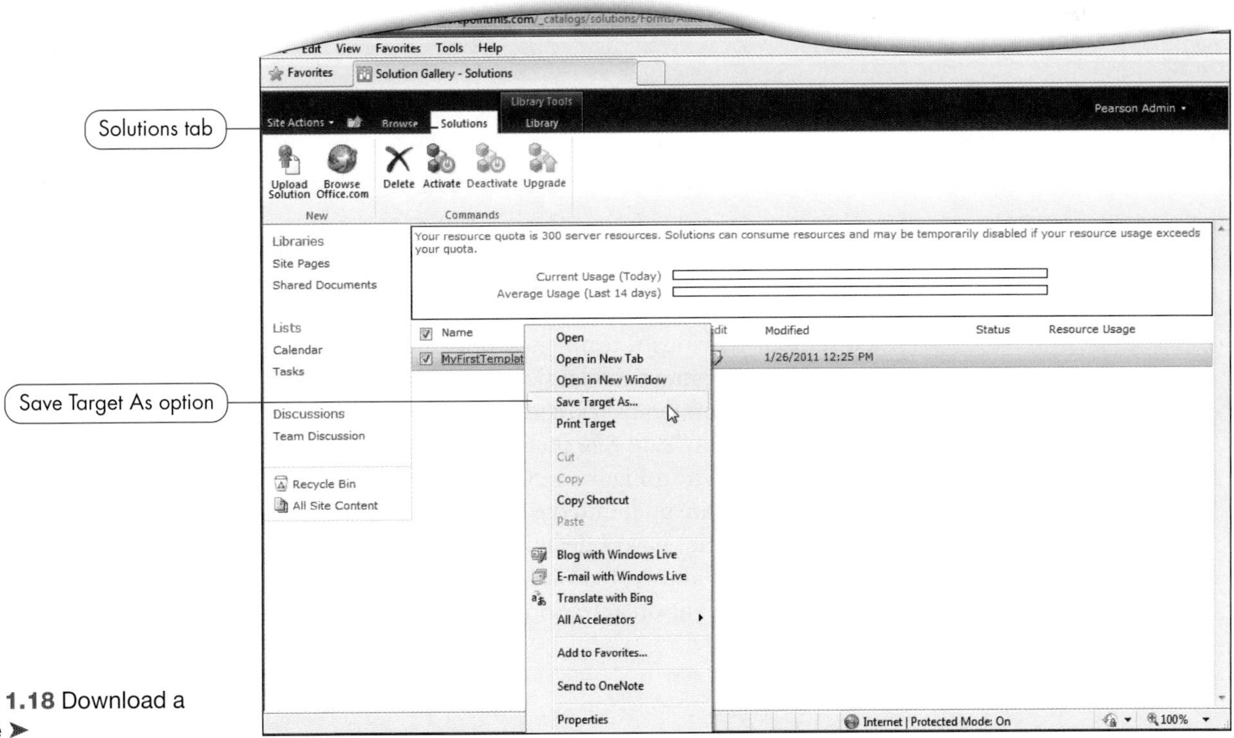

FIGURE 1.18 Download a Template ➤

Identifying SharePoint Site Layouts

As you begin to work with templates, you will notice that some, such as Team Sites, Documents Workspaces, and Group Work Sites, contain consistent tools. The layouts of the sites will also be alike. For instance, on all three of these templates, you will find a discussion board, announcements, and the various libraries. This is because the tools are needed to facilitate work and collaboration. Conversely, meeting workspaces require different tools, such as agendas, objectives, and tracking. The Blog site template is unique from the other types of templates because it must facilitate the gathering of postings and comments. In Chapter 2, you will learn in depth about all SharePoint Foundation templates.

The default Team Site template or the Blank Site template can be used to create new team sites with the appropriate tools, as shown in Figure 1.19. Each of the other types of sites has one default template available. The location of the templates varies based on whether you have Microsoft Silverlight plug-in installed on the local computer. Microsoft Silverlight is a development platform for creating multimedia objects. These objects, played on browsers and mobile devices, provide interactive experiences for the user. The Silverlight plug-in can be downloaded, free of charge, from the Microsoft Web site.

If the Silverlight plug-in is installed, as required by this textbook, you will find the template on the Collaboration tab on the New SharePoint Site page.

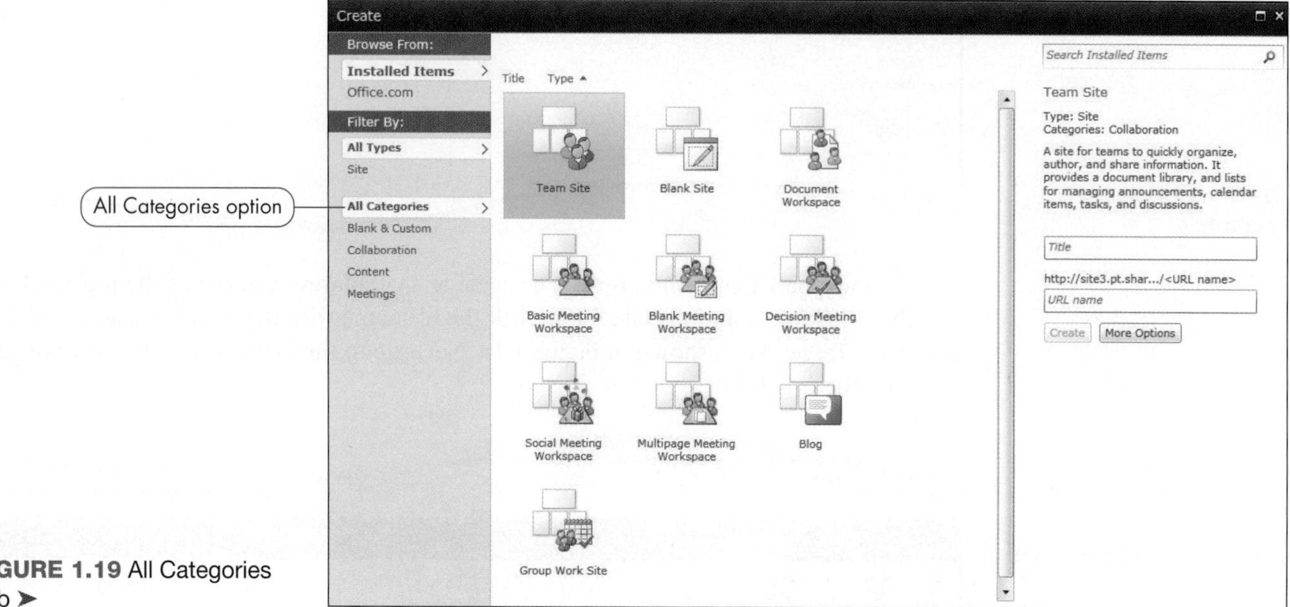

FIGURE 1.19 All Categories Tab ➤

Identify Team Sites, Document Workspaces, and Group Work Sites Layouts

As discussed previously, team sites, document workspaces, and group work sites created using templates contain similar default features and layouts. The Team Site, one of the most popular SharePoint templates, enables teams to quickly organize, create, and share information. Features of a Team Site include libraries, such as the Document, Picture, and Pages libraries, as shown in Figure 1.20. SharePoint lists, such as Announcements, Calendars, Links, and Tasks, are built into the Team Site template. You also have the option to create custom lists. Team sites have a default discussion board, called the Team Discussion, enabling members to post and reply to forums. You can create custom discussion boards to fit the unique needs of your organization.

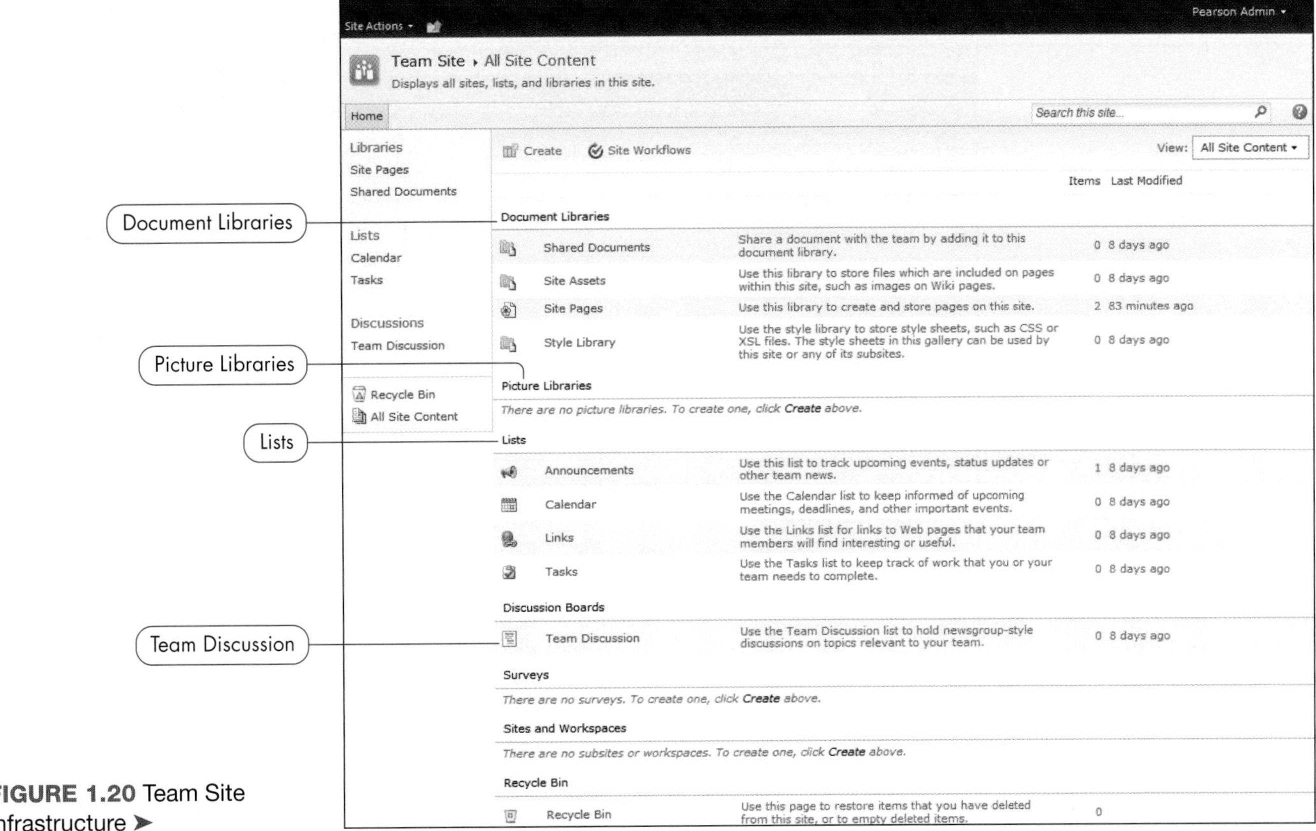

FIGURE 1.20 Team Site Infrastructure ➤

A Document Workspace site, as shown in Figure 1.21, focuses on features that enable the sharing and updating of documents. The template's default Shared Documents library is used to store documents and supporting files. Using the Tasks feature, responsibilities related to the document can be assigned. The Links feature can be used to record resource listings that are related to the document. The Members feature, included on the Document Workspace homepage, shows a list of the members; Document Workspace shows who has access to the site, and can be used to send e-mail alerts. For instance, a government agency might create an annual report, placing the original document in the Shared Documents library. Tasks might be assigned to the workspace members including collecting links to current court case rulings that might have affected the agency. A calendar can be established giving benchmark dates for completion of the various tasks. As you can see, the Document Workspace brings together most of the requirements for collaboration on a large-scale document such as an annual report. Keep in mind that Document Workspaces based on a template are easily modified to meet the needs of the members and the organization.

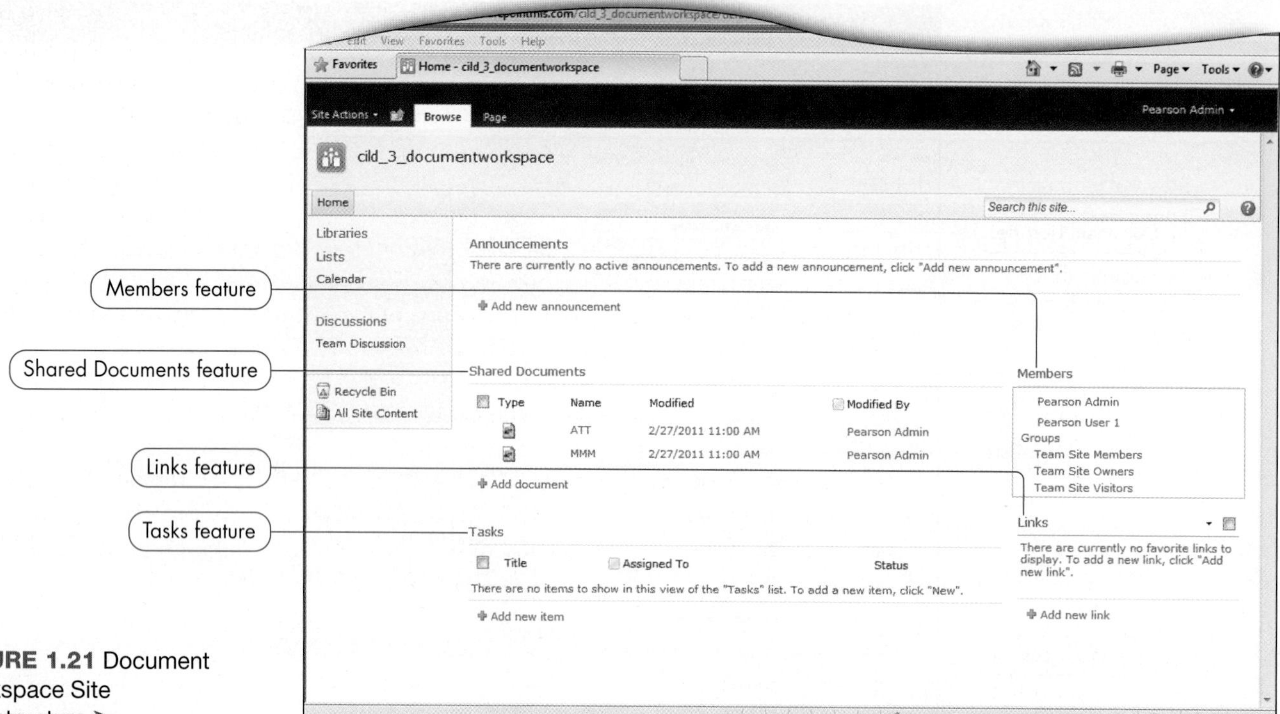

FIGURE 1.21 Document Workspace Site Infrastructure ➤

The **Global links bar** appears across the very top of the SharePoint page, and includes five links that are not related to the user location in the site hierarchy.

The **Breadcrumb navigation** trail enables you to see the path leading to the current page, and to easily keep track of the current page location within its site.

The Group Work template, new to SharePoint 2010, facilitates remote group collaboration which is common in today's business world. Unique to this template are the Group Calendar, Circulations, Phone Call Memo, and Whereabouts, as shown in Figure 1.22. The Group Calendar can be used to keep track of upcoming dates for scheduling and reservations. You can use, for example, a site built on the Group Work template for reserving cars, meeting rooms, books, or anything else you might need to track. The Phone Call Memo feature enables people to record the details of phone calls that may have an impact on the work of the group. The Whereabouts feature can be used to track the location of group members throughout the day, for instance, tracking where the sales manager is as she attends various meetings. The Group Work template also contains the basic SharePoint lists, such as Announcements, Links, and Tasks, and libraries such as the Share Document.

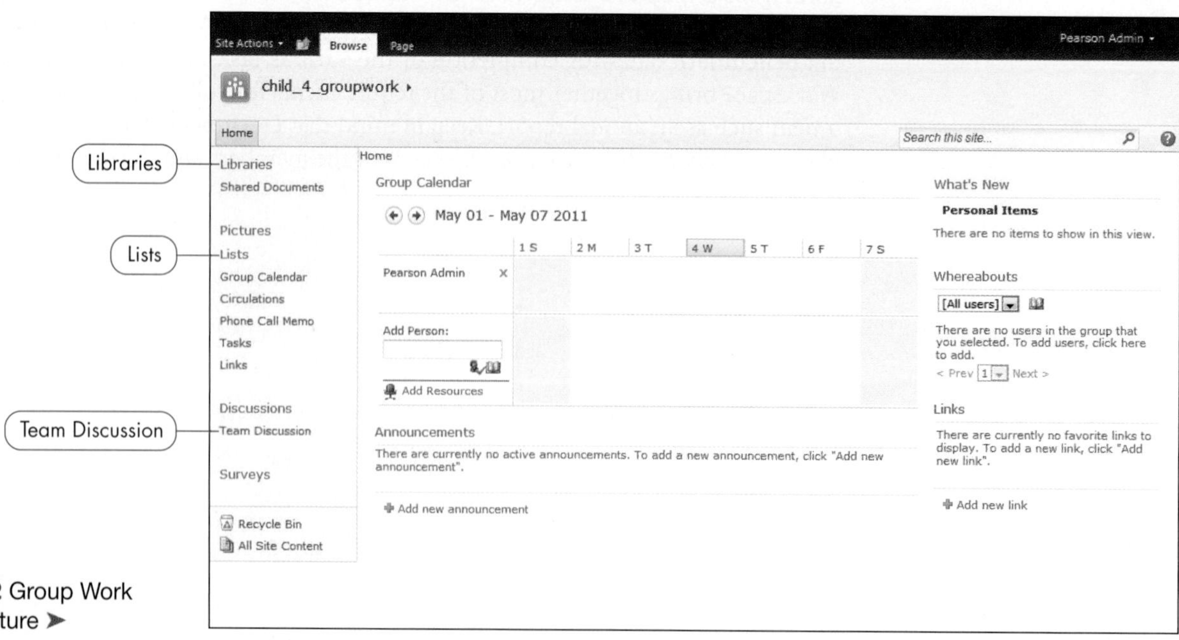

FIGURE 1.22 Group Work Site Infrastructure ➤

The **User menu** displays the name of the user and a menu enabling you to personalize SharePoint.

The **Title area** initially lists the title of the site or page you are currently viewing, and is dynamically updated to include the title of the site and the breadcrumb menu leading you down to the page within the site being viewed.

The **Top Link bar** usually shows the links to the home page of the site and subsites of the current site.

The **Quick Launch area** is located in the left pane of a site, provides easy access to elements that are available within the site including libraries, lists, sites, and members, and includes links to the site's Recycle Bin and to access all of the site content.

The **Content section**, located to the right of the Quick Launch area, is the main body of the site page and includes all the elements you want to make available through the site (such as documents, lists, and web parts).

Team sites, Document Workspaces, and Group Work sites have consistent layouts, as shown in Figure 1.23 on the Team Site template. The ***Global links bar*** appears across the very top of the SharePoint page, and includes Site Actions, Navigate Up, Edit, Browse, and Page. The Site Actions link opens the Site Actions menu that enables you to edit the current page, create a new site or a site component, configure site permissions, and change the settings for your site. The Navigate Up button gives you access to a global navigation path maintained by SharePoint showing you the trail from the top-level site to the current page. The ***Breadcrumb navigation*** trail enables you to see the path leading to the current page and to easily keep track of the current page location within its site. This menu appears at the top of every page within the site. You can click on the various parts of the breadcrumb menu to jump directly to that page. The ***User menu*** displays the name of the user and a menu enabling you to personalize SharePoint. The ***Title area*** initially lists the title of the site or page you are currently viewing, and is dynamically updated to include the title of the site and the breadcrumb menu leading you down to the page within the site being viewed. If you select a tab on the Ribbon, the title area will update to contain the commands of the selected Ribbon tab. The ***Top Link bar*** usually shows the links to the home page of the site and subsites of the current site. On the same bar, the search box enables you to search for information contained by the current site. The help link, for online SharePoint context-sensitive support, is also on the Top Link bar.

The ***Quick Launch area*** is located in the left pane of a site; provides easy access to elements that are available within the site including libraries, lists, sites, and members (for the Document Workspace); and includes links to the site's Recycle Bin and to access all of the site content. The ***Content section***, located to the right of the Quick Launch area, is the main body of the site page, and includes all the elements you want to make available through the site (such as documents, lists, and web parts). Web Part zones and Wiki zones are used to house the content of the pages. We will discuss Web Part pages later in this chapter and in more detail in Chapters 2 and 3.

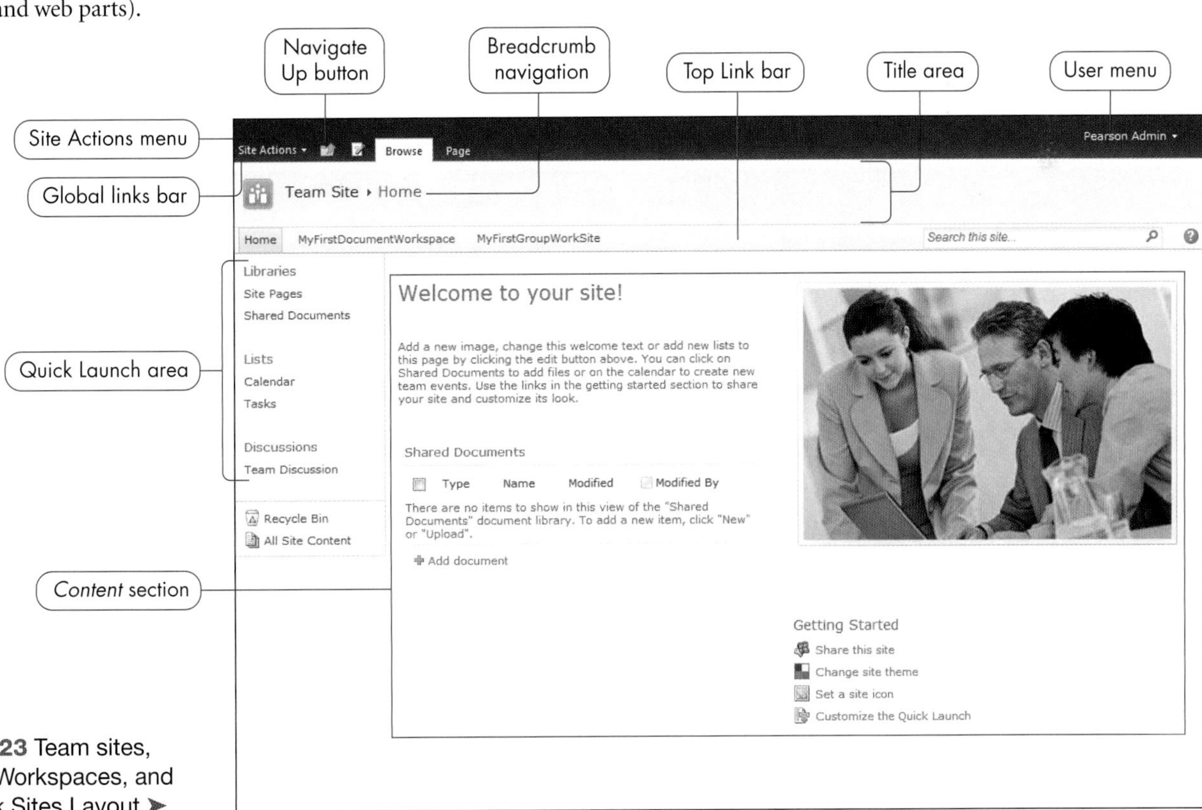

FIGURE 1.23 Team sites, Document Workspaces, and Group Work Sites Layout ➤

Explore Meeting Workspace Layouts

The layout and tools of the Multipage Meeting Workspaces site template, shown in Figure 1.25, are designed to help improve communication before, during, and after a meeting. The site provides a place to store information relevant to the meeting so it can be accessed by all attendees. This can help make meetings more efficient for both large and small organizations.

Features of the Meeting Workspace site can be used to collect and organize needed documents such as agendas, attendee lists, and libraries for documents. The development and publishing of an agenda before the meeting enables participants to prepare. Libraries containing documents enable people to review the documents prior to the meeting. Action items can be developed to serve as objectives for the meeting so that everyone understands what constitutes progress.

During the meeting, participants can continue to access the documents, track the action items, and document decisions as they are being made. Once the meeting is over, the minutes can be posted to the site. Participants can add follow-up documents to the libraries and share ideas on the discussion board. The Meeting Workspace can further be used to track the progress on tasks assigned during the meeting.

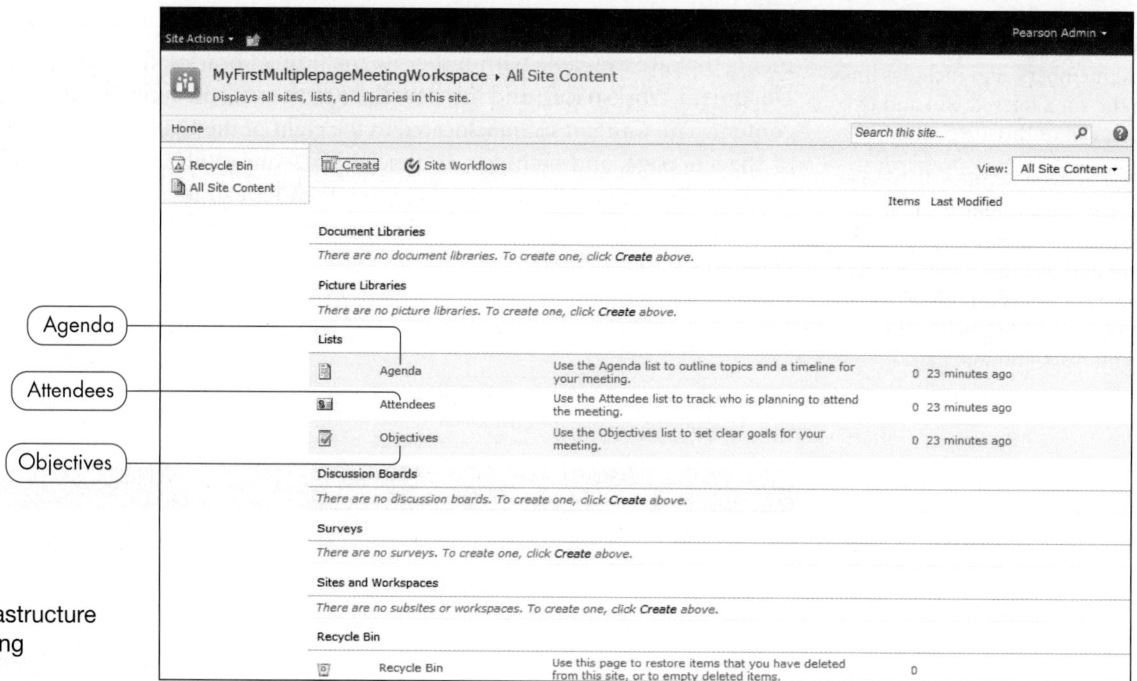

FIGURE 1.24 Infrastructure of Multipage Meeting Workspace ➤

You cannot create subsites under Meeting Workspaces. Meeting workspaces have a different layout than other types of sites, but feature similar tools and menus, as shown in Figure 1.25. The Global links bar, Title area, and navigation bar are the same as discussed in the previous section. The Quick Launch area is located on the left pane and provides access to additional meeting pages and site content. The content section is divided into zones, which allow the organization of Web parts, such as the agenda or attendees, to be arranged in a one, two, or three column structure, as shown in Figure 1.26.

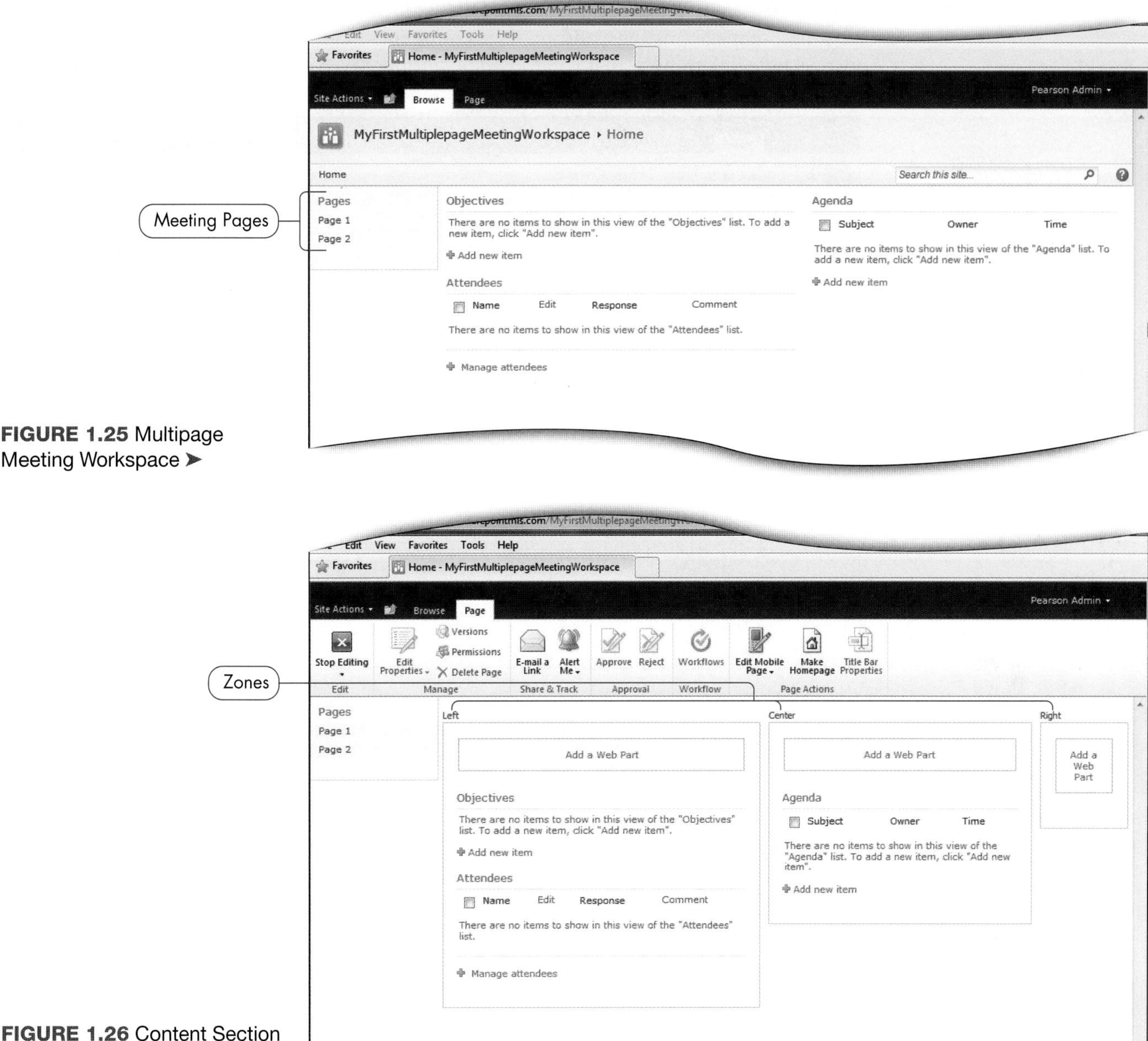

FIGURE 1.25 Multipage Meeting Workspace ➤

FIGURE 1.26 Content Section for a Multipage Meeting Workspace ➤

Explore Blog Site Layouts

The SharePoint Blog site template enables you to create a site which can be used as a journal. Users of the blog site can discuss topics, and because of the archiving features of the blog, previously discussed items can be reviewed. Blog postings are organized by date and topic so if someone remembers the approximate date of the discussion or the topic title, they can quickly find that portion of the discussion. Organizations use blog sites as a way to distribute news, gain consensus on topics through discussion, and tap into the collective knowledge of the team by asking and responding to questions. In addition, blog postings can be e-mailed to others from within the blog. Settings enable the site owner to monitor postings prior to the comments being publically posted.

The layout of blog sites is similar to the sites discussed previously, as shown in Figure 1.27. Blog sites contain a Global links bar, Title area, and navigation bar. The left pane, known as the Blog Navigator, provides ways to access the content by category or date. Additional Web Parts, as shown in Figure 1.28, can be added to the Blog Navigator. The content section is divided into two zones. The blog description and postings are displayed in the left zone, whereas the Blog Tools are located in the right zone. The Blog Tools enable you to create new postings, manage postings, and manage comments made on the postings. The Blog Tools also include link tools so that you can add additional Web Parts to the blog.

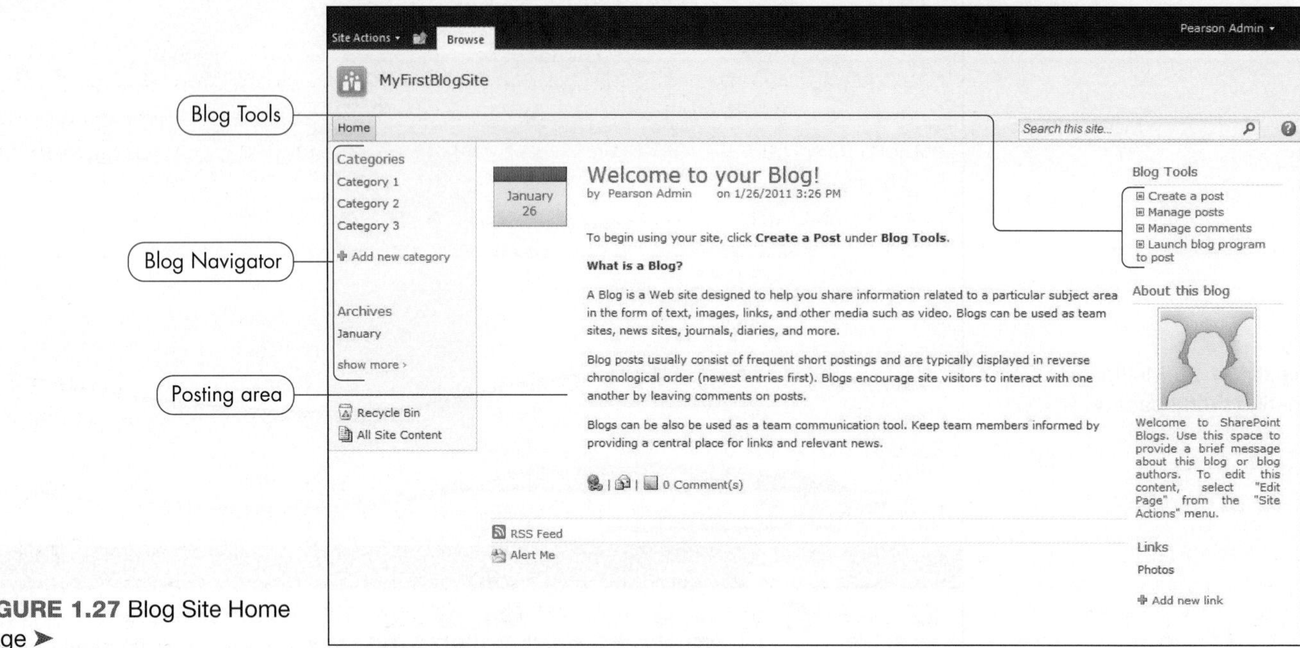

FIGURE 1.27 Blog Site Home Page ➤

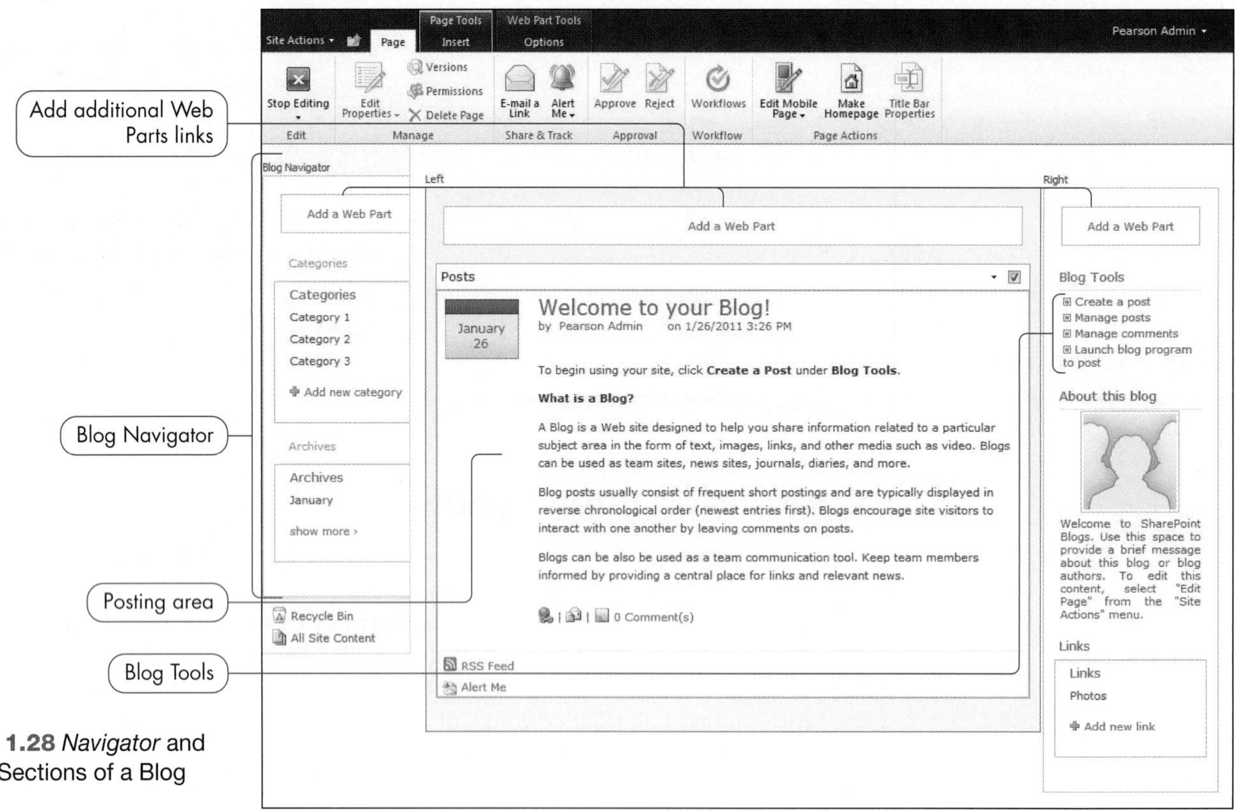

FIGURE 1.28 *Navigator* and *Content* Sections of a Blog Site ➤

Understanding the Relationship between SharePoint Foundation and SharePoint Server

As discussed earlier, SharePoint Server 2010 is a more complex platform, built on the SharePoint Foundation applications. It is recommended for organizations that need both an internal and external collaboration tool. SharePoint Server provides the services needed to host Web pages and allow customers, business partners, and employees to share information. Keep in mind that SharePoint Server is expensive but it supports business goals involving having a virtual presence and competing in the global marketplace.

As you might expect, the SharePoint Server provides additional site templates and libraries to support businesses and organizations. For instance, the Workflow site capabilities are extended in SharePoint Server to enable the smooth transfer of data between the processes of a company. On a basic level, this allows inventories to be viewed in real time and can assure customers that orders they place will be delivered quickly. Online tracking of purchases is an example of how data from one company (the shipping company) can be integrated into a Web site of another company (the one selling the goods).

Whereas the Central Administration site is the only special site that comes with SharePoint Foundation 2010, SharePoint Server 2010 offers more features, as shown in Figure 1.29, and a few more special sites, as shown in Figure 1.30. The one you will most certainly come across is MySite. ***MySite*** is a site that all users can define for themselves (unless it was blocked by the administrator), as shown in Figure 1.30. It can be used for the dual role of having a personal page containing information that the user wants to make available to others, and a more personal page that serves as his usual entry to the system and that contains the information that the user does not want to make available to others.

MySite is a site that all users can define for themselves (unless it was blocked by the administrator).

The following reference table lists additional default templates available in SharePoint Server 2010. These templates support large-scale use within the organization.

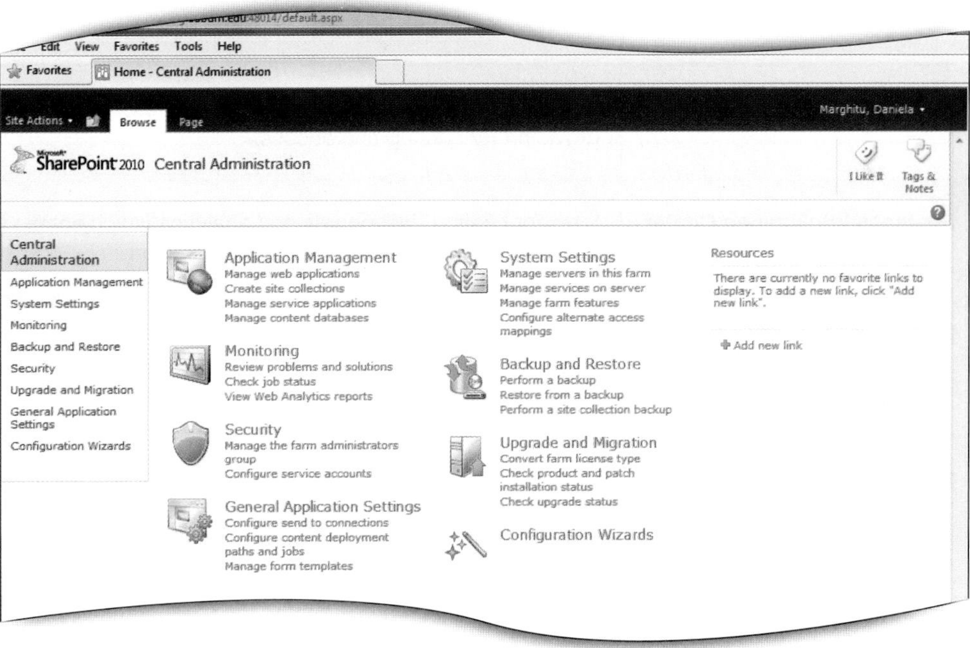

FIGURE 1.29 SharePoint Central Administration Site ➤

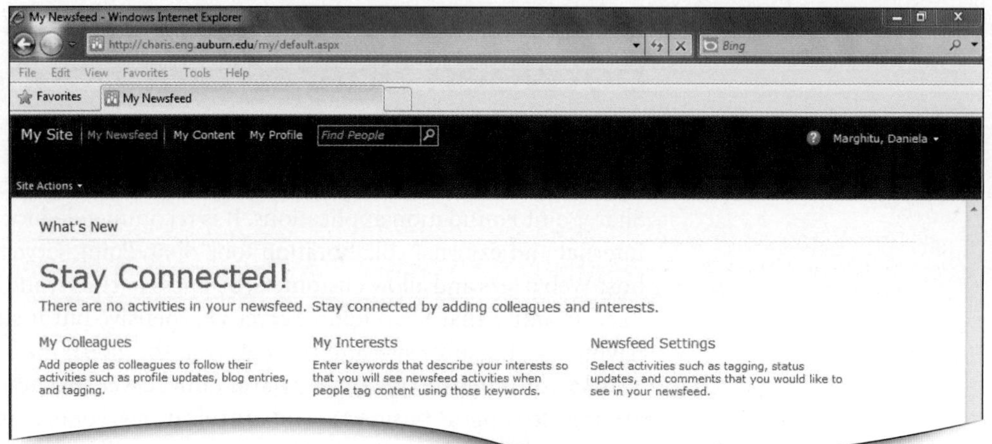

FIGURE 1.30 SharePoint Server MySite ➤

REFERENCE SharePoint Server Templates

SharePoint 2010 Server Template	Use
Visio Process Repository Template	Site for the management of Visio process diagrams.
Enterprise Wiki Template	Wiki site for collaboration in the writing of documents by the entire organization.
Document Center Template	Site for document storage and management within the entire organization. Enables more control over who can access the documents and store documents.
Records Center Template	Sites for indexing and routing files to libraries and folders in order to archive them, providing for backup and access.
Business Intelligence Center Template	Sites for hosting dashboards and analytics which enable the organization to track their return on investment, data mine, and forecast.
Personalization Site Template	Personalized sites based on the user's information as they access the site. This could be as simple as displaying the user's name, or as complex as displaying all of the data available to the organization.
Enterprise Search Center Template	Sites for performing SharePoint searches. This template features tabs which enable users to select either a general search or a search of the people within the organization. The tabs can be customized to include other options.
Basic Search Center Template	Sites for performing SharePoint site searches. It does not include any of the tabs found in the Enterprise Search Center Template.
FAST Search Center Template	Search sites using the FAST (Fast Search & Transfer) search engine rather than the SharePoint search engine. Like the Enterprise Search Center template, you can customize the tabs.

1 Introduction to SharePoint Technologies

Stephanie is eager to get acquainted with the SharePoint 2010 features and tools. You built a SharePoint collection for her that includes some of the most popular SharePoint sites so you can start exploring and learning how she can take advantage of all the SharePoint built-in features and tools.

Skills covered: Log On to Your SharePoint Foundation Collection • Explore the SharePoint Foundation UI • Discover SharePoint Foundation Site Templates Components and Site Permission Levels • Manage Templates • Explore the SharePoint Foundation Collection and SharePoint Foundation Site Layouts

STEP 1 LOG ON TO YOUR SHAREPOINT FOUNDATION COLLECTION

Before you can start exploring the SharePoint Foundation capabilities, you must learn to log on to the SharePoint Collection created for you. Refer to Figure 1.31 as you complete Step 1.

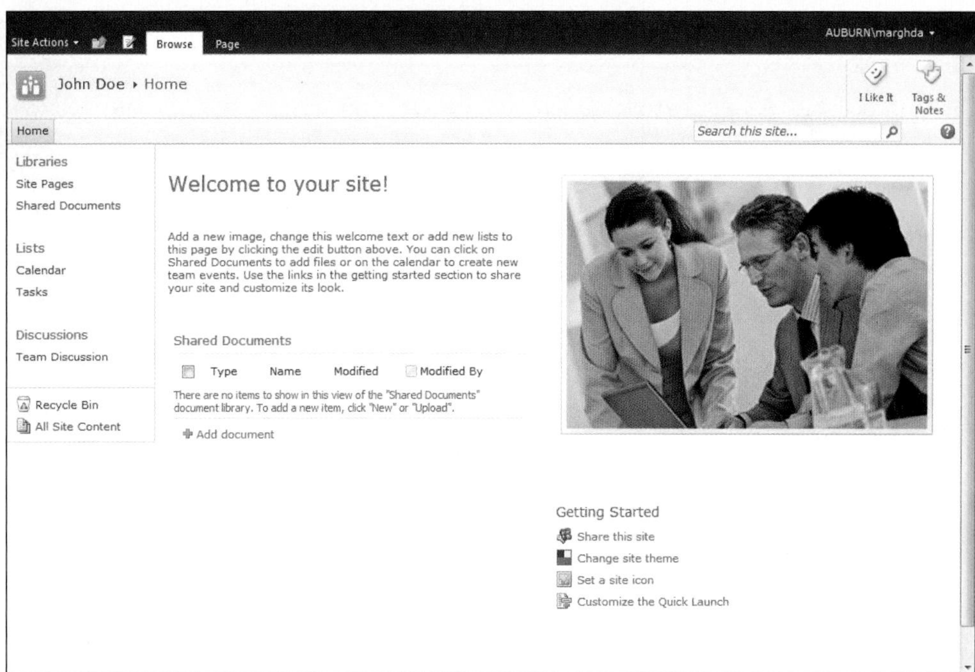

FIGURE 1.31 Top-Level Site Home Page ➤

a. Click **Start** to display the Start menu. Click **All Programs**, and then click **Internet Explorer** to open the program.

> **TROUBLESHOOTING:** Check with instructor for the URL of your top-level site, user name, and password.

b. Go to the top-level site provided by your instructor, which will be in the format of http://pt.sharepointmis.com/SitePages/yourname.

> **TROUBLESHOOTING:** It might take a few seconds to access your top-level site on your Internet connection.

c. Enter the user name and password provided by your instructor.

If you logged in correctly, the home page of the top-level site displays in Internet Explorer. Your screen will look similar to the one shown in Figure 1.31.

STEP 2 EXPLORE THE SHAREPOINT FOUNDATION UI

You will now explore some of the core elements of the SharePoint Foundation 2010 Ribbon using the top-level site of your collection. You will identify the Site Settings page main categories of settings, and you will explore the Page and Edit tabs on the Ribbon. Refer to Figure 1.32 as you complete Step 2.

FIGURE 1.32 SharePoint Foundation UI ➤

a. Identify the Share Point interface components described in the *Working with the SharePoint 2010 Ribbon User Interface* section.

b. Click **Site Actions**, and then click **Site Settings** to display the Site Settings page. Identify each category of settings.

c. Click **Back** on the Internet Explorer Address bar. The home page of your top-level site should now again display.

d. Click the **Page tab** to display the Page Ribbon.

e. Click **Edit** in the Edit group to display the Editing Tools tab.

f. Click **Check Out** in the Edit group, and then notice the Status bar and the Notification area.

Your screen will look similar with the one shown in Figure 1.32. The notification will show on the Status bar only for few seconds.

g. Click **Check In** in the Edit group. Press **Continue** to complete the Check-in process, and then notice the Status bar and the Notification area.

STEP 3 DISCOVER SHAREPOINT FOUNDATION SITE TEMPLATES COMPONENTS AND SITE PERMISSION LEVELS

In order to decide if you should use a SharePoint template for developing your site, you need to start getting acquainted with the components of a SharePoint Site template and the site group permissions levels. You will explore the core components of a Team site using the top-level site of your collection. Then, you will check your site level permission. Refer to Figure 1.33 as you complete Step 3.

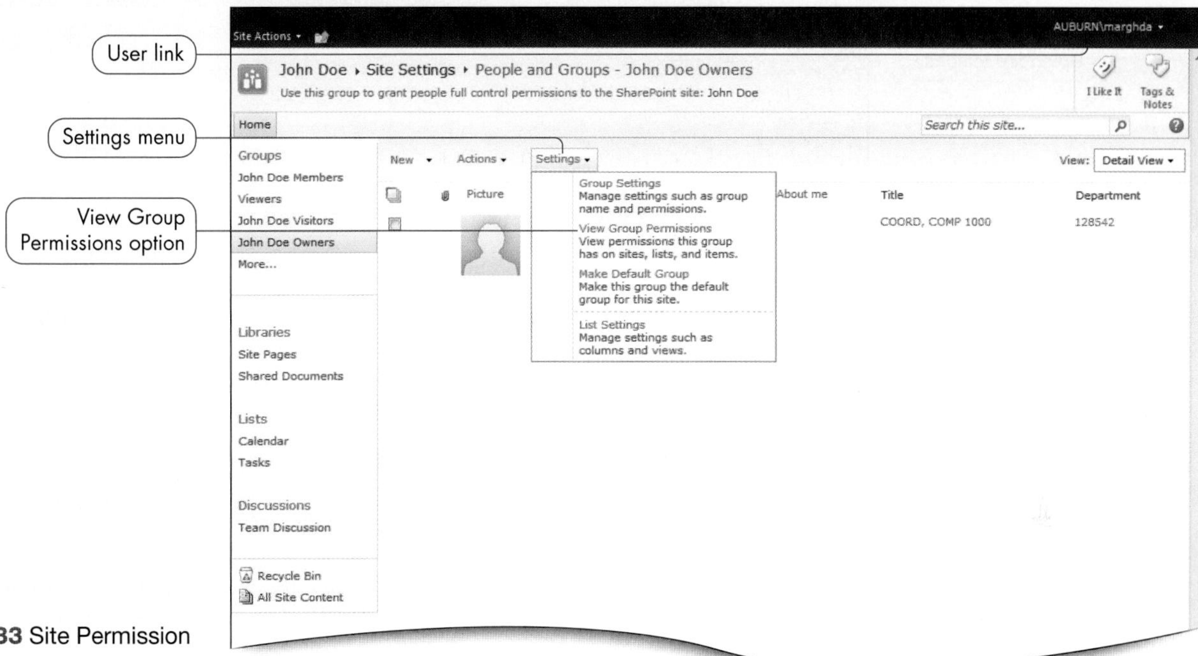

FIGURE 1.33 Site Permission Levels ➤

a. Click **Site Actions**, and then click **View All Site Content** to display the All Site Content page. Identify each category of components.

b. Identify the Share Point Team site template components.

c. Click **Site Actions**, and then click **Site Settings** to display the Site Settings page.

d. Click the **People and groups link** in the *Users and Permissions* section to display the People and Groups page.

e. Click the **Owners link** under Groups in the left pane.

   You should now see your information as owner of this site.

f. Click the **Settings arrow**, and then select **View Group Permissions**.

   You should now see the View Site Collection Permissions window.

g. Click **OK** to close the Site Collection Permissions window.

STEP 4 MANAGE TEMPLATES

You can always use a SharePoint custom template, previously created by someone, to create a new SharePoint site. You will upload a site template, change its name, and then activate it again. Refer to Figure 1.34 as you complete Step 4.

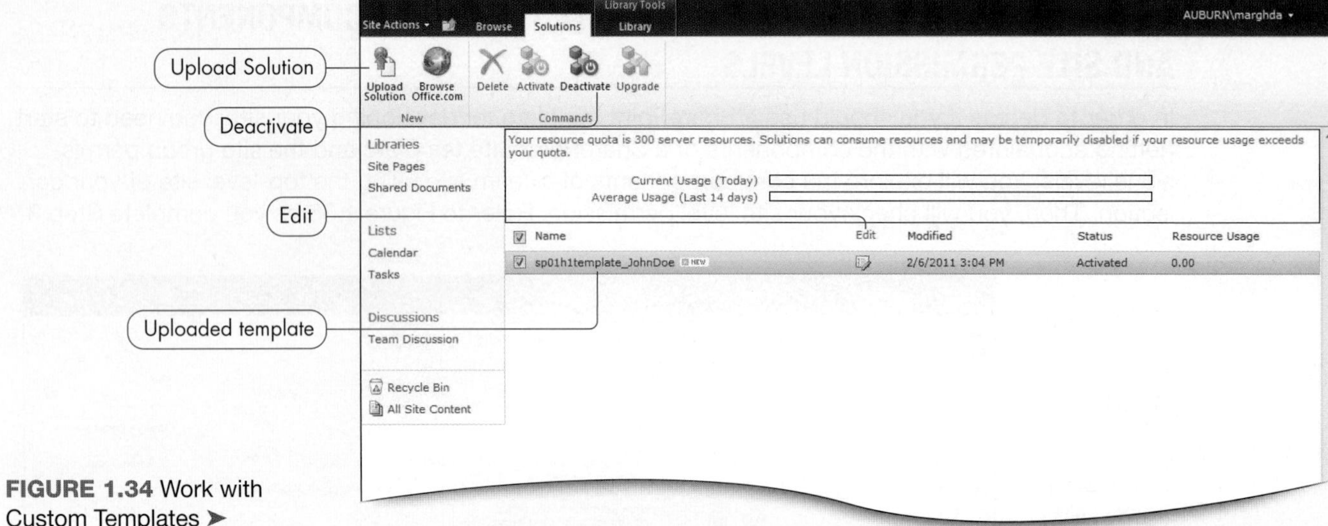

FIGURE 1.34 Work with Custom Templates ➤

a. Click **Site Actions**, and then click **Site Settings** to display the Site Settings page.

b. Click the **Solutions link** in the *Galleries* section.

   The Solution Gallery page should now display.

c. Click the **Solutions tab** on the Solution Gallery page. Click **Upload Solution** in the New group of the Solutions tab.

   The Upload Document dialog box should now display.

d. Click **Browse** to display the Choose File to Upload dialog box and navigate to the *sp01h1template.wsp* document corresponding to the template you want to upload.

e. Click the name of the *sp01h1template.wsp* document, click **Open** to close the Choose File to Upload Document dialog box, and then click **OK** to close the Upload Document dialog box. Click **Close** on the Solution Gallery – Activate Solution dialog box.

   The Solution Gallery is updated to reflect the upload of the new site template.

f. Point to the name of the uploaded template, and then click the check box on the left.

g. Click **Edit** to the right of the uploaded template to display the Solution Gallery dialog box. Type **sp01h1template_LastNameFirstName** in the **Name box**, and then click **Save**.

   The Solution Gallery is updated to reflect the new name of the uploaded site template.

h. Point to the name of the uploaded template, and then click the check box on the left, if it is not already checked. Click **Activate** in the Commands group of the Solutions tab, and then click **Activate** in the Commands group on the Solution Gallery dialog box.

STEP 5 EXPLORE THE SHAREPOINT FOUNDATION COLLECTION AND SHAREPOINT FOUNDATION SITE LAYOUTS

In order to be able to choose the appropriate SharePoint Foundation site templates, you will need to get acquainted with the three core categories of SharePoint Foundation site layouts. You will explore the layout of your top-level team site, a Multipage Meeting Workspace, and a blog site. Refer to Figure 1.35 as you complete Step 4.

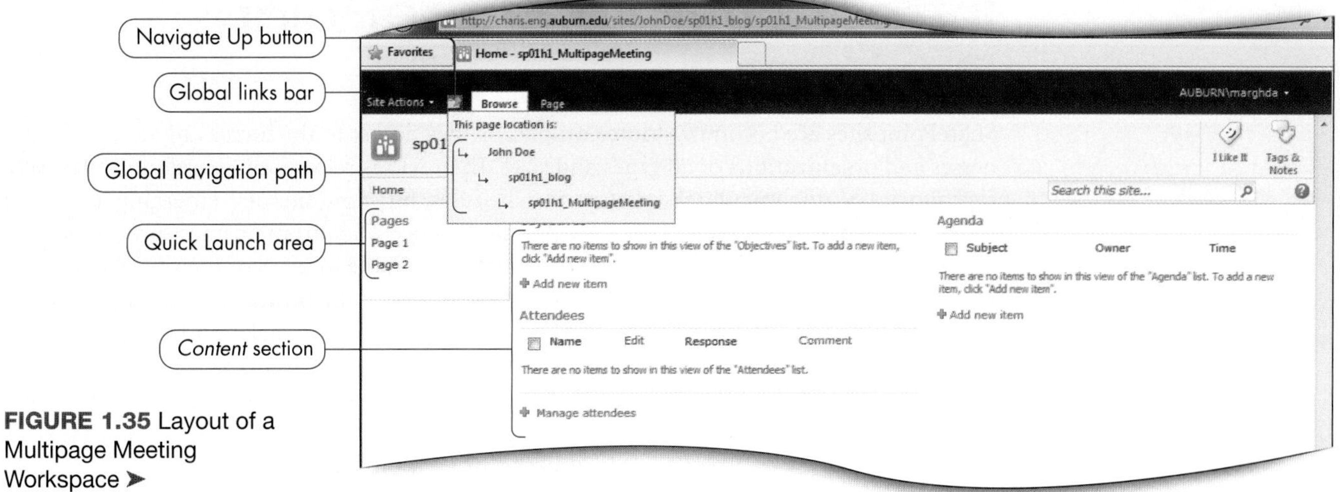

FIGURE 1.35 Layout of a Multipage Meeting Workspace ➤

a. Go to the http://pt.sharepointmis.com/SitePages/*yourname* top-level site provided by your instructor.

b. Identify the five main components of the top-level team site infrastructure: Global links bar, Title area, Navigation bar, Quick Launch area, and *Content* section.

c. Click the **All Site Content link** in the Quick Launch area.

d. Click **sp01h1_blog** in the *Sites and Workspace* section of the All Site Content page.

   The sp01h1_blog site now displays.

e. Identify the three main components of the top-level team site infrastructure: Global links bar, Blog Navigator, Blog Tools, and *Content* section.

f. Click the **sp01h1_MultipageMeeting link** on the Top Link bar.

   The sp01h1_MultipageMeeting workspace now displays.

g. Identify the three main components of the sp01h1_MultipageMeeting workspace infrastructure: Global links bar, Quick Launch area, and *Content* section.

h. Click the **Navigate Up button** on the Global Links bar. The global navigation path should look like the one shown in Figure 1.35 and it is showing the parent sites up to your top-level site.

i. Click the name of your top-level site.

   Your top-level site should now display.

j. Close Internet Explorer.

Introduction to SharePoint Designer

SharePoint sites are becoming more complex as they adjust to the increasing needs of businesses and organizations of all types and sizes. In previous releases of SharePoint, sites were repositories of documents, task lists, and schedules, but now sites are emerging as critical tools on which organizations build their online presence. Data from business processes, such as inventory or ordering systems, is made instantly available to users of the site. Therefore, a SharePoint site designer needs to understand the needs of the business, the complex structure of the SharePoint site and the wide range of elements that make up the site, the relationships between the many elements of the site, and the ability to manage all of this in one place. SharePoint Designer 2010 is a user-friendly, free design tool for configuring and customizing SharePoint 2010 sites. For simple tasks such as adding static content (text or images) to your pages, uploading documents, or creating list items, you should always use the SharePoint Foundation browser interface.

SharePoint Designer 2010 is a user-friendly, free design tool for configuring and customizing SharePoint 2010 sites.

In this section, you will explore SharePoint Designer capabilities, get started with the SharePoint Designer User Interface (UI) components and tools, and learn how you can customize the SharePoint Designer UI. Then, you will learn how to get help while working with SharePoint Designer.

> **TIP** More About SharePoint Designer 2010
>
> You can use SharePoint Designer 2010 only with sites running on SharePoint Foundation 2010 or SharePoint Server 2010. SharePoint Designer 2010 cannot be used with earlier versions of SharePoint. You can download SharePoint Designer free of charge and access up-to-date information from the official Microsoft SharePoint Designer Web site.

Exploring SharePoint Designer 2010 Capabilities

... SharePoint Designer enables the designer to use tools to create more complex sites and effectively manage all of the sites within SharePoint.

SharePoint Designer 2010 provides a consolidated environment where you can work on your SharePoint site, all of its lists and libraries, pages, data sources, workflows, permissions, and more. SharePoint Designer 2010 can be used to perform basically any level of site customization in SharePoint. Whereas SharePoint Foundation provides methods for basic site customization using a browser interface, SharePoint Designer enables the designer to use tools to create more complex sites and effectively manage all of the sites within SharePoint.

The following five categories cover the core site customizations that you perform as you design and build solutions using SharePoint Designer 2010:

- Data Sources: You can connect to data sources, including lists and libraries, external databases, master pages, page layouts, Cascading Style Sheets, and more, and then integrate that data into your SharePoint site. You can learn more about Data Sources in other chapters of this textbook.
- Views: SharePoint Designer enables you to create views of live data that are relevant to your organization. Views of data can be customized so that only certain fields are displayed. Additional functions can sort and/or filter the data. Calculations using the data can produce outcomes. Conditional formatting can be applied to the data view. View Styles, available in SharePoint Designer under the Data View feature, enable you to quickly create customized views. You can learn more about Data View in other chapters of this textbook.

- Forms: A built-in form editor enables you to create forms to display, edit, and create data which then flows into data sources. You can learn more about Forms in other chapters of this textbook.
- Workflows: Both business application processes, such as data automatically flowing from one data source into another and human processes, such a document signatures, can be created as workflows using SharePoint Designer 2010.
- Designing and Branding: SharePoint Designer enables you to apply the desired look and feel to your SharePoint site. In large organizations or businesses, a Web designer may have responsibility for branding a site. Using SharePoint Designer, you can create a custom look and feel for your sites using master pages, page layouts, and CSS. You can learn more about designing and branding in other chapters of this textbook.

TIP Configure SharePoint Designer Settings

Master pages, page layouts, and CSS are all disabled by default for all users except site collection administrators. In SharePoint 2010, there is a single page, accessed via Central Administration or Site Collection Administration pages, where you can specify exactly what can and cannot be done with SharePoint Designer 2010 (see Figure 1.36).

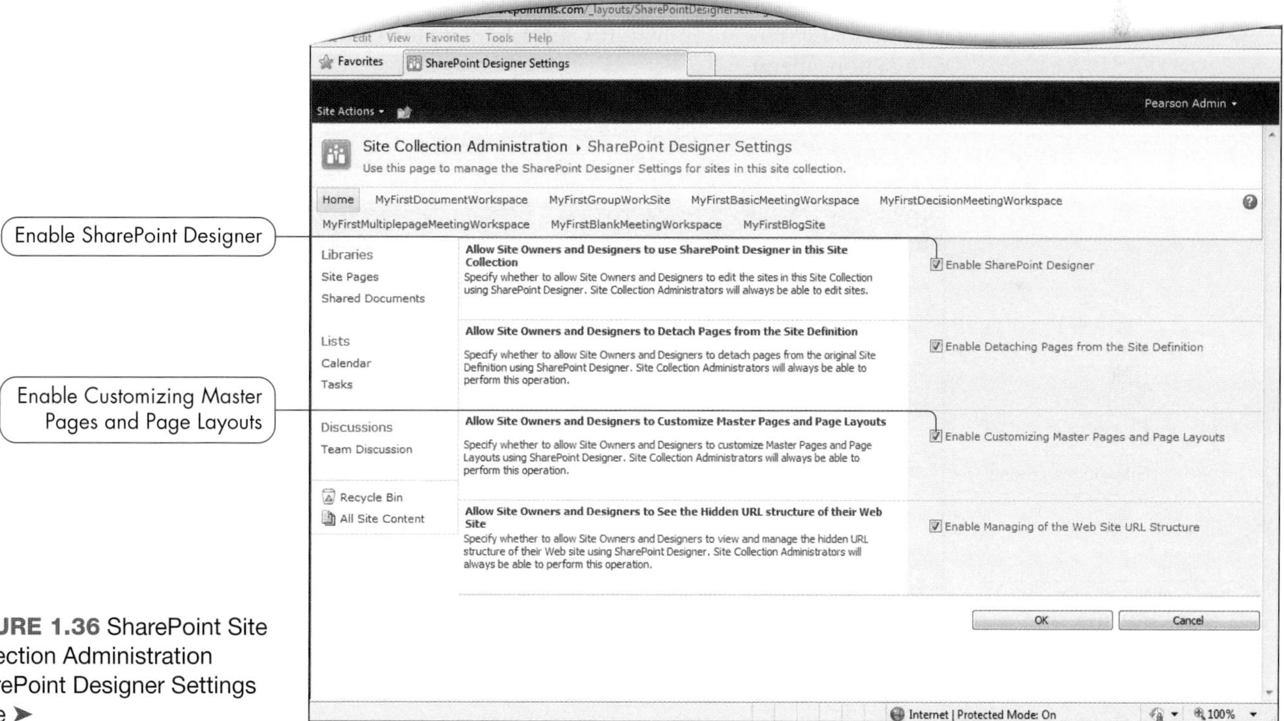

FIGURE 1.36 SharePoint Site Collection Administration SharePoint Designer Settings Page ➤

Identifying the SharePoint Designer Default Interface Components and Tools

SharePoint Designer 2010 is a premier desktop application for customizing SharePoint sites. SharePoint Designer 2010 provides an enhanced user experience with a fully redesigned UI that enables you to:

SharePoint Designer 2010 is a premier desktop application for customizing SharePoint sites.

- Edit SharePoint content
- Create and modify lists, libraries, and data views
- Create and edit master pages and page layouts
- Create and edit CSS
- Connect SharePoint to a wide range of data sources
- Design and edit workflows

Many of the SharePoint Designer features, such as creating and editing master pages or designing and editing workflows, are not available via the SharePoint Foundation browser interface.

Open SharePoint Designer

SharePoint Designer 2010 can be launched directly from the Windows Start menu, or from within SharePoint. As shown in Figure 1.37, SharePoint Designer can be accessed from the Site Actions menu.

FIGURE 1.37 SharePoint Site Actions Menu ➤

If you have not installed SharePoint Designer 2010 yet, the first time you launch it from SharePoint using the Site Actions menu, you will be prompted to download and install it from the Web. When you open SharePoint Designer 2010 next time from within SharePoint, it will open immediately.

TIP More About Opening SharePoint Designer

Depending on the installation method used, you might have a SharePoint Designer icon on your Windows desktop. If so, you can save time by double-clicking this icon to start SharePoint Designer. If SharePoint Designer was recently used on your computer, you can start SharePoint Designer by selecting Microsoft Office SharePoint Designer 2010 from the Start menu.

The **SharePoint Designer Backstage view** enables you to view and access larger site or application settings.

When you open SharePoint Designer 2010 from the Windows Start menu, the first thing you see is the File tab that displays the SharePoint Designer Backstage view. The ***SharePoint Designer Backstage view***, shown in Figure 1.38, enables you to view and access larger site or application settings. This includes creating a new site, opening another site, adding pages, importing files, and changing SharePoint Designer 2010 application settings. If you open SharePoint Designer 2010 from the browser view of a SharePoint site, you will not see the File tab screen, and your site opens in the Site tab of SharePoint Designer 2010 interface (see Figure 1.39), which displays a summary of the site, including its title, description, current permissions, and subsites.

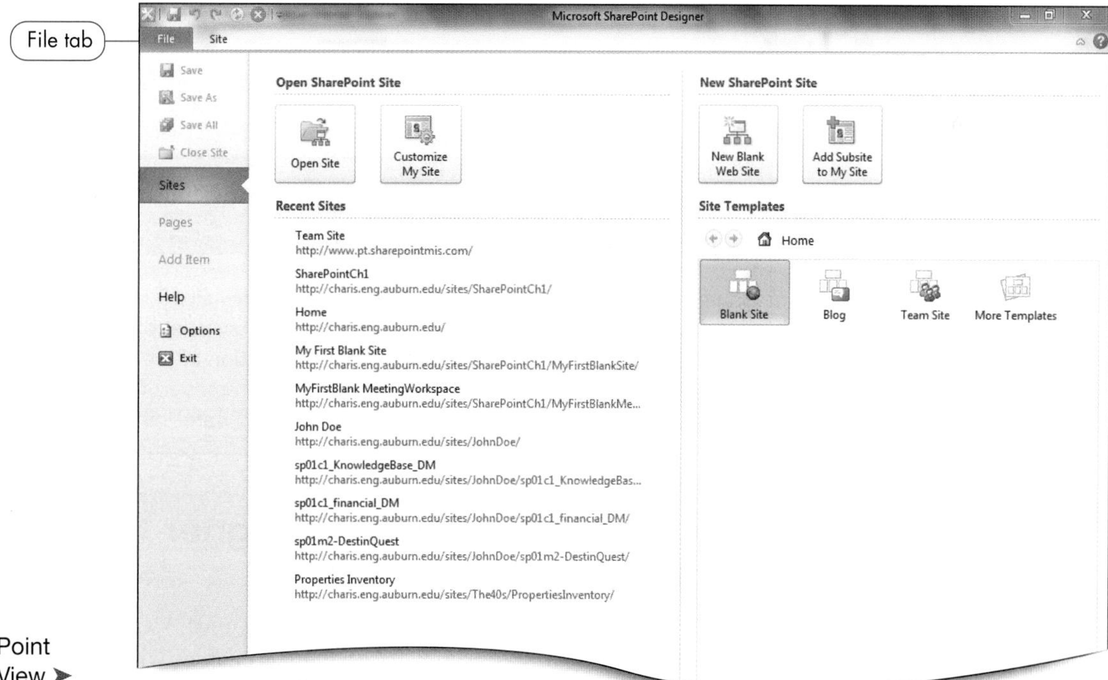

FIGURE 1.38 SharePoint Designer Backstage View ➤

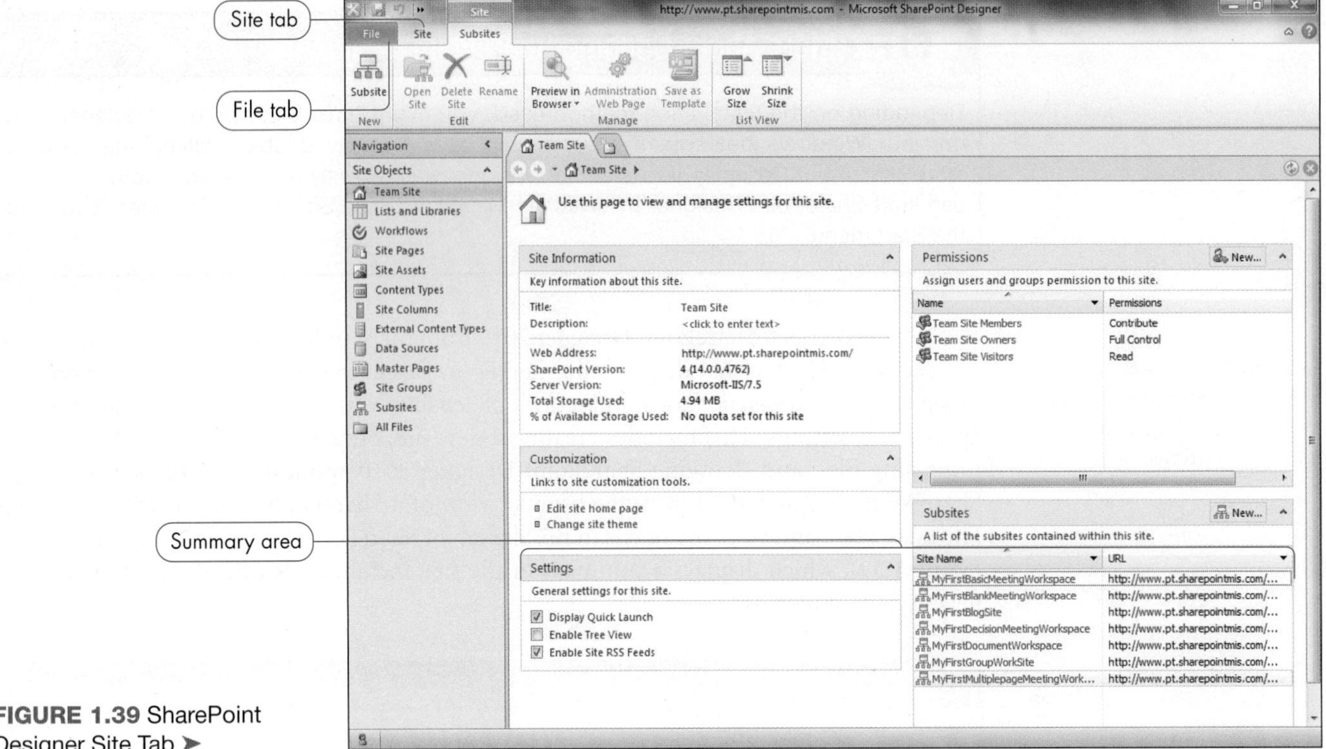

FIGURE 1.39 SharePoint Designer Site Tab ➤

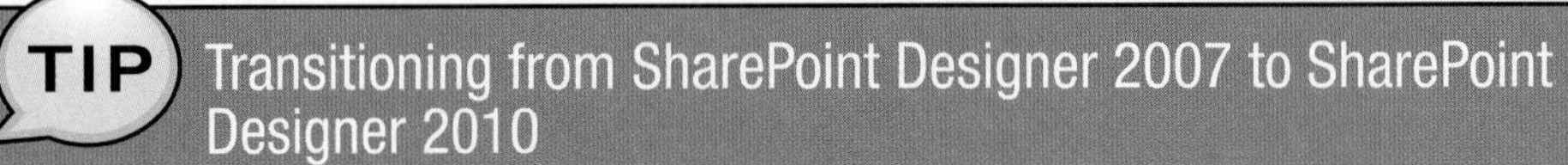

TIP
Transitioning from SharePoint Designer 2007 to SharePoint Designer 2010

SharePoint Designer 2007 and SharePoint Designer 2010 user interfaces do have major differences. If you used SharePoint Designer 2007, you should consider using the *Microsoft Reference SharePoint Designer 2007 to 2010* section of the Student Resources which shows you, for example, the SharePoint Designer 2007 removed features and the SharePoint 2010 features that replace them, as the new enhanced SharePoint 2010 features.

Identify the SharePoint Designer User Interface Components

The **Quick Access Toolbar** enables you to save, undo, redo, and refresh with a single mouse click.

The SharePoint Designer UI is composed of the Quick Access Toolbar and three main areas, as shown Figure 1.40. The ***Quick Access Toolbar*** enables you to save, undo, redo, and refresh with a single mouse click. You can add buttons to the toolbar, and the tools are always available regardless of which tab is displayed on the Ribbon. The Quick Access Toolbar can be displayed next to the Microsoft Office button, or below the Ribbon. Commands available on the Ribbon can be added to the Quick Access Toolbar for convenience. For instance, you may find yourself using the Spell Check command often. You can add it to the Quick Access Toolbar by right-clicking the command on the Ribbon, and then selecting Add to Quick Access Toolbar.

The three main areas of the SharePoint Designer Default UI that you will use when designing and building SharePoint sites and pages are the following:

- Navigation Pane is used to navigate the major parts, or components, of your site.
- Gallery and Summary pages to see lists of each component type and summaries of one particular component.
- Ribbon to perform actions on the selected component. When you click on any components listed in the Navigation Pane, a contextual tab on the Ribbon is displayed, as shown in Figure 1.40. In addition to the default options in the tab on

the Ribbon, new tabs may be added to the Ribbon as specific objects on the page are selected. In Figure 1.41, the photograph, which is inside of a table structure, is selected. So as a result, the Ribbon shows two additional tabs: one for Picture Tools and the other for Table Tools. The Ribbon will only display the options available to the user based on their set of permissions on the site.

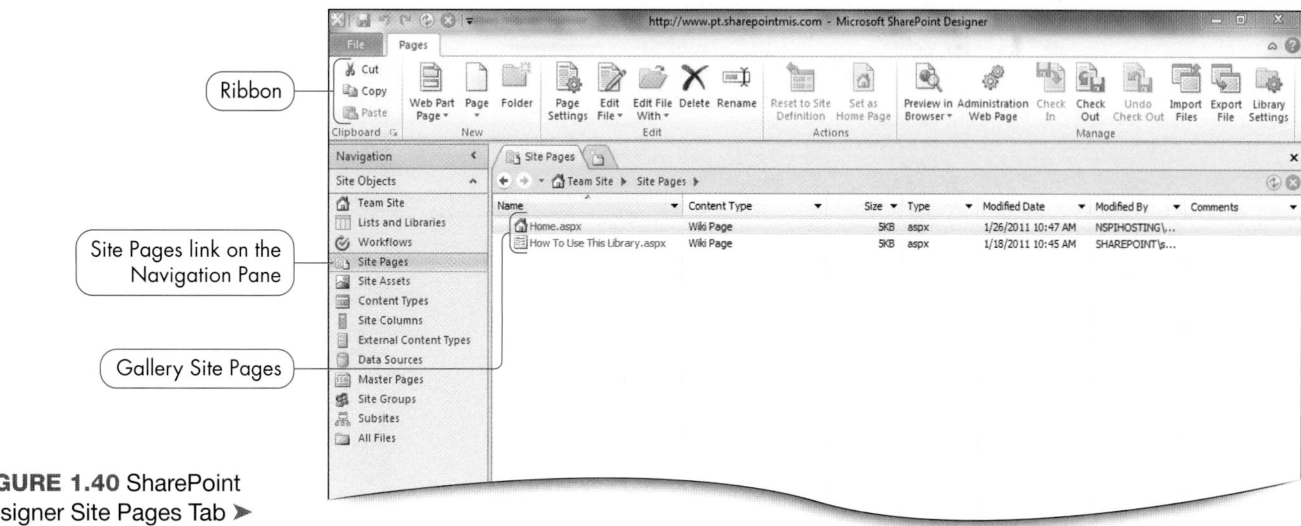

FIGURE 1.40 SharePoint Designer Site Pages Tab ➤

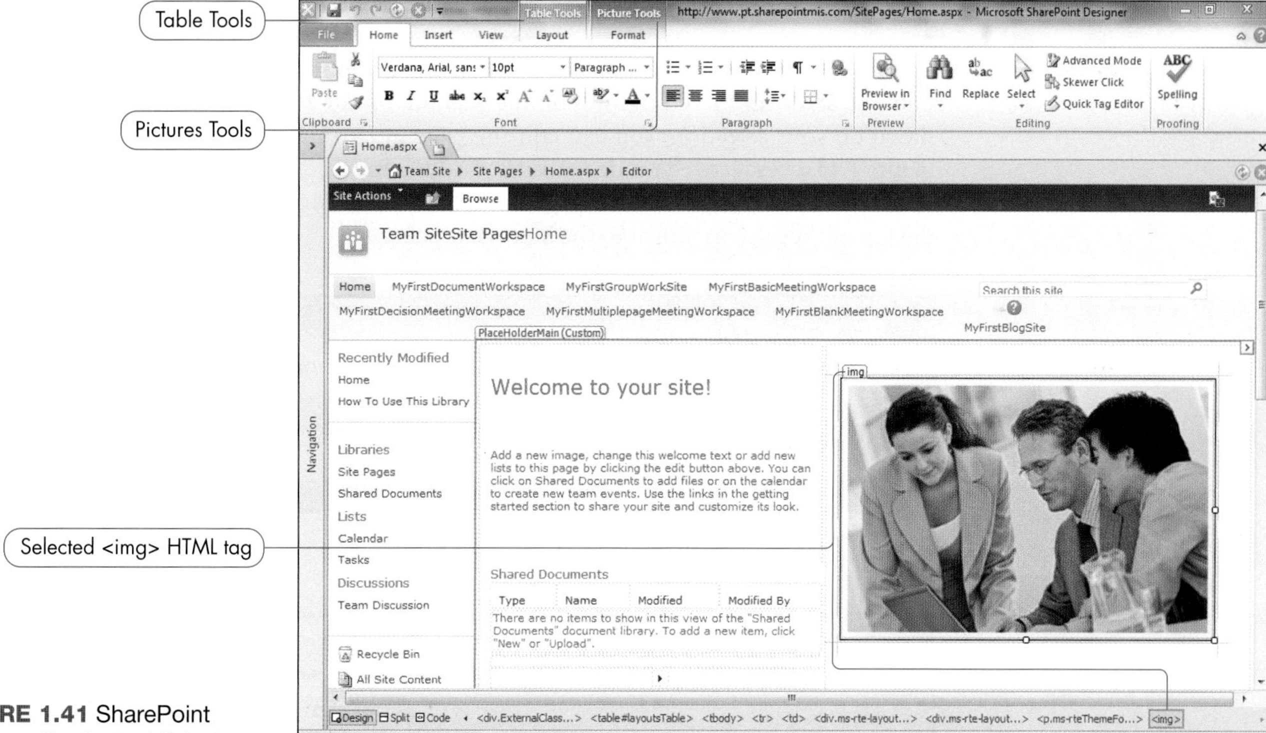

FIGURE 1.41 SharePoint Designer Contextual Tabs ➤

The **Navigation Pane** shows the core components of a SharePoint site, such as Lists and Libraries, Content Types, Data Sources, Workflows, Site Pages, Master Pages, Subsites, and more.

The ***Navigation Pane*** shows the core components of a SharePoint site, such as Lists and Libraries, Content Types, Data Sources, Workflows, Site Pages, Master Pages, Subsites, and more. You can collapse the Navigation Pane by clicking on the Collapse the Navigation Pane button to the right of Navigation, and then you can expand it by clicking the Expand the Navigation Pane button to the right of Navigation, as shown in Figure 1.43. To edit one of the components, a site page for example, click Site Pages, and a Gallery page showing all site pages is displayed. From there, you can open a specific page in the site by double-clicking its name on the Gallery page. This displays a Summary page for the page you selected. The Page tab is automatically displayed when you open a page within a site. On the Summary page, you see its associated File Information, Customization, Permissions, and Version History, as shown in Figure 1.42.

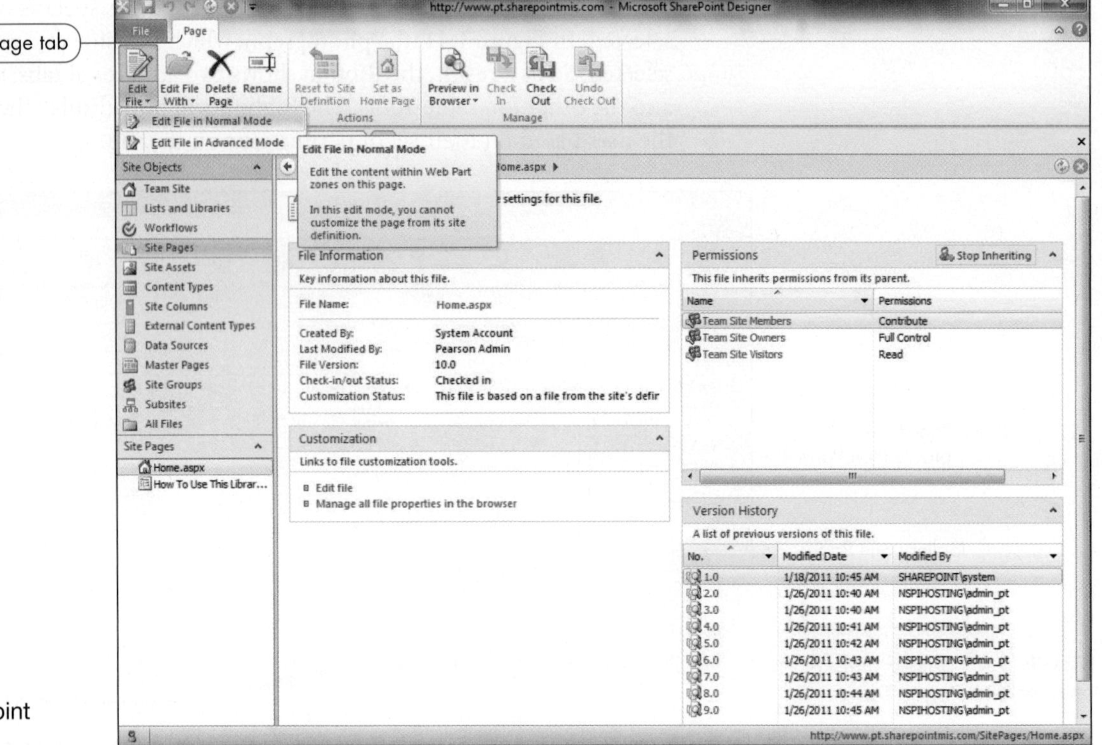

FIGURE 1.42 SharePoint Summary Page ➤

To edit the selected page, double-click the page on the Gallery page, and then click the Edit File arrow in the Edit group on the Ribbon, on the Page tab, as shown in Figure 1.42. Based on your selection, you can edit the page in Normal Mode (Editor Page), shown in Figure 1.43, or Advanced Mode (Advanced Editor Page).

When you finish editing the page, click the Back button or the breadcrumb navigation at the top of the page to return to the Summary page.

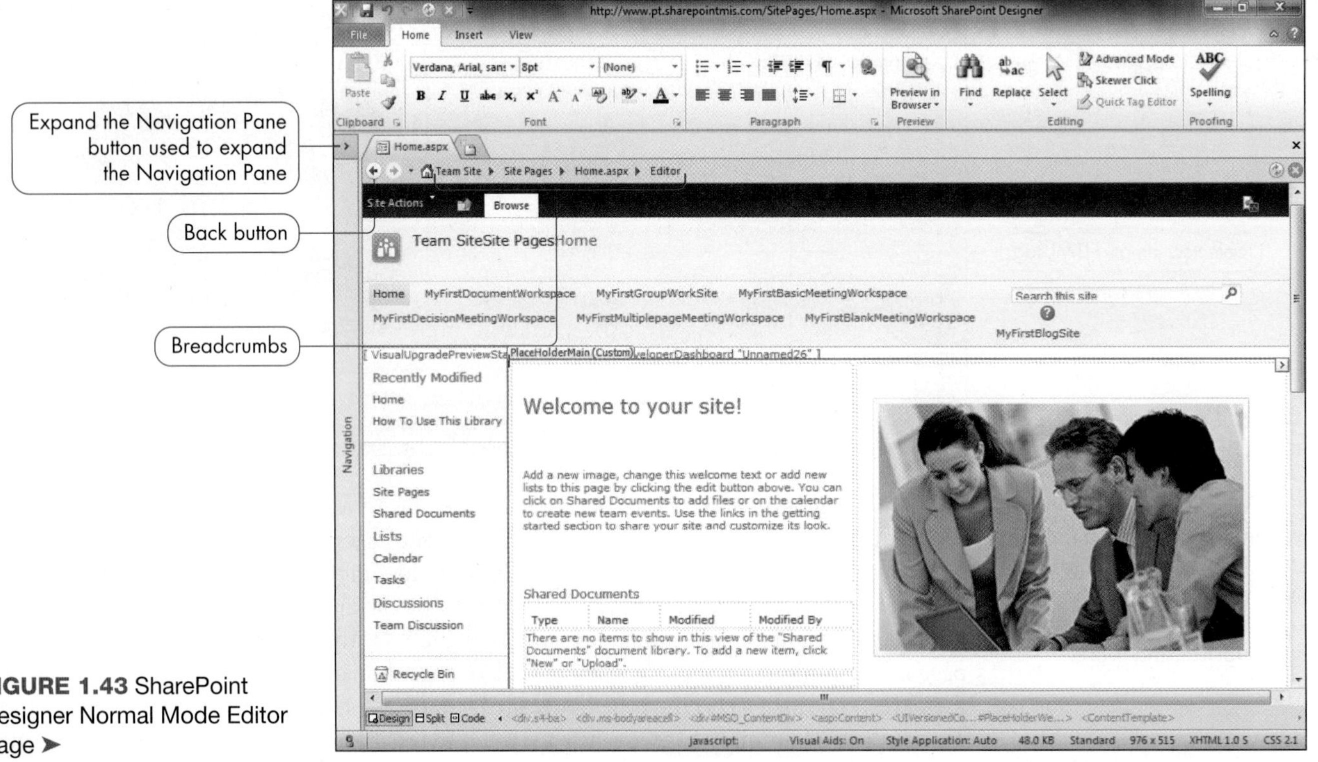

FIGURE 1.43 SharePoint Designer Normal Mode Editor Page ➤

The Task Panes menu displays task panes organized in five groups, described in Table 1.2. Click Task Panes on the Workspace group of the View tab to display the list of task panes, as shown in Figure 1.44. These five groups are also part of the SharePoint Designer default workspace. When you open task panes from the same group, they are displayed by default as merged task panes that cover the same space and are laid one behind the other. Each merged task pane is available by clicking its corresponding tab.

FIGURE 1.44 Task Panes Menu ➤

TABLE 1.2 SharePoint Designer Core Task Panes	
SharePoint Designer Task Pane	**Options**
Tag Properties/CSS Properties	Apply HTML properties (attributes) and CSS properties (styles) to HTML tags using just the WYSIWYG interface.
Apply Styles/Manage Styles	Apply CSS styles. Manage CSS styles.
Behaviors	Add built-in SharePoint Designer behaviors (scripting code that can assist you when adding interactivity to your Web pages).
Layers	Add, delete, and modify layers.
Toolbox	Add HTML tags, form controls, ASP.NET, and SharePoint controls.
Clipart	Search for a clipart.
Clipboard	View a thumbnail of any item, such as text and graphics that can be copied or pasted. Collect up to 24 copied items. Paste all copied items at once or one at a time. Delete all copied items.

Use the SharePoint Designer Page Views

SharePoint Designer 2010 includes four types of page views ... Design view, Code view, Split view ... and the Preview in Browser view.

SharePoint Designer 2010 includes four types of page views (see Table 1.3). The first three views—Design view, Code view, Split view—are available via the Page views group of the View tab and the Preview in Browser view is available via the Preview group of the Home tab.

Double-click the Web page name that you wish to open on the Site Pages tab. The Summary Page is displayed, including information about the page you just opened. For each opened page, SharePoint Designer displays a tab positioned to the right of the Site Summary page tab. Click the Edit File link in the *Customization* section of the Summary page. The SharePoint Designer Design view displays the Web page that is being edited which is also referred to as the current or active page.

TABLE 1.3 SharePoint Designer Web Page Views

View	Description
Design	• You design and edit Web pages in Design view with just minimal WYSIWIG authoring experience. • When you open a Web page, this is the default view, as shown in Figure 1.45.
Code	• You view, add, and edit HTML tags in Code view, as shown in Figure 1.46.
Split	• You can simultaneously display the Code view and Design view of the Web page content in a split screen format. • You use this view to make changes in Code view and immediately see the changes in Design view, or vice versa, as shown in Figure 1.47.
Preview in Browser	• You can see what a Web page will look like in one or more Web browsers without having to first save or publish your page, as shown in Figure 1.48. • You can use all SharePoint Foundation UI functions from this view.

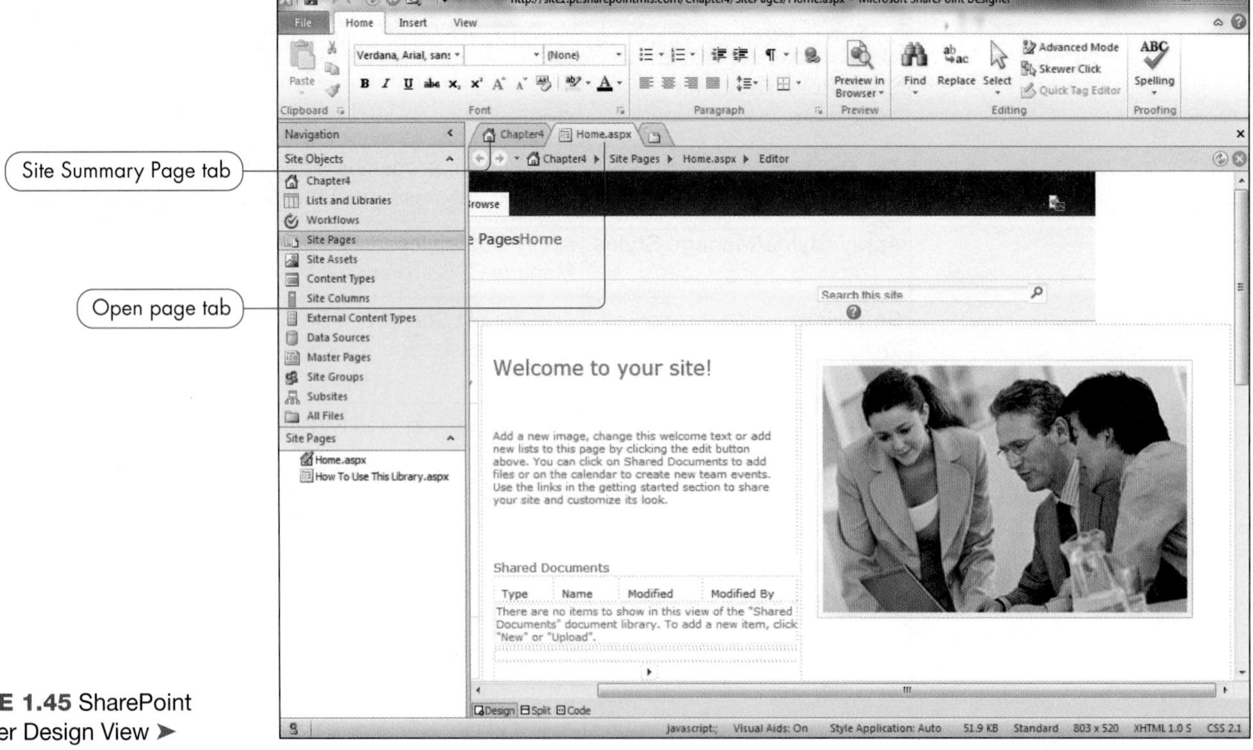

FIGURE 1.45 SharePoint Designer Design View ➤

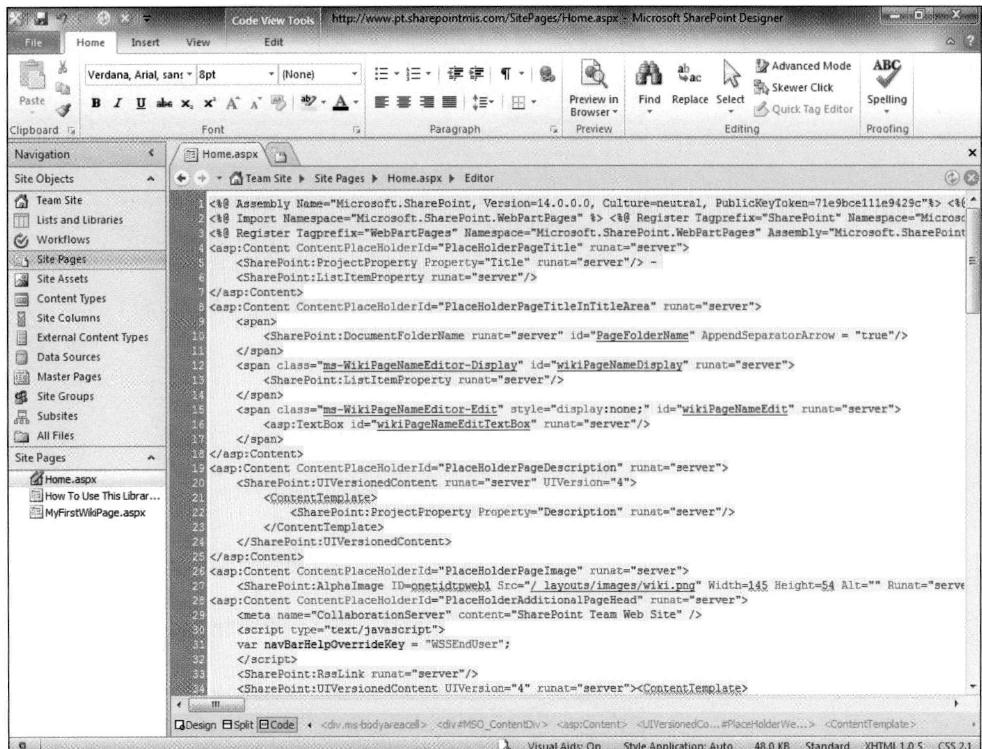

FIGURE 1.46 SharePoint Designer Code View ➤

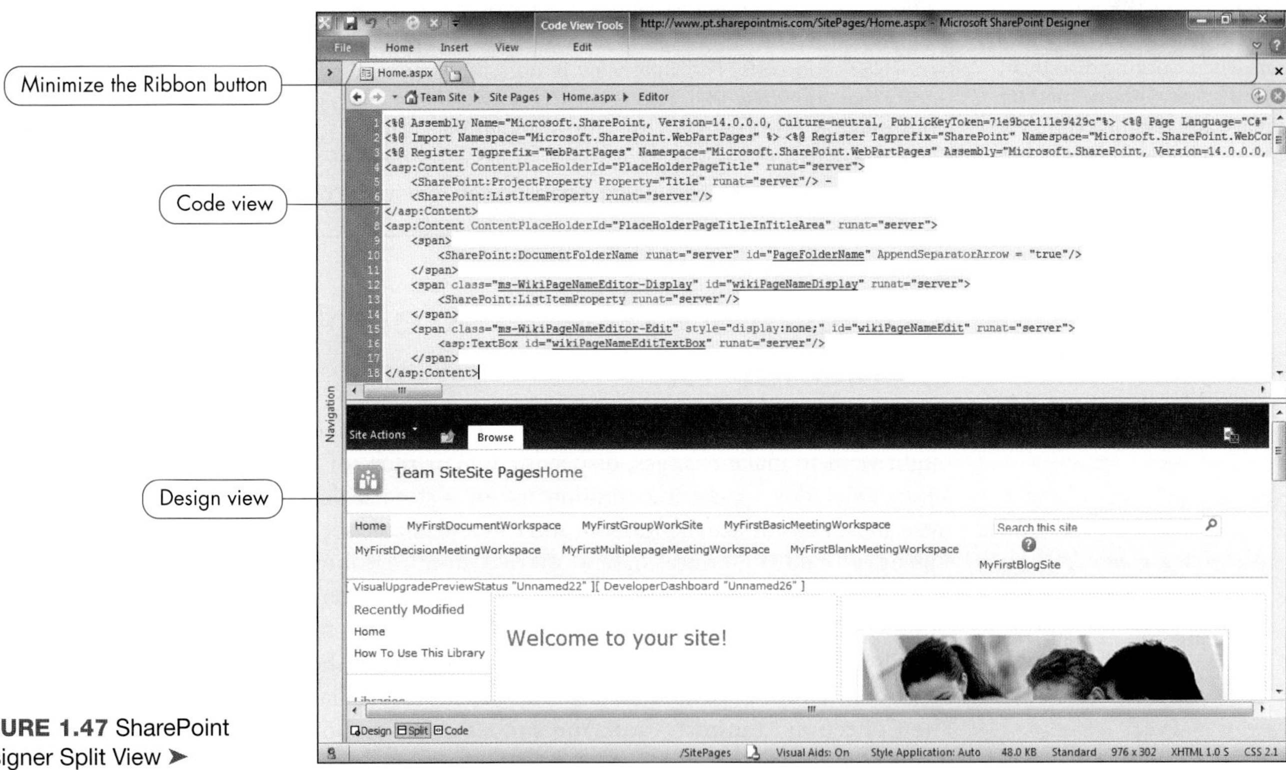

FIGURE 1.47 SharePoint Designer Split View ➤

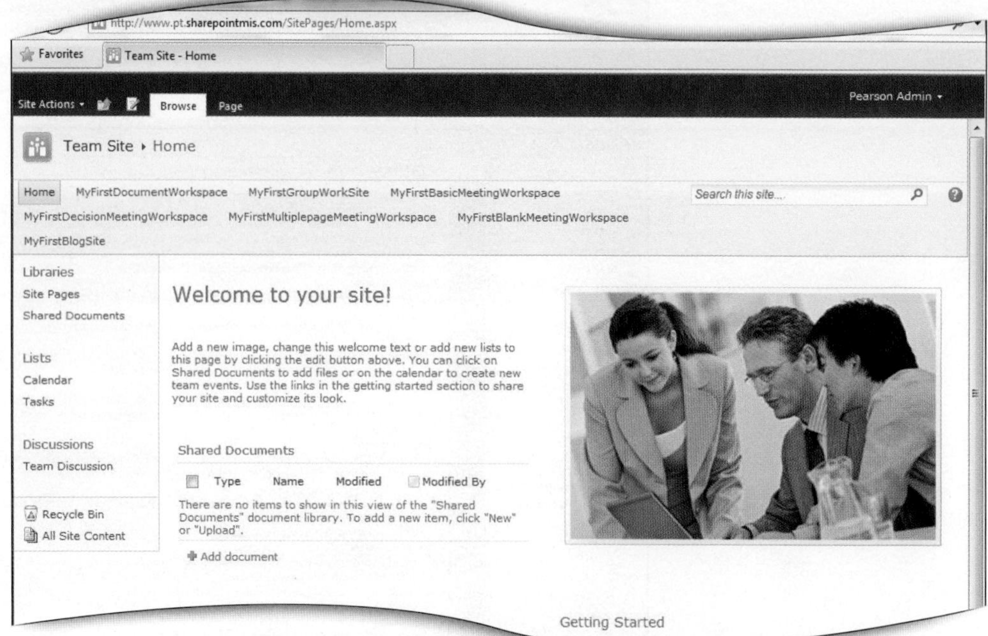

FIGURE 1.48 SharePoint Designer Preview in Browser View ➤

Microsoft IntelliSense technology helps you minimize errors when working directly in the Code view with the markup language and tags that comprise the site, including HTML, XHTML, ASP.NET, and CSS.

TIP SharePoint Designer IntelliSense Technologies

Microsoft IntelliSense technology helps you minimize errors when working in the Code view with the markup language and tags that comprise the site, including HTML, XHTML, ASP.NET, and CSS. The Split view feature provides a WYSIWYG view of the portion of the code that you are working on and a Code view in the same pane. The Tag Inspector validates the markup code and points out irregularities. When editing a page in the SharePoint Designer 2010 Code view, Microsoft IntelliSense technology can also suggest commands based on the work you are doing, enabling you to develop pages more quickly and efficiently.

Customizing the SharePoint Designer UI

Figure 1.39 shows how the SharePoint Designer Site Tab looks the first time it is opened. You might want to make changes, displaying one or more of the task panes in the SharePoint Designer window, change the position and/or customize the Quick Access Toolbar, and minimize and/or customize the Ribbon. You can also enable speech and handwriting recognition. The user-friendly interface enables you to customize features to suit your needs.

The links displayed in the Navigation Pane depend on your permissions on the site and can restrict your access to tools. You will not even see the tools that you do not have permissions to use. For example, the Master Pages link will not show if Enable Customizing Master Pages and Layout Pages option was unchecked in the SharePoint Designer Settings within Site Collection Administration. You can learn more about the Navigation Pane in other chapters of this textbook.

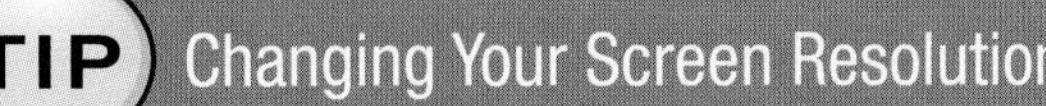

Changing Your Screen Resolution

You can change the resolution of your computer screen if your specific needs and preferences require it. Your needs could be based on accessibility issues (such as vision) or editing and authoring requirements. If you work on a computer with Windows 7, choose Start, Control Panel, Appearance and Personalization, and then Personalization. Click Display, and then click Adjust Resolution to modify your screen resolution and other display settings. If you work on a computer with Windows Vista, choose Start, Control Panel, Appearance and Personalization, and then Personalization. Click Display Settings to modify your screen resolution and other display settings.

To change the position and/or customize the Quick Access Toolbar, minimize and/or customize the Ribbon, right-click anywhere within the Ribbon, and then click one of the options displayed on the fly-out menu explained in Table 1.4. The corresponding tab of the SharePoint Designer Options dialog box will display.

If you click the Minimize the Ribbon button, as shown in Figure 1.47, the Ribbon will be minimized. This provides more room for the display of the page. You can also minimize the Ribbon by clicking the down arrow on the top-right near the Help icon. To maximize the Ribbon, click the up arrow on the top right near the Help icon.

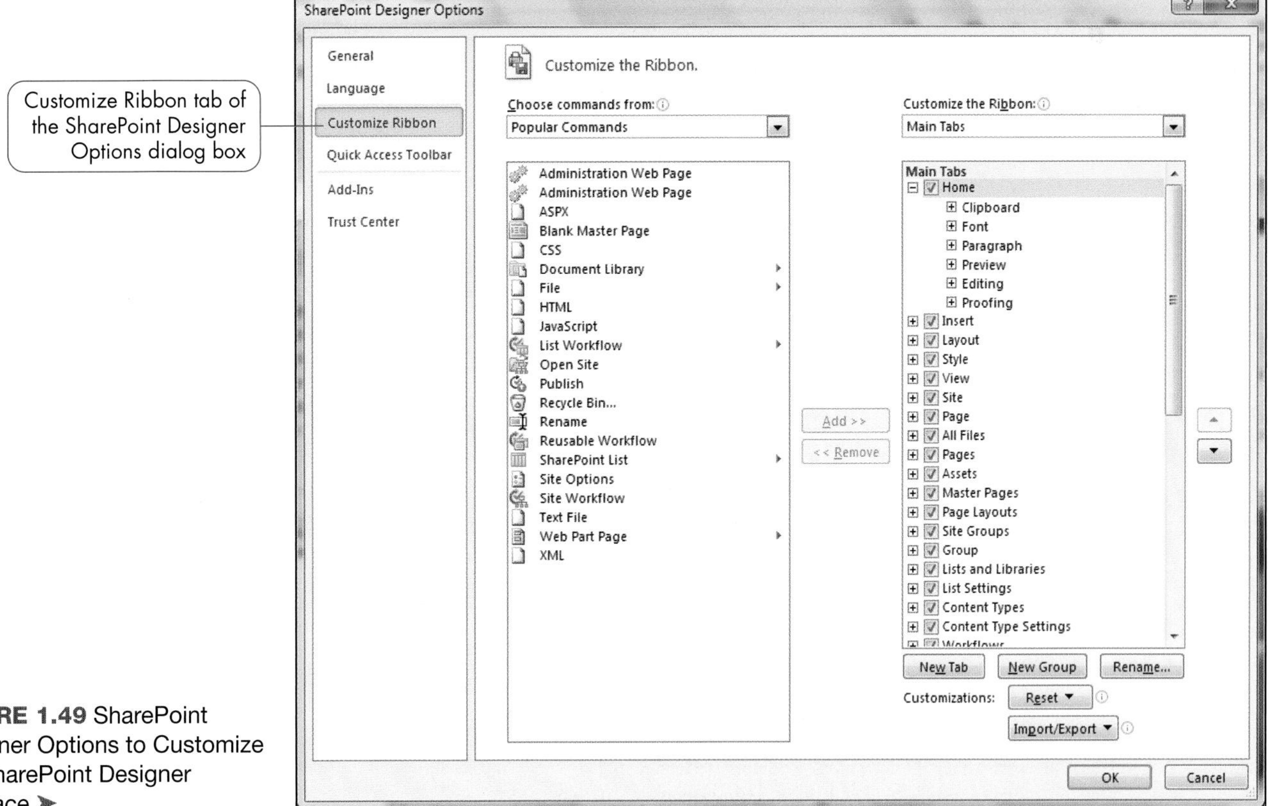

FIGURE 1.49 SharePoint Designer Options to Customize the SharePoint Designer Interface ➤

If you right-click a specific button on the Ribbon, and then select Add to Quick Access Toolbar, that specific button will be added to the Quick Access Toolbar.

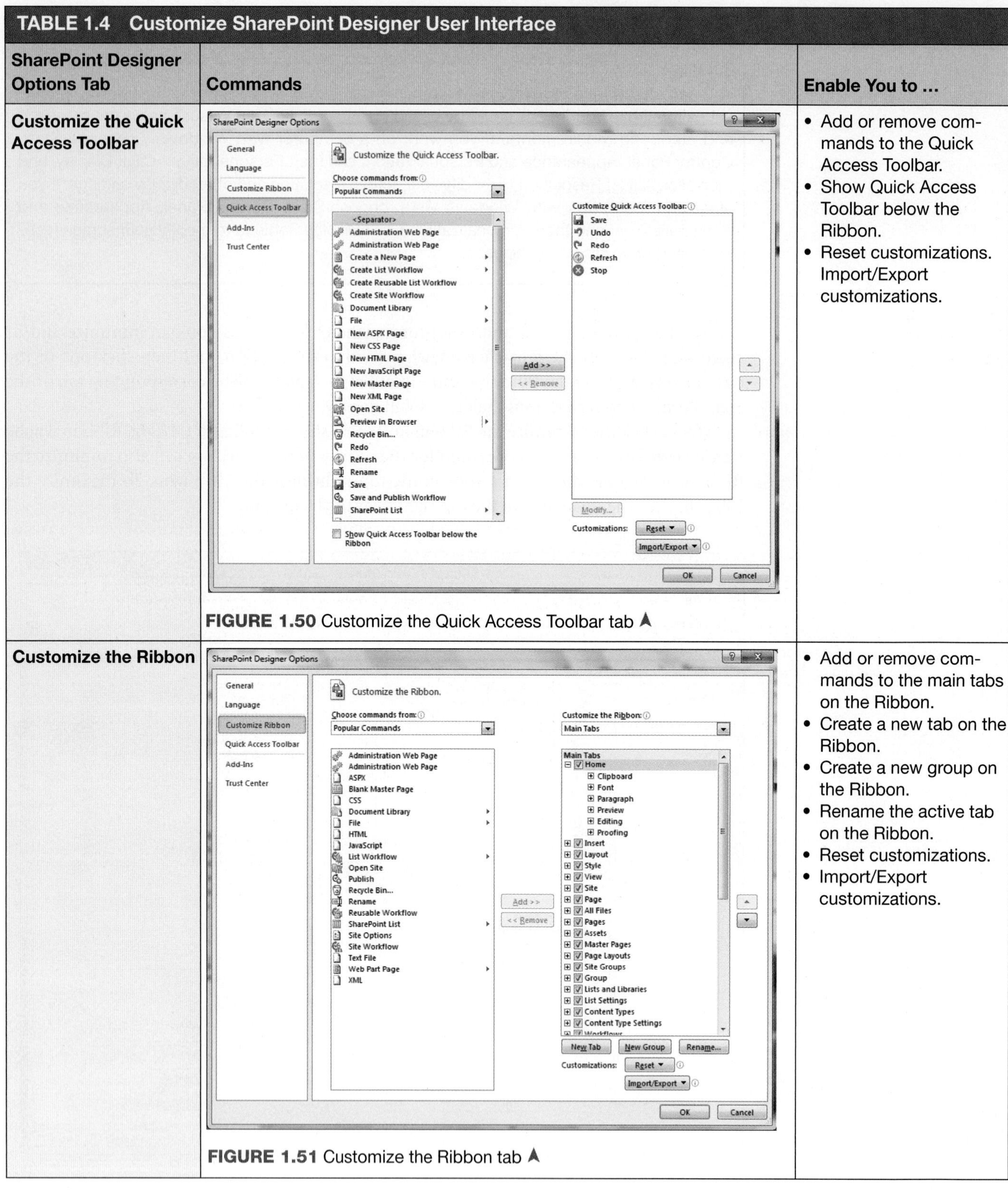

TABLE 1.4 Customize SharePoint Designer User Interface

SharePoint Designer Options Tab	Commands	Enable You to ...
Customize the Quick Access Toolbar	**FIGURE 1.50** Customize the Quick Access Toolbar tab	• Add or remove commands to the Quick Access Toolbar. • Show Quick Access Toolbar below the Ribbon. • Reset customizations. Import/Export customizations.
Customize the Ribbon	**FIGURE 1.51** Customize the Ribbon tab	• Add or remove commands to the main tabs on the Ribbon. • Create a new tab on the Ribbon. • Create a new group on the Ribbon. • Rename the active tab on the Ribbon. • Reset customizations. • Import/Export customizations.

The **Language bar** appears on your desktop automatically when you add text services, such as input languages, speech recognition, handwriting recognition, or Input Method Editors (IME).

When working in Windows 7, the ***Language bar*** appears on your desktop automatically when you add text services, such as input languages, speech recognition, handwriting recognition, or Input Method Editors (IME), a program that enables users to enter East Asian text by converting regular keystrokes into East Asian characters. The Language bar is displayed on the top-right on the Ribbon when you add text services to the computer. The Language bar, shown in Figure 1.52, makes it easy to switch between the text services.

TIP Speech Recognition Features

To use speech recognition features, such as speaking the names of menu commands, toolbar buttons, dialog box commands, and so on, you will first need to set up Windows 7 using the Ease of Access Center. At the time when this manuscript was written, Windows 7 speech recognition tool does not work for SharePoint Designer, but it works with all Microsoft applications that come with Windows 7, such as Microsoft Word and PowerPoint. Ease of Access Center can be found in the Accessories folder of the Start/All Programs menu. To learn more about accessibility features of the Microsoft Office 2010 System see the *Microsoft Accessibility in the 2010 Microsoft Office System* Web site (www.microsoft.com/enable/products/office2010/default.aspx).

If the Language bar is not shown in Windows 7, you will need to add an input language using the Keyboards and Languages tab of the Region and Language dialog box. If the Language bar is not showing in Windows Vista, you will need to check Show the Language bar on the desktop in the Language Bar Settings dialog box within the Regional and Language Options. When you are finished using the Language bar features, you can close it by right-clicking the Language bar to open the shortcut menu, clicking Close, and then clicking OK in the Language Bar dialog box, as shown in Figure 1.52.

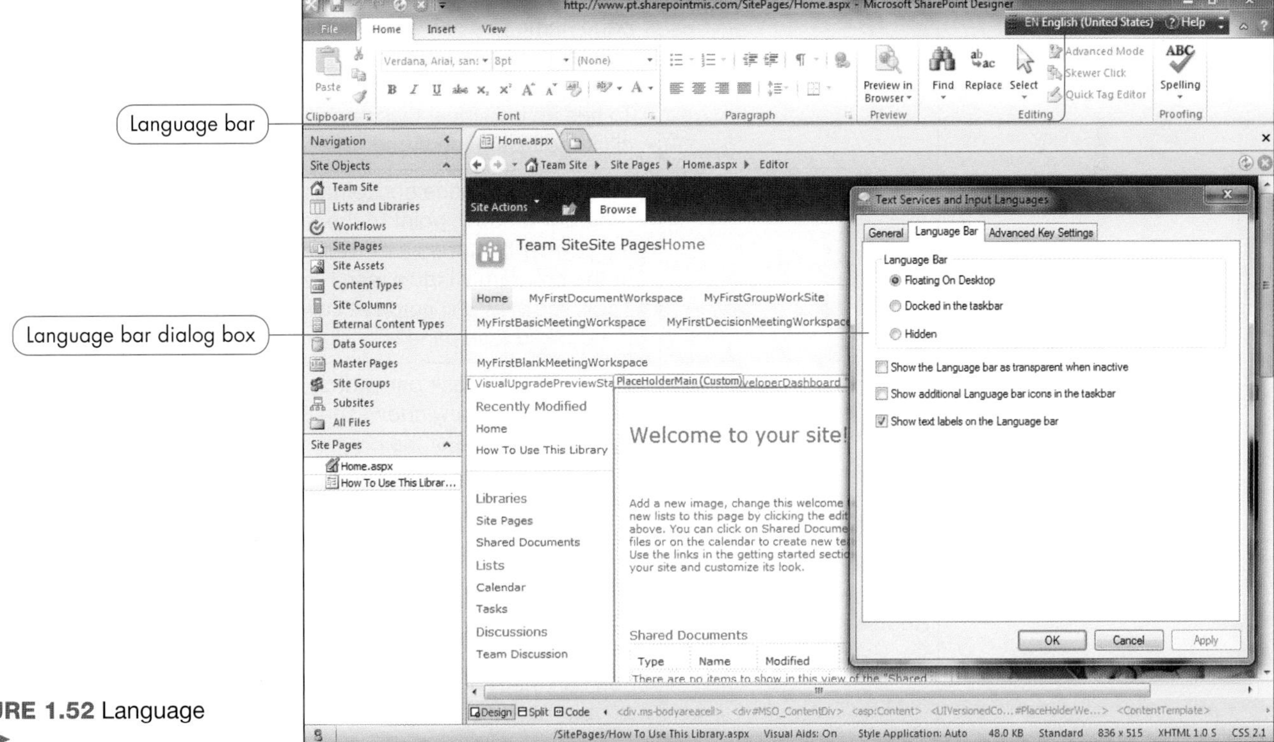

FIGURE 1.52 Language Bar ➤

Work with SharePoint Designer Task Panes

In SharePoint Designer, you can have multiple task panes open simultaneously. To create your custom layout you can open and close a task pane, or you can close a group of task panes.

SharePoint Designer also enables you to merge, dock, float, stack, and resize task panes, as described in Table 1.5. Once you have arranged the task pane in a layout that meets your preferences, SharePoint Designer automatically uses this layout the next time the application is launched. You can restore the default task pane layout at any time by clicking Reset Workspace Layout on the Task Panes menu on the Workspace group of the View tab.

TABLE 1.5 Arrange the SharePoint Designer Task Panes

Task Panes Layout Arrangement Options	Description
Open	• To open a task pane click Task Panes on the View tab, as shown in Figure 1.44. • A task pane always opens in the position in which it was most recently closed. • A check mark next to a task pane name on the Task Panes menu indicates that the task pane is visible. • If a task pane is open but not visible that is because it is merged with other task panes. Therefore, to make it visible you will need to click that task pane on the Task panes menu.
Close	• To close an individual task pane, click the Close (X) button (see Figure 1.53). • To close a group of task panes, click the Close (X) button on the task pane name title bar (see Figure 1.53).
Merge	• To merge a task pane or a group of task panes, point to the task pane name title bar, and when the pointer becomes a move pointer (four-headed arrow), drag the title bar onto another task pane. • To see an individual task pane in a group of merged task panes, click the task pane name tab (see Figure 1.54).
Dock	• To dock a task pane horizontally or vertically to an edge of the program window, point to the task pane name title bar, and when the pointer becomes a move pointer, drag the title bar to an edge of the program window (see Figure 1.55). • The Page view will automatically adjust its size to include the docked task pane.
Float	• You can float a task pane, drag, and place it anywhere, even outside the program window (see Figure 1.56). If you drag the task pane to the edge of the program window, it might become docked. To avoid this, hold down CTRL while you drag.
Stack	• You can stack individual or groups of task panes so they cover the same vertical or horizontal space along the edge of the SharePoint Designer window.
Resize	• You can resize a docked pane when the pointer becomes a split line, as shown in Figure 1.57. • You can resize a floating pane when the pointer becomes a double-headed arrow.

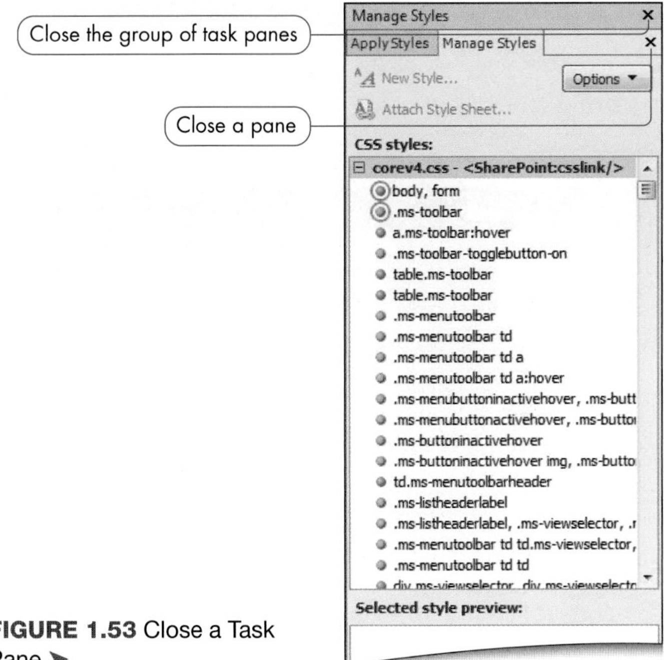

FIGURE 1.53 Close a Task Pane ➤

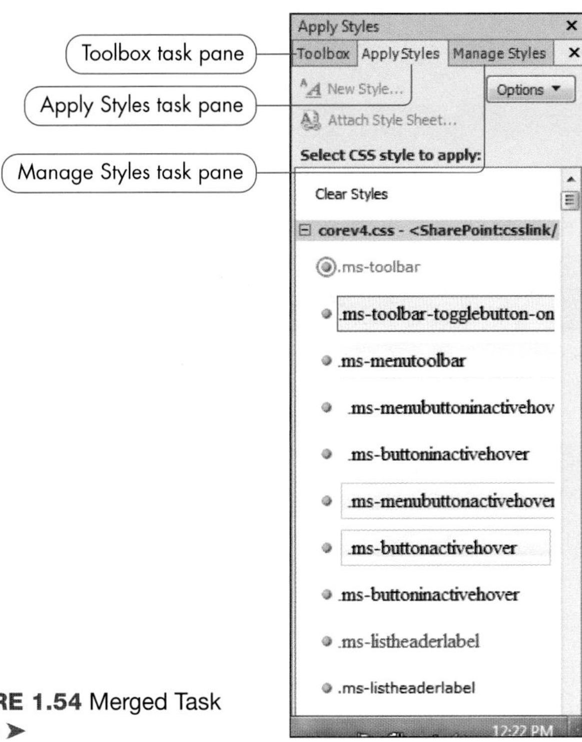

FIGURE 1.54 Merged Task Panes ➤

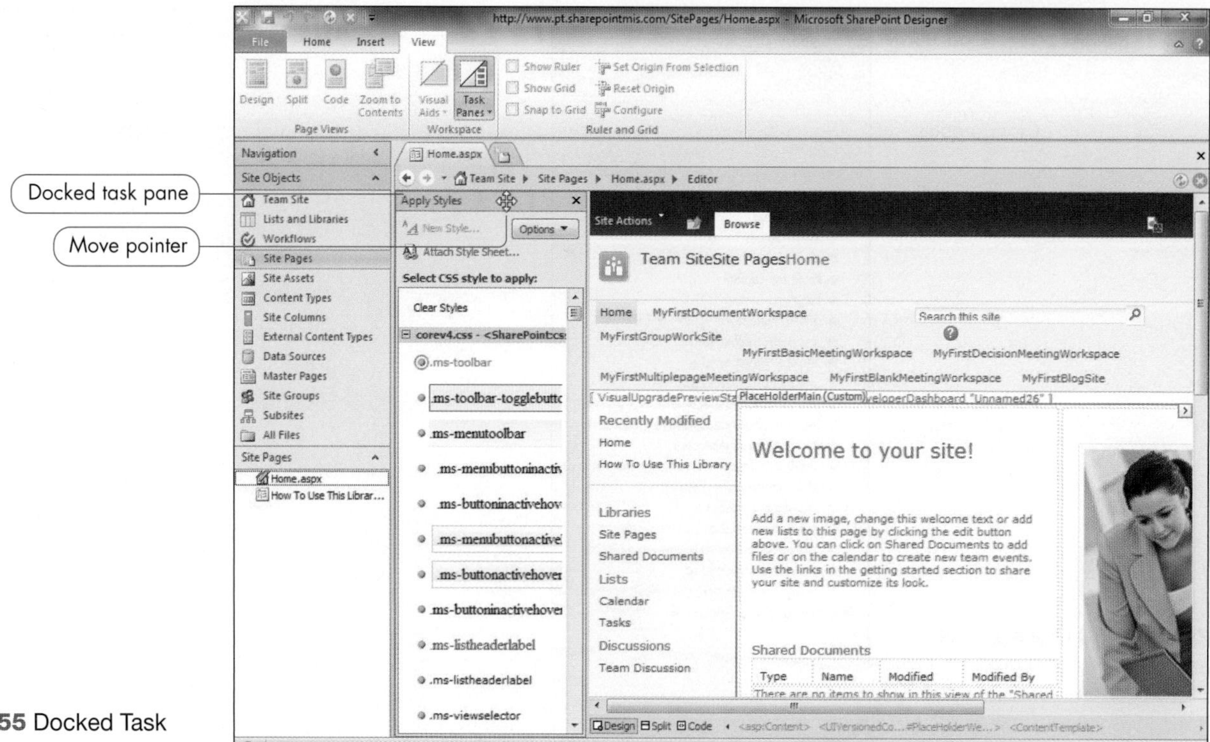

FIGURE 1.55 Docked Task Pane ➤

FIGURE 1.56 Floated Task Pane ➤

FIGURE 1.57 Resizing a Docked Task Pane ➤

Use SharePoint Designer Help

SharePoint Designer, as with all Microsoft Office 2010 applications, includes a wide range of features that assist you in accomplishing anything from a simple task to a complex project. Help files are automatically saved on your computer when you install SharePoint Designer. Microsoft Office Online also provides, via the Microsoft Web site, extensive help and access to up-to-date products, files, and graphics.

To access the SharePoint Designer Help window, as shown in Figure 1.58, you can press F1 (on the majority of keyboards), or click the Help button in the top-right corner of the Ribbon.

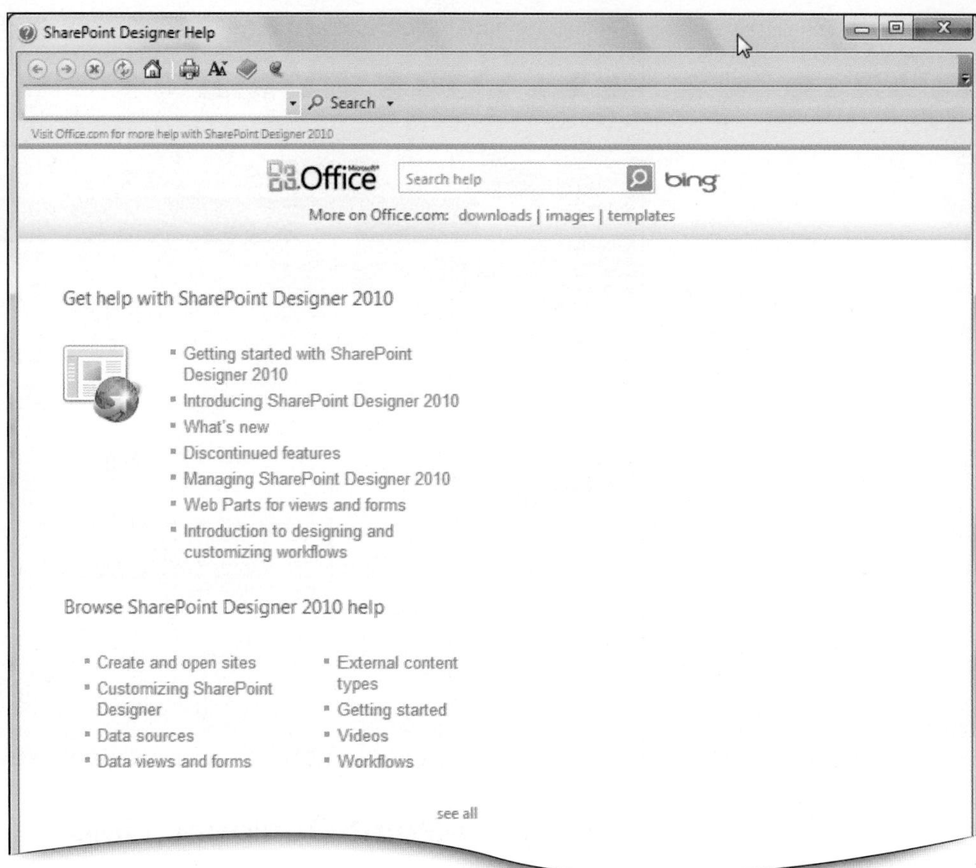

FIGURE 1.58 SharePoint Designer Help Window ➤

Within the SharePoint Designer Help window, you can browse general topics, access more information on Office Online, or, if you know the topic you need help with, you can type a key term in the Search box to display relevant help files. To display a comprehensive table of contents, click the Show Table of Contents button. Once you have located the needed help information, you can print a hard copy by clicking the Print button. Figure 1.59 shows all of these methods.

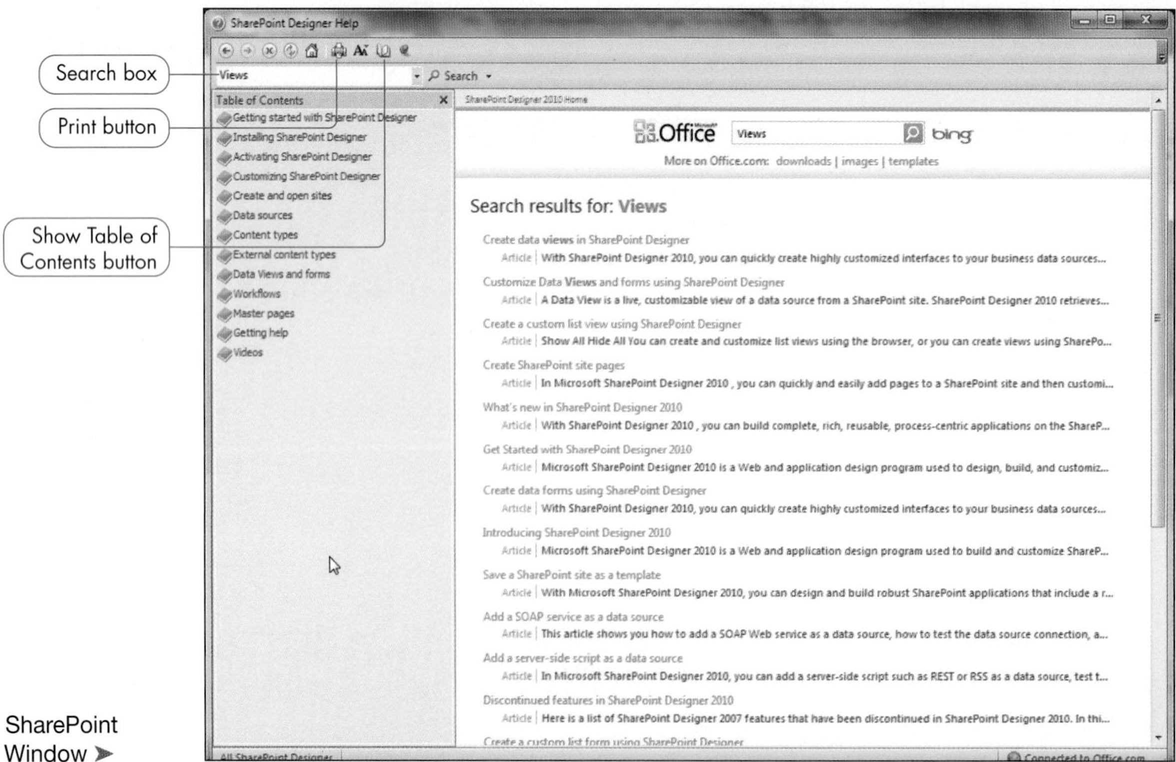

FIGURE 1.59 SharePoint Designer Help Window ➤

A **ScreenTip** displays small boxes with descriptive helpful text when you point to a command or control.

As you work with a dialog box, you might need help with some of the numerous options contained in it. For example, if you open the Picture Properties dialog box and want help with the Alternate Text, click the Help button on the title bar of the dialog box to display specific help, as shown in Figure 1.60.

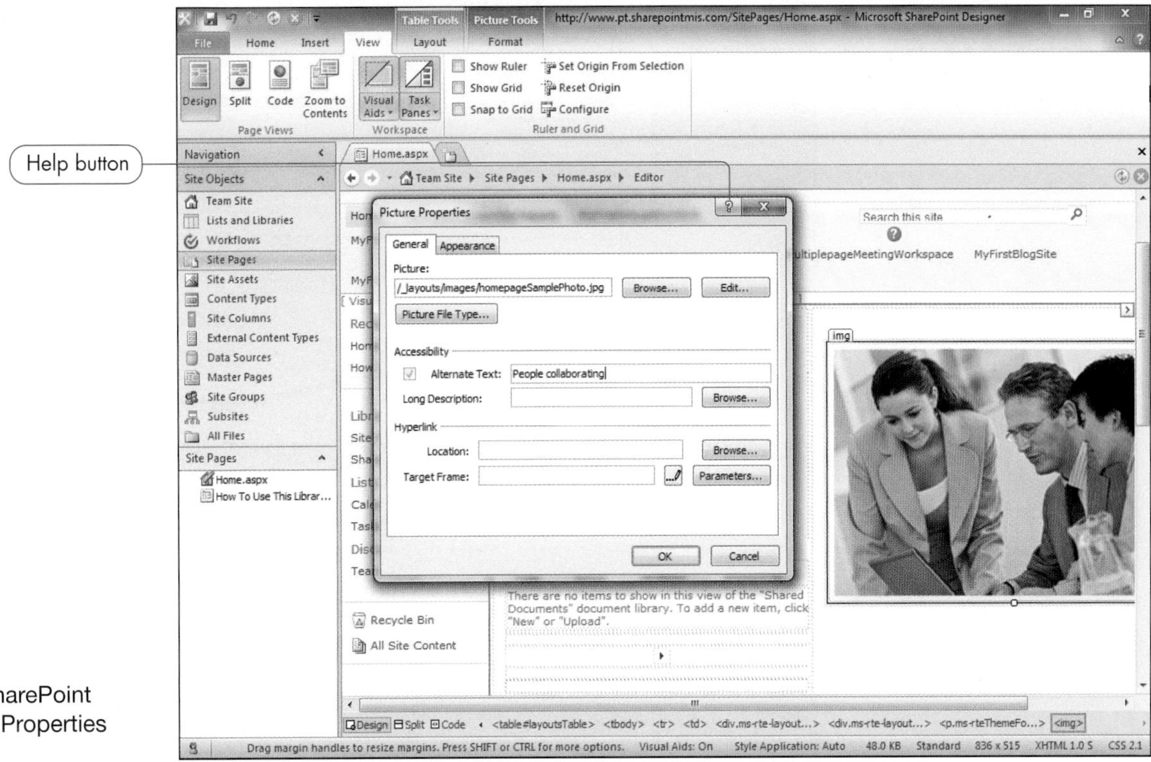

FIGURE 1.60 SharePoint Designer Picture Properties Dialog Box ➤

ScreenTips and Enhanced ScreenTips are very useful features of the SharePoint Designer UI.

ScreenTips and Enhanced ScreenTips are very useful features of the SharePoint Designer UI. ***ScreenTips***, shown in Figure 1.61, display small boxes with descriptive, helpful text when you point to a command or control. ***Enhanced ScreenTips***, shown in Figure 1.62, display additional descriptive text and can have a link to a Help topic. You can show or hide ScreenTips on the File tab. Click the Options tab under Help, and then click General on the General tab if necessary. Select the ScreenTip style under the User interface options. The options include displaying both ScreenTips and Enhanced ScreenTips, displaying only ScreenTips, or not displaying ScreenTips or Enhanced ScreenTips.

An **Enhanced ScreenTip** displays additional descriptive text and can have a link to a Help topic.

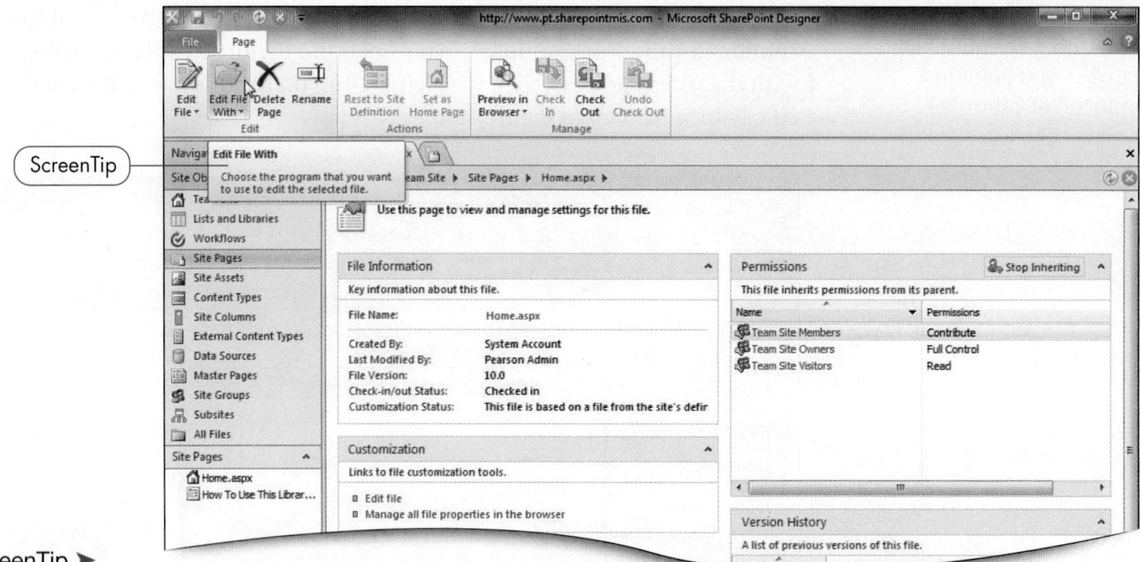

FIGURE 1.61 ScreenTip ➤

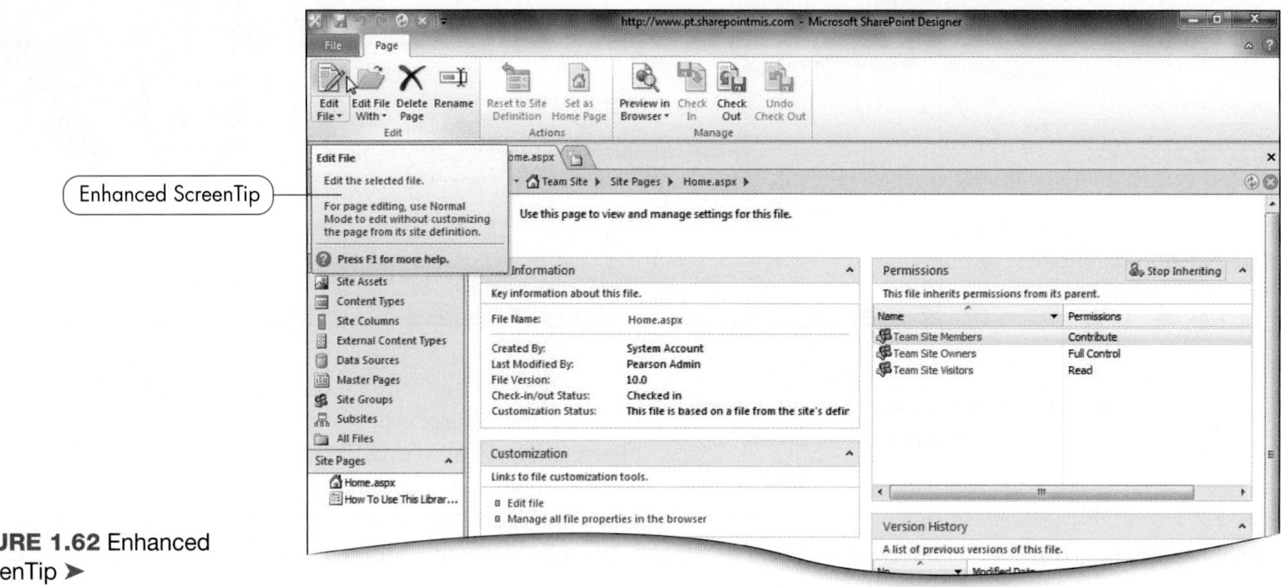

FIGURE 1.62 Enhanced ScreenTip ➤

2 Introduction to SharePoint Designer

Stephanie is eager to get acquainted with the SharePoint Designer features and tools. Using your SharePoint collection you start exploring and learning how you can take advantage of all the SharePoint Designer built-in features and tools.

Skills covered: Open SharePoint Designer • Explore the SharePoint Designer UI • Customize the SharePoint Designer UI • Work with SharePoint Designer Task Panes • Use SharePoint Designer Help

STEP 1 OPEN SHAREPOINT DESIGNER

Before you can start exploring the SharePoint Designer capabilities, you must learn how you can log on, using SharePoint Designer Backstage view, to the SharePoint Collection created for you. Refer to Figure 1.63 as you complete Step 1.

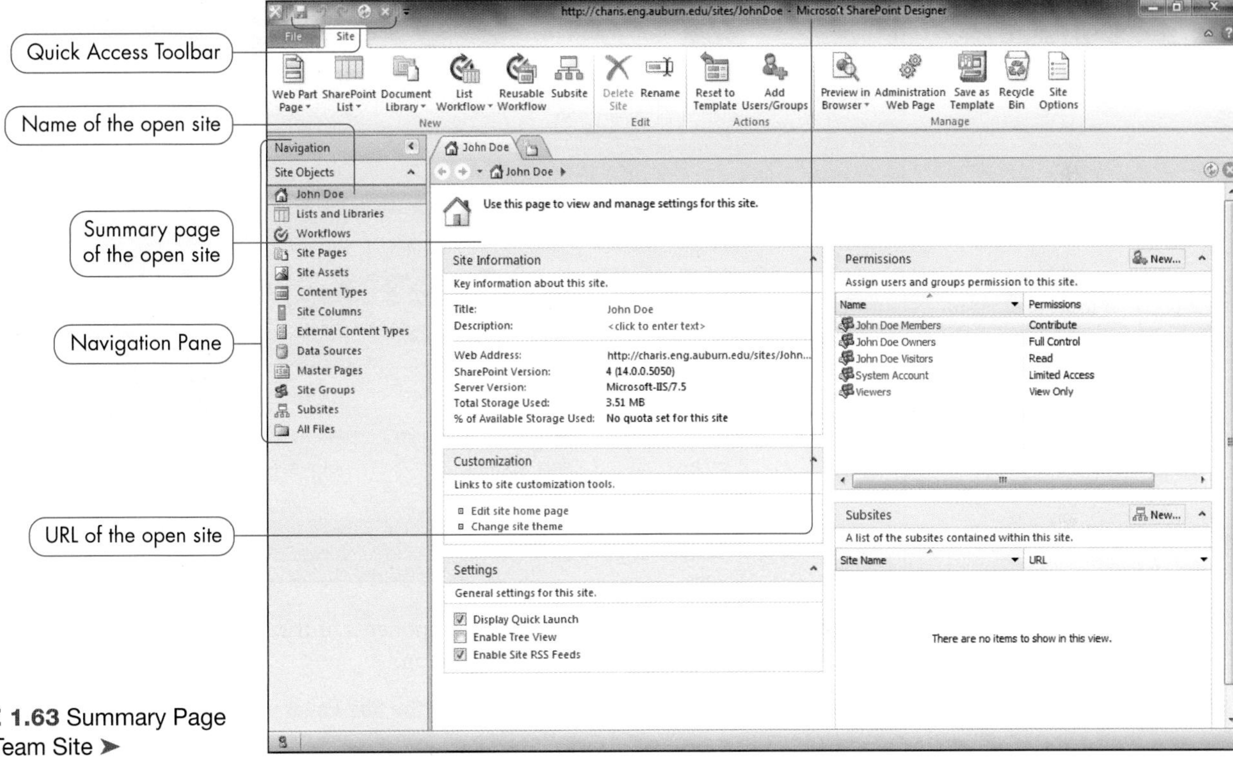

FIGURE 1.63 Summary Page of your Team Site ➤

a. Click **Start** to display the Start menu. Click **All Programs**, click **SharePoint**, and then click **SharePoint Designer** to open the program.

   The SharePoint Designer Backstage view displays.

b. Click **Open Site** to display the Open Site dialog box. Type the URL of your top-level site in the **Site name box**, and then click **Open**.

> **TROUBLESHOOTING:** Check with your instructor for the URL of your top-level site, user name, and password.

c. Enter the user name and password provided by your instructor.

> **TROUBLESHOOTING:** It might take a few seconds to access your top-level site on your Internet connection.

If you logged in correctly, the Site tab screen of the top-level site now displays. Your screen will look similar to Figure 1.63.

STEP 2 EXPLORE THE SHAREPOINT DESIGNER UI

In order to fully take advantage of the powerful SharePoint Designer UI, you will first need to identify the location of the four main components of the SharePoint Designer UI, and the three SharePoint Designer Web page views. Refer to Figure 1.64 as you complete Step 2.

FIGURE 1.64 SharePoint Designer UI ➤

a. Identify the location of the four main components of the SharePoint Designer UI: the Quick Access Toolbar, Navigation Pane, and Ribbon.

b. Double-click the **Site Pages link** to display the Site Pages gallery page.

   You should now see all pages included in the top-level site of your collection.

c. Click **home.aspx** on the Site Pages gallery page to display its related Summary page. Explore all the displayed info associated with the home.aspx page.

d. Click the **Edit File arrow** in the Edit group on the Ribbon, and then select **Edit File in Normal Mode**. Observe the Ribbon groups.

e. Click the **Back button** on the Navigation bar, click the **Edit File arrow** on the Edit group, and then select **Edit File in Advanced Mode**. Observe the enhanced Ribbon groups.

f. Click the **View tab** on the Ribbon. Click the the **Task Panes arrow** in the Workspace group on the Ribbon and explore the five categories of task panes (see Figure 1.64).

g. Click **Split**, and then click **Code** in the Page Views group of the View tab and explore the three Web page Views as described in Table 1.3.

STEP 3 CUSTOMIZE THE SHAREPOINT DESIGNER UI

Although the SharePoint Designer UI is user-friendly, you want to learn how you can customize it in order to better assist you. You will explore the SharePoint Designer UI customizing options using the SharePoint Collection created for you. Refer to Figure 1.65 as you complete Step 3.

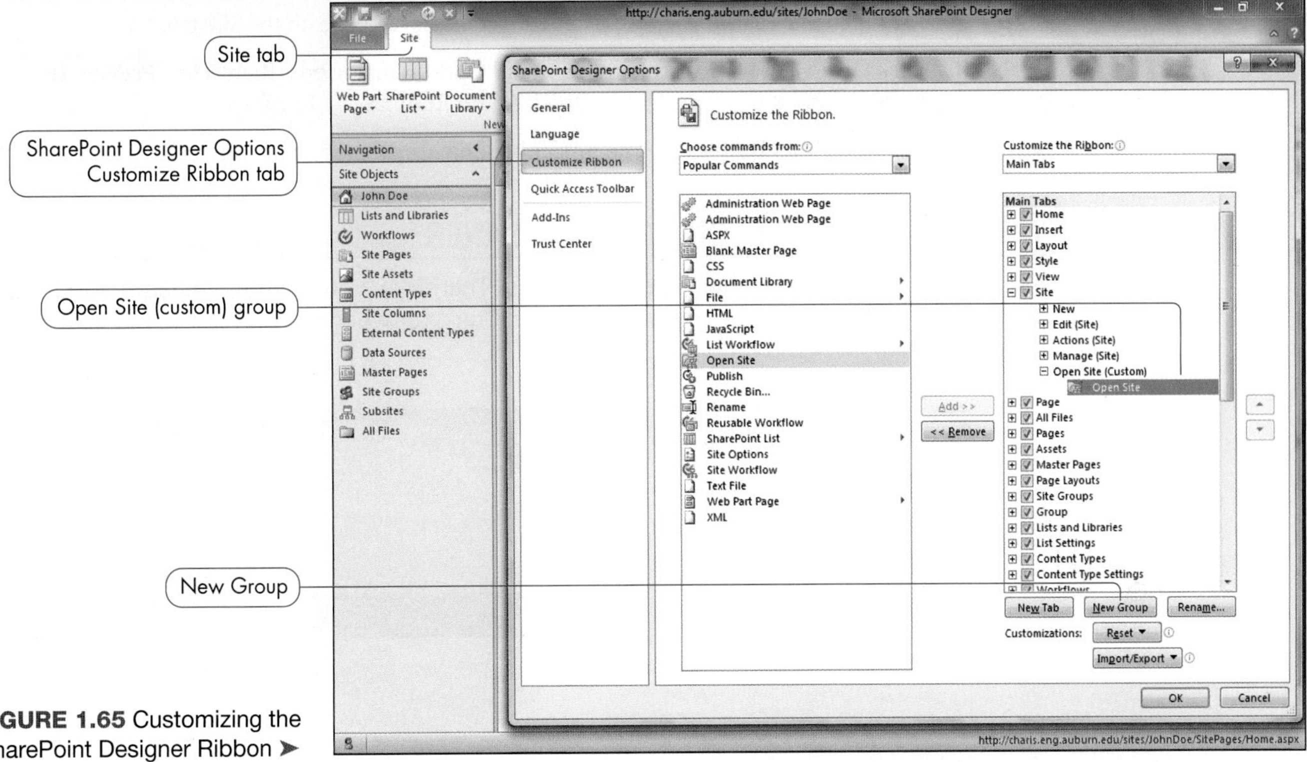

FIGURE 1.65 Customizing the SharePoint Designer Ribbon ➤

a. Click the site name in the Navigation Pane, click the **Site tab**, right-click **Preview in Browser**, and then select **Add to Quick Access Toolbar**.

   A second Preview in Browser should now show on the Quick Access Toolbar.

b. Right-click anywhere on the Ribbon, and then select **Customize Quick Access Toolbar**.

   The SharePoint Designer Options dialog box should now display.

c. Click **Preview in Browser** under the Customize Quick Access Toolbar, click **Remove**, and then click **OK** to close the SharePoint Designer Options dialog box. Repeat step 5 for the second Preview in Browser.

   Preview in Browser should no longer show on the Quick Access Toolbar.

d. Right-click anywhere on the Site tab on the Ribbon, and then select **Customize the Ribbon**.

   The Customize Ribbon tab of the SharePoint Designer Options dialog box should now display.

e. Click **Open Site** under *Choose commands from*, and then click **New Group**.

   A New Group (Custom) should now display beneath the Site tab.

f. Click **Rename**, type **Open Site** in the **Display name box**, and then click **OK**.

g. Click **Open Site** under *Choose commands from*, and then click **Add**.

   The Open Site command should now display beneath the Open Site (Custom) group, as shown in Figure 1.65.

h. Click **OK** to close the SharePoint Designer Options dialog box.

   The Open Site group should now be showing on the Site tab on the Ribbon.

i. Right-click anywhere on the Site tab on the Ribbon, and then select **Customize the Ribbon.**

   The Customize Ribbon tab of the SharePoint Designer Options dialog box should now display.

j. Click the **Open Site (Custom)** group in the *Customize the Ribbon* section, click **Reset**, and then select the **Reset only selected Ribbon tab**.

   The Open Site (Custom) group is no longer displayed beneath the Site tab.

k. Click **OK** to close the SharePoint Designer Options dialog box. Right-click **Preview in Browser**, and then select **Add to Quick Access Toolbar.**

   The Open Site group should no longer be showing on the Site tab on the Ribbon.

STEP 4 WORK WITH SHAREPOINT DESIGNER TASK PANES

Task panes are very complex SharePoint Designer tools. Therefore, you will need to learn about how you can show and close a Task pane on the SharePoint Designer workspace. Refer to Figure 1.66 as you complete Step 4.

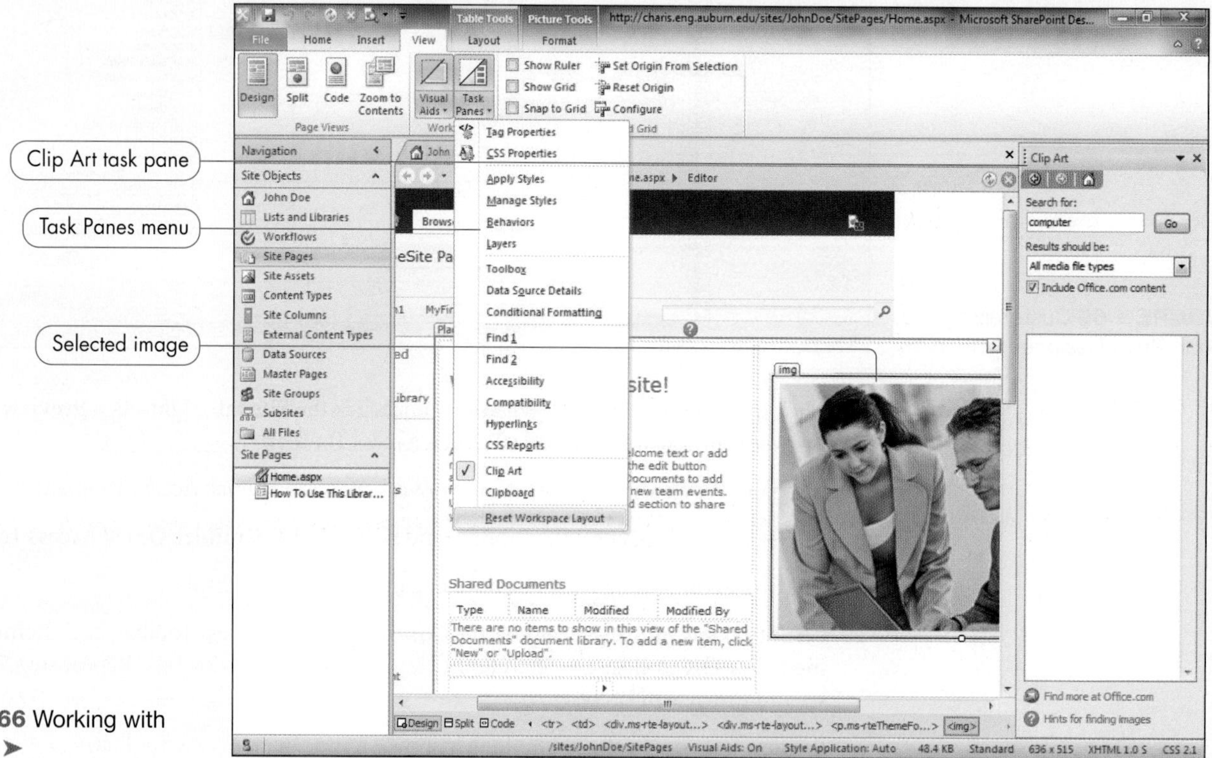

FIGURE 1.66 Working with Task Panes ➤

a. Click the **Edit site home page link** in the *Customization* section of the Site settings page.

   The home page of the site should now display in Design view.

b. Click the image included in the *Content* section of the home page. Click the **View tab** to display the View tab on the Ribbon. Click **Task Pane arrow** in the Workspace group on the Ribbon, and then select **Clip Art.**

   The Clip Art task pane should now display on the SharePoint Designer workspace.

c. Click **Task Pane arrow** in the Workspace group on the Ribbon, and then select **Reset Workspace Layout.**

   The Clip Art task pane should no longer display, and the SharePoint Designer default workspace should display.

STEP 5 USE SHAREPOINT DESIGNER HELP

From beginner to advanced level, all SharePoint Designer users will need at some point in time to take advantage of the built-in Help features. You will learn how to use SharePoint Designer Help features. Refer to Figure 1.67 as you complete Step 5.

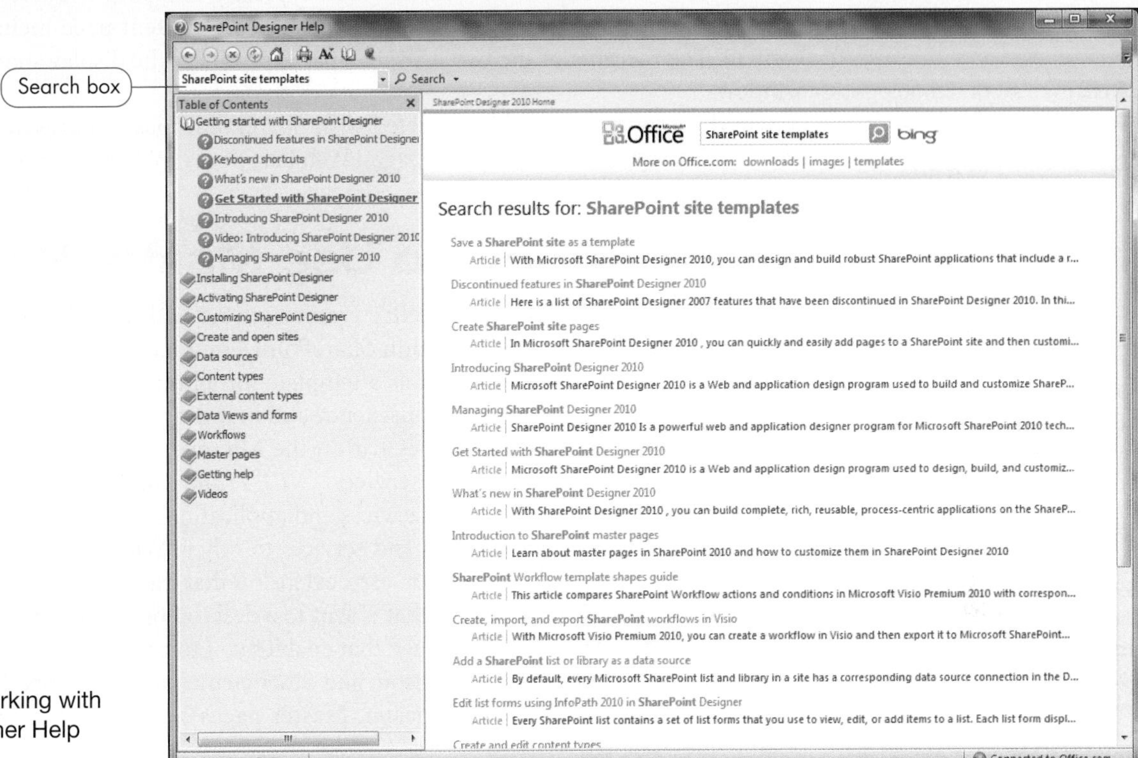

FIGURE 1.67 Working with SharePoint Designer Help Tools ➤

a. Click the **Site name** in the Navigation Pane to display the Site tab on the Ribbon. Press **F1** to display the SharePoint Designer Help window, including content related with Get Started with SharePoint Designer.

b. Scroll down, and then click the **Introducing SharePoint Designer 2010 link** in the WHERE TO GO column of the displayed table.

   Content related to Introducing SharePoint Designer 2010 should now display.

c. Type **SharePoint site templates** in the **Search box**, and then click **Search**.

   A page with the title *Search results for: SharePoint site Templates* should now display.

d. Click the **Close (X) button** in the top-right corner of the SharePoint Designer Help window to close the window.

e. Close the top-level site, and then exit SharePoint Designer.

Introduction to SharePoint Pages

Every time you view a page on a SharePoint site, you are actually viewing two ASP.NET pages: a master page and a content page.

Every time you view a page on a SharePoint site, you are actually viewing two ASP.NET pages: a master page and a content page. The master page provides the common layout and navigation elements (which typically make up the left, top, and bottom portions of the page). The content page includes page-specific content. The merging of the two ASP.NET pages produces the display shown in the browser window.

ASP.NET is a set of technologies within the Microsoft .NET Framework for building Web applications and XML Web services.

In this section, you will get started with SharePoint master pages and learn about the three core categories of SharePoint pages: Web Part pages, Wiki pages, and Publishing pages.

.NET Framework is a platform for building, deploying, and running XML Web services and applications.

An **XML Web service** is a module of application logic providing data and services to other Web applications.

An **ASP.NET page** is a dynamic web page saved with an .aspx extension that executes on the server and generates markup (such as HTML, or XML) that is sent to a desktop or mobile browser.

A **master page** is an ASP.NET page that enables you to create consistent elements within a site.

Learning How to Use Master Pages

SharePoint Foundation is built on .NET Framework 3.5 and ASP.NET 3.5. Master pages are a feature of ASP.NET included within SharePoint Foundation for designing the layout of your site. Master pages can be used as a template for all other pages within the site, and in other SharePoint sites, to provide consistency and branding to the sites.

ASP.NET is a set of technologies within the Microsoft .NET Framework for building Web applications and XML Web services. ***.NET Framework*** is a platform for building, deploying, and running XML Web services and applications. ***XML Web services*** are modules of application logic providing data and services to other Web applications. ***ASP.NET pages*** are dynamic Web pages saved with an .aspx extension that execute on the server and generate markup (such as HTML, or XML) that is sent to a desktop or mobile browser.

A ***master page*** is an ASP.NET page that enables you to create consistent elements within a site. The layout, font styles, navigation, and other elements are specified in the master page file. The file name extension is .master. Master pages can only be viewed and edited in SharePoint Designer.

SharePoint site designers leverage master pages by using them to build sets of pages that have the same structure and layout. Changes made to a master page are reproduced in all of the pages associated with that master page. This makes it a very efficient way to update pages. CSS, linked or embedded in master pages, control the site elements such as color schemes, font styles, and backgrounds. If an element requires adjusting, CSS can be changed and the changes would flow through the master page and into the entire site.

Changes made to a master page are reproduced in all of the pages associated with that master page.

Another advantage of master pages is that graphic elements (such as logos) and text (such as copyright notices or contact information) can be placed so that they appear on all pages. These static elements become part of every site page based on the master page. In order to place content that varies onto the pages, content placeholders are added to the master page, as shown in Figure 1.68. ***Content placeholders*** delineate areas where the content of a page will appear.

A **content placeholder** delineates areas where the content of a page will appear.

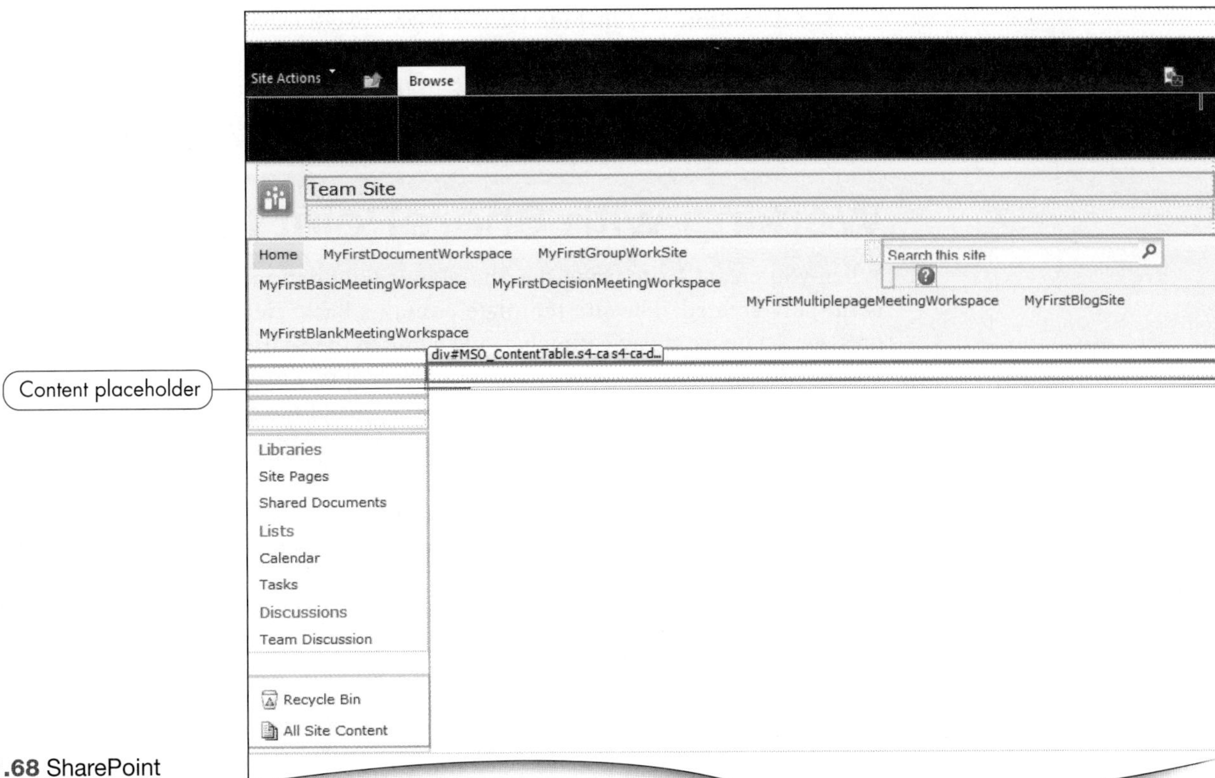

FIGURE 1.68 SharePoint Foundation v.4 Master ➤

SharePoint contains four master pages to use as beginning points for your own customizations. The primary master page (named v4.master) is used for building content and administration pages, and contains all of the SharePoint tools on the Ribbon. Team site pages, list and library pages, and site settings pages can all be based on this master page. The minimal master page (named minimal.master) is a scaled-back version of the primary master page. It can be used to create embedded elements on a page, such as the search results page, and for full-screen functionality. The 2007 default master page (named default.master) is available to support SharePoint sites that have not yet been upgraded to SharePoint 2010. The publishing master (named nightandday.master) is used for pages on a SharePoint Server publishing-enabled site. This type of site supports frequent news updates or press releases to intranets, extranets, and the Web.

TIP Starter Master Page

A starter master page can be downloaded (http://code.msdn.microsoft.com/odcSP14StarterMaster/Release/ProjectReleases.aspx?ReleaseId=3861) from the Microsoft Developer Network (MSDN). This master page contains the minimum elements to render a page in SharePoint and serves as a good starting point for designing a new master page.

SharePoint Foundation uses v4.master ... as its primary master page; therefore, all content pages use v4.master.

SharePoint Foundation uses v4.master, as shown in Figure 1.68, as its primary master page; therefore, all content pages are based on the v4.master. This means that all of the pages in all of the sites have the same layout and visual elements. For instance, the content placeholders will be shown in the same place on every page of every site. When elements change on a master page, the edited master is stored in a content database.

Site definition files include master pages, pages used by libraries to create new documents, and CSS files. These files are stored on the server. SharePoint Designer enables you to customize and later reset all these pages to their original site definitions if you change your mind and want to begin with the original pages.

Working with SharePoint Pages

When you create a site using the SharePoint Foundation site template, only a home page is initially created. The site template contains basic elements such as a welcoming text message, an image, a navigation bar, and a link to the Shared Documents library, as shown in Figure 1.48, and other figures throughout the chapter. If you are using SharePoint Server site templates, more pages are initially available as part of the created site.

Additional pages are added to sites and customized to fit the needs of the users. Three types of pages can be added to SharePoint sites. SharePoint allows you to expand the sites by creating additional pages. These pages can then be customized to display information. Three types of pages are available to add to your sites: Web Part page, Wiki page, and Publishing page.

Work with Web Part Pages

A **Web Part page** is a Web page that contains one or more Web Parts.

The simplest site template available is the Web Part page. ***Web Part pages***, shown in Figure 1.69, are Web pages that contain one or more Web Parts. Web Parts are components that provide a function, such as a video player, a database search function, or a form that collects information from the user. Web Parts are placed within Web Part zones on the Web page. Most often, you will use the Web Part page for information or media content Web pages. The Quick Launch navigation area is not displayed on Web Part pages, giving you more space to place Web Parts on the page. It is useful to know that Web Parts can be used on other types of pages, too. We will discuss Web Part pages and Web Parts in more detail in Chapters 2 and 3.

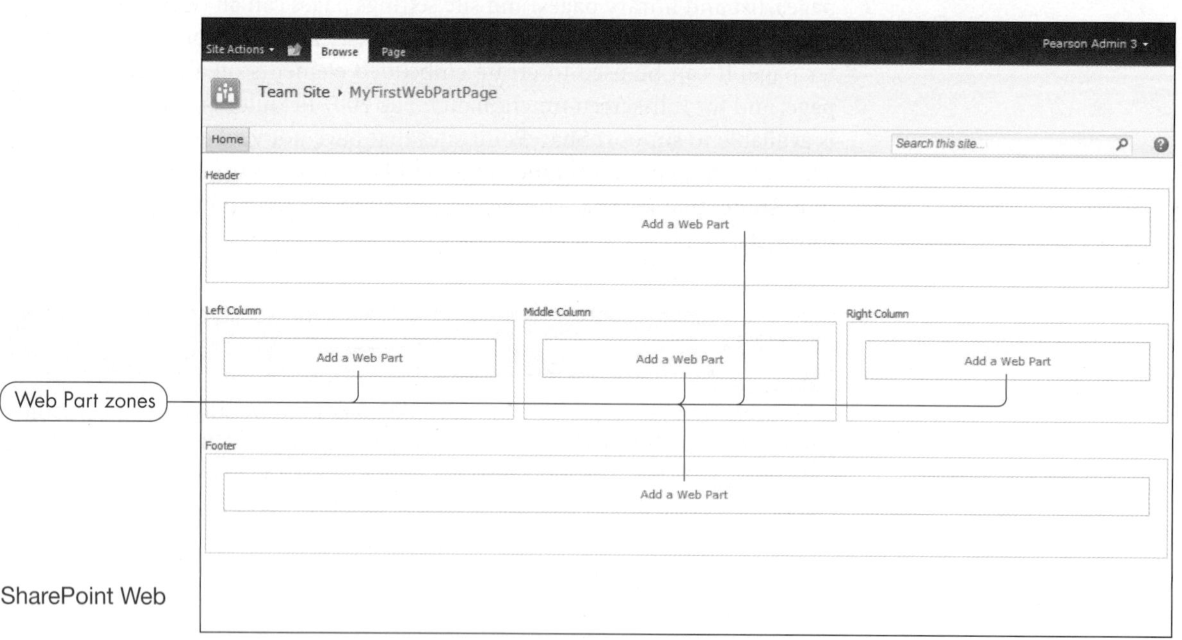

FIGURE 1.69 SharePoint Web Part Page ➤

Work with Wiki Pages

A **Wiki page** is the most flexible page type, made up of a large content area that allows for the editing of rich text, including formatting, tables, and most importantly, linking to other wiki pages.

"Wiki" is the Hawaiian word for "quick" and it is used to describe sites that make content available immediately. Wiki pages are built on a site template type new to SharePoint.

Wiki pages are the most flexible page type, made up of a large content area that allows for the editing of rich text, including formatting, tables, media, links, and Web Parts, in a very easy, customizable format. An important feature is the ability to link to other Wiki

A **Wiki page library** is a customized and specialized document library that enables users to collaborate on the development of shared documents.

pages. Wiki pages, as shown in Figure 1.70, do not restrict you on placing Web Parts in Web Part zones such as on a Web Part page. ***Wiki page libraries*** are customized and specialized document libraries that enable users to collaborate on the development of shared documents. Wiki page libraries only contain Wiki pages.

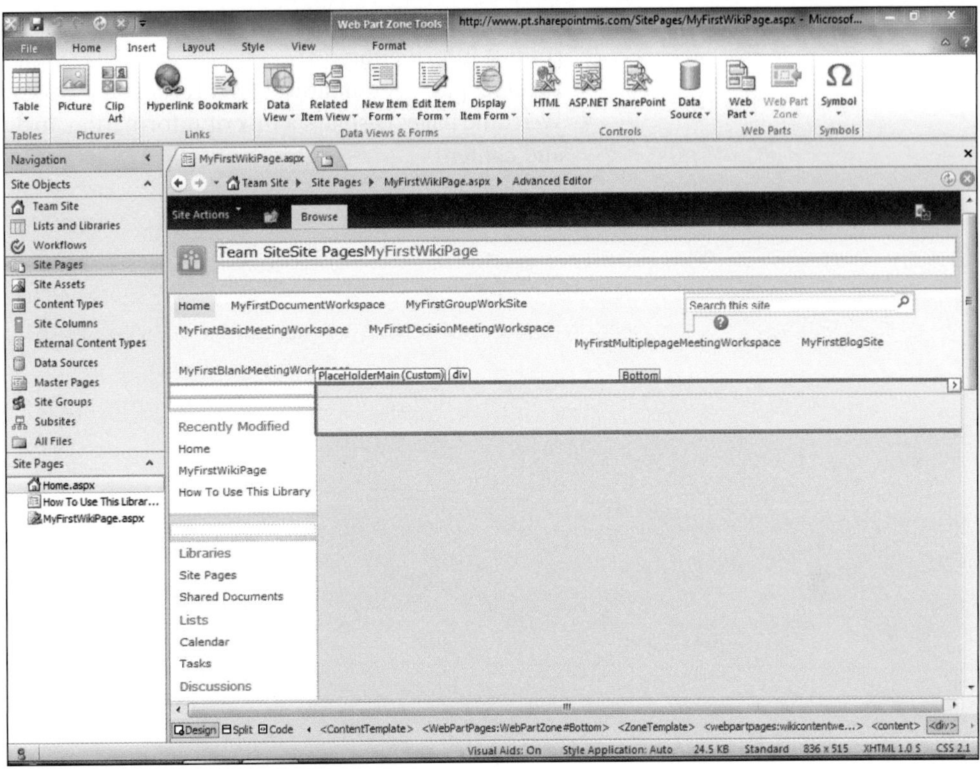

FIGURE 1.70 Wiki Page ➤

In SharePoint sites, by default, Wiki pages are everywhere. On many new SharePoint sites you will create, the home page is now a Wiki page. On Team Sites, all new pages that you create are Wiki pages by default. All Wiki pages are stored in the Site Pages library, which is a Wiki page library.

Other site templates support the creation of one or more Wiki page libraries. If you want to share information in a collaborative way that allows others to add content, and you do not require complete ownership of the page, use a Wiki page from a Wiki library in your SharePoint site.

TIP Working with Wiki Page Libraries

In the Wiki page library, the first page shown is the home page. Using links on the home page, users can navigate to other pages. A navigational bar is on the left side of the page that can be used to access additional pages in the Wiki page library. You can also click the Page tab, and then click View All Pages in the Page Library group to see the pages in the Wiki library.

Work with Publishing Pages

The **Publishing page** type enables the creation and update of pages used to distribute information, such as news releases, in various display formats.

The ***Publishing page*** type, available only on SharePoint Server 2010, enables the creation and update of pages used to distribute information, such as news releases, in various display formats. The site or page designer creates the layout specifying where the content will be displayed on the page by utilizing content types. People who have the content and the proper permissions can publish the pages using a browser. Five content types are available for a Publishing page:

- Article page: Includes areas for published article information, such as a byline, date, and content
- Enterprise Wiki page: Used in the Enterprise Wiki site template; provides content, categorization, and ratings
- Project page: Used in the Enterprise Wiki site template; provides task status and contact information
- Redirect page: Automatically redirects users to a configurable Web page
- Welcome page: Displays a mix of information, including images, links, Web Parts, and content

3 Introduction to SharePoint Pages

Stephanie is eager to get acquainted with all categories of pages built in SharePoint Foundation. Using your SharePoint collection, you can start exploring these pages and their attached master templates using SharePoint Foundation UI and SharePoint Designer UI.

Skills covered: Explore a Wiki Page with the SharePoint Foundation Ribbon • Explore a Web Part Page with SharePoint Designer UI • Explore the v4.master Master Page in SharePoint Designer

STEP 1 EXPLORE A WIKI PAGE WITH THE SHAREPOINT FOUNDATION RIBBON

Before you can start to create SharePoint pages, you need to explore the SharePoint category of pages, using the SharePoint Foundation Ribbon and SharePoint Designer UI along with the SharePoint Collection created for you. Refer to Figure 1.71 as you complete Step 1.

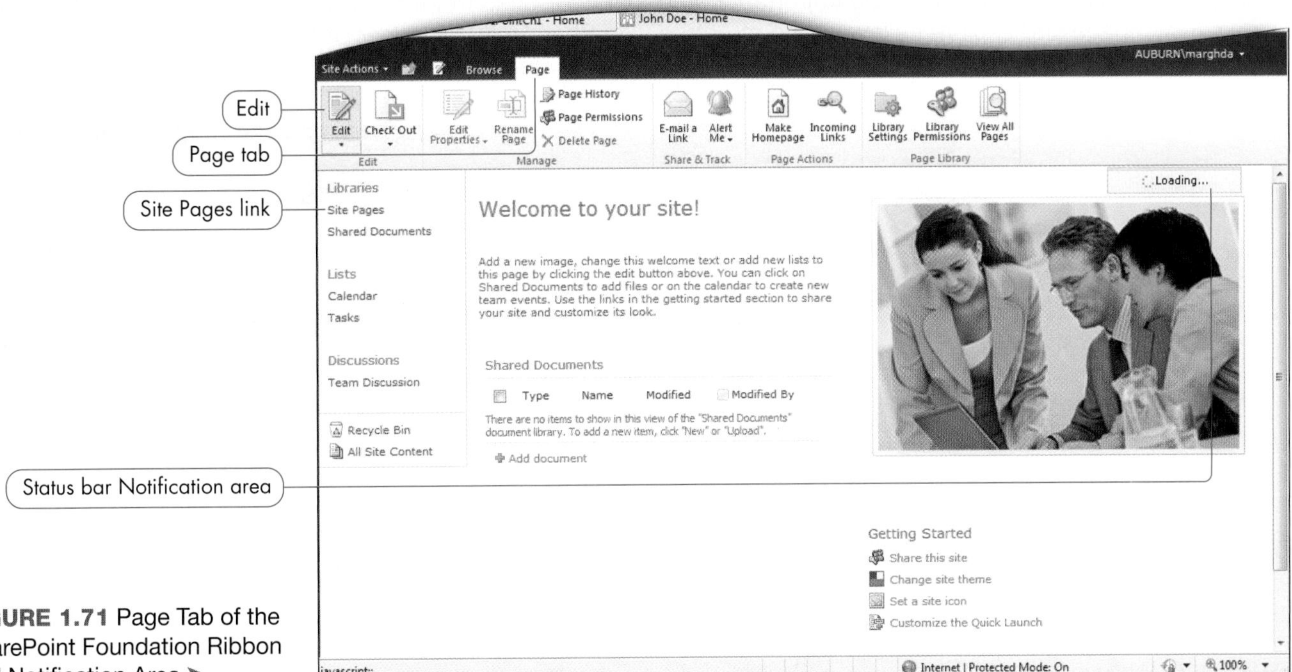

FIGURE 1.71 Page Tab of the SharePoint Foundation Ribbon and Notification Area ➤

a. Click **Start** to display the Start menu. Click **All Programs**, and then double-click **Internet Explorer** to open the program.

b. Go to the top-level site provided by your instructor, which will be in the format of http://pt.sharepointmis.com/SitePages/*yourname*.

> **TROUBLESHOOTING:** Check with your instructor for the URL of your top-level site, user name, and password.

c. Enter the user name and password provided by your instructor.

> **TROUBLESHOOTING:** It might take a few seconds to access your top-level site on your Internet connection.

If you logged in correctly, the home page of the top-level site now displays in Internet Explorer. Your screen will look similar to Figure 1.31 from Hands-On Exercise 1.

d. Click the **Site Pages link** in the Quick Launch area.

The *Content* section should now display the two default Wiki pages: Home and How to Use This Library.

e. Click the **Home link**.

The home page of the top-level site is displayed.

f. Click the **Page tab** to display the Page tab on the Ribbon.

g. Click **Edit** in the Edit group of the Page tab.

The Notification area should appear on the right side of the page underneath the Ribbon, showing the text *Loading ...* for as long as the page is loaded into the SharePoint Foundation Editor, as shown in Figure 1.71. A new Editing Tools tab will show now.

h. Explore the groups and commands of the Editing Tools tab.

i. Click the **Browse tab**.

STEP 2 EXPLORE A WEB PART PAGE WITH SHAREPOINT DESIGNER UI

Web Part pages are very important components of SharePoint sites. You will create a new Web Part page and explore its layout and structure with SharePoint Designer UI tools and the top-site of your SharePoint Collection. Refer to Figure 1.72 as you complete Step 2.

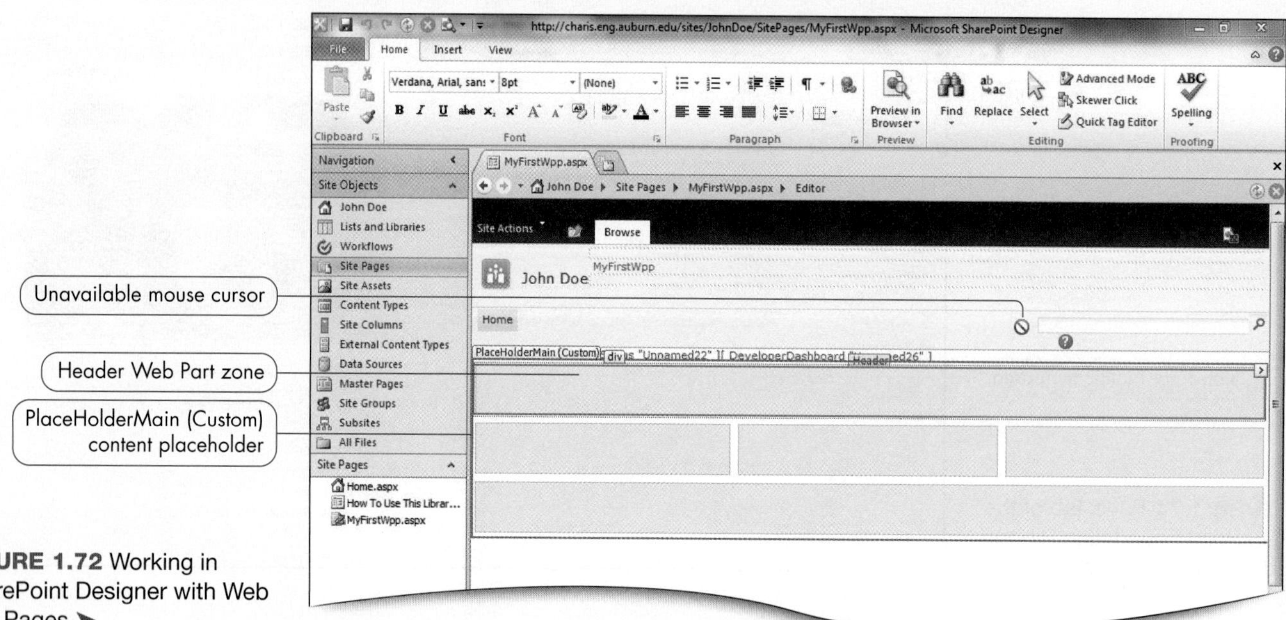

FIGURE 1.72 Working in SharePoint Designer with Web Part Pages ➤

TROUBLESHOOTING: Check with your instructor and make sure all options are enabled on the SharePoint Designer Settings page under the Site Collection Administration.

a. Click **Site Actions**, and then click **Edit in SharePoint Designer**. Enter your password if required.

SharePoint Designer window will display, including the Site Summary page.

b. Click **Web Part Page** in the New group on the Site tab, hover the mouse over the layouts menu, look for a *Header, Footer, 3 Columns layout screen tip*, and select it.

The New Web Part page dialog box should now display.

TROUBLESHOOTING: Each dark-blue section and the rectangular light-blue shapes on the Web Part page selection of layouts of possible Web pages are Web Part zones.

c. Type **MyFirstWpp** in the **Enter a name for this new Web Part page box**, and then click **OK** to close the New Web Part page dialog box.

The new MyFirstWpp page should now display in Design view and it should look similar to Figure 1.72. Click on the page. The borders of the PlaceHolderMain(Custom) content placeholder should now be highlighted with one color (purple in Figure 1.72) and the border of the Header Web Part zone should be highlighted with another color (blue in Figure 1.72).

d. Click all the remaining rectangular shapes one-by-one and observe as the borders of the LeftColumn, MiddleColumn, RightColumn, and Footer Web Part zones are highlighted.

e. Move the mouse toward the top of the page, outside the PlaceHolderMain(Custom) content placeholder and observe how the cursor icon changes into the Unavailable cursor as shown in Figure 1.72. That indicates that you are moving your mouse into the area controlled by the master template that cannot be edited using the Normal Editor.

f. Click the **Advanced Mode** on the Editing group on the Home tab. Move the mouse toward the top of the page, outside the PlaceHolderMain(Custom) content placeholder and observe that the cursor icon remains unchanged. That indicates that now you can edit the master page.

STEP 3 EXPLORE THE V4.MASTER MASTER PAGE IN SHAREPOINT DESIGNER

Explore the v4.master master page layout and structure with SharePoint Designer UI tools and use the SharePoint Collection created for you. Refer to Figure 1.73 as you complete Step 3.

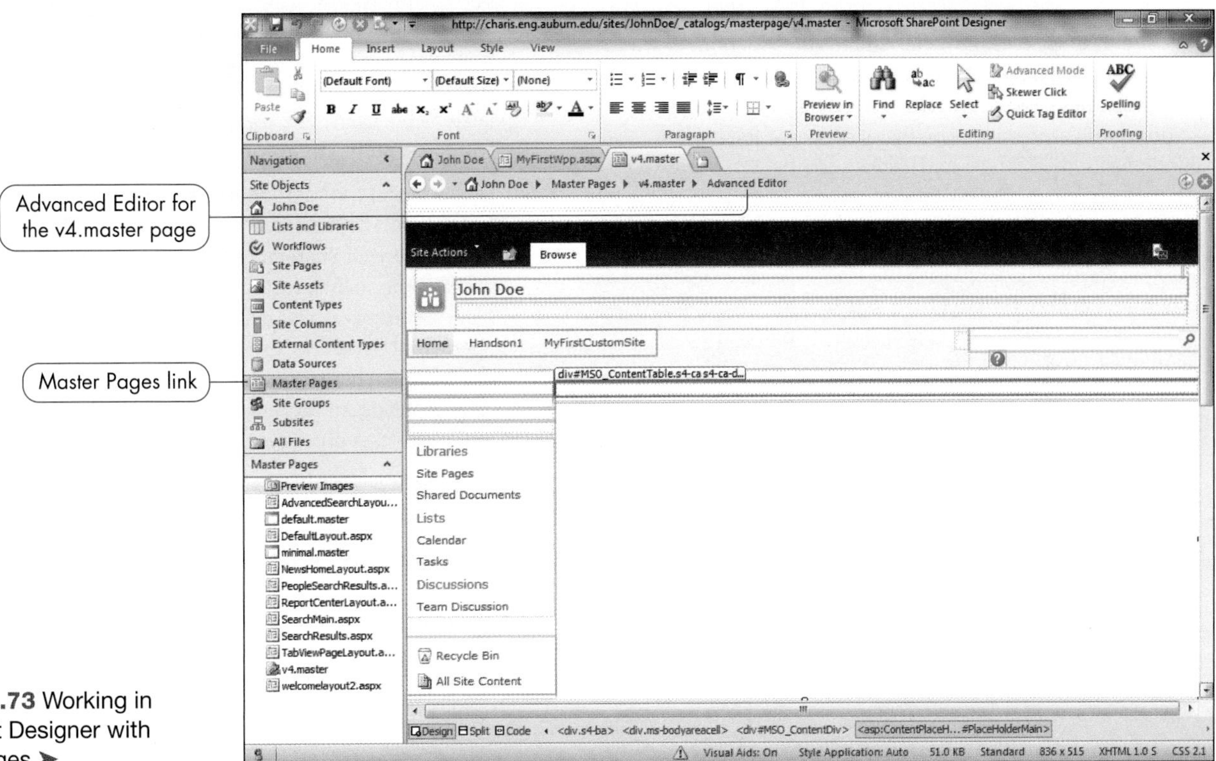

FIGURE 1.73 Working in SharePoint Designer with Master Pages ➤

a. Click the **Master Pages link** on the Navigation Task pane. The Master Pages summary page now displays. Locate the .master files.

b. Click **v4.master** on the Master Pages summary page.

The v4.master summary page now displays.

c. Click the **Edit file link** in the *Customization* section of the v4.master summary page.

The Advanced Editor for the v4.master page now displays, as shown in Figure 1.73.

d. Click the **File tab**, and then click **Close Site** to close the site.

e. Click **Exit** to close the SharePoint Designer window.

CHAPTER OBJECTIVES REVIEW

After reading this chapter, you have accomplished the following objectives:

1. **Explore SharePoint 2010 capabilities.** SharePoint 2010 tools enable you to create any kind of site. Site management is implemented through a single infrastructure. The SharePoint capabilities used to create solutions that bring together people, information, systems, and business processes are summarized by Microsoft into six categories: Sites, Communities, Content, Search, Insights, and Composites. The SharePoint 2010 building blocks are sites and workspaces, libraries, workflows, records management, alerts, Web Parts, navigation, and search.
2. **Work with the SharePoint 2010 Ribbon user interface.** The SharePoint Ribbon is formed by three categories of components: tabs, groups, and commands. The Browse tab will be the tab visible when you display a site page. This tab does not show any commands. The Ribbon contains context-related commands that are populated depending on the part of the type of page you are viewing and the permissions you have for working on the site. The Site Actions menu, available to you on every page, contains functions that you can apply to the features of the site. The Site Actions menu extends the functions past what are available on the Ribbon. The Status bar gives the user information, in context, such as page status or version. The Notification area appears on the right side of the page underneath the Ribbon, and displays transient messages that communicate the progress of an operation.
3. **Prepare to install a SharePoint Foundation 2010 environment.** Microsoft does not charge for SharePoint Foundation. However, to install it, you need to pay full product and licensing costs for an appropriate operating system (a version of 64-bit Windows Server 2008 or, for learning, testing, and development only, a copy of 64-bit Windows 7).
4. **Use SharePoint Foundation site templates.** Sites constitute the foundation of all SharePoint installations and include a variety of components and services that represent the core elements of business solutions. A SharePoint site is a collection of related Web pages, Web Parts, lists, and document libraries. Sites enable you to share and manage documents, create ways for people to collaborate, and utilize data in business environment workflows. SharePoint Foundation includes five different categories of sites to meet the needs of organizations: Team sites, Document workspaces, Group work sites, Meeting workspaces, and Blog sites. SharePoint Foundation's site templates enable you to create sites with a common set of tools or components. The core components of the SharePoint sites are Lists, Libraries, Workflows, Web Parts, Web Parts Zones, and the Recycle Bin.
5. **Use SharePoint collections and permission levels.** SharePoint sites are made up of a top-level site with one or more subsites. A top-level site, usually created from the Team site template, is a separate site hierarchy. A subsite is created inside of the top-level site as a child site. Permission levels determine what the users can manipulate or access within SharePoint. The five default permission levels available within SharePoint Foundation are Full control, Design, Contribute, Read, and Limited Access. When a new top-level site is created, three default site permission groups are also created: Owners, Members, and Visitors.
6. **Work with site templates.** Sites that you create can be saved as templates for future use. Templates provide the framework for the site, including the specific lists and libraries used, the views and forms available, and the workflows. You can include the contents of the site in the template; for example, the documents stored in the document libraries or organizational branding. Saved templates are stored in the Solution Gallery of the SharePoint site collection. You can deactivate and activate site templates as necessary. You can edit, save, and delete any custom template. Custom templates can be uploaded to the Solution Gallery from other sources.
7. **Identify SharePoint site layouts.** Team sites, document workspaces, and group workspaces share a similar layout and many of the same components. Meeting workspaces, by the nature of the problems they solve, are quite different in layout and components. Blog sites also differ from all other types of sites because of the way discussions are constructed and manipulated by the users. The components of sites vary based on the template and modifications you make.
8. **Understand the relationship between SharePoint Foundation and SharePoint Server.** SharePoint Server extends beyond SharePoint Foundation and provides additional components, customization, and scalability. Larger companies, enterprise deployments, and portal scenarios utilize SharePoint Server because of the added capabilities, provided by additional libraries and templates. SharePoint Server enables the organization's information to be incorporated into businesses processes.

   SharePoint Server offers special sites such as MySite, which is a portal that the user can customize.
9. **Explore SharePoint Designer 2010 capabilities.** SharePoint Designer provides a consolidated environment where you can work on your SharePoint site, all of its lists and libraries, pages, data sources, workflows, permissions, and more. SharePoint Designer can be used to perform basically any level of site customization in SharePoint. Although some site customizations are available through the browser, SharePoint Designer extends these capabilities, giving you more control of the site.
10. **Identify the SharePoint Designer default interface components and tools.** The SharePoint Designer UI is composed of the Quick Access Toolbar and three main areas: Navigation Pane, Gallery and Summary pages, and the Ribbon. The Task Panes menu displays task panes organized in five groups, which are also part of the SharePoint Designer default workspace. SharePoint Designer includes four page views: Design view, Code view, Split view, and Preview in Browser view. Microsoft IntelliSense technologies helps you minimize errors when working directly in the Code view with the

markup language and tags that comprise the site, including: HTML, XHTML, ASP.NET, and CSS.

11. **Customize the SharePoint Designer UI.** You can customize the SharePoint Designer UI, such as changing the position, and/or customizing the Quick Access Toolbar, and minimizing and/or customizing the Ribbon. You can also enable speech and handwriting recognition. Help files are automatically saved on your computer when you install SharePoint Designer. Microsoft Office Online also provides, via its dedicated Microsoft Web site, extensive help and access to up-to-date products, files, and graphics.

    To access the SharePoint Designer Help window, you can press F1 or click the Help button on the right edge on the Ribbon. As you work with a dialog box, you can click the Help button on the title bar of the dialog box to display specific help. ScreenTips and Enhanced ScreenTips are very useful features of the SharePoint Designer UI.

12. **Learn how to use Master Pages.** Every time you view a page on a SharePoint site, you are viewing two ASP.NET pages merged together: a master page and a content page. The master page defines the common layout and navigation (which typically make up the left, top, and bottom portions of the page). The content page includes page-specific content. When you change a master page all of the site pages associated with that master page will automatically change. Master pages contain static elements, such as text and graphics that appear on all pages, and one or more content placeholders which hold the information to be displayed on the page. SharePoint Foundation uses v4.master as its primary master page; therefore all content pages use v4.master. As long as this master page is not customized, its page definition is shared across sites. If the master page is edited, the edited copy is stored in a content database.

13. **Work with SharePoint pages.** SharePoint enables you to create and customize additional pages in sites. The three types of pages that are available to add to your sites are: Web Part page, Wiki page, and Publishing page (available only on the SharePoint Server). Web Part pages display information or media, such as videos, but have limited capabilities for collaboration. The Web Parts that you find on Web Part pages depend on the type of site. Wiki pages are the most flexible page type made up of a large content area that allows for the editing of text, including formatting, tables, and most importantly, linking to other Wiki pages. Wiki page libraries allow users to collaboratively contribute and edit information on specific topics through the use of specialized document libraries. Wiki page libraries do not contain documents, forms, or picture files, and they store only Wiki pages.

KEY TERMS

ASP.NET ***p.62***
ASP.NET page ***p.62***
Blog site ***p.12***
Breadcrumb navigation ***p.24***
Content placeholder ***p.62***
Content section ***p.25***
Document Library ***p.14***
Document workspace ***p.12***
Enhanced ScreenTip ***p.55***
Global links bar ***p.24***
Group ***p.4***
Group work site ***p.12***
Home page ***p.12***
Language bar ***p.49***
Library ***p.13***
List ***p.13***
Master page ***p.62***
Meeting workspace ***p.12***
Menu ***p.4***
Microsoft IntelliSense technology ***p.46***
Microsoft Office System ***p.2***
Microsoft Visual Studio 2010 ***p.10***
MySite ***p.29***
Navigation Pane ***p.41***
.NET Framework ***p.62***
Notification area ***p.9***
Office Web Apps ***p.14***
Permission levels ***p.16***
Publishing page ***p.65***
Quick Access Toolbar ***p.40***
Quick Launch area ***p.25***
Recycle Bin ***p.13***
ScreenTip ***p.55***
SharePoint 2010 ***p.3***
SharePoint 2010 Ribbon ***p.4***
SharePoint Designer 2010 ***p.10***
SharePoint Designer Backstage view ***p.39***
SharePoint Foundation 2010 ***p.3***
SharePoint Server 2010 ***p.4***
SharePoint site ***p.4***
Site Actions menu ***p.6***
Site collection ***p.16***
Site hierarchy ***p.16***
Solution ***p.18***
Solution file ***p.18***
Status bar ***p.9***
Subsite ***p.16***
Tab ***p.4***
Team site ***p.12***
Template ***p.11***
Title area ***p.25***
Top-level site ***p.15***
Top Link bar ***p.25***
User menu ***p.25***
Web Part ***p.4***
Web Part page ***p.64***
Web Part zone ***p.13***
Wiki page ***p.64***
Wiki page library ***p.65***
Workflow ***p.13***
XML Web service ***p.62***

MULTIPLE CHOICE

1. Which of the following is false?
   (a) The SharePoint Ribbon includes tabs.
   (b) The SharePoint Ribbon includes dialog boxes.
   (c) The SharePoint Ribbon includes groups.
   (d) The SharePoint Ribbon includes commands.

2. The Site Actions menu:
   (a) Is the same for all sites.
   (b) Is the same for all level of users.
   (c) Is not available on all SharePoint pages.
   (d) Includes a link to the Site Settings page.

3. What is the effect of activating a custom template?
   (a) It can be used to create a SharePoint site.
   (b) It can be edited.
   (c) It can be deleted.
   (d) It cannot be downloaded.

4. SharePoint Designer does not support:
   (a) Creation of a new SharePoint collection.
   (b) Branding of a SharePoint site.
   (c) Creation of Views.
   (d) Creation of Forms.

5. When using the SharePoint Designer Backstage view, you cannot:
   (a) Open a site.
   (b) Create a new site.
   (c) Customize the workspace.
   (d) Add Pages to a site.

6. When using SharePoint Designer Ribbon, you cannot:
   (a) Edit a master template.
   (b) Create a top-level site.
   (c) Delete a subsite.
   (d) Reset the workspace to its default settings.

7. Which of the following is false?
   (a) You can edit a master template using the Ribbon.
   (b) You can customize a master template.
   (c) A change made to a master page is reflected across all of the site pages that are associated with that master page.
   (d) SharePoint Foundation uses v4.master as its primary master page.

8. Which of the following statements about Web Part pages is false?
   (a) They include Web Part zones.
   (b) They include Web Parts.
   (c) They display a Quick Launch Navigation area.
   (d) They usually do not include content such as text and images.

9. A Wiki page cannot:
   (a) Include a Web Part.
   (b) Include a Web Part zone.
   (c) Be customized.
   (d) Be included in any other library than a Wiki page library.

10. Which of the following is not a SharePoint Foundation master page?
    (a) default.master
    (b) v4.master
    (c) minimal.master
    (d) collaboration.master

PRACTICE EXERCISES

1 Introduction to Management Information Systems Business Course

Two years ago, as an undergraduate student in the Personal Computer Applications course, you learned about SharePoint Services 3.0. As a result of your excellent work in this class, you have been hired as an undergraduate teaching assistant in the Introduction to Management Information Systems course and, as part of your new assignment, you will help students working on their assignments in the course laboratory. Your faculty supervisor is giving you administrator access to a SharePoint Foundation top-level site so that you can start getting acquainted with SharePoint Foundation and SharePoint sites layouts. This exercise follows the same set of skills as used in Hands-On Exercise 1 in the chapter. Refer to Figure 1.74 as you complete this exercise.

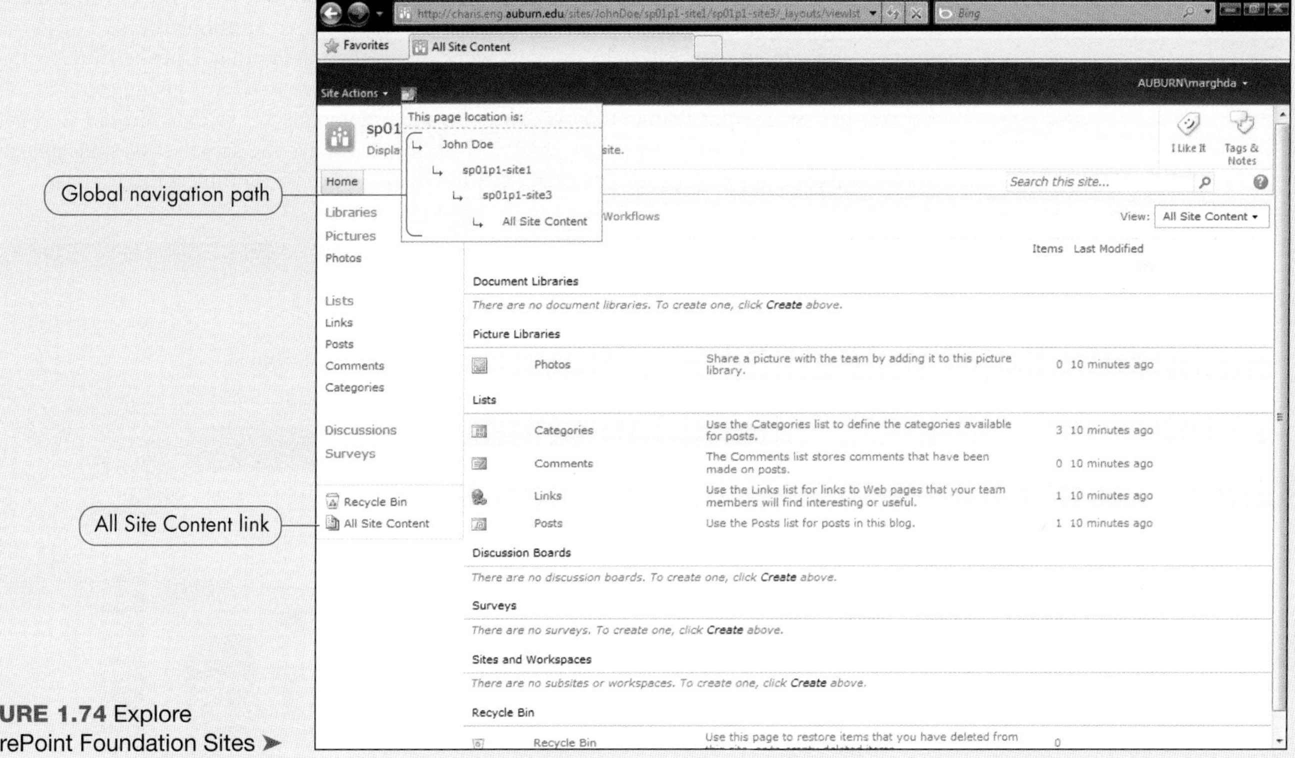

FIGURE 1.74 Explore SharePoint Foundation Sites ➤

a. Click **Start**, click **All Programs**, and then select **Internet Explorer** to start Internet Explorer.

b. Type the URL of the top-level site in the **Address bar**, and then enter your user name and password.

c. Identify the five main components of the top-level team site layout: Global links bar, Title area, Navigation bar, Quick Launch area, and *Content* section.

d. Click the **All Site Content link** on the Quick Launch area. Can you see all Libraries, Lists, Sites, and Workspaces included in the top-level site? Click **sp01p1-site1** in the *Sites and Workspaces* section.

e. Identify the five main components of the Work site layout: Global links bar, Title area, Navigation bar, Quick Launch area, and *Content* section. Compare them with the five main components of the top-level team site layout. Launch Microsoft Word, and then save the blank document as **sp01p1-report_LastNameFirstName**. Write your findings.

f. Click **sp01p1-site2** on the Navigation bar. Identify the components of the sp01p1-site2 layout.

g. Compare the layout of the sp01p1-site2 site with the layout of the top-level site. Write your findings in *sp01p1-report_LastNameFirstName.*

h. Click **Site Actions** on the Global links bar. Can you see the New Site link? Explain in your *sp01p1-report_LastNameFirstName* report what you see and why.

i. Click the **Navigate Up button** on the Global links bar. The global navigation path should look like the one in Figure 1.74. Select **sp01p1-site1** on the global navigation path.

j. Click the **All Site Content link** in the Quick Launch area. Click **sp01p1-site3** in the *Sites and Workspaces* section. Compare the layout of this site with the layout of sp01p1-site1 and sp01p1-site2. Write your findings in your *sp01p1-report_LastNameFirstName* report.
k. Click **Site Actions** on the Global links bar.
l. Click the **All Site Content link** on the Quick Launch area.
m. Click **Home** on the Navigation bar. The home page of the sp01p1-site3 site should now be displayed.
n. Click the **Close (X) button** to close the Internet Explorer window.

2 Introduction to Personal Computer Applications IT Course

As an undergraduate student in the Personal Computer Applications course, you also learned SharePoint Designer so you already know that SharePoint Designer is a powerful tool for designing SharePoint sites. As a result of your excellent work in this class, you have been hired as an undergraduate teaching assistant in the Introduction to Personal Computer Applications course and, as part of your new assignment, you will help students working on their assignments in the Introduction to Personal Computer Applications course laboratory. Your faculty supervisor is giving you administrator access to a SharePoint Foundation top-level site and a notebook PC so that you can start getting acquainted with SharePoint Designer 2010. This exercise follows the same set of skills as used in Hands-On Exercises 2 and 3 in the chapter. Refer to Figure 1.75 as you complete this exercise.

FIGURE 1.75 Explore SharePoint Designer UI ➤

a. Click **Start**, click **All Programs**, click **SharePoint**, and then click **Microsoft Office SharePoint Designer 2010** to start SharePoint Designer. You should see the SharePoint Designer Backstage view.
b. Click **Open Site**. Type the URL of the top-level site of your SharePoint collection, and then click **Open**. Type your credentials in the **Windows security box**, if required, and then click **OK** to close it. The SharePoint Designer Site Tab should now display.
c. Identify the four areas of the SharePoint Designer UI: Quick Access Toolbar, Navigation Pane, Gallery and Summary Page, and the Ribbon. Identify the groups of the Site tab.
d. Double-click the **Site Pages link**. Identify the groups of the Pages tab of the SharePoint Designer Ribbon.

e. Double-click **Home.aspx**.
f. Click the **Edit File arrow** in the Edit group of the Page Ribbon, and then select **Edit in Normal Mode**.
g. Click the **View tab.** Click the image included in Home.aspx.
h. Click the **Task Panes arrow**, and then select the **Tag Properties task pane name.** Now the Tag Properties task pane displays properties of the <img> tag associated with the pictures you selected.
i. Compare the SharePoint Designer workspace displayed on your computer with Figure 1.75.
j. Click the **Task Panes arrow**, and then select **Reset Workspace Layout**.
k. Click the **Close (X) button** in the top-right corner of the document window to close the Home.aspx page.
l. Click the **File tab**, and then click **Close Site** to close the Web site.
m. Click **Exit** to close SharePoint Designer.

MID-LEVEL EXERCISES

1 Hope Hospital Business Office Management

The push towards Electronic Medical Records requires a host of solutions to streamline and improve processes, which will take hospitals through the evolution from paper- and people-driven models to automated evidence-based, results-driven practices.

You work for the Hope Hospital, and your supervisor has asked you to carefully review SharePoint 2010 capabilities and see if your company should consider using it for implementing the hospital financial and medical services. He is providing you with a custom template that could be used by the Business Office. You need to upload the template and create a new subsite using this custom template. Figure 1.76 shows the Browse view of the new subsite. You will then explore the layout and components of this new subsite. This exercise follows the same set of skills as used in Hands-On Exercise 1 in the chapter. Refer to Figure 1.76 as you complete this exercise.

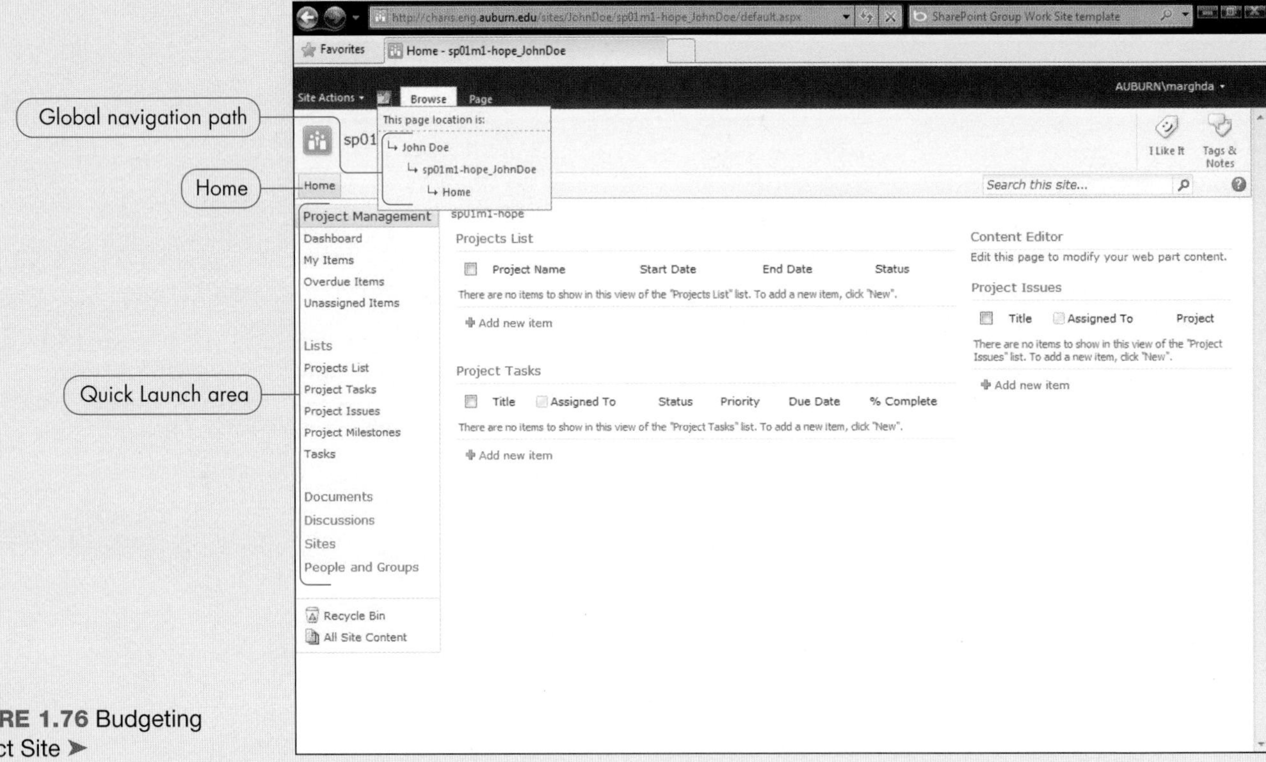

FIGURE 1.76 Budgeting Project Site ➤

a. Start Internet Explorer.
b. Type the URL of the top-level site in the **Address bar**.
c. Select **Site Settings** on the Site Actions menu.
d. Click **Solutions** under the *Galleries* section. Click the **Solutions tab.**
   - Click **Upload Solution** in the New group of the Solutions tab. Click **Browse** on the **Upload Document dialog box**. Navigate to the Exploring SharePoint folder, and then double-click the name of the *sp01m1-hope.wsp* solution. Click **OK** to start uploading the solution (custom template).
   - Click **Activate** on the Solution Gallery – Activate Solution dialog box. Close the dialog box. The new *sp01m1-hope* solution should now show on the Solution Gallery page.

e. Select **New Site** on the Site Actions menu. Locate and click **sp01m1-hope** in the gallery.
   - Type **sp01m1-hope_LastnameFirstName** in the **Title box.**
   - Type **sp01m1-hope_LastnameFirstName** in the **URL box.**
   - Click **Create.**

f. Explore the links to the elements included in the Quick Launch area.

g. Click the **All Site Content link** on the Quick Launch area. Explore all lists included on the All Site Content page.

h. Click **Home** on the Navigation Bar.

i. Compare the layout, content, and functionalities of this custom template with the Group Work Site Template. Write a report about your conclusions and submit it to your instructor.

j. Close Internet Explorer.

2 DestinQuest Co.

You work for DestinQuest, a vacation rental hospitality and resort real estate company, and your supervisor has asked you to carefully review SharePoint 2010 capabilities and see if your company should consider using it for implementing the company vacation rental and real estate services. He is providing you with a custom template that could be used to manage the inventory of the Properties Maintenance department. You need to upload the template, and then create in SharePoint Designer a new subsite using this custom template. Figure 1.77 shows the Browse view of the new subsite. You will explore in SharePoint Designer the layout, components, and the master page of this new subsite. You will make changes on the site pages and save the site as a new template. You will then download the template. This exercise follows the same set of skills as used in Hands-On Exercises 2 and 3 in the chapter. Refer to Figure 1.77 as you complete this exercise.

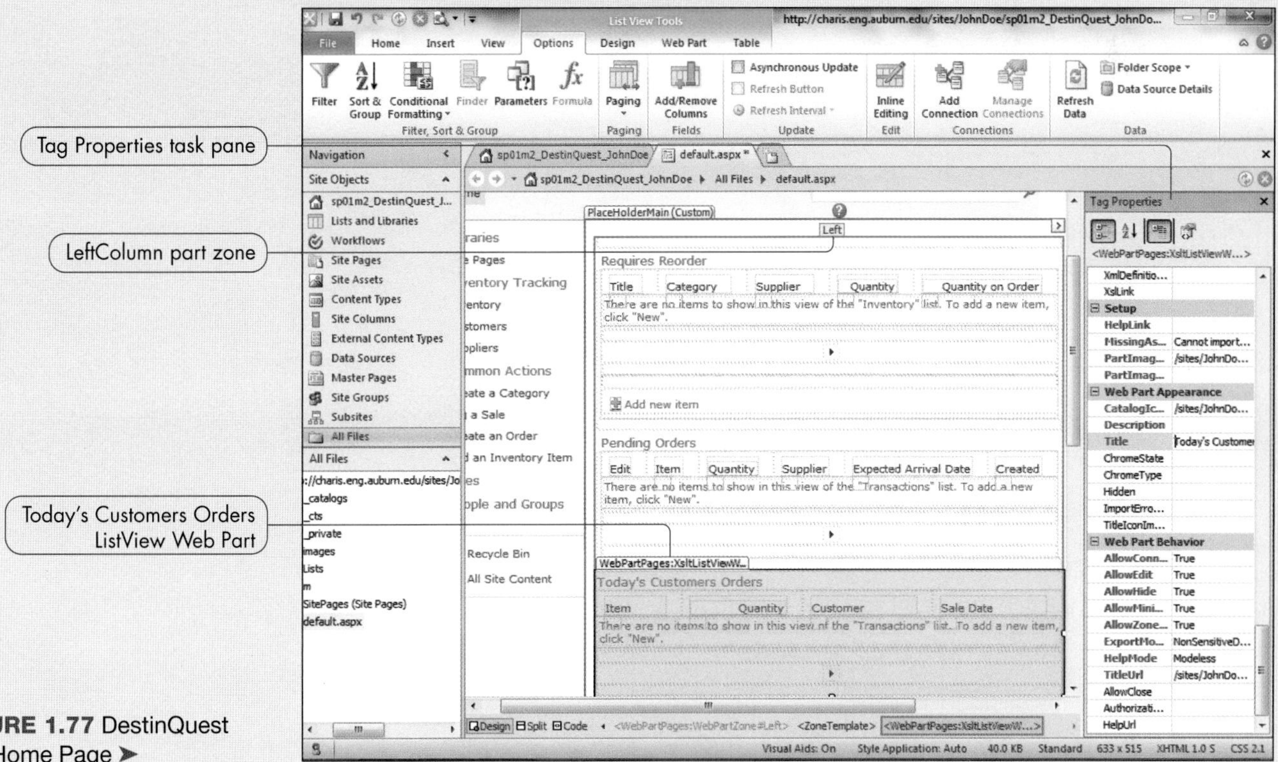

FIGURE 1.77 DestinQuest site Home Page ➤

a. Start Internet Explorer.

b. Type the URL of the top-level site in the **Address bar**.

c. Click the **Site Actions menu** in the Quick Launch area. Using the instructions from steps d–e in Mid-Level Exercise 1, upload the *sp01m2-DestinQuest* template and create the *sp01m2-DestinQuest_LastNameFirstName* child site of the top-level site.

d. Select **Edit in SharePoint Designer** on the Site Actions menu.

e. Click the **Edit site home page link** in the *Customization* section of the Site Summary page.

f. Click the white space near the left border of the PlaceHolderMain(Custom) content placeholder borders. The LeftColumn part zone borders should now be highlighted. Click the white space near the right border of the PlaceHolderMain(Custom) content placeholder borders. The RightColumn part zone borders should now be highlighted.

g. Click the **View tab**. Click the **Task Panes arrow** in the Workspace group of the View tab, and then select **Tag Properties**.

DISCOVER 

h. Click anywhere on the *Today's Sale* text in the LeftColumn part zone. Replace *Today's Sale* in the Tag Properties task pane with **Today's Customers Orders**. Compare the image on your computer screen with the one shown in Figure 1.77.

i. Save your work. Click **sp01m2-DestinQuest** in the Navigation Pane.

DISCOVER

j. Click the name of the site in the Navigation task pane, and then click **Save as Template** on the manage group on the Ribbon.
    - Type **sp01m2-DestinQuest_LastNameFirstName** in the **File name box**.
    - Type **sp01m2-DestinQuest_LastNameFirstName** in the **Template name box**.
    - Check the **Include Content check box**. Close the Save as Template page and the Operation Successful page.

k. Click the **Navigate up button**, and then select the top-level site of your collection. Select **Site Settings** on the Site Actions menu. Click **Solutions** in the *Galleries* section of the Site Settings page. The *sp01m2-DestinQuest_LastNameFirstName* file should be displayed in the Solutions page.

l. Right-click **sp01m2-DestinQuest_LastNameFirstName**, and then select **Save Target As**. Save the template in your Exploring SharePoint folder.

m. Close Internet Explorer.

n. Close the site, and then close SharePoint Designer.

CAPSTONE EXERCISES

You work for a major Financial Management and Advisory Company, and your supervisor has asked you to start getting acquainted with the new generation of SharePoint Technologies and see how your company can extend and align its rich sets of capabilities to your company's key business processes and objectives. You are provided with a custom template that you will use to create a searchable Knowledge Base for your company Global Research site. You will use Internet Explorer and SharePoint Designer2010 to explore the newly created site, and then create a report.

Upload a Template, Create a Subsite, and Explore It Using Internet Explorer Browser

You are to upload a solution file. You create a subsite of your top-level site using the uploaded custom template.

a. Launch Internet Explorer browser and navigate to the top-level site of your site collection.

b. Upload and activate the *sp01c1_KnowledgeBase.wsp* solution file in your collection Solution Gallery.

c. Create a new *sp01c1_KnowledgeBase_LastNameFirstName* site using the uploaded template.

d. Click the **All Site Content link** in the Quick Launch area. Carefully review all the listed libraries and lists and decide in which of the three main categories of SharePoint templates this custom template would fit in.

e. Create a new *sp01c1_Report_LastNameFirstName* document in Microsoft Word and write a short report of your findings in step d.

Explore a SharePoint Customized Site Using SharePoint Designer

You are to explore the layout and components of the customized team site and compare it with the layout and components of the top-level team site.

a. Select **Edit in SharePoint Designer** on the Site Actions menu.

b. Click **All Files** in the Navigation Pane. Double-click **default.aspx** on the All Files Summary page to display default.aspx in Design view.

c. Click **Master Pages** in the Navigation Pane. Double-click **default.master** on the Master Pages Summary page.

d. Click **Edit File** in the Edit group of the Page tab to open default.master in SharePoint Designer Advanced Editor.

e. Add a paragraph to the new *sp01c1_Report_LastNameFirstName* document indicating what type of page default.aspx is (e.g., Web Part page or Wiki page) and describing what is included in the content page of default.aspx (e.g., part zones, Web Parts).

f. Click **Site Pages** on the Navigation Pane. Click **Home.aspx**, and then click **Edit File** in the *Customization* section on the Site Pages Summary page to display Home.aspx in Design view.

g. Add a paragraph to the new *sp01c1_Report_LastNameFirstName* document indicating what type of page Home.aspx is (e.g., Web Part page or Wiki page) and describing what is included in the content page of Home.aspx.

h. Close the *sp01c1_KnowledgeBase_LastNameFirstName* site and exit SharePoint Designer. Close the Internet Explorer window.

i. Submit the *sp01c1_Report_LastNameFirstName* report to your instructor.

Communication Skills Class

GENERAL CASE 

You are taking a Communication Skills class and must develop an end-of-semester demonstration speech that will demonstrate your stronger communication and collaboration skills, and potential to work confidently with others. A demonstration speech is one in which you teach or direct the class on how to do something. Because SharePoint 2010 is a relatively new technology, you decide to demonstrate some of its features. You will use PowerPoint to develop your presentation. After completing your notes, save the document as **sp01b1speech_LastnameFirstname** in a location as directed by your instructor. In a 1, 2, 3 fashion (listing your points in numerical order), provide directions to the class on:

- Understanding SharePoint Foundation Sites Templates and Sites Collections.
- Working with Site Templates.
- Using the SharePoint Designer UI and Tools.
- Customizing the SharePoint Designer UI.
- Understanding SharePoint Pages.

The Microsoft Office Forums

RESEARCH CASE 

A large international community of SharePoint developers help each other through online forums. One of the most professional and helpful SharePoint 2010 set of forums are organized by Microsoft. Use Microsoft Internet Explorer to open the Microsoft SharePoint Developer Center home page (http://msdn.microsoft.com/en-us/sharepoint/). Click Forums in the top navigational bar, and then click SharePoint 2010 - General Questions and Answers. Search for your most relevant 10 topics (key terms) covered in this chapter, and then print or save the most useful information. Provide your instructor with a copy of your printed or uploaded report. You can also post a new question, but be aware that you will be required to have a .NET Passport, which you can obtain free of charge.

SharePoint Sites Recovery Tools

DISASTER RECOVERY 

The *sp01b3_SiteBackup* solution file in the Exploring SharePoint folder was the last site backup completed by your predecessor prior to his unfortunate dismissal. The backup was not properly created, which caused your company to loose relevant Word, Excel, and Adobe files posted on that site. Upload the *sp01b3_SiteBackup* solution file, and then create a *sp01b3_SiteBackup_LastnameFirstname* site using this solution file and the New Site command on the Site Actions menu. Explore the content of the new site and write a memo to your instructor describing the nature of the error. Include suggestions in the memo on how to avoid mistakes of this nature in the future.

SHAREPOINT
2 WEB SITES

Working with SharePoint Sites

CASE STUDY | The DestinQuest Company Web Site

Nadia, Leslie, and Conner are three intelligent and enthusiastic best friends who, as soon as they graduated from college five years ago, decided to build their own real estate company, named DestinQuest, based in Destin, Florida. Initially they planned to provide services related to buying, selling, and renting properties situated in the little paradise surrounding the Destin area. Since then they opened three more offices in Vail, Colorado; Catalina Island, California; and Blowing Rock, North Carolina.

One of the important things they learned in school was how much a well-developed e-business Web site can help in promoting, publicizing, and managing their business. In one of their college computer courses, they were introduced to SharePoint 2007 and its powerful, friendly tools and features for designing, developing, publishing, and managing professional Web sites. Five years ago, they hired Andy to help them develop a SharePoint site. Thanks to their efforts and Andy's skills, they have a functional Web site, and their DestinQuest Company is slowly but surely expanding, making a constant progress in the Destin, Vale, Catalina Island, and Blowing Rock real estate market. Now, they have hired you to fully upgrade their e-business Web site using SharePoint Foundation 2010 and SharePoint Designer 2010.

You will create a top-level, parent site for the DestinQuest Company and create subsites using SharePoint site templates that better match the functionality needed for those subsites. You will create new Lists and Libraries using the SharePoint templates and will create new folders within Libraries to better organize the DestinQuest Company documents stored on SharePoint. You will add new .ASPX pages, using SharePoint templates and master pages, to customize pages to better meet your needs or reghost customized pages as needed. You will set new home pages for your sites and delete sites that are no longer needed.

OBJECTIVES AFTER YOU READ THIS CHAPTER, YOU WILL BE ABLE TO:

Tools for Creating a SharePoint Site

Studies show that a successful twenty-first-century professional must learn to innovate. Developing creative adaptations using emerging technology, and being able to collaborate successfully toward gaining competitive advantages, has proven to be a very successful approach towards building a successful professional career. SharePoint Technologies are one of the fastest-growing products in Microsoft's history, having a tremendous impact on the Web developer community, and enabling small or large businesses and organizations to develop innovative business applications.

The content of this chapter builds upon the knowledge covered in previous chapters and appendices of this textbook. You will learn to create, brand, back up, and delete SharePoint sites. You will learn in depth about SharePoint site capabilities and navigation systems. After you have mastered these concepts, you will learn about working with Lists and Libraries, and about the management of SharePoint sites documents.

This section introduces you to SharePoint tools for creating sites, adding new Web pages to a site, custom branding sites, and resetting custom pages to their site definition. You will then learn how to delete, back up, and restore SharePoint content.

Planning the Development of a SharePoint Site

In the planning stage, you need to carefully analyze all of the requirements related to the business or organizational processes you want to build....

In the planning stage, you need to carefully analyze all of the requirements related to the business or organizational processes you want to build, so you will be able to use the appropriate SharePoint tools and features in developing a new SharePoint site or workspace.

You will need to take into consideration some core marketing, technical, usability, and social requirements while planning to develop a new SharePoint site.

- Determine the reasons for developing a new site. Has your business undergone a change that leads to a new business model? Is your previous Web site not meeting the expectations of management or users? Do you need to provide more services or information to your users? Does your site need to attract a wider audience with more diverse interests?
- Determine short-term and long-term objectives for the Web site. Do you need to increase sales by a certain percentage through your Web site? Do you want to increase the awareness of your brand? Do you need an additional marketing outlet?
- Determine how often the site will be updated and who will be responsible for the content and the updating of the Web site.
- Determine, in concrete numbers, how you will measure the success of the Web site. Will an increase in site visitors constitute success? How much money will the site need to generate in order to be considered successful?
- Determine the characteristics of the people using your Web site. How often are they online? What are they doing while on the Web?
- What are their basic characteristics such as age, occupation, educational level, income, and purchasing habits, and how will these impact the content or organization of the Web site? What is their level of technical proficiency?
- What is the corporate structure? What security is needed? How much time will they allot to maintaining the site?
- Determine what a site visitor should do on the site. Will they make a purchase? Join a cause? Search for information that is important to them?
- Determine what value your organization has to the Web site visitors. Are they looking for a better price? A specific product or service? Relevant, timely information?

- Determine the daily, weekly, or monthly usage of your site. How will you track the usage?
- Determine the source of the content and how it is organized. Will you use existing content? How is that content structured? Is it already in an electronic format? What visual elements, such as a logo, color scheme, and navigation, will you use?
- Determine the type of browser used by your potential audience.
- Determine the need for third-party technologies, such as JavaScript or Flash.
- Determine the potential for database functionality. Will you have personalization? Will the site users be required to log on to the site? Will content be generated from the database, for example for a catalog of products?
- Determine how your organization will be paid for your products or services. Will you need to use secured online transactions?
- Determine other specific programming needs. Will personalization be a necessary part of the Web site experience for the users? Will the users have the ability to search your Web site for information or products?

TIP SharePoint Sites Compatibility and Portability

Although SharePoint has historically supported the Microsoft Internet Explorer browser, SharePoint 2010 also supports Firefox, Safari, and micro-browsers (such as found on mobile devices). Using these browsers, people can create, view, and edit sites, and effectively work with content by manipulating Office documents, browsing SharePoint document libraries, and searching for content or people.

The next important planning step in the process of developing a SharePoint site is to secure a SharePoint hosting account or Uniform Resource Locator (URL) from a hosting service, such as an Internet Service Provider (ISP). Once all planning steps have been accomplished, you can initiate the design stage. For now, let us identify the SharePoint tools for creating sites.

Identifying Tools for Creating Sites

You can create SharePoint sites and components through the Web browser or SharePoint Designer 2010. From SharePoint Designer you can view any SharePoint 2010 site in a Web browser using the SharePoint Designer Preview in the browser tool.

Web application is any Windows Internet Information Services (IIS) Web site in the SharePoint system.

A ***Web application*** is any Windows Internet Information Services (IIS) Web site in the SharePoint system. The SharePoint system administrator provides you with a SharePoint Web application so that you can design a site. The initial top-level site, created in a SharePoint Foundation site collection, can only be created using the SharePoint Central Administration site, as shown in Figure 2.1. A SharePoint administrator follows these steps to create a new collection:

The initial top-level site, created in a SharePoint Foundation site collection, can only be created using the SharePoint Central Administration site....

1. Open the SharePoint Central Administration site in a browser. Click the Application Management link, as shown in Figure 2.1, to open the Application Management tab, as shown in Figure 2.2, and then click the Create site collections link, as shown in Figure 2.2, to display the Create Site Collection page.
2. Fill in the title and description, Web site address, primary site collection administrator, and secondary site collection administrator sections on the Create Site Collection page, as shown in Figure 2.3.
3. Select Team Site in the *Template Selection* section (if it is not already selected), and then click OK. Click OK again on the Top-Level Site Successfully Created page.
4. Click the *View all site collections* link on the Application Management tab. The new site collection is displayed on the Site Collection List page.

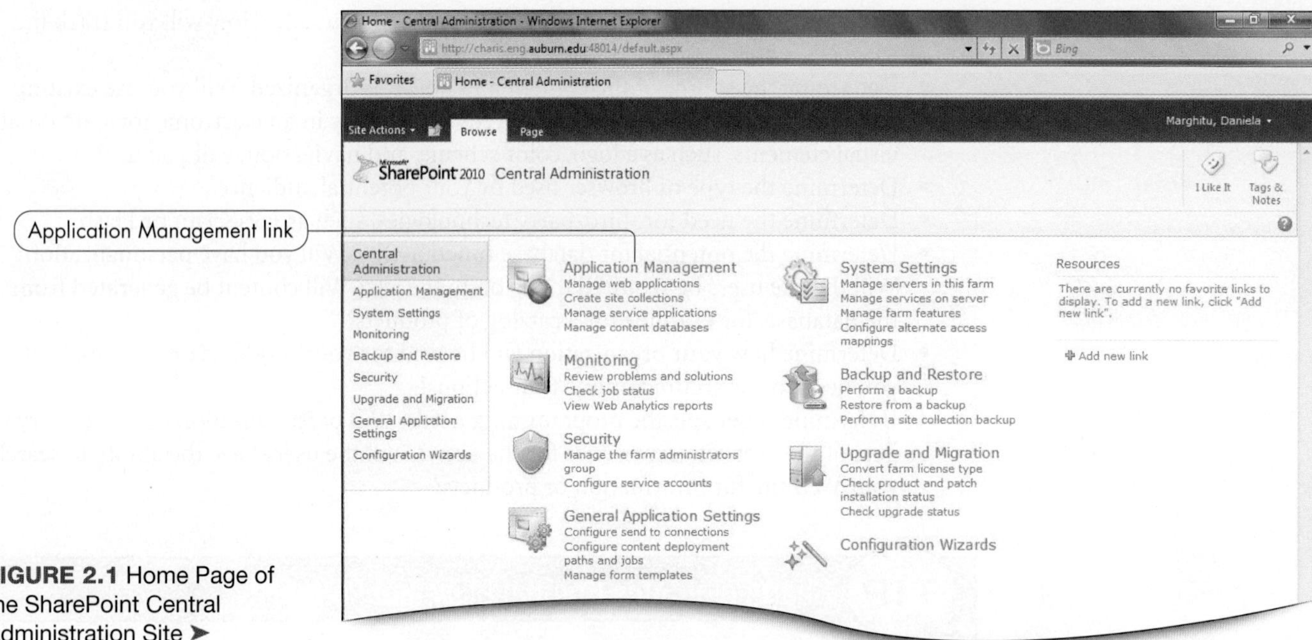

FIGURE 2.1 Home Page of the SharePoint Central Administration Site ➤

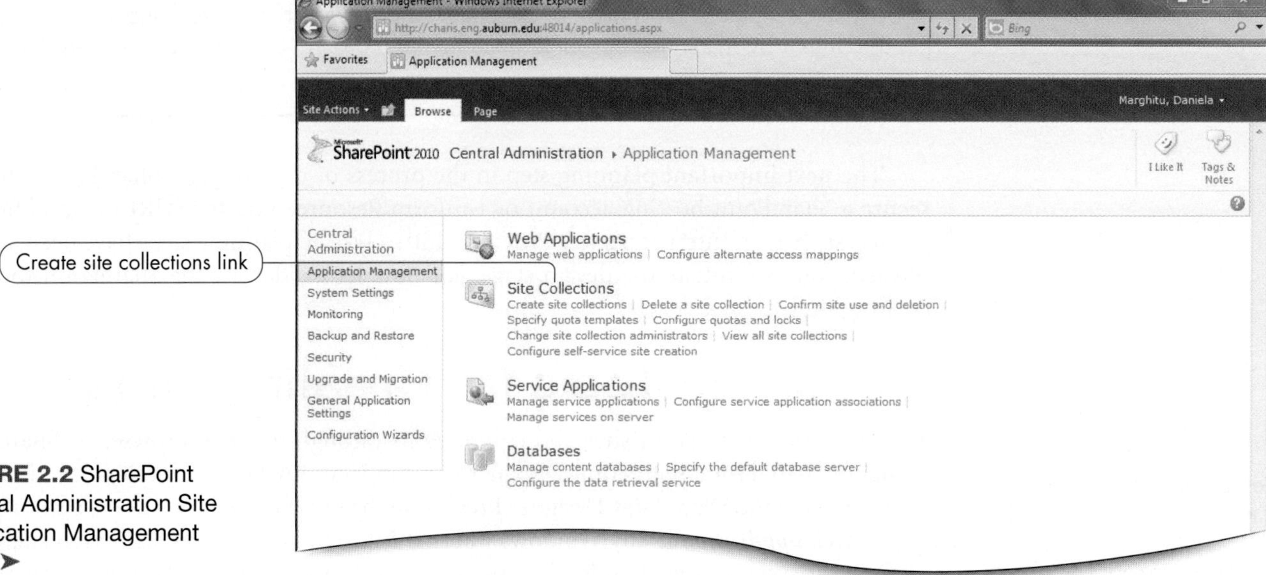

FIGURE 2.2 SharePoint Central Administration Site Application Management Page ➤

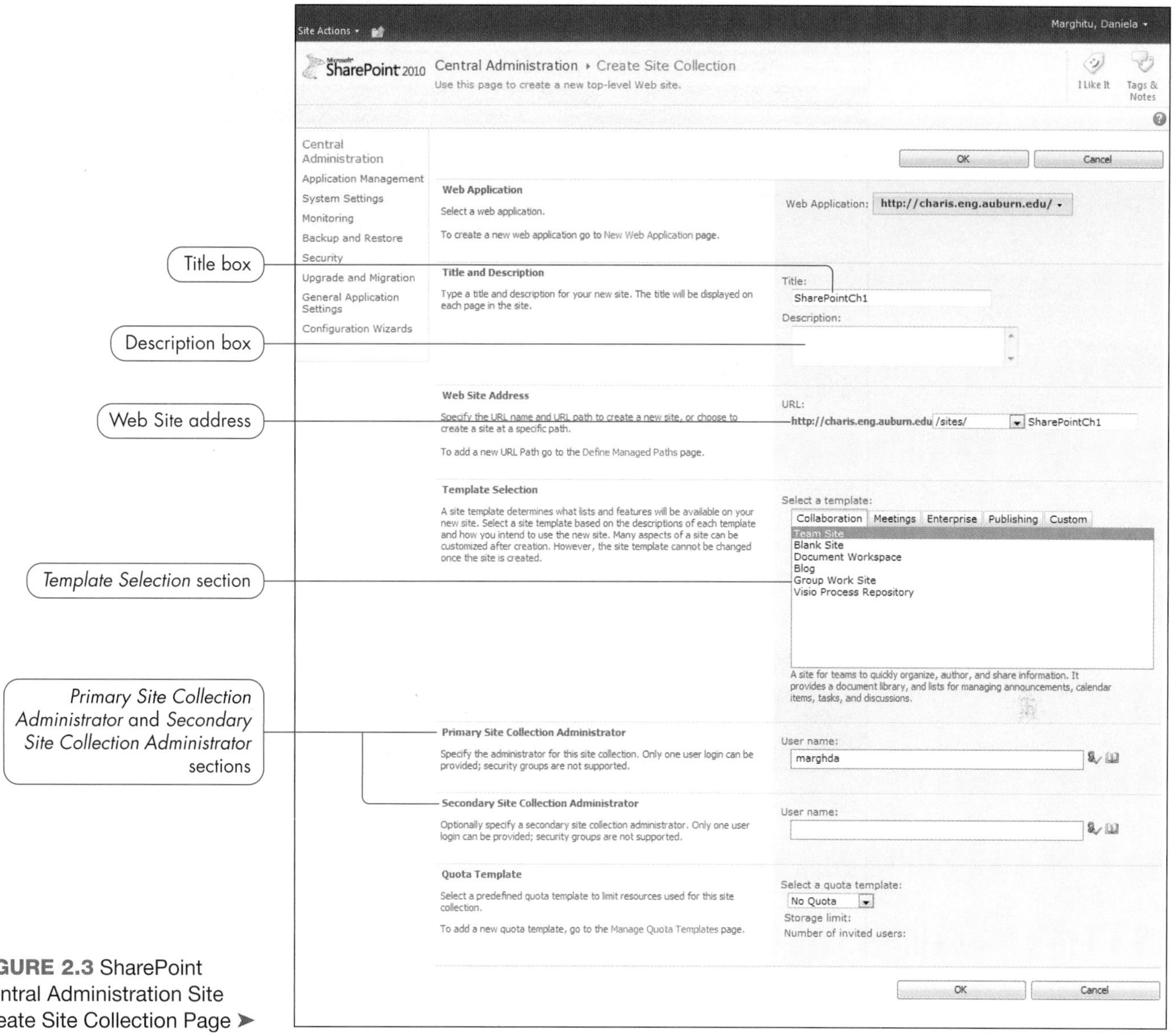

FIGURE 2.3 SharePoint Central Administration Site Create Site Collection Page ➤

The top-level site includes the functionality of all child sites, and it also enables you to manage site collections via the Site Collection Administration links included in the Site Settings page, as shown in Figure 2.4. You can access the top-level Site Settings page, if you are signed on as Administrator, from the Site Settings of any subsite included in the collection, as shown in Figure 2.5.

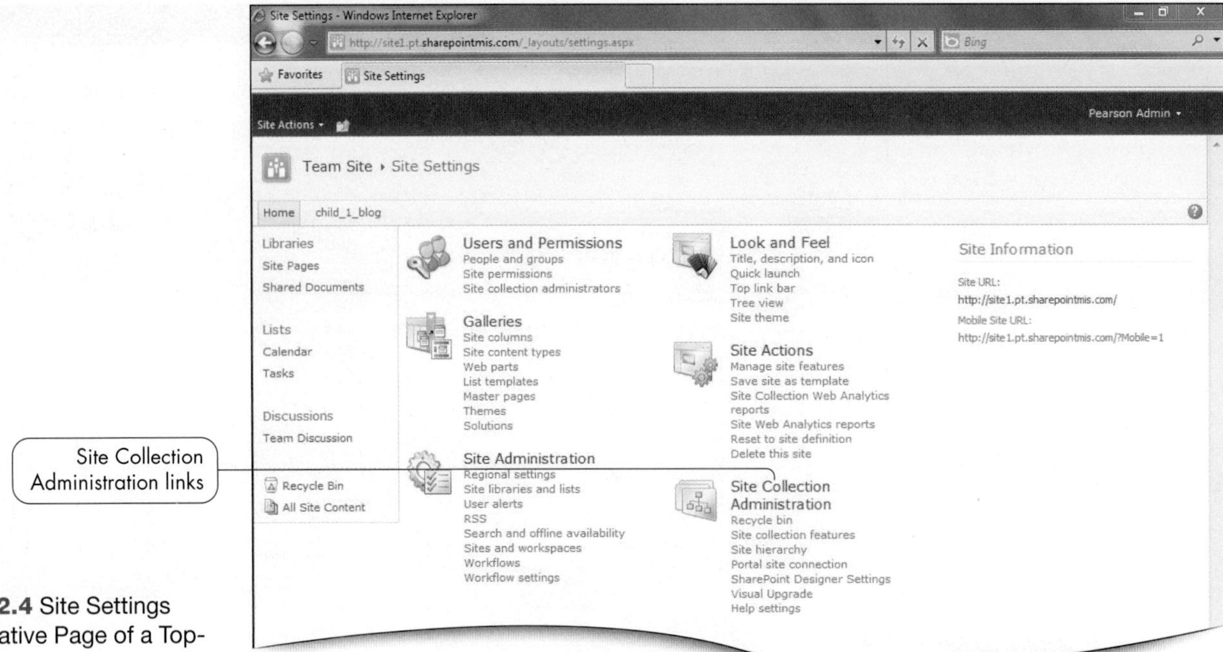

FIGURE 2.4 Site Settings Administrative Page of a Top-Level Site ➤

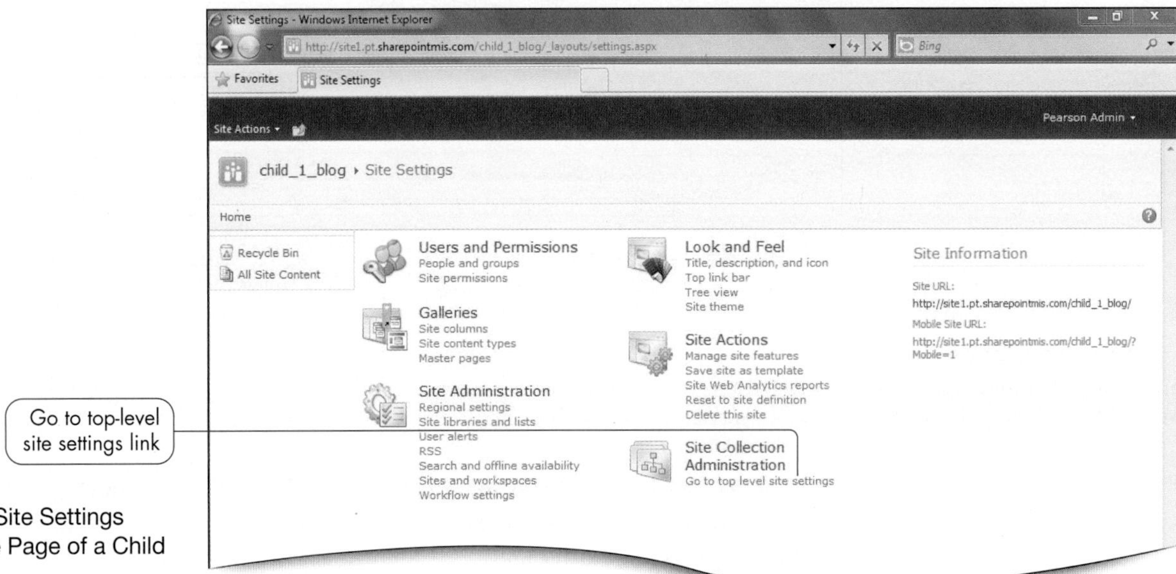

FIGURE 2.5 Site Settings Administrative Page of a Child Site ➤

When a new top-level parent site is created by the Site Administrator or Secondary Administrator, that person is the only one initially with rights to the site. This person sets up the security so that other people can access the site. As subsites or child sites are created within the top-level site, permissions can be assigned in one of two ways. Subsites can inherit the permissions that the top-level site is assigned. This means that the security of the subsite cannot be managed from the subsite. Subsites can also be set up with unique permissions that are individually assigned to users of the subsite. When you create a subsite, the default choice is that whoever can access the top-level site can also access the subsite and has the same security rights.

The Site Actions menu contains various site management tools, as shown in Figure 2.6. The options on the menu may vary for a number of reasons. You will notice different options when SharePoint Foundation is installed versus SharePoint Server. The features within the site will also affect the Site Actions menu. Your permission level within the site will also enable or disable some of the site management options. The Site Actions menu can include:

- Edit Page: Enables you to update the content of the current page.
- Sync to SharePoint Workspace: Enables you to create a synchronized copy of the site on your computer.
- New Page: Enables you to create a new page based on the type of site you have open. For example, Wiki page sites cause Wiki pages to be created, whereas publishing page sites create publishing pages.
- New Document Library: Enables you to create a new storage location for documents within the site.
- New Site: Enables you to create a new subsite to the current site by selecting options on the New SharePoint Site page.
- More Options: Enables you to create additional libraries, lists, pages, and sites using the Create screen.
- View All Site Content: Displays the All Site Content page, showing the libraries, lists, and subsites associated with the current site.
- Edit in SharePoint Designer: Enables you to use SharePoint Designer to create and edit site content. This option will open the site in SharePoint Designer to allow for editing. SharePoint Designer must be installed on the computer used to access SharePoint.
- Site Permissions: Displays the Site Permissions page, enabling you to provide access to the site to other individuals or groups.
- Site Settings: Displays the Site Settings page.

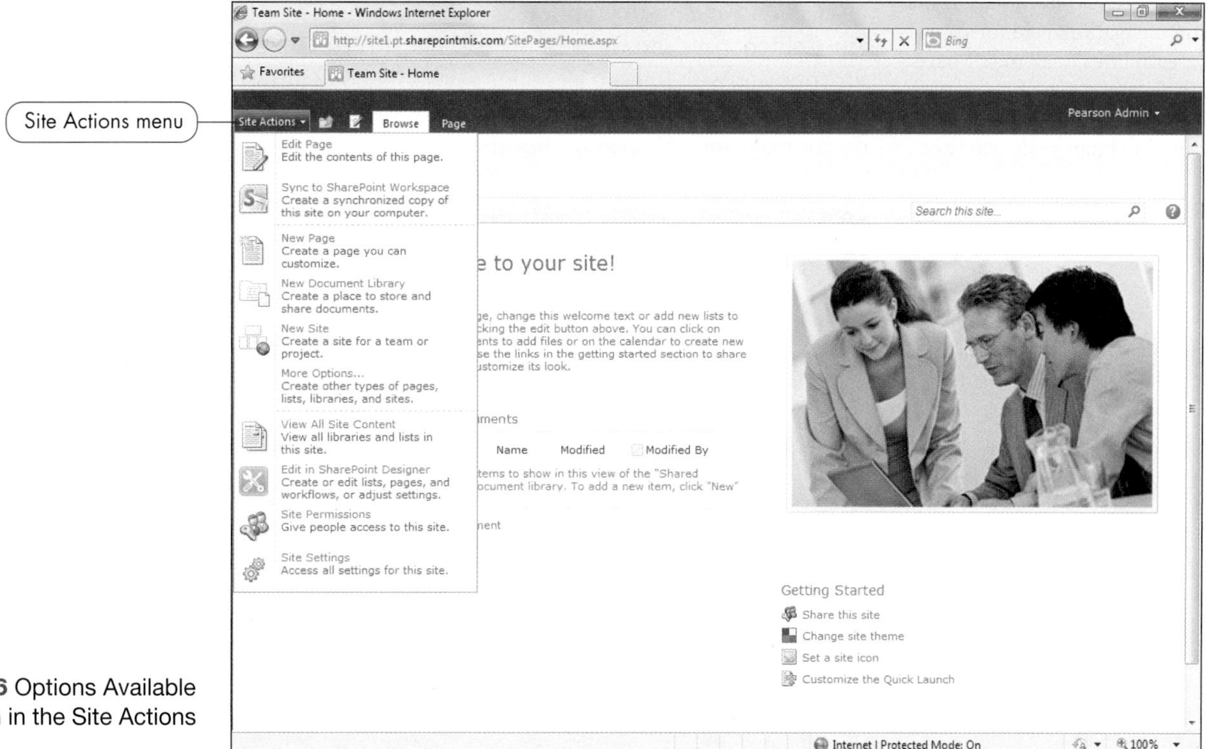

FIGURE 2.6 Options Available for Inclusion in the Site Actions Menu ➤

In a discussion on creating and managing SharePoint sites, two core topics should be considered: top-level sites and subsites. Top-level sites feature their own hierarchy and are at the top of the hierarchy in the site collection. Subsites are created within another SharePoint site, either in the top-level site or nested within another subsite.

The entire site hierarchy can be viewed from the top-level site by clicking Site Settings on the Site Actions menu, and then clicking the Site Hierarchy link in the Site Collection Administration section. The Site Hierarchy page, as shown in Figure 2.7, displays the URL and title for each site in the site collection. Click the URL to navigate to a site.

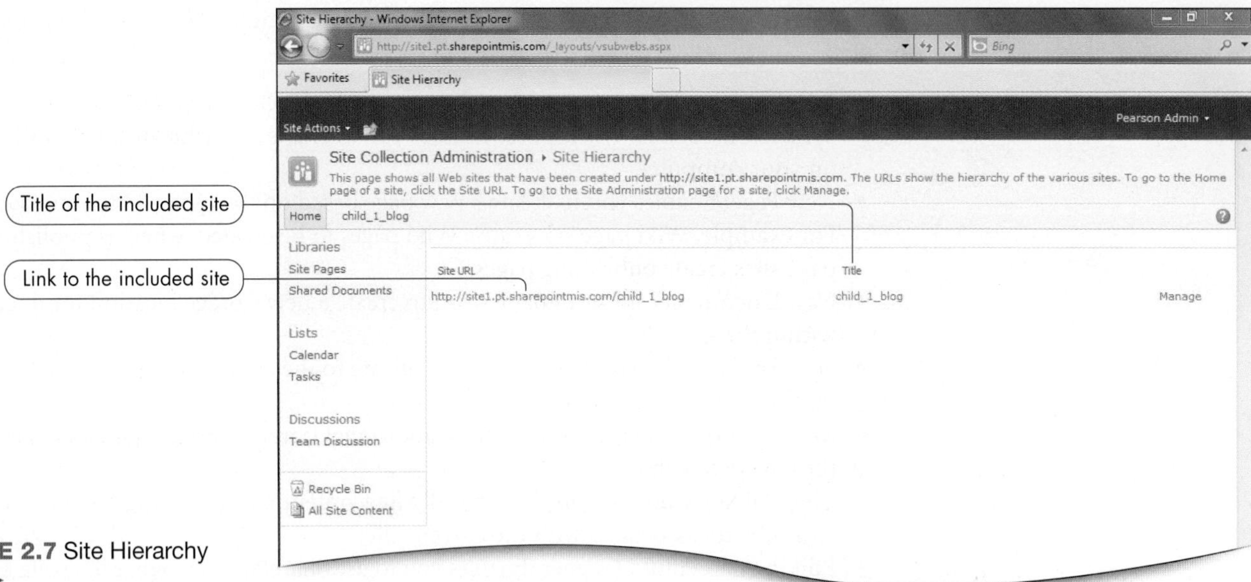

FIGURE 2.7 Site Hierarchy Page ➤

Create Subsites or Child Sites

The SharePoint Foundation hierarchy data structure, built upon parent and child sites, is conceptually similar to organizing your Windows file system data in folders.

The **All Site Content** page is the main navigational aid for your site, with links to all major parts of the site infrastructure, as well as all of the libraries, lists, discussion boards, and surveys.

Start creating a new subsite (or child site) by clicking the All Site Content link on the left Navigation Pane on the top-level site home page. The All Site Content link displays the All Site Content page shown in Figure 2.8. The ***All Site Content*** page is the main navigational aid for your site, with links to all major parts of the site infrastructure (such as child sites, workspaces, and the Recycle Bin), and lists all of the libraries, lists, discussion boards, and surveys on your site and child sites. Click the Create link to open the Create dialog box.

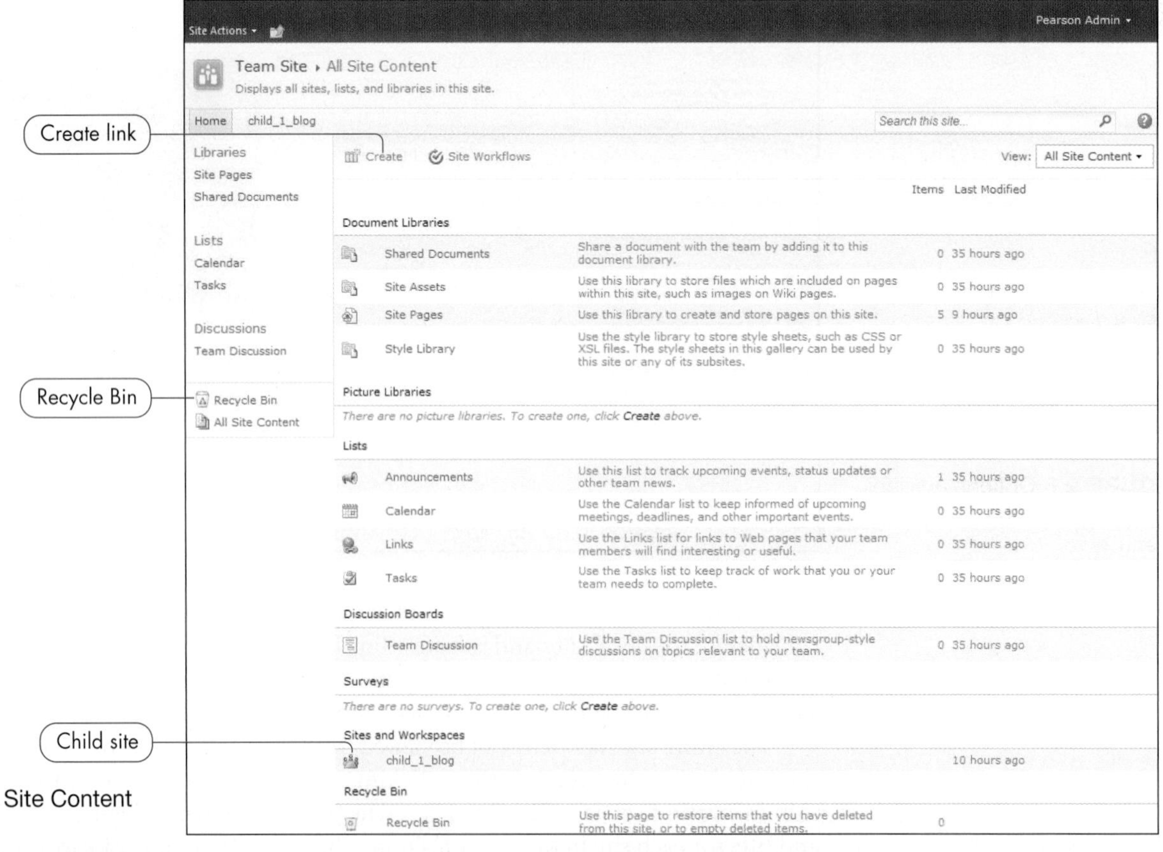

FIGURE 2.8 All Site Content Page ➤

If you have the Silverlight plug-in installed in your browser, the animated Create page will be displayed. Click the *Site link in the Filter By* section to display only the site templates, as shown in Figure 2.9a. The templates are clustered in categories, such as Collaboration, Communication, and Meetings. Click the template you want to use, enter the title for the site and the Web address in the URL field, and then click More Options to display additional navigational inheritance and inherit permissions settings for the new site, as shown in Figure 2.9b, and Create Page Sections Reference table.

> **TIP** Working without Silverlight Plug-in in Your Browser
>
> If you do not have the Silverlight plug-in installed on the browser, the Create dialog box will look similar to the Create Site Collection page of the SharePoint Central Administration site, as shown in Figure 2.1.

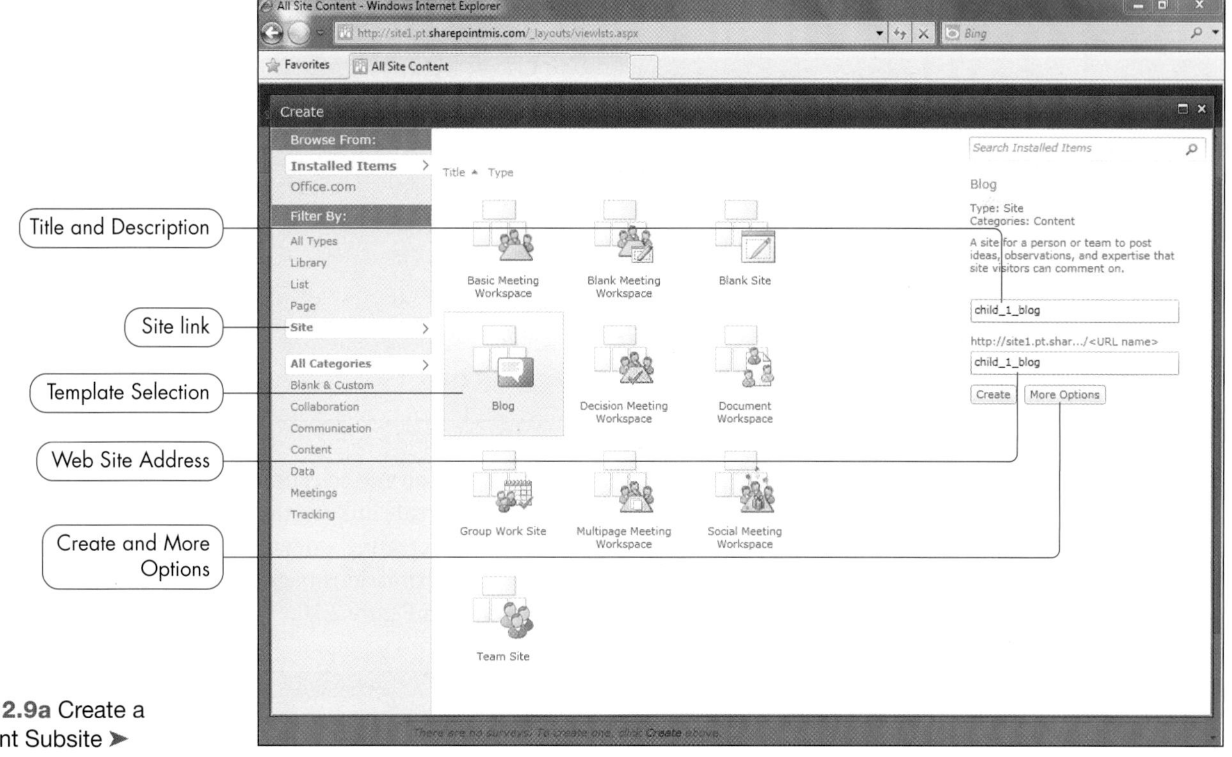

FIGURE 2.9a Create a SharePoint Subsite ➤

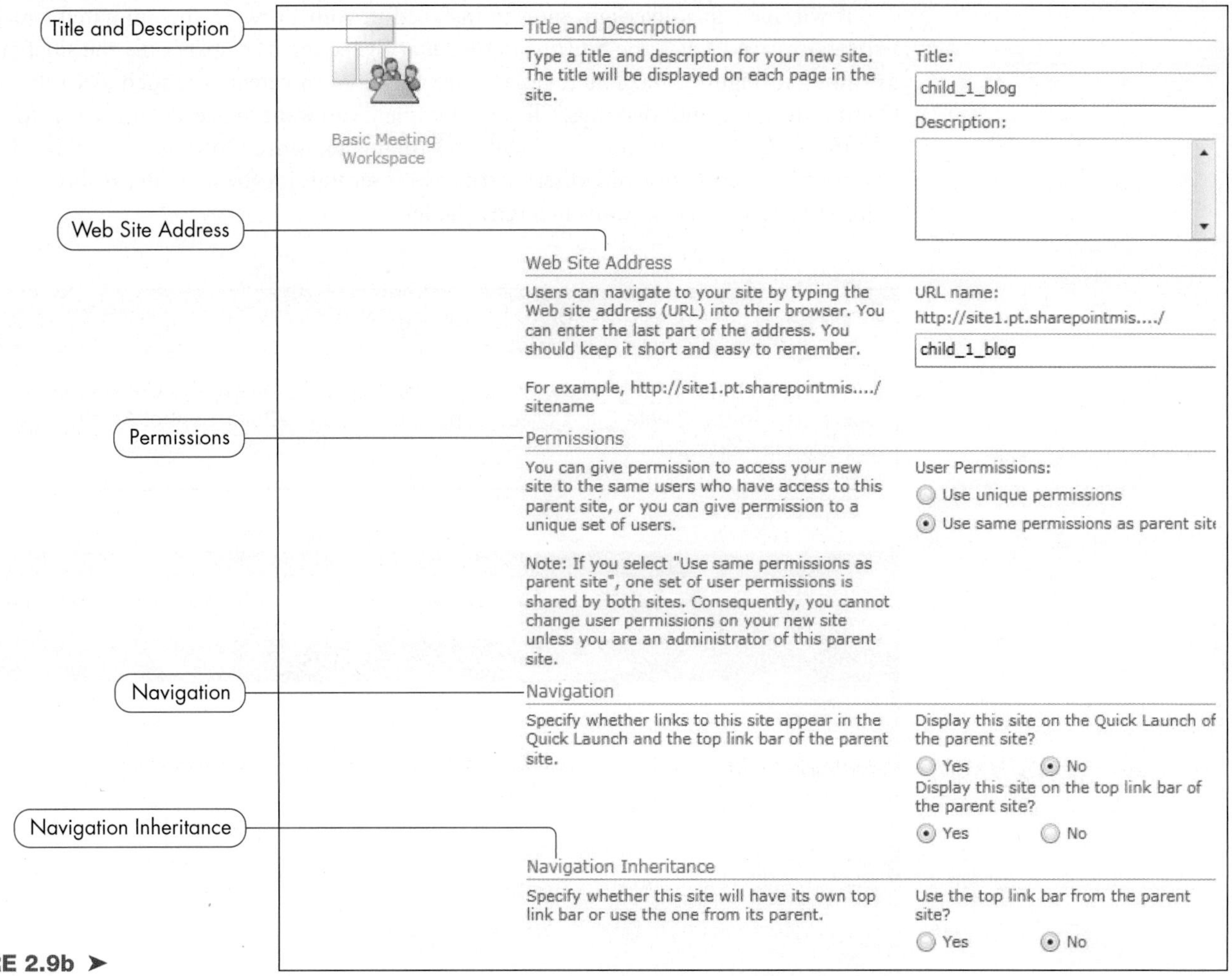

Title and Description
Web Site Address
Permissions
Navigation
Navigation Inheritance
Basic Meeting Workspace
Title and Description
Type a title and description for your new site. The title will be displayed on each page in the site.
Title:
child_1_blog
Description:
Web Site Address
Users can navigate to your site by typing the Web site address (URL) into their browser. You can enter the last part of the address. You should keep it short and easy to remember.
For example, http://site1.pt.sharepointmis..../sitename
URL name:
http://site1.pt.sharepointmis..../
child_1_blog
Permissions
You can give permission to access your new site to the same users who have access to this parent site, or you can give permission to a unique set of users.
Note: If you select "Use same permissions as parent site", one set of user permissions is shared by both sites. Consequently, you cannot change user permissions on your new site unless you are an administrator of this parent site.
User Permissions:
Use unique permissions
Use same permissions as parent sit
Navigation
Specify whether links to this site appear in the Quick Launch and the top link bar of the parent site.
Display this site on the Quick Launch of the parent site?
Yes
No
Display this site on the top link bar of the parent site?
Yes
No
Navigation Inheritance
Specify whether this site will have its own top link bar or use the one from its parent.
Use the top link bar from the parent site?
Yes
No

FIGURE 2.9b ➤

After supplying the required information and selecting the permissions, navigation, and navigation inheritance options, click the Create link to create a new child site, or click Cancel to return to the Create dialog box without creating a new site. You can adjust the navigation and permission settings later on the Site Permissions page (click the Site Actions menu, and then the Site Permissions link), as shown in Figure 2.10.

Permissions: child_1_blog - Windows Internet Explorer
http://site1.pt.sharepointmis.com/child_1_blog/_layouts/user.aspx
Favorites
Permissions: child_1_blog
Permission Tools
Site Actions
Browse
Edit
Pearson Admin
Manage Parent
Stop Inheriting Permissions
Grant Permissions
Create Group
Check Permissions
Inheritance
Grant
Check
This Web site inherits permissions from its parent. (Team Site)
Recycle Bin
All Site Content
Name
Type
Permission Levels
Pearson Admin (NSPIHOSTING\admin_pt)
User
Full Control
Pearson User 1 (NSPIHOSTING\pearsouse_pt)
User
Contribute
Team Site Members
SharePoint Group
Contribute
Team Site Owners
SharePoint Group
Full Control
Team Site Visitors
SharePoint Group
Read

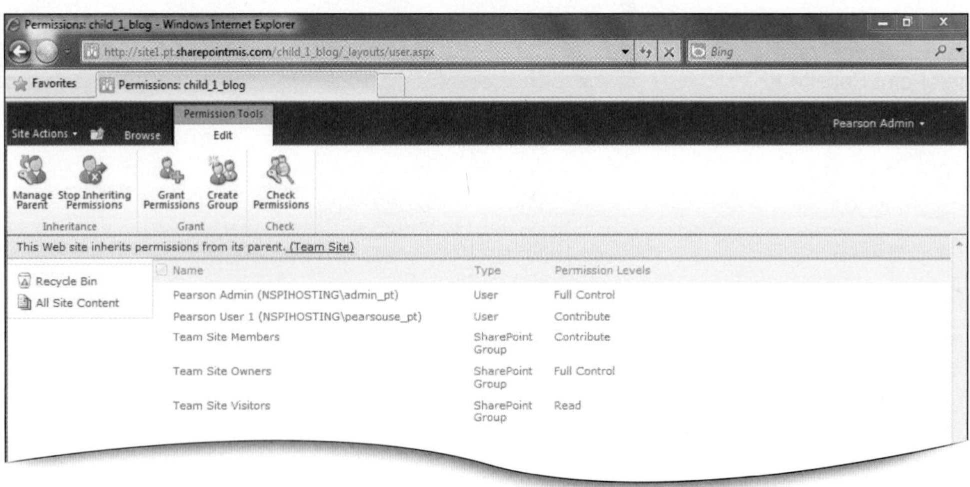

FIGURE 2.10 Site Permissions Page ➤

REFERENCE Create Page Sections

Section	Components	Description
Title and Description	Title box Description box	Type a title for the new site. Type a relevant description of the new site.
Web Site Address	URL name box	Type the last part of the value in the Internet browser's address bar that users will see when they visit this new site.
Permissions	Use unique permissions Use same permissions as parent site	Select to give permissions to a unique group of users. Select to give the same set of permissions to the parent and child sites.
Navigation	Display this site on the Quick Launch of the parent site Display this site on the top link bar of the parent site	Select Yes if you want the links to the new site to appear in the Quick Launch list. Select Yes if you want the links to the new site to appear on the top link bar of the parent site.
Navigation Inheritance	Use the top link bar from the parent site	Select Yes if you want the new site to share the same link bar with the parent site.

Change the Default Home Page for a SharePoint Site

You can set a page as the new SharePoint site home page using SharePoint Designer or the SharePoint Foundation Ribbon. To set a page as the site home page in SharePoint Designer, click Site Pages in the Navigation Pane, select the name of the page, and then click Set as Home Page in the Actions group of the File tab. You can also right-click the page name, and then select the Set as Home Page option from the context menu, as shown in Figure 2.11a. The icon of the home page will be displayed to the left of the new site home page.

To set a page as the site home page using the SharePoint Foundation Ribbon, open the page in a browser, click Make Homepage in the Page Actions group on the Page tab, and then click OK on the *Message from webpage alert* box, as shown in Figure 2.11.

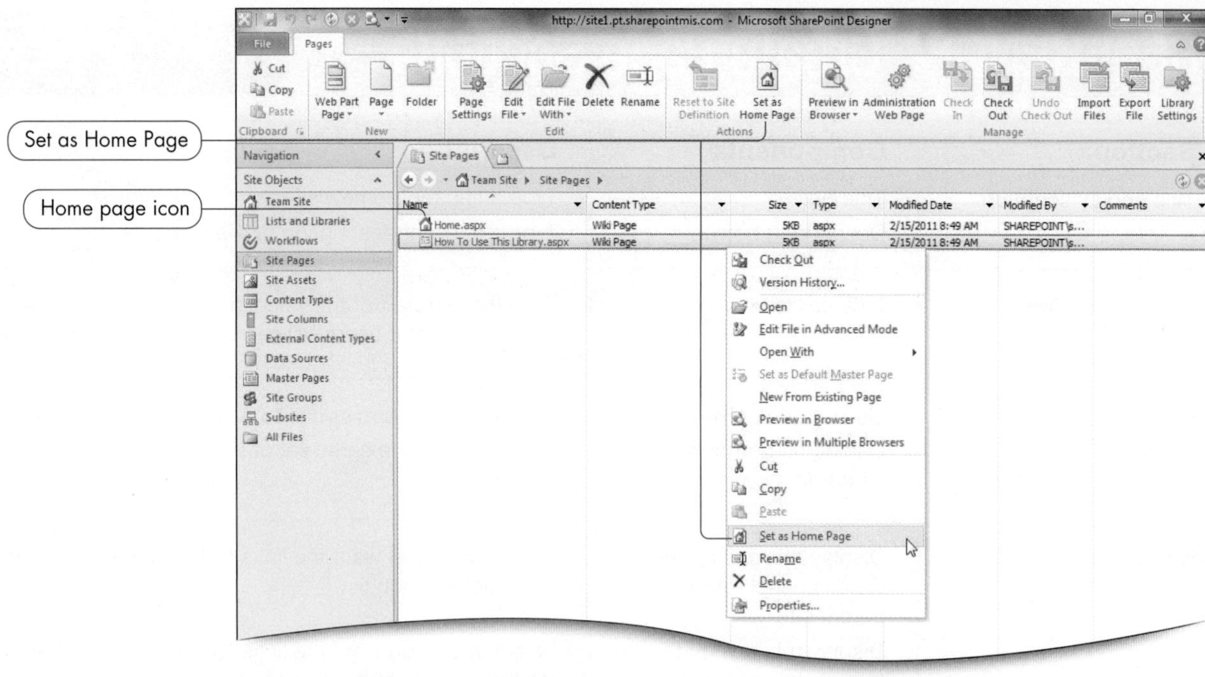

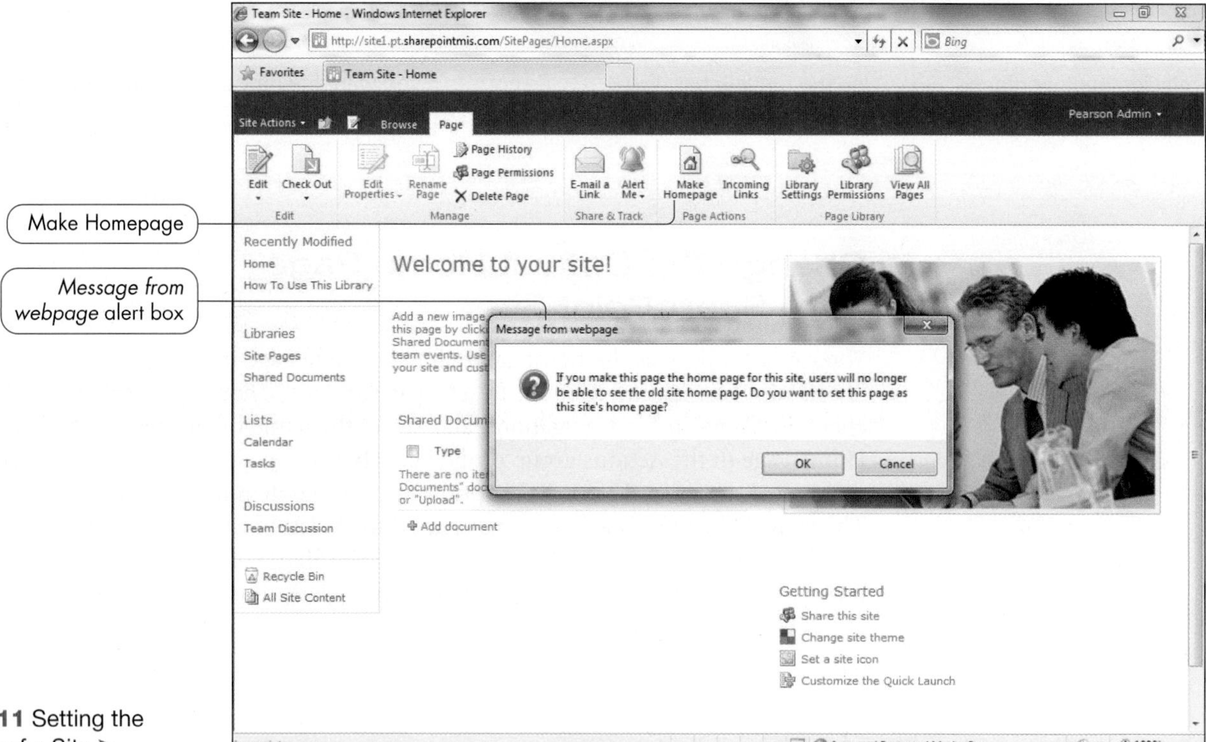

FIGURE 2.11 Setting the Home Page of a Site ➤

Adding New Web Pages

You can add new pages to SharePoint sites to fit the needs of your organization. The pages of the site can be customized using SharePoint Designer, the text entry tools, and Web Parts.

New SharePoint site pages are created using a Web browser or SharePoint Designer. When using SharePoint Designer, new pages can be created using the Backstage view or the Ribbon. The Pages section of the Add Item page of the SharePoint Designer Backstage view enables you to:

- Add a Web Part page
- Add a Wiki page

- Add a New Page from Master
- Add More Pages : HTML, ASPX, CSS, Master Page, Java Script, XML, or Text File

Add an ASPX and HTML Page

The Pages tab of SharePoint Designer Ribbon is used to easily add a new ASPX or HTML page. Open the site, click Site Pages on the Navigation Pane, click Page in the New group of the Pages tab, and then select ASPX to add a new ASP.NET (.aspx) page or select HTML to add a new HTML (.html) page, as shown in Figure 2.12. A new Untitled_1.aspx or Untitled_1.html page will open in the document window.

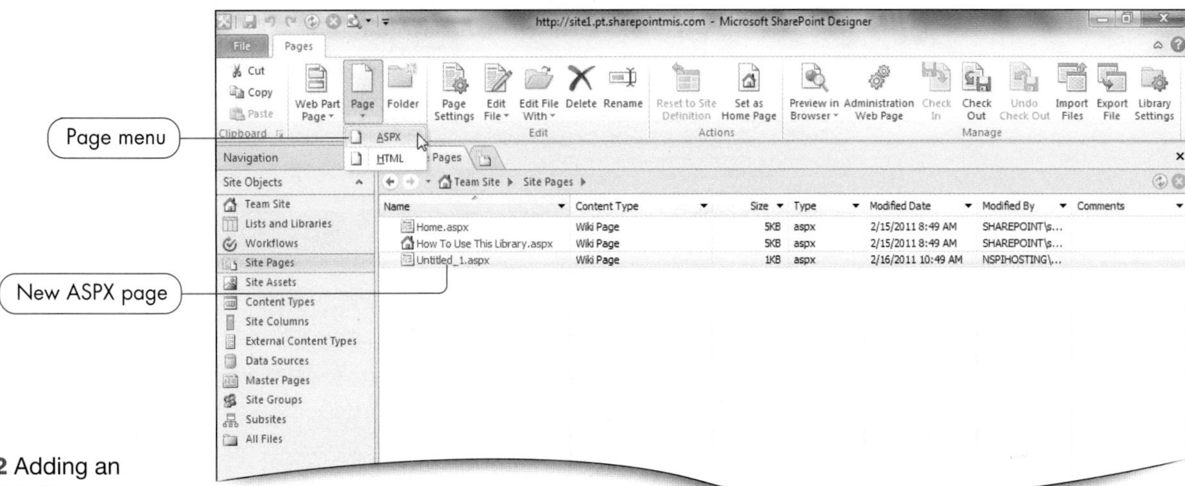

FIGURE 2.12 Adding an ASPX and HTML Page ➤

Attach and Detach a Master Page

Master pages provide consistency between the pages of a Web site by providing common layouts and font styles. You can create a new master page from a blank page in a site. In SharePoint Designer, click Untitled_1.aspx, as shown in Figure 2.12, and then click Edit file in the *Customization* section of the Untitled_1.aspx Summary page to open the page in Advanced Edit mode. The Style tab of the SharePoint Designer Advanced Editor Ribbon (displayed when a Web page is visible in the SharePoint window) enables you to attach or detach a master page, as shown in Figure 2.13.

Click Attach in the Master Page group of the Style tab, and then select a master page from the list, as shown in Figure 2.13. It is a good practice to click Save on the Quick Access Toolbar to save the file before making changes to the page.

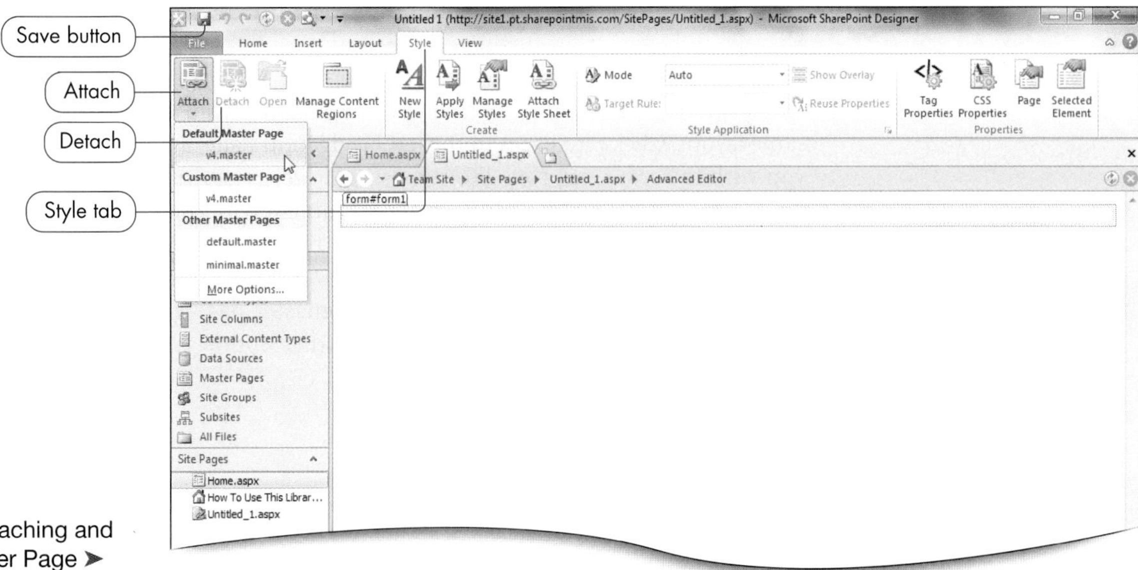

FIGURE 2.13 Attaching and Detaching a Master Page ➤

Add a Web Part Page

Web Parts are components that are added to Web Part pages and are dependent on the type of site you are creating. Some examples of Web Parts are content, images, viewers, forms, and more. Web Part pages require a Document Library; therefore, you must ensure that a library is available before creating new pages for a site.

Web Parts are placed within the layout in Web Part zones. People with the appropriate permissions (full control or design levels) can place the Web Parts in columns and rows on the page. In the SharePoint Foundation browser interface, click More Options on the Site Actions menu, and then select the Web Part Page icon on the Installed Items section of the Create window. Click the Create link to display the New Web Part page, as shown in Figure 2.14. Type a name for the page, and then select the layout template for the Web Part zones. Select the Save Location for the page, and then click the Create link to finalize your selections.

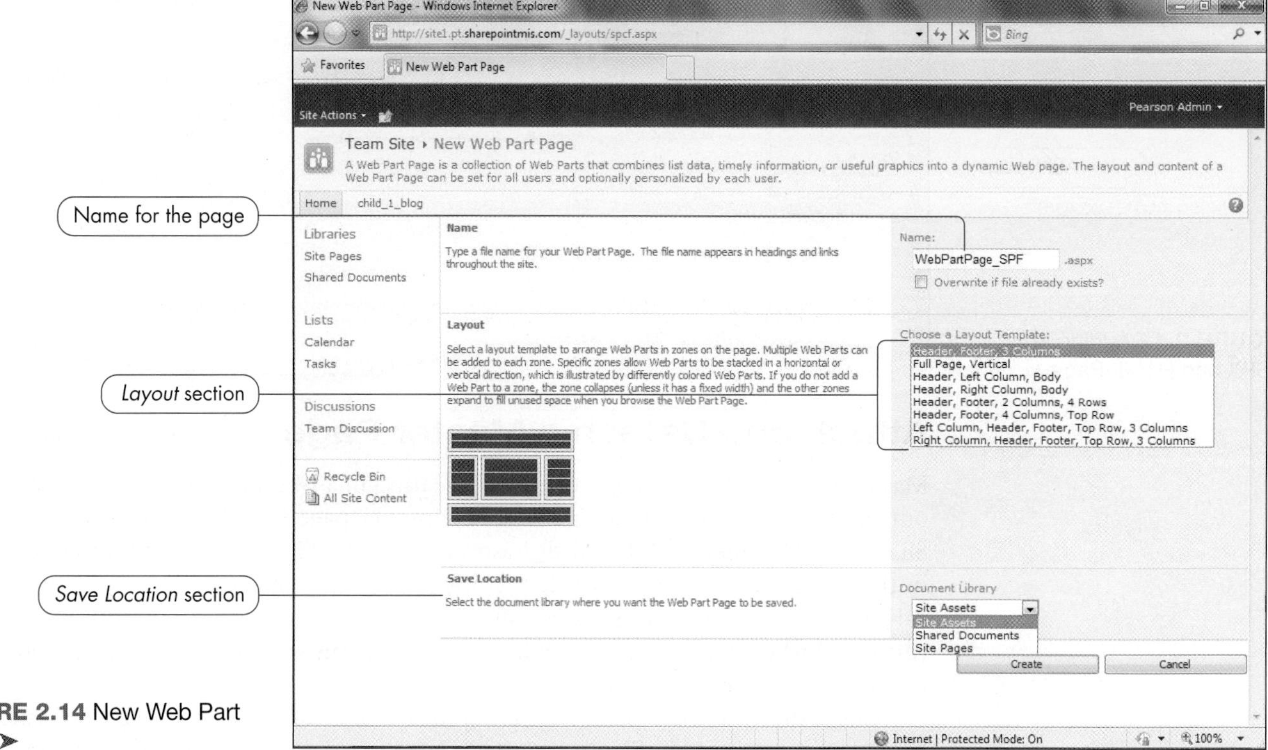

FIGURE 2.14 New Web Part Page ➤

Some features of a Web Part page, such as the page layout, cannot be changed using the SharePoint Foundation browser user interface once the page is created. You will need to use SharePoint Designer for further customization.

In SharePoint Designer, you can add a new Web Part page by copying an existing Web Part page. This method creates cohesiveness within your site by producing pages with the same layout. Click Site Pages in the left Navigation Pane, and then right-click the page name you wish to copy. Click New From Existing Page, as shown in Figure 2.15a. A new Web Part page (Untitled_1.aspx) will open in the document window.

You can also add a new Web Part page based on an ASPX page by attaching a master page and then inserting Web Part zones and Web Parts. Click Master Pages in the left Navigation Pane, and then right-click the master page you wish to use. Click New from Master Page, as shown in Figure 2.15b. Another option is to click Page from Master in the New group of the Master Pages tab.

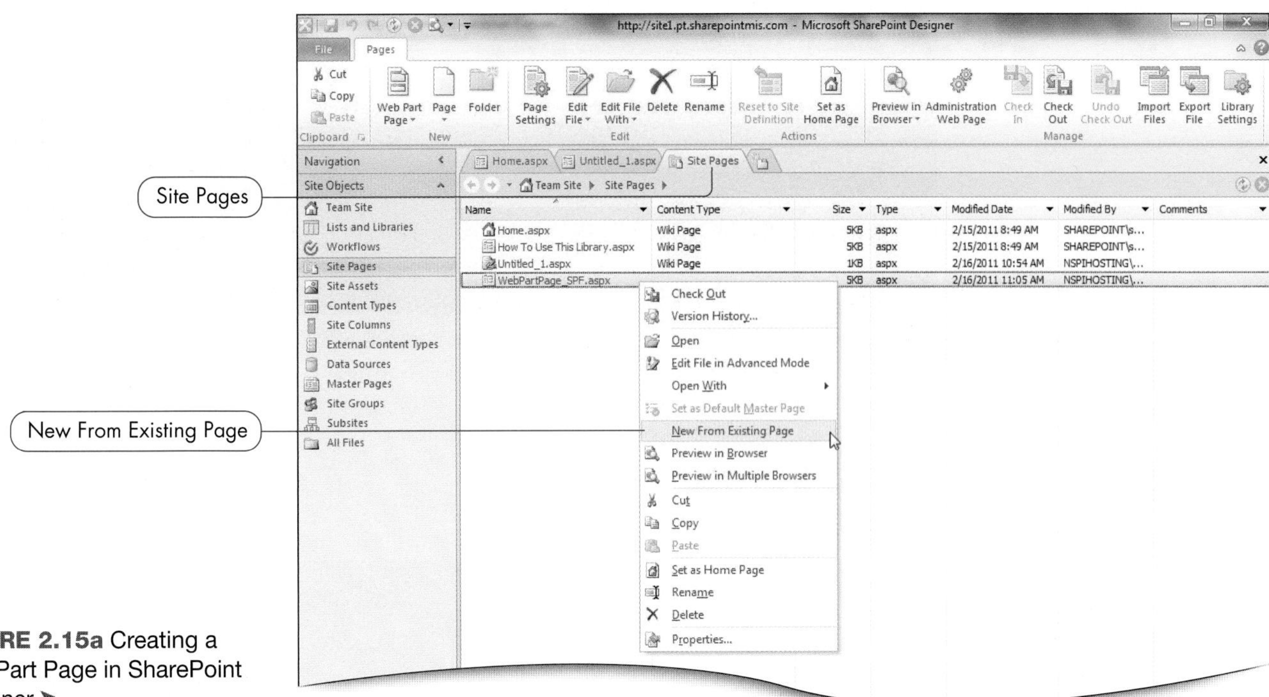

FIGURE 2.15a Creating a Web Part Page in SharePoint Designer ➤

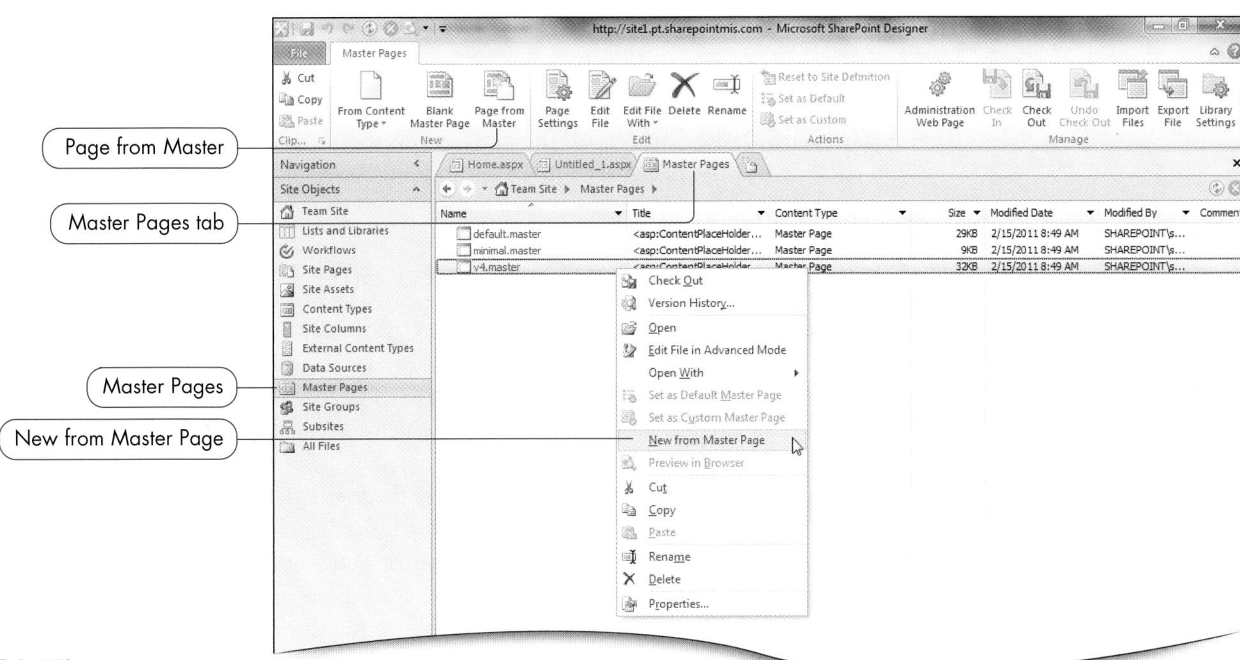

FIGURE 2.15b ➤

Add a Wiki Page

Wiki Pages are stored, by default, in the Site Pages Document Library. Media content is stored in an assets library. If these libraries do not exist the first time you choose to create a Wiki page, a dialog box asking if you want the libraries to be created will appear. This is not necessary to some site templates, such as the Team Site template, because these libraries are a part of the template by default. In the SharePoint Foundation browser user interface, click the New Page link on the Site Actions menu from the site's home page. Enter the name of the page in the New Page dialog box, as shown in Figure 2.16, and then click Create.

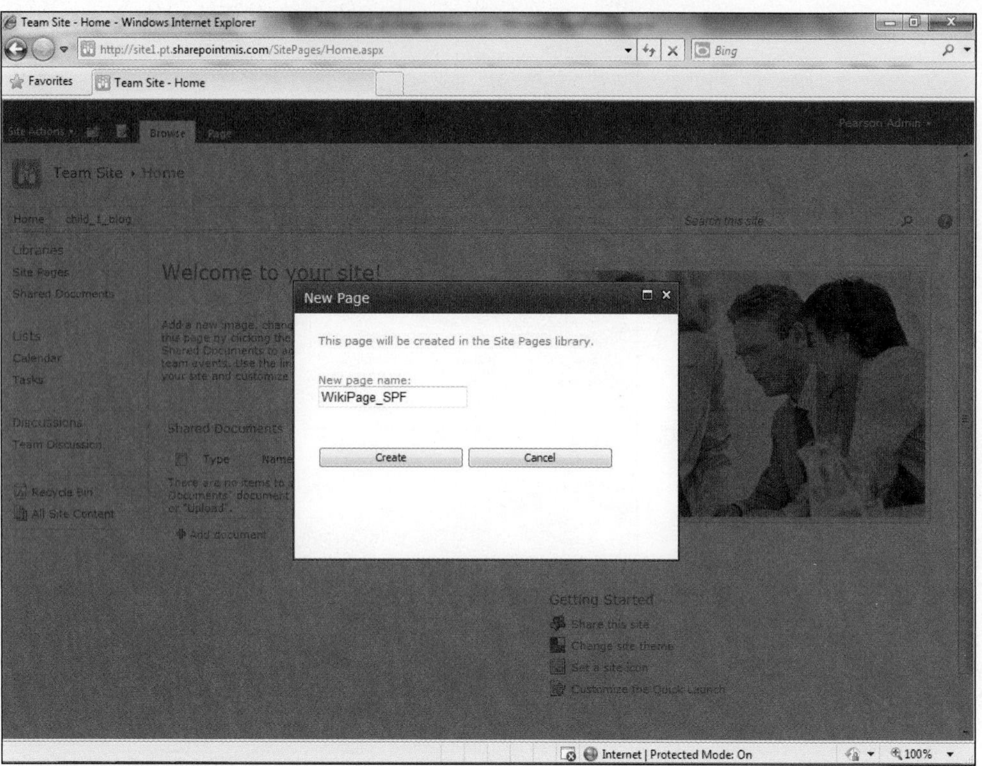

FIGURE 2.16 Creating a Wiki Page ➤

You will notice that other site templates do not have the New Page link on the Site Actions menu. If you want to create a Wiki page on one of these sites, the Blank Site for instance, click More Options on the Site Actions menu, and then select the Page icon. When you click Create, the necessary Site Pages and Site Assets libraries will be created.

Reset SharePoint Pages to Site Definitions

You will most certainly want and/or need to customize the look, feel, and functionalities of your SharePoint site toward meeting the objectives of your organization. SharePoint Designer is the perfect tool to make these types of changes.

Pages on a site are based on templates which have a site definition. The site definition, and therefore the template page, is shared across all of the pages within the site collection in a concept called "ghosting." As you customize these site pages, only the differences between the original site definition and the changes you made are saved into the content libraries. This improves the loading performance of your Web page because the template page loads from the cache memory and then the changes are added to the page.

An **unghosted** page is a customized page that does not contain the characteristics of the standard configuration and layout of the site definition.

Reghost means to reset the pages to the original site definition.

As you use SharePoint Designer to update the site pages, they become unghosted. ***Unghosted*** pages are customized pages that do not contain the characteristics of the standard configuration and layout of the site definition. These unghosted pages are stored in the content libraries of the site and loaded from the libraries when requested by a browser. This slows the performance of the Web site. To regain the advantage of the ghosting concept, you can reghost all or part of the pages within a site. ***Reghost*** means to reset the pages to the original site definition. This removes any customization, reverting the page back to the configuration and layout of the template. From the site home page, using the SharePoint foundation browser user interface, click Site Settings on the Site Actions menu, and then click the *Reset to site definition* link. If you only wish to reset one page, click *Reset specific page to site definition version*, as shown in Figure 2.17, type the URL of the page you wish to reghost, and then click Reset. To reghost all of the pages in a site, click Reset all pages in this site to site definition version. Click Reset to complete the action. Using SharePoint Designer, you can display the Reset Page to Site Definition page by clicking Reset to Template on the File tab.

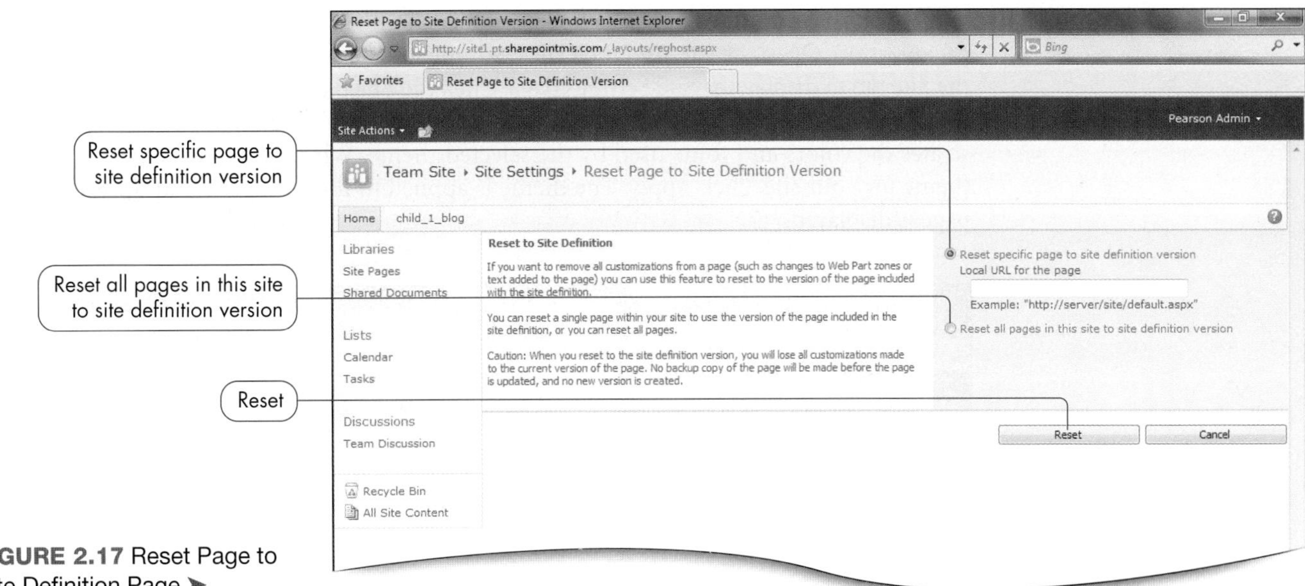

FIGURE 2.17 Reset Page to Site Definition Page ➤

Branding SharePoint Foundation Sites

As a site designer, you can create a custom brand for your sites using Master pages, Cascading Style Sheets (CSS), and site themes.

A **site theme** defines the font and color schemes for a site.

As a site designer, you can create a custom brand for your sites using Master pages, Cascading Style Sheets (CSS), and site themes. A ***site theme***, similar to other Microsoft themes, defines the font and color schemes for a site. Only users with design or full control permission levels can customize site themes.

SharePoint Foundation sites use CSS to apply colors, graphics, and positioning to the various objects on a page. Multiple style sheets can be applied to a single page. To customize these styles, you can modify them directly in the master page or site page, or modify the styles directly in the CSS file attached to the page.

Themes enable you to make color and font selections for page elements that you can quickly apply to the complete site. If you make modifications to the theme, they will be reflected on all pages of the site. This provides a consistent look and feel to all of the pages in the site. Color themes affect page elements such as backgrounds, text, hyperlinks, and some graphic elements such as bullets and horizontal rules (or lines). Font themes dictate the fonts used for titles and body text. Themes can be applied to SharePoint Foundation 2010 site template pages or to custom master pages.

As you plan for a site, you consider the look and feel of the site and how you might brand it to reflect your organization. For instance, if you are planning a university Web site, you will probably use the school's colors as a basis for selecting theme colors for the site. You will probably also consider the skills of your Web development team as you decide whether to use themes, CSS files, or custom master pages. A combination of these three options provides a high level of customization to a site. Table 2.1 describes different levels of customization and recommends the solution best suited for each level.

TABLE 2.1 SharePoint Sites Levels of Customization

Customization Criteria	Solution
Allow site owners to change colors and fonts	Themes
Make changes to other design elements such as font size and spacing	CSS
Completely change the page structure and design	Master Pages

Using SharePoint Designer, you can modify the theme to effectively brand it for your organization. Open the site, and then click Administration Web Page in the Manage group of the Site tab to display the Site Settings page. Click the *Site theme* link in the *Look and Feel* section. Select the theme to apply from the list, as shown in Figure 2.18. The preview demonstrates the colors and fonts used by the selected theme. When you have settled on the best theme for your site, click Apply. The theme is applied to the entire site and the Site Settings page is displayed.

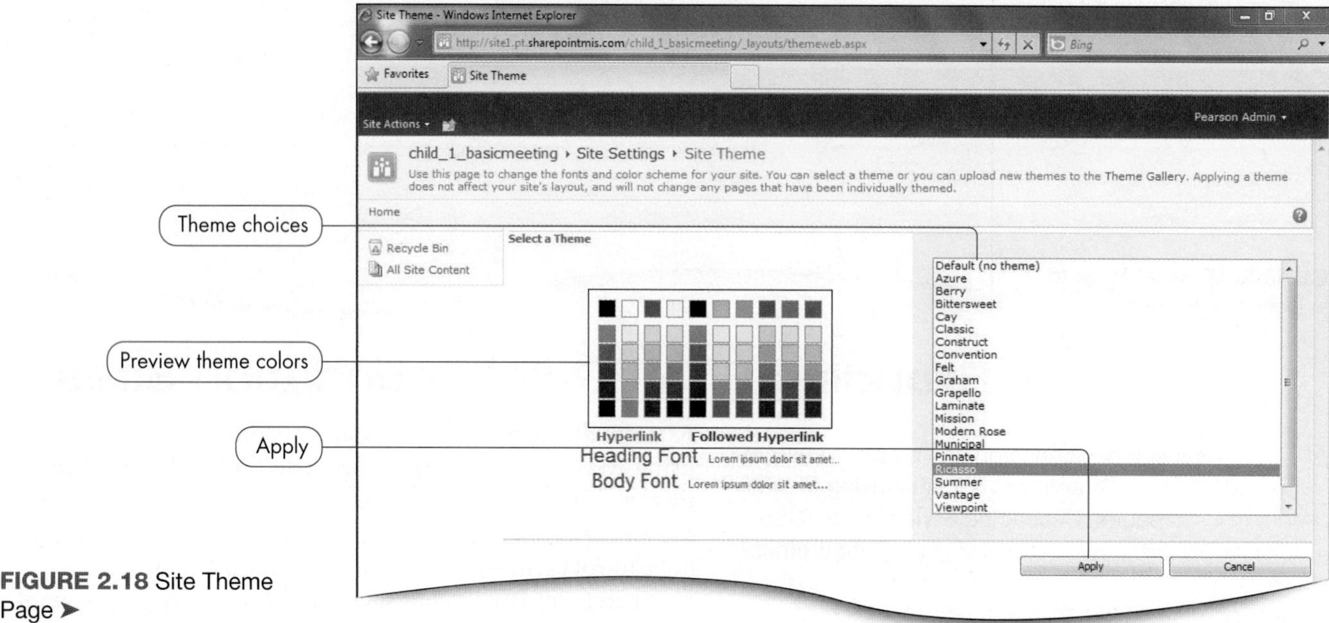

FIGURE 2.18 Site Theme Page ➤

In SharePoint 2010, you can create a SharePoint theme without any CSS knowledge, easily deploy it to your server, and apply it using just your Internet browser (of course you can do that as well using SharePoint Designer).

The Ribbon of the SharePoint Designer Editor page enables you to edit just some of the content page elements, such as Wiki fields and Web Part zones, and includes three tabs, Home, Insert and View, as shown in Figure 2.19a. If you move the mouse pointer over page areas that cannot be changed, the pointer changes into an Unavailable cursor (see Figure 2.19a). For this reason, editing a page using the SharePoint Designer Editor page is also known as the Safe Editing mode.

The Ribbon of the SharePoint Designer Advanced Editor page enables you to edit the content page, as well as the master page, and includes two more tabs—the Layout tab and the Style tab, as shown in Figure 2.19b. For this reason, editing a page using the SharePoint Designer Advanced Editor page is also known as the Advanced Editing mode. You will always use the Advanced Editing mode when you need to create or modify the layout and style of pages. Appendices of this textbook introduce you to CSS and SharePoint Designer tools you can use to work in the Advanced Editing mode.

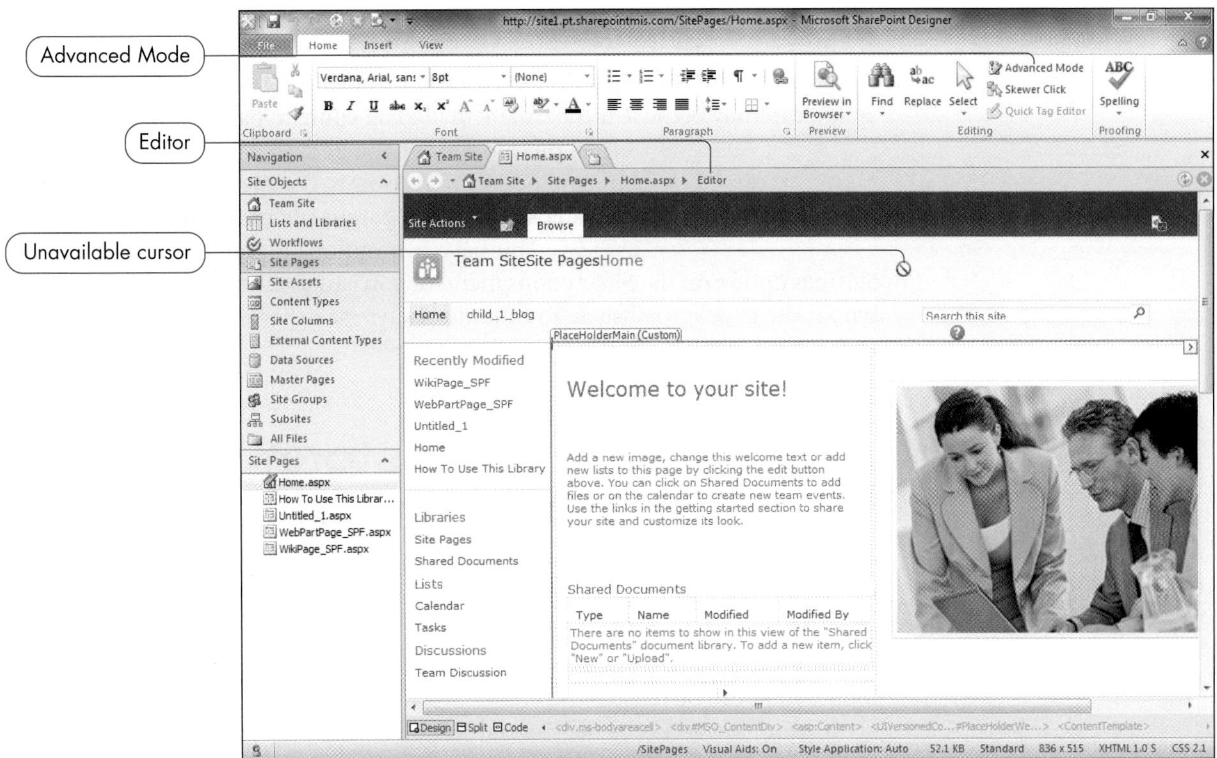

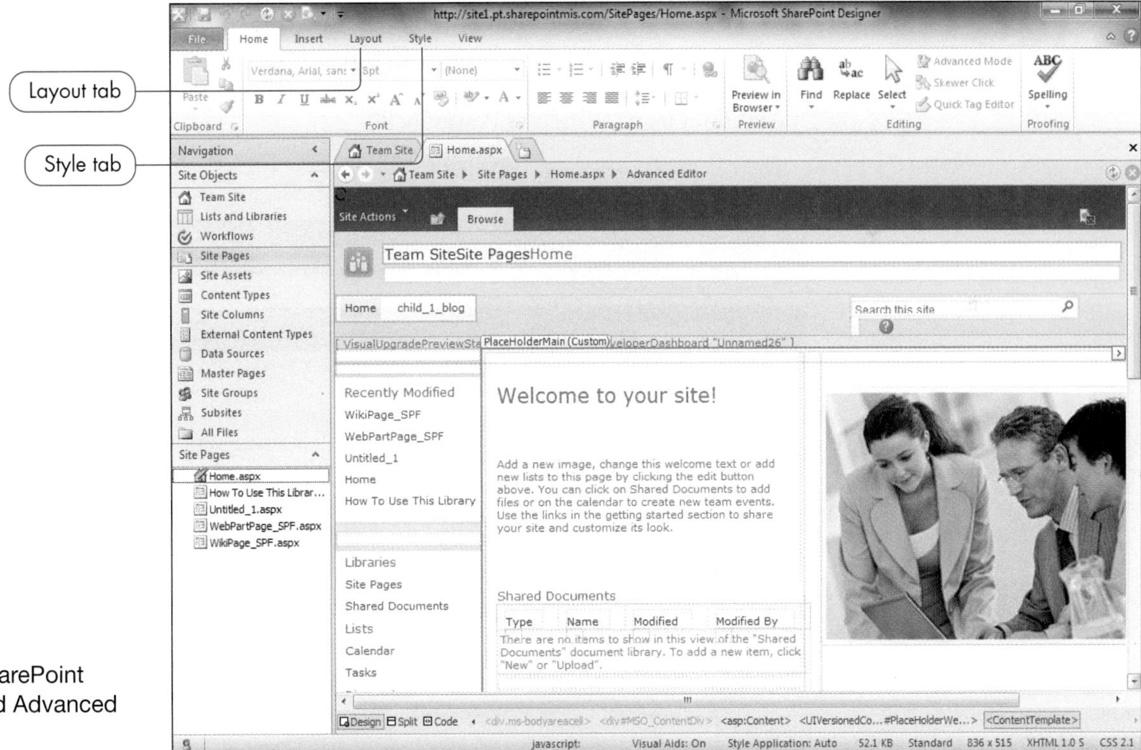

FIGURE 2.19 SharePoint Designer Safe and Advanced Editing Modes ➤

Deleting Sites

After some time, you may decide you want to delete a site from SharePoint. Consider this action carefully because it is permanent, and all content, pages, and the site itself are deleted. A deleted site will not be stored in the Recycle Bin; hence, you will not be able to recover it. If a site contains subsites, you will not be able to delete the parent site until you have deleted the subsites.

A deleted site will not be stored in the Recycle Bin; hence, you will not be able to recover it.

You have two options for site deletion. You can use the Site Settings option on the Site Actions menu or you can use the Sites and Workspaces page of the parent site to delete subsites. You should always make backups of your sites in order to avoid the loss of hours and hours of work.

Backing Up and Restoring SharePoint Sites and Content

SharePoint systems have always offered a wide range of backup and restore tools. You can back up and restore SharePoint sites using the SharePoint Foundation browser interface or SharePoint Designer. You can also use the Save List as Template and Save Site as Template functions to manually generate ad hoc copies of lists and sites that can be used to create models that can be reused.

If you have access to the Central Administration site, you can back up a whole site collection (as a .bak file) and export a site or a list (as a .cmp file), as shown in Figure 2.20. Using the Central Administration Backup and Restore page, you cannot restore sites collections, sites, and lists. A restoration requires the use of Windows PowerShell (see the Microsoft "Getting Started with Windows PowerShell for SharePoint Server 2010 Administrators" video (http://technet.microsoft.com/en-us/sharepoint/ee518673.aspx) if you wish to learn more about using Windows PowerShell.

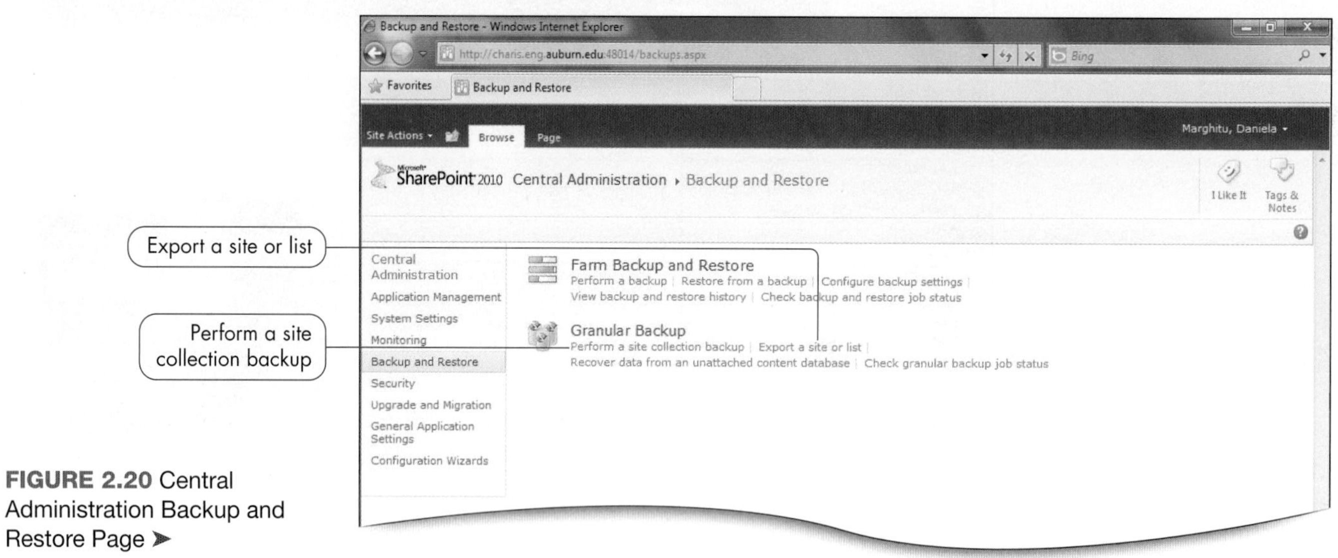

FIGURE 2.20 Central Administration Backup and Restore Page ➤

HANDS-ON EXERCISES

1 Tools for Creating a SharePoint Site

Nadia, Leslie, and Conner are eager to start working with you on creating the new DestinQuest SharePoint 2010 site. You will learn how to create new sites using SharePoint Foundation templates, add a new Wiki page to a site, change the default home page of a site, and change a site theme using SharePoint Designer. Then, you will learn how to customize a master page and create a new page from it. Finally, you will learn how to reset all pages to the original site definition.

Skills covered: • Log On to Your SharePoint Collection • Create a Site Using the Blank Site Template and Add a Wiki Page • Set the New Page as the Site Home Page • Change the Site Theme Using SharePoint Designer • Create a Page from v4.master and Customize It • Delete a Site

STEP 1 LOG ON TO YOUR SHAREPOINT COLLECTION

Before you can start creating a SharePoint Foundation site, you must log on to your SharePoint Collection. Refer to Figure 2.21 as you complete Step 1.

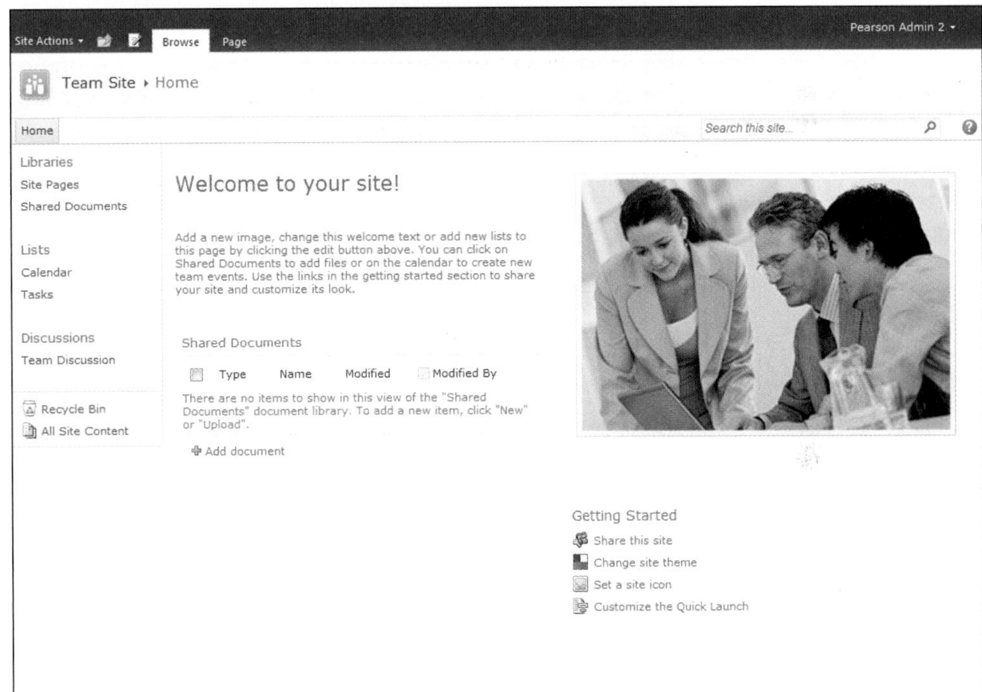

FIGURE 2.21 Logging on to a SharePoint Collection Collections ➤

a. Click **Start** to display the Start menu. Click **All Programs**, and then click **Internet Explorer** to open the program.

> **TROUBLESHOOTING:** Check with instructor for the URL of your top-level site, user name, and password.

b. Go to the top-level site provided by your instructor, which will be in the format of http: //pt.sharepointmis.com/SitePages/*yourname*.

> **TROUBLESHOOTING:** It might take a few seconds to access your top-level site on your Internet connection.

c. Enter the user name and password provided by your instructor.

If you logged in correctly, the home page of the top-level site is now displayed in Internet Explorer. Your screen will look similar with the one shown in Figure 2.21.

STEP 2 CREATE A SITE USING THE BLANK SITE TEMPLATE AND ADD A WIKI PAGE

You will now create a site using the Blank Site template, and then add a Wiki page. Refer to Figure 2.22 as you complete Step 2.

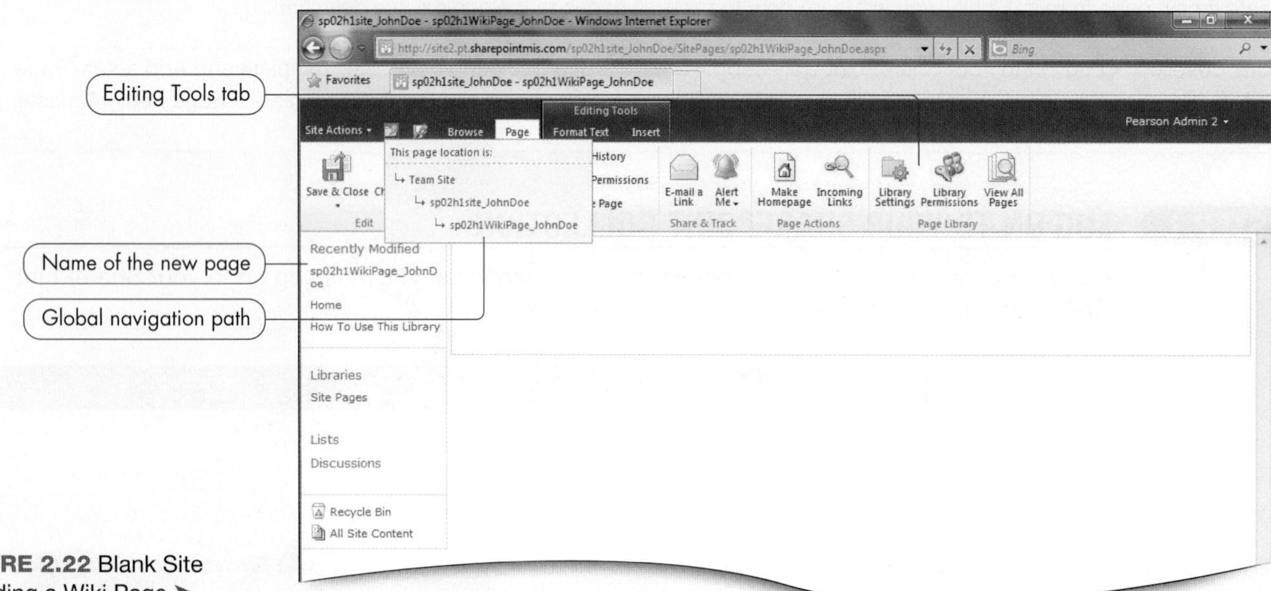

FIGURE 2.22 Blank Site Including a Wiki Page ➤

a. Click the **All Site Content link** on the Navigation Pane of the top-level site.

The All Site Content page is now displayed.

b. Click the **Create link** to open the Create dialog box.

The Create dialog box is now displayed.

c. Click **Site** in the *Filter By* section of the Create dialog box.

Only the site templates are now displayed.

d. Click **Blank Site**, type **sp02h1site_LastNameFirstName** in the **Title** and **URL name boxes**, and then click **More Options**.

e. Review all the listed options. Click **Create**.

The *sp02h1site_LastNameFirstName* page should now be displayed.

f. Click **Site Actions**, and then click **More Options**.

The Create dialog box is now displayed.

g. Click **Page** in the *Filter By* section of the Create dialog box, and then click the **Page icon**. Type **sp02h1WikiPage_LastNameFirstName** in the **Title box**, and then click **Create**.

The New Page alert box is now displayed, indicating that there must be a default Wiki page library and a site assets library.

h. Click **Create**. Click the **Page tab**, and then click **Navigate Up** to display the global navigation path.

Your screen should now look similar to Figure 2.22.

STEP 3 SET THE NEW PAGE AS THE SITE HOME PAGE

You will set as the home page the Wiki page created in Step 2. Refer to Figure 2.23 as you complete Step 3.

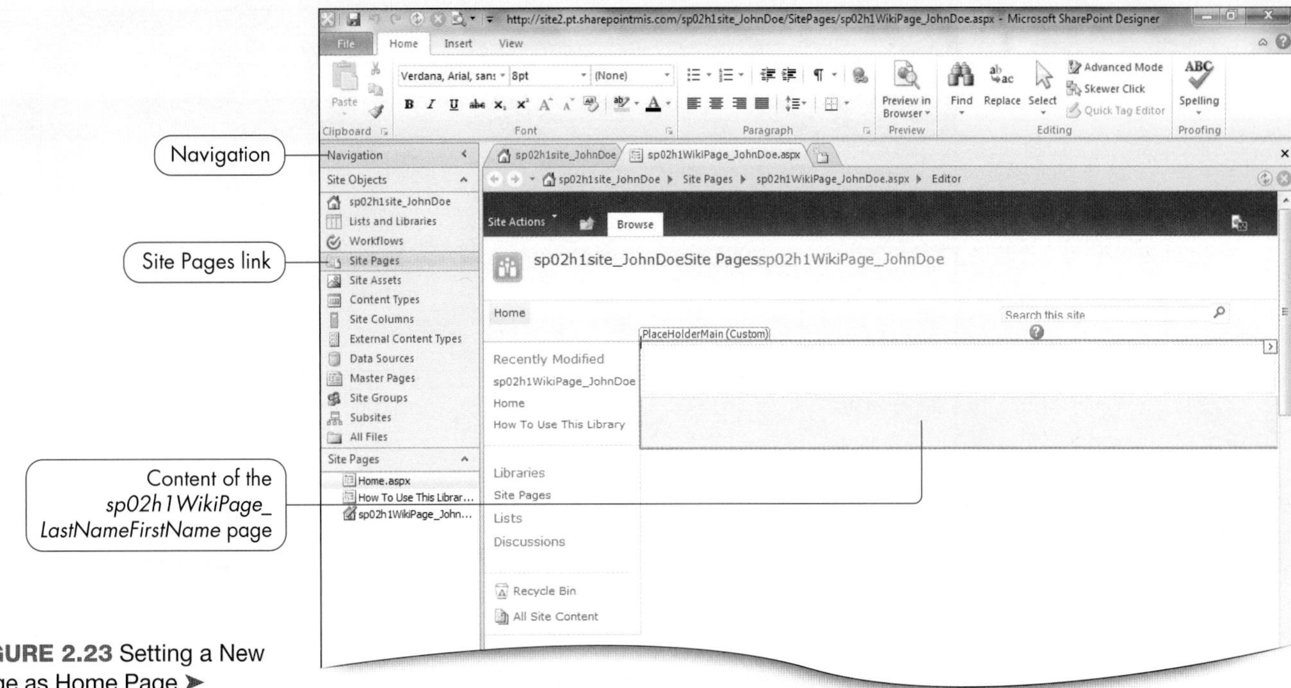

FIGURE 2.23 Setting a New Page as Home Page ➤

a. Click **Make Home Page** in the Page Actions group on the Page tab.

b. Click **OK** in the *Message from webpage* alert box.

c. Click **View All Pages** in the Page Library group.

d. Click **Site Actions**, and then click **Edit in SharePoint Designer** on the Site Actions menu. Enter the password provided by your instructor, if required, and then click **OK.**

   The Site Settings page of the *sp02h1site_LastNameFirstName* site is now displayed in the SharePoint Designer window.

e. Click **Edit site home page** in the *Customization* section of the Site Settings page.

   You should now see the *sp02h1WikiPage_LastNameFirstName* page in Editor mode and Design view. Your screen should look similar to Figure 2.23.

f. Click **Site Pages** on the Navigation Pane.

   You should now see the *sp02h1WikiPage_LastNameFirstName* page with the home page icon to the left of its name.

STEP 4 CHANGE THE SITE THEME USING SHAREPOINT DESIGNER

You will change the theme of the site created in Step 2. Refer to Figure 2.24 as you complete Step 4.

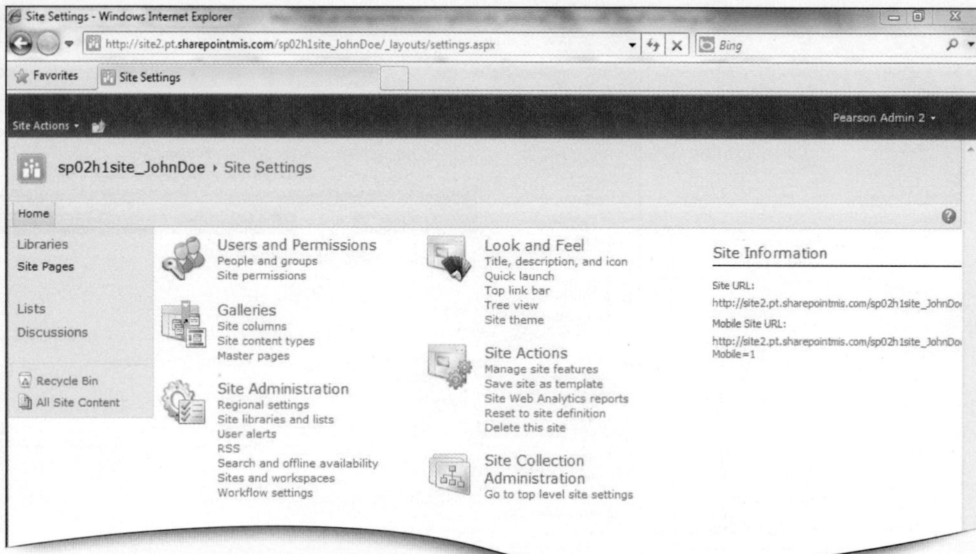

FIGURE 2.24 Changing the Theme of a SharePoint Site Using SharePoint Designer ➤

a. Click **sp02h1site_LastNameFirstName** on the Navigation Pane.

   The Site Settings page is now displayed

b. Click **Change site theme** under the Customization link of the Site Settings page.

   The Site Theme page is now displayed in the browser.

c. Click the **Azure theme**, and then click **Apply**.

   The Site Settings page is now displayed in the browser using the Azure theme. Your screen should look similar to the image in Figure 2.24.

d. Click the **Navigate Up button**, and then select **Team Site**.

   The home page of the top-level site is still displayed using the default theme.

e. Close the SharePoint Designer window.

STEP 5 CREATE A PAGE FROM V4.MASTER AND CUSTOMIZE IT

You will create a new page from the v4.master page. Refer to Figure 2.25 as you complete Step 5.

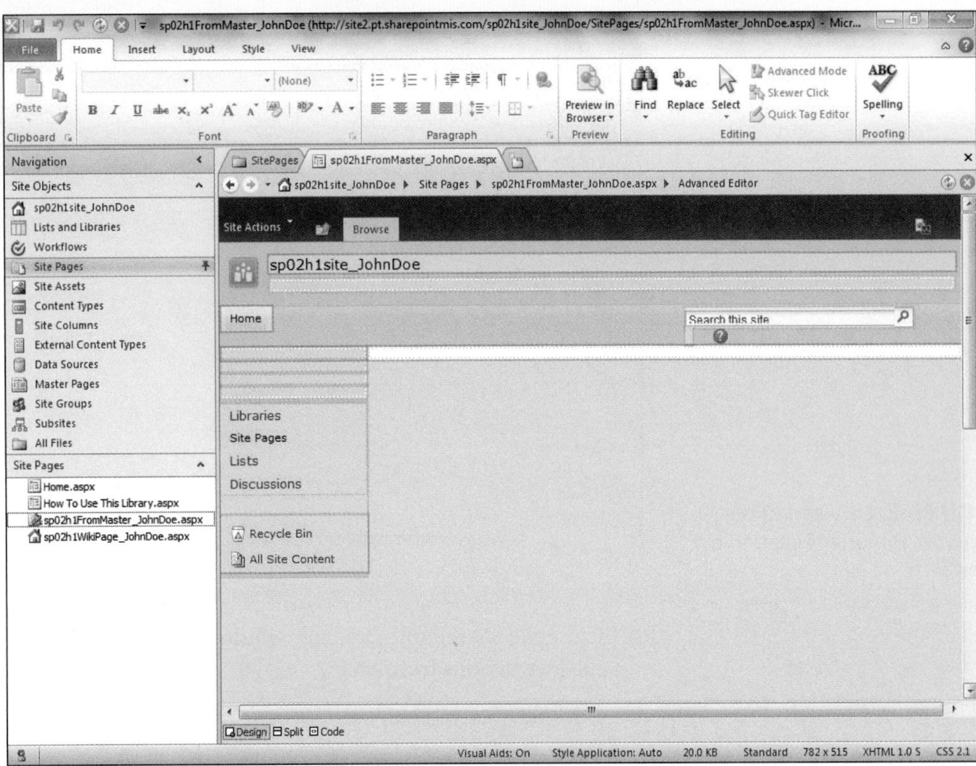

FIGURE 2.25 Creating a Page from the v4.master and Customizing It ➤

a. Click the **Edit in SharePoint Designer link** on the Site Actions menu, and then enter your credential in the Windows Security dialog box.

   The SharePoint Site Setting page should now be displayed.

b. Click the **File tab.**

   The SharePoint Designer Backstage view should now be displayed.

c. Click **Add Item** to display the Add Item page if it is not already displayed.

d. Click the **New Page from Master** in the *Pages* section of the Add Item page.

   The Create Page from Existing Master Page is now displayed.

e. Click **v4.master (Default)**, and then click **Create** on the Create Page from Master Page.

   The New Web Part Page dialog box is now displayed.

f. Type **sp02h1FromMaster_LastNameFirstName** in the **Enter a name for this new Web Part Page: box**, and then click **OK**. Click **Yes** in the Microsoft SharePoint Designer alert box.

   You should now see the *sp02h1FromMaster_LastNameFirstName* page in Advanced Editor mode and Design view. Your screen should look similar to Figure 2.25.

STEP 6 DELETE A SITE

You will create and delete a site. Refer to Figure 2.26 as you complete Step 6.

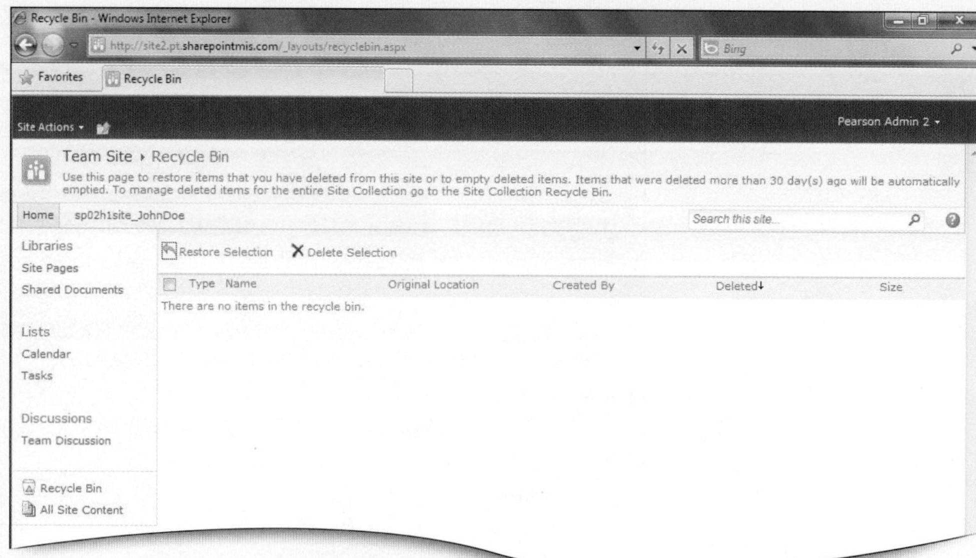

FIGURE 2.26 Viewing the Recycle Bin after Deleting a Site ➤

a. Close the SharePoint Designer window. Create a *sp02h1delete_LastNameFirstName* site using the instructions from Step 2.

b. Click **Site Settings** on the *sp02h1delete_LastNameFirstName* Site Actions menu.

   The Site Settings page of the *sp02h1delete_LastNameFirstName* site is now displayed.

c. Click **Delete this site** in the *Site Actions* section of the Site Settings page.

d. Click **Delete** on the *Delete this Site* page. Click **OK** in the *Message from the webpage* alert box. Click **Go back to site** on the Delete Web page.

   The home page of your top-level site is now displayed.

e. Click the **Recycle Bin link** on the Quick Launch.

   The Recycle Bin page should now be displayed and it should look similar to Figure 2.26. It does not contain the name of the *sp02h1delete_LastNameFirstName* site.

f. Close all the Internet Explorer, and then exit these applications.

SharePoint Built-in Site Templates Layout, Structure, and Capabilities

SharePoint sites foster and encourage team collaboration through the use of discussions, shared documents, files, contacts, events, calendars, tasks, blogging, knowledge bases (such as using Wikis), and surveys. As you have seen, SharePoint site templates are the starting point in the design and development of a variety of sites. As you select the template for the site, consider the layout, structure, and capabilities of the template, and how they fit the needs identified in the planning stage. As previously discussed in Chapter 1, in addition to the SharePoint built-in templates, you can also create new templates and have them appear either under the existing Collaboration and Meetings group names or under a group name that you specify.

As you select the template for the site, consider the layout, structure, and capabilities of the template, and how they fit the needs identified in the planning stage.

In this section, you will learn about the structure and functionalities of the SharePoint built-in site templates. Then, you will learn how to navigate SharePoint sites using an Internet browser or SharePoint Designer.

Working with Team Site, Document Workspace, and Group Work Site Templates

Team sites, document workspaces, and group work sites look similar and have similar functions. These types of sites are designed to enable groups of people to productively work together.

Team Site Template

The ***Team Site template*** is designed to provide the core set of capabilities needed in a site that will be used to support team collaboration and information sharing. This site template has the Wiki Page Home Page feature enabled, which results in Wiki pages being available within the site. The home page is also a Wiki page.

The **Team Site template** is designed to provide the core set of capabilities needed in a site that will be used to support team collaboration and information sharing.

TIP Wiki Page Home Page Site Feature

If you have a site that does not already have a Wiki page as the home page, you can apply the Wiki Page Home Page feature to the page to change it. To activate this feature, using the SharePoint Foundation browser interface, click the *Manage site features* link under the *Site Actions* section of the Site Settings page, and then click Activate corresponding to the Wiki Page Home Page feature. The activation of this feature will create a pages library (if there is none within your site), create a Wiki page in the library, and set the newly created Wiki page as the site home page.

The default Team Site home page has two Wiki zones, the left and right, that serve as content holders, as shown in Figure 2.27. You can modify this page template to better fit your needs by using other Wiki page configurations. More detailed information about this process appears in Chapter 3. The team site created from the Team Site template, as shown in Figure 2.27, includes the components listed in Table 2.2.

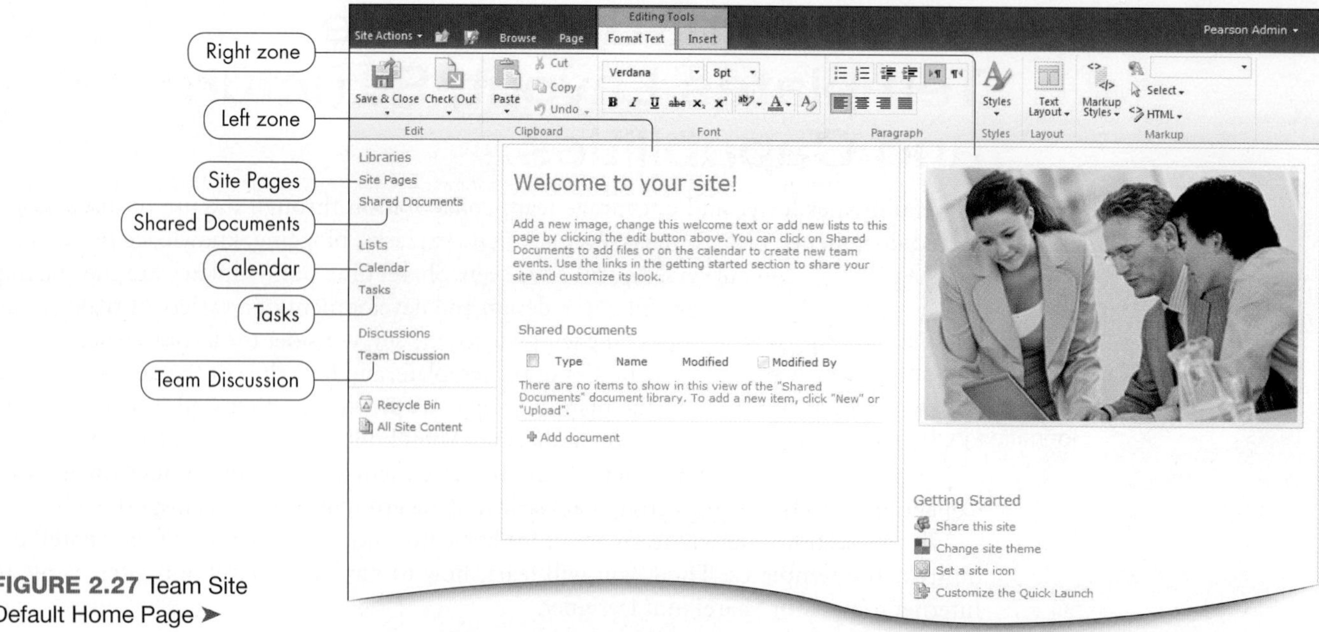

FIGURE 2.27 Team Site Default Home Page ➤

TABLE 2.2 Team Site Template Components

Item	Type	Location
Calendar	Calendar list	Quick Launch
Shared Documents	Document library	Quick Launch Left zone of the Content
Site Pages	Wiki Page library	Quick Launch
Tasks	Tasks list	Quick Launch
Team Discussion	Discussion board	Quick Launch

Blank Site Template

A **Blank Site template** has no lists or libraries and should be used when you do not need most of the items in the Team Site template.

The Blank Site is also a default site template that is used to develop a team site. A ***Blank Site template*** has no lists or libraries and should be used when you do not need most of the items in the Team Site template. This template is very flexible, enabling you to add the Web Parts you need to support the objectives of your organization or team.

The Wiki Page Home Page is not enabled on the Blank Site template. A Web Part site page is used as the home page of the site. As shown in Figure 2.28, the home page of a Blank site has Web Part zones on the left and the right.

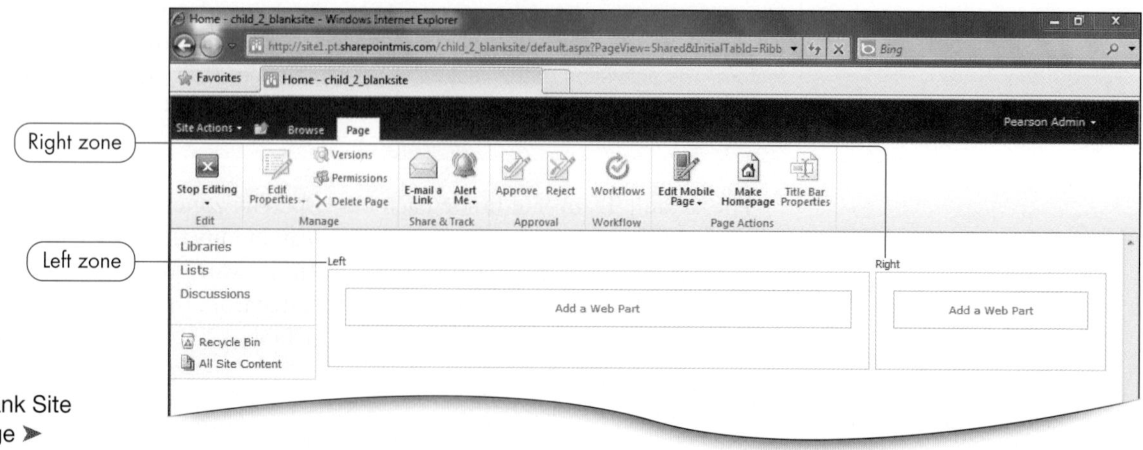

FIGURE 2.28 Blank Site Default Home Page ➤

Document Workspace Template

The only Document Workspace template available by default in SharePoint 2010 is the Document Workspace template. This template is designed to enable people to work together in the creation of a document or documents, such as the manuscript for this book, an annual report, or product information. The ***Document Workspace template*** provides the tools needed to manage a collaborative effort in the creation of a document. This workspace has features for storing the document, notifying people when changes are made, making announcements, conducting team discussions, and assigning tasks.

The **Document Workspace template** provides the tools needed to manage a collaborative effort in the creation of a document.

The Document Workspace template has three Web Part zones. The top zone typically contains announcements because of its prominence on the page. Below that is a left and right zone that contains links to other content and tools within the site, as shown in Figure 2.29. The document workspace shown was created with the Document Workspace template, and includes the components listed in Table 2.3.

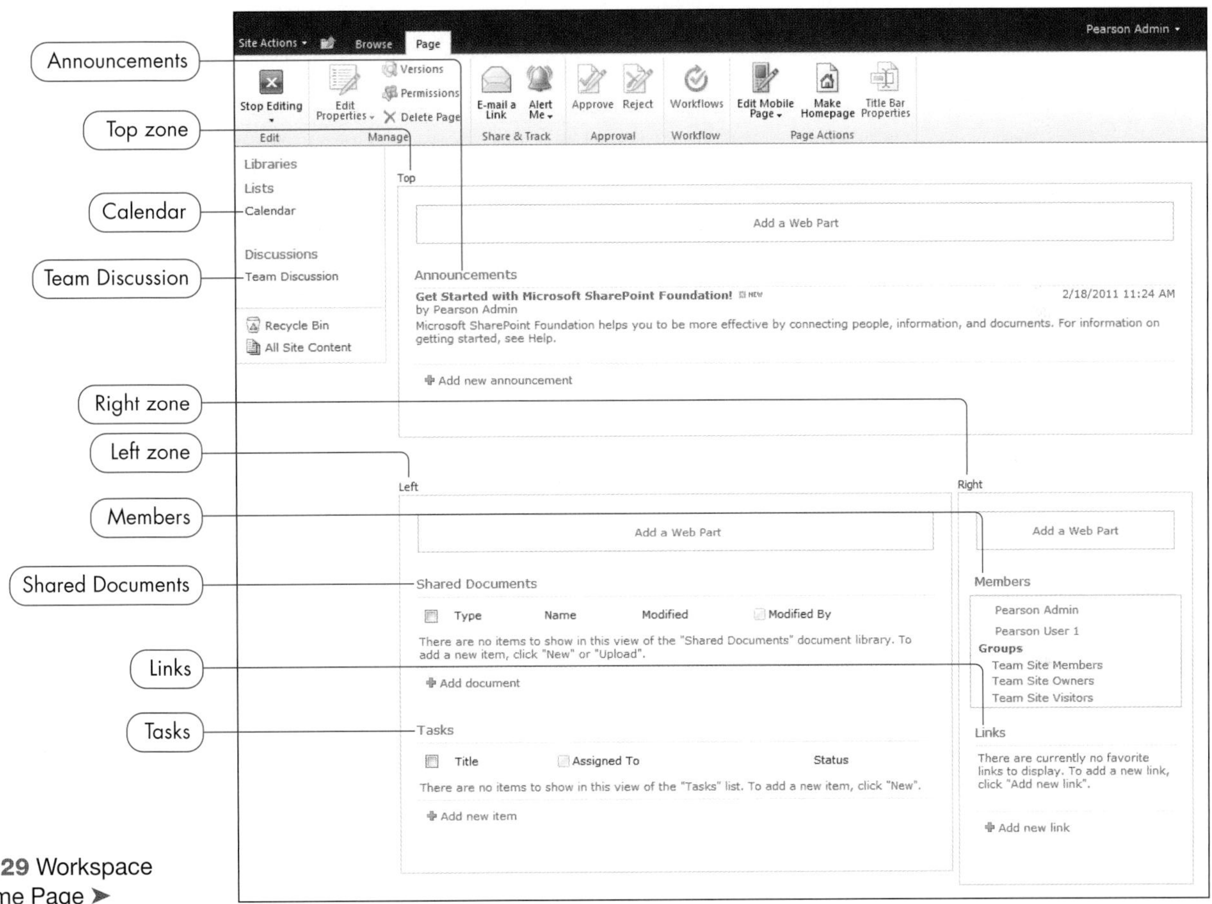

FIGURE 2.29 Workspace Default Home Page ➤

TABLE 2.3 Document Workspace Template Components

Item	Type	Location
Announcements	Announcements list	Top zone
Calendar	Calendar list	Quick Launch
Links	Links list	Right zone
Shared Documents	Document library	Left zone
Tasks	Tasks list	Left zone
Team Discussion	Discussion board	Quick Launch
Members	Site Users web part	Right zone

Group Work Site Template

The **Group Work Site template** provides tools that enable the management of a team.

The Group Work Site category includes only one default site template. It is a new SharePoint 2010 template. The ***Group Work Site template*** provides tools that enable the management of a team.

Using the default Web Part site page as a home page, this template features Web Part zones on the left and the right, as shown in Figure 2.30. The components of a group work site created from the Group Work Site template are listed in Table 2.4. Notice the robust tools available on the Quick Launch list in comparison to the previously discussed site templates.

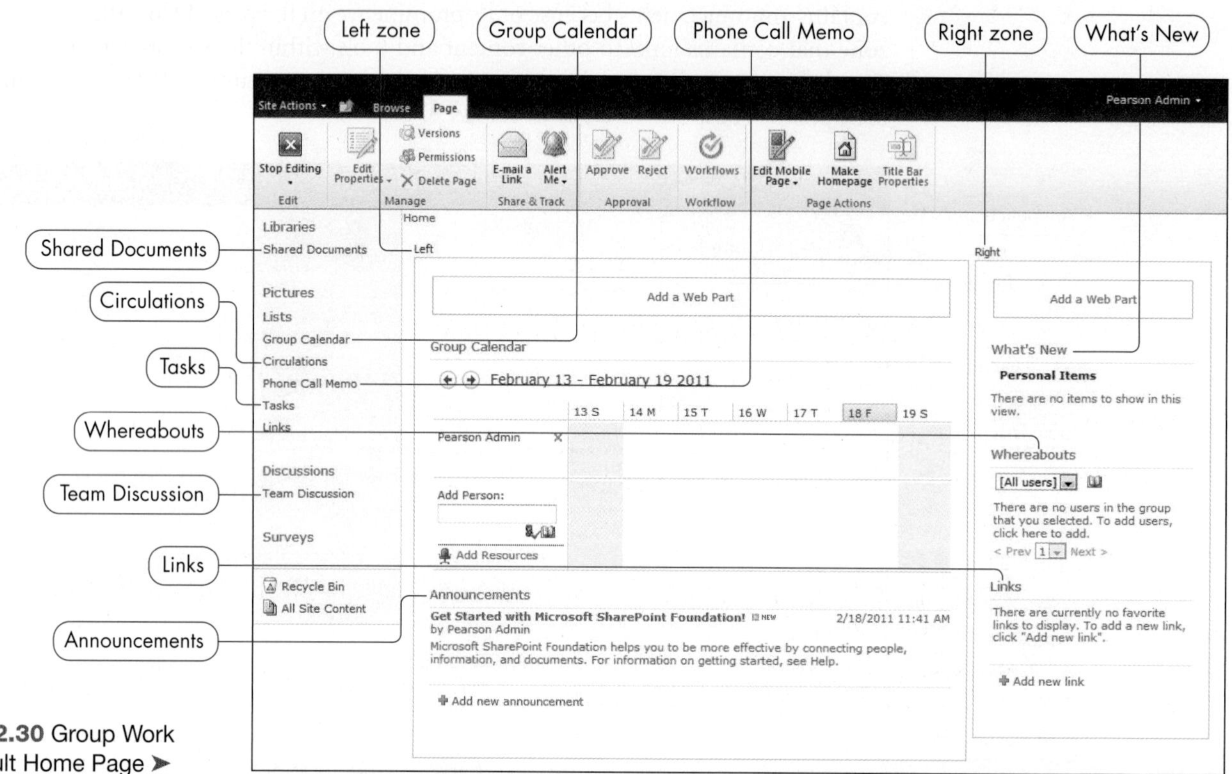

FIGURE 2.30 Group Work Site Default Home Page ➤

TABLE 2.4 Document Group Work Site Template Components		
Item	**Type**	**Location**
Announcements	Announcements list	Left zone
Circulations	Circulations list	Quick Launch
Group Calendar	Calendar list	Quick Launch Left zone
Links	Links list	Quick Launch Right zone
Phone Call Memo	Phone call memo list	Quick Launch
Shared Documents	Document Library	Quick Launch
Tasks	Tasks list	Quick Launch
Team Discussion	Discussion board	Quick Launch
Whereabouts	Whereabouts list	Right zone
What's New	What's new list	Right zone

Working with Meeting Workspace Templates

The purpose of the Meeting Workspace templates is to enable an organization or a company to organize a meeting, facilitate the meeting, and follow up on the meeting objectives. As preparations are made for the meeting, documents can be collected and reviewed by the participants prior to the meeting. The Meeting Workspace can store the agenda for the meeting. Participants (attendees) can be invited and their responses tallied. During the meeting, the documents can be presented and reviewed from within the workspace, ensuring that everyone is working with the same copy. Action times and decisions can be tracked and logged in the workspace. After the meeting, the minutes can be stored in the workspace along with follow-up materials. Tracking of the progress of the implementation of the decisions made at the meeting can continue so that everyone is aware of the progress being made.

The default templates for meeting workspaces include the Basic Meeting Workspace, Blank Meeting Workspace, Decision Making Workspace, Social Meeting Workspace, and Multipage Meeting Workspace. As with other templates, you can customize each type of template so that it fits the needs of the group or organization.

Basic Meeting Workspace Template

The **Basic Meeting Workspace template** is used to create sites with tools to enable members to plan, conduct, and document meetings.

The Basic Meeting Workspace is the most generic meeting site in SharePoint Foundation, as shown in Figure 2.31. The ***Basic Meeting Workspace template*** is used to create sites with tools to enable members to plan, conduct, and document meetings.

The components of the Basic Meeting Workspace site are listed in Table 2.5.

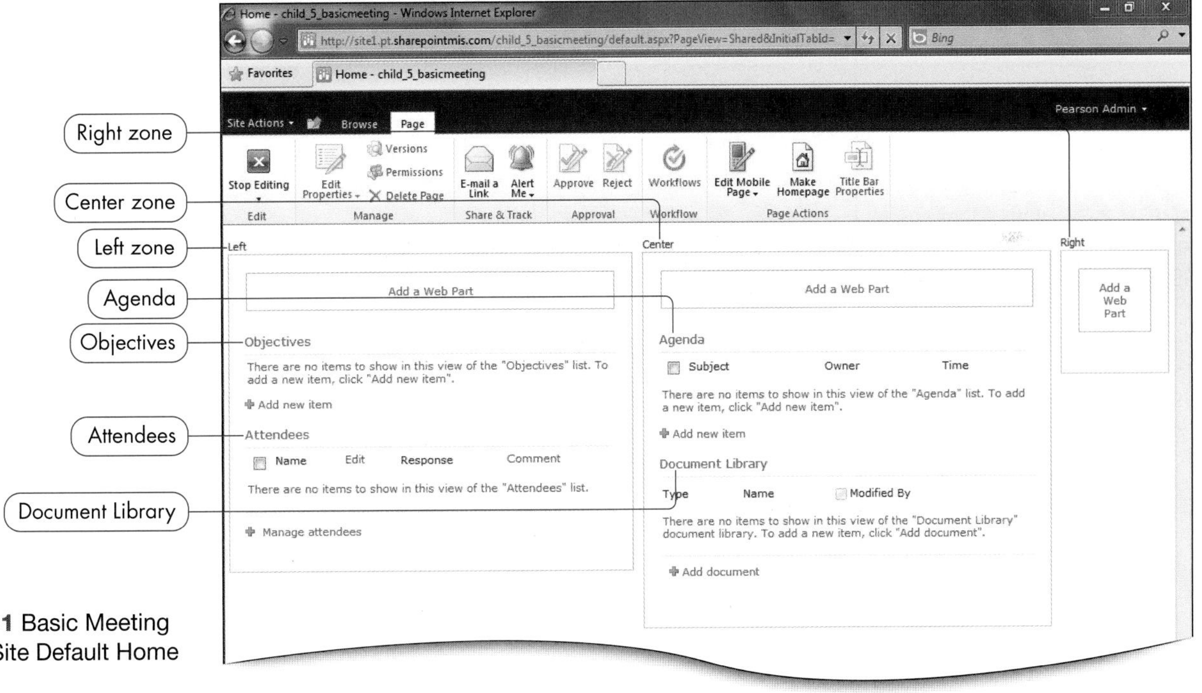

FIGURE 2.31 Basic Meeting Workspace Site Default Home Page ➤

TABLE 2.5 Basic Meeting Workspace Site Template Components

Item	Type	Location
Agenda	Agenda list	Center zone
Attendees	Attendees list	Left zone
Document Library	Document Library	Center zone
Objectives	Objectives list	Left zone

Blank Meeting Workspace Template

The **Blank Meeting Workspace template** is used to create an empty meeting workspace that does not include any site pages containing Web Parts.

In some cases, you may want to create a meeting workspace that you can fully customize with Web Parts that fit the needs of your team or organization. The ***Blank Meeting Workspace template*** is used to create an empty meeting workspace that does not include any site pages containing Web Parts. With this template, you add tools that support your specific requirements. Another advantage is that you will not spend time removing elements that you do not need.

Only an Attendees list is initially displayed on a site created with the Blank Meeting Workspace template. This template uses the default Web Part site page as home page. This default Web Part page is divided into a left zone, center zone, and right zone where Web Parts can be placed, as shown in Figure 2.32.

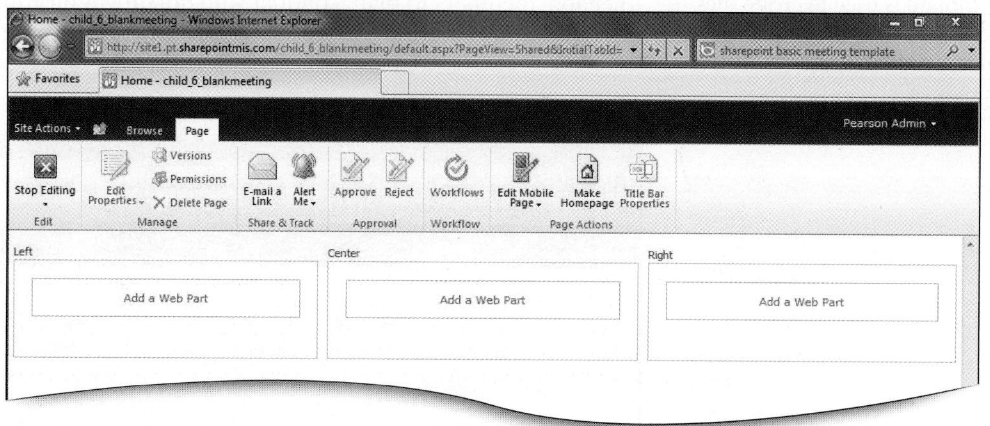

FIGURE 2.32 Blank Meeting Workspace Site Default Home Page ➤

Decision Meeting Workspace Template

The **Decision Meeting Workspace template** is used to create sites to support and track the decision-making process.

The ***Decision Meeting Workspace template*** is used to create sites to support and track the decision-making process. Tools included in the template are attendee lists, task lists, and objective lists. Document libraries are used to store the supporting documentation used to make the decisions. This template includes three Web Part zones. Figure 2.33 shows the default layout of a Decision Meeting Workspace. A default Decision Meeting Workspace contains the components included in Table 2.6.

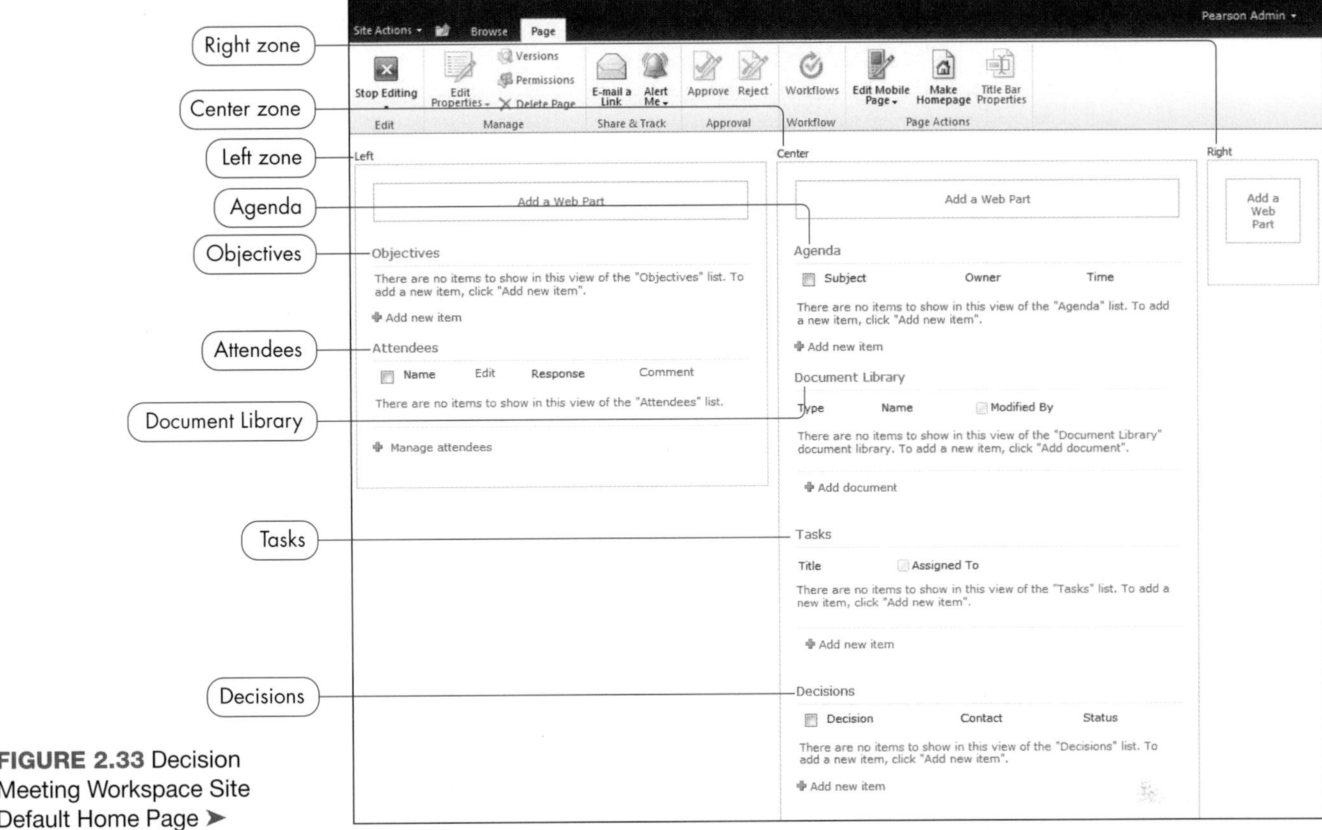

FIGURE 2.33 Decision Meeting Workspace Site Default Home Page ➤

TABLE 2.6 Decision Meeting Workspace Site Template Components

Item	Type	Location on Home Page
Agenda	Agenda list	Center zone
Attendees	Attendees list	Left zone
Decisions	Decisions list	Center zone
Document Library	Document Library	Center zone
Objectives	Objectives list	Left zone
Tasks	Task list	Center zone

Social Meeting Workspace Template

The **Social Meeting Workspace template** provides the tools necessary to facilitate informal social meetings.

The Social Meeting Workspaces support informal social meetings such as birthday, wedding, retirement, or graduation parties. The ***Social Meeting Workspace template*** provides the tools necessary to facilitate informal social meetings. In addition to an attendee list, there are Web Parts for providing directions, listing items to bring, and a discussion board. Figure 2.34 shows the default layout of a meeting workspace created from the Social Meeting Workspace template. The components of a default Social Meeting Workspace, shown in Table 2.7, are made available throughout multiple pages.

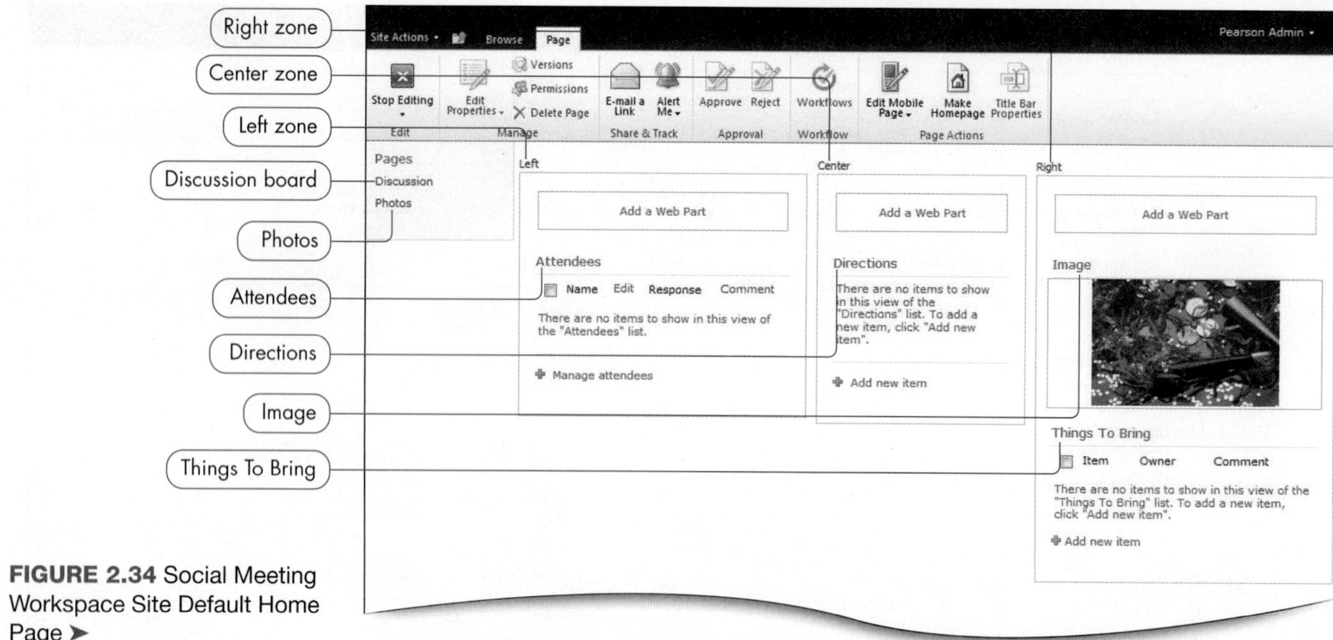

FIGURE 2.34 Social Meeting Workspace Site Default Home Page ➤

TABLE 2.7 Social Meeting Workspace Site Template Components

Item	Type	Page	Location
Attendees	Attendees list	Home	Left zone
Directions	Text box list	Home	Center zone
Discussion board	Discussion board	Discussion	Left zone
Photos	Picture library	Photos	Left zone
Things To Bring	Things to bring list	Home	Right zone
Image	Image Web Part	Home	Right zone

Multipage Meeting Workspace

The **Multipage Meeting Workspace template** provides the resources for creating meeting workspaces that will require more than one page.

The Multipage Meeting Workspace template tools and structure are the same as the Basic Meeting Workspace template. In addition, two blank pages are added to the site. The ***Multipage Meeting Workspace template*** provides the resources for creating meeting workspaces that will require more than one page. The additional pages are used to track subsequent meetings in the same topic area.

Figure 2.35 shows the layout of a Multiple Meeting Workspace. The components of the Multiple Meeting Workspace are shown in Table 2.8.

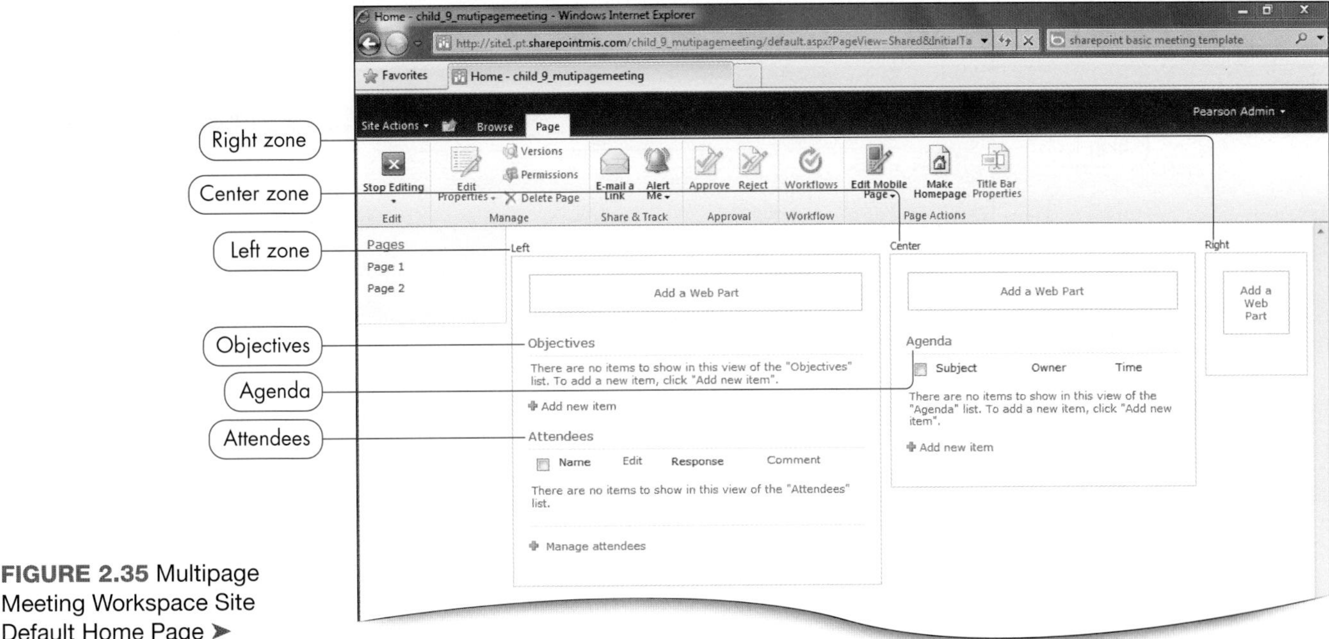

FIGURE 2.35 Multipage Meeting Workspace Site Default Home Page ➤

TABLE 2.8 Multiple Meeting Workspace Site Template Components

Item	Type	Location on Home Page
Agenda	Agenda list	Center zone
Attendees	Attendees list	Left zone
Objectives	Objectives list	Left zone

Working with Blog Site Templates

The Blog site template is commonly used to build news sites, journals, and diaries. A blog usually focuses one or more interests of the site owner and is often used to state an opinion.

The **Blog Site template** provides the tools needed for managing blog postings and comments.

SharePoint Foundation includes only one default blog site template. The ***Blog Site template*** provides the tools needed for managing blog postings and comments. A Blog site, shown in Figure 2.36, created from the Blog Site template, includes the default components listed in Table 2.9.

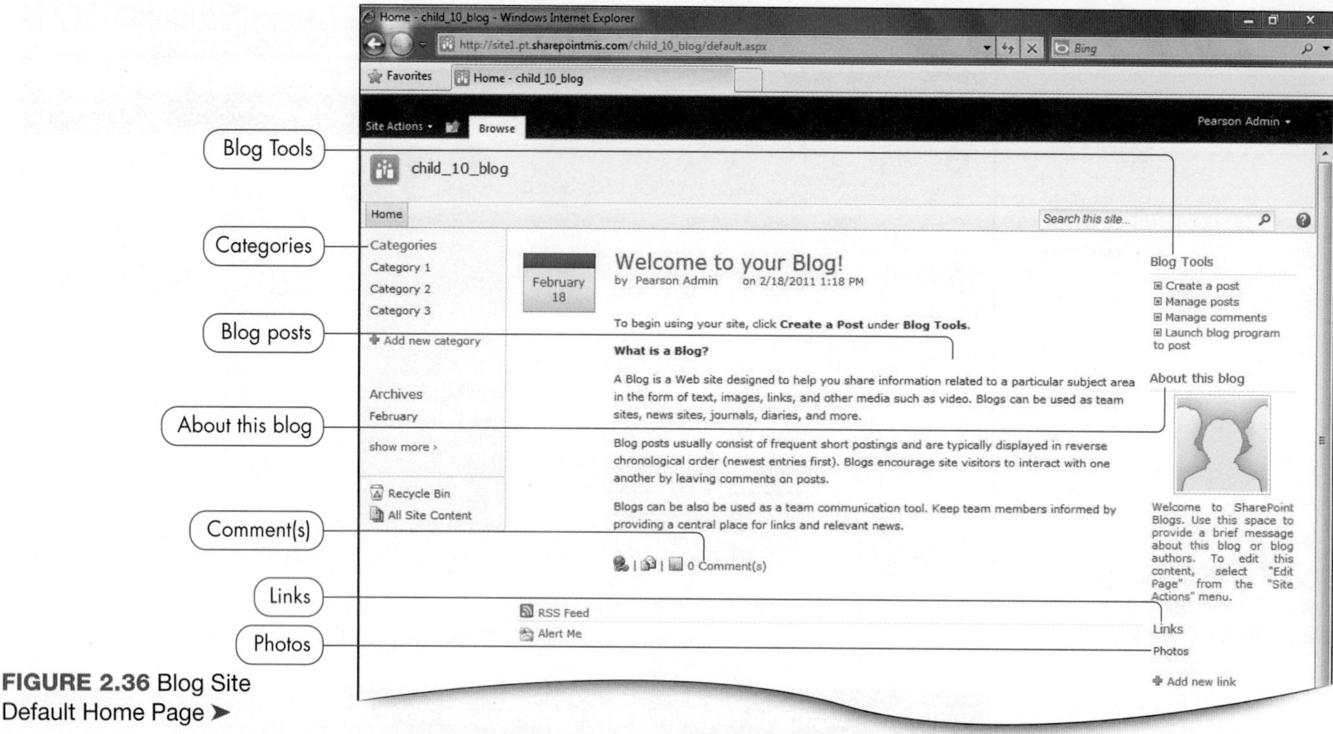

FIGURE 2.36 Blog Site Default Home Page ➤

TABLE 2.9 Blog Site Template Components

Item	Type	Location
Categories	Categories list	Quick Launch
Comments	Comments list	Left zone
Links	Links list	Right zone
Photos	Picture library	Right zone
Posts	Posts list	Left zone
Blog Tools	Blog tools Web Part	Right zone
About this blog	Content Editor Web Part	Right zone
Archives	List	Quick Launch

A **Post** (or article) is a thought published on a blog Web site.

A blog owner creates posts to which other users can comment. ***Posts*** (or articles) are thoughts published on a blog Web site. As posts accumulate, they are archived and removed from display on the home page. Past posts can be accessed through the Archive links on the Quick Launch list.

Blogs can be used for keeping project team members informed. For instance, the department head of the research and development group may make postings to a blog to inform the sales team about new product developments. Blog site content can be syndicated using a Really Simple Syndication (RSS) feed. ***RSS*** feed-aggregating software enables people to subscribe to the content they are interested in and have new and updated posts automatically delivered to them. Using these tools, people can aggregate the content from many blogs (or any SharePoint Foundation list) into one common reader where posts can be sorted, filtered, and grouped. Microsoft Office Outlook 2010 can aggregate RSS feeds; there are also many vendors that give away or sell RSS feed-aggregating software.

RSS feed-aggregating software enables people to subscribe to the content they are interested in and have new and updated posts automatically delivered to them.

Navigating SharePoint Sites

You can navigate SharePoint sites in a Web browser or in SharePoint Designer. The user-friendly methods can be used to navigate between all SharePoint sites within a SharePoint hierarchy, as well as among the elements within a site. As a site owner, you can manage site navigation options.

Use a Web Browser to Navigate a SharePoint Site

The first method used to navigate among sites in a Web browser focuses on the navigation bar, shown in Figure 2.37. This bar contains the list of navigational links created by the site owner. The navigation bar provides links to subsites and elements within the site, such as lists or libraries. When a site visitor clicks a site link, the browser displays the subsite home page or content element. A highlighted tab on the navigation bar indicates where you are in the site.

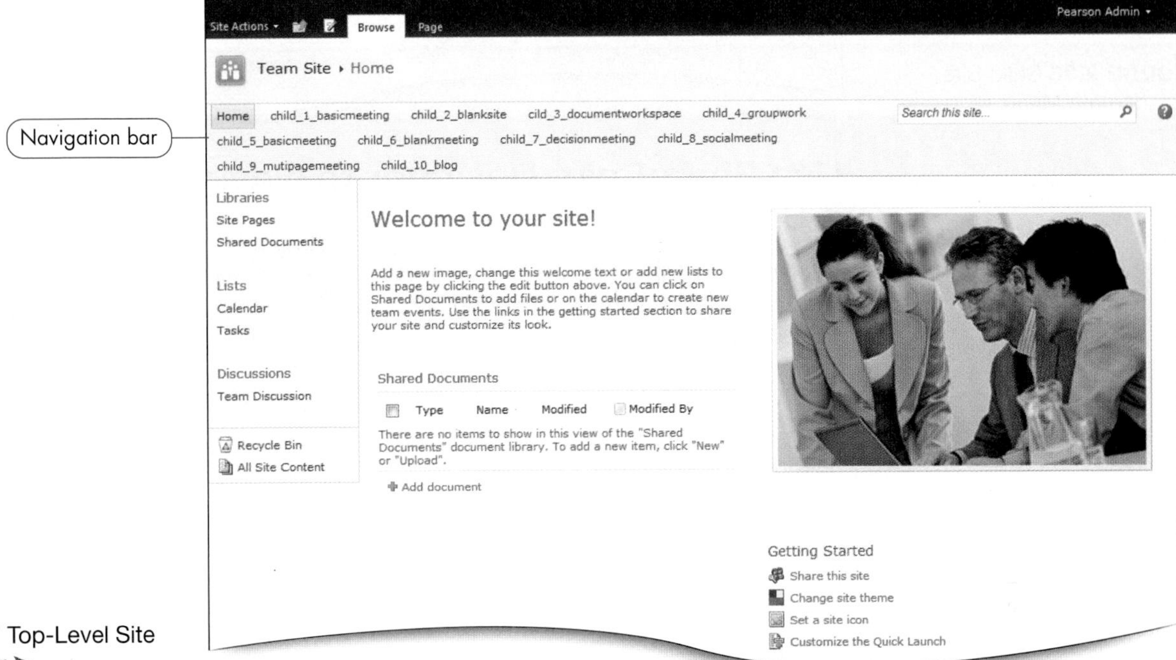

FIGURE 2.37 Top-Level Site Navigation Bar ➤

> **TIP** Navigation Bar on SharePoint Server Sites
>
> The navigation bar available when you are using a SharePoint Server adds drop-down menus to the bar, enabling you to move more efficiently to the content you are trying to access. You also have more options for adding links to and deleting subsites from the navigation bar when working in the SharePoint Server environment.

The Navigate Up button, located in the global links bar, enables you to quickly navigate to previous places that you have visited in the site hierarchy, while viewing the site with a Web browser. Click the Navigate Up button on the global links bar to display the Global navigation path. As shown in Figure 2.38, the navigation menu includes the global navigation for the current site, and if there were a number of subsites nested together, this list would display additional parent sites. Simply click on one of the links in the global navigation path to return to a parent site.

FIGURE 2.38 Child Site Breadcrumb Menu ➤

Use SharePoint Designer to Navigate a SharePoint Site

In SharePoint Designer, the Navigation Pane provides access to all of the components of a SharePoint site, organized into groups of related items, such as Lists and Libraries, Content Type, and Site Columns. When you click on one of the group links on the Navigation bar, SharePoint Designer automatically creates a tab at the top of the window. The majority of these tabs include a breadcrumb menu enabling you to navigate through the site hierarchy, while displaying the pages you have viewed, as well the position of the current item in the hierarchy, as shown in Figure 2.39.

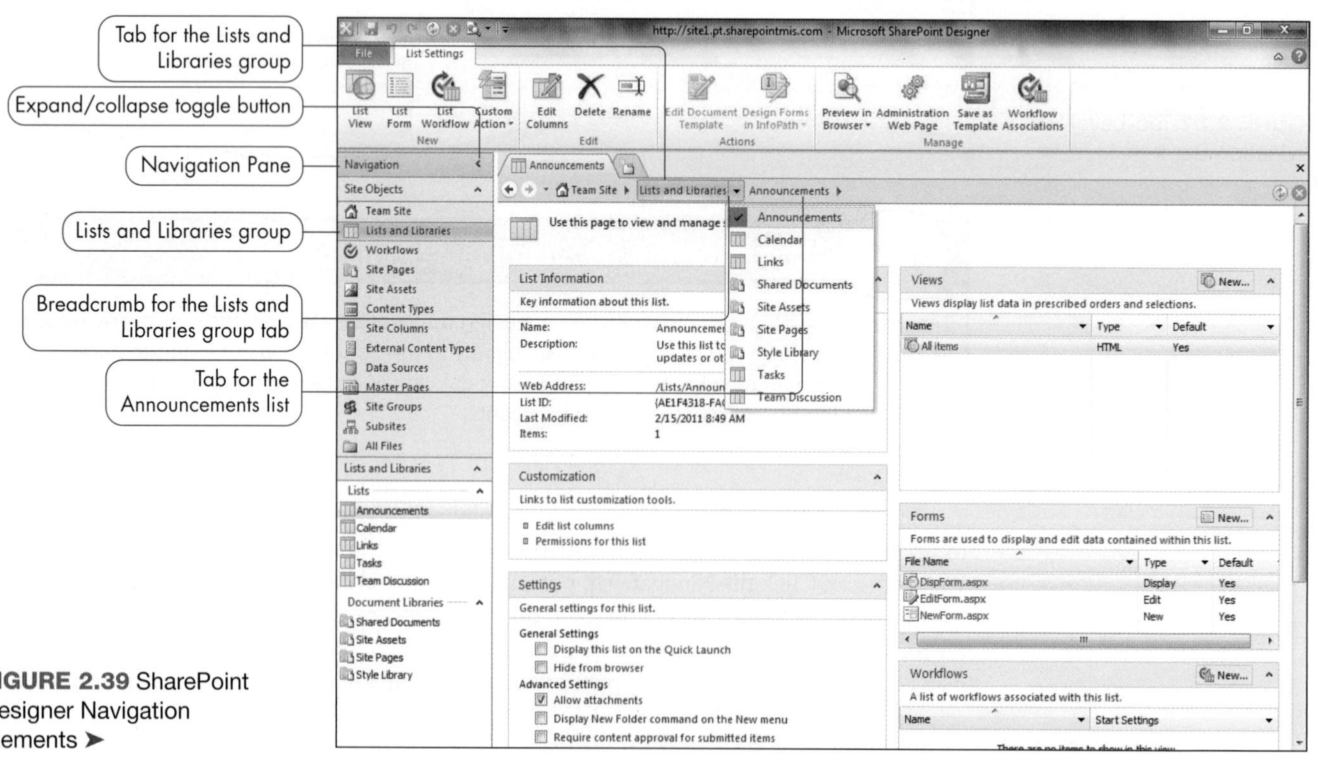

FIGURE 2.39 SharePoint Designer Navigation Elements ➤

You can expand or collapse the Navigation Pane as needed by clicking the expand/collapse toggle button to the right of the word Navigation in the page, as shown in Figure 2.39. The following reference table includes the options in the Navigation Pane and a brief explanation for each.

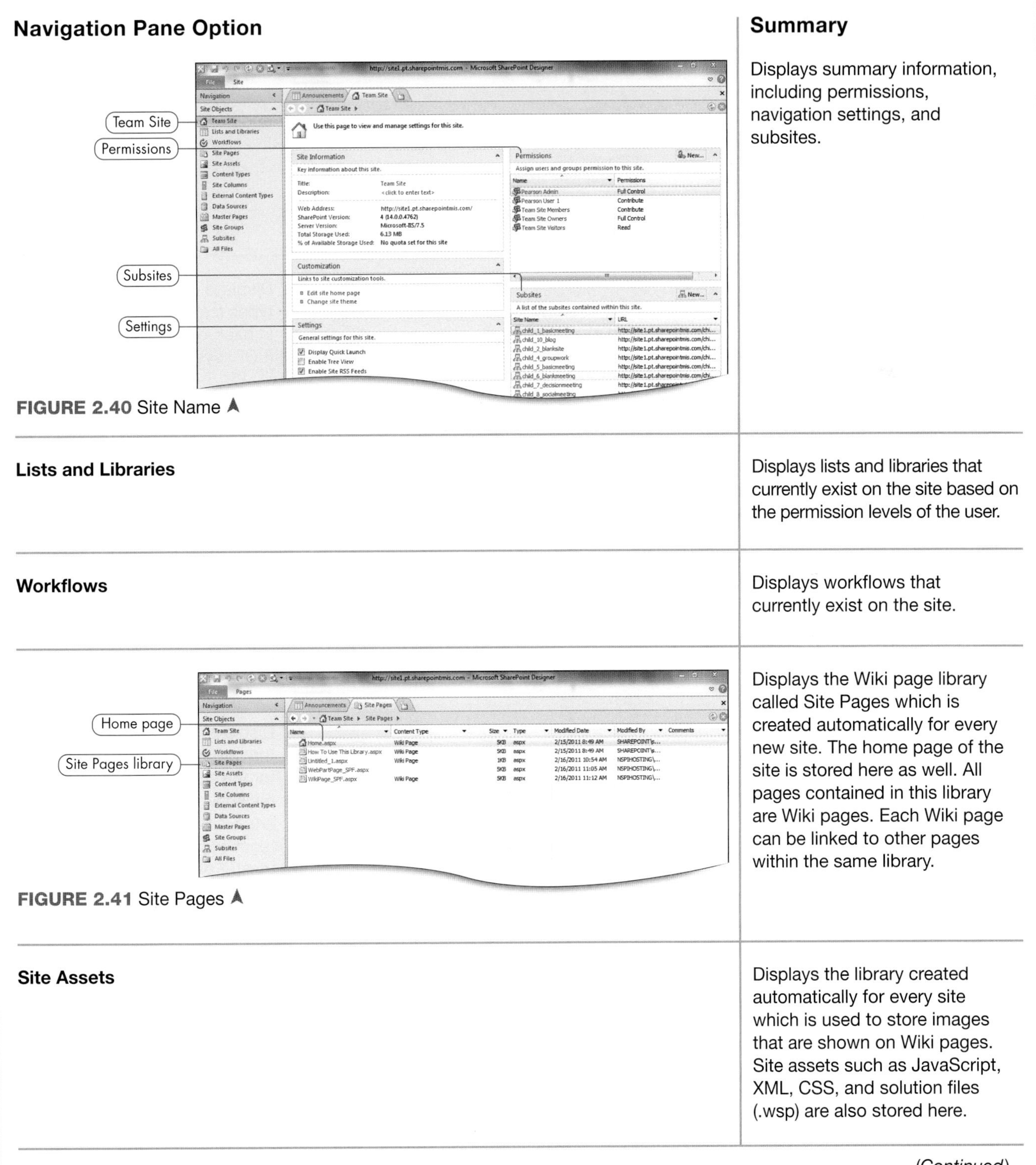

REFERENCE SharePoint Designer Navigation Pane Options

Navigation Pane Option	Summary
FIGURE 2.40 Site Name	Displays summary information, including permissions, navigation settings, and subsites.
Lists and Libraries	Displays lists and libraries that currently exist on the site based on the permission levels of the user.
Workflows	Displays workflows that currently exist on the site.
FIGURE 2.41 Site Pages	Displays the Wiki page library called Site Pages which is created automatically for every new site. The home page of the site is stored here as well. All pages contained in this library are Wiki pages. Each Wiki page can be linked to other pages within the same library.
Site Assets	Displays the library created automatically for every site which is used to store images that are shown on Wiki pages. Site assets such as JavaScript, XML, CSS, and solution files (.wsp) are also stored here.

(Continued)

Navigation Pane Option	Summary
Document Content Types (Figure 2.42)	Displays the content types in galleries and includes parent site content types.
Site Columns (Figure 2.43)	Displays columns for this site and the parent site.
External Content Types	Displays external content types (connections to data in back-end Line of Business (LOB) systems).
Data Sources (Figure 2.44)	Displays connections to external data sources such as databases, web services, and XML files, and connections to lists and libraries.
Master Pages (Figure 2.45)	Displays the master pages that are available to be used for the site. Default.master, minimal.master, and v4.master are available by default in a team site. If other custom master pages are created, they would appear here as well.

Document Content Types

Name	Group	Parent	Source	Description
Document Content Types				
Basic Page	Document Content Types	Document	http://site1.pt.sharepoint...	Create a new basic page.
Document	Document Content Types	Item	http://site1.pt.sharepoint...	Create a new document.
Dublin Core Columns	Document Content Types	Document	http://site1.pt.sharepoint...	The Dublin Core metadata element set.
Form	Document Content Types	Document	http://site1.pt.sharepoint...	Fill out this form.
Link to a Document	Document Content Types	Document	http://site1.pt.sharepoint...	Create a link to a document in a different location.
List View Style	Document Content Types	Document	http://site1.pt.sharepoint...	Create a new List View Style
Master Page	Document Content Types	Document	http://site1.pt.sharepoint...	Create a new master page.
Picture	Document Content Types	Document	http://site1.pt.sharepoint...	Upload an image or a photograph.
Web Part Page	Document Content Types	Basic Page	http://site1.pt.sharepoint...	Create a new Web Part page.
Wiki Page	Document Content Types	Document	http://site1.pt.sharepoint...	Create a new wiki page.
Folder Content Types				
Discussion	Folder Content Types	Folder	http://site1.pt.sharepoint...	Create a new discussion topic.
Folder	Folder Content Types	Item	http://site1.pt.sharepoint...	Create a new folder.
Summary Task	Folder Content Types	Folder	http://site1.pt.sharepoint...	Group and describe related tasks that you or your team n...
Group Work Content T...			http://site1.pt.sharepoint...	Add a new Circulation.

FIGURE 2.42 Content Types

Extended Columns			
Company Phonetic	Single line of text	Extended Columns	http://site1.pt.sharepointmis.com/
First Name Phonetic	Single line of text	Extended Columns	http://site1.pt.sharepointmis.com/
Issue Status	Choice (menu to choose from)	Extended Columns	http://site1.pt.sharepointmis.com/
Last Name Phonetic	Single line of text	Extended Columns	http://site1.pt.sharepointmis.com/
Related Issues	Lookup (information already on thi...	Extended Columns	http://site1.pt.sharepointmis.com/
Task Group	Person or Group	Extended Columns	http://site1.pt.sharepointmis.com/
UDC Purpose	Choice (menu to choose from)	Extended Columns	http://site1.pt.sharepointmis.com/

FIGURE 2.43 Site Columns

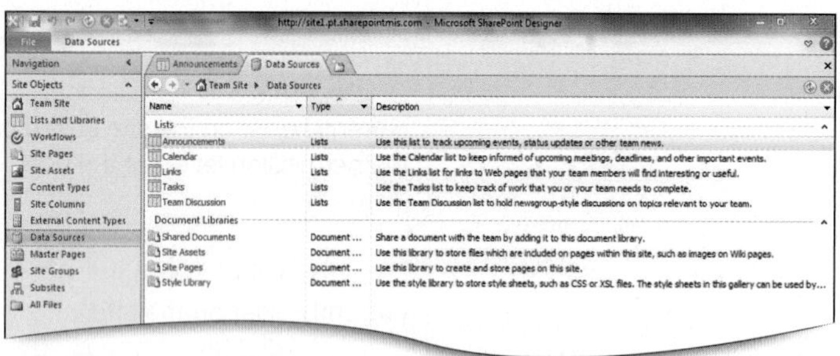

FIGURE 2.44 Data Sources

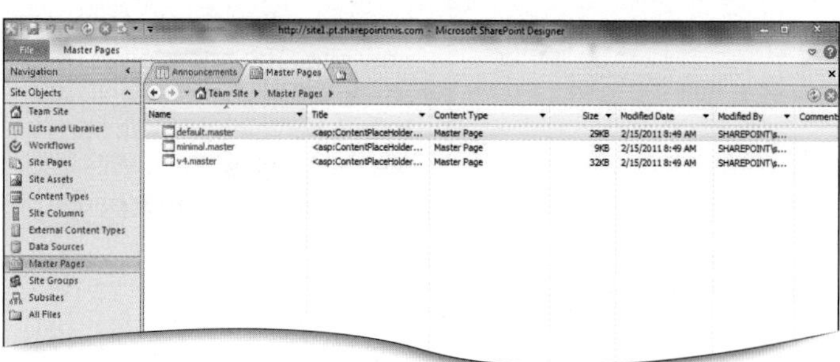

FIGURE 2.45 Master Pages

Navigation Pane Option	Summary
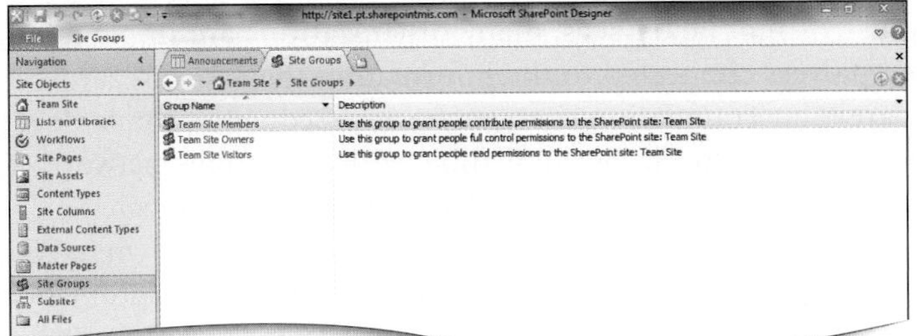 **FIGURE 2.46** Site Groups	Displays the SharePoint groups and the permission level of the groups.
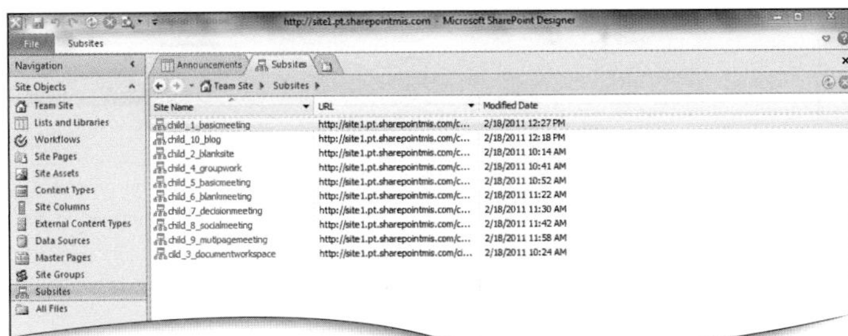 **FIGURE 2.47** Subsites	Displays subsites directly below this site based on the users permission level.
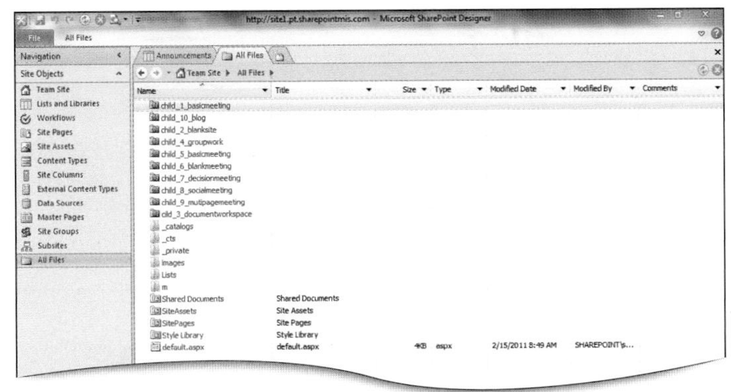 **FIGURE 2.48** All Files	Displays the URL structure of the Web site. The sub-sites, lists, libraries, hidden folders, and more all appear within this folder tree view.

Navigate SharePoint Foundation Sites Using Mobile Devices

With the ever-expanding use of mobile devices, many organizations are implementing SharePoint sites to keep employees connected to the information they need regardless of where they are located. SharePoint Foundation sites can be accessed with mobile devices, such as cell phones, if the server is set up to be compatible with the mobile network. The mobile device will also need a browser application in order to open SharePoint sites.

SharePoint mobile pages display the information in a single column, as shown in Figure 2.49, so that it can be read on the smaller screens of mobile devices. SharePoint automatically switches to the mobile page view when a mobile device requests site access. Using the links, you can navigate to the content of the site selecting different views, such as the Details view. You can also view documents when you click the name of the document.

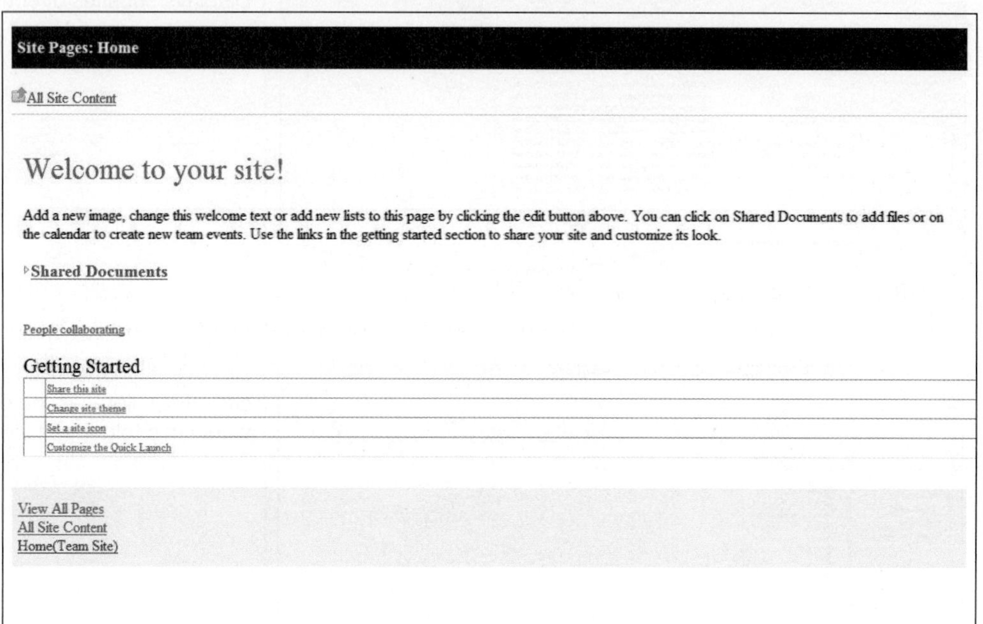

FIGURE 2.49 Site in a Single-Column Format ➤

Navigate Team Sites, Document Workspaces, Group Work Sites

Team sites, document workspaces, and group work sites have additional navigation methods which provide access to subsites. For instance, you may have a team site for the marketing department of your company. That site might contain a number of subsites, including a subsite where scripts for TV spots are worked on by the team, a budget subsite, and a FAQ that is added to by everyone in the group to inform others about the company and products. Because of the similarity in the navigation options, team sites, document workspaces, and group work sites are discussed as one in this section.

The quickest way to access a subsite from a top-level site is to click the name on the navigation bar or Quick Launch list. You can also use the All Site Content page to access the names of all of the subsites within the parent site, clicking the one you want in the *Sites and Workspaces* section. You can also use the Site Actions menu, if it is available, to access the Sites and Workspaces page through the Site Settings page, as shown in Figure 2.50.

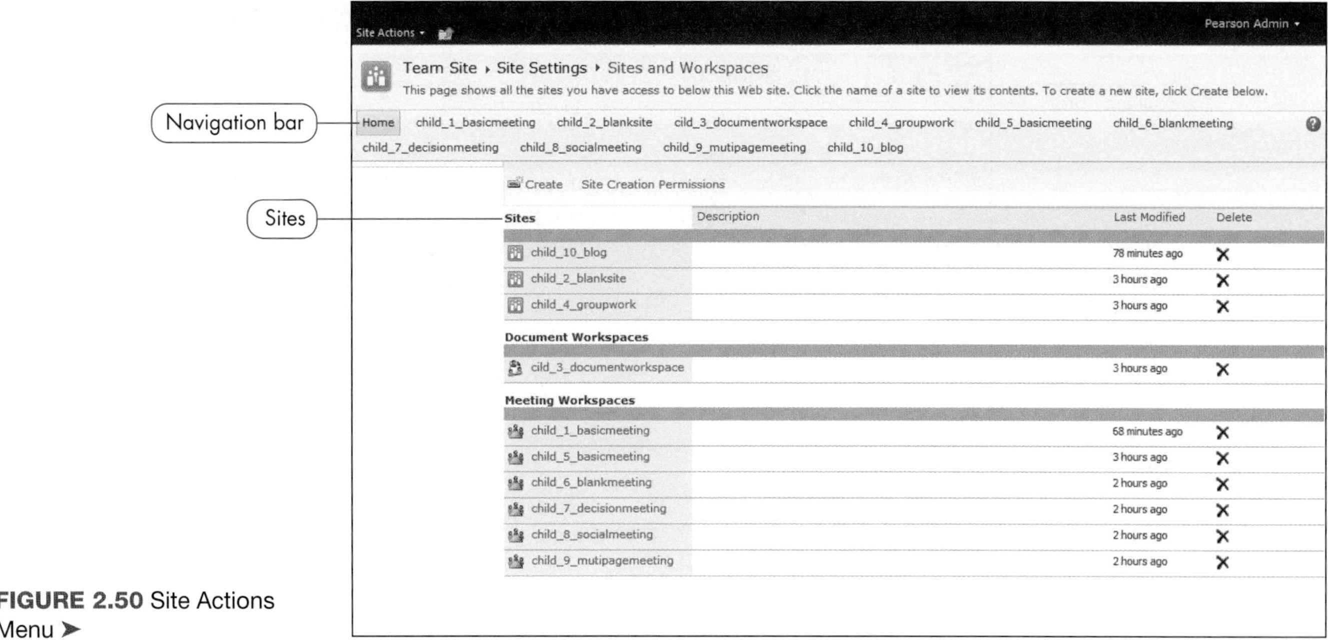

FIGURE 2.50 Site Actions Menu ➤

Navigate Meeting Workspaces

Meeting workspaces potentially have additional pages because of the unique features of the template that enable the meeting functions. For example, if the site is for a committee that meets often, the additional pages could represent each meeting that they have, storing the minutes, attendees, and related documents within each meeting page. These pages are accessed using Quick Launch, as shown in Figure 2.51.

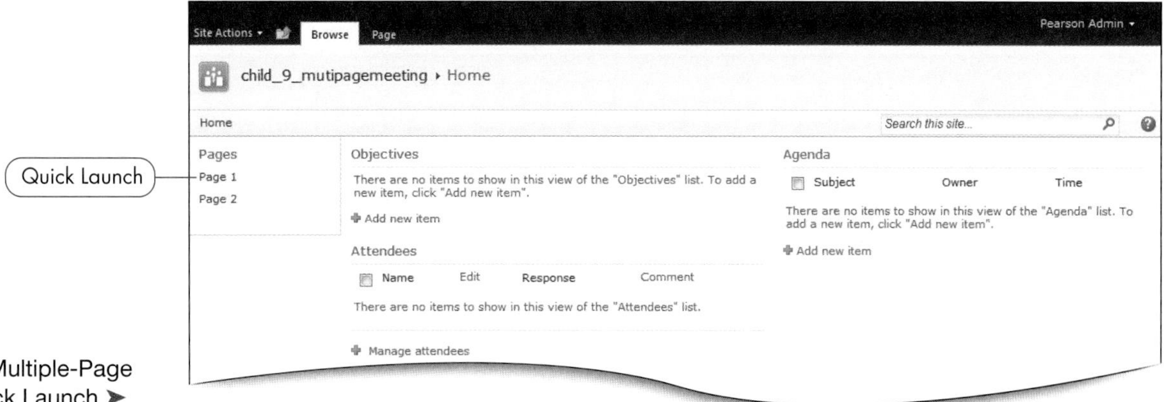

FIGURE 2.51 Multiple-Page Workspace Quick Launch ➤

Navigate Blog Sites

Blog sites enable access to the content through headers and lists. Just as with team sites, the Quick Launch list (or the Blog navigator, if viewing the home page) provides for navigation throughout the site. At the bottom of Quick Launch, the All Site Content link opens a page that displays all of the components within the site as links that you can click to navigate to the items. Additional document pages, stored in the Document Library, as shown in Figure 2.52, are displayed by first accessing the Document Library and then clicking the page you want from the library list.

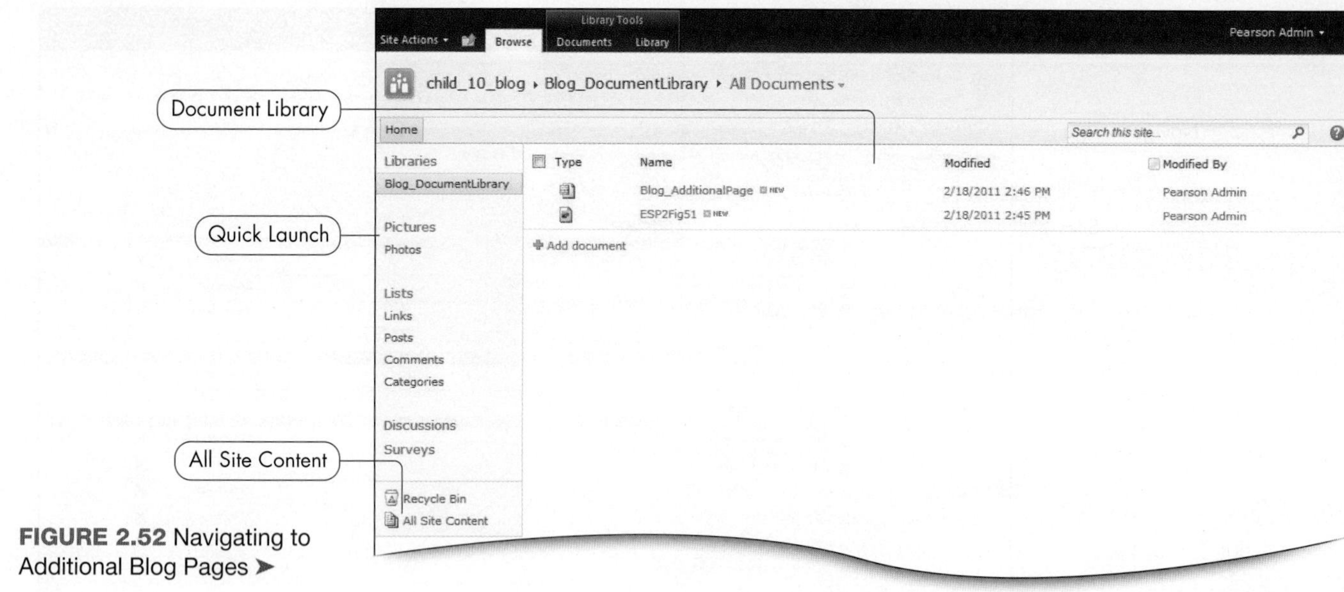

FIGURE 2.52 Navigating to Additional Blog Pages ➤

HANDS-ON EXERCISES

2 SharePoint Built-in Site Templates Layout, Structure, and Capabilities

Before you start building the new and enhanced DestinQuest Web site, you need to carefully review all the SharePoint build-in site templates structure, layout, and functionality. That will help you choose, as startup points, the templates that better match your needs. You will first create a subsite using the Team Site template. Then, you will create a subsite of the team site using the Group Work Site template. Next, you will create two subsites of the group work site, one using the Decision Meeting Workspace template and the other one using the Blog template. You will navigate and explore all the components of these subistes using the browser and SharePoint Designer.

Skills covered: • Log On to Your SharePoint Collection • Create a Site Using the Team Site Template • Create a Subsite Using the Group Work Site Template • Create a Subsite Using the Decision Meeting Workspace Template • Create a Subsite Using the Blog Template • Navigate Sites in a Browser and Using SharePoint Designer

STEP 1 LOG ON TO YOUR SHAREPOINT COLLECTION

Before you can start exploring the SharePoint Foundation sites capabilities, you need to log on to your SharePoint Collection. Refer to Figure 2.53 as you complete Step 1.

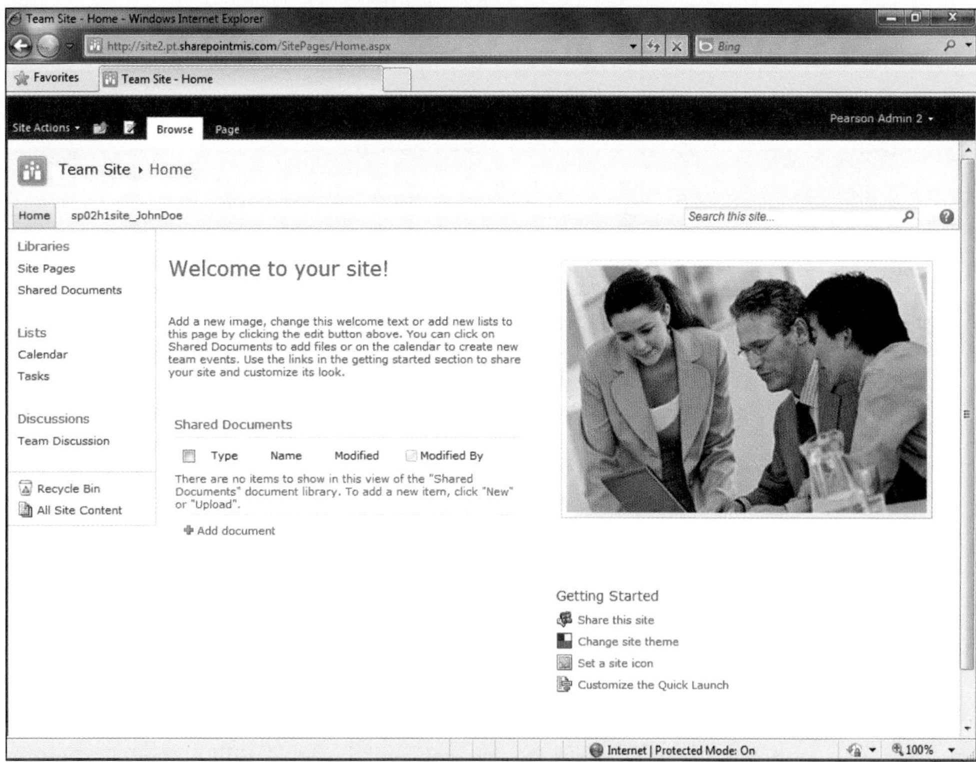

FIGURE 2.53 Logging On a SharePoint Collection ➤

a. Click **Start** to display the Start menu. Click **All Programs**, and then click **Internet Explorer** to open the program.

b. Go to the top-level site provided by your instructor, which will be in the format of http://pt .sharepointmis.com/SitePages/*yourname*.

c. Enter the user name and password provided by your instructor.

> **TROUBLESHOOTING:** It might take a few seconds to access your top-level site on your Internet connection.

If you logged in correctly, the home page of the top-level site is now displayed in Internet Explorer. Your screen will look similar with the one shown in Figure 2.53.

STEP 2 CREATE A SITE USING THE TEAM SITE TEMPLATE

You will build a site using the Team Site template, and you will carefully review its structure and layout. Refer to Figure 2.54 as you complete Step 2.

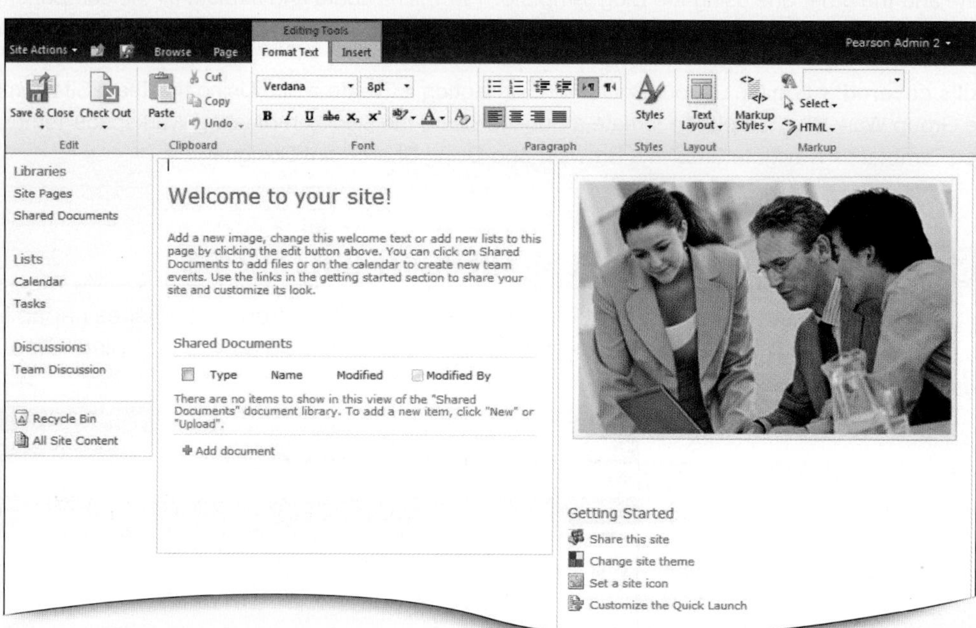

FIGURE 2.54 Home Page of a Team Site ➤

a. Click **All Site Content** on the Quick Launch of the top-level site.

   The All Site Content page is now displayed.

b. Click **Create** to open the Create dialog box.

   The Create dialog box is now displayed.

c. Click **Site** in the *Filter By* section of the Create dialog box.

   Only the site templates are now displayed.

d. Click **Team Site**, type **sp02h2teamsite_LastNameFirstName** in the **Title** and **URL name boxes**, and then click **More Options**.

e. Review all the listed options. Click **Create**.

   The *sp02h2teamsite_LastNameFirstName* home page should now be displayed.

f. Click the **Page tab**, and then click **Edit** in the Edit group.

   Your screen should look similar to Figure 2.54.

g. Carefully review the layout of the site home page along with all the site components, using Table 2.2.

STEP 3 CREATE A SUBSITE USING THE GROUP WORK SITE TEMPLATE

You will build a subsite using the Group Work Site template, and you will carefully review its structure and layout. Refer to Figure 2.55 as you complete Step 3.

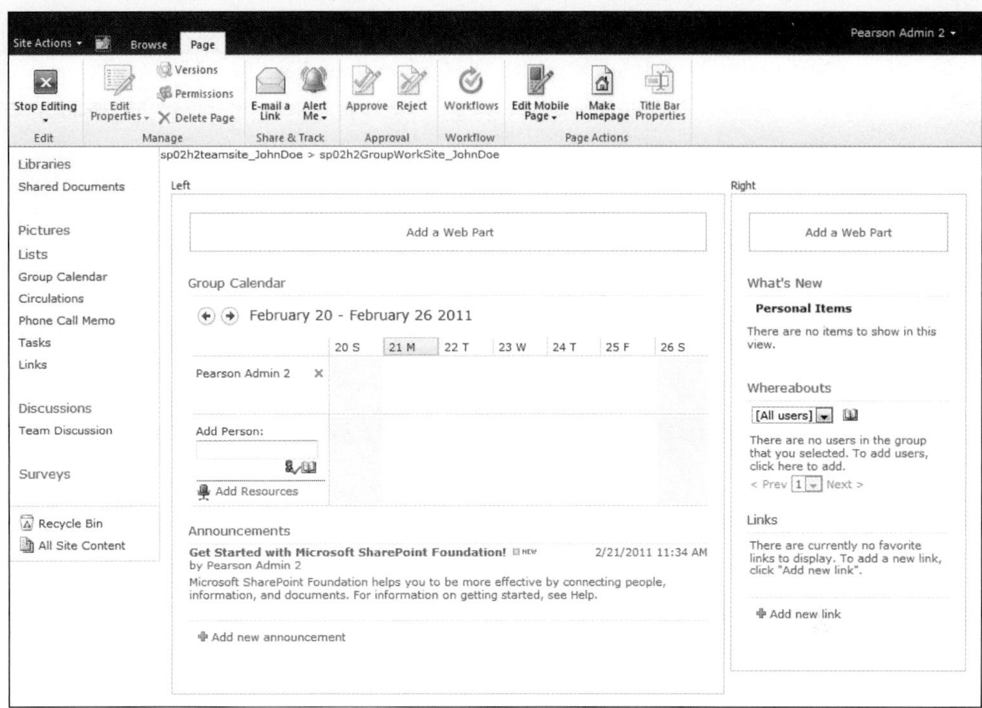

FIGURE 2.55 Home Page of a Group Work Site ➤

a. Click **All Site Content** on the Quick Launch of the *sp02h2teamsite_LastNameFirstName* site.

   The All Site Content page is now displayed.

b. Click **Create** to open the Create dialog box.

   The Create dialog box is now displayed.

c. Click **Site** in the *Filter By* section of the Create dialog box.

   Only the site templates are now displayed.

d. Click **Group Work Site**, type **sp02h2GroupWorkSite_LastNameFirstName** in the **Title** and **URL name boxes**, and then click **More Options**.

e. Review all the listed options. Click **Yes** in the *Navigation Inheritance* section of the Create dialog box. Click **Create**.

   The *sp02h2GroupWorkSite_LastNameFirstName* page should now be displayed.

f. Review all the site components, using Table 2.4.

g. Click the **Page tab**, and then click **Edit Page** in the Edit group.

   Your screen should look similar to Figure 2.55.

h. Review the layout of the site home page.

STEP 4 CREATE A SUBSITE USING THE DECISION MEETING WORKSPACE TEMPLATE

You will build a subsite using the Decision Meeting Workspace template, and you will carefully review its structure and layout. Refer to Figure 2.56 as you complete Step 4.

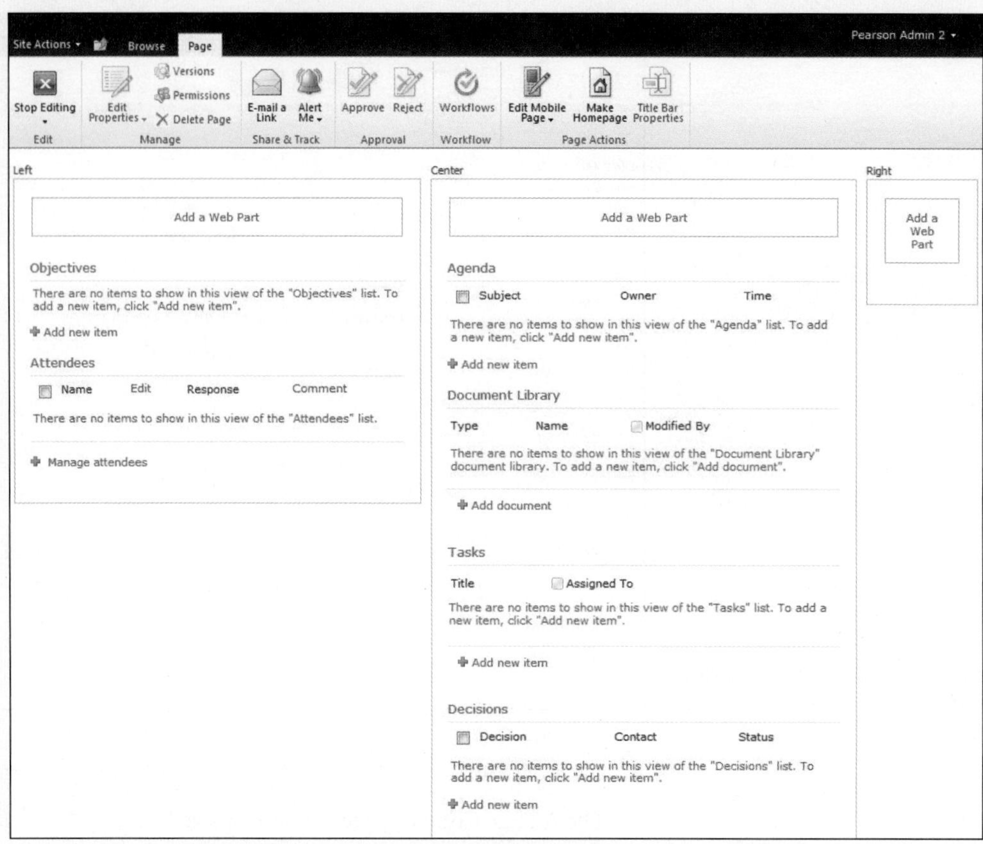

FIGURE 2.56 Creating a Subsite Using the Decision Meeting Workspace Template ➤

a. Click **All Site Content** on the Quick Launch of the *sp02h2GroupWorkSite_LastNameFirstName* site.

   The All Site Content page is now displayed.

b. Click **Create** to open the Create dialog box.

   The Create dialog box is now displayed.

c. Click **Site** in the *Filter By* section of the Create dialog box.

   Only the site templates are now displayed.

d. Click **Decision Meeting Workspace**, type **sp02h2DecisionMeeting_LastNameFirstName** in the **Title** and **URL name boxes**, and then click **More Options**.

e. Review all the listed options. Click **Create**.

   The *sp02h2DecisionMeeting_LastNameFirstName* page should now be displayed.

f. Review all the site components, using Table 2.6.

g. Click the **Page tab**, and then click **Edit Page** in the Edit group.

   Your screen should look similar to Figure 2.56.

h. Review the layout of the site home page.

i. Click the **Browse tab**.

STEP 5 CREATE A SUBSITE USING THE BLOG TEMPLATE

You will build a subsite using the Blog template, and you will carefully review its structure and layout. Refer to Figure 2.57 as you complete Step 5.

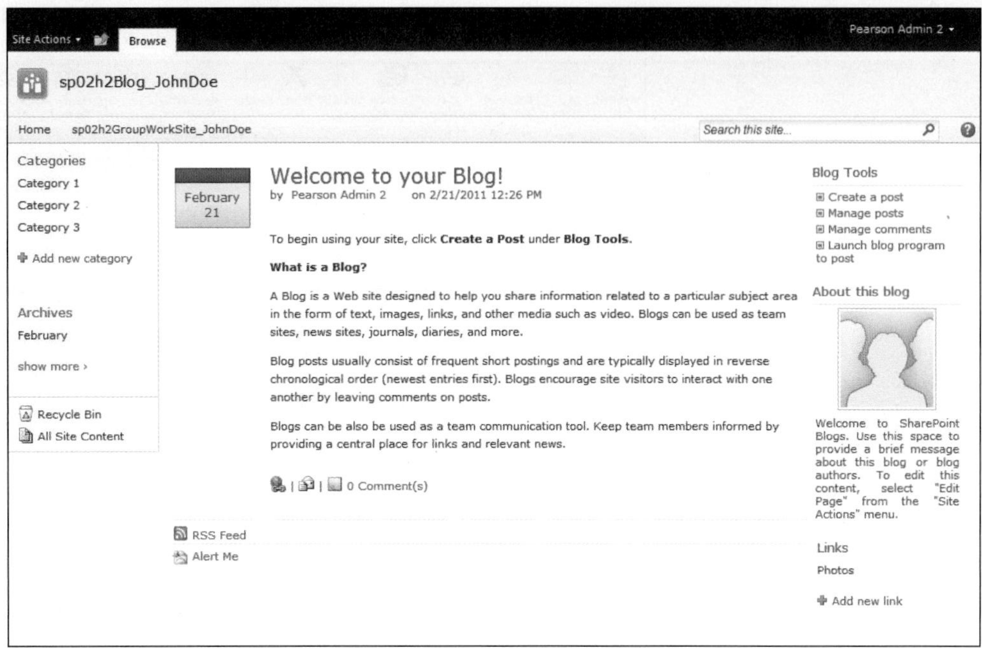

FIGURE 2.57 Create a Subsite Using the Blog Template ➤

a. Click **sp02h2GroupWorkSite_LastNameFirstName** on the *sp02h2DecisionMeeting_LastNameFirstName* link bar.

   The home page of *sp02h2GroupWorkSite_LastNameFirstName* is now displayed.

b. Click **All Site Content** on the Quick Launch, and then click **Create** to open the Create dialog box.

   The Create dialog box is now displayed.

c. Click **Site** in the *Filter By* section of the Create dialog box.

   Only the site templates are now displayed.

d. Click **Blog**, type **sp02h2Blog_LastNameFirstName** in the **Title** and **URL name boxes**, and then click **More Options**.

e. Review all the listed options. Click **Yes** in the *Navigation Inheritance* section of the Create dialog box. Click **Create**.

   The *sp02h2Blog_LastNameFirstName page* should now be displayed. Your screen should look similar to Figure 2.57.

f. Review all the site components, using Table 2.9.

g. Review the layout of the site home page.

STEP 6 NAVIGATE SITES IN A BROWSER AND USING SHAREPOINT DESIGNER

You will navigate the sites created in previous steps of this exercise using the browser and SharePoint Designer. Refer to Figure 2.58 as you complete Step 6.

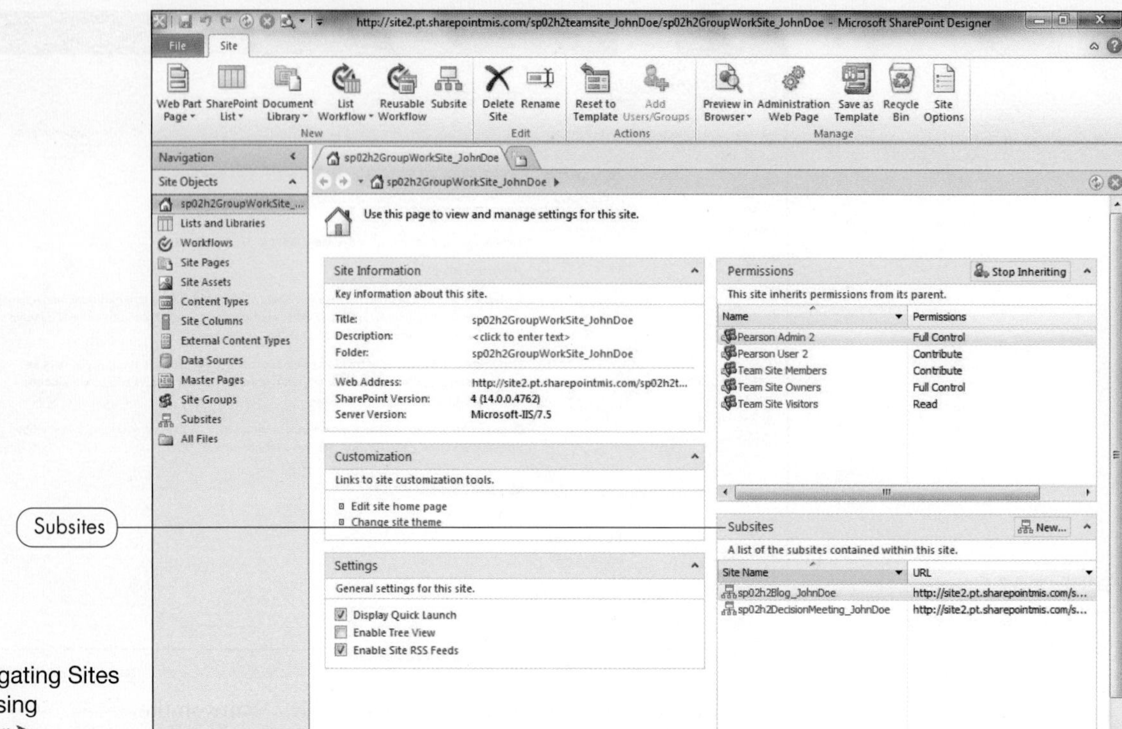

FIGURE 2.58 Navigating Sites in a Browser and Using SharePoint Designer ➤

a. Click **sp02h2GroupWorkSite_LastNameFirstName** on the *sp02h2DecisionMeeting_LastNameFirstName* Navigation bar.

   The home page of *sp02h2GroupWorkSite_LastNameFirstName* is now displayed.

b. Click **Site Settings** on the Site Actions menu. Click **Sites and Workspaces** in the *Site Administration* section of the Site Settings page.

   The Sites and Workspaces page of the *sp02h2GroupWorkSite_LastNameFirstName* site is now displayed.

c. Click **sp02h2DecisionMeeting_LastNameFirstName** on the Site Settings Sites and Workspaces page.

   The home page of the *sp02h2DecisionMeeting_LastNameFirstName* is now displayed.

d. Click the **Navigate Up button** on the Global Links bar of the *sp02h2DecisionMeeting_LastNameFirstName* site, and then select **Team Site**.

   The home page of the Team Site top-level site is now displayed.

e. Click **sp02h2teamsite_LastNameFirstName** on the Navigation bar of the top-level site.

   The home page of the *sp02h2teamsite_LastNameFirstName* site is now displayed.

f. Click **Edit in SharePoint Designer** on the Site Actions menu of *sp02h2teamsite_LastNameFirstName*. Type your password in the **Windows Security dialog box**.

   The Site Settings page of the *sp02h2teamsite_LastNameFirstName* site is now displayed.

g. Click **All Files** on the Navigation Pane.

   The All Files page is now displayed.

h. Double-click **sp02h2GroupWorkSite_LastNameFirstName** on the All Files page of the *sp02h2teamsite_LastNameFirstName* site.

SharePoint Designer opens the *sp02h2GroupWorkSite_LastNameFirstName* page in a new window. Your screen should now look similar to Figure 2.58.

i. Right-click **SharePoint Designer tab** on the Windows task bar, and then click **Close All windows.** Close the browser window.

SharePoint Foundation Lists and Libraries

In normal business operations documents can be difficult to collaborate upon as a group. One person may make changes that do not filter out to other people who are simultaneously making changes on their copies of the same document. Using SharePoint Foundation, you can collaborate in real time with other team members to create and update documents stored and accessed from lists and in libraries within sites. The Web-based interface reflects changes made to the documents while maintaining a single centralized copy in the lists or libraries. Lists are structured in a familiar table-based layout, with columns and rows. This makes it easy for everyone to understand how items on the list are related.

Using SharePoint Foundation, you can collaborate in real time with other team members....

In this section, you will learn about SharePoint Lists and Libraries structure and functionalities, how to create a new List or Library based on the SharePoint built-in templates and change their settings, and how to create folders.

TIP Columns and Rows

In SharePoint, columns are also referred to as fields and rows are referred to as items.

Working with SharePoint Lists and Libraries Templates

SharePoint Foundation enables you to create new Lists and Libraries based on a rich set of built-in list and library templates. When you create a new site using a SharePoint template, template-specific lists, libraries, and pages necessary to support the use of the list or library will be created by default. The pages will enable you to create, review, update, and delete documents in the list or library. New lists and libraries can be created if you have a sufficient permission level. As previously discussed in this chapter, the availability of types of lists and libraries is controlled by the features activated. Here are the List and Library templates built into SharePoint Foundation:

- Agenda
- Announcements
- Attendees
- Calendar
- Categories
- Circulations
- Comments
- Contacts
- Custom list
- Custom list in Datasheet view
- Decisions
- Directions
- Discussion Board
- Document Library
- External Data
- Form Library
- Group Calendar
- Import Spreadsheet
- Issue Tracking
- Links

- Objectives
- Phone Call Memo
- Picture Library
- Posts
- Project Tasks
- Resources
- Survey
- Tasks
- Text Box
- Things to Bring
- Whereabouts
- Wiki Page Library

Creating a List or a Library

A list or a library can be created using the SharePoint Foundation Ribbon in an Internet browser, or using the SharePoint Designer Ribbon. As mentioned earlier in this chapter, when using an Internet browser, Microsoft Silverlight affects how components can be created. When Silverlight is not installed on the computer, the Create page displays links to the list types. With Silverlight installed, you have options which enable you to filter the lists by type and category on the Create page.

The Create Announcement page, shown in Figure 2.59, enables you to create a new list based on the installed components. For instance, you can create a new list for announcing milestones on a project by basing the list on the Announcements type in the Communication category.

When Silverlight is available on the computer and a browser is used to create a new list or library, the Create dialog box is accessed by clicking the More Options link on the Site Actions menu. You select the appropriate component from the Installed Items list. If you select the Custom List option, the page shown in Figure 2.59 will request the Name and Description of the list. You will also have the option to display the name on the Quick Launch.

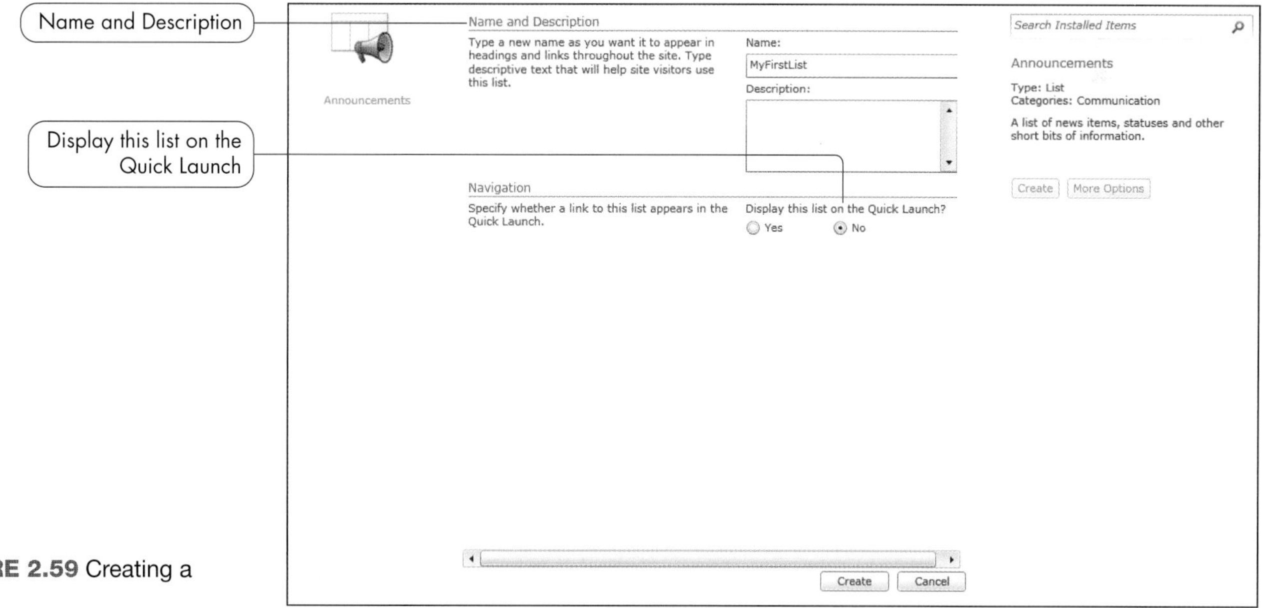

FIGURE 2.59 Creating a List ➤

Depending on the type of list or library you want to create, you may need to select more options. For example, for many libraries the Item Version History will be another option, as shown in Figure 2.60. By default, new libraries do not support versions. Hence, when you make changes to documents in the library, the changes replace the previous copy stored in the library. Selecting No in Version History minimizes the amount of storage space, but it leaves you unable to retrieve a previous document version to compare changes or to revert back to a previous version should you accidentally delete a section of text and need to retrieve it.

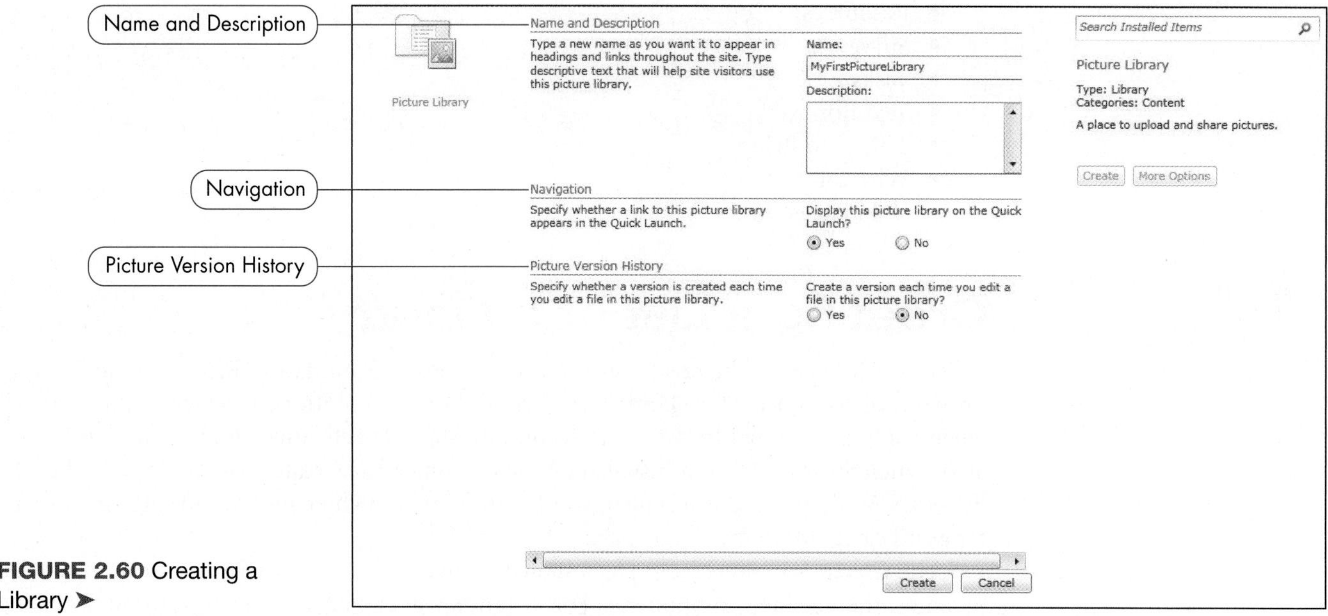

FIGURE 2.60 Creating a Library ➤

SharePoint Designer can also be used to create lists and libraries. Use the Navigation Pane and click Lists and Libraries to display the page shown in Figure 2.61. Click SharePoint List or Document Library depending on the template you wish to use. You can also create a Custom List by clicking the Custom List button. The Create List or Library dialog box will request the name and description for the list or library. The list settings are accessed and modified using the List Settings button.

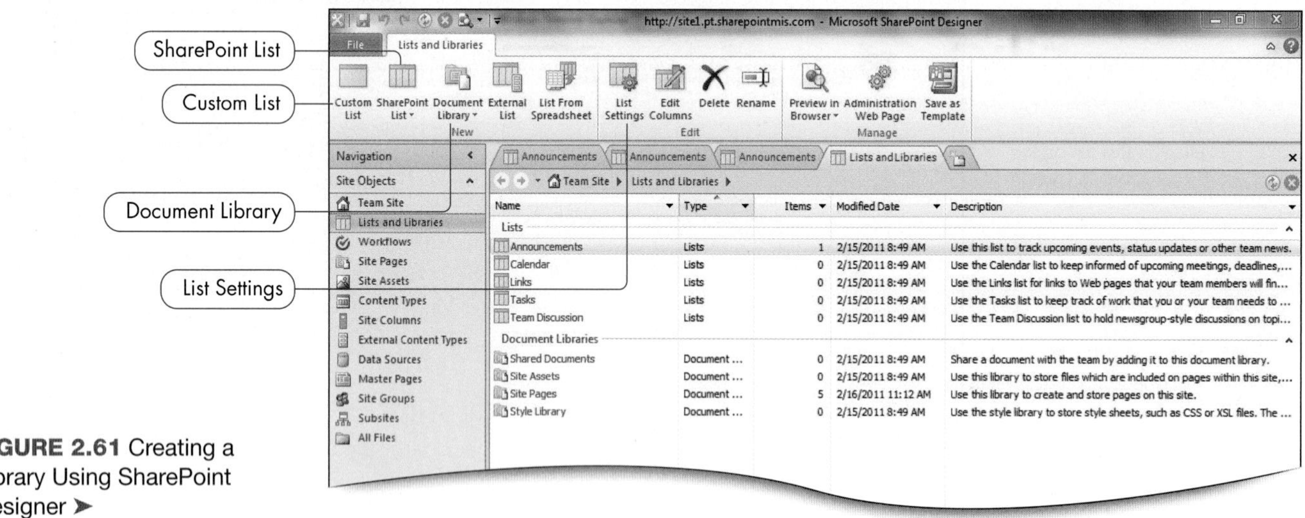

FIGURE 2.61 Creating a Library Using SharePoint Designer ➤

In the following chapters of this textbook, you will learn about how to provide the content in a list or library, editing and deleting items, and how to locate items in an efficient manner.

> **TIP** Lists and Libraries Permissions
>
> Lists and libraries inherit permissions from their parent site. You can change the permissions only in a browser. In a process called breaking permissions inheritance, you can assign individual permissions to the lists and libraries. Keep in mind that changes made to the parent site permissions will not affect the lists and libraries where you have broken the permissions inheritance.

Working with Lists

Almost all the data that you create or use within SharePoint sites is contained in a list of similar information.

Almost all the data that you create or use within SharePoint sites is contained in a list of similar information. Each list has a particular set of attributes that describe an item in the list. SharePoint lists enable you to:

- Control how the information is displayed.
- Assign permissions for modifications to the information or for viewing the list content.
- Decide if new content must be approved before it appears in the list.
- Manage the structure and data using the Lists tools tab.

Various categories on the List Settings page enable you to manage the list. Using a browser, select a list in the Navigation Pane, click the Lists Tools–List tab, and then click List Settings on the List tab, as shown in Figure 2.62a. The List Settings page, shown in Figure 2.62b, contains categories for General Settings, Permissions and Management, Communications, Content Type, Columns, and Views. General Settings enable you to name and describe the list so that users can understand the purpose, as shown in Figure 2.62c. You can also provide for navigation, versioning, approval, and other advanced features using the General Settings category. Permissions and Management enable you to delete a list, save the list as a template, modify the permissions for a list, and alter the Workflow settings. In the Communications category, you can configure the list to enable advanced information integration. Content Types are used to provide the information you want to display about an item, including its policies, workflows, or other behavior. Columns determine how the information is stored and enable you to require certain types of information for the list. You can also alter the format of the types of information; for instance, specifying single lines of text or multiple lines. Through the Views category, you can give access to the information on the list to users with different devices, such as mobile phones, and you can create new views to customize the way information is displayed to users.

Just as folders help you to organize files in your computer system, SharePoint enables you to create a hierarchy of folders for lists. Lists are initially created without folders, and folders must be enabled on the Advanced Settings page of the list in order to create the folders. Click List Settings in the Lists group on the List Tools–List tab, and then click Advanced Settings in the General Settings of the List Settings page. Using the same Advanced Settings page, you can allow attachments to the list, enabling users to store content within the folders.

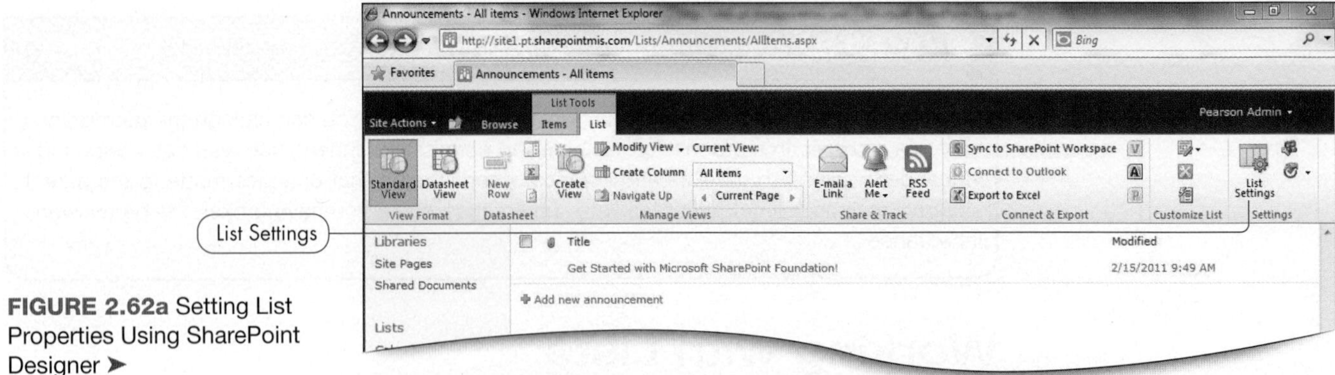

FIGURE 2.62a Setting List Properties Using SharePoint Designer ➤

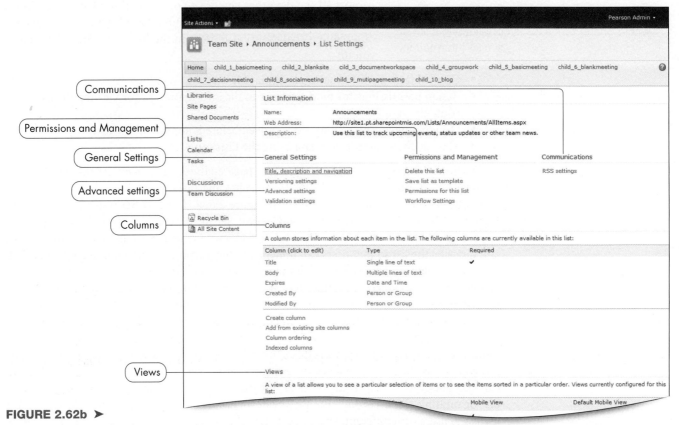

Communications

Permissions and Management

General Settings

Advanced settings

Columns

Views

FIGURE 2.62b ➤

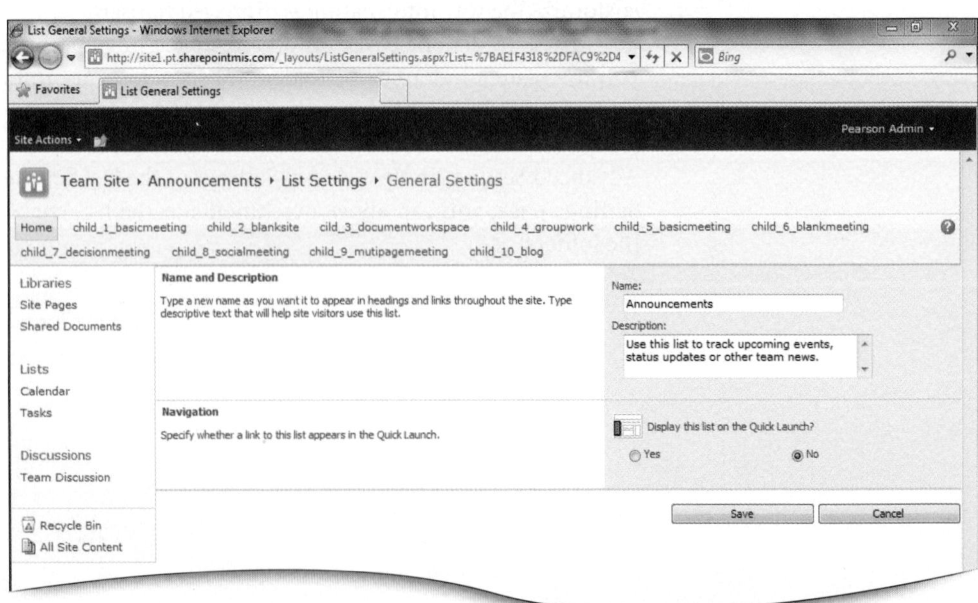

FIGURE 2.62c ➤

You can also modify the settings of a list (or a library) using the SharePoint Designer Ribbon. Click the name of the list, and then click List Settings on the Edit group of the Lists and Libraries tab, as shown in Figure 2.61. On the List Settings page, modify the settings as needed.

You can add a new folder only using the SharePoint Foundation browser interface. Once you have enabled folders on a site, you can create a new folder by selecting the list, and then clicking New Folder. You will provide a name for the folder, and then save it. The resulting folder will appear as a folder icon that you normally see in Windows, as shown in Figure 2.63.

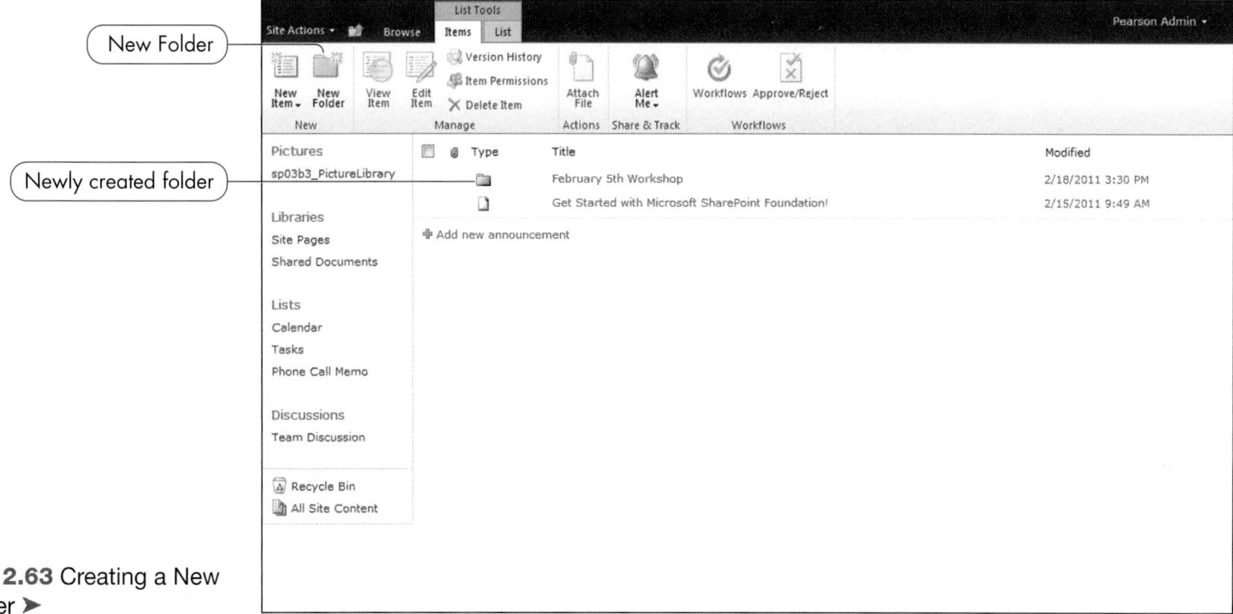

FIGURE 2.63 Creating a New List Folder ➤

Working with Libraries

In SharePoint, document management is based on libraries.

In SharePoint, document management is based on libraries. Libraries are built on the same philosophy as lists; hence they enable you to customize the way in which they store and present information to the user. The main difference between a library and a list is that an item in a library must contain a file and the accompanying metadata to the file. Metadata is information about the file, such as who created it and when. Document management has some unique requirements, but includes some list features such as columns, views, versioning, and content approval. Fortunately, after learning about lists, you will be very comfortable working with libraries because they are very similar.

Libraries are managed on the Sharepoint Foundation Library Settings page, as shown in Figure 2.64. To start the process of managing a library, click the link to the library on the All Site Content page, click the Library Tools–Library tab, and then click Library Settings on the Settings group. The Library Setting page contains options categorized into sections with tools similar to the List Settings page (shown in Figure 2.62).

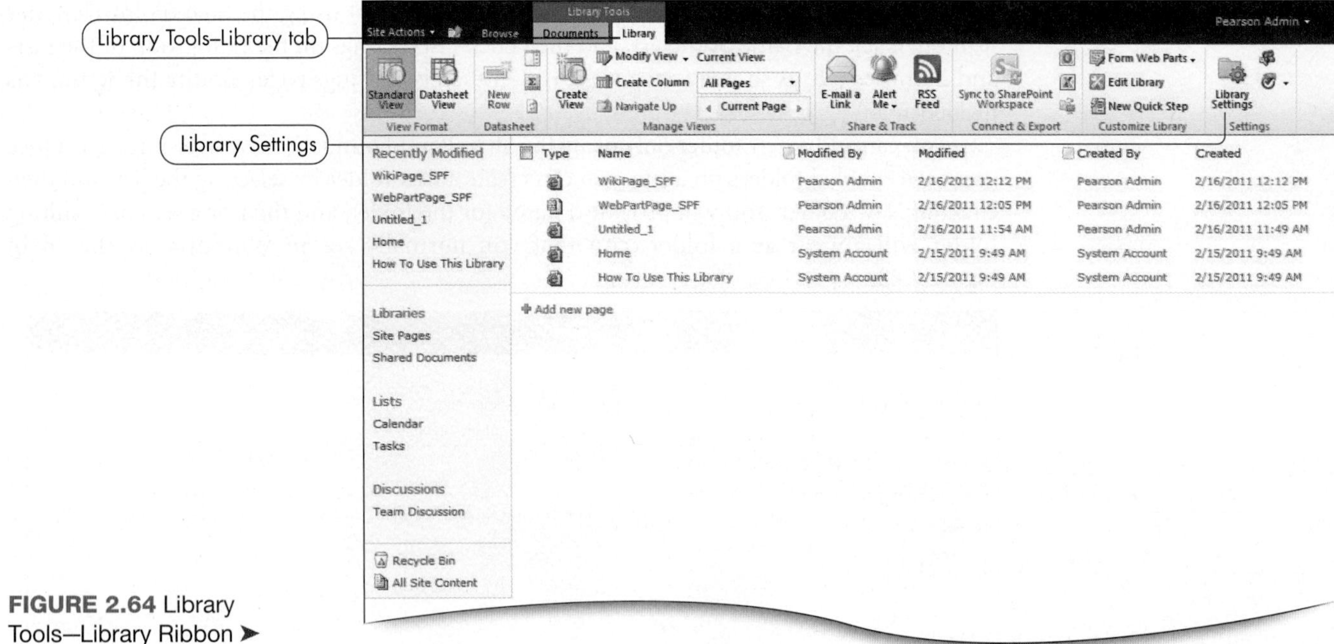

FIGURE 2.64 Library Tools–Library Ribbon ➤

To assist users in the organization of documents in a library, you can add folders to the library. On the Library Tools–Documents tab, click New Folder. Provide a descriptive name for the folder in the dialog box, and then click Save. Notice that you can also create new documents from this tab. To place the new document in the folder, select the folder, and then click New Document.

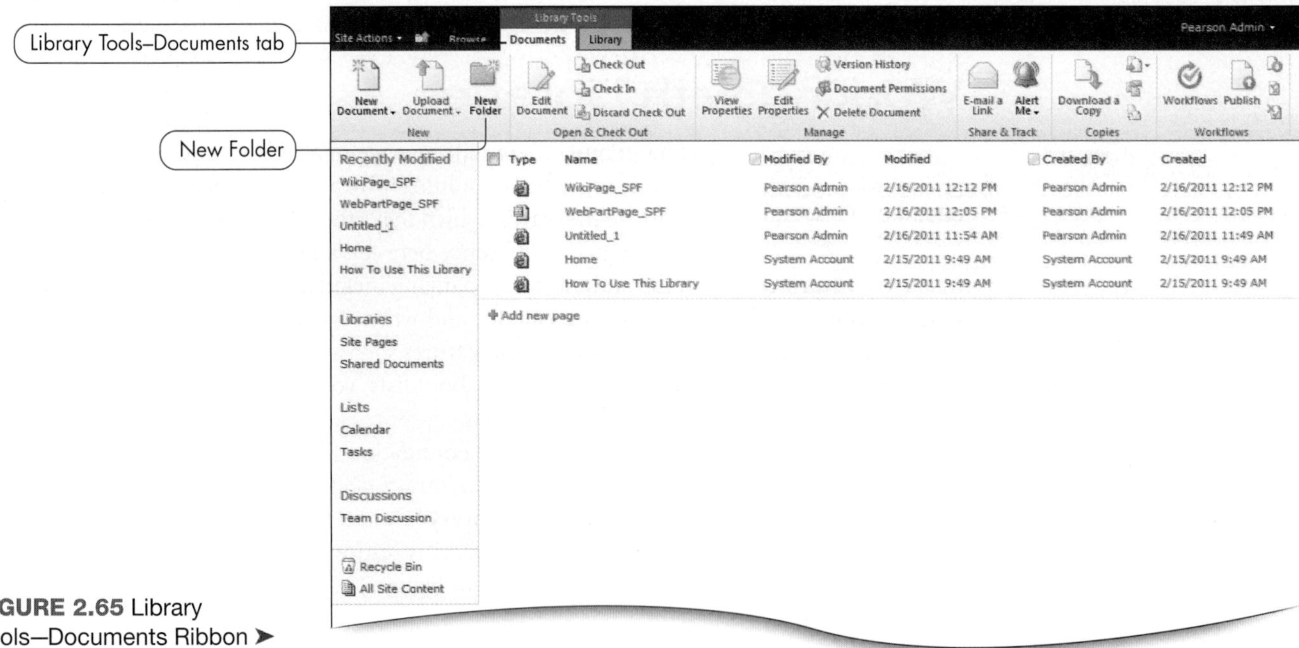

FIGURE 2.65 Library Tools–Documents Ribbon ➤

The Management of SharePoint Sites Documents

SharePoint Foundation provides you with a set of user-friendly tools for working with documents. You can upload documents and move them within the site. You can edit the document properties. Documents can be checked in or out. You can also delete and restore documents as needed. All these tools are available through the SharePoint Foundation browser interface and SharePoint Designer.

When working through the browser, SharePoint enables you to work with documents using the Edit Menu or the Documents tab of the SharePoint Foundation Ribbon. If you use SharePoint Designer, you work with documents using the Edit and Manage groups of the File tab.

In this section, you learn how to upload documents and edit their properties within a SharePoint site, and how to use the check-in and check-out options. You will then learn about deleting, restoring, and exchanging documents between SharePoint sites.

Uploading Documents

Using the Library Tools–Documents tab in SharePoint Foundation, you can upload a single document or multiple documents. To access the Documents tab, browse to the Document Library where you want to upload documents by clicking the Libraries link on the SharePoint left Navigation Pane, shown as Shared Documents in Figure 2.66. Click the Upload Document arrow in the New group of the Library Tools–Documents tab.

To upload a single document, click Upload Document to display the Shared Documents – Upload Document dialog box, as shown in Figure 2.66, click Browse, and then select the file you want to upload. If versioning is turned on for the site, you will have an option to add the file as a new version. If versioning is turned off and you check *Overwrite existing files*, the new file replaces the old. If you uncheck Overwrite existing files, the new file will not be uploaded if another file with the same name is available in the library. Click OK to upload the file. The uploaded file displays in the Document Library.

To upload multiple documents, click Upload Multiple Documents to display the Shared Documents – Upload Multiple Documents dialog box, as shown in Figure 2.66. Drag and drop files from your computer or network file system into the Upload Multiple Documents window, or click the *Browse for files instead* link to display *Open dialog box to select the files you want to upload.* Decide if you wish to overwrite files with the same name, and then appropriately check *Overwrite existing files.* The upload progress bar of the Upload Multiple Documents window shows you the uploading status. Click Done to return to the Documents tab. The uploaded files are displayed in the Document Library.

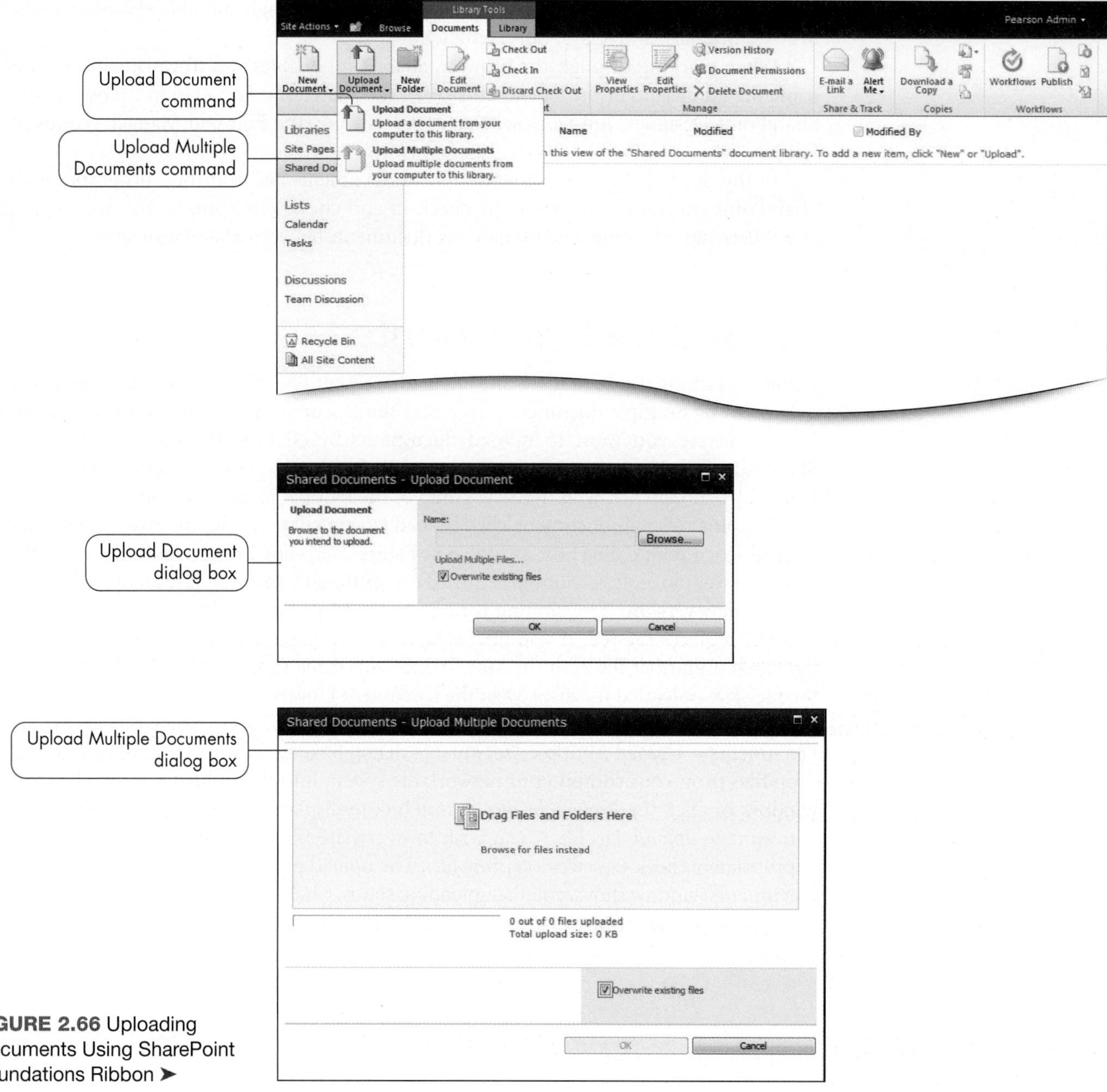

FIGURE 2.66 Uploading Documents Using SharePoint Foundations Ribbon ➤

If you are using SharePoint Designer to upload documents, click the All Files link on the Navigation Pane, and then double-click the library in which you wish to upload the document. Click Import Files in the Manage group of the All Files tab, as shown in Figure 2.67. Click Add File in the dialog box, select the documents you want to upload, and then click Open. Click OK to upload the documents and they will display in the Document Library you have selected.

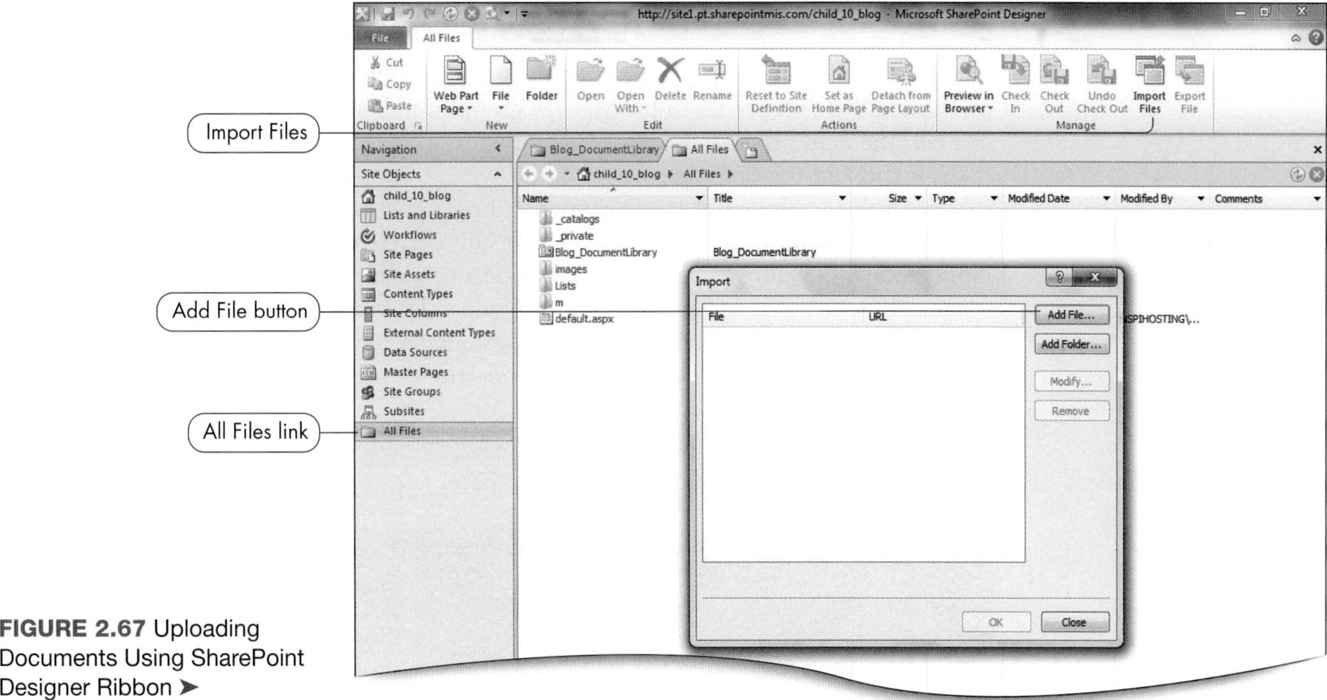

FIGURE 2.67 Uploading Documents Using SharePoint Designer Ribbon ➤

TIP Upload Size and Document Version

As you are uploading files, SharePoint displays the number of files you are about to upload and the total upload size. This is important to you because limits on the size of uploads may be in place. The default total size limit is 50 MB.

After you finish uploading a document to a library, you can perform further actions on that document. For each document, SharePoint Foundation provides an Edit menu that enables you to view and edit the properties, edit the document, check the file in or out, manage permissions, or delete the file. To display the Edit menu, point to the name of your document, and then click on the arrow to the right of the document, as shown in Figure 2.68.

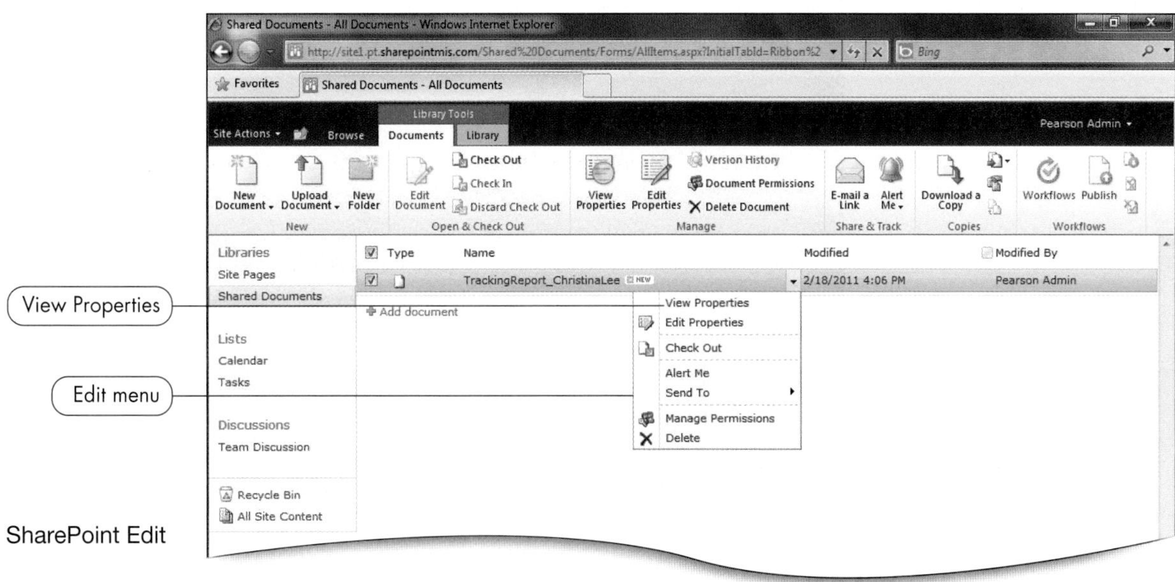

FIGURE 2.68 SharePoint Edit Menu ➤

Editing Documents Properties

You can view the properties of the documents included in your site using the Edit menu, or by clicking View Properties in the Manage group of the Library Tools–Documents tab. You can edit the item properties, view version history (if available), manage permissions, and manage check in/out options.

Select the document in the Document Library, and then click View Properties to open the View tab, as shown in Figure 2.69a. Click Edit Item to edit the properties using the Edit tab, as shown in Figure 2.69b. You can provide a new name for the file, much as you would rename a file in other applications and provide a descriptive title for the file. Descriptive titles are helpful to users where file names are sometimes more cryptic. For instance, the file name *RVSD_Budget_4-12* is not as easy to understand as the title *Revised Budget April 2012*.

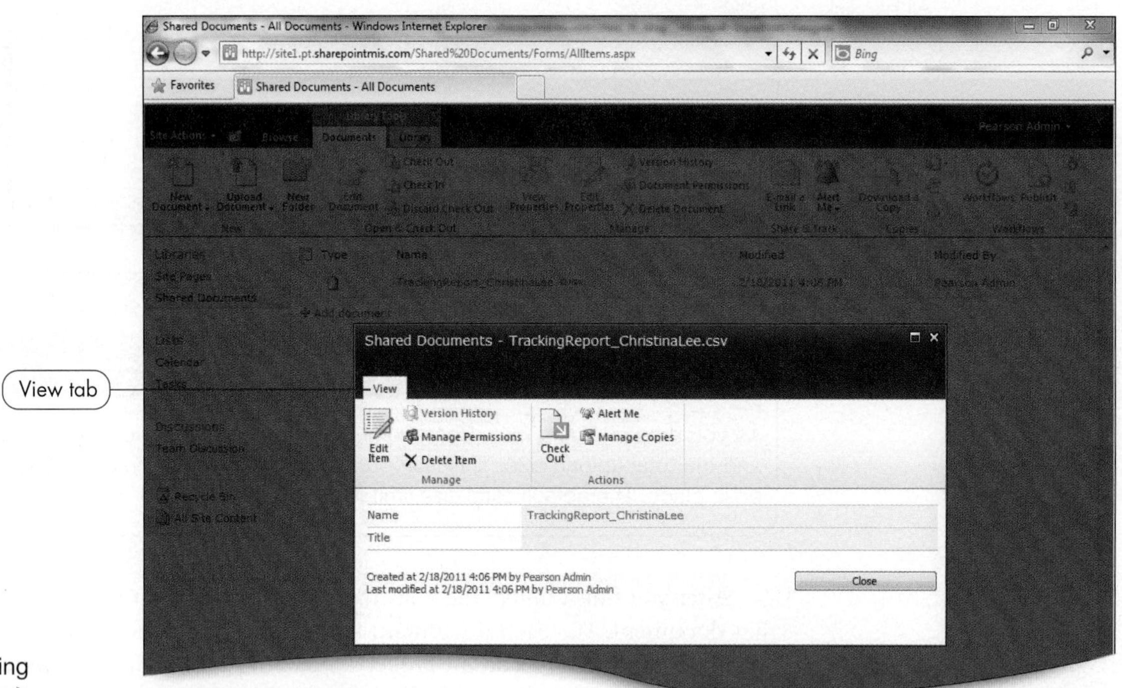

FIGURE 2.69a Editing Document Properties ➤

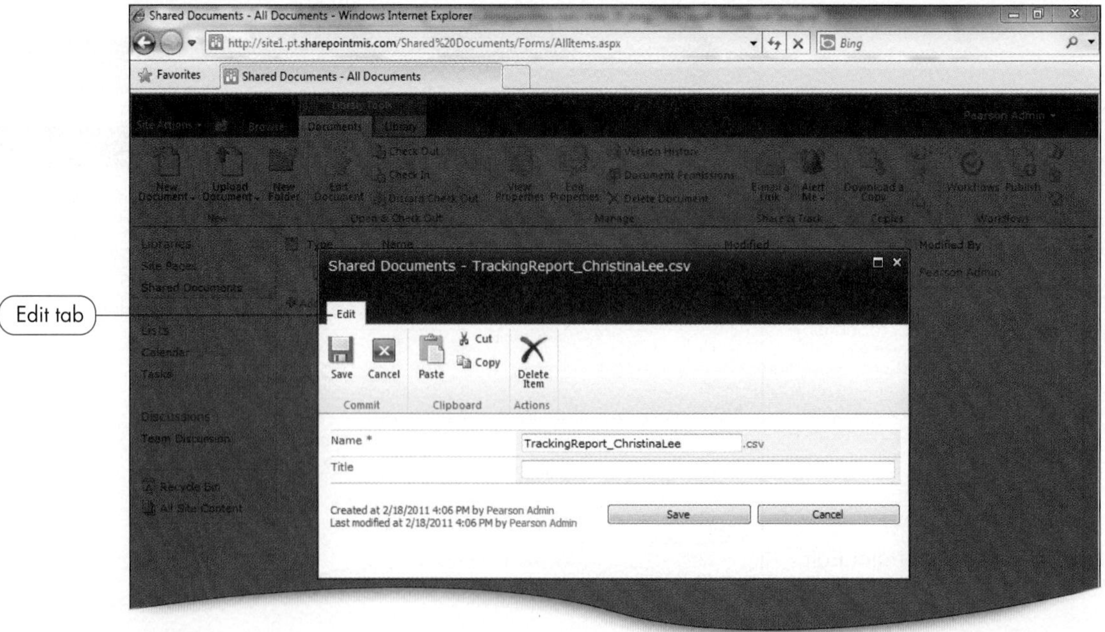

FIGURE 2.69b ➤

More About Document Properties

As a site owner, you can add more properties to describe a document. Each property of a document corresponds to a column in the Document Library or list.

Checking Documents In and Out

SharePoint enables you to check out documents that you need to work on for a longer time. Other users will not be able to work on that document and they will not see your changes until you check in the document.

When you check out a document using a Web browser, the Check Out flag is set to Yes and stores the user name of the person who checked out the document, as shown in Figure 2.70a. You should always remember to check in a document when you finish editing the document, as shown in Figure 2.70b.

When using a browser, you can Check Out, Check In, and Discard Check Out for a document either using the related buttons on the Open & Check Out group of the Library Tools–Documents tab or the context drop-down menu, as shown in Figure 2.70b. Using SharePoint Designer, Check Out, Check In, and Undo Check Out are on the Manage group of the Page tab, as shown in Figure 2.71b.

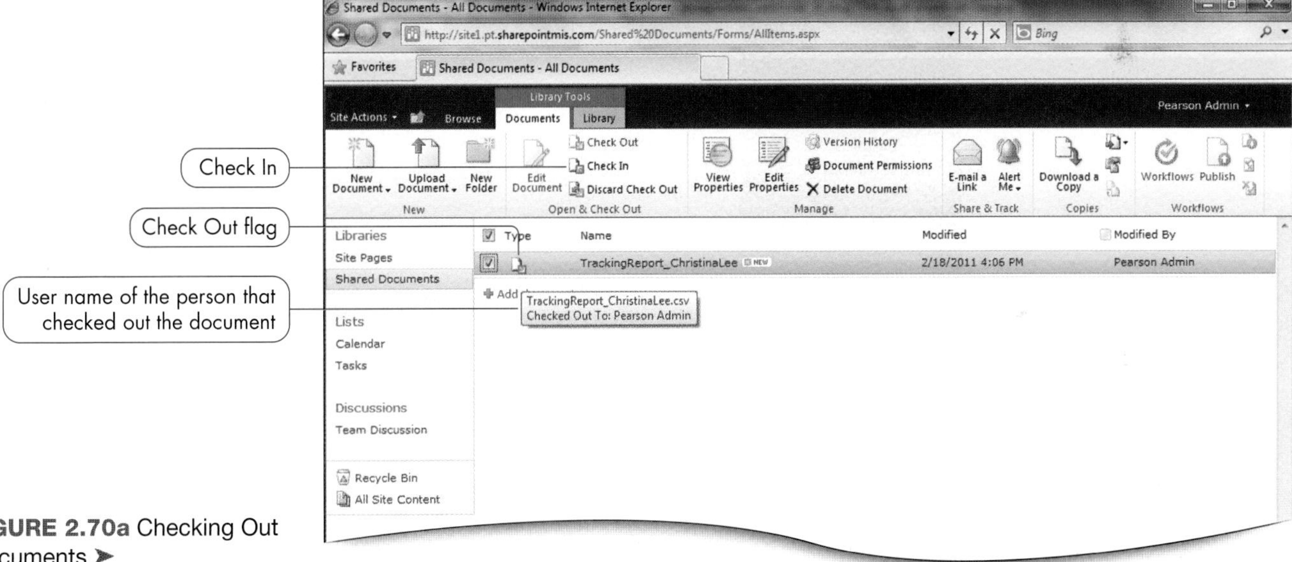

FIGURE 2.70a Checking Out Documents ➤

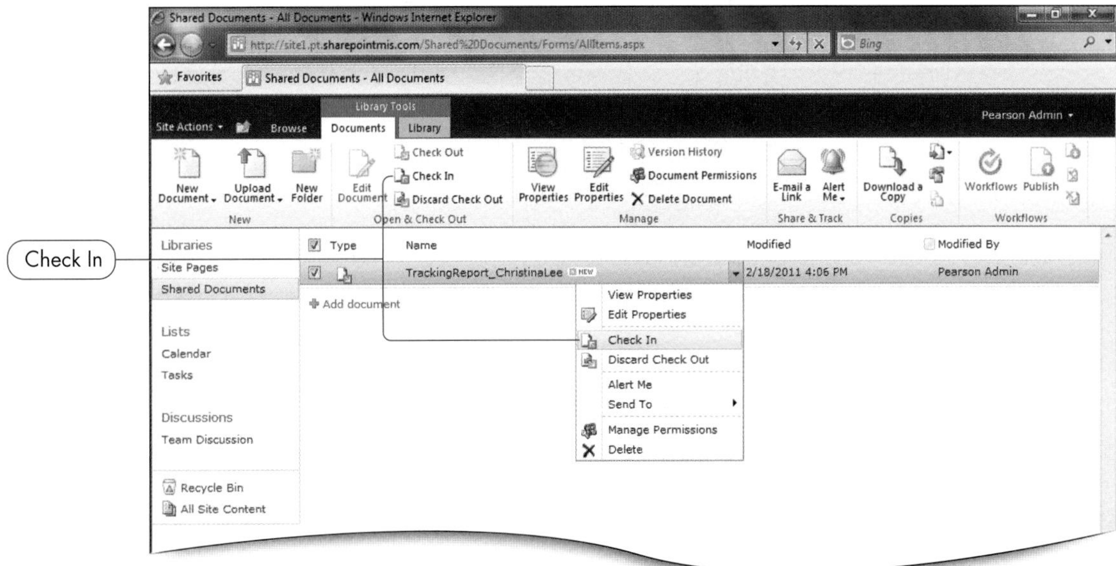

FIGURE 2.70b ➤

If you check in the document using the SharePoint Foundation Ribbon or the context drop-down menu, the Check In dialog box enables you to retain the check out and add comments on the changes made to the document, as shown in Figure 2.71a. When you retain the check out, you make the document changes available for others to view, but they cannot modify the document because it will still be checked out to you. If you checked out a document and do not want to keep any record of this action, click Discard Check Out or Undo Check Out in the Manage group. When you check in the document using the SharePoint Designer Ribbon, the Check In dialog box only allows comments about the changes you made to the document, as shown in Figure 2.71b.

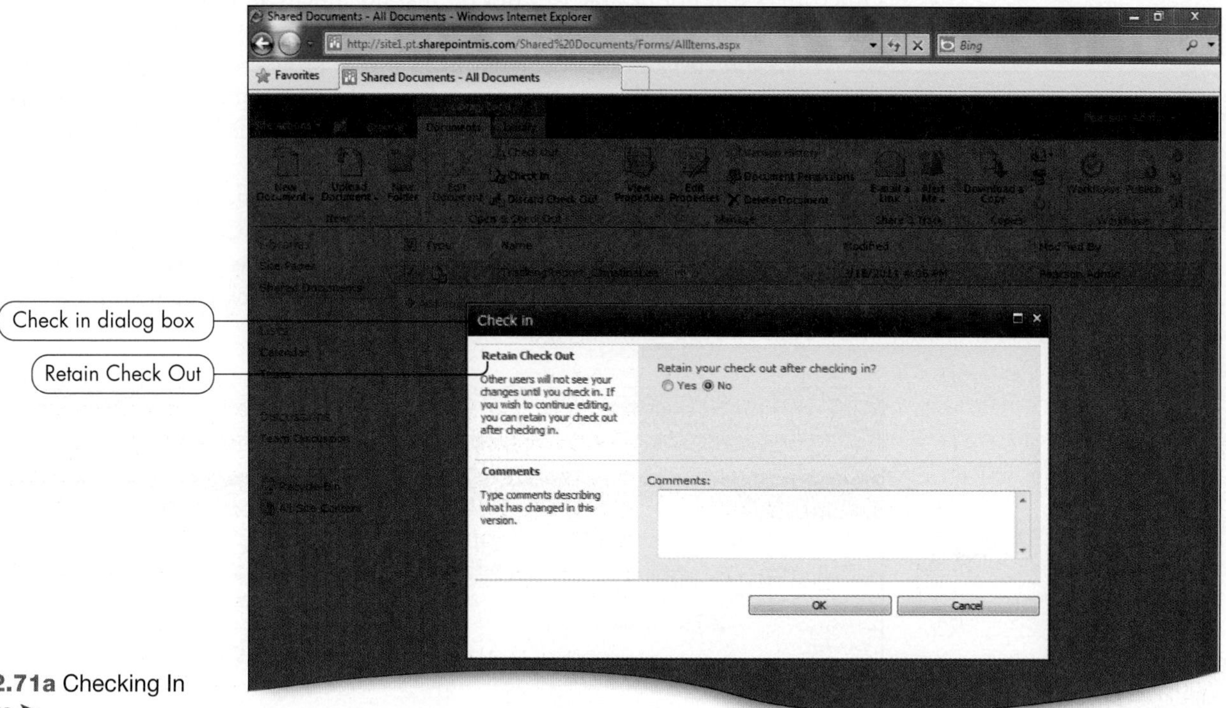

FIGURE 2.71a Checking In Documents ➤

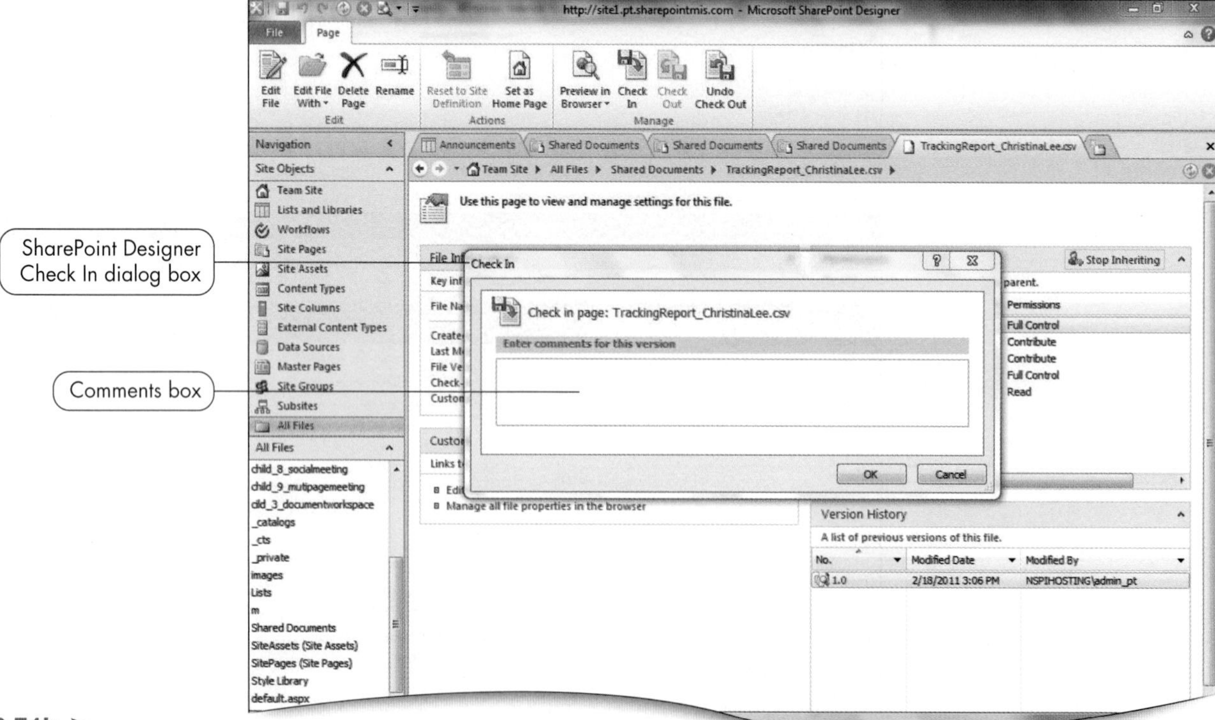

FIGURE 2.71b ➤

TIP Overwriting Checked Out Documents Setting

Imagine, for example, a scenario where your team needs to make a time-sensitive modification to a document, and the team member who has the document checked out is not immediately available. With Full Control permission, you can check in documents that other users have checked out. If you are the site owner, select Check In from the context menu of the checked-out document or its Ribbon. When you click OK on the Check In window, a warning will be displayed naming the user who has the document checked out, with the check-out date and time. Click Yes on the warning. The document status will change to checked in, and other users can view and modify the most recent version.

Deleting and Recovering Deleted Documents

Every time you delete a document from a List or a library, you are not losing it forever. Documents that you delete are stored in the Recycle Bin of your site which functions in a similar way to the Recycle Bin in Windows. The Recycle Bin enables you to either restore a deleted document to its original location or to remove it permanently from the Recycle Bin.

Using SharePoint Designer, you can delete a document from a library either by clicking Delete in the Edit group on the All Files tab, or by right-clicking the document name in the All Files report and selecting the Delete command, as shown in Figure 2.72. You can also delete a document by clicking Delete Document in the Manage group of the SharePoint Foundation Documents tab or using the Edit menu, as shown in Figure 2.70.

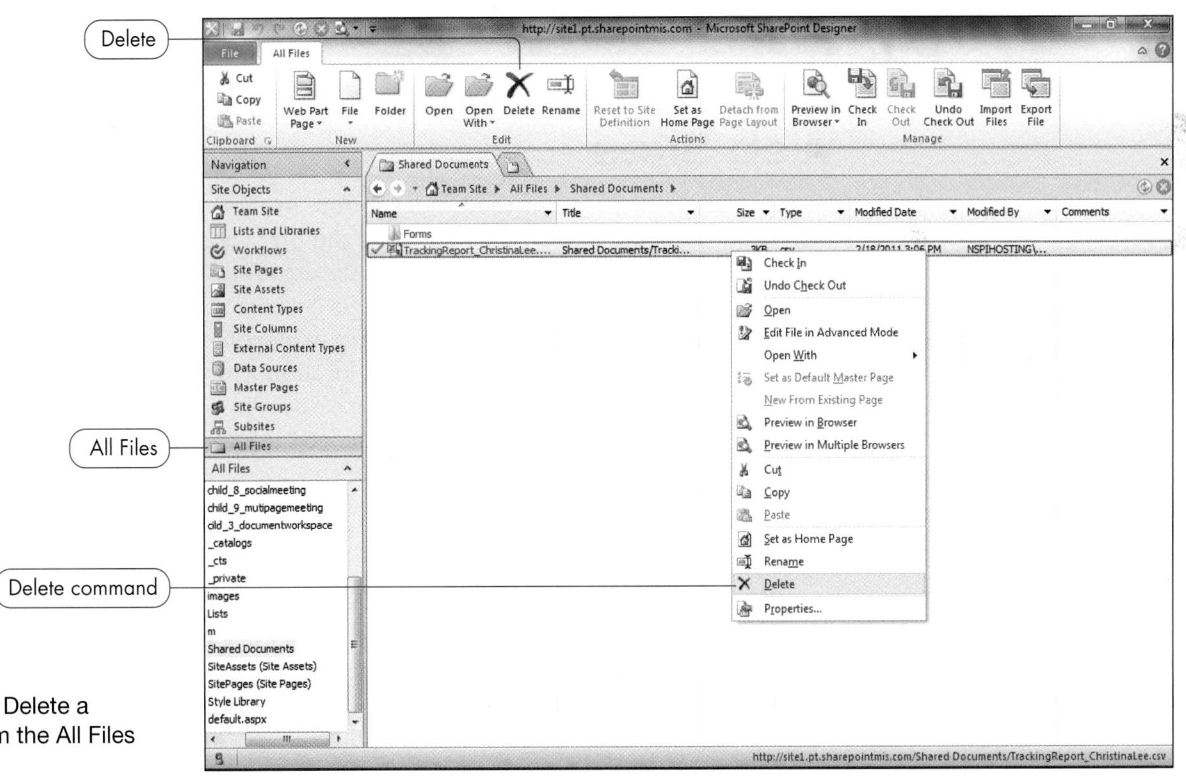

FIGURE 2.72 Delete a Document from the All Files Report ➤

It is sometimes necessary to undelete a file that was deleted. If you are using a browser, click the Recycle Bin link on the Navigation Pane of the site, and click the check box next to the file you want to restore, as shown in Figure 2.73. You can select multiple files to restore if necessary. Click Restore Selection and the file will be returned to the location from which it was deleted.

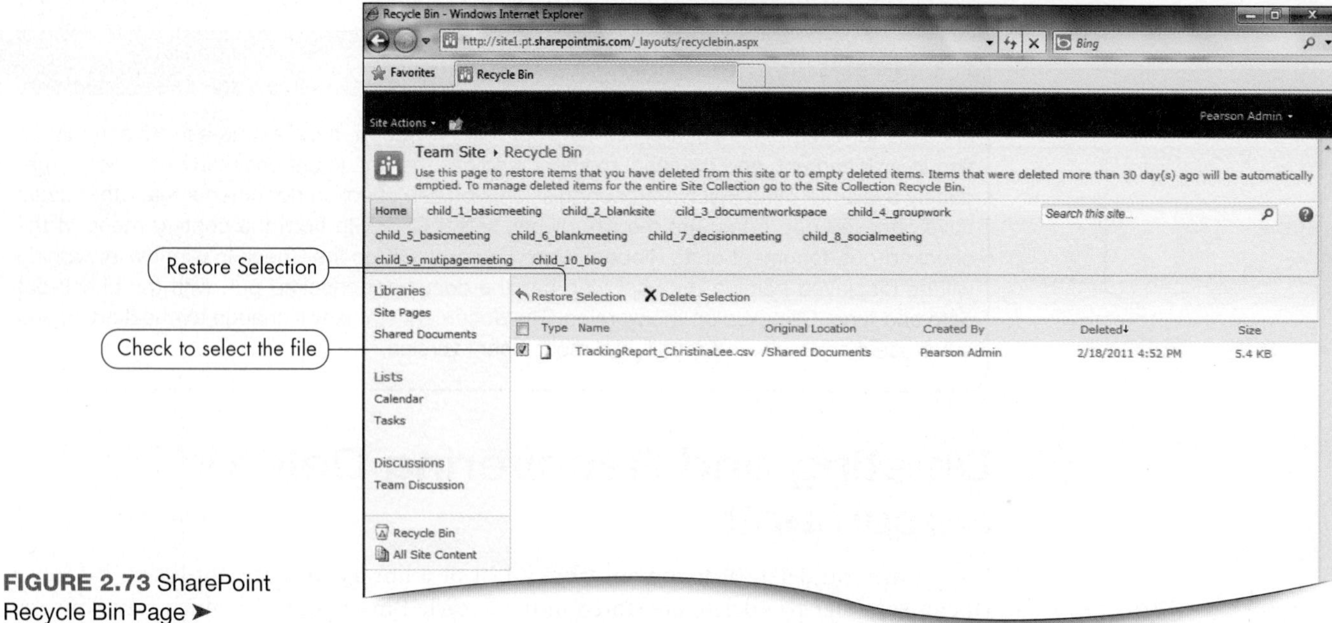

FIGURE 2.73 SharePoint Recycle Bin Page ➤

If instead of clicking the Restore Selection link, you click the Delete Selection link, the selected files will be removed from the site Recycle Bin and moved to the Recycle Bin of the site collection in which your site is included. This adds a second layer of security in the deletion process. Files moved to the site collection Recycle Bin will remain there for 30 days (or length of time set by the site administrator) or until they are deleted by the site collection administrator.

Exchanging Documents Between Web Sites

The commands included in the Copies group, in the Library Tools–Documents tab in SharePoint Foundation, enable you to create and manage copies of the documents included in a library. This fosters collaboration across the organization, and saves time because multiple documents can be created based on a single document.

The **Send To** command is used to distribute documents to other libraries.

The ***Send To*** command is used to distribute documents to other libraries, making it available for other teams or in a centralized location. Using Send To, you copy the original file, called the *source file*, into a different library. The copy can be edited independently of the source file, but you have the option to send updates from the source to the copies. For example, you have a budget template that departments across the company must complete. You can copy it to multiple libraries and each department can fill in the data on their own library copy. If a formula is changed in the source document, the update can be sent to the other copies throughout the company.

With Contribute permission in the library where you will store the file, you locate the source document file in your library and send it to the URL for the library where the copy will be displayed. Select the file you want to copy, click the Send To arrow in the Copies group of the Library Tools–Documents tab, and then click Other Location to display the Copy dialog box shown in Figure 2.74. Type the full URL of the SharePoint library where the copy will be stored, including http://, the server name, the site name, the library name, and the folder name (if applicable). You can specify a new name for the copy, if desired. Selections related to updating the copies include whether a prompt will be made when an updated source file is checked in and whether an alert will be issued when the source file is updated. E-mail must be enabled on the server in order to send these alerts.

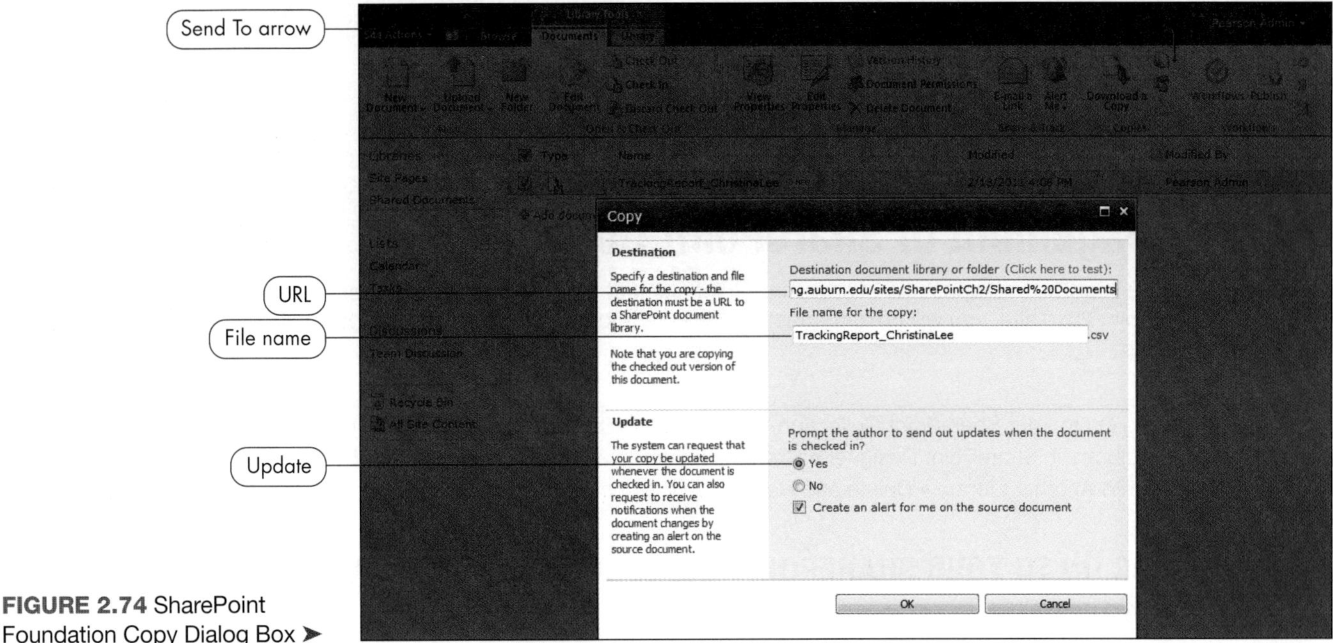

FIGURE 2.74 SharePoint Foundation Copy Dialog Box ➤

TIP More About Send To Command Options

If you use an application, such as Microsoft Office Word 2010, to create documents that you store in a SharePoint library and send to other libraries, you will not receive prompts to update the copies in that application.

3 SharePoint Foundation Lists and Libraries and The Management of SharePoint Documents

Lists and libraries are important components of any SharePoint site that allow you to manage documents. For developing the DestinQuest SharePoint 2010 site, you will need to master concepts and hands-on skills for working with Lists and Libraries and Managing documents.

Skills covered: • Log On to Your SharePoint Collection, Create a New Document Workspace Site, and Create a New Contacts List • Create a New Library in SharePoint Designer • Create a Folder in a List Using SharePoint Designer • Upload a Document in a Library and Move It to Another Library • Delete and Restore a Document

STEP 1 LOG ON TO YOUR SHAREPOINT COLLECTION, CREATE A NEW DOCUMENT WORKSPACE SITE, AND CREATE A NEW CONTACTS LIST

Before you can start exploring how you can manage the Destin Quest company documents using Lists and Libraries, you will need to log on to your SharePoint Collection. You will create a new site, as a location for storing and sharing the company documents, using the Document Workspace template, and you will create a new List using the Contacts template to manage the company contact information. Refer to Figure 2.75 as you complete Step 1.

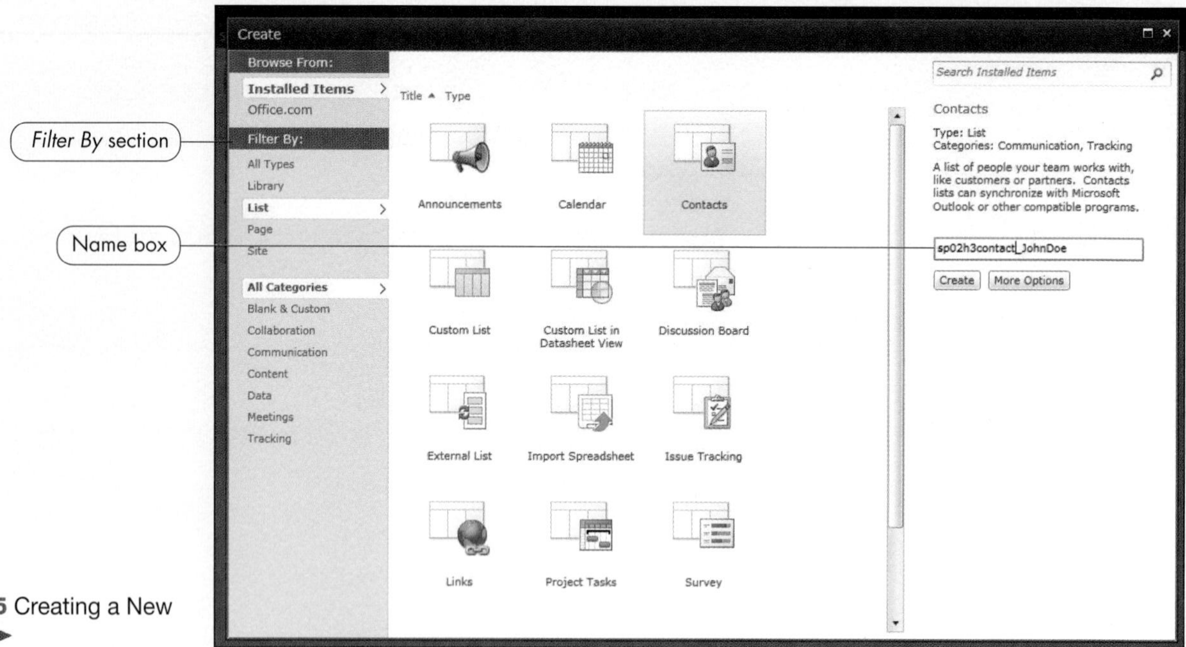

FIGURE 2.75 Creating a New Contact List ➤

a. Click **Start** to display the Start menu. Click **All Programs**, and then click **Internet Explorer** to open the program.

b. Go to the top-level site provided by your instructor, which will be in the format of http://pt.sharepointmis.com/SitePages/*yourname*. Enter the user name and password provided by your instructor.

c. Click **All Site Content** on the Quick Launch of the top-level site.

   The All Site Content page is now displayed.

d. Click **Create** to open the Create dialog box. Click **Site** in the *Filter By* section of the Create dialog box. Click **Document Workspace**, type **sp02h3docworkspace_LastNameFirstName** in the **Title** and **URL name boxes**, and then click **Create**.

   The *sp02h3docworkspace_LastNameFirstName* workspace is now displayed.

e. Click **Lists** on the Quick Launch, and then click **Create** to open the Create dialog box.

   Your screen should now look similar to Figure 2.75.

f. Click **List** in the *Filter By* section of the Create dialog box. Click **Contacts** type **sp02h3contacts_LastNameFirstName** in the **Name box**, and then click **Create**.

   The List Tools – List tab is now displayed and the link to the *sp02h3contacts_LastNameFirstName* page is displayed on the Quick Launch.

STEP 2 CREATE A NEW LIBRARY IN SHAREPOINT DESIGNER

You will create a Library in SharePoint Designer, using the Pictures template, where you can store company relevant pictures. Refer to Figure 2.76 as you complete Step 2.

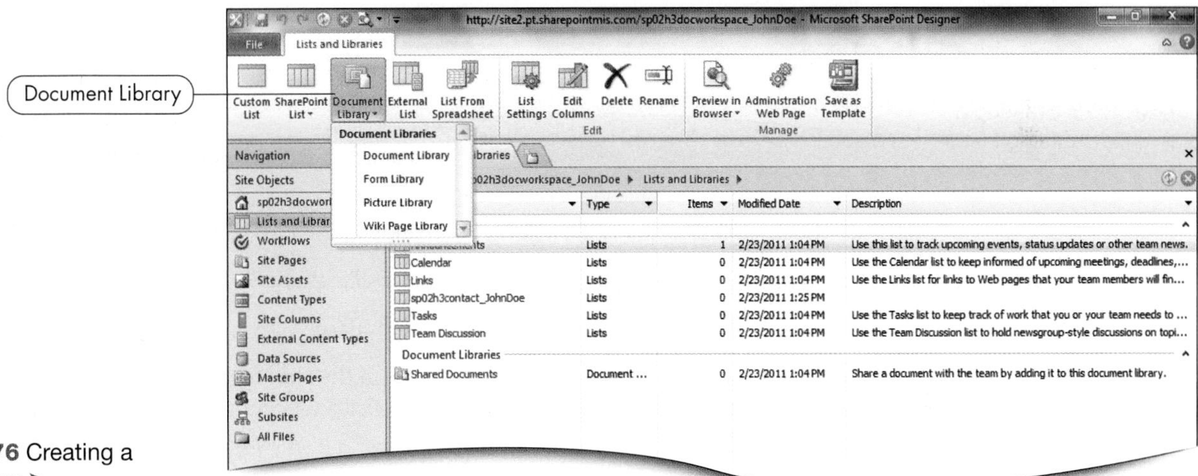

FIGURE 2.76 Creating a Picture Library ➤

a. Click **Edit in SharePoint Designer** on the Site Actions menu of the *sp02h3docworkspace_LastNameFirstName* page. Type your password in the Windows security dialog box.

   The Site Settings page of the *sp02h3docworkspace_LastNameFirstName* page is now displayed in SharePoint Designer.

b. Click **Lists and Libraries** on the Navigation Pane.

   The Lists and Libraries tab is now displayed.

c. Click **Document Library** in the New group of the Lists and Libraries tab, and then click **Picture Library**, as shown in Figure 2.76.

   The Create list or Document Library page is now displayed.

d. Type **sp02h3pictures_LastNameFirstName** in the **Name box**, and then click **OK**.

   The link to the new *sp02h3pictures_LastNameFirstName* library is displayed in the *Documents Libraries* section of the Lists and Libraries page.

STEP 3 CREATE A FOLDER IN A LIST USING SHAREPOINT DESIGNER

You will create a Folder in the *sp02h3contacts_LastNameFirstName* Contacts List, using SharePoint Designer, to better organize the company contacts information. Refer to Figure 2.77 as you complete Step 3.

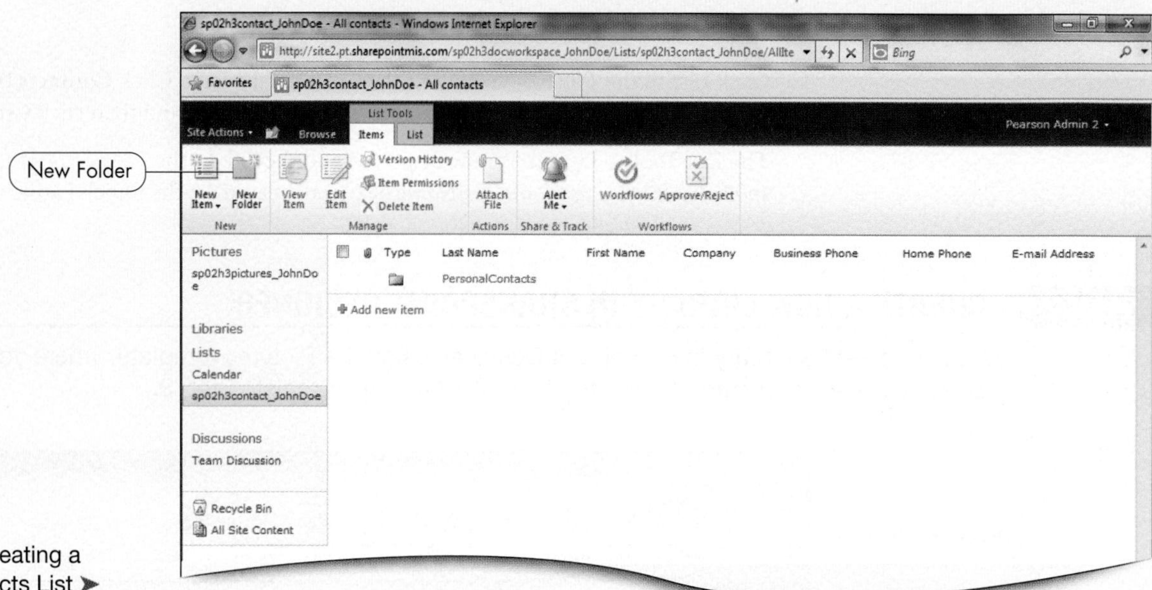

FIGURE 2.77 Creating a Folder in a Contacts List ➤

a. Click **sp02h3contacts_LastNameFirstName** in the *Lists* section of the List and Libraries page.

The List Settings page for the *sp02h3contact_LastNameFirstName* site is now displayed.

b. Review all the options from the List Settings page.

c. Check the **Display New Folder command** on the New Menu in the *Advanced Settings* section of the List Settings page, and then click **Save** on the Quick Access Toolbar.

d. Click **Preview in Browser** in the Manage group of the List Settings tab. Click the **List Tools–Items tab.**

The Items tab is now displayed.

e. Click **New Folder** on the New group of the Items tab.

The New Folder dialog box is now displayed.

f. Type **PersonalContact** in the **Name box** of the New Folder dialog box, and then click **Save.**

The link to the new PersonalContact folder is now displayed on the All contacts page, as shown in Figure 2.77.

STEP 4 UPLOAD A DOCUMENT IN A LIBRARY AND MOVE IT TO ANOTHER LIBRARY

You will upload a document to the Shared Documents library and send a copy of this file to the *sp02h3Pictures_LastNameFirstName* library. Refer to Figure 2.78 as you complete Step 4.

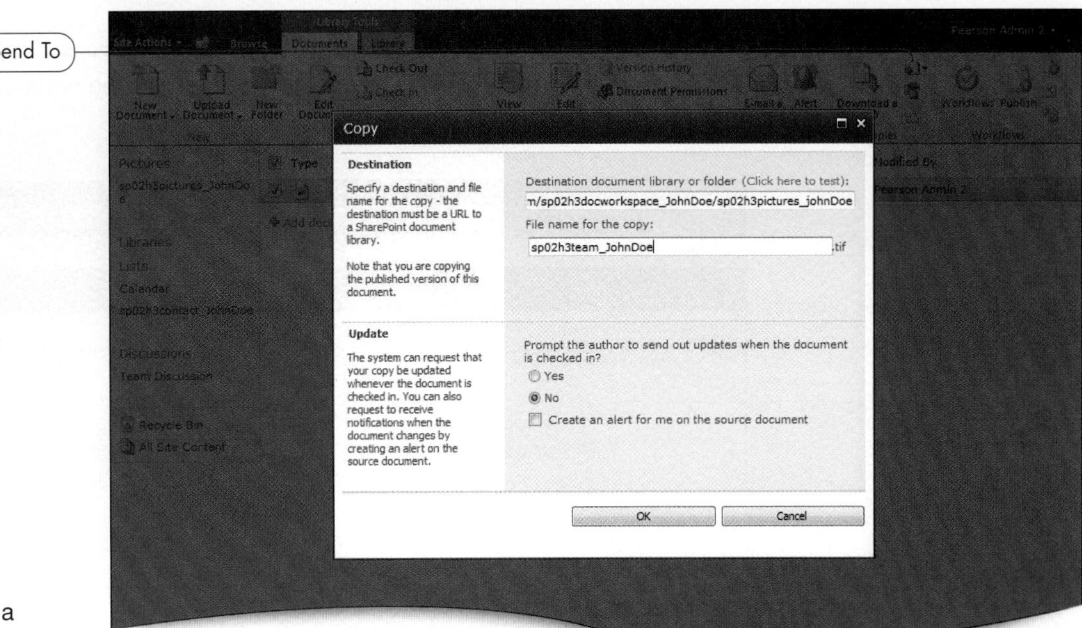

FIGURE 2.78 Sending a Document to Another Library ➤

a. Click **Libraries** on the Quick Launch in the browser view of the All Site Content page within the *sp02h3docworkspace_LastNameFirstName* site.

   The All Site Content page is now displayed.

b. Click **Shared Documents** in the *Document Libraries* section of the All Site Content page.

   The All Documents page of the **Shared Documents library** is now displayed.

c. Click the **Library Tools–Documents tab** to display the Library Tools–Documents options.

d. Click **Upload Document** in the New group of the Library Tools–Documents tab.

   The Upload Document dialog box is now showing.

e. Click **Browse**, navigate to the *sp02h3team* file in your Exploring folder, and then double-click its name. Click **OK.**

   The *sp02h3team* file is now shown on the All Documents page of the Shared Documents library.

f. Select the check box to the left of the *sp02h3team* file name, which appears when the pointer is placed over the document link. Click **Send To** in the Copies group of the Library Tools–Documents tab, and then click **Other Location**.

   The Copy page is now displayed.

g. Add **/sp02h3Pictures_LastNameFirstName** to the URL of the *sp02h3docworkspace_LastNameFirstName* site. Add **_LastNameFirstName** to the name shown in the **File name for the copy box**, as shown in Figure 2.78. Click **OK**.

h. Click **OK** on the Copy Progress box. Click **Done** on the Copy Progress box when you see the *Copy operation was successful* message.

i. Click **sp02h3Pictures_LastNameFirstName** on the Quick Launch.

   The All Pictures page of the *sp02h3Pictures_LastNameFirstName* library is now displayed including the link to the *sp02h3team_LastNameFirstName* file.

STEP 5 DELETE AND RESTORE A DOCUMENT

You will delete a document from the Shared Documents library, and then restore it using the Recycle Bin. Refer to Figure 2.79 as you complete Step 5.

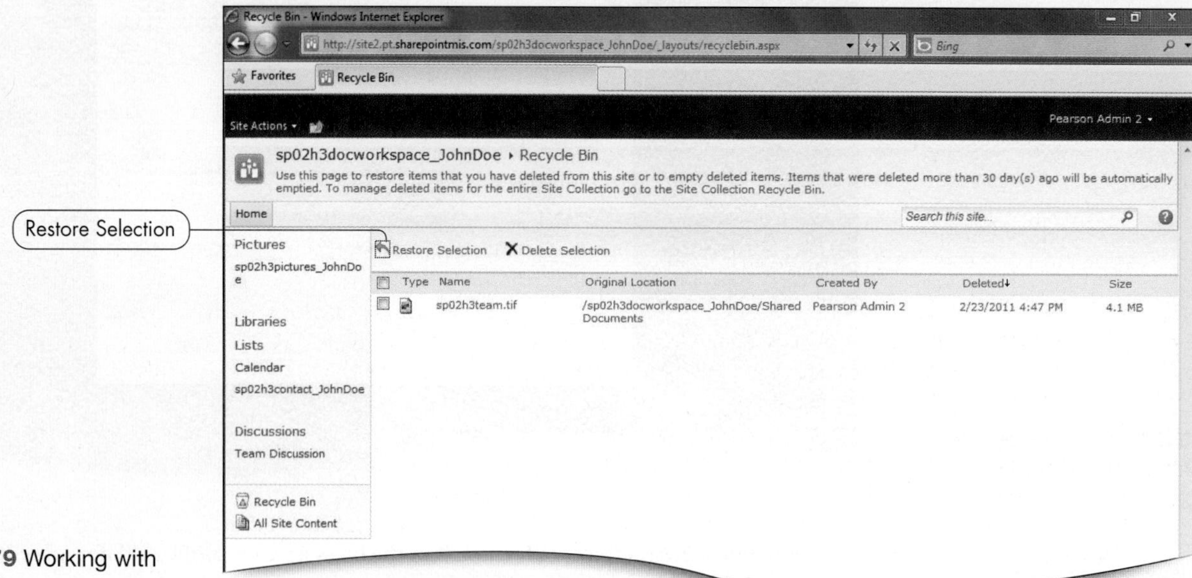

FIGURE 2.79 Working with Recycle Bin ➤

a. Click **Libraries** on the Quick Launch in the All Pictures page of the *sp02h3Pictures_LastNameFirstName* library.

   The All Site Content page is now displayed.

b. Click **Shared Documents** in the *Document Libraries* section of the All Site Content page.

   The All Documents page of the Shared Documents library is now displayed.

c. Select the check box to the left of *sp02h3team*, and then click **Delete** in the Manage group of the Library Tools–Documents Ribbon.

d. Click **OK** on the *Message from webpage* alert box.

   The *sp02h3team* file is no longer shown on the All Items page of the Shared Documents library.

e. Click **Recycle Bin** on the Quick Launch.

   The Recycle Bin page is now shown.

f. Select the check box to the left of *sp02h3team.tif*, as shown in Figure 2.79. Click **Restore Selection**, and then click **OK** on the *Message from webpage* alert box.

   The *sp02h3team* file is no longer shown on the Recycle Bin page.

g. Click **Libraries** on the Quick Launch, and then click **Shared Documents** on the All Site Content page.

   The *sp02h3team* file is now shown on the All Documents page of the Share Documents library.

h. Close all Internet Explorer windows, and then exit Internet Explorer.

i. Close the SharePoint Designer window.

CHAPTER OBJECTIVES REVIEW

After reading this chapter, you have accomplished the following objectives:

1. **Plan the development of a SharePoint site.** In the planning stage, you need to carefully analyze all the requirements related with the business or organization processes you want to build, so you will be able to use the appropriate SharePoint tools and features in developing a new SharePoint site or workspace. The next important planning step is to secure a SharePoint hosting account or Uniform Resource Locator (URL) from a hosting service, such as an Internet Service Provider (ISP). Once all planning steps have been accomplished, you can initiate the design stage.
2. **Identify tools for creating sites.** You can create SharePoint sites and components through the Web browser or SharePoint Designer 2010. The initial, top-level site can be created only using the SharePoint Central Administration site. The top-level site includes the functionality of all child sites, and it also enables you to manage site collections via the Site Collection Administration links included in the Site Settings page. By default, when a new top-level, parent site is created, the Site administrator is the only person with access to the site. Subsites inherit the top-level site permissions or subsite users can be assigned unique permissions. The top-level site can be used to view the site structure within the site collection. You can set a page as the new SharePoint site home page using SharePoint Foundation or SharePoint Designer.
3. **Add new Web pages.** You can add new pages to a SharePoint site, using a Web browser or SharePoint Designer, Web Part pages, Wiki pages, a New Page from Master, or other types of pages such as HTML, ASPX, CSS, Master Page, Java Script, XML, or Text File. As you make changes to the pages of a site, they are unghosted, which means they no longer contain the characteristics of the standard configuration and layout. You can reghost pages to reset them to the original site definition.
4. **Brand SharePoint Foundation sites.** As a site designer, you can create a custom brand for your sites using Master pages, CSS, and site themes. A site theme defines the font and color schemes for a site. People with design or full control permission levels have the ability to change site themes. Themes enable you to apply a consistent look and feel to the pages in a site and enable you to maintain consistency with custom branding. Usually, Web designers develop alternative CSS or Master pages to complement the company's brand. You can use a combination of these options to fit the site into the overall organizational brand.
5. **Delete sites.** Site deletions do not have a Recycle Bin. It is a permanent action, with which you delete all content, pages, and the site itself. You should always make backups of sites before deleting. Parent sites cannot be deleted until the child sites are deleted.
6. **Back up and restore SharePoint sites and content.** You can back up and restore SharePoint Foundation sites using a Web browser or using SharePoint Designer. If you have access to the Central Administration site, you can back up a whole site collection (as a .bak file) and export a site or a list (as a .cmp file). Using the Central Administration Backup and Restore page, you cannot restore sites collections, sites, and lists. A restoration requires the use of Windows PowerShell.
7. **Work with Team Site, Document Workspace, and Group Work Site templates.** Team sites, document workspaces, and group work sites look similar, have similar functions, and are designed to allow groups of people to productively work together. The Team Site template is designed to provide the core set of capabilities needed in a site that will be used to support team collaboration and information sharing. The Blank Site template has no lists or libraries and should be used when you do not need most of the items in the Team Site template. The Document Workspace template enables people to work together on the creation of documents. The Group Work Site template contains components which enable the management of a team. The Social Meeting Workspace template provides the tools necessary to facilitate informal social meetings.
8. **Work with Meeting Workspace templates.** The purpose of the Meeting Workspaces is to enable an organization or a company to organize a meeting, facilitate the meeting, and follow up on meetings objectives. The Basic Meeting Workspace template is used to create sites with tools to enable members to plan, conduct, and document meetings. The Blank Meeting Workspace template is used to create an empty meeting workspace that does not include any site pages. The Decision Meeting Workspace template is used to create sites to support and track the decision-making process. The Multipage Meeting Workspace template provides the resources for creating meeting workspaces that will contain more than one page.
9. **Work with Blog Site templates.** Blogs are commonly used as news sites, journals, and diaries. A blog focuses one or more interests of the site owner and is often used to state an opinion. A blog owner creates posts on which others can comment. Posts (or articles) are thoughts published on a blog Web site. RSS feed-aggregating software enables people to subscribe to the content they are interested in and have new and updated posts delivered to them.
10. **Navigate SharePoint sites.** You navigate through SharePoint sites using a Web browser or SharePoint Designer 2010. In SharePoint Designer, the Navigation Pane provides access to all of the components of a SharePoint site organized by groups of related items such as Lists and Libraries, Content Type, and Site Columns. When you click on such a group link, SharePoint Designer automatically creates a tab at the top of the page. The majority of these tabs include a breadcrumb that enables you to navigate the site hierarchy, showing you the position of the current item in the hierarchy. SharePoint sites can be accessed with mobile devices if the server is set up to be compatible with the mobile network and the appropriate mobile application is available on the device.

11. **Work with SharePoint Lists and Libraries templates.** SharePoint Foundation enables you to create new lists and Libraries based on 22 built-in list templates (14 List templates and 8 Library Templates). All of the Web pages needed to create, review, update, delete, and manage a list or a library and its data are automatically and dynamically generated by SharePoint. When you create a new site using a SharePoint template, template specific lists and libraries will be created, by default. If your user account has an appropriate level of permission, you can also create new lists and libraries. The availability of list and library types is controlled by the features activated.
12. **Create a List or a Library.** A List or a Library can be created using SharePoint Foundation, via an Internet browser, or SharePoint Designer. When using an Internet browser, Microsoft Silverlight affects how components are created.
13. **Work with Lists.** Almost all the data that you create or use within SharePoint sites is contained in a list of similar information. You can use templates to create standard list sites or create your own custom list. You can to decide how to display information, who has permission to view or alter the information, what content approval controls are in place, and manage the structure and data using the Lists Tools tab. Various categories on the List Settings page enable you to manage the list. Just as folders help you to organize files in your computer system, SharePoint enables you to create a hierarchy of folders for lists. Lists are initially created without folders, and folders must be enabled on the Advanced Settings page of the list in order to create the folders. Using the same Advanced Settings page, you can enable attachments to the List.
14. **Work with Libraries.** The main difference between a Library and a List is that an item in a Library must contain a file and the accompanying metadata to those files. The SharePoint document management is based on libraries. Libraries use display and management components that are much like lists. Libraries provide the tools necessary to manage documents, including versioning, content approval, and searching. Similar to lists, folders can be created to assist in the organization of information in the libraries.
15. **Upload documents.** Using the Documents tab of SharePoint Foundation, you can upload a single document or multiple documents. You have the option to keep previous versions of the file(s) uploaded.
16. **Edit documents properties.** You can view the properties of the documents included in your site using the Edit menu or by clicking View Properties in the Manage group of the SharePoint Foundation Documents tab.
17. **Check documents in and out.** SharePoint enables you to check out documents that you need to work on for a longer time. Other users will not be able to work on that document and they will not see your changes until you check in the document. You can Check Out, Check In, or Discard Check Out using SharePoint Designer or SharePoint Foundation in a browser.
18. **Delete and recover deleted documents.** Every time you delete a document from a list or a library, you are not losing it forever. Deleted documents are stored in the Recycle Bin of your site. The Recycle Bin enables you to either restore a deleted document to its original location or to remove it from the Recycle Bin.
19. **Exchange documents between sites.** The Send To command is used to distribute documents to other libraries, making it available in other sites or in a centralized location. Using Send To, you copy the original file, called the source file, into a different library. The copy can be edited independently of the source file, but you have the option to send updates from the source to the copies.

KEY TERMS

All Site Content ***p.88***
Basic Meeting Workspace template ***p.111***
Blank Meeting Workspace template ***p.112***
Blank Site template ***p.108***
Blog Site template ***p.115***
Decision Meeting Workspace template ***p.112***
Document Workspace template ***p.109***
Group Work Site template ***p.110***
Multipage Meeting Workspace template ***p.114***
Post ***p.116***
Reghost ***p.96***
RSS ***p.116***
Send To ***p.146***
Site theme ***p.97***
Social Meeting Workspace template ***p.113***
Team Site template ***p.107***
Unghosted ***p.96***
Web application ***p.83***

MULTIPLE CHOICE

1. Which of the following statements about top-level sites is false?
   - (a) The top-level sites do not include the functionality of all child sites.
   - (b) You can access the top-level Site Settings page from the Site Settings of any subsite included in the collection.
   - (c) The top-level sites can be created only using the SharePoint Central Administration site.
   - (d) By default, when a new top-level site is created, the user who created it is the only person who has access to the site.

2. Which of the following options is never included in the SharePoint Foundation Site Actions menu?
   - (a) View All Site Content
   - (b) Edit Page
   - (c) All Files
   - (d) New Site

3. Which of the following statements about subsites is false?
   - (a) You can restore a deleted subsite using the Recycle Bin.
   - (b) You can change the default home page of a subsite.
   - (c) You can manually generate ad hoc copies of sites that can be used, as well, to create models that could be reused elsewhere.
   - (d) By default, whoever can access the top-level site can also access the subsite and with the same rights.

4. Which of the following statements about Blog sites is false?
   - (a) Blogs can be used as a one-way communication tool for keeping project stakeholders and/or team members informed.
   - (b) Blog site content can be syndicated using a RSS (Really Simple Syndication) feed.
   - (c) A Blog site template cannot be used to create a top-level site.
   - (d) A Blog site can have subsites.

5. You cannot customize SharePoint Foundation pages using:
   - (a) Themes.
   - (b) CSS.
   - (c) A combination of a theme and one or more CSS files.
   - (d) Layout pages.

6. Which of the following statements about navigating SharePoint sites is false?
   - (a) You can navigate among sites in a Web browser using the Navigation bar.
   - (b) The SharePoint navigation inheritance options cannot be used to determine which options are available on the navigation bar.
   - (c) The link for the Mobile Site URL of a SharePoint site is listed in the Site Information section of the Site Settings page.
   - (d) Additional pages available in a meeting workspace are referenced in the Quick Launch.

7. SharePoint Foundation does not allow you to:
   - (a) Create new lists based on its built-in templates.
   - (b) Change the settings of an existing list.
   - (c) Store forms.
   - (d) Create multiple views of a list.

8. Which of the following statements about SharePoint sites is false?
   - (a) A site built on a SharePoint template includes by default some specific libraries.
   - (b) You are never allowed to create folders within a library.
   - (c) You can create a custom library.
   - (d) An item in a library always includes a file.

9. When working with SharePoint Foundation sites you cannot:
   - (a) Edit a document checked out by another user.
   - (b) Maintain different versions of a document included in a library.
   - (c) Upload multiple files.
   - (d) Export documents to another library within another site.

10. Which of the following statements about SharePoint sites is false?
    - (a) You can restore a deleted site.
    - (b) You can restore a deleted document.
    - (c) You can restore a deleted List.
    - (d) You can back up a Library.

PRACTICE EXERCISES

1 Start Developing a SharePoint Site for an Introduction to Management Information Systems Business Course

You have been hired as a graduate teaching assistant in the Introduction to Management Information Systems course and, as part of your new assignment, you will develop a SharePoint site for the course. Your faculty supervisor gave you administrator access to a SharePoint Foundation top-level site and provided you with a description of the required functionalities of the site. This exercise follows the same set of skills as used in Hands-On Exercise 1 in the chapter. Refer to Figure 2.80 as you complete this exercise.

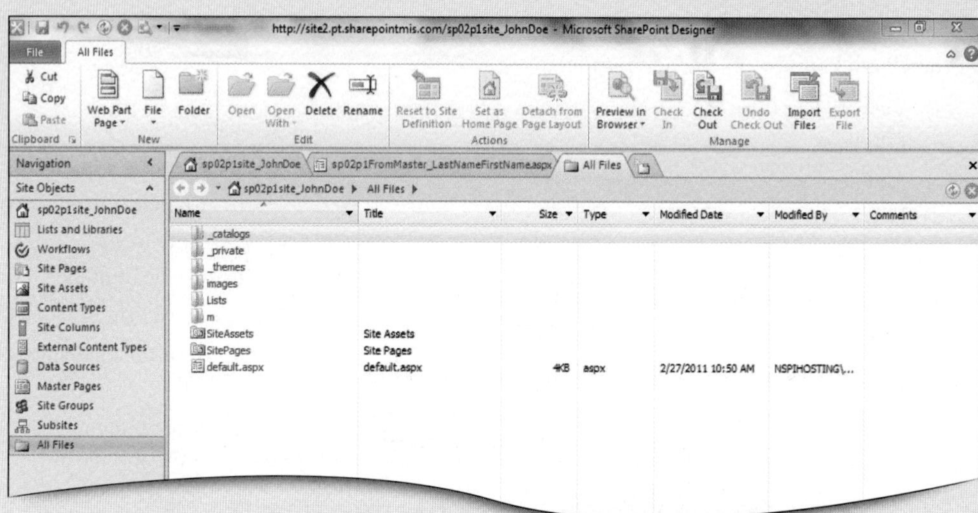

FIGURE 2.80 Develop a Course Site ➤

a. Click **Start**, click **All Programs**, and then select **Internet Explorer** to start Internet Explorer.
b. Click **File** on the Menu bar, and then click **Open**. Type the URL of the top-level site in the **Open box.**
c. Click **All Site Content** on the Quick Launch. Click **Create link**, and then create a new *sp02p1site_LastNameFirstName* site using the Blank Site template.
d. Click **Site Actions**, and then click **More Options**.
e. Create a new *sp02p1WikiPage_LastNameFirstName* Wiki page library. Click **Save&Close**.
f. Click **Make Home Page** in the Page Actions group of the Page tab. Click **OK**.
g. Click **Edit in SharePoint Designer** in the Site Actions menu.
h. Click **Site Pages** on the Navigation Pane. You should now see the *sp02hp1WikiPage_LastNameFirstName* added to the left of its name the home page icon.
i. Click **sp02p1psite_LastNameFirstName** on the Navigation Pane.
j. Click **Change site theme** under the *Customization* section of the Site Settings page.
k. Click **Classic**, and then click **Apply**.
l. Click **SharePoint Designer** on the Windows task bar.
m. Click the **File tab** on the SharePoint Designer Ribbon. Click **Add Item** to display the Add Item page if it is not already displayed.
n. Click **New Page from Master** in the *Pages* section of the Add Item page.
o. Click **v4.master (Default)**, and then click **Create**.
p. Type **sp02p1FromMaster_LastNameFirstName** in the **Enter a name for this new Web Part Page: box**, and then click **OK**. Click **Yes** on the Microsoft SharePoint Designer alert box.
q. Click **All Files** on the Navigation Pane. The All Files report page should look similar to Figure 2.80.
r. Click **Internet Explorer** on the Windows task bar, and then click the **sp02p1site_LastNameFirstName Site Setting window.**

s. Create a *sp02p1delete_LastNameFirstName* Blog site as a subsite of the *sp02p1site_LastNameFirstName* page using the instructions from steps c–e.

t. Click **SharePoint Designer** on the Windows task bar, and then click **Refresh** on the Quick Access Toolbar. The All Files report page should now include the *sp02p1delete_LastNameFirstName* site.

u. Click **Internet Explorer** on the Windows task bar.

v. Click **Site Settings** on the Site Actions menu, click **Delete this Site**, and then click **Delete** on the Delete this Site page. Click **OK** on the *Message from webpage* alert box. Click **Go back to site** on the Delete Web page.

w. Click **SharePoint Designer** on the Windows task bar, and then click **Refresh** on the Quick Access Toolbar. The All Files report page should now not include the *sp02p1delete_LastNameFirstName* site.

x. Close all the Internet Explorer and SharePoint Designer windows, and then close both applications.

2 Start Developing a SharePoint Site for a University Research Lab

You have been hired as a graduate research assistant in the Educational and Assistive Technology Research lab and, as part of your new assignment, you will help to develop a SharePoint site for the lab. Your faculty supervisor gave you administrator access to a SharePoint Foundation top-level site, a description of the needed functionalities of the site, and a notebook. You will use SharePoint Designer 2010 in developing the site. This exercise follows the same set of skills as used in Hands-On Exercises 1–3 in the chapter. Refer to Figure 2.81 as you complete this exercise.

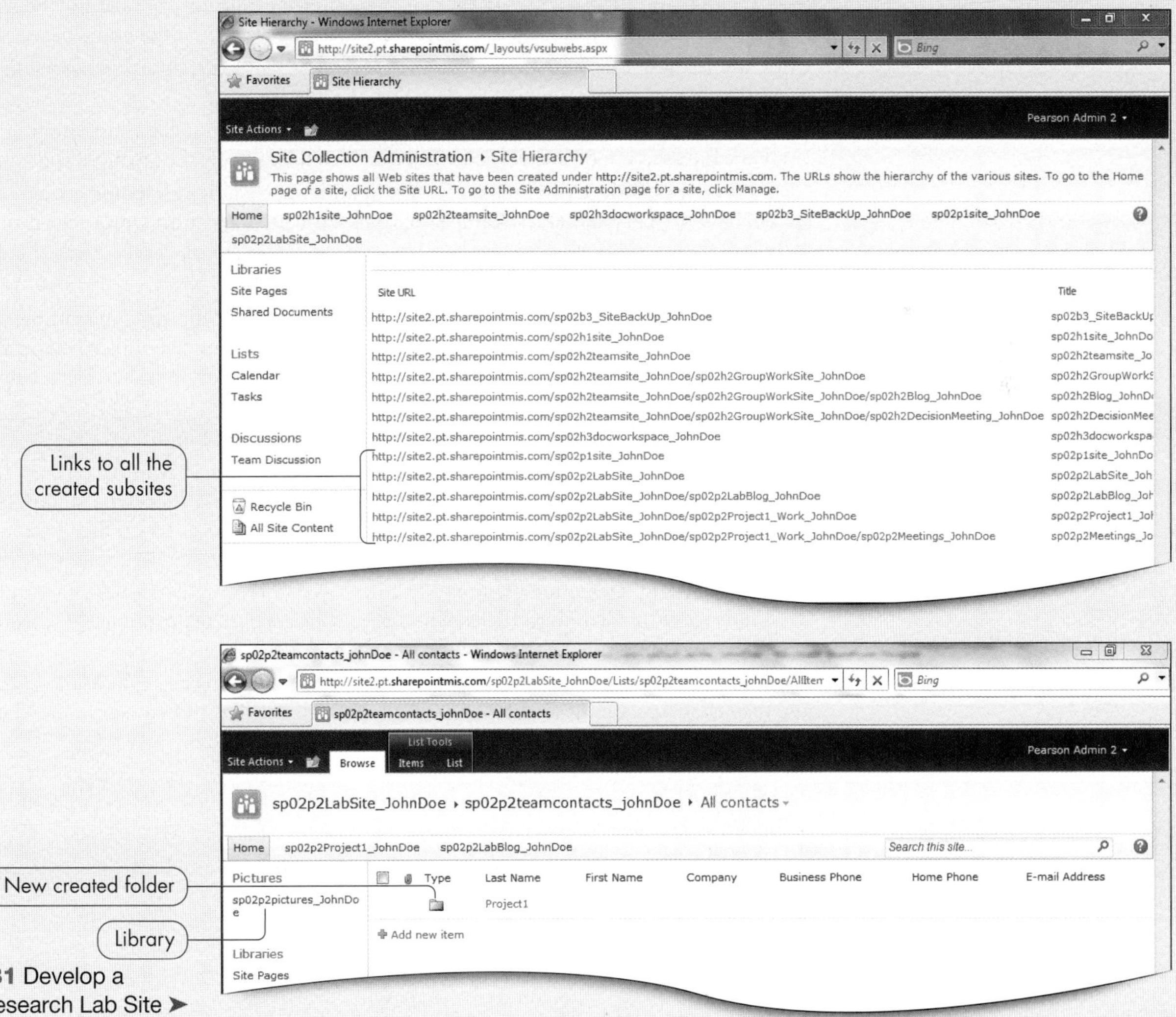

FIGURE 2.81 Develop a University Research Lab Site ➤

a. Click **Start**, click **All Programs**, and then select **Internet Explorer** to start Internet Explorer. Click **File** on the Menu bar, and then click **Open**. Type the URL of the top-level site in the **Open box**.
b. Click **All Site Content** on the Quick Launch. Click **Create**, and then create a new *sp02p2LabSite_LastNameFirstName* site using the Team Site template.
c. Click **All Site Content** on the Quick Launch. Click **Create**, and then create a new site named *sp02p2Project1_LastNameFirstName* using the Group Work Site template.
d. Click **All Site Content** on the Quick Launch. Click **Create**, and then create a new site workspace called *sp02p2Meetings_LastNameFirstName* using the Multipage Meeting Workspace template.
e. Click the **Navigate Up button**, and then select **sp02p2LabSite_LastNameFirstName**. Click **All Site Content** on the Quick Launch. Click **Create**, and then create a new site named *sp02p2LabBlog_LastNameFirstName* using the Blog template.
f. Click the **Navigate Up button**, and then click the **Team Site top-level site**. Click **Site Settings** in the Site Actions menu. Click **Site hierarchy** in the Site Collection Administration of the Site Settings page. The Site Hierarchy page should look similar to Figure 2.81.
g. Locate the links to the four sites created in steps b–e. Carefully review all the built-in components of the four sites created in steps b–e in the order they are listed on the Site Hierarchy page.
h. Click the link to **sp02p2Meetings_LastNameFirstName** in the site hierarchy page. Click the **Page tab**, and then click **Edit Page** in the Edit group of the Page tab for the *sp02p2Meetings_LastNameFirstName* home page. Carefully review the layout of the home page.
i. Click the **Navigate Up button**, and then select **sp02p2Project1_LastNameFirstName**. Click the **Page tab**, and then click **Edit Page** in the Manage group of Page tab for the *sp02p2Project1_LastNameFirstName* home page. Carefully review the layout of the home page.
j. Click the **Navigate Up button**, and then select the **sp02p2LabSite_LastNameFirstName site**. Click the **Page tab**, and then click **Edit Page** in the Manage group of Page tab for the *sp02p2LabSite_LastNameFirstName* site home page. Carefully review the layout of the home page.
k. Click the **Browse tab**, and then click the *sp02p2LabBlog_LastNameFirstName* link on the top Navigation bar of the *sp02p2LabSite_LastNameFirstName* site.
l. Click **Edit in SharePoint Designer** on the Site Actions menu. Click **Edit site home page** in the *Customization* section of the Site Settings page. Carefully review the layout of the home page.
m. Click **Preview in Browser** in the Preview group. Click the **Navigate Up button**, and then select the **sp02p2LabSite_LastNameFirstName site**. Click **Edit in SharePoint Designer** on the Site Actions menu.
n. Click **Lists and Libraries** on the Navigation Pane.
o. Click **Document Library** in the New group of the Lists and Libraries tab, and then click **Picture Library**. Type **sp02p2pictures_LastNameFirstName** in the **Name box**, and then click **OK**. The link to the new *sp02p2pictures_LastNameFirstName* library is displayed in the *Documents Libraries* sections of the Lists and Libraries page.
p. Click **Preview in Browser** in the Manage group of the List and Libraries tab.
q. Click **Lists** on the Quick Launch, and then click **Create** to open the Create dialog box. Click **List** in the *Filter By* section of the Create dialog box. Click **Contacts**, and then type **sp02p2teamcontacts_LastNameFirstName** in the **Name box**. Click **Create**. The link to the *sp02p2teamcontacts_LastNameFirstName* is displayed on the Quick Launch.
r. Click **SharePoint Designer** on the Windows task bar, and then select the **sp02p2LabSite_LastNameFirstName window**. Refresh the screen. Click **sp02p2teamcontacts_LastNameFirstName** in the *Lists* section of the Lists and Libraries setting page.
s. Check the **Display New Folder checkbox** in the *Advanced Settings* section of the List Settings page, and then click **Save** on the Quick Access Toolbar. Click **Preview in Browser** in the Manage group of the List Settings Ribbon. Click the **Items tab** on the List Tools tab.
t. Click **New Folder** in the New group of the List Tools–Items tab. Type **Project1** in the **Name box** of the New Folder dialog box, and then click **Save**. The link to the new Project1 folder is now displayed on the All Items page. Your screen should look similar to Figure 2.81b.
u. Close all SharePoint Designer and Internet Explorer windows, and then close both applications.

1 Hope Hospital Business Office Management SharePoint Site

You work for the Hope hospital, and after carefully analyzing all the SharePoint capabilities at your supervisor's request, you decided to develop a pilot SharePoint site for the hospital business office. You will create a new team site and create a new subsite using the Blank Site template. You will add a new Wiki page to the subsite and make it the subsite home page. You will change the theme of the parent team site. Then you will create a new Document Library, a new folder, and then upload an Excel Document in the new folder. You will edit the uploaded Excel document. This exercise follows the set of skills as used in Hands-On Exercises 1–3 in the chapter. Refer to Figure 2.82 as you complete this exercise.

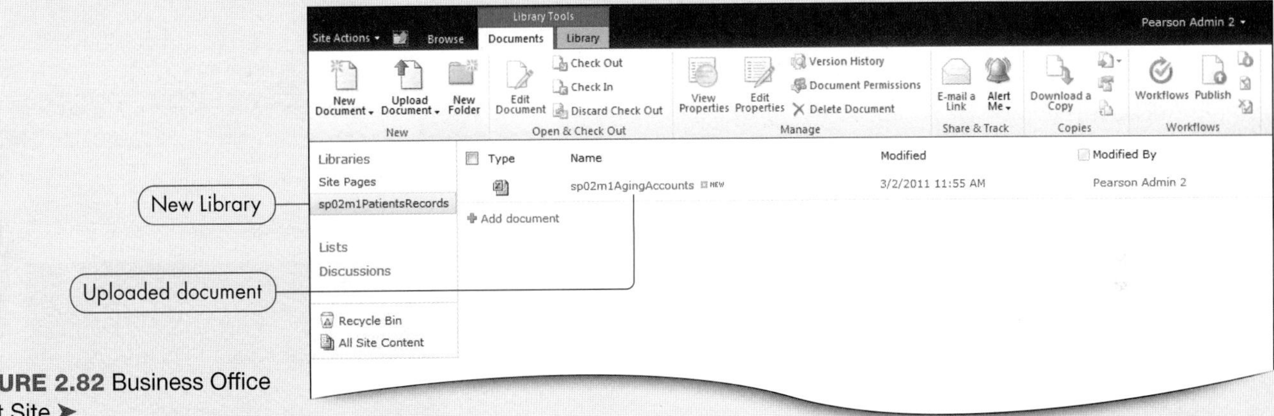

FIGURE 2.82 Business Office Pilot Site ➤

a. Start Internet Explorer.

b. Open the top-level-site.

c. Create a *sp02m1Hope_LastNameFirstName* subsite of the top-level site using the Team Site template.

d. Create a *sp02m1AccAccountsReceivableAging_LastNameFirstName* subsite of the *sp02m1Hope_LastNameFirstName* site using the Blank Site template. Display the *sp02m1AccAccountsReceivableAging_LastNameFirstName* subsite on the Quick Launch of the *sp02m1Hope_LastNameFirstName* subsite.

e. Add a new *sp02m1home page_LastNameFirstName* Wiki page to the *sp02m1AccAccountsReceivable Aging_LastNameFirstName* subsite.

f. Make the new *sp02m1home page_LastNameFirstName* Wiki page the home page of the *sp02m1AccAccountsReceivableAging_LastNameFirstName* subsite.

g. Navigate to the *sp02m1Hope_LastNameFirstName* site. Open the *sp02m1Hope_LastNameFirstName* site in SharePoint Designer.

h. Change the theme of the *sp02m1Hope_LastNameFirstName* site to **Municipal**.

i. Navigate to the *sp02m1AccAccountsReceivableAging_LastNameFirstName* subsite.

j. Open the *sp02m1home page_LastNameFirstName* Wiki page.

k. Create a new *sp02m1PatientsRecords_LastNameFirstName* Document Library in SharePoint Designer.

l. Click the **Preview in Browser button**. Create a new ActiveAccounts folder in the *sp02m1Patients Records_LastNameFirstName* Document Library.

m. Upload the *sp02m1AgingAccounts* Excel file in the *ActiveAccounts folder*. Your screen should now look similar to the one in Figure 2.82.

n. Select the *sp02m1AgingAccounts* Excel file, and then click **Edit Document** in the Open and Check Out group. Type your name in the Patient column of the file, and then save the file.

o. Close the Excel window. Close all SharePoint Designer and Internet Explorer windows, and then close all three applications.

2 DestinQuest Co.

You work for DestinQuest, a vacation rental hospitality and resort real estate company, and after carefully reviewing SharePoint 2010 capabilities at your supervisor request, you decided to implement, as a start, the site available only to the company employees on the SharePoint Foundation platform. You need to create a parent site using the Team Site template, and three subsites using the Decision Meeting Workspace, Social Meeting Workspace, and Group Work Site template. The subsite created based on the Decision Meeting Workspace will be dedicated to the company executive board meetings and members should not inherit from the parent site the access permissions. You will upload a document into the Share Documents library of a subsite, and then send a copy to the Shared Documents of the parent site. You will unghost the home page of a subsite and reghost all pages of that subsite. This exercise follows the set of skills as used in Hands-On Exercises 1–3 in the chapter. Refer to Figure 2.83 as you complete this exercise.

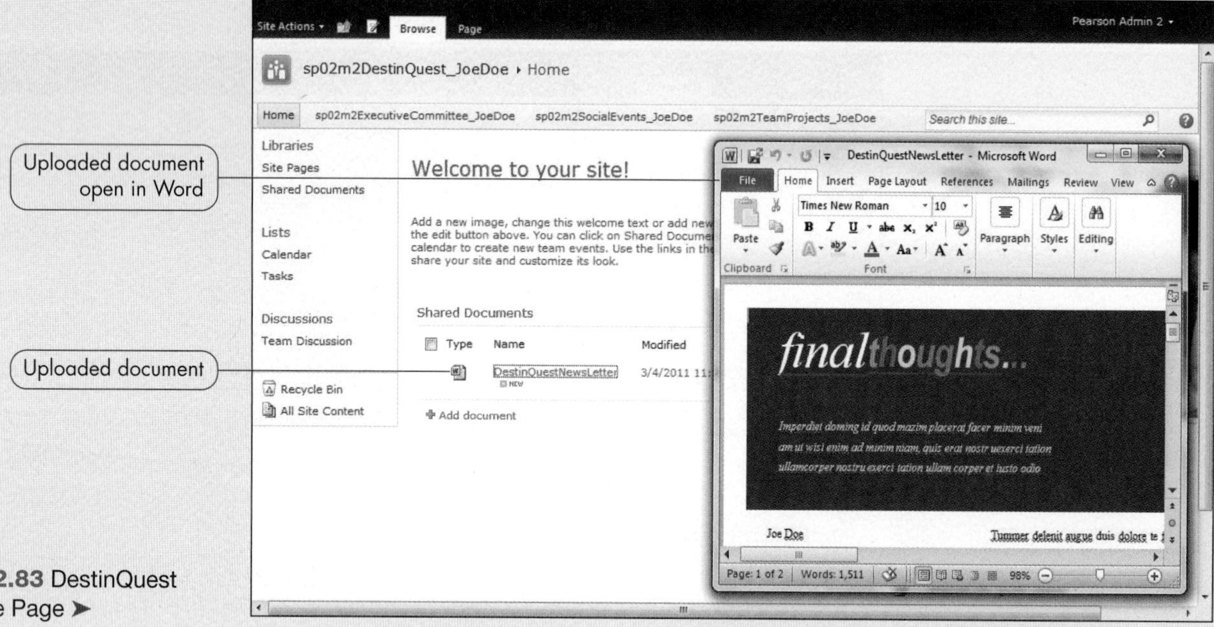

FIGURE 2.83 DestinQuest Site Home Page ➤

a. Start Internet Explorer.

b. Open the top-level site.

c. Create a *sp02m2DestinQuest_LastNameFirstName* subsite of the top-level site using the Team Site template.

DISCOVERY 

d. Create a *sp02m2BoardMeetings_LastNameFirstName* subsite of the *sp02m2DestinQuest_LastNameFirstName* site using the Decision Meeting Workspace template. Click **More options**, and then select **Use unique permissions** in the *Permissions* section. Click **Create**, and then, in all sections of the Set Up Groups for this Site page, select the **Use an existing group**, and then select the **Team Site Owners group**.

e. Navigate to the *sp02m2DestinQuest_LastNameFirstName* parent site. Create a *sp02m2SocialEvents_LastNameFirstName* subsite using the Social Meeting Workspace template.

f. Navigate to the *sp02m2DestinQuest_LastNameFirstName* parent site. Create a *sp02m2TeamProjects_LastNameFirstName* subsite using the Group Work Site template.

g. Upload the *DestinQuestNewsLetter.docx* document from the Exploring folder into the Shared Documents library.

h. Send a copy of the *DestinQuestNewsLetter.docx* document to the Shared Documents library of the *sp02m2DestinQuest_LastNameFirstName* parent site. Check the **Create an alert for me on the source document** in the Copy dialog box.

i. Navigate to the *sp02m2DestinQuest_LastNameFirstName* parent site. Click the link to the DestinQuestNewsLetter.docx. Click Edit in the browser. Type your name in the most top-left box on the first page, and then save the document.

j. Navigate to the *sp02m2TeamProjects_LastNameFirstName* subsite. Click the link to the *DestinQuestNewsLetter.docx* document. Delete the most top-left box on the first page, and then save the document.

k. Navigate to the *sp02m2DestinQuest_LastNameFirstName* parent site. Click the link to the *DestinQuestNewsLetter.docx* document. The document should be unchanged. Your screen should now look similar to the one in Figure 2.83.

l. Navigate to the *sp02m2BoardMeetings_LastNameFirstName* subsite. Open the subsite in SharePoint Designer. Open the site home page in Advanced Mode Editor. Type **This site has restricted access only for the DestinQuestCo. Board members** within the purple border of the PlaceHolderPageDesciption at the top of the page. The home page of the *sp02m2BoardMeetings_LastNameFirstName* subsite is now unghosted. Save the unghosted page.

m. Activate the Internet Explorer browser, and then reghost all pages of the *sp02m2BoardMeetings_LastNameFirstName* subsite.

n. Close all SharePoint Designer, Internet Explorer, and Word windows, and then close all of the applications.

CAPSTONE EXERCISE

You work for a major financial management and advisory company. At your supervisor's request, you start developing a pilot site for all categories of company clients from individual investors to institutions and corporate clients. You will create sites and a List using SharePoint Foundation templates, create new folders in a Shared Documents library, and send copies of it to Shared Documents libraries in other sites. You will add a new ASPX page, attach a master page, customize it, and make it the site home page.

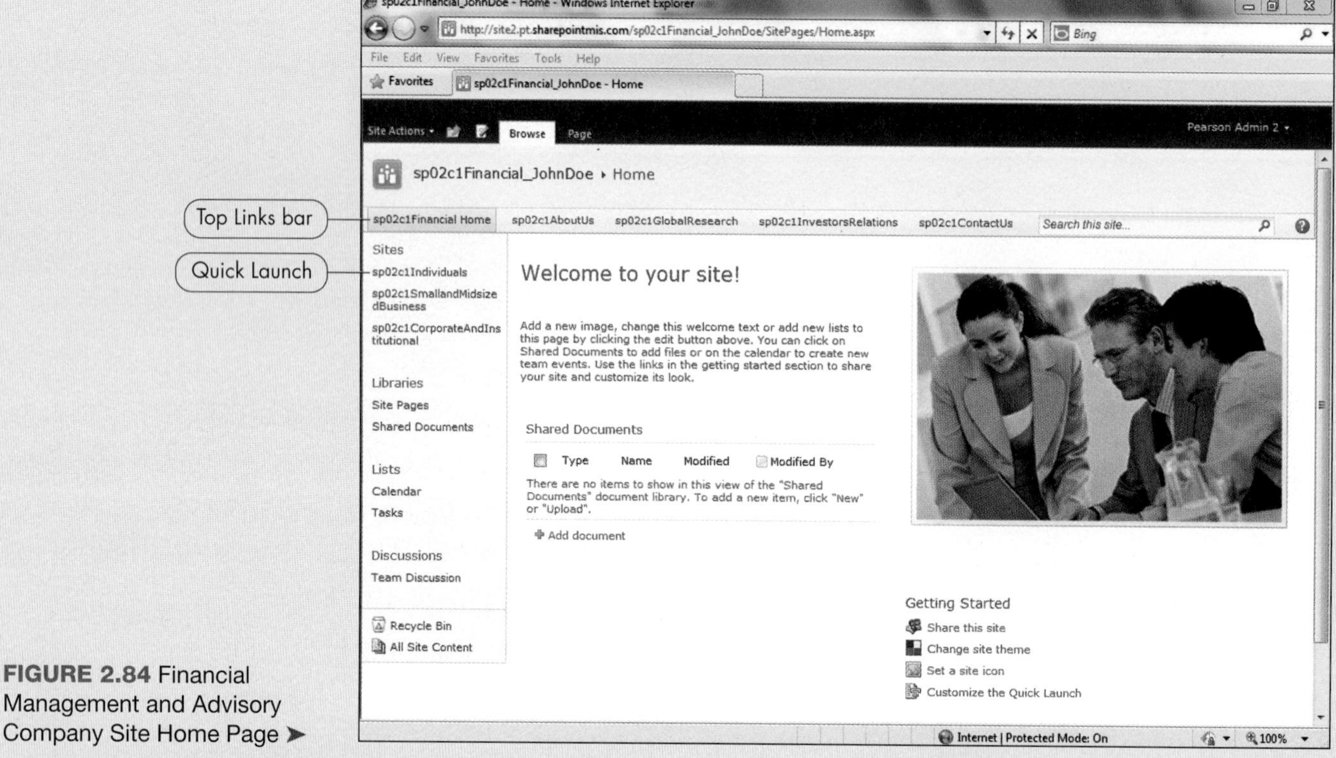

FIGURE 2.84 Financial Management and Advisory Company Site Home Page ➤

Create a Parent Site and Subsites Using SharePoint Foundations and Navigate Using Internet Explorer Browser and SharePoint Designer

You are to create a parent site for your company. You create multiple subsites of your top-level site using the SharePoint Foundations template. You navigate all these sites using the Internet Explorer browser and SharePoint Designer.

a. Launch Internet Explorer, and then navigate to the top-level site of your site collection.

b. Create a *sp02c1Financial_LastNameFirstName* subsite of your top-level site using the Team Site template.

c. Create a *sp02c1Individuals* subsite of the *sp02c1Financial_LastNameFirstName* site using the Team Site template.

d. Navigate to the *sp02c1Financial_LastNameFirstName* site, and then create a *sp02c1SmallAndMidsizedBusiness* subsite of *sp02c1Financial_LastNameFirstName* site using the Team Site template.

e. Navigate to the *sp02c1Financial_LastNameFirstName* site, and then create a *sp02c1CorporateAndInsititutional* subsite of *sp02c1Financial_LastNameFirstName* site using the Team Site template.

f. Navigate to the *sp02c1Financial_LastNameFirstName* site, and then create an *sp02c1AboutUs* subsite of the *sp02c1Financial_LastNameFirstName* site using the Blank Site template.

g. Navigate to the *sp02c1Financial_LastNameFirstName* site, and then create an *sp02c1GlobalReserach* subsite of the *sp02c1Financial_LastNameFirstName* site using the Document Workspace template.

h. Navigate to the *sp02c1Financial_LastNameFirstName* site, and then create an *sp02c1InvestorsRelations* subsite of *sp02c1Financial_LastNameFirstName* site using the Blog template.

i. Navigate to the *sp02c1Financial_LastNameFirstName* site, and then create an *sp02c1ContactUs* subsite of the *sp02c1Financial_LastNameFirstName* site using the Blank Site template.

j. Navigate to the *sp02c1Financial_LastNameFirstName* site, and then change the text of the Home link on the Top link bar to **sp02c1Financial Home**.

k. Open the *sp02c1Financial_LastNameFirstName* site in SharePoint Designer. Navigate to all subsites of the *sp02c1Financial_LastNameFirstName* site using their links displayed in the *Subsites* sections of the *sp02c1Financial_LastNameFirstName* site Site Settings page. The last subsite that you will open should be *sp02c1ContactUs.*

Create a List and Three List Folders, Upload a Document, and Send It to Another Library

You are to create a new list using the SharePoint Foundation Contacts List template, create three new folders, upload the document in one of the folders, and then send copies to the other two folders.

a. Create a new Contact Us list using the SharePoint Foundation Contacts List template.

b. Check the **Display New Folder** command, and then save the file.

c. Create three new folders of the Contact Us list (**Individuals**, **Business**, and **Institutions and Corporations**).

d. Navigate to the Shared Documents Library of the *sp02c1Individuals* subsite, and then upload the *sp02c2StockPresentation* file from the Exploring SharePoint 2010 folder.

e. Send copies of the *sp02c2StockPresentation* file to the Shared Documents Library of the *sp02c1SmallAndMidsizedBusiness* subsite and *sp02c1CorporateAndInstitutional* subsite.

f. View all the copies made of the *sp02c2StockPresentation* file.

Add a New Page, Attach a Master, Customize It, and Make It the Site Home Page

You are to create a new ASPX page, attach to it the v4.master master page, customize the page, and then set it as the site home page.

a. Open the *sp02c1AboutUs* subsite in SharePoint Designer.

b. Create a new AboutUs ASPX page.

c. Attach v4.master to the AboutUs.ASPX page, and then save the page.

d. Click the > **button** on the right edge of the PlaceHolderPageDesciption PlaceHolder; at the top of the page, select **Create Custom Content**, and then type **We are one of the USA's largest financial institutions, serving individual consumers, small and middle market businesses and large corporations with a full range of banking, investing, asset management and other financial and risk-management products and services.** Save the page.

e. Click **Site Pages**, and then make the AboutUs.ASPX page the home page of the *sp02c1AboutUs* subsite.

f. Navigate to the *sp1c1Financial_LastNameFirstName* page. Your screen should look similar to Figure 2.84.

g. Close all Internet Explorer browser windows, and then exit Internet Explorer. Close all SharePoint Designer windows, and then exit SharePoint Designer.

Communication Skills Class

GENERAL CASE 

You are taking a communication skills class and must develop an end-of-semester demonstration speech that will demonstrate your stronger communication and collaboration skills and potential to work confidently with others. A demonstration speech is one in which you teach or direct the class on how to do something. Because SharePoint 2010 is a relatively new technology, you decide to demonstrate some of its features. You will use PowerPoint to develop your presentation. After completing your notes, save the document as **sp02b1speech_LastnameFirstname** in a location as directed by your instructor. In a 1, 2, 3 fashion (listing your points in numerical order), provide directions to the class on:

- Creating a SharePoint site.
- Working with SharePoint sites.
- Working with Lists and Libraries.
- Managing of SharePoint sites documents.

The Microsoft Office Case Studies

RESEARCH CASE 

SharePoint is used by a large international community of companies for developing their portals. One of the most professional and helpful sites where you can find examples of how SharePoint 2010 is used by different companies is created by Microsoft. Use Microsoft Internet Explorer to open the Microsoft Case Studies home page (www.microsoft.com/casestudies/default.aspx). Type **SharePoint Designer 2010** in the **Search box**. Select two case studies, and then create a report, using Word 2010, on your findings about how SharePoint 2010 helped the organizations included in the case studies. After completing your report, save the document as **sp02b2casestudies_LastnameFirstname.docx** in a location as directed by your instructor.

SharePoint Sites Recycle Bin

DISASTER RECOVERY 

The *sp02b3_SiteBackUp* solution file in the Exploring SharePoint folder was the last site backup completed by your predecessor. The backed-up site initially included three stock analyses reports AFLAC.TIFF, ATT.TIFF, and MMM.TIFF Your predecessor deleted the AFLAC.TIFF file from the Shared Documents library before creating the backup. Upload and activate the *sp02b3_SiteBackUp* solution file, and then create a *sp02b3_SiteBackUp_LastNameFirstName* subsite using this solution file. Explore the content of the new site, check if AFLAC.TIFF is in the Recycle Bin, and then write a memo to your instructor describing the nature of the error. Include suggestions in the memo on how to avoid mistakes of this nature in the future.

SHAREPOINT

3 WEB PAGES

Working with SharePoint Web Pages

CASE STUDY | The Center for Woman in Science, Technology, Engineering, and Math (STEM)

Women constitute 46.5% of the workforce in the United States, but hold just 25% of mathematical and computer science jobs and 11% of engineering jobs. (National Science Foundation, 2007; U.S. Department of Labor, 2008). Women account for 53% of all biological scientists, 31% of all physicians and surgeons, 33% of all chemists and material scientists, and 29% of all environmental scientists and geoscientists (U.S. Department of Labor, 2009). Many women across the state of Alabama and nationwide are not aware of the opportunities available to them in the STEM fields. The Alabama Center of Women in STEM goals are to:

- Maximize access to shared resources with public- and private-sector organizations and institutions that are interested in expanding women's participation in STEM.
- Strengthen the capacity of existing and evolving projects by sharing promising practice research and program models, outcomes, and products.
- Use the leverage of a network or collaboration of individual women serving STEM programs to promote gender equity in STEM.

You have been hired by the Center to develop a SharePoint site that will provide user-friendly support for the Center's mission and goals. The new site should provide a professional virtual environment where women in STEM can communicate, access STEM resources, participate in virtual seminars, register for live events, apply for grants, and learn about new STEM academic and business job opportunities.

OBJECTIVES

AFTER YOU READ THIS CHAPTER, YOU WILL BE ABLE TO:

Work with SharePoint Page Contents

Now that you know how to add a new page to a Web site, you can start working with SharePoint Web page content. Each Web page has its own individual design and functionality. However, they all use a combination of generic Web page elements, such as text, images, hyperlinks, lists, tables, and forms, to name a few. SharePoint pages also have some specific elements such as SharePoint Controls. The SharePoint Foundation browser interface and SharePoint Designer empower you with a complex set of user-friendly tools for inserting any of these elements into a page and modifying their characteristics so that they display and function the way you want.

In this section, you will learn about editing SharePoint pages. You will check the spelling of the text included in your pages using SharePoint Designer. You will organize page content using hyperlinks and lists. You will also learn when and how you should use tables in developing SharePoint pages.

Editing SharePoint Page Content

The SharePoint Foundation browser interface, as the main SharePoint Web content editing tool, provides a comprehensive set of user-friendly page editing functionalities. If you have permissions to edit the page and the page is not checked out by another user, you can edit the contents of the page using the browser interface. You edit a page by clicking the Page tab, and then clicking Edit Page in the Edit group. You can also click Site Actions, and then select Edit Page from the menu. Depending on the type of page you are editing, each page displayed in editing mode will look different, as shown in Figure 3.1. On the Wiki page type, you can only type in the page body control, whereas in a Web Part page you can add new Web Parts using Web Part zones and edit the existing Web Parts.

The method used for saving the changes depends on the configuration of the library in which the page is included; you will click Stop Editing on the Page tab or click Save & Close on the Page tab, and then click Check In, as shown in Figure 3.1.

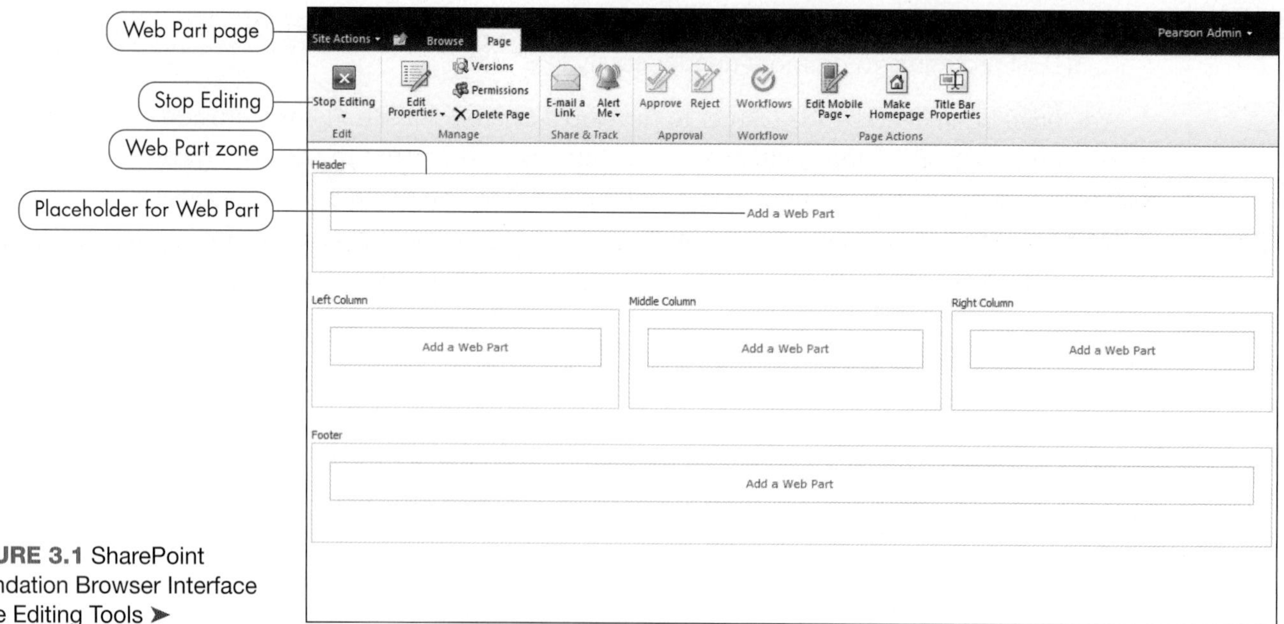

FIGURE 3.1 SharePoint Foundation Browser Interface Page Editing Tools ➤

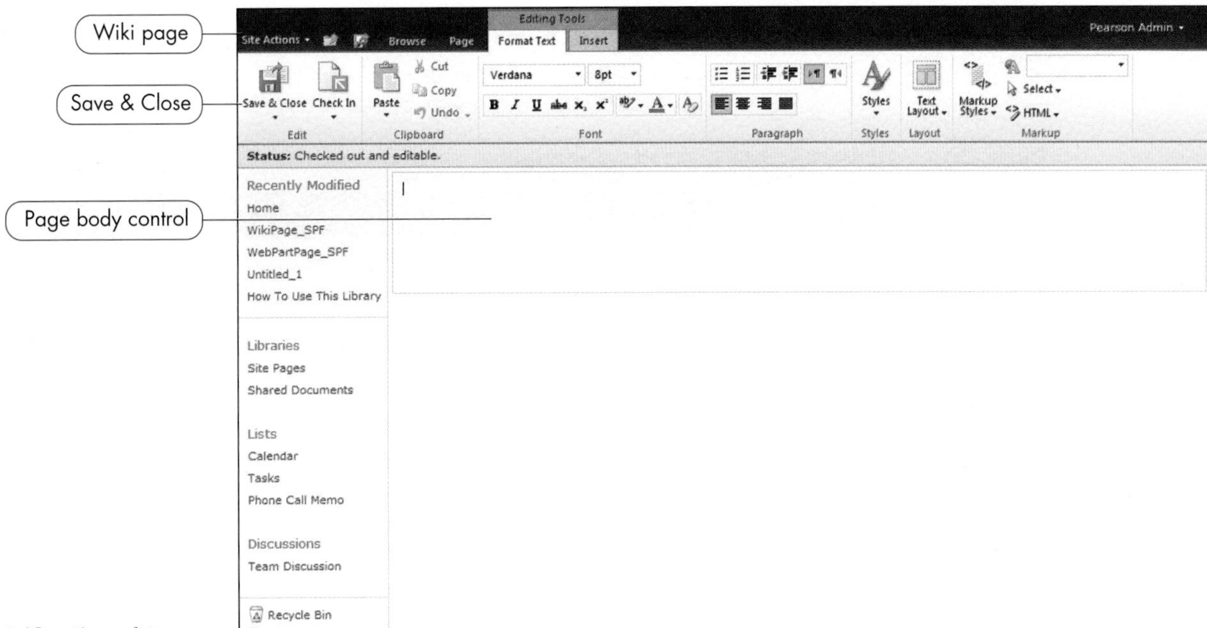

FIGURE 3.1 *(Continued)* ➤

> **TIP** Editing the Content of Wiki Pages and Web Part Pages
>
> When using a browser to edit a Wiki page, you can modify only the content included in the EmbeddedFormField SharePoint control, which is contained by the PlaceHoldermain(Custom) region. When using a browser to edit a Web Part page, you can modify only the content included in Web Part zones and you cannot add or remove Web Parts. In contrast to editing in a browser, SharePoint Designer enables you to edit any content on all SharePoint pages.

The SharePoint Designer editing workspace includes the Ribbon, editing window (or document window), status bar, and task panes. The editing window offers three views: Design, Code, and Split. You select the view on the View tab or Page Mode toolbar. The SharePoint Designer Page Editor includes the editing window, tab bar, Page Mode toolbar, Quick Tag Selector, and status bar, as shown in Figure 3.2a. Using the tab bar you can display any file or summary view that is currently open by clicking on the tab. The Page Mode toolbar enables you to switch between the three editing modes. As you click on HTML tags displayed in the Quick Tag Selector, the corresponding element is selected within the page. If you then click the arrow next to the tag and click the Tag Properties command, you can change the properties of the element, as shown in Figure 3.2b. The status bar displays information about the open files, and enables you to customize the SharePoint Designer interface and functions. Table 3.1 includes a concise description of the information and tools provided on the five sections of the status bar.

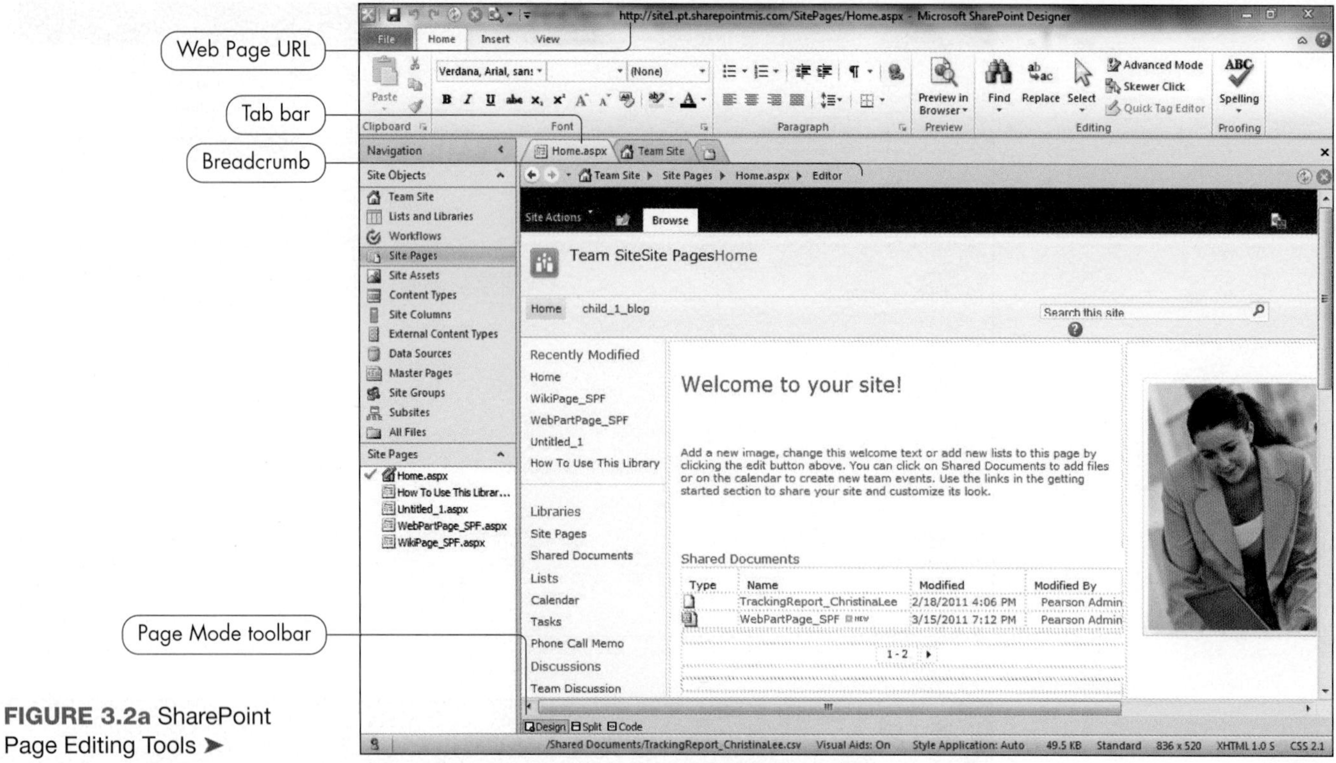

FIGURE 3.2a SharePoint Page Editing Tools ➤

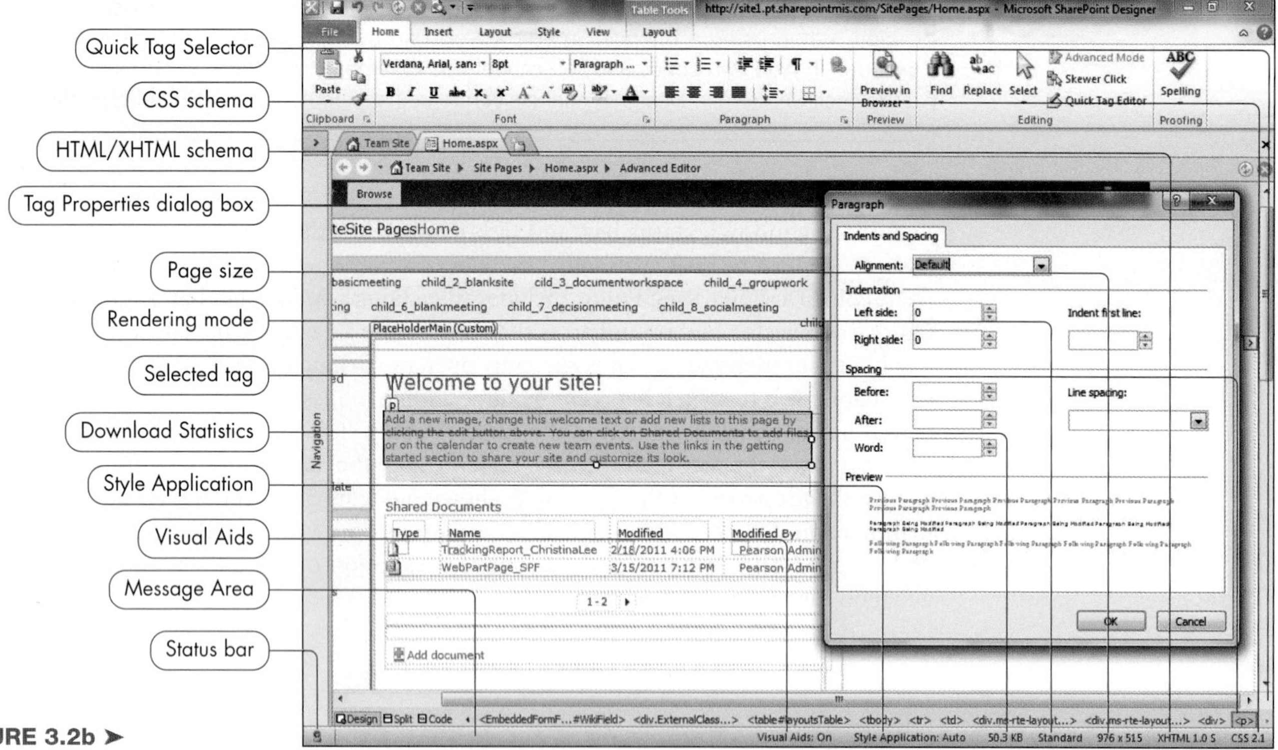

FIGURE 3.2b ➤

TIP Navigating Using the Tab Bar and the Breadcrumb

You can easily switch between the tabs included in the tab bar by pressing Ctrl+Tab or Ctrl+Shift+Tab. The SharePoint Designer breadcrumb, as shown in Figure 3.2a, enables you to easily navigate backward and forward, and know where you are at all times.

TABLE 3.1 SharePoint Designer Status Bar	
SharePoint Designer Status Bar Areas	**Options**
Message Area	Located on the left side of the status bar, the message area displays information about hyperlinks, file names, locations, and more.
Visual Aids	When Visual Aids indicators are OFF, the Web page layout in Design view looks almost identical to the Web page layout in the browser. When the Visual Aids indicators are ON, empty elements and properties are displayed.
Style Application	Enables you to view and customize the SharePoint Designer Cascading Style Sheet (CSS) settings using the CSS tab of the Page Editor Options dialog box. Click the indicator, and then click CSS Options to display the Page Editor Options dialog box, as shown in Figure 3.3a.
Download Statistics	Displays the size of the HTML page, the size of the data linked to the HTML page, the size of the total download, and the number of files linked to the HTML page, as shown in Figure 3.3b.
HTML/XHTML schema	Enables you to view the Default Document Type and choose a Doctype and a Secondary Schema for the authoring document using the Authoring tab of the Page Editor Options dialog box. Click indicator to display the Authoring tab of the Page Editor Options dialog box, as shown in Figure 3.3c.
CSS schema	Enables you to see and set the CSS schema available in CSS IntelliSense, as shown in Figure 3.3c.

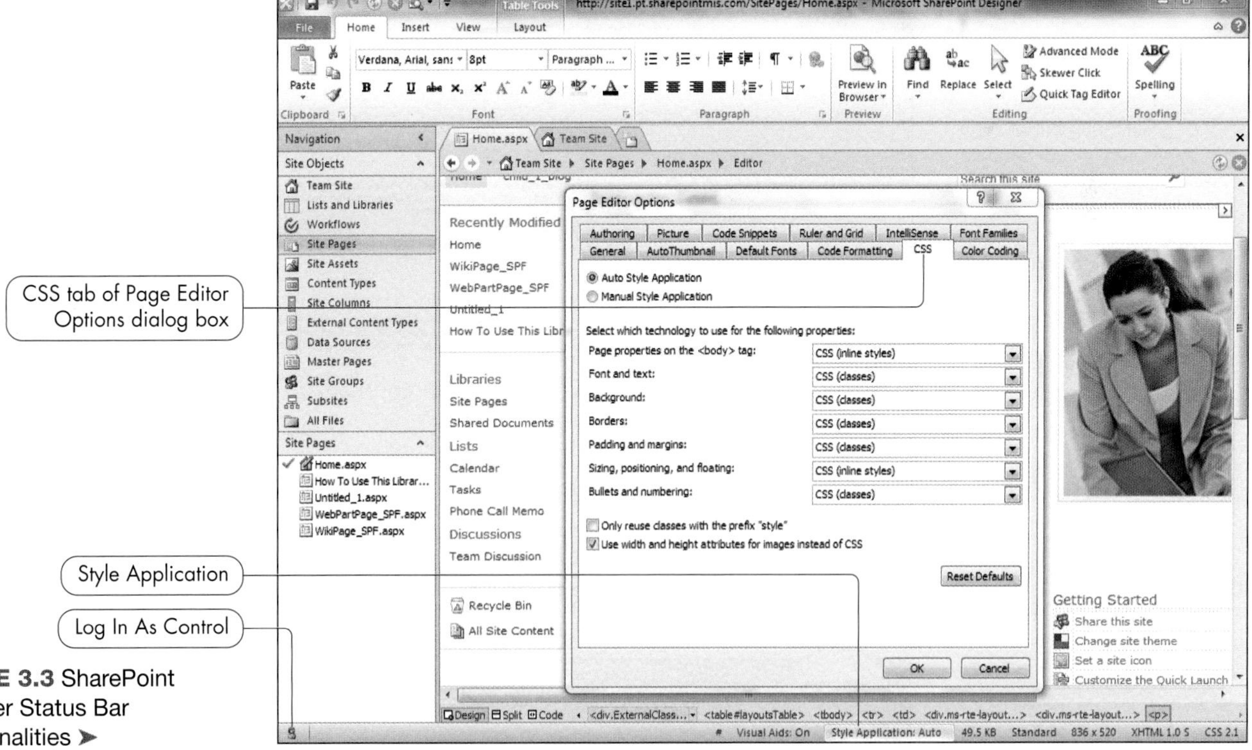

FIGURE 3.3 SharePoint Designer Status Bar Functionalities ➤

Download Statistics Information

Authoring tab of Page Editor Options dialog box

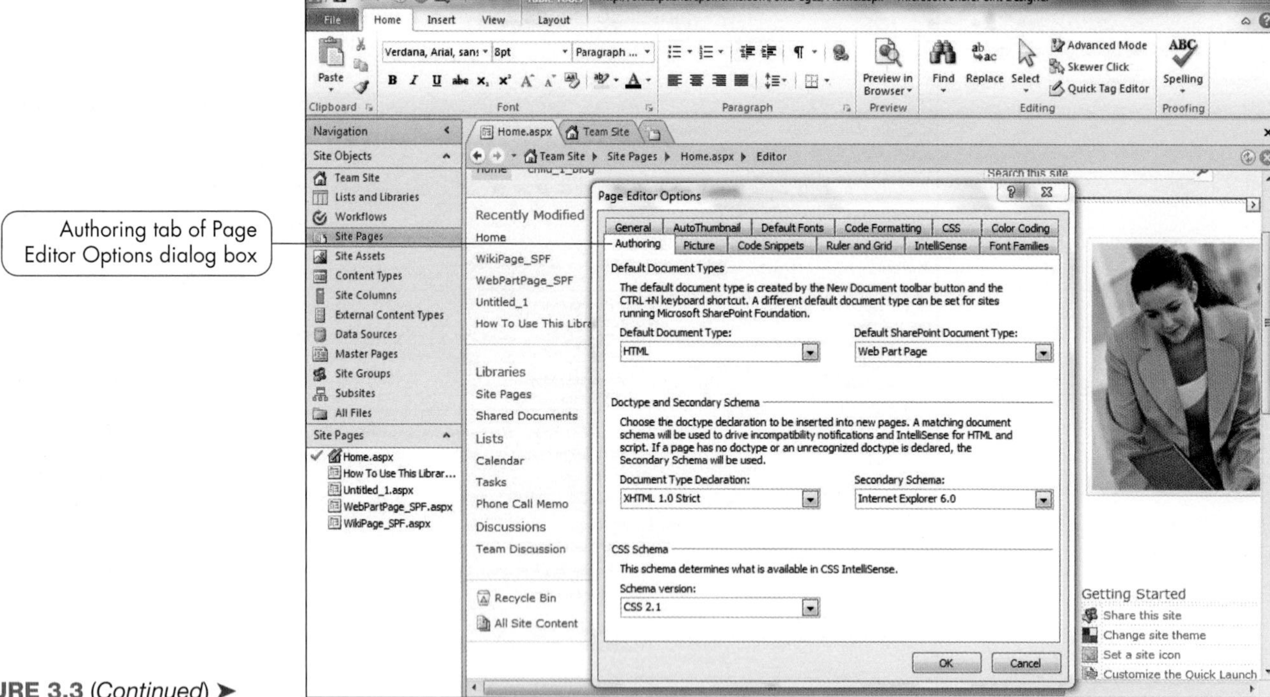

FIGURE 3.3 *(Continued)* ➤

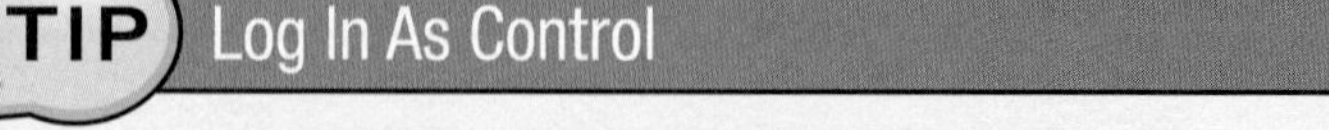

TIP Log In As Control

The Log In As Control is on the left side of the status bar and enables you to log in as another user.

Add, Edit, and Format Text

You can type text directly onto the Web page, import the content of a text file, or copy and paste text from another file.

The most common element of Web page content is text. Text appears in many different ways on a Web page, including normal body text, headings, links, and formatted as ordered or unordered lists. You can type text directly onto the Web page, import the content of a text file, or copy and paste text from another file. Using SharePoint Foundation or SharePoint Designer, text can be also edited and formatted to emphasize the purpose of the Web page and enhance its appearance. SharePoint Designer also provides a spell checker that you should always use to check the spelling of your Web page text before publishing it.

Designers begin the process of editing Web pages by selecting a layout. The Text Layout gallery on the Editing Tools–Format Text tab in SharePoint Foundation enables you to select a suitable page layout, as shown in Figure 3.4. This applies the layout to the current page.

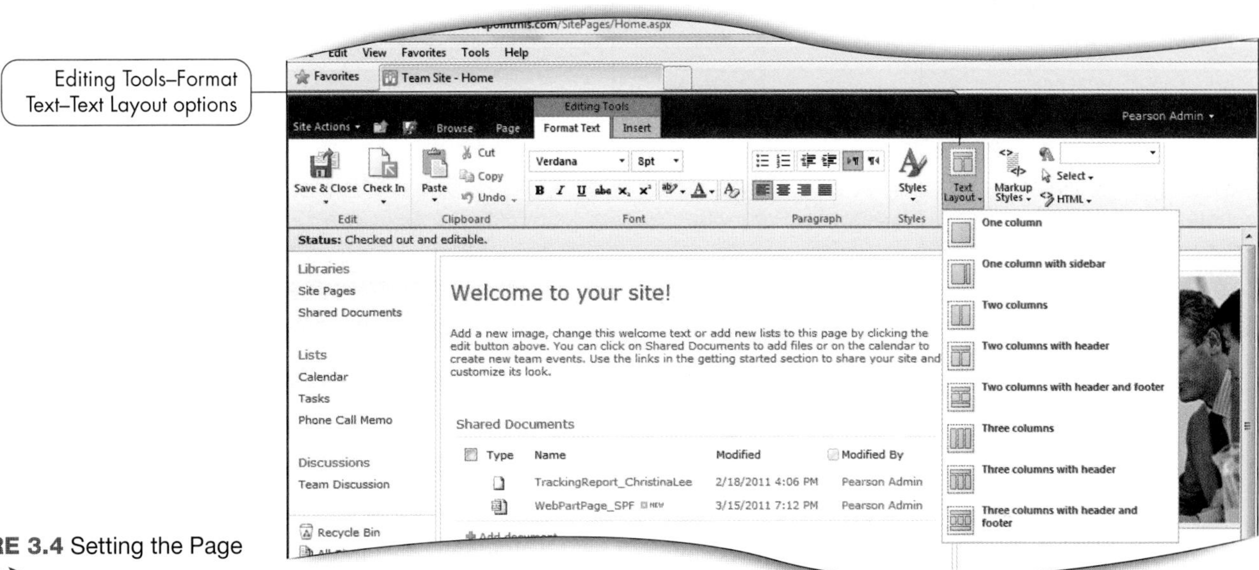

FIGURE 3.4 Setting the Page Layout ➤

Whether you type text, or copy and paste it, it is entered in the content areas of the layout. Text formatting is similar to other Microsoft Office applications, using the Font, Paragraph, and Styles groups on the Editing Tools–Format Text tab. When you type text directly on a Web page, position the insertion point where you want the text to appear and begin typing the text. When you reach the end of the line, the insertion point is automatically positioned at the beginning of the next line. Press Enter when you want to start a new paragraph.

If you want to insert a character that is not available on your keyboard, such as the copyright symbol, click the Insert tab, and then click Symbol in the Symbols group. Click the symbol in the gallery to insert it on your page at the cursor position. A wide variety of symbols are available, as shown in Figure 3.5, and you can access more by clicking More Symbols at the bottom of the gallery.

FIGURE 3.5 Inserting Symbols ➤

TIP Symbols and Cross-Platform Issues

Symbols inserted in SharePoint Designer might not display properly on other computer platforms, such as Macintosh.

You can copy and paste (or move) text from one document to another, or within the same page. You can copy and paste text within the same page using the Copy and Paste commands in the Clipboard group on the Editing Tools–Format Text tab using the SharePoint Foundation browser interface, or by using the Clipboard Group in the Home Tab menu in SharePoint Designer. Highlight the desired text, right-click, and then click Copy in the Clipboard Group to copy the text. Position the insertion point where you want the text to appear, right-click, and then select Paste in the Clipboard group to paste the text.

To copy text from another application, open the source file, highlight the desired text, and then click Copy on the Clipboard group of the Home tab. To paste the copied text in the Web page, open the Web page, click to position the insertion point where you want to paste the text, right-click, and then select Paste on the shortcut menu to paste the text. You can also paste the copied text by clicking the arrow on the Paste command in the Clipboard group, and then selecting the Paste plain text command. Once you paste the text, you can format it as desired.

When you paste text onto a SharePoint Designer page, you see the Paste Options button, as shown in Figure 3.6. This button enables you to decide how you want the pasted content to appear in its new location. Move your mouse pointer over the Paste Option button, click the arrow, and then select an option.

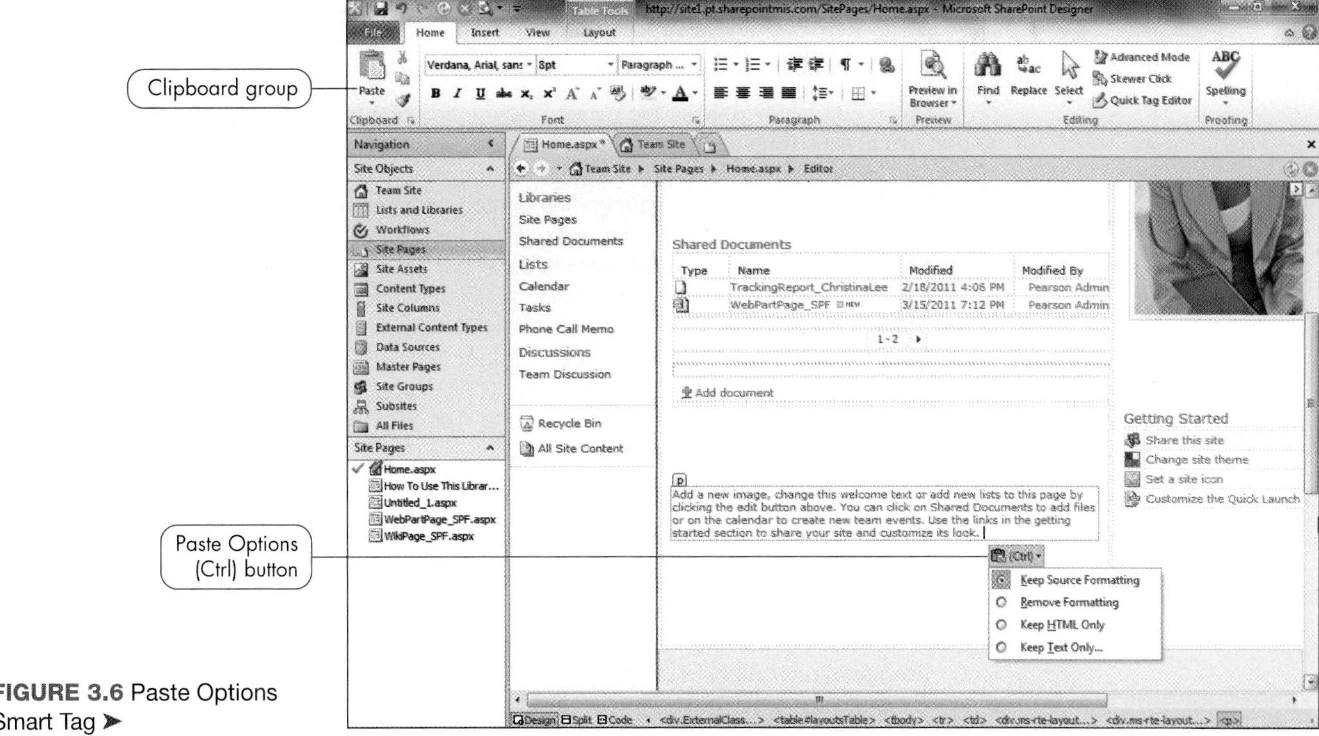

FIGURE 3.6 Paste Options Smart Tag ➤

When you paste text using the Paste command, an excess of tags are included within the text, which increases the risk of creating a Web page with compatibility and accessibility errors. If you want to import text without maintaining any previous formatting, use the Keep Text Only option on the Paste Options menu. When you click the Keep Text Only command, the Paste Text dialog box opens, as shown in Figure 3.7. Any option displayed will enable you to paste the text with no compatibility problems.

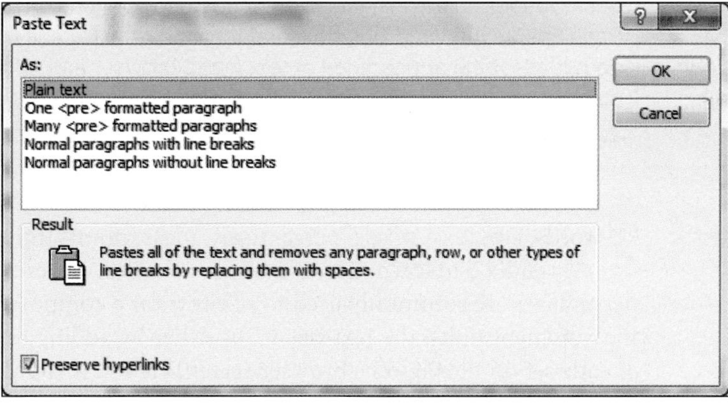

FIGURE 3.7 Paste Text Dialog Box ➤

After you have placed text on the Web page, you might want to edit and format it. The SharePoint Foundation browser interface and SharePoint Designer enable you to move, replace, or delete text and change its appearance. In SharePoint Designer, all of these changes are usually applied in Design view. Select the text, and then right-click to access to the shortcut menu commands such as Cut or Copy.

To replace text, select it, and then type the new text. To delete text, select it, and then press Delete. If you make mistakes while working on your Web page, use the Undo button on the SharePoint Designer Quick Access Toolbar or Ctrl+Z. On the SharePoint Foundation Ribbon, the Undo button is in the Clipboard group. You can undo the 30 most recent consecutive actions. If you accidentally undo the wrong thing, the Redo button on the Quick Access Toolbar (or Ctrl+Y) enables you to reverse the result of the most recent Undo command. Redo is also available for the previous 30 consecutive actions.

TIP Generic Font Families and Fonts

A generic font family defines the general description of a font's appearance. Browsers support five generic fonts: serif (a more formal font, used mostly for body text), sans-serif (a less formal font with no serifs, used mostly as a heading font on Web pages), cursive (a font that looks more like pen or brush writing than printed text), fantasy (a more decorative font), and monospace (a font in which all characters have the same width). Each of these generic font families is available in all CSS implementations, but this does not mean that you can assume they will be the same font on all browsers. A specific font is a font actually installed on your computer, such as Arial, Courier, or Times New Roman. To read more about generic font families and specific fonts that fit each generic font family description, see the W3C Web site (www.w3.org/ and search the Web site for "CSS2 Fonts"). To read more about Microsoft-specific fonts see the Microsoft Typography Web site (www.microsoft.com/typography/default.mspx).

The font can be changed three ways, using the SharePoint Foundation browser interface or SharePoint Designer ribbon:

- Select the text where the font changes will be applied, and then click the Font arrow on the Font group to select a font family, and then use the Font group options to change the specification properties.
- Position the insertion point where you want to insert text, and then make selections from the Font group.
- Select existing text, and then click the appropriate options from the Font group.

TIP Change the Default Font Used in Design and Code Views

Using SharePoint Designer in the Design and Code views, you can change the default fonts. Click Options on the File tab, click Page Editor Options on the Options dialog box to open the Page Editor Options dialog box, and then click the Default Fonts tab. However, these settings do not affect the appearance of text in the browser and affect only how SharePoint Designer displays text when you work in a SharePoint Designer window.

The text size can be expressed in HTML and CSS using a rather wide selection of units: keywords, ems, exs, pixels, percentages, picas, points, inches, centimeters, and millimeters (see Appendix B to learn more about this selection of units). Only pixels, keywords, ems, and percentages are commonly used to size text for a computer monitor. When using these four measurement units, the text size is set either by adding to or subtracting from the text size already set on the viewer's browser screen. Hence, if you do not specify a size for text using CSS, Web browsers apply their base font size, which is 16 pixels for most browsers. For more information about fonts, see the reference table on the next page.

TIP Accessible Text Content

One way to make sure an uncommon font used in your Web page is properly displayed by all browsers is to create graphic text (a graphic file that captures the actual text and inserts it in the Web page body). From an accessibility point of view, plain text is better than graphic text because graphic text cannot be customized. Plain text that uses style sheets provides increased flexibility for styling and customizing, such as higher contrast and different combinations of size, color, and typeface.

REFERENCE The Font Specification Properties

Font Specification Property	Description
Font Type	Five generic font families are supported by browsers: sans serif, serif, cursive, fantasy, and monospace. Arial is probably the best-known sans serif font. Times New Roman, which is also the default SharePoint Designer font, is the best-known serif font. Courier is the most common monospace font.
Font Style	Font styles can be used to enhance text and emphasize the message. The most frequently used font styles are bold and italic. You can apply more than one font style to a selected text. (The most popular combination of styles is bold and italic.)
Font Color	The default font color of a Web page is black. You can alter the font color to emphasize a word or an entire paragraph. You can create custom colors with SharePoint Designer.
Font Size	In SharePoint Designer, you use the CSS seven keywords (xx-small, x-small, small, medium, large, x-large, and xx-large) to set the text size relative to the base text size and the corresponding measure in points.
Text Effects	Some of the better known text effects, in addition to underline, are superscript and subscript. You can apply text effects using the Font group on the Home tab in SharePoint Designer or the Editing Tools–Format Text tab in SharePoint Foundation.

TIP Hyperlinks and the Underline Text Effect

Because hyperlinks often display as underlined text, you should avoid using underlined text on Web pages.

Style is a SharePoint Designer feature that enables Web designers to format text using built-in HTML styles.

Style is a SharePoint Designer feature that enables Web designers to format text using built-in HTML styles. Among the styles included in the Style list on the Font group, as shown in Figure 3.8, are headings and some of the more popular styles for formatting lists and applying alignment. Having the styles grouped together this way enables Web designers to give more consistency to their Web page content. You can use six levels of headings in Web design, from Heading 1 to Heading 6. Each heading level has a distinct HTML tag. The <h1> tag creates the largest Heading 1 font, and the <h6> tag creates the smallest. All these heading levels are included in the SharePoint Designer built-in styles and can be accessed by clicking the Style arrow in the Font group, as shown in Figure 3.8.

FIGURE 3.8 Heading 5 Further Aligned Center ➤

> **TIP** Format Painter
>
> With SharePoint Designer, you can copy the format of specific characters or even an entire paragraph that was previously created and formatted, and then apply it to other characters or paragraphs using Format Painter, available in the Clipboard group on the Home tab. Select the characters or paragraphs that have the formatting you want to copy, and then click Format Painter. Next, select the text that you want formatted. If you want to apply the format to more than one area of text, double-click Format Painter and it applies the format to any text you select. Click Format Painter again to turn off the feature.

Check the Spelling of Your Text Using SharePoint Designer

SharePoint Designer enables you to check the spelling of a highlighted section of a Web page, an entire Web page, a group of selected Web pages, or an entire Web site.

It is always important to check your document for spelling errors. The SharePoint Foundation browser interface does not provide you with a spell checker tool. SharePoint Designer enables you to check the spelling of a highlighted section of a Web page, an entire Web page, a group of selected Web pages, or an entire Web site. Open the Spelling dialog box by clicking Spelling in the Proofing group of the Home tab. The Spelling dialog box displays the first misspelled word along with suggestions for correcting it, as shown in Figure 3.9. Choose the best option for correcting the misspelled word or type the word correctly in the Change to box, and then click one of the following options:

- Click Change to change the selected instance of the word.
- Click Ignore to ignore the selected instance.
- Click Change All to change every instance of the word.
- Click Ignore All to ignore every instance of the word.

After you make your selection, the Spelling dialog box shows the next error in your page.

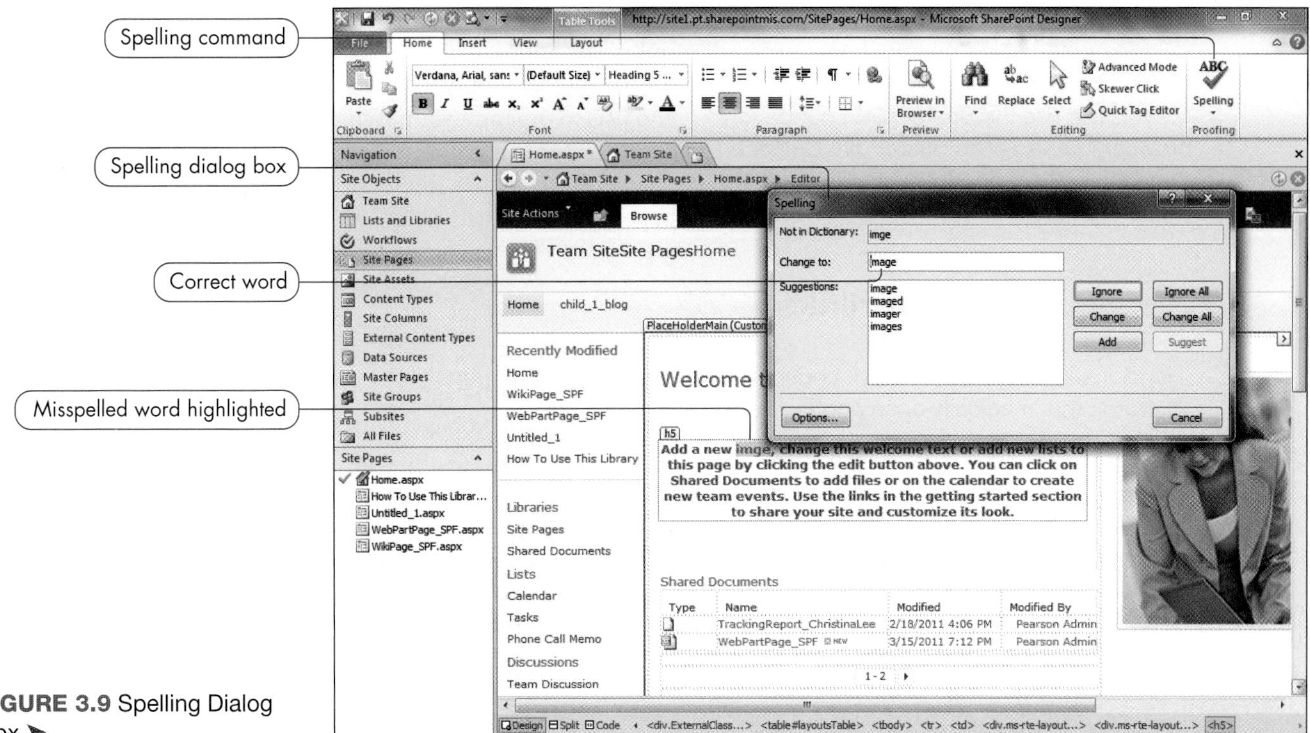

FIGURE 3.9 Spelling Dialog Box ➤

Although you can wait until your Web page is finished to check your spelling, SharePoint Designer shows you your mistakes as soon as they occur. SharePoint Designer uses the Check Spelling as You Type feature to mark each misspelled word with a wavy red line so that you can fix your spelling errors on the spot. When you find a word on your page with the wavy red line under it, right-click the word to see a selection of possible corrections. From this shortcut menu, you can click one of the word choices, choose to ignore all instances of that particular word, or choose to add the word to a personal dictionary. Alternatively, you can simply choose to click the word in the main text and make your correction there.

Although you can wait until your Web page is finished to check your spelling, SharePoint Designer shows you your mistakes as soon as they occur.

TIP Turning Off the Check Spelling as You Type Feature

The Check Spelling as You Type feature is turned on by default, but if you decide you do not want to use it, you can turn it off by clicking Options on the File tab, clicking Page Editor Options, and then clicking Spelling Options on the General tab to display the Spelling Options dialog box. Deselect the *Check Spelling as You Type* check box in the *When correcting spelling* area in SharePoint Designer.

Using Hyperlinks and Lists in Organizing a Web Page

Nobody likes to explore a cluttered and confusing document. Most people instinctively prefer clear, well-organized, and easy-to-navigate Web pages. Keeping your Web pages clean and organized is an important design consideration. Hyperlinks and lists are two features that can help Web authors achieve these goals.

Hyperlinks can help designers break the contents of a large, difficult-to-navigate Web page into a set of Web pages that are connected. Alternatively, designers can reduce the amount of jumping back and forth between different Web pages by using bookmark links and bookmarks to give users access to the content.

Lists are great tools for organizing Web page content in a concise and consistent fashion. You can choose ordered (numbered), unordered (bulleted), and definition lists.

... you can use the SharePoint Foundation browser interface and SharePoint Designer for adding, editing, and formatting hyperlinks and lists.

In this section, you learn when and how to use hyperlinks and lists to organize your Web pages. You will also learn how you can use the SharePoint Foundation browser interface and SharePoint Designer Ribbon for adding, editing, and formatting hyperlinks and lists.

Hyperlinks

Hyperlinks are not just colored, underlined words that magically open another Web page.

Hyperlinks are not just colored, underlined words that magically open another Web page. The HTML code contains a tag with the URL of the linked page, which the browser requests from the server when you click the link. As you will learn in Appendix A, a URL can include an address for a Web page or file on the Internet, on your computer, on a local network, a bookmark within a Web page, or an e-mail address.

An **absolute URL** provides the full path to a Web page or file.

A **relative URL** provides the path to a Web page or a file relative to another file.

Two different kinds of URLs exist: absolute and relative. An ***absolute URL*** provides the full path to a Web page or file, whereas a ***relative URL*** provides the path to a Web page or a file in relation to another file. The HTML code in Figure 3.10 shows how typical absolute and relative URLs look. Notice that relative URLs are often shorter than absolute ones are.

FIGURE 3.10 Absolute and Relative URL ➤

```
Absolute URL http://www.eng.auburn.edu/users/daniela/
Relative URL images/access/daniela_access_2012.jpg
```

Absolute URLs are required to access Web pages or files outside your Web site. When Web sites include multiple Web pages and many folders and subfolders, they can be confusing and difficult to remember and type correctly; you should use relative URLs in these situations. In addition to being shorter, there are other significant advantages to using relative URLs, such as when relocating a Web site to another place on the same Web server or on another Web server. Using relative URLs cuts down on the time required to adjust links from the previous location.

SharePoint Designer assists you in creating hyperlinks to existing files or even to files that have not been created yet. You can also decide in which browser window the hyperlink target should display.

SharePoint Designer assists you in creating hyperlinks to existing files or even to files that have not been created yet. You can also decide in which browser window the hyperlink target should display. The file that opens when a hyperlink is clicked is called the ***hyperlink target***. When you move the mouse pointer over a hyperlink, the target URL displays on the Status bar. To create a hyperlink targeting an existing file, position the insertion point where you want the hyperlink to appear. Click Insert Hyperlink in the Paragraph group of the Home tab or in the Links group of the Insert tab. The Insert Hyperlink dialog box displays, enabling you to choose a file from the Current Folder, Browsed Pages, and Recent Files areas. You can also type an address in the Address box or locate the desired target file using the *Look in* list. The *Browse the Web* button opens a browser window, enabling you to browse the Internet for a Web page. The *Browse for file* option opens the *Link to File* dialog box, enabling you to search for a file on your computer or network. You also need to type the display text for the hyperlink in the *Text to Display* box (see Figure 3.11). Click OK to close the Insert Hyperlink dialog box.

Hyperlink target is the file that opens when a hyperlink is clicked.

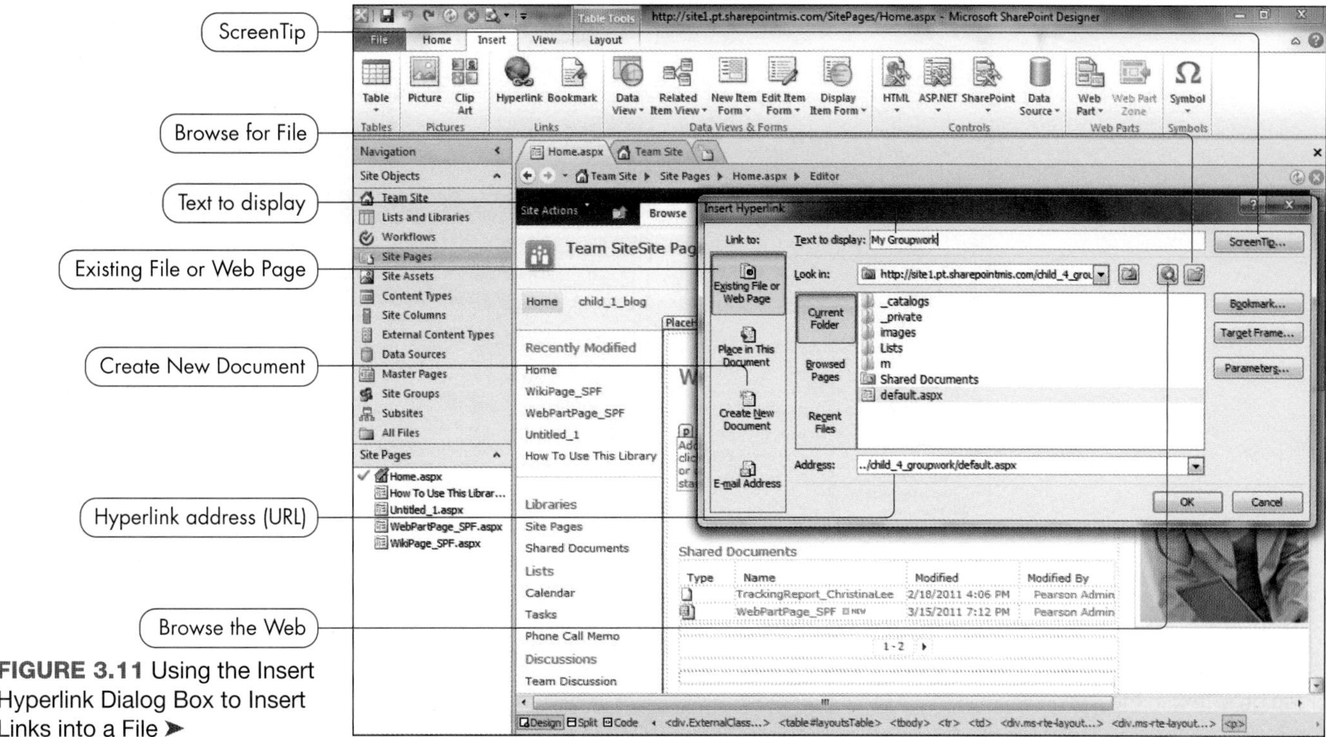

FIGURE 3.11 Using the Insert Hyperlink Dialog Box to Insert Links into a File ➤

To create a link to a file that has not been created yet, click Create New Document, as shown in Figure 3.11. Type the name of the file you want to create in the *Name of New Document* box or, if you want to change the path of the new file, click the Change button.

TIP SharePoint Designer and URLs

If you type a URL (such as http://www.eng.auburn.edu or just www.eng.auburn.edu) in your text, SharePoint Designer automatically converts it into a hyperlink.

A **ScreenTip** is text that displays in the body of the Web page whenever the mouse pointer is moved over the hyperlink.

For all types of links, you can also add a ScreenTip. A ***ScreenTip*** is text that displays in the body of the Web page whenever the mouse pointer is moved over the hyperlink. To set up a ScreenTip, click ScreenTip in the Insert Hyperlink dialog box to open the Set Hyperlink Screen Tip dialog box, as shown in Figure 3.12. Type the desired text in the *ScreenTip text:* box, and then click OK to close the dialog box. The ScreenTip text displays every time the mouse pointer moves over the link, as shown in Figure 3.13, in Preview view or when viewing the Web page in a browser. Designers use ScreenTip text to provide users with more information about the related hyperlink.

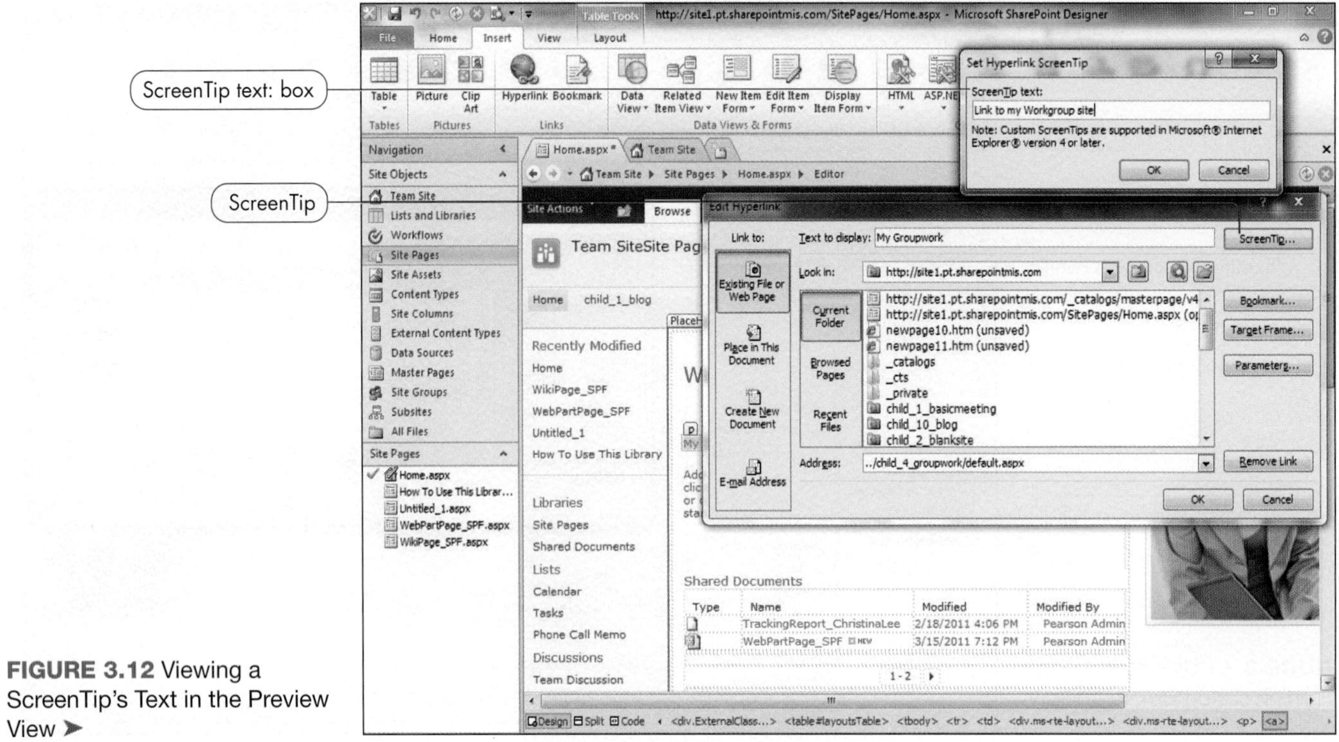

FIGURE 3.12 Viewing a ScreenTip's Text in the Preview View ➤

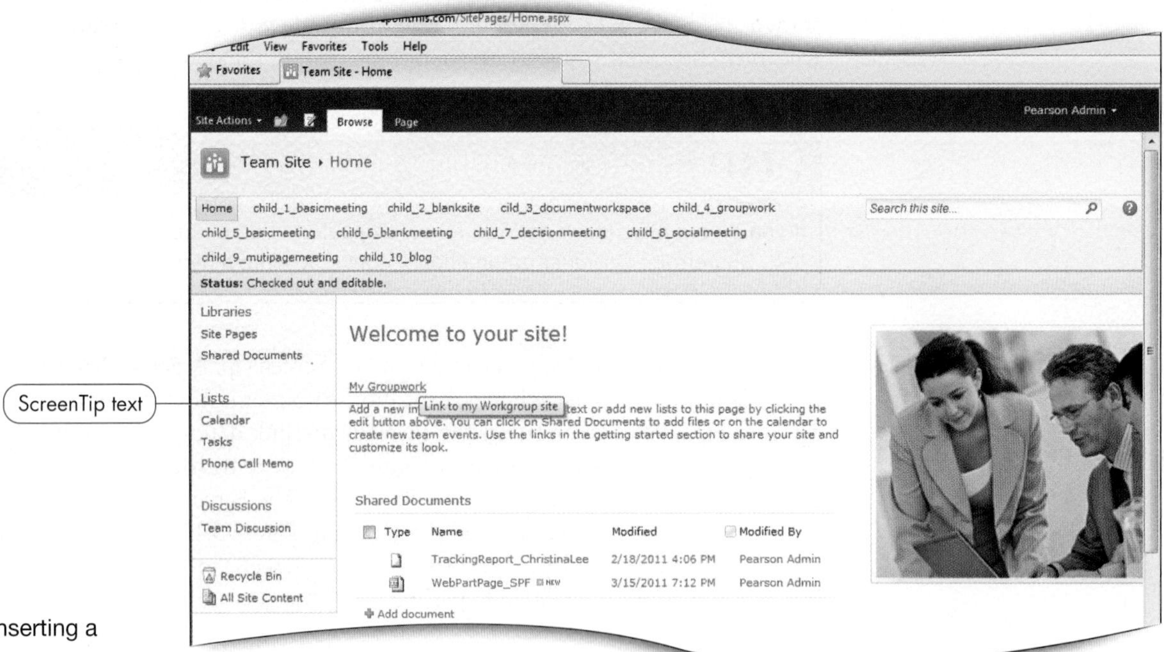

FIGURE 3.13 Inserting a ScreenTip ➤

TIP Editing a Hyperlink's Display Text

If the hyperlink's display text has been previously added to the Web page, you can change it by editing the hyperlink. Highlight the text, and then open the Insert Hyperlink dialog box. The selected text is automatically displayed in the *Text to Display* box.

After a hyperlink has been created, you can change its URL or its text message anytime. To edit a hyperlink, click the text of the hyperlink, and then click Insert Hyperlink to open the Edit Hyperlink dialog box.

You can remove a hyperlink in one of two ways: by deleting the text and the associated link from the page or by keeping the text on the page but removing the associated link.

You can remove a hyperlink in one of two ways: by deleting the text and the associated link from the page or by keeping the text on the page but removing the associated link. To delete a hyperlink and its text completely from the page, double-click the hyperlink to select the text, right-click, and then click Cut. Alternatively, you can select the linked text, and then press Delete. To preserve the hyperlink text on the page but delete the link associated with it, click Hyperlink to open the Edit Hyperlink dialog box (see Figure 3.14). Click Remove Link in the bottom right of the dialog box.

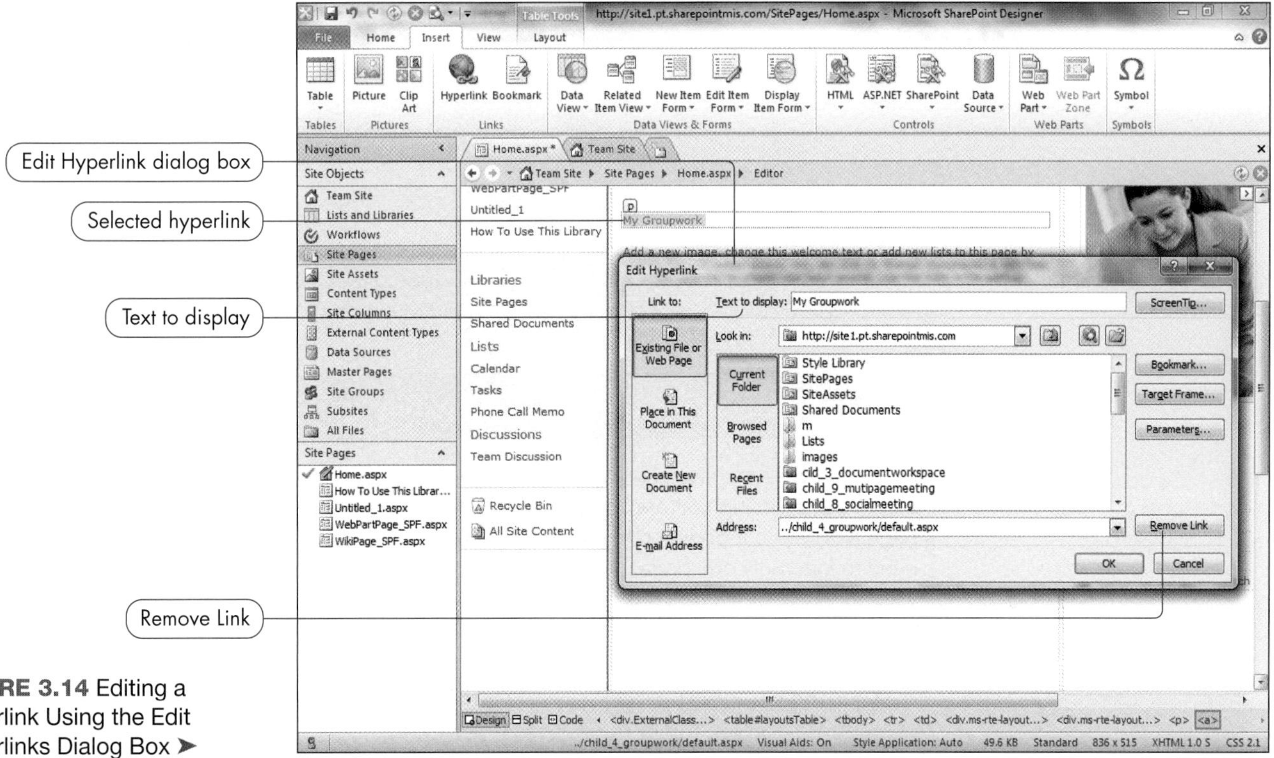

FIGURE 3.14 Editing a Hyperlink Using the Edit Hyperlinks Dialog Box ➤

Bookmark link is a link to a specific position within the same document or another document.

A link to a specific position within the same document or another document is called a ***bookmark link.*** Bookmark links are helpful navigation tools, especially when you are dealing with long pages, because they replace the slower scrolling (using the vertical and horizontal scrollbars) method of working through the text. Before you can create a bookmark link, you need to create the bookmark targets within a page. To create a bookmark, place the insertion point or select text where the bookmark target will be, click the Insert tab, and then click Bookmark in the Links group to open the Bookmark dialog box, as shown in Figure 3.15. If you just placed the insertion point, type the bookmark name in the Bookmark name box (bookmark names cannot contain spaces). If you selected text before opening the Bookmark dialog box, the bookmark text appears in the Bookmark name box. When you have the Bookmark name text the way you want it, click OK to close the Bookmark dialog box. You should always use a descriptive name for each bookmark target so you can identify it easily when you add a link to it.

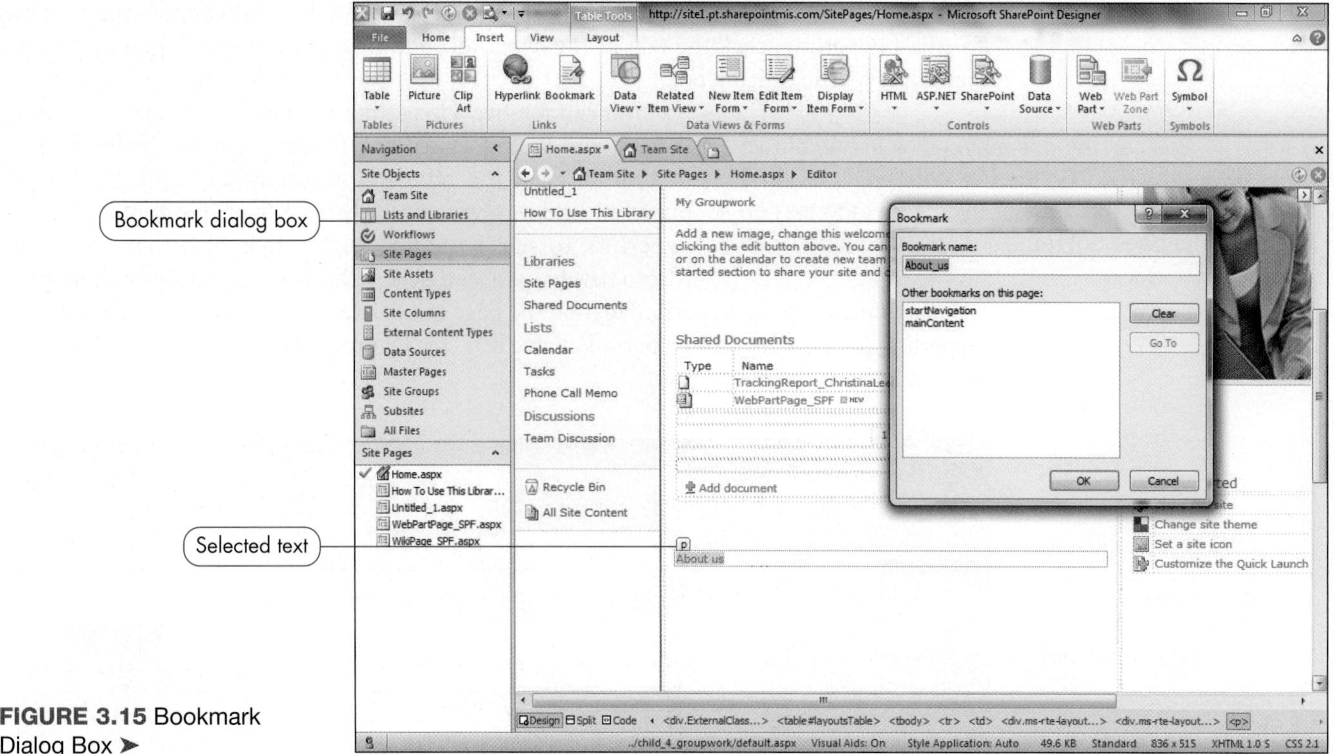

FIGURE 3.15 Bookmark Dialog Box ➤

TIP Why and When to Use Bookmarks

Often it is wise to have one long Web page, instead of spreading the content among many Web pages forcing visitors to jump back and forth among them. When you have a single-page site, you cut down on the time required for users to browse your Web site because they need to load only one page into the browser window. Bookmarks are the best solution to help visitors navigate a long Web page.

After the bookmark target is created, the second step is to create the link that points to the bookmark target. Open the Insert Hyperlink dialog box, click *Place in This Document* to display the list of available bookmarks (as shown in Figure 3.16), and then click the desired bookmark. If you want to display text that is different than the name of the bookmark, type the desired text in the Text to Display box, and then click OK to close the Insert Hyperlink dialog box. When the hyperlink is clicked, the cursor jumps to the bookmark target position whether it is in the same file or another. If a bookmark is placed in an external file, you select the external file in the Insert Hyperlink dialog box before you select the bookmark to use.

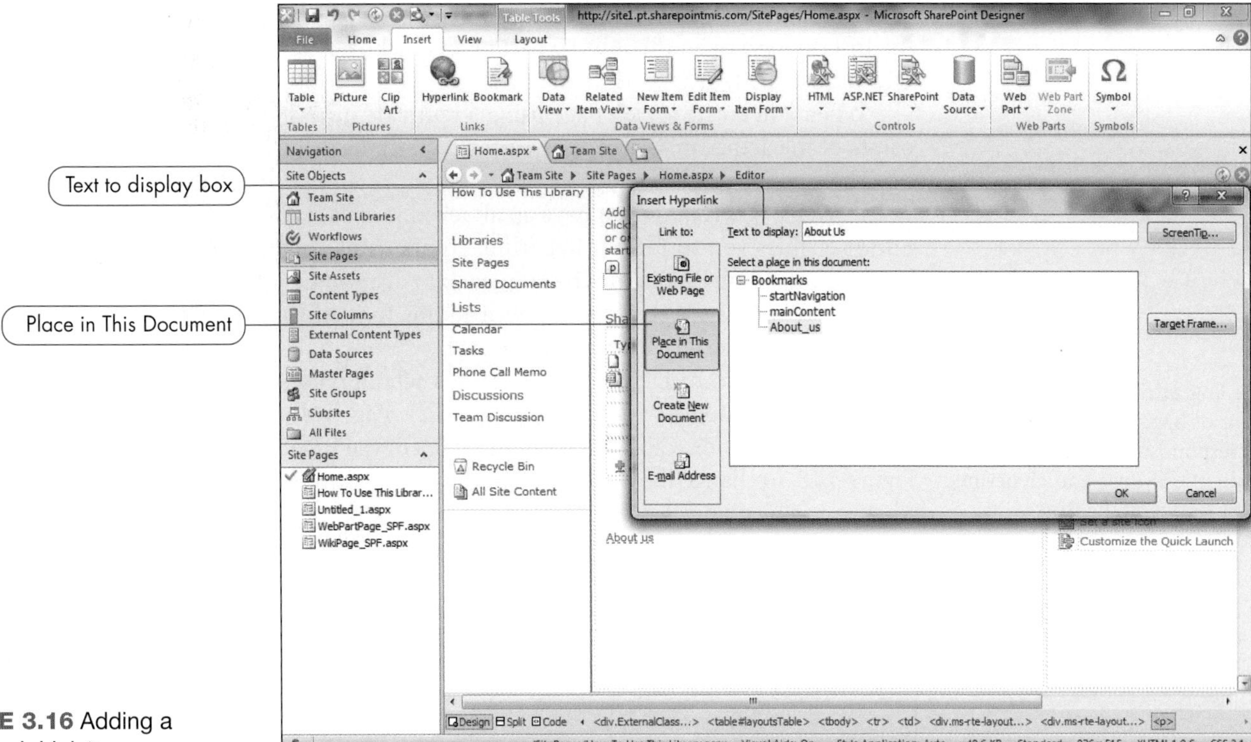

FIGURE 3.16 Adding a Bookmark Link ➤

A **mailto link** is a common type of hyperlink that connects the user to an e-mail address.

Another common type of hyperlink, called a ***mailto link***, connects the user to an e-mail address. When users click a mailto link, their default e-mail application opens a new message window and the target address of the link is already entered in the To address box. Create a mailto link by clicking E-mail Address on the left side of the Insert Hyperlink dialog box. The Insert Hyperlink dialog box displays the mailto options, as shown in Figure 3.17. Type the desired address in the E-mail address field. Observe that SharePoint Designer automatically enters mailto: into the address field preceding the address as you type. If you want, you can also enter a Subject for the e-mail. Often, the text displayed on the Web page is not the e-mail address, but rather a phrase like Contact Us. Type the text you want displayed in the *Text to display* box. If you type an e-mail address directly in a document, SharePoint Designer automatically formats it as a mailto link.

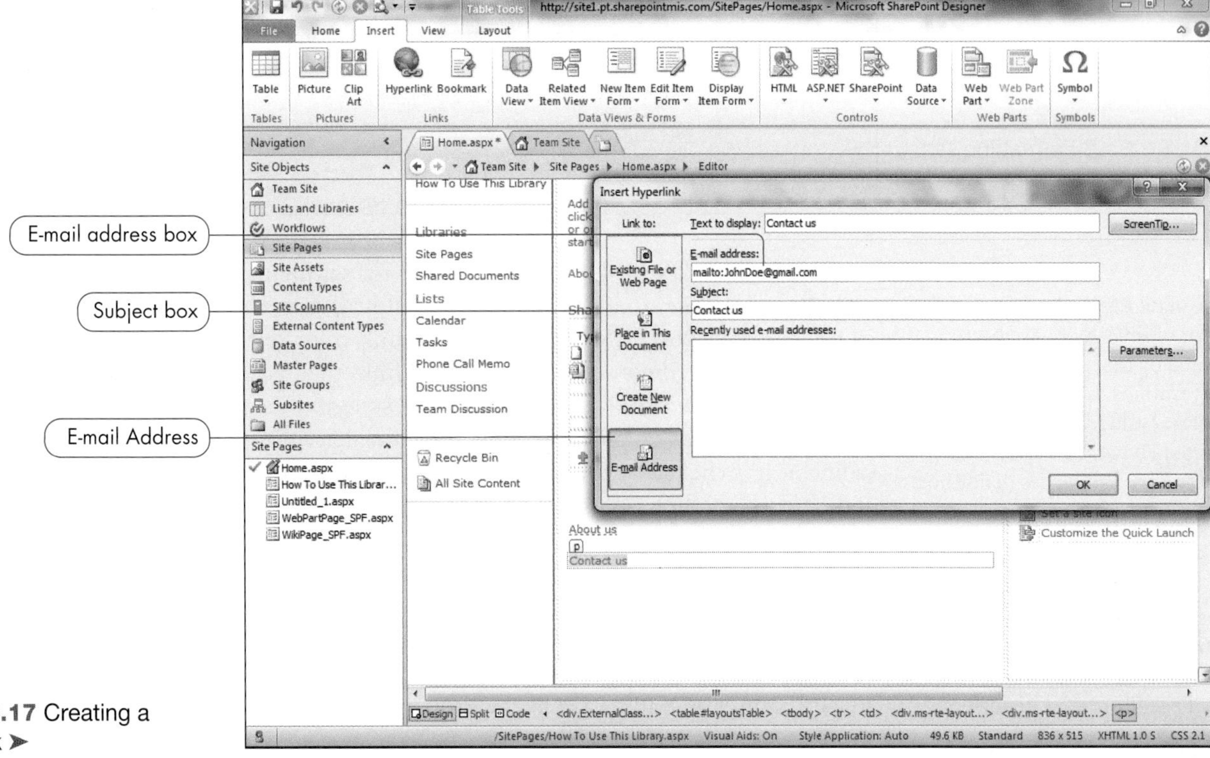

FIGURE 3.17 Creating a Mailto Link ➤

To edit a mailto link, select the hyperlink, and then click Hyperlink in the Links group of the Insert tab to open the Edit Hyperlink dialog box. After you finish making changes, click OK to close the Edit Hyperlink dialog box.

When you create a Web page using a template or a CSS external style sheet, the default colors of the active, unvisited, and visited hyperlinks included in your Web page are usually set. These colors can be changed by modifying the template or the CSS external style sheet.

In Web pages that do not have an attached template, the SharePoint Designer Advanced Editor enables you to format hyperlink colors using the Page Properties. Click Advanced Mode in the Editing group on the Home tab to display the Advanced Editor page. SharePoint Designer also assists Web designers with adding font effects to hyperlinks in Web pages with or without a CSS external style sheet linked.

The **link attribute** defines the color of hypertext links and corresponds to the a:link {color: #value;) CSS style and Hyperlink color setting in the Page Properties dialog box.

Using SharePoint Designer, you can set default colors for active, unvisited, and visited hyperlinks included in your Web page. Click Page on the Style tab to display the Page Properties dialog box. Click the Formatting tab of the Page Properties dialog box, as shown in Figure 3.18, to change the colors of each type of hyperlink. The selected colors should be distinctive and blend nicely into the design of your Web page. If after customizing the hyperlink colors you apply a theme to your Web page, your settings will be overwritten by the theme.

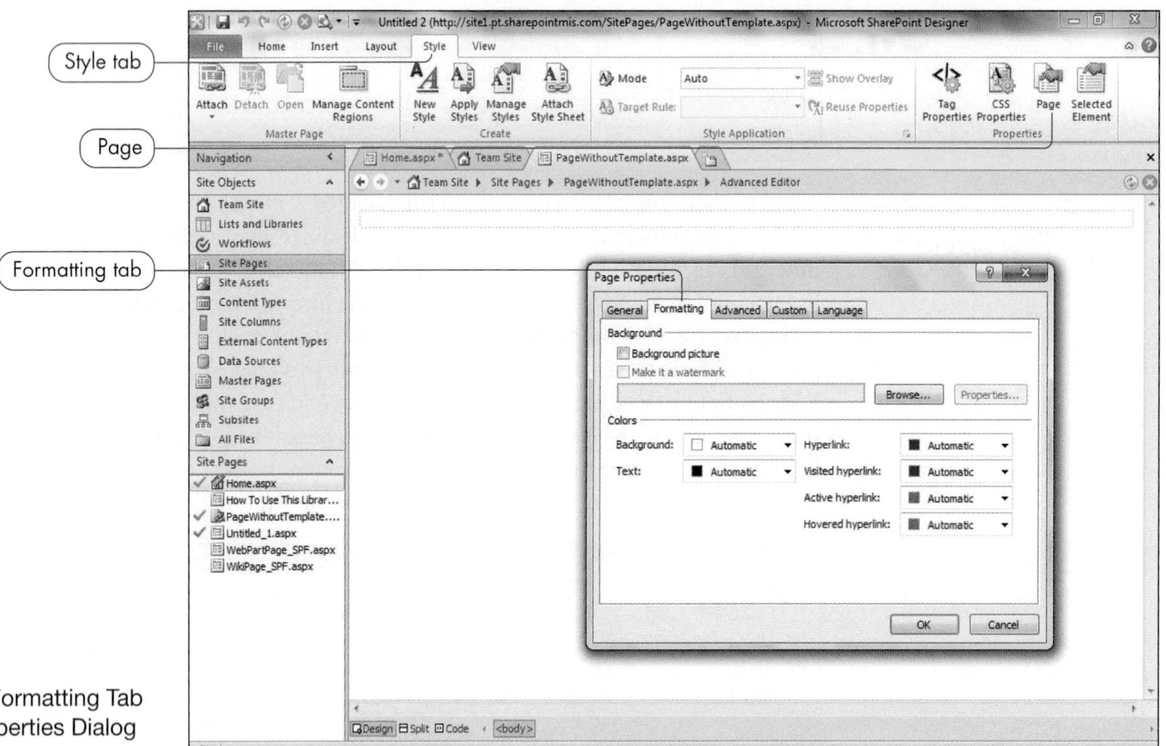

FIGURE 3.18 Formatting Tab of the Page Properties Dialog Box ➤

The **vlink attribute** defines the color of links that have been visited by the user and corresponds to the a:visited {color: #value;} CSS style and Visited Hyperlink Color setting in the Page Properties dialog box.

The **alink attribute** determines the color of an active hyperlink (a link as it is clicked by the user) and corresponds to the a:active {color: #value;} CSS style and Active Hyperlink Color setting in the Page Properties dialog box.

The HTML <a> tag has three attributes for setting the colors of hyperlinks: link, vlink, and alink. The ***link attribute*** defines the color of hypertext links and corresponds to the a:link {color: #value;} CSS style and Hyperlink color setting in the Page Properties dialog box. The ***vlink attribute*** defines the color of links that have been visited by the user and corresponds to the a:visited {color: #value;} CSS style and Visited Hyperlink Color setting in the Page Properties dialog box. The ***alink attribute*** determines the color of an active hyperlink (a link as it is clicked by the user) and corresponds to the a:active {color: #value;} CSS style and Active Hyperlink Color setting in the Page Properties dialog box.

In SharePoint Designer, you cannot set color effects for a hyperlink if the page uses a template. Therefore, the color formatting options are not available in the Page Properties dialog box. However, you can set many color effects on these Web pages by customizing the attached template. In the Editing group of the SharePoint Designer Home tab, click Advanced mode to display the Style tab. Click Open in the Master Page group to open the attached template. Click Page in the Properties group to display the Page Properties dialog box. You can set hyperlink colors using the Formatting tab of the Page Properties dialog box, shown in Figure 3.19. In the Colors area, click the arrows next to the link colors to select the colors you want to use for the color of a link. Each of the colors for the Hyperlink, Visited Hyperlink, and Active Hyperlink can be set to the same color or different colors.

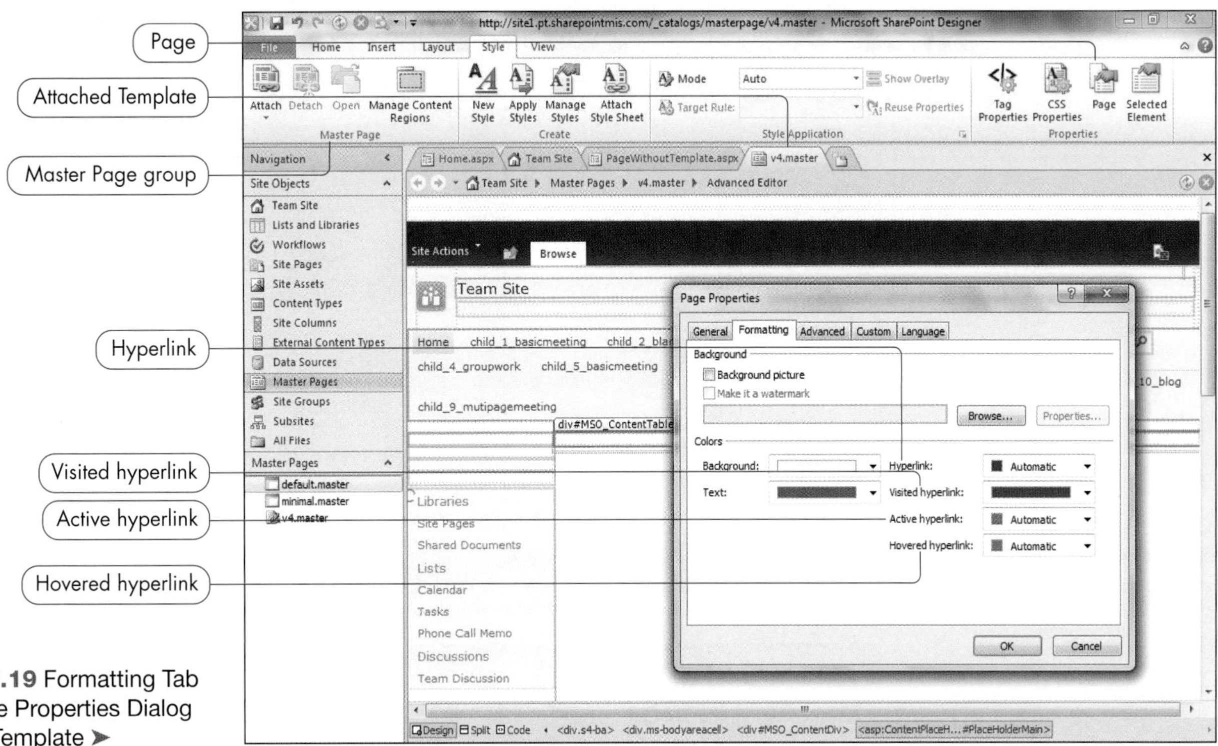

FIGURE 3.19 Formatting Tab of the Page Properties Dialog Box for a Template ➤

You can add rollover effects to hyperlinks so that when a Web site visitor moves the mouse pointer over the hyperlink, the font attribute changes. You can add a hover color effect using the Formatting tab of the Page Properties dialog box (see Figure 3.19) by selecting a different color than the one used for the Hyperlink font. This should help your Web page visitors be aware of the current position of the mouse and add a little dynamic charm to your Web page.

Dynamic HTML (DHTML) is an extension of HTML that enables changes to the styles and attributes of page elements based on user actions.

Hyperlink rollover effects use Dynamic HTML (DHTML). ***Dynamic HTML (DHTML)*** is an extension of HTML that enables changes to the styles and attributes of page elements based on user actions.

TIP Restrictions on Applying Effects to a Hyperlink

Some Web browsers might not support DHTML, so the hyperlink rollover effects will not display properly on the user's computer.

To further format hyperlinks (for example, to change the hyperlink text to a smaller, bold, orange font on hover), click New Style in the Create group on the Style tab, and then make selections using the New Style dialog box, shown in Figure 3.20. SharePoint Designer enables you to apply the changes just to the current page, to create a new style sheet, or to add the new style to an existing external style sheet that can also be linked to other pages using the *Define in* box. After you add the new style, you see the style attribute within the current page (see Figure 3.21) and the rollover effect when you view the Web page in browser and hover the mouse pointer over the hyperlink (see Figure 3.22).

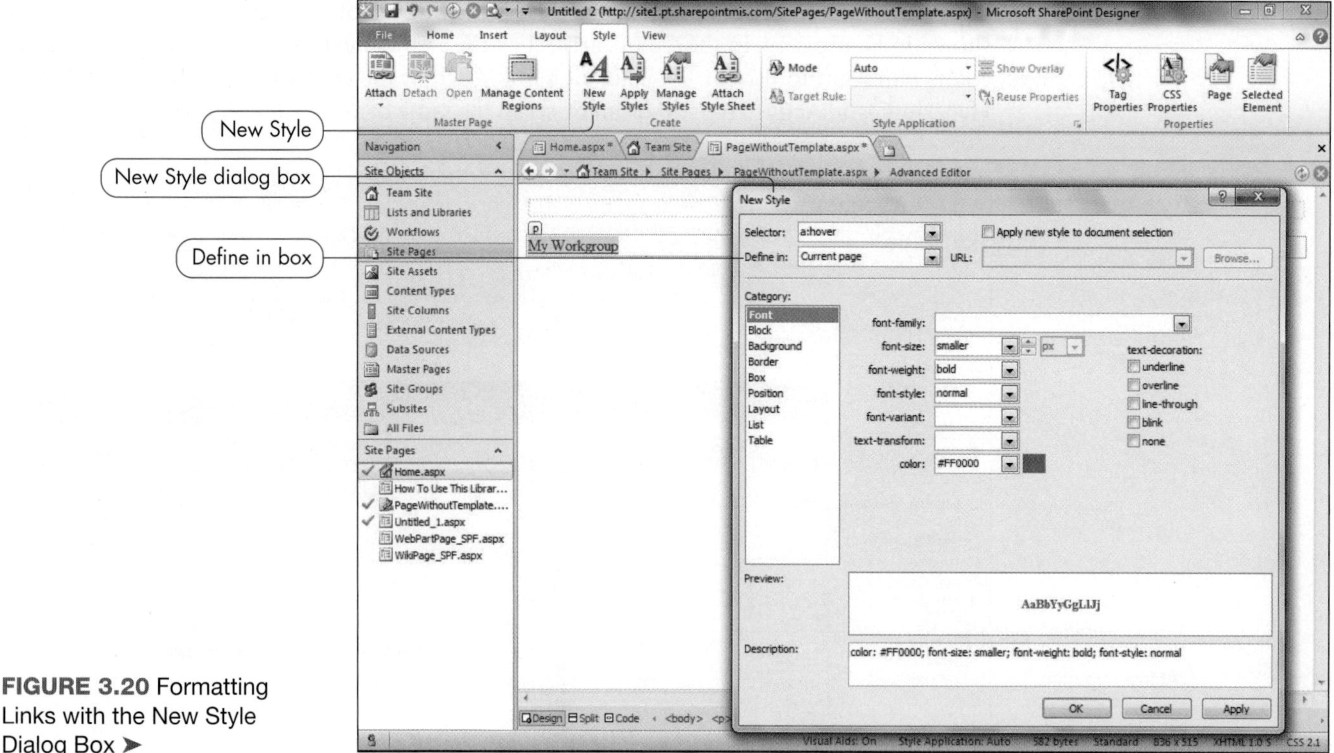

FIGURE 3.20 Formatting Links with the New Style Dialog Box ➤

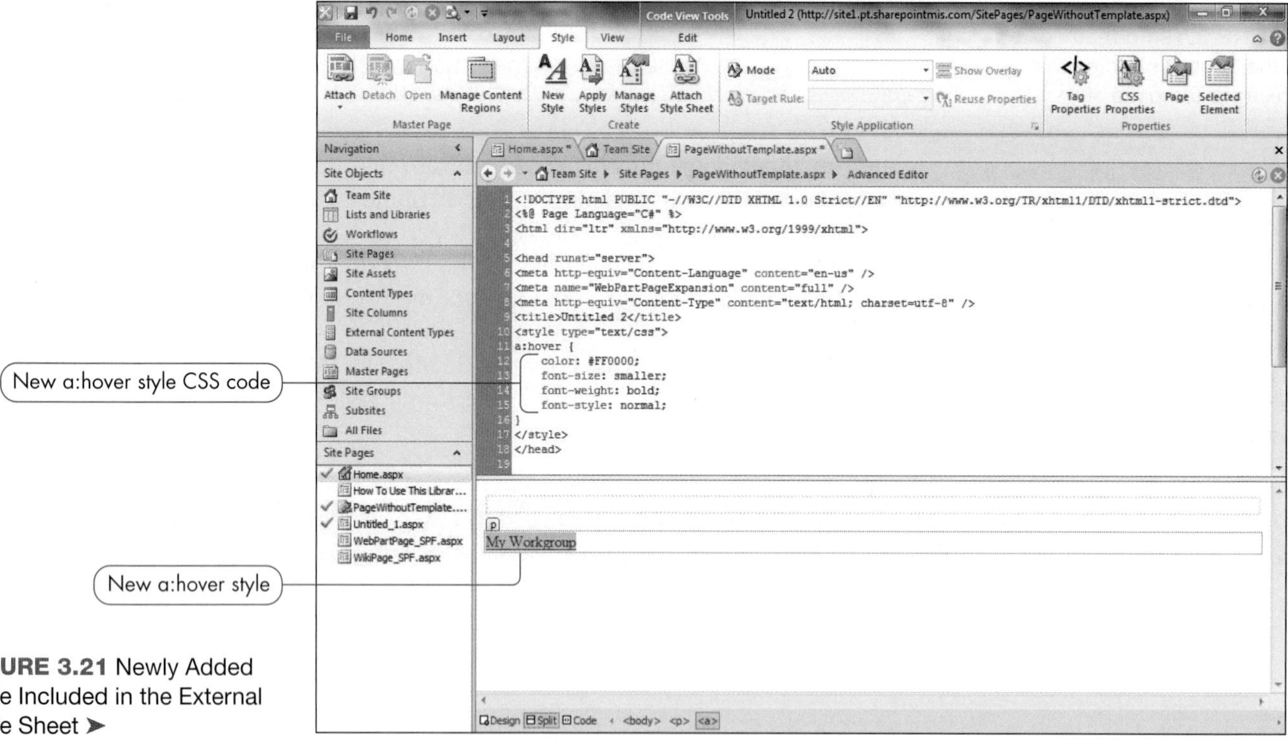

FIGURE 3.21 Newly Added Style Included in the External Style Sheet ➤

FIGURE 3.22 Hover Effect Viewed in Browser ➤

Lists

The most popular SharePoint Designer list styles are numbered and bulleted. Use a numbered list when the order in which elements appear is important, such as a list of meetings scheduled for a day, or a list of instructions included in a software application tutorial. If the order of the elements is not important, use a bulleted list.

The **list format** is a common format, seen on almost any Web page, that helps you organize and present your content in a consistent and concise fashion.

The ***list format*** is a common format seen on almost any Web page. Lists help you organize and present your content in a consistent and concise fashion. Figure 3.23 shows an example of text formatted as numbered and bulleted lists.

In HTML, each line from either type of list is included between the pair tags <li> and </li>. The HTML tags for creating lists using picture bullets are the pair tags <ul> and </ul> (for unordered list), whereas for creating lists using numbers, the pair tags are <ol> and </ol> (for ordered list), as shown in Figure 3.23.

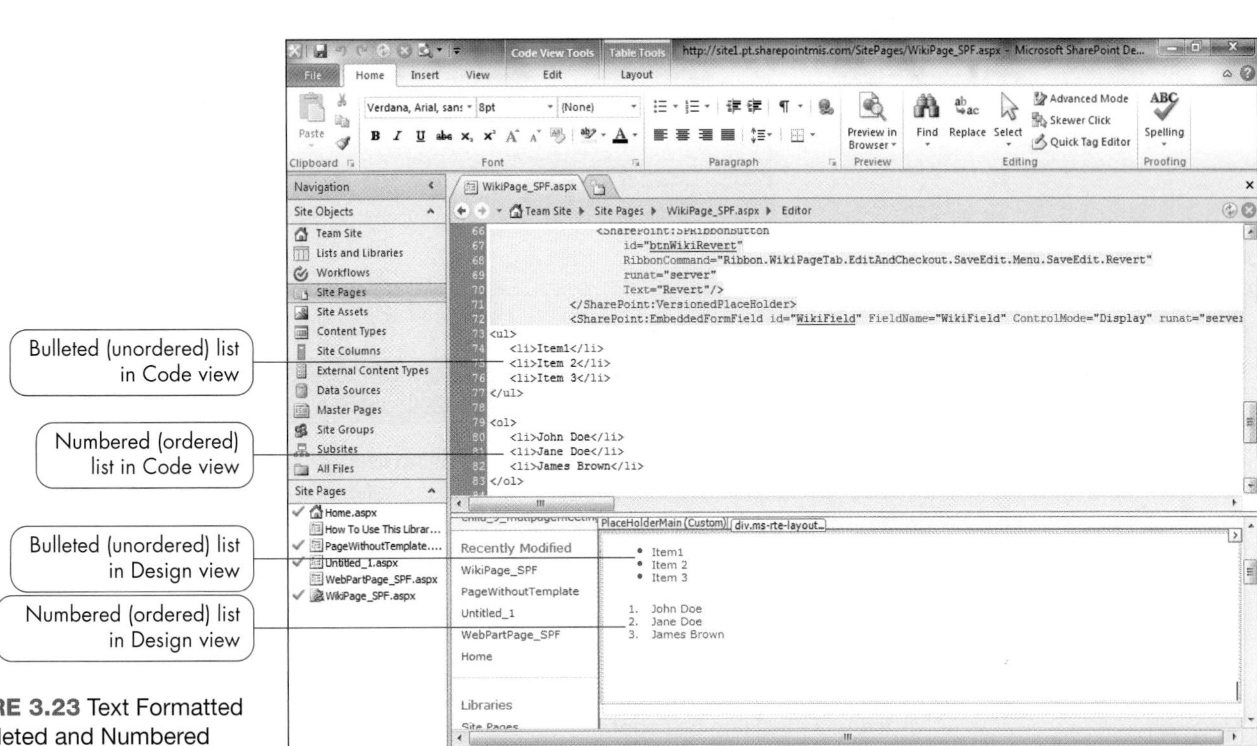

FIGURE 3.23 Text Formatted as Bulleted and Numbered Lists ➤

Among the elements usually preset in a Web page template or included within CSS external style sheets are the small graphics used in bulleted lists. Thus, if a page has an attached template or is linked to a CSS external style sheet, you can create an unordered list that uses the template's preset picture by selecting the text and simply clicking the Bullets arrow in the Paragraph group of the Home tab and selecting a graphic bullet from the list. These buttons apply the list style directly without going through a dialog box, as shown in Figure 3.24.

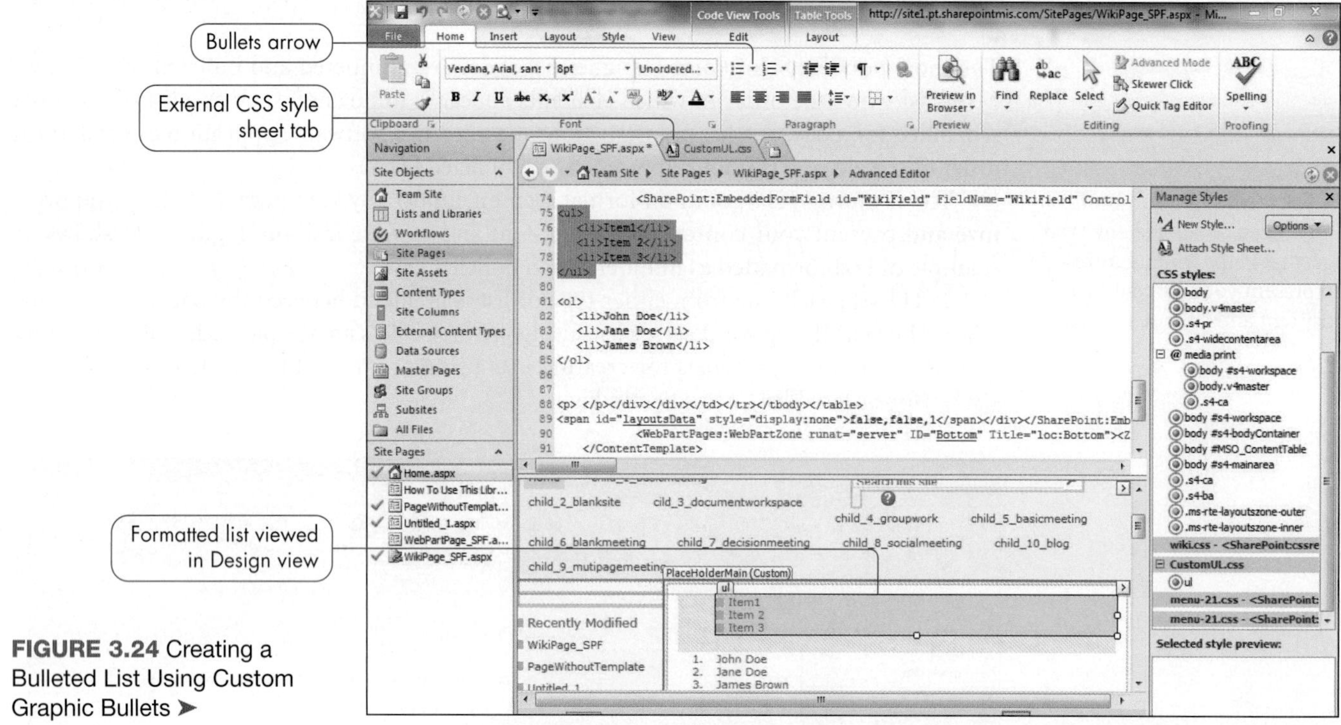

FIGURE 3.24 Creating a Bulleted List Using Custom Graphic Bullets ➤

TIP Styling Lists

You can read more about creating and formatting lists using CSS styles from the W3Schools CSS2 Reference at www.w3schools.com/css/css_reference.asp#list, as well as in Appendix B.

If your Web page does not have an attached template, you can customize a list using the Bullets and Numbering dialog box available from the Paragraph group of the Home tab. Click the Bullet arrow, and then click Picture Bullets to open the dialog box. You can use this dialog box to format your list into a numbered list or a bulleted list using either plain bullets or icons. The dialog box contains the following three tabs:

- Picture Bullets: Use the Picture Bullets tab, as shown in Figure 3.25, to use a graphic as the bullet. Click Specify Picture in the Picture area and click Browse to locate and select the desired picture.

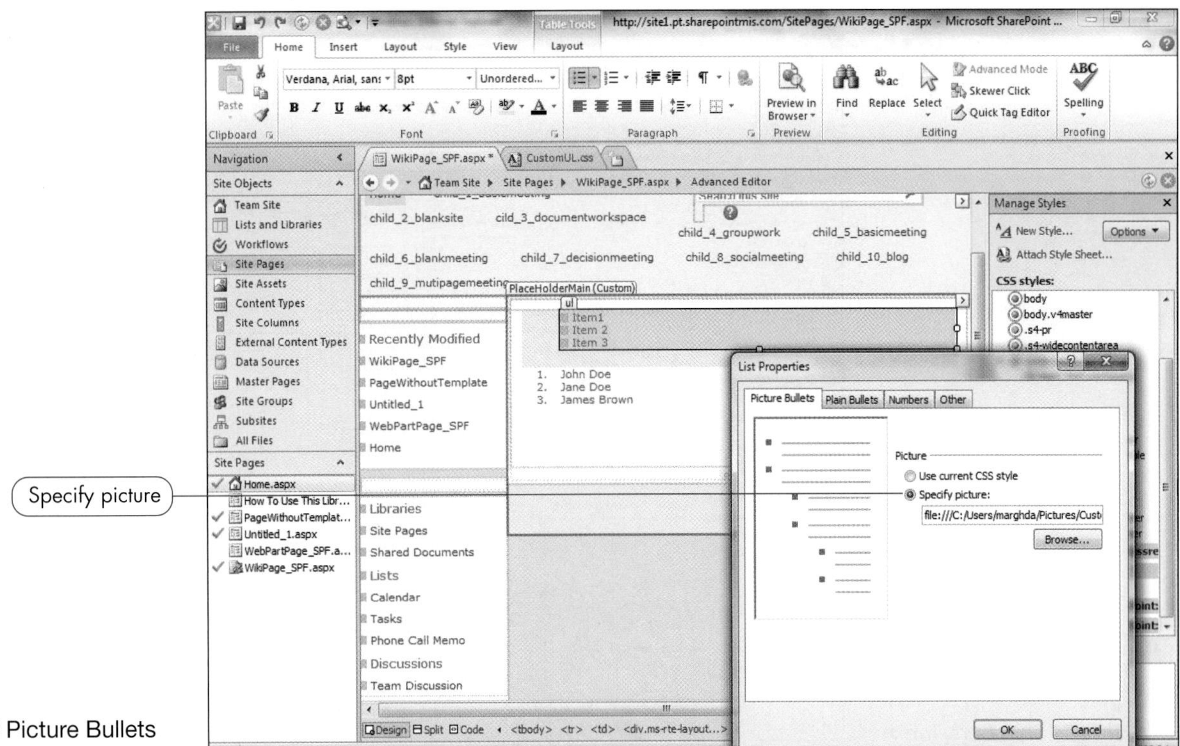

FIGURE 3.25 Picture Bullets Tab ➤

- Plain Bullets: Use the Plain Bullets tab to choose a standard symbol as a bullet, such as a circle, open circle, or square. Click the box for the bullet style you prefer from the styles available, as shown in Figure 3.26.

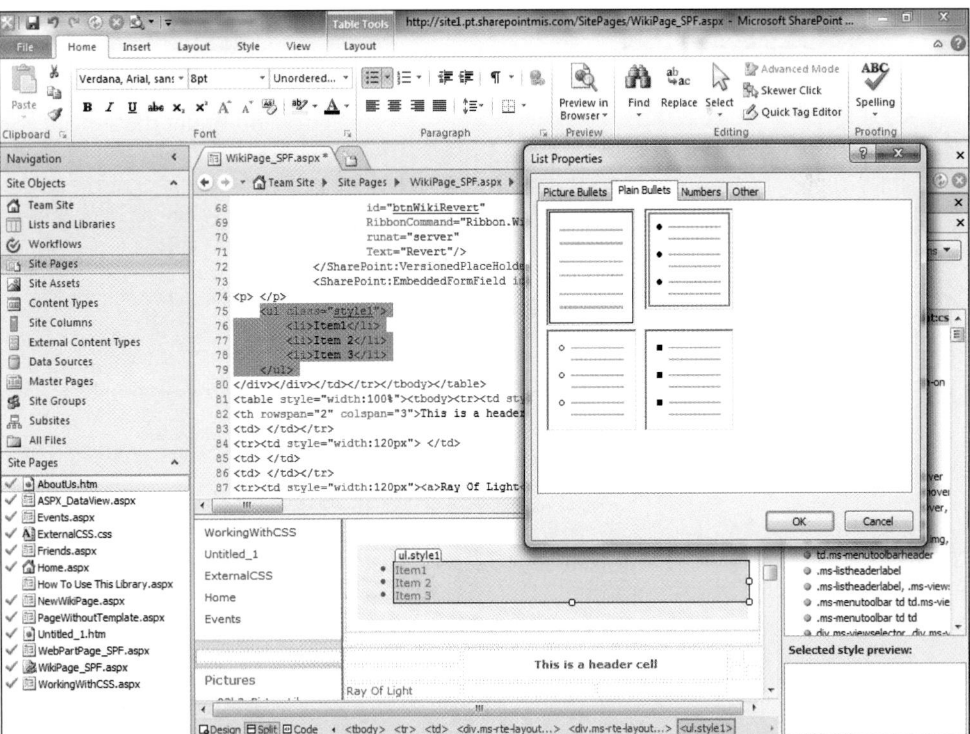

FIGURE 3.26 Plain Bullets Tab ➤

- Numbers: Use the Numbers tab to create an ordered list. You can choose to use consecutive numbers or letters. Click the box of the numbering style you prefer from the styles available, as shown in Figure 3.27. Use the *Start at* box to set the value of the number or letter you want to use as the first item in the list.

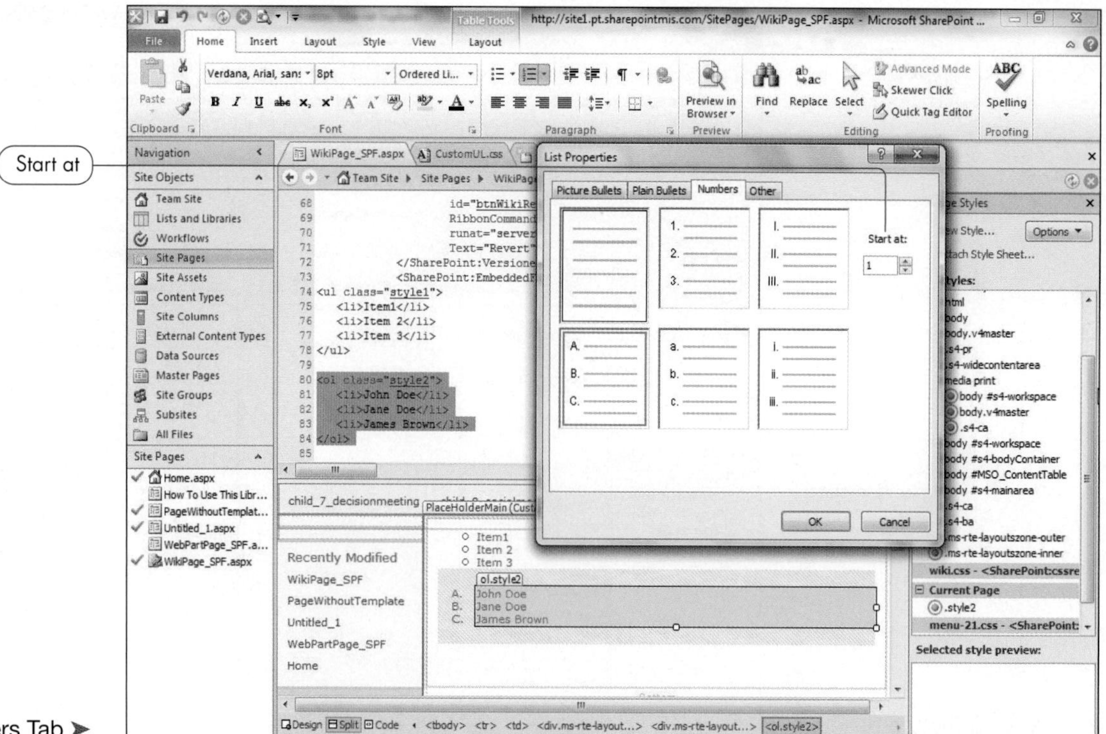

FIGURE 3.27 Numbers Tab ➤

After you have created a list, you can edit it by right-clicking any line of the list, clicking List Properties, and then selecting an option from the List Properties dialog boxes discussed previously. Use the Other tab from the List Properties dialog box to create other types of lists such as the Definition list.

Nested lists are popular features used by Web designers to emphasize text categories and subcategories.

Nested lists are popular features used by Web designers to emphasize text categories and subcategories. In SharePoint Designer, you can create nested lists, including the same styles or different styles of lists. For instance, you can letter the major category and bullet the subcategory, as shown in Figure 3.28.

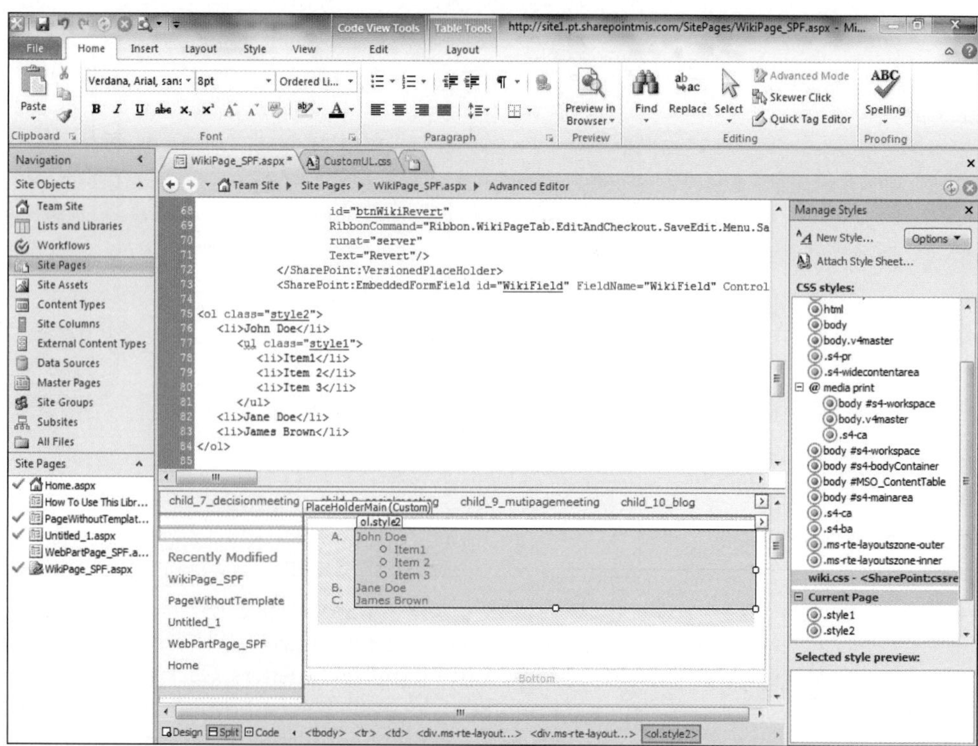

FIGURE 3.28 Nested Lists ➤

Working with Tables and Layout Tables

The fact that tables are supported by all browsers and are similar to the tables used in many other desktop applications makes them attractive to Web designers from beginners to professionals.

Tables have always played an important role in Web development. The fact that tables are supported by all browsers and are similar to the tables used in many other desktop applications makes them attractive to Web designers from beginners to professionals. SharePoint Designer has a comprehensive set of tools for adding and formatting tables.

TIP SharePoint Designer Uses CSS to Create Tables

The Microsoft SharePoint Designer 2010 CSS layout features have replaced the layout tables feature available in previous versions of SharePoint and FrontPage. SharePoint Designer 2010 will open previously created pages with layout tables, and they will function correctly, but you cannot use SharePoint Designer 2010 to create a new layout table. You must use CSS to create new tables.

Create a Standard Table

A **table** is a collection of rows having one or more columns.

A **cell** is the intersection of a column and a row.

A **nested table** is a table inserted within the cell of a table.

A ***table*** is a collection of rows having one or more columns. A ***cell*** is the intersection of a column and a row. A ***nested table*** is a table inserted within the cell of a table. Because tables and cells can have 0-pixel borders, they are not necessarily visible when a Web page is displayed in a browser.

TIP HTML Tables

An HTML table is created using the <table> </table> tag pair. Each row in a table is added using the <tr> </tr> (for table row) tag pair and each cell within a row is added using <td> </td> (for table data) tag pairs for regular cells, or <th> </th> (for table header) tag pairs for header cells. Appendix B introduces you to the HTML tags that are used to create an HTML table.

Before creating a table, consider how many rows and columns you need, the elements that will be placed in the table cells, and the total width and height of the table. SharePoint Designer enables Web designers to establish the size of a table in pixels or as a percentage of the browser window.

TIP Setting the Dimensions of a Table

Setting the dimensions of a table as a percentage of the browser window is highly recommended because it ensures the proper display of all elements included in the table regardless of the size of the browser window.

In the SharePoint Designer Design view, you create a table by clicking Table in the Tables group of the Insert tab. You can also use Table when you are in Code view and Split view.

The **Insert Table grid** is a graphical table that enables you to select the number of rows and columns for your table.

To create a table, click Table on the Insert tab to display the Insert Table grid. The ***Insert Table grid*** is a graphical table that enables you to select the number of rows and columns for your table. If the Insert Table grid displays too few rows or columns, you can add more rows and columns by clicking anywhere within the table grid, and then continuing to move the mouse while keeping the left mouse button pressed. For example, to create a three-row table with three columns, display the Insert Table grid, and then position the arrow mouse pointer in the third column of the third row, as shown in Figure 3.29. Release the mouse to complete the table.

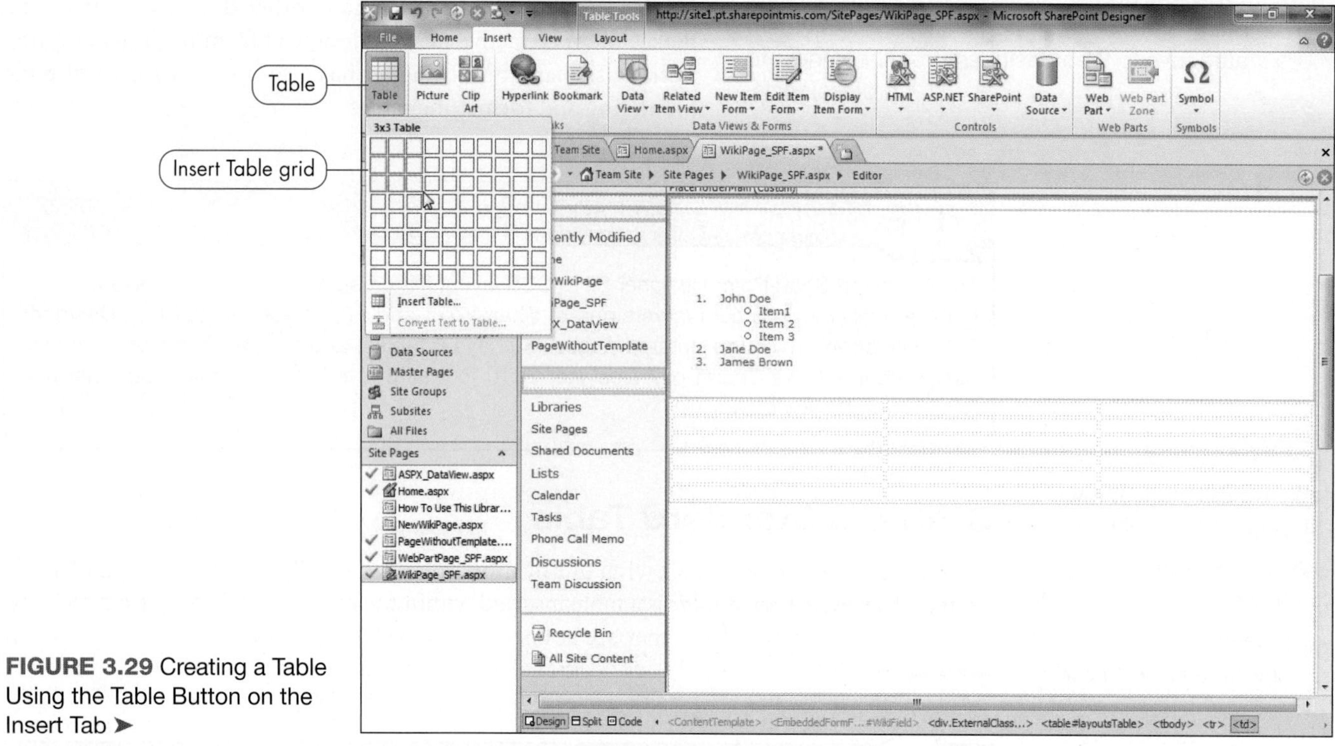

FIGURE 3.29 Creating a Table Using the Table Button on the Insert Tab ➤

Insert Rows and Columns

After inserting a table in a Web page you can always add more rows or columns.

After inserting a table in a Web page, you can always add more rows or columns. Position the insertion point in the last column of the last row, and then press Tab to add another row. You can add more rows and columns anywhere within the table by positioning the insertion point in the desired location, clicking the Table Tools–Layout tab, and then clicking one of the four buttons in the Rows and Columns group: Insert Above, Insert Below, Insert Left, or Insert Right, as shown in Figure 3.30. You can also add more rows and columns anywhere within the table by positioning the insertion point in the desired location, right-clicking, pointing to Insert, and then selecting Rows and Columns to display the Insert Rows and Columns dialog box, also shown in Figure 3.30. Select whether to add Rows or Columns, and then increase the number to match your needs. You also have the option to select the Location of the new rows, either above or below the current selection in the table.

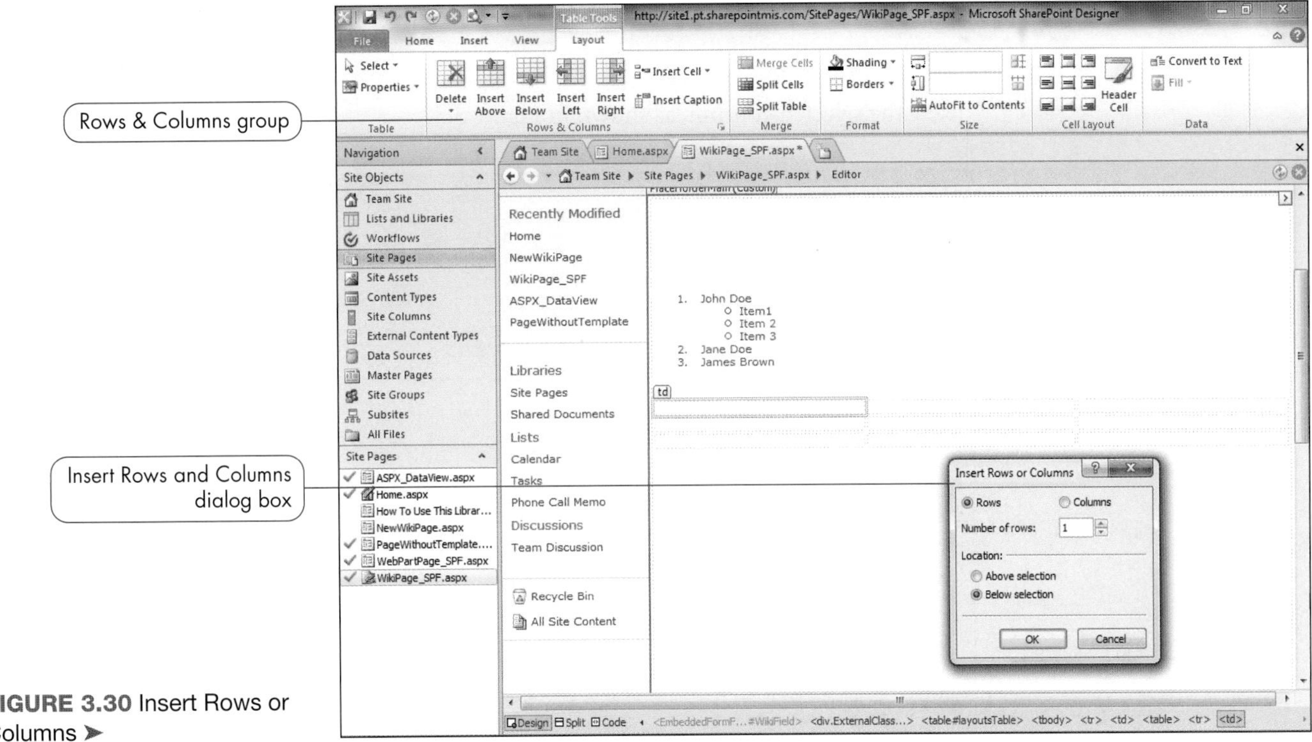

FIGURE 3.30 Insert Rows or Columns ➤

Select and Delete Rows and Columns

... you can delete a row or a column from a table at any time.

As careful as you might be when creating a table or inserting rows or columns into a table, it is only human to make mistakes. Fortunately, you can delete a row or a column from a table at any time. To delete a row, move the mouse pointer over the left border of the row and when the pointer changes into a black arrow, click. The row is selected and highlighted, as shown in Figure 3.31. Right-click anywhere within the selected row, point to Delete, and then click Delete Rows to delete the selected row.

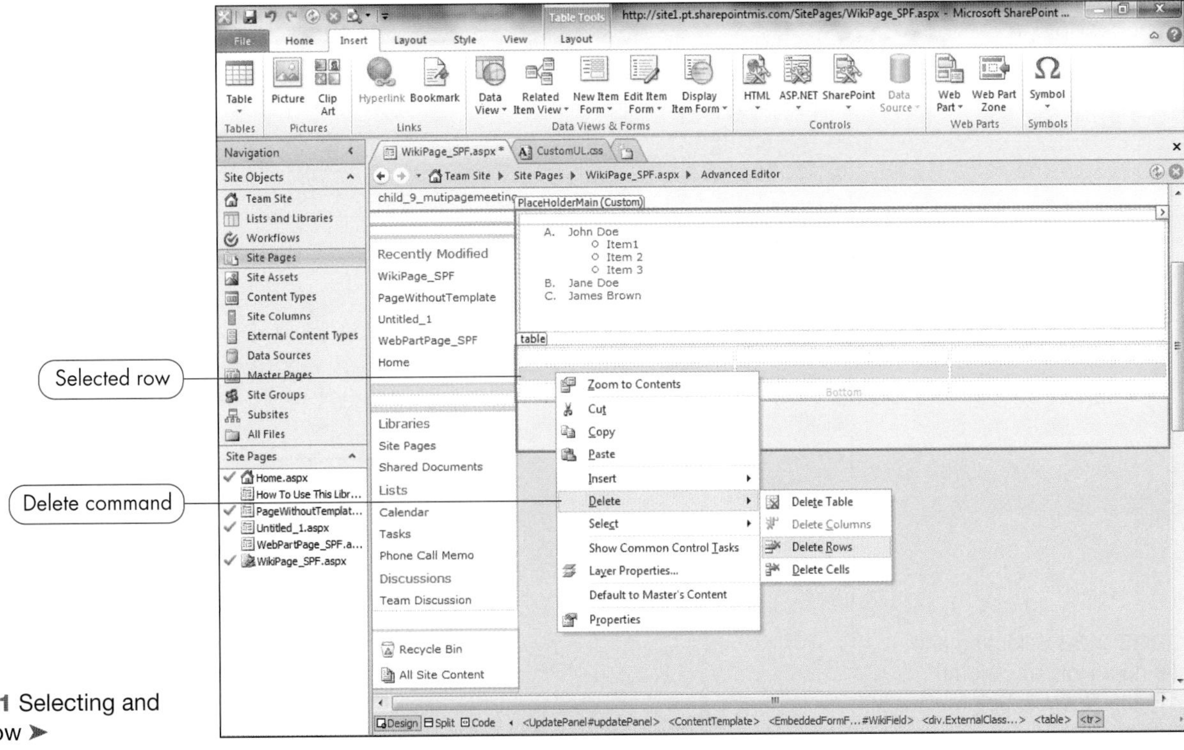

FIGURE 3.31 Selecting and Deleting a Row ➤

To delete a column, position the pointer over the top border of the column and when the pointer changes into a black arrow, click. The column is selected and highlighted. Right-click anywhere within the selected column, select Delete, and then select Delete Columns to delete the selected column, as shown in Figure 3.32.

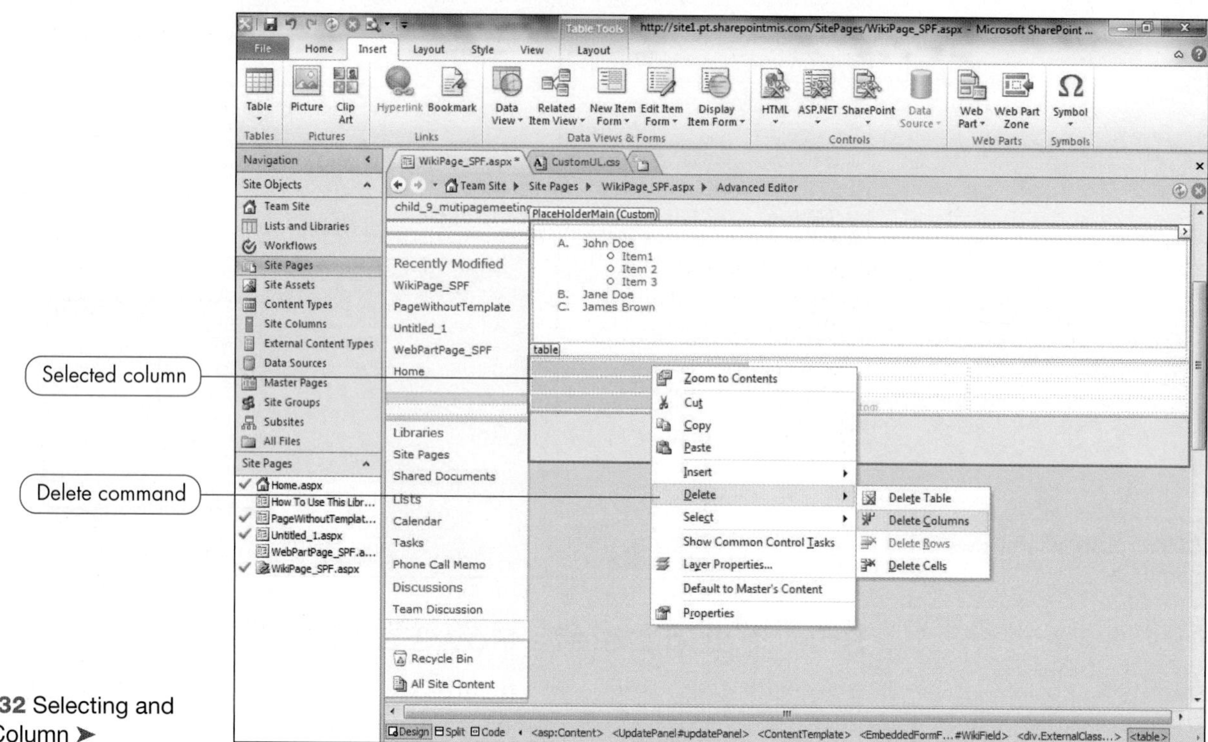

FIGURE 3.32 Selecting and Deleting a Column ➤

Another method of selecting and deleting rows and columns uses the Delete command in the Rows & Columns group of the Table Tools–Layout tab. Select the column or a row you want to delete by positioning the insertion point anywhere within the row or the column, and then click Delete, as shown in Figure 3.33. To delete the selected row or column, click Delete Rows or Delete Columns command as needed.

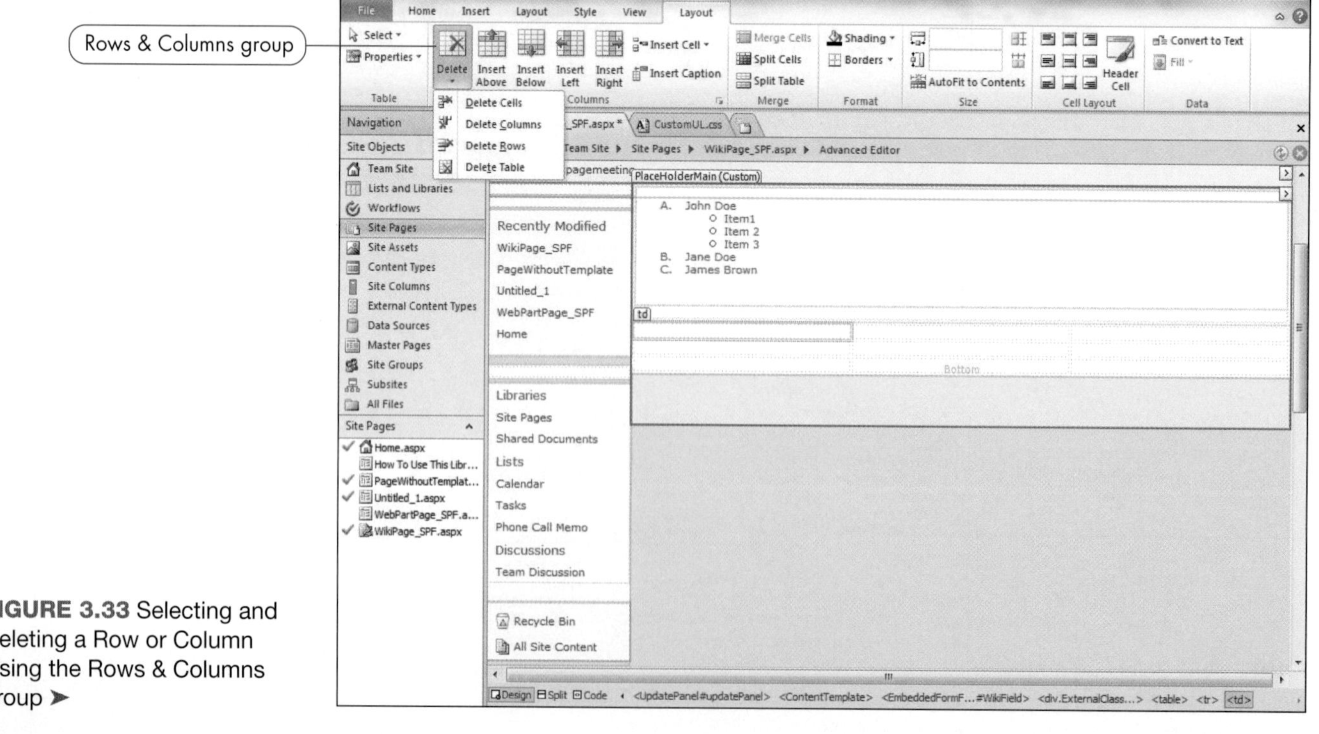

FIGURE 3.33 Selecting and Deleting a Row or Column Using the Rows & Columns group ➤

SharePoint Designer enables you to select multiple rows and columns for deletion. To select multiple, adjacent, or nonadjacent rows or columns, select a row or column, and then select additional rows or columns while pressing Ctrl. Another method for selecting adjacent rows or columns is to drag along the left border (to select rows) or along the top border (to select columns). After rows and columns are selected, press Delete to delete them. After selecting one or more rows or columns, click anywhere in the Web page body outside the table to deselect the rows or columns.

> **TIP Using Undo and Redo**
>
> Another way to eliminate errors when working with tables is to use the Undo feature, which enables you to undo as many as 30 past actions. The Redo feature enables you to restore up to the last 30 changes you made. Undo and Redo commands can be used by clicking Undo and Redo on the Quick Access toolbar.

Enter Data in a Table

As previously discussed in this chapter, you can add text to a Web page in three ways: type directly in the page, copy and paste text into your page, or insert a previously formatted file into your page. You can use the same methods for entering text into a table.

When you want to enter text directly in the cell of a table, you first position the insertion point where you want the text to appear, and then type the text. Press Enter when you want to start a new paragraph or click the Insert tab, click HTML on the Controls group, and then click Break in the *Tags* section of the All HTML Controls, to break the line, as shown in Figure 3.34. You can also create a break by pressing Shift as you press Enter.

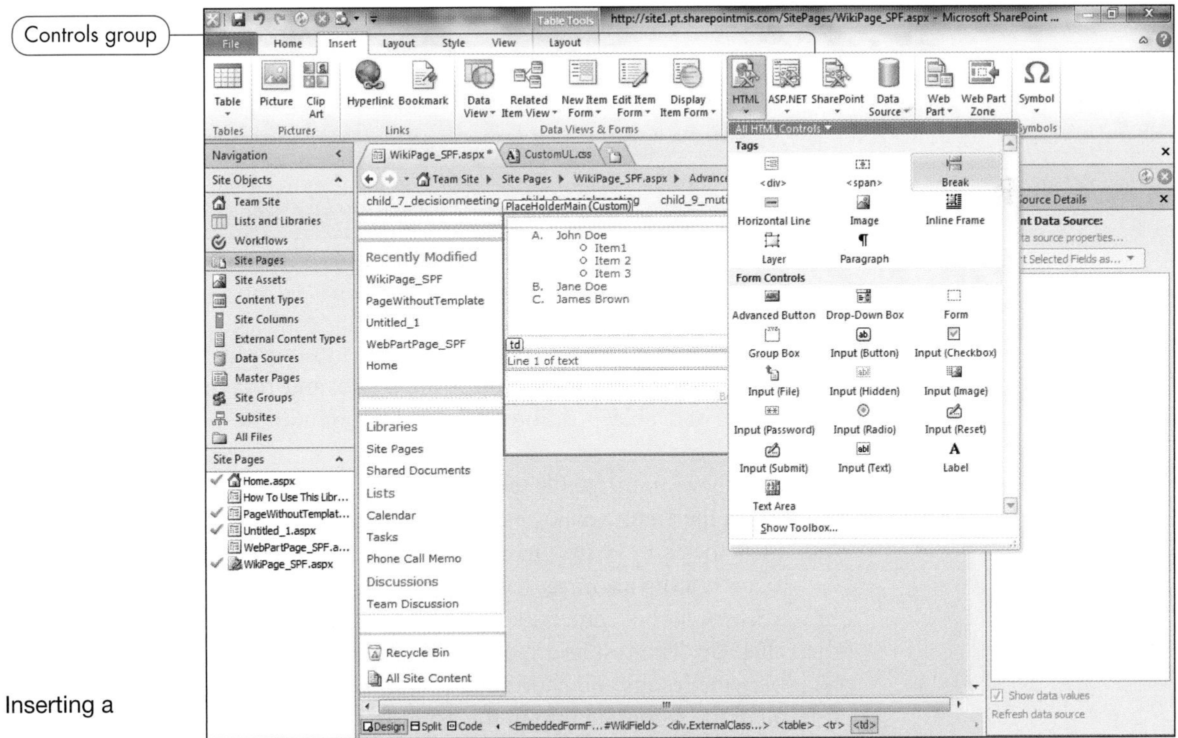

FIGURE 3.34 Inserting a Break ➤

TIP Converting Text to Table

You can also convert an existing table into regular text. This feature is available via the Data group commands on the Table tools tab. When you copy an Excel or Word table and paste it to a Web page, SharePoint Designer automatically converts it into an HTML table. In Chapter 4, you will learn more about how to integrate Excel and Word tables in a Web page.

To copy and paste text into a table cell, copy the text from the original location, and then position the insertion point in the cell where you want the text to appear, right-click, and then click Paste, as shown in Figure 3.35.

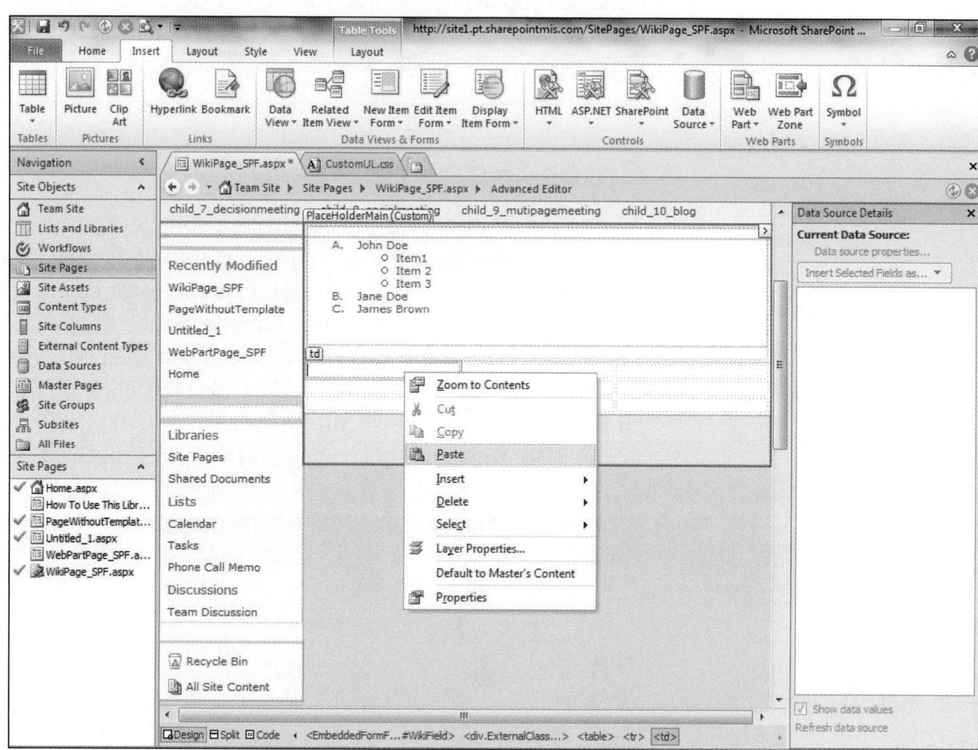

FIGURE 3.35 Pasted Text in a Cell ➤

Insert an Image

You can insert an image from clip art or a file into the cell of a table using the Pictures group of the Insert tab. You can also position, resize, and resample an image. To insert an image into the cell of a table, position the insertion point in the cell in which you want the image to appear.

If you have an image file to place in a cell, such as a .jpg or .gif, click Picture on the Insert tab to open the Picture dialog box. Using the *Look in* list, locate the folder that contains the picture. Click the name of the picture, and then click Insert. The image appears in the table cell.

To insert a clip art image, click Clip Art on the Insert tab to display the Clip Art task pane. In the *Search for* box, enter a keyword that describes the clip that you are searching for, and then click Go. The results are displayed in the Clip Art pane, as shown in Figure 3.36. After reviewing the results and choosing the clip you want, click the arrow that appears on its right side, fill in the requested info in the Accessibility Properties dialog box, and then click OK.

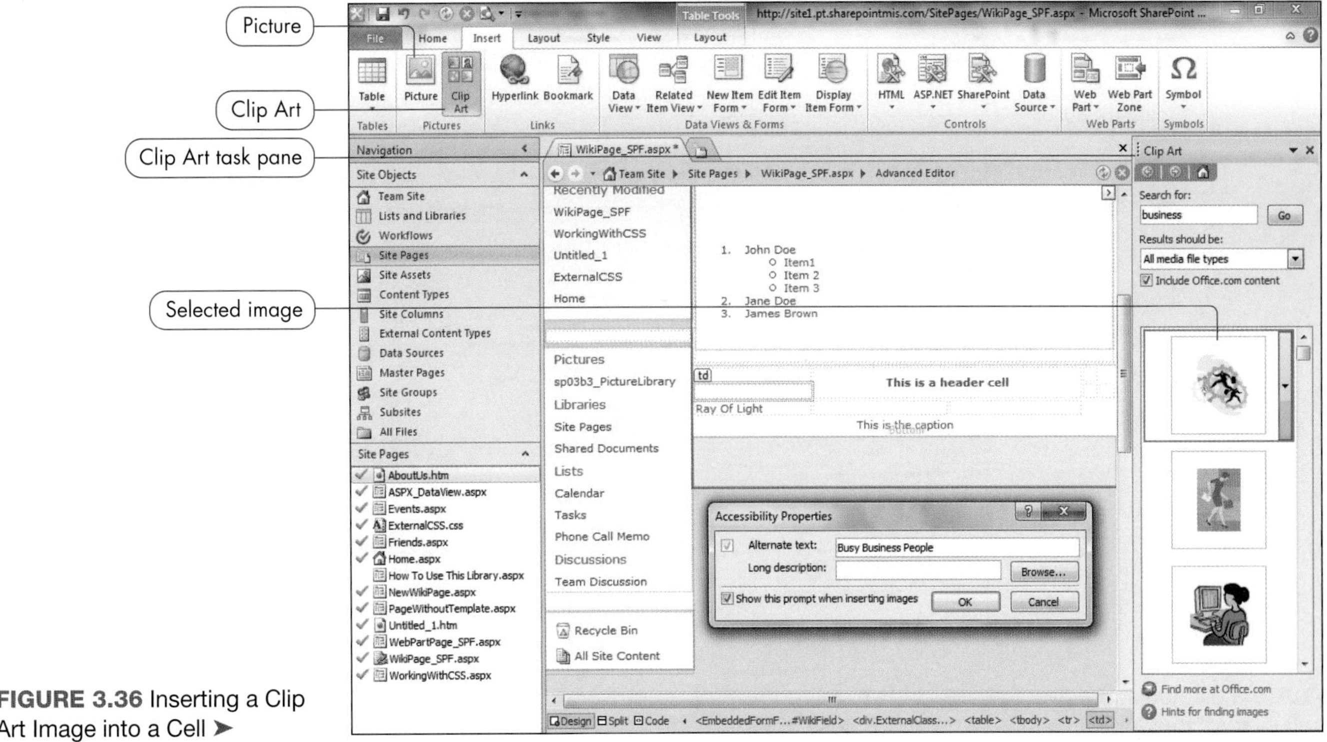

FIGURE 3.36 Inserting a Clip Art Image into a Cell ➤

TIP
Copy and Paste an Image in a Table

Using a procedure similar to copying and pasting text, you can copy and paste an image into the cell of a table.

Add a Table Caption

A caption can be a word or a phrase and, in general, identifies the content of the table.

SharePoint Designer enables you to add a caption to a table. A caption can be a word or a phrase and, in general, identifies the content of the table. By default, the caption is positioned at the top of the table and centered. However, you can position it at the top or bottom of the table, and set the alignment to left, center, right, or justified.

To add a table caption, click anywhere within the table, click the Table Tools–Layout tab, click Insert Caption, and then type the caption text. To change the position of the caption, right-click the caption, and then click Caption Properties to display the Caption Properties dialog box, as shown in Figure 3.37. Select the appropriate option, and then click OK to close the dialog box. To change the alignment of the caption, click the caption, and then click Align Right, Align Left, Align Center, or Justified on the Home tab. To remove a caption, highlight the caption text, right-click, and then click Cut.

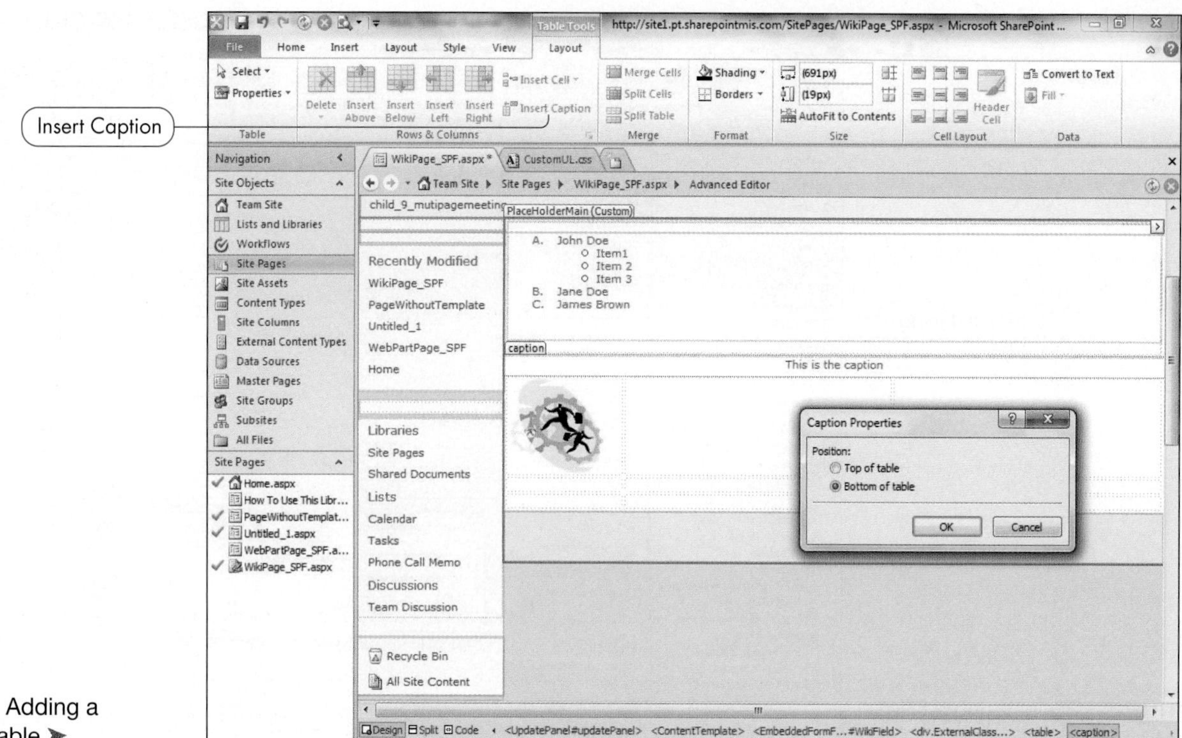

FIGURE 3.37 Adding a Caption to a Table ➤

Edit Table Properties

SharePoint Designer makes it easy to modify tables using the Table Properties dialog box.

It is rather common for a Web designer to change the table and cell properties in the process of developing a table. SharePoint Designer makes it easy to modify tables using the Table Properties dialog box. You can modify the table alignment, width, border size and color, and table background color or background picture, as shown in Figure 3.38, and modify the individual cells in similar ways. Two other common ways in which Web designers modify the structure of a table and further refine the position of elements within the table, are splitting and merging cells, using the Split Cells and Merge Cells commands on the Merge Group of the Table Tools–Layout tab.

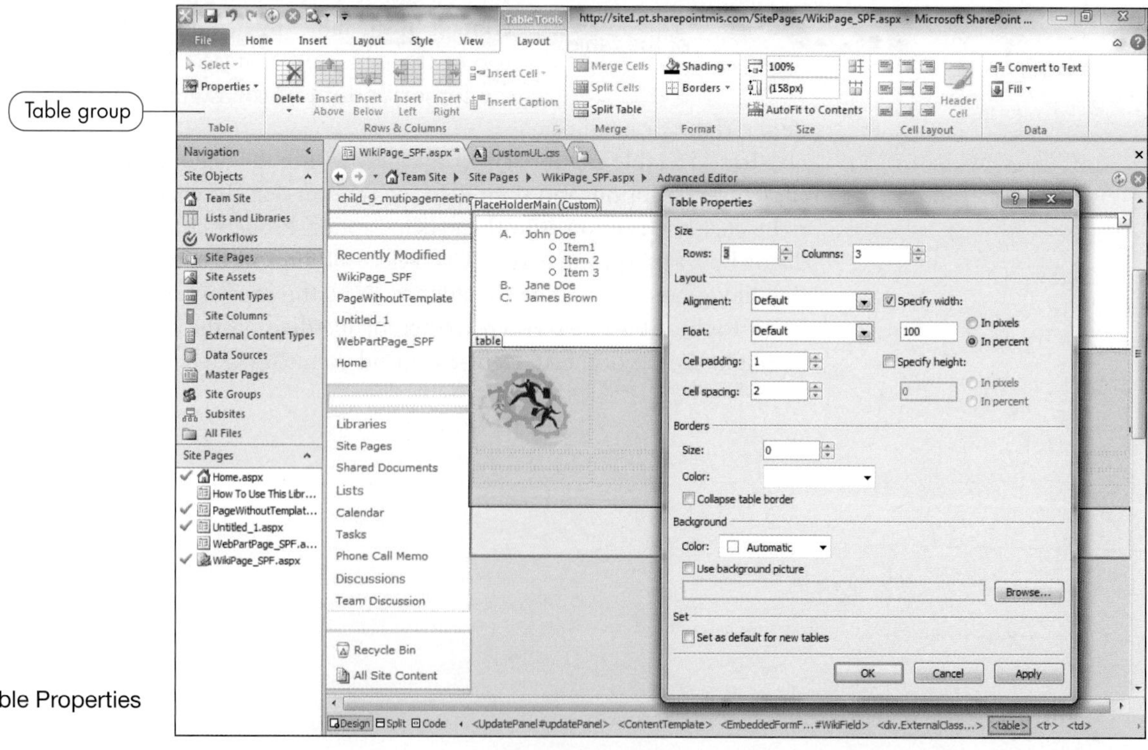

FIGURE 3.38 Table Properties Dialog Box ➤

To edit the properties of a table, click anywhere within the table, click the arrow to the right of Properties in the Table group of the Table Tools–Layout tab, and then select Table to display the Table Properties dialog box. Select the desired properties for the table, and then click OK to close the Table Properties dialog box (see the Reference table below).

REFERENCE Table Properties dialog box

Table Properties Dialog Box Option	Functionality
Size	Size is determined by setting the number of rows and columns.
Alignment	A table that is smaller than 100 percent of the browser window can be aligned left, right, or center. If the default value is selected, the table aligns according to the page content that you place around it.
Float	The way that Web page elements, such as text or graphics, float around a table that is smaller than 100 percent of the browser window.
Cell Padding	In pixels, the amount of empty space surrounding the content of cells.
Cell Spacing	In pixels, the amount of empty space between the cells of a table.
Specify Width and Specify Height	Size of a table in pixels or as a percentage of the browser window.
Borders	Size and color properties of the table border and the color of the light and dark table border. If the Collapse table border option is checked, it enables you to collapse the table border. (A collapsed border uses only one line.) The Collapse table border option might not be available depending on the browser compatibility settings. A setting of 0 removes the border from the browser view of the table (you will see a dotted line).
Background	A color for the table background or a picture for the table background.
Set	You can set your selections to be the default for all new tables.

Edit Cell Properties

In many tables, you want different cells to have different properties. When editing the properties of selected cells, the table-level properties are overridden. To edit the properties of a cell, click the cell you want to change, click the arrow to the left of Properties in the Table group of the Table Tools–Layout tab, and then select Cell to display the Cell Properties dialog box, as shown in Figure 3.39. Select the desired properties for the table cell, and then click OK to close the Cell Properties dialog box. Using the options included in the Cell Properties dialog box, you can modify a wide range of cell properties (see the Reference table on the next page).

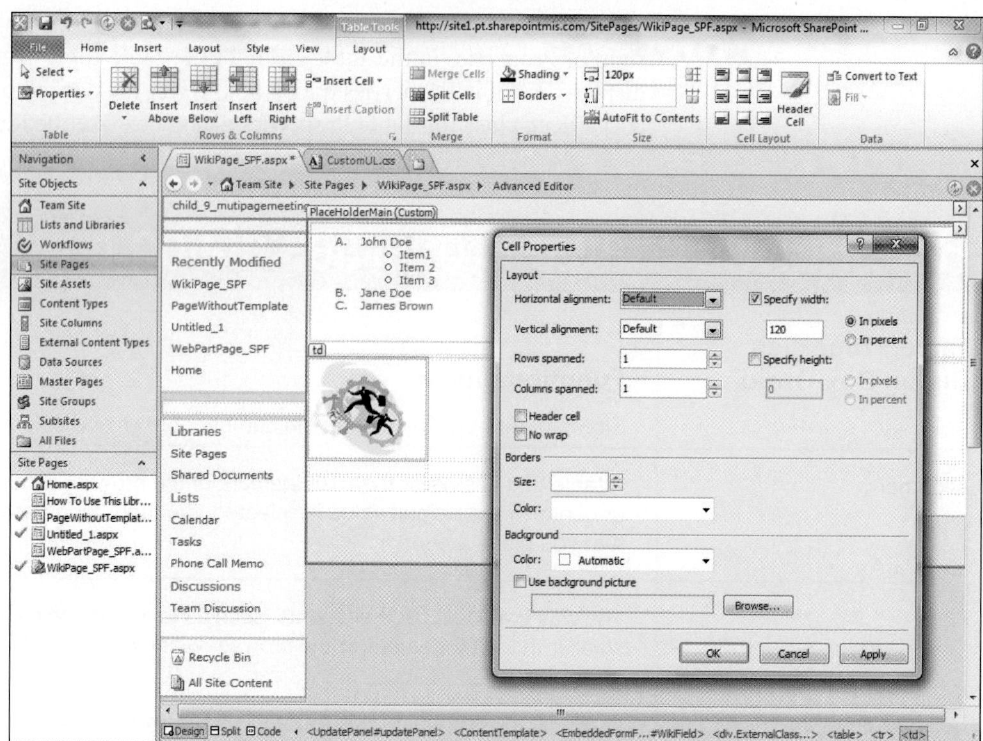

FIGURE 3.39 Cell Properties Dialog Box ➤

REFERENCE Cell Properties Dialog Box

Cell Properties Dialog Box Option	Functionality
Horizontal Alignment	Determines the horizontal alignment of the cell contents (Left, Right, Center, and Justified).
Vertical Alignment	Determines the vertical alignment of the cell contents (Top, Middle, Baseline, and Bottom).
Rows Spanned	Sets the number of rows the cell will span (without deleting any cells), as shown in Figure 3.40.
Columns Spanned	Sets the number of columns the cell will span (without deleting any cells), as shown in Figure 3.40.
Specify Width and Specify Height	Specifies the width and the height of the cell in pixels or as a percentage of the table's total width and height.
Header Cell	Automatically applies a bold and centered format to any text typed within the cell, as shown in Figure 3.40.
No Wrap	Prevents cell contents from wrapping, which results in the cell expanding to fit the contents inserted in the cell.
Borders Color	Defines the color of the cell borders, including Light border and Dark border settings.
Background Color	Changes the background color of a cell (the default background color is white).
Use Background Picture	Enables you to use a picture as the cell background.

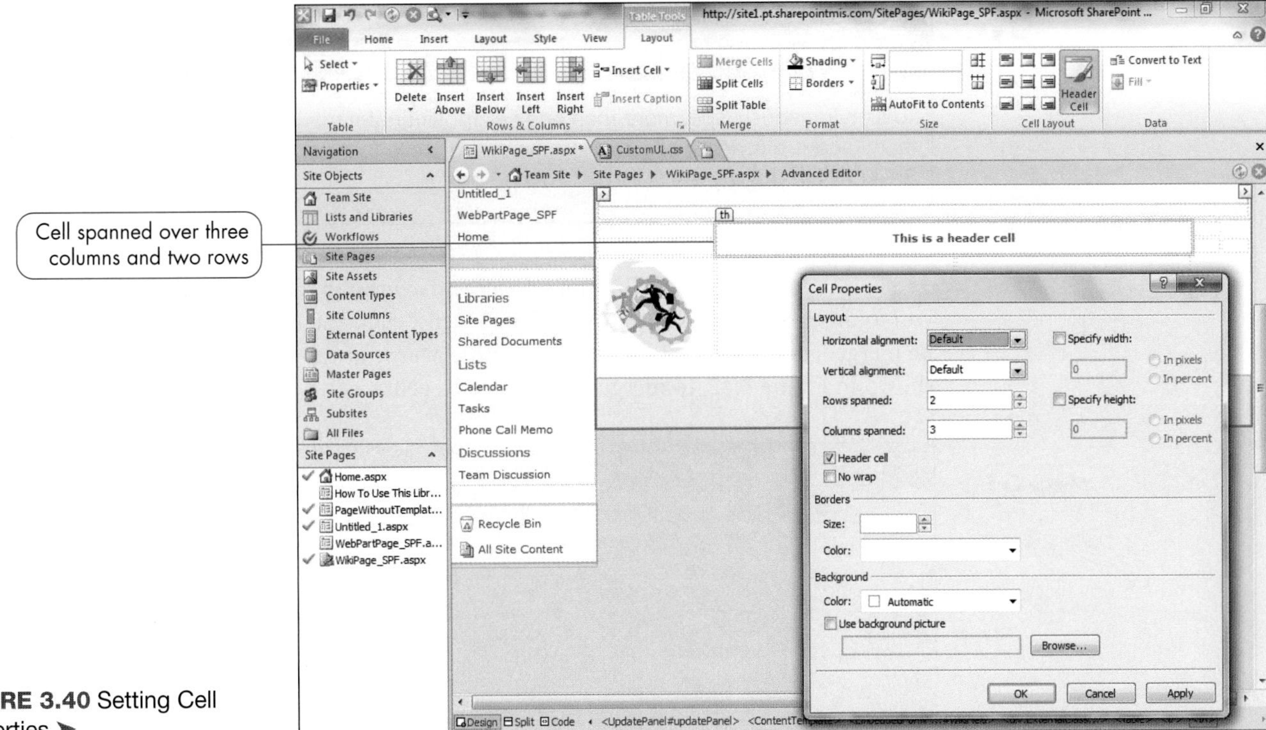

FIGURE 3.40 Setting Cell Properties ➤

Split and Merge Cells

Web designers commonly choose to split or merge cells to position elements within a table.

Web designers commonly choose to split or merge cells to position elements within a table. Theoretically, you can split a cell into as many distinct cells as needed. Likewise, you can merge as many distinct cells as needed into one combined cell.

To split a cell, click anywhere inside it, and then click Split Cells on the Merge group of the Table Tools–Layout tab to display the Split Cells dialog box, as shown in Figure 3.41. Click the Split into Columns or Split into Rows option, as needed, and then choose the number of rows or columns to split. Click OK to close the Split Cells dialog box.

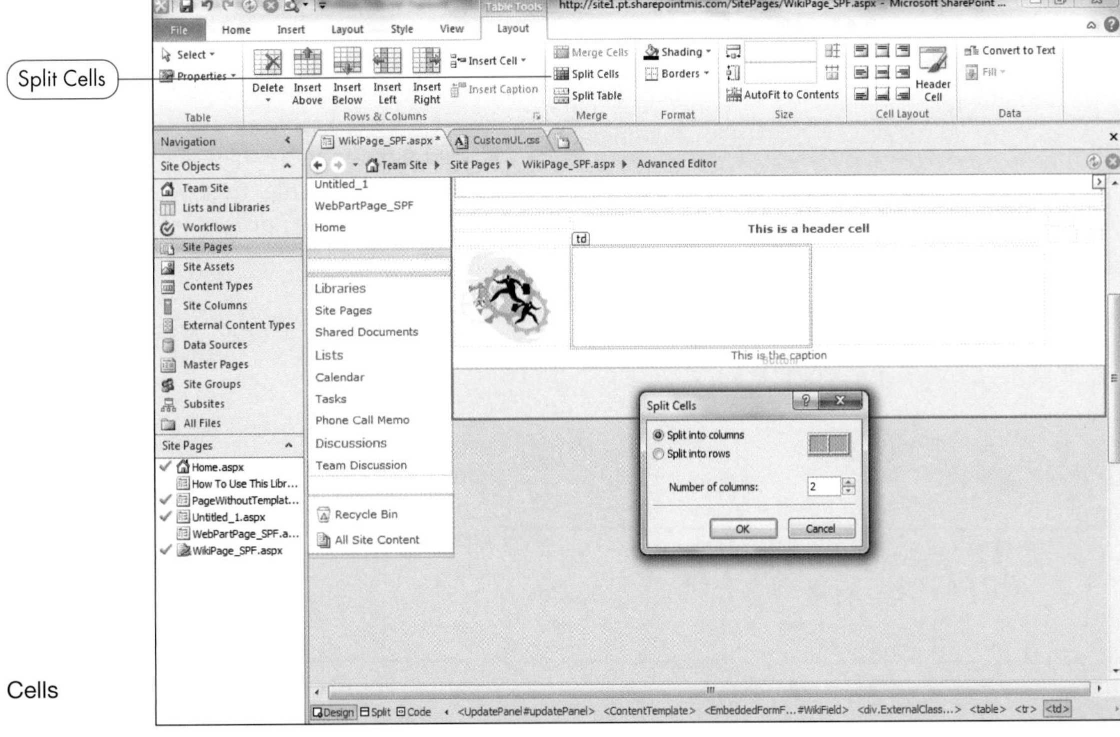

FIGURE 3.41 Split Cells Dialog Box ➤

> **TIP Split Multiple Cells**
>
> To simultaneously split more than one cell, position the mouse in the first cell, press Ctrl, and then keep it pressed while clicking the rest of cells to be split. After selecting the cells, click Split cells to display the Split Cells dialog box.

For a more precise positioning of elements within a table, SharePoint Designer enables you to merge adjacent table cells. To merge cells, click and drag the mouse across the cells to be merged, and then click Merge Cells in the Merge group of the Table Tools–Layout tab, as shown in Figure 3.42, to merge all the selected cells.

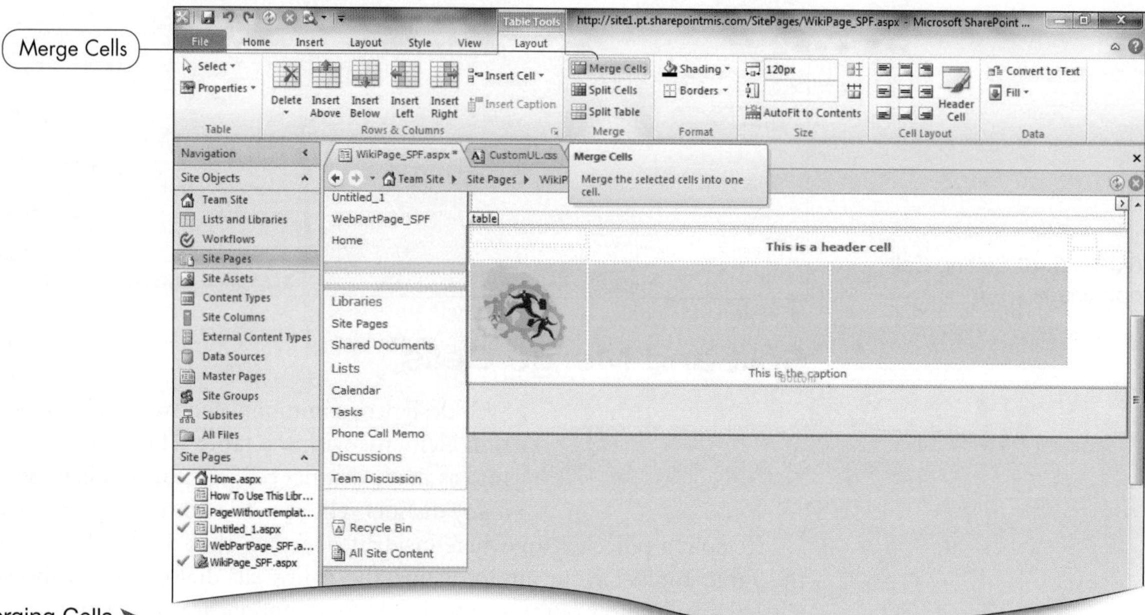

FIGURE 3.42 Merging Cells ➤

Nested Tables

Nested tables are used by Web designers to further refine the position of elements within a Web page.

Nested tables are used by Web designers to further refine the position of elements within a Web page. Theoretically, you can insert a nested table in any cell of a table, but in reality, you should not add more than one or two nested levels of tables. To insert a nested table, first position the insertion point in the desired location (cell) and follow the regular procedure for creating a table. Figure 3.43 shows a nested table.

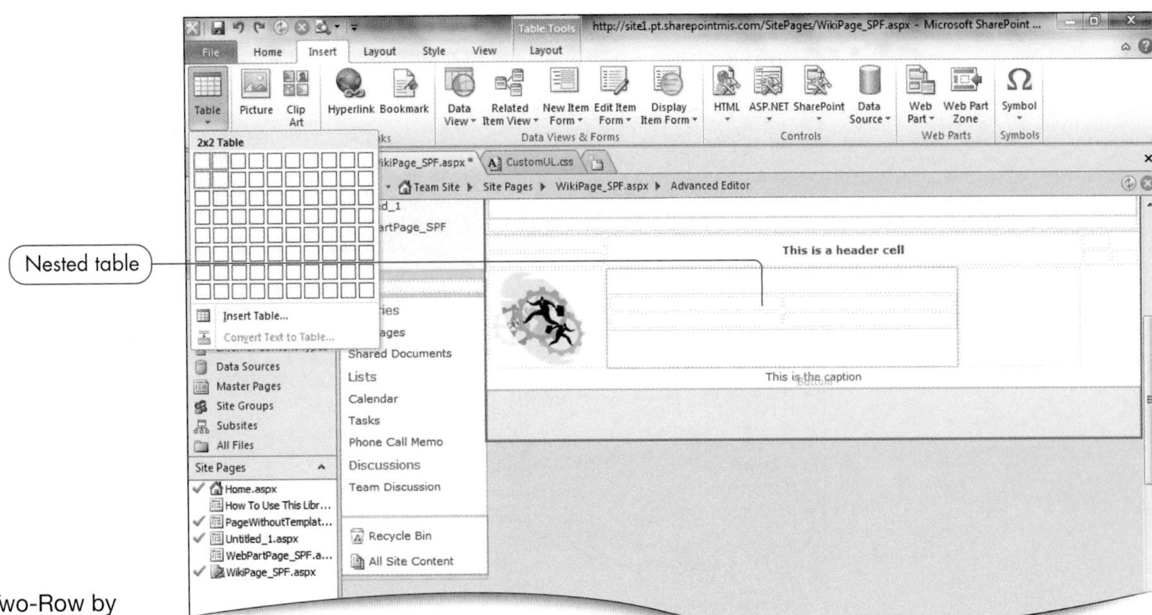

FIGURE 3.43 Two-Row by Two-Column Nested Table ➤

Select and Delete Tables

To select a table, right-click anywhere within the table, click the arrow to the right of Select on the Table Tools–Layout tab, and then click Table, as shown in Figure 3.44. All of the table's cells are automatically highlighted (selected), including any nested tables. If you click within a nested table, only the nested table is selected.

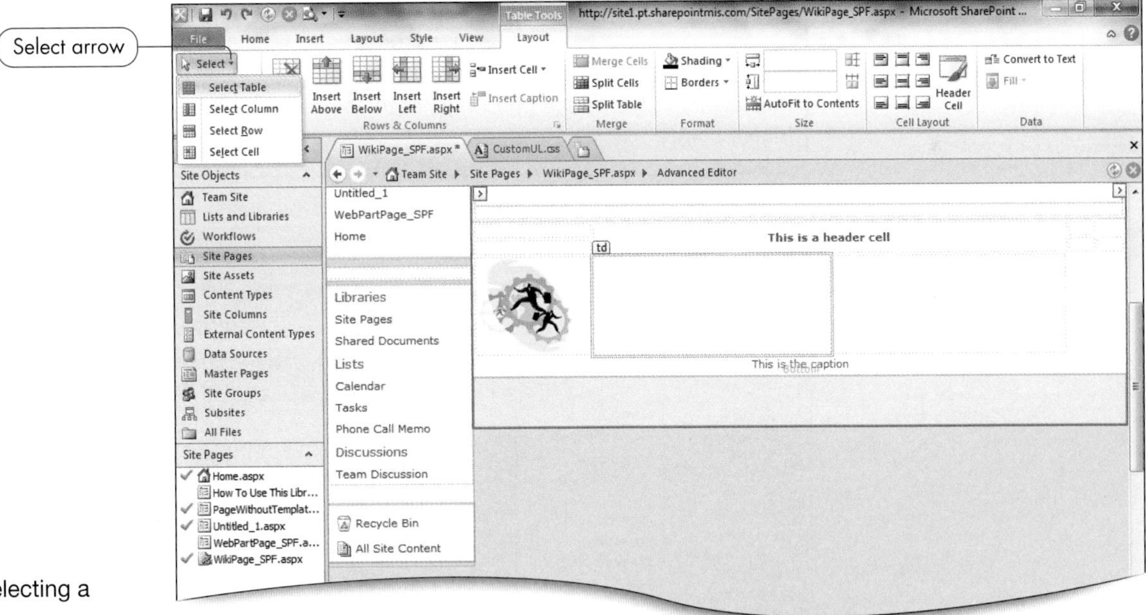

FIGURE 3.44 Selecting a Table ➤

> **TIP** Dragging a Table
>
> After a table is selected, you can click and hold the pointer anywhere on the table, and then drag it anywhere you want within the Web page.

If you want to delete the selected table, click within the table, click Delete in the Rows & Columns group, and then select Delete Table, as shown in Figure 3.45.

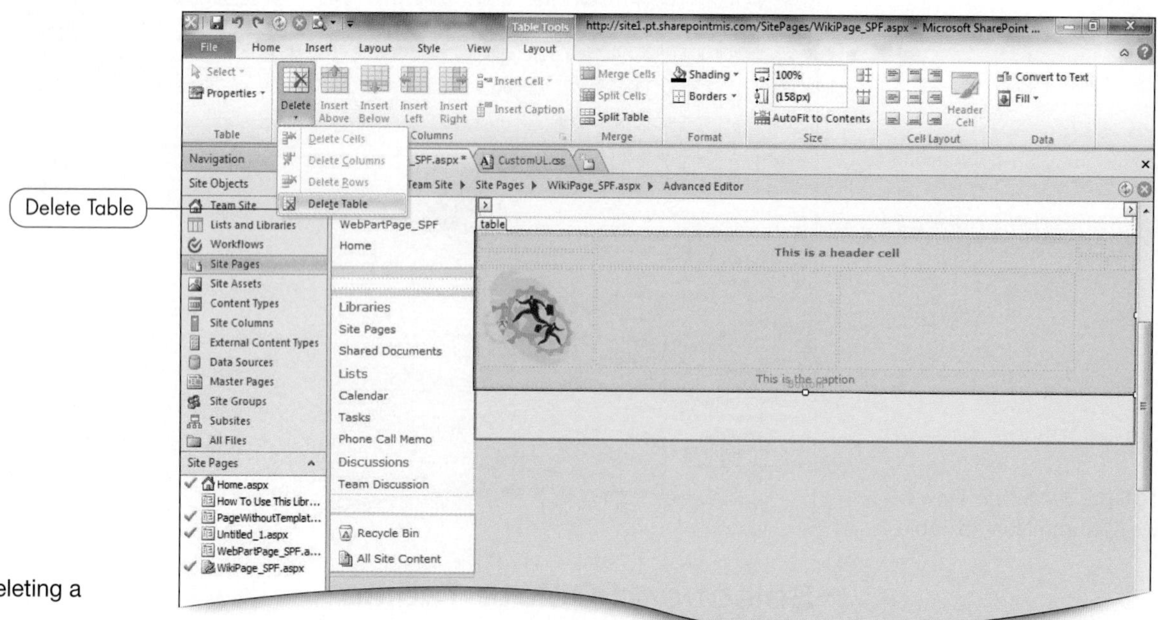

FIGURE 3.45 Deleting a Table ➤

TIP Quick Tag Selector

You can also select a table, row, cell, or nested table using the Quick Tag Selector. When you click a tag on the Quick Tag Selector, its color automatically changes, depending on the color scheme, and the corresponding table, row, cell, or nested table is selected. Click the arrow at the right of each tag when you point to it, and then click Tag Properties on the menu that is displayed to change the properties of the element that corresponds to that tag, as shown in Figure 3.46.

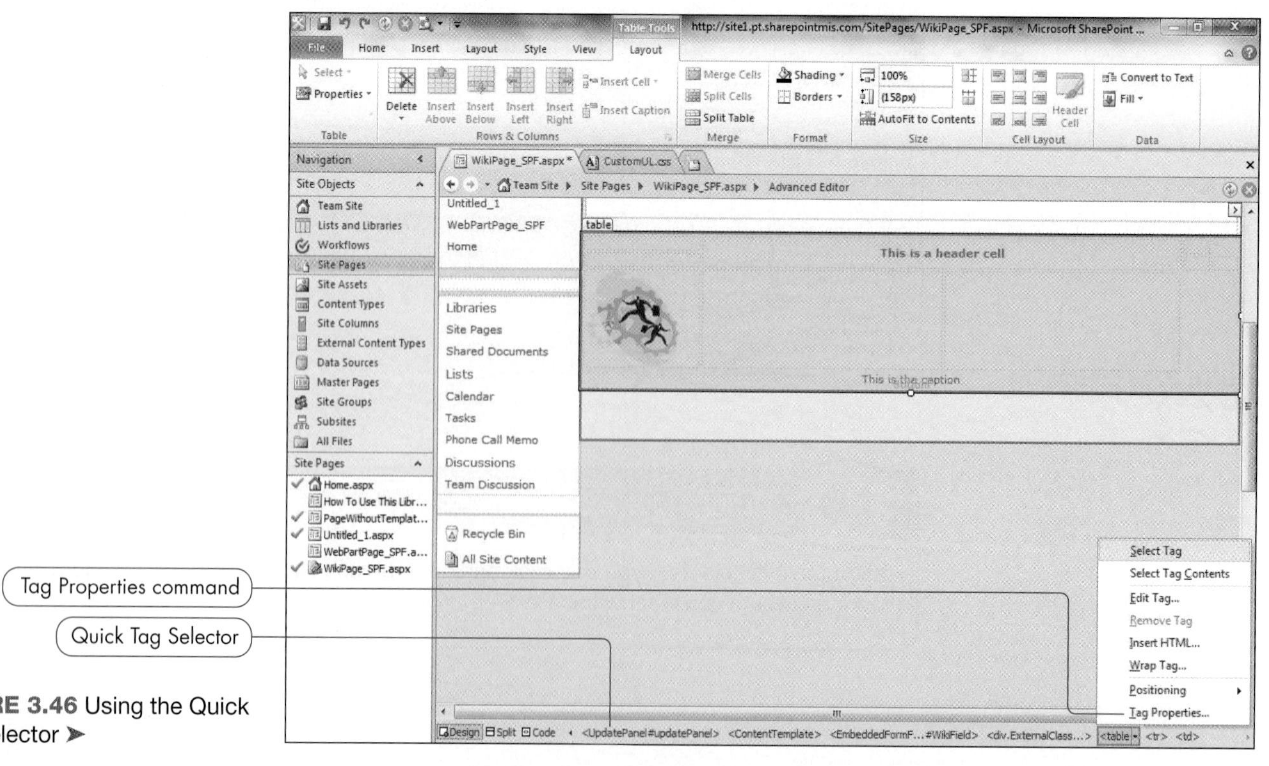

FIGURE 3.46 Using the Quick Tag Selector ➤

TIP Accessible Tables

Two major requirements exist for building accessible tables in compliance with the W3C requirements: identify row and column headers by placing them in the first row and first column, and use the <th> tag for all header cells. To read more about building accessible tables, visit the W3C Web site (www.w3.org/) and search the Web site for "accessible tables." Appendix B will provide you with more information as well.

Enhance a Web Page Using Graphics and Multimedia

> As a great Web developer, you need good computer knowledge, practical skills, the imagination of Picasso, and the clear vision of Leonardo DaVinci.

SharePoint empowers Web designers to increase the attractiveness of their Web sites by using graphics and multimedia elements. As a great Web developer, you need good computer knowledge, practical skills, the imagination of Picasso, and the clear vision of Leonardo DaVinci. Web designers need to balance the demanding requirements of developing highly technical, usable, accessible, and attractive Web pages. (Appendix C includes the top 10 do's and don'ts of Web design, along with references to a few great Web sites that synthesize these tips.) When combining these elements, Web designers follow a set of Web style guidelines including, but not limited to, the following recommendations:

- Use graphic, audio, and video files only when they support your Web page's message. Overusing such files makes your Web pages cumbersome and difficult to navigate.
- As a general rule, audio files should not be used as background sound for your Web pages. Many Web page visitors find it irritating to have background sound.
- Provide captions or transcripts of relevant audio content.
- Provide text or audio descriptions for relevant video content.
- When using graphics, keep in mind that people with different visual impairments might not be able to see every graphic. Consider including brief paragraphs describing the information that the graphics convey, as recommended by Access Board Section 508 standards (http://www.access-board.gov/508.htm). For image maps, consider assigning text to each hot spot.
- Avoid graphic animations that run continuously because they distract and irritate Web site visitors.
- Do not include large multimedia files on the main page. Larger files should appear on secondary pages that users can access from the main pages of your site.
- Give users a clear idea about the content of multimedia files before they begin to download them. Include descriptive information about the multimedia files, on the main page, with previews such as still shots from the video. List the run time for media, and the file size for downloadable materials.
- Clearly explain the software requirements for accessing the multimedia files, such as media players, and provide a download link to the software.
- Store audio and video files on a streaming media server, which is a server that ensures high quality when delivering audio and video files via the Internet. Such servers enable users to quickly load and play these files in a browser.

In this section, you will learn about adding graphics to SharePoint pages and using video and audio files to enhance pages.

Adding Graphics to a Web Page

Now that you know how to create a Web site and a Web page, you are ready to learn how to enhance a Web site using Clip Art and images from files, position and format the images, add links to images, and create thumbnails and image maps. Later in this chapter, you will learn how to add graphics to a Web page using Web Parts. The following two image file formats are supported by most Web browsers:

Graphics Interchange Format (GIF) supports transparent colors, is most often used to create animated images, can display only 256 colors, and tends to have large file sizes compared, for example, to the Joint Photographic Experts Group (JPEG) format. Animated GIFs combine several images and display them one after the other in rapid succession.

Joint Photographic Experts Group (JPEG) does not support animation and transparent colors, displays all 17.6 million colors that are available in the color palette, and uses an image compression algorithm.

Portable Network Graphics (PNG) supports transparent colors, can be used for animated graphics and can display all 17.6 million colors available in the color palette, but is not yet fully supported by all browsers.

Interlacing is a technology used for displaying images in stages.

Adobe Flash is a popular application used to create Flash-animated graphics.

- ***GIF (Graphics Interchange Format)*** GIF files are most often used for drawn graphics and are still the preferred standard. GIFs are often used for animated images. You can easily create animated GIFs by combining several images and displaying them one after the other in rapid succession. You can create these animations using most graphic applications, including many of the graphic and animation programs that can be downloaded from the Internet for free. GIFs support transparent colors, which you can use to simulate motion. However, there are some drawbacks to using GIFs. They can display only 256 colors and tend to have large file sizes. The large file size can increase the time required to display GIFs in a browser.
- ***JPEG (Joint Photographic Experts Group)*** JPEGs can display all 17.6 million colors that are available in the color palette, and JPEG is the format most often used for photographs. JPEGs use an image compression algorithm. Although increasing the degree of compression can considerably reduce the file size, it often reduces the quality of the image. Another drawback of JPEGs is that they do not support animation and transparent colors.

A more recent graphic file format, called ***Portable Network Graphics (PNG)***, is becoming popular and might eventually replace the GIF file format. PNGs can be used for animated graphics. They support transparent colors and can display all 17.6 million colors available in the color palette. Unfortunately, older browsers do not support the new PNG format, which causes some compatibility problems.

Interlacing is a technology used for displaying images in stages. For example, every third line of the image is displayed, then every fifth line, followed by every sixth line, and so on until the whole image is displayed. This technology can be used with GIF, JPEG, and PNG files on the Internet, which enables users (especially those with a slow connection) to get a general idea of what the image is going to look like before it is fully displayed.

More and more Web sites include Adobe Flash (or simply Flash) multimedia content, usually for animated graphics. ***Adobe Flash*** is a popular application used to create Flash-animated graphics. To view a Flash-animated graphic, the user needs the Flash player, which can be downloaded free of charge from the Adobe Web site (www.adobe.com/products/flashplayer/). SharePoint supports Flash files.

> **TIP** BMP, XPM, and XBM Images and Browsers
>
> BMP, XPM, and XBM images can cause some cross-browser problems. Of these three graphic file formats, Internet Explorer can display graphic files only in the BMP format. Consequently they are not commonly used in Web design.

The **Clip Art task pane** provides you with media files, generically called clips, stored in a comprehensive group of collections.

Images affect the content, style, and online performance of your Web page. When choosing images that you want to add to a Web page, never forget that each image you add increases the amount of time required for the Web page to display on your visitors' browsers. The Pictures group of the SharePoint Designer Insert tab includes commands through which you can insert a Clip Art image, or an image from a file. The Media group of the SharePoint Foundation Insert tab includes commands through which you can insert a picture From Computer (a file on the local computer) or From Address (from a URL).

Using the SharePoint Designer ***Clip Art task pane***, you can insert a wide variety of media files, generically called clips. These clips are stored in a comprehensive group of col-

Office Collections includes media files stored in the Office Collections folder when SharePoint Designer was installed.

Web Collections includes media files downloaded from the Web and stored in the Web Collections folder.

My Collections includes your personal collection of media files.

lections that include the ***Office Collections*** (media files stored in the Office Collections folder when SharePoint Designer was installed), the ***Web Collections*** (media files downloaded from the Web and stored in the Web Collections folder), and ***My Collections*** (your personal collection of media files). Click the Insert tab, and then click Clip Art in the Pictures group to display the Clip Art task pane used to search for and insert a clip. Type a keyword that describes the clip you want in the *Search for* box, and then click Go. The results are displayed in the Clip Art task pane. After browsing the results and choosing the clip you want, click the arrow on the right side of the clip, and then click Insert on the displayed menu. If the Accessibility Properties dialog box is displayed, as shown in Figure 3.47, type concise descriptive text in the Alternate text box, and then click OK to close the dialog box.

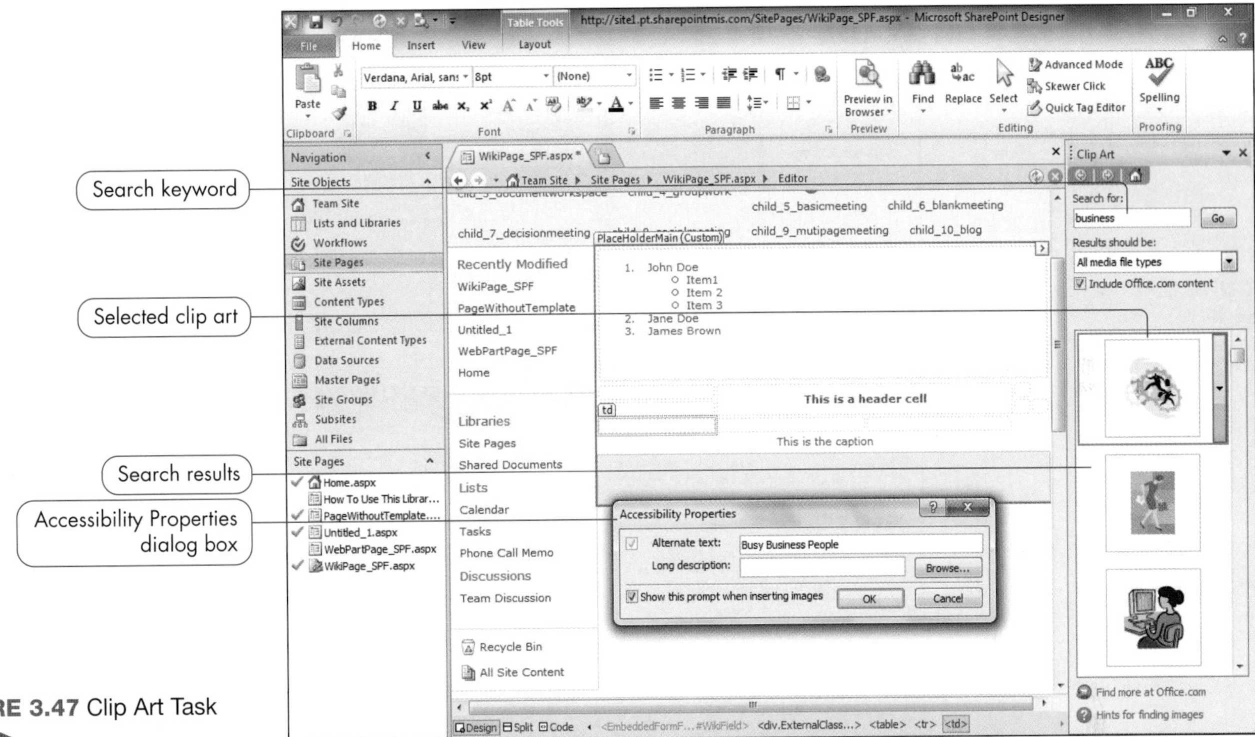

FIGURE 3.47 Clip Art Task Pane ➤

TIP Clip Art Online

You can always find more images by using the Find more at Office.com link at the bottom of the Clip Art pane. That link opens the Microsoft Office Clip Art and Media Home Page in your default browser. From there, you can search for, preview, and download more clips.

In addition to Clip Art media you can also use graphics, photographs, and videos that have been captured and stored as files on your local computer. To insert a picture from a file, click Picture in the Pictures group of the Insert tab to open the Picture dialog box. Using the *Look in* list, navigate to locate the folder that contains the media. Click the name of the media you want, and then click Insert, as shown in Figure 3.48. If the Accessibility Properties dialog box appears, type concise descriptive text in the Alternate text box, and then click OK to close the dialog box. The media appears on the body of your Web page, as shown in Figure 3.49.

FIGURE 3.48 Picture Dialog Box ➤

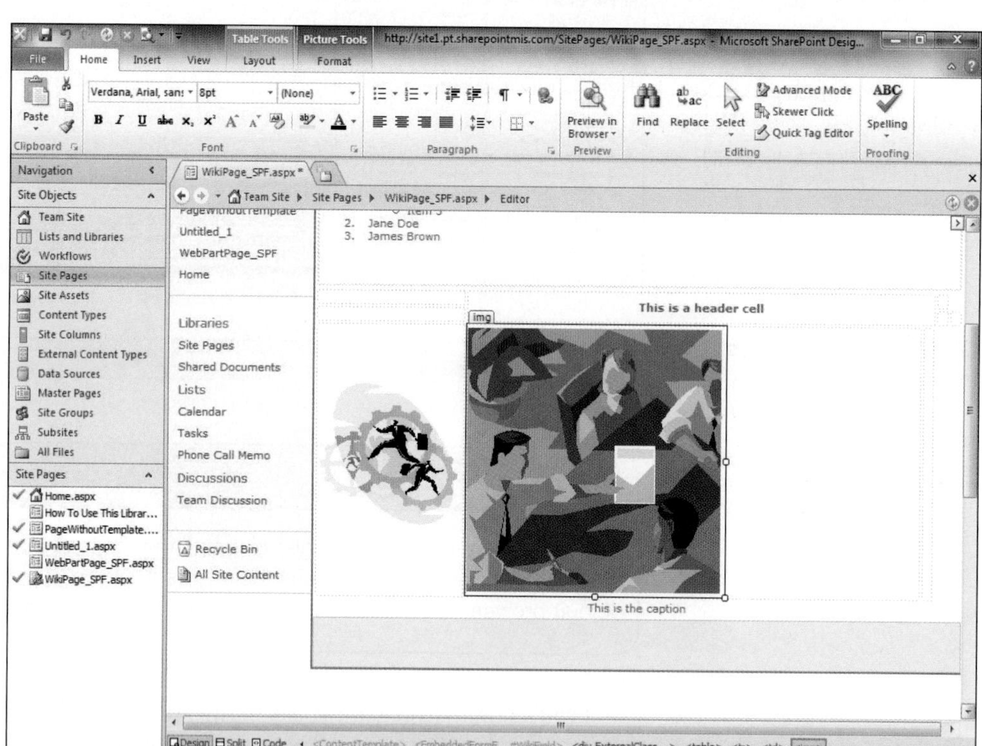

FIGURE 3.49 Web Page Including the Picture ➤

TIP SharePoint Designer Image Conversion Tool

If you insert an image that has a format other than GIF or JPEG, SharePoint Designer automatically converts it to a GIF or JPEG file format, depending on the original number of colors. If, after inserting the image, you want to change its file format, you can easily do that using the Picture Tools–Format tab or the Picture Properties dialog box.

To **resize** a picture means to modify its display size.

To **resample** a picture means to modify its physical size.

A **sizing handle** is a small square evenly distributed around the picture that enables you to resize the picture.

An image that has been included in a Web page can be characterized by the size it is when displayed in the Web page and by its actual physical size (the size of the file that stores the picture). SharePoint Designer enables you to modify the display size of each picture (***resize*** it) and modify the physical size of the picture in the file (***resample*** it). When you click a picture that has already been added to a Web page, sizing handles are displayed. A ***sizing handle*** is a small square evenly distributed around the picture, as shown in Figure 3.50. You can resize the picture by dragging one of the corner handles to another position. The pointer changes to a double arrow when you click a sizing handle. If you click and drag one of the side handles, only the width of the picture changes. Similarly, if you click and drag on a top or bottom handle, only the height of the picture changes.

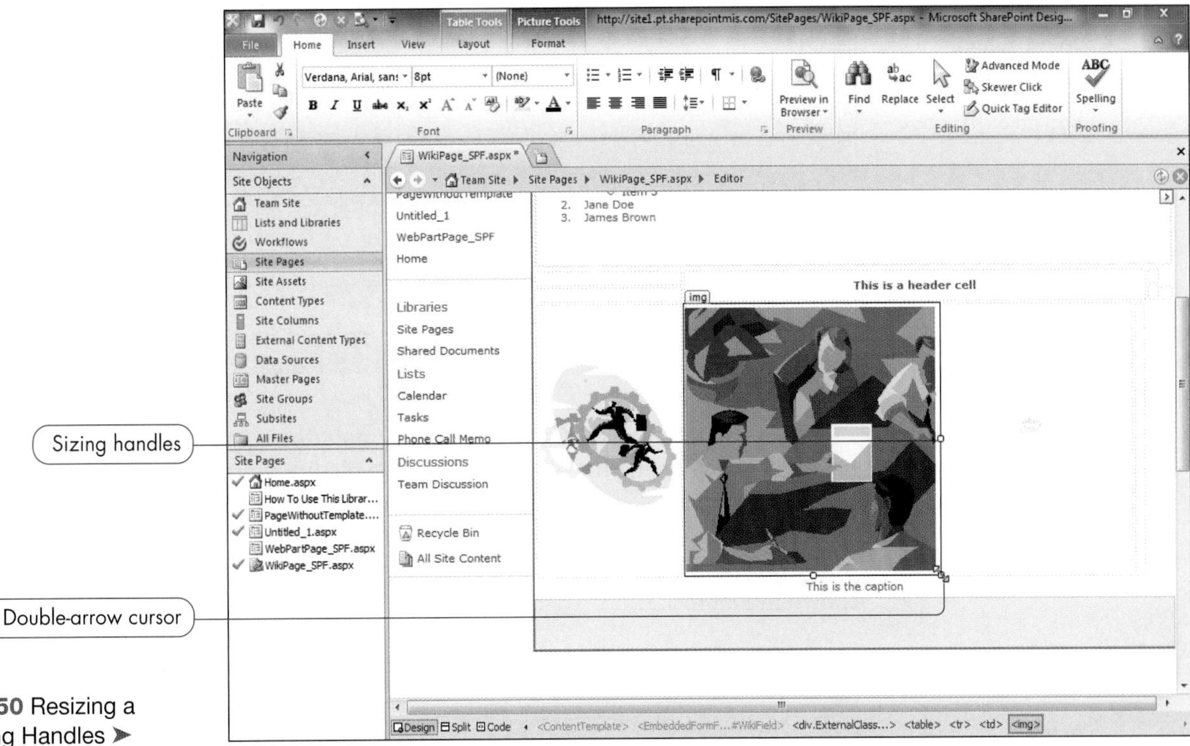

FIGURE 3.50 Resizing a Picture Using Handles ➤

The **Keep aspect ratio** check box enables you to maintain the aspect ratio of the picture as you resize it.

Another feature you can use to resize a picture is the Picture Properties dialog box. To access this dialog box, select the image, and then click Properties in the Picture group of the Pictures Tool–Format tab. Click the Appearance tab, and then use the options in the Size area to change the width and height of the picture. To maintain the aspect ratio of the picture, the width versus the height proportions of the picture, as you resize it, select the ***Keep aspect ratio*** check box, as shown in 3.51.

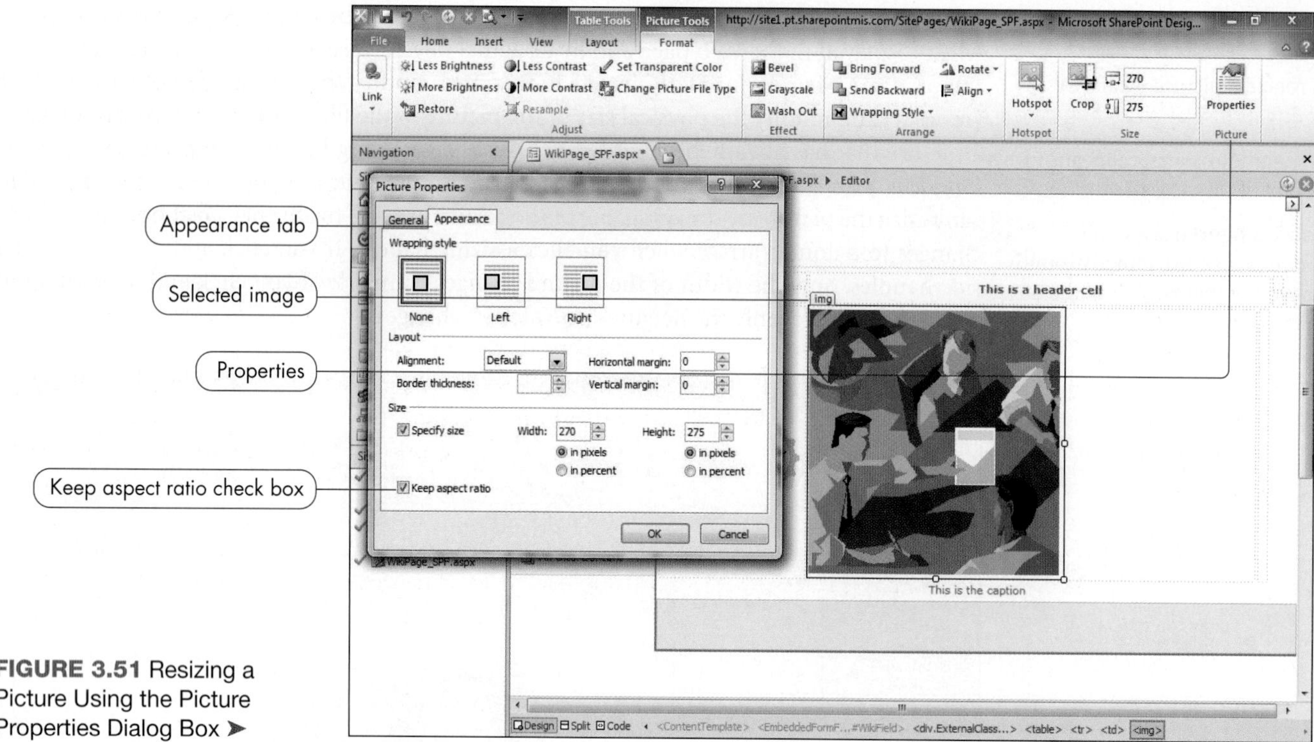

FIGURE 3.51 Resizing a Picture Using the Picture Properties Dialog Box ➤

The two options described here change only the way the picture appears on the Web page without affecting the physical size of the picture itself. The only way to change the size of the file that stores the picture is to resample the original picture file so that it is the size you want it to appear on the page. To resample the image, adjust the physical appearance of the image on your page, click Picture Actions, and then click Resample Picture to Match Size, as shown in Figure 3.52.

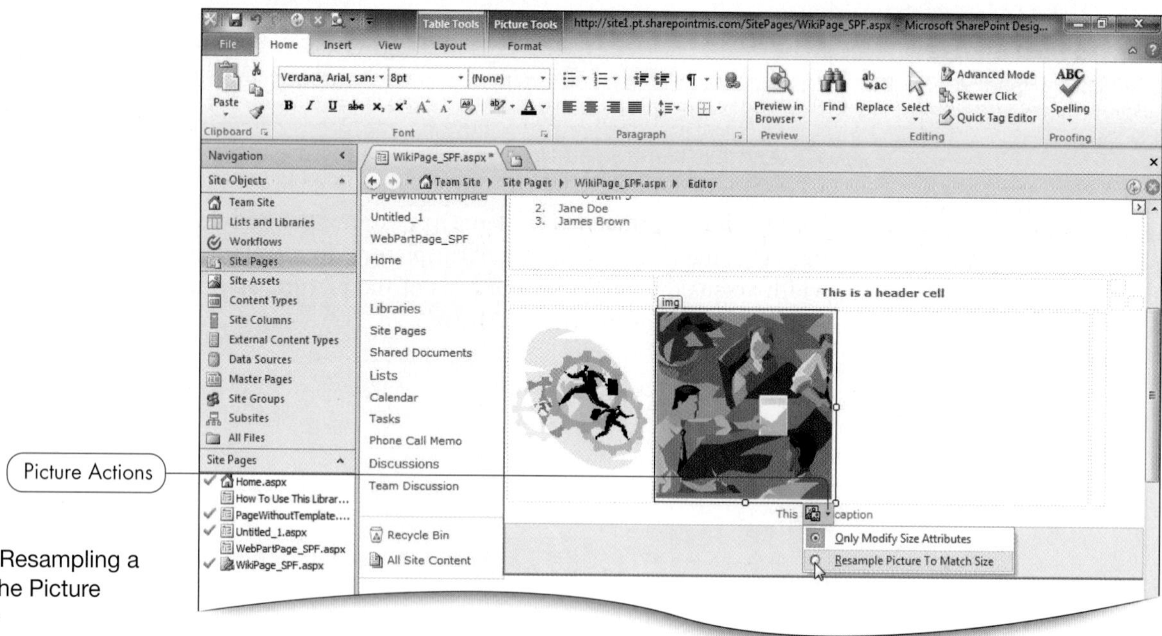

FIGURE 3.52 Resampling a Picture Using the Picture Actions Icon ➤

TIP Resampling a Picture

You can click Undo to undo the resampling of a picture.

The SharePoint Designer Picture Tools–Format tab includes a collection of tools giving you access to a comprehensive set of features....

Modifying an image goes beyond resizing and resampling it. The SharePoint Designer Picture Tools–Format tab includes a collection of tools giving you access to a comprehensive set of features for creating thumbnails, rotating images, controlling the contrast and brightness of images, cropping images, adding hotspots to images, and more. You can display the Picture Tools tab, as shown in Figure 3.53, by clicking an image when editing the Web page using the normal or advanced editor.

If you want to use only a portion of the image and remove the rest, use Crop in the Size group of the Picture Tools–Format tab. Click the picture, and then click the Crop group to display a dashed border cropping box with its own set of handles that appears around the image, as shown in Figure 3.53. Drag the handles to position the dashed box over the area that you want to keep. When you are satisfied with the position of the box, click Crop again or double-click one of the crop box handles to complete the cropping process. Any part of the image that was outside the dashed border cropping box is deleted. The cropped picture is displayed on the Web page, as shown in Figure 3.54.

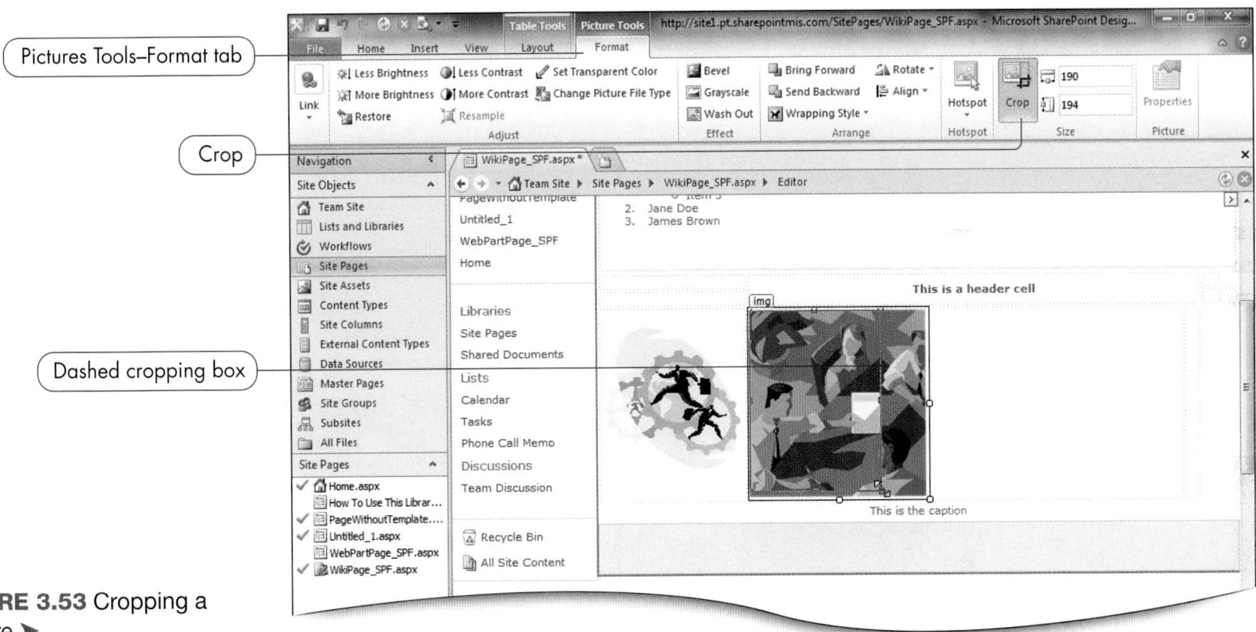

FIGURE 3.53 Cropping a Picture ➤

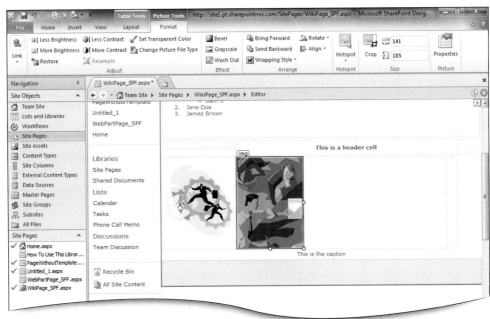

FIGURE 3.54 Cropped Picture ➤

TIP Rotating a Picture

Using SharePoint Designer, you can easily rotate an image to the left or right using the Rotate Left or Rotate Right options by clicking Rotate in the Arrange group on the Picture Tools–Format tab. To reverse an image, click Flip Horizontal or Flip Vertical.

SharePoint Designer has useful features that enable you to adjust the appearance of an image by improving the contrast and brightness, by changing an image to black and white only, and by making it appear washed out. To adjust the contrast of an image, click More Contrast or Less Contrast in the Adjust group of the Picture Tools–Format tab until the desired contrast is reached. To adjust the brightness of a picture, click More Brightness or Less Brightness in the Adjust group. You can change a picture to black and white or make it appear washed out by clicking Grayscale or Wash Out in the Effect group on the Picture Tools–Format tab.

You can change the background color of an image (or any specific color within the image) to transparent. Select the image, click Set Transparent Color in the Adjust group, shown in Figure 3.55, and then click a color in the image. All of the pixels in the image with that color will become transparent. When a picture has a transparent color, the Web page background color or image becomes visible within the picture.

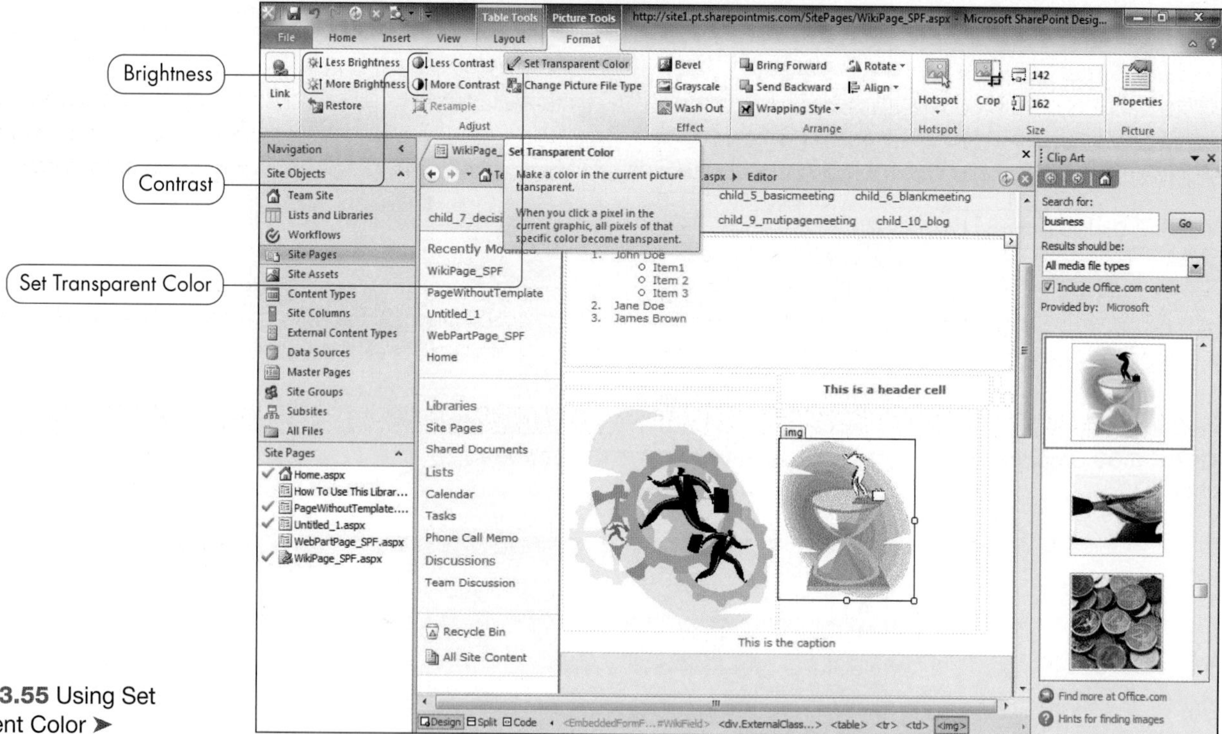

FIGURE 3.55 Using Set Transparent Color ➤

TIP Transparent Picture

If you try to make a .jpg format picture transparent, SharePoint Designer will alert you to the fact that it will first need to convert it into a .gif format picture.

It is not unusual to be unhappy with the look of a image after you have made a number of changes to it. The good news is that you can reverse the changes you made to a picture (including resizing, cropping, and applying colors, but excluding resampling) by clicking Restore in the Adjust group of the Picture Tools–Format tab, as shown in Figure 3.56.

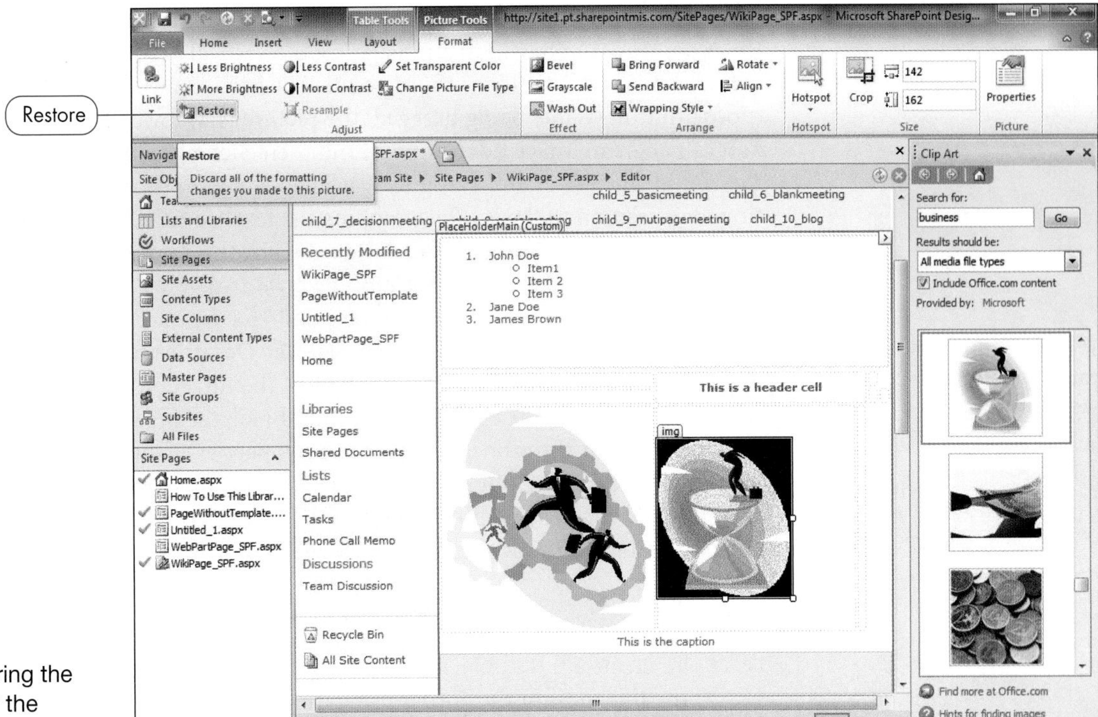

FIGURE 3.56 Restoring the Original Properties of the Picture ➤

After adding images to a Web page, saving a Web page that includes the newly embedded files requires a few more steps. When you click Save to save a Web page that includes embedded images, the Save Embedded dialog box appears. Figure 3.57 displays a picture preview, with a list of all the embedded files, and the following buttons:

- *Rename*—Enables you to rename the embedded picture.
- *Change Folder*—Enables you to save the embedded picture in a different folder.
- *Set Action*—Enables you to maintain the previous copy of the picture or overwrite it.
- *Picture File Type*—Enables you to convert the picture to another format.

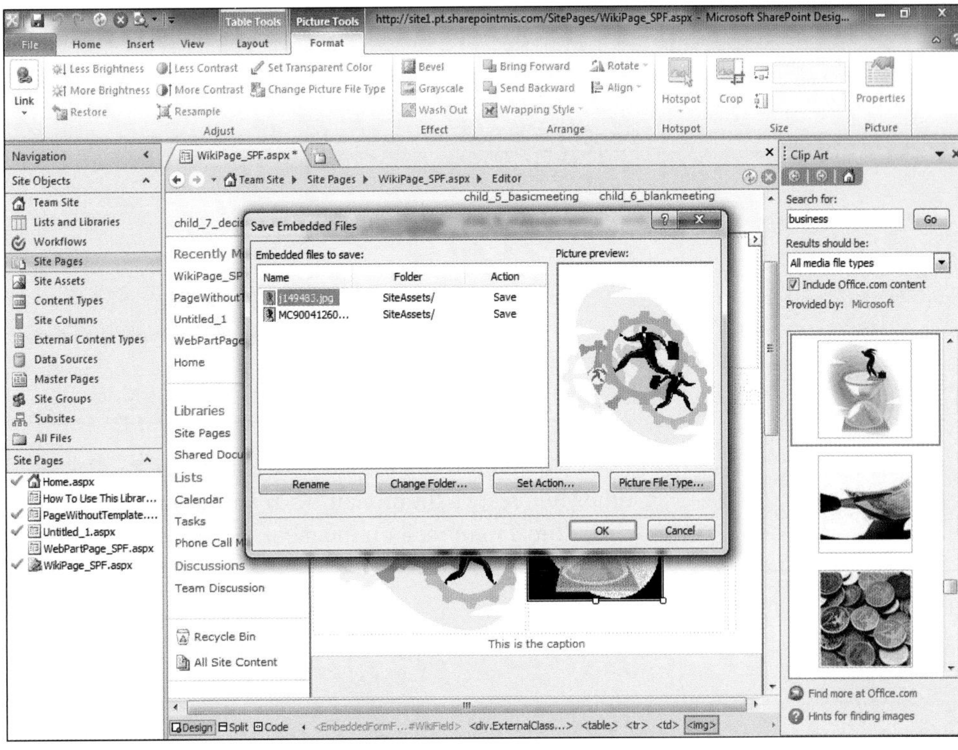

FIGURE 3.57 Save Embedded Files Dialog Box ➤

As you work with your Web page, you might want to change the position of an image on the page. You can reposition an image, on the vertical axis, by clicking and dragging the picture up or down. When the mouse pointer is where you want the image to appear, release the mouse button. While being dragged, the picture is followed by a small square-shaped icon. You can align an image by clicking it, and then clicking Center, Right Align, or Left Align on the Home tab. SharePoint Designer also enables you to decide how a picture should be positioned in relation to the text by wrapping the text around the image. Double-click the image to open the Picture Properties dialog box. Click the Appearance tab, if necessary, and then click None, Left, or Right in the Wrapping style area.

The **Auto Thumbnail** feature creates a small version of the image.

When you need to use a large image and you are concerned that the size of the file will make your page load too slowly, SharePoint Designer has an option for you. The ***Auto Thumbnail*** feature creates a small version of the image. You then add the necessary HTML coding so that when the user clicks the thumbnail, the image is loaded in its true size. Before creating an auto thumbnail, you set the properties using the AutoThumbnail tab of the SharePoint Designer Options dialog box. To access this dialog box, click Options on the File tab, and then click Page Editor Options. Click the AutoThumbnail tab, shown in Figure 3.58, choose from the options there, and then click OK to close the Page Options dialog box.

- To change the size of the thumbnail, use Set; select the desired width, height, shortest side, or longest side settings; and then use the Pixels box to specify the size.
- To create a thumbnail border, check the Border Thickness check box, and then set the thickness of the border using the Pixels box.
- To create a beveled effect for the thumbnail, check the *Beveled edge* check box.

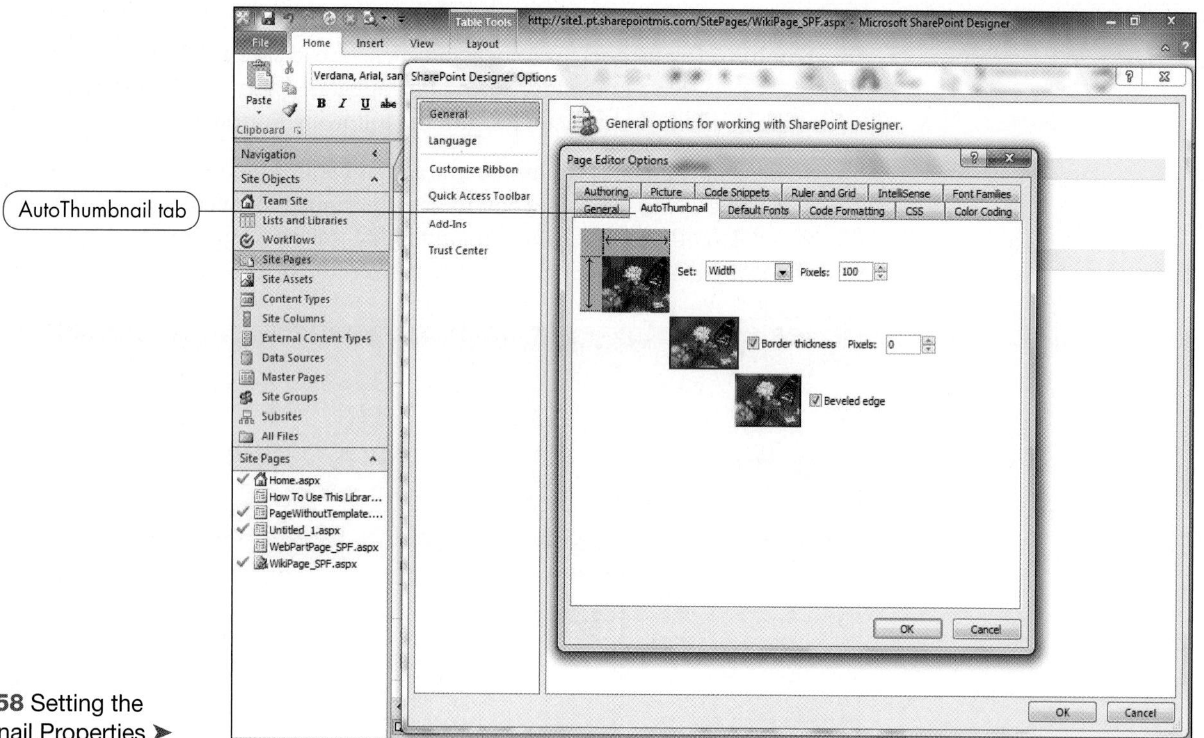

FIGURE 3.58 Setting the AutoThumbnail Properties ➤

If you do not change the AutoThumbnail properties, these properties will be used every time you create a thumbnail. To create a thumbnail image, right-click the picture, and then click Auto Thumbnail on the menu, as shown in Figure 3.59.

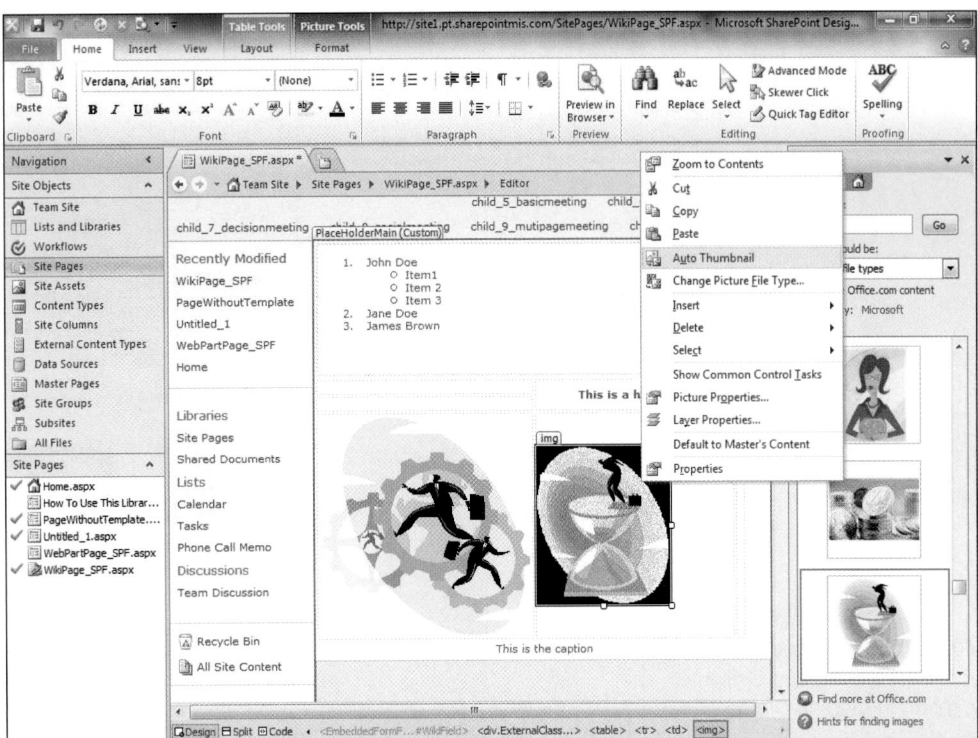

FIGURE 3.59 Creating an AutoThumbnail ➤

You can add a hyperlink to an image by selecting the image, and then clicking Properties on the Picture group of the Picture Tools–Format tab. Click the General tab, as shown in Figure 3.60. In the Location box of the *Hyperlink* section, type the URL of the hyperlink, and then click OK to close the Picture Properties dialog box.

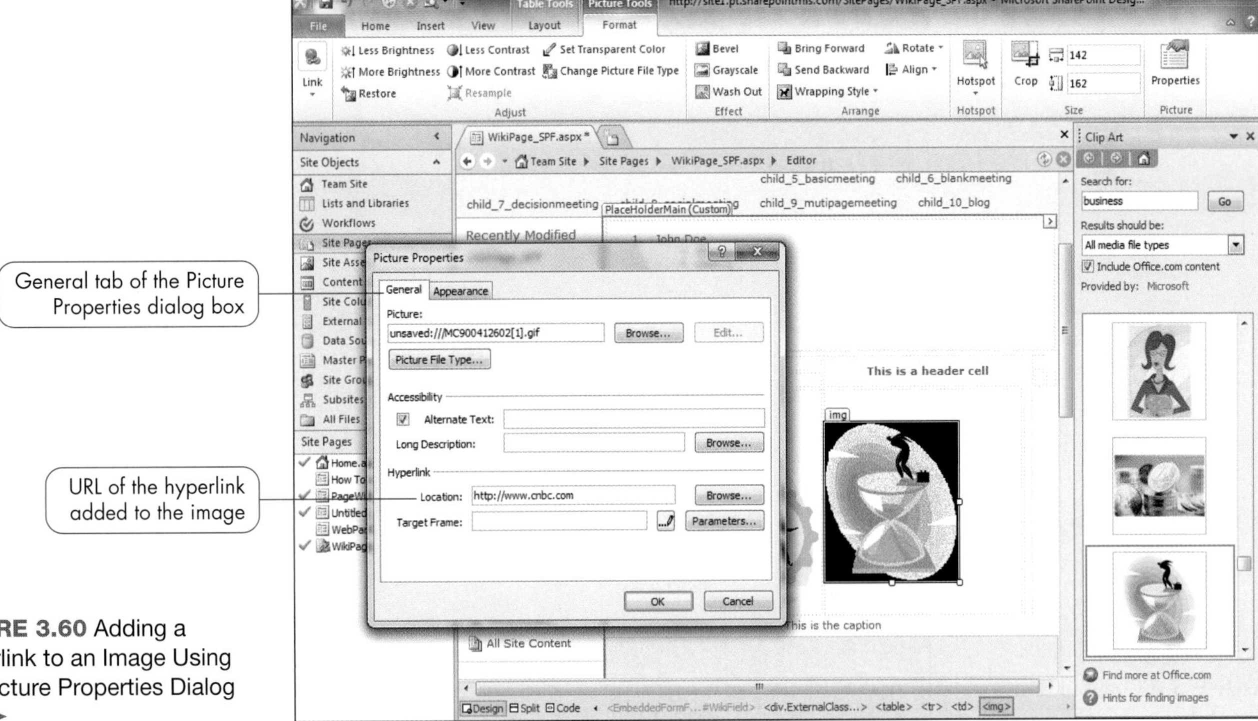

FIGURE 3.60 Adding a Hyperlink to an Image Using the Picture Properties Dialog Box ➤

Another method for adding a hyperlink to an image is to click the arrow below Link on the Picture Tools–Format tab, and then click Hyperlink to display the Insert Hyperlink dialog box, as shown in Figure 3.61. In the Address box, type the URL of the hyperlink, and then click OK to close the Insert Hyperlink dialog box.

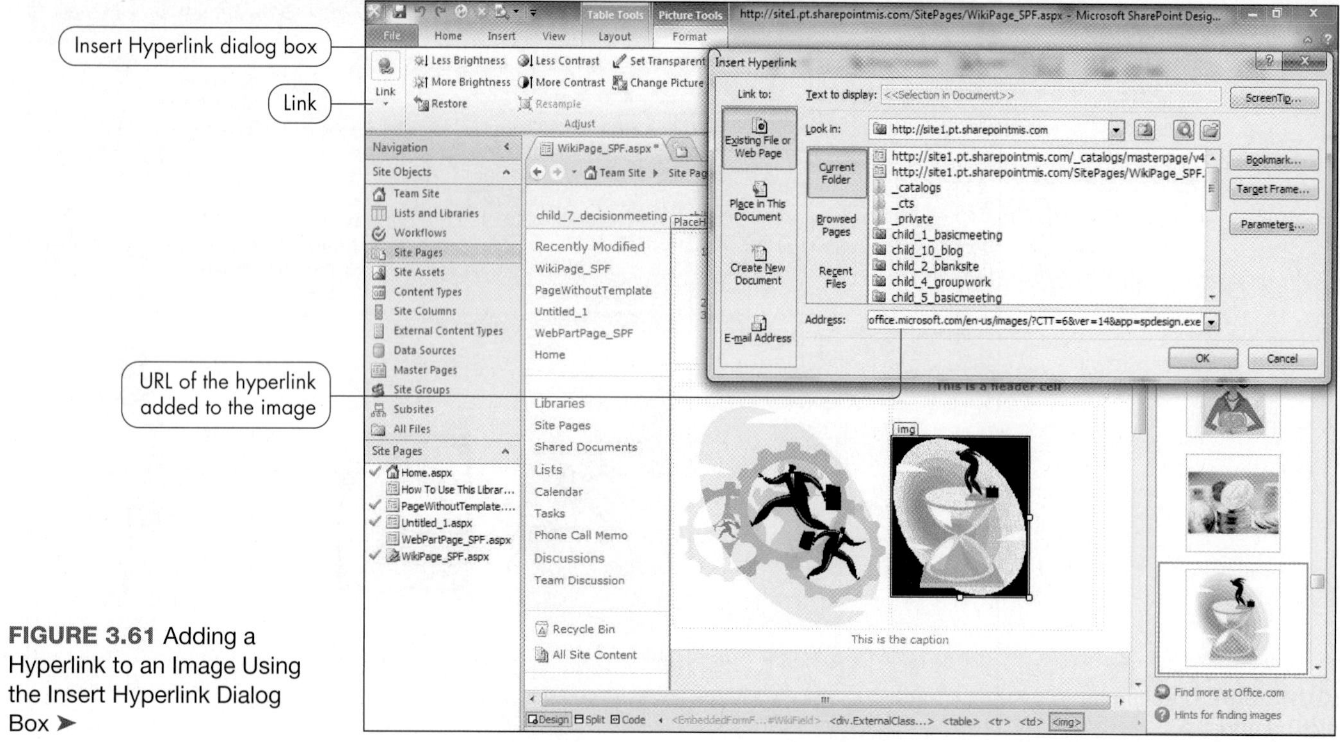

FIGURE 3.61 Adding a Hyperlink to an Image Using the Insert Hyperlink Dialog Box ➤

To arrange Web page content, after including images, it is highly recommended that you use CSS styles. Figure 3.62 will be used as an example to learn more about images and Web page layout. In the highlighted section of the Web page, text is too close to and unevenly wrapped around the picture.

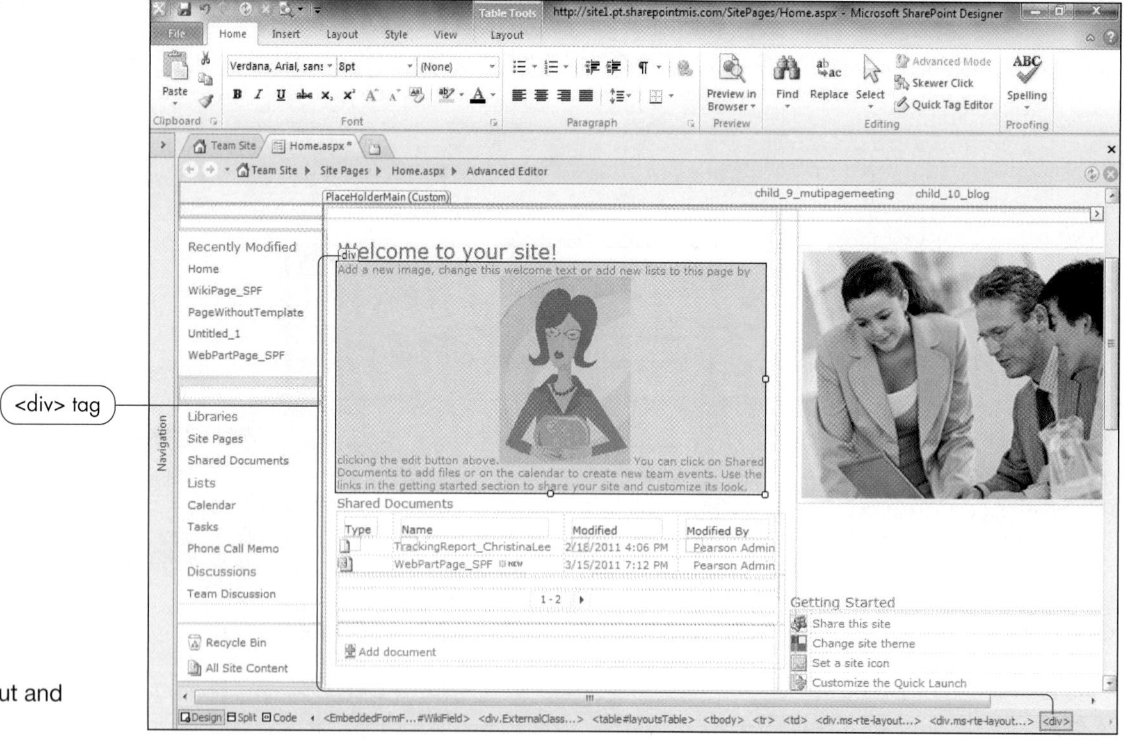

FIGURE 3.62 Layout and Images ➤

You can adjust the position of the image in the layout by floating the image to the right or left of the adjacent content using the float property. In Design view, using the HTML command from the Insert tab, insert a <div> tag just above the selected section. Then, keeping the mouse button pressed, drag and drop the selected section within the <div> </div>, as shown in Figure 3.62. Select the image, click the Style tab, and then click New Style in the Create group to open the New Style dialog box.

> **TIP** The <div> Tag
>
> The <div> tag is commonly used in Web design to define Web page document sections. A unique ID is given to each <div> tag to which you can apply styles. These styles will apply to all Web page elements contained within the section.

To create a new class style, type a period and an appropriate name, such as .floatimageleft, in the Selector box. To save the new class style in the style sheet already linked to the Web page, select New style sheet in the *Define in* box, and then check the *Apply new style to document* selection in order to automatically apply the new style to the selected image. Select Layout in the Category list, select the appropriate direction for the float in the Float list (left, in this case), and then click OK to close the dialog box, as shown in Figure 3.63. Now drag the image before the first word of the adjacent text and observe how the text now wraps around the image. After wrapping, the picture may still be too close to the right edge of the text content.

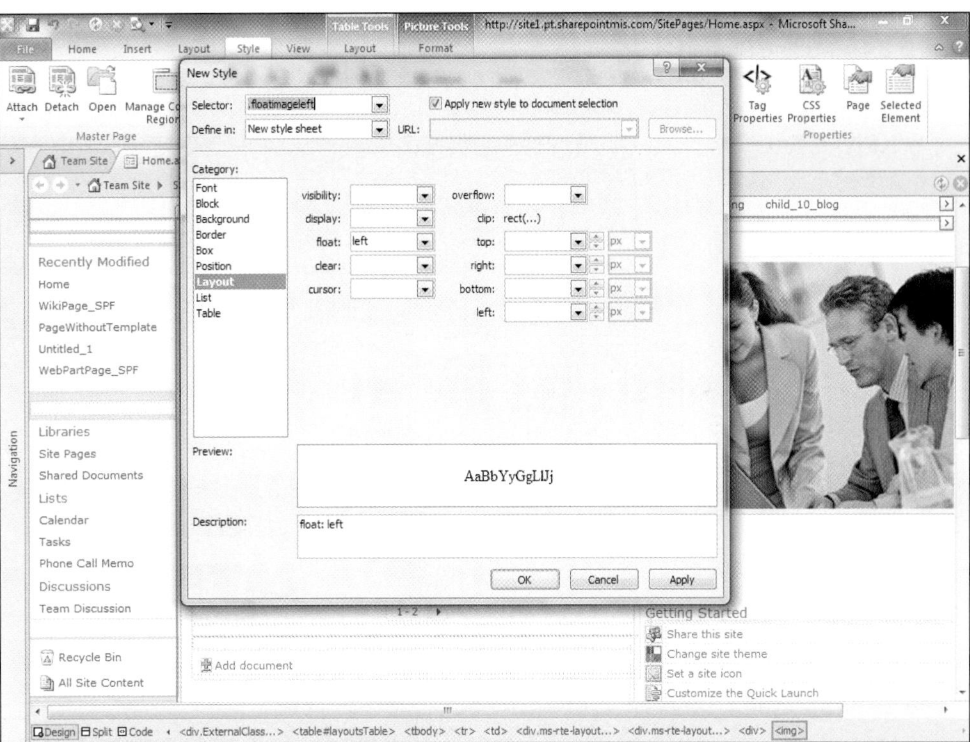

FIGURE 3.63 Creating a Floating Layout ➤

Padding increases the space between any element content ... and its borders, whereas margins represent the space outside the element border.

You can further refine the layout of your page by applying padding and margins to the image, as well as visible borders. Padding increases the space between any element content (the image in the example) and its borders, whereas margins represent the space outside the element border. To add visible borders to the image, right-click the style name (in this case, .floatimageleft) in the Manage Styles task pane, and then select Modify Style to open the Modify Style dialog box. Click Border in the Category list, and then select the values for the Border styles, as shown in Figure 3.64. Click Box in the Category list, select the values for the image padding and margins, as shown in Figure 3.65, and then click OK to close the Modify Style dialog box.

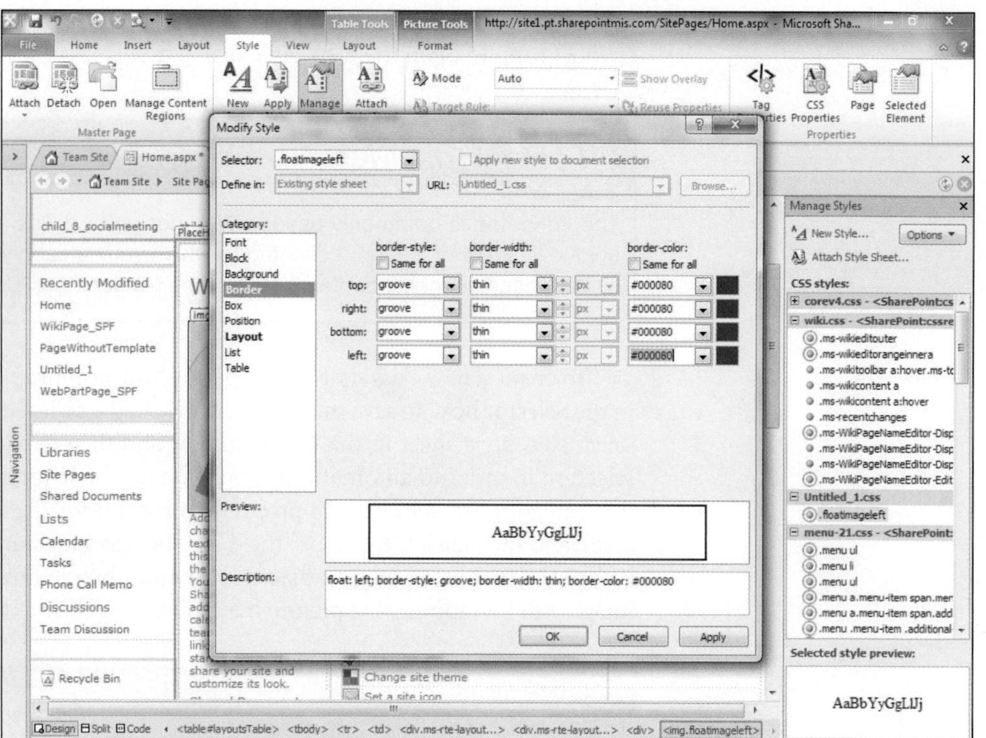

FIGURE 3.64 Adding Borders to an Image ➤

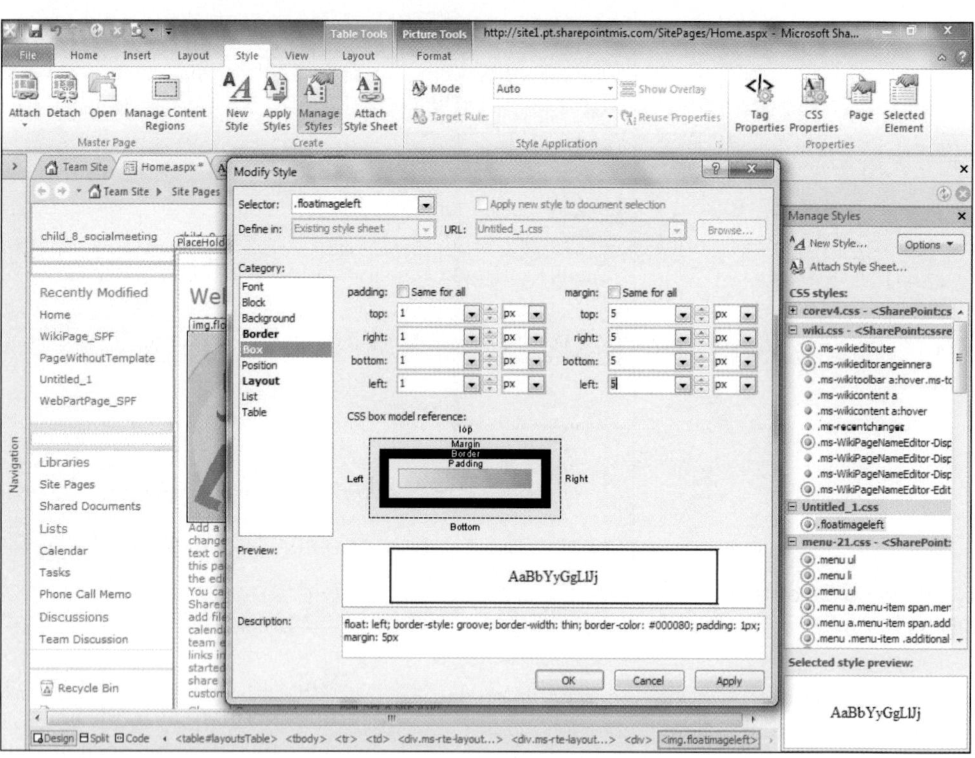

FIGURE 3.65 Adding Padding and Margins to an Image ➤

Select the <div> tag that contains the image, and then in the Tag Properties, type a name (.team_member is used in the example) as a value of the id attribute. In the Manage Styles task pane, click New Style to open the New Style dialog box. Type the same id attribute (.team_member) in the Selector box, and then select Current page in the *Define in* box. Check the *Apply new style to document* selection. Click Font in the Category list, and then select the values for the font family and color. Click Apply to see the changes made to the <div> tag, as shown in Figure 3.66, and then click OK to close the Modify Style dialog box. If you wish to further edit the newly created style, right-click the style name in the Manage Styles task pane, and then select Modify Style to open the Modify Style dialog box.

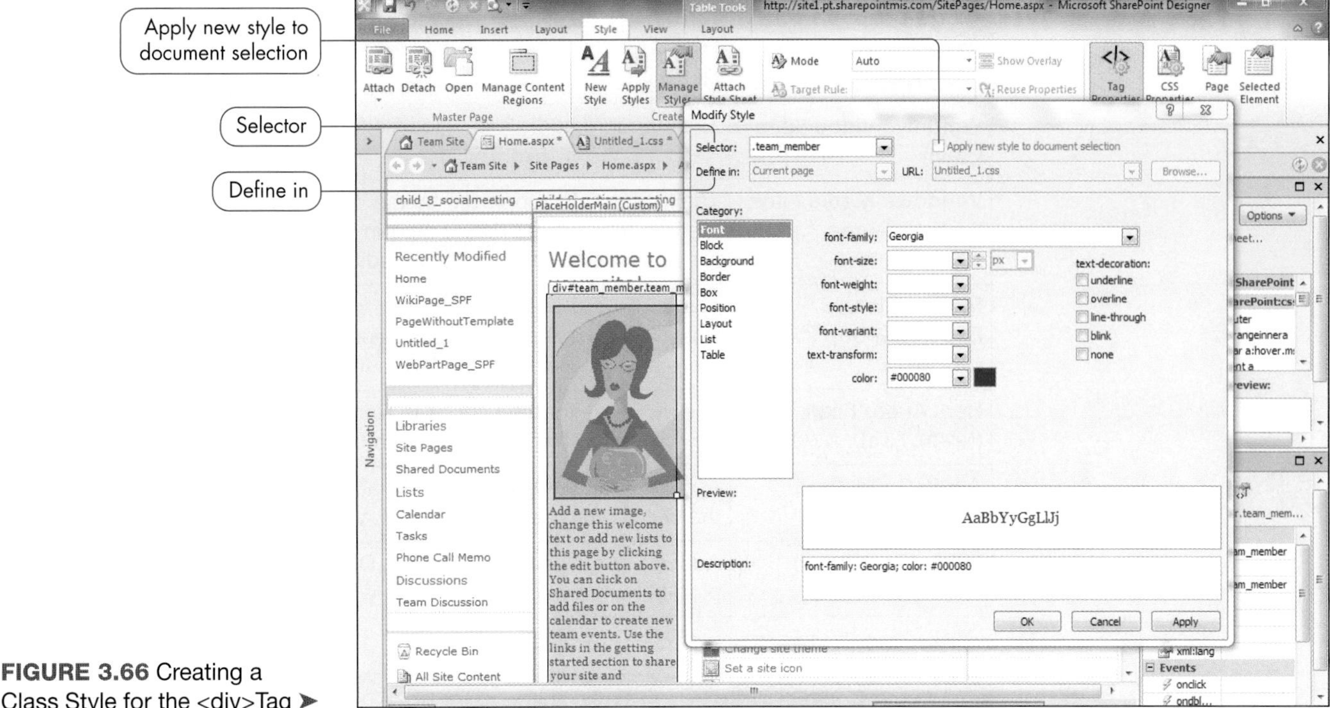

FIGURE 3.66 Creating a Class Style for the <div>Tag ➤

Working with Multimedia Files

If you choose to add audio and video elements to your Web sites, you can make the multimedia available in two formats.

Using sound and video is another way Web designers enhance their Web pages. If you choose to add audio and video elements to your Web sites, you can make the multimedia available in two formats. You can incorporate sound and video files that can be downloaded and played, or create streaming audio and video files that enable users to hear and view these files while they are downloading. A streaming video file is sent in compressed form to the browser and displayed as it arrives, as a sequence of images. If your Web page is stored on a Web server that cannot stream the content of audio and video files, your visitors must completely download them before they can see or listen to them.

> **TIP** Using Sounds
>
> Just because you can add sounds to your Web page does not mean you should. Like graphic files, audio files can increase the size of your Web page and the time required to load your Web page in a browser.

A **plug-in** is a software application that can be an integral part of a browser or give the browser additional multimedia capabilities.

Today's technology still requires the use of programs called plug-ins to interact with (view or play) some multimedia files. A ***plug-in*** is a software application that can be an integral part of a browser or give the browser additional multimedia capabilities. Plug-ins are downloaded from the software developer's Web site (usually at no charge) and installed. Table 3.2 shows the audio and video file types that SharePoint Designer supports.

TABLE 3.2 Audio and Video File Types Supported by SharePoint Designer

File Type	Description
Windows Video Files (*.avi)	The standard audio and video file format for Microsoft Windows.
Windows Media Files (*.wmv, *.wma, *.asf)	The file formats supported by the Windows Media Player. Download the Windows Media Player plug-in from www.microsoft.com/windowsmedia/.
Motion Picture Experts Group (*.mpg, *.mpeg)	The audio and video format used with Windows Media Player and Real Networks RealPlayer. Download the Windows Media Player plug-in or the Real Player plug-in from www.real.com.
Real Audio Files (*.ram, *.ra)	The audio file format used with Real Networks Real Player. Download the Real Player plug-in from www.real.com.
Apple QuickTime (*.mov, *.qt)	Apple's audio and video file format. Windows users can download the QuickTime plug-in from www.apple.com/quicktime.
Flash Files (*.swf)	Adobe's audio and video format. Download the Adobe Flash Player plug-in from www.adobe.com/downloads/.

TIP Multipurpose Internet Mail Extension (MIME) Types

Multipurpose Internet Mail Extension (MIME) types enable the exchange of different kinds of files on the Internet. Normally the MIME types are preset in the browser, but it is possible that these will need to be manually configured. The MIME type for a WMV file is video/x-ms-wmv, and for WMA, it is audio/x-ms-wma. The MIME type for ASF video is video/x-ms-asf. To display Windows Media files and live broadcasts, both the Web browser and Web server must have the MIME types configured to recognize Windows Media file types. MIME types usually have to be configured manually on a Web server. To learn more about MIME types, see the Microsoft "MIME Type Settings for Windows Media Services" (http://support.microsoft.com/kb/288102).

SharePoint Designer enables you to add a link to an audio file on your Web page or to place an audio file on your Web page.

SharePoint Designer enables you to add a link to an audio file on your Web page or to place an audio file on your Web page. To insert a link to an audio file, click Hyperlink in the Links group of the Insert tab. In the Insert Hyperlink dialog box, type the text you want to display for the link, and then select the audio file. Click OK to close the Insert Hyperlink dialog box and see the link and player added to the Web page, as shown in Figure 3.67 a & b.

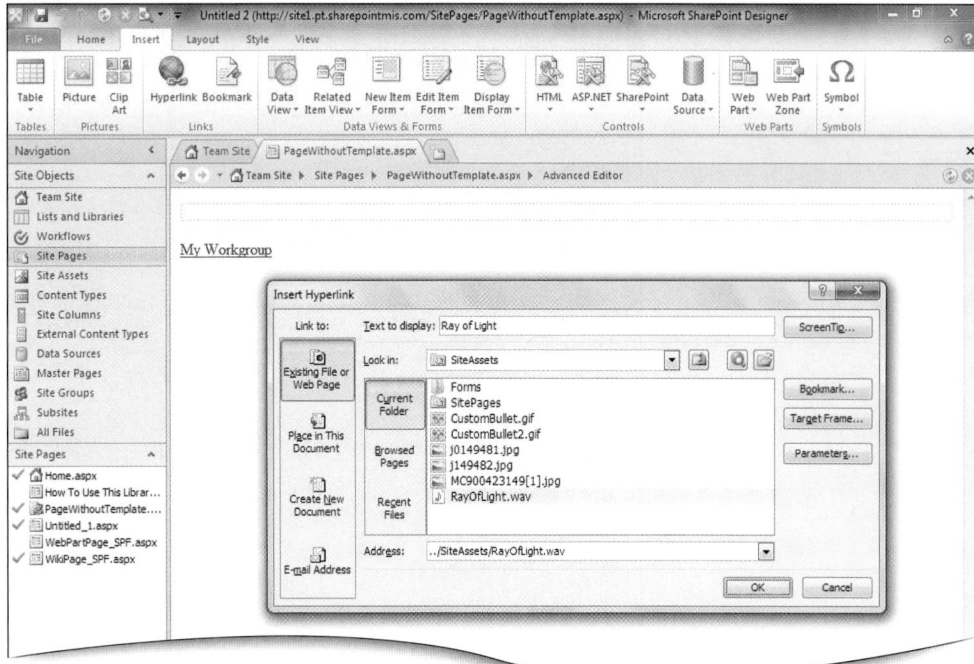

FIGURE 3.67a Adding a Link to an Audio File ➤

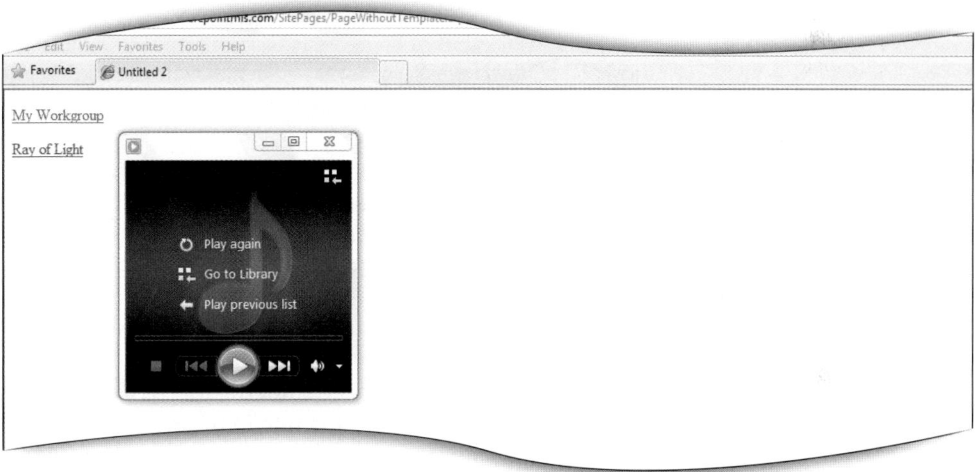

FIGURE 3.67b ➤

TIP User-Friendly Web Design

Whenever you include audio or video files in your Web page, it is a good practice to add a link to the Web site that contains the download for the plug-in that your visitors need to play the media files.

Background sound is an audio file that plays for as long as a Web page is open in a browser or for a limited number of loops, or cycles, depending on the designer's preference.

SharePoint Designer enables you to add background sound to a Web page that is not attached to a template. A ***Background sound*** is an audio file that plays for as long as a Web page is open in a browser or for a limited number of loops, or cycles, depending on the designer's preference. To add a background sound to your Web page, click Page in the Properties group of the Advanced Editor Style tab to display the Page Properties dialog box. Click the General tab, as shown in Figure 3.68. Type the name of the audio file you want to use or click Browse to locate it, select the number of loops, and then click OK.

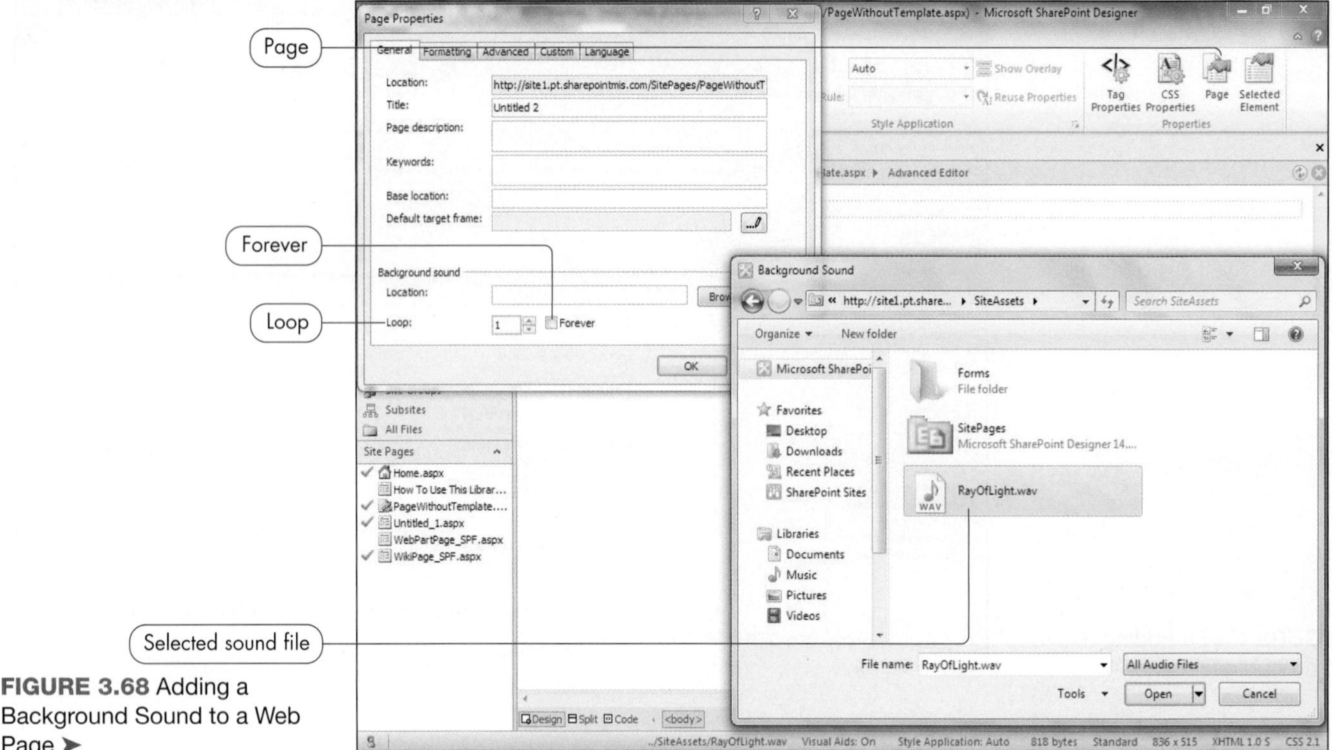

FIGURE 3.68 Adding a Background Sound to a Web Page ➤

> **TIP** Changing the Properties of an Audio File
>
> In the General tab of the Page Properties dialog box, if you check the Forever box, the sound will play, as it says, forever, or as long as the Web page is open in the browser. If the Forever box is not checked, you can choose the number of loops.

For the past few years, the technology of video streaming has developed and improved. Powerful companies, such as Microsoft and Real Media, are investing in research dedicated to improving the performance standards for Web-based video. The popularity of Web-based video is also driven by the reduction in the prices of digital video cameras, which enables more people and businesses to create their own video clips and post them on the Web. However, the size of video files is still rather large and the quality of delivery is not always the best.

> **TIP** Live Broadcast
>
> Streaming video is usually sent from preexisting video files. However, it can be distributed as part of a live broadcast in which the video signal is converted into a compressed digital signal and transmitted from a special Web server that can multicast (send the same file to multiple users at the same time).

As with audio, the main ways to use video on your Web page are to insert a link to a video file or to place a video file directly onto your Web page as streaming media. To insert a link to a video file on your Web page, click Hyperlink on the Insert tab to open the Insert Hyperlink dialog box. Type the hyperlink display text, select the video file, and then click OK to close the Insert Hyperlink dialog box. When the dialog box closes, the link is displayed on the Web page, as shown in Figure 3.69.

As with audio, the main ways to use video on your Web page are to insert a link to a video file or to place a video file directly onto your Web page as streaming media.

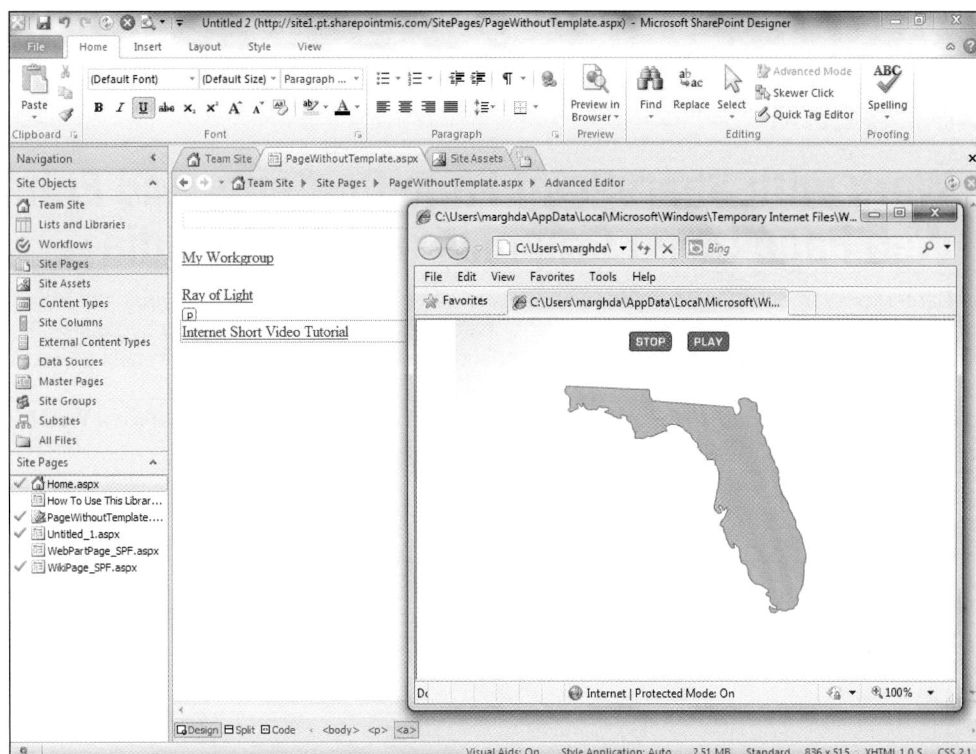

FIGURE 3.69 Video Flash File (.swf) Added to a Web Page ➤

Later in this chapter, you will learn about using Web Parts for displaying images and media content.

HANDS-ON EXERCISES

1 Work with SharePoint Page Contents and Enhance a Web Page Using Graphics and Multimedia

The Center for Women in STEM board members are eager to start working with you on creating the new and enhanced SharePoint 2010 site. You will learn how to edit SharePoint page content and use hyperlinks, lists, and tables to organize the content of pages. Then, you will learn how to enhance your site content using graphics and multimedia files.

Skills covered: Edit SharePoint Page Content • Use Hyperlinks and Lists to Organize a Web Page • Work with Tables and Layout Tables • Add Graphics to a Web Page • Work with Multimedia Files

STEP 1 EDIT SHAREPOINT PAGE CONTENT

You will add text to the Center for Women in STEM site's Wiki page using different tools made available by the SharePoint Foundation Browser interface and SharePoint Designer. Refer to Figure 3.70 as you complete Step 1.

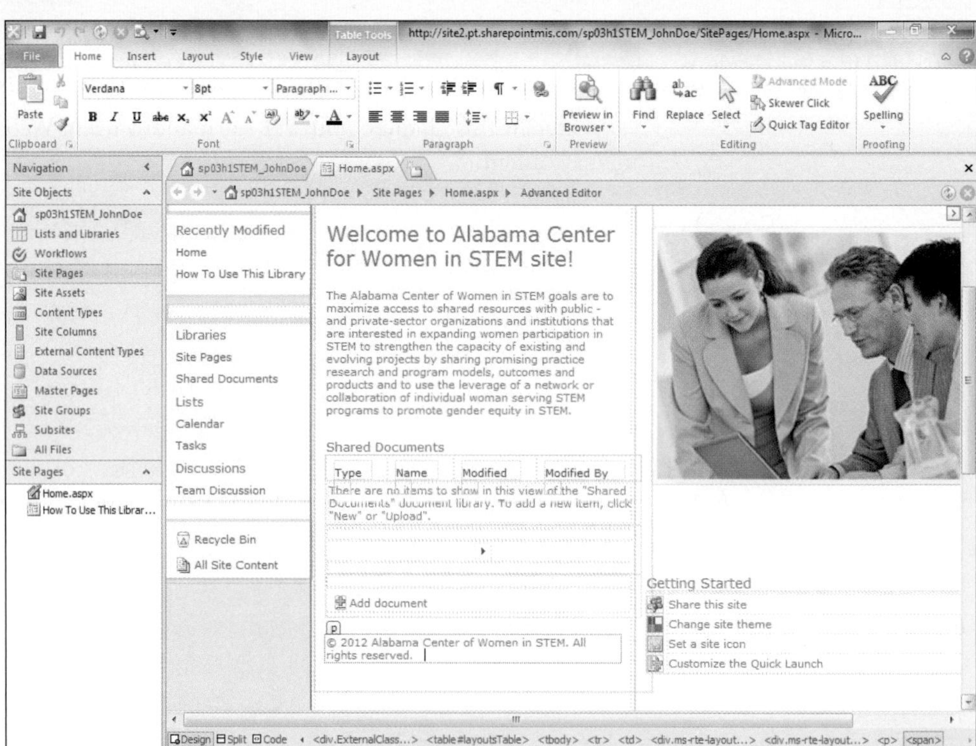

FIGURE 3.70 Edit SharePoint Pages Content in SharePoint Designer ➤

a. Click **Start** to display the Start menu. Click **All Programs**, and then click **Internet Explorer** to open the program. Go to the top-level site provided by your instructor, which will be in the format of *http://pt.sharepointmis.com/SitePages/yourname*. Enter the user name and password provided by your instructor.

   If you logged in correctly, the home page of the top-level site is now displayed in Internet Explorer.

b. Click **All Site Content** on the Quick Launch of the top-level site. Click **Create** on the All Site Content page to open the Create page.

c. Click **Site** in the *Filter By* section of the Create page. Click **Team Site**, and then type **sp03h1STEM_LastNameFirstName** in the **Title** and **URL name boxes**. Click **Create**.

   The *sp03h1STEM_LastNameFirstName* site is now displayed.

d. Click the **Page tab**, and then click **Edit** in the Edit group. Highlight the text *your site* and then type **Alabama Center for Women in STEM site.**

e. Launch the Microsoft Word application, and then open the *AlabamaCenterOf WomenIn STEMGoals.docx* file from your Exploring folder. Highlight the first paragraph, right-click, and then click **Copy**. Activate the Internet Explorer window, highlight the first paragraph on the home page of the *sp03h1STEM_LastNameFirstName* site, click the **Paste arrow** on the Clipboard group, and then click **Paste plaintext**. Click **Save & Close** in the Edit group.

TROUBLESHOOTING: Click Allow Access on the Internet Explorer alert window if it shows up.

   The home page, including the new text, is now displayed in the browser.

f. Click **Edit in SharePoint Designer** on the Site Actions menu. Type the password provided by your instructor.

   The Site settings page of your *sp03h1STEM_LastNameFirstName* site should now be displayed in the SharePoint Designer window.

g. Click the **Edit site home page** in the *Customization* section of the Site Summary page.

   The SharePoint Designer editing window displays Home.aspx in Design view.

h. Review all elements of the SharePoint Designer editing workspace carefully, using Figure 3.2 and Table 3.1.

i. Click to the right of *Add document*, and then press the down arrow twice.

   A highlighted <p> tag should now show on the Quick Tag Selector.

j. Click the **Insert tab**, click **Symbol** on the Symbol group of the Insert tab, and then select the **Copyright Sign (©) symbol.**

k. Activate the Microsoft Word application window, highlight the second paragraph, right-click, and then click **Copy**.

l. Activate the SharePoint Designer window. Press the Space bar to insert a blank space after the Copyright Sign symbol, click the **Home tab** if it is not already displayed, click the **Paste arrow**, select **Plain text**, and then click **OK** in the Paste Text dialog box.

m. Click **Save** on the QuickAccess Toolbar. Click **Yes** in the dialog boxes.

   Your screen should now look similar to Figure 3.70.

STEP 2 USE HYPERLINKS AND LISTS TO ORGANIZE A WEB PAGE

You will add a hyperlink to the Center's Wiki page and format it. Then, you will create an HTML page, paste text into the page content from a Microsoft Word document, and format text as a list. Finally, you will also format the list using the Apply Styles task pane. Refer to Figure 3.71 as you complete Step 2.

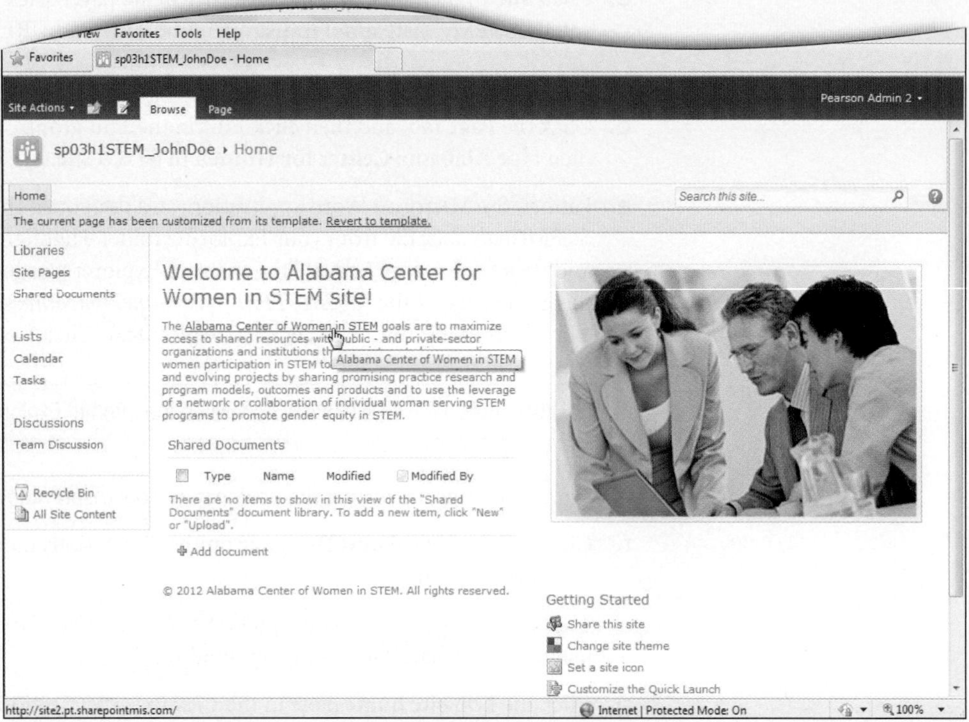

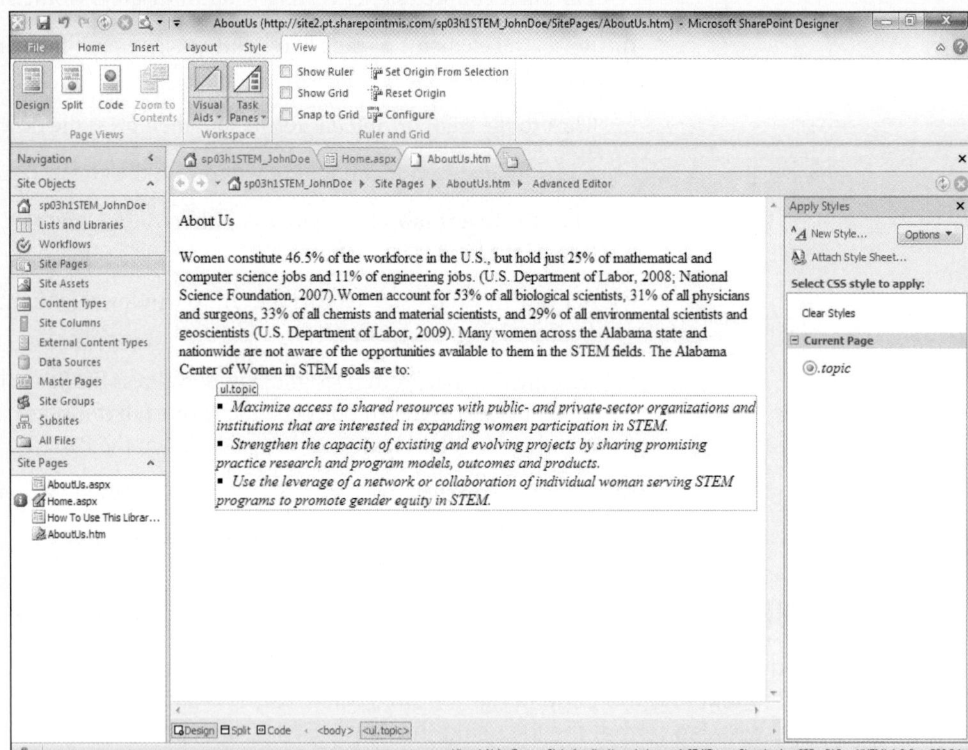

FIGURE 3.71 Format Text Using Hyperlinks and Lists ➤

a. Place the insertion point in the first paragraph added in Step 1 in SharePoint Designer, and then highlight **Alabama Center of Women in STEM**. Click the **Insert tab**, and then click **Hyperlink** in the Links group of the Ribbon.

   The Insert Hyperlink dialog box is now displayed.

b. Type the URL of your collection top-level site in the **Address box**. Click **ScreenTip**, type **Alabama Center of Women in STEM** in the **ScreenTip text box**, and then click **OK** twice to close the two open dialog boxes.

   An asterisk should now show on the Home.aspx tab.

c. Click **Save** on the Quick Access Toolbar. Click **Yes** in the Microsoft SharePoint Designer dialog box, alerting you that SharePoint may remove unsafe content, and in the Site Definition Page Warning dialog box, alerting you your changes will customize the page.

   No asterisk should now show on the Home.aspx tab.

d. Click the **Home tab**, and then click **Preview in Browser** in the Preview group of the Ribbon.

   Home.aspx is now displayed in the browser, including a yellow bar *Important* message that the current page has been customized from its template.

e. Move the mouse over the hyperlink created. The ScreenTip is now displayed and your screen should look like Figure 3.71a. Click the hyperlink.

   The home page of your top-level site is now displayed in the same browser window.

f. Activate the SharePoint Designer window, and then click the **File tab** to open the Backstage view. Click **More Pages** in the *Pages* section of the Add Item tab, click **HTML**, if it is not already selected, and then click **Create**. Type **AboutUs** in the **Enter a name for this new HTML page: box**, and then click **OK**.

   The AboutUs.htm page is now displayed in Design view.

g. Open the *AboutUs.docx* file from your Exploring folder, highlight all the text, right-click, and then click **Copy**. Activate the SharePoint Designer window, click the **Paste arrow** in the Clipboard group of the Home tab, and then click **Paste**. Move your mouse pointer over the Paste Option smart tag, click the down arrow, and then select **Remove Formatting**.

h. Highlight the last three paragraphs, and then click the **Bullets button** in the Paragraph group of the Home tab.

   The bulleted list is now displayed.

i. Click the **View tab**, click the **Task Panes arrow** in the Workspace group, and then select **Apply Styles**.

   The Apply Styles task pane is now displayed.

j. Click **New Style** in the Apply Styles task pane.

   The New Style dialog box is now displayed.

k. Click the **Selector arrow**. Click **ul** in the Selector box, and then click **List** in the *Category* section. Click **square** in the list-style-type list, click **inside** on the list-style-position list, and then click **OK** to close the New Style dialog box.

l. Click **New Style** in the Apply Styles task pane. Type **.topic** in the **Selector box**, and then click **Font** in the *Category* section. Click **italic** on the font-style list, and then click **OK** to close the New Style dialog box.

   The new .topic style is now showing the *Current Page* section of the Manage Styles task pane.

m. Highlight the three lines of the <ul> list, click the arrow to the right of the .topic style, and then click **Apply Style** from the menu.

   The three lines of the <ul> list are now italicized.

n. Click **Save** on the Quick Access Toolbar to save the AboutUs.htm.

   Your screen should now look similar to Figure 3.71b.

STEP 3 WORK WITH TABLES AND LAYOUT TABLES

You will create a page for the Center's site from the default master and will add a table to the page content. Then, you will format the table cells, insert a caption, and insert text into the table cells. Refer to Figure 3.72 as you complete Step 3.

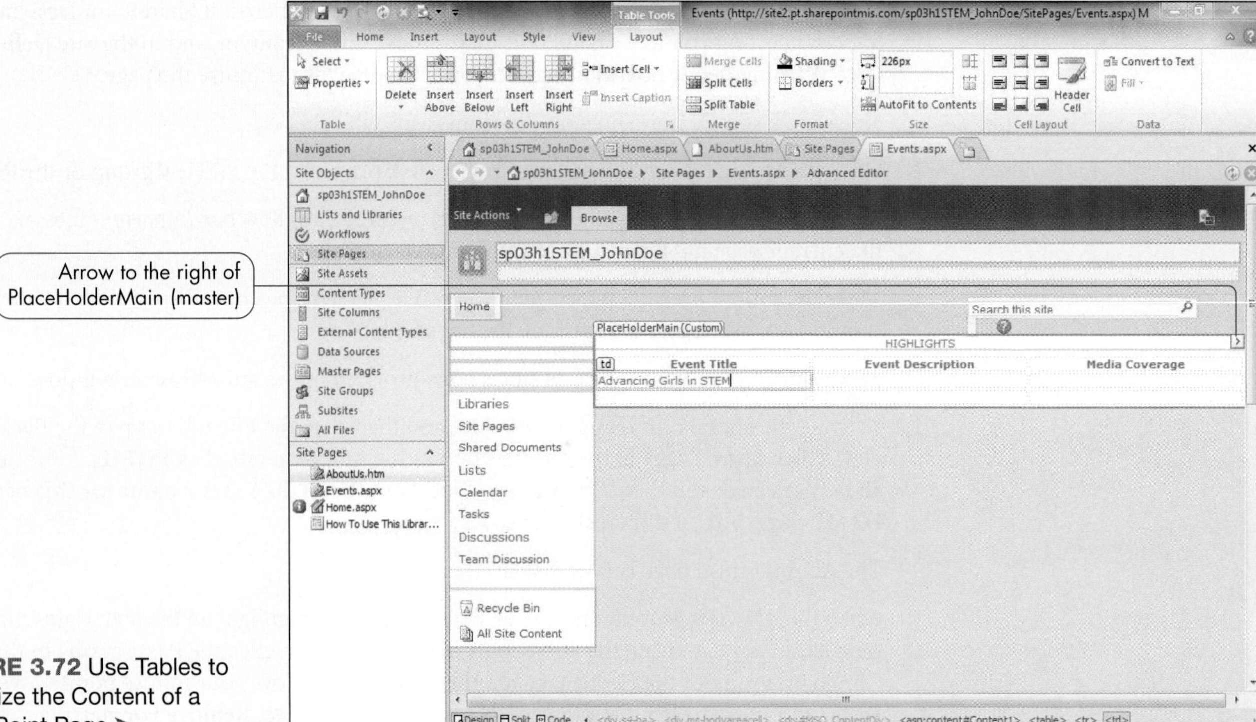

FIGURE 3.72 Use Tables to Organize the Content of a SharePoint Page ➤

a. Click the **File tab** to open the Backstage view. Click **New Page from Master** in the *Pages* section of the Add Item tab, click **v4.master (Default)**, and then click **Create**. Type **Events** in the **Enter a name for this new Web Part Page: box**, and then click **OK**. Click **Yes** in the Microsoft SharePoint Designer dialog box to edit in Advanced Mode.

   The Events.aspx page is now displayed in Advanced Editor mode.

b. Click the arrow to the right of the PlaceHolderMain (master), see Figure 3.72, and then select **Create Custom Content**.

c. Click anywhere within the purple borders of the PlaceHolderMain (custom), and then click the **Insert tab**.

d. Click **Table** in the Tables group, move the mouse pointer over the Insert Table grid to create a table with three rows and three columns, and then click on the highlighted area of the Insert Table grid.

   The new table is now displayed in the placeholder.

e. Position the insertion point in row one column one, click, and then click on the remaining two cells in the row while pressing **Shift**. Click **Header Cell** in the Cell Layout group of the Table Tools–Layout tab.

   The cells of the first row are now header cells.

f. Position the insertion point in row one column one, click, press **Shift**, and then click in row three column three. Click the **Distribute Columns button** in the Size group of the Table Tools–Layout tab. The columns will have the same width whichever will be the size of the future inserted content.

g. Click **Insert Caption** in the Rows and Columns group of the Table Tools–Layout tab, and then type **HIGHLIGHTS** in the caption area of the table.

h. Position the insertion point in row one column one, click, type **Event Title**, and then press **Tab**.

   The insertion point is now in the row one column two cell.

i. Type **Event Description**, and then press **Tab**. Type **Media Coverage**, and then press **Tab**. Position the insertion point in row two, column one, and then type **Advancing Girls in STEM**.

j. Click **Save** on the Quick Access Toolbar.

   The Web page should look similar to Figure 3.72.

STEP 4 ADD GRAPHICS TO A WEB PAGE

You will insert a picture into the cell of a table on the Center's site, format the cell properties, and then create an Auto Thumbnail. Refer to Figure 3.73 as you complete Step 4.

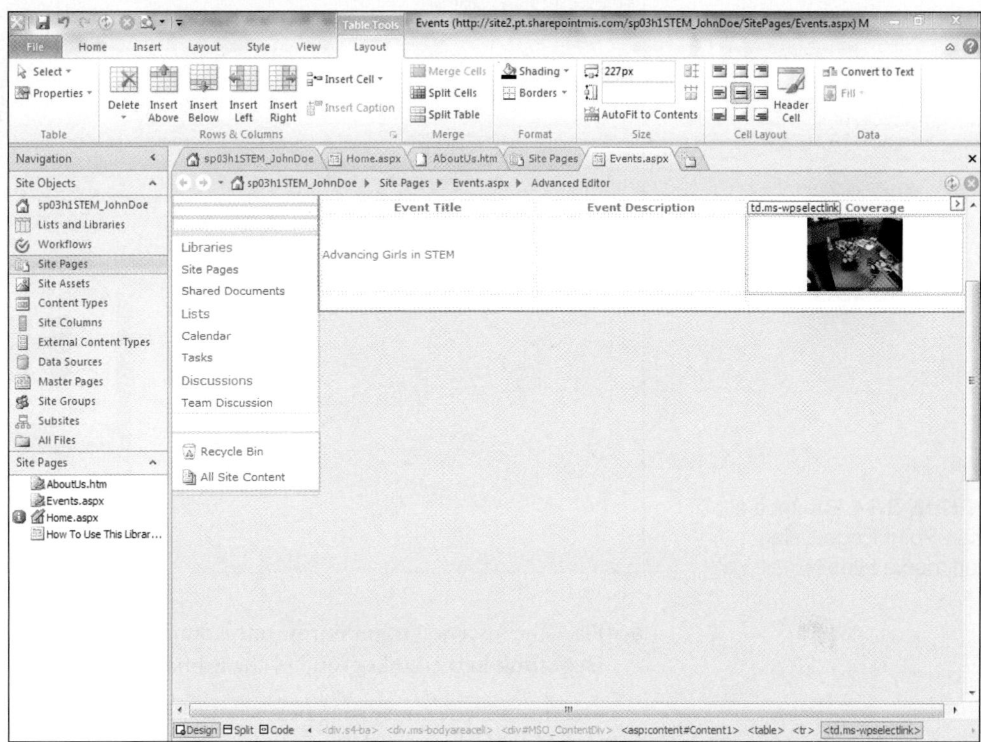

FIGURE 3.73 Enhance a SharePoint Page Using Graphics ➤

a. Place the insertion point in row one, column three. Click the **Insert tab**, and then click **Picture** in the Pictures group of the Insert ribbon.

   The Picture dialog box is now displayed.

b. Navigate to the Exploring folder, click **robotics.jpg**, and then click **Insert** in the Picture dialog box.

   The Accessibility Properties dialog box is now displayed.

c. Type **Advancing Girls in STEM** in the **Alternate text box**, and then click **OK** to close the Accessibility Properties dialog box.

d. Right-click the picture, and then click **Auto Thumbnail**.

   The thumbnail picture is now displayed.

e. Click the **Table Tools–Layout tab**, if the Layout tab is not already displayed, and then click **Center Vertically** in the Cell Layout group.

   The thumbnail picture is now centered in the cell.

f. Click **Save** on the Quick Access Toolbar, and then click **OK** in the Save Embedded Files dialog box.

   The Web page should look similar to Figure 3.73.

STEP 5 WORK WITH MULTIMEDIA FILES

You will insert a hyperlink to a YouTube video file created by the Center into a table cell. Refer to Figure 3.74 as you complete Step 5.

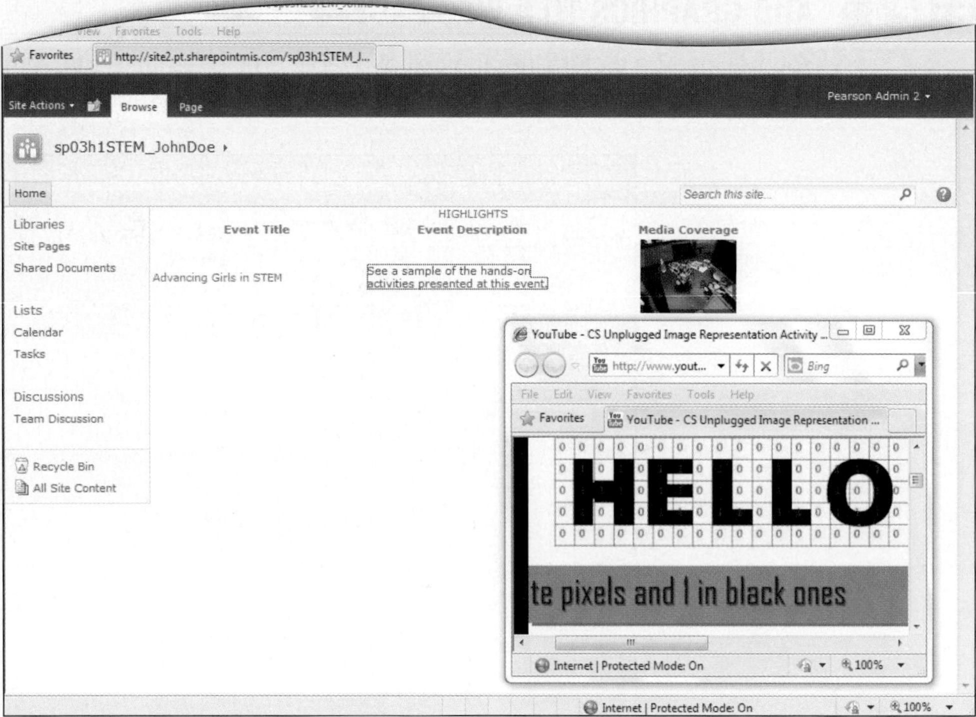

FIGURE 3.74 Enhance a SharePoint Page Using Multimedia Files ➤

a. Place the insertion point in row one, column two. Click the **Insert tab**, and then click **Hyperlink** in the Links group of the Ribbon.

   The Insert Hyperlink dialog box is now displayed.

b. Type **See a sample of the hands-on activities presented at this event** in the **Text to display: box**, and then type **http://www.youtube.com/watch?v=2zQDAcBzIKU** in the **Address: box**.

c. Click **Target Frame**, click **New Window** in the Target Frame dialog box, and then click **OK** twice to close the Target Frame dialog box and the Insert Hyperlink dialog box.

d. Click **Save** on the Quick Access Toolbar, click the **Home tab**, and then click **Preview in Browser** in the Preview group. Click the link to display the video.

   The Web page should look similar to Figure 3.74.

e. Close all Internet Explorer browser windows. Close all Word and SharePoint Designer windows, and then exit the application.

Work with Web Part Zones and Web Parts

As discussed in previous chapters of this textbook, Web Part pages are SharePoint Web pages that contain one or more Web Parts. Web Parts are very important SharePoint components, especially when deciding how information is presented to SharePoint users. This technology enables SharePoint sites to be flexible and highly customizable.

A Web Part page displays Web Part zones with blue borders in a grid pattern. Web Part zones are containers for Web Parts. Web Parts are components that can be reused. They can contain any type of Web-based information, including analytical, collaborative, and database information. Web Parts can be used to search and manage data in external databases and file systems. You can also develop Custom Web Parts to provide functions found in other applications, enabling you to integrate your SharePoint environment with other existing systems within the organization.

In this section, you will learn how to insert a Web Part zone into a page. Then, you will learn how to add or remove SharePoint Foundation 2010 built-in Web Parts from your pages, modify, import, and export one of the SharePoint Foundation 2010 built-in Web Parts.

Getting Started with the SharePoint Foundation Default Installation Web Parts

SharePoint Foundation 2010 comes with a number of built-in Web Parts that are available for you to add to your pages. The built-in Web Parts, as well as ones you might create, are organized into categories. Click Web Part in the SharePoint Foundation Web Parts group on the Editing Tools–Insert tab to display the Web Part bar.

In a default installation, the 13 SharePoint Foundation 2010 Web Parts are grouped into five categories, as shown in Figure 3.75. Each category contains a number of different Web Parts. For instance, the Lists and Libraries category contains Web Parts such as Announcement, Calendar, Links, and more. With the Content Rollup Web Parts, you can merge information from multiple locations and display them within a single Web Part. The Forms category enables the collection and submission of data. You can add images, video, and other media to the Web page using the Media and Content Web Part category. The Social Collaboration Web Parts enable you to make contact and collaborate with people within the SharePoint environment.

In a default installation, the 13 SharePoint Foundation 2010 Web Parts are grouped into five categories....

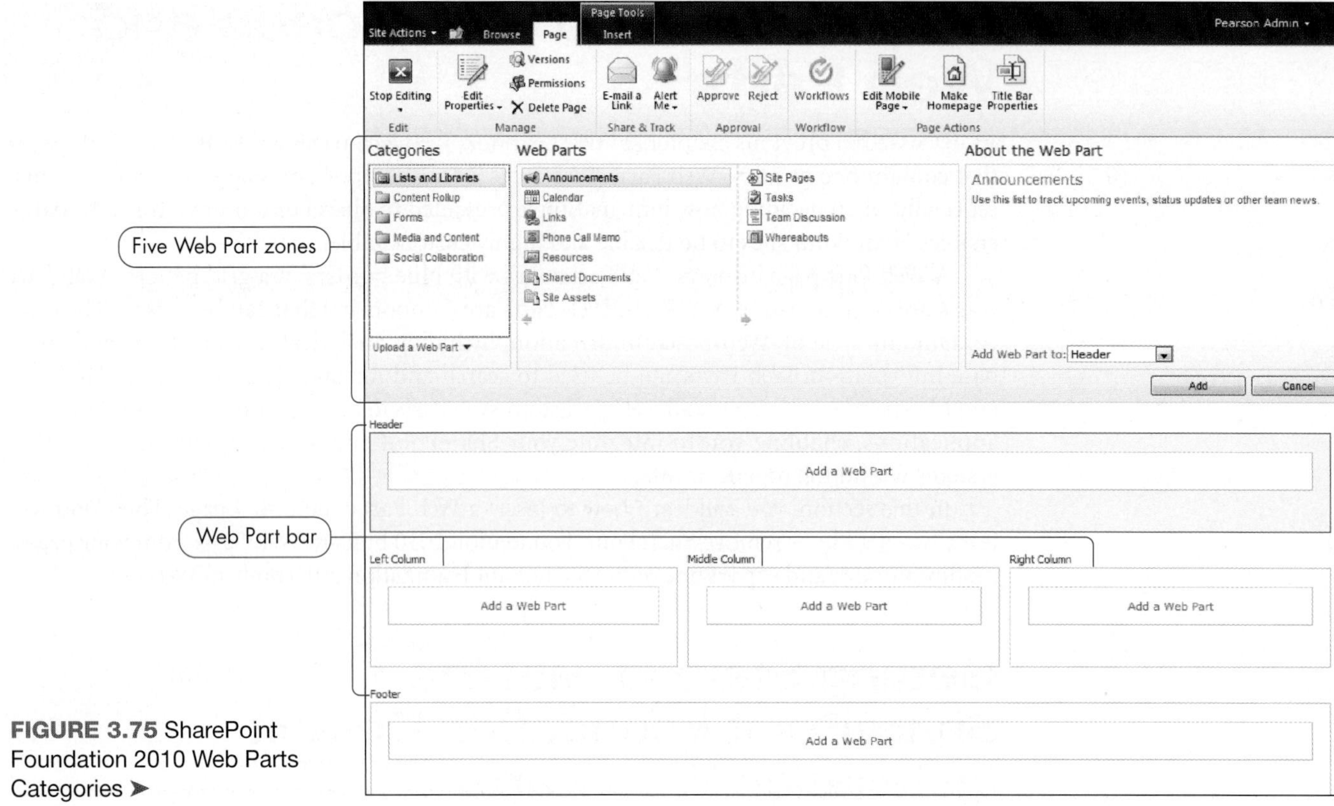

FIGURE 3.75 SharePoint Foundation 2010 Web Parts Categories ➤

You can also display and modify data that comes from other sources supported by SharePoint. You can create a Data View Web Part (DVWP) or a Data Form Web Part (DFWP) to make this data available. Later in this chapter, you will learn how to use a DVWP to display information from SharePoint Lists and Libraries. You will learn, in the following chapter, how to create a DVWP for types of data sources other than SharePoint List and Libraries.

Inserting a Web Part Zone

Web Part zones are containers only for Web Parts; thus, you cannot insert other elements, such as text or an image, into a Web Part zone.

Web Part zones are containers only for Web Parts; thus, you cannot insert other elements, such as text or an image, into a Web Part zone. Web Part zone properties control the actions that site visitors can take using a browser. The way Web Parts are displayed is also affected by the Web Part zone properties, described in Table 3.3 (see the Web Part zone properties dialog box in Figure 3.78).

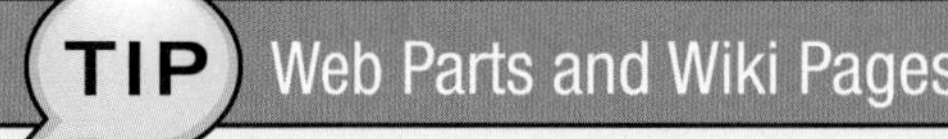

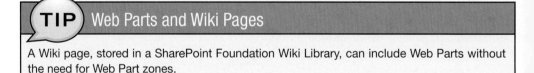

TIP Web Parts and Wiki Pages

A Wiki page, stored in a SharePoint Foundation Wiki Library, can include Web Parts without the need for Web Part zones.

TABLE 3.3 SharePoint Foundation Web Part Zone Properties	
Property	**Description**
Zone Title	Stores information about the Web Part zone in the SQL server content database.
Frame Style	Defines the default frame style for all Web Parts included in the Web Part zone.
Layout of Web Parts Contained in the Zone	Sets the layout as Top-To-Bottom for a vertical layout or Side-By-Side for a horizontal layout.
Browser Settings for Web Parts Contained in the Zone	Sets browser properties, enabling user access to the Web Parts included in the Web Part zone.

A Web Part zone can only be inserted into an ASP.NET page using SharePoint Designer. Click on the page where you wish to insert a new Web Part zone, and then click Web Part Zone in the Web Parts group on the Insert tab, as shown in Figure 3.76. The Web Part Zone Tools–Format tab appears, along with a new Web Part zone labeled Zone 1. A tag label displays *webpartpages:wikicontentweb*, as does the Quick Tag Selector. Type a title in the Zone Title box, as shown in Figure 3.77, to change the name of the zone. Click Zone Layout in the Layout group to select the layout you want. Click Properties in the Web Part Zone group to display the dialog box shown in the figure. Here, you can change the zone title, frame style, layout, and settings for the user's browser.

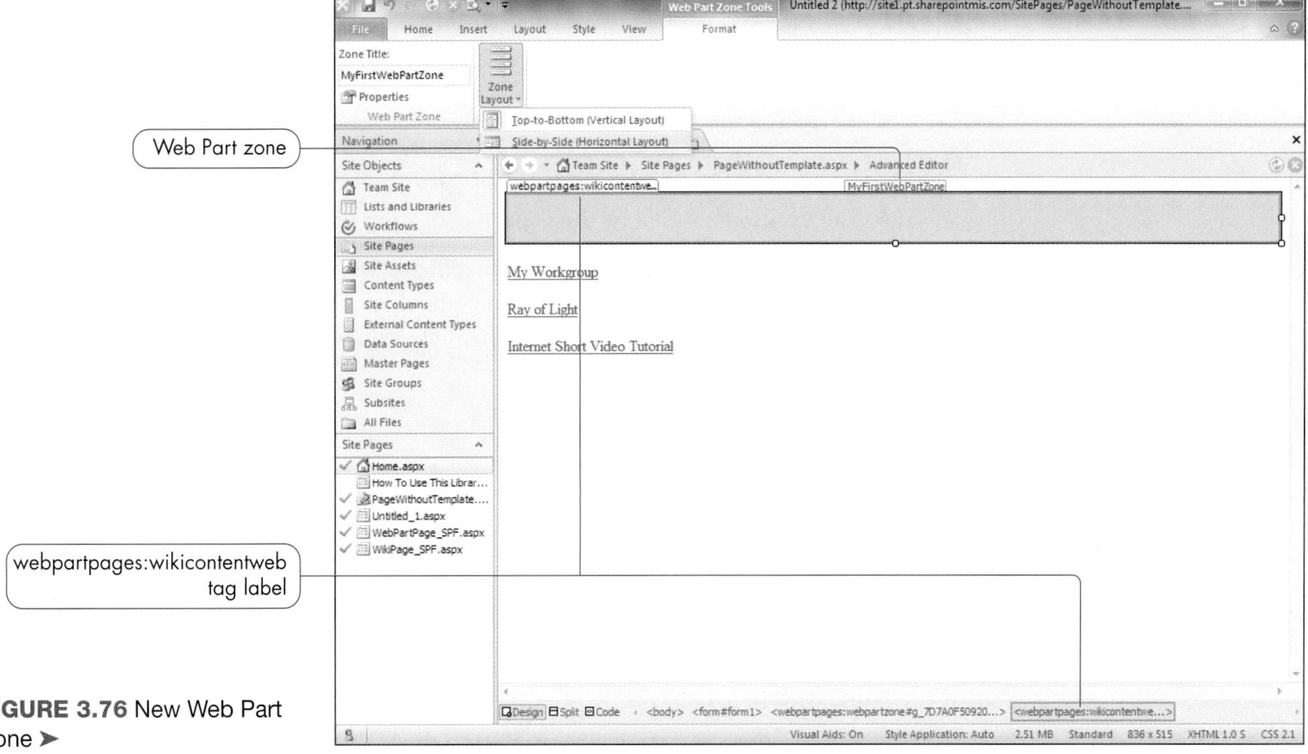

FIGURE 3.76 New Web Part Zone ➤

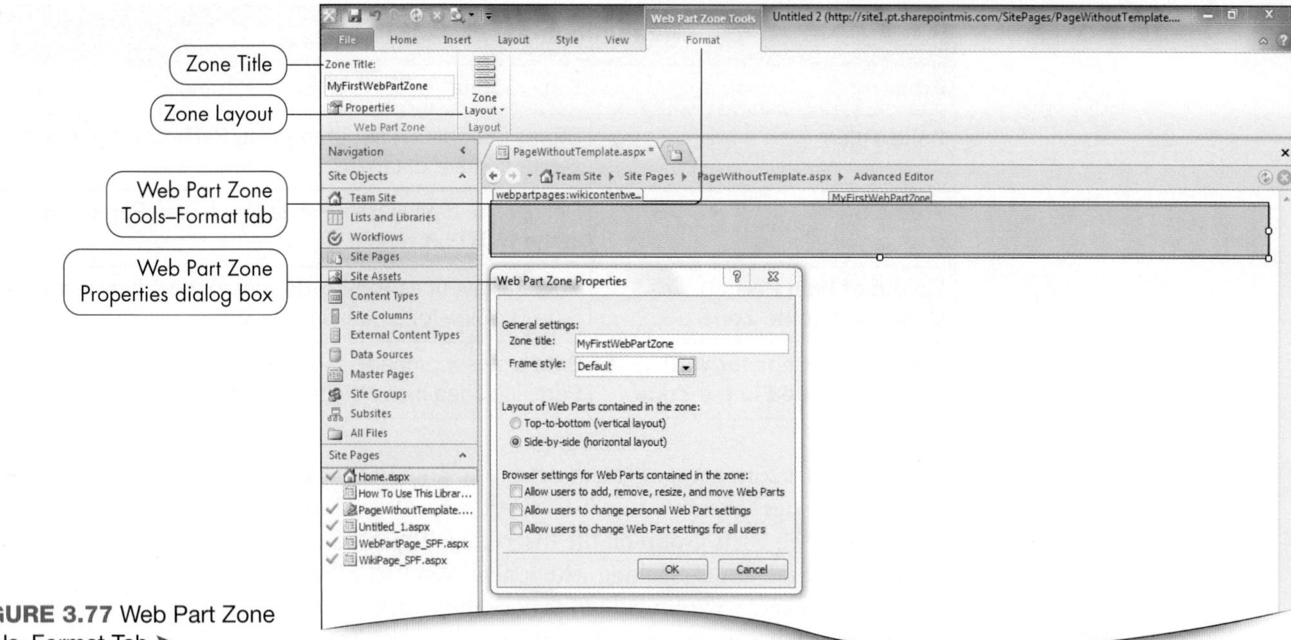

FIGURE 3.77 Web Part Zone Tools–Format Tab ➤

> **TIP** Positioning the Cursor in SharePoint Designer
>
> In SharePoint Designer, the easiest way to navigate and position the cursor in the desired location on a page is by pressing ESC with the up arrow, down arrow, left arrow, and right arrow.

Adding and Modifying a Web Part

Web Parts can be also classified by their specific location within a page:

A **Dynamic Web Part** is a part that can be placed using SharePoint Designer or the browser or in a Web Part zone on Web Part pages. It is saved separately from the page in the SQL Server content database.

A **Static Web Part** is a part that can be placed using SharePoint Designer in Advanced Edit Mode or outside a Web Part zone on Web Part pages. It is saved as part of the page.

- ***Dynamic Web Parts*** can be placed using SharePoint Designer or the browser with the EmbeddedFormShield SharePoint control on a Wiki page, or in a Web Part zone on Web Part pages. They are saved separately from the page in the SQL Server content database.
- ***Static Web Parts*** can be placed only using SharePoint Designer in Advanced Edit mode, outside of the EmbeddedFormShield SharePoint control on a Wiki page, or outside a Web Part zone on Web Part pages. They are saved as part of the page.

Add Web Parts to SharePoint Pages

After creating a site or adding either a Web Part page or general content page to an existing site, you may want to further customize the page by utilizing Web Parts. You can use either the SharePoint Foundation or the SharePoint Designer to add Web Parts.

To add a Web Part to a Web Part page in a team site using the SharePoint Foundation, click Edit Page on the Site Actions menu. Within the Web Part page, click *Add a Web Part* in the Web Part zone where you want the Web Part displayed. Select the category from the *Categories* section, and then select the Web Part you want to use from the *Web Parts* section, as shown in Figure 3.78. At the bottom of the *About the Web Part* section, select the desired Web Part zone in the *Add Web Part to* box. Click Add, and then click Stop Editing in the Edit group on the Page tab.

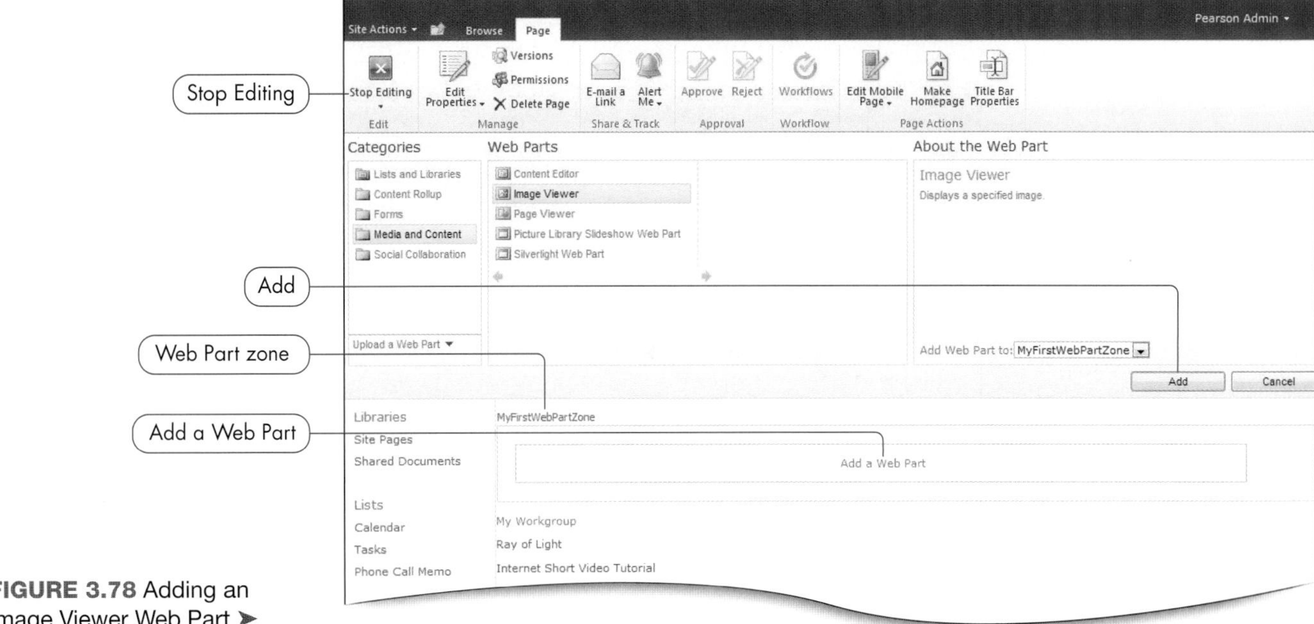

FIGURE 3.78 Adding an Image Viewer Web Part ➤

Page Content areas on Wiki pages give you more flexibility when adding Web Parts. Again, begin to add Page Content by clicking Edit Page on the Site Actions menu in SharePoint Foundation. Click within a content area where you want to place the Web Part. Click Web Part in the Web Parts group on the Editing Tools–Insert tab. Select from the *Categories* section, and then select the Web Part from the *Web Parts* section. Click the appropriate type of content in the *Add Web Part to* box, and then click Add. Click Save & Close in the Edit group on the Page tab.

Modify a Web Part

Each Web Part has settings that establish its functions and how it displays information. SharePoint enables you to make changes in the behavior of a Web Part in order to further customize it. You do this by editing the Web Part properties. You can modify three major categories: Appearance, Layout, and Advanced. In the Appearance category, you can display a title, alter the height and width, and change whether the Web Part appears minimized (Chrome State) and how the title is displayed (Chrome Type). The Layout category enables you to hide the Web Part, change the direction of the text and data in the Web Part, and determine which zone the Web Part is in and its relationship to other Web Parts in the zone (Zone Index). The Advanced category contains settings for enabling the user to adjust the layout, the display properties of the title, the Help options, the display of icon images on the title bar and catalog, and the error messages provided to the user as he or she works on the page.

Using SharePoint Foundation, you can edit the properties of the Web Parts. Click the title bar of the Web Part you want to change. Click the arrow on the right side of the title bar, and then click Edit Web Part on the menu, as shown in Figure 3.79a. Change the appropriate properties in the Web Part Properties pane, as shown in Figure 3.79b, and then click OK. In Figure 3.79b, notice the three major categories discussed above: Appearance, Layout, and Advanced. You can click the plus sign next to each to display the additional settings for the category.

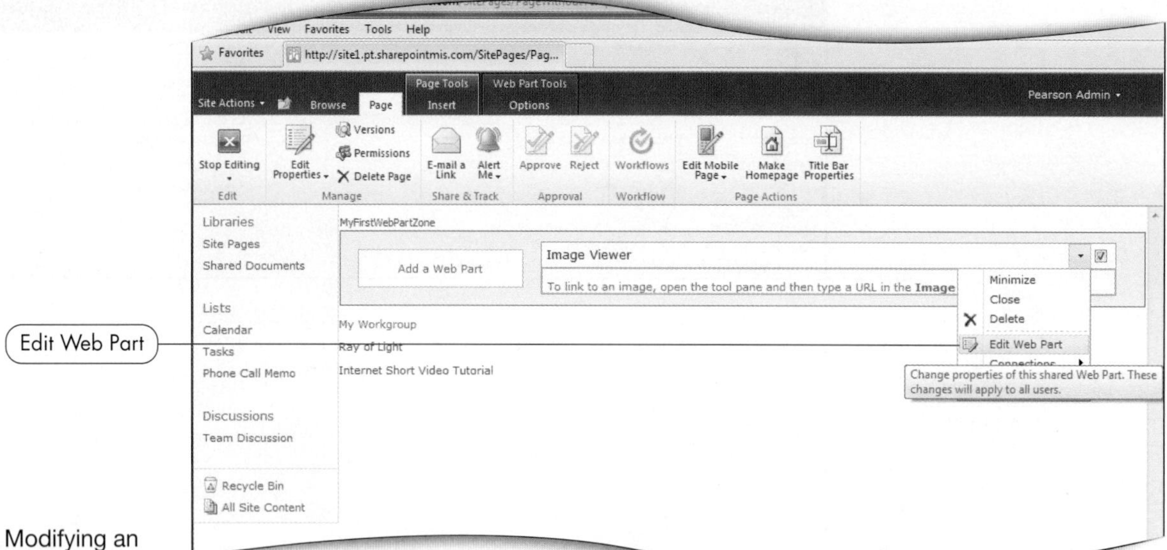

FIGURE 3.79a Modifying an Image Viewer Web Part ➤

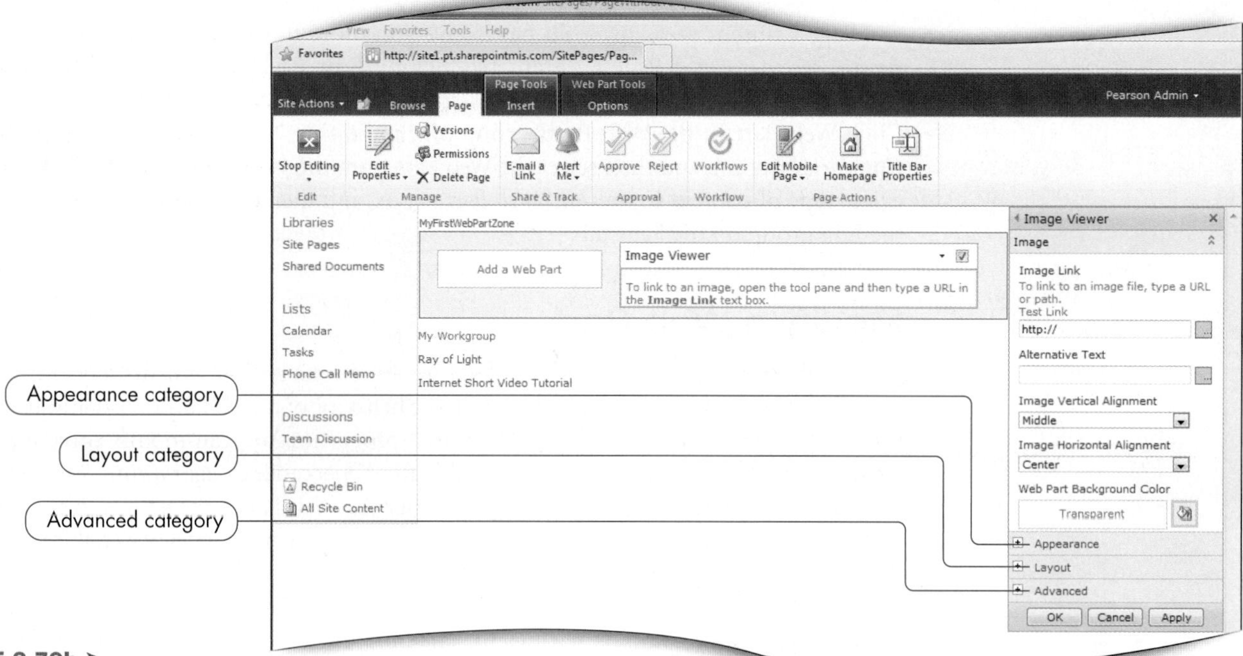

FIGURE 3.79b ➤

The List Views pane contains additional properties. The Selected View property enables you to select a view for the list affecting the display of the items. You can also customize the list view of the Web Part by clicking *Edit the current view* below the selection box, as shown in Figure 3.80. The Toolbar Type property controls the display of functional links on the Web Part. For example, the Summary Toolbar displays an Add Item/New Document link below the list. Show Toolbar displays a link and a menu bar above the list with Actions and Settings commands. The No Toolbar option removes the links from the Web Part display.

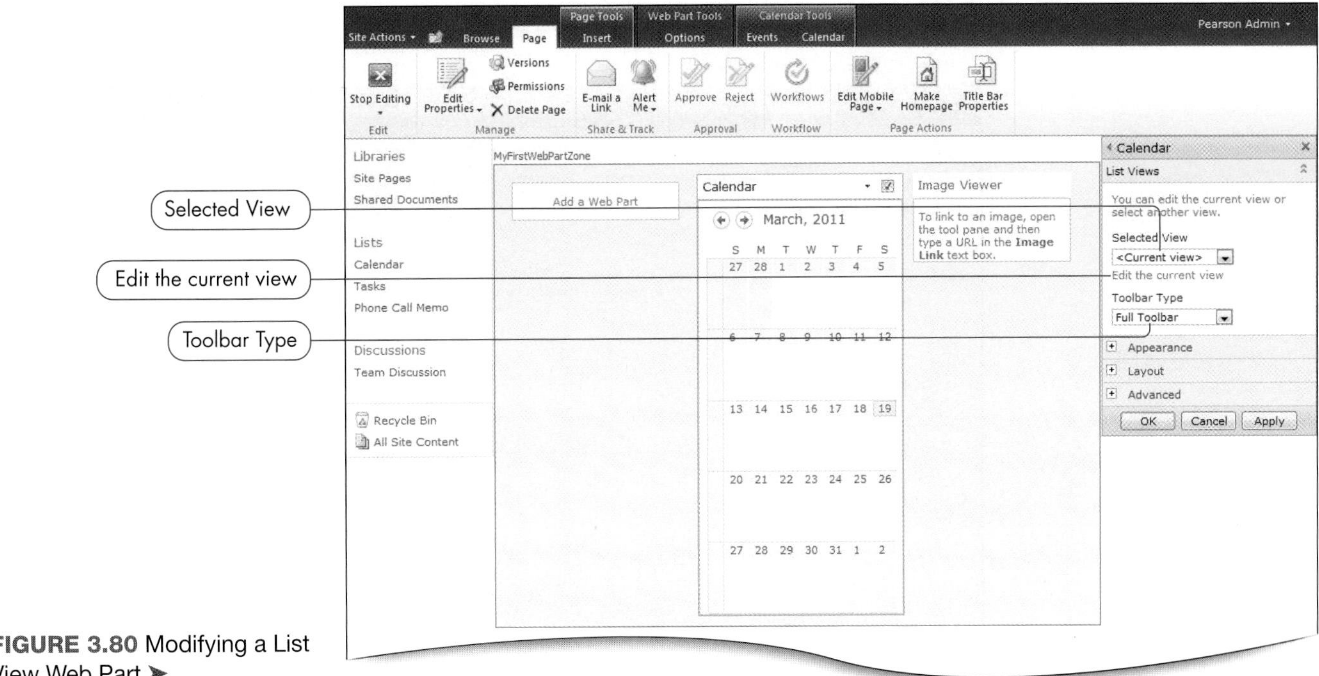

FIGURE 3.80 Modifying a List View Web Part ➤

Exporting and Importing Web Parts

SharePoint enables you to export and import most Web Parts.

Once you finish configuring a Web Part, including both common and unique properties, you may want to reuse the Web Part, with the same settings, in other sites or pages. SharePoint enables you to export and import most Web Parts.

When you export a Web Part, an XML file is created. The XML file extension for exported files is .webpart or .dwp. When you export Web Parts, you have the option to export Non-Sensitive Data Only which protects sensitive information, such as passwords, from being exported. Using SharePoint Foundation, click Edit Page on the Site Actions menu. Click the title bar of the Web Part you want to export, and then click the arrow on the right side of the title bar to display the Web Part menu. Click Export, and then click Save in the File Download dialog box, as shown in Figure 3.81. Browse to the directory where you want to save the Web Part file, and then click Save.

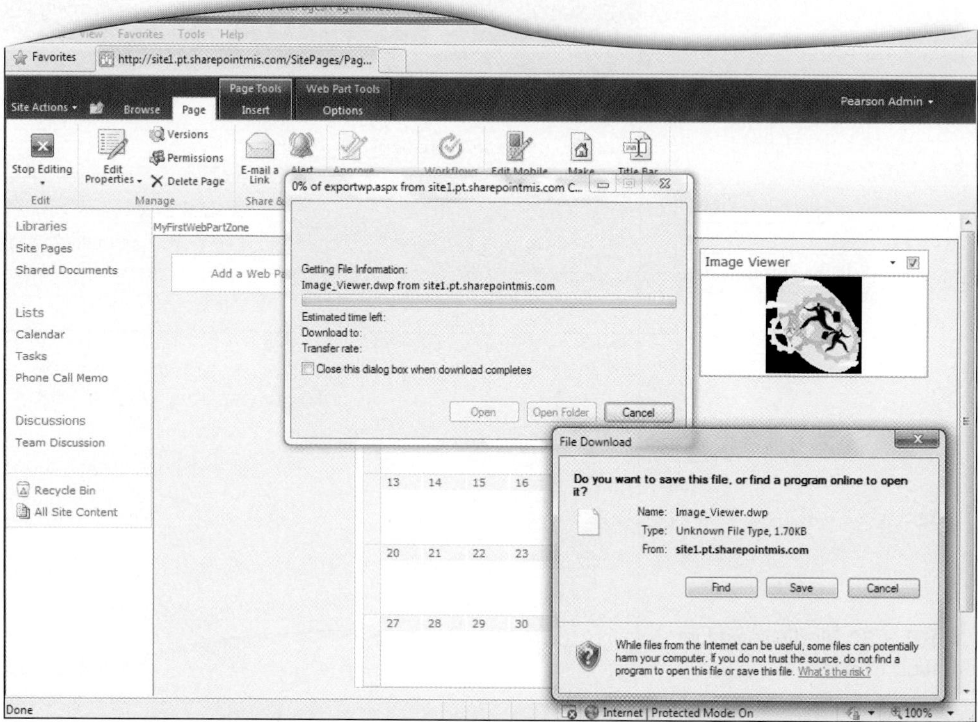

FIGURE 3.81 Exporting a Web Part ➤

To import a .webpart or .dwp file into a site Web Part, the Full Control permission level is required. You have two options for importing the Web Part; one prevents others from using the Web Part, whereas the other enables users to reuse the Web Part. If you decide to prevent others from using the Web Part, you must import it each time you want to add it to a page.

You import Web Parts using Edit Page on the Site Actions menu of SharePoint Foundation. Click Web Part in the Web Parts group of the Editing Tools–Insert tab. Click Upload a Web Part at the bottom of the Categories list, and then click Browse. Locate and select the .webpart or .dwp file, and then click Open. Click Upload. The Web Part will appear in the Imported Web Parts Category; from there, you can add it to the page.

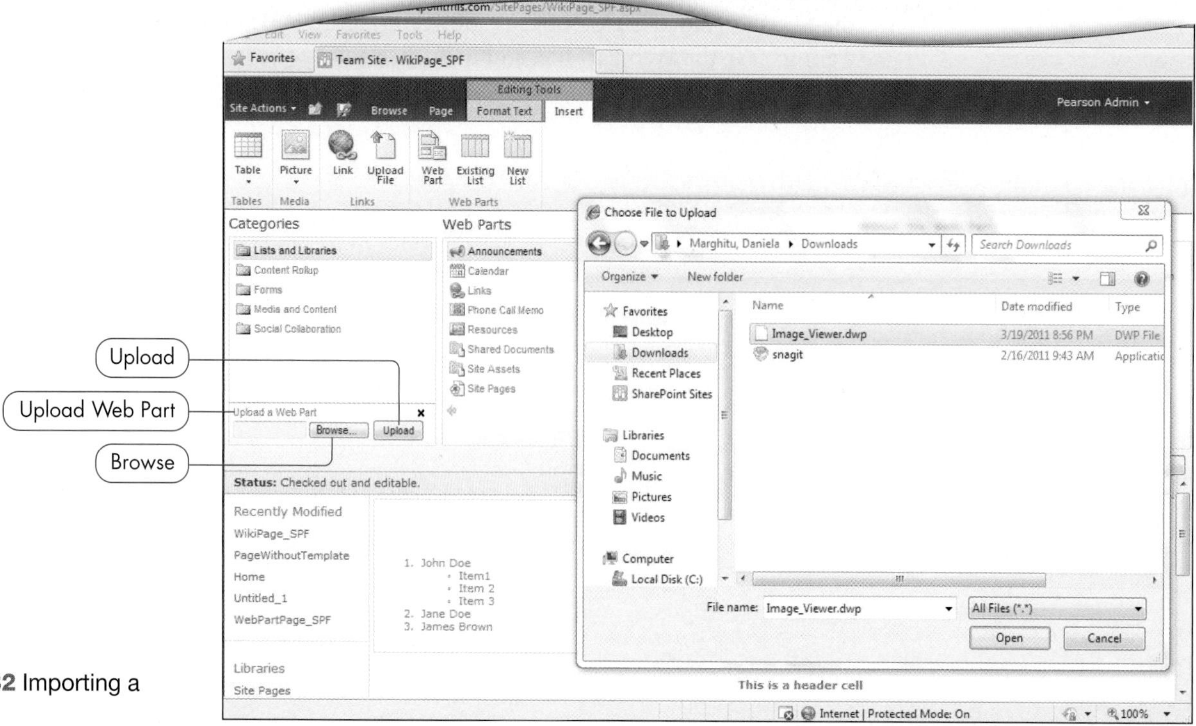

FIGURE 3.82 Importing a Web Part ➤

When you import a Web Part, as described above, it is not available to other users. You can import the file so that it is available in other categories on the Web Parts bar. For this import, you begin at the Site Settings on the Site Actions menu of SharePoint Foundation. The import is made on the top-level site, so you may have to navigate to that level using the Go to Top Level Site Settings link on the *Site Collection Administration* section. On the Site Settings page, click Web Parts in the *Galleries* section. Select Upload Document in the New group of the Library Tools–Document tab. Browse to the .webpart or .dwp file, click Open, and then click OK, as shown in Figure 3.83. In the Edit Item window, shown in Figure 3.84, change the name, title, and description as needed. Select the Group and appropriate Recommendation Settings to organize and display the imported Web Part to users. Click Save to complete the import operation. The imported file will appear in the Web Part Gallery (as shown previously in Figure 3.75). Using the Web Part Gallery, you can edit, delete, and manage security for the Web Parts.

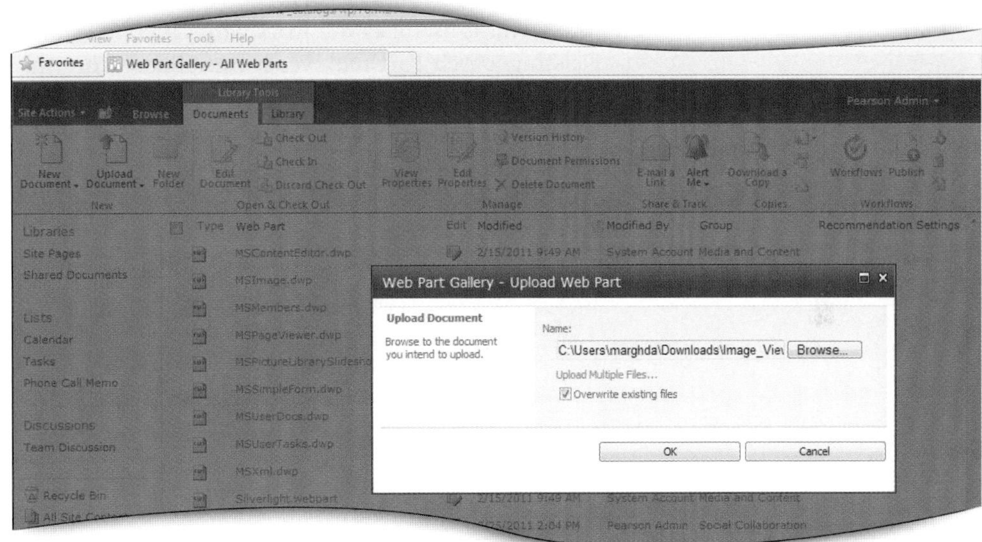

FIGURE 3.83 Importing a Web Part Using the Web Part Gallery ➤

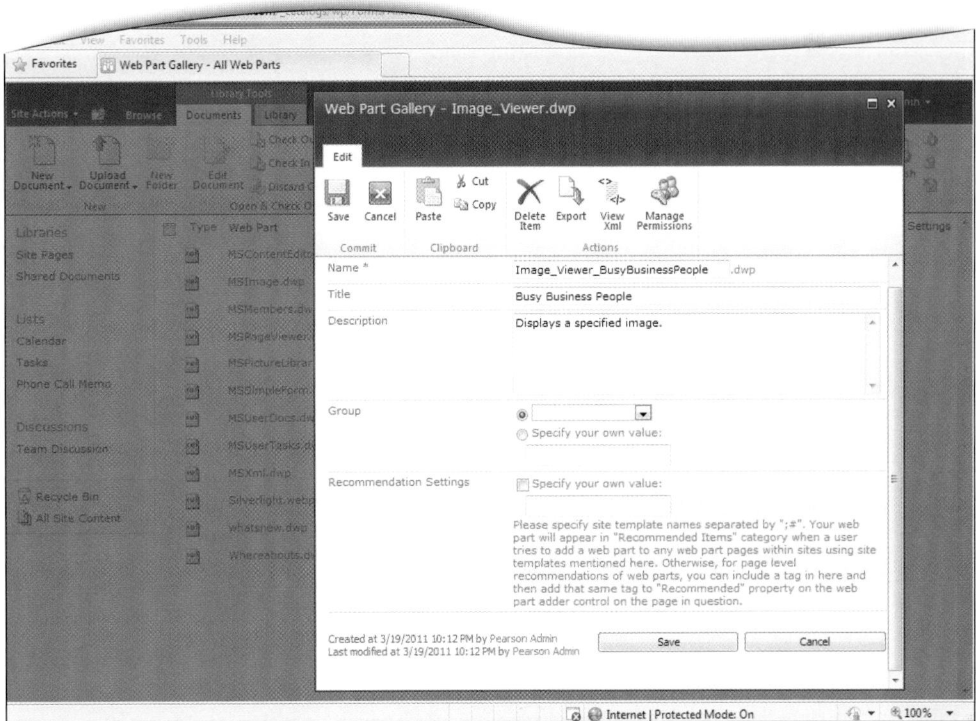

FIGURE 3.84 Edit Item Window ➤

Removing a Web Part

It is not uncommon that, at some point in time, you will need to remove Web Parts from your pages. You can remove Web Parts in one of three ways. First, you can minimize the Web Part, displaying only the title bar to the user. Second, you can close the Web Part, which makes it available through the Closed Web Parts category so it can be added back in later. Finally, you can delete it completely from the Web page.

To minimize a Web Part, using SharePoint Foundation while viewing the Web Part page, click Edit Page on the Site Actions menu. Click the title bar of the Web Part, and then click the arrow on the title bar to open the Web Part menu. Click Minimize in the State group on the Web Part Tools–Option tab.

If you close the Web Part, users will not see it unless they view the Closed Web Parts category on the Web Parts bar. Repeat the steps for minimizing the Web Part, but select Close from the State Group on the Web Part Tools–Option tab. Keep in mind that using this strategy for removing a Web Part makes it readily available to add back onto the Web page at a later time. This is useful as you work with different layouts of the elements on the page.

Deleting a Web Part removes it completely from the page. If you need it on the page later, you must add it from the *Categories* section on the Web Parts bar, and then reset any properties that you might have changed for the Web Part. As with the other two methods of removing Web Parts, follow the same methods, but select Delete from the Web Part Tools–Option tab.

2 Work with Web Part Zones and Web Parts

The Center for Women in STEM is built on a SharePoint Foundation server, and you want to take full advantage of all the powerful built-in components for implementing the site's functionalities. You will create an add Web Part zone and format it. You will also add Web Parts to this Web Part zone, and format them. Finally, you will export a Web Part, import it to another subsite, and then remove a Web Part.

Skills covered: Insert a Web Part Zone • Add and Modify a Web Part • Export and Import a Web Part • Remove a Web Part

STEP 1 INSERT A WEB PART ZONE

You will use SharePoint Designer to create an ASPX Web page for the Center for Women in STEM. Then, you will insert a Web Part zone and format it. Finally, you will attach the default master to the .ASPX page so you will be able to use the SharePoint Foundation browser interface. Refer to Figure 3.85 as you complete Step 1.

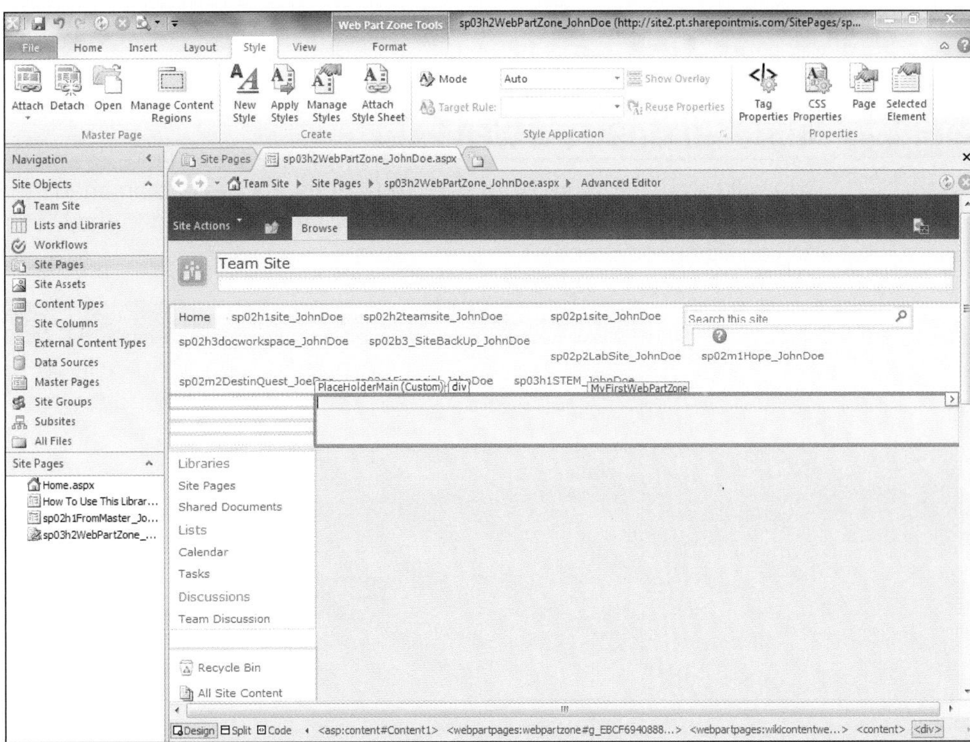

FIGURE 3.85 Insert a Web Part Zone in SharePoint Designer ➤

a. Click **Start** to display the Start menu. Click **All Programs**, and then click **Internet Explorer** to open the program. Go to the top-level site provided by your instructor, which will be in the format of *http://pt.sharepointmis.com/SitePages/yourname*. Enter the user name and password provided by your instructor. Click **Edit in SharePoint Designer** on the Site Actions menu. Type the password in the **Windows Security dialog box**.

b. Click the **File tab** to open the Backstage view. Click **More Pages** in the *Pages* section of the Add Item tab, click **ASPX**, and then click **Create**. Type **sp03h2WebZone_LastNameFirstName** in the **Enter a name for this new ASPX page: box**, and then click **OK**. Click **Yes** in the Microsoft SharePoint Designer dialog box asking if you want to open this page in Advanced Editor mode.

   The *sp03h2WebPartZone_LastNameFirstName.aspx* page is now displayed in Advanced Editor mode.

c. Position the insertion point just below *<form#Form1>* if you are not already there. Click the **Insert tab**, and then click **Web Part Zone** in the Web Parts group of the Insert ribbon. Click the **Web Part Zone Tools–Format tab.**

   The Web Part Zone Tools–Format tab is now displayed and a new Web Part zone labeled Zone 1 appears at the top of the *sp03h2WebPartZone_LastNameFirstName.aspx* page.

d. Type **MyFirstWebPartZone** in the **Zone Title: box** in the Web Part zone group. Click **Properties** in the Web Part zone group.

   The Web Part Zone Properties dialog box is now displayed.

e. Review all settings in the Web Part Zone Properties dialog box using Table 3.3, and then click **OK** to close the Web Part Zone Properties dialog box.

f. Click the **Style tab**, click the **Attach arrow** in the Master Page group, and then select **v4.master under Default Master Page**. Click **OK** in the Match Content Regions dialog box, if needed. Click **Save** on the Quick Access Toolbar.

   Your screen should now look similar to Figure 3.85.

> **TROUBLESHOOTING:** You attach the v4.master master page so you can further edit the page using the SharePoint Foundation browser interface.

g. Click **Save** on the Quick Access Toolbar.

STEP 2 ADD AND MODIFY A WEB PART

You will create a Picture Library for the Center and upload an image to it. Then, you will insert a Picture Library Slideshow Web Part that will be connected to the Picture Library. Refer to Figure 3.86 as you complete Step 2.

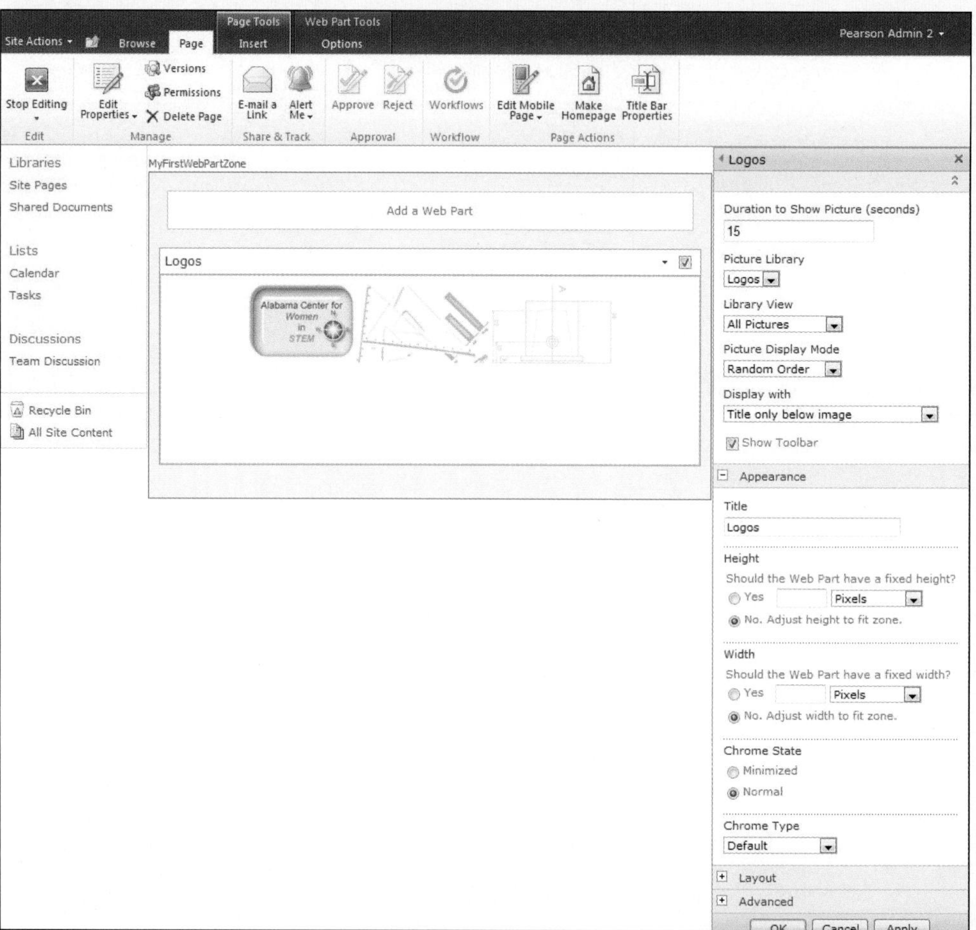

FIGURE 3.86 Enhance a SharePoint Page Using a Picture Library Slideshow Web Part ➤

a. Click the **Home tab**, and then click **Preview in Browser** in the Preview group of the Ribbon.

   The *sp03h2WebPartZone_LastNameFirstName.aspx* page is now displayed in the browser.

b. Create a Logos library using the Picture Library template that will not show on the Quick Launch, and then upload *stem-banner.jpg* to it from your Exploring folder.

c. Click **Site Pages** on the Quick Launch, click **sp03h2WebPartZone_LastNameFirstName**, and then click **Edit Page** on the Site Actions menu.

d. Click **Add a Web Part** in the MyFirstWebPartZone Web Part zone created in Step 1.

   The Web Part bar is now displayed.

e. Click **Media and Content** under *Categories*, and then click **Picture Library Slideshow Web Part** under *Web Parts*. Click **Add**.

   The Picture Library Slideshow Web Part is now placed in the MyFirstWebPartZone Web Part zone.

f. Click the arrow on the title bar of the Picture Library Slideshow Web Part, and then select **Edit Web Part**.

   The Web Part Properties pane is now displayed.

g. Review all Web Part properties. Type **Logos** in the **Title box** under *Appearance*. Scroll down, and then click **OK** in the Web Part Properties pane.

   Your screen should now look similar to Figure 3.86.

h. Click **Stop Editing**.

STEP 3 EXPORT AND IMPORT A WEB PART

You will export a Web Part to a local folder, and then you will import it into another one of the Center's subsites. Refer to Figure 3.87 as you complete Step 3.

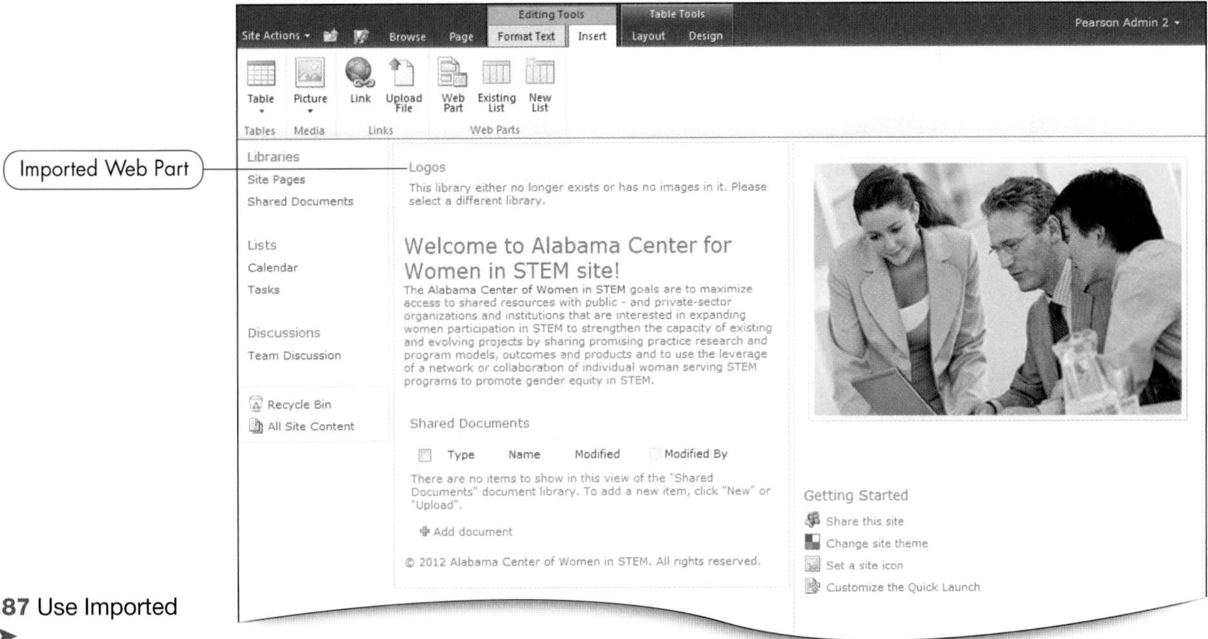

FIGURE 3.87 Use Imported Web Parts ➤

a. Click **Edit Page** on the Site Actions menu on the *sp03h2WebPartZone_LastNameFirstName* page.

b. Click the arrow on the title bar of the Logos Web Part, and then select **Edit Web Part**.

   The Web Part Properties pane is now displayed.

c. Click **Advanced** on the Web Part Properties pane, and then click **Export all data** on the Export Mode list. Click **OK**.

d. Click the arrow on the title bar of the Logos Web Part, and then select **Export**. Click **Save** in the File Download dialog box. Browse to the Exploring folder. Click **Save** in the Save As dialog box.

TROUBLESHOOTING: Click Close on the Download Complete dialog box if needed.

The *Logos.webpart* file should now be stored in your Windows Exploring folder.

e. Click **Site Pages**, and then click **Home** to open the home page of your top-level site. Click the link to the *sp03h1STEM_LastNameFirstName* subsite.

The home page of the subsite is now displayed in the browser.

f. Click **Edit Page** on the Site Actions menu. Click the **Editing Tools–Insert tab.**

g. Click **Web Part** in the Web Parts group of the Editing Tools–Insert tab.

The Web Part bar is now displayed.

h. Click the **Upload a Web Part arrow** under *Categories*. Click **Browse** to display the Choose File to Upload dialog box. Navigate to the *Logos.webpart* file, click, and then click **Open** to close the Choose File to Upload dialog box. Click **Upload**.

The Imported Web Part folder now shows under Categories.

i. Click the **Imported Web Part folder** under *Categories*, click **Logos** under *Web Parts*, and then click **Add**.

Your screen should now look similar to Figure 3.87.

STEP 4 REMOVE A WEB PART

You will remove a Web Part from the Center's site. Refer to Figure 3.88 as you complete Step 4.

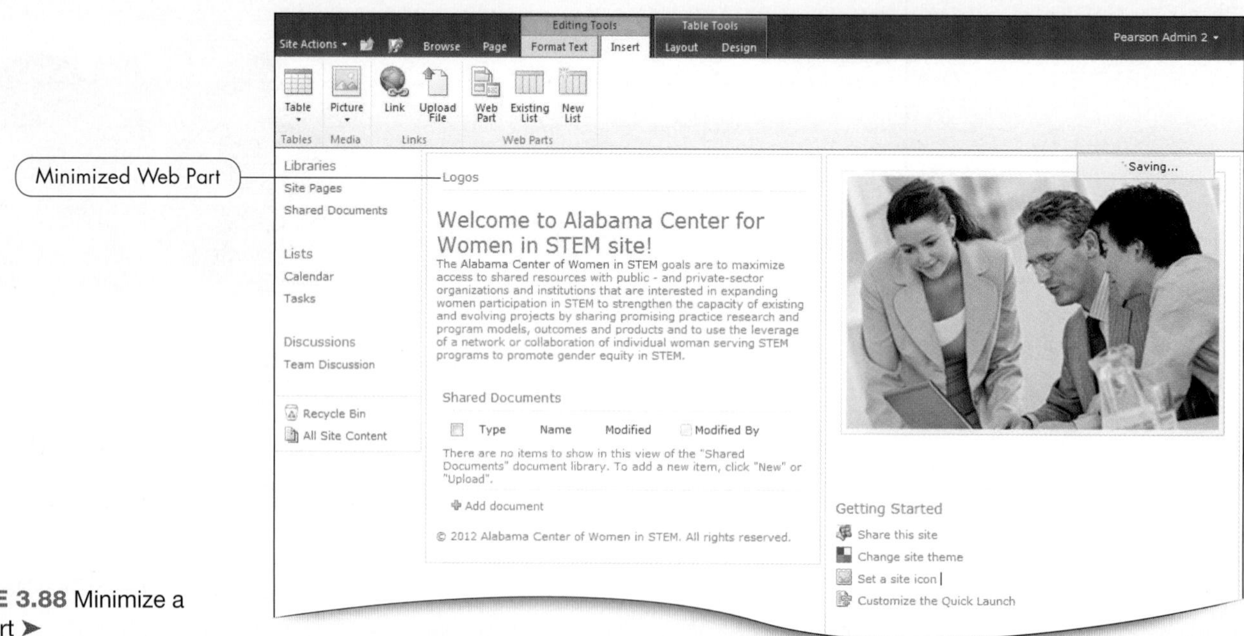

FIGURE 3.88 Minimize a Web Part ➤

a. Click the arrow on the title bar of the Logos Web Part, and then select **Minimize**.

   Your screen should look similar to Figure 3.88.

b. Click the arrow on the title bar of the Logos Web Part, and then select **Restore**.

   Your screen should look similar to Figure 3.87.

c. Click the arrow on the title bar of the Logos Web Part, select **Delete**, and then click **OK** to confirm the deletion.

   Your screen should no longer display the **Logos Web Part**.

d. Click the **Page tab,** and then click **Save & Close**. Close all browser windows, close all SharePoint Designer windows, and then exit the application.

Work with Data Views in SharePoint Designer

Data View Web Parts and Data Form Web Parts enable you to display data from a variety of sources in your SharePoint sites. Also known as Data View, data from a SharePoint list or library can be shown, along with data from XML files or other external data sources. Users can access the information they need to solve business problems and increase productivity. SharePoint Designer is used to show and hide fields, sort and filter data, and more. Built-in View Styles enable you to quickly create Data Views. Not only can Web page users view the data, they can write to data sources, such as database queries, XML documents, and SharePoint lists and libraries.

Data is retrieved from the data source as Extensible Markup Language (XML) and displayed in HTML by using Extensible Stylesheet Language Transformations (XSLTs). The WYSIWYG tools in SharePoint Designer can be used to modify the Data View. You can change the layout, modify the fonts, add or remove columns from the data, filter and sort the data, and group fields. SharePoint Designer updates the Extensible Stylesheet Language (XSL) automatically as you modify the Data Views.

In this section, you will learn how to create in SharePoint Designer Data Views, form libraries and lists, and how to modify a Data View using SharePoint Designer and SharePoint browser interface.

Creating Data Views

SharePoint Designer is used to add a Data View to an .ASPX page or a Web Part page.

SharePoint Designer is used to add a Data View to an .ASPX page or a Web Part page. The easiest way to do this is to click Data View on the Insert tab, and then select the data source. When using this option, if you select a list or library as the data source, a List View is displayed on the page. If you choose a different data source (other than a list or library), a Data Form Web Part (DFWP) is displayed. Other data sources include XML files, databases, server-side scripts, and more. In this section, we will create a Data View for a list or library. In Chapter 4, you will learn about creating Data Views for other types of data sources.

The method for creating a Data View from a list or library begins by selecting the page where you want to add the Data View in SharePoint Designer. Click Edit File in the Edit group on the Page tab, and then click inside the <div> tag or form box. The <div> tag option is shown in Figure 3.89a, and the form box is shown on an .ASPX page in Figure 3.89b. Click the Insert tab, and then click Data View in the Data Views & Forms group. Select the data source from the gallery. Figure 3.90 shows an example of a Data View.

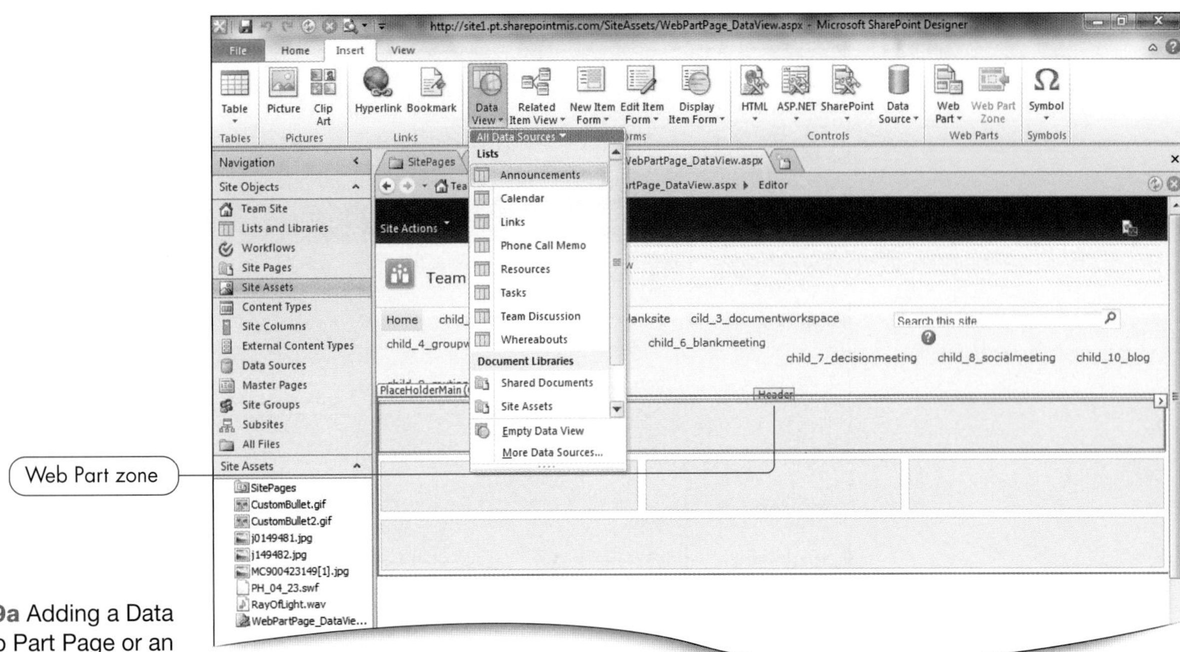

FIGURE 3.89a Adding a Data View to a Web Part Page or an ASPX Page ➤

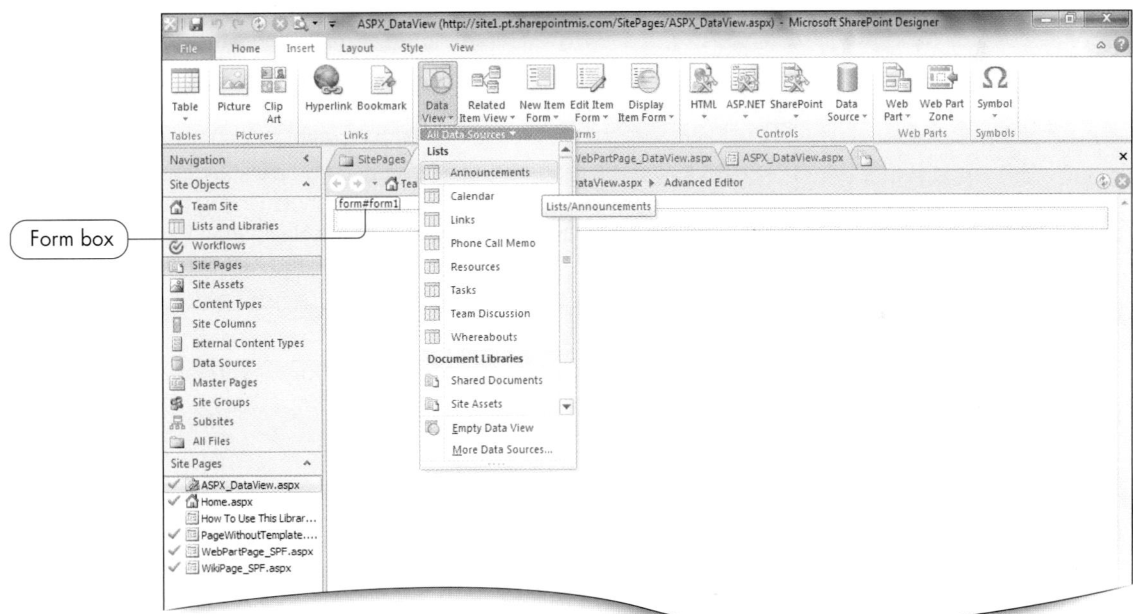

FIGURE 3.89b ➤

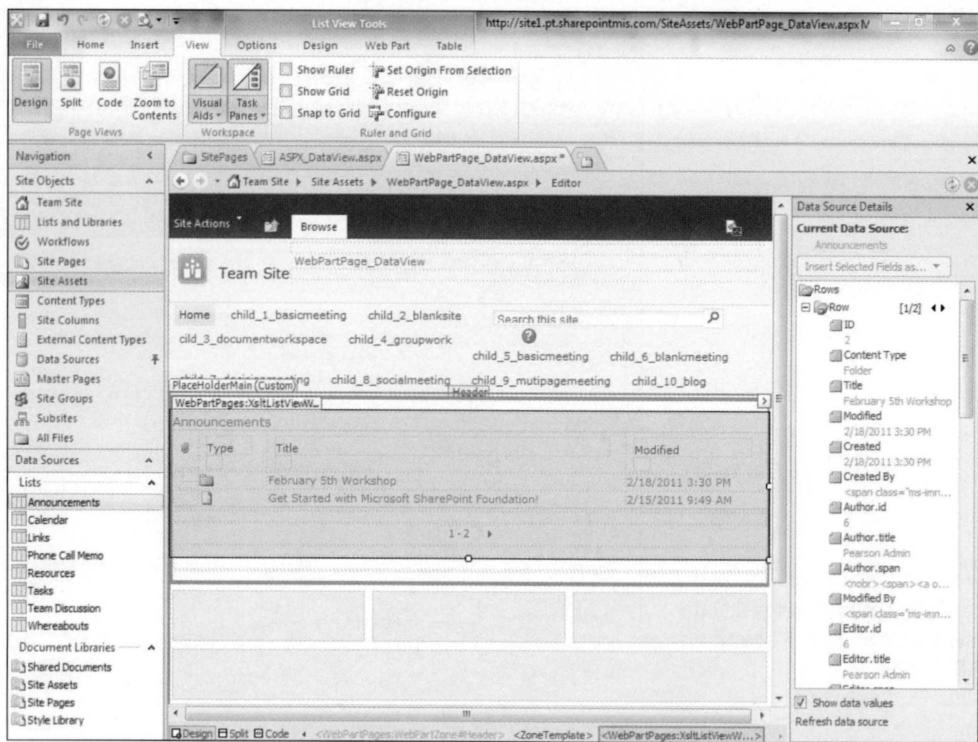

FIGURE 3.90 Data View ➤

TIP Dragging Data Sources from the Navigation Pane

You can also use a drag-and-drop action to add a Data View to a page. Click the pushpin next to Data Sources on the Navigation Pane, as shown in Figure 3.91. The files and available data sources will be displayed at the bottom of the Navigation Pane. Drag the data source onto the page. Depending on the data source, the required XLV or DFWP will be automatically created.

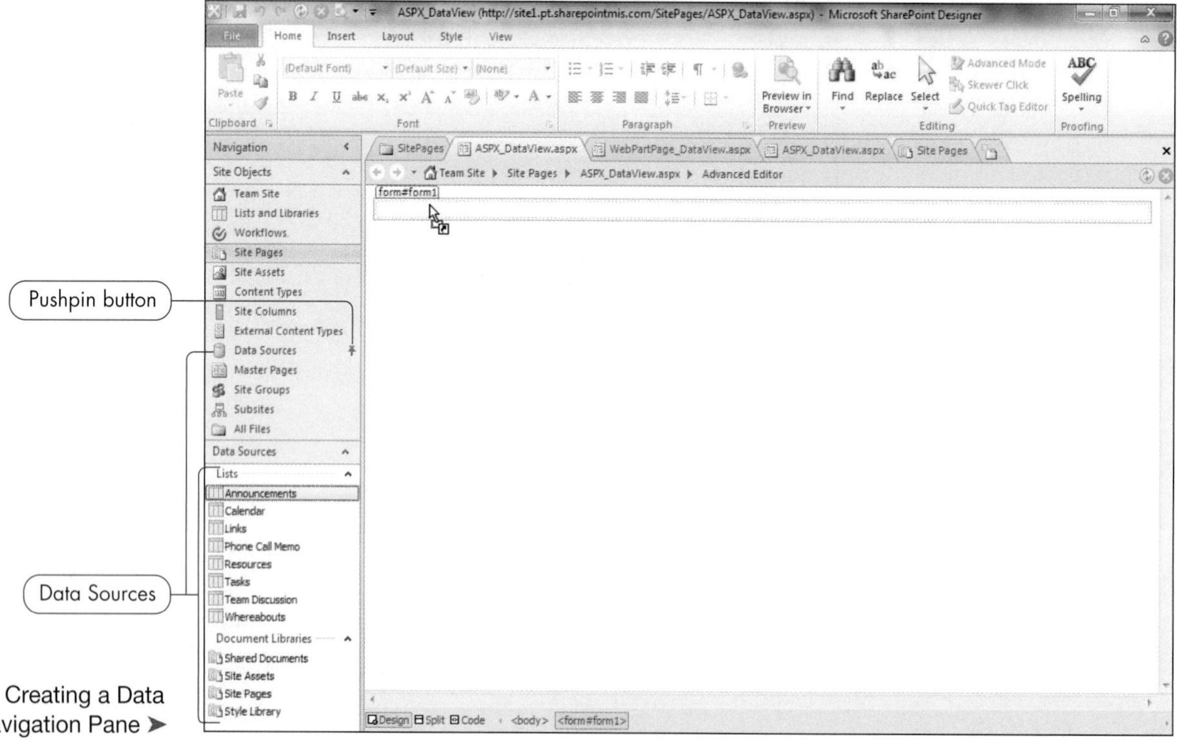

FIGURE 3.91 Creating a Data View Using Navigation Pane ➤

Modifying Data Views

SharePoint enables you to customize a Data View by taking advantage of its user-friendly Data View tools. For example, you can add, rearrange, and remove columns; sort and filter data; apply conditional formatting; and change the overall layout.

SharePoint enables you to customize a Data View by taking advantage of its user-friendly Data View tools.

Add, Remove, and Rearrange Columns

The most common type of customization you will do to a Data View is adding, rearranging, and removing the fields to be displayed. Later in this section, you will learn about how you can modify columns using the table editing commands on the Table tab.

The Displayed Fields dialog box enables you to modify the fields that appear in the Data View. Select the Data View on the Web page, and then click the Options tab, as shown in Figure 3.92. Click Add/Remove Columns in the Fields group to open the Displayed Fields dialog box. The fields shown in the *Available fields* column are the fields in the data that is selected for the Data View. If you want to add a column to the display, select the field, and then click Add. This moves it to the *Displayed fields* column on the right. To remove a field, select it in the *Displayed fields* list, and then click Remove. The fields can be reordered by selecting them, and then clicking Move Up or Move Down. You can select a number of fields at once by pressing Ctrl, and then clicking the fields to select them. Click OK when the Displayed fields list is in the correct order and contains the appropriate fields.

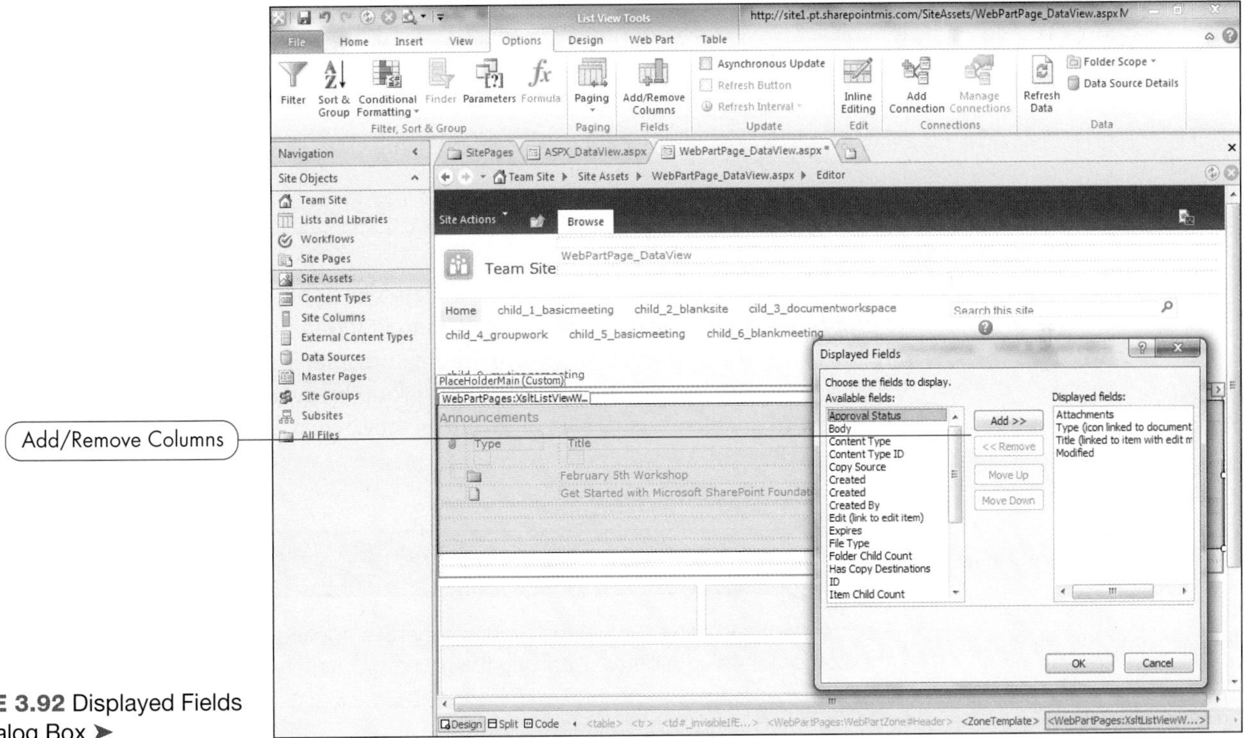

FIGURE 3.92 Displayed Fields Data Dialog Box ➤

Sort and Group

SharePoint Designer enables you to sort data in a Data View. You can sort the data alphabetically or numerically. You can produce customized sort orders using the Advanced Sort dialog box. You also have options for grouping the data once it is sorted. As the data is grouped, you can expand or collapse it in the Data View, as well as show column names or totals for each group.

It is important to keep in mind that you must sort first and then group. Using SharePoint Designer, click the Data View on the Web page. Click the Options tab, and then click Sort & Group, as shown in Figure 3.93. From the *Available fields* column, select the field to sort, and then click Add to move it to the *Sort order* column. Select whether the sort on that field should be ascending or descending. You can select more fields and rearrange them using Move Up or Move Down, and they can have different specifications for ascending and descending. For example, in a Data View, you may sort by Content Type ID in ascending order, while also sorting by modification date (Modified) in descending order to see the most recently updated materials first in alphabetical order.

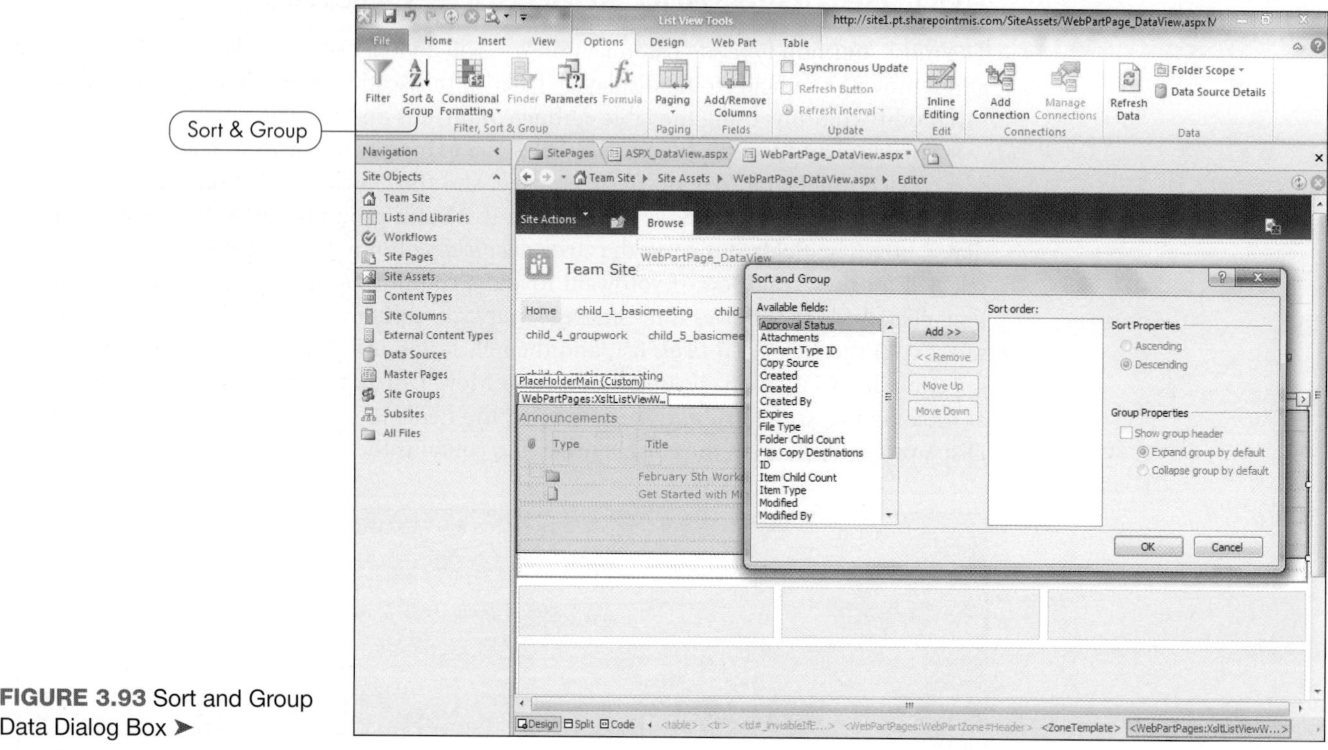

FIGURE 3.93 Sort and Group Data Dialog Box ➤

Once you have created the sort for the Data View, you can select the fields that you want to group. Select the field, and then in the *Group Properties* section of the Sort and Group dialog box, click the appropriate options. You can display a header at the top of each group, expand the group by default, or collapse the group by default. Later in this section, you will learn how to enable users to sort or group as they access the page in a browser by adding a toolbar to the Data View.

More About Group Properties

Each sorted field can have unique group properties applied to it. Select the individual field in the Sort order column before applying the group properties you want.

Filter

Filtering causes only the data that meet specific criteria to be displayed in the Data View. For instance, if you only want to display files with a certain file extension, such as .docx, you can filter the file type field by making a comparison to the value you want to show. Files that do not match the filtering criteria will not be shown in the Data View. Filters are expressions where you name the field you want to filter, provide an operator that is the state of the field you want checked, and provide the value you want to have present after the filtering. For example, the field would be File Type, with an expression of equal and a value of .docx.

Create a filter by selecting the Data view on the Web page using SharePoint Designer. Click the Options tab, and then click Filter to display the Filter Criteria dialog box, as shown in Figure 3.94. Click the Field Name of the field you want to filter from the list. Click the operator you want to use in the Comparison box. Select or type the criteria of the filter in the Value box. Click OK to activate the filter on the Data View.

Additional filtering criteria can be added to the filter using And and Or. If you are using And, the data Field Name must match the criteria for both expressions. For instance, if you filter .docx file types and modified dates for the current date, only Word files modified today would be shown. If you use Or, you generally obtain more results because they are displayed if they meet either criteria. In this case, if you created a filter using Or expressions to find file types of .docx or a current date, you would see all Word files that were in the Data View, as well as files of all file types that were created today. You can extend the filtering by mixing And and Or expressions, but carefully evaluate the results before releasing the page to the users.

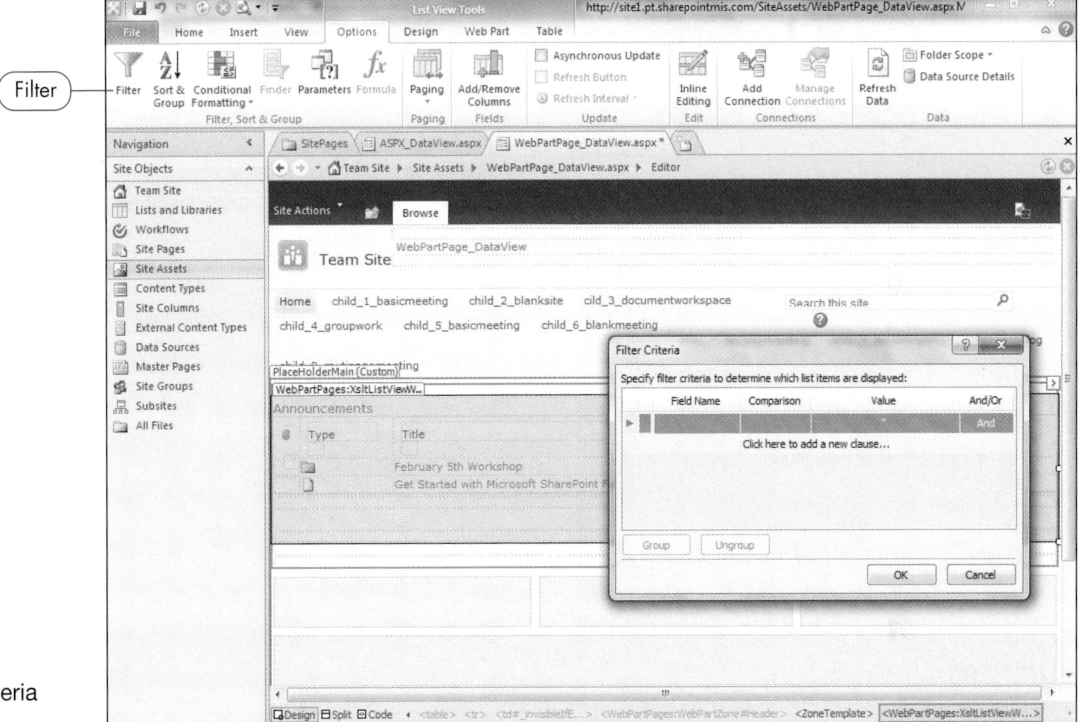

FIGURE 3.94 Filter Criteria Dialog Box ➤

A filter is very useful when you have a Data View that contains thousands of records because you can focus attention on the more pertinent filtered information. You can also enable the users to create their own sorts, groups, and filters of the data by adding a toolbar to their Web page view in a browser, as described later in this section.

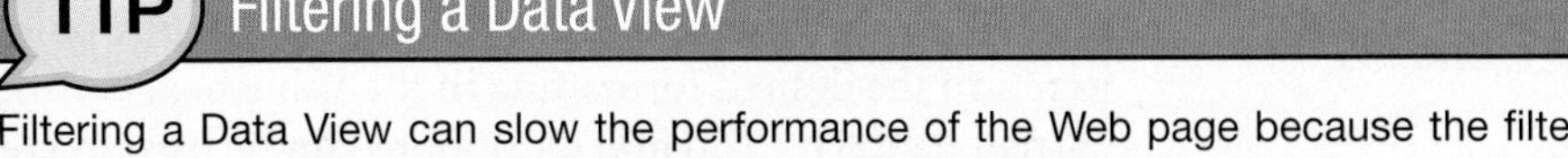

Filtering a Data View

Filtering a Data View can slow the performance of the Web page because the filtering just described is applied to the Data View completely before any of the data is shown. Numerous records in the Data View can take time to process through a filter.

Conditional Formatting

Conditional formatting is used to call attention to Data View items that require an action by the user. Using SharePoint Designer, you can display these items with formatted text, different background colors, custom icons, and more, to make them stand out from the other data in the Data View. Using a data value or a selected HTML tag, a criterion is set for comparison. You can further extend conditional formatting to hide or display data based on the conditions. For instance, the calendar appointments for the current date could be highlighted in the Data View so that the users could focus on the day's agenda.

Just as with other formatting of the Data View, you select the Data View in the Web page using SharePoint Designer. In addition to selecting the Data View, you must also select the row or column to which the conditional formatting will be applied. Click the Options tab, and then click Conditional Formatting to display the gallery of formatting options, as shown in Figure 3.95.

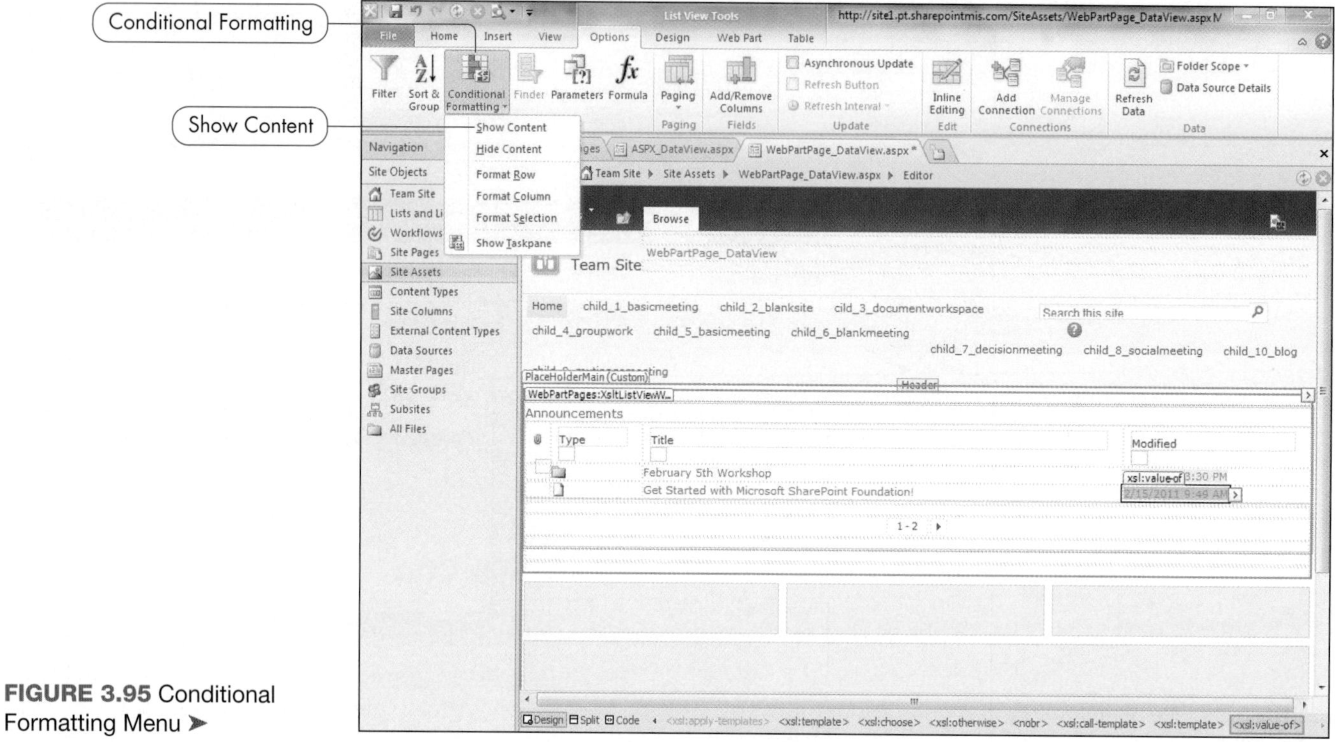

FIGURE 3.95 Conditional Formatting Menu ➤

The Show Content option displays the data that meet the criteria you specify for conditional formatting, whereas Hide Content removes the data from the current view. Formatting can be applied to columns or rows that meet the criteria. You can also apply formatting to a selection if you highlight a portion of the Data View first. After making a selection from the formatting options, the Condition Criteria dialog box opens, as shown in Figure 3.96, for you to set the conditional statements for formatting. Click the field with the values you want to display, for instance Date. In the Comparison box, click the operator you want to use; in the case of the calendar example, it would be equal. Type or select the criteria to return the desired formatting in the Value box. For the calendar example, it would be the current date. The And and Or options can be used to create more complex conditional formatting criteria as needed. Click Set Style when the criteria are complete or OK if you are showing or hiding data.

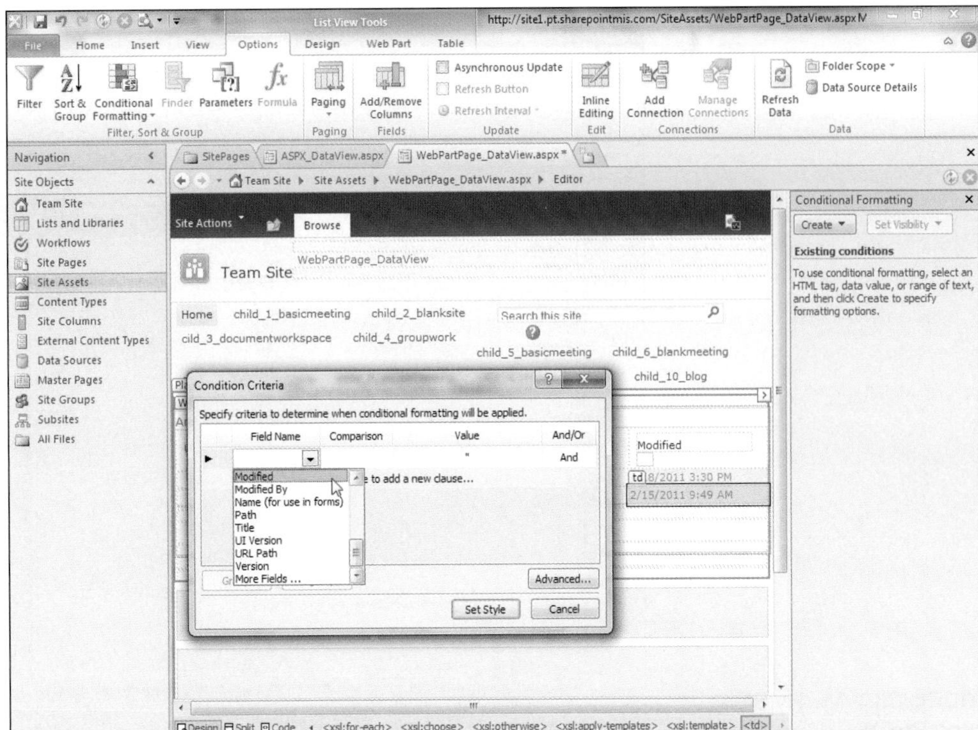

FIGURE 3.96 Conditional Criteria Dialog Box ➤

> **TIP** Advanced Conditions
>
> XPath expressions can be used to provide even more complex conditional criteria to the Data View. Click Advanced to display the Advanced Condition dialog box and set additional conditional formatting criteria.

After specifying the criteria for conditional formatting, the style must be selected so that the data you want to focus on is highlighted. The Modify Style dialog box enables you to make the custom formatting choices, as shown in Figure 3.97. Select from the Category column, and then click the formatting options you want for that category. When you click OK, the Design View automatically updates to display the conditional formatting for the criteria you have set.

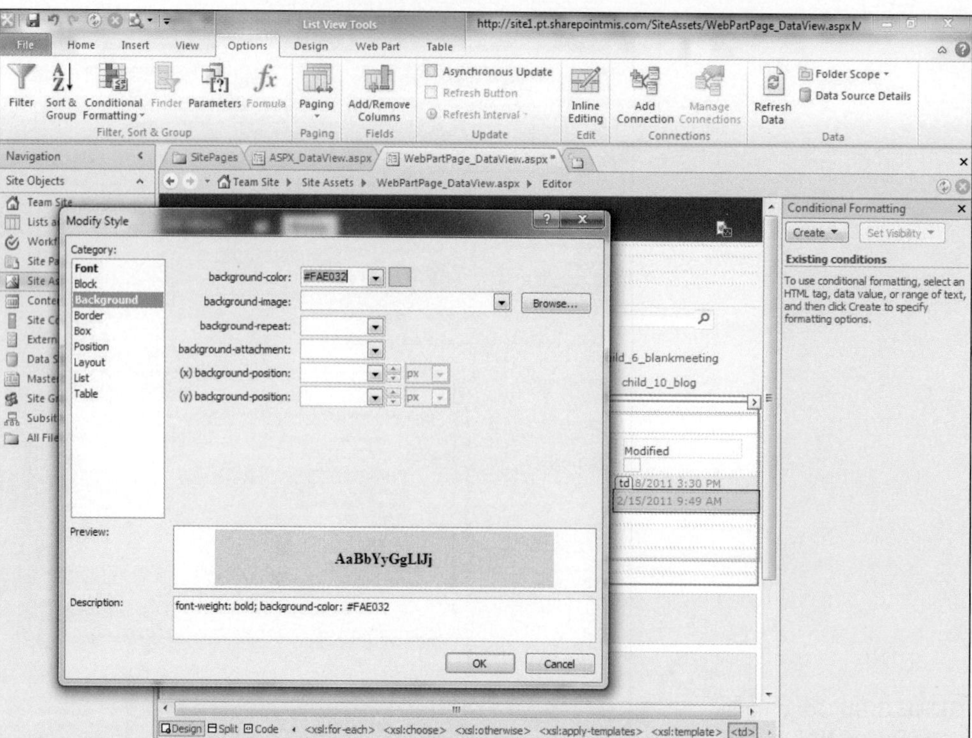

FIGURE 3.97 Modify Style Dialog Box ➤

Paging

Using the Paging option from the Options tab in SharePoint Designer, you can specify the number of records that are displayed at one time in the Data View. When the Data View contains more than the number of records you have set, the browser will display links that enable the users to move forward and backward through the data. You can also specify the maximum number of records to display. For instance, you can display task deadlines that are in the future, showing five deadlines at a time in the Data View, but not more than 20 in all, to focus the users on the current tasks for a project. The users can click links to move through the Data View, but cannot go beyond the number you set as a maximum.

Click the Data View to which you want to apply Paging options. Click the Options tab, and then click Paging to display the Paging menu, as shown in Figure 3.98. Make a selection from the menu indicating the number of items in a Display Set and/or the Limit of Items to display, or click Choose More Paging Options to set values not displayed on the menu. The Data View Properties dialog box enables you to set different numbers of pages on the Paging tab, as shown in Figure 3.99. It also gives you a clue as to the number of records in the Data View by the default values shown in the boxes. If there are more than 25 records in the Data View, the default value for the Display items in sets option will be 10. If there are less than 25 records, the default value will be 6. Click OK to apply paging to the Data View.

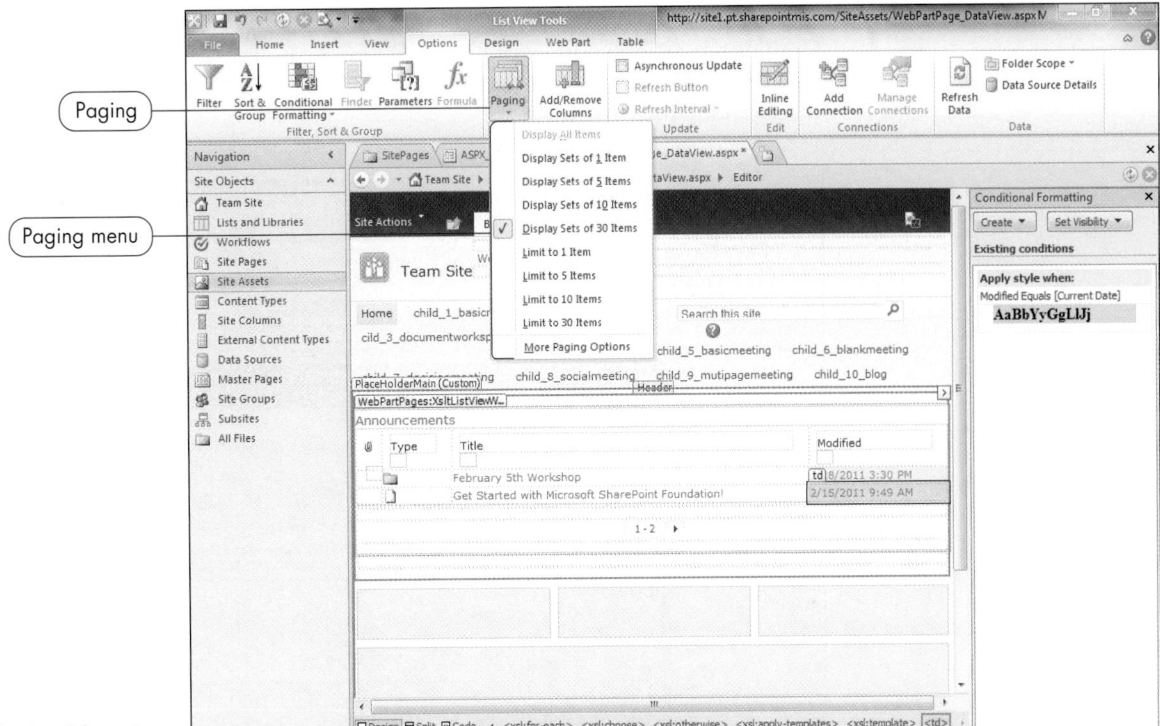

FIGURE 3.98 Paging Menu ➤

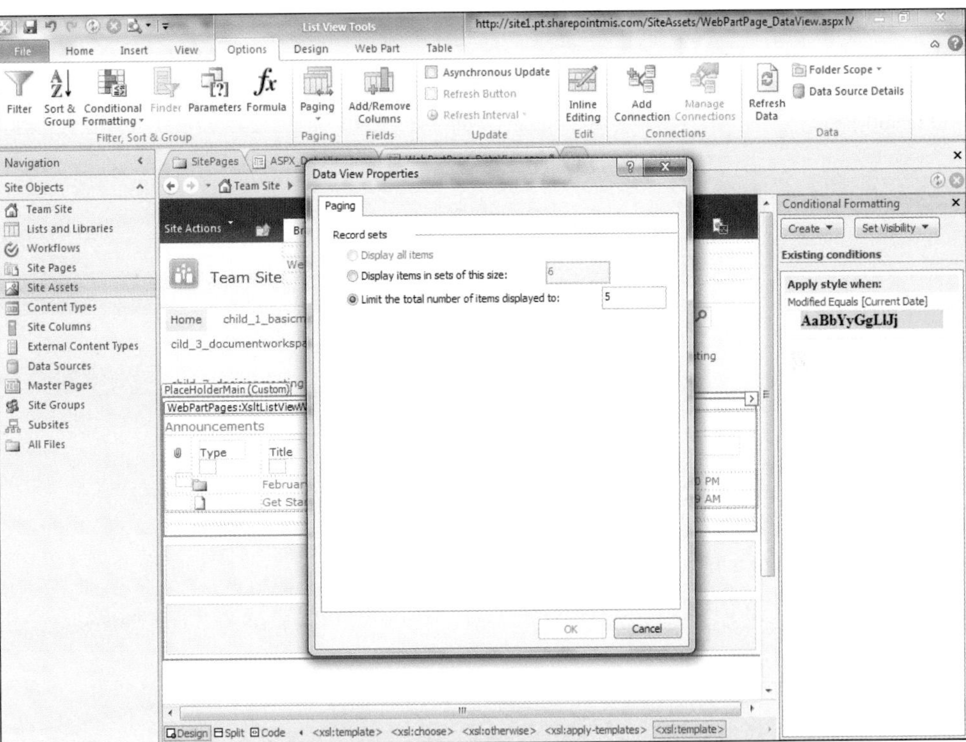

FIGURE 3.99 Data View Properties Dialog Box ➤

Enable Inline Editing

If the users need to be able to edit records within the context of the Data View without leaving the page or opening a new window, you can enable inline editing. This provides an edit button for the column or row that the user clicks to change the value. For instance, a task Data View can contain inline editing which enables the users to mark the status of the tasks so that everyone knows what is in progress or complete. Think of inline editing as an on-demand form that instantly applies to a Data View. Just as forms have text boxes, menus, and field controls, inline editing provides the same functionality to the Data View.

Select the Data View where you want to enable inline editing. Click Inline Editing on the Options tab, as shown in Figure 3.100. When the user accesses the Data View, the Edit button appears, as shown in Figure 3.101a. The user clicks the Edit button and can begin editing, as shown in Figure 3.101b.

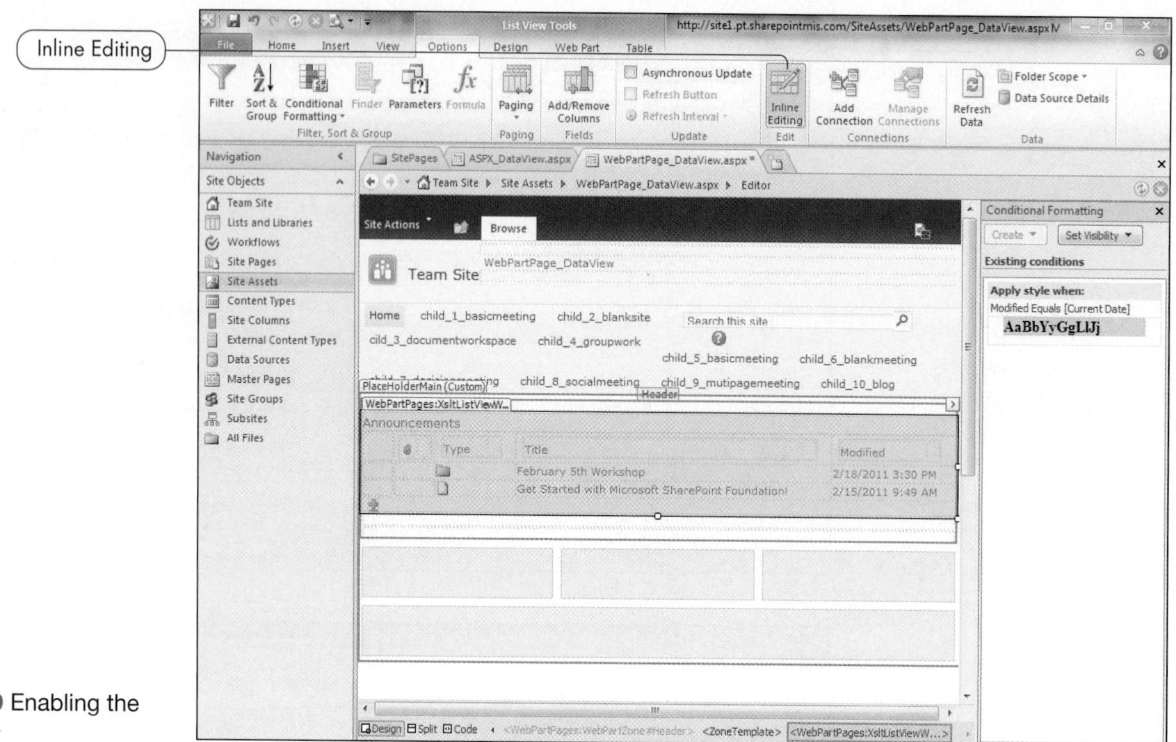

FIGURE 3.100 Enabling the Inline Editing ➤

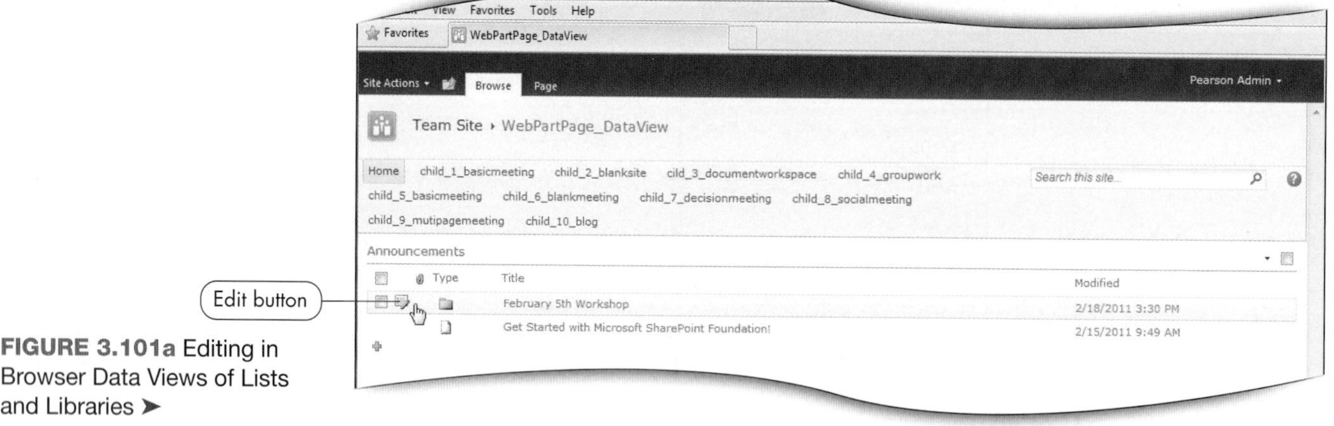

FIGURE 3.101a Editing in Browser Data Views of Lists and Libraries ➤

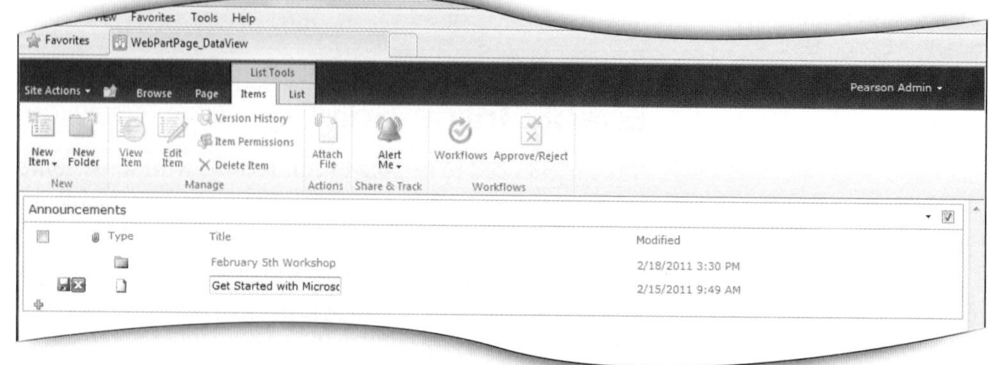

FIGURE 3.101b ➤

Apply View Styles

Typically, Data Views are displayed in an easy-to-understand table layout, with rows and columns used to arrange the data. SharePoint Designer enables you to select a different layout and apply it to the Data View. For instance, you may wish to show a list of tasks as a bulleted list, rather than in a table. It is important to note that when you apply a View Style, it removes previous customizations and Web Part connections.

Select the Data View you want to restyle, and then click the Design tab on the List View Tools tab. Click the desired style from the View Styles gallery, as shown in Figure 3.102, or click the More button to display additional style options. A warning message alerts you that your selection will override previous formatting, so click Yes to proceed. Click Save on the Quick Access Toolbar to save the changes to the Data View.

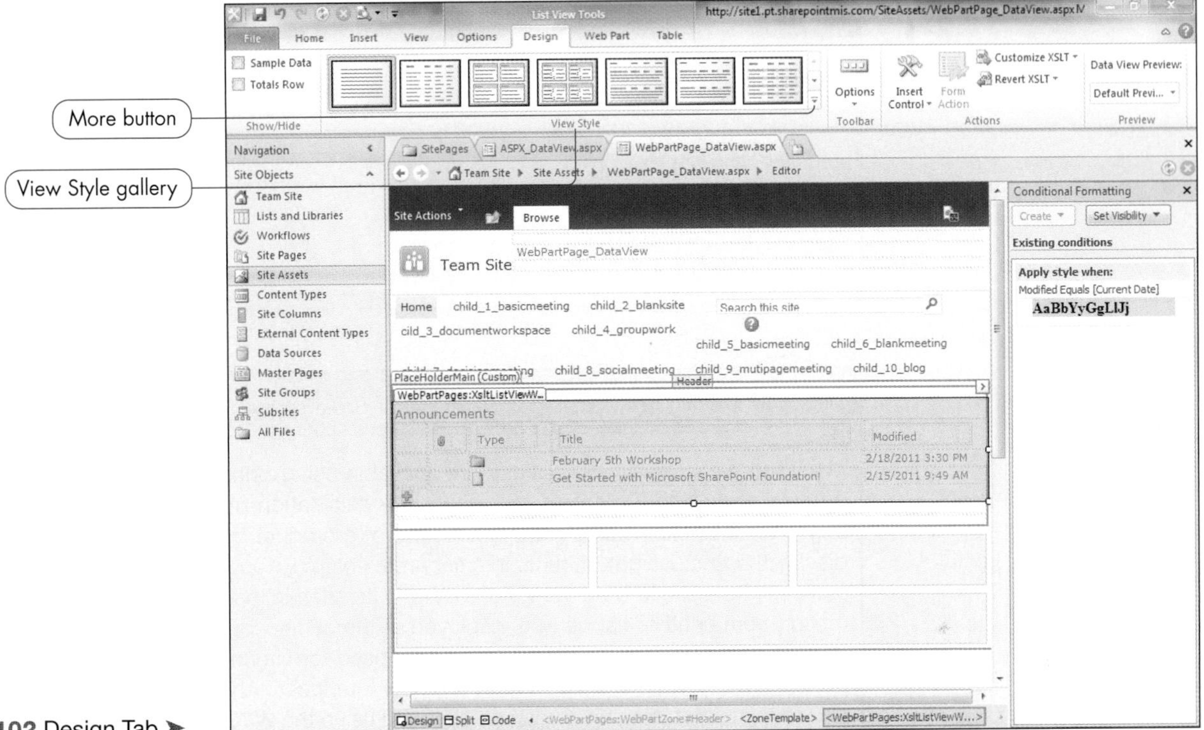

FIGURE 3.102 Design Tab ➤

> **TIP** More About Data View Styles
>
> The styles displayed in the Styles Gallery depend on what has been uploaded to the site collection. Styles with fewer fields than in the original Data View will remove the extra fields from the view.

Add Toolbar Options

SharePoint Designer enables you to add a SharePoint list toolbar to the Data View of lists and libraries, giving users additional options for editing and grouping when using the data. The Full Toolbar provides the editing options so that users can add and modify items and list properties in the Data View. The Summary Toolbar enables filtering, sorting, and grouping of the Data View.

In SharePoint Designer, click the Data View to which you want to add a toolbar, and then click the Design tab of the List View Tools tab. Click Options to display the menu shown in Figure 3.103. Click the type of toolbar to make available. If you wish to remove a toolbar from a Data View, click None. Click Save on the Quick Access Toolbar to save the changes to the Web page.

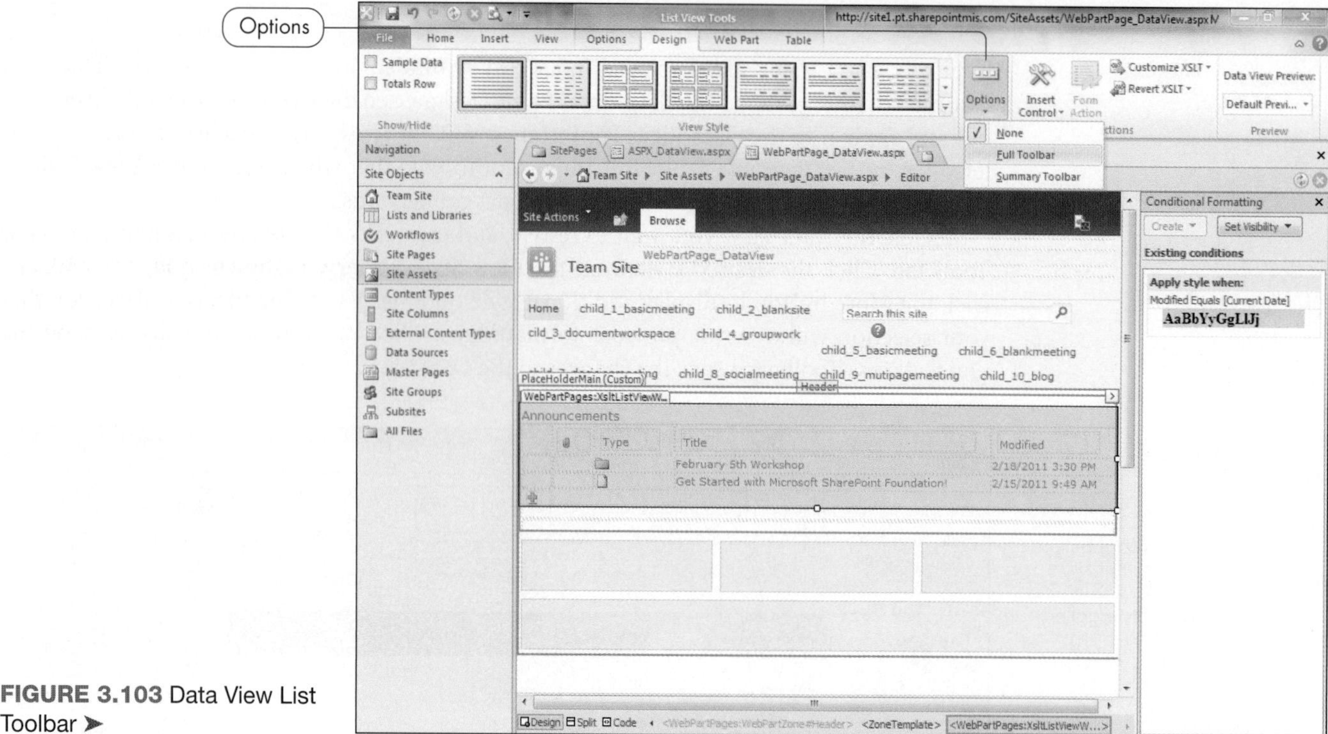

FIGURE 3.103 Data View List Toolbar ➤

TIP More Customization Options

Many more customization options are available using SharePoint Designer. You can add a formula column that displays the result of a calculation performed on other columns. You might, for example, multiply the unit weight of a product by the number of units in stock to display the total weight of items in a separate column. You can combine views from multiple sources into a single Data View. For example, academic majors from one list and major information from another list can be displayed in the same view. Parameters can be added and passed between Data Views. This could be used for filtering data. You can add server controls to a Data View to create interactive user interfaces. And, as you learned earlier, the font and formatting of Data Views can be changed using the WYSIYG tools or CSS styles, and you can customize table layouts in Data Views using the table editing options.

HANDS-ON EXERCISES

3 Work with Data Views in SharePoint Designer

You will continue developing the Center for Women in STEM site built on a SharePoint Foundation server. You will upload a custom template that includes a custom list. You will also create a subsite using this custom template and will create a data view for the built in custom list. Finally, you will modify the newly added data view.

Skills covered: Create a Subsite from a Given Custom Template • Create Data Views • Modify Data Views

STEP 1 CREATE A SUBSITE FROM A GIVEN CUSTOM TEMPLATE

Before you can start working with Data Views, you must log on to your SharePoint Collection and create a new subsite for the Center using a given custom template. Refer to Figure 3.104 as you complete Step 1.

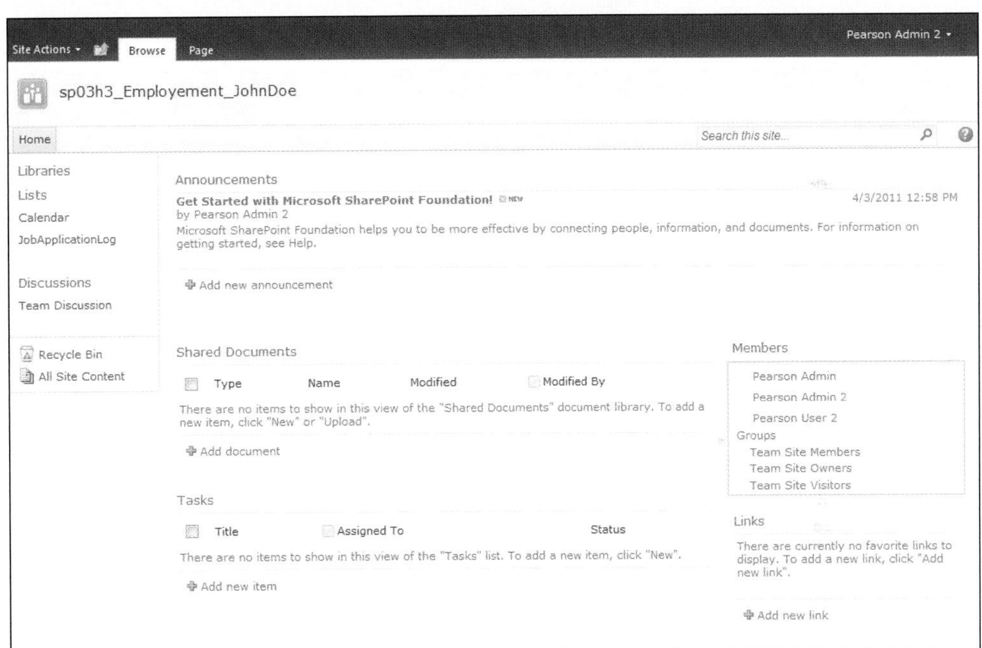

FIGURE 3.104 Create a Subsite from a Given Custom Template ➤

a. Click **Start** to display the Start menu. Click **All Programs**, and then click **Internet Explorer** to open the program.

b. Go to the top-level site provided by your instructor, which will be in the format of *http://pt.sharepointmis.com/SitePages/yourname*. Enter the user name and the password provided by your instructor.

c. Upload the *sp03h3_JobApplicationLogo.wsp* solution file from your Exploring folder into your collection Solution Gallery, and then activate it.

d. Create a *sp03h3_Employment_YourLastNameFirstName* subsite using the *sp03h3_JobApplication.wsp* solution file.

   Your screen should now look similar to Figure 3.104.

STEP 2 CREATE DATA VIEWS

You will use SharePoint Designer to create a data view for a custom list of job applicants at the Center. Refer to Figure 3.105 as you complete Step 2.

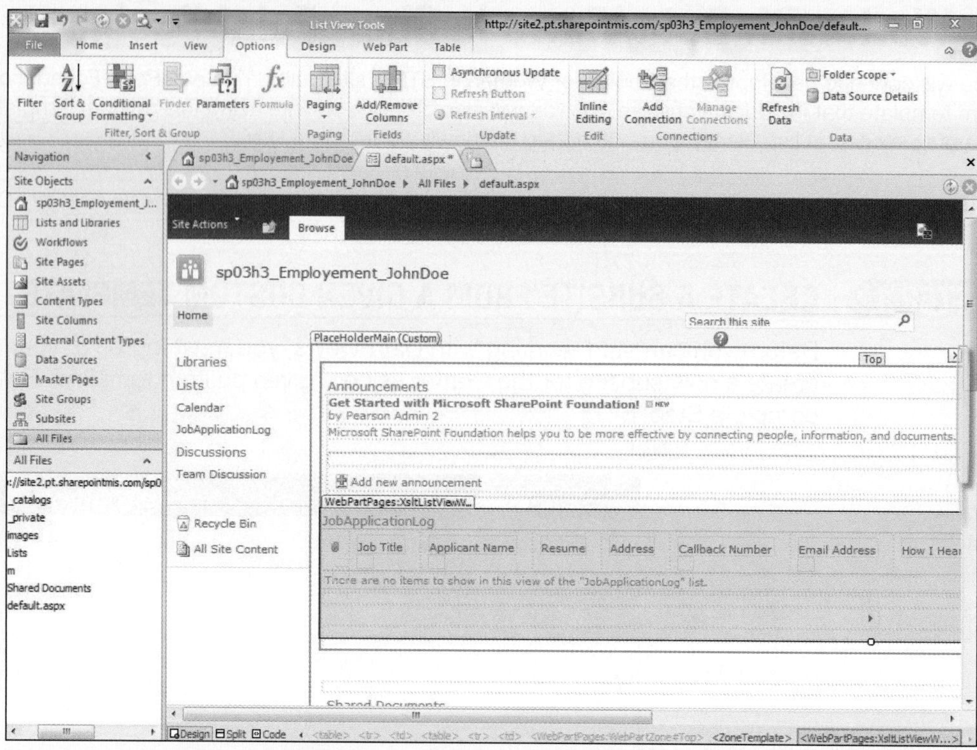

FIGURE 3.105 Create Data Views ➤

a. Click **Edit in SharePoint Designer** on the Site Actions menu. Type the password in the **Windows Security dialog box.**

   The Site Settings page of the *sp03h3_Employement_YourLastNameFirstName* site is now displayed in SharePoint Designer workspace.

b. Click **Edit site home page** in the *Customization* section.

   The default.aspx is now displayed in Design view.

c. Click inside the <div> box below the *Add new announcement* text within the Top Web Part zone.

d. Click the **Insert tab**, click **Data View** in the Data View & Forms group, and then select **JobApplicationLog** on the All Data Sources list.

TROUBLESHOOTING: If the Data View command on the Insert menu is not active, you did not position the insertion point in the correct position.

   The <WebPartPages:XSLTViewWebPart> is now selected and the <WebPartPages:XSLTViewWebPart> tag is highlighted in orange on the *Quick Tag Selector* section of the Status bar, as shown in Figure 3.105.

e. Click **Save** on the Quick Access Toolbar.

STEP 3 MODIFY DATA VIEWS

You will modify the data view created in Step 2 by adding a column, creating a group, and then allowing users at the Center to edit the Data view using the SharePoint Foundation browser interface. Refer to Figure 3.106 as you complete Step 3.

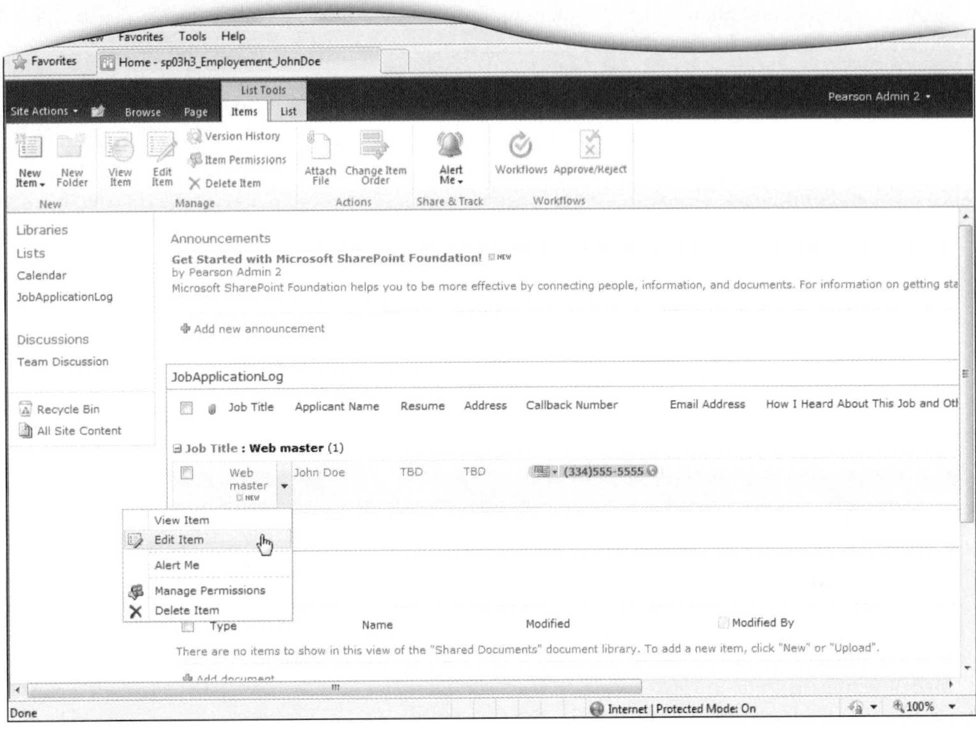

FIGURE 3.106 Modify Data Views ➤

a. Click the **Options tab**, and then click **Add/Remove Columns** in the Fields group.

   The Displayed Fields dialog box is now showing.

b. Click **Approval Status** in the *Available fields* section, and then click the **Add button**.

   The Approval Status field is now displayed in the *Displayed fields* section.

c. Click **OK** to close the Displayed Fields dialog box.

   The Approval Status field is now displayed within the Data view.

d. Click **Sort & Group** in the Filter, Sort & Group group.

   The Sort & Group dialog box is now displayed.

e. Click **Job Title** in the *Available fields* section, and then click the **Add button**.

   The Job Title field is displayed in the Sort Order section.

f. Click **Show group header** in the *Group Properties* section, and then click **OK** to close the Sort & Group dialog box.

g. Click **Inline Editing** in the Edit group, and then click **Save** on the Quick Access Toolbar. Click the **Home tab**, and then click **Preview in Browser**.

   The home page of your subsite is now displayed in browser.

h. Click **Add New item link** in the Job ApplicationLog. Fill in the information in the JobApplicationLog–New Item dialog box using your own name, etc., and then click **Save**.

   The new item is now displayed.

i. Point to the Job Title column, and then click the arrow.

   The Edit Item is now displayed on the menu, as shown in Figure 3.106.

CHAPTER OBJECTIVES REVIEW

After reading this chapter, you have accomplished the following objectives:

1. **Edit SharePoint page content.** The SharePoint Foundation browser interface and SharePoint Designer empower you with a complex set of user-friendly tools for inserting page elements into a page and modifying their characteristics so that they display and function the way you want. Using SharePoint Foundation in a browser limits some of the editing actions, whereas SharePoint Designer enables you to edit any content on all SharePoint pages. The SharePoint Designer editing workspace includes the Ribbon, the editing window (or document window), the status bar, and the task panes. The editing window offers three views: Design, Code, and Split. The SharePoint Designer Page Editor page includes the editing window, tab bar, Page Mode toolbar, Quick Tag Selector, and status bar. You can type text directly onto the Web page, import the content of a text file, or copy and paste text from another file. Text formatting is similar to other Microsoft Office applications, using the Font, Paragraph, and Styles groups on the Editing Tools–Format Text tab. The SharePoint Foundation browser interface and SharePoint Designer enable you to move, replace, or delete text and change its appearance. Special characters or symbols, such as the copyright symbol, can be inserted onto pages using the Insert tab. Style is a SharePoint Designer feature that enables Web designers to format text using built-in HTML styles. SharePoint Designer enables you to check the spelling of a highlighted section of a Web page, an entire Web page, a group of selected Web pages, or an entire Web site.
2. **Use hyperlinks and lists in organizing a Web page.** Hyperlinks can help designers break the contents of a large, difficult-to-navigate Web page into a set of Web pages that are connected. Alternatively, designers can reduce the amount of jumping back and forth between different Web pages by using bookmark links and bookmarks to give users access to their content. A URL can include an address for a Web page or file on the Internet, on your computer, on a local network, a bookmark within a Web page, or an e-mail address. Two different kinds of URLs exist: absolute and relative. An absolute URL provides the full path to a Web page or file, whereas a relative URL provides the path to a Web page or a file relative to another file. The file that opens when a hyperlink is clicked is called the hyperlink target. SharePoint Designer assists you in creating hyperlinks to existing files or even to files that have not been created yet. For all types of links, you can also add a ScreenTip. A ScreenTip is text that displays in the body of the Web page whenever the mouse pointer is moved over the hyperlink. After a hyperlink has been created, you can change its URL or its display text anytime. You can remove a hyperlink in one of two ways: by deleting the text and the associated link from the page, or by keeping the text on the page but removing the associated link. A link to a specific position within the same document or another document is called a bookmark link. Bookmark links are helpful navigation tools, especially when you are dealing with long pages, because they replace the slower scrolling (using the vertical and horizontal scrollbars) method of working through the text. Another common type of hyperlink, called a mailto link, connects the user to an e-mail address. When users click a mailto link, their default e-mail application opens a new message window and the target address of the link is already entered in the To address box. When you create a Web page using a template or a CSS external style sheet, the default colors of the active, unvisited, and visited hyperlinks included in your Web page are usually set. These colors can be changed by modifying the template or the CSS external style sheet. In Web pages that do not have an attached template, the SharePoint Designer Advanced Editor enables you to format hyperlink colors using the Page Properties. SharePoint Designer also assists Web designers with adding font effects to hyperlinks in Web pages with or without a CSS external style sheet linked. Lists are great tools for organizing Web page content in a concise and consistent fashion. The list format is a common format seen on almost any Web page. Lists help you organize and present your content in a consistent and concise fashion. You can choose ordered (numbered), unordered (bulleted), and definition lists. Use a numbered list when the order in which elements appear is important. If the order of the elements is not important, use a bulleted list. Among the elements usually preset in a Web page template or included within CSS external style sheets are the small graphics to be used in bulleted lists. Thus, if a page has an attached template or is linked to a CSS external style sheet, you can create an unordered list that uses the template's preset picture by selecting the text and simply clicking the Bullets arrow on the Paragraph group of the Home tab and selecting a graphic bullet from the list. After you have created a list, you can edit it by right-clicking any line of the list, clicking the List Properties command, and then selecting an option from the List Properties dialog boxes discussed previously. Nested lists are popular features used by Web designers to emphasize text categories and subcategories. In SharePoint Designer, you can create nested lists, including the same styles or different styles of lists.
3. **Work with tables and layout tables.** Tables have always played an important role in Web development. The fact that tables are supported by all browsers and are similar to the tables used in many other desktop applications makes them attractive to Web designers from beginners to professionals. SharePoint Designer has a comprehensive set of tools for adding and formatting tables. A table is a collection of rows having one or more columns. A cell is the intersection of a column and a row. A nested table is a table inserted within a cell of a table. Before creating tables, consider how many rows and columns you need, the elements that will be placed in the table cells, and the total width and height of the table. SharePoint Designer enables Web designers to establish the size of a table as pixels or as a percentage of the browser window. The Insert Table grid is a graphical table that enables you to select the number of rows and columns for your table. You can add columns or rows after creating a table, and delete rows and columns at any time. SharePoint Designer enables you to add a caption to a table. It is rather common for a Web designer to change the table and cell properties in the process of developing a table. SharePoint

Designer makes it easy to modify tables using the Table Properties dialog box. You can modify the table alignment, width, border size and color, and table background color or background picture and modify the individual cells in similar ways. When editing the properties of selected cells, the table-level properties are overridden. Web designers commonly choose to split or merge cells to position elements within a table. Nested tables are used by Web designers to further refine the position of elements within a table. To select a table, right-click anywhere within the table, click the arrow to the right of the Select button on the Table Tools–Layout tab, and then click Table. After a table is selected, you can click and hold the mouse pointer anywhere on the table and drag it anywhere you want within the Web page. If you click within a nested table, only the nested table is selected.

4. **Add graphics to a Web page.** GIF and JPEG are the two image file formats supported by most Web browsers. The Pictures group of the SharePoint Designer Insert tab includes commands through which you can insert a clip art image or an image from a file. The Media group of the SharePoint Foundation Insert tab includes commands through which you can insert a picture From Computer (a file on the local computer) or From Address (from a URL). In addition to clip art images, you can also use graphics and photographs that have been captured and stored as files on your local computer. An image that has been included in a Web page can be characterized by the size it is when displayed in the Web page and by its actual physical size (the size of the file that stores the picture). SharePoint Designer enables you to modify the display size of each picture (resize it) and modify the physical size of the picture in the file (resample it). When you click a picture that has already been added to a Web page, sizing handles are displayed. The sizing handles are small squares evenly distributed around the picture. The SharePoint Designer Picture Tools–Format tab includes a collection of buttons, giving you access to a comprehensive set of features for creating thumbnails, rotating images, controlling the contrast and brightness of images, cropping images, adding hotspots to images, and more. It is not unusual to be unhappy with the look of a picture after you have made a number of changes to it. The good news is that you can reverse the changes you made to a picture (including resizing, cropping, and applying colors, but excluding resampling) by clicking Restore in the Adjust group of the Picture Tools–Format tab. After adding images to a Web page, saving a Web page that includes newly embedded files requires a few more steps. When you click Save to save a Web page that includes embedded images, the Save Embedded dialog box appears. You can reposition an image, on the vertical axis, by clicking and dragging the picture up or down. When you need to use a large image and you are concerned that the size of the file will make your page load too slowly, the Auto Thumbnail feature enables you to create a small version of the image. You then add the necessary HTML coding so that when the user clicks the thumbnail, the image is loaded in its true size. You can add a hyperlink to an image. To arrange Web page content, after including images, it is highly recommended that you use CSS styles.

5. **Work with multimedia files.** Using sound and video is another way Web designers enhance their Web pages. If you choose to add audio and video elements to your Web sites, you can make the multimedia available in two formats. You can incorporate sound and video files that can be downloaded and played, or create streaming audio and video files that enable users to hear and view these files while they are downloading. A streaming video file is sent in compressed form to the browser and displayed as it arrives, as a sequence of images. If your Web page is stored on a Web server that cannot stream the content of audio and video files, your visitors must completely download them before they can see or listen to them. Today's technology still requires the use of programs called plug-ins to interact with (view or play) some multimedia files. A plug-in is a software application that can be an integral part of a browser or give the browser additional multimedia capabilities. Plug-ins are downloaded from the software developer's Web site (usually at no charge) and installed. SharePoint Designer enables you to add a link to an audio file on your Web page or to place an audio file on your Web page. SharePoint Designer enables you to add background sound to a Web page that is not attached to a template. As with audio, the main ways to use video on your Web page are to insert a link to a video file, or to place a video file directly onto your Web page as streaming media.

6. **Get started with the SharePoint Foundation default installation Web Parts.** SharePoint Foundation 2010 comes with a number of built-in Web Parts that are available for you to add to your pages. The built-in Web Parts, as well as ones you might create, are organized into categories. In a default installation, the 13 SharePoint Foundation 2010 Web Parts are grouped in five categories: Lists and Libraries, Content Rollup, Forms, Media and Content, and Social Collaboration.

7. **Insert a Web Part zone.** Web Part zones are containers only for Web Parts; thus you cannot insert other elements, such as text or image, into a Web Part zone. Web Part zone properties control the actions that site visitors can take using a browser. The way Web Parts are displayed is also affected by the Web Part zone properties. A Web Part zone can only be inserted into an ASP.NET page using SharePoint Designer.

8. **Add and modify a Web Part.** Web Parts can also be classified by their specific location within a page as Dynamic Web Parts and Static Web Parts. After creating a site or adding either a Web Part page or general content page to an existing site, you may want to further customize the page by utilizing Web Parts. You can use either the SharePoint Foundation or the SharePoint Designer to add Web Parts. SharePoint enables you to make changes in the behavior of a Web Part in order to further customize it. You do this by editing the Web Part properties. You can modify three major categories: Appearance, Layout, and Advanced.

9. **Export and import Web Parts.** Once you finish configuring a Web Part, including both common and unique properties, you may want to reuse the Web Part, with the same settings, in other sites or pages. SharePoint enables you to export and import most Web Parts. You have two options for importing the Web Part; one prevents others from using the Web Part, whereas the other enables users to reuse the Web Part. If you decide to prevent others from using the Web Part, you must import it each time you want to add it to a page. You can also import the file so that it is available in other categories on the Web Parts bar.

10. **Remove a Web Part.** It is not uncommon that, at some point in time, you will need to remove Web Parts from your pages.

You can remove the display of Web Parts in one of three ways. First, you can minimize the Web Part, displaying only the title bar to the user. Second, you can close the Web Part, which makes it available through the Closed Web Parts category so it can be added back in later. Finally, you can delete it completely from the Web page.

11. **Create data views.** Data View Web Parts and Data Form Web Parts enable you to display data from a variety of sources in your SharePoint sites. Also known as Data View, data from a SharePoint list or library can be shown, along with data from XML files or other external data sources. Users can access the information they need to solve business problems and increase productivity. SharePoint Designer is used to show and hide fields, sort and filter data, and more. Built-in View Styles enable you to quickly create Data Views. Not only can Web page users view the data, but they can write to data sources, such as database queries, XML documents, and SharePoint lists and libraries. SharePoint Designer is used to add a Data View to an .ASPX page or a Web Part page. The easiest way is to click Data View on the Insert tab, and then select the data source. When using this option, if you select a list or library as the data source, a List View is displayed on the page. If you choose a different data source (other than a list or library), a DFWP is displayed.

12. **Modify data views.** SharePoint enables you to customize a Data View by taking advantage of its user-friendly Data View tools. For example, you can add, rearrange, and remove columns; sort and filter data; apply conditional formatting; and change the overall layout. SharePoint Designer enables you to sort data in a Data View. You can sort the data alphabetically or numerically. You can produce customized sort orders using the Advanced Sort dialog box. If you only want to display files with a certain criteria, you can filter a field by making a comparison to the value you want to show. Filters are expressions where you name the field you want to filter, provide an operator that is the state of the field you want checked, and provide the value you want to have present after the filtering. A filter is very useful when you have a Data View that contains thousands of records because you can focus attention on the more pertinent filtered information. If the users need to be able to edit records within the context of the Data View without leaving the page or opening a new window, you can enable inline editing. This provides an edit button for the column or row that the user clicks to change the value. Think of inline editing as an on-demand form that instantly applies to a Data View. Just as forms have text boxes, menus, and field controls, inline editing provides the same functionality to the Data View. Typically, Data Views are displayed in an easy-to-understand table layout, with rows and columns used to arrange the data. SharePoint Designer enables you to select a different layout and apply it to the Data View. SharePoint Designer enables you to add a SharePoint list toolbar to the Data View of lists and libraries, giving users additional options for editing and grouping when using the data. The Full Toolbar provides the editing options so that users can add and modify items and list properties in the Data View. The Summary Toolbar enables filtering, sorting, and grouping of the Data View. Many more customization options are available using SharePoint Designer, such as creating a formula column, displaying data from multiple sources, adding parameters, adding server controls, changing fonts and formatting, and customizing table layout.

KEY TERMS

Absolute URL ***p.178***
Adobe Flash ***p.206***
Alink attribute ***p.184***
Auto Thumbnail ***p.214***
Background sound ***p.221***
Bookmark link ***p.181***
Cell ***p.191***
Clip Art task pane ***p.206***
Dynamic HTML (DHTML) ***p.185***
Dynamic Web Part ***p.234***
Graphics Interchange Format (GIF) ***p.206***
Hyperlink target ***p.178***
Insert Table grid ***p.191***
Interlacing ***p.206***
Joint Photographic Experts Group (JPEG) ***p.206***
Keep aspect ratio ***p.209***
Link attribute ***p.184***
List format ***p.187***
Mailto link ***p.183***
My Collections ***p.207***
Nested table ***p.191***
Office Collections ***p.207***
Plug-in ***p.219***
Portable Network Graphics (PNG) ***p.206***
Relative URL ***p.178***
Resample ***p.209***
Resize ***p.209***
ScreenTip ***p.179***
Sizing handle ***p.209***
Static Web Part ***p.234***
Table ***p.191***
Vlink attribute ***p.184***
Web Collections ***p.207***

MULTIPLE CHOICE

1. When using a browser to edit a Wiki page, you can:
   (a) Modify any content anywhere within the page.
   (b) Insert Web Part zones anywhere within the page.
   (c) Insert Symbols anywhere within the page.
   (d) Modify content included in the EmbeddedFormField SharePoint Control.

2. When using a browser to edit a Web Part page, you can:
   (a) Modify any content anywhere within the page.
   (b) Insert Web Part zones anywhere within the page.
   (c) Insert Symbols anywhere within the page.
   (d) Modify content included in the Web Part zones.

3. The SharePoint Designer Editor does not include the:
   (a) Navigation Pane.
   (b) Status bar.
   (c) Quick Tag Selector.
   (d) Tab bar.

4. The SharePoint Foundation browser interface includes a(n):
   (a) Spelling tool.
   (b) Find and Replace tool.
   (c) Text Layout tool.
   (d) Insert Symbol tool.

5. Which of the following statements about hyperlinks is false?
   (a) You can format the hyperlink color in any type of SharePoint page using SharePoint Designer.
   (b) You can modify the URL of the hyperlink anytime after is created.
   (c) You can add a hyperlink to a file that is not yet created.
   (d) You can set a hyperlink to open the targeted page in a new browser window.

6. Which of the following statements about lists and tables is true?
   (a) Using the SharePoint Designer Bullets and Numbers dialog box, you can format a list in any type of SharePoint page.
   (b) Using the SharePoint Foundation browser interface, you can insert a table caption.
   (c) Using the SharePoint Foundation browser interface, you can format cells as <th>.
   (d) Using SharePoint Designer, you can merge cells of a table.

7. Which of the following statements about Web Part zones and Web Parts is false?
   (a) You can insert a Web Part zone using the SharePoint Foundation browser interface.
   (b) In Web Part pages, you can insert a Web Part only within Web Part zones.
   (c) In Wiki pages, you can insert a Web Part outside a Web Part zone.
   (d) Exporting a Web Part creates an XML file.

8. Which of the following commands cannot be performed on an image?
   (a) Resizing
   (b) Resampling
   (c) Condensing
   (d) Cropping

9. You cannot organize the text of your Web pages using:
   (a) A hierarchical list.
   (b) A numbered list.
   (c) Nested lists.
   (d) A bulleted list.

10. When working in SharePoint Designer with an existing Data View, you cannot:
    (a) Import data from another data source.
    (b) Add or remove columns.
    (c) Sort or filter data.
    (d) Create a conditional criteria.

PRACTICE EXERCISES

1 Editing and Enhancing a SharePoint Site for an Introduction to Management Information Systems Business Course

You have been hired as a graduate teaching assistant in the Introduction to Management Information Systems course and, as part of your new assignment, you have been working on the development of a SharePoint site for the course. Your faculty supervisor gave you administrator access to a SharePoint Foundation top-level site and provided you with a description of the required functionalities of the site. This exercise follows the same set of skills as used in Hands-On Exercise 1 in the chapter. Refer to Figure 3.107 as you complete this exercise.

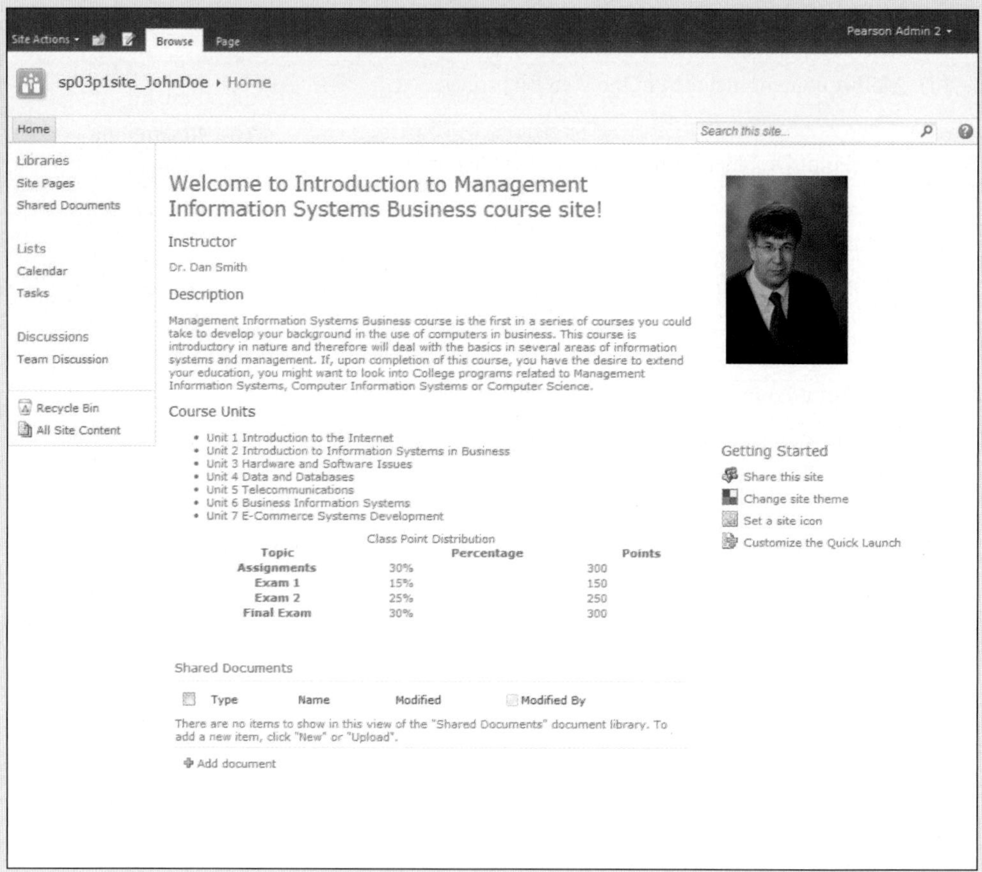

FIGURE 3.107 Edit and Enhance a Course Site ➤

a. Click **Start**, click **All Programs**, and then select **Internet Explorer** to start Internet Explorer.

b. Click **File** on the Menu bar, and then click **Open Site**. Type the URL of the top-level site in the **Open box**.

c. Click **All Site Content** on the Quick Launch area. Click **All Site Content**. Click **Create**, and then create a new site *sp03p1site_LastNameFirstName* using the Team Site Template.

d. Click the **Page tab**, and then click **Edit** in the Edit group. Highlight the "site" text, and then type **Introduction to Management Information Systems Business Course.**

e. Launch the Microsoft Word application, and then open the *MISB_CourseInfo.docx* file from your Exploring folder. Highlight the first paragraph including the instructor, description, and course units information (through the course description paragraph), right-click, and then click **Copy**. Activate the Internet Explorer window, highlight the first paragraph on the home page of the *sp03p1site_LastNameFirstName* site, click the **Paste arrow** in the Clipboard group, and then select **Paste plaintext.**

f. Highlight the word *Instructor*, click **Markup Styles** in the Markup group of the Ribbon, and then select **Colored Heading 2**. Highlight the word *Description*, click **Markup Styles** in the Markup group of the Editing Tools–Format Text tab, and then select **Colored Heading 2**. Click **Save & Close** in the Edit group.

g. Click **Edit in SharePoint Designer** on the Site Actions menu.
h. Click **Edit site home page** in the *Customization* section.
i. Position the insertion point below the Description paragraph, and then activate the Microsoft Word application. Highlight the Course Units paragraph and the Units 1 through 7 paragraphs, right-click, and then click **Copy**. Activate the SharePointDesigner window, right-click, and then click **Paste**. Click the **Paste Options Smart Tag**, and then select **Remove Formatting**.
j. Highlight the seven paragraphs below the *Course Units* heading, and then click the **Bullets button** in the Paragraph group of the Home tab.
k. Highlight the word *Description*, click **Format Painter** in the Clipboard group, and then highlight the words *Course Units*. Click **Save** on the Quick Access Toolbar to save the Home.aspx page.
l. Highlight the words *Dr. Dan Smith*, click the **Insert tab,** and then click **Hyperlinks** in the Links group of the Ribbon. Click **Email Address**, type **DanSmith@gmail.com** in the **E-mail address box**, and then click **OK**.
m. Position the insertion point below the Course Units bulleted list, click the **Insert tab**, click **Table** in the Tables group, move the mouse pointer over the Insert Table grid to create a table with five rows and three columns, and then click on the highlighted area of the Insert Table grid.
n. Position the insertion point in row one, column one, click, press **Shift**, and then click on the remaining cells from the first row while keeping **Shift** pressed. Click **Header Cell** in the Cell Layout group of the Table Tools–Layout tab.
o. Click **Insert Caption** in the Rows and Columns group of the Table Tools–Layout tab, and then type **Class Point Distribution** in the caption area of the table. Type in the cells of the table the text showing in the Class Point Distribution table from *MISB_CourseInfo.docx.*
p. Click the image included in the PlaceHolderMain(Custom) placeholder, click the **Insert tab,** and then click **Picture** in the Pictures group of the Insert ribbon.
q. Navigate to the Exploring folder, click **smith-dan.jpg**, and then click **Insert** in the Picture dialog box. Type **Instructor** in the **Alternate text box**, and then click **OK** to close the Accessibility Properties dialog box.
r. Click **Save** on the Quick Access Toolbar. Click **OK** in the **Save Embedded Files dialog box** to save the picture to the Site Assets folder. Click **Yes** if the Alert dialog box appears.
s. Click the **Home tab**, and then click **Preview in Browser**. Your screen should look similar to Figure 3.107.
t. Close the browser, and then close SharePoint Designer.

2 Adding Web Parts to a SharePoint Site for a University Research Lab

The Laboratory for Educational and Assistive Technology (LEAT) Research offered you a position as a graduate research assistant and, as part of your assignment, you have been working on developing the SharePoint site for the lab. One of the reasons for choosing SharePoint as a platform for the LEAT site was the very rich collections of built-in components, such as Web Parts, that can help you minimize the time required to implement different site functionalities. This exercise follows the same set of skills as used in Hands-On Exercises 1–2 in the chapter. Refer to Figure 3.108 as you complete this exercise.

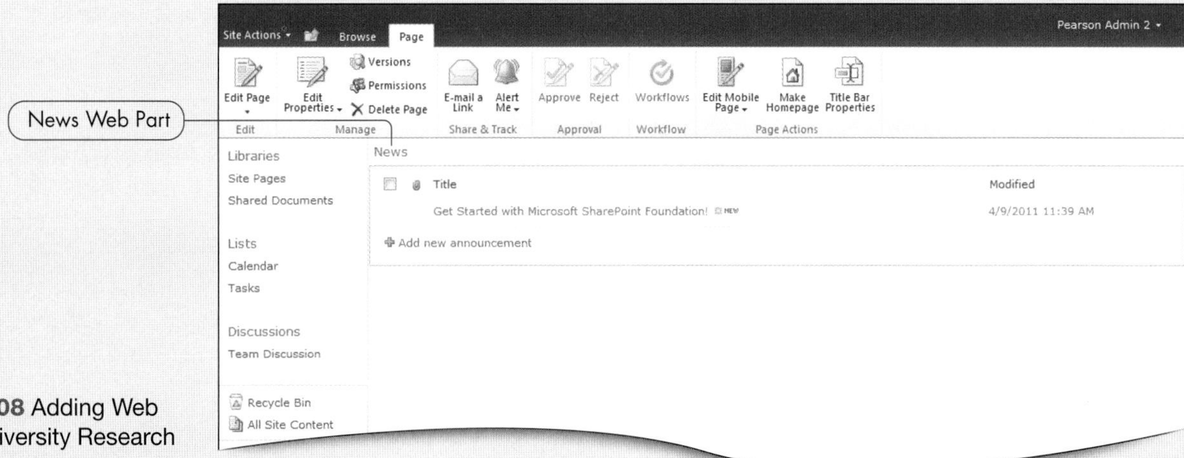

FIGURE 3.108 Adding Web Parts to a University Research Lab Site ➤

a. Click **Start**, click **All Programs**, and then select **Internet Explorer** to start Internet Explorer. Click **File** on the Menu bar, and then click **Open Site**. Type the URL of the top-level site in the **Open box**.
b. Click **All Site Content** on the Quick Launch area to open the All Site Content page. Click **Create**, and then create a new site *sp03p2LEAT_LastNameFirstName* using the Team Site Template.
c. Click the **Page tab**, and then click **Edit** in the Edit group. Highlight the text *your*, and then type **LEAT**. Click **Save & Close** in the Edit group.
d. Click **Edit in SharePoint Designer** on the Site Actions menu. Use the SharePoint Designer File tab to create a new ASPX page named **News.aspx**. Click **Yes** to display *News.aspx* in Advanced Editor mode.
e. Click the **Insert Tab**, and then click **Web Part Zone** in the Web Parts group of the Insert tab. Click the **Web Part Zone Tools–Format tab**.
f. Type **News** in the **Zone Title: box** in the Web Part zone group. Click **Save** on the Quick Access Toolbar.
g. Click the **Style tab**, and then attach the Default Master Page (v4.master) to the *News.aspx* page. Click **OK** in the Match Content Regions dialog box. Click **Save** on the Quick Access Toolbar. Click the **Home tab**, and then click **Preview in Browser** in the Preview group.
h. Click the **Page tab**, and then click **Edit Page** in Edit group. Click the **Add a Web Part link** in the news Web Part zone and if they are not already selected, select **Lists and Libraries** in the *Categories* section and **Announcements** in the *Web Parts* section of the Web Parts bar. Click **Add**.
i. Click the arrow on the title bar of the Announcements Web Part, and then click **Edit Web Part**. Type **News** in the **Title box** under *Appearance*. Click **Stop Editing** in the Edit group. Your screen should now look similar to Figure 3.108.
j. Activate the SharePoint Designer window, click **Refresh**, and then click anywhere within the newly added Web Part.
k. Click the **Web Part tab** on the List View Tools tab, and then click **To Site Gallery** in the Save Web Part group. Click **OK** in the Save Web Part to Site Gallery dialog box. Click **No** in the Microsoft SharePoint Designer alert dialog box.
l. Activate the Internet Explorer window, and then click **Site Settings** on the Site Actions menu. Click **Go to top level site settings** under *Site Collection Administration* on the Site Settings page.
m. Click **Web parts** under *Galleries* on the Site Settings page of the top-level site.
n. Click **sp03p2LEAT_JohnDoe** on the top navigation bar.
o. Keep the Internet Explorer and SharePoint Designer windows open for the next exercise.

3 Adding Data Views to a SharePoint Site for a University Research Lab

Data Views represent another very powerful SharePoint feature that enable you to easily display the data included in lists and libraries on your site pages in the way you need it to appear. As developer and Web master of the Laboratory for Educational and Assistive Technology Research site, you want to take advantage of this feature and are eager to learn how to create and modify Data Views using SharePoint Designer 2010 and the SharePoint Foundation browser interface. This exercise follows the same set of skills as used in Hands-On Exercise 3 in the chapter. Refer to Figure 3.109 as you complete this exercise.

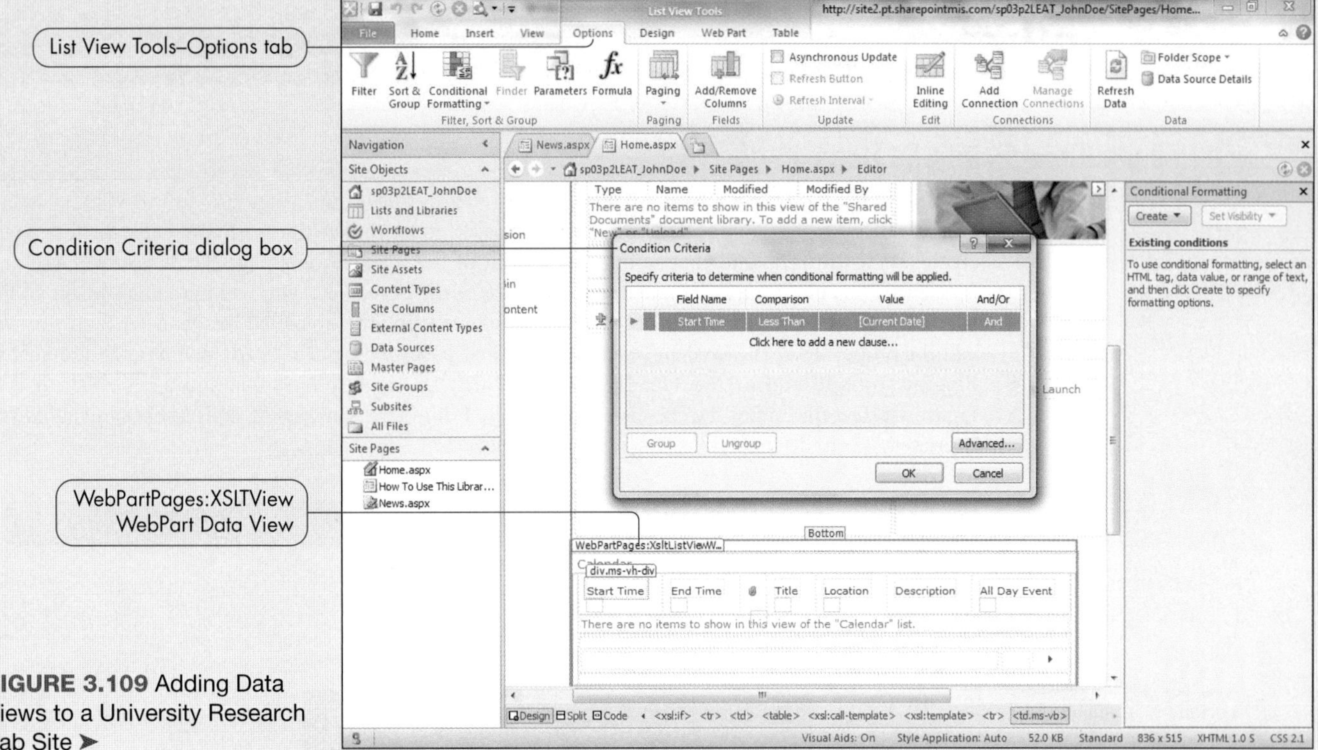

FIGURE 3.109 Adding Data Views to a University Research Lab Site ➤

a. Activate the SharePoint Designer window. Click **Site Pages** on the Navigation Pane, click **Home.aspx**, and then click **Edit File** in the *Customization* section.
b. Position the insertion point inside the <div> box within the Bottom Web Part zone.
c. Click **Insert tab**, click **Data View** in the Data View & Forms group, and then select **Calendar** on the All Data Sources list.
d. Click the **Options tab**, and then click **Add/Remove Columns** in the Fields group.
e. Press **Ctrl**, and then select **Workspace** and **Recurrence** in the *Displayed fields* section of the Displayed Fields dialog box. Click **Remove**, and then click **OK**.
f. Click **Sort & Group** in the Filter, Sort & Group group. Click **Start Time** in the *Available fields* section, and then click the **Add button**. Click **OK**.
g. Click the **Start Time column**, click **Conditional Formatting** in the Filter, Sort & Group group, and then select **Hide Content**.
h. Select **Start Time** in the Field name, and then select **Less Than** in the Comparison field. Your screen should look similar to Figure 3.108.
i. Click **OK**, and then click **Save** on the Quick Access Toolbar. Activate Internet Explorer, and then click **Refresh** to refresh the screen.
j. Click **Add new event** and add two new events. They should display in ascending order of the Start Time.
k. Click **Add new event**, and then add a new event with a Start Time before the current date. The event will not be displayed.
l. Close all SharePoint Designer and Internet Explorer windows, and then exit the two applications.

MID-LEVEL EXERCISES

1 Hope Hospital SharePoint Site Home Page

You work for Hope Hospital, and you have been asked to customize the site home page. First, you will create a new team site and change the Text Layout of the subsite home page. Then, you will edit and format the text and images included in the subsite home page. Next, you will upload an image to the assets library and create a new Image Viewer Web Part using the uploaded image. After that, you will edit the properties of the Image Viewer Web Part and paste text from a Word document and format it. Finally, you will add a New Heading to the Quick Launch. Your screen should look similar to Figure 3.110 at the end of the exercise. This exercise follows the same set of skills as used in Hands-On Exercises 1–2 in the chapter.

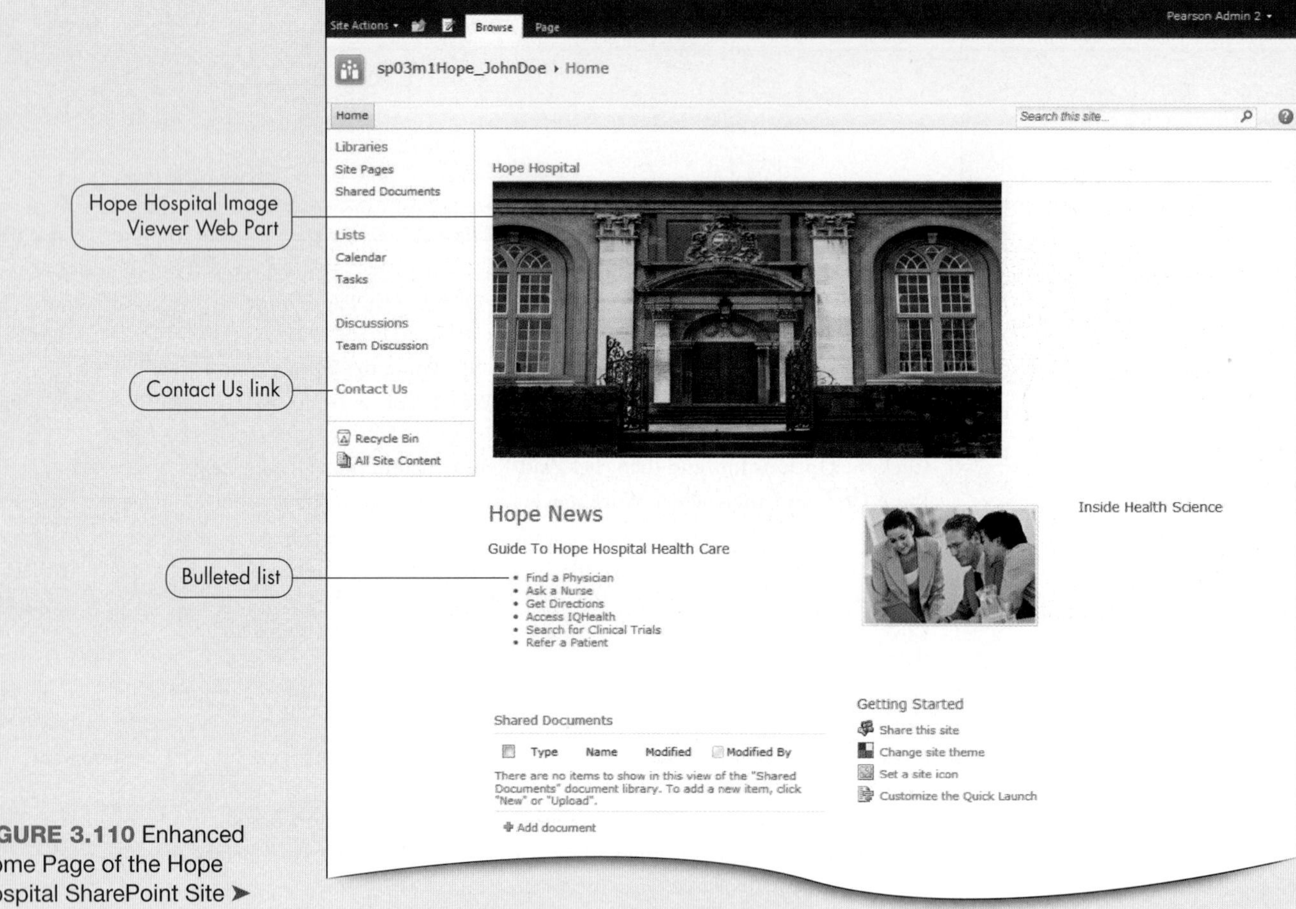

FIGURE 3.110 Enhanced Home Page of the Hope Hospital SharePoint Site ➤

a. Start Internet Explorer.
b. Click **File** on the Menu bar, and then click **Open Site**. Type the URL of the top-level site in the **Open box**.
c. Create a *sp03m1Hope_LastNameFirstName* subsite of the top-level site using the Team Site template.
d. Change the Text Layout of the *sp03m1Hope_LastNameFirstName* subsite home page to the **Three columns with header and footer layout**.
e. Click the **People Collaborating image**, and then change the size of the picture to 181 px (horizontal size) and 121 px (vertical size).
f. Replace *Welcome to your site!* with **Hope News**. Type **Inside Health Science** in column three, and then change the text format to **Color Heading 2**. Save the page.
g. Upload *HopeMain1.jpg* in the Site Assets Library.

h. Insert an Image Viewer Web Part in the top zone. Change the title of the Web Part to **Hope Hospital**.

i. Open the Web Part Properties dialog box, select **Left** in the Image Horizontal Alignment down list, and then type:
   - **../SiteAssets/HopeMain1.jpg** in the **Image Link type box**.
   - **Hope Hospital Central Building** in the **Alternate text box**.

j. Open *GuideHopeHospitalHealthCare.docx*, copy all the text, highlight the first paragraph below the *Hope News* heading, and then paste the copied text.

k. Highlight the last six lines of the text, and then format them as a bulleted list.

l. Highlight the Inside Health Science text, and then format *Guide To Hope Hospital HealthCare* to **Color Heading 2**. Save the page.

m. Click **Customize the Quick Launch** in the center zone to display the Quick Launch page. Click the **New Heading link**, type **Contact Us** in the **Type the description box**, and then type **YourSiteURL/SitePages/ContactUs.aspx**.

n. Navigate to the home page of your site. The new Contact Us link shows on the Quick Launch. Your screen should now look like Figure 3.110. You will not need to create a ContactUs.aspx page.

o. Close all SharePoint Designer and Internet Explorer windows and exit the applications.

2 DestinQuest Co.

You work for DestinQuest, a vacation rental, hospitality, and resort real estate company, and at your supervisor's request, you are enhancing the home page of the DestinQuest parent site and developing a marketing subsite for DestinQuest's Vacation Rentals. You need to create both the parent site and the subsite using the Team Site template. You will create a Picture Library, upload pictures from a local folder, and insert a Picture Library Slideshow Web Part on the home page of the parent site. Then you will export the Picture Library Slideshow Web Part and the Picture Library and import it within DestinQuest's Vacation Rentals subsite. Figure 3.110a shows the Browse view of the parent site. You will also upload images in the Assets Library and an audio file in the Share Documents Library. After that, you will insert a layout table on the home page of DestinQuest's Vacation Rentals subsite and use it to place text and images. Finally, you will insert the Picture Library Slideshow Web Part. This exercise follows the same set of skills as used in Hands-On Exercises 1–3 in the chapter. Refer to Figure 3.111 as you complete this exercise.

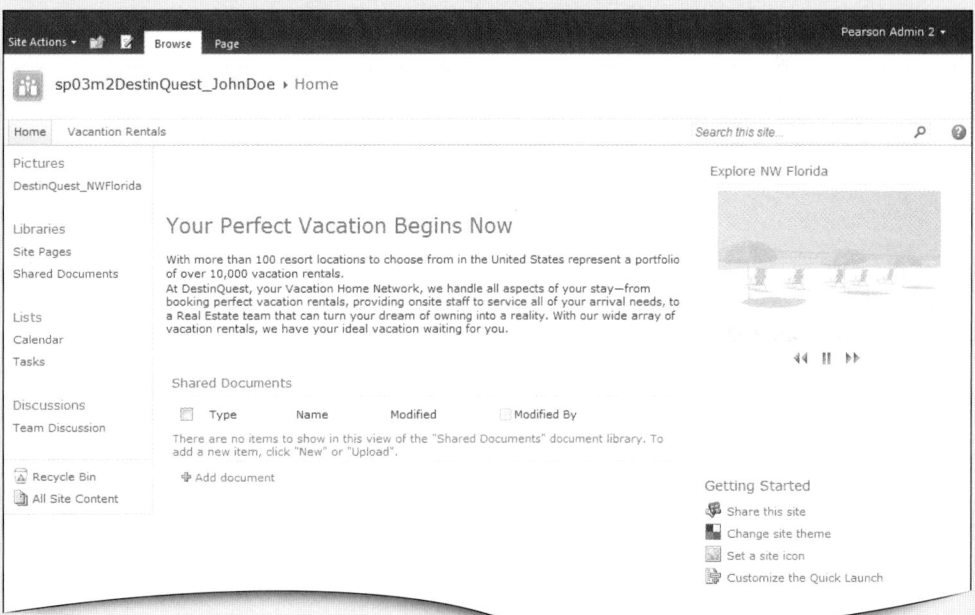

FIGURE 3.111 Enhanced Pages of the DestinQuest Site ➤

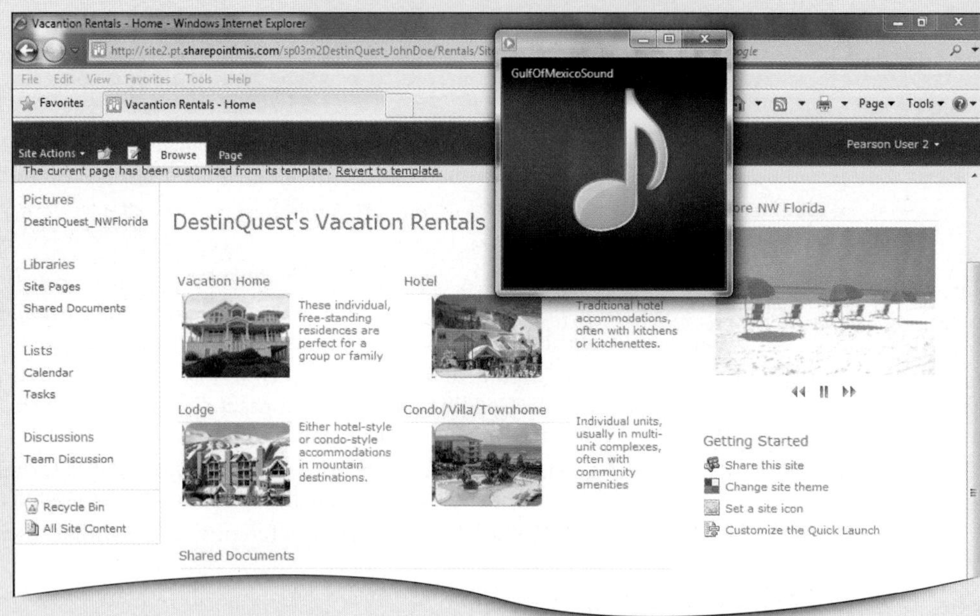

FIGURE 3.111 *(Continued)* ➤

a. Start Internet Explorer.
b. Click **File** on the Menu bar, and then click **Open Site**. Type the URL of the top-level site in the **Open box**.
c. Create a *sp03m2DestinQuest_LastNameFirstName* subsite of the top-level site using the Team Site template.
d. Create a Vacation Rentals subsite of the *sp03m2DestinQuest_LastNameFirstName* site using the Team Site template.
e. Navigate to the *sp03m2DestinQuest_LastNameFirstName* parent site. Open the site home page in Edit mode. Open the *DestinQuestRentals.docx* document, and then copy the first title and the two paragraphs underneath the title. Paste the text over the first title and paragraph on Home.aspx. Format the new title using the **Color Heading 1 Markup Style**.
f. Create a new DestinQuest_NWFlorida Picture Library, and then upload all pictures from the *DestinPictures* folder to this folder.
g. Open *sp03m2DestinQuest_LastNameFirstName* in SharePoint Designer, and then open *Home.aspx* in Edit mode. Remove the People Collaborating picture, and then insert a Picture Library Slideshow Web Part with the following properties:
   - No Title or Description under *Display with.*
   - Explore **NW Florida** under *Appearance/Title.*
   - Export all data under *Advanced/Export Mode.*
h. Export the Explore NW Florida Web Part to Site Gallery. Save as **Template DestinQuest_NWFlorida Picture Library** and make sure you select the Include Content option on the Save as Template page.
i. Save *Home.aspx*, preview in browser *sp03m2DestinQuest_LastNameFirstName*, and then navigate to the vacation rentals subsite. Create a DestinQuest_NWFlorida Picture Library using the template created at step h.
j. Open the Vacation Rentals subsite home page in SharePoint Designer Edit mode. Remove the People Collaborating picture, and then insert the Explore NW Florida Custom Web Part.
k. Highlight the text *Welcome to your site!*, and then type **DestinQuest's Vacation Rentals**.
l. Upload all pictures from the RentalsPictures folder to the Assets Library, and then upload the *GulfOfMexicoSound.wma* file to the Shared Documents Library.
m. Insert a table similar to the one included in the *DestinQuestRentals.docx* file below the DestinQuest's Vacation Rentals title as shown in Figure 3.110b:
   - For each image, use an Image Viewer Web Part.
   - Copy and paste the text from *DestinQuestRentals.docx.*
n. Remove the Modified and Modified by columns of the Shared Documents XsltListViewPart.
o. Save *Home.aspx*, and then open it in the browser. Click the **GulfofMexicoSound link**. Your screen should now look similar to Figure 3.110b.
p. Close all SharePoint Designer and Internet Explorer windows and exit the applications.

CAPSTONE EXERCISE

You have being working for a major financial management and advisory company on developing a site for all categories of company clients from individual investors to institutions and corporate clients. You will create a parent site for the financial management and advisory company and enhance its home page, using the SharePoint Foundation Browser interface, by adding and formatting text, and adding links, images, and audio files. You will also add a new ASPX page, dedicated to the crisis in Japan, and enhance the page by adding a table, adding and formatting text, and using bookmarks. Then, you will insert a Web Part zone, create a Picture Library, and insert a Picture Library Slideshow Web Part that will display pictures from Japan's most devastated areas. You will then upload a custom list template and will create a new list, using this template, dedicated to Tax Income Brackets for 2010. Finally, you will add a new Web Part page, and then insert and modify a Data View.

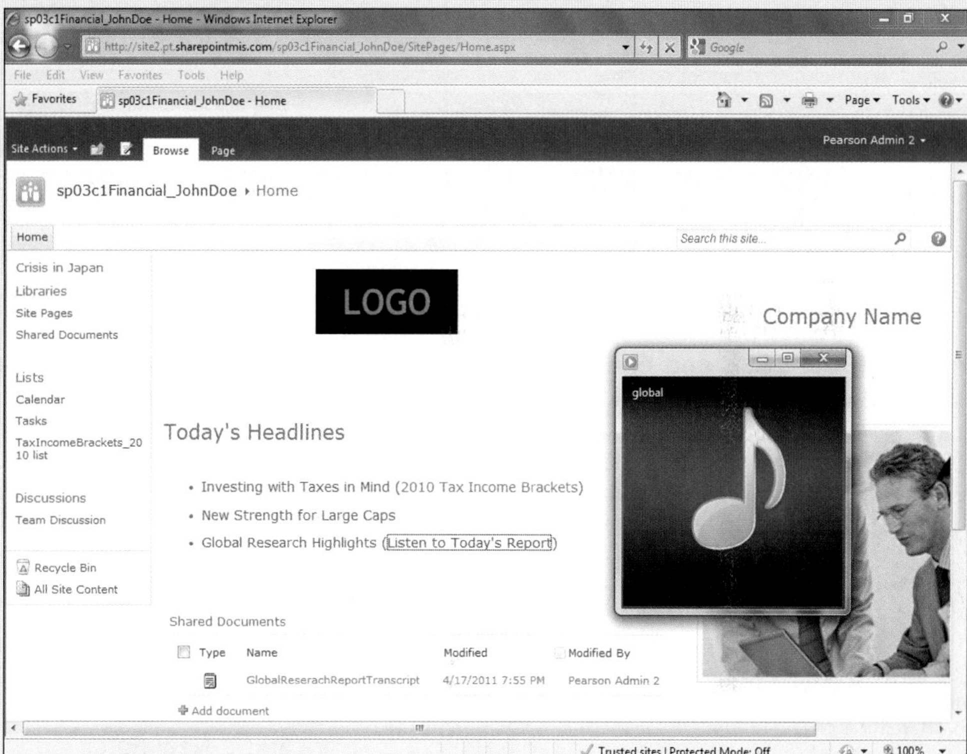

FIGURE 3.112 Financial Management and Advisory Company Site ➤

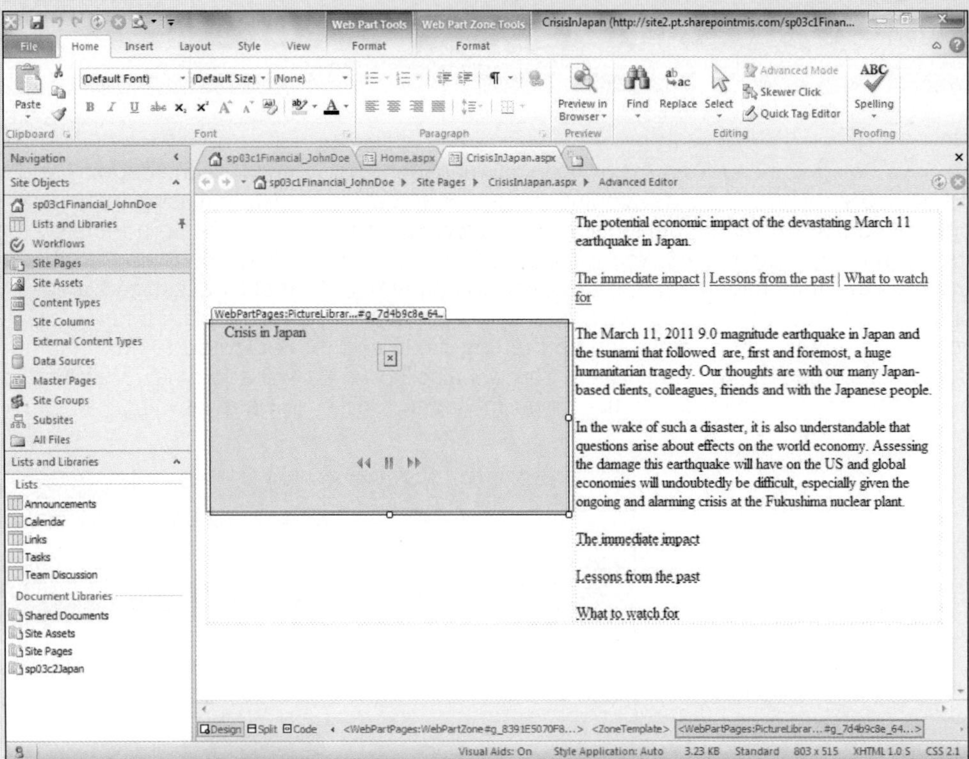

FIGURE 3.112 *(Continued)* ➤

Create a Parent Site and Enhance Its Home Page Using the SharePoint Foundation Browser Interface

You will create a parent site for your company. You will change the Text Layout of the home page and add a table to create an interesting site. You will also add lines of text to the home page and format those using Markup Styles. Additionally, you will upload documents in the Assets and Shared Documents libraries, insert an image in the new table, and then format the table. Finally, you will add and format a link to an audio file.

a. Launch the Internet Explorer browser, and then navigate to the top-level site of your site collection.

b. Create a *sp03c1Financial_LastNameFirstName* subsite of your top-level site using the Team Site template.

c. Change the Text Layout of the Home.aspx to **Two columns with header and footer**.

d. Insert a table with one row and two columns in the header layout area. Type **Company Name** in column two, and then format the text as **Heading 1 <h1>**.

e. Replace the text *Welcome to your site!* with **Today's Headlines**. Replace the paragraph placed just below with **Investing with Taxes in Mind**, and then format the text as **Color Heading 2**. Type another text line: **New Strength for Large Caps**, and then format the text as **Color Heading 2**. Save *Home.aspx*.

f. Upload *logo.gif* and *global.wma* into the Site Assets Library. Upload *GlobalResearchReportTranscript.rtf* in the Shared Documents library.

g. Insert *logo.gif* in column one of the table created in step e. Apply the **Table Style 1–Clear style**.

h. Type **Global Research Highlights (Listen to Today's Report)** above the Shared Documents link, and then format it as **Colored Heading 2**. Highlight *Listen to Today's Report*, and then insert a hyperlink to the *global.wma* audio file (the absolute URL should be **http://the URL of sp03c1Financial_LastNameFirstName/SiteAssets/global.wma**.

i. Select the Display icon in the Behavior group on the Link Tools–Format tab. Format the three Color Heading 2 text lines as a bulleted list. Save *Home.aspx*.

j. Click the **Listen to Today's Report hyperlink**. Your screen should look similar to Figure 3.112a.

Add a New Page, Add a Table and Text, Format the Text Using Bookmarks, Insert a Web Part Zone, Create a Picture Library, and Insert a Web Part

You will create a new ASPX page, add and format a table, paste text in the table, format the text using bookmarks, create a Picture Library, and then insert a Web Part zone and a Picture Library Slideshow Web Part.

a. Open the **sp03c1Financial_LastNameFirstName** site in SharePoint Designer, and then create a new *CrisisInJapan.aspx* page.

b. Insert a table with one row and two columns. Click **Distribute Columns**. Open the *TheCrisisInJapan.docx* file from your Exploring folder, select all text, and then copy the text. Paste the text in column two of the table. Remove text formatting.

c. Add bookmarks, see Figure 3.15, to the last three lines in the text. Add hyperlinks to these three bookmarks using the corresponding text placed below the title of the text.

d. Create a *sp03c2Japan* Picture Library and upload *files japan_*.jpg* from your Exploring folder.

e. Create a Japan Web Part zone in column one of the table. Insert a Crisis in Japan Picture Library Slideshow Web Part.

f. Save the *CrisisInJapan.aspx* page. Your screen should now look similar to Figure 3.112b.

Upload a Custom List Template, Create a Custom List, Create a Web Part Page, Add a Data View, and Format It

You will create and upload a custom List Template, create a Custom List Template, and then create a new Web Part page. Add to the new page a Data View of the Custom List Template and format it. Add a link to the new Web Part page in the site home page.

a. Activate your Internet Explorer window, and then navigate to your top-level site.

b. Display the Site Settings page, click **List Templates** in the *Galleries* section, click **Upload Document**, and then upload *sp03c3_Year2010IncomeBracketsAndTaxes.stp*.

c. Navigate to *sp03c1Financial_LastNameFirstName* site, display the All Site Content page, and then create a *TaxIncomeBrackets_2010* list. Do not display a link to the new list on the Quick Launch.

d. Navigate to the All Site Content page, and then create a TaxIncomeBrackets_2010 Web Part Page using the Header, Footer, 2 Columns, 4 Rows Layout Template.

e. Open the *TaxIncomeBrackets_2010.aspx* file in SharePoint Designer.

f. Insert a Data View for the TaxIncomeBrackets_2010 list in the Zone Template Row1. Click **Inline Editing**.

g. Click the **List View Tools–Web Part tab**, click **Properties**, and then modify the following properties:
   - New Title : **2010 Tax Income Brackets**
   - New Chrome Type : **Title and Border**
   - Deselect all six check boxes in the *Advanced* section.

h. Save the page and preview it in the browser. Navigate to the home page of the *sp03c1Financial_LastNameFirstName* site.

i. Type the following text at the end of the first line in the bulleted list: **2010 Tax Income Brackets**. Highlight the newly added text, and then insert a hyperlink to *http://the URL of sp03c1Financial_LastNameFirstName/SiteAssets/TaxIncomeBrackets_2010.aspx.*

j. Type **2010 Tax Income Brackets** in the **Description box** on the Link Tools–Format tab. Save the page. Your screen should now look similar to Figure 3.112a.

k. Close all Explorer windows and exit Internet Explorer. Close all SharePoint Designer windows and exit SharePoint Designer.

BEYOND THE CLASSROOM

Communication Skills Class

GENERAL CASE 

You are taking a communication skills class and must develop an end-of-semester demonstration speech that will demonstrate your strong communication and collaboration skills and your potential to work confidently with others. A demonstration speech is one in which you teach or direct the class how to do something. Because SharePoint 2010 is a relatively new technology, you decide to demonstrate some of its features. You will use PowerPoint to develop your presentation. After completing your notes, save the document as **sp03b1speech_LastnameFirstname** in a location as directed by your instructor. In a 1, 2, 3 fashion (listing your points in numerical order), provide the class with directions about the following topics:

- Working with SharePoint Page Contents.
- Enhancing a Web Page Using Graphics and Multimedia.
- Working with Web Part zones and Web Parts.
- Working with Data Views in SharePoint Designer.

The Microsoft Office Case Studies

RESEARCH CASE 

One of the most professional and helpful sites for finding up-to-date technical documentation on SharePoint 2010 is Microsoft TechNet Library. Use Microsoft Internet Explorer to open the Microsoft TechNet Library home page (http://technet.microsoft.com/en-us/library/default.aspx). Search for your 12 most relevant topics (key terms) covered in this chapter and print or save the most useful articles. Using the information you have found, write a report including the most relevant findings about these topics. After completing your report, save the document as **sp03b2TechNet_LastnameFirstname.docx** in a location as directed by your instructor.

SharePoint Sites Web Parts

DISASTER RECOVERY 

The *sp03b3_SiteBackUp* solution file in the Exploring SharePoint folder was the last site backup you completed for your personal blog. The backed-up site included an imported *Friends* Picture Library Slideshow Web Part initially built on a *sp03b3_PictureLibrary* that included a few pictures of your friends. Upload and activate the *sp03b3_SiteBackUp* solution file and create a *sp03b3_SiteBackUp_LastNameFirstName* subsite using this solution file. Open in the browser the home page of the *sp03b3_SiteBackUp_LastNameFirstName* subsite and observe the message displayed below the Friends Web Part included in the Right Web Part zone. Explore the content of the new site, check if *sp03b3_PictureLibrary* or another Picture Library is in the *sp03b3_SiteBackUp_LastNameFirstName* subsite, and then write a memo to your instructor describing the nature of the error. Include suggestions in the memo on how to avoid mistakes of this nature in the future.

SHAREPOINT

4 MICROSOFT OFFICE 2010

Integrating Microsoft Office 2010 Documents with SharePoint Sites

CASE STUDY | Building a SharePoint Portal for a Statewide K12 Robotics Outreach Initiative

Three major universities from Alabama have decided to join their collective experience in robotics, smartphone applications development, Computer Science education, community outreach, and implementation of assistive technologies in the educational process toward building a project titled "Robotics Across Alabama (RAA)" that will foster advanced computer technology education to the kindergarten through twelfth-grade students (K12) of Alabama.

The principal investigators want to take full advantage of the SharePoint technology to develop the statewide portal for this project. The proposed portal will implement important project related functionalities, such as disseminating and archiving any project relevant documents and events, providing real-time collaboration between all educators involved in this project, and administering surveys to stakeholders.

You have been hired by the RAA project to develop a SharePoint portal that will provide user-friendly support for the RAA mission and goals. The portal should help the RAA team to process and archive any type of financial documents and records. The portal should also provide a friendly, virtual environment where K12 teachers in STEM can communicate, access robotics educational resources, participate in the RAA robotics competitions, participate in virtual seminars, register for live events, apply for mini-grants, and learn about new robotics academic and business opportunities.

OBJECTIVES AFTER YOU READ THIS CHAPTER, YOU WILL BE ABLE TO:

1. Add a New Document Library ***p.279***
2. Add a document to a Document Library ***p.282***
3. Display documents in Lists and Libraries ***p.287***
4. Work with SharePoint Foundation built-in list types ***p.299***
5. Open, edit, and save a Microsoft Office documents to a SharePoint Document Library ***p.323***
6. Work with Word documents ***p.328***
7. Integrate Word documents with blog sites ***p.329***
8. Work with PowerPoint 2010 documents ***p.331***
9. Use Excel 2010 in SharePoint ***p.345***
10. Use Access 2010 documents in SharePoint ***p.358***
11. Work with data sources and Data Views ***p.375***

SharePoint Tools for Working with Microsoft Office 2010 Documents

SharePoint 2010 tools enable you to effectively work with various Microsoft Office and Windows client applications. This can solve many problems, especially if you travel and experience low bandwidth, because you can link to the client applications via the SharePoint Ribbon of the SharePoint Foundation browser interface or SharePoint Designer. This gives you the option to work with SharePoint in the context of the application. The following Office and Windows client applications are supported:

- Access:
  - Export or link tables to a SharePoint 2010 List
  - Incorporate SharePoint data into Access data sources and use it for queries and reports
  - Transfer databases to a shared, managed platform
- Excel:
  - Enhanced integration with SharePoint for saving documents, adding metadata, checking in/out, and workflow
  - Office Web Application enables viewing, editing, and coauthoring of spreadsheets in the browser platform
- Office Upload Center:
  - Per-document level caching and central access to see recently viewed and pending check-in SharePoint files
  - Synchronize changes only between the client and server applications across the Office suite
- PowerPoint:
  - Enhanced integration with SharePoint for saving documents, adding metadata, checking-in/out
  - Office Web Application for viewing and editing of presentations in the browser platform
  - Coauthoring support for concurrent editing
  - Add videos and manipulate layout on the slide from SharePoint
  - Broadcast presentation by publishing it to SharePoint or Windows Live, enabling slide transitions, builds, and other multimedia features of PowerPoint
- Windows Explorer:
  - Integration for uploading and copying documents between SharePoint and another file storage location
- Word:
  - Enhanced integration for saving documents, adding metadata, checking in/out, and workflow.
  - Office Web Application provides tools for browser-based viewing and editing of documents. Client supports coauthoring so multiple people can edit the same document concurrently.
- SharePoint Workspace:
  - Offline site content and data, at site or per list
  - Synchronizes changes only
- Office 2010 client applications:
  - Backstage can be launched from the File button enabling updates to authoring permissions, metadata, and tagging
- Office Web Apps for Word, Excel, PowerPoint, and OneNote
  - Integrated with SharePoint providing read and edit access to documents using popular browsers
- Office Mobile Applications for SharePoint, Word, Excel, PowerPoint, and OneNote:
  - Windows Mobile device access to content
  - Microbrowser support on other non-Windows Mobile device platforms

SharePoint Document libraries can contain thousands of documents created with Microsoft Office or other applications. In addition to documents from Access, Excel, PowerPoint, and Word, you can store non-Microsoft files such as text files, PDFs, and files from other applications. Within the SharePoint libraries, the files can be grouped in folders or by their creator.

TIP SharePoint 2010 Document Sets

SharePoint 2010 Document Sets can be used to create different views of the document library. These views show only the documents in the set by using a column in the library to filter the files.

SharePoint Designer enables you to work with several types of data sources such as lists, libraries, XML files, and databases. As previously discussed, the two main Web Parts that you can use in order to display data from all of these data sources are XSLT List View Web Parts and XSLT Data Form Web Parts (DFWP).

In this section, you will learn about the enhanced tools and features provided by the Microsoft SharePoint 2010 browser interface and SharePoint Designer for working with Word, PowerPoint, Excel and Access.

Adding a New Document Library

You will usually need more than one document library in a site. This enables you to assign different access rights to documents to different groups of people at different stages in the life of the document.

A travel reimbursement document is an example of one where different people will need different access rights at different times. In most businesses, anyone can submit a travel reimbursement document, and, when using SharePoint, it can be stored in the main shared documents library. Once the travel reimbursement is signed by the department head, it should be moved into another document library so that only the department head and administrative assistant can edit it. This protects the document from being modified later by the person who originally submitted it. Access rights to this document library might enable people to only view the document so they will know it is being processed. Once the travel reimbursement is completely processed, it should be moved to yet another document library and the access rights should change to read-only for all groups.

Using multiple document libraries also allows you to define different default document types, as will be discussed in the next section. Content types can also be used to organize libraries, as discussed later in this chapter.

Create a New Document Library

When you create a collaboration site, a default document library (Shared Documents) is created. As you create additional document libraries, be sure to use descriptive names that enable you and others to understand the purpose of the library. This will help keep things organized.

The All Site Content page displays all of the document libraries and lists for a site. Open the All Site Content page by clicking All Site Content from the Quick Launch area, or View All Site Content from the Site Actions menu.

Add a new document library by clicking Create, which displays the Create dialog box. To see the available types of libraries, select the Filter By object type of Library. From that list, click Document Library. Name the library with a descriptive, meaningful name. The additional settings are optional. Figure 4.1 shows the options for the new document library. You can provide a more detailed description and place the library on the Quick Launch menu (as discussed in previous chapters of this textbook). Other options are available if you click More Options on the column on the right.

The **default template** defines the default content type for that library.

The ***default template*** option defines the default content type for that library. This is the type of file SharePoint creates when you press New Document in the New group while viewing the library's contents. Only one default template can be specified per library. Keep in mind that even with a default template defined, you can still store many types of files within the document library. The default list of available templates is shown in Figure 4.1 and includes Word, Excel, PowerPoint, OneNote, and Web page options. The Document Template option is used to define the default template.

Only one default template can be specified per library.

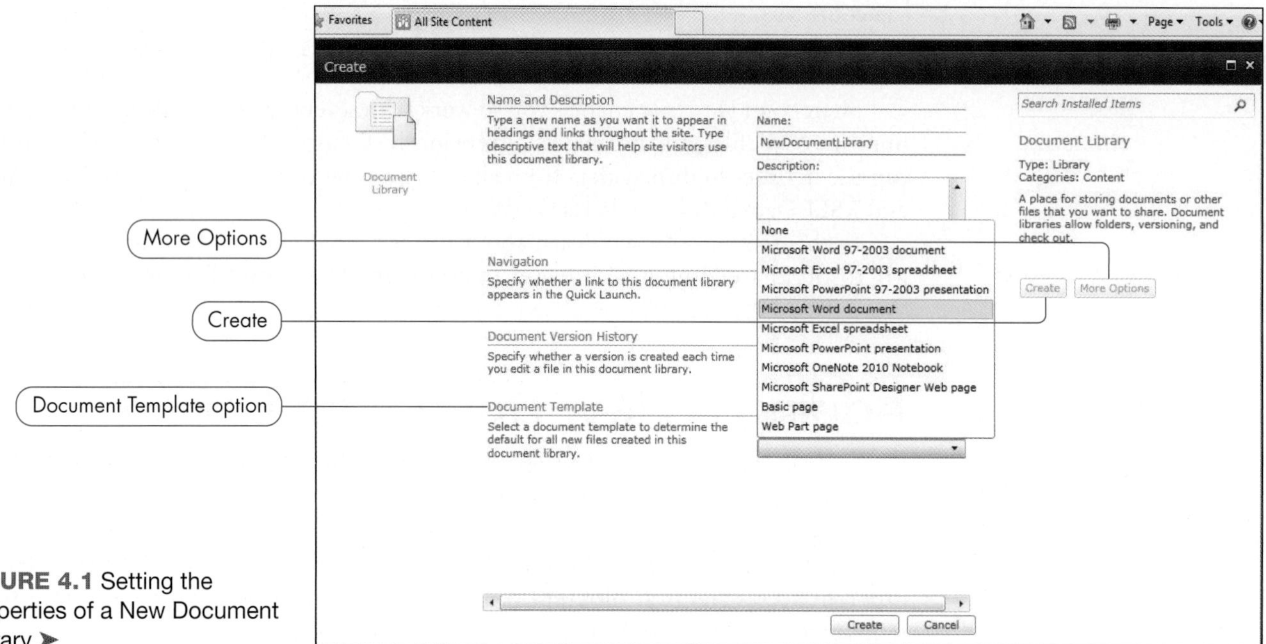

FIGURE 4.1 Setting the Properties of a New Document Library ➤

TIP Default Document Templates

You might wonder why some Office applications are shown twice in the Document Template option list. The various versions of Office use different file formats. For example Word 2007 and 2010 use the .docx format, whereas Word 97 and 2003 use the .doc format.

The selected Document Template option opens a blank template or Web page when the user clicks New in the library view. You are not locked into just Office application templates for this option. The SharePoint administrator can add other document templates, such as the travel reimbursement form discussed earlier, which can be set to open as the default template.

Once you have selected the options for the library, click Create and the library will automatically open. Two sub-tabs will appear under the Library Tools tab, as new tabs:

The **Documents tab** contains options for managing and editing documents.

The **Library tab** enables you to manage the way your new library appears on the screen.

- The ***Documents tab*** contains options for managing and editing your documents. You can add documents from your local computer or network drive. New documents can be created using the default template using the New group of the Documents tab.
- The ***Library tab*** enables you to manage the way your new library appears on the screen. You can define different views, permissions, additional columns, filters, and sort orders.

Change the Default Template for a Document Library

...the default template can be changed to any type of document that a user's computer recognizes.

As previously indicated, the default template can be changed to any type of document that a user's computer recognizes. For instance, the default template in a SharePoint library for the accounting department might be set to open an Excel document or other accounting software application document.

To change the default template for a document library that has already been created, begin by creating the document you want to use as a template. Open the library, and then on the Library Tools–Library tab, click *Open with Explorer* in the Connect & Export group. In a different window, browse to the template you created (as shown in Figure 4.2a), and then copy the file by right-clicking the file and selecting Copy. Using the window that contains the library, locate the library's Forms folder, right-click in a blank area, and then paste the template. You can then close the window from which you copied the template.

TIP Showing Hidden Files

If you do not see the library's Forms folder, you will need to select Folder and search options in the Organize menu, click the View tab, and then click the Show hidden files and folders option.

Now the settings need to be changed so that the copied file is assigned as the default template. Click Library Settings in the Settings group, and then click Advanced settings under the General Settings column. Update the URL in the *Document Template* section to point to the location of the template file you just copied and pasted into the Forms folder, as shown in Figure 4.2b. When the user creates a new document in the library, the default document will be the template you created, as shown in Figure 4.2c.

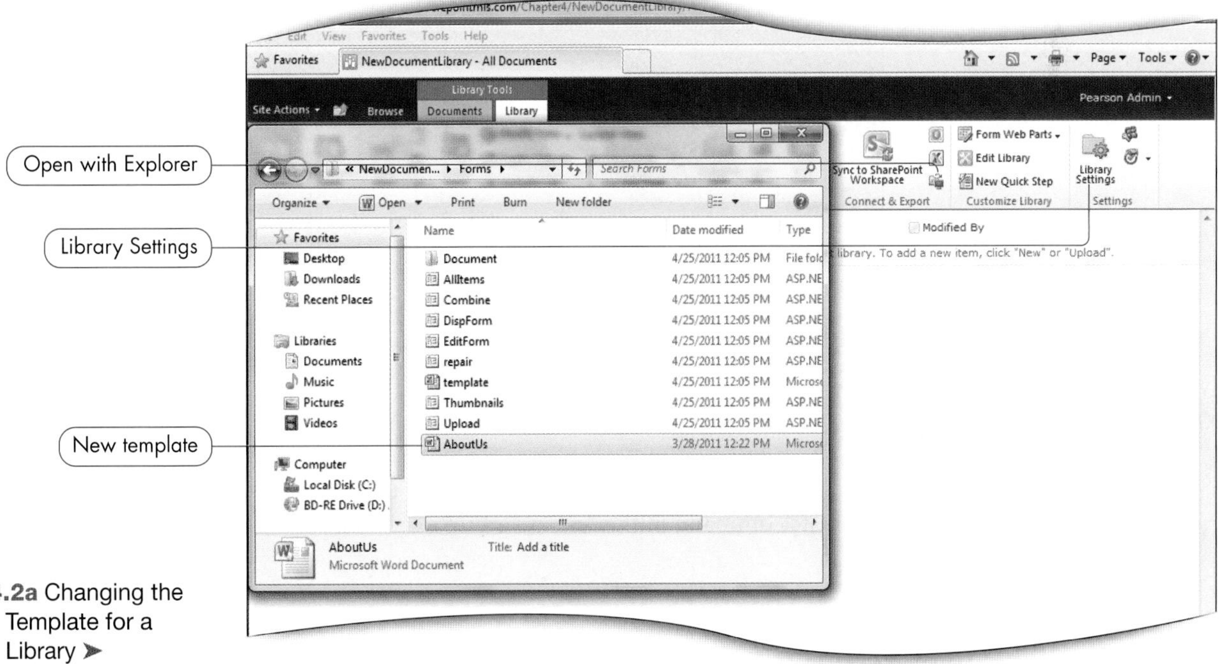

FIGURE 4.2a Changing the Document Template for a Document Library ➤

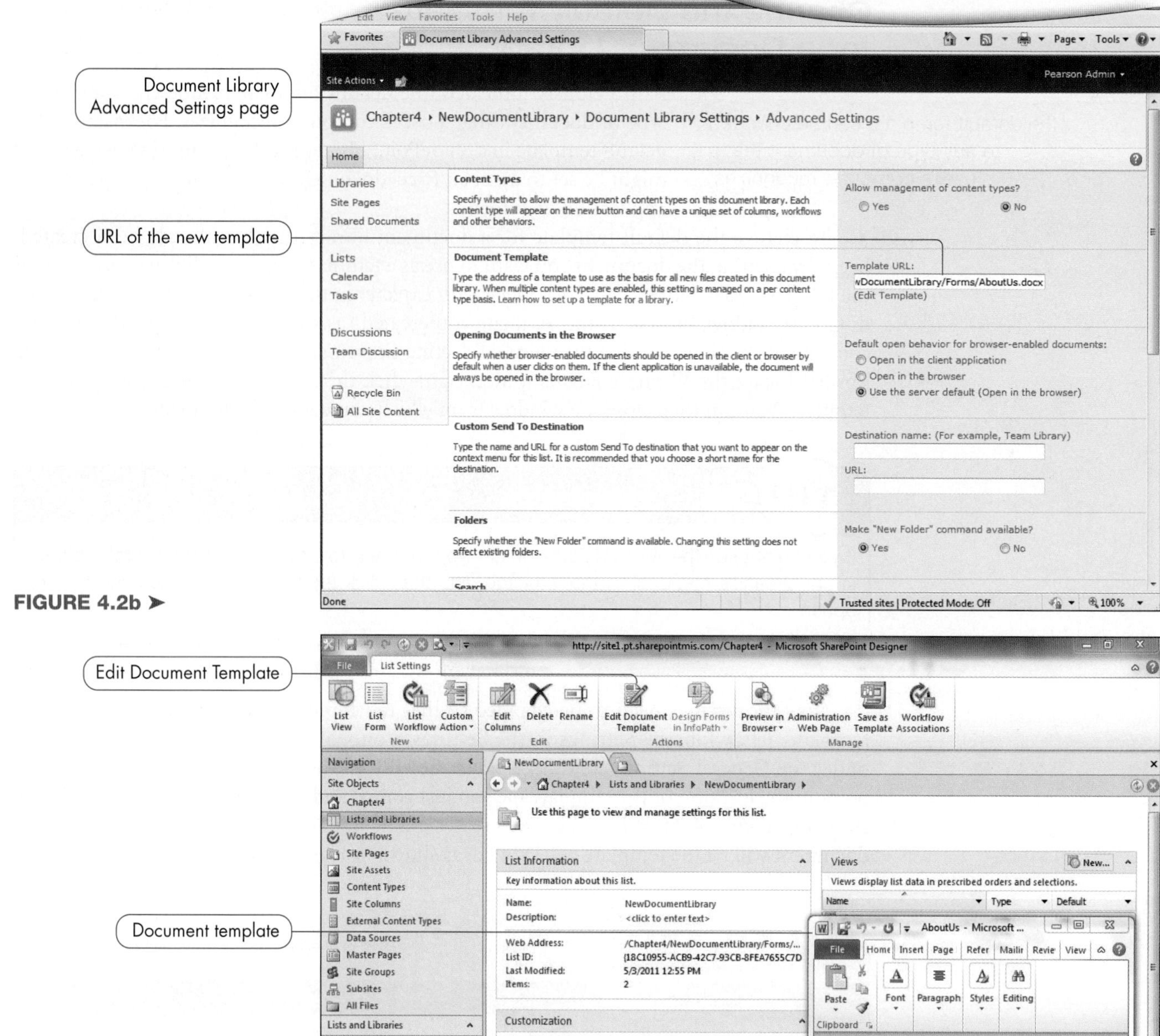

FIGURE 4.2b ➤

FIGURE 4.2c ➤

SharePoint Designer enables you to edit the document template via the Edit Document template command in the Actions group on the List Settings tab (see Figure 4.2c).

Adding a Document to a Document Library

Depending on whether the new document library was set up to appear on the Quick Launch, you may or may not be able to see it when working with the site. If it is visible under the Documents section of the Quick Launch, click it to open it; otherwise, click All Site Content on the Quick Launch, and then click the library name. Because it is a new library, no documents are available in it.

Create a New Document

To create a new document, click the Library Tools–Documents tab in SharePoint Foundation, and then click New Document in the New group. Edit the document, adding, deleting, and updating the content as necessary. When you have completed the work, click Save on the Word Quick Access Toolbar. In the Save As dialog box, as shown in Figure 4.3a, provide a file name. Notice that the location where the file will be saved is in the document library of the site and the document type is the default template type, selected for the library. The saved document is shown in the document library in Figure 4.3b. Notice the properties for the document:

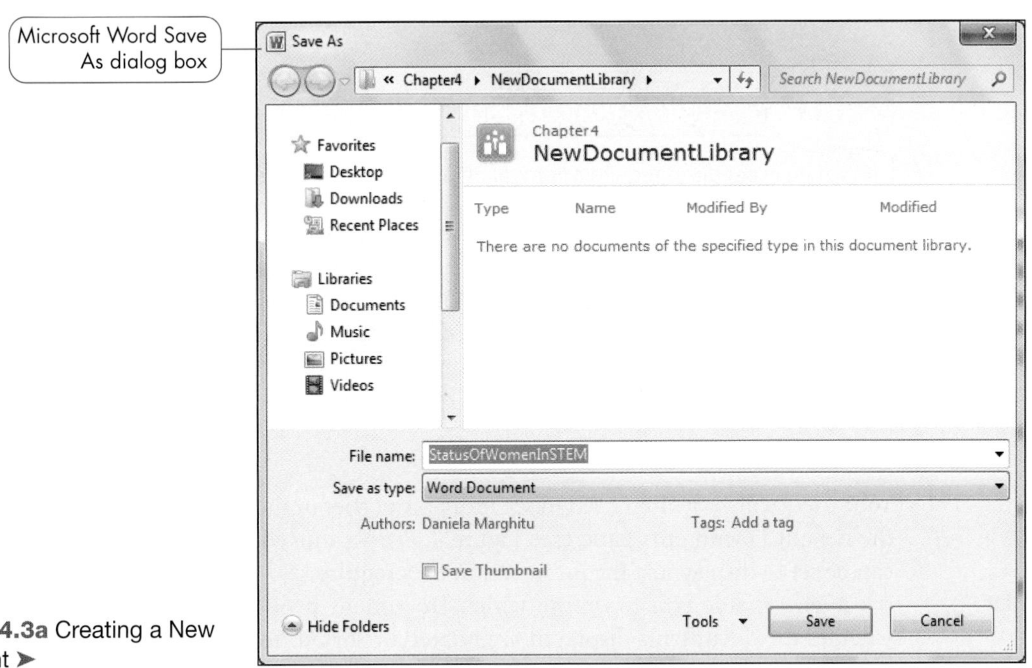

FIGURE 4.3a Creating a New Document ➤

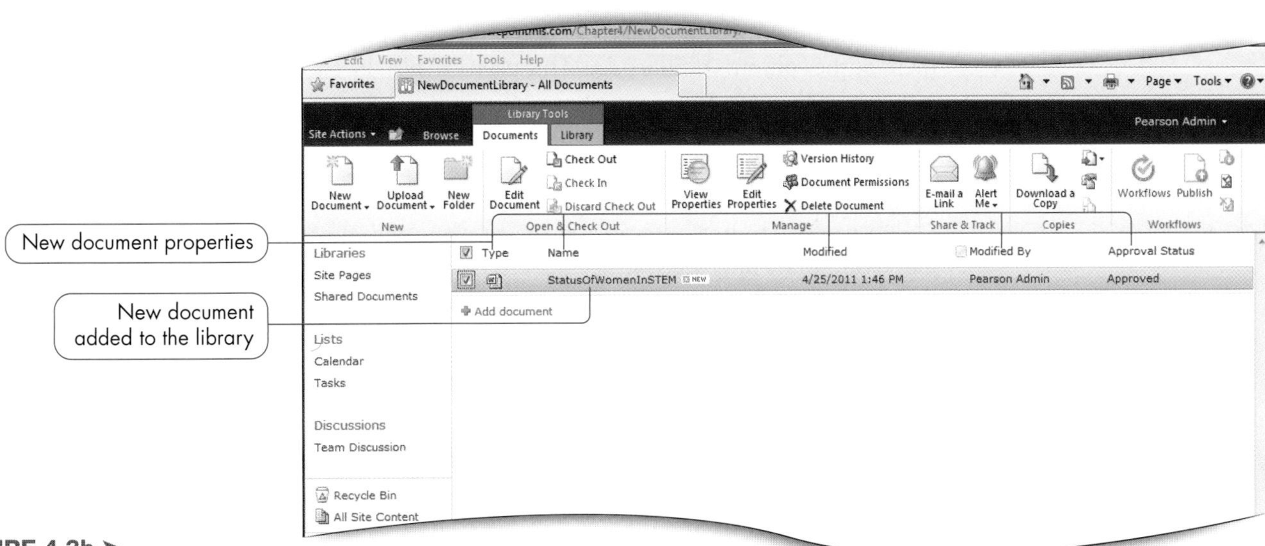

FIGURE 4.3b ➤

- The Type column displays a familiar Windows Explorer icon that represents the document type. Click the icon to open the document file.

- The document name for a new document is highlighted with a New icon, as shown in Figure 4.3b, indicating a recently added file. This icon is automatically added and later removed (after two days).
- The *Date and Time* column displays when the file was last modified.
- The Modified By column displays the SharePoint name of the person who last saved the file to the document library. Click the SharePoint name to view the profile information about the user.
- A Check Out To column will appear if the library requires checking out the document to edit it. It also tracks who has this document currently locked for editing.
- The Approval column appears if the document library is set to require content approval before publishing the document. This column displays the current status of the document as it goes through the approval process.

TIP Require Content Approval

If the site is set up to require approval of documents before they are published on the site, the Approval column will be displayed as a document property. The column displays the word *Draft* if the document is unpublished. Draft will also be displayed if changes have been made and saved to an existing document but it has not been submitted for publication. The word *Pending* in the Require Content Approval column indicates that the document has been submitted for approval. The word *Approved* appears in the column when the document is approved and published.

Add Columns to a View

Your users will very often need to see more properties of the documents than are displayed in the default Documents pane (see Figure 4.3b). Various views of the Document properties can be set to display just the information they require.

Views enable you to define which Document property columns are displayed and whether the documents displayed are filtered or sorted.

Views enable you to define which Document property columns are displayed and whether the documents displayed are filtered or sorted. You can add additional columns to the Document view using the Library Tools–Library tab. Click All Documents in the *Views* section. You can add a number of additional columns to this view, as shown in Figure 4.4a. Check the columns you want to add to the view. Click the list arrow to change the arrangement of the columns on the page. This page can also be used to set up filters and sorting. You can change the name of the view, as well.

As shown in Figure 4.4b, the new column (Checked Out To in this case) is displayed. Now it will be easy to figure out who has a document checked out, and you can contact them for additional information on the status of the document.

As you add more columns to the view, some columns shrink in width, and often the file name cannot be fully seen. To see the full file name, point to the document icon. A box with the file name will appear. The file name will also be displayed on the Status bar.

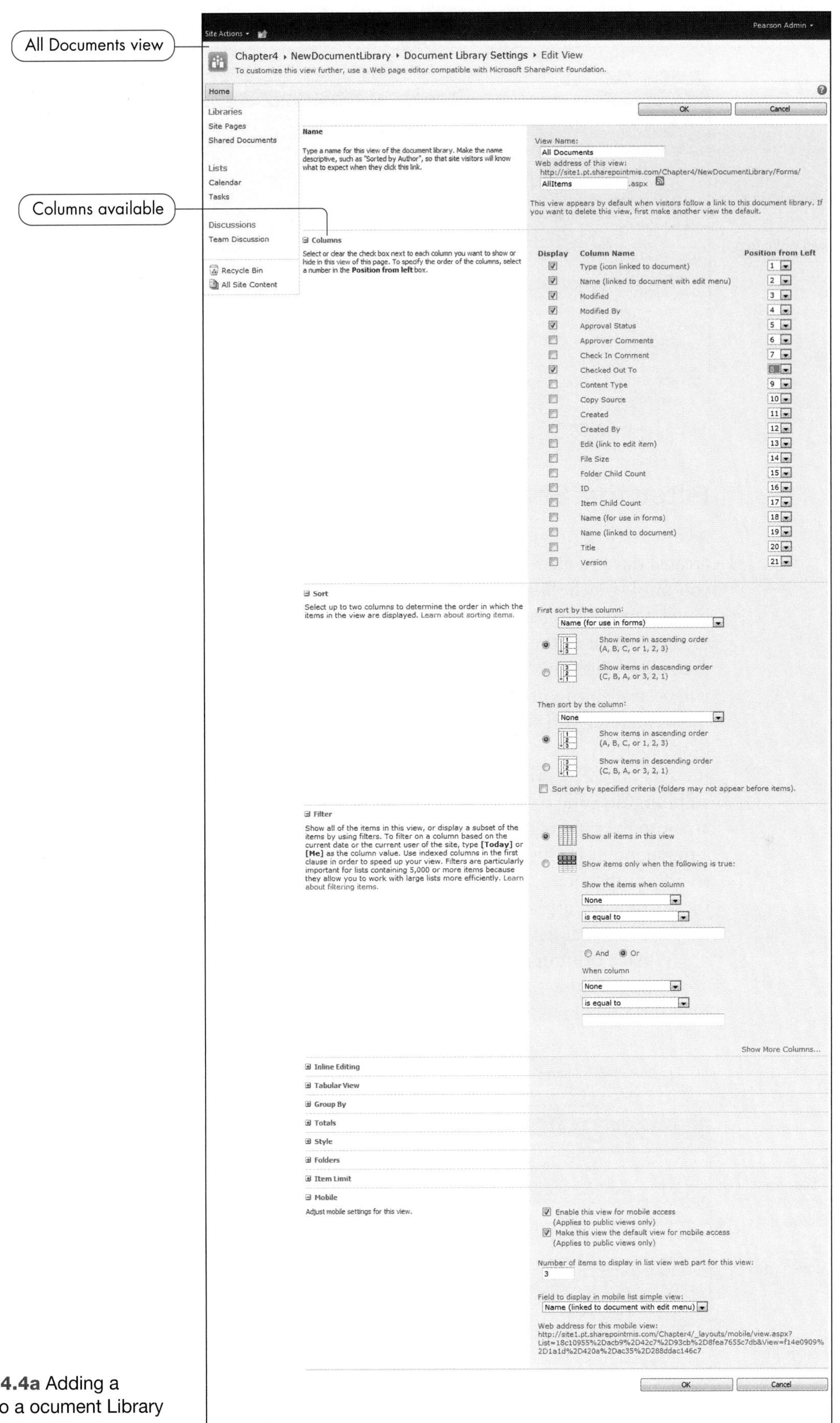

FIGURE 4.4a Adding a Column to a ocument Library View ➤

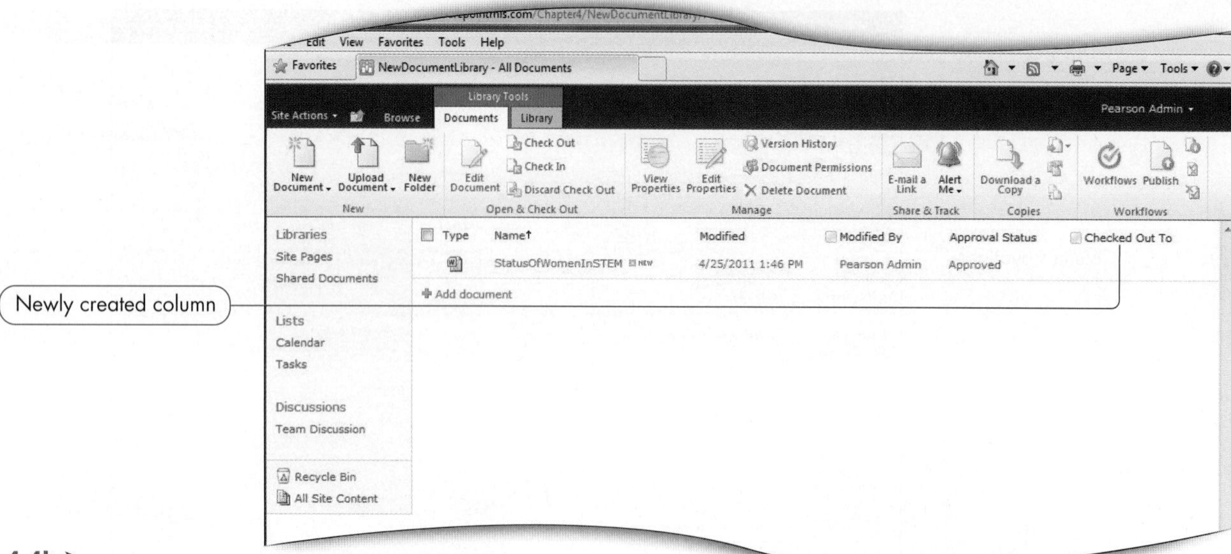

FIGURE 4.4b ➤

Filter the Shared Documents in a Library

As discussed in previous chapters of this textbook, SharePoint enables you to upload already created documents to your Shared Documents library. These documents are checked out to you until you check them in. You can select individual items to check in by pointing to the item's name and selecting the Check In command from the menu that appears. If you want to check in all of the items you uploaded, click the check box next to each document, and then click Check In on the Documents tab. Once you have checked in the documents they will be available to other people who have access to the site.

Whenever you want to change the sorting order of the documents in the Document pane, click the column header of the column you want to use as the sort field (also known as the sort key). The documents will appear in ascending sorted order, based on the sort field column. Click the column header again to display the column in descending order. A small arrow to the right of the column name indicates the direction of the sort. If you prefer to use a menu, point to the column header and click the arrow that appears. Select the sort direction from the menu, as shown in Figure 4.5. Notice that this menu also enables you to filter the documents displaying only the ones that meet a certain criteria. For instance, you can filter the document list to show only Excel files, or ones that were modified on a certain date.

When a column is currently filtered, a funnel appears to the right of the column name, as shown in Figure 4.5. Point to the column header, and then select Clear Filter to remove the filter (also shown in Figure 4.5).

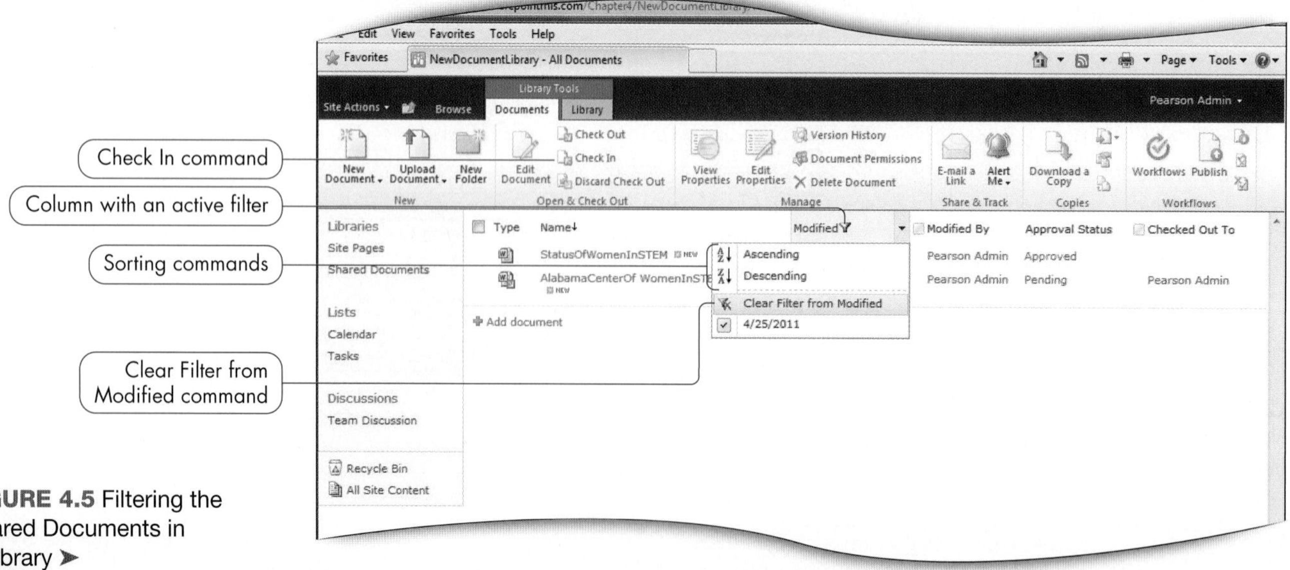

FIGURE 4.5 Filtering the Shared Documents in a Library ➤

Displaying Documents in Lists and Libraries

Built-in lists and libraries in SharePoint Foundation contain at least one default view, but many contain additional built-in views, such as Standard view, Datasheet view, Calendar view, Gantt view, and Access view. Using SharePoint Designer, you can customize views to suit the needs of your users.

To add a new view to a document library, click the Library Tools–Library tab in SharePoint Foundation, and then click Create View in the Manage Views group to display the Create View page, as shown in Figure 4.6. Select the view you want to apply to the Document library.

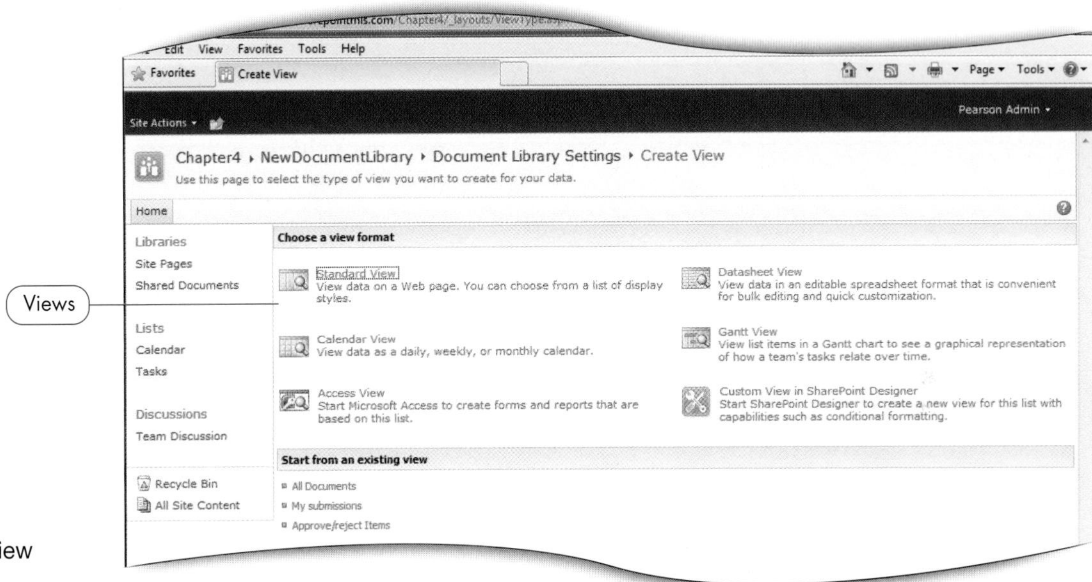

FIGURE 4.6 Create View Page ➤

> **TIP Gantt View**
>
> A Gantt chart (www.ganttchart.com/) is very often used in order to provide a graphical representation for a project timeline. Excel enables you to build Gantt charts. The SharePoint Gantt view is the default view for the Project Tasks lists. It is available for all SharePoint list and library types except the Picture Library, External List, Discussion Board, and Survey types.

Work with a Standard View

Standard view displays contents of lists and libraries as lists included in a Web page.

Standard view displays contents of lists and libraries as lists included in a Web page. In previous chapters of this textbook, the default Standard view of lists and libraries was used. The Standard view is available for all SharePoint Foundation lists and libraries (including custom ones) other than Surveys and Discussions.

If you are using SharePoint Foundation, display the Document Library Settings page, and then click Create view. Click Standard view on the Create View page, shown in Figure 4.6, type the name of the new view in View Name box, select the appropriate options, as shown in Figure 4.7a, and then click OK to create the new view. The library page will display in the new view. You can customize the view in SharePoint Designer by clicking the Modify View command in the Manage Views group of the Library Tools–Library tab, as shown in Figure 4.7b.

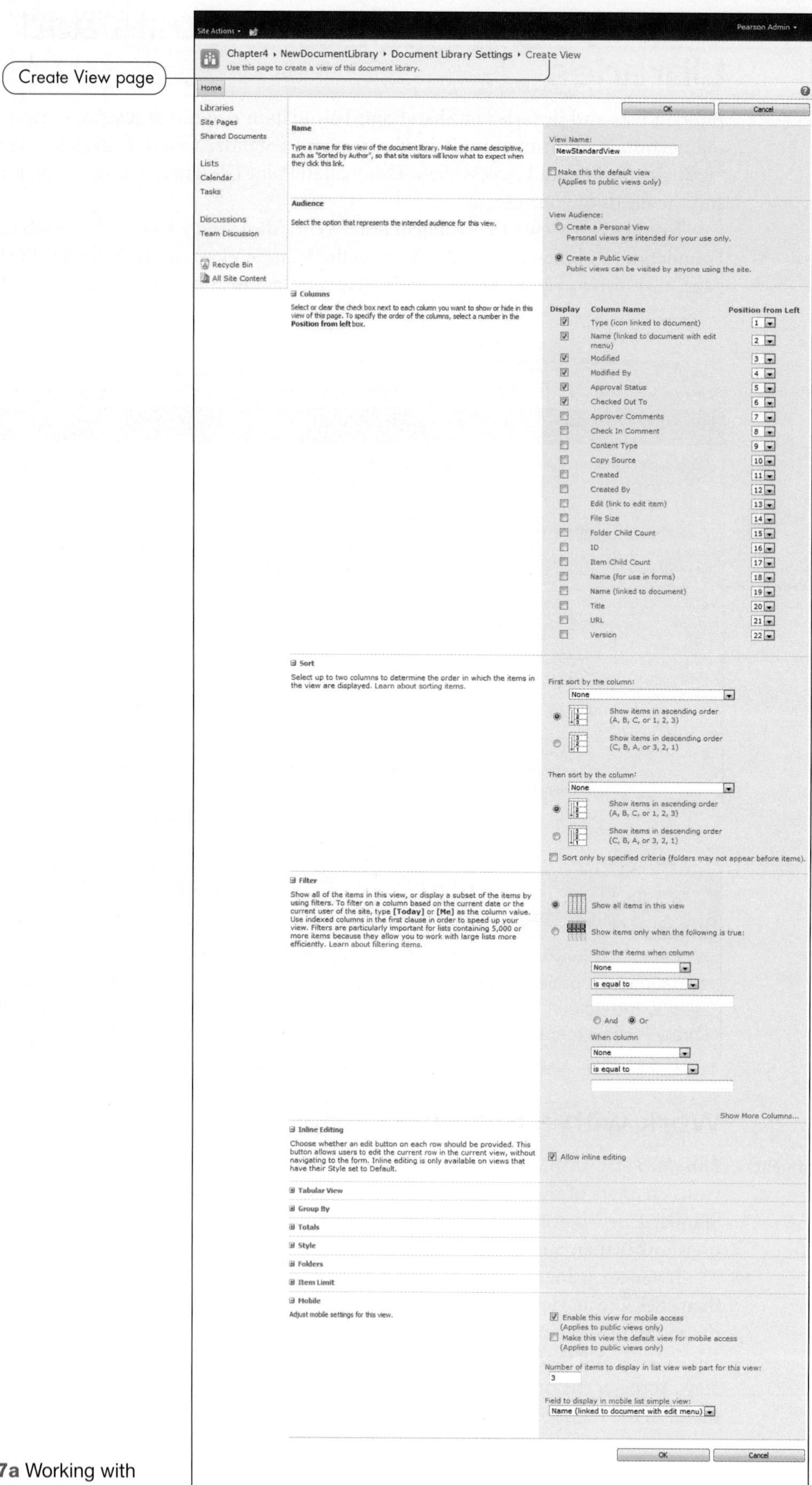

FIGURE 4.7a Working with Library Standard View ➤

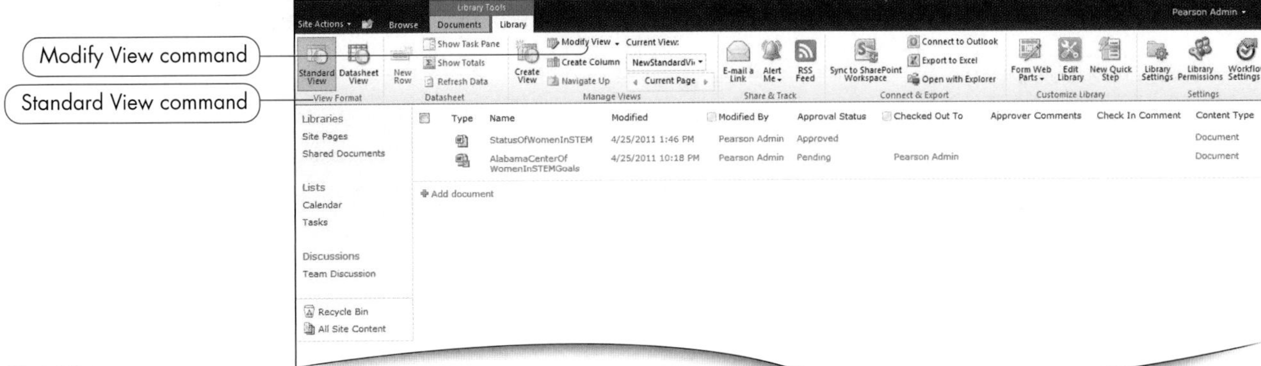

FIGURE 4.7b ➤

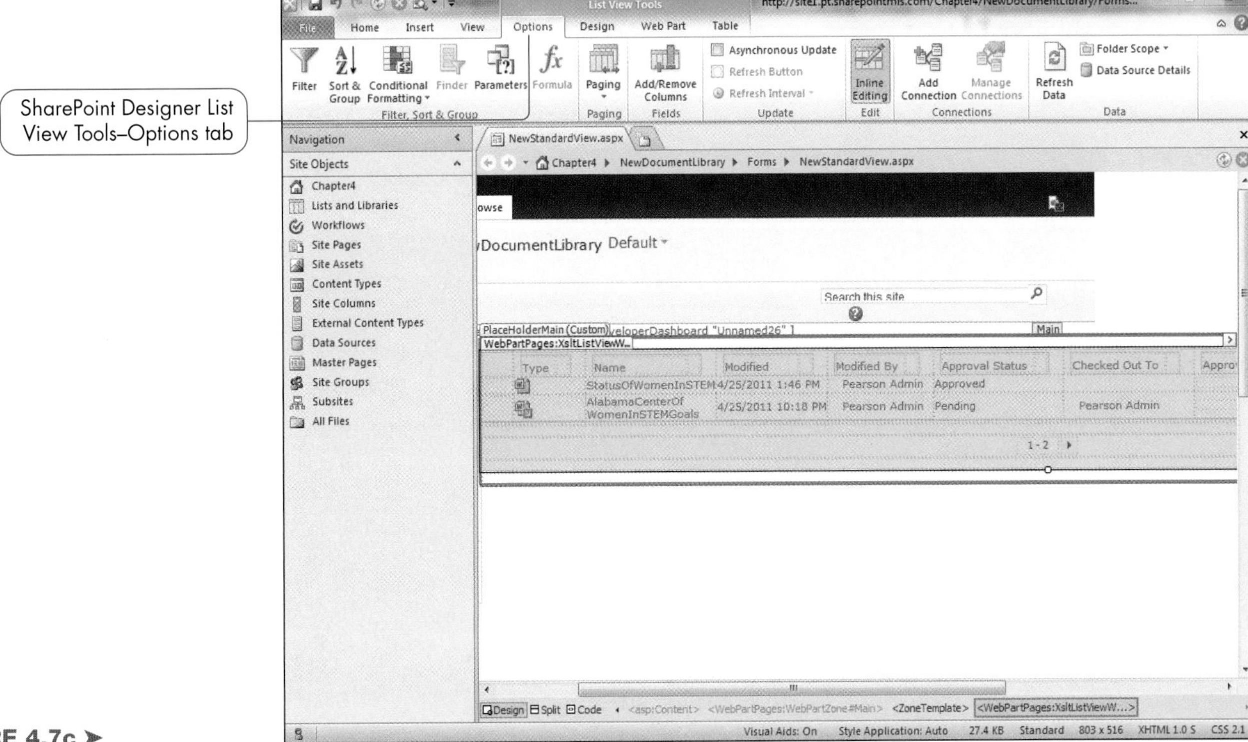

FIGURE 4.7c ➤

If you select Modify View in SharePoint Designer (Advanced), SharePoint Designer will be launched and the List View Tools–Options tab of SharePoint Designer will be displayed, as shown in Figure 4.7c. The steps for creating and modifying a Standard view for a list are the same, as shown in Figures 4.8a–c.

Create View page

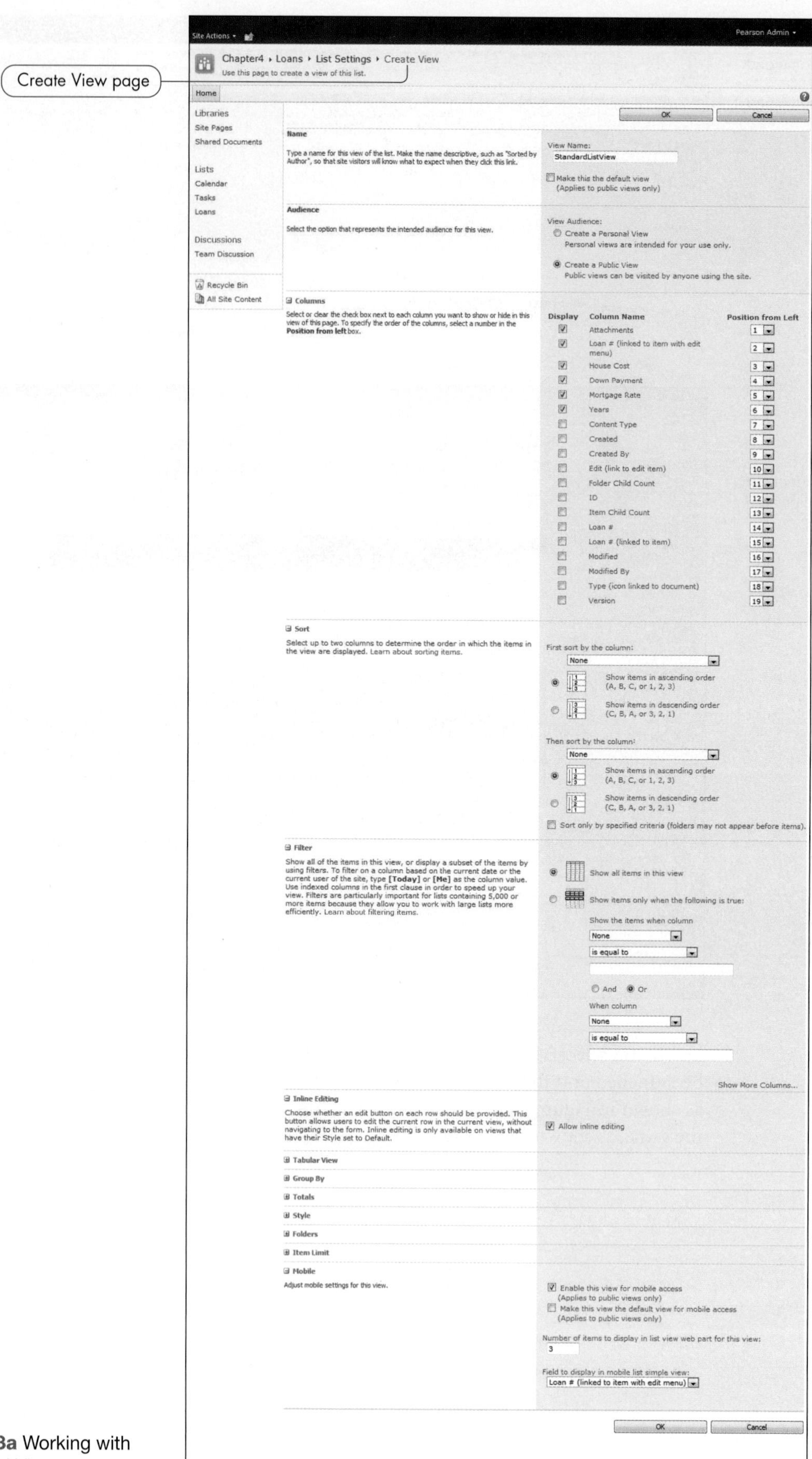

FIGURE 4.8a Working with List Standard View ➤

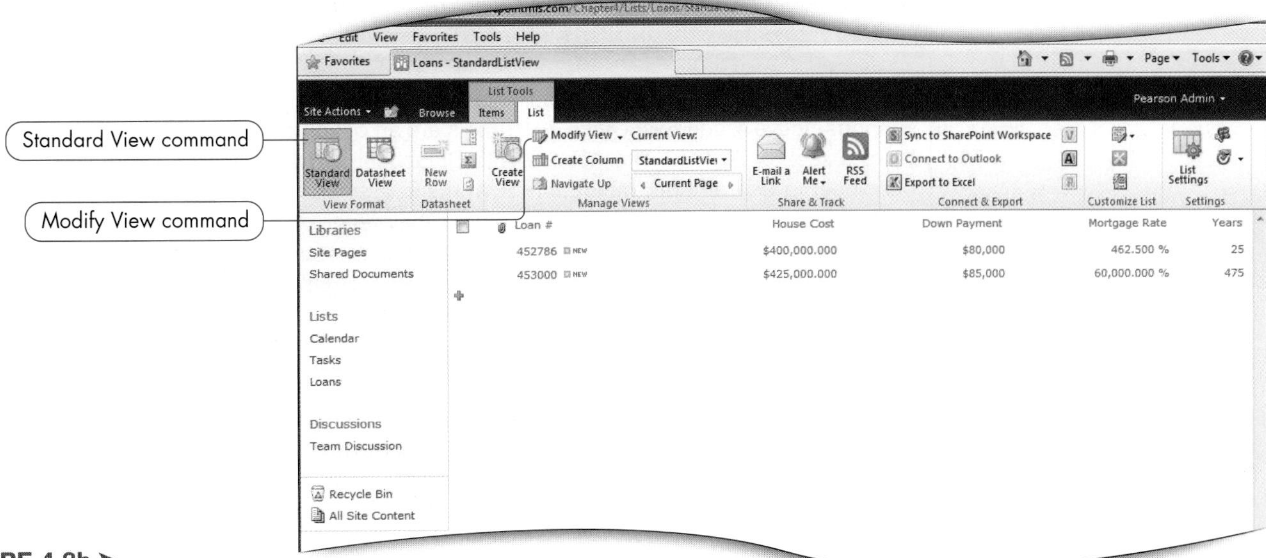

FIGURE 4.8b ➤

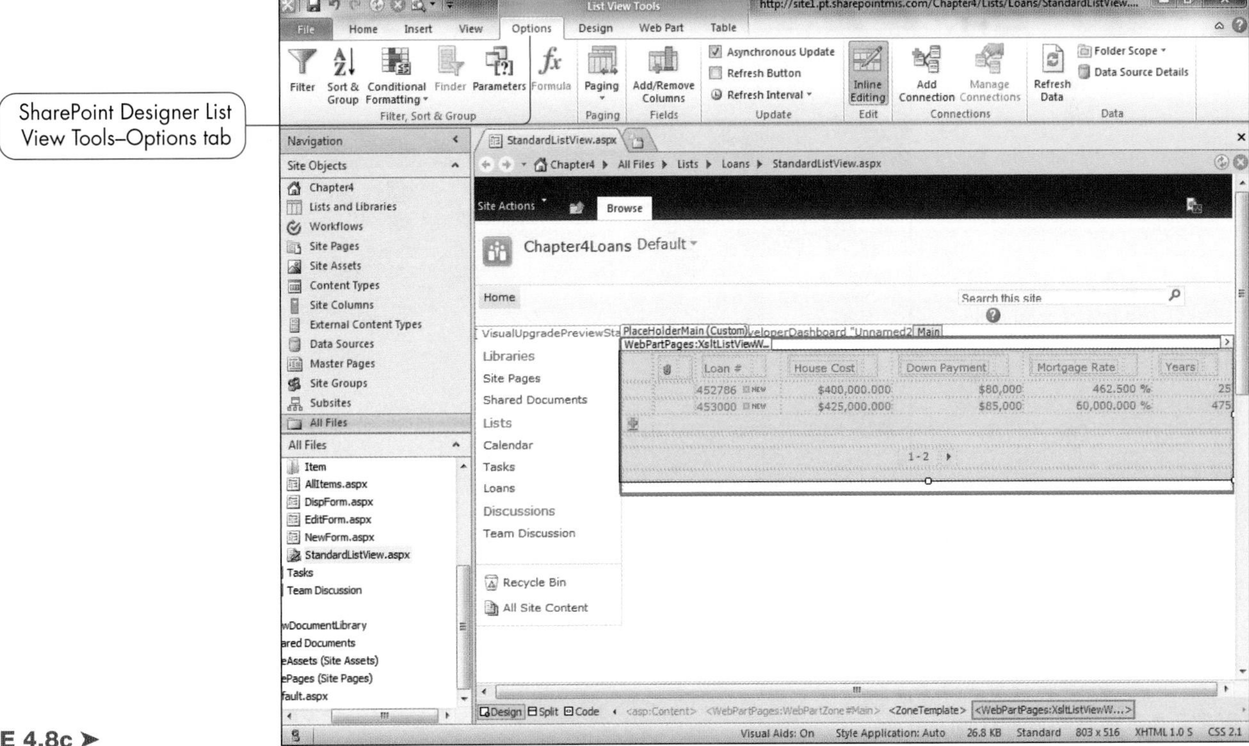

FIGURE 4.8c ➤

Work with a Datasheet View

Datasheet view displays a list or library items using a gridlike layout that enables you to easily edit the whole table.

Datasheet view displays a list or library items using a gridlike layout that enables you to easily edit the whole table. The arrow on each of the column headings can be used to filter and sort data, as described previously. Datasheet view can be used with any list or library type other than the Picture Library, External List, and Survey types.

TIP Using Datasheet View

The Datasheet view requires the installation of Microsoft Office 2010 tools and a browser that supports Active X controls. Office 2010 Tools are an option during the installation process of Word, Excel, or Access. The Access Web Datasheet is the framework used to display the datasheet in SharePoint Foundation. It works in a similar fashion to Access. If you use a 64-bit version of Microsoft Office 2010, you may receive an error when trying to use the Datasheet view. Carefully read the Microsoft support article "You cannot view a list in Datasheet view after you install the 64-bit version of Office 2010" article (http://support.microsoft.com/kb/2266203).

In a library, you can edit and delete items only using the Datasheet view. Click Datasheet View in the View Format group of the Library Tools–Library tab to display the view in SharePoint Foundation. You can select any row using the keyboard, or your mouse to move from cell to cell. When you move to another row, the changes made to the previous row are automatically saved. In a list, as shown in Figure 4.9, you can also add items using the Datasheet view. In the Access Web Datasheet, the last row (which contains an asterisk * in the left column) is used to add new content to the list.

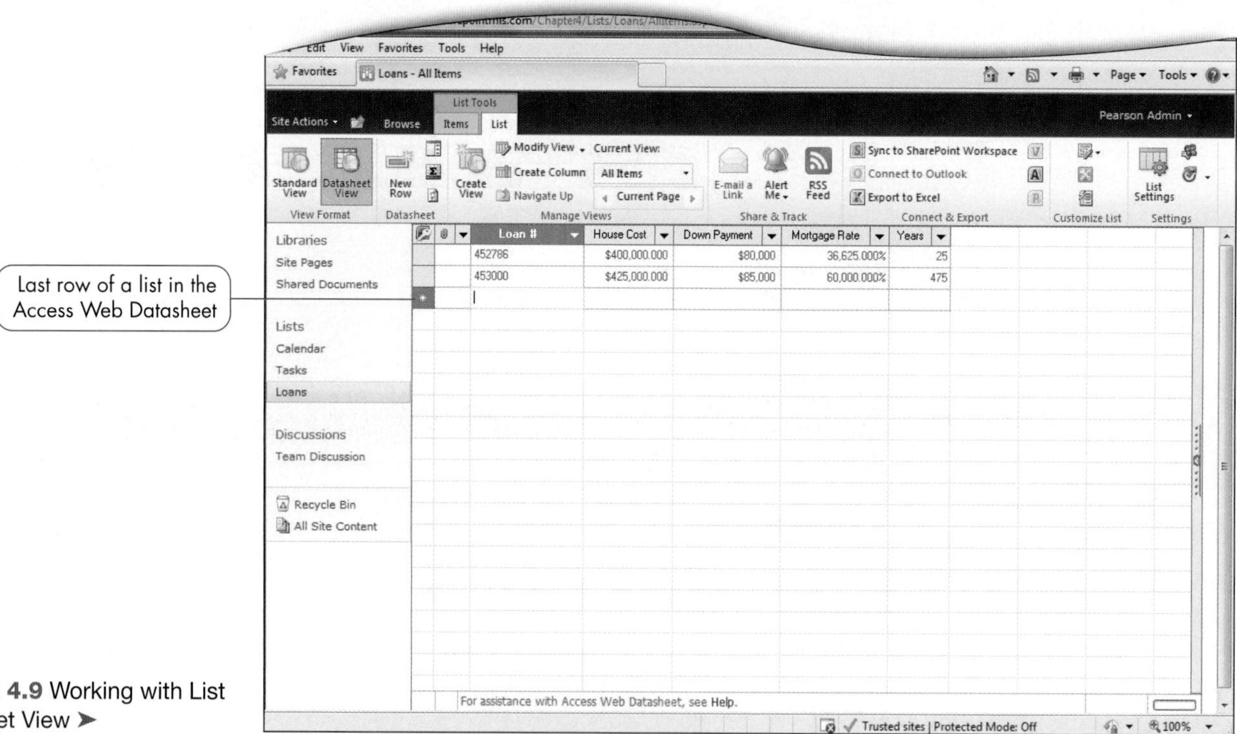

FIGURE 4.9 Working with List Datasheet View ➤

When using the Access Web Datasheet, regardless of the size of the list or library, all items are displayed within one Web page. For performance reasons, you should not use Access Web Datasheet to work with very large lists or libraries of more than 5,000 items. Filter and sort the data using the column headers, as described previously and shown in Figure 4.10.

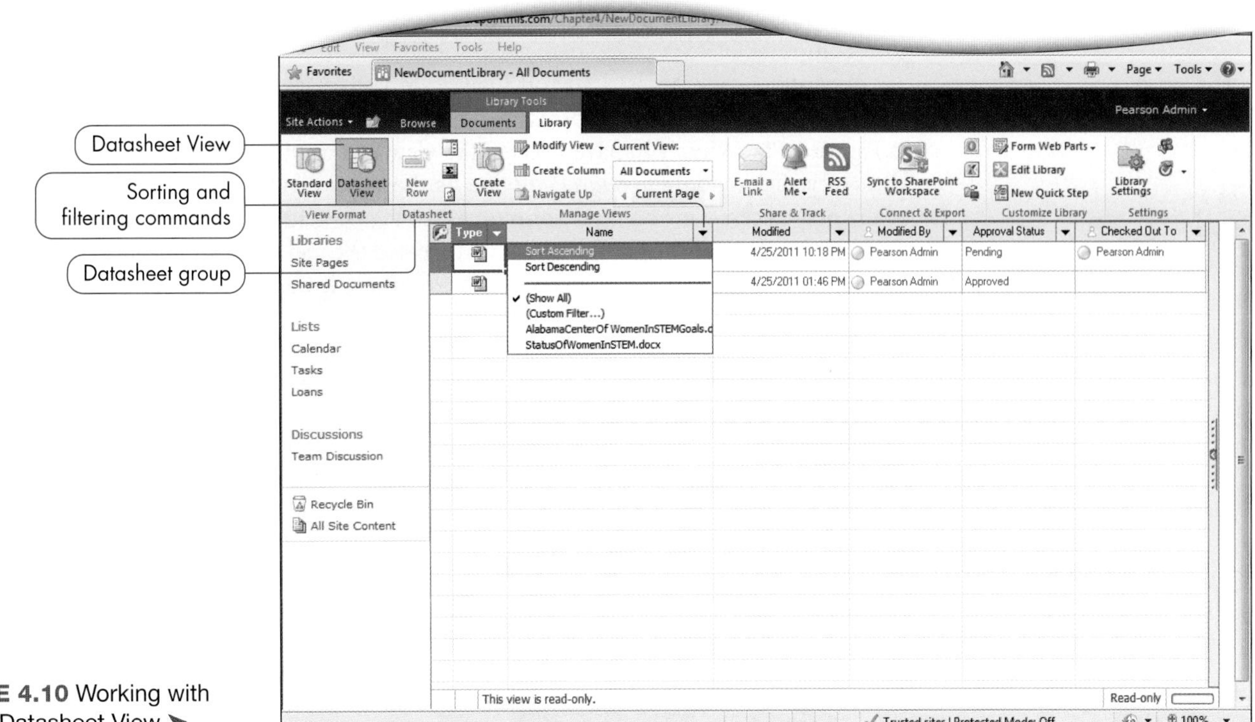

FIGURE 4.10 Working with Library Datasheet View ➤

The process of creating and modifying a list or library in Datasheet view is similar to the process used in the Standard view. Once you display a list or library in a Datasheet view, the Datasheet group of commands is activated on the List or Library Tools tab (see Figures 4.9 and 4.10). Click Show Task Pane, in the Datasheet group, to display the Task Pane, shown in Figure 4.11, that enables you to easily integrate data with Excel 2010 and Access 2010. Help on the Task Pane gives you access to Access Web Datasheet help topics.

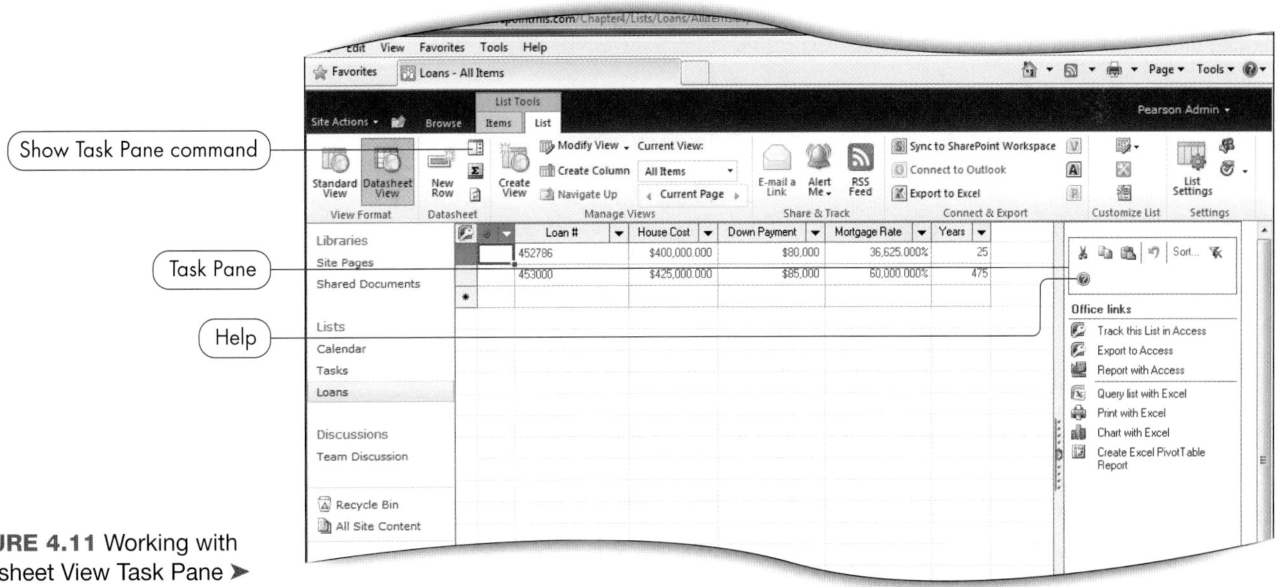

FIGURE 4.11 Working with Datasheet View Task Pane ➤

Work with an Access View

Access view enables you to fully take advantage of the Access advanced tools for generating reports and views.

SharePoint Foundation enables you to create a list or library view using Access 2010 or 2007. ***Access view*** enables you to fully take advantage of the Access advanced tools for generating reports and views. Data in the lists and libraries will be automatically updated when you edit content in the Access view. You can use Access view for all SharePoint Foundation lists and libraries, except the External List and Survey. For instance, you can create an Access view to use on a Task List file. It is important to note that you will need the Access client installed on your computer.

When you click Access View on the Create View page, the list opens in an Access client window, and you can then choose what view you want to use to display the list data, as shown in Figure 4.12a. When you have selected the view you want to use, save the file to a document library by clicking *Save to SharePoint Site*, as shown in Figure 4.12b. You can also save a copy of the new Access view on your computer (see Figure 4.12c). Access view does not appear in the existing views of the list for which you created the view. You will need to open the Access file corresponding to the view from the library where it was saved, as shown in Figure 4.12d.

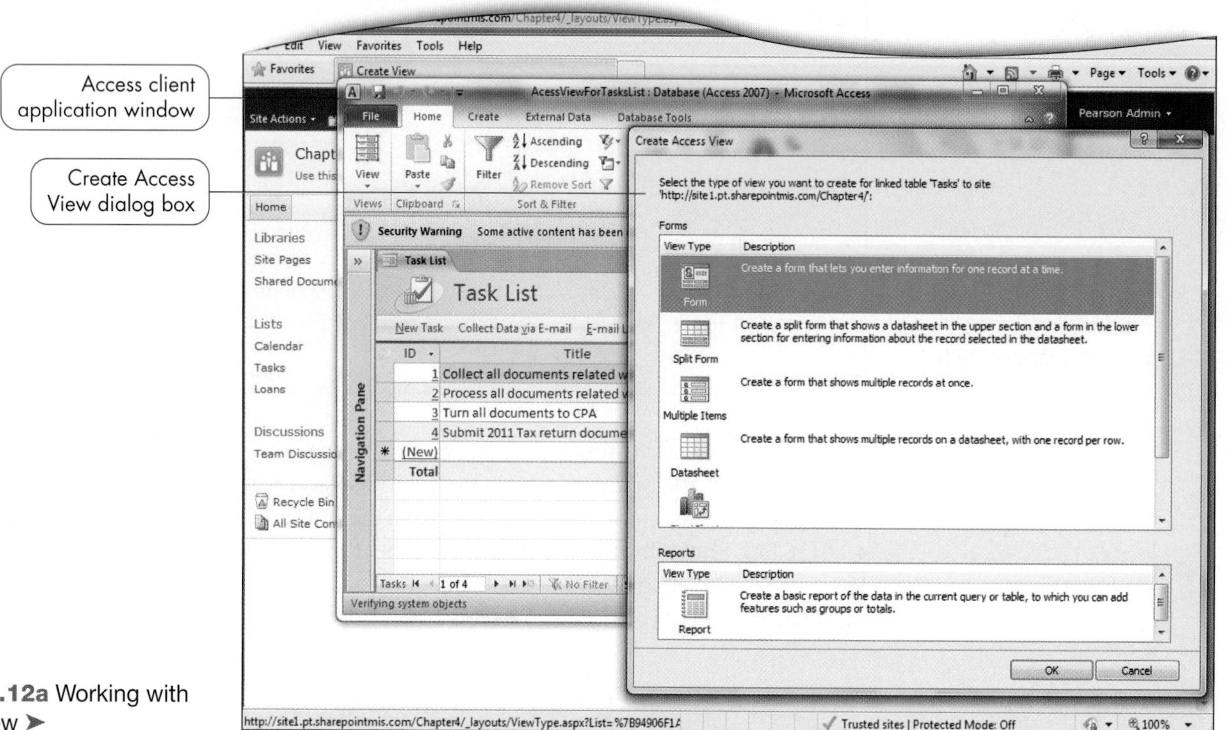

FIGURE 4.12a Working with Access View ➤

FIGURE 4.12b ➤

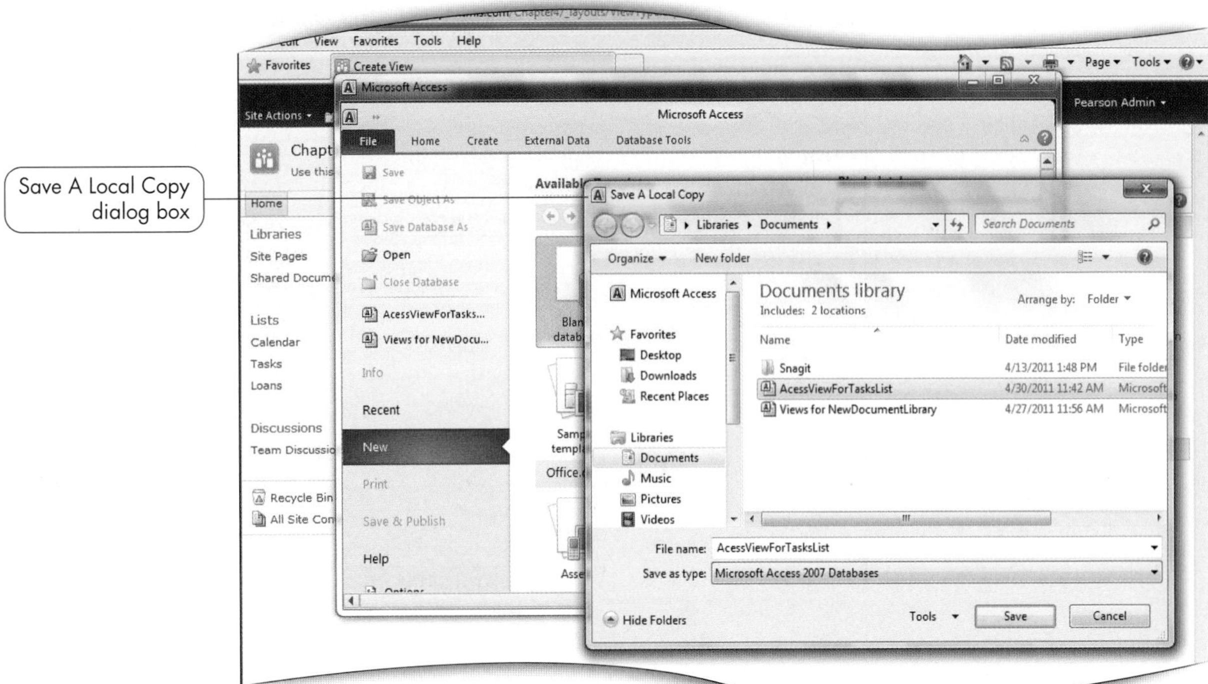

FIGURE 4.12c ➤

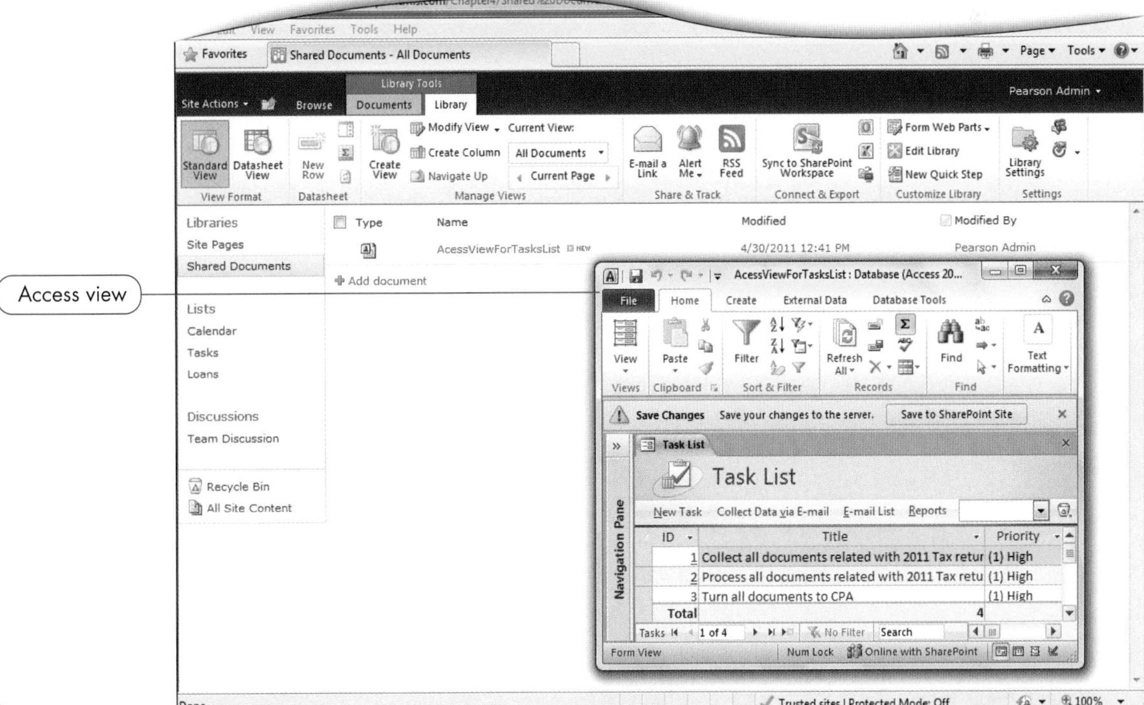

FIGURE 4.12d ➤

Work with a Calendar View

With SharePoint Foundation you can create a Calendar view for data that includes at least one date field, except in the External List, Discussion Board, and Survey. The Calendar view is the default view for the Calendar List.

When you click Calendar View on the Create View page, the Create Calendar View page is displayed, as shown in Figure 4.13a. The options include renaming the calendar view, specifying the audience, selecting the time frame to display, and more. Select the options you want, and then click OK to see the list displayed in the Calendar view, as shown in Figure 4.13b. The Calendar Tools–Calendar tab (see Figure 4.13c) enables you to further customize the view.

Create Calendar View page

Site Actions ▾ Pearson Admin ▾

Chapter4 ▸ Tasks ▸ List Settings ▸ Create Calendar View
Use this page to create a view of this list.

Home

Libraries
Site Pages
Shared Documents

Lists
Calendar
Tasks
Loans

Discussions
Team Discussion

Recycle Bin
All Site Content

OK Cancel

Name

Type a name for this view of the list. Make the name descriptive, such as "Sorted by Author", so that site visitors will know what to expect when they click this link.

View Name:
TaskListCalendarView
Make this the default view
(Applies to public views only)

Audience

Select the option that represents the intended audience for this view.

View Audience:
Create a Personal View
Personal views are intended for your use only.
Create a Public View
Public views can be visited by anyone using the site.

Time Interval

Specify the columns used to place items in the calendar.

Begin:
Start Date
End:
Due Date

Calendar Columns

Specify columns to be represented in the Calendar Views. The Title fields are required fields. The Sub Heading fields are optional fields.

Month View Title:
% Complete
Week View Title:
Predecessors
Week View Sub Heading:
Priority
Day View Title:
Status
Day View Sub Heading:
Optional

Default Scope

Choose the default scope for the view.

Default scope:
Day
Week
Month
You can change this at any time while using the calendar.

Filter

Show all of the items in this view, or display a subset of the items by using filters. To filter on a column based on the current date or the current user of the site, type **[Today]** or **[Me]** as the column value. Use indexed columns in the first clause in order to speed up your view. Filters are particularly important for lists containing 5,000 or more items because they allow you to work with large lists more efficiently. Learn about filtering items.

Show all items in this view
Show items only when the following is true:
Show the items when column
None
is equal to
And Or
When column
None
is equal to

Show More Columns...

Mobile

Adjust mobile settings for this view.

Enable this view for mobile access
(Applies to public views only)
Make this view the default view for mobile access
(Applies to public views only)

Number of items to display in list view web part for this view:
3

OK Cancel

FIGURE 4.13a Working with Calendar View ➤

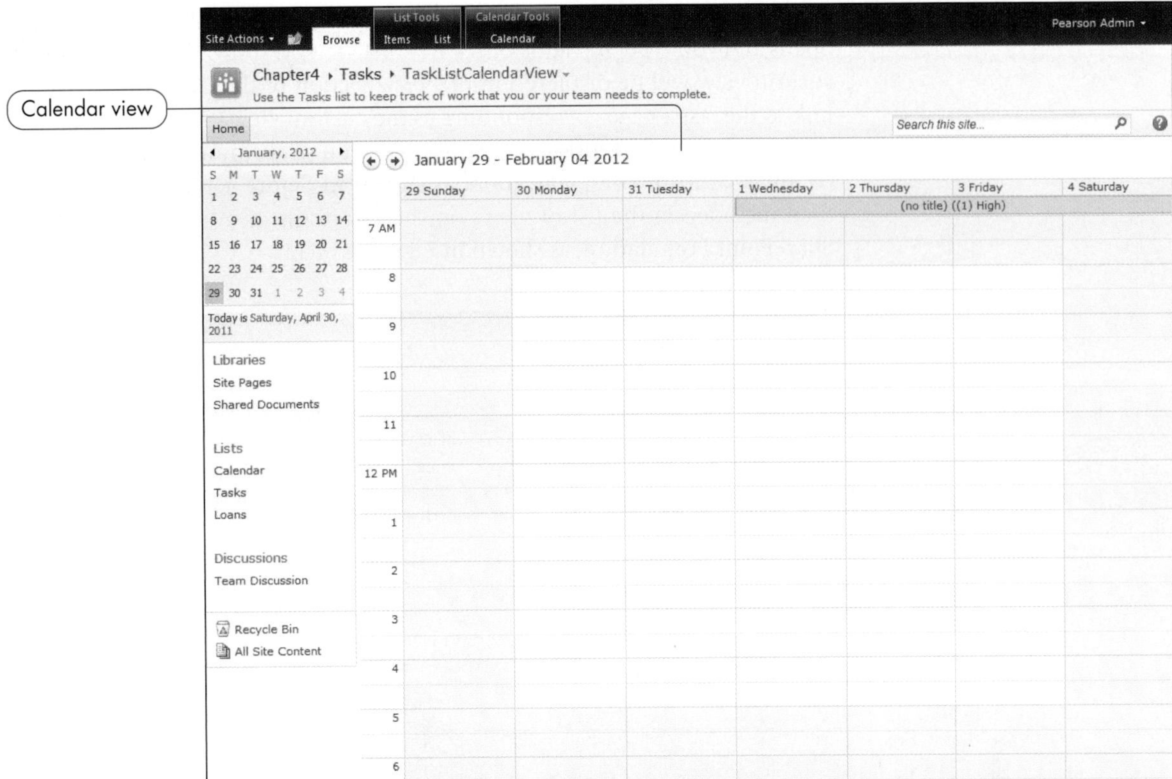

FIGURE 4.13b ➤

FIGURE 4.13c ➤

Work with a SharePoint Designer Custom View

The Custom View in SharePoint Designer option on the Create View page enables you to create a custom view of your list or library. When you click Custom View in SharePoint Designer, in the *Choose a view format* section of the Create View page, SharePoint Designer will launch and display the summary page of the list. The Create New List View dialog box opens and you type the name of the new list view, as shown in Figure 4.14a. A link to the new custom view will be displayed in the *View* section of the list summary page. If you click the link to the .aspx page corresponding to the custom view you created, it will be displayed and the List View Tools–Options tab will enable you to customize the view with filtering, sorting, conditional formatting, and more as shown in Figure 4.14b. The new custom view will be then included in the list of views on the List Tools–List tab in the Manage Views group in SharePoint Foundation, as shown in Figure 4.14c.

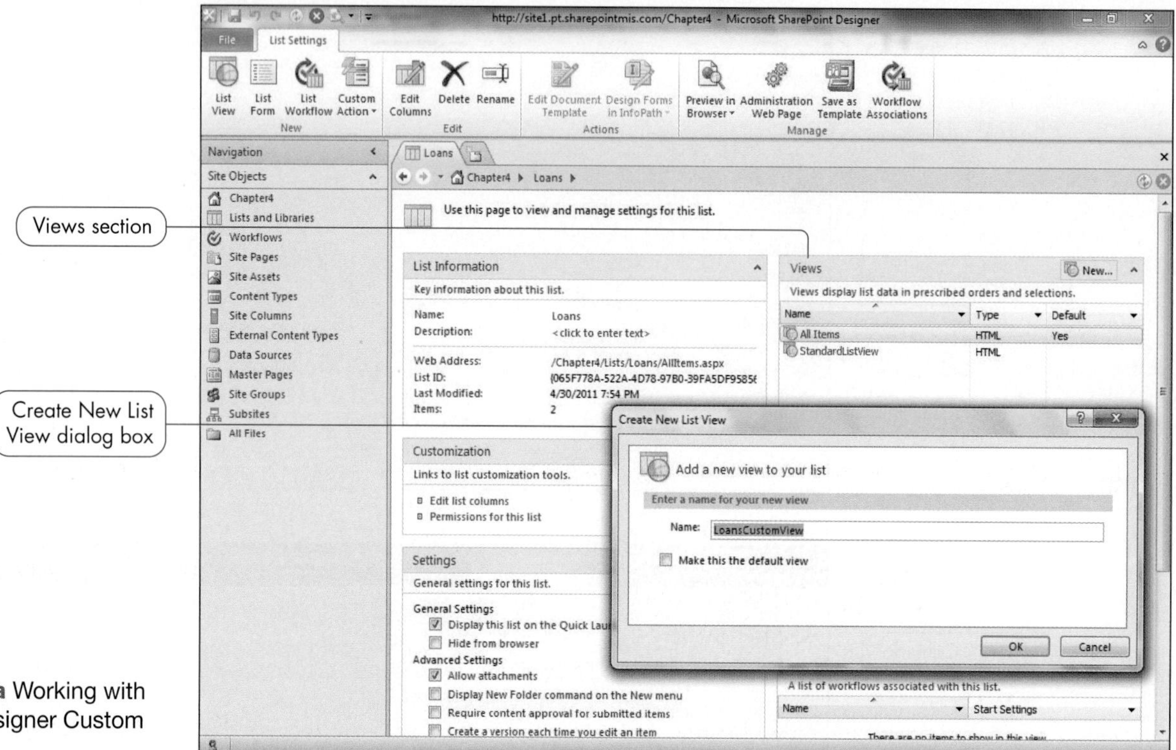

FIGURE 4.14a Working with SharePoint Designer Custom View ➤

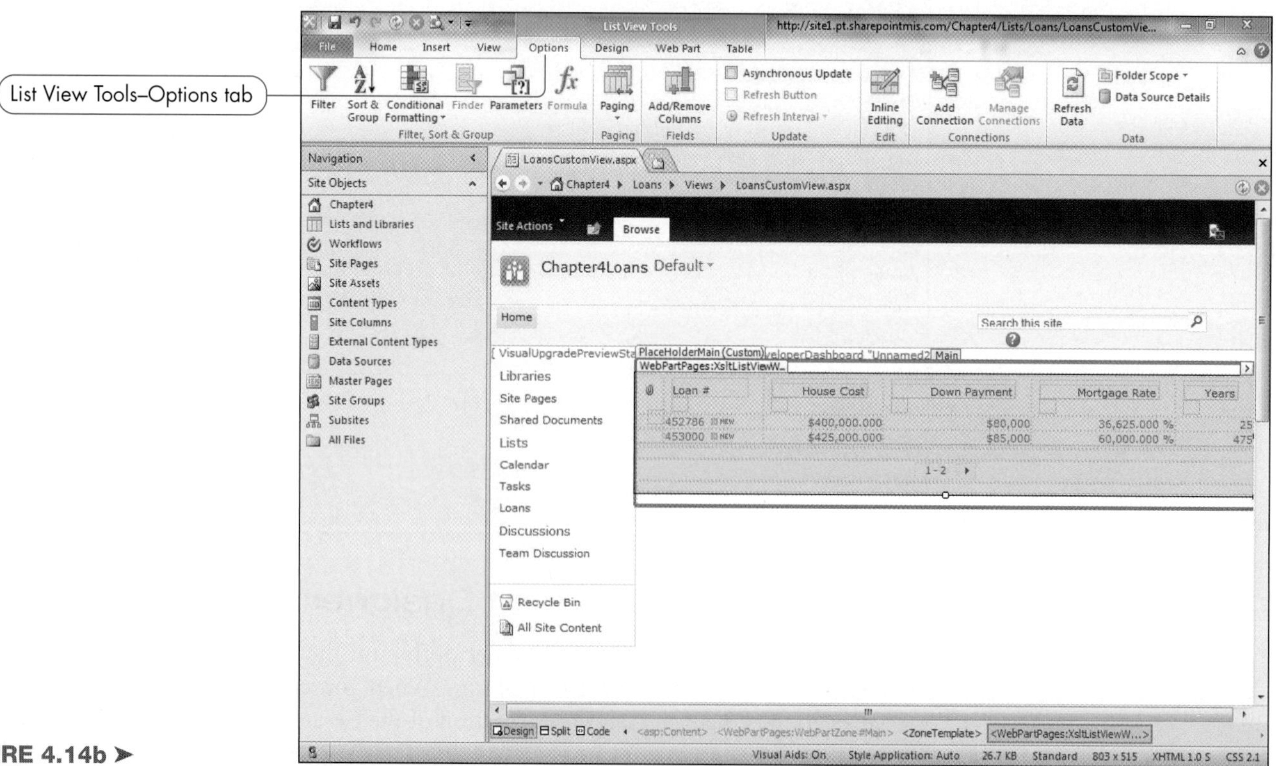

FIGURE 4.14b ➤

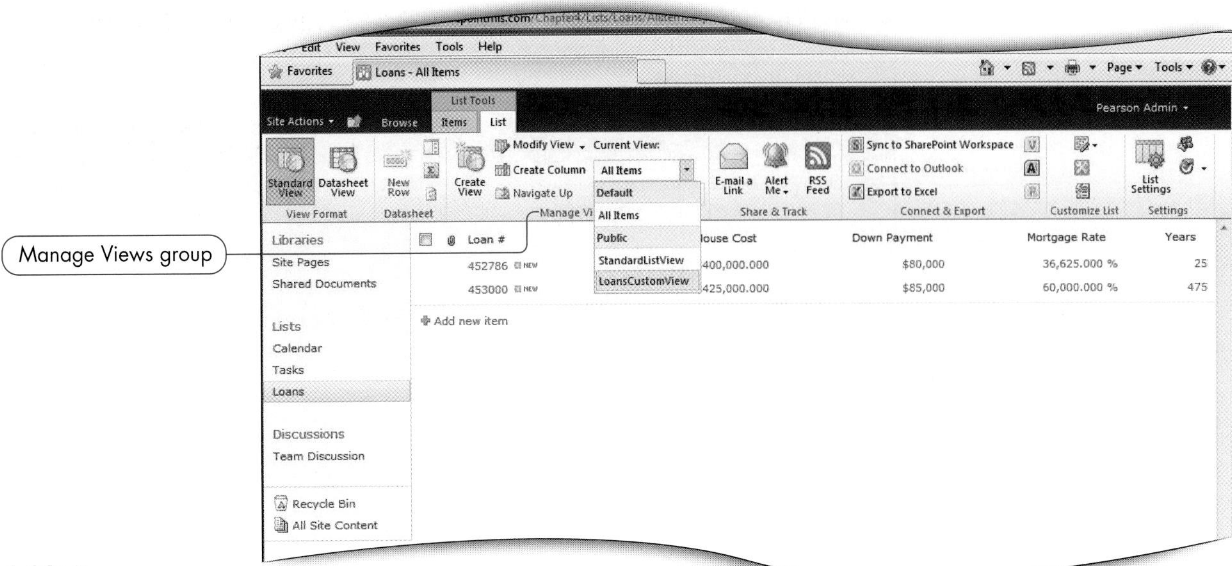

FIGURE 4.14c ➤

Working with SharePoint Foundation Built-In List Types

Lists provide the easiest way to store information in SharePoint, using a rather familiar list paradigm such as important work tasks at the office, grocery items to buy on your way home, and home improvement projects for the weekend. As discussed in previous chapters of this textbook, SharePoint provides a variety of ways to keep this information electronically in predefined lists grouped into six categories: Blank & Custom, Collaboration, Communication, Content, Data, and Tracking.

Each SharePoint list is arranged in columns. Some columns appear in almost every list, whereas other columns add unique capabilities to a list. Site templates have specialized libraries or lists designed specifically for the type of site, but you can also create custom lists for the site. The only required column is the Title column, which you should give a descriptive name. Additional columns can be added to meet the requirements of the users. In this section, you will explore some popular predefined lists.

An **Announcements list** can be used to inform your site users about upcoming events, news, or activities.

An **announcement item** initially contains columns for a title, a body, and an expiration date.

Announcements List

An ***Announcements list*** can be used to inform your site users about upcoming events, news, or activities. This is a popular type of list that is available in a number of collaboration site templates. This list contains columns to enable users to organize and view the posted announcements. An ***announcement item*** initially contains a title, body, and an optional expiration date but attachments can also be added to the item. Figure 4.15a shows one default event on the Announcements list with the initial columns created.

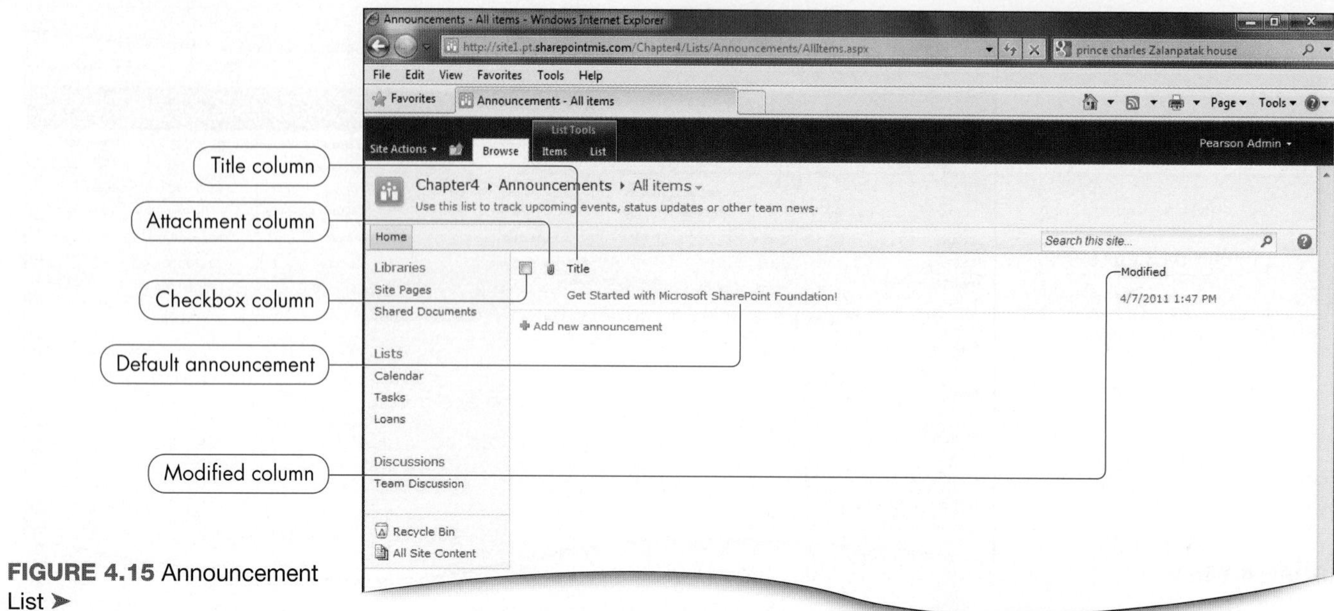

FIGURE 4.15 Announcement List ➤

- The Checkbox column is used to select list items and perform an operation, such as deleting them. You can select one or more items at a time. If you do not want to make this column available to users, you can customize the list by turning the column off.
- The Attachment column displays a paperclip when a document has been attached to the list item. For instance, the default item shown in Figure 4.15, *Get Started with Microsoft SharePoint Foundation!*, could have a document with written instructions attached to it. This list column can also be turned off if it is not useful to the users of the site.
- The Title column provides a descriptive title that users will click to open the item. It is the link to the edit page where information can be changed for the item. When announcements are posted, a new icon appears for a period of time to indicate the status to the users.
- The Modified column displays the date and time of the last modification of the item.

Click an announcement item title to open and view the information in the View dialog box, as shown in Figure 4.16a. Additional columns, Created By and Modified By, are added to the Announcement list by SharePoint when someone adds or modifies an item on the list. If you have editing permissions, as discussed in previous chapters in the textbook, click Edit Item to modify the title, add text to the body, add an attachment to the announcement, and then set up an expiration date, as shown in Figure 4.16b.

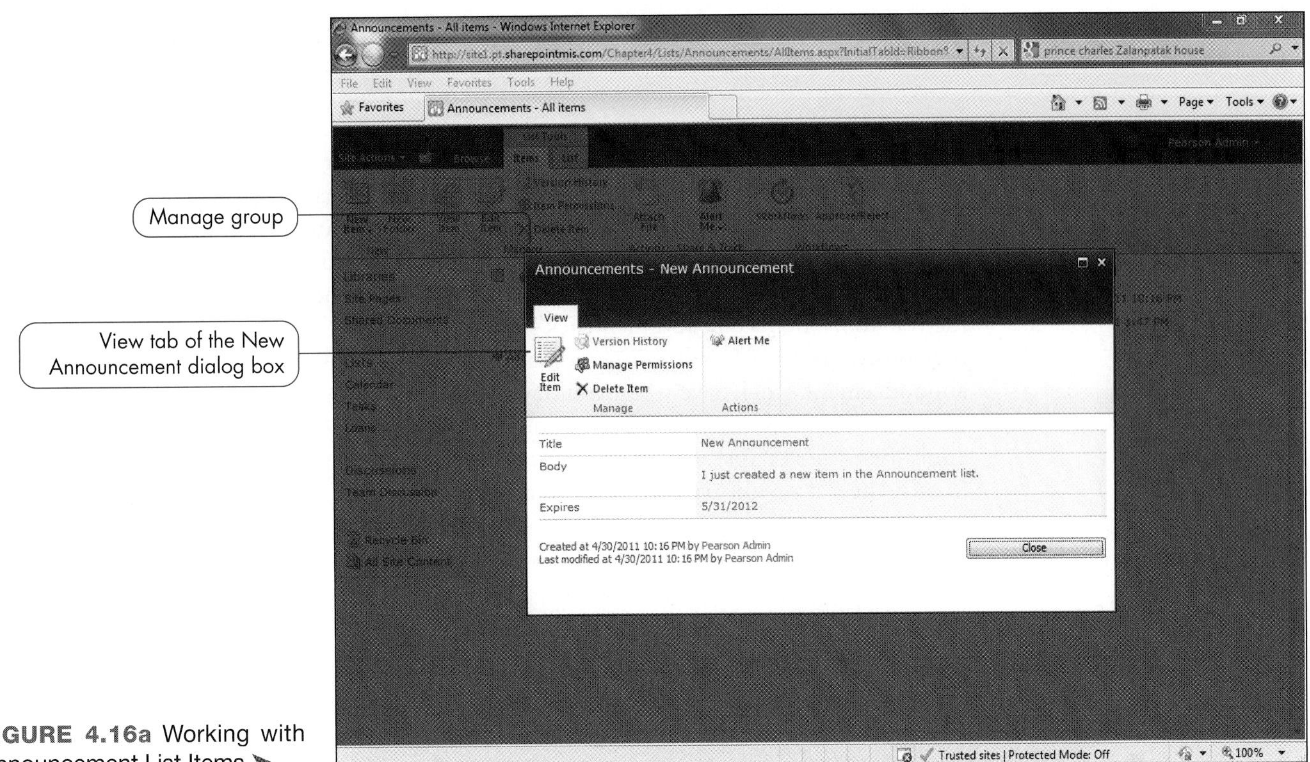

FIGURE 4.16a Working with Announcement List Items ➤

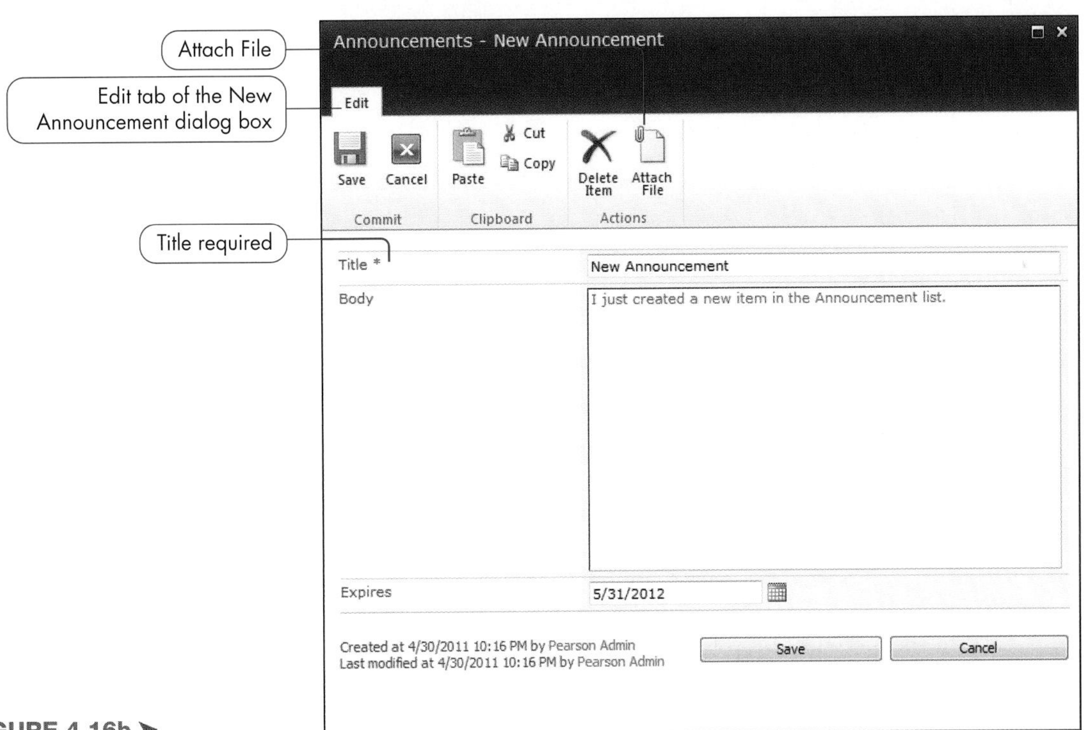

FIGURE 4.16b ➤

The title is required (as shown with a red asterisk) but the other fields on the Edit tab are optional. The body field on the Edit tab provides space for text. For example, the text might give the details of an event that will take place, such as a party, meeting, or seminar. The Expires field enables you to set a date for the announcement to expire, typically after the event takes place or after a certain period of time if the announcement is not related to an event. This field is actually only used to remove an announcement from the list, if a custom view is set up using the expiration date field. Otherwise, SharePoint will not automatically remove past events from your announcements list. To add an attachment to the announcement, such as a Word document or Excel worksheet, click Attach File on the Edit tab, as shown in Figure 4.16b. The file must be uploaded to a library on the SharePoint site, prior to attaching it to an announcement.

Using the Clipboard options of cut, copy, and paste, you can add text to any of the fields on the Edit tab. When you click in the Body field, familiar tabs for formatting the text and inserting objects, such as pictures, tables, and links, appear at the top of the Edit tab. Click Save to add the announcement to the list. Click Cancel to discard any changes you made and return to the Announcement list. Click Delete to remove an item from the Announcement list (attachments will not be deleted from their location in a library by this action).

With the Announcements list displayed, you can add additional announcements. Click the List Tools–Items tab, and then click New Item in the New group. The Edit tab, discussed previously, opens to enable you to add a title, body, attachment, and expiration date to the announcement. Click Save when you have completed the announcement and it will be displayed on the Announcement list, as shown in Figure 4.17. Additional options on the List Tools–Items tab enable you to set up permissions for an item, and view the history of the item if the list or library tracks the versions of the items. Items can be edited from the Announcements list or any page that displays the list in the page content.

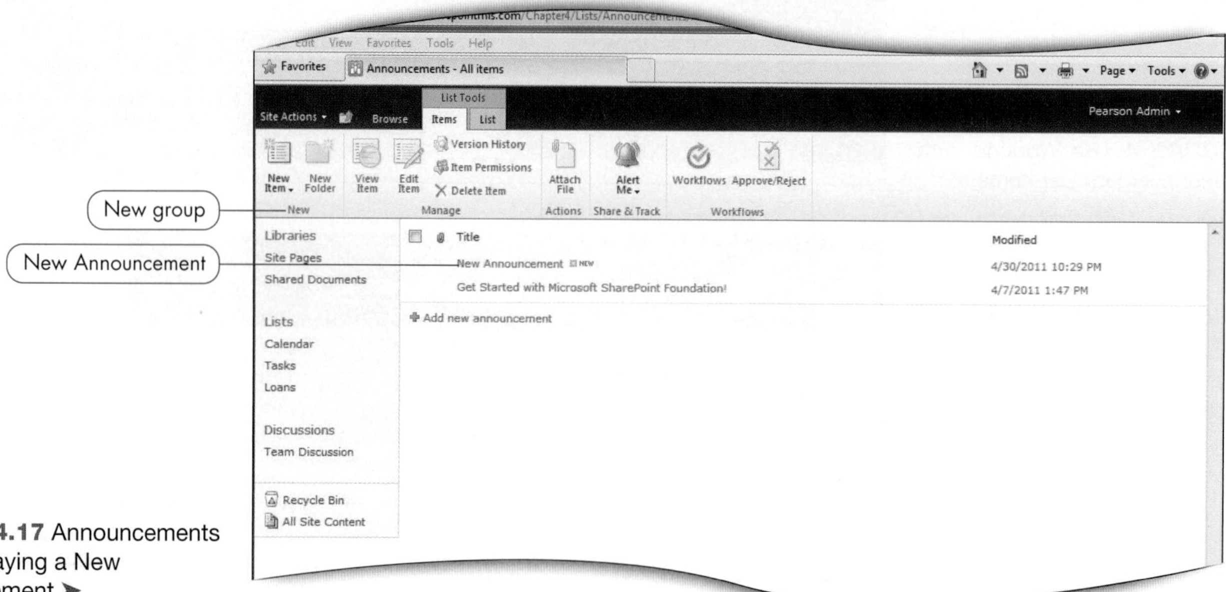

FIGURE 4.17 Announcements List Displaying a New Announcement ➤

Contacts List

On a team site, a Contacts list must be created from the Contact list template before you can use it. The Contacts list contains columns that enable you to manage contact information, such as first and last name, company, phone numbers, e-mail address, and much more.

You can add columns to the Contacts list using the List Tools–List tab. Click List Settings in the Settings group to display the page shown in Figure 4.18. Six areas are shown on the Contacts List Settings page. You cannot change the name or location of the list; just view the information in the *List Information* section. The General Settings enable you to change the title, description, and navigation, as well as make some other advanced settings. In the *Permissions and Management* area, you can modify the permissions to the list and manage workflow settings for the list. The RSS settings are modified in the Communications area, and depend on whether the RSS is enabled at the administrator level. Columns are edited, deleted, and specified in the *Column* section of the Contacts List Settings page. You can also change the order of the columns and create new columns in this section. The *Views* section displays the Contact List views that are currently defined.

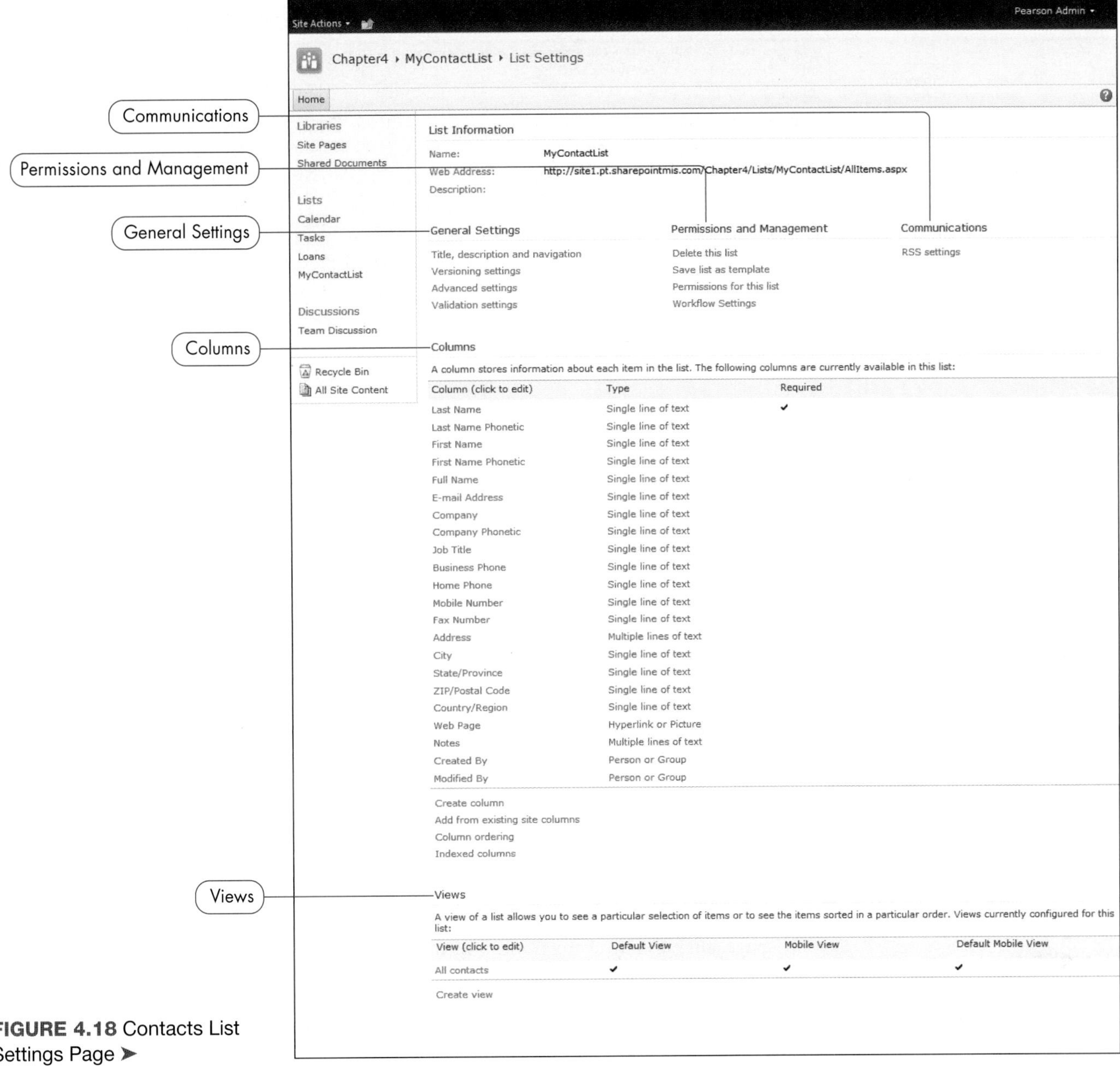

FIGURE 4.18 Contacts List Settings Page ➤

Often, you will want to add or modify a column in a view to contain information specific to the use of the list. You may need additional columns for alternative phone numbers or addresses, for instance. Click the column header to open the Change Column page, as shown in Figure 4.19. Change the Column Name as needed. Select the default type of information that will be displayed in the column: Single line of text, Multiple lines of text, Choice, Number, Currency, or Date and Time. The example in Figure 4.19 selects Choice, so that a user can select an option from a menu that you provide in the Description area. Select the way the menu will be displayed: Drop-down Menu, Radio Buttons, or Check boxes. Type a default value to display in the Default value area. Click OK when you have finished making adjustments to the page.

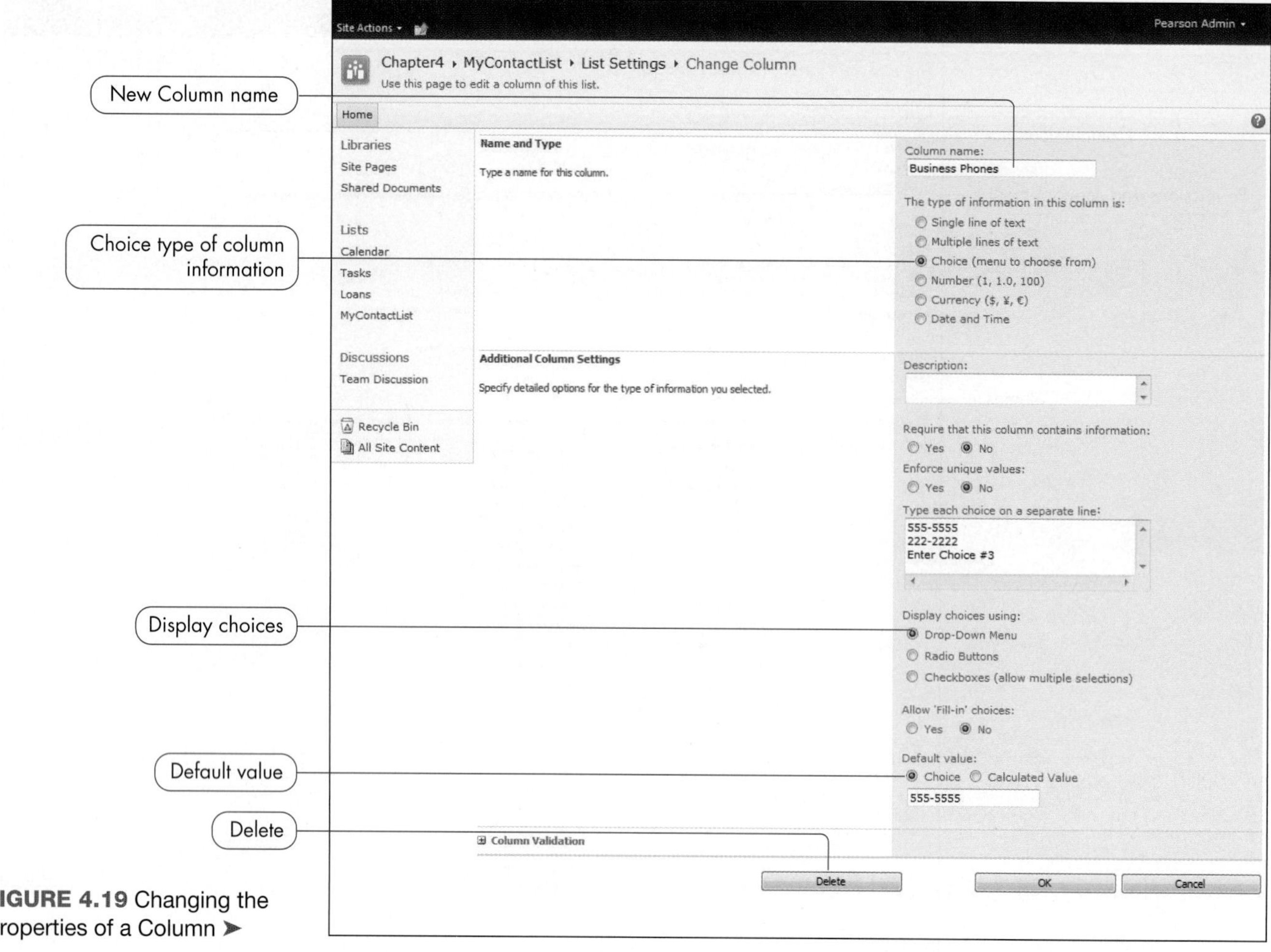

FIGURE 4.19 Changing the Properties of a Column ➤

SharePoint enables you to not display a column. You can accomplish this in two ways:

- Delete a column: After selecting the column name to display the Change Column page, click Delete at the bottom of the page (see Figure 4.19) to completely remove the column from the list. This is a rather drastic option, so consider it carefully before deleting the column.
- Hide a column: Using the List Settings page, you can alter the view, and hide the column from the users of that view. Click the view name in the *Views* section to display the view definition, as shown in Figure 4.20. Select or deselect the check boxes next to the column names to display or hide the columns. Click OK to save your changes.

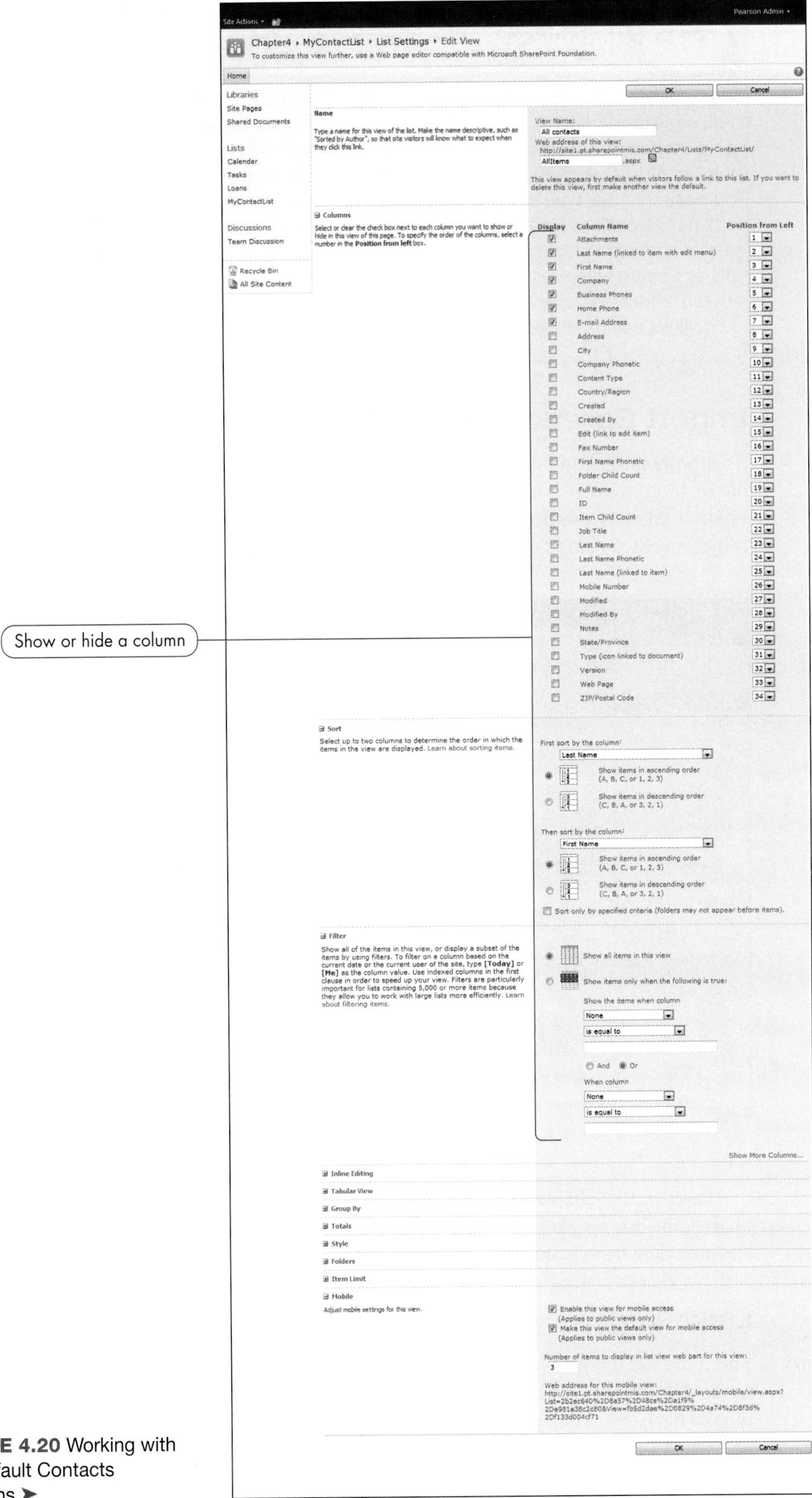

FIGURE 4.20 Working with the Default Contacts Columns ➤

TIP Hyperlinks Fields

As items are added to a list, SharePoint creates a hyperlink that enables the user to open the edit page to display the content. This happens for all list items, usually on the column named Title. As you have seen, you can rename the columns as necessary. In the Contacts list, you may want to change the Title to Last Name so that your users more clearly understand the purpose. Another type of hyperlink column that can be displayed in a list is an e-mail address column. Hyperlinks have two parts: a descriptive name displayed to the user, and the actual e-mail address link that opens the default e-mail client when a user clicks the link. E-mail links always begin with mailto:. Yet another type of hyperlink column links to Web addresses. These addresses can be SharePoint addresses or other URLs on the Internet. These hyperlinks begin with http:// or https://, depending on the security settings of the site.

Import Spreadsheet List

Excel worksheets can be used to quickly populate data into SharePoint, saving you the trouble of retyping the data. When creating an Import Spreadsheet custom list, as shown in Figure 4.21, you can decide if you want to import all the data included in a worksheet, a range of cells, a named range, or an Excel table.

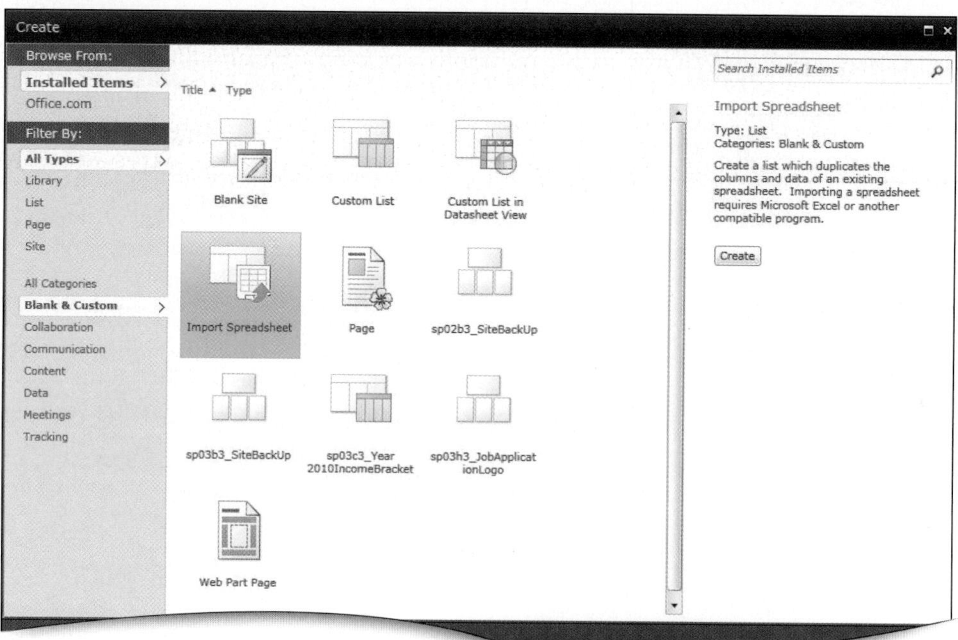

FIGURE 4.21 Creating a Custom Import Spreadsheet List ➤

Later in this chapter, we will discuss in depth about how to import Excel data into a SharePoint list, how to export a SharePoint List to an Excel spreadsheet, and how to synchronize data from a SharePoint list to Excel spreadsheets.

Links List

The **Links list** is a group of links to other pages or Web sites.

The ***Links list*** is a group of links to other pages or Web sites. It is available in the Content group. It is convenient to use this list type to display the links to Web pages in the site as a type of navigational menu to the pages.

The All Links view displays the linked items and contains columns for the Web address and Notes. The built-in columns of the Links list template are:

- URL: Includes the WWW address for the link and text that shows as the name. It can be implemented using a hyperlink or graphic image.

- Notes: Includes a long description of the link.
- Additional columns: Created By and Modified By columns are added automatically as items are added or edited.

Using Links lists enable you to arrange links in a long list, or you can group them in folder or additional lists. This can become quite cumbersome, so a better option is to create a custom column that provides views that filter the links.

A good implementation of the Links list is including it on a Web Part page of a site, as shown in Figure 4.22. This way you can provide users with a list of the most relevant site-related links. The Change Item Order option for the Links list enables you to change the order of the items, so that you can place the more important ones at the top of the list. Because people usually begin scanning at the top of the list, this is helpful. Each view of the Links list can display a different order of items. On the Edit view page of the Links list, you can modify this option so that users can manually set the order of the items on the list. When this feature is available, Change Item Order is available in the Actions group of the List Tools–Items tab, as shown in Figure 4.22.

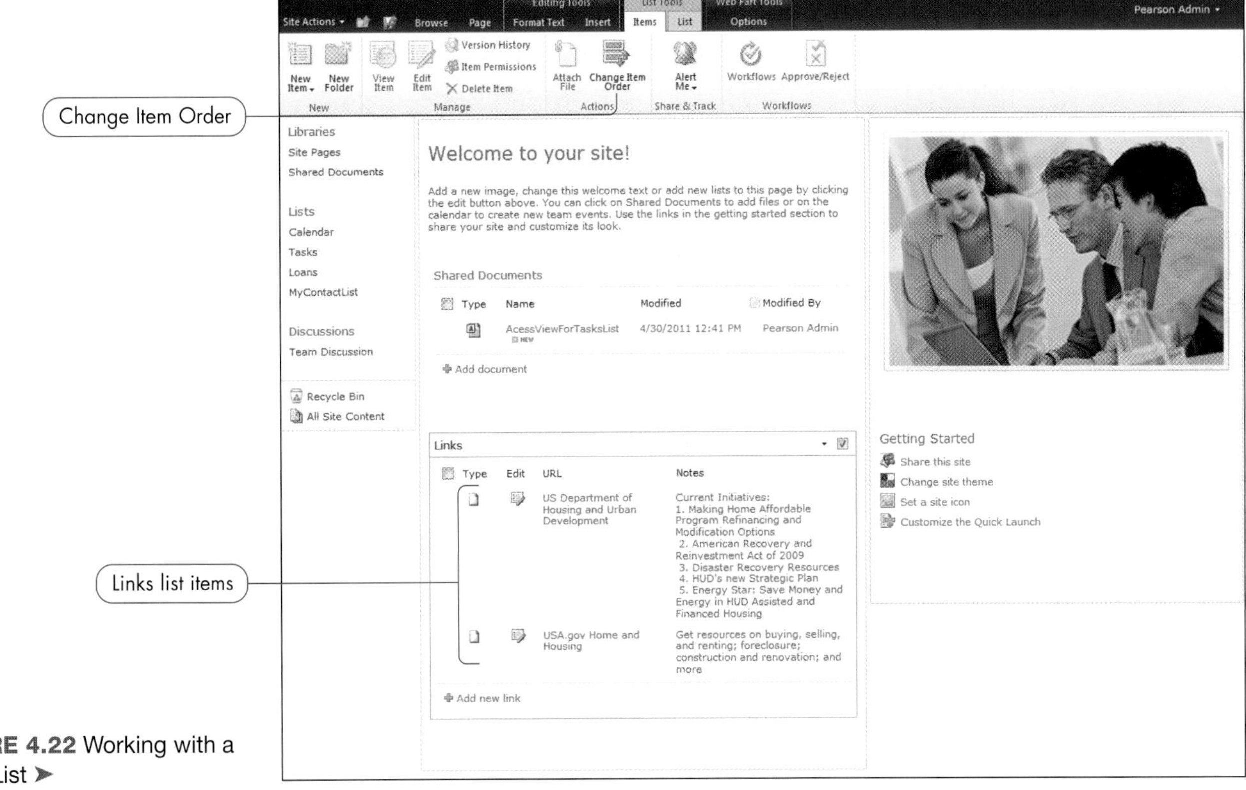

FIGURE 4.22 Working with a Links List ➤

> **TIP More About Links List**
>
> The Wiki page template, used to build collaboration pages, enables you to link to other page sites without using a Links list. For external links to other Web sites, you should consider using a Links list to make the link easy to find and use.

Survey List

The **Survey list** displays columns as a questionnaire or a poll rather than a list of columns and rows.

The ***Survey list*** displays columns as a questionnaire or a poll rather than a list of columns and rows. Begin a new Survey list by naming and describing the survey on the Create form, as shown in Figure 4.23. You can specify whether the survey will appear on the Quick Launch.

Survey lists feature two options that are unique to this type of list, but that support the use of the survey:

- Show user name in survey results: With this option you can decide to make the survey anonymous or not. As you may know, sometimes people tend to share their opinions more freely in an anonymous survey, but there are times when knowing who is commenting is helpful, especially in order to provide customer service. Consider your motives for the survey carefully as you select this option.
- Allow multiple responses: Multiple responses may taint the results of your survey if a person answered it more than once. If the user logs in to the site, a hidden field tracks them, and the responses can be limited to one response per survey.

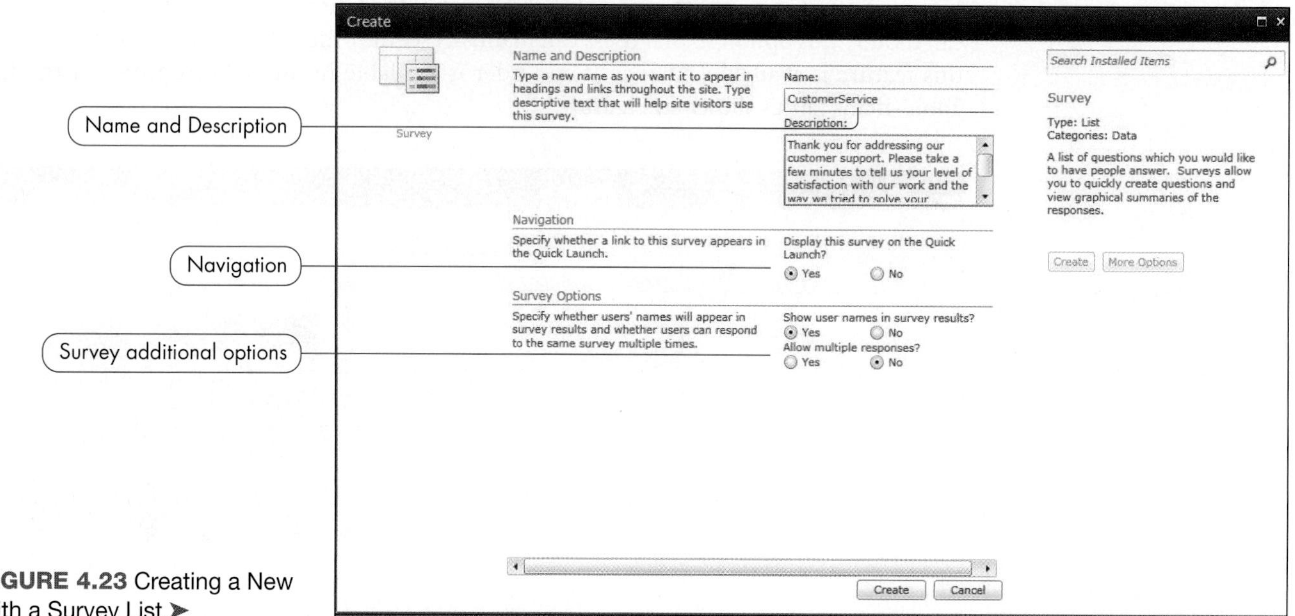

FIGURE 4.23 Creating a New with a Survey List ➤

TIP Survey Advance Settings

The Advanced Settings options enable you to display the results of the survey to everyone, or limit the view to the user's own responses. The person who creates the survey and the site owners can always access the survey results. Consider whether you want people to view the responses before answering the survey. This could sway the responses you receive from people who review the answers of others.

After creating the Survey list, you populate the survey with questions. Type the text of the question in the Question box, and then select the type of answers that you will accept. There are 12 built-in answer types, as shown in Figure 4.24, ranging from text, rating scales such as a Likert scale (http://en.wikipedia.org/wiki/Likert_scale), Yes/No, Number, Date and Time, to Lookup, and External Data. Additional settings enable you to require that questions be answered. Some questions, such as multiple choice and rating scales, require that you add the text of the answers. For example, a rating scale question would have text answers such as "Strongly agree," "Neutral," and "Strongly disagree." Minimum and maximum value limits can be added to numeric answers. You can set the answer lists to display as drop-down menus, radio buttons, or check boxes. Surveys in SharePoint enable branching based on the responses someone makes. As you add questions to the survey, you can determine branching triggers to customize the survey.

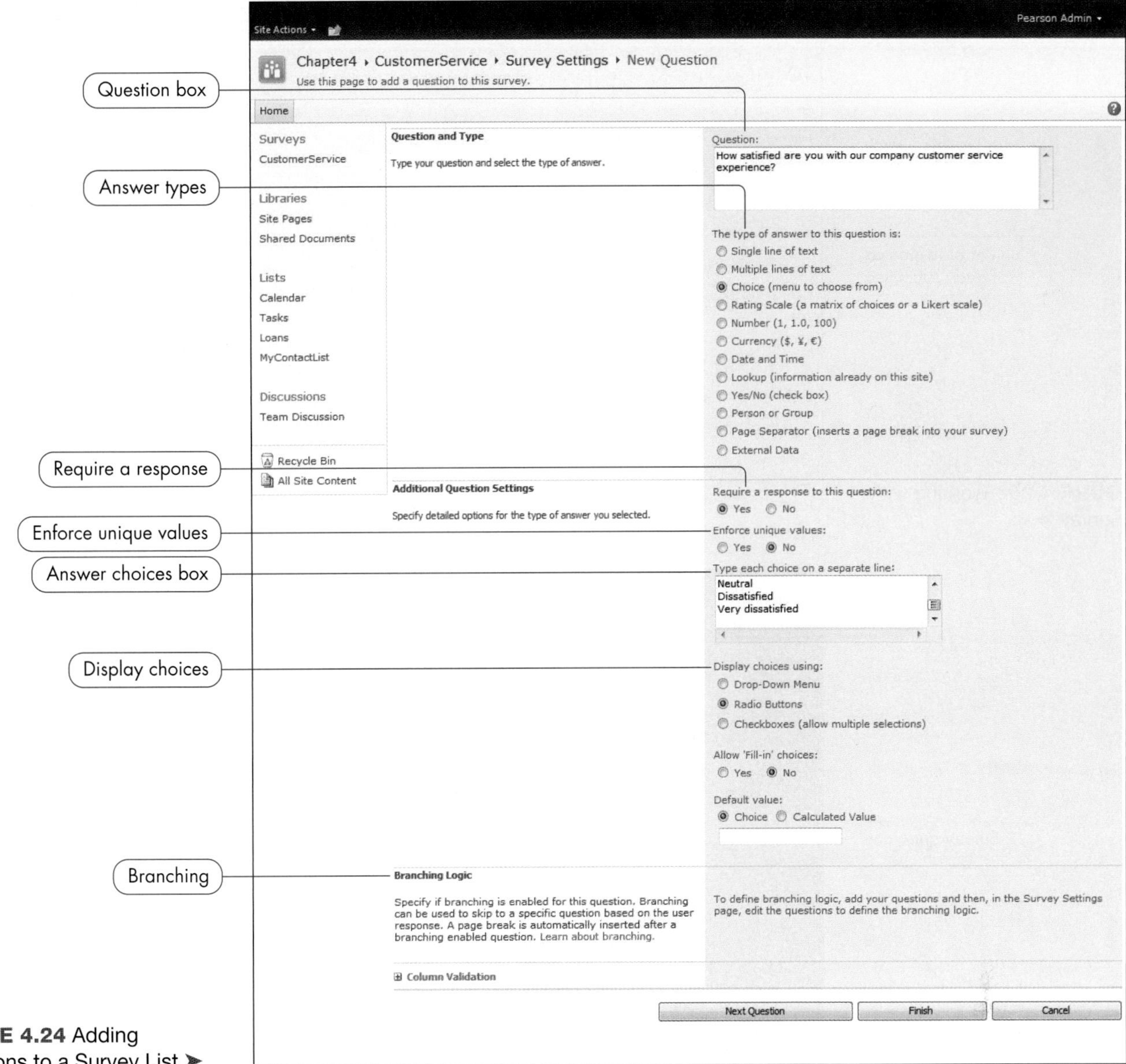

FIGURE 4.24 Adding Questions to a Survey List ➤

When a user views the Survey list, the name of the survey, a description, and the date it was created is displayed, as shown in Figure 4.25. If answers have been made by other people, a number will indicate the number of responses to the survey. By clicking the title of the survey or the *Respond to this Survey* link, the user displays the actual survey on a new page, as shown in Figure 4.25b. The user selects the appropriate answers, and then clicks Finish when they have completed the survey, or Cancel to discard any changes made to the survey.

The Actions menu, see Figure 4.25c, enables you to:

- Export to Spreadsheet: The export option moves the results of the survey to Excel so that you can complete analysis of the items.
- View RSS Feed: This option enables you to add an RSS feed to the survey so you can be notified when users complete the survey.
- Alert Me: Sends you a notification when items change.

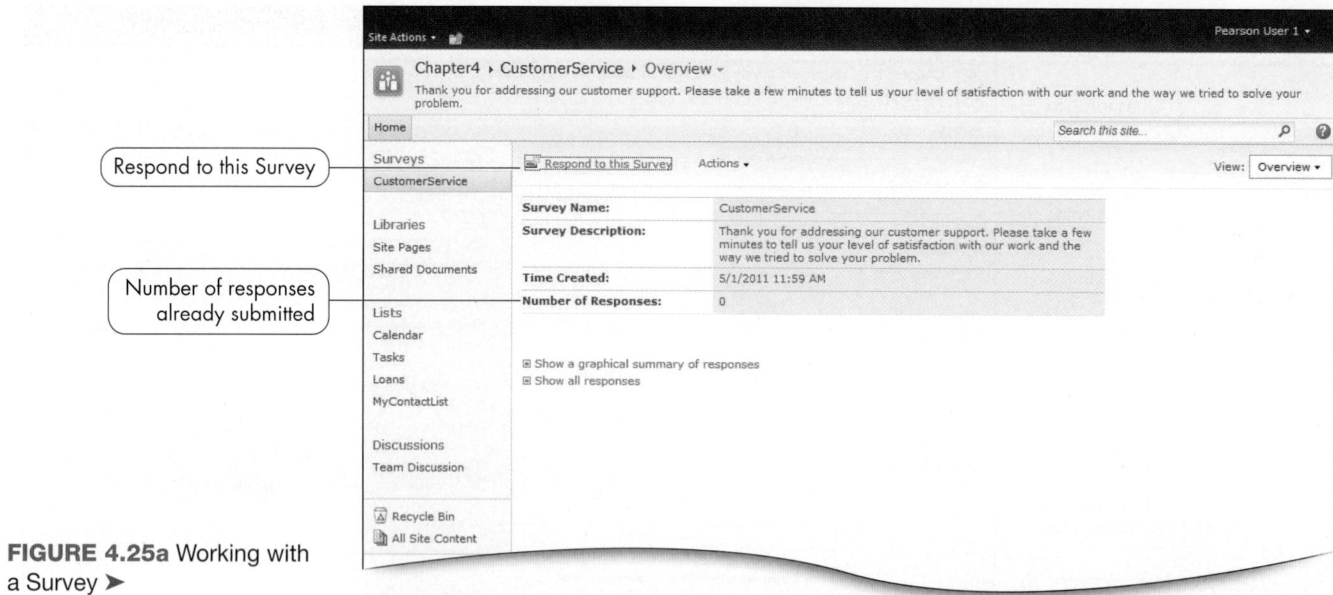

FIGURE 4.25a Working with a Survey ➤

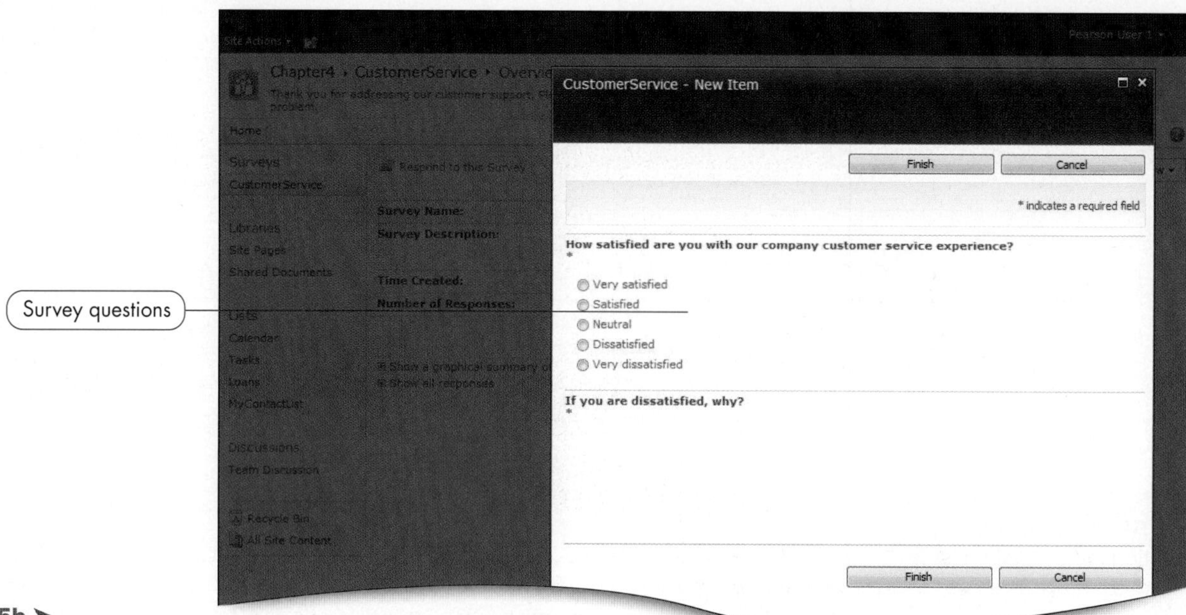

FIGURE 4.25b ➤

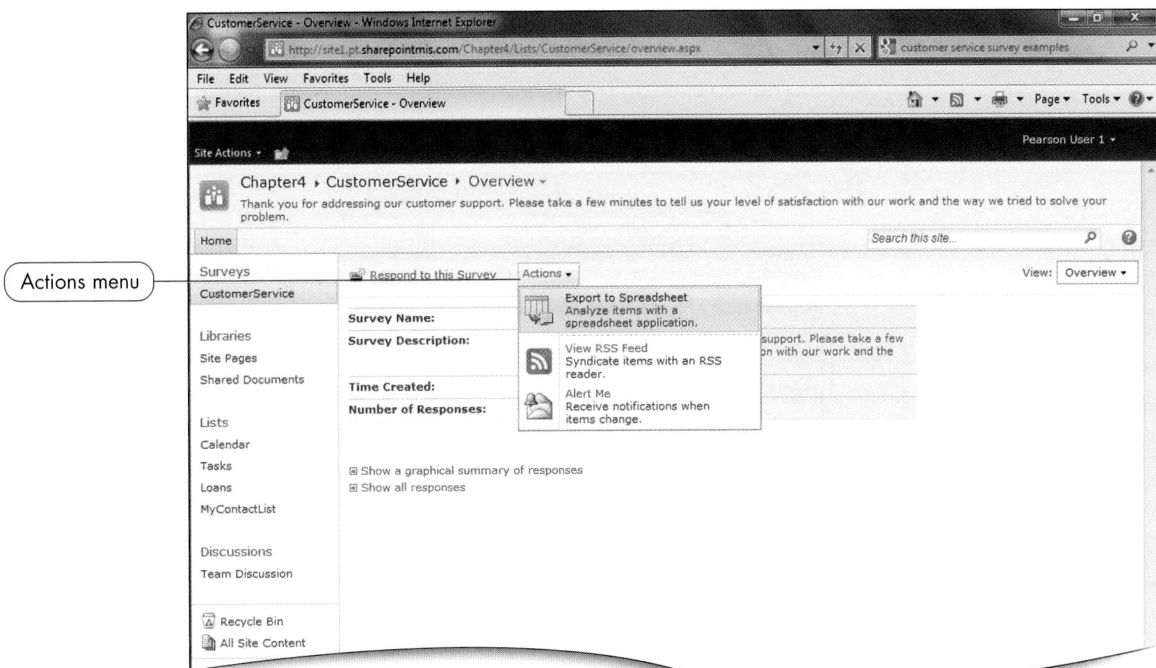

FIGURE 4.25c ➤

TIP Survey Yes/No Questions

When Yes/No questions are specified for a question type, the Yes default value is automatically selected as the survey is displayed. You can change the default value to No. Unfortunately, because of the defaults, you can never be sure whether the user actually responded, or simply skipped the question leaving the default answer. For this reason, you may wish to write Yes/No questions using the Choice question type, leaving the default option as NA. This will leave a blank value if the user does not select an answer.

Discussion Board List

The **Discussion Board list** supports message postings related to list topics.

The ***Discussion Board list*** supports message postings related to list topics. If you have used newsgroups, social media, or educational learning management systems, you have probably participated in discussion boards. A Discussion Board list enables you to group messages and responses in the order in which they arrived, or by threads. The built-in Discussion Board list has columns for the subject, body, the name of the user who created the message, and the date the message was created. Additional columns can be added to the Discussion Board lists. Team, Document Workspaces, and Social Meeting Site templates include a Discussion Board list.

If you have used newsgroups, social media, or educational learning management systems, you have probably participated in discussion boards.

A Discussion Board list enables you to elicit feedback, questions, answers, and ideas from your users. Figure 4.26 shows a discussion board for students regarding upgrading a course. Figure 4.26a shows the topics listed by subject, in Subject view, with responses made to the first topic. The response is viewed by clicking the subject title. A new page will display the messages related to the topic clicked, as shown in Figure 4.26b. This page displays a flat view of the messages.

In a **flat view** postings appear in a sequence based on the date and time they were added to the Discussion Board list.

A **threaded view** displays messages in a hierarchical view.

By default, the messages are displayed in a ***flat view***, where the postings appear in sequence based on the date and time they were added to the Discussion Board list. This enables the users to view the conversation as it occurred. The ***threaded view***, shown in Figure 4.26, displays the messages in a hierarchical view, which groups the responses to the actual topic they are addressing. This enables the users to view a conversation about a topic without having to sift through a list of responses. Indentations on the reply lists are used to indicate replies to a message, with multiple replies to a single user having the same indent. The List Tools–List tab can be used to change to a different defined view of the Discussion Board list, or you can click on the last entry in the breadcrumb trail and select a different view, as shown in Figure 4.26c.

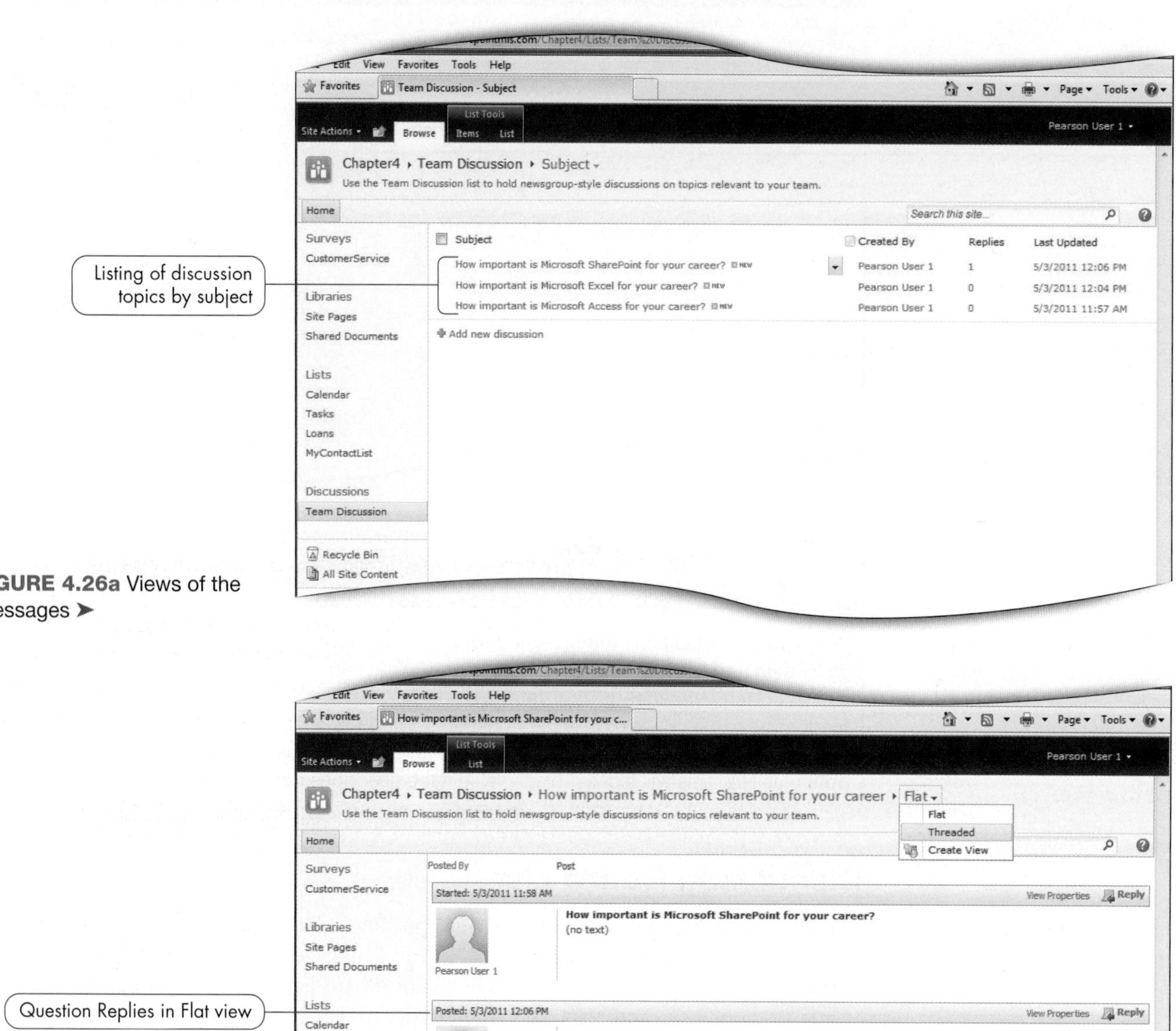

FIGURE 4.26a Views of the Messages ➤

FIGURE 4.26b ➤

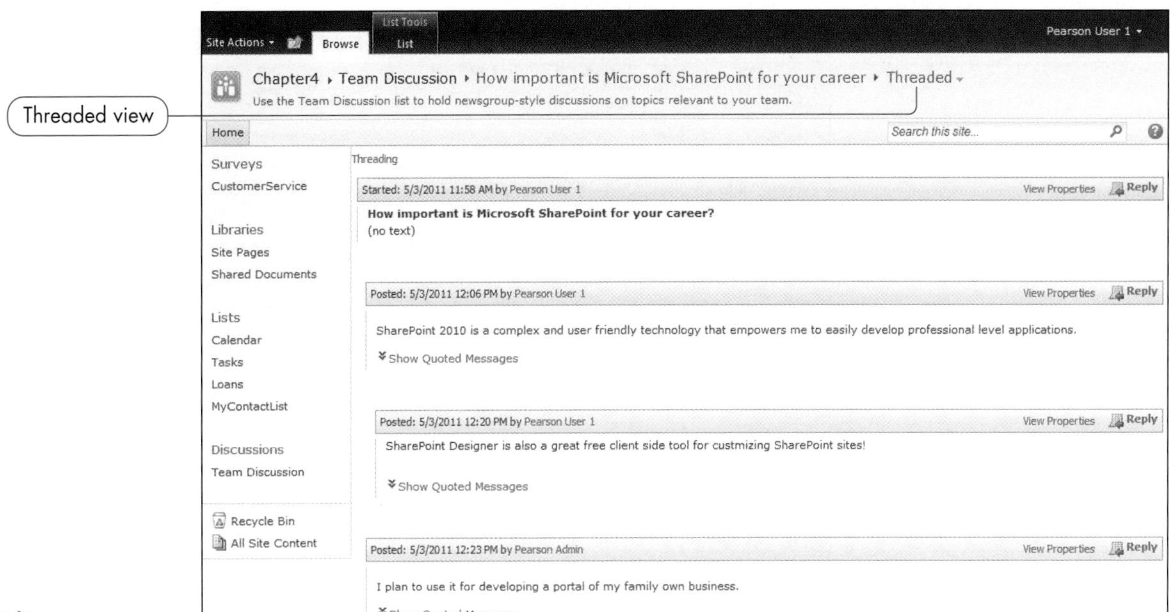

FIGURE 4.26c ➤

Calendar List

The **Calendar list** displays events and activities in a month, week, or daily layout.

All Events view displays all past, present, and future events.

Current Events view displays all present and future events.

The ***Calendar list*** displays events and activities in a month, week, or daily layout, as shown in Figure 4.27. It is similar to an Announcements list in that it displays a title, description, and time and date information when an event is displayed.

Figure 4.27a shows the default calendar list view displaying the event title, description, date, and time. Two additional built-in views enable you to display ***All Events*** (past, present, and future), as shown in Figure 4.27b, or ***Current Events*** (present and future), as shown in Figure 4.27c. Special views of the calendar display the events by month, week, or day, as shown in the month view in Figure 4.27d.

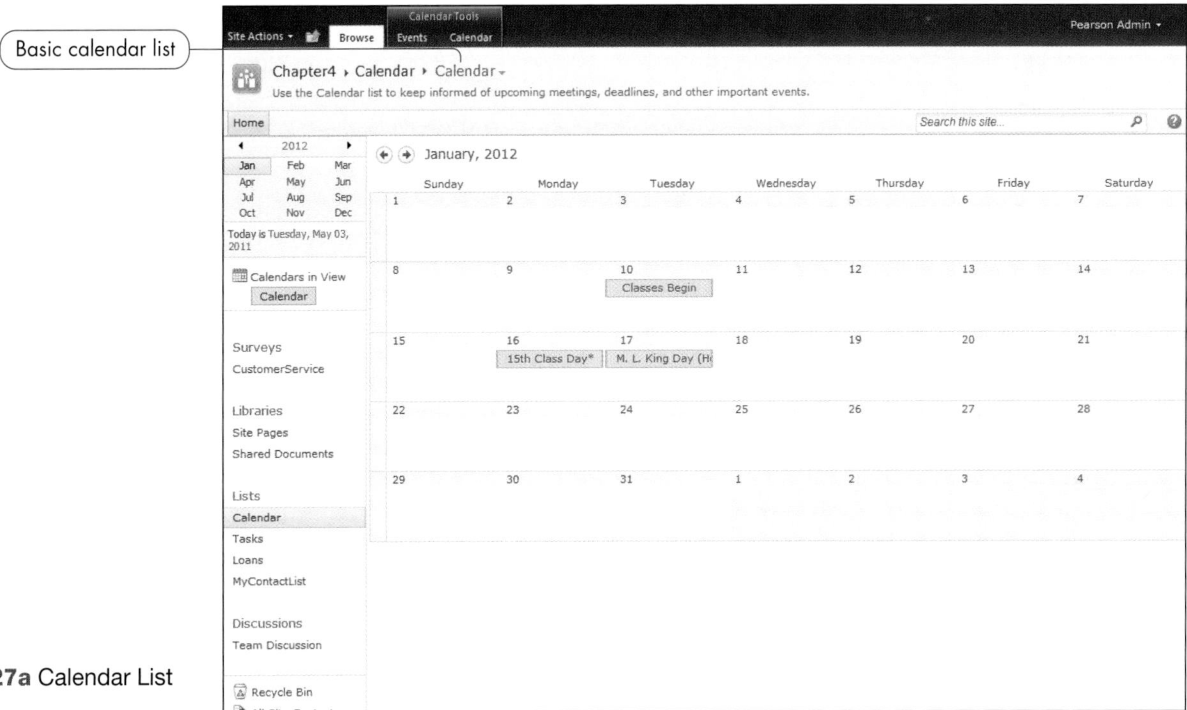

FIGURE 4.27a Calendar List Views ➤

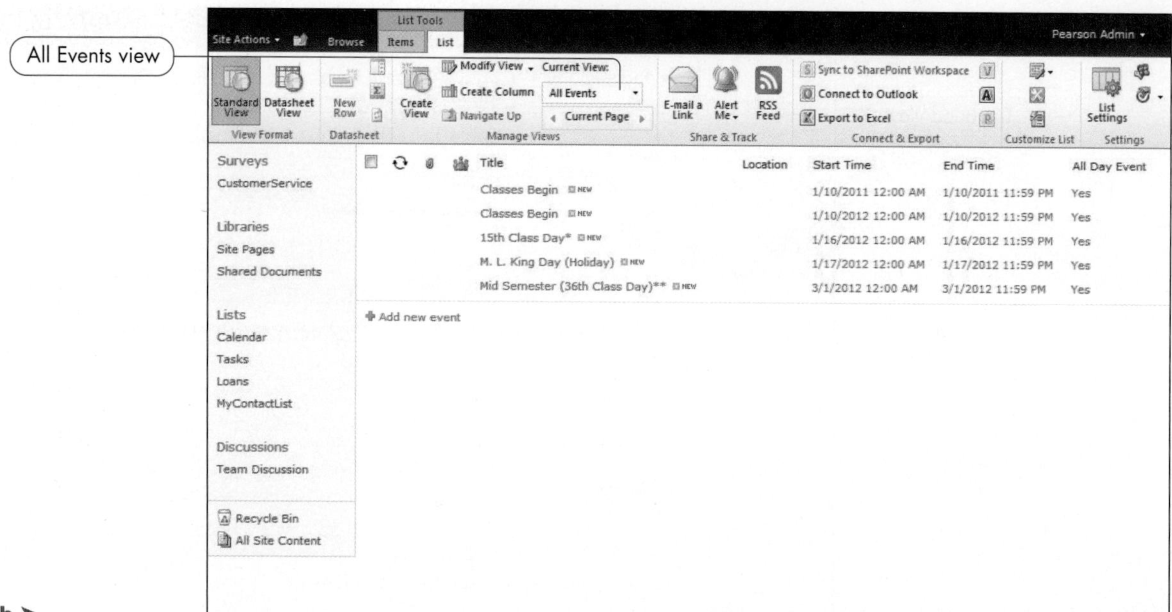

FIGURE 4.27b ➤

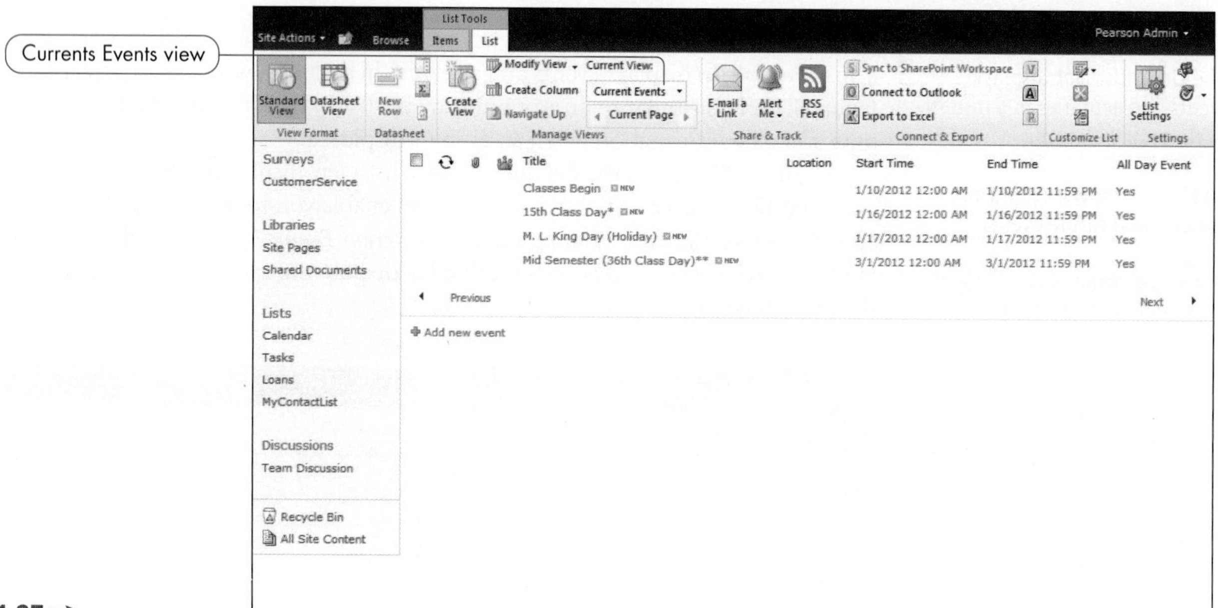

FIGURE 4.27c ➤

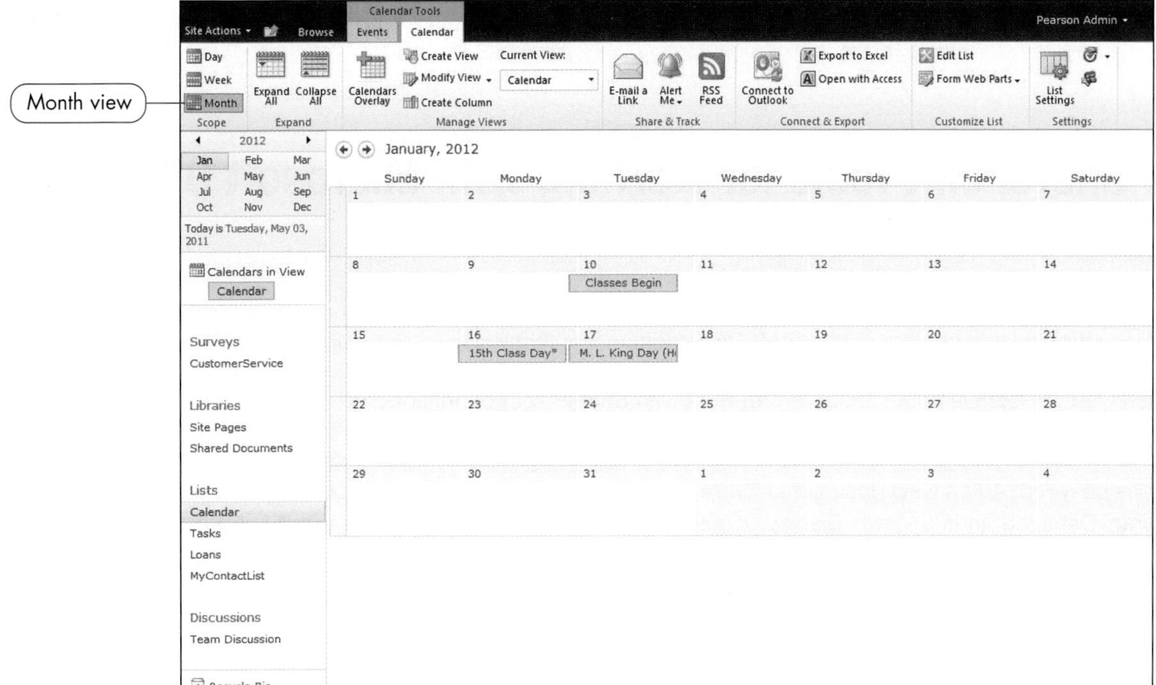

FIGURE 4.27d ➤

1 SharePoint Tools for Working with Microsoft Office 2010 Documents

The RAA investigators are eager to start working with you on creating the new SharePoint 2010 portal for their project. They already have a large number of Microsoft Office documents that will need to be uploaded and displayed on the portal pages. You will learn how to add a new Document Library, upload documents, and how to display documents contained in lists and libraries. Then, you will learn in depth about how to work with SharePoint Foundation Built-in List Types so that you will know when and how to integrate them into the RAA site.

Skills covered: Add a New Document Library • Add a Document to a Document Library and Add a Column to the Document Library Default Standard View • Display Documents in Lists and Libraries • Work with SharePoint Foundation Built-In List Types

STEP 1 ADD A NEW DOCUMENT LIBRARY

You will create a new Document Library and change its default document template. Refer to Figure 4.28 as you complete Step 1.

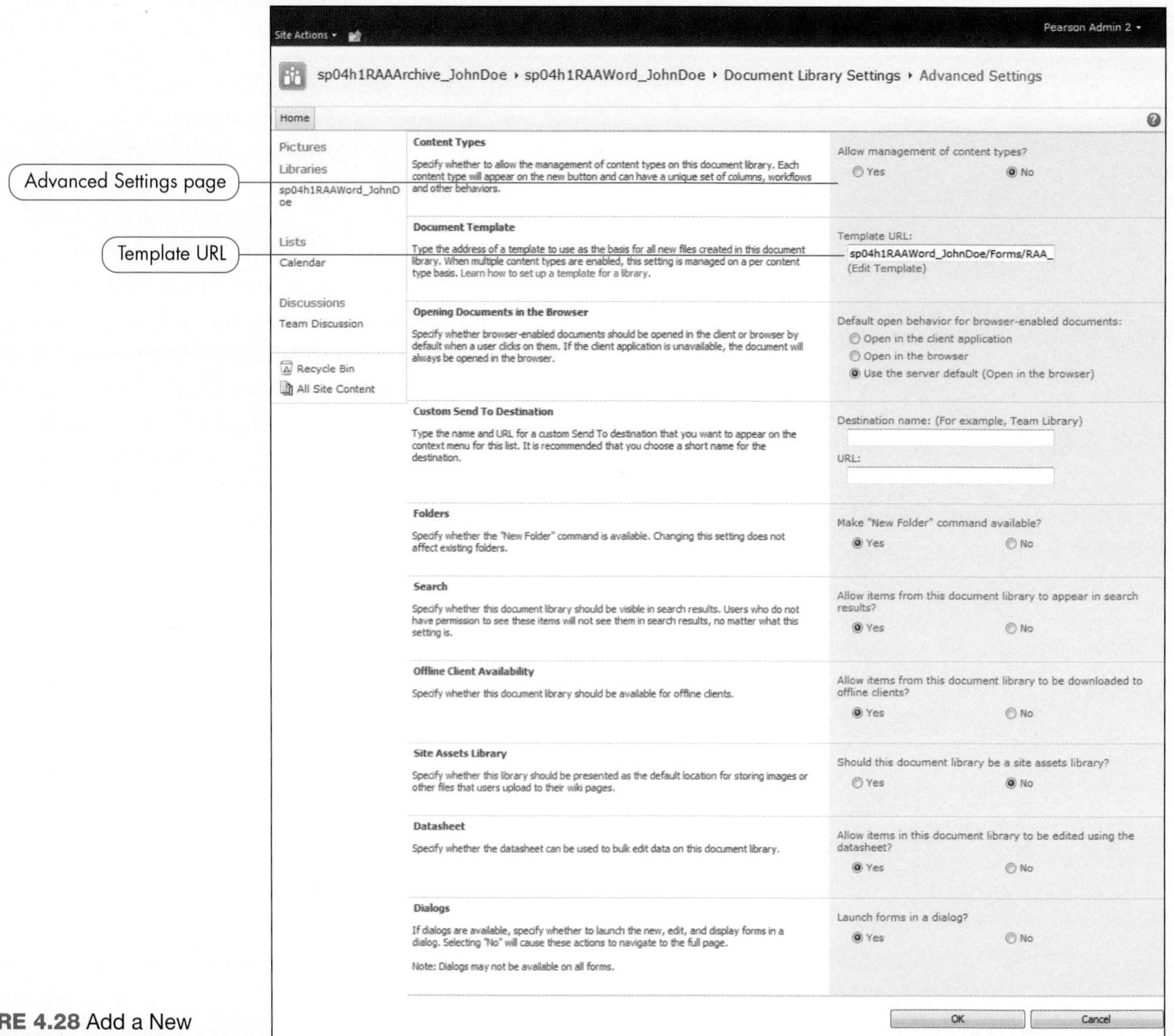

FIGURE 4.28 Add a New Document Library ➤

a. Click **Start** to display the Start menu. Click **All Programs**, and then click **Internet Explorer** to open the program. Go to the top-level site provided by your instructor, which will be in the format of *http://pt.sharepointmis.com/SitePages/yourname.* Enter the user name and password provided by your instructor.

   If you logged in correctly, the home page of the top-level site is now displayed in Internet Explorer.

b. Click the **All Site Content link** on Quick Launch in the top-level site. Click **Create** on the All Site Content page to open the Create dialog box. Click **Site** in the *Filter By* section of the Create page. Click the **Document Workspace template**, and then type **sp04h1RAAarchive_LastNameFirstName** in the **Title and URL name box**. Click **Create.**

   The *sp04h1RAAarchive_LastNameFirstName* site is displayed.

c. Click the **All Site Content link** on Quick Launch in the *sp04h1RAAarchive_LastNameFirstName* site, click **Create**, and then click **Library** in the *Filter By* section of the Create dialog box. Click **Document Library**, and then type **sp04h1RAAWord_LastNameFirstName** in the **Title box**. Click **More Options.**

   The *Create page* of the *sp04h1RAAWord_LastNameFirstName* library is displayed.

d. Type **This Library will include all RAA Word documents** in the **Description box**. Check **Yes** in the *Document Version History* section. Click **Create.**

   The *sp04h1RAAWord_LastNameFirstName* library is displayed in the default Standard view.

e. Click **Open with Explorer** in the Connect & Export group. Open a separate Windows Explorer window, browse to *RAA_WordTemplate.docx* in your Exploring folders, right-click the file, and then select **Copy**. Click in the window opened by *Open with Explorer*, double-click the **Forms folder**, right-click in a blank area, and then select **Paste.**

   The *RAA_WordTemplate.docx library* template is listed in the window.

f. Activate the browser window, and then click **Library Settings** in the Settings group of the Library Tools–Library tab. Click **Advanced settings** in the *General Settings* section of the Document Library Settings page.

   The Advanced Settings page of the library template is displayed in the window.

g. Highlight *template.dotx* in the **Template URL box**, and then type **RAA_WordTemplate.docx**, as shown in Figure 4.28. Click **OK**. Click **sp04h1RAAWord_LastNameFirstName** in the breadcrumb.

   The *sp04h1RAAWord_LastNameFirstName* library is now displayed in the default Standard view.

STEP 2 ADD DOCUMENTS TO A DOCUMENT LIBRARY AND ADD A COLUMN TO THE DOCUMENT LIBRARY DEFAULT STANDARD VIEW

You will create a new document based on the default template of the Document library. You will upload a document into the Document library. Refer to Figure 4.29 as you complete Step 2.

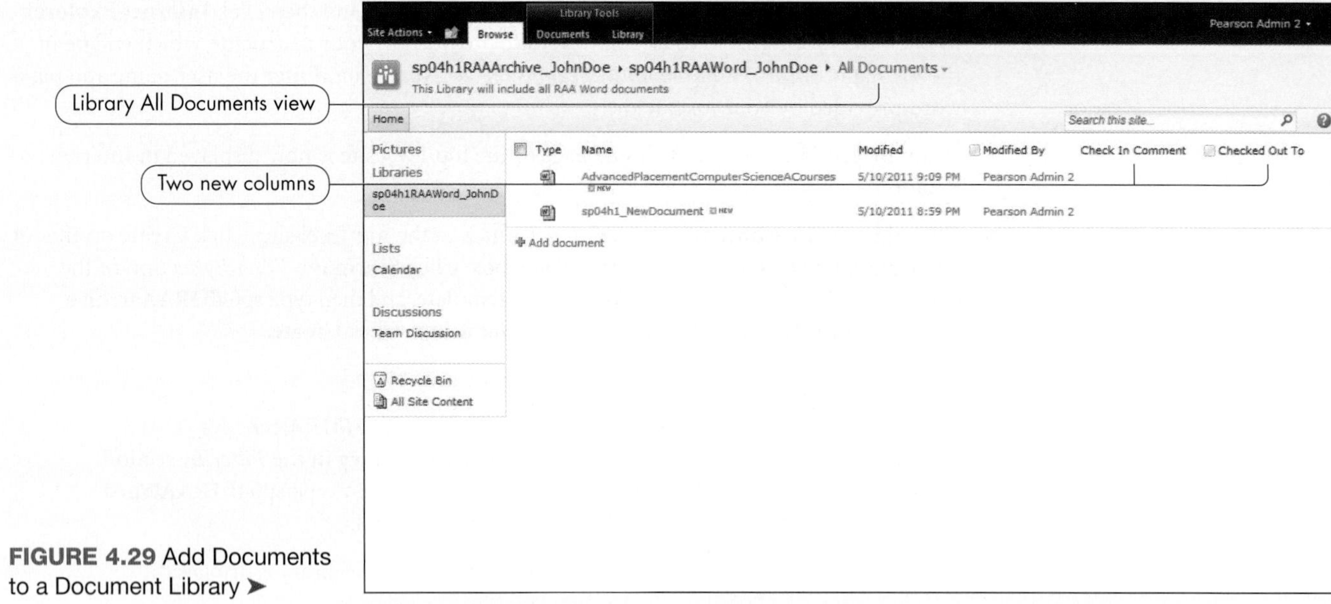

FIGURE 4.29 Add Documents to a Document Library ➤

a. Click **New Document** on the New group on the Library Tools–Documents tab.

   A new document built upon the Library document template is displayed in the Word window.

b. Type your name, and then click **Save**. Type **sp04h1_NewDocument** in the **File name box** of the Save As dialog box, and then click **Save**. Activate the browser window.

TROUBLESHOOTING: Enable Editing if needed.

   The *sp04h1_NewDocument* is now displayed in the built-in All Documents view of the *sp04h1RAAWord_LastNameFirstName* library.

c. Click the **Upload Document arrow**, and then select **Upload Document**. Browse for the *AdvancedPlacementComputerScienceCoursesACourses.docx* document, click Open, and then click OK to upload it.

   The *AdvancedPlacementComputerScienceACourses.docx* document is displayed in the built-in All Documents view of the *sp04h1RAAWord_LastNameFirstName* library.

d. Click **Library Settings** in the Settings group on the Library Tools–Library tab.

   The Document Library Settings page is displayed.

e. Click **All Documents** in the *Views* section of the Document Library Settings page. Check the **Check In Comment** and **Checked Out To check boxes** in the *Columns* section of the Edit View page, and then click **OK**.

   The two new columns are shown on the browser view of the *sp04h1RAAWord_LastNameFirstName* library. Your screen should look similar to Figure 4.29.

STEP 3 DISPLAY DOCUMENTS IN LISTS AND LIBRARIES

You will upload a custom list template and will build a custom list. You will create a Datasheet view for the custom list. Then, you will create in SharePoint Designer a custom view of the custom list. Refer to Figure 4.30 as you complete Step 3.

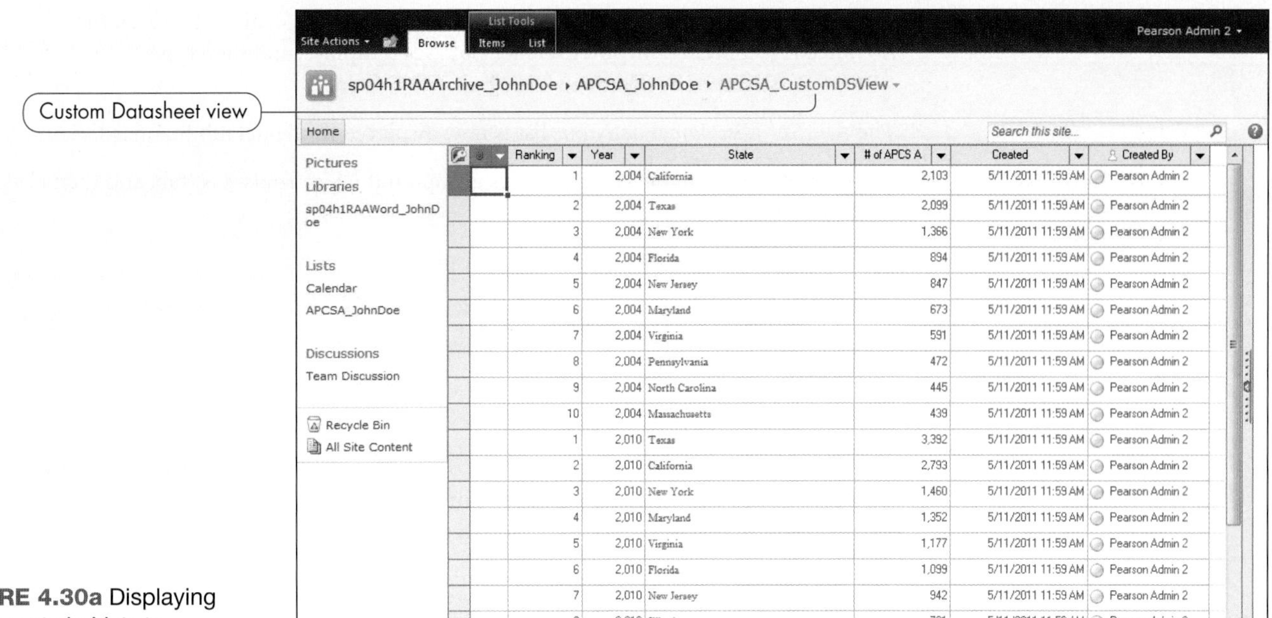

FIGURE 4.30a Displaying Documents in Lists ➤

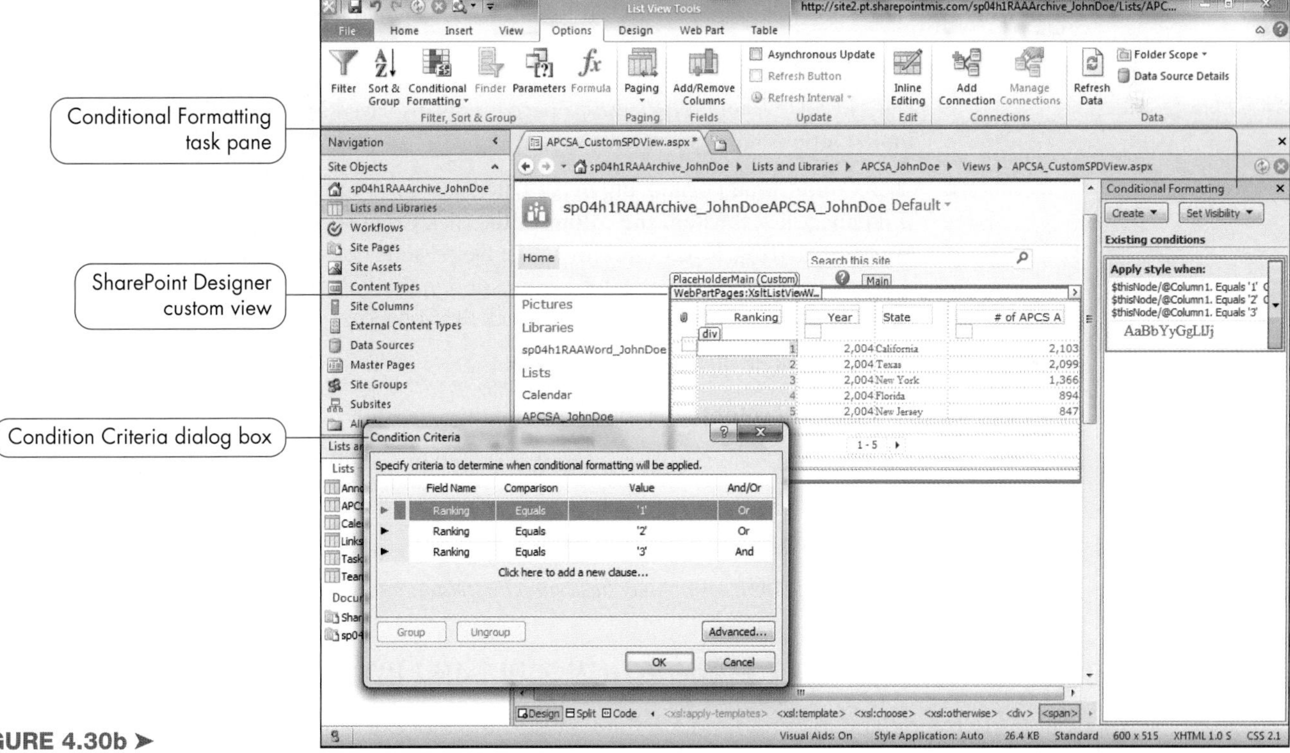

FIGURE 4.30b ➤

a. Click the **Navigate Up button**, and then select **Team Site**. Click **Site Setting**s on the Site Actions menu, click **List templates** in the *Galleries* section, and then click **Upload Document** in the New group of the Library Tools–Documents tab. Browse for the *AdvancedPlacementComputerScienceACourses.stp* document in your Exploring folder, click the file, click **Open**, click **OK**, and then click **Save** on the Edit tab of the List Template Gallery dialog box.

   The *AdvancedPlacementComputerScienceACourses* List template is now available in the top-level site List Template gallery.

b. Click the **Navigate Up button**, select **Team Site**, and then click **sp04h1RAAarchive_LastNameFirstName** on the Top link navigation bar. Click the **All Site Content link** on Quick Launch. Click **Create** on the All Site Content page to open the Create page.

c. Click **Blank & Custom** in the *All Categories* section of the Create page. Click the **AdvancedPlacementComputerScienceCourses template**, and then type **APCSA_LastNameFirstName** in **Title box**. Click **Create**.

   The *APCSA_LastNameFirstName* list is now displayed in the default Standard View.

d. Click **Create View** in the Manage Views group on the List Tools–List tab, and then click **Datasheet View** on the Create view page.

   The Create Datasheet View page is now displayed.

e. Type **APCSA_CustomDSView** in the **View Name box**, check the **Created** and **Created By check boxes** in the *Columns* section, and then click **OK**.

   The APCSA_CustomDSView Custom Data View is now displayed in a browser window similar to Figure 4.30a.

f. Click **Edit in SharePoint Designer** on the Site Actions menu. Click **Lists and Libraries** on the Navigation Pane. Click **APCA_LastNameFirstName** in the *Lists* section of the Lists and Libraries summary page, click in the *Views* section, and then click **New**.

   The Create New List View dialog box should be now displayed.

g. Type **APCSA_CustomSPDView** in the **Name box** of the Create New List View dialog box, and then click **OK**.

   The APCSA_CustomSPDView Custom Data View should now be displayed in the *Views* section.

h. Click **APCSA_CustomSPDView** in the *Views* section.

   The *APCSA_CustomSPDView.aspx* page is now displayed in Design view and the List View Tools–Options tab is activated.

i. Click **Conditional Formatting** in the Filter, Sort & Group group, and then select **Show Taskpane**. Click the **Ranking column title**, click **Create** on the task pane, and then select **Apply formatting**. Select **Ranking** in the Field Name box, select **Equals** in the Comparison box, and then build a 1 OR 2 OR 3 expression in the *Value* section, as shown in Figure 4.30b of the Condition Criteria dialog box. Click **Set Style**.

   The Modify Style dialog box is displayed.

j. Select the **Red color** in the color box, and then click **OK**.

   The *APCSA_CustomSPDView.aspx* page should now look similar with the one shown in Figure 4.30b.

k. Click **Save** on the Quick Access Toolbar.

l. Close the *sp04h1RAAarchive_LastNameFirstName* site, and then exit SharePoint Designer.

STEP 4 WORK WITH SHAREPOINT FOUNDATION BUILT-IN LIST TYPES

You will delete the default item and modify the views to the site built-in Announcements list. You will create a new Survey list, customize it, and add a question to it. Refer to Figure 4.31 as you complete Step 4.

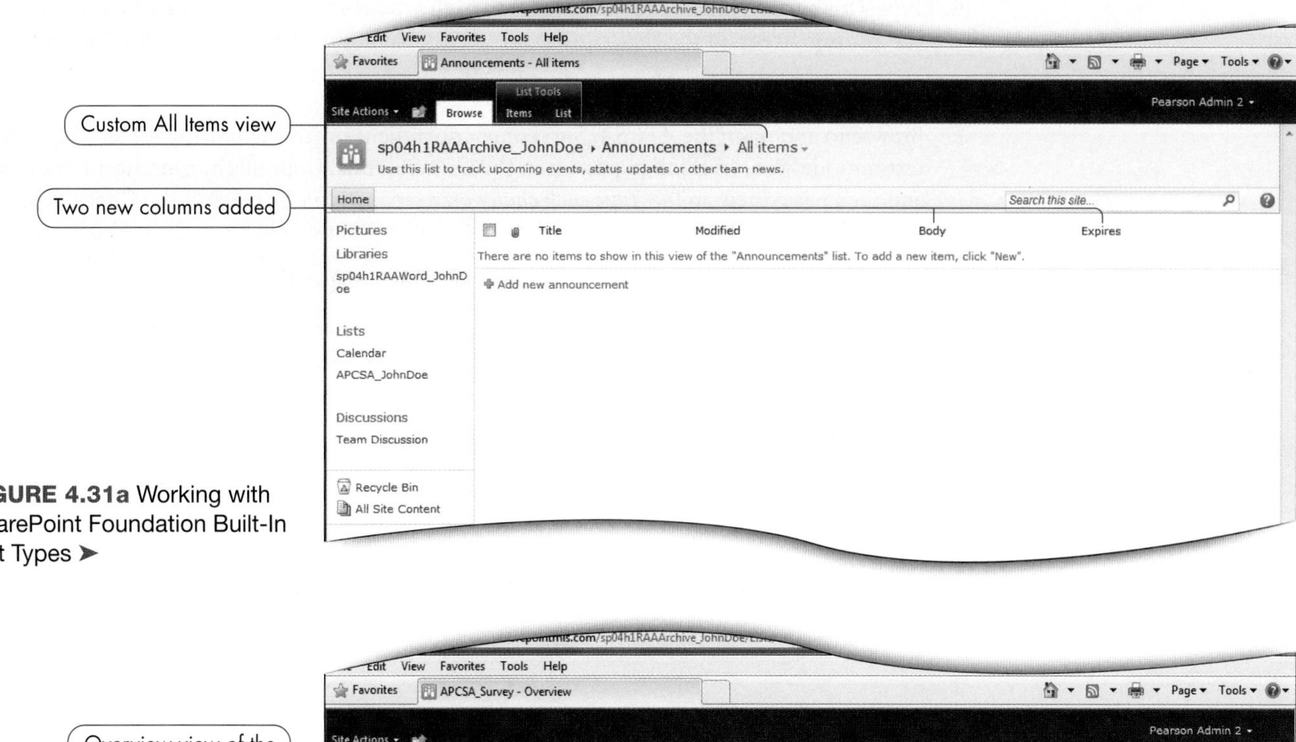

FIGURE 4.31a Working with SharePoint Foundation Built-In List Types ➤

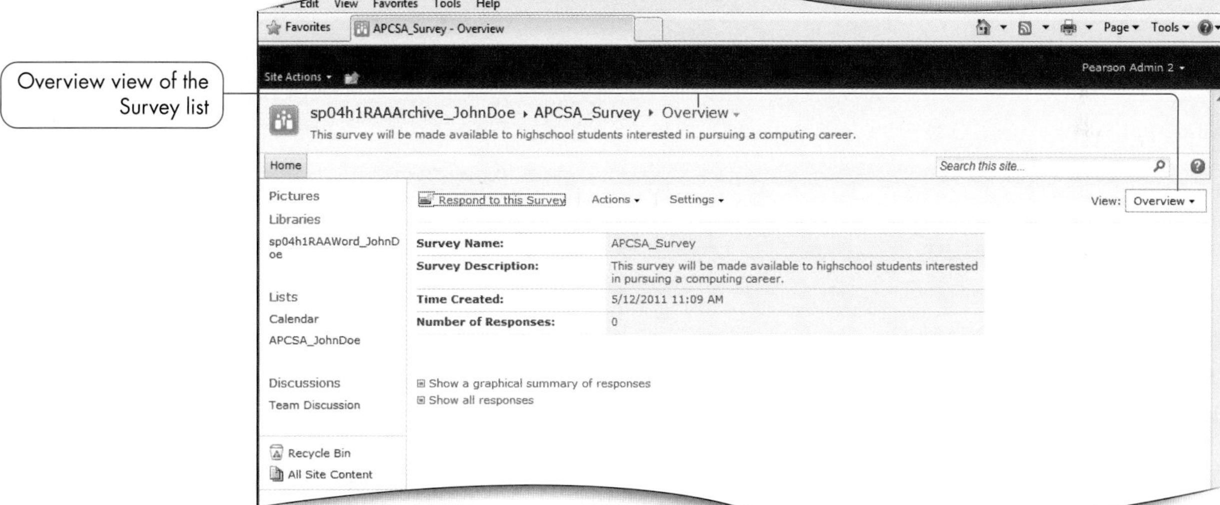

FIGURE 4.31b ➤

a. Activate the browser window. Your screen should look similar to Figure 4.30a. Click **Home**.

b. Click **Announcements**. Point to the default item, select the check box in the list first column, and then click **Delete Item** in the Manage group of the List Tools–Items tab. Click **OK** on the dialog box.

c. Click **Modify View** in the Manage Views group on the List Tools–List tab**.** Select the check boxes to the left of the Body and Expires columns in the *Columns* sections on the Edit View page, and then click **OK**.

   The *AllItems.aspx* page of the Announcements list is displayed and the Body and Expires columns are showing.

d. Click **All Site Content** on Quick Launch in the top-level site. Click **Create** on the All Site Content page to open the Create page. Click **List** in the *Filter By* section on the Create page. Click **Survey**, and then type **APCSA_Survey** in the **Name box**. Click **More Options**.

   The Create Survey page is displayed.

e. Type **This survey will be made available to high school students interested in pursuing a computing career**. in the **Description box**. Select **No** in the *Navigation* section. Click **Create**.

The New Question page is displayed.

f. Browse to and open the *APCSA_Survey.docx* document in your Exploring folder. Copy the text for Question 1, and then paste it in the Question box. Copy all the Question 1 choices, and then paste them in the *Type each choice on a separate line* box. Select the **Check boxes (allow multiple selections) option** in the *Display choices using* section. Click **Finish**.

The Survey Settings page is now displayed including the question.

g. Click **Advanced settings**. Select the **None option** in the *Create and Edit access* section. Select the **No option** in the following three sections on the Advanced Settings page. Then click **OK**.

The Survey Settings page is displayed including the question.

h. Click **APCSA-Survey** on the navigation breadcrumb. The Overview page of the APCSA_Survey list should now be displayed similar to what is shown in Figure 4.31b.

i. Click **Close**.

Integration of Word and PowerPoint 2010 Files in SharePoint Foundation Sites

One of the biggest strengths of SharePoint Foundation is its integration with Microsoft Office applications, including Word, PowerPoint, and Excel. New features in Office 2010 enhance document sharing with SharePoint 2010. When you store documents in a SharePoint document library, users can open the document and see who else is editing the document on the status bar. SharePoint Foundation enables you to take content offline so you can work on both documents and list items without an Internet connection. You can collaborate simultaneously, with other users, in editing Word or PowerPoint files, in a process known as "coauthoring." PowerPoint presentations can also be streamed over the Web using SharePoint Foundation sites.

Word and PowerPoint support a large number of file formats (see the Microsoft Web page "File formats supported in Office 2010," http://technet.microsoft.com/en-us/library/dd797428.aspx, for comprehensive information) that can be integrated into a SharePoint site. For example, the Portable Document Format (PDF) and XML Paper Specification (XPS) are supported by both Word and PowerPoint, and can be easily integrated into a SharePoint site.

Portable Document Format (PDF) is a fixed-layout file format that preserves document formatting and enables file sharing.

XML Paper Specification (XPS) is a fixed-layout file format that preserves document formatting and enables file sharing.

Portable Document Format (PDF) and ***XML Paper Specification (XPS)*** are both fixed-layout file formats that preserve document formatting and enable file sharing. The PDF and XPS formats ensure that whether the file is viewed online or printed, the format remains exactly as you created it. In addition, the data in the file cannot be easily changed. The PDF format is used when the document will be commercially printed.

TIP — More About Microsoft Office 2010, PDF and XPS

To read more about the Microsoft XPS format see the Microsoft XML Paper Specification Overview (www.microsoft.com/whdc/xps/default.mspx). The add-in used to create the PDF and XPS file formats is a part of Office 2010, so no additional downloads or applications are needed to create documents in these formats.

In this section, you will learn how you can work with SharePoint Foundation, SharePoint Designer, Word, and PowerPoint to integrate Word and PowerPoint documents into SharePoint sites.

Opening, Editing, and Saving Microsoft Office Documents to a SharePoint Document Library

You can open a Microsoft application document included in a SharePoint library in two different ways. If you have administrator access to your computer, you can add a mapped drive to your Windows Vista or Windows 7 operating system, as shown in Figure 4.32a. To start creating a mapped drive, right-click Network in the Windows Explorer window. You can use your mapped drive from within a Microsoft Office application to open or save documents (see Figure 4.32b), but you cannot use it as a browser to open a SharePoint site.

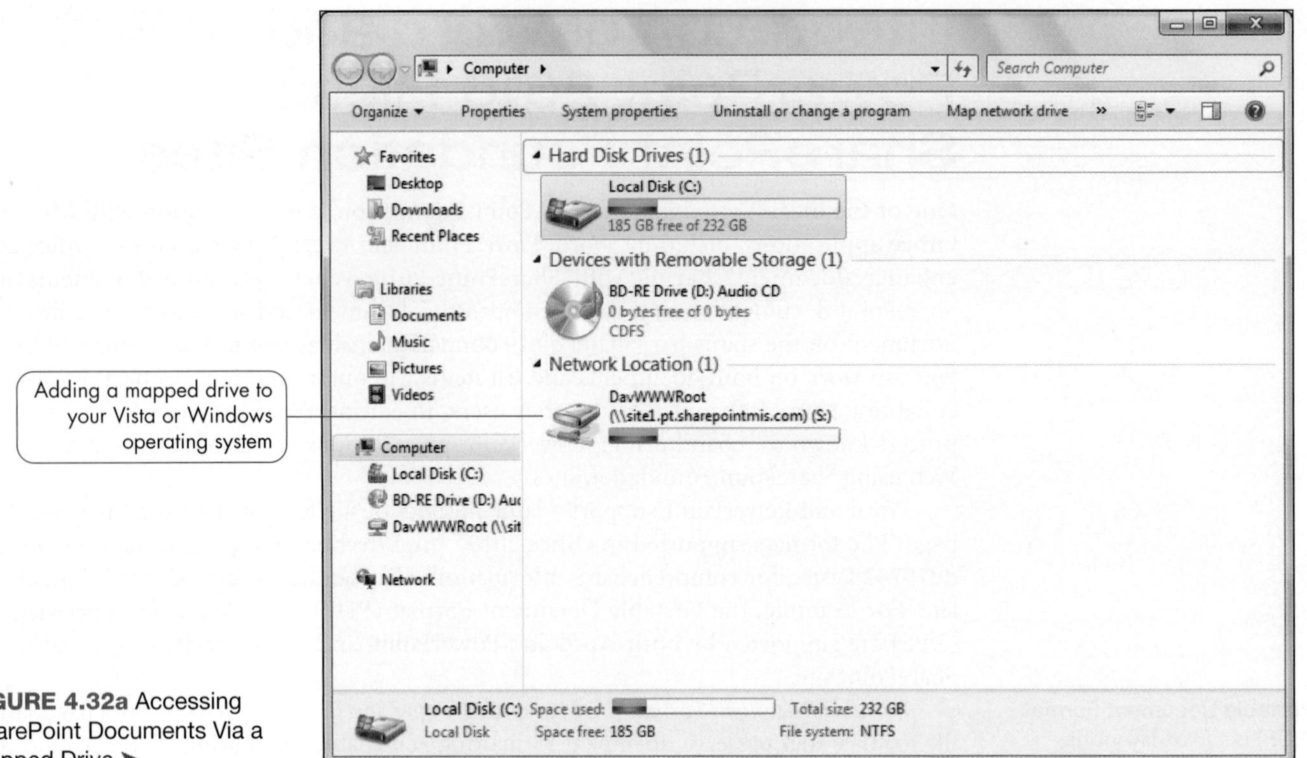

FIGURE 4.32a Accessing SharePoint Documents Via a Mapped Drive ➤

Using a mapped drive

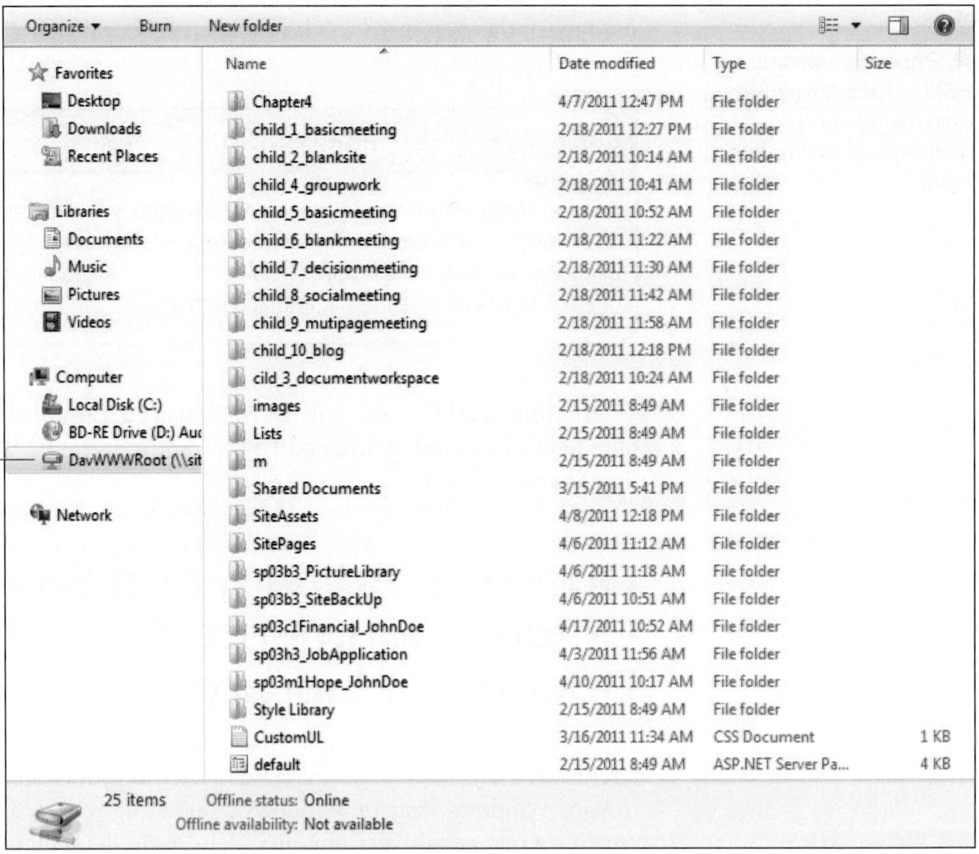

FIGURE 4.32b ➤

Even if you do not have administrator access to your computer, you can still directly open SharePoint documents using the URL of your SharePoint site and the library names. Figure 4.33a shows the Microsoft Open dialog box with the site Document Libraries listed.

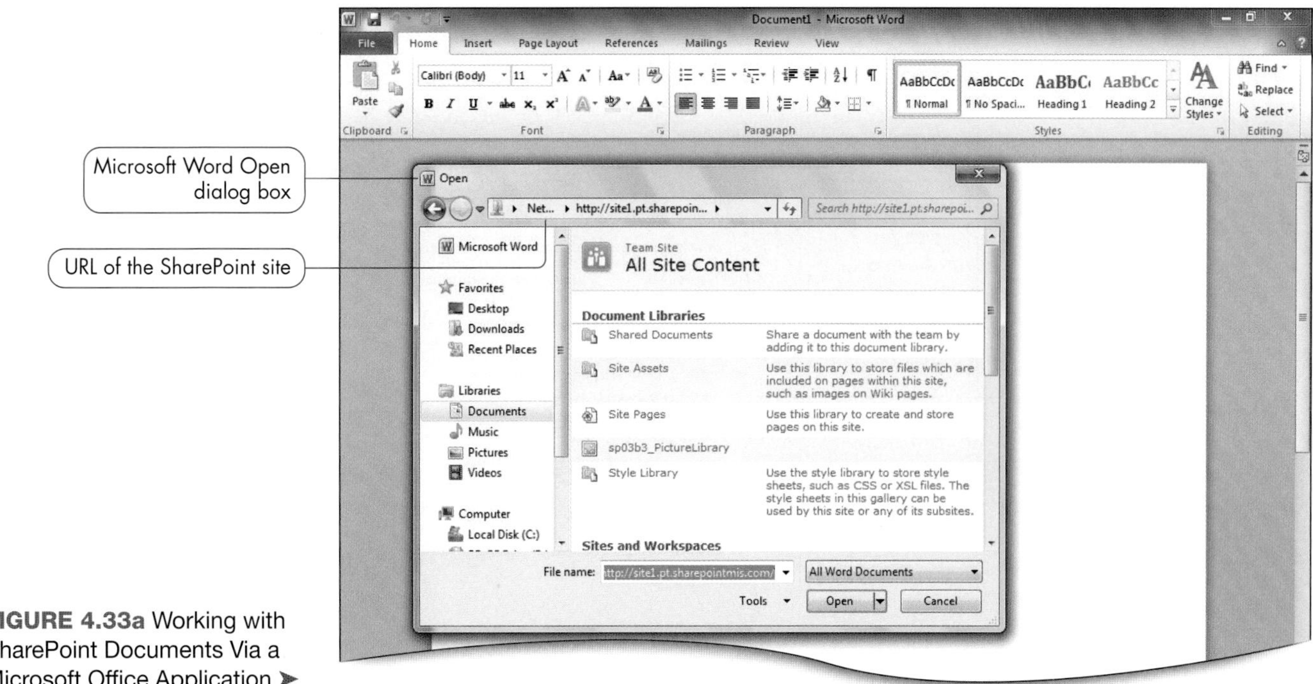

FIGURE 4.33a Working with SharePoint Documents Via a Microsoft Office Application ➤

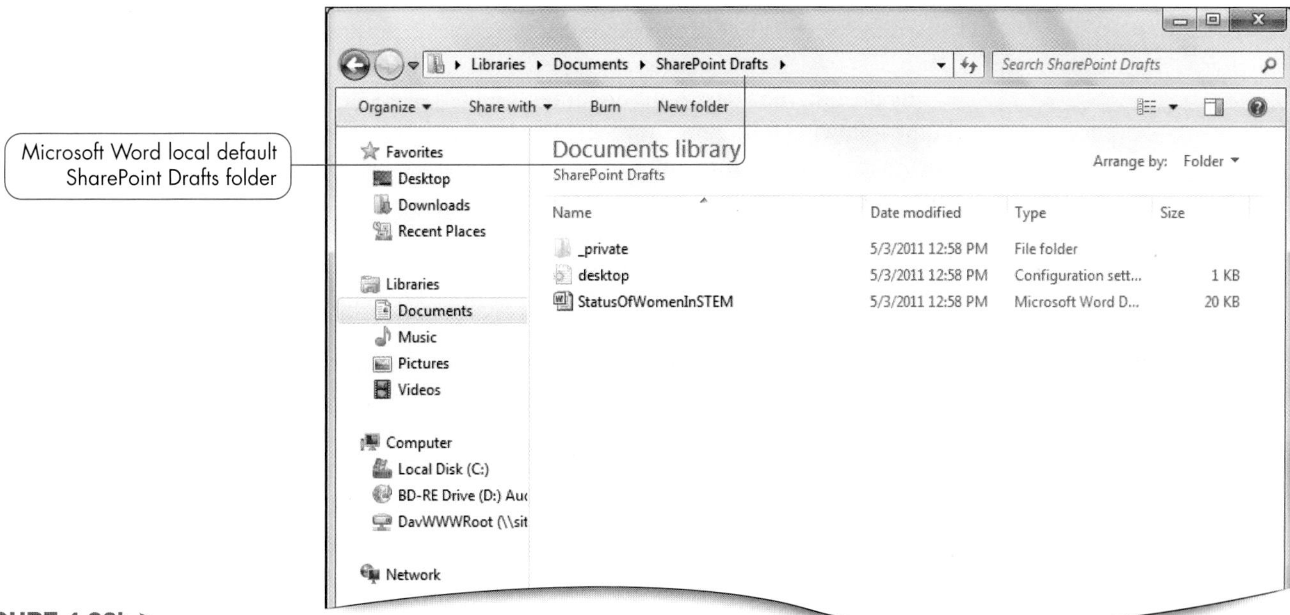

FIGURE 4.33b ➤

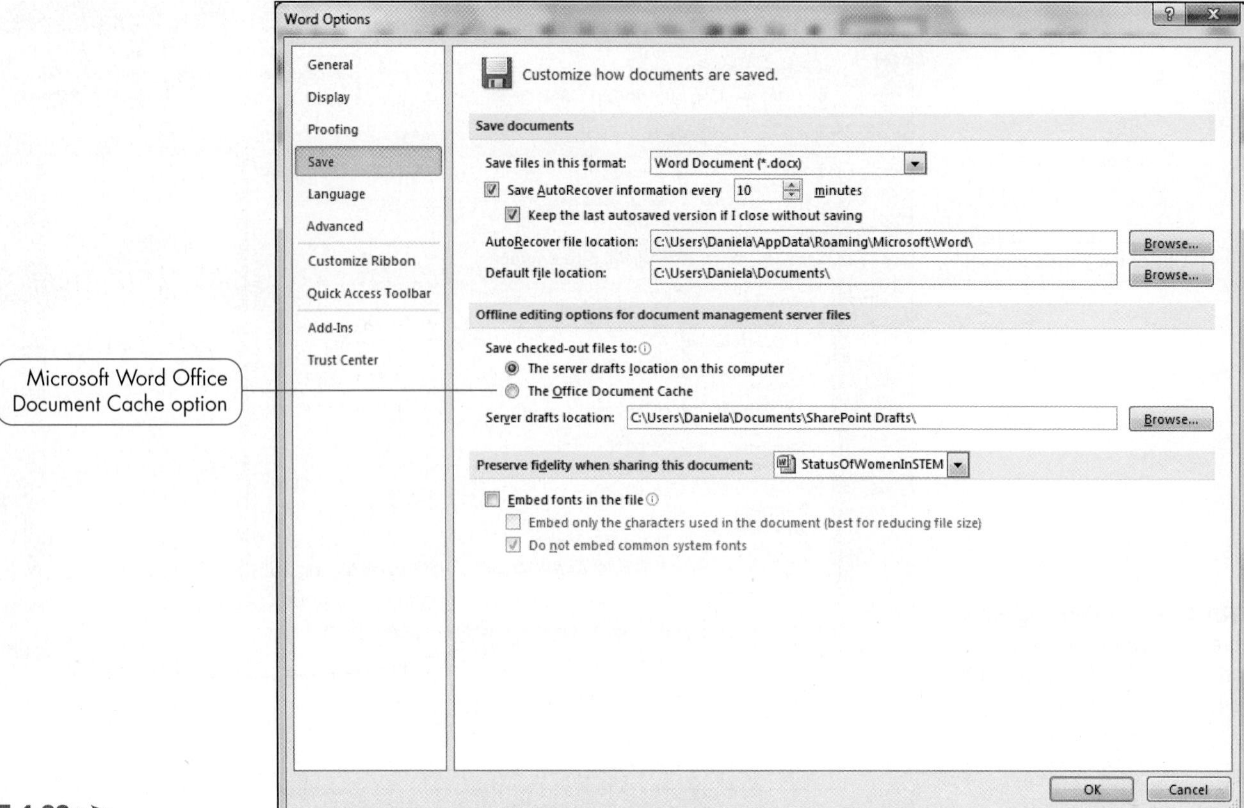

FIGURE 4.33c ➤

By default, the SharePoint documents edited in a Microsoft Office application are saved on the following folder on your local hard disk: local hard disk drive:\Users\YourUserName\Documents\SharePoint Drafts, as shown in Figure 4.33b. You can also see this address on the Save tab of your Microsoft Office Application Options dialog box, as shown in Figure 4.33c. To set a different location for saving drafts, select The Office Document Cache (see Figure 4.33c) in the Backstage view of the application, using the Save tab.

If you use Windows Explorer to open a Microsoft Office document, Word in our example, you will receive no information about the document being checked out by another user. However, if you use the Microsoft Office application (continuing with Word in our example) to open a document that was checked out by somebody else, a checked out symbol will appear in the bottom-right corner of the file icon in the Type column, as shown in Figure 4.34a.

If you open a file that was already checked out, the File in Use dialog box will display the options you have for working with the file, as shown in Figure 4.34b:

- Read Only: Enables you to view or print the document.
- Notify: When the document becomes available you will receive a notification, shown in Figure 4.34c, if you leave the application window open.
- Cancel: Cancels your request to access the document.

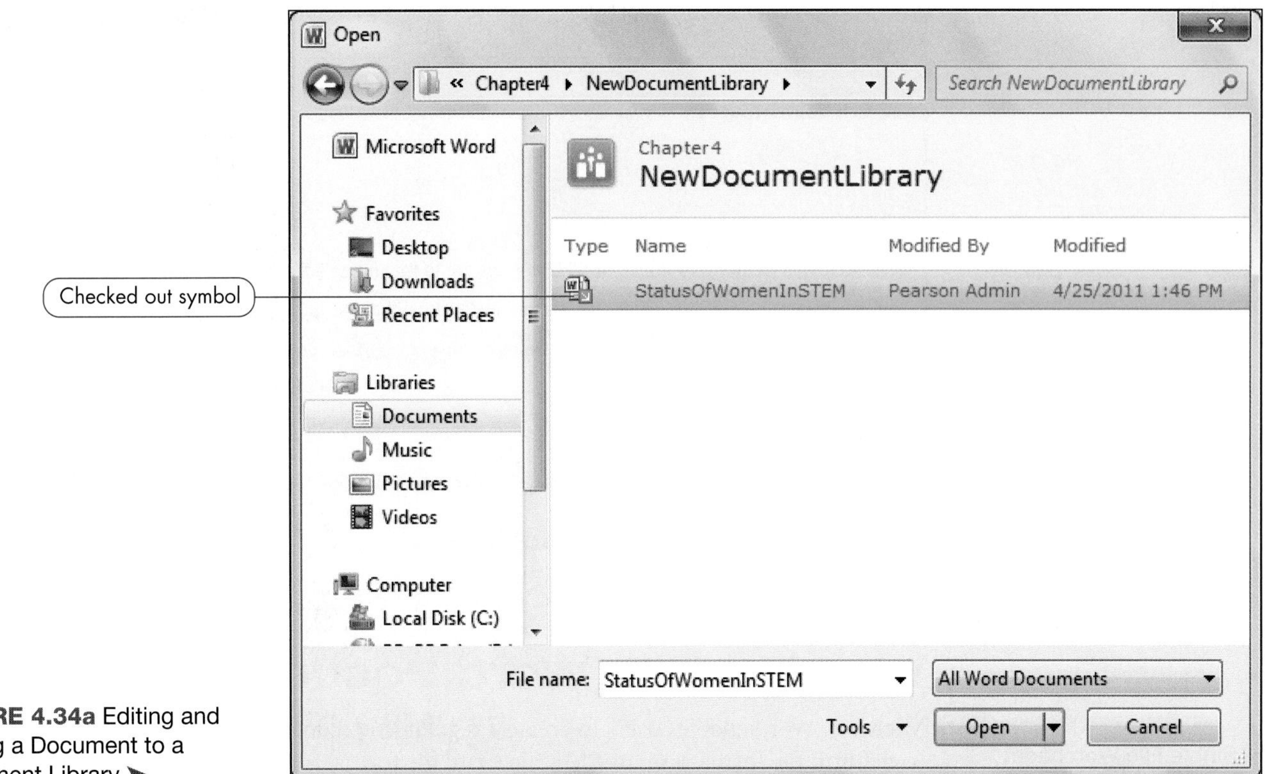

FIGURE 4.34a Editing and Saving a Document to a Document Library ➤

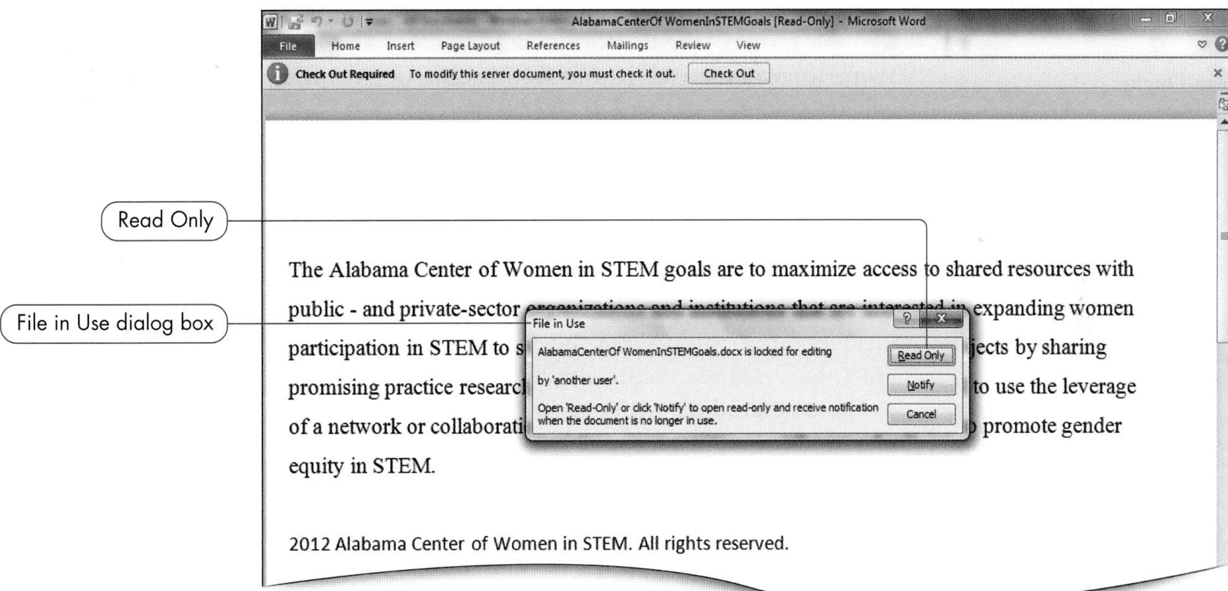

FIGURE 4.34b ➤

Notification received when the document becomes available

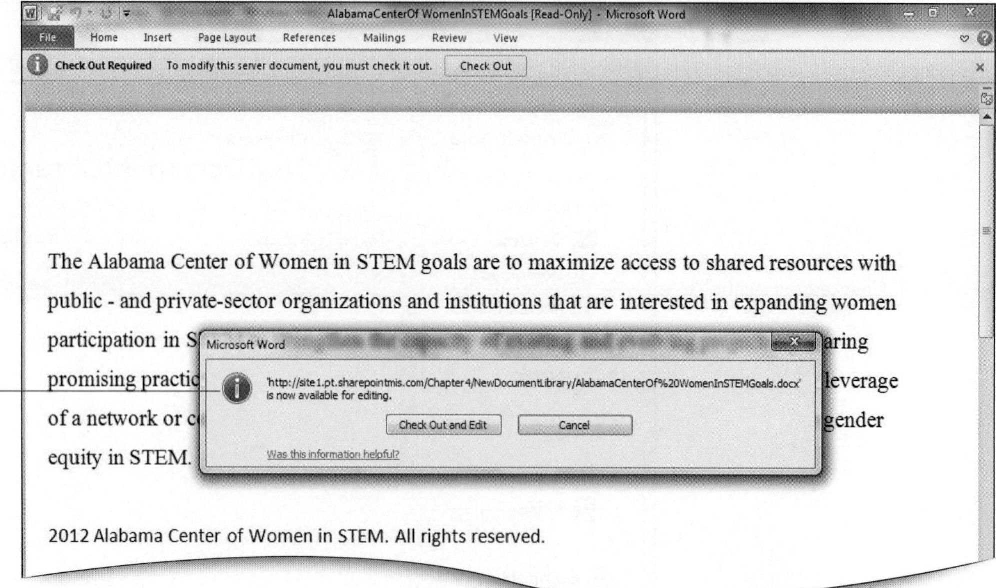

FIGURE 4.34c ➤

Working with Word Documents

The **Single File Web page option** saves the entire document into a single .mht format file, which is supported only by Internet Explorer version 6.0 and higher.

The **Web page option** saves the document as an .htm file with a set of files grouped in a folder that that enables you to rebuild the original Word document.

The **Web page, Filtered option** saves the document in an .htm file format, and saves an additional set of files grouped in a folder, but filters and removes all the Word-specific metadata.

Microsoft Word enables users to create a regular Word document (.docx file format), a Web page (.htm file format), or an XML file (.xml file format). It also offers three options for saving a Word document as a Web page: Single File Web Page, Web Page, and Web page, Filtered. Starting with Microsoft Word 2007, you can also save and export a Word document as a PDF (.pdf file format) or XPS Document (.xps file format). When you are creating a Web page in Word, work in the Web Layout view because it gives you a good idea of how the document will look when it is viewed in a Web browser.

The ***Single File Web page option*** saves the entire document into a single .mht format file, which is supported only by Internet Explorer versions 6.0 and higher. The ***Web page option*** saves the document as an .htm file with a set of files (grouped in a folder having the same name as that of the .htm file), which enables you to rebuild the original Word document (for example, but not limited to, all graphic files included in the original Word document, and .xml files defining the color scheme used by the original Word document). Word metadata includes information about the document, such as the full name, path, smart tags, hyperlinks, track changes, comments, hidden text, and the last 10 authors. The ***Web page, Filtered option*** saves the document in an .htm file format, and saves an additional set of files grouped in a folder, but it filters and removes all the Word-specific metadata.

Add Word Documents to a SharePoint Site

SharePoint enables you to upload any Word file format to a document library.

SharePoint enables you to upload any Word file format to a document library. From a developer's point of view, the process of uploading a document saved as a PDF, XPS Document, and Single File Web page is identical. The graphic files are embedded in these documents so there is no need to upload/import them separately.

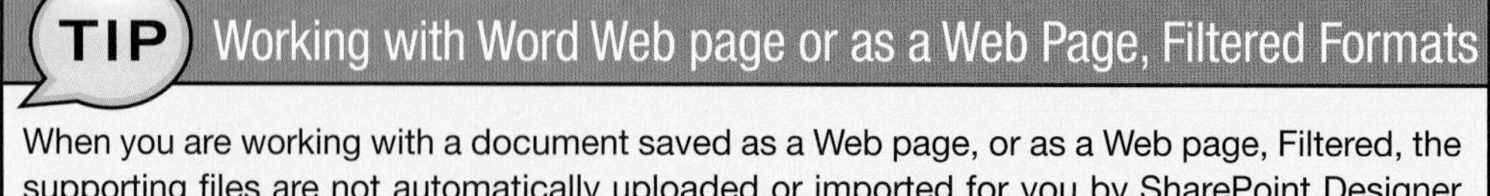

TIP
Working with Word Web page or as a Web Page, Filtered Formats

When you are working with a document saved as a Web page, or as a Web page, Filtered, the supporting files are not automatically uploaded or imported for you by SharePoint Designer from the *filename_files* folder. Therefore, you must upload/import this folder as well.

When any Word document is opened in SharePoint Foundation Web interface or SharePoint Designer, the document is opened, by default, in Word. In SharePoint Designer, you can overwrite this default option using the General tab of the Application Options dialog box (click Application Options on the SharePoint Designer Options page, click the General tab, and then deselect the Open Web pages in the Microsoft Office application that created them check box).

To open an uploaded .pdf or .xps file in SharePoint Foundation Web interface or SharePoint Designer, double-click the file name in the browser or on the SharePoint Designer All Files page. The .pdf file will display in an Adobe Reader window, and the .xps file will display in an XPS Viewer window.

If you need to modify any uploaded document created in Word's .mht file format, edit the original .docx source file of the Web page in Word...

If you need to modify any uploaded document created in Word's .mht file format, edit the original .docx source file of the Web page in Word, save it again as a .mht file, and then import the updated file into the Web site, replacing the existing files. You can also edit these files in SharePoint Designer with the Word editor and save them directly on the Web site, replacing the existing files. Edit these files directly in SharePoint Designer only if there is no other option because you will not be able to use all the tools in the Word editor, such as ones on the Review tab.

If you need to modify any uploaded document created in Word's .pdf or .xps file format, edit the original .docx source file of the Web page in Word, save it again as a .pdf or .xps file, and then import the updated file into your Web site, replacing the existing files.

Integrate Word Documents with Blog Sites

Microsoft Word enables you to create a blog entry for a SharePoint blog site that will maintain all the formatting features already applied to the text in Word. Launch the Word application, click New on the File menu, select the Blog post template in the *Available Templates* section, and then click Create. If this is your first time creating a blog post, the Register a Blog Account dialog box will be displayed, as shown in Figure 4.35a. Click Register Now, on the Blog menu in the New Blog Account dialog box, select SharePoint blog, and then click Next. Type or paste the URL of your SharePoint blog in the Blog URL box of the New SharePoint Blog Account (see Figure 4.35b), and then click OK. If you see a Microsoft privacy box, click Yes. A Microsoft confirmation box indicating that your account was successfully registered will appear. The Blog Post tab displays on the Word window, as shown in Figure 4.35c. Type the title and text you want to post on the blog, and then click Publish in the Blog group. A banner confirmation of your posting appears at the top of the Word document. Click Home Page in the Blog group to see your posting on the Blog site, as shown in Figure 4.35d.

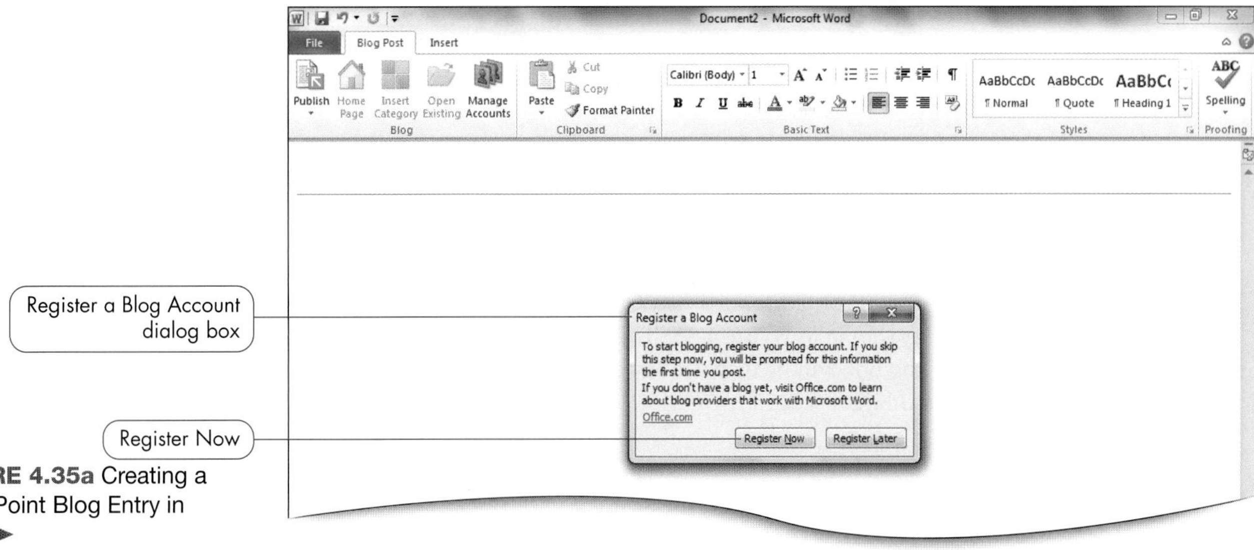

FIGURE 4.35a Creating a SharePoint Blog Entry in Word ➤

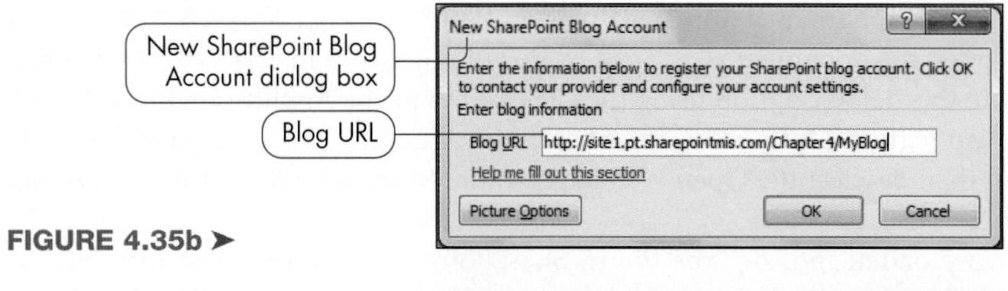

FIGURE 4.35b ➤

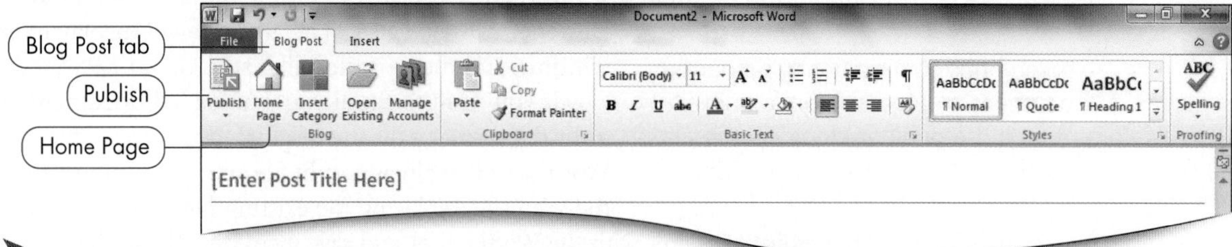

FIGURE 4.35c ➤

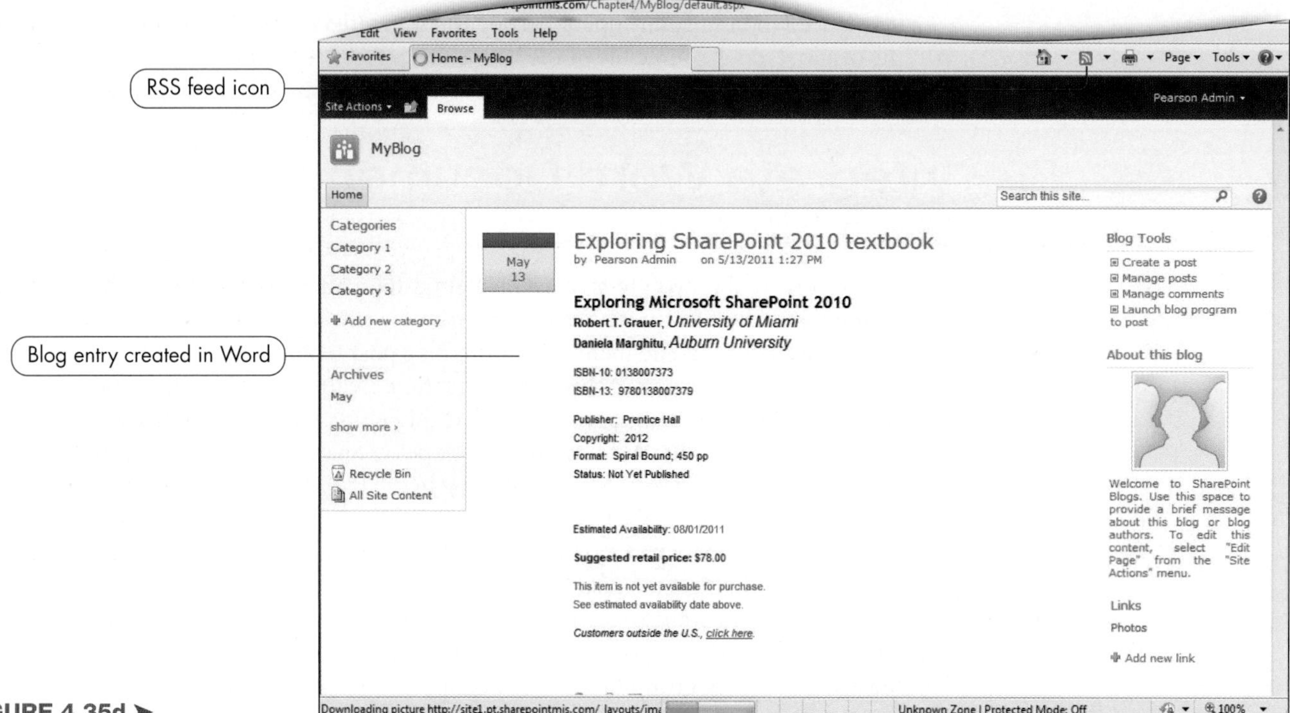

FIGURE 4.35d ➤

TIP SharePoint Blog Sites RSS Feeds

By default, RSS feeds are enabled for SharePoint blog sites. When the RSS feed icon is orange, as shown in Figure 4.35d, users can subscribe to this RSS feed.

If the SharePoint Blog site has Categories, click Insert Category in the Blog group on the Blog Post tab to display a Category list enabling you to select the category for your posting, as shown in Figure 4.36. If you click Manage Accounts in the Blog group, a Blog Account dialog box will be displayed enabling you to add new, change, or remove an account, as shown in Figure 4.36.

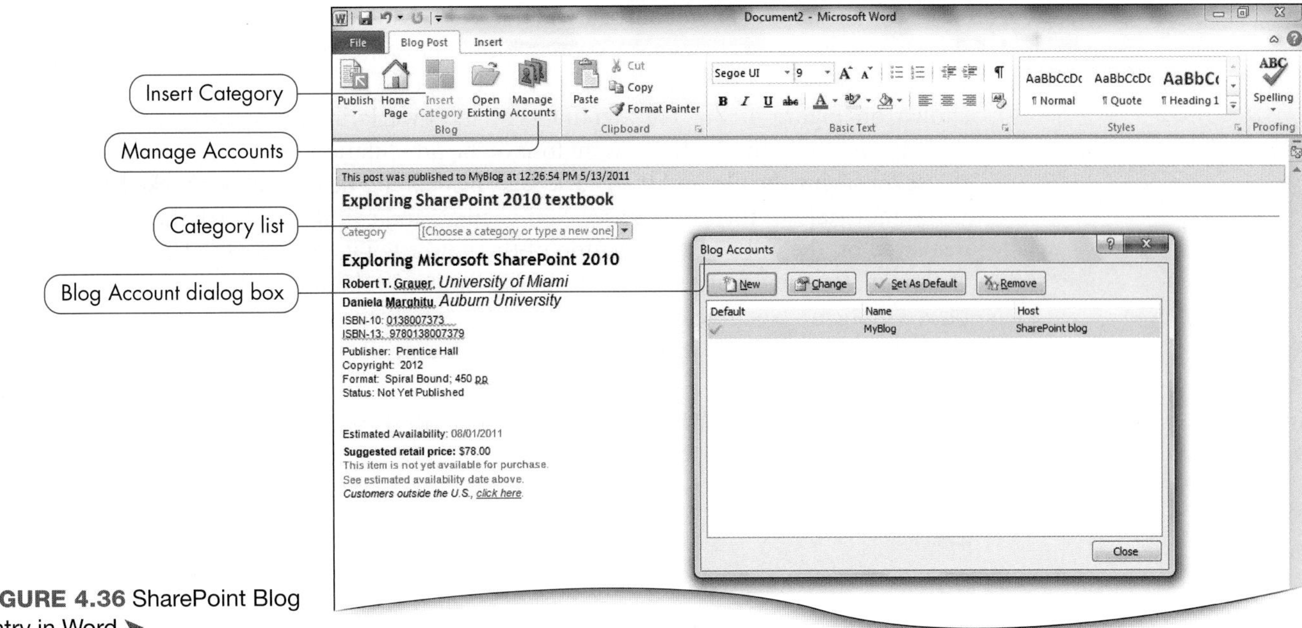

FIGURE 4.36 SharePoint Blog Entry in Word ➤

Working with PowerPoint 2010 Documents

PowerPoint is another popular Microsoft Office application. It is so versatile that a nine-year-old child could use it to prepare a show-and-tell school presentation, a PhD candidate could use it to prepare his or her thesis dissertation, or a corporate CEO could use it to prepare a company's annual report. You can make PowerPoint slides or an entire presentation available to users of SharePoint sites. PowerPoint enables you to save a whole presentation to a SharePoint Documents library or to publish slides, as individual PowerPoint files, into a SharePoint Documents Library. You can also add a link to a PowerPoint presentation.

The Save & Send tab of the PowerPoint Backstage view enables you to either save an entire presentation to a SharePoint library using the Save to SharePoint command, or to publish slides from a presentations, using the Publish Slides command, as shown in Figure 4.37.

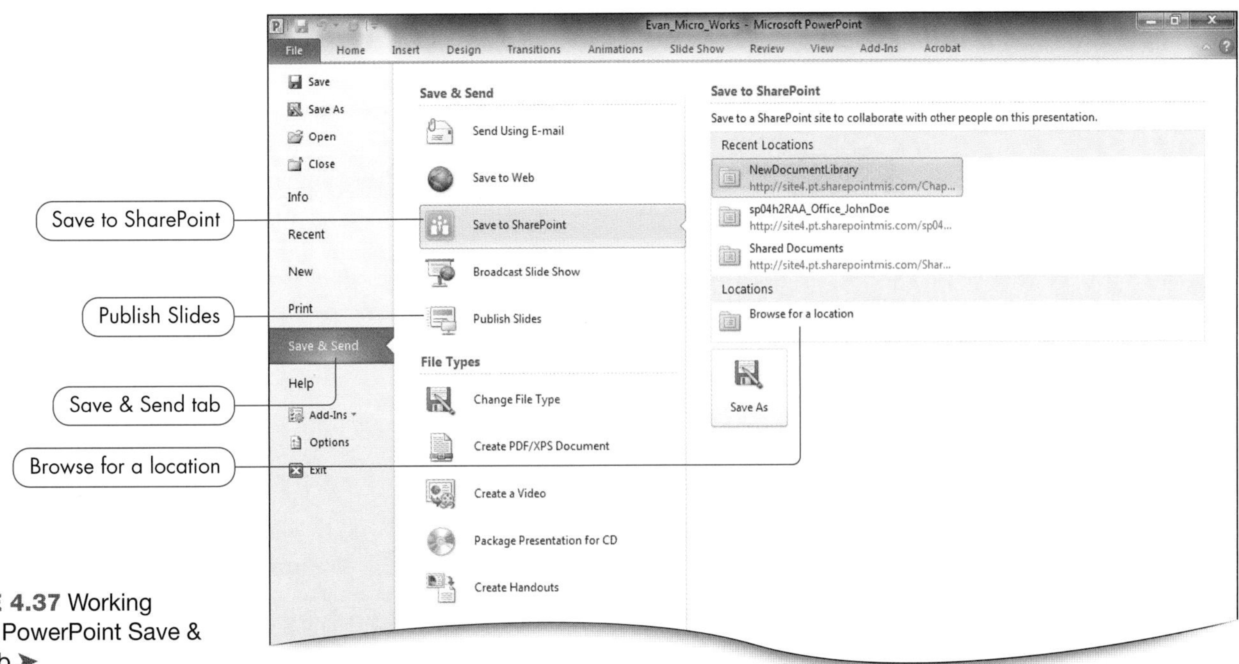

FIGURE 4.37 Working with the PowerPoint Save & Send Tab ➤

Click the Save to SharePoint command, and double-click Browse for a Location to open the Save As dialog box that enables you to locate the SharePoint Documents Library in which you want to save the presentation. You will also specify the type of file in this dialog box, as shown on Figure 4.38a. The default type is PowerPoint Presentation. Browse for the SharePoint library in which you want to save the presentation, select the type of file you want to use for saving the file, and then click Save. By default, the file will be checked out to you. If you want to allow other users to see your changes and edit the file, click the *Check in* button displayed on the yellow bar at the top of the Power Point workspace. Click OK on the Edit Offline dialog box in order to allow editing offline in the file. The presentation file is displayed in the All Documents page of the destination library, as shown in Figure 4.38b. If you click the name of the presentation, the corresponding file will open in PowerPoint.

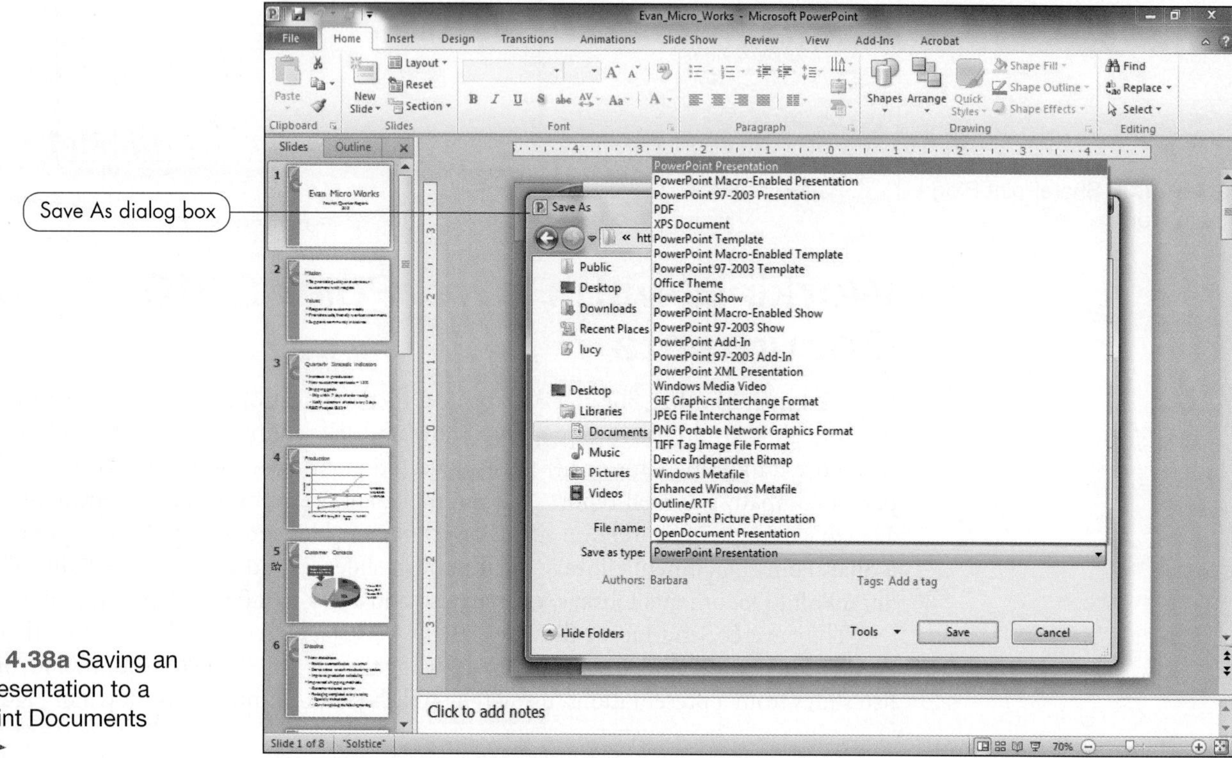

FIGURE 4.38a Saving an Entire Presentation to a SharePoint Documents Library ➤

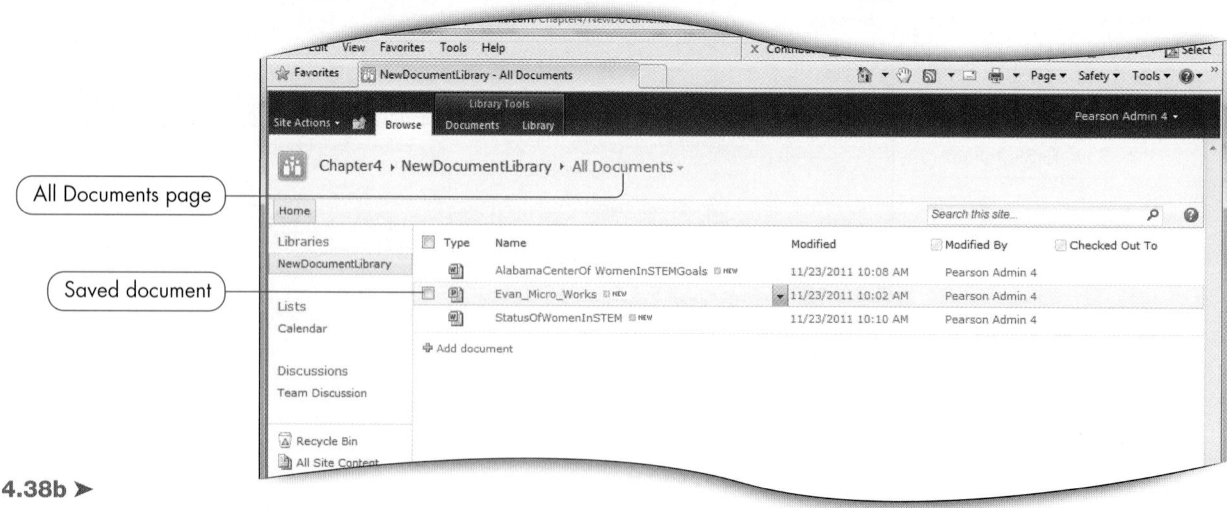

FIGURE 4.38b ➤

You can publish all slides or selected slides from a presentation as individual PowerPoint files, using the Publish Slides command. It is wise to create a dedicated folder, within the destination library, for slides included in the same presentation. You can also create topic-based folders in which you can publish slides from different presentations that have the same main topic; this way, you will be able to easily find these slides and use them for other future presentations. In the example for Figure 4.38, a folder was created for slides that focus on Degas, an impressionist painter. Only this set of slides is published in the folder.

To display the Publish Slides dialog box, click the Publish Slides command, and then click Publish Slides, as shown in Figure 4.39a. Click Browse to display the Select a Slide Library dialog box that will enables you to locate the library where you wish to publish the slides. Click Select All if you wish to publish all slides or click the check boxes placed to the right of the slides you want to publish. Click Publish. The slides are displayed in the destination library and folder. Navigate to the location to see the selected slides, as shown in Figure 4.39b. If you click the name of each presentation (corresponding to one slide), its corresponding file will open in a separate PowerPoint window, as shown in Figure 4.39c.

FIGURE 4.39a Publishing Selected Slides as Individual PowerPoint Files to a SharePoint Document Library ➤

FIGURE 4.39b ➤

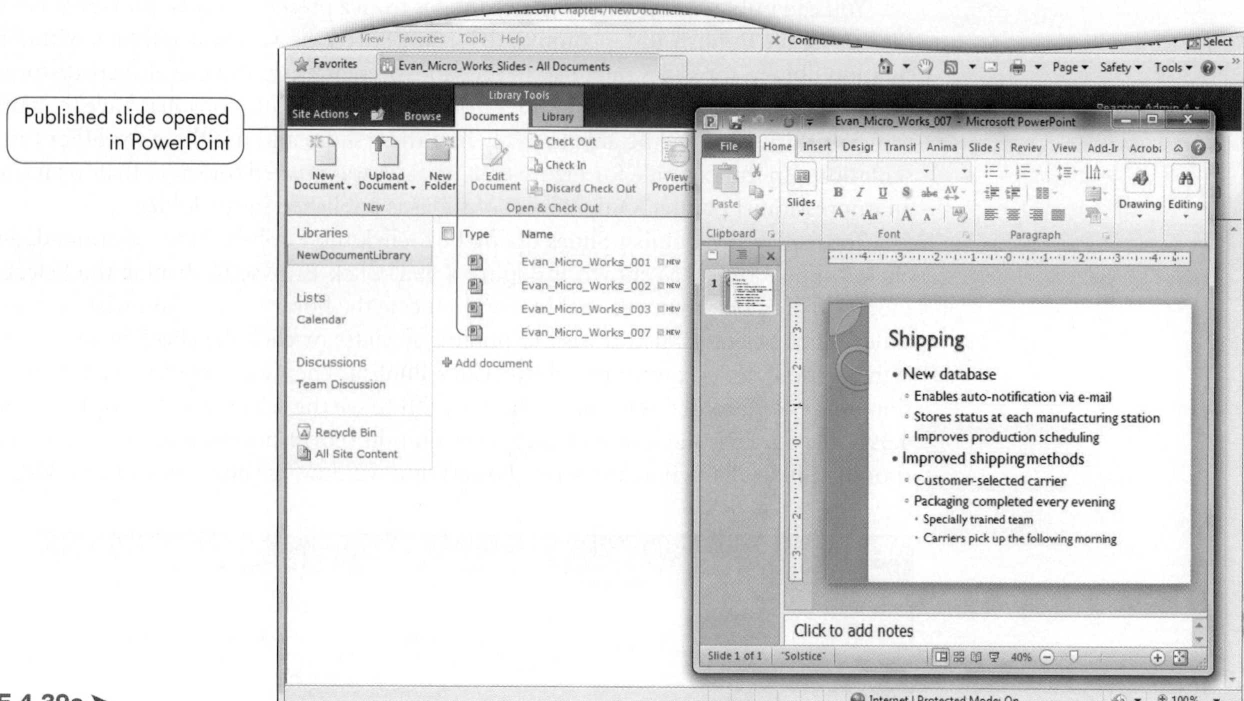

FIGURE 4.39c ➤

To further work with the individual slides, point to the name of the slide you want to work with, and click the arrow that is displayed to the right of the name. Click this arrow to display the item menu, as shown in Figure 4.40a.

You can easily move a published slide from one library to another using the Windows Explorer view of the library. Click Open with Explorer in the Connect & Export group on the Library Tools Library tab, to display the Windows Explorer view of the library, shown in Figure 4.40b. Right-click the name of the PowerPoint slide, select Copy, and then navigate to the destination library and folder and paste it there by pressing Ctrl+V.

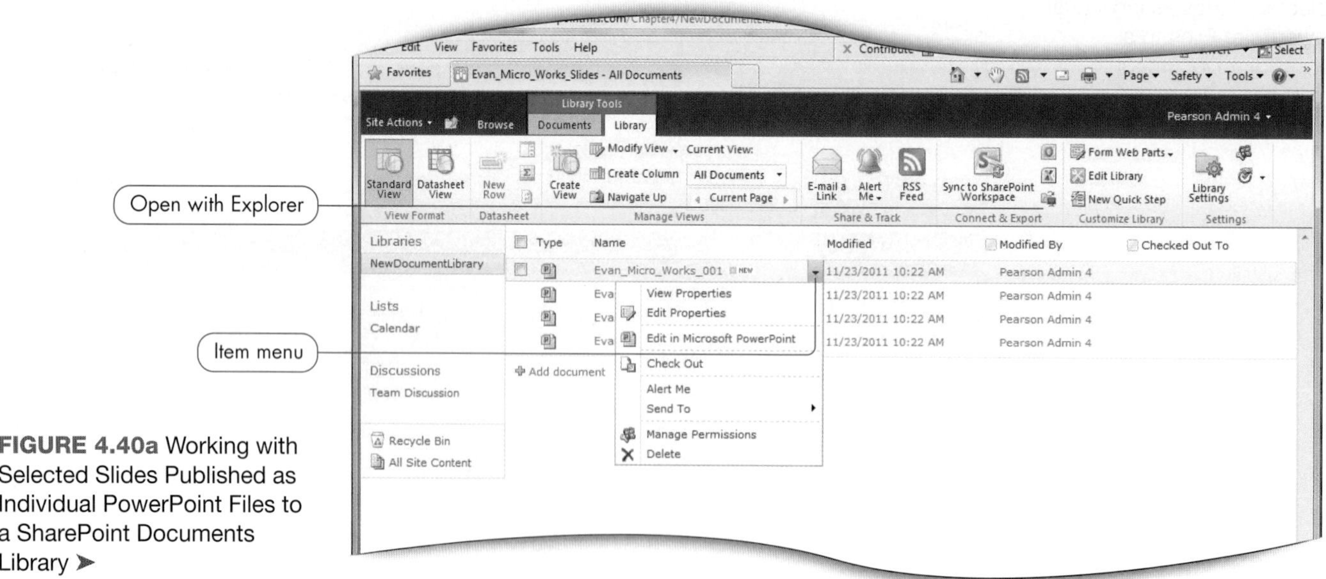

FIGURE 4.40a Working with Selected Slides Published as Individual PowerPoint Files to a SharePoint Documents Library ➤

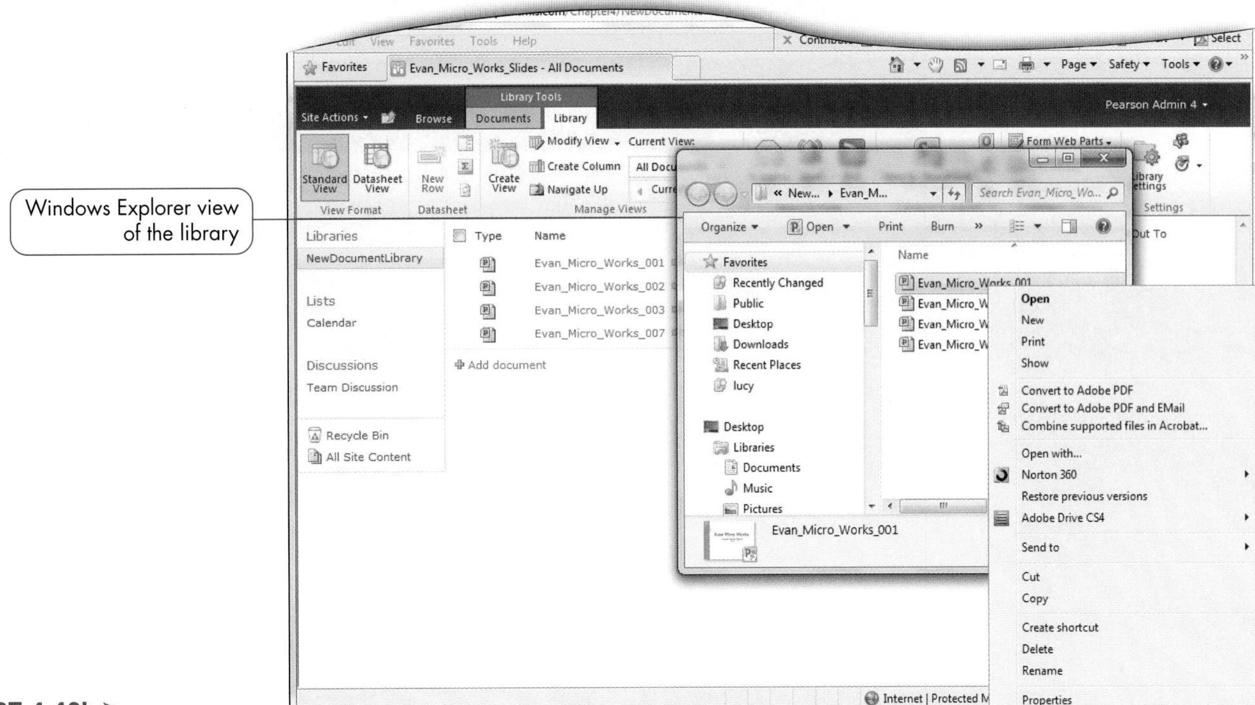

FIGURE 4.40b ➤

TIP SharePoint Server Slide Library

If you have access to a SharePoint server, you can publish presentation slides in a specialized Slide Library. For each published slide in the Slide Library, a thumbnail image is created, as shown in Figure 4.41a. If you click on the thumbnail image for a slide, a View tab is displayed, enabling you to further work with the slide, as shown in Figure 4.41b. If you click on the name of the slide, the file is opened in the Microsoft PowerPoint Web App, as shown in Figure 4.41c.

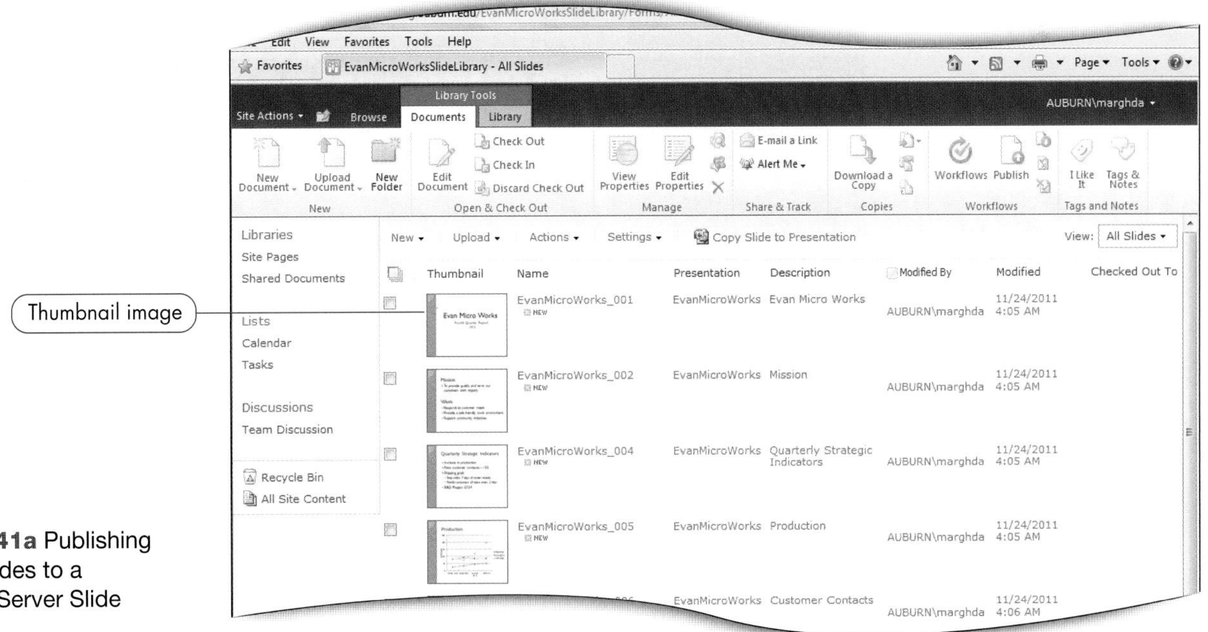

FIGURE 4.41a Publishing Selected Slides to a SharePoint Server Slide Library ➤

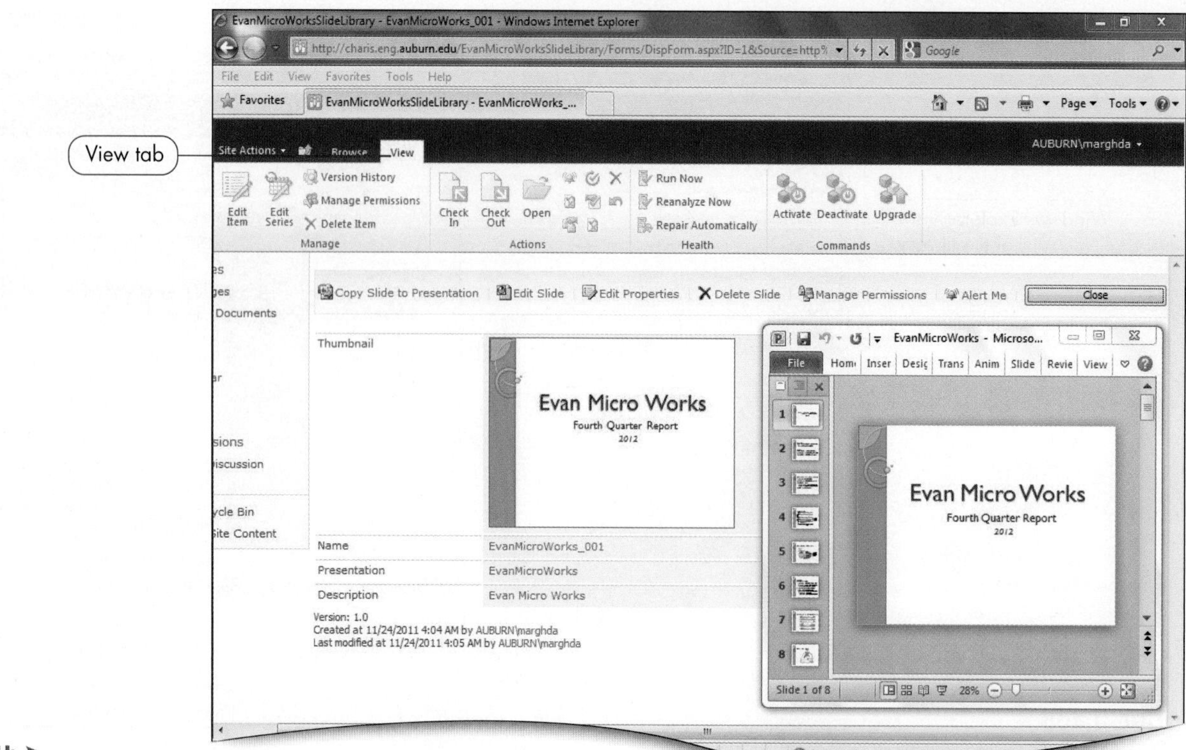

FIGURE 4.41b ➤

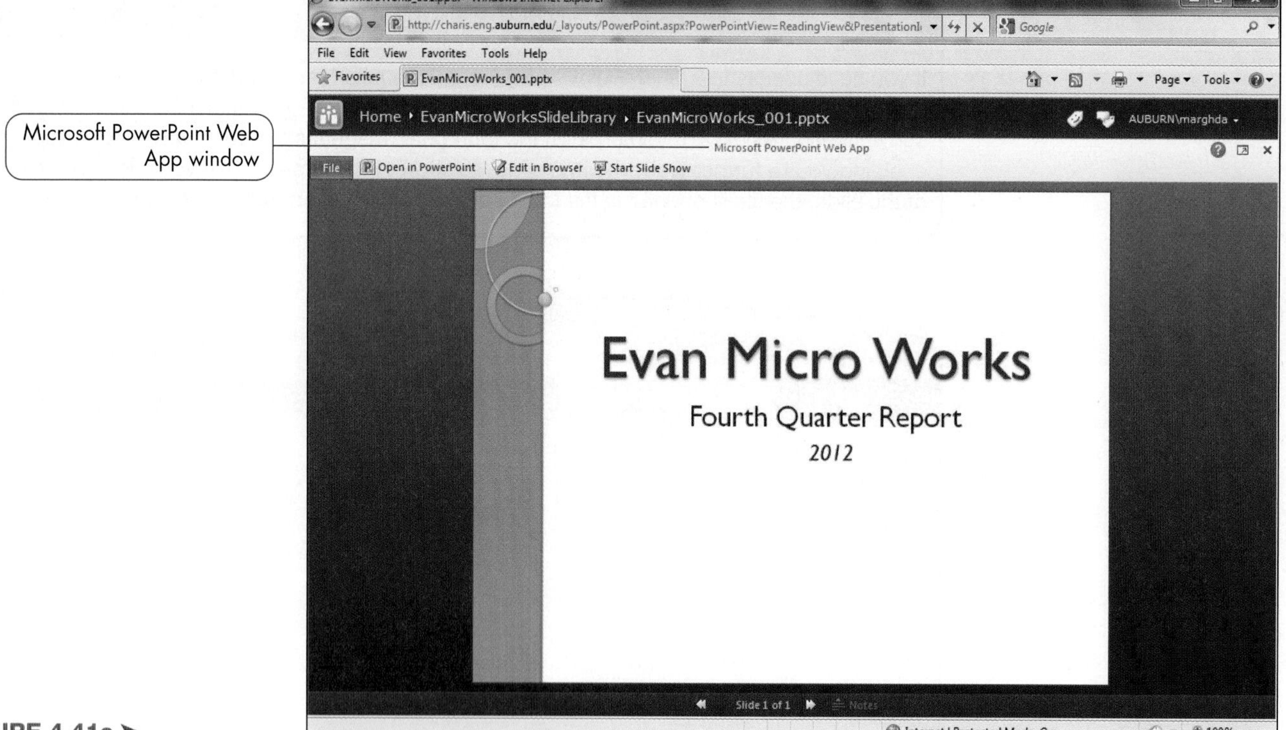

FIGURE 4.41c ➤

You can add a link to a PowerPoint presentation (saved in original PowerPoint format (.pptx) or PowerPoint Slideshow (.ppsx)) on a SharePoint page using SharePoint Designer. Position the insertion point in the location where you want to add the link, and click Hyperlinks in the Links group to open the Insert Hyperlink dialog box, shown in Figure 4.42a. Navigate to the presentation file, click its name, and then click OK. Save the page, and then click Preview in Browser in the Preview group on the Home tab. Click the link; the linked PowerPoint file will open in PowerPoint, as shown in Figure 4.42b.

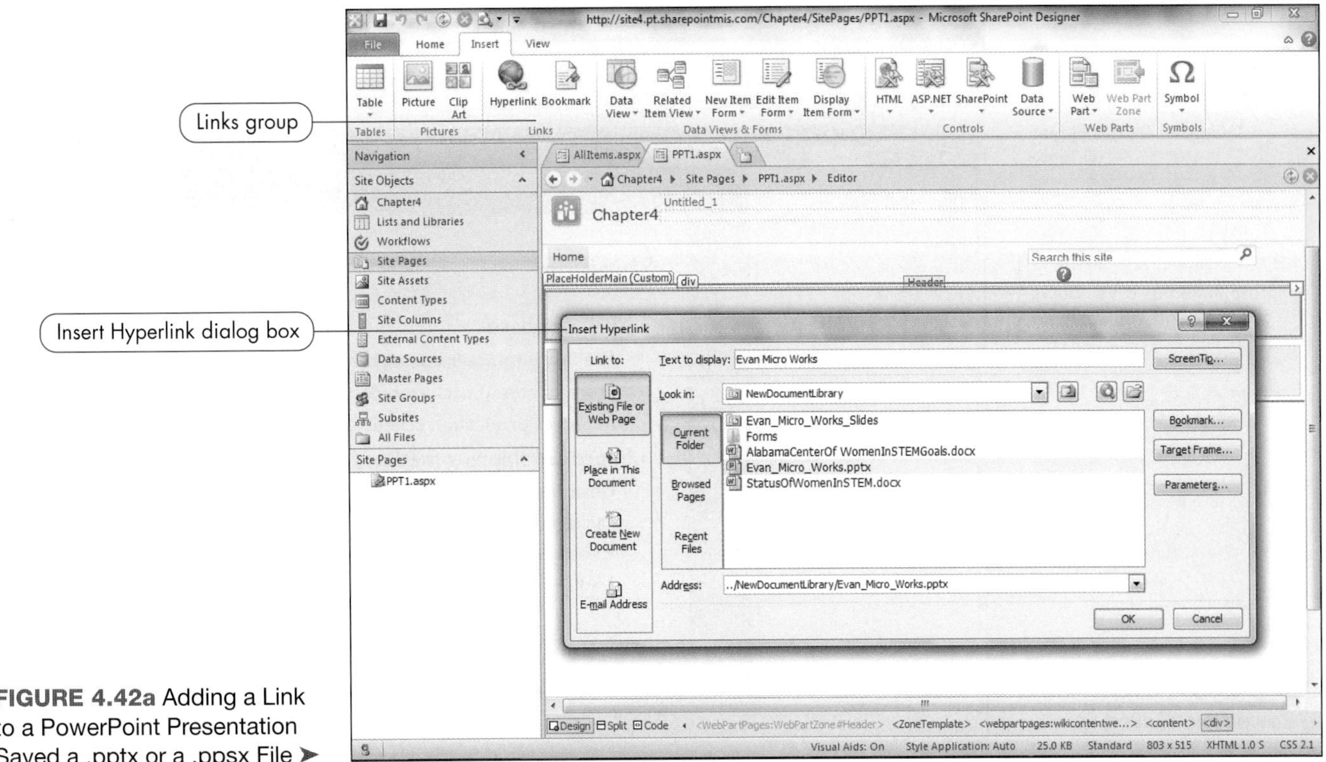

FIGURE 4.42a Adding a Link to a PowerPoint Presentation Saved a .pptx or a .ppsx File ➤

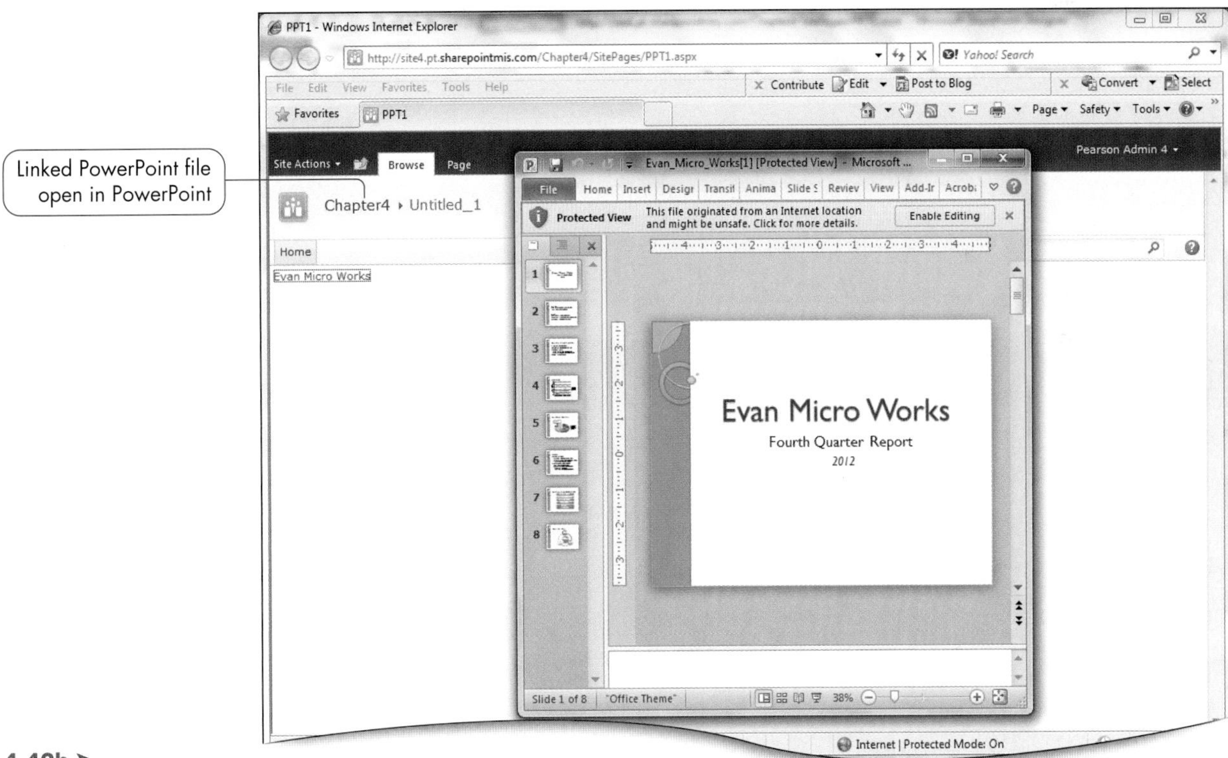

FIGURE 4.42b ➤

You can also save a PowerPoint presentation as a Windows Media Video (.wmv) file, retaining the animations, narrations, and other multimedia elements. You can then upload the file into a SharePoint Assets library and add a link on a Web page. When you click the link, a window of the Windows Media Player will be displayed, enabling the user to play the .wmv video file, as shown in Figure 4.43.

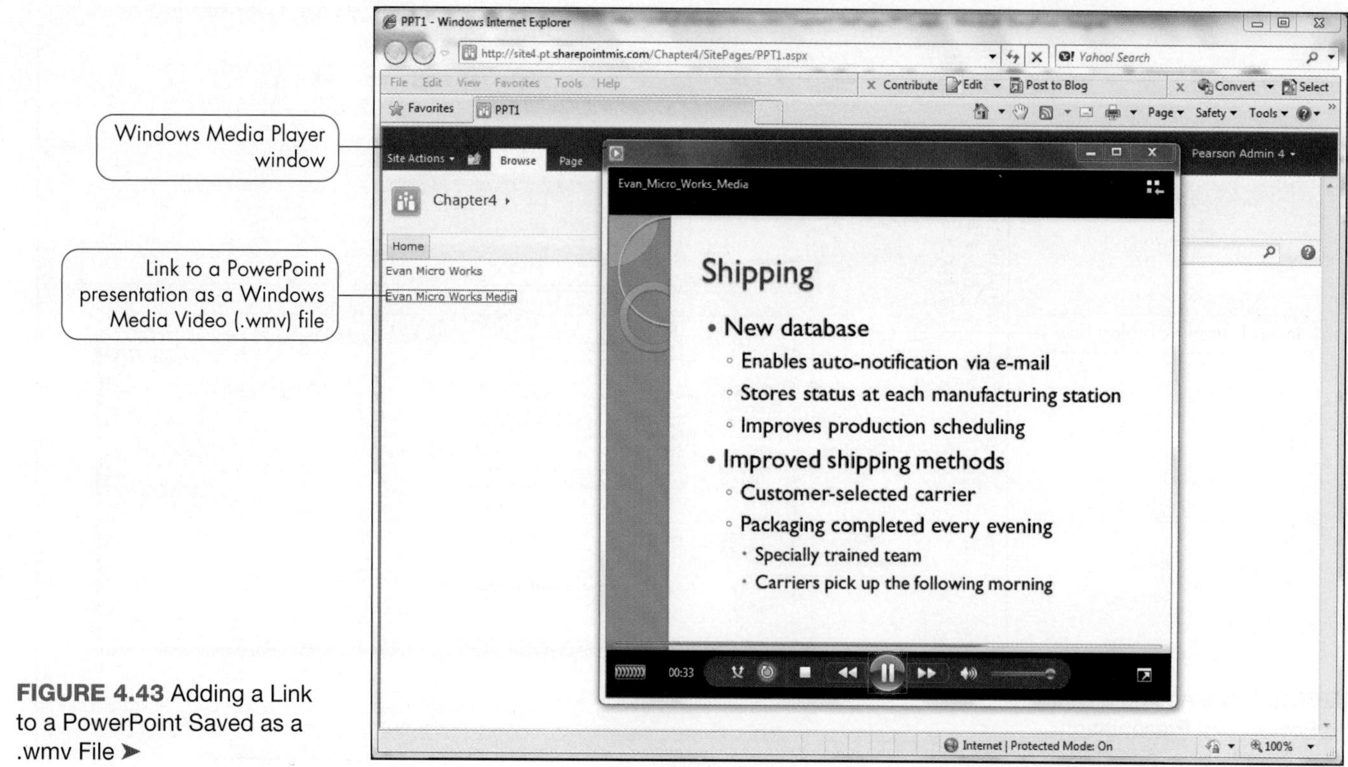

FIGURE 4.43 Adding a Link to a PowerPoint Saved as a .wmv File ➤

2 Integration of Word and PowerPoint 2010 Files with SharePoint Foundation Sites

The RAA portal is built on a SharePoint Foundation server, so you want to take full advantage of all the powerful built-in components for implementing all the portal functionalities. You have many Word and PowerPoint documents that will need to be included in the RAA portal pages and you also need to create a Blog site where you can easily integrate content from Word documents. You will open, save, and edit Microsoft documents to a SharePoint Document library. You will add Word documents to a SharePoint site. You will integrate Word documents with Blog sites. You will integrate PowerPoint documents into a Team site and Blog site.

Skills covered: Open, Save, and Edit Microsoft Documents from a SharePoint Document Library • Add Word Documents to a SharePoint Site • Integrate Word Documents with Blog Sites • Work with PowerPoint Documents

STEP 1 OPEN, SAVE, AND EDIT MICROSOFT DOCUMENTS FROM A SHAREPOINT DOCUMENT LIBRARY

Before you start integrating Microsoft Office documents into your portal, you will learn how to open, save, and edit Microsoft Office documents included in SharePoint libraries. Refer to Figure 4.44 as you complete Step 1.

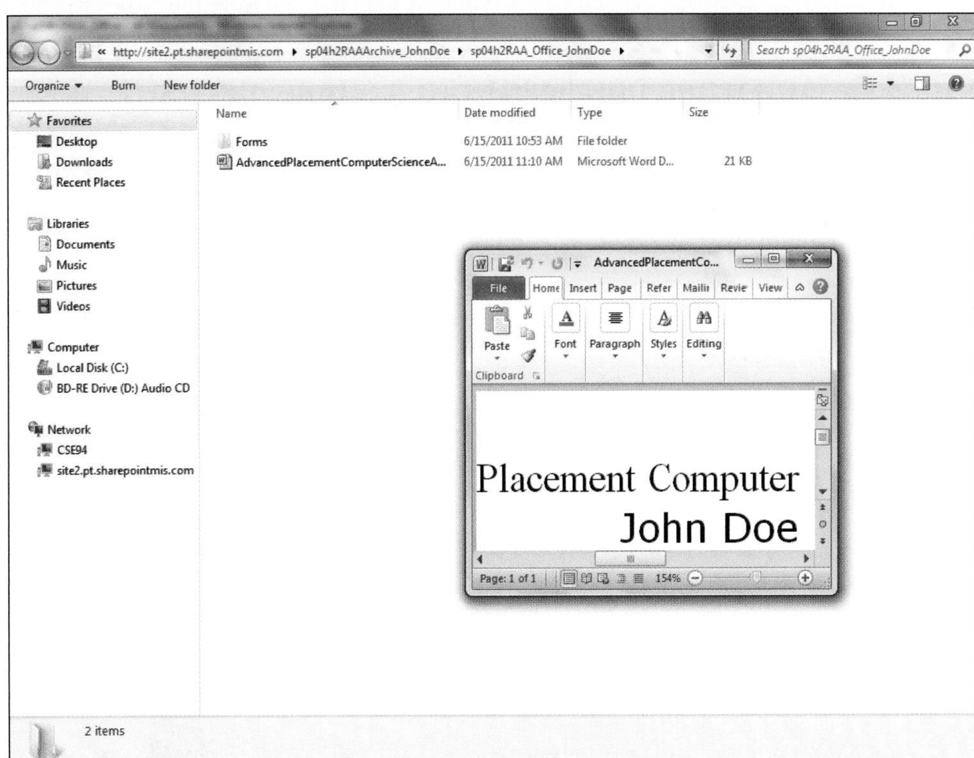

FIGURE 4.44 Open, Save and Edit Microsoft Documents from a SharePoint Document Library ➤

a. Click **Start** to display the Start menu. Click **All Programs**, and then click **Internet Explorer** to open the program. Go to the top-level site provided by your instructor which will be in the format of *http://pt.sharepointmis.com/SitePages/yourname.* Enter the user name and password provided by your instructor.

b. Use the *sp04h2RAAArchive.wsp* solution file from your Exploring folder to create a *sp04h2RAAArchive_LastNameFirstName* subsite.

   The *sp04h2RAAArchive LastNameFirstName* site is now displayed in the browser and the name of the *sp04h2RAA_Office* document library appears on the Quick Launch.

c. Click **sp04h2RAA_Office** on the Quick Launch. Click the URL of the *sp04h2RAA_Office* library in the browser Address bar, right-click, and then click **Copy**.

d. Click **Start** to display the Start menu. Click **All Programs**, and then click **Microsoft Word** to open the program. Click the **File tab** to open the Backstage view, and then click **Open** to display the Microsoft Word Open dialog box.

e. Right-click in the **File name box**, and then click **Paste**. Remove from the URL */Forms/AllItems.aspx*. Click **Open**. Click the **AdvancedPlacementComputerScienceACourses name** of the Word document displayed in the Open dialog box, and then click **Open**.

   The Word document is now displayed in the Microsoft Word window.

TROUBLESHOOTING: Enable Editing if necessary.

f. Type your name under the title of the document, and then click **Save** on the Quick Access toolbar.

g. Close the Word window, activate the browser window, click the **Library Tools–Library tab**, and then click **Open with Explorer** in the Connect & Export group.

   The *sp04h2RAA_Office* document library is now displayed in Windows window.

h. Double-click the **AdvancedPlacementComputerScienceACourses name** of the Word document. The Word document is now displayed in Word window. Click the **Restore Down button**.

   Your screen should now look similar to Figure 4.44.

i. Close the Windows Explorer and leave the browser window and the Word window open for the following step.

STEP 2 ADD WORD DOCUMENTS TO A SHAREPOINT SITE

Very often you will need to save your Word documents, especially for sharing purposes, as PDF files. You will save a .docx file as a .pdf file, and then upload it to in the SharePoint document library. Then, you will open the .pdf file using the SharePoint Foundation Web interface and SharePoint Designer. Refer to Figure 4.45 as you complete Step 2.

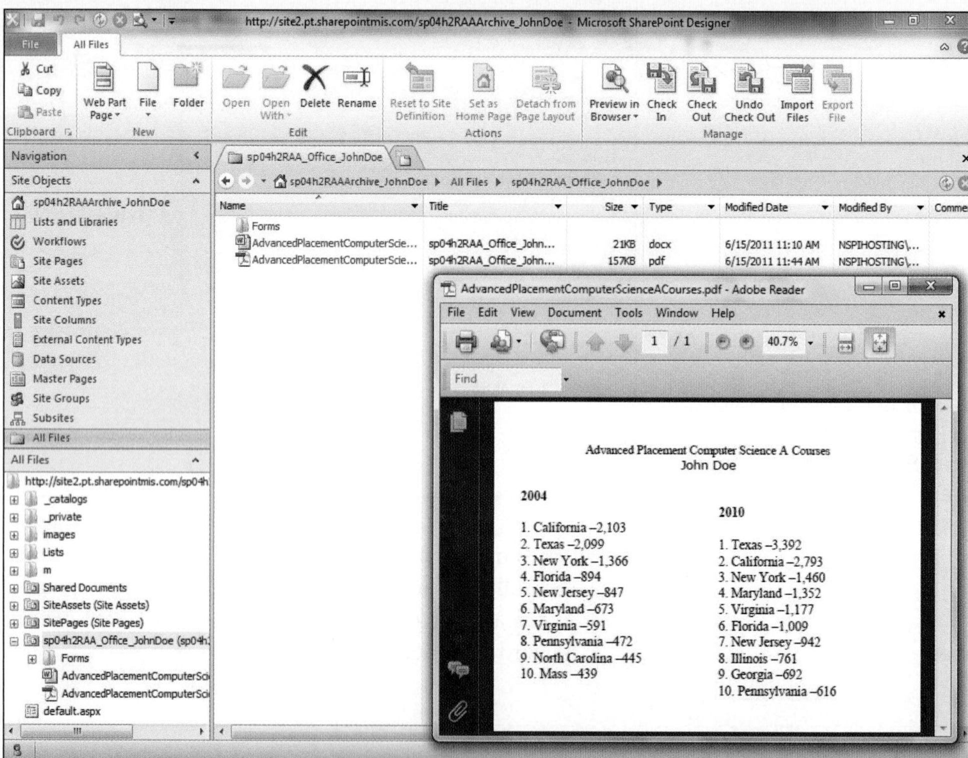

FIGURE 4.45 Add Documents to a SharePoint Site ➤

a. Click the **File tab** to open the Word Backstage view, and then click **Save As** to display the Microsoft Save As dialog box. Select the **PDF format** in the Save as type box, and then click **Save.**

   The Saving dialog box displays while the file is saved.

b. Click **Cancel** in the File Download dialog box to display the Save As dialog box.

c. Click **Refresh** in the browser window.

   The name of the .pdf file is now displayed in the All Documents page.

d. Click **Edit in SharePoint Designer** on the Site Actions menu. Type your password in the **Windows Security dialog box**, and then click **OK.**

   The *sp04h2RAAArchive_ LastNameFirstName* subsite is now open in SharePoint Designer.

e. Click **All Files** on the Navigation Pane. Click **sp04h2RAA_OfficeJohnDoe**. Right-click the name of the .pdf file, click **Open With**, and then select **Adobe Reader.**

   The .pdf file is now displayed in the Adobe Reader window.

f. Click the **Restore Down button.** Your screen should now look similar to Figure 4.45.

g. Close the Adobe Reader window and the SharePoint Designer window. Leave the Word window open for the next step.

STEP 3 INTEGRATE WORD DOCUMENTS WITH BLOG SITES

Your RAA portal will include several dedicated blog sites. One of them will be for K12 teachers. For the RAA staff, it will be much easier if they can create new blog entries in Word, and then post them on the blog site. You will create a new blog site. You will create in Word a blog entry, and then you will publish the new entry on the new blog site. Refer to Figure 4.46 as you complete Step 3.

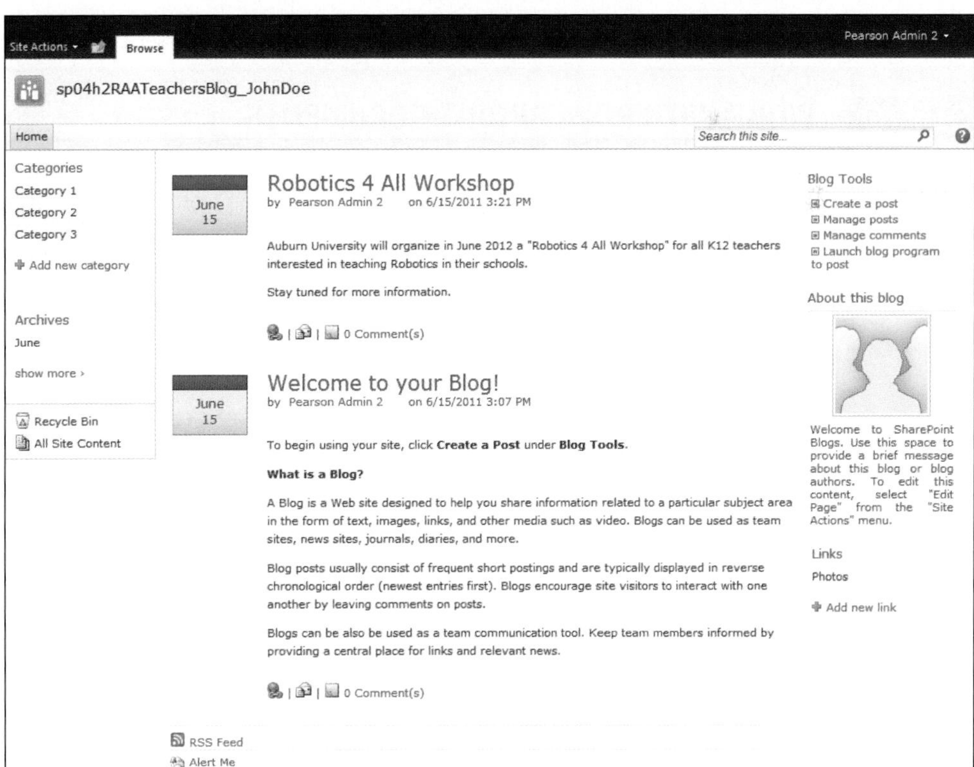

FIGURE 4.46 Integrate Word Documents with Blog Sites ➤

a. Activate the browser window, click the **Navigate Up button**, and then select the **sp04h2RAAArchive_LastNameFirstName site.**

b. Create a *sp04h2RAATeachersBlog_LastNameFirstName* blog subsite. Display the site on the Quick Launch of the *sp04h2RAAArchive_LastNameFirstName* site. Copy the URL of the new subsite from the browser Address box.

   The home page of the *sp04h2RAATeachersBlog_LastNameFirstName* blog subsite is now displayed in browser.

c. Activate the Word window, click the **File tab**, and then click **New** in the Backstage view.

TROUBLESHOOTING: Click Cancel in the Register the Blog Account dialog box if necessary.

d. Click **Blog post** in the *Available Templates* section, and then click **Create.**

   A Document 1 is open now and the Blog Post tab is displayed.

e. Click the **Enter Post Title Here text**, and then type **Robotics 4 All Workshop.** Place the insertion point below the horizontal line, and then type **Auburn University will organize in June 2012 a "Robotics 4 All Workshop" for all K12 teachers interested in teaching Robotics in their schools. Stay tuned for more information!**

f. Click **Manage Accounts** in the blog group, and then click **Change** in the Blog Accounts dialog box. Paste the URL of the *sp04h2RAATeachersBlog_LastNameFirstName* blog subsite in the Blog URL box, and then click **OK.** Click **Yes** in the Microsoft alert box. Click **Close** to close the Blog Accounts dialog box.

g. Click **Publish** in the Blog group. Click **Yes** in the Microsoft alert box. Type your password in the **Windows security Alert box.**

h. Activate the browser window, and then click **Refresh.** Your screen should look similar to Figure 4.46.

i. Close all Word windows and exit the browser application.

STEP 4 WORK WITH POWERPOINT DOCUMENTS

You will certainly need to disseminate, via your portal, RAA presentations delivered as PowerPoint files. You will also need to reuse slides from previous presentations in future presentations. You will publish selected slides from an RAA presentation as individual PowerPoint files. You will save an RAA PowerPoint presentation as a Windows Media file and add a link to a page to this file so the portal users can easily view it. Refer to Figure 4.47 as you complete Step 4.

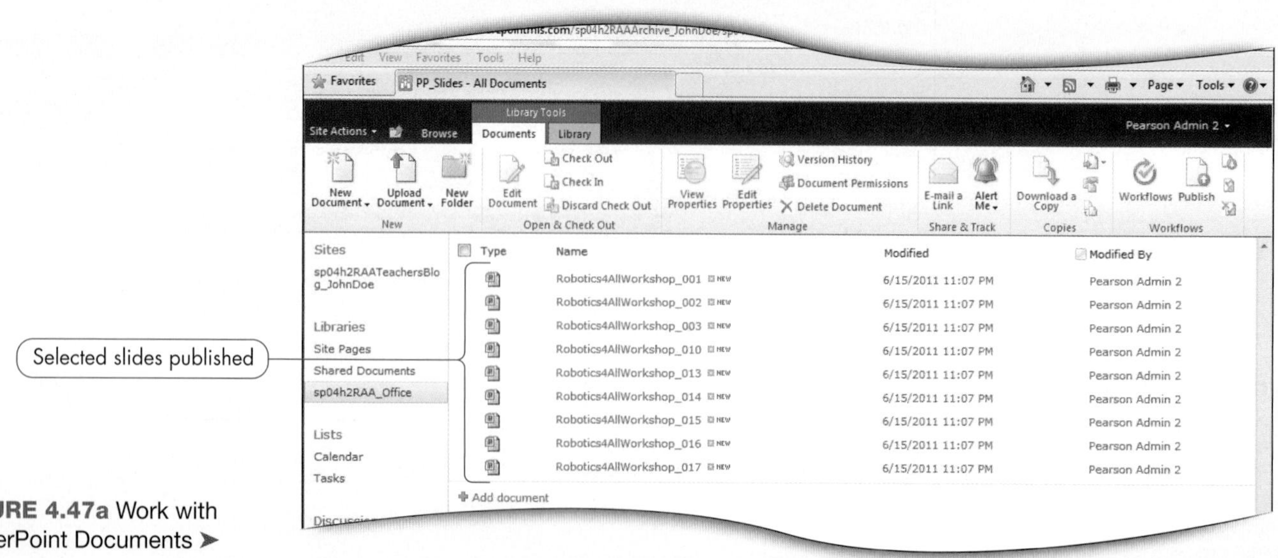

FIGURE 4.47a Work with PowerPoint Documents ➤

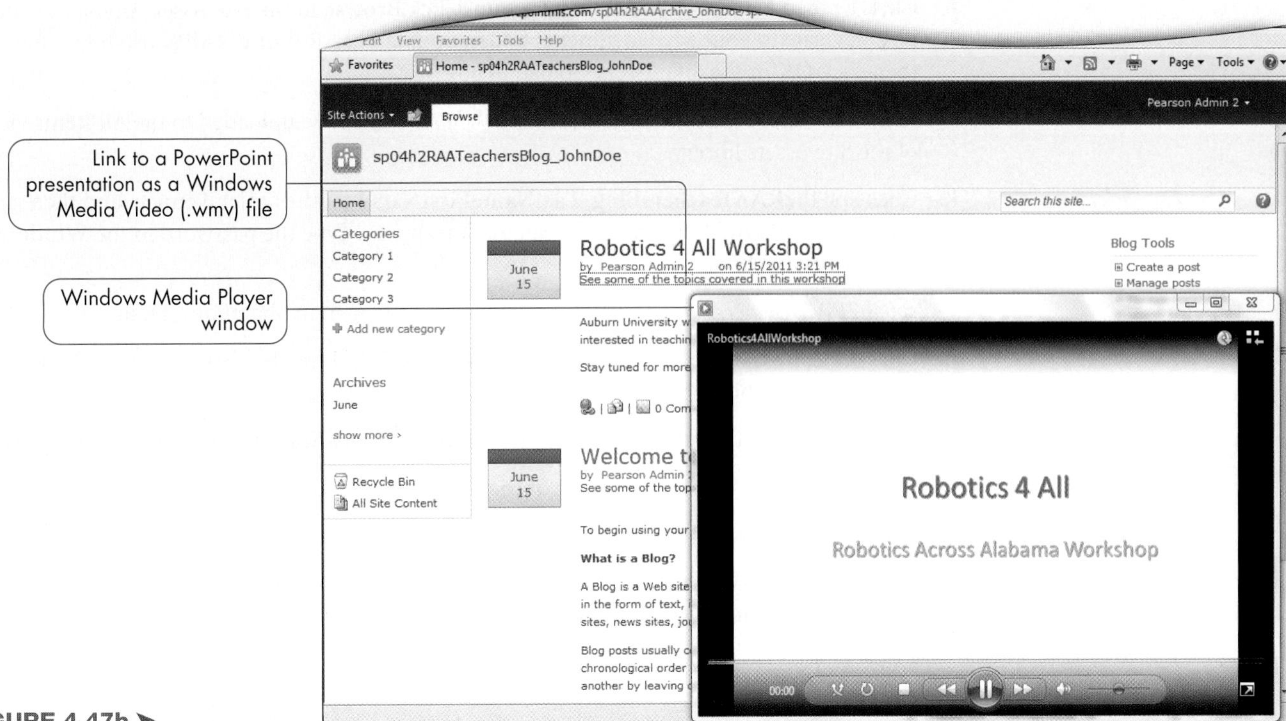

FIGURE 4.47b ➤

a. Click the **Navigate Up button**, and then select the **sp04h2RAAArchive_LastNameFirstName site**. Click **sp04h2RAA_Office** in Quick Launch.

b. Click the **Library Tools–Documents tab**, and then create a new *PP_Slides* folder in the *sp04h2RAA_Office* library. Double-click **PP_Slides** on the All Documents page.

c. Click **Start** to display the Start menu. Click **All Programs**, and then click **Microsoft PowerPoint** to open the program. Open the *Robotics4AllWorkshop* file from your Exploring folder.

d. Click the **File tab**, click **Save & Send** on the PowerPoint Backstage view, click **Publish Slides** in the *Save & Send* section, and then click **Publish Slides**.

   The Publish Slides dialog box is now displayed.

e. Click **Select All**, and then type the URL of the *PP_Slides* folder (*sp04h2RAA_Office library/PP_Slides*) in the **Publish to box**. Click **Publish**.

TROUBLESHOOTING: It takes a few moments to load the files onto the server.

f. Activate the browser window, and then click **Refresh**. Your screen should now look similar to Figure 4.47a.

g. Activate the PowerPoint window, click the **File tab**, and then click **Save As**.

   The PowerPoint Save As dialog box is now displayed.

h. Click **Windows Media Video** in the *Save as type* list, and then navigate to your My Documents folder. Click **Save**.

   Robotics4AllWorkshop.wmv is now saved in your My Documents folder.

i. Activate the browser window, click **Libraries** in the Quick Launch, click **Site Assets** under the Document Libraries of the All Site Content page, and then click the **Library Tools–Documents tab**.

   The Library Tools–Documents tab is now displayed.

j. Click **Upload Document** in the New group. Click **Browse** in the Site Assets Upload dialog box, navigate to your My Documents folder, double-click **Robotics4AllWorkshop.wmv**, and then click **OK** in the Site Assets Upload dialog box.

   After a few moments, the *Robotics4AllWorkshop.wmv* is now uploaded to the All Items view of the Site Assets library.

k. Click **sp04h2RAATeachersBlog_LastNameFirstName** on the Quick Launch, and then click **Edit** in SharePoint Designer on the Site Actions menu. Type the password in the **Windows Security dialog box.**

   sp04h2RAATeachersBlog_LastNameFirstName is now open in SharePoint Designer.

l. Click **Edit site home page** in the *Customization* section. Type the password in the **Windows Security dialog box.**

   The home page of *sp04h2RAATeachersBlog_LastNameFirstName* is now open in Editor mode.

m. Position your cursor below the title of the first post.

   A <div> tag is now selected.

n. Click the **Insert tab**, and then click **Hyperlink** in the Links group. Type **See some of the topics that will be covered in this workshop** in the **Text to display box**. Type **../SiteAssets/Robotics4AllWorkshop.wmv** in the **Address box**, and then click **OK**. Click **Save** in the Quick Access Toolbar.

o. Click the **Home tab**, and then click **Preview in Browser** in the Preview group.

   The home page of *sp04h2RAATeachersBlog_LastNameFirstName* is now displayed in browser.

p. Click **See some of the topics that will be covered in this workshop**.

   Robotics4AllWorkshop.wmv should play in a new Windows Media Player window, as shown in Figure 4.47b.

q. Close the browser, SharePoint Designer, and Windows Media Player windows.

Integration of Excel and Access 2010 Files in SharePoint Foundation Sites

Whereas Excel provides only one-way synchronization between SharePoint lists and Excel spreadsheets, Access empowers developers with two-way synchronization between SharePoint lists and Access databases.

SharePoint Foundation is the designated collaboration platform for the Microsoft Office suite. Excel and Access 2010 enable you to easily import data from and export data to SharePoint lists. Whereas Excel provides only one-way synchronization between SharePoint lists and Excel spreadsheets, Access empowers developers with two-way synchronization between SharePoint lists and Access databases. Access also enables developers to develop SharePoint data-driven applications.

In this section, you will learn about the different approaches you can take in order to integrate Excel and Access with SharePoint Foundation sites, from copying and pasting content to a SharePoint page, to importing and exporting data from Excel and Access files into SharePoint lists. You will also learn how you can use Access files as data sources in order to develop SharePoint data-driven applications.

Using Excel 2010 in SharePoint

Excel is one of the most in-demand Microsoft applications. Its versatility enables students from second grade through college, home and business owners, or scientists to fulfill a wide variety of tasks. With its friendly user interface and comprehensive set of features, Excel can assist you in building a spreadsheet for keeping track of your household expenses or sophisticated business and scientific statistical studies and charts.

Excel enables integration with other applications. Its capability to create documents that can be cut and pasted into a Web page, or even to create a document ready to be published on the World Wide Web, has consistently improved in the past few years. Excel 2010 enables you to export to and import data from a SharePoint list. You can also edit Excel file data offline, and then synchronize it with the SharePoint list.

Add Excel Content to a Web Page

A **spreadsheet** is the computerized version of a ledger, and consists of rows and columns of data.

A **worksheet** is a single spreadsheet consisting of a grid of columns and rows that can contain descriptive labels, numeric values, formulas, functions, and graphics.

A **workbook** is a set of related worksheets contained within a file.

A **range** is a group of adjacent or contiguous cells.

A **table** is a range that contains related data, structured to allow easy management and analysis.

You can take advantage of the Microsoft Excel and SharePoint Designer content integration features and use content created in Excel in your Web pages. A ***spreadsheet*** is the computerized version of a ledger, and consists of rows and columns of data. A ***worksheet*** is a single spreadsheet consisting of a grid of columns and rows that can contain descriptive labels, numeric values, formulas, functions, and graphics. A ***workbook*** is a set of related worksheets contained within a file. A ***range*** is a group of adjacent or contiguous cells. A ***table*** is a range that contains related data, structured to allow easy management and analysis.

The easiest way to add Excel content to a SharePoint Web page is by using traditional Copy and Paste commands. To copy and paste content from an Excel worksheet to a Web page using SharePoint Designer, use the Clipboard task pane. Launch Excel, and then open the document containing the content you want to use. Click the first cell in the cell range you want to copy and drag the mouse pointer over the remaining cells you want to select. Right-click, and then click Copy, as shown in Figure 4.48a. The selected cell range is copied to the Clipboard.

After you have copied the Excel content, launch SharePoint Designer and create a new Web page or open an existing one. Click the Task Panes arrow in the Workspace group on the View tab, and then select Clipboard on the Task Panes menu. You will see the copied content on the Clipboard task pane, as shown in Figure 4.48b. Position the insertion point in the body of the Web page where you want the Excel content to appear, click to the right of the copied content in the Clipboard task pane, and then click Paste. SharePoint Designer automatically converts the Excel content into HTML. Using the Paste Options list (see Figure 4.48b), you can format the pasted content in different ways. If you click the Keep Text Only button, the Paste Text dialog box, shown in Figure 4.48c, opens.

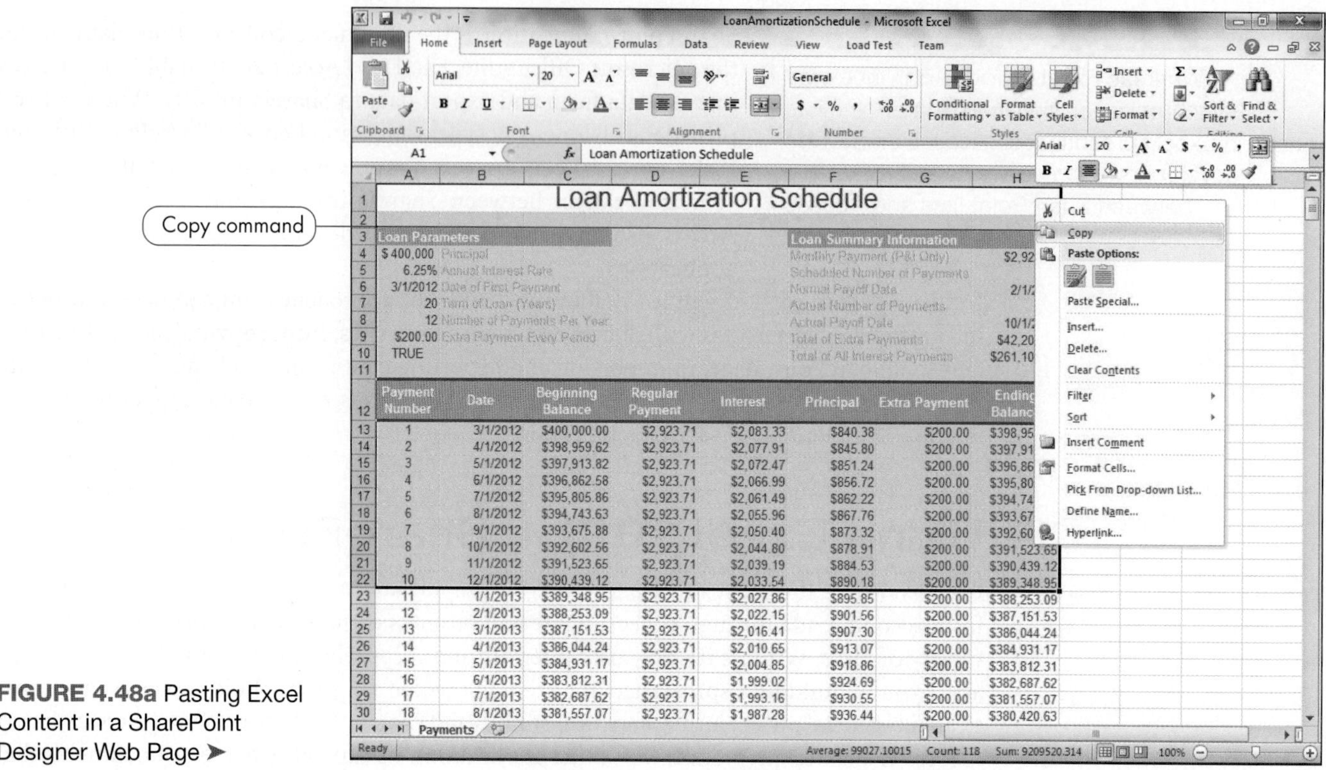

FIGURE 4.48a Pasting Excel Content in a SharePoint Designer Web Page ➤

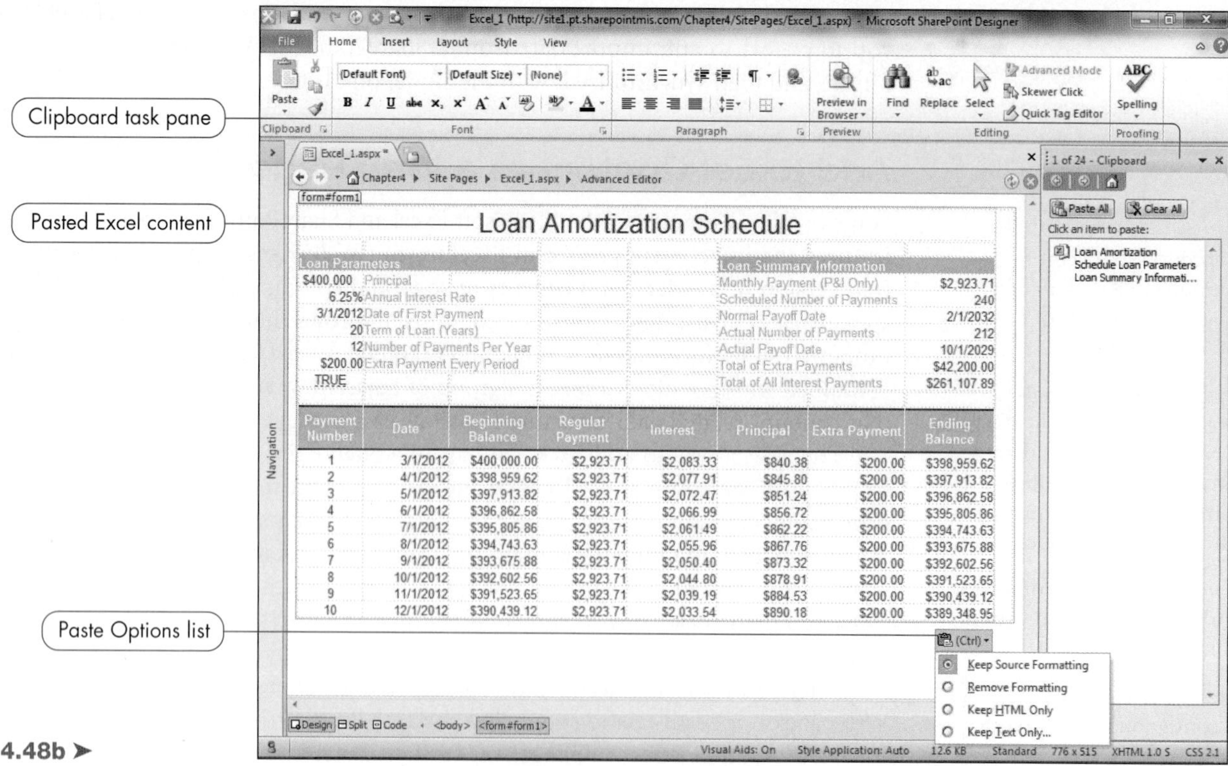

FIGURE 4.48b ➤

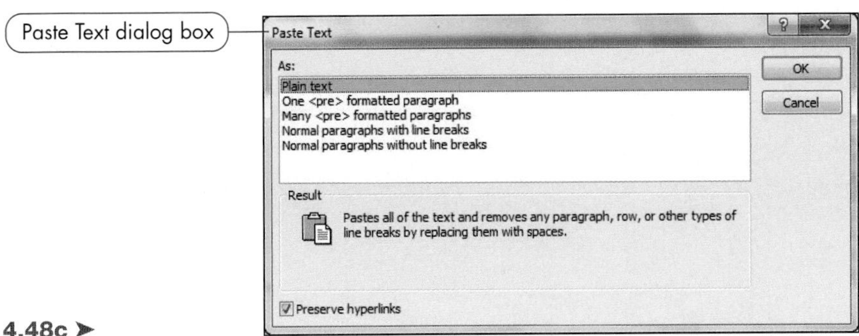

FIGURE 4.48c ➤

REFERENCE Paste Options

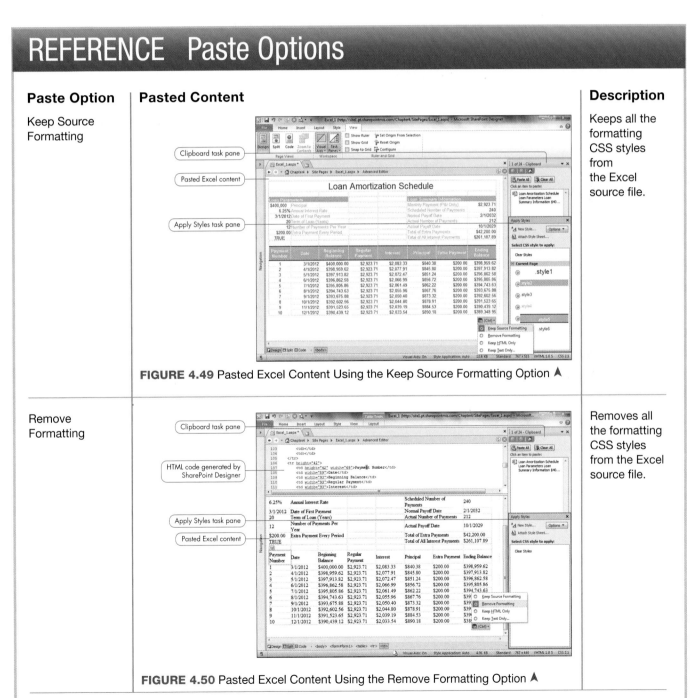

Paste Option	Pasted Content	Description
Keep Source Formatting	Clipboard task pane Pasted Excel content Apply Styles task pane **FIGURE 4.49** Pasted Excel Content Using the Keep Source Formatting Option ▲	Keeps all the formatting CSS styles from the Excel source file.
Remove Formatting	Clipboard task pane HTML code generated by SharePoint Designer Apply Styles task pane Pasted Excel content **FIGURE 4.50** Pasted Excel Content Using the Remove Formatting Option ▲	Removes all the formatting CSS styles from the Excel source file.

(Continued)

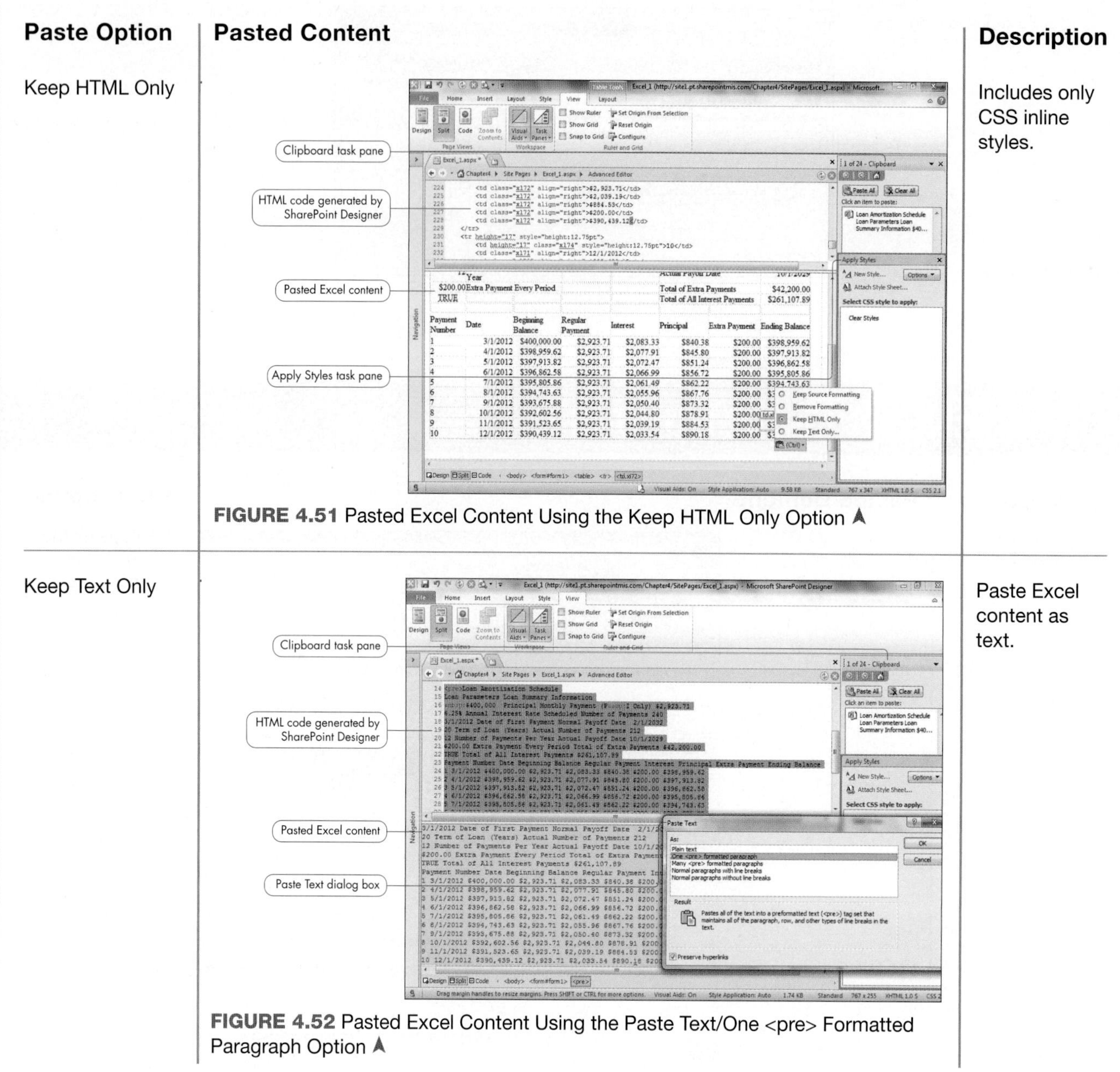

Paste Option	Pasted Content	Description
Keep HTML Only	**FIGURE 4.51** Pasted Excel Content Using the Keep HTML Only Option	Includes only CSS inline styles.
Keep Text Only	**FIGURE 4.52** Pasted Excel Content Using the Paste Text/One <pre> Formatted Paragraph Option	Paste Excel content as text.

Upload Excel Files to a SharePoint Library

SharePoint enables you to upload any Excel file format into a library. Microsoft Excel 2010 enables users to create XML formats such as Excel Workbook (*.xlsx). Many options are available for saving or exporting an Excel document as an Excel Binary Workbook (*.xlsb), as XML Data, as a Web page (*.htm, *.html) or Single File Web page (*mht, *.mhtml), or as a PDF (*.pdf) or XPS document (.xps). When you create a Web page in Excel, work in the Web Layout view, because it gives you a good idea of how the document will look when it is viewed in a Web browser.

SharePoint enables you to upload any Excel file format into a library.

If you use the Web page option, the document is saved as an .htm or .html file with a set of files grouped in a *filename_files* folder that includes Excel metadata that enables you to rebuild the original Excel document. Excel metadata includes information about the document, such as the full name, path, smart tags, hyperlinks, track changes, comments, hidden text, and the last 10 authors.

The Single File Web page option saves the entire Excel document into a single .mht format file, which is supported only by Internet Explorer version 6.0 and higher. When you save an Excel document as a Single Web page or Web page you can choose to save the Entire Workbook, or a Selection: Sheet (the active Worksheet). When you click Publish, the Publish as Web Page dialog opens, enabling you to select the AutoRepublish check box so the Web page is automatically republished every time the corresponding workbook is saved, as shown in Figure 4.53.

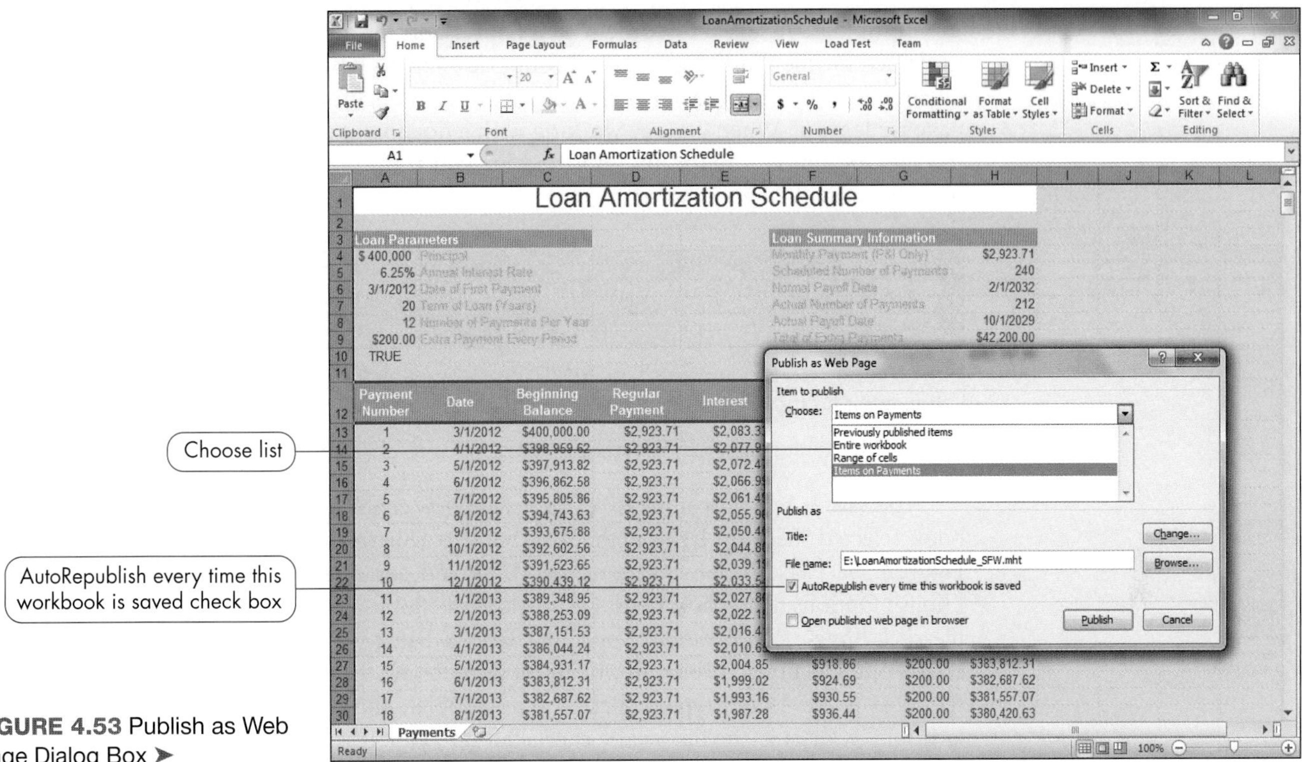

FIGURE 4.53 Publish as Web Page Dialog Box ➤

When you save an Excel document as a PDF or XPS Document, click Options to open the Options dialog box, as shown in Figure 4.54. Within the sections of this dialog box, you can select the Page range, if you want to publish the Active sheet(s), the Entire workbook, or just a selection (range cell) within a worksheet.

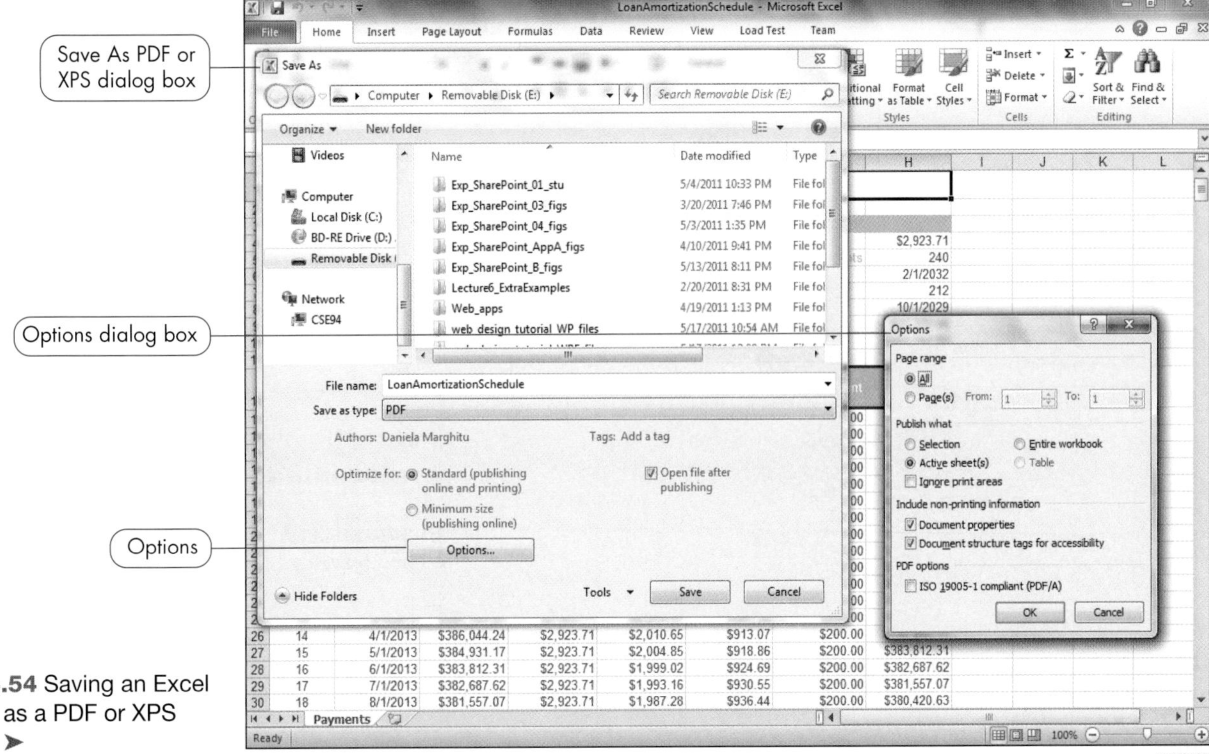

FIGURE 4.54 Saving an Excel Document as a PDF or XPS Document ➤

TIP Saving an Excel Document as a PDF or XPS Document

If the Excel table is wider than the screen, you may prefer to use the Landscape Orientation in the Excel Page Setup dialog box to fit the entire table onto the page.

To upload an Excel document to a SharePoint library, you apply the same procedure explained for the Word documents. From a developer's point of view, the process of importing an Excel document saved as an XLSX, PDF, XPS document, Single File Web page, or Web page is identical. When you are working with a document saved as a Web page, the supporting files are not automatically imported for you from the *filename_files* folder. These files must be individually uploaded.

TIP Graphic Files and Imported .xlsx, .mht, .pdf, or .xps Excel Documents

If you import a .xlsx, .mht, .pdf, or .xps Excel document, the graphic files are embedded in the document so there is no need to import them separately.

The Save & Send tab of the Excel Backstage view enables you to directly save a whole workbook, selected Sheets, or Items in the Workbook to a SharePoint Document library, as shown in Figure 4.55a. Click the *Save to SharePoint* command, and then click Publish button to open the Publish Options dialog box. Click OK to close the Publish Options dialog box, and then double-click *Browse for a Location* to open the Save As dialog box that enables you to browse for the SharePoint Document library in which you want to save the presentation, and select the type of file (.xlsx is the default type). Click Save to complete the saving of the file to the SharePoint location. By default, the file will be checked out to you. If you want to allow other users to see your changes and edit the file, click Check in displayed on the yellow bar at the top of the Excel workspace, as shown in Figure 4.55c. Click OK on the Edit Offline dialog box in order to allow file editing offline. The Excel file is displayed on the All Documents page of the destination library, as shown in Figure 4.55d. If you click the name of the file, the file will open in Excel.

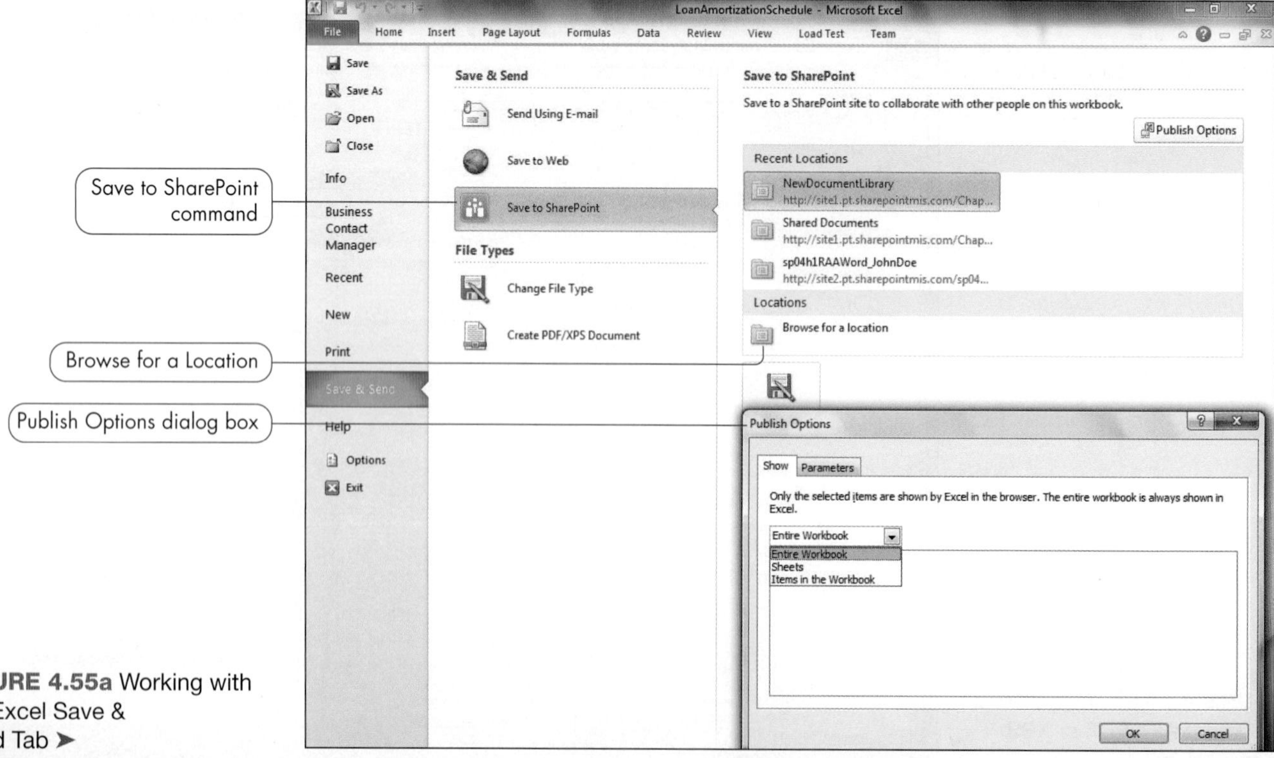

FIGURE 4.55a Working with the Excel Save & Send Tab ➤

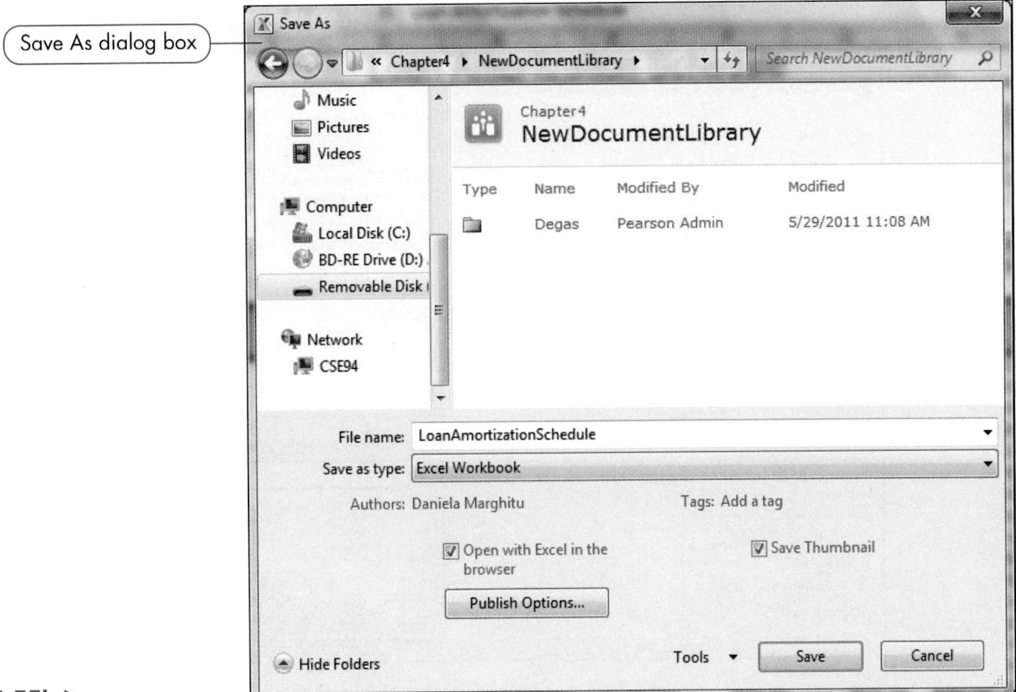

FIGURE 4.55b ➤

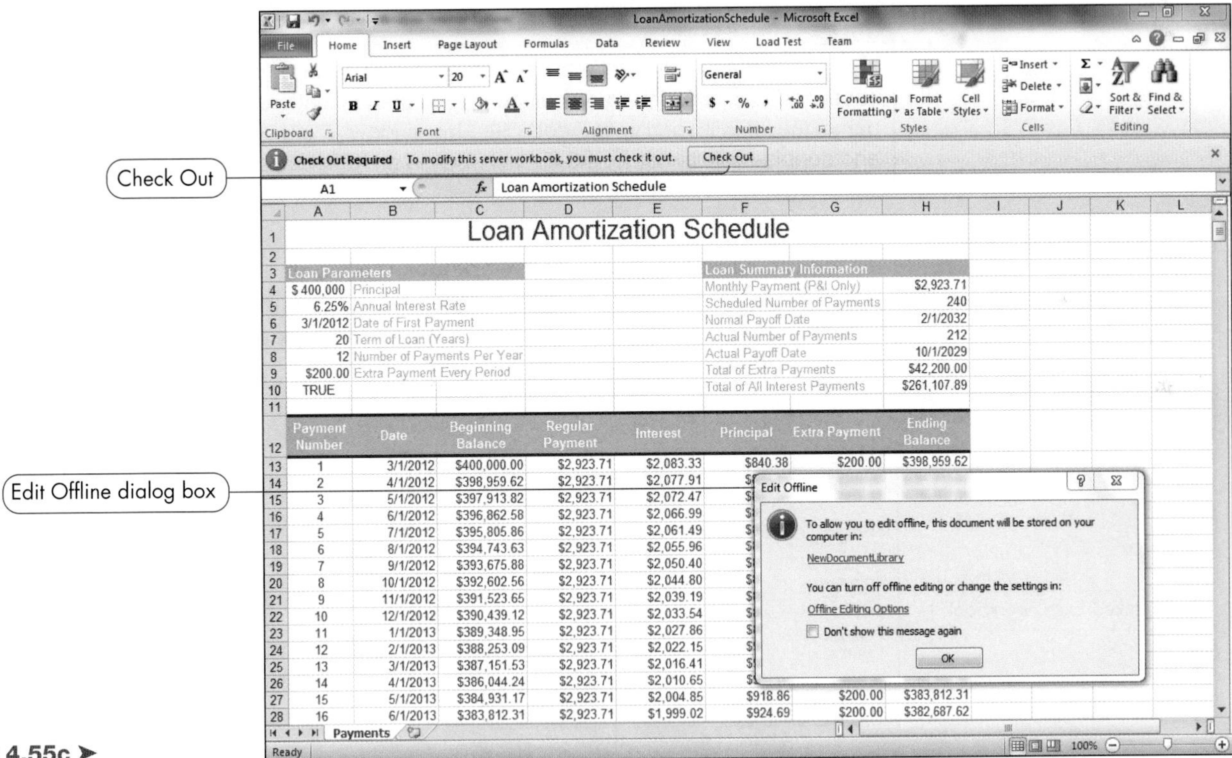

FIGURE 4.55c ➤

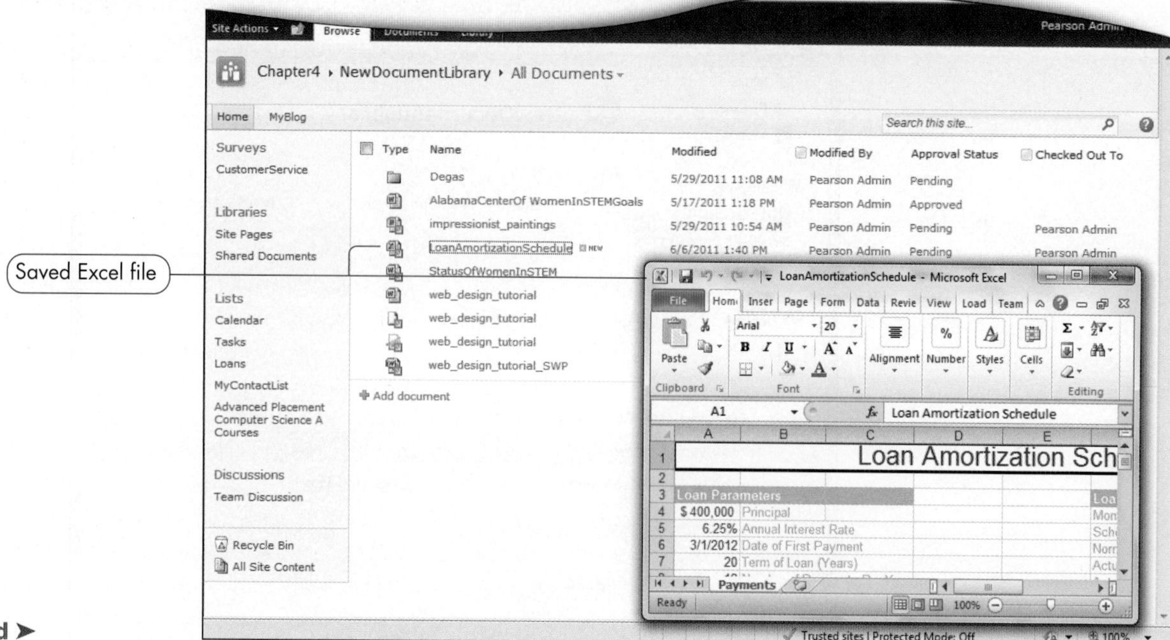

FIGURE 4.55d ➤

TIP Opening Single File Web Page, .pdf, .xps Files Created in Excel

If you upload a Single File Web Page created in Excel and double-click its name, the spreadsheet will open in Excel. If you upload a .pdf spreadsheet created in Excel and double-click its name, the file will open in an Adobe Reader window. If you upload an .xps file created in Excel and double-click its name, the file will open in an XPS viewer window.

You can add a link to an Excel Workbook (*.xlsx) that you have previously uploaded to a SharePoint Document library using a procedure similar to the one introduced for PowerPoint files, as shown in Figure 4.56. When you click the link, the Excel file will open in an Excel window.

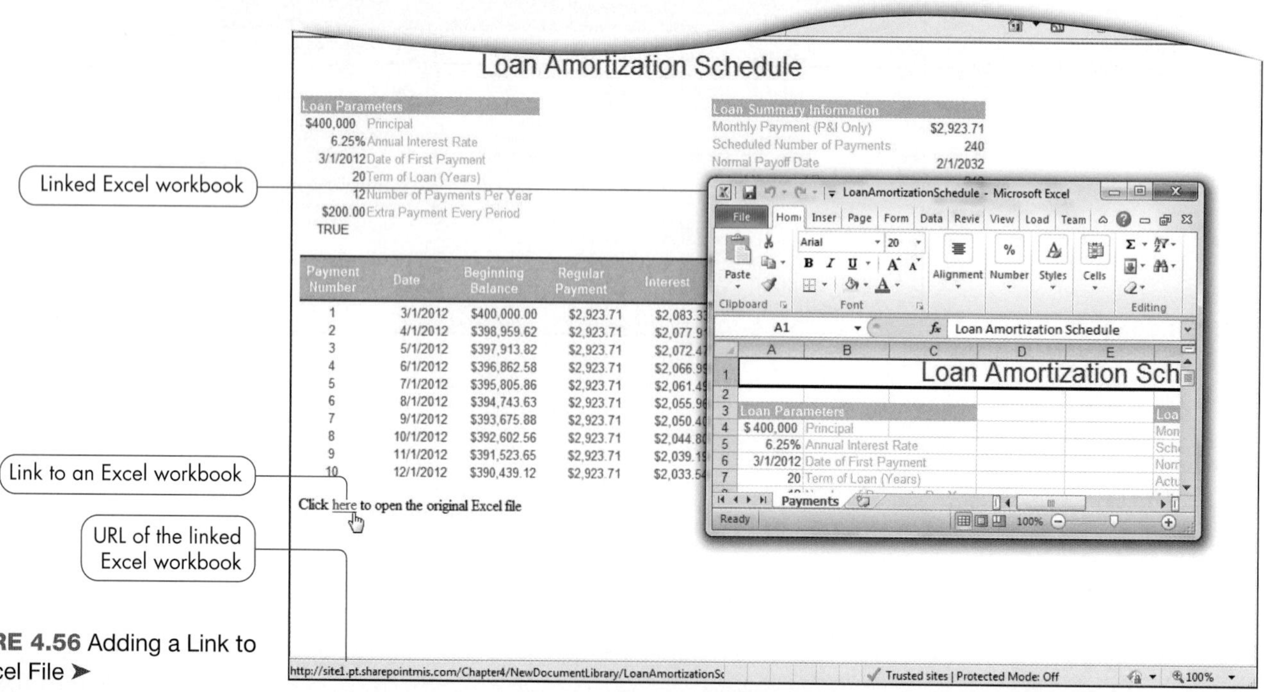

FIGURE 4.56 Adding a Link to an Excel File ➤

Import Data from Excel to a SharePoint List

With SharePoint, you can import data contained in an Excel spreadsheet, range, or table into a SharePoint list.

With SharePoint, you can import data contained in an Excel spreadsheet, range, or table into a SharePoint list. Depending on their permissions level, other users will be able to read, revise the list, or enter new data.

Open the site in which you wish to import Excel data in a browser, click Site Actions, and then click More options to open the Create dialog box. Click Blank & Custom in the *All Categories* section, click Import Spreadsheet, and then click Create to open the New page. Type the name of the new custom list in the Name box, type a short description of the list content in the Description box, and then click Browse to open the *Choose File to Upload* dialog box. Navigate to the Excel file, double-click its name, and then click Import, as shown in Figure 4.57a. The spreadsheet will open in an Excel window and the Excel Import to Windows SharePoint Services list dialog box opens, too. Select the Range Type, and then select the data you wish to import using the Select Range list (in Figure 4.57b, the import a Table Range option was selected along with the Payments!Table 1 Excel table). Click Import on the Excel Import to Windows SharePoint Services list dialog box. The All Items view of the new list is displayed, as shown in Figure 4.57c. You can further customize the list using the List Settings page (click the List tab, and then click List Settings in the Settings group to display the Setting page), as shown in Figure 4.57d.

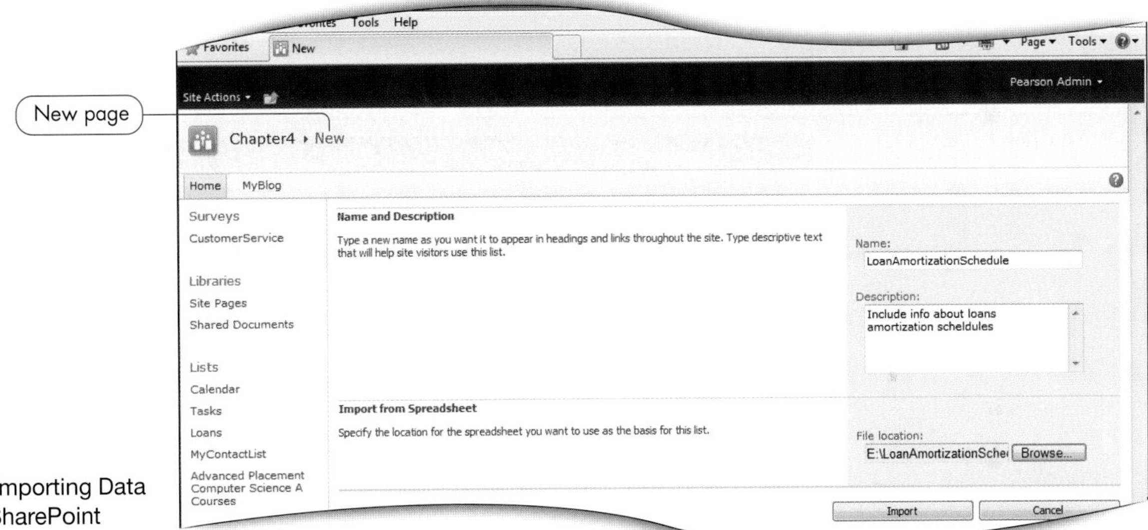

FIGURE 4.57a Importing Data from Excel to a SharePoint List ➤

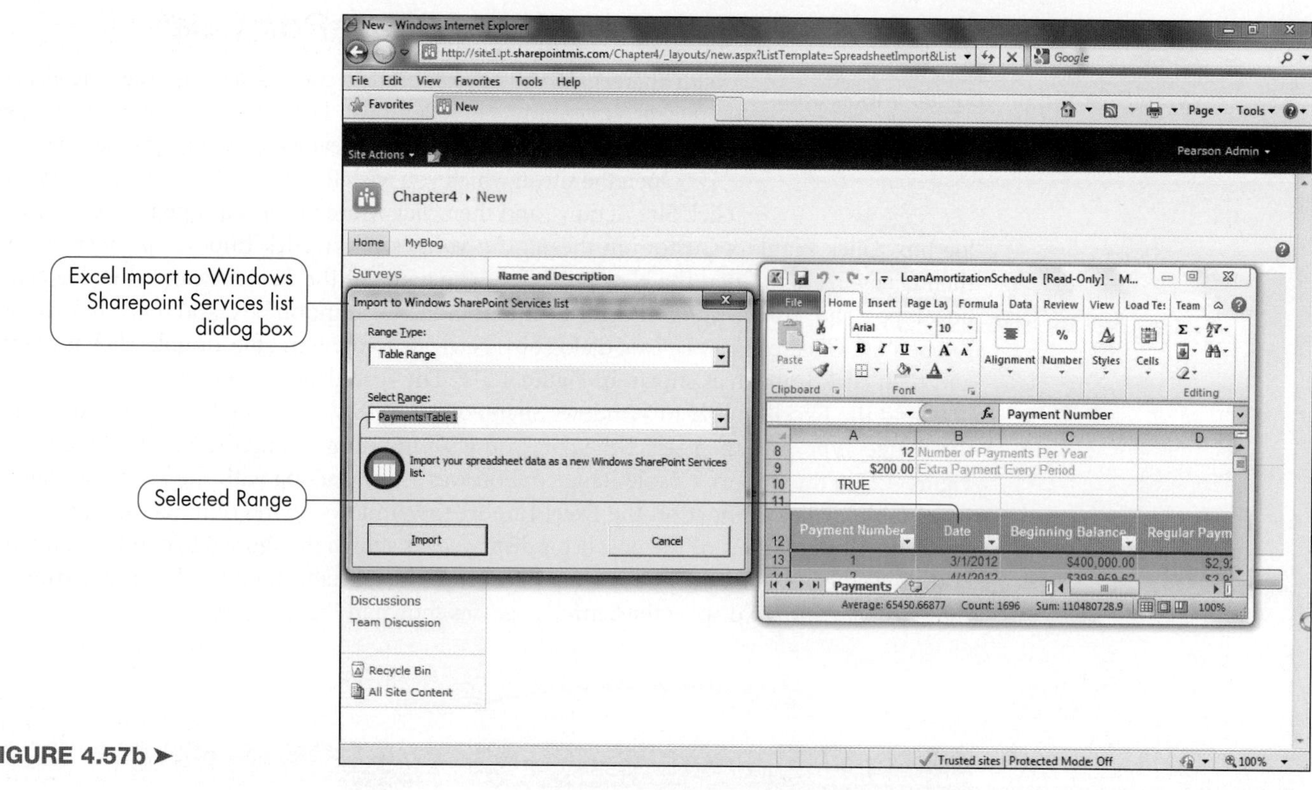

FIGURE 4.57b ➤

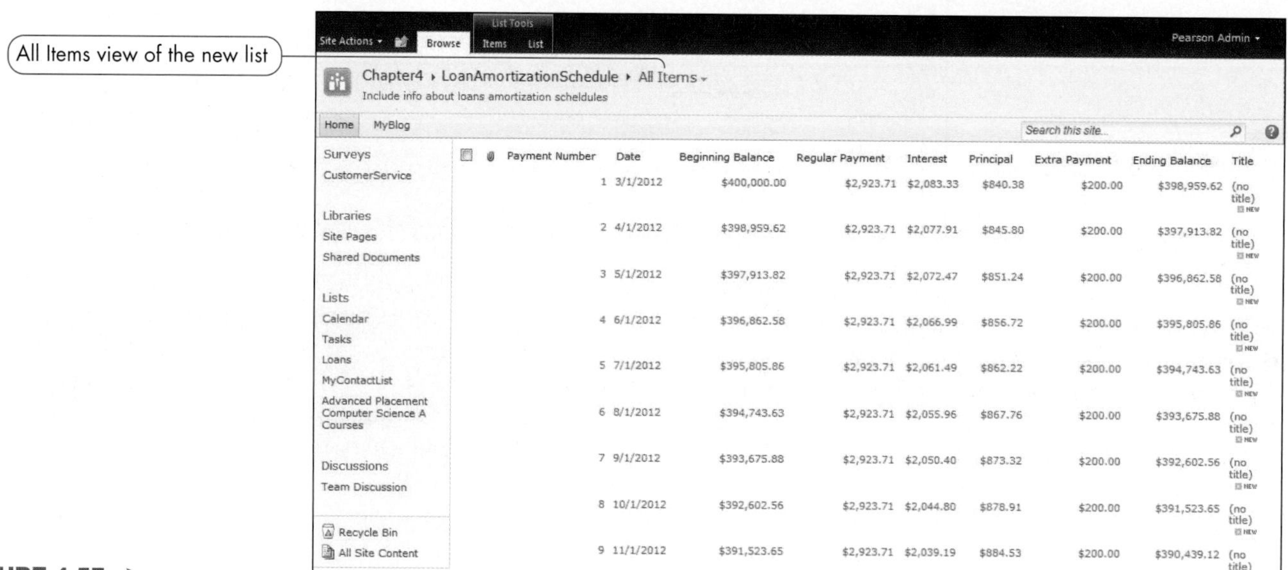

FIGURE 4.57c ➤

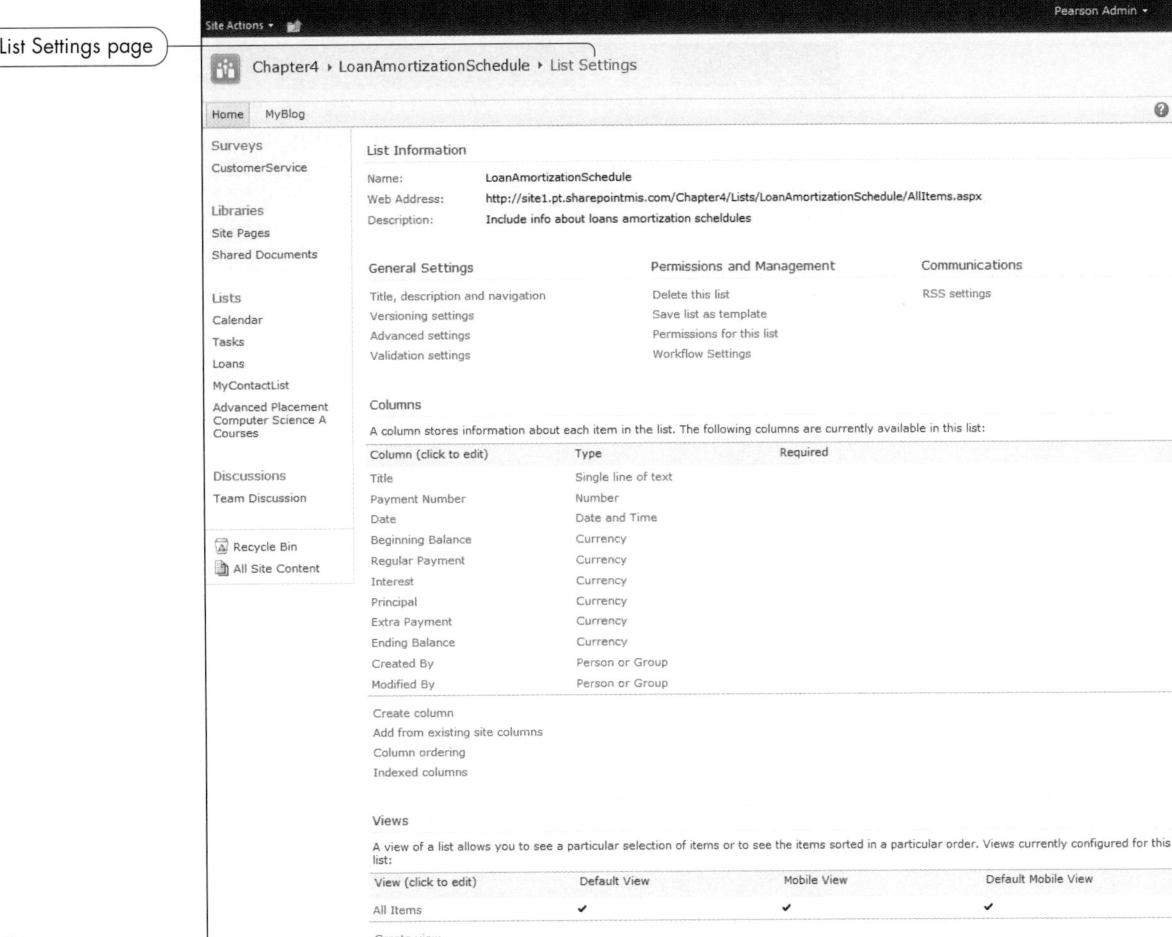

FIGURE 4.57d ➤

Export Data from a SharePoint list to an Excel File

A **Web query (.iqy)** extracts data from text or tables on a Web page and imports that data into Excel.

Microsoft Excel enables you to create a saved ***Web query (.iqy)***, which extracts data from text or tables on a Web page and imports that data into Excel. With SharePoint, you can export the contents of SharePoint lists, document libraries, and survey results to an Excel worksheet as an Excel Web query that will be automatically updated anytime you make changes to the original list or library. This automatic update is realized by a connection maintained by Excel between the spreadsheet that becomes a linked object and the SharePoint list.

With SharePoint, you can export the contents of SharePoint lists, document libraries, and survey results to an Excel worksheet....

This export method applies only to the columns and rows included in the current view of the list. That means you will need to create a List view that includes all the columns and rows that you want to export, or export one existing view and then filter the data in Excel.

To start exporting data from a SharePoint list to an Excel spreadsheet, open the SharePoint site in a browser, and then click the link to the list in the Quick Launch. Click the List Tools–List tab, and then click *Export to Excel* in the Connect & Export group, as shown in Figure 4.58a. The File Download dialog box, shown in Figure 4.58b, opens while SharePoint generates an Excel Web query. Click Save in the File Download dialog box. The Save As dialog box opens, enabling you to export the SharePoint list in an owssvr.iqy web query file, as shown in Figure 4.58c. Click Save in the Save As dialog box, and then click Open in the Download Complete dialog box. Click Enable in the displayed Microsoft Excel Security Notice dialog box, indicating that the data connection has been blocked.

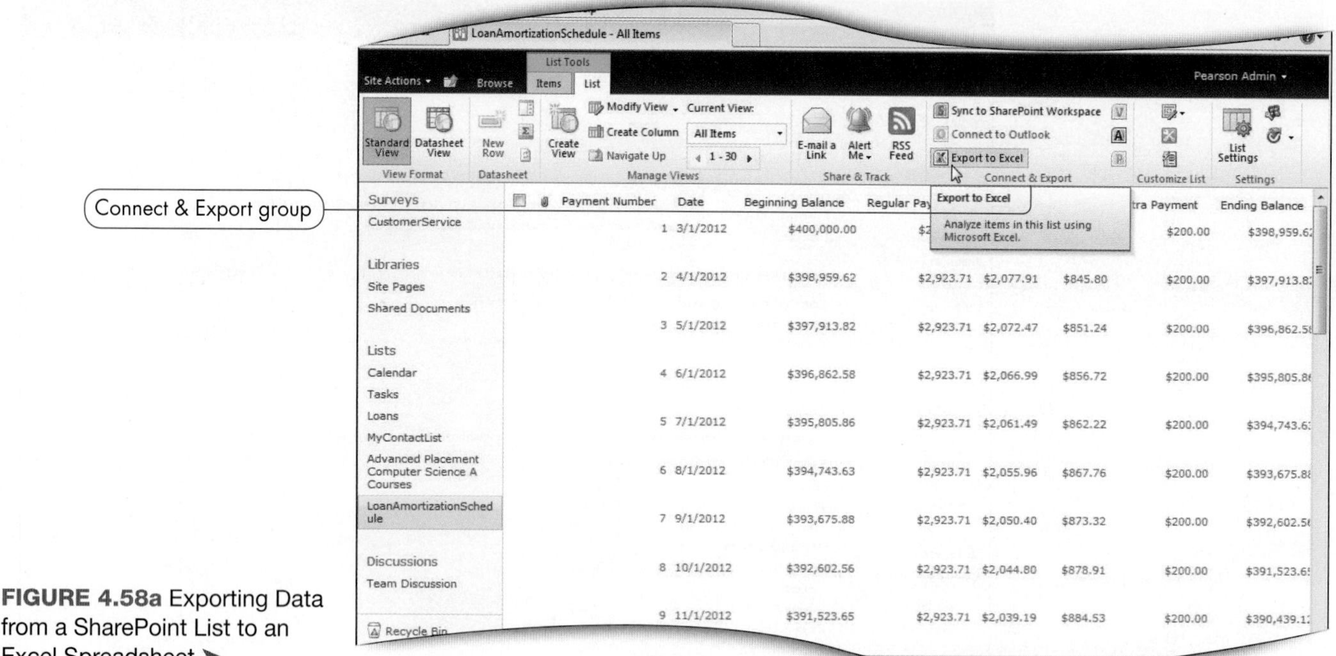

FIGURE 4.58a Exporting Data from a SharePoint List to an Excel Spreadsheet ➤

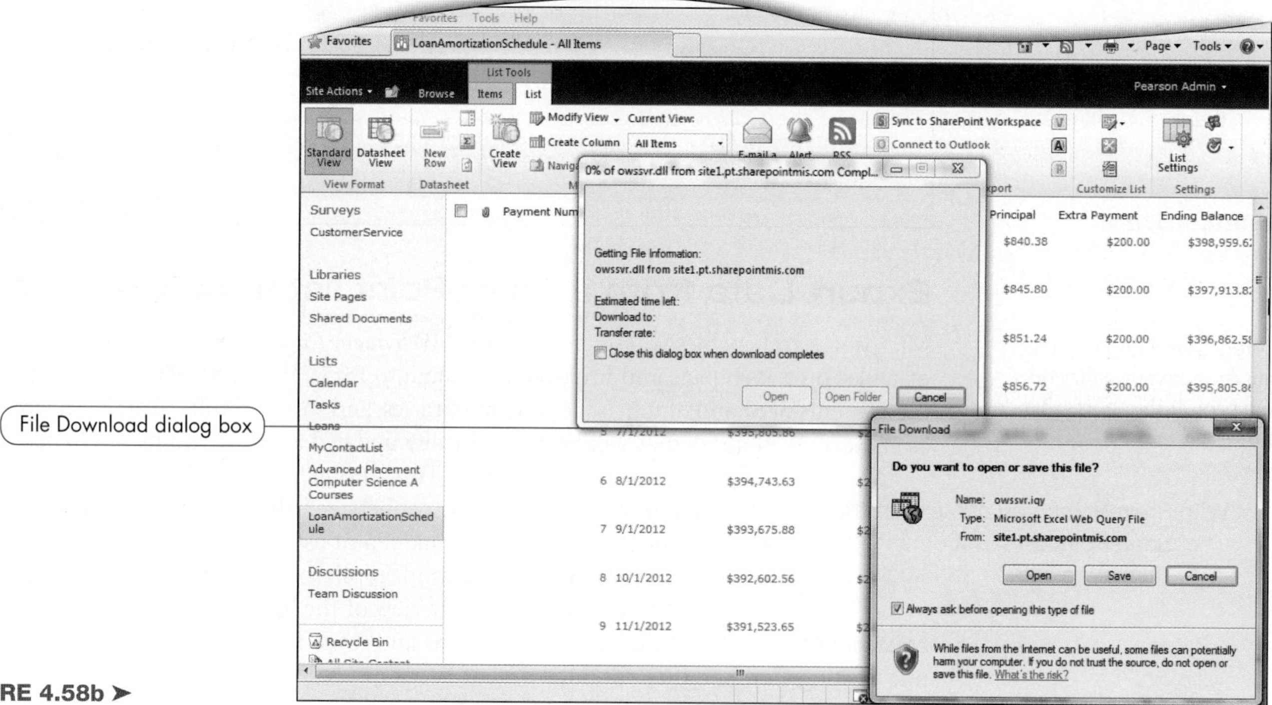

FIGURE 4.58b ➤

FIGURE 4.58c ➤

A new workbook is displayed in Excel, including an *owssvr* worksheet, shown in Figure 4.59, in which the Excel Web query results are displayed. The Table Tools–Design tab is active. Each column has an AutoFilter arrow in its header row, enabling you to further refine the display of the exported data.

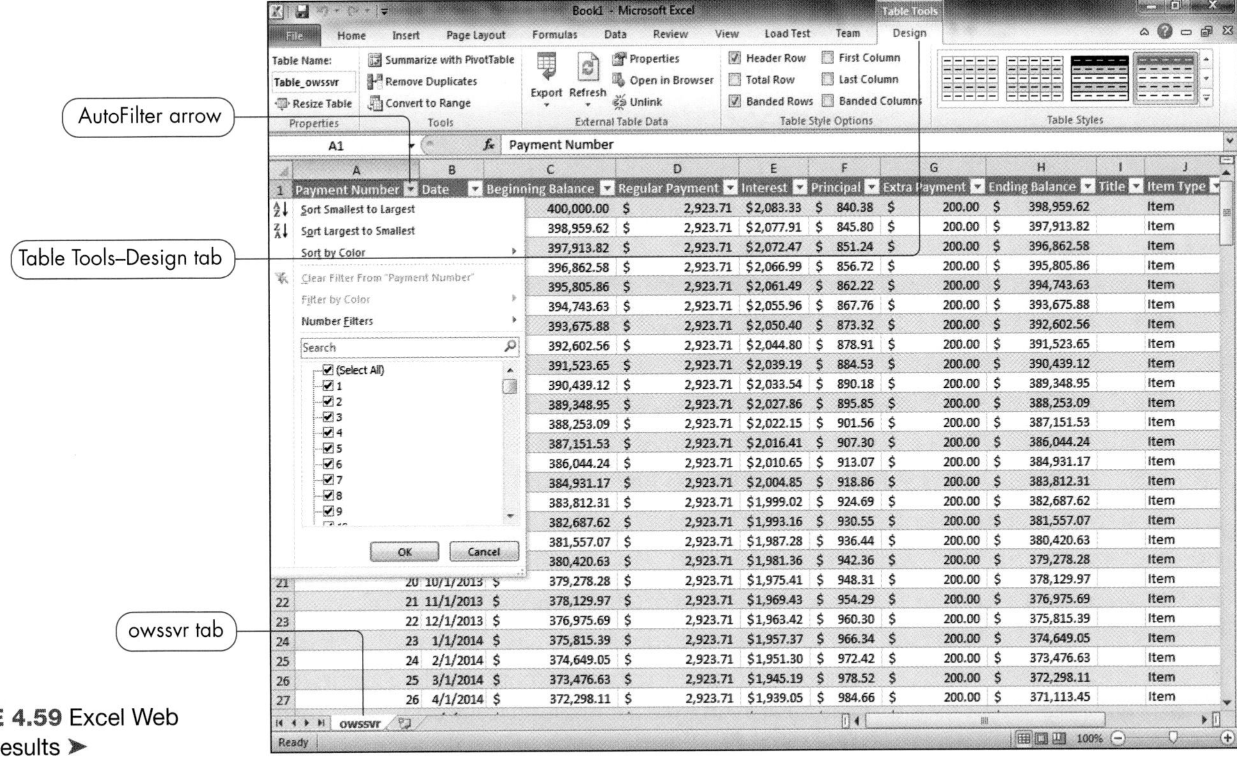

FIGURE 4.59 Excel Web Query Results ➤

Any change you make in the Excel spreadsheet will not show in the source SharePoint list. However, any changes you make to the SharePoint list will be automatically made to the linked worksheet.

Excel enables you to modify the way data will be synchronized between the SharePoint list and the linked Excel spreadsheet. Click the Data tab, and then click Properties in the

Connections group, as shown in Figure 4.60, to display and modify the settings in the the External Data Properties dialog box.

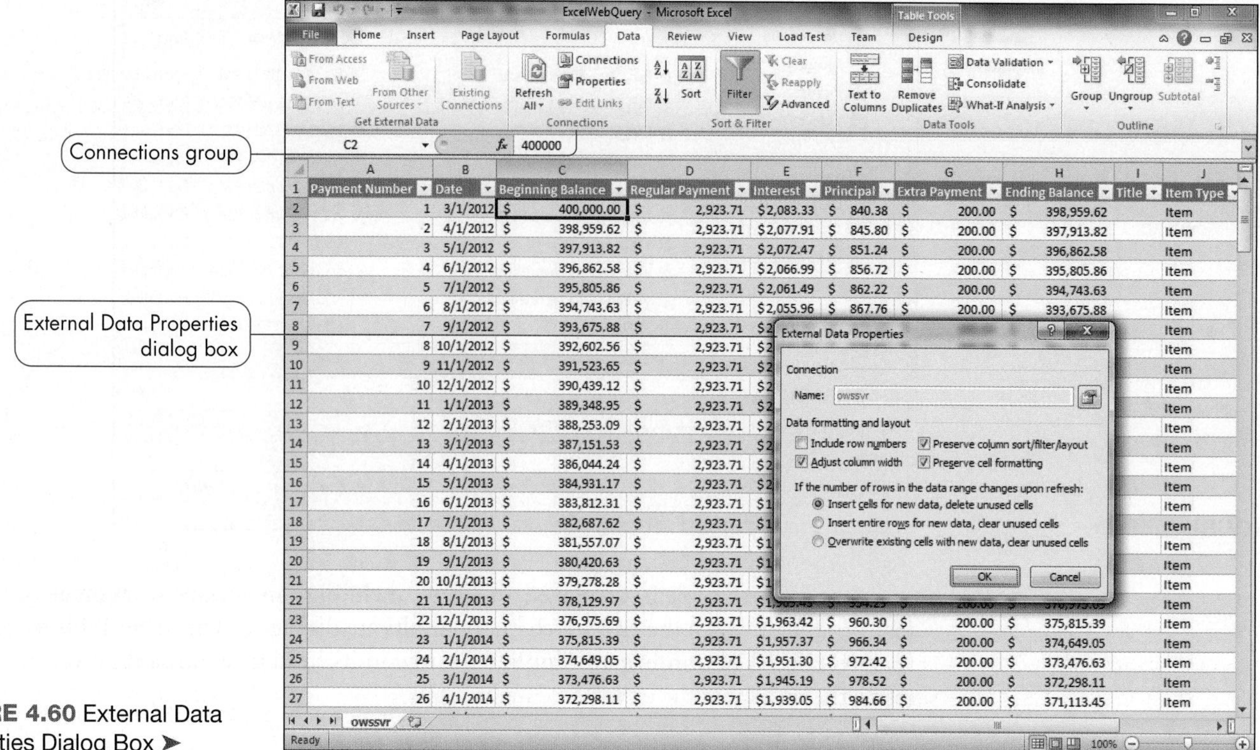

FIGURE 4.60 External Data Properties Dialog Box ➤

Using Access 2010 Documents in SharePoint

In response to the boom of the Internet, with applications built on real-time access to databases for e-commerce and e-trading in recent years, the SharePoint database capabilities have been upgraded.

Access is one of the most in-demand, powerful, yet easy-to-use relational databases. It requires a Windows environment to run. Access provides “wizards” that walk users through the setup of simple relational databases. Access is a product suitable for the development of small-scale databases that are used in office workgroups with relatively few numbers of users. However, because of its ease of use, Access is often used to develop prototypes of larger-scale databases. Migration of data from an Access database to another database (such as SQL Server or Oracle) can be accomplished relatively easily. Therefore, Access can be a good choice for small-scale databases that will eventually require a more robust environment.

Profit and non-profit organizations use databases to keep track of their employees, volunteers, events, sales, product inventories, and acquisitions.

Access 2010 provides you with considerable SharePoint connectivity enhancements and a wizard that enables you to fully take advantage of SharePoint 2010 list improvements.

Access 2010 enables you to export a table, a report, or a query object to a wide range of formats, such as an external file, an Excel workbook, a Rich Text Format (RTF) file, a text file, a PDF, or XPS file. You can also export into formats for an email attachment, an Extensible Markup Language (XML) document, an Open Database Connectivity (ODBC) data source, or a Hypertext Markup Language (HTML) document. You can also export a table to a SharePoint site by creating a new list.

Access 2010 enables you to create a new table by importing data from an external data source, such as a dBase database, an Excel workbook, an XML document, an ODBC data source, or a SharePoint website.

Access and SharePoint do not provide any data synchronization between their two data locations.

Access and SharePoint do not provide any data synchronization between their two data locations. If you do not need to keep copies of the data in both locations, and you just need content synchronized access to a SharePoint list, you can use Access linked tables. A ***linked table*** provides only the connection to a SharePoint list and synchronizes data changes.

Linked table provides only the connection to a SharePoint list and synchronizes data changes.

A **database** is a set of related data containing records or rows.

A **database table** is formed by columns, each of which is attached to a database field.

Add Access Content to a SharePoint Page

You can take advantage of the Access and SharePoint Designer content integration features, and use content created in Access on your Web pages. A ***database*** is a set of related data containing records or rows. All records in a database consist of the same set of database fields. Usually databases display their records as rows within tables. A ***database table*** is formed by columns, each of which is attached to a database field.

The easiest way to add Access content to a SharePoint Designer Web page is by using the traditional Copy and Paste commands. You can also use the Clipboard task pane. Open an Access file database containing the content you want to use in a SharePoint site. In the Navigation Pane, double-click the desired Access object such as a table, query, form, or report. If, for example, you wish to copy the whole content of an Access table object, click Select in the Find Group, and then click Select All. If you wish to copy only a selection from the Access table object, click the row selector to highlight the first record, navigate to the last record, press Shift, and then click the row selector, as shown in Figure 4.61a. Right-click within the selected records, and then click Copy from the shortcut menu. The highlighted section is copied to the Clipboard.

After you have copied the Access content, launch SharePoint Designer and create a new Web page or open an existing one. Click Clipboard on the Task Panes menu (on the View tab) and you will see the copied text on the Clipboard task pane. Position the insertion point in the body of the Web page where you want the Access content to appear, click the arrow to the right of the copied Access content, and then click Paste. SharePoint Designer automatically converts the Access content into HTML (see Figure 4.61b) and places it on the SharePoint page. Using the Paste Options list, you can format the pasted content in different ways. If you click the Keep Text Only button, the Paste Text dialog box opens.

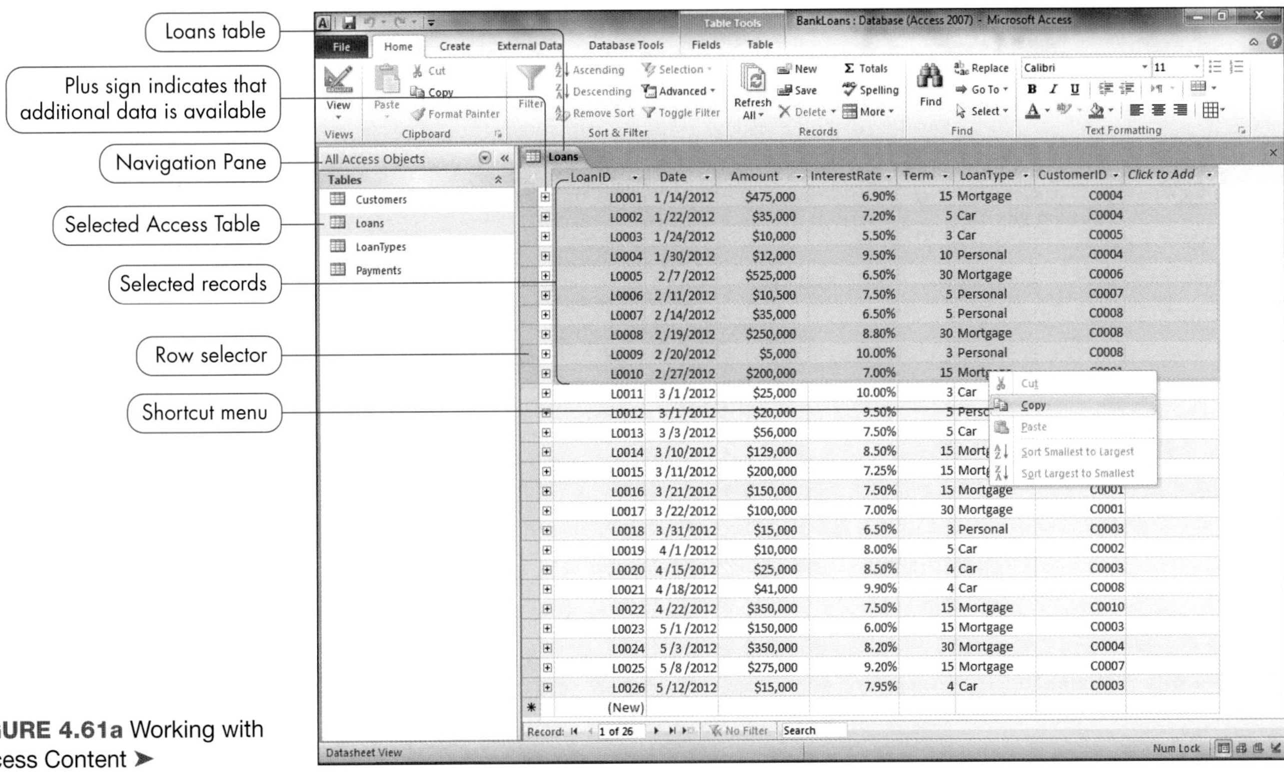

FIGURE 4.61a Working with Access Content ➤

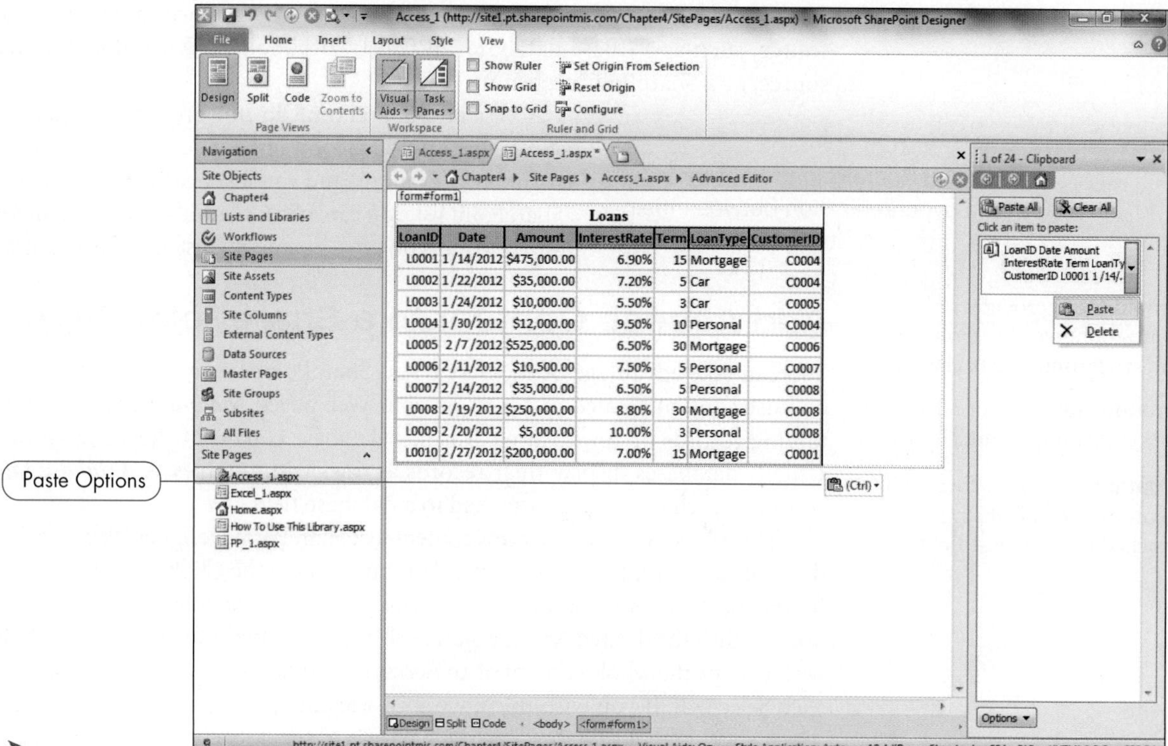

FIGURE 4.61b ➤

Upload Access Files to a SharePoint Library

When you export an Access document as an HTML Document (.html), the Export-HTML Document dialog box enables you to specify export options, as shown in Figure 4.62a. When you click OK, the HTML Output Options dialog box opens, as shown in Figure 4.62b, enabling you to select an HTML Template, as well as the encoding you wish to use for saving the file, making any further export from the document easier (see Figure 4.62c). The Access object will then be displayed on the SharePoint page.

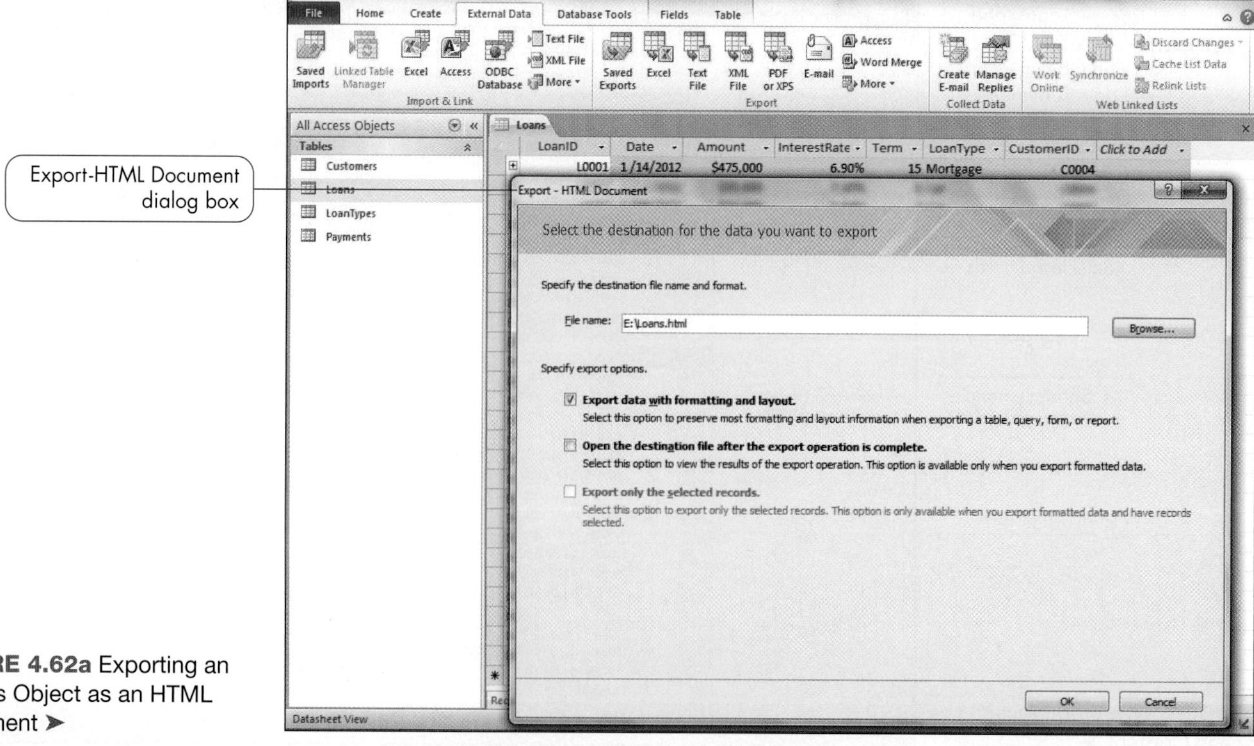

FIGURE 4.62a Exporting an Access Object as an HTML Document ➤

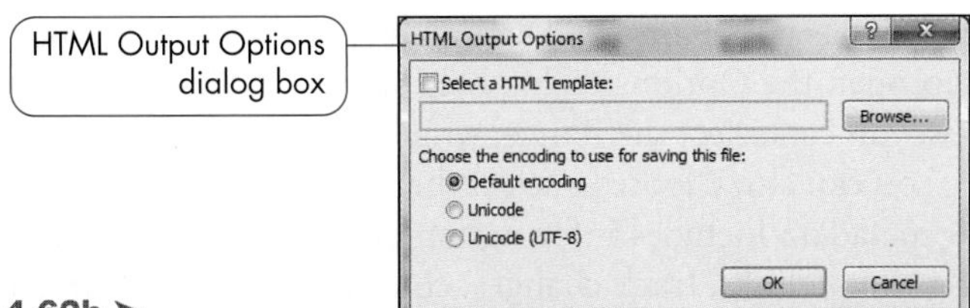

FIGURE 4.62b ➤

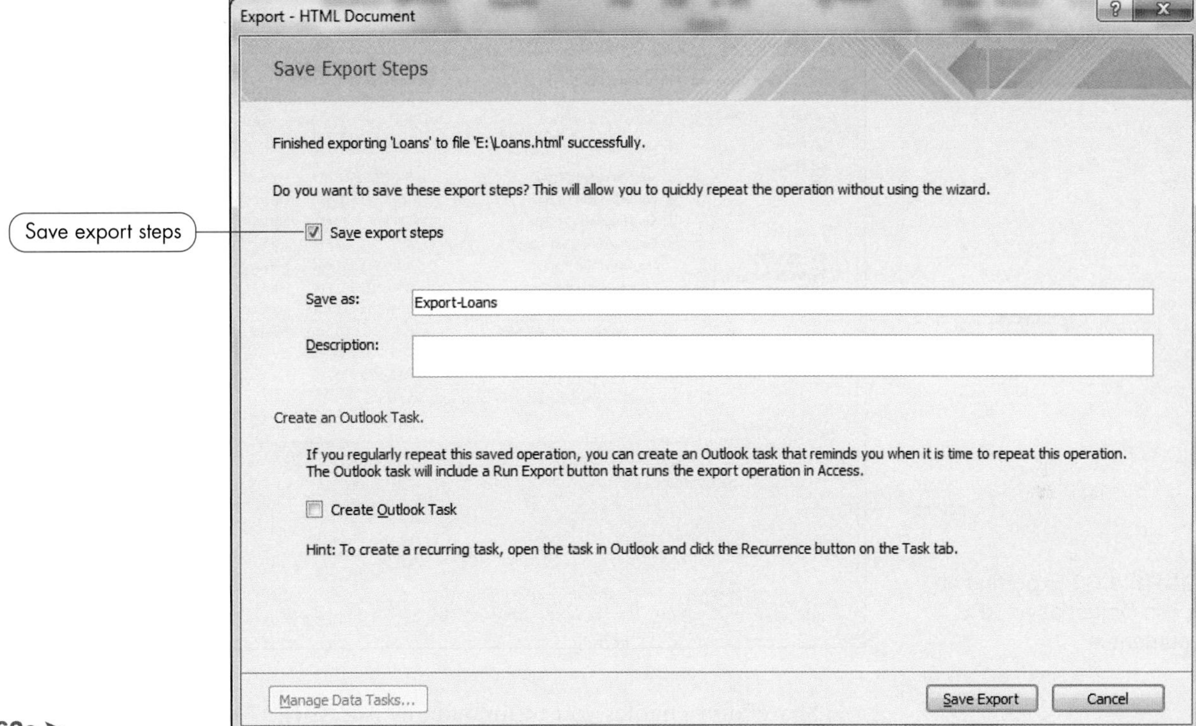

FIGURE 4.62c ➤

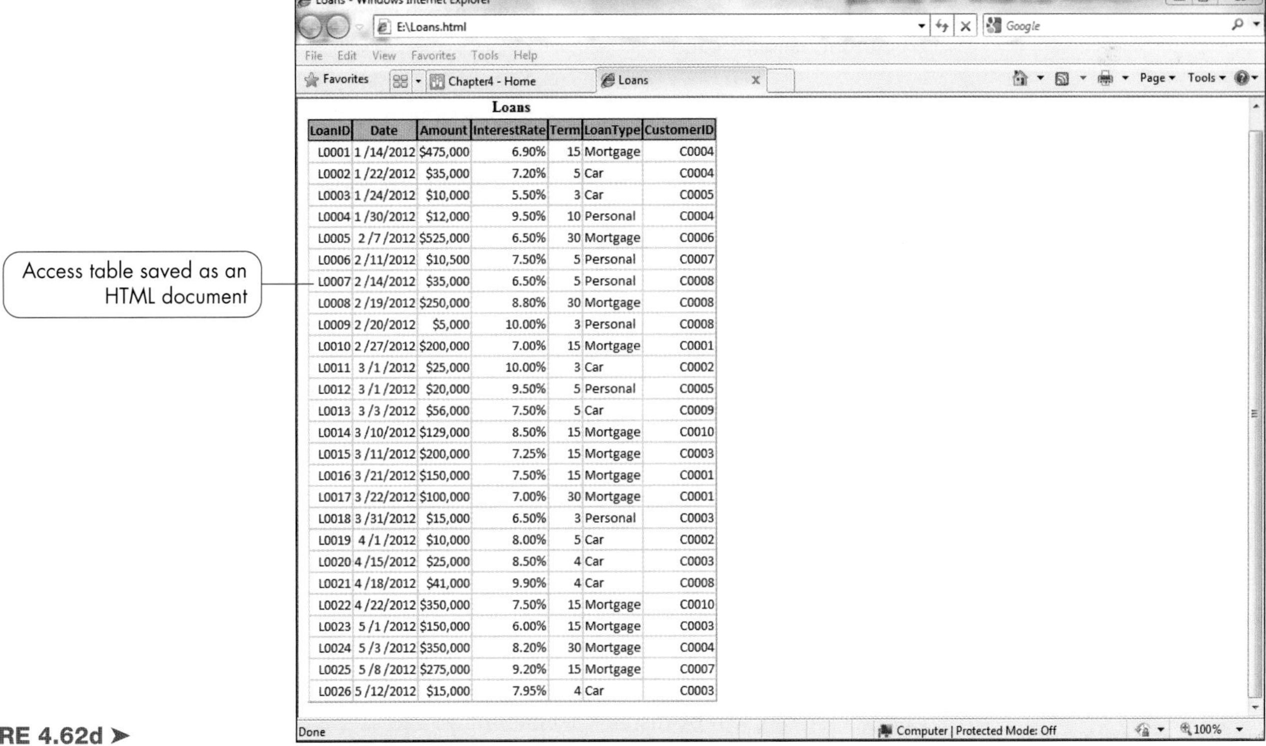

Loans

LoanID	Date	Amount	InterestRate	Term	LoanType	CustomerID
L0001	1/14/2012	$475,000	6.90%	15	Mortgage	C0004
L0002	1/22/2012	$35,000	7.20%	5	Car	C0004
L0003	1/24/2012	$10,000	5.50%	3	Car	C0005
L0004	1/30/2012	$12,000	9.50%	10	Personal	C0004
L0005	2/7/2012	$525,000	6.50%	30	Mortgage	C0006
L0006	2/11/2012	$10,500	7.50%	5	Personal	C0007
L0007	2/14/2012	$35,000	6.50%	5	Personal	C0008
L0008	2/19/2012	$250,000	8.80%	30	Mortgage	C0008
L0009	2/20/2012	$5,000	10.00%	3	Personal	C0008
L0010	2/27/2012	$200,000	7.00%	15	Mortgage	C0001
L0011	3/1/2012	$25,000	10.00%	3	Car	C0002
L0012	3/1/2012	$20,000	9.50%	5	Personal	C0005
L0013	3/3/2012	$56,000	7.50%	5	Car	C0009
L0014	3/10/2012	$129,000	8.50%	15	Mortgage	C0010
L0015	3/11/2012	$200,000	7.25%	15	Mortgage	C0003
L0016	3/21/2012	$150,000	7.50%	15	Mortgage	C0001
L0017	3/22/2012	$100,000	7.00%	30	Mortgage	C0001
L0018	3/31/2012	$15,000	6.50%	3	Personal	C0003
L0019	4/1/2012	$10,000	8.00%	5	Car	C0002
L0020	4/15/2012	$25,000	8.50%	4	Car	C0003
L0021	4/18/2012	$41,000	9.90%	4	Car	C0008
L0022	4/22/2012	$350,000	7.50%	15	Mortgage	C0010
L0023	5/1/2012	$150,000	6.00%	15	Mortgage	C0003
L0024	5/3/2012	$350,000	8.20%	30	Mortgage	C0004
L0025	5/8/2012	$275,000	9.20%	15	Mortgage	C0007
L0026	5/12/2012	$15,000	7.95%	4	Car	C0003

FIGURE 4.62d ➤

To export an Access object as a PDF or XPS Document, click Options in the Publish as PDF or XPS dialog box to open the Options dialog box, shown in Figure 4.63. Within the sections of this dialog box, you can select the Range, which can include all records, selected records, or specific pages. You can also choose to select the *Document structure tags for accessibility* check box. Access metadata includes information about the document, such as the full name, path, smart tags, hyperlinks, track changes, comments, hidden text, and the last 10 authors.

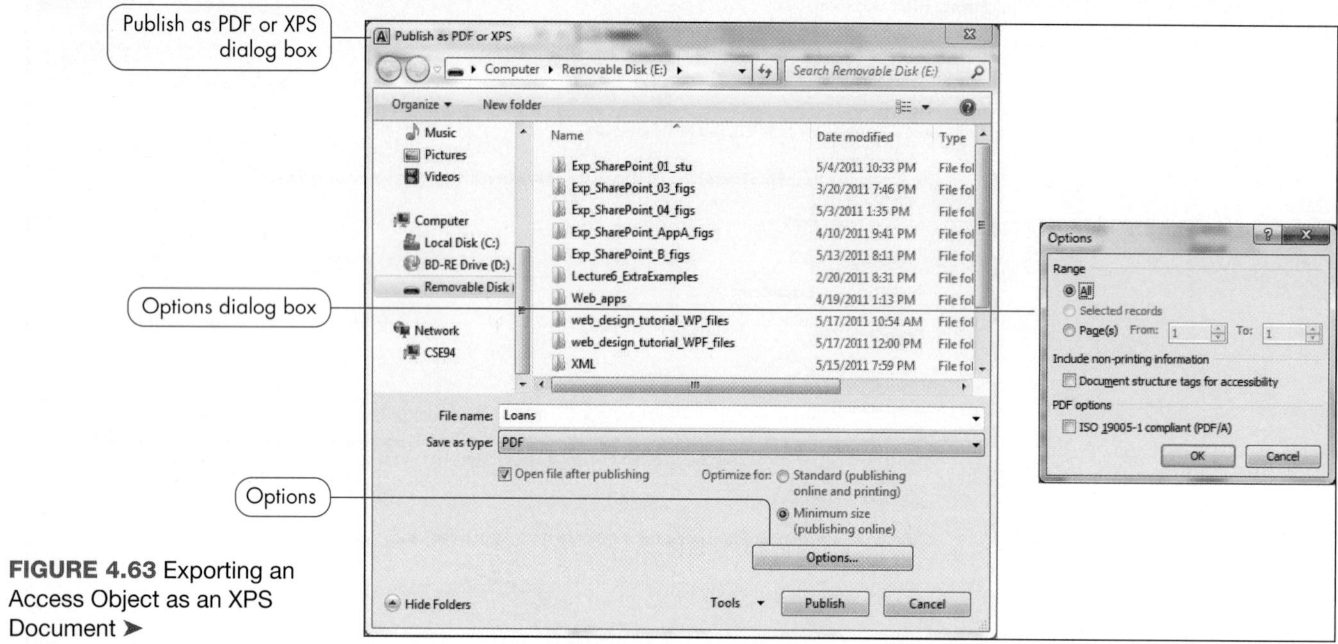

FIGURE 4.63 Exporting an Access Object as an XPS Document ➤

SharePoint enables you to upload any Access file format to a Document library. To upload an Access document in a SharePoint library, you apply the same procedures explained previously for Word and Excel documents. From a developer's point of view, the process of uploading an Access document saved as a PDF, XPS Document, or HTML Document is identical.

TIP
Graphic Files and Imported .accdb, .html, .pdf, or .xps Access Documents

If you import a .accdb, .html, .pdf, or .xps Access document, the graphic files are embedded in the document so there is no need to import them separately.

> The Save & Publish tab of the Access Backstage view enables you to directly save the whole database to a SharePoint Document library....

The Save & Publish tab of the Access Backstage view enables you to directly save the whole database to a SharePoint Documents library, as shown in Figure 4.64a. Click the Save Database As tab, select the SharePoint option, and then click Save As to open the *Save to SharePoint* dialog box that enables you to locate the SharePoint Document library in which you want to save the file. Browse for the SharePoint library in which you want to save the file, and then click Save, as shown in Figure 4.64b. The Access file will now be included in the All Documents page of the destination library, as shown in Figure 4.64c. If you click the name of the file, its corresponding file will open in Access. The first time you do this, the *Save a Local Copy* dialog box will be displayed, enabling you to save a copy of the database on your local machine. When you finish editing the file, click *Save to SharePoint Site* (shown in Figure 4.64d) displayed on the yellow bar at the top of the Access workspace.

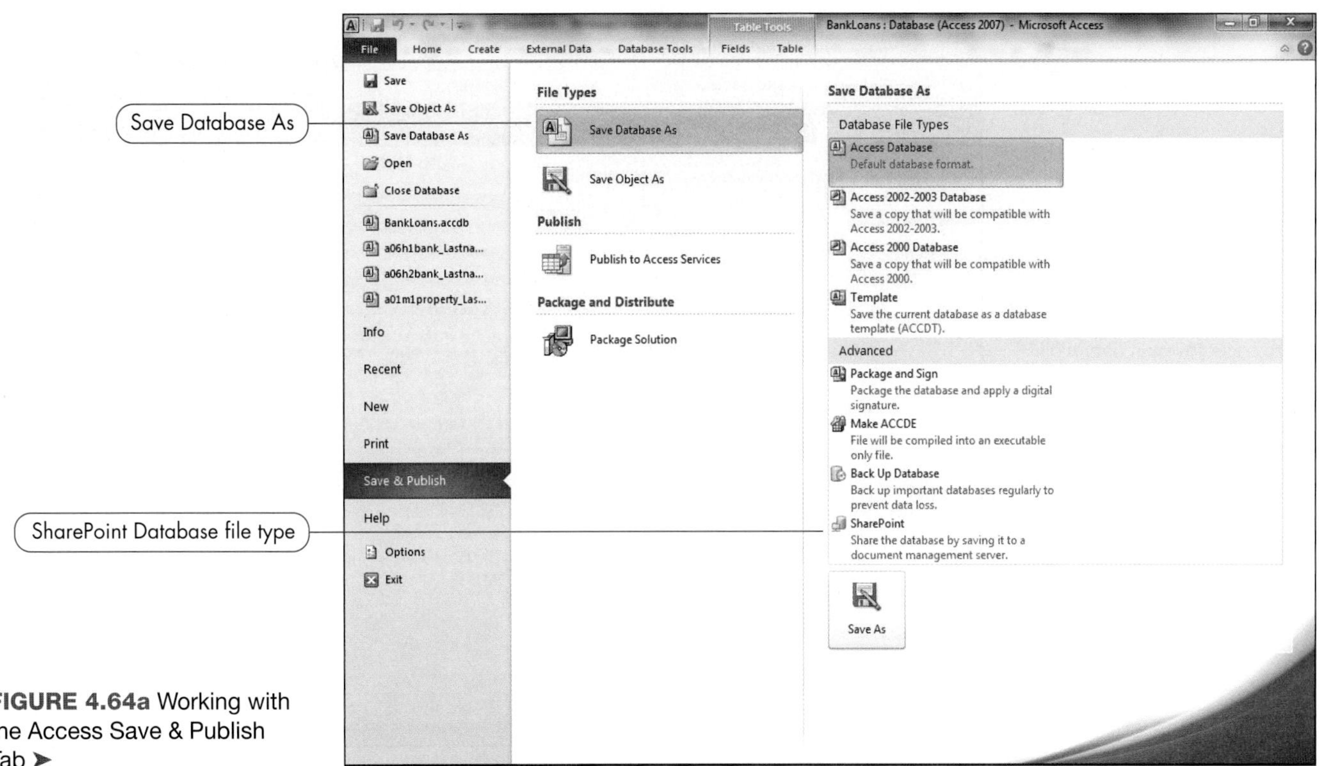

FIGURE 4.64a Working with the Access Save & Publish Tab ➤

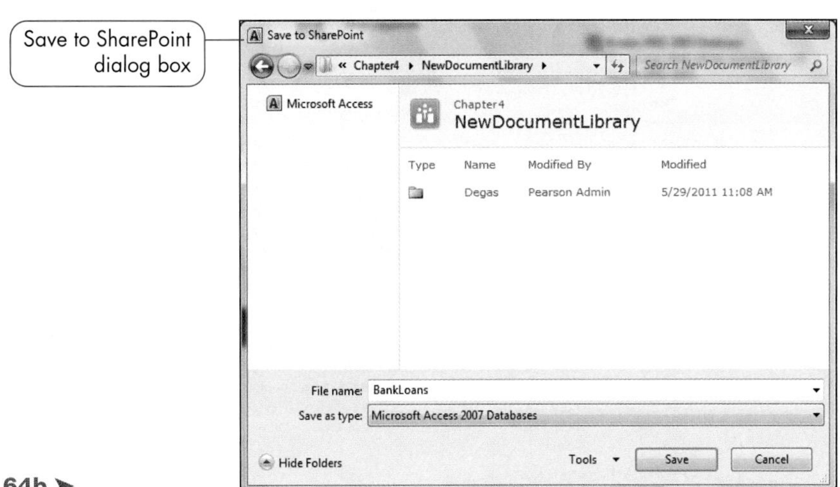

FIGURE 4.64b ➤

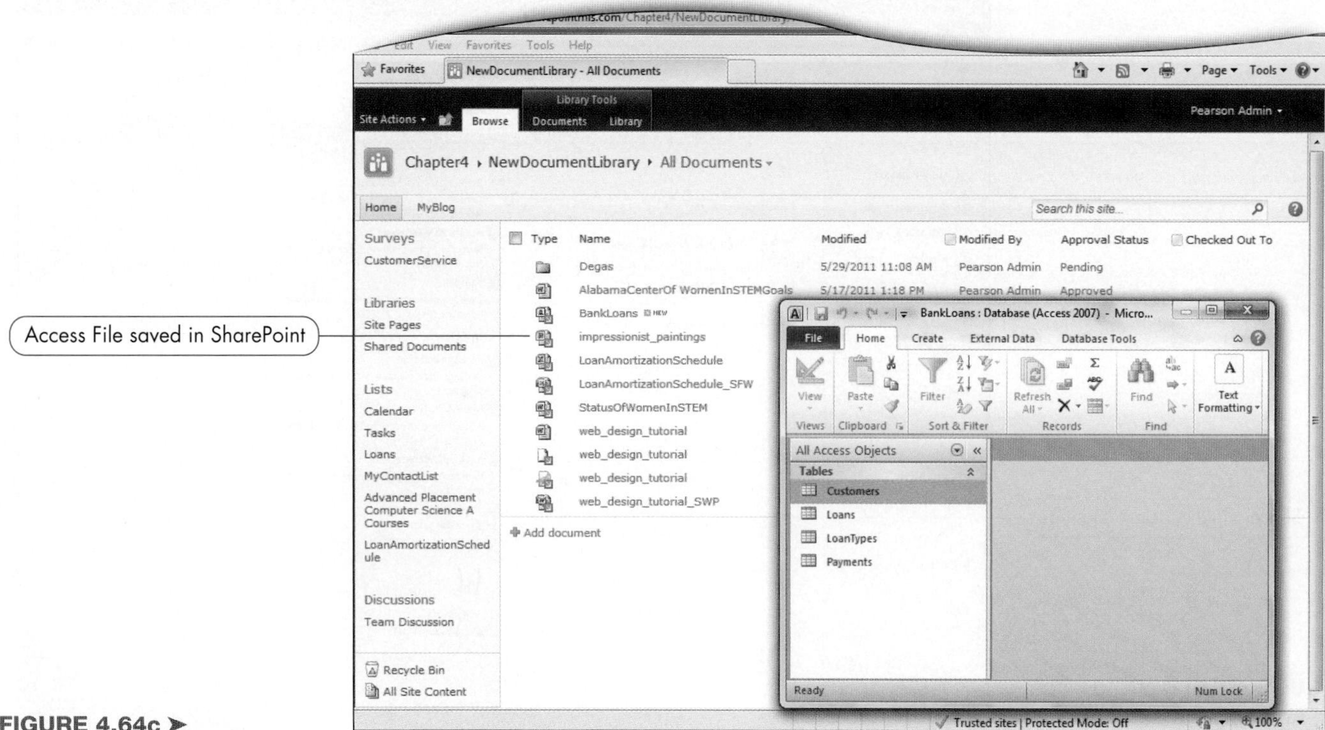

FIGURE 4.64c ➤

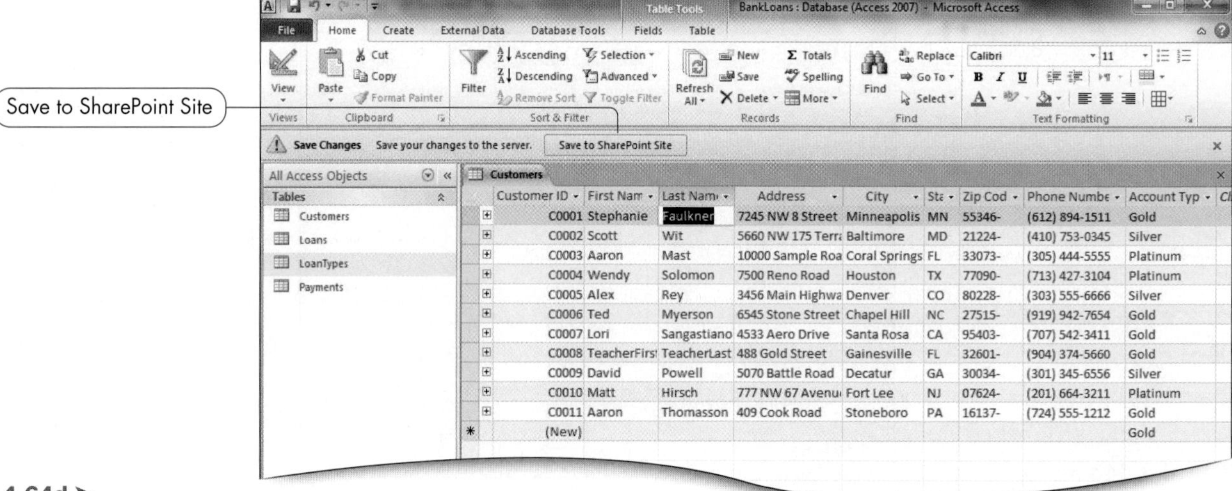

FIGURE 4.64d ➤

Export Access Data to a SharePoint Lists

The Access 2010 Ribbon includes a number of tabs that enable you to easily integrate Access data with SharePoint sites and lists:

- The SharePoint Lists arrow (see Figure 4.65a) in the Tables group of the Create tab enables you to create a SharePoint list, and a table within the current Access database which is linked to the new list.
- The More arrow (see Figure 4.65b) in the Import & Link group on the External Data tab enables you to import from or link data to a SharePoint list.
- The More arrow (see Figure 4.65c) in the Export group of the External Data tab enables you to export a selected Access object into a SharePoint list.
- SharePoint (see Figure 4.65d) in the Move Data group of the Database Tools tab enables you to move an Access table to a SharePoint list and add links to this table within the database.

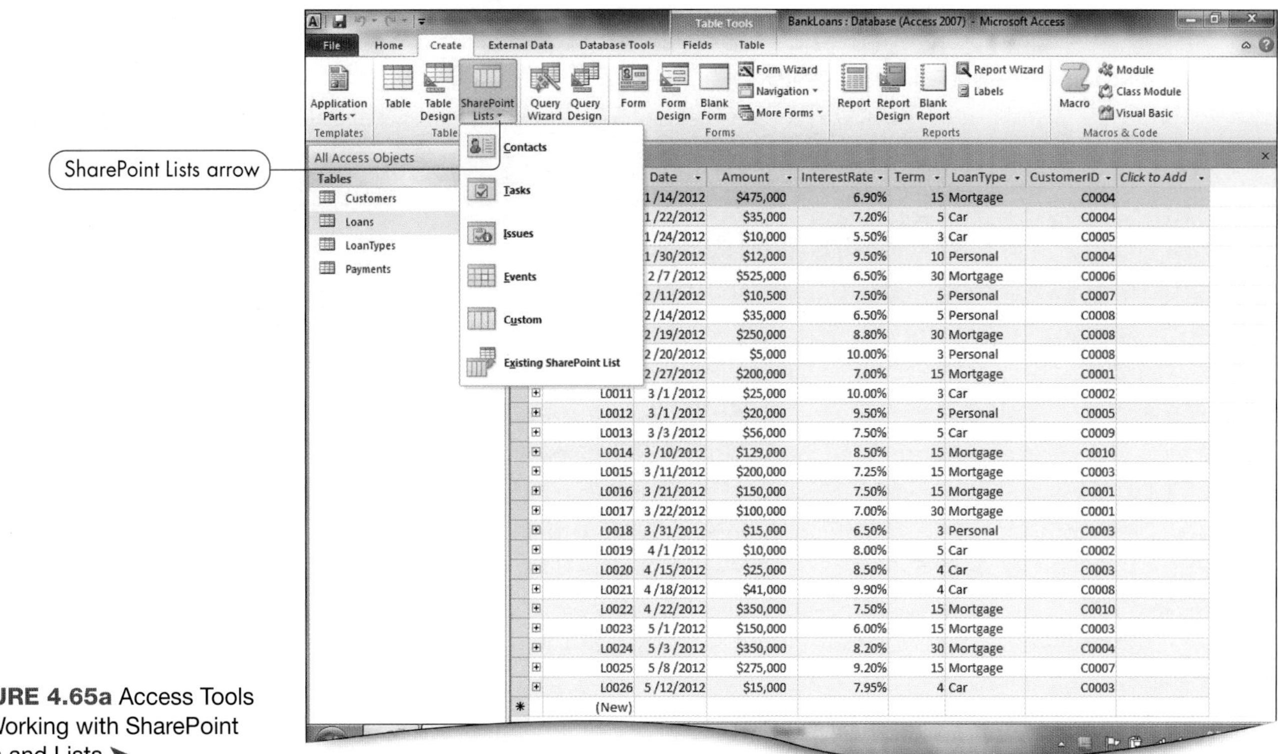

FIGURE 4.65a Access Tools for Working with SharePoint Sites and Lists ➤

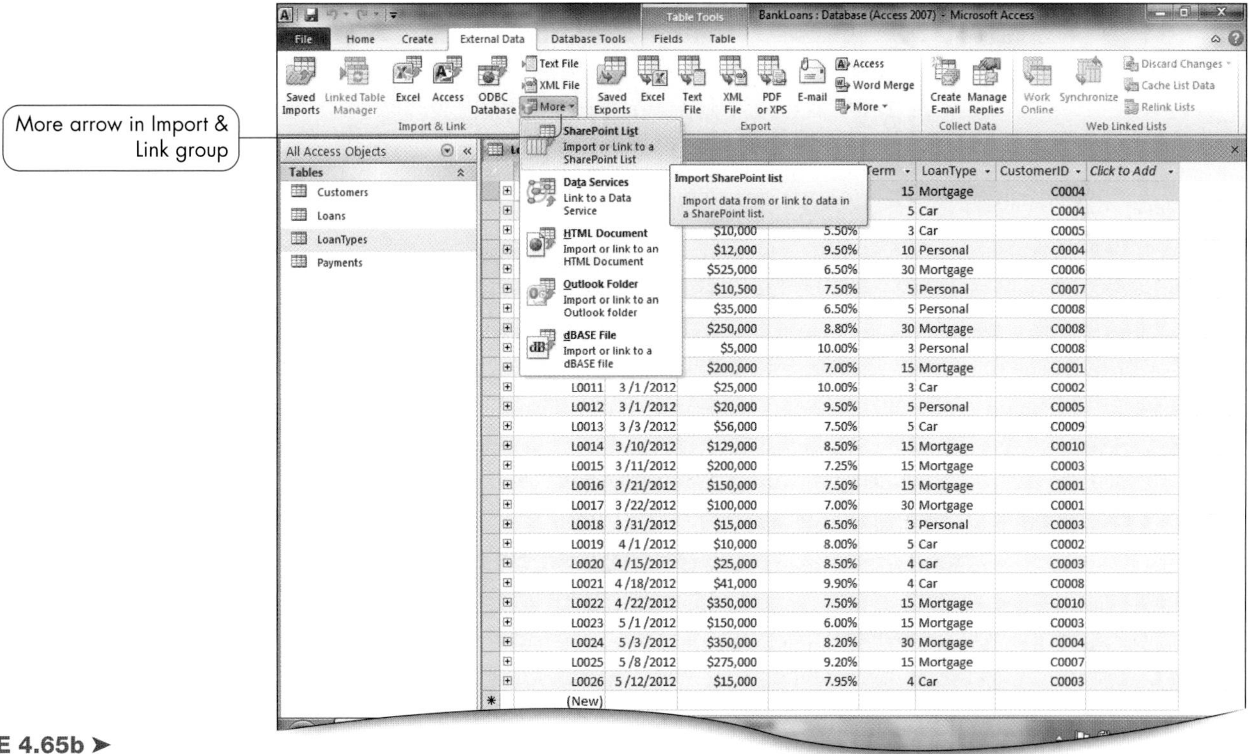

FIGURE 4.65b ➤

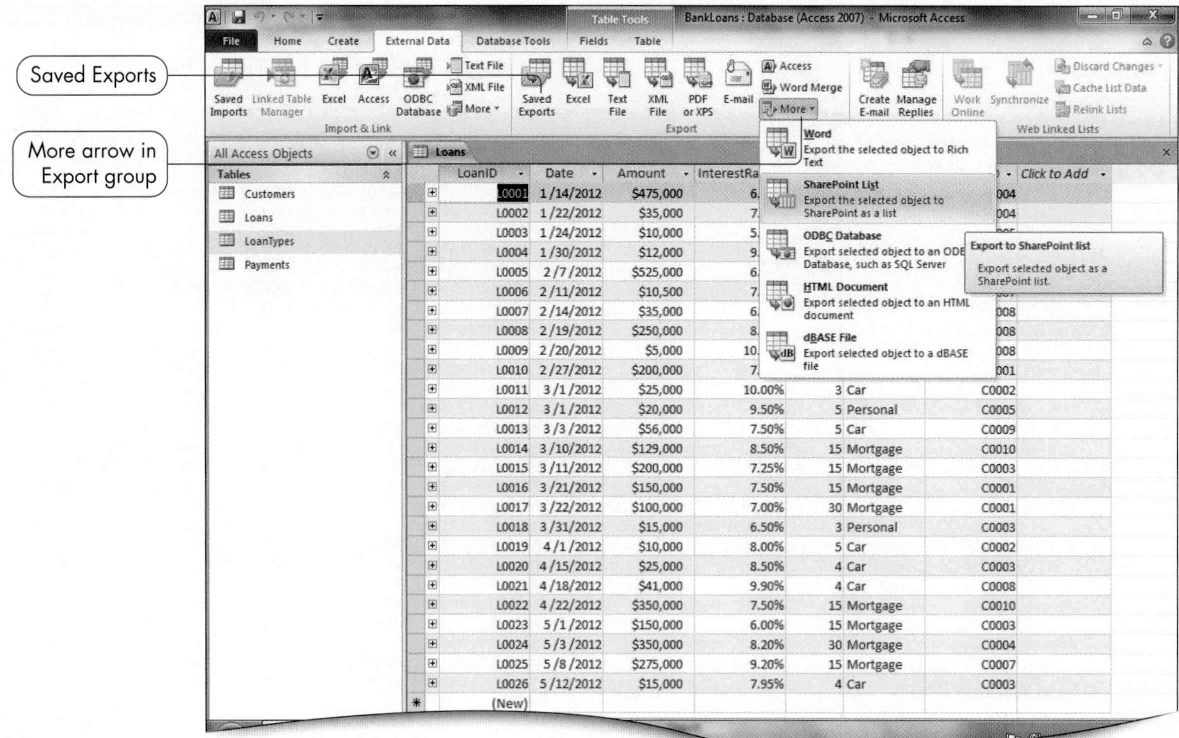

FIGURE 4.65c ➤

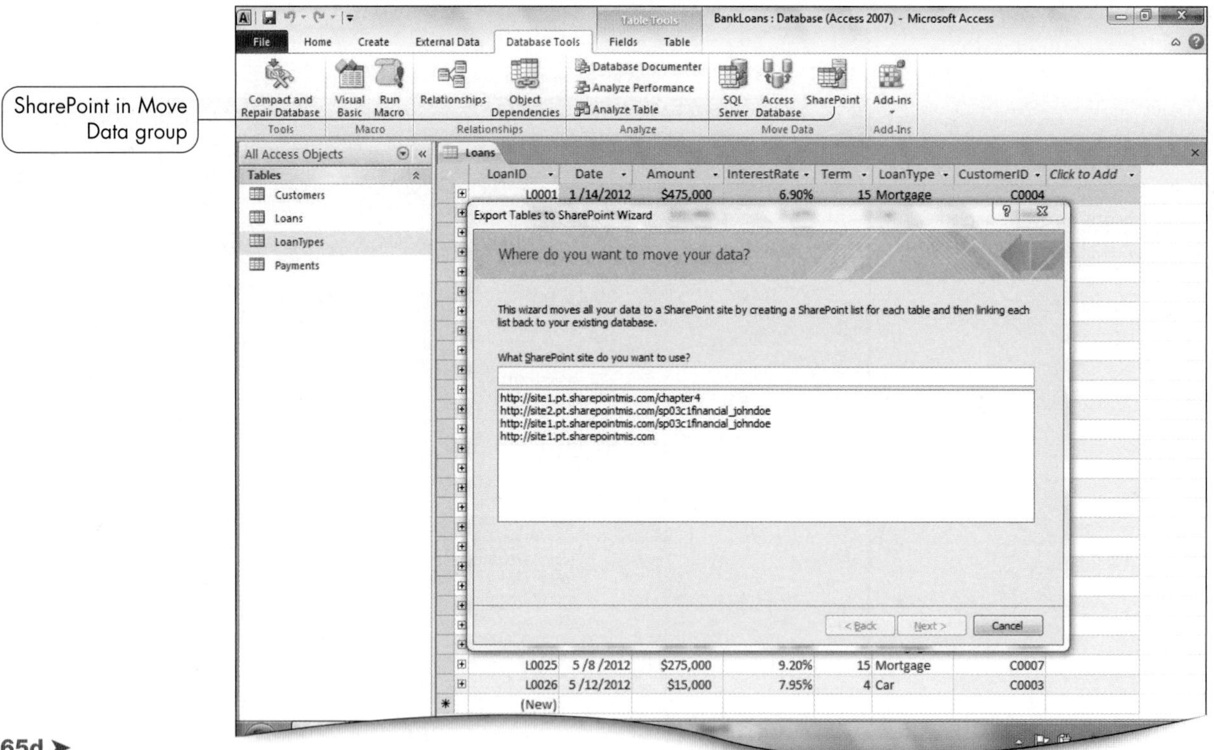

FIGURE 4.65d ➤

You can export an Access table to SharePoint. In Access, open the table you want to export to a SharePoint list, click the External Data tab, click More in the Export group, and then click SharePoint List. The Export - SharePoint Site dialog box is displayed. Select the site in the *Specify a SharePoint* section or type the URL in the text box. Type a name for the new list in the *Specify a name for the new list* box, leave the *Open list when finished* check box checked, and then click OK. The All Items view of the new list is displayed in a new browser window (see Figure 4.66a). Activate the Save Export page of the Access Export - SharePoint

Site dialog box, if you want to save the steps for future use, as shown in Figure 4.66b, select the Save Export steps check box, and then click Save Export.

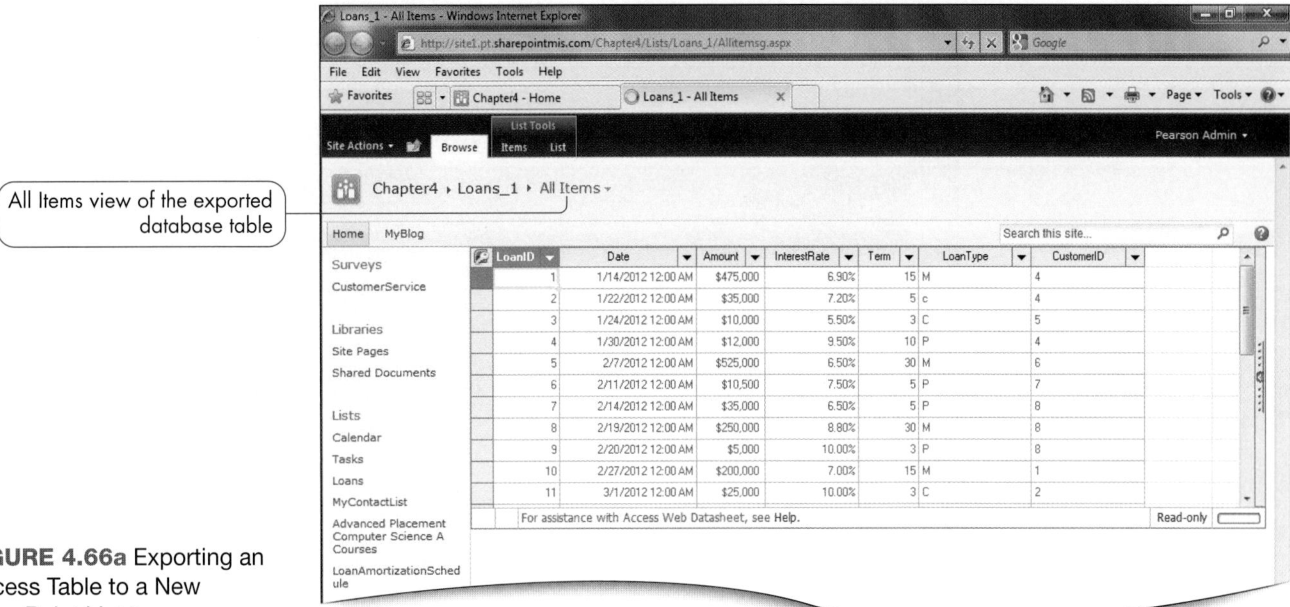

FIGURE 4.66a Exporting an Access Table to a New SharePoint List ➤

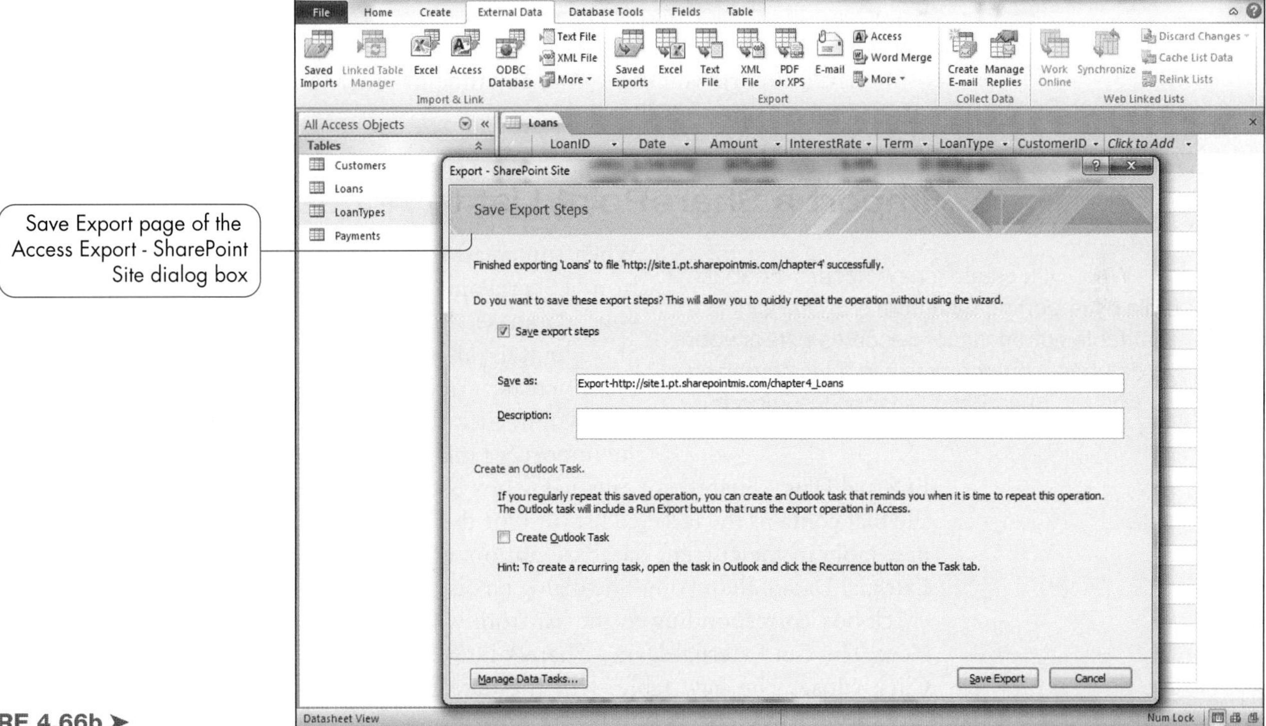

FIGURE 4.66b ➤

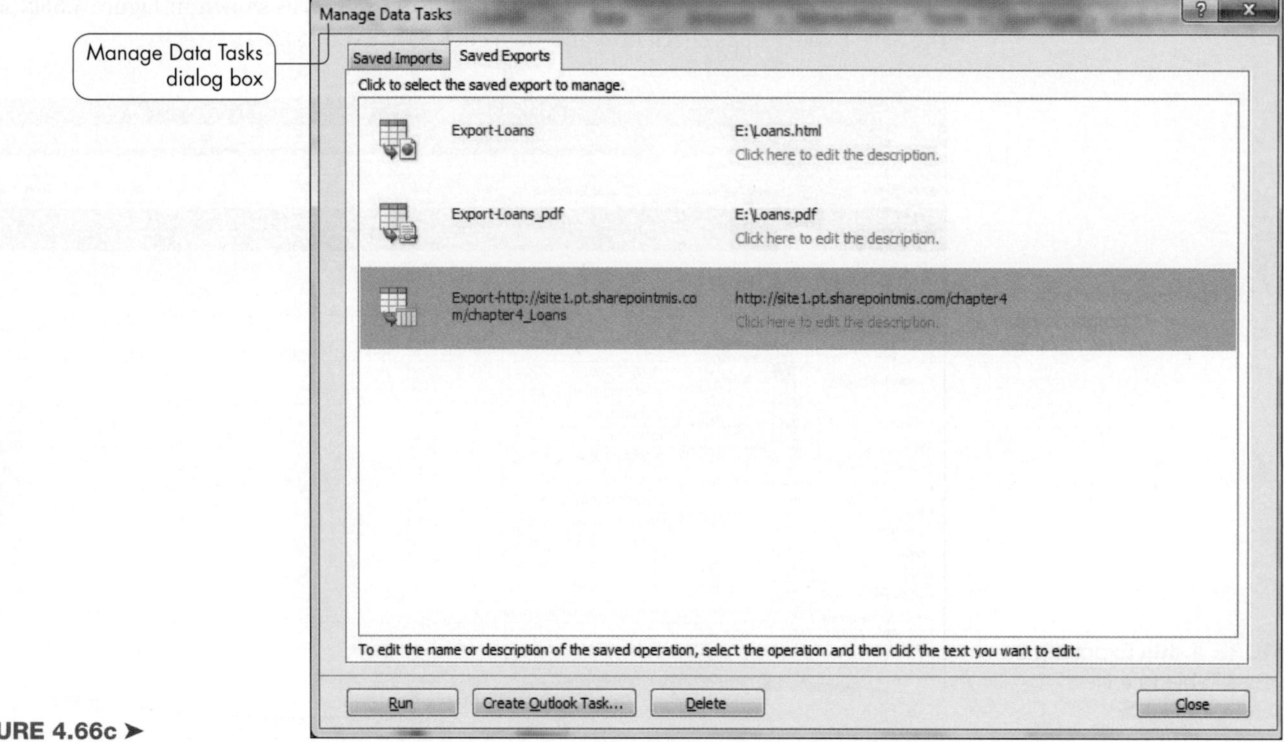

FIGURE 4.66c ➤

All previously saved exports can be found using the Saved Exports command in the Export group on the External Data tab. Click Saved Exports (see Figure 4.65c) to display the Saved Exports tab of the Manage Data Tasks dialog box, as shown in Figure 4.66c, listing all of the saved exports you can run at any time in order to repeat the steps included in each selected export.

Import a SharePoint List to Access

When you create a new Access database table by importing data from a SharePoint list, that table automatically becomes part of your database, but the data is not synchronized with the SharePoint list after it is imported.

When you create a new Access database table by importing data from a SharePoint list, that table automatically becomes part of your database, but the data is not synchronized with the SharePoint list after it is imported.

To create a new blank Access database table with data from SharePoint, click the External Data tab in Access, click More in the Import & Link group, and then click SharePoint list. The Get External Data - SharePoint Site dialog box is displayed, as shown in Figure 4.65a. Select the site that contains the targeted list (or type the URL), select the Import the source data into a new table in the current database option, and then click Next. In the next step, the Get External Data - SharePoint Site dialog box is displayed, as shown in Figure 4.67b. Select the check box corresponding to the list from which you want to import data, and then click Next. The Get External Data - SharePoint Site Save Import Steps dialog box is displayed. Click Close. The new table with the data from SharePoint is displayed in the Access Navigation Pane, as shown in Figure 4.67c.

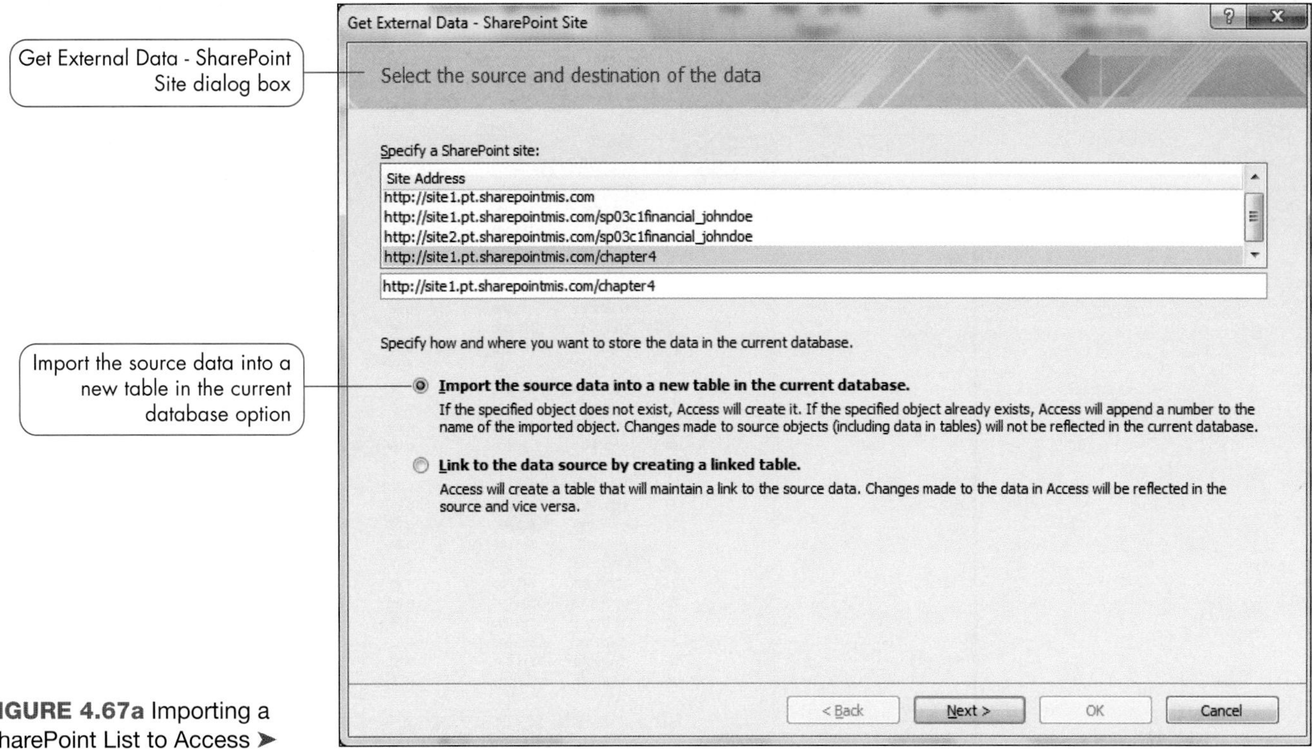

FIGURE 4.67a Importing a SharePoint List to Access ➤

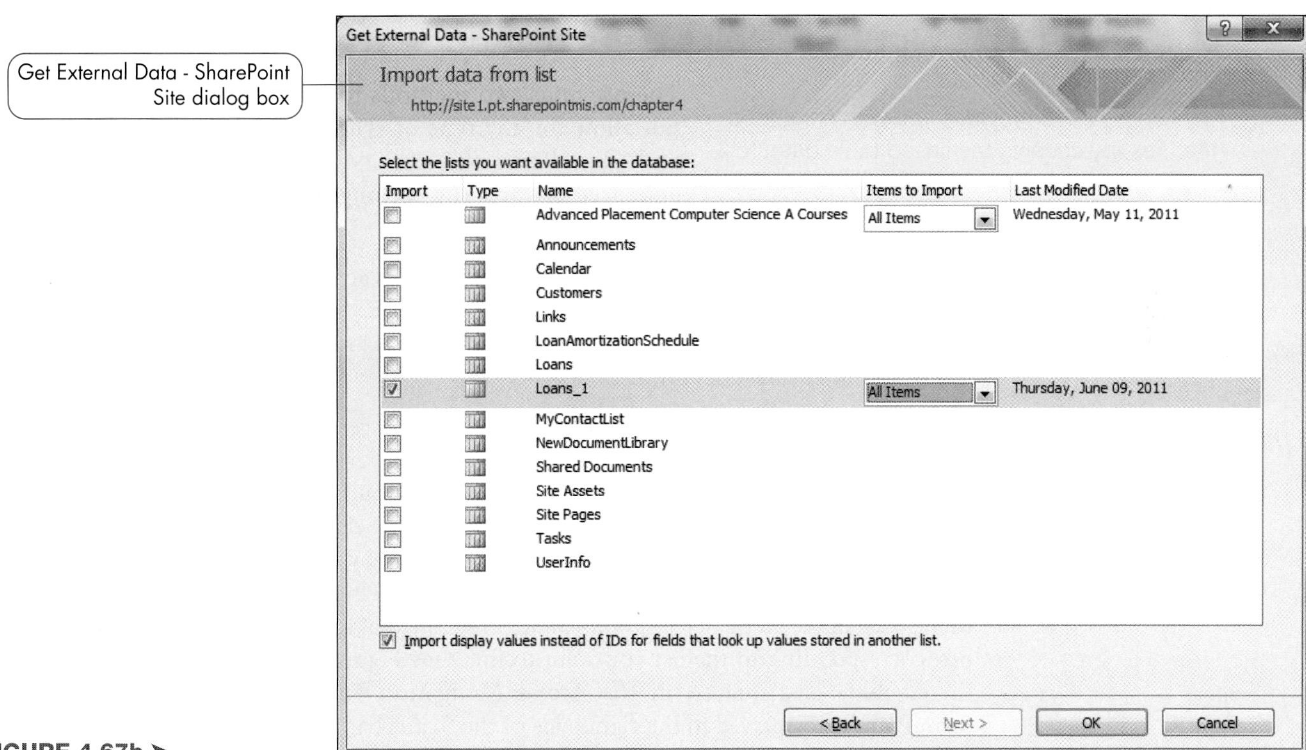

FIGURE 4.67b ➤

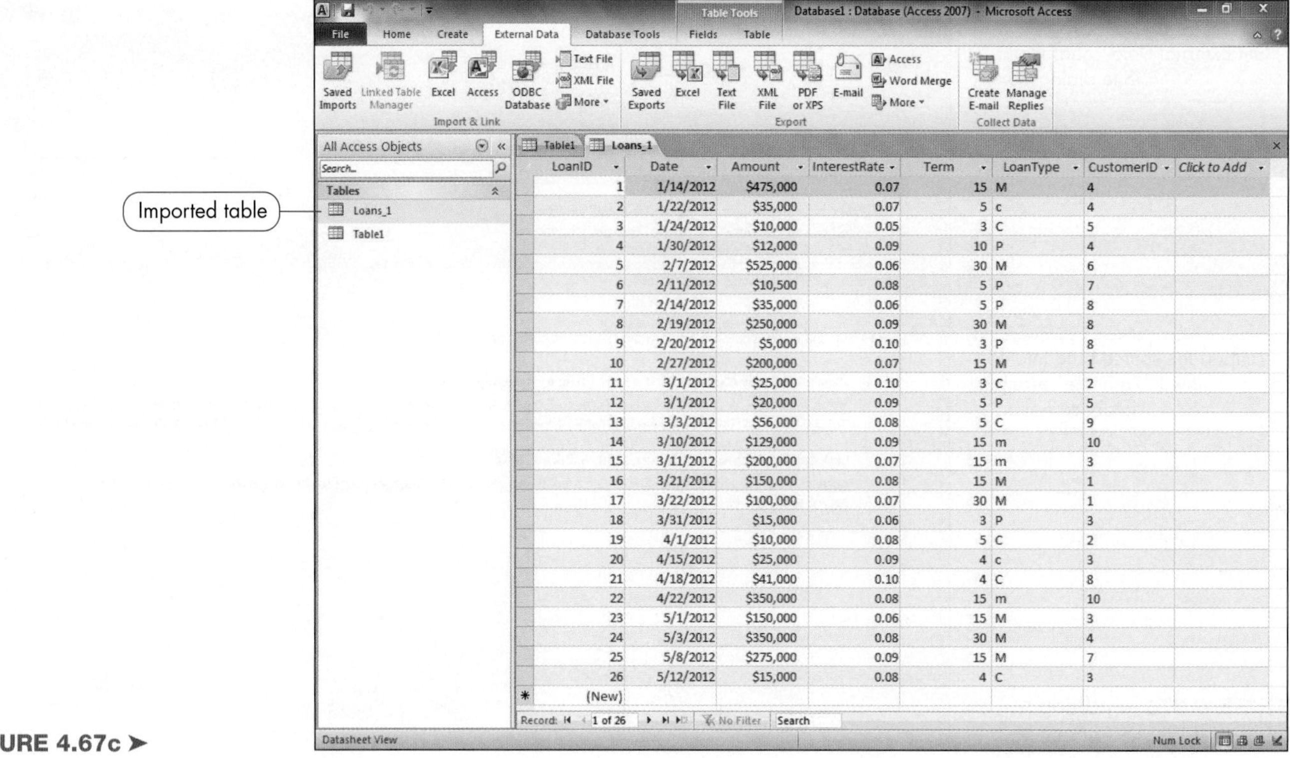

LoanID	Date	Amount	InterestRate	Term	LoanType	CustomerID
1	1/14/2012	$475,000	0.07	15	M	4
2	1/22/2012	$35,000	0.07	5	c	4
3	1/24/2012	$10,000	0.05	3	C	5
4	1/30/2012	$12,000	0.09	10	P	4
5	2/7/2012	$525,000	0.06	30	M	6
6	2/11/2012	$10,500	0.08	5	P	7
7	2/14/2012	$35,000	0.06	5	P	8
8	2/19/2012	$250,000	0.09	30	M	8
9	2/20/2012	$5,000	0.10	3	P	8
10	2/27/2012	$200,000	0.07	15	M	1
11	3/1/2012	$25,000	0.10	3	C	2
12	3/1/2012	$20,000	0.09	5	P	5
13	3/3/2012	$56,000	0.08	5	C	9
14	3/10/2012	$129,000	0.09	15	m	10
15	3/11/2012	$200,000	0.07	15	m	3
16	3/21/2012	$150,000	0.08	15	M	1
17	3/22/2012	$100,000	0.07	30	M	1
18	3/31/2012	$15,000	0.06	3	P	3
19	4/1/2012	$10,000	0.08	5	C	2
20	4/15/2012	$25,000	0.09	4	c	3
21	4/18/2012	$41,000	0.10	4	C	8
22	4/22/2012	$350,000	0.08	15	m	10
23	5/1/2012	$150,000	0.06	15	M	3
24	5/3/2012	$350,000	0.08	30	M	4
25	5/8/2012	$275,000	0.09	15	M	7
26	5/12/2012	$15,000	0.08	4	C	3

FIGURE 4.67c ➤

Link SharePoint Lists to Access

Access 2010 provides you with enhanced features (by caching the linked table data) for using linked tables.

The previous two methods for importing/exporting data did not allow for any type of synchronization between the Access and SharePoint site data. Access 2010 provides you with enhanced features (by caching the linked table data) for using linked tables:

- When connectivity with the SharePoint server is activated, Access automatically synchronizes data changes.
- When connectivity with the SharePoint server is lost, the Access database automatically goes offline.

The linking process begins with closing all the Access objects in the Access database. Click the External Data tab, click More in the Import & Link group, and then click SharePoint List. The Select the source and destination page of the data page of the Get External Data - SharePoint Site dialog box is displayed. Select the site that contains the list to which you need to link, select the Link to data source by creating a linked table option, as shown in Figure 4.68a, and then click Next. The Choose the SharePoint lists you want to link to the page of the Get External Data - SharePoint Site dialog box is displayed. Select the check box corresponding to the list you want to link (see Figure 4.68b), and then click OK. The linked table is displayed in the Access Navigation Pane, and the text "Online with SharePoint" is displayed to the right edge of the Status bar, as shown in Figure 4.68c.

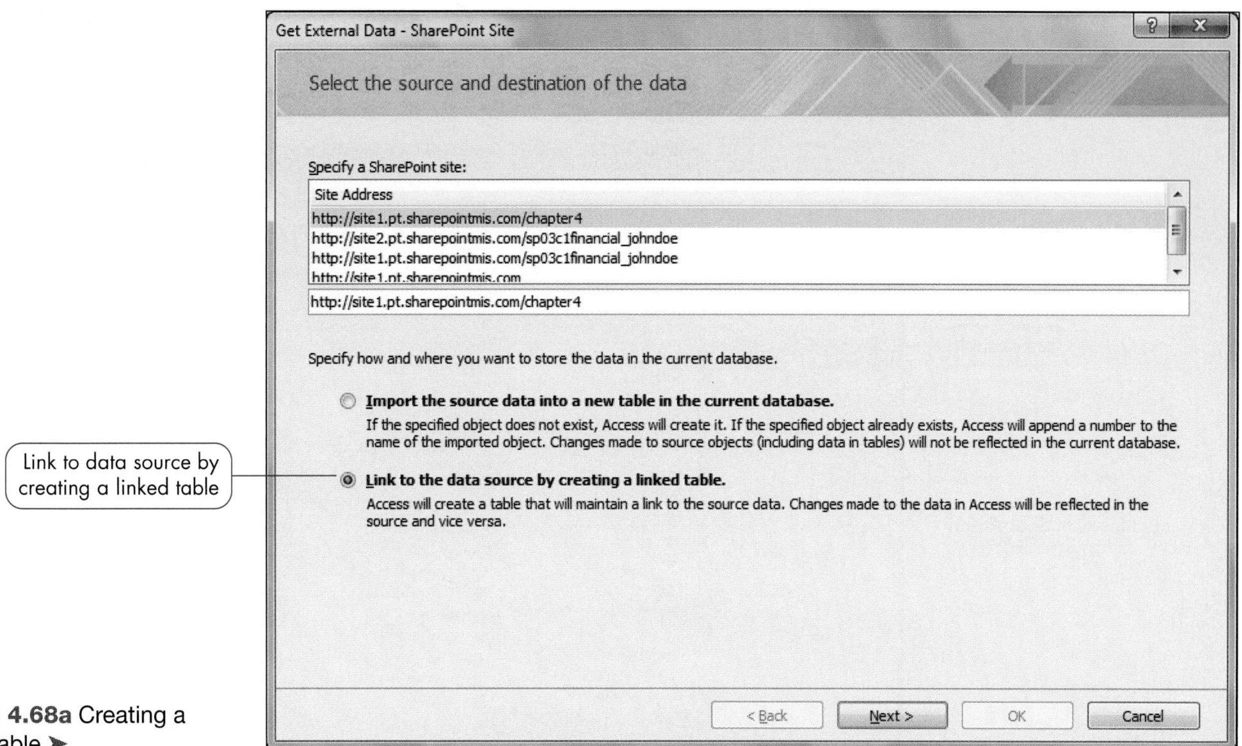

FIGURE 4.68a Creating a Linked Table ➤

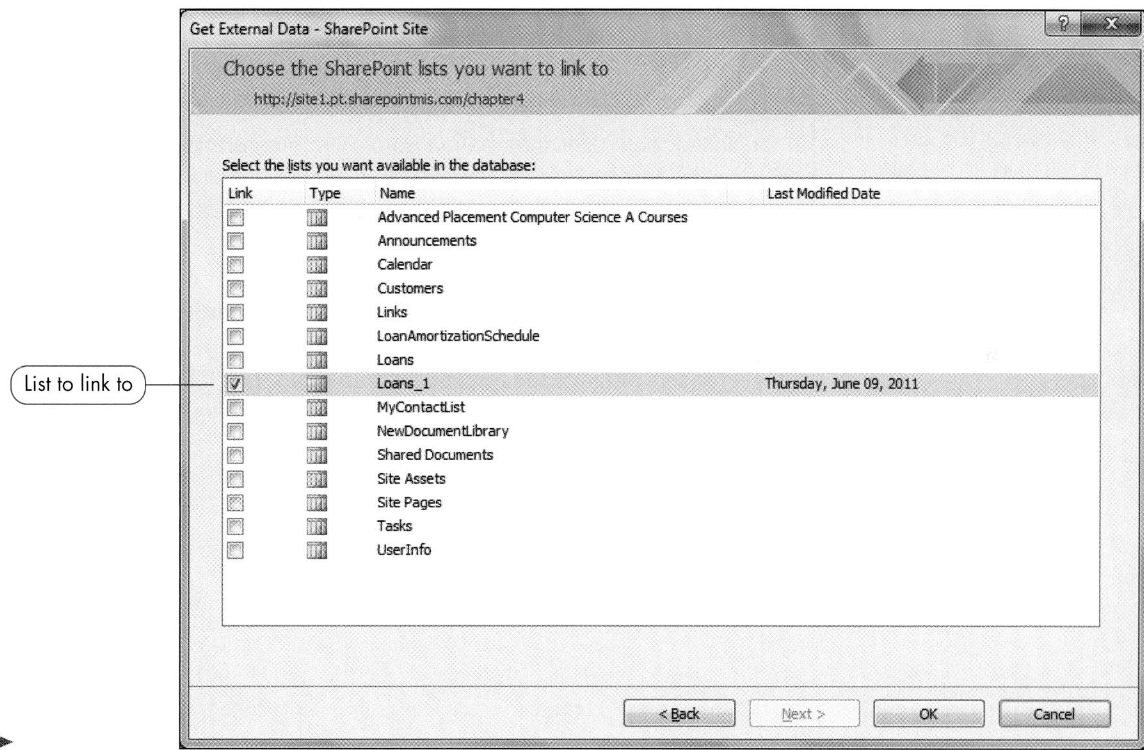

FIGURE 4.68b ➤

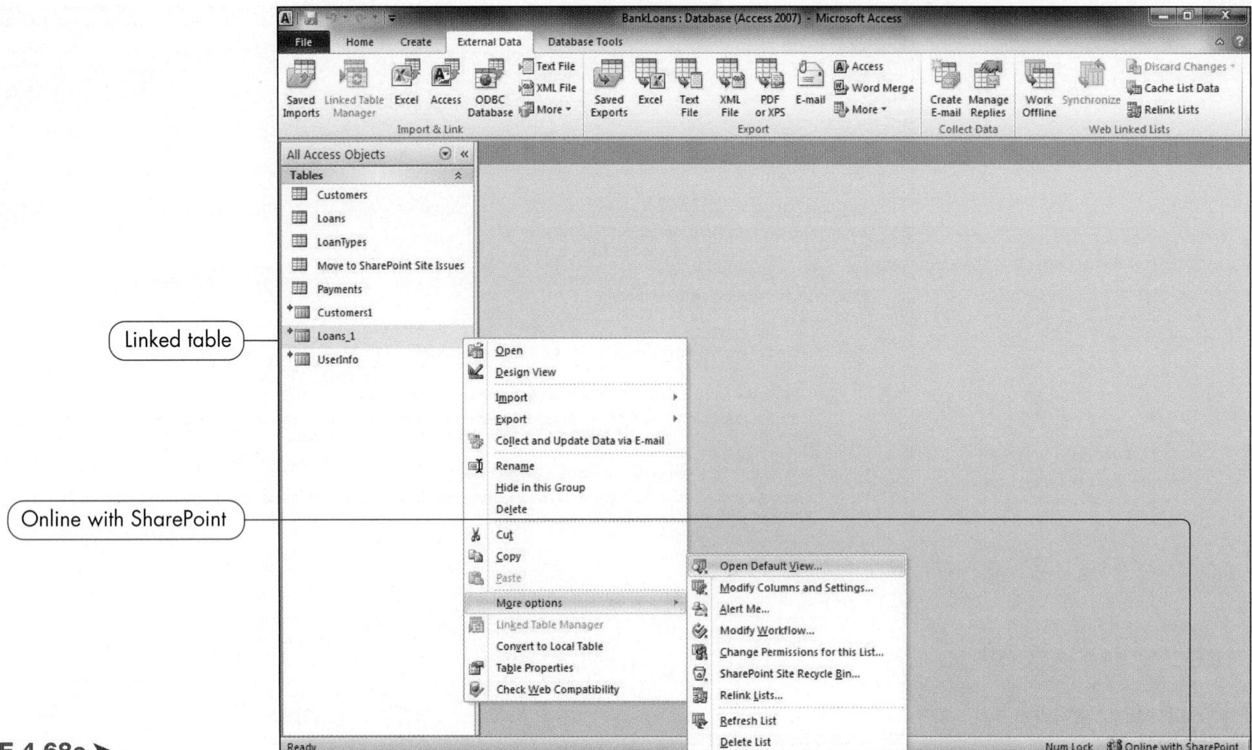

FIGURE 4.68c ➤

Linked Table

If the linked table uses information from other supporting tables, all those tables will also show on the Access Navigation Pane as linked, as shown in Figure 4.68c.

To see the results of a linked Access and SharePoint object, right-click the linked table, click More, and then click Open Default View. The SharePoint list is displayed in a browser window. In the Access window, double-click the name of the linked table, and then make a change in a cell. Activate the browser window, and then click Refresh. The value of the modified cell will now show the same value in the SharePoint browser window, as shown in Figure 4.69.

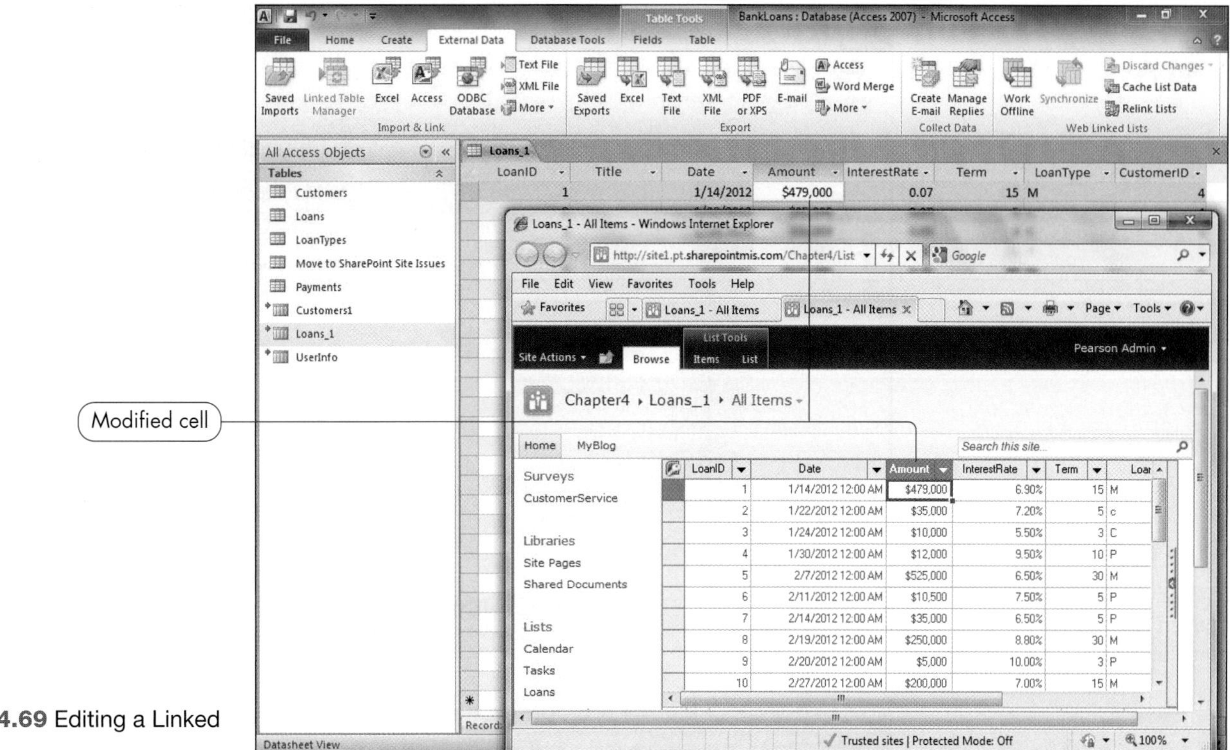

FIGURE 4.69 Editing a Linked Table ➤

Moving an Access Database to SharePoint

> Moving Access databases to SharePoint sites enables you to take advantage of both Access and SharePoint tools for managing and sharing data.

Although Access is a powerful application for managing data, it was not designed to enable users to work concurrently on the same project. Moving Access databases to SharePoint sites enables you to take advantage of both Access and SharePoint tools for managing and sharing data.

In Access, click the Database Tools tab, and then click SharePoint in the Move Data group. The Export Tables to SharePoint Wizard is launched and the *Where do you want to move your data?* page is displayed. Select the target site in the *What SharePoint site do you want to use* section (or type the URL of the site), as shown in Figure 4.70a, and then click Next. The Moving Data to SharePoint site dialog box displays the progress of this process in the following steps:

- A SharePoint list is created for each Access table, as shown in Figure 4.70b.
- Data is moved from each Access table to their corresponding SharePoint list. Each row of an Access table is moved to an item in the corresponding list.
- The Access tables are replaced by linked tables that target their corresponding SharePoint lists, as shown in Figure 4.70c.
- A backup copy of the database is created on your computer.

Click the Show Details check box, and then click Finish, as shown in Figure 4.70d. The Access database now functions as a user interface to the data moved into SharePoint. Your users will be able to take advantage all of the SharePoint functionalities, including check-in and check-out functions, secure access to data, and restoring deleted items using the Recycle Bin.

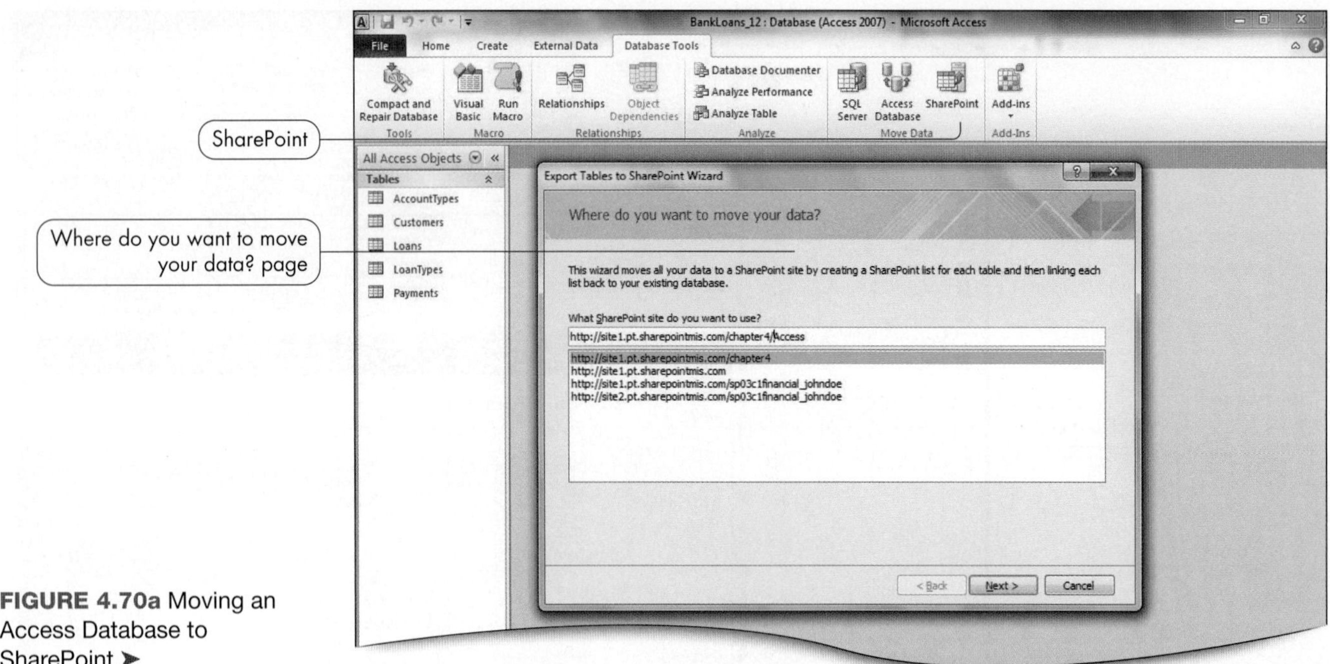

FIGURE 4.70a Moving an Access Database to SharePoint ➤

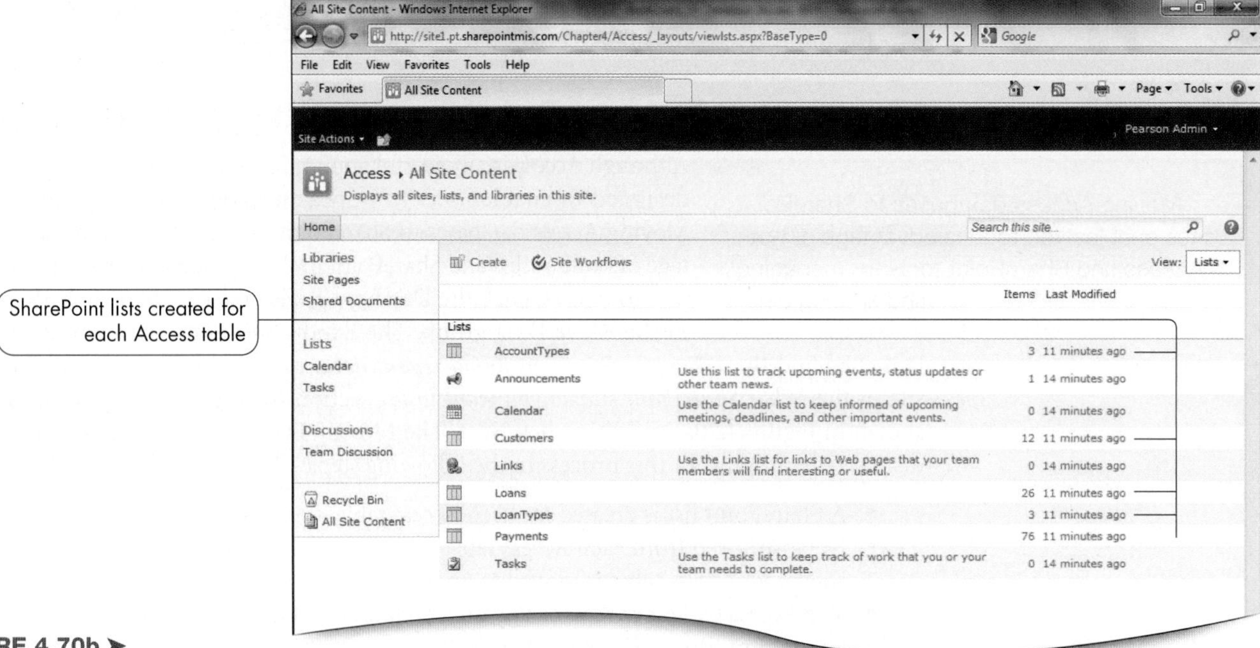

FIGURE 4.70b ➤

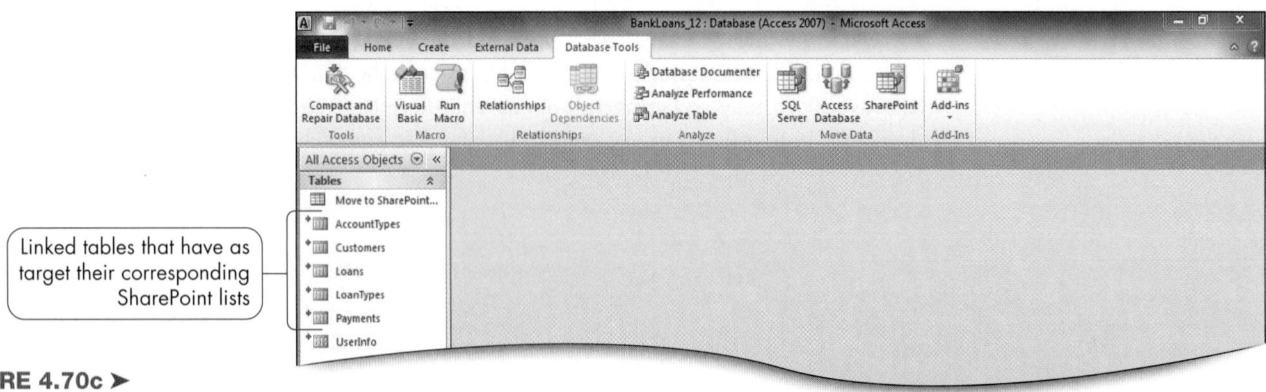

FIGURE 4.70c ➤

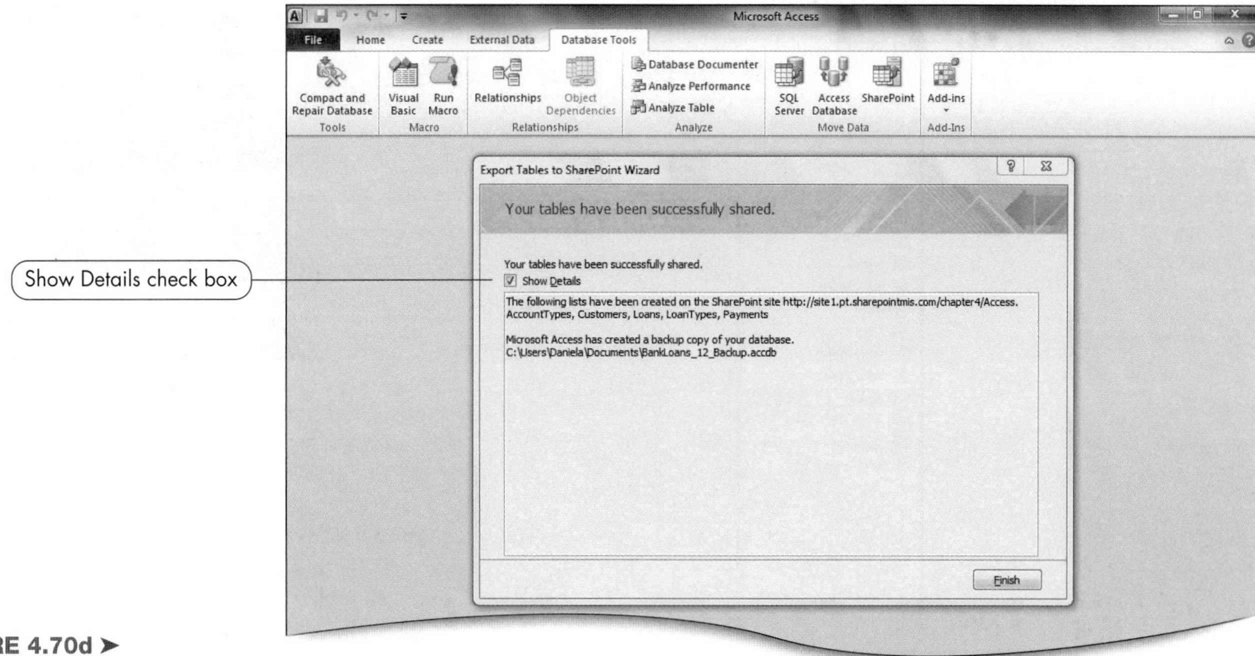

FIGURE 4.70d ➤

Working with Data Sources and Data Views

> By default, documents, worksheets, and presentations that you create in Office 2010 are saved in XML format....

By default, documents, worksheets, and presentations that you create in Office 2010 are saved in XML format, with a file name extension that adds an "x" or an "m" to the extensions with which you are already familiar. The "x" signifies an XML file that has no macros, and the "m" signifies an XML file that contains macros. All Microsoft Office 2010 files can be exported as XML files.

SharePoint Designer includes tools that enable you to connect, read, and modify the content of different type of data sources, such as XML files. These tools enable you to create dynamic, data-driven Web pages.

Export Microsoft Office 2010 Access Data in XML Files

The Access 2010 user interface enables you to export a table as XML files, and generates the data file (.xml), schema file (.xsd), and presentation file (.xsl). If you choose a client-side transformation, an .html file will be generated, whereas if you choose a server-side transformation an .asp file will be created.

To export an Access table to XML, select the table you want to export in the Navigation Pane. Click the External Data tab, and then click XML File in the Export group. The Export-XML File dialog box opens, as shown in Figure 4.71a. Click Browse and navigate to the location where the files will be stored, specifying the name and format. Click OK to continue; the Export XML dialog box appears. Click all three check boxes to select them, as shown in Figure 4.71b, and then click More Options. Click the Presentation tab on the Export XML dialog box. If you want to generate a client-side transformation, click the Client (HTML) option. If you want a server-side transformation, click the Server (ASP), as shown in Figure 4.71c. Click Browse and navigate to the location where the export will be stored, clicking OK to close the Browse dialog box when you are finished. Click OK to close the Export XML dialog box. So that you can later reuse the export, click the Save export steps check box, and then click Save Export. The transformation is completed and the files are shown in the destination location. Preview the .xml file in a browser, as shown in Figure 4.71d. The content of the .xml file is an accurate representation of the original Access data.

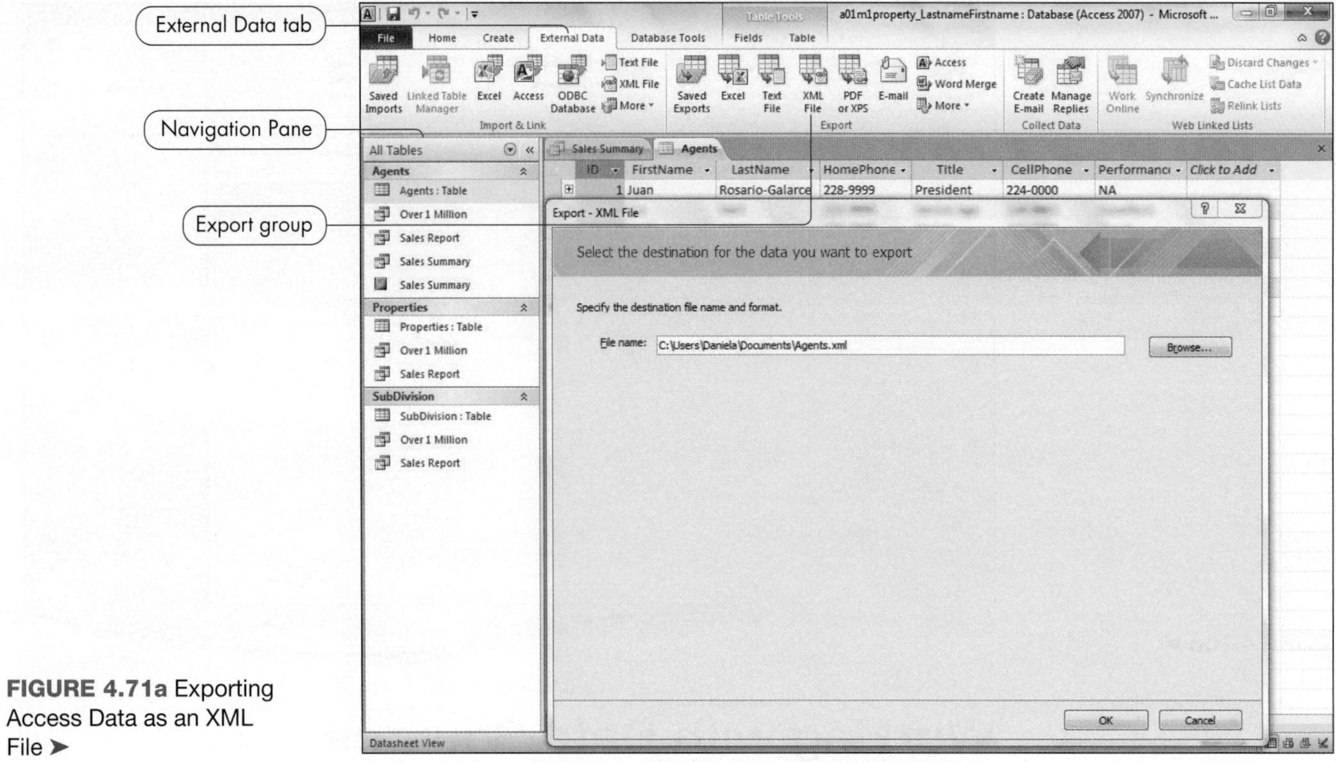

FIGURE 4.71a Exporting Access Data as an XML File ➤

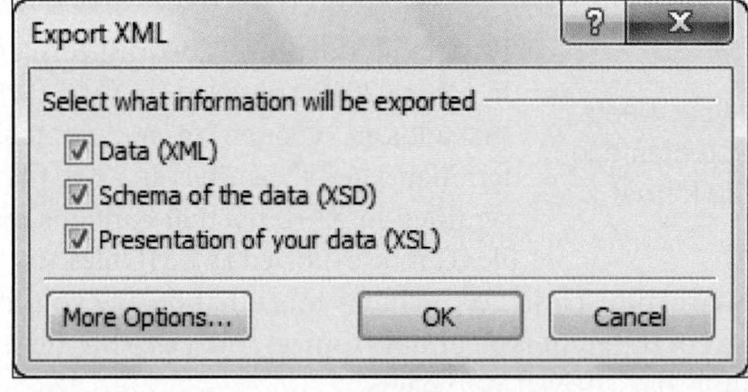

FIGURE 4.71b ➤

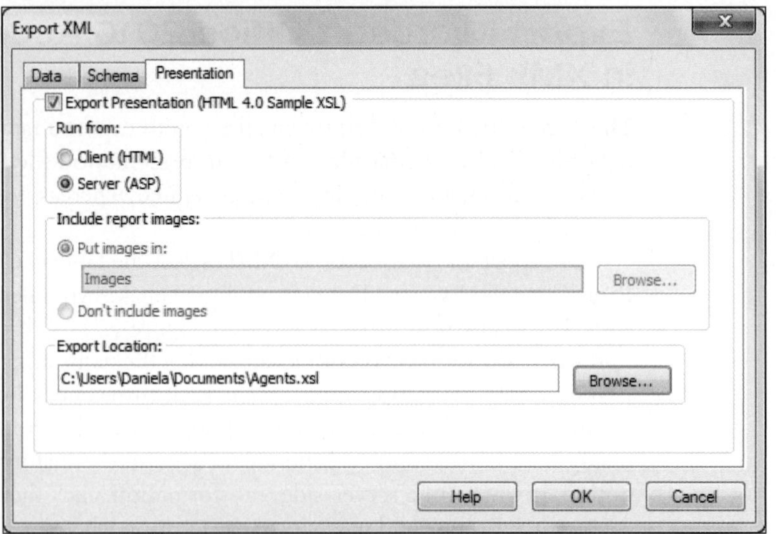

FIGURE 4.71c ➤

```
<?xml version="1.0" encoding="UTF-8" ?>
- <dataroot xmlns:od="urn:schemas-microsoft-com:officedata" xmlns:xsi="http://www.w3.org/2001/XMLSchema-instance"
  xsi:noNamespaceSchemaLocation="Agents.xsd" generated="2011-06-11T10:19:18">
  - <Agents>
      <ID>1</ID>
      <FirstName>Juan</FirstName>
      <LastName>Rosario-Galarce</LastName>
      <HomePhone>228-9999</HomePhone>
      <Title>President</Title>
      <CellPhone>224-0000</CellPhone>
      <PerformanceReview>NA</PerformanceReview>
    </Agents>
  - <Agents>
      <ID>2</ID>
      <FirstName>Kia</FirstName>
      <LastName>Hart</LastName>
      <HomePhone>222-9999</HomePhone>
      <Title>Senior Age</Title>
      <CellPhone>224-0001</CellPhone>
      <PerformanceReview>Excellent</PerformanceReview>
    </Agents>
  - <Agents>
      <ID>3</ID>
      <FirstName>Keith</FirstName>
      <LastName>Mast</LastName>
      <HomePhone>226-9999</HomePhone>
      <Title>Agent</Title>
      <CellPhone>224-0002</CellPhone>
      <PerformanceReview>Good</PerformanceReview>
    </Agents>
  - <Agents>
      <ID>4</ID>
      <FirstName>Ko-Yun</FirstName>
      <LastName>Yang</LastName>
      <HomePhone>221-9999</HomePhone>
      <Title>Agent</Title>
      <CellPhone>224-0003</CellPhone>
      <PerformanceReview>Good</PerformanceReview>
    </Agents>
  - <Agents>
      <ID>5</ID>
      <FirstName>Steven</FirstName>
      <LastName>Lookabil</LastName>
      <HomePhone>222-0000</HomePhone>
      <Title>Agent Trai</Title>
      <CellPhone>224-0004</CellPhone>
      <PerformanceReview>Satisfactory</PerformanceReview>
    </Agents>
  - <Agents>
      <ID>6</ID>
      <FirstName>Angela</FirstName>
      <LastName>Scott</LastName>
      <HomePhone>228-0000</HomePhone>
      <Title>Agent Trai</Title>
      <CellPhone>223-0005</CellPhone>
      <PerformanceReview>Good</PerformanceReview>
    </Agents>
  </dataroot>
```

FIGURE 4.71d ➤

TIP Create an XML Data File and XML Schema File from Excel Worksheet Data

The process of creating an XML data file and XML schema file from a cell range on an Excel worksheet is a little more complicated. You can use version 1.1 of the Excel 2003 XML Tools Add-in to enhance the existing XML features in Microsoft Excel 2010. To learn about this process see the comprehensive Microsoft article "Create an XML data file and XML schema file from worksheet data" (http://office.microsoft.com/en-us/excel-help/create-an-xml-data-file-and-xml-schema-file-from-worksheet-data-HA010342365.aspx).

Use an XML Document as a Data Source for a SharePoint Data View

SharePoint Foundation includes a basic version of Business Connectivity Services. This means that users can work in SharePoint with external data

SharePoint Foundation includes a basic version of Business Connectivity Services. This means that users can work in SharePoint with external data. All you need is SharePoint Designer 2010 to create the connection to the data and define what you want to display. In Chapter 3, you created Data Views of lists and libraries. Now you are ready to learn how to connect to an XML file so it becomes a data source and create a Data View of the data included in the XML file.

Launch SharePoint Designer, open a Wiki page, click inside the PlaceHolderMain (custom) placeholder to place an insertion point in the placeholder, click the Insert tab, and then click Data View in the Data Views & Forms group, as shown in Figure 4.72a. By default, all the lists and libraries within a site are listed as Data Sources. You can add an Empty Data View and later on add a source, as shown in Figure 4.72b, or you can click More Data Sources to open the Data Sources Picker dialog box, as shown in Figure 4.72c.

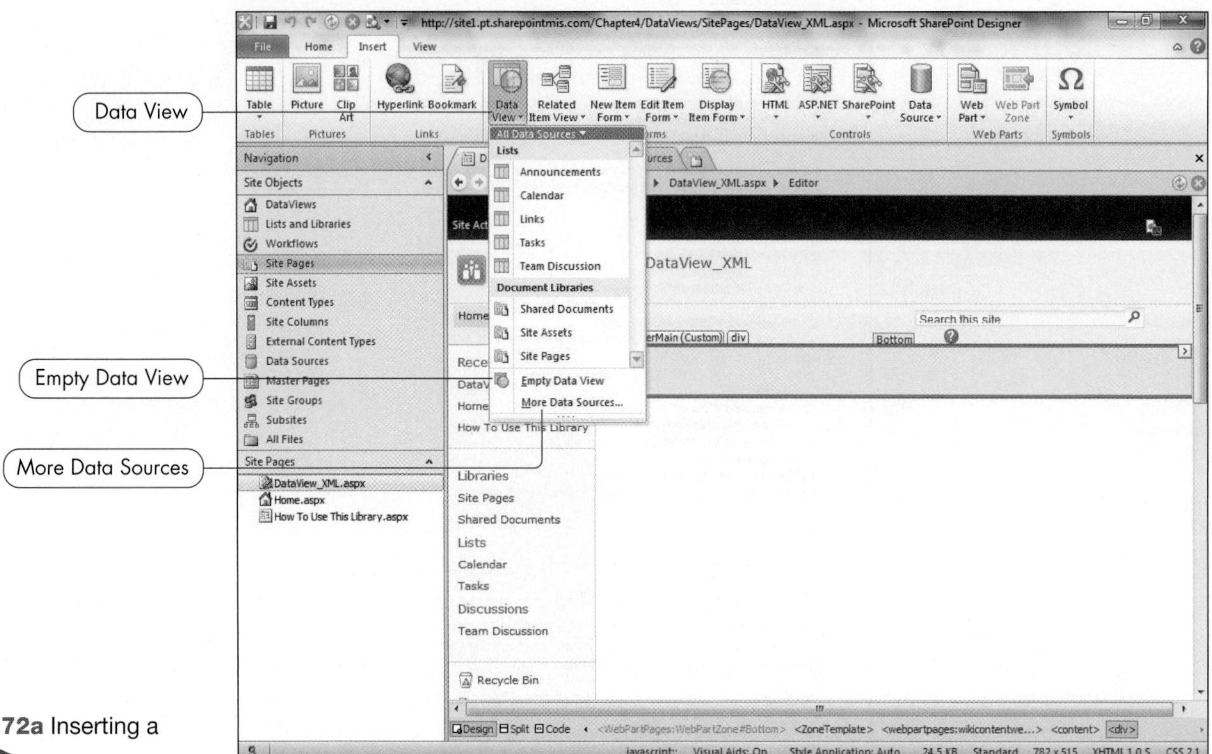

FIGURE 4.72a Inserting a Data View ➤

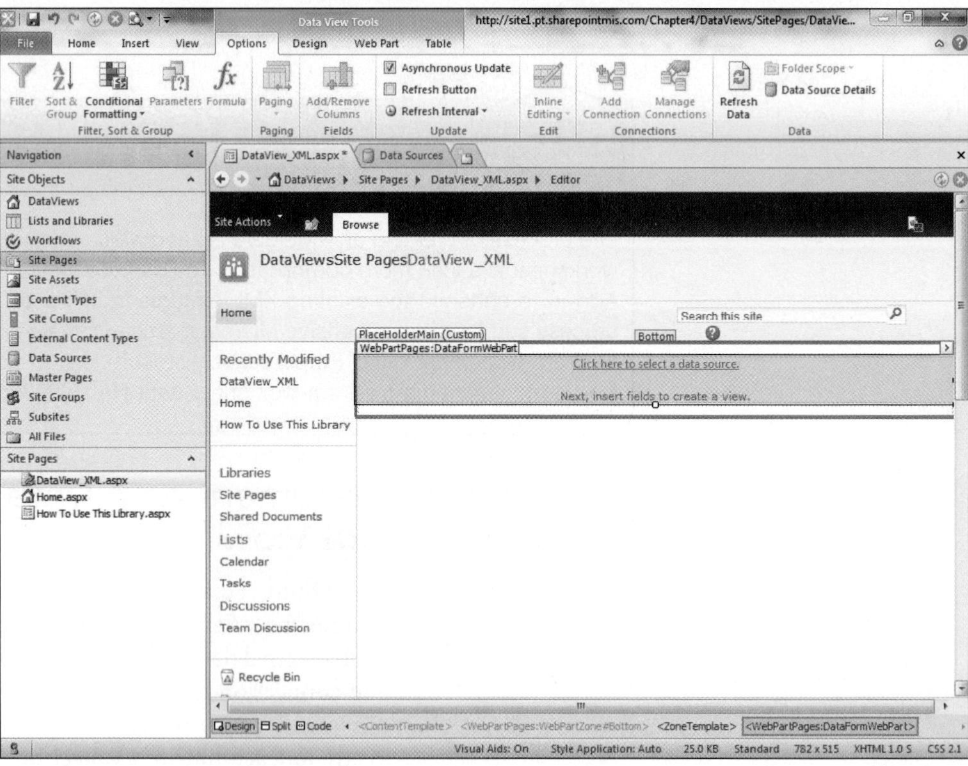

FIGURE 4.72b ➤

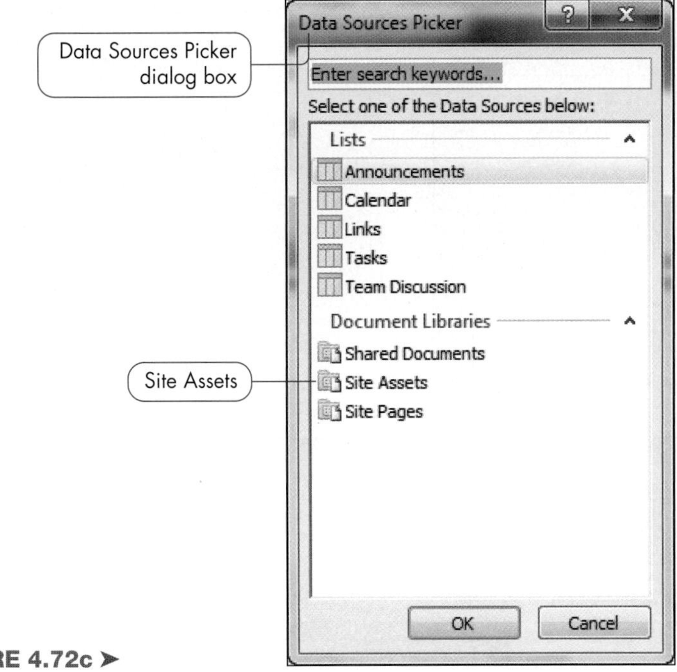

FIGURE 4.72c ➤

SharePoint Designer then queries the root of the current site and the Site Assets Library for XML files. These files will be automatically added to the Data Sources gallery, as shown in Figure 4.72c. Click Site Assets in the Navigation Pane, and then click Import in the New group to display the Import dialog box, as shown in Figure 4.73a. Click Add File to display the Add File to Import List dialog box, press Ctrl, and select the .xml and its associated .xsd and .xsl files, and then click Open, as shown in Figure 4.73b. Click OK to close the Import dialog box.

Open the Wiki page again, position an insertion point inside the PlaceHolderMain (custom) placeholder, click the Insert tab, and then click Data View in the Data Views & Forms group. The imported XML file is now displayed in the XML Files section of the All Data Sources list, as shown in Figure 4.73c. Click the name of the imported XML file. The content of the XML file is displayed as an HTML table within the DataForm WebPart control, and the Data Source Details task pane is visible, as shown in Figure 4.73d. The Data View Tools–Options tab is displayed, enabling you to further customize the Data View (as previously discussed in Chapter 3).

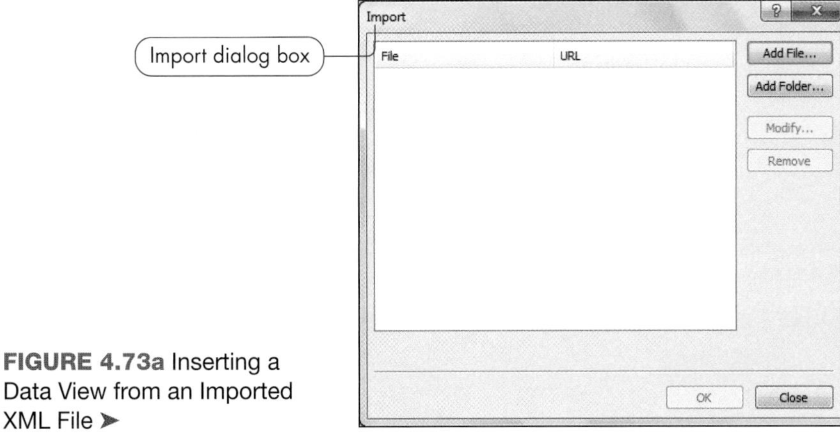

FIGURE 4.73a Inserting a Data View from an Imported XML File ➤

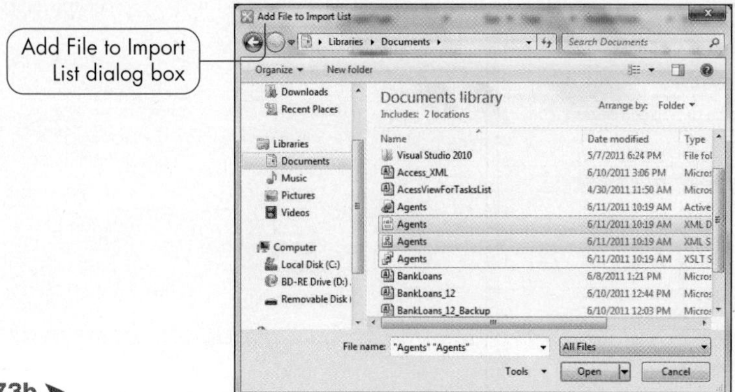

FIGURE 4.73b ➤

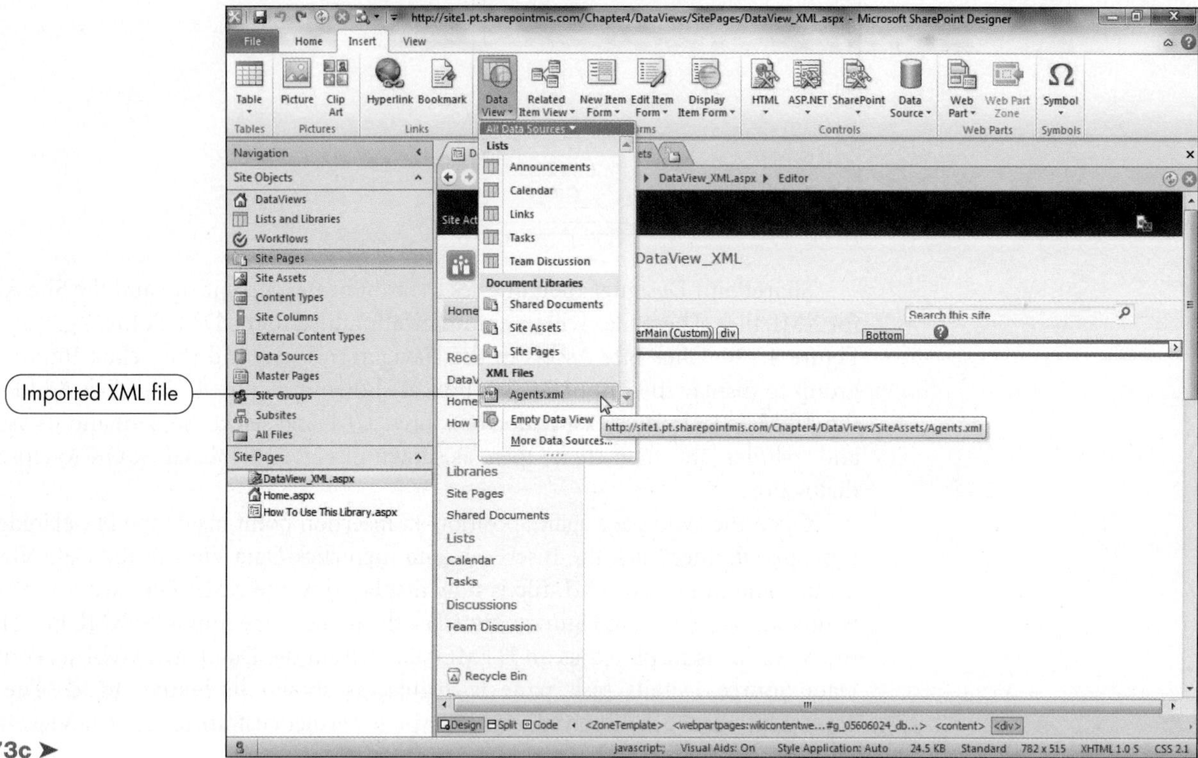

FIGURE 4.73c ➤

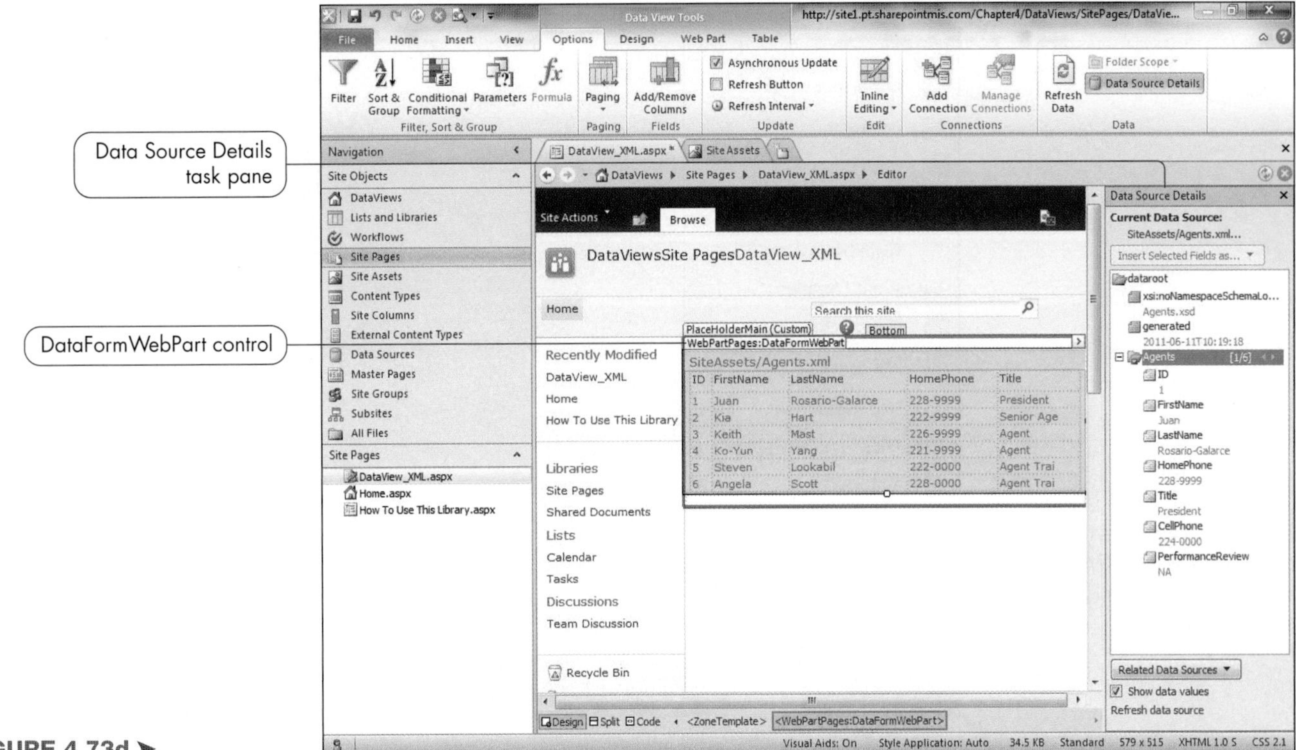

FIGURE 4.73d ➤

You can also create a Data View of an XML file from another library or site by using the XML File Connection command.

You can also create a Data View of an XML file from another library or site by using the XML File Connection command. Consider a situation when you have an XML file uploaded in the Shared Documents library, and you want to create a Data View of this file in a Wiki page. Launch SharePoint Designer, open a Wiki page, and then position an insertion point inside the PlaceHolderMain (custom) placeholder. Click the Insert tab, and then click Data View in the Data Views & Forms group. The XML file uploaded in the Shared Documents library will not be displayed on the All Data Sources menu, as shown in Figure 4.74a. Click Empty Data View. A DataFormWebPart control, shown in Figure 4.74b, is added to the page. Click Data Sources in the Navigation Pane. Click the icon to the left of the Shared Documents library in the Data Sources gallery page, and then click XML File Connection in the New group. Click Browse in the Source tab of the Data Sources Properties dialog box. Locate the XML file in the File Open dialog box, as shown in Figure 4.74c, and then double-click its name. Click OK to close the Data Sources Properties dialog box. The .xml file will now be displayed in the *XML Files* section of the Data Sources gallery page, as shown in Figure 4.74d. Open the Wiki page again, and then click the *Click here to select a data source* link in the PlaceHolderMain. Click the name of the XML file in the Data Source Picker dialog box, as shown in Figure 4.74e, and then click OK. The Data Source Details task pane displays the structure of the XML file. Select all fields, click Insert Selected Fields as, and then select Multiple Item View. Collapse the Navigation Pane to see the data included now in the Data View, as shown in Figure 4.74f.

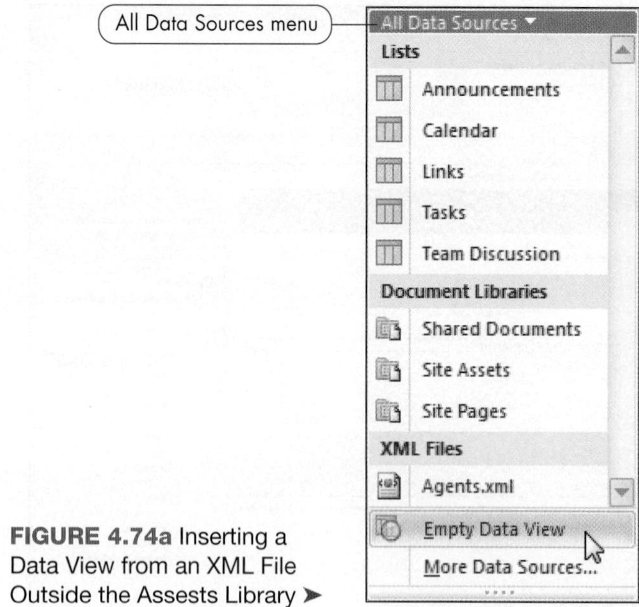

FIGURE 4.74a Inserting a Data View from an XML File Outside the Assests Library ➤

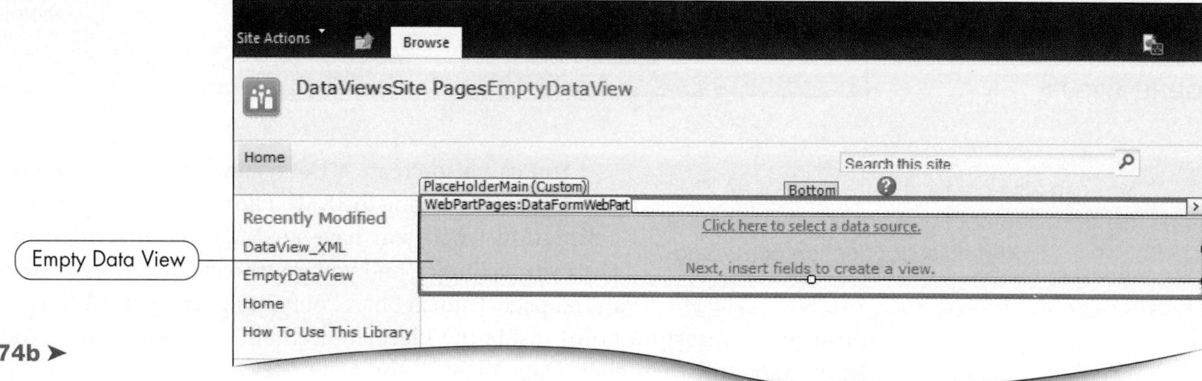

FIGURE 4.74b ➤

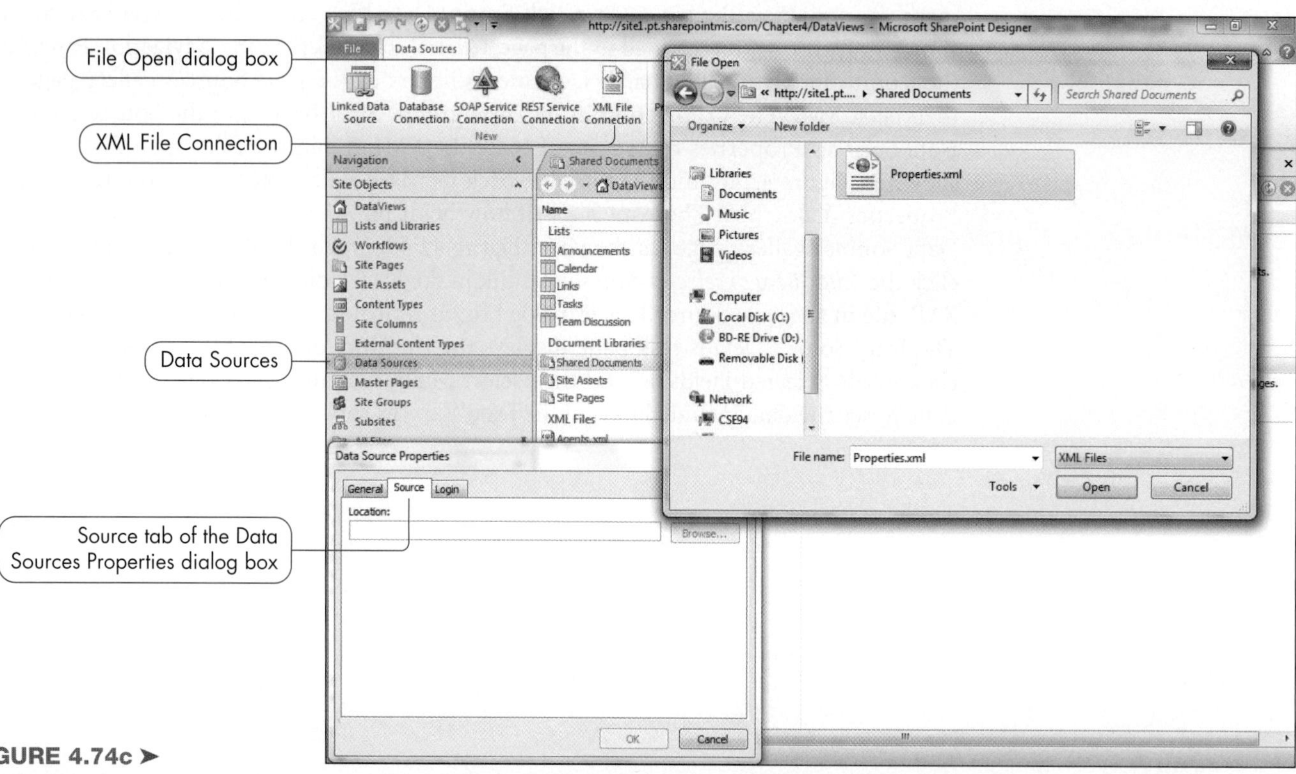

FIGURE 4.74c ➤

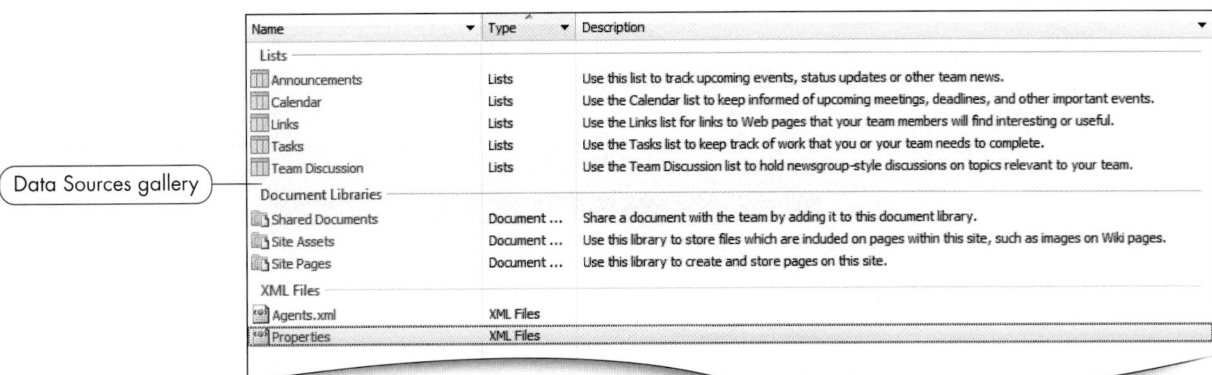

FIGURE 4.74d ➤

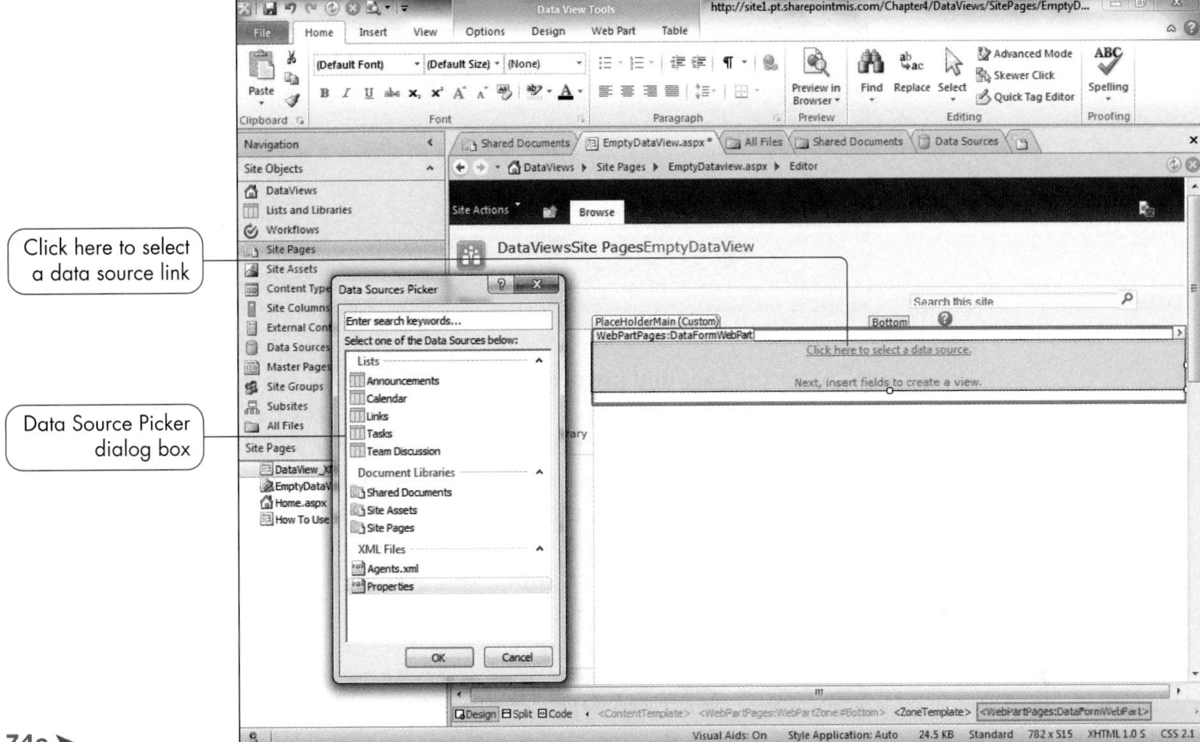

FIGURE 4.74e ➤

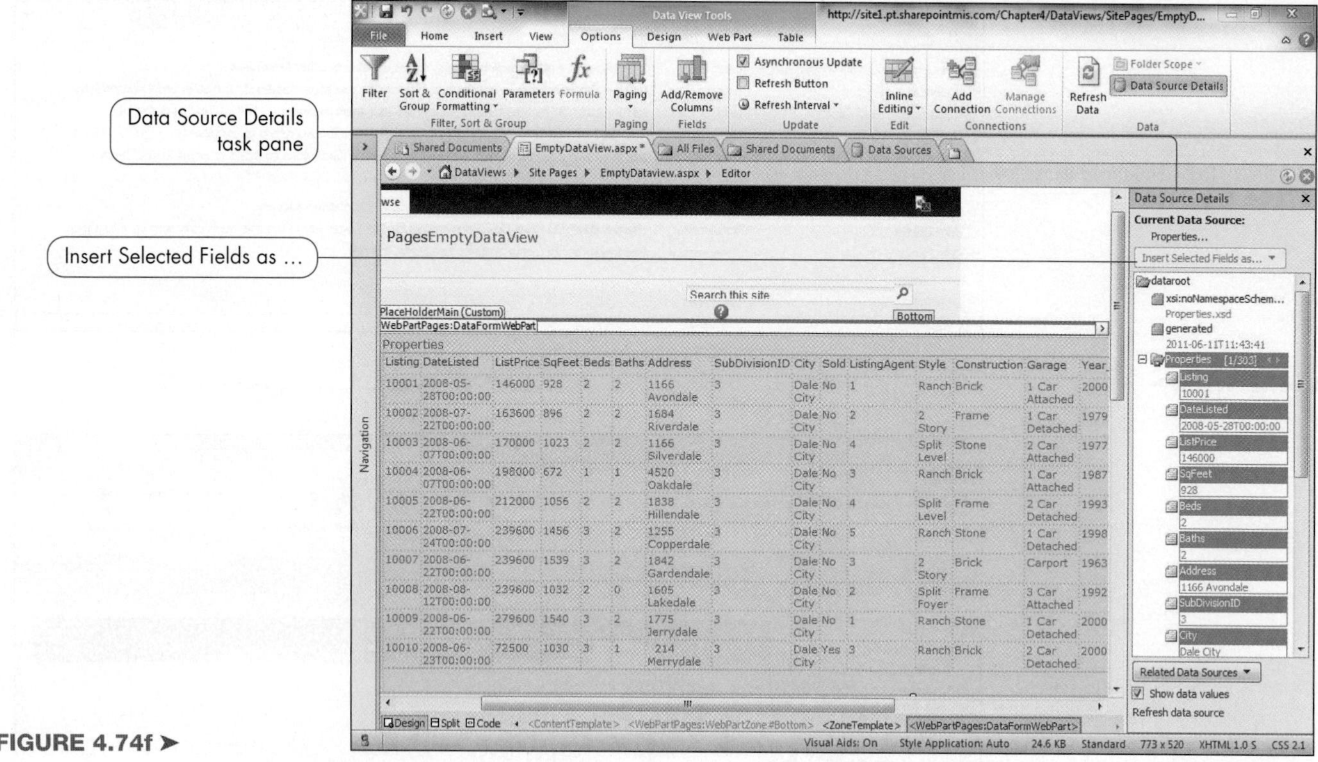

FIGURE 4.74f ➤

Save the page and preview it in browser, as shown in Figure 4.75a. At this stage you cannot do any online editing of the displayed data. Activate the SharePoint Designer window, click anywhere within the Data View, and then click Inline Editing in the Edit group on the Data View Tools–Option tab, as shown in Figure 4.75b. Select the Show Item Links and Show Insert Item Links options, and save the page. Click the browser window, and then refresh the page. As shown in Figure 4.75c, each row contains an edit link to the left of the row that enables you to edit the data in that row. An insert link appears at the bottom of the table, enabling you to add new rows of data to the table.

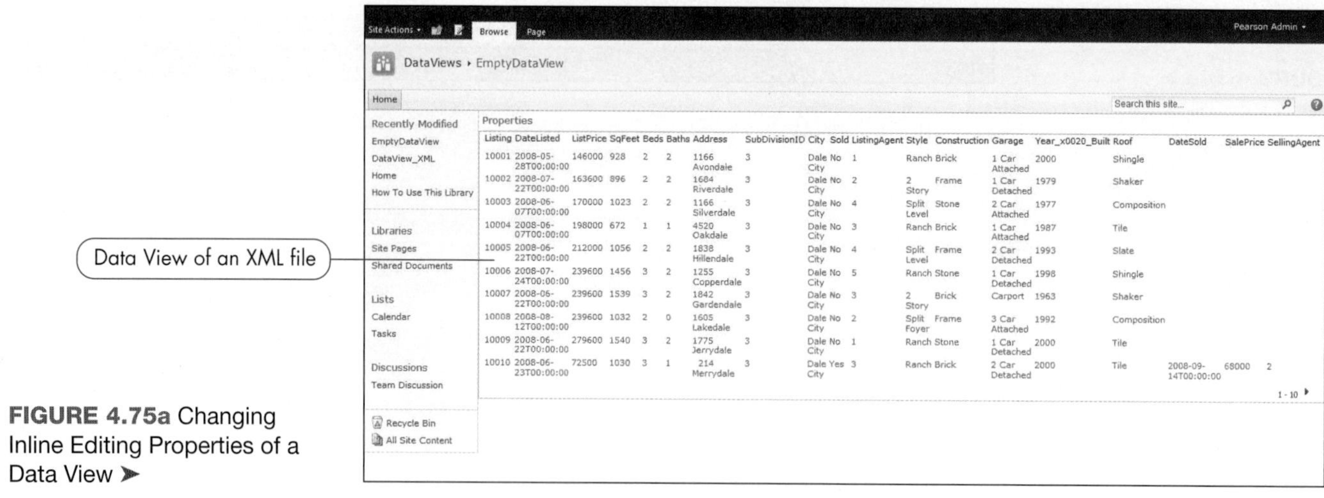

FIGURE 4.75a Changing Inline Editing Properties of a Data View ➤

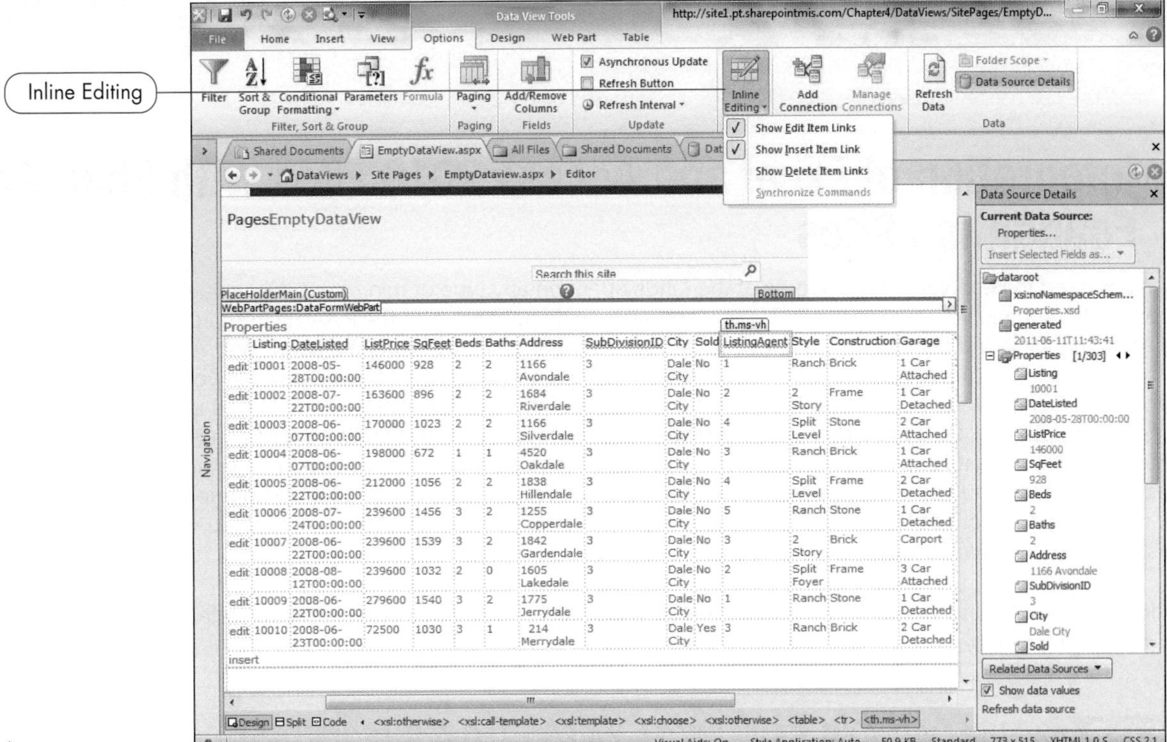

FIGURE 4.75b ➤

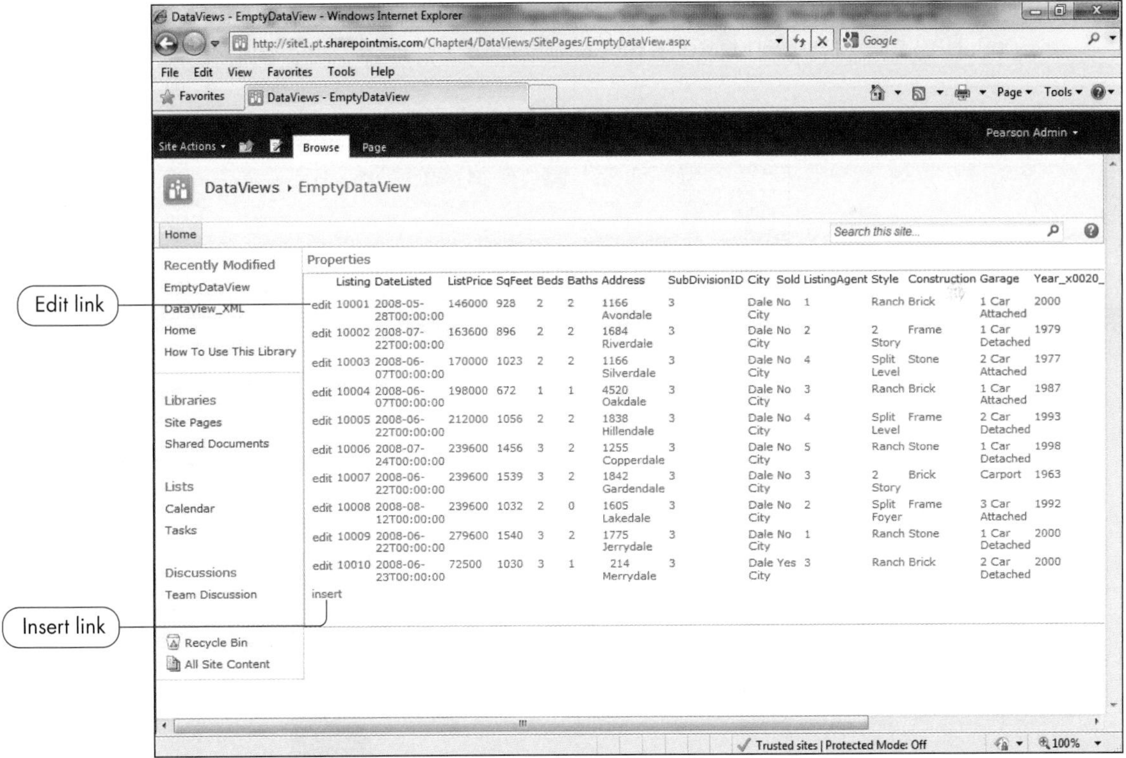

FIGURE 4.75c ➤

3 Integration of Excel and Access 2010 Files with SharePoint Foundation Sites

RAA will need to keep very good records of the funds spent on any type of mini-grant they award and event they will organize or sponsor. Integrating their business office Excel and Access documents with the RAA SharePoint portal will allow them more flexibility in managing and sharing documents between all their team members and collaborators. You will create a subsite that will be accessible only to RAA-selected employees. You will create a new document library in which you will create a folder for the .xlsx Excel documents and another folder for the .pdf format Excel documents. You will then import and export RAA Excel data, saved in .xlsx and .pdf formats, in and from a SharePoint Import Spreadsheet list. You will publish an RAA Access database to a SharePoint Document library. You will export an Access table to a new SharePoint list. You will import a SharePoint List to an Access database and you will link a SharePoint list to an Access file. In order to take advantage of the powerful SharePoint tools for managing XML format files as data sources you will export a table as an XML file. Then you will use this XML file as a source for a SharePoint Data View.

Skills covered: Upload and Save Excel Files into a SharePoint Document Library • Import Data from and Export Excel Data to a SharePoint List • Use Access 2010 in SharePoint • Work with Data Sources and Data Views

STEP 1 UPLOAD AND SAVE EXCEL FILES INTO A SHAREPOINT DOCUMENT LIBRARY

You will create a subsite that will be accessible only to RAA-selected employees and will create a new document library. You will create a folder for the .xlsx documents and another folder for .pdf versions of the Excel document. You will upload an .xlsx file including the final budget report for a RAA mini-grant, and save it as .pdf. Refer to Figure 4.76 as you complete Step 1.

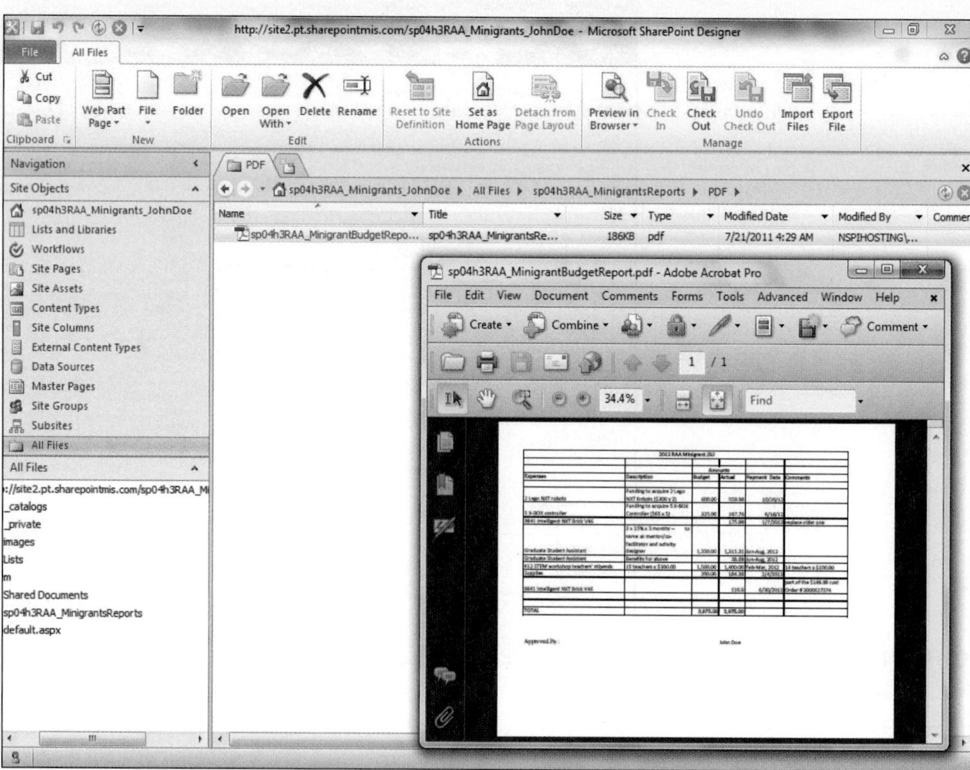

FIGURE 4.76 Upload and Save Excel Files into a SharePoint Document Library ➤

a. Click **Start** to display the Start menu. Click **All Programs**, and then click **Internet Explorer** to open the program.

b. Go to the top-level site provided by your instructor which will be in the format of *http://pt.sharepointmis.com/SitePages/yourname*. Enter the user name and password provided by your instructor.

c. Create a *sp04h3RAA_Minigrants_LastNameFirstName* subsite with unique permissions (only the Team Site Owners group should have access to it) and using the Document Workspace template.

   The *sp04h3RAA_Minigrants_LastNameFirstName* subsite is displayed in browser.

d. Create a *sp04h3RAA_MinigrantsReports* Document library, selecting Microsoft Excel spreadsheet as Document Template.

   The name of the *sp04h3RAA_MinigrantsReports* Document library appears on Quick Launch.

e. Click the **Library Tools–Documents tab**, and then create a *PDF* and a *XLSX* folder in the *sp04h3RAA_MinigrantsReports* Document library.

f. Click the **XLSX link** to open the *XLSX* folder. Upload the *sp04h3RAA_MinigrantBudgetReport .xlsx* file from your Exploring folder. Click the **sp04h3RAA_MinigrantBudgetReport.xlsx link**. Select the Edit mode if necessary.

   The *sp04h3RAA_MinigrantBudgetReport.xlsx* is displayed in a new Microsoft Excel window.

g. Click **Enable Editing** on the yellow band shown at the top of the Excel window.

h. Click in **cell A20**, and then type **Approved By:**. Click in **cell D20**, and then type your name. Save the document. Click the **Page Layout tab**, click **Orientation** in the Page Setup group, and then click **Landscape**.

i. Click the **File tab**, and then click the **Save As tab** on the Excel File menu to display the Save As dialog box. Navigate to the *sp04h3RAA_MinigrantsReports/PDF* folder. Click the **Save as Type arrow**, and then select **PDF**. Click **Save**. Click **Cancel** in the File Download dialog box.

   The *sp04h3RAA_MinigrantBudgetReport.pdf* file name is now included in the *sp04h3RAA_MinigrantsReports/PDF* folder.

j. Click **Edit in SharePoint Designer** on the Site Actions Menu. Type your password in the **Windows Security dialog box**.

   The *sp04h3RAA_Minigrants_LastNameFirstName* subsite is now open in SharePoint Designer.

k. Click **All Files** in the Navigation Pane. Click **sp04h3RAA_MinigrantsReports**, and then click **PDF**. Right-click the name of the .pdf file, click **Open With**, and then select **Adobe Reader**.

   The .pdf file is now displayed in the Adobe Reader window. Your screen should look similar to Figure 4.76.

l. Close the SharePoint Designer, Adobe Reader, and Excel windows.

STEP 2 IMPORT AND EXPORT EXCEL DATA IN AND FROM A SHAREPOINT LIST

In order to take advantage of the SharePoint lists features for handling Excel data you will import the .xlsx file, including the final budget report for an RAA mini-grant into an Import Spreadsheet list. Then in order to maintain a fully synchronized local version of the data exported in the Import Spreadsheet list, you will export the data from the Import Spreadsheet list into a local Excel spreadsheet, creating a Web Query. Refer to Figure 4.77 as you complete Step 2.

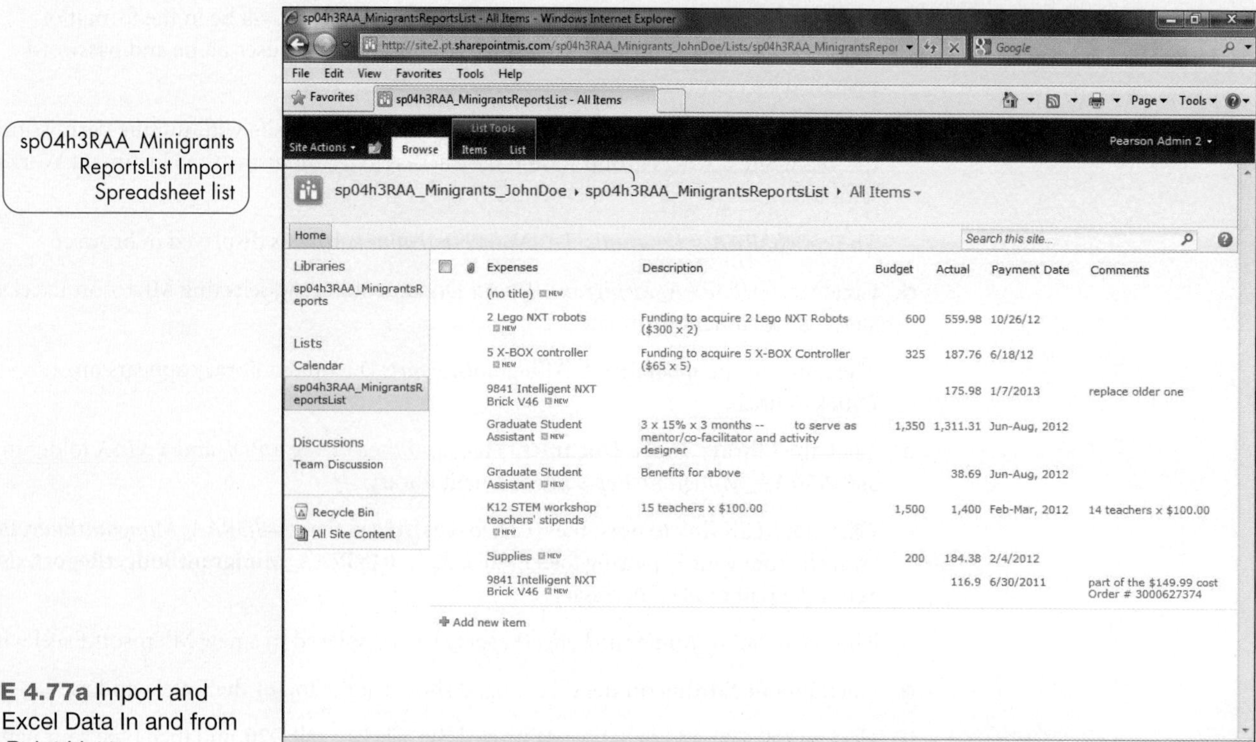

FIGURE 4.77a Import and Export Excel Data In and from a SharePoint List ➤

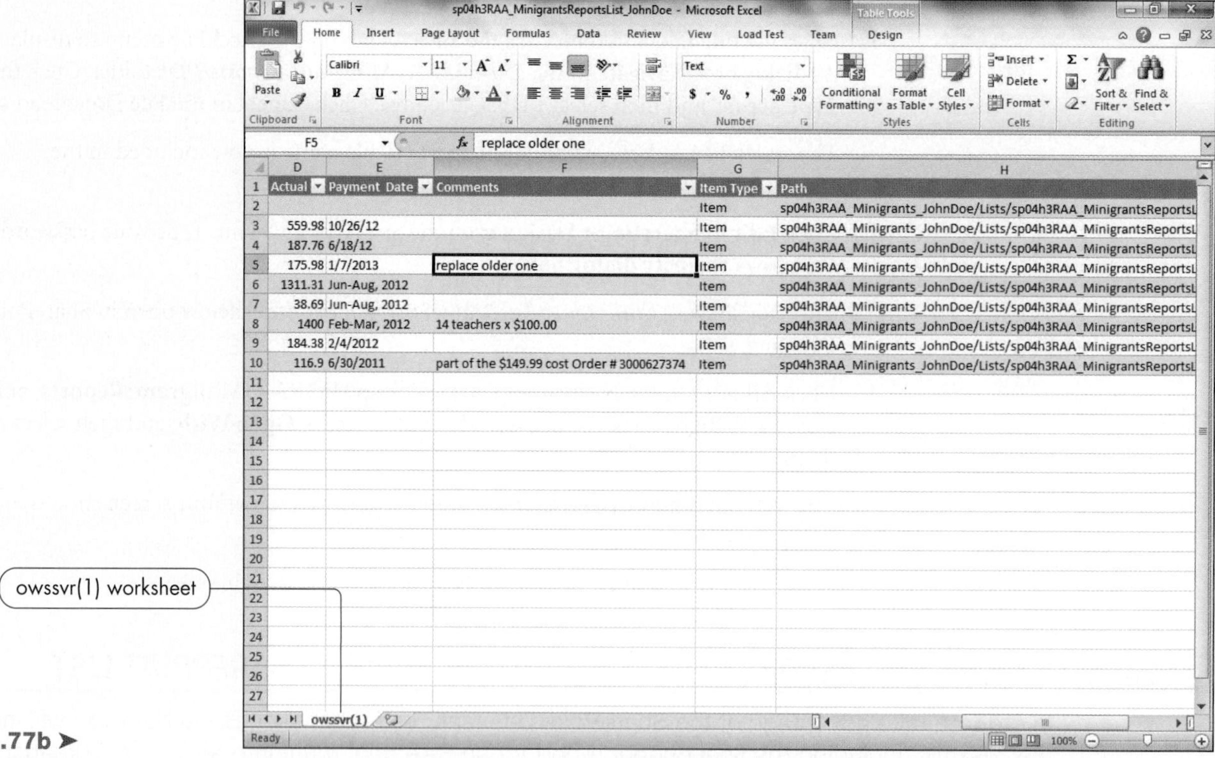

FIGURE 4.77b ➤

a. Activate the browser window, click **Site Actions**, and then click **More Options** to open the Create dialog box. Click **Blank & Custom** in the *All Categories* section, click **Import Spreadsheet**, and then click **Create** to open the New page.

b. Type **sp04h3RAA_MinigrantsReportsList** in the **Name box**, and then click **Browse** to open the Choose File to Upload dialog box. Navigate to the *sp04h3RAA_MinigrantBudgetList.xlsx* file in the Exploring folder, double-click its name, and then click **Import**.

   The *sp04h3RAA_MinigrantBudgetList.xlsx* file opens in a new Excel window and the Excel Import to Window SharePoint Services list dialog box opens.

c. Select **Table Range** in the Range Type: list and **FinalReport!BudgetReport** in the Select Range: list. Click **Import.**

   The All Items page of the new *sp04h3RAA_MinigrantsReportsList* list is now displayed in the browser.

d. Click the **List Tools–List tab**, and then click **List Settings** in the Settings group. Click **Title, Description and Navigation** under the *General Settings* section of the List Settings page.

e. Click the **Yes option** in the *Navigation* section of the General Settings page to display the list on the Quick Launch. Click **Save** on the General Settings page. Click the **sp04h3RAA_MinigrantsReportsList link** on the breadcrumb.

   The All Items view of the *sp04h3RAA_MinigrantsReportsList* list is now displayed. Your screen should look similar to Figure 4.77a.

f. Click the **List Tools–List tab**, and then click **Export to Excel** in the Connect & Export group. Click **Open** in the File Download dialog box.

   Excel 2010 opens a new workbook that includes the owssvr(1) worksheet and an Excel Security Notice dialog box is displayed indicating the data connections have been blocked.

g. Click **Enable in** in the Excel Security Notice dialog box.

   The Excel Web query results are now displayed in the owssvr(1) worksheet.

h. Delete *replace older one* text from **cell F5**. Click the **Data tab**, and then click **Refresh All** in the Connections group.

   The spreadsheet is updated with a copy of the data from the *sp04h3RAA_MinigrantsReportsList* SharePoint list and the data changes you just made are lost. Your screen should look similar to Figure 4.77b.

i. Save the spreadsheet on your local computer as **sp04h3RAA_MinigrantsReportsList_FirstNameLastName.xlsx**.

j. Exit Excel.

STEP 3 USE ACCESS 2010 IN SHAREPOINT

You will publish an Access database to a SharePoint document library. You will export an Access table in a new SharePoint list. You will import a SharePoint List to an Access database and you will link a SharePoint list to an Access file. Refer to Figure 4.78 as you complete Step 3.

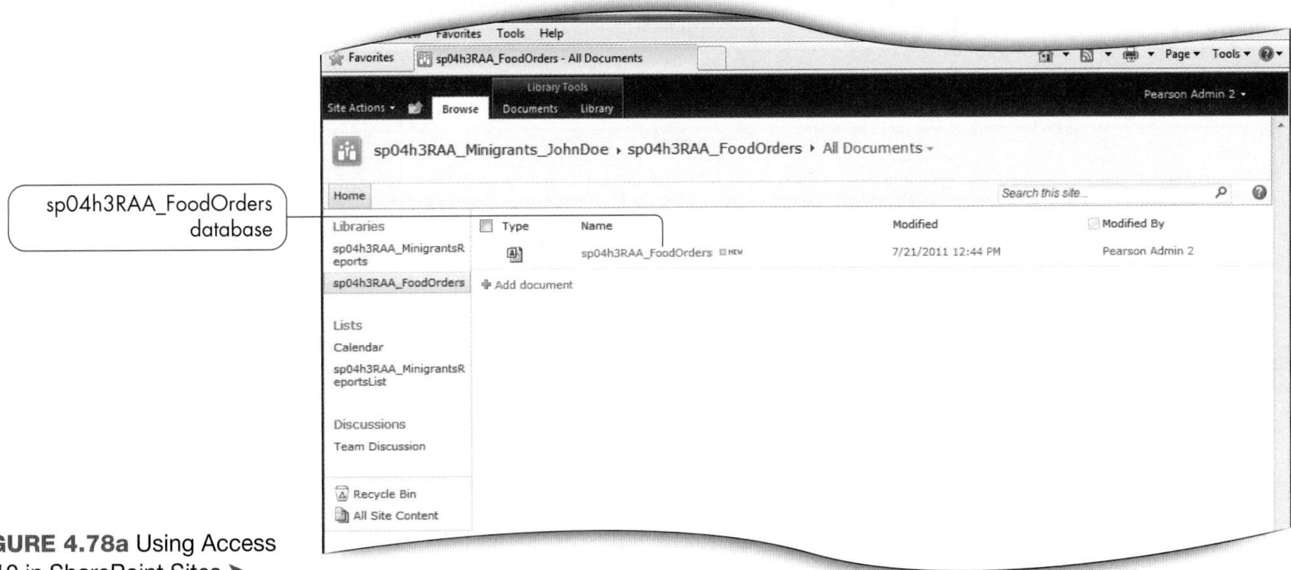

FIGURE 4.78a Using Access 2010 in SharePoint Sites ➤

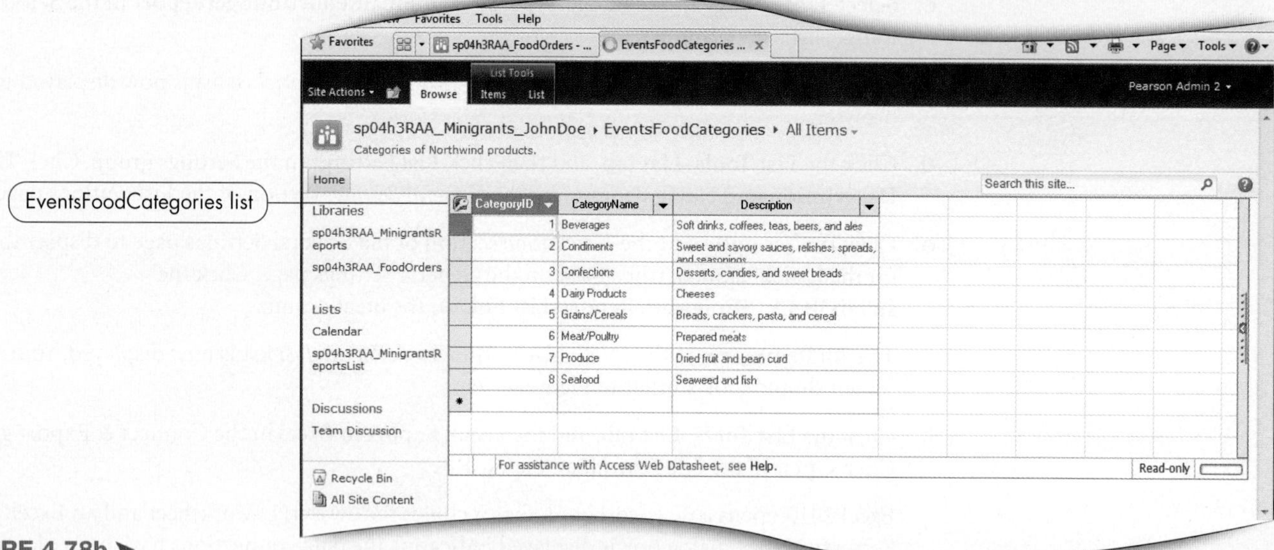

FIGURE 4.78b ➤

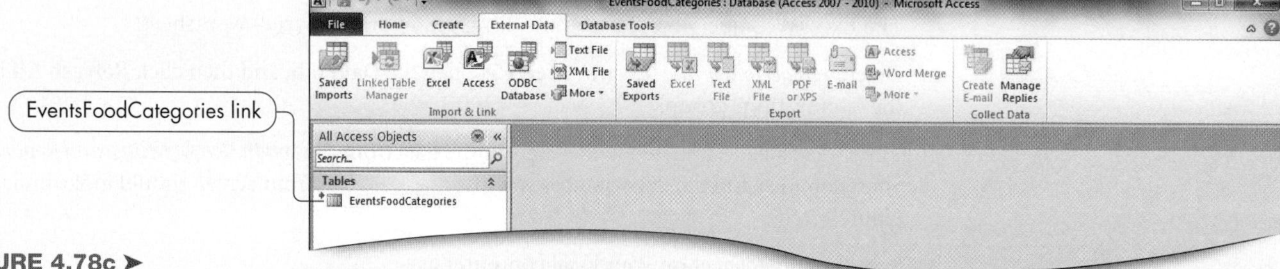

FIGURE 4.78c ➤

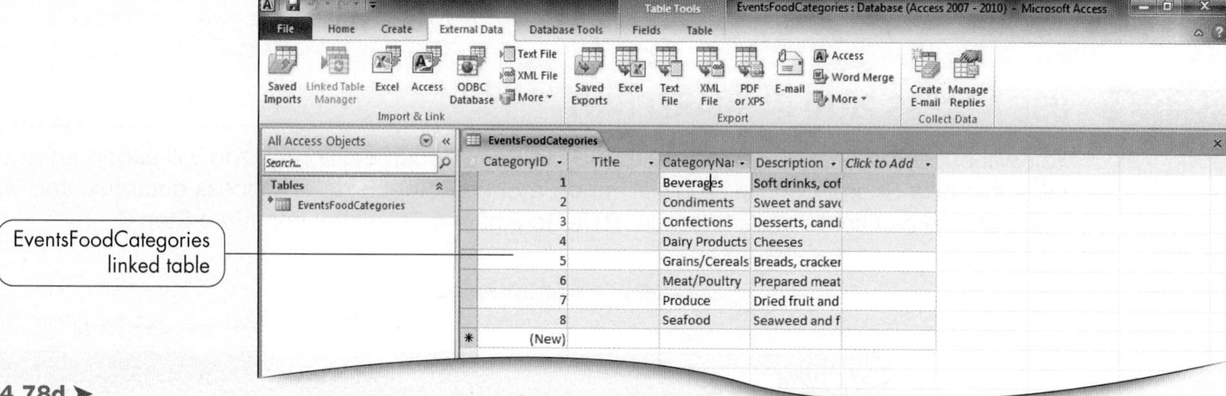

FIGURE 4.78d ➤

a. Activate the browser window, and then create a new *sp04h3RAA_FoodOrders* document library in the *sp04h3RAA_Minigrants_LastNameFirstName* subsite.

b. Navigate on your local computer to your Exploring folder, and then double-click **sp04h3RAA_FoodOrders**.

   The database *sp04h3RAA_FoodOrders* opens in a new Microsoft Access window.

c. Click **Enable Content**, click the **File tab**, and then click **Save & Publish** in the the Access Backstage view. Click **Save Database As** in the *File Types* section, select **SharePoint** in the *Save Database As* section, and then click **Save As**.

   The Save to SharePoint dialog box is now open.

d. Navigate to the *sp04h3RAA_FoodOrders* document library, and then click **Save**. Activate the browser window, and then click **Refresh (F5)**.

The *sp04h3RAA_FoodOrders* database is now included in the *sp04h3RAA_FoodOrders* document library. Your screen should now look similar to Figure 4.78a.

e. Close the Access window. Navigate on your local computer to your Exploring folder, and then double-click **sp04h3RAA_FoodOrdersList**. Click **Enable Content**, if needed, and then double-click **Categories** in the Navigation Pane.

The *Categories* table is now displayed.

f. Click the **External Data tab**, click **More** in the Export group, and then click **SharePoint List** on the More gallery.

The Export-SharePoint Site dialog box is now displayed.

g. Select the **sp04h3RAA_Minigrants_LastNameFirstName subsite** in the Specify a SharePoint site area, type **EventsFoodCategories** in the **Specify a name for the new list box**, and then click **OK**.

The Exporting Table to-SharePoint Site List dialog box is now open, showing the progress of the import.

h. Select **Save Exports Steps check box** in the Save Export Steps page of the of the Export - SharePoint Site dialog box. Click **Save Export**.

The Export - SharePoint Site dialog box closes and your screen should be similar to Figure 4.78b.

i. Close the *sp04h3RAA_FoodOrdersList.accdb* database. Close the browser window. Navigate on your local computer to your Exploring folder, and then double-click **sp04h3RAA_FoodOrdersList**. Click the **External Data tab**. Click **More** in the Import & Link group, and then click **SharePoint List**.

The Get External Data - SharePoint Site dialog box is now shown.

j. Select the **sp04h3RAA_Minigrants_LastNameFirstName subsite**, in the *Specify a SharePoint site* area, select the **Import the source data in a new table in the current database option**, and then click **Next**.

The Get External Data - SharePoint Site dialog box is now displayed.

k. Select the check box to the left of the EventsFoodCategories list, and then click **OK**. Check the **Save import steps check box** in the Save Import Steps page of the Get External Data - SharePoint Site dialog box, and then click **Save Import**.

The *EventsFoodCategories* table is now shown in the All Access Objects pane. The EventsFoodCategories list is not synchronized with the *EventsFoodCategories* table.

l. Create a new blank database named *EventsFoodCategories.* Click the **External Data tab**. Click **More** in the Import & Link group, and then click **SharePoint List**.

The Get External Data - SharePoint Site dialog box is now showing.

m. Select the **sp04h3RAA_Minigrants_LastNameFirstName subsite** in the Specify a SharePoint site area, make sure **Link to the date source by creating a linked table option** is selected, and then click **Next**.

The *Choose the SharePoint lists you want to link to* page of the Get External Data - SharePoint Site dialog box is now displayed.

n. Select the check box to the left of the EventsFoodCategories list, and then click **OK**.

The EventsFoodCategories linked table is shown in the Navigation Pane and the text *Online with SharePoint* is displayed to the right edge of the Access Status bar. Your screen should look similar to Figure 4.78c.

o. Right-click the **EventsFoodCategories linked table**, select **More options**, and then click **Open Default View**.

The All Items view of the EventsFoodCategories list is now displayed in the browser.

p. Click the **List Tools–Items tab**, and then click **New Item** in the New Item group. Type **Breads** in the **Category box**, type **Assorted breads** in **Description box**, and then click **Save**.

The new item is now displayed in the All Items view of the EventsFoodCategories list.

q. Switch back to the Access window, and then double-click the **EventsFoodCategories linked table**.

The new item is also displayed in the All Items view of the EventsFoodCategories list.

r. Delete the new item from the **EventsFoodCategories linked table**, and then click in any other row of the table.

Your screen should now look similar to Figure 4.78d.

s. Switch back to the browser window, and then click **Refresh (F5)**.

The item deleted in the EventsFoodCategories linked table is no longer displayed in the All Items view of the EventsFoodCategories list.

t. Close the browser and Access windows.

STEP 4 WORK WITH DATA SOURCES AND DATA VIEWS

You will export a table as an XML file. Then, you will use this XML file as a source for a Data View. Refer to Figure 4.79 as you complete Step 3.

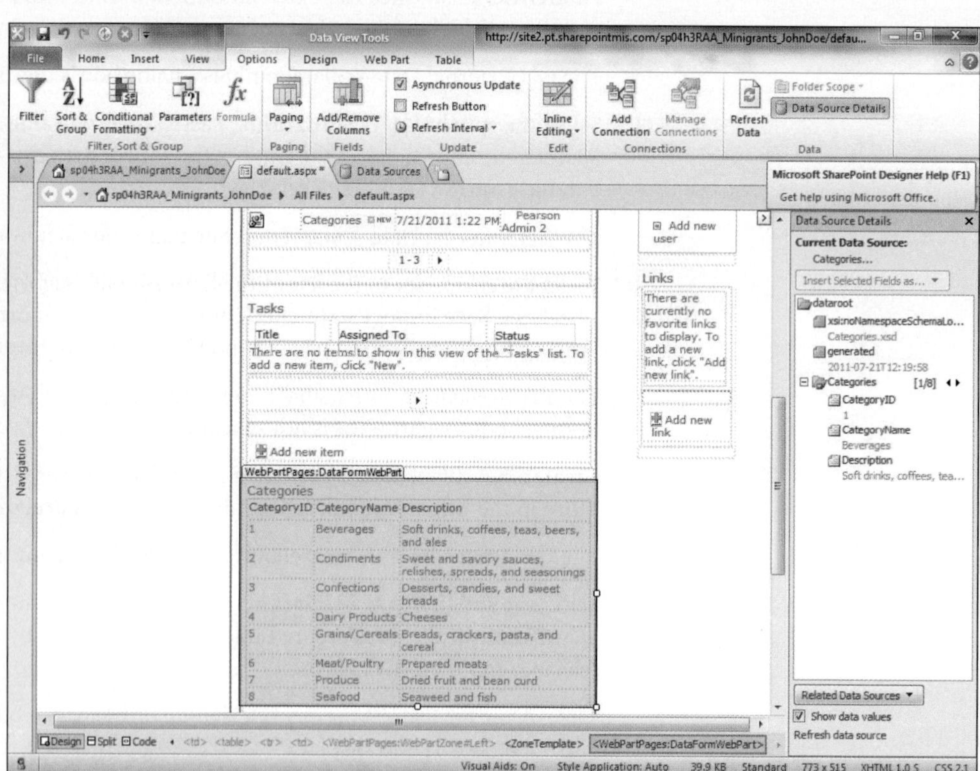

FIGURE 4.79 Work with Data Sources and Data Views ➤

a. Navigate on your local computer to your Exploring folder, and then double-click **sp04h3RAA_FoodOrders**. Double-click **Categories** in the Navigation Pane.

b. Click the **External Data tab**, and then click **XML File** in the Export group.

The Export - XML File dialog box is displayed.

c. Click **Browse**, and then navigate to your local Documents folder. Click **Save**, and then click **OK**.

The Export-XML dialog box is now displayed.

d. Check all three check boxes, and then click **More Options**. Click the **Presentation tab**. Check **Server (ASP)**, and then click **OK**.

e. Click the **Save exports steps check box**, and then click **Save Export**. The *Categories.xml*, *Categories.xsd*, and *Categories.xsl* files are now shown in the destination location.

f. Click **Start** to display the Start menu. Click **All Programs**, and then click **Internet Explorer** to open the program. Go to the *sp04h3RAA_Minigrants_LastNameFirstName* subsite. Enter the user name and password provided by your instructor.

g. Click the **Shared Documents link**, click the **Library Tools–Documents tab**, click **Upload Document** in the New group, and then import the *Categories.xml*, *Categories.xsd*, and *Categories.xsl* files.

h. Click **Edit in SharePoint Designer** in the Site Actions menu. Click **Edit site home page** in the *Customization* section of the Site Settings page. Position your mouse below the Left Web Part Zone.

The <div> tag is now selected.

i. Click the **Insert tab**, click **Data View** in Data View & Forms group, and then click **Empty Data View** on the All Data Sources gallery.

A DataFormWebPart control is added to the page.

j. Click **Data Sources** in the Navigation Pane. Click the icon to the left of the Shared Documents library in the Data Sources gallery page, and then click **XML File Connection** on the New tab on the Data Sources tab.

The Source tab of the Data Sources Properties dialog box is now displayed.

k. Click **Browse**, and then navigate to the *Categories.xml* file in the File Open dialog box. Double-click **Categories.xml**, and then click **OK** in the Data Sources Properties dialog box.

The *Categories.xml* file is now shown in a new *XML Files* section of the Data Sources gallery page.

l. Click the **default.aspx tab** to display the default.aspx page, and then click the **Click here to select a data source link** inside the DataFormWebPart control.

The Data Sources Picker dialog box is now open.

m. Click the **Categories file** in the *XML Files* section of the Data Sources Picker dialog, and then click **OK**.

The Data Source Details task pane shows now the structure of the XML file.

n. Select all fields of the XML file, click **Insert Selected Fields as ...**, and then select the **Multiple Item view option** on the Insert Selected Fields drop-down menu. Collapse the Navigation Pane.

Your screen should now look similar to Figure 4.79.

o. Save **Default.aspx**, and then close the SharePoint Designer, Access, and browser windows.

CHAPTER OBJECTIVES REVIEW

After reading this chapter, you have accomplished the following objectives:

1. **Add a New Document Library.** SharePoint Document libraries can contain thousands of documents. You can store different types of documents in a library, including Office documents, such as Word, Excel, and PowerPoint files; text files; PDFs; XMLs; and many other file types. Files can be grouped into folders to organize them. In a collaboration site, the only document library created by default is the Shared Documents library. In addition to folders, document libraries, with descriptive names, can be created to organize the site documents. Document libraries can only have one default template, which also defines the default content type for the library. This is important because the default content type of the document library determines the type of file SharePoint creates when you click New. Other types of documents can be stored in the library, regardless of the default content type. Documents are uploaded to the library from local computer drives or network drives. You can also create documents in SharePoint with the default template. The default template can be changed to a different template, and you can even create and upload your own customized template to a document library.
2. **Add a document to a Document Library.** New documents are added to the document library using the Documents tab in SharePoint, with the library's default document template as a basis for the document. Documents can have many more properties than the ones displayed by default, but SharePoint does not display some document properties unless you make the proper settings. When you look at a list or library you actually see a view of the list or library, and not the actual list or library. Views enable you to define which columns appear, as well as whether you see all the items or just selected items based on a filter and sort criteria. You can change the sort order of the columns in ascending or descending order. You can also filter columns based on values in the column.
3. **Display documents in Lists and Libraries.** SharePoint Foundation provides at least one default view for each built-in list and library, but in most cases, additional views are available. Views enable you to display the data in a meaningful way. The built-in views include: Standard view, Datasheet view, Calendar view, Gantt view, and Access view. The Standard view displays the contents of lists and libraries as lists and is available for all SharePoint Foundations lists and libraries except Surveys and Discussions. The Datasheet view displays list or library items using a table layout, which enables you to easily edit the whole table. The Datasheet view is available in all lists and libraries except the Picture Library, External List, and Survey. Items are added, edited, or deleted in Datasheet view, which automatically saves the changes as you move from row to row. With the Access view, you take advantage of the Access advanced tools for generating reports and views, but you will need the Access client installed on your computer. Data in the lists and libraries automatically updates when you edit the content in Access. The Access view can be used for all SharePoint Foundation lists and libraries except the External List and Survey. A Calendar view can be used for the data in all lists and libraries (as long as it contains at least one date field), except the External List, Discussion Board, and Survey. You can also create a Custom view. Views are created using the Library Tools Library tab.
4. **Work with SharePoint Foundation Built-in List Types.** SharePoint provides predefined lists, grouped into six categories: Blank & Custom, Collaboration, Communication, Content, Data, and Tracking. Each SharePoint list contains column types, that may appear in every type of list or not, depending on the list. Site templates often feature specialized libraries that support the function for that type of site. You can also create custom lists to fit the needs of your users. Only the Title column is required on a list, but the title can be changed to something more descriptive of the data displayed in the column. By adding columns, you can customize the list. Popular built-in lists include: Announcements, Contacts, Links, and Survey. An Announcements list displays events, news, or activities to the users. An announcement item consists of a title, a body, and an expiration date. Created By and Modified By columns are automatically added as the items are added or modified. Attachments, used to distribute documents, can also be added to announcement items. A Contacts list, by default, contains columns for Last Name, First Name, Company, Business Phone, Home Phone, and E-mail Address. Data to populate this list can be imported from an Excel worksheet, a range of cells, or an Excel table. The Links list is a collection of links to other pages in the site or other Web sites. Often, it is used like a navigational menu on a site. The Links list contains the All Links built-in view, which displays all of the items in a list and provides a way to edit the items. The built-in columns on the Links list are URL and Notes, with Created By and Modified By columns added automatically as items are added or modified. The order of the list items can be changed as needed. The Survey list displays columns as a questionnaire or a poll rather than a list of columns. Surveys can be set up to be anonymous or not depending on the uses of the survey. You can also specify that the survey can only be taken once, rather than multiple times. Twelve question types are available in SharePoint Survey lists with each question type having unique settings. Surveys in SharePoint also support branching, which displays different questions based on the previous responses of the user.
5. **Open, edit, and save Microsoft Office documents to a SharePoint Document Library.** Documents can be opened from a mapped drive on the Windows Vista or Windows 7 operating systems, or with a browser using the URL of the SharePoint site and the libraries' names. By default, the SharePoint documents edited in a Microsoft Office application are saved on your local hard disk to this folder: local hard disk drive: \Users\YourUserName\Documents\SharePoint Drafts. If you need to set a different location for saving your drafts, select The Office Document Cache. When you open an Office document using Windows Explorer, you will not receive information about checked out status of the document. If you use a Microsoft Office application, to open a checked out document,

the checked out symbol displays in the bottom-right corner of the file icon in the Type column. If you attempt to open a checked out file, the *File in Use* dialog box offers you options for continuing to working with that document.

6. **Work with Word documents.** You can upload any Word file format, including documents saved as a PDF, XPS, or Single File Web page, to a Document library. The graphic files are embedded in these documents, so there is no need to separately upload or import them. When you open a Word document in SharePoint, it is opened in Word by default. This default can be overridden using the General tab of the Backstage view. To open a PDF or XPS file in SharePoint Foundation, double-click the file name in the browser or on SharePoint Designer All Files page. The PDF file will be displayed in an Adobe Reader window, whereas the XPS file will be displayed in an XPS Viewer window. Word also enables you to create a blog entry for a SharePoint blog site that will maintain all the formatting features already applied to the text.

7. **Work with PowerPoint documents.** The Save & Send tab of PowerPoint Backstage view enables you to either save an entire presentation to a SharePoint library (using the Save to SharePoint), or to publish all slides or selected slides from a presentation (using the Publish Slides). It is wise to create a dedicated folder, within the destination library, for slides included in the same presentation. You can also create topic-based folders in which you can publish slides from different presentations that have the same main topic; this way you will be able to easily find the slides and use them for future presentations. You can add a link to a PowerPoint presentation (saved in the original PowerPoint format (.pptx), or the PowerPoint Slideshow format (.ppsx)) to a SharePoint page. You can also save a PowerPoint presentation as a Windows Media Video (.wmv) file which will be displayed to the user in the Windows Media Player with all of the animations, narration, and multimedia originally added to the presentation.

8. **Use Excel 2010 in SharePoint.** Data can be exported and imported to a SharePoint list using Excel 2010. You can edit an Excel file offline and synchronize it with the SharePoint list when you are online. The easiest way to add Excel content to a SharePoint Web page is by using the Copy and Paste commands. You can also use the Clipboard task pane in SharePoint by copying data to the clipboard, and then selecting it for pasting as needed. Any Excel file format, including XML formats, Excel Binary Workbooks, Web Page formats, Single File Web pages, PDF, or XPS Documents can be uploaded into a library. When you are creating a Web page in Excel, you should work in the Web Layout view, because it gives you a good idea of how the document will look when it is viewed in a Web browser. When you save an Excel document as a Single Web page or Web page, you can choose to save the entire workbook, or just the active worksheet. As you save, you will have the option to AutoRepublish every time the workbook is saved. Excel documents are uploaded to a SharePoint library using the same procedures described for Word documents. The Save & Send tab of Excel Backstage view enables you to directly save to a SharePoint Documents library. You can add a link to an Excel Workbook (*.xlsx) previously uploaded to a SharePoint Documents library using a procedure similar with the one introduced for PowerPoint files. With Excel, you can create a saved Web query (.iqy) which extracts data from text or tables on a Web page, and then imports that data into Excel. SharePoint enables you to export the contents of SharePoint lists, document libraries and survey results to an Excel worksheet as an Excel Web query that will be automatically updated anytime you make changes to the original list or library. This automatic update is realized by a connection maintained by Excel between the spreadsheet that becomes a linked object and the SharePoint list. This export method applies only to the columns and rows included in the current view of the list. You can create a List view that includes all the columns and rows that you wish to export, or you can export one existing view and then filter the data in Excel. Any change you make in the Excel spreadsheet will not show in the source SharePoint list, but changes you make to the SharePoint list will automatically be made in the linked worksheet. Excel enables you to modify the way data will be synchronized between the SharePoint list and the linked Excel spreadsheet.

9. **Use Access 2010 documents in SharePoint.** Access 2010 enables you to export a table, a report or a query object to a wide range of formats, such as an external file, an Excel workbook, a Rich Text Format (RTF) file, a text file, a PDF or XPS file, an email attachment, an Extensible Markup Language (XML) document, an Open Database Connectivity (ODBC) data source, or a Hypertext Markup Language (HTML) document. You can also export a table into a new list on a SharePoint site. You can create a new table by importing data from an external data source, such as a dBase database, an Excel workbook, an XML document, an ODBC data source, or a SharePoint Web site. No data synchronization is between the two Access and SharePoint data locations. If you do not need to keep copies of the data in both locations, and you just need content synchronized access to a SharePoint list, you can use Access linked tables. A linked table provides the connection to a SharePoint list and synchronizes data changes. The easiest way to add Access content to a SharePoint Designer Web page is by using Copy and Paste commands. You can also use the Clipboard task pane to place content on the clipboard and then paste it as needed into the SharePoint site. SharePoint enables you to upload any Access file format to a Document library. To upload an Access document in a SharePoint library, you apply the same procedure explained for the Word and Excel documents. The Save & Publish tab of Access Backstage view enables you to directly save the whole database to a SharePoint Document library. The Access 2010 Ribbon includes a number of tabs that enable you to easily integrate Access data with SharePoint sites and lists. You can save exports, and later reuse them. When you create a new Access database table by importing data from a SharePoint list, that table automatically becomes part of your database but the data is not synchronized with the SharePoint list after it is imported. Although Access is a powerful application for managing data, it was not designed to enable more users to work concurrently on the same project, but moving Access databases to SharePoint sites enable you to take advantage of both Access and SharePoint tools for managing and sharing data.

10. **Work with Data Sources and Data Views.** The Access 2010 user interface enables you to export a table as an XML file, and generates data (.xml), schema (.xsd), and presentation (.xsl) files. If you choose a client-side transformation, an

.htm file will be generated, whereas if you choose a server-side transformation, an .asp file will be created. SharePoint Foundation includes a basic version of Business Connectivity Services. This means that you can take advantage of external data in SharePoint by creating a connection to the data and defining what you want to display. SharePoint Designer queries the root of the current site and the Site Assets Library for XML files. These files will be automatically added to the Data Sources gallery page. You can also create a Data view of an XML file from another library or site by using the XML File Connection command. In order to edit a Data view in the browser, use SharePoint Designer and click anywhere within the Data view, and then click Inline Editing in the Edit Group. Select Show Item Links and Show Insert Item Links options, and then save the page. Activate the browser window, and then refresh the page. An edit link is now placed at the left of each row and an insert link is placed at the bottom of the table.

KEY TERMS

Access view ***p.293***
All Events view ***p.313***
Announcement item ***p.299***
Announcements list ***p.299***
Calendar list ***p.313***
Current Events view ***p.313***
Database ***p.359***
Database table ***p.359***
Datasheet view ***p.291***
Default template ***p.280***
Discussion Board list ***p.311***
Documents tab ***p.280***
Flat view ***p.311***
Library tab ***p.280***
Linked table ***p.359***
Links list ***p.306***
Portable Document Format (PDF) ***p.323***
Range ***p.345***
Single File Web page option ***p.328***
Spreadsheet ***p.345***
Standard view ***p.287***
Survey list ***p.307***
Table ***p.345***
Threaded view ***p.311***
Views ***p.284***
Web page option ***p.328***
Web page, Filtered option ***p.328***
Web query (.iqy) ***p.355***
Workbook ***p.345***
Worksheet ***p.345***
XML Paper Specification (XPS) ***p.323***

MULTIPLE CHOICE

1. Which of the following statements about a SharePoint document library is false?
   (a) A document library can have only one default template.
   (b) You can upload multiple types of files within a document library.
   (c) The default document template defines the type of files SharePoint you can use to create new documents.
   (d) You can create new multiple types of files within a document library.

2. Which of the following statements about a SharePoint library is false?
   (a) SharePoint enables you to change the sort order of your documents list.
   (b) SharePoint Foundation provides you, for all its built-in libraries, with at least one default view.
   (c) The Standard view is available for all SharePoint Foundation libraries.
   (d) Datasheet view displays library items using a gridlike layout that enables you to easily edit the whole table.

3. Which of the following statements about SharePoint Designer is false?
   (a) You can create a Custom View only in SharePoint Designer.
   (b) You can create a Data View only in SharePoint Designer.
   (c) You can create a data connection only in SharePoint Designer.
   (d) SharePoint Designer queries the root of the current site and all the site libraries for XML files.

4. Which of the following statements about SharePoint Foundation built-in list types is false?
   (a) SharePoint will not automatically remove past events from Announcements list.
   (b) SharePoint does not allow you to hide a column of a list.
   (c) SharePoint Survey list allows the developer to determine whether other users can see everyone's responses or just their own.
   (d) By default, SharePoint displays the messages included in a Discussion Board list in a flat view.

5. Which of the following statements about Excel and SharePoint is not correct?
   (a) SharePoint Designer automatically converts the Excel content into HTML.
   (b) Excel enables you to directly save a whole workbook, selected Sheets or Items in the Workbook to a SharePoint Documents library.
   (c) When you save an Excel document as a PDF or XPS Document you can publish only the Active sheet or a selection (range cell) within a worksheet.
   (d) When you publish an Excel document as a Web Page you may select the AutoRepublish option.

6. Which of the following statements about PowerPoint and SharePoint is not correct?
   (a) PowerPoint enables you to save a whole presentation to a SharePoint Document library or to publish slides, as individual PowerPoint files, into a SharePoint Document Library.
   (b) You can also save a PowerPoint presentation as a Windows Media Video (.wmv) file.
   (c) If you import a .pptx, .ppsx, .mht, .pdf, or .xps PowerPoint document, the graphic files are not embedded in the document.
   (d) To add a link into a Web page to a PowerPoint presentation saved as a PDF (*.pdf) or XPS Document (*.xps), you will first need to import the files into the Web site.

7. Which of the following statements about Access and SharePoint Designer is not correct?
   (a) To copy and paste content from Access to SharePoint Designer, you can use the Clipboard task pane.
   (b) The Save & Publish tab of Access Backstage view enables you to directly save the whole database to a SharePoint Documents library.
   (c) When you export an Access Object as a PDF or XPS Document, you can choose to publish All records, Selected Records, or Pages.
   (d) No methods for importing/exporting data provide synchronization between the Access and SharePoint site data.

8. Which of the following statements about the Access Export Tables to SharePoint Wizard is not correct?
   (a) It creates a SharePoint list for each Access table.
   (b) It moves data from each Access tables to their corresponding SharePoint lists.
   (c) It replaces Access tables with linked tables.
   (d) It does not enable you to back up a copy of the database.

9. Which of the following statements about Excel and SharePoint is not correct?

   (a) Excel data is synchronized with the Import Spreadsheet custom list in which it was imported.
   (b) SharePoint lists content exported to an Excel worksheet, as an Excel Web query, and it will be automatically updated anytime you make changes to the SharePoint original list.
   (c) Excel enables you to modify the way data is synchronized between the SharePoint list and the linked Excel spreadsheet.
   (d) You can edit an Excel workbook published to a SharePoint library offline.

10. Which of the following statements about the SharePoint Survey lists is not correct?

   (a) SharePoint enables you to export the results of a survey to a spreadsheet.
   (b) Surveys support branching logic.
   (c) A survey enables you to see the number of responses already submitted.
   (d) The respondent's name can never be displayed in a survey.

1 Archiving Microsoft Office Documents into a SharePoint Site for an Introduction to Management Information Systems Business Course

As a graduate teaching assistant in the Introduction to Management Information Systems course, you have been working on the development of a SharePoint site for the course. Your faculty supervisor gave you different types of Microsoft Office files that will need to be uploaded to the site. Some of these files will be displayed on the site pages using different formats. You will also format the view of the Announcements list and add a class survey. This exercise follows the same set of skills as used in Hands-On Exercise 1 in the chapter. Refer to Figures 4.80a–d as you complete this exercise.

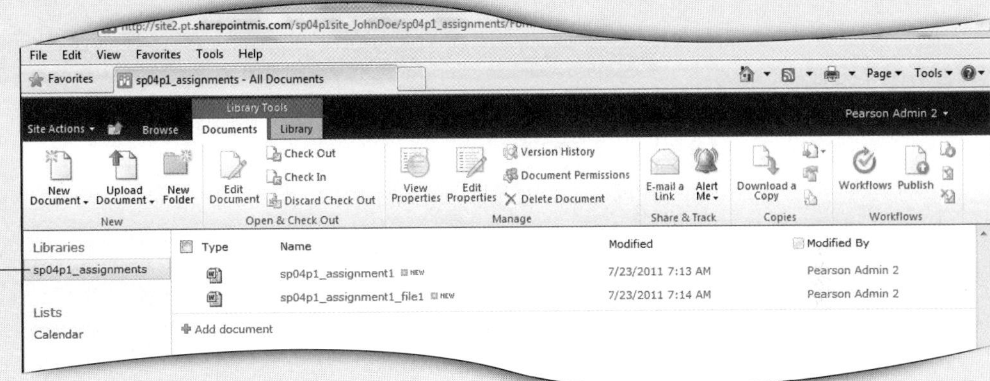

FIGURE 4.80a Archiving Microsoft Office Documents into a SharePoint Site ➤

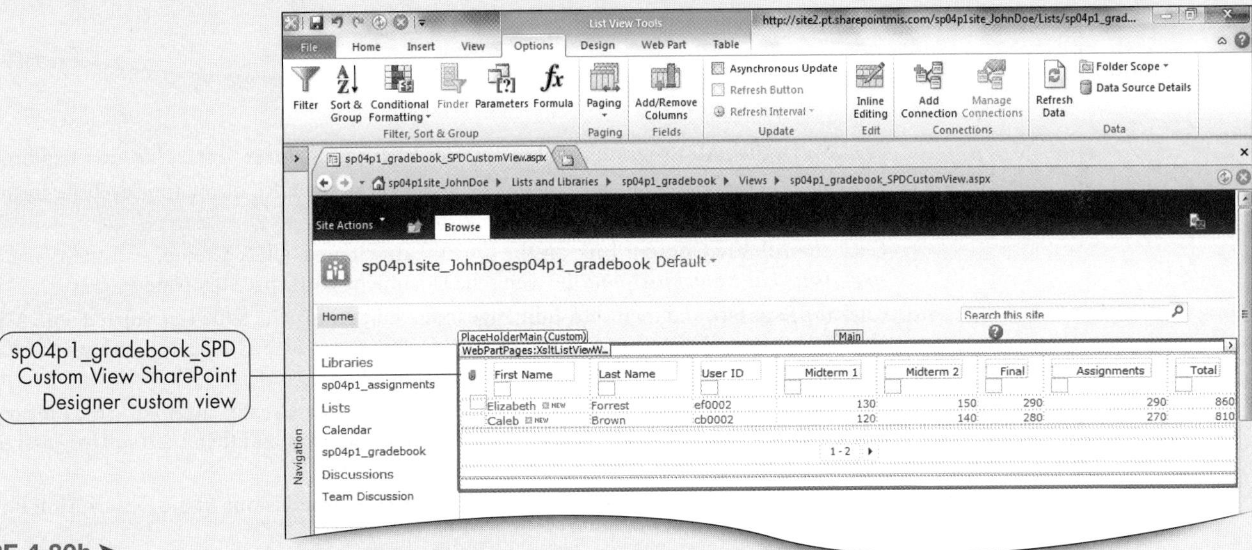

FIGURE 4.80b ➤

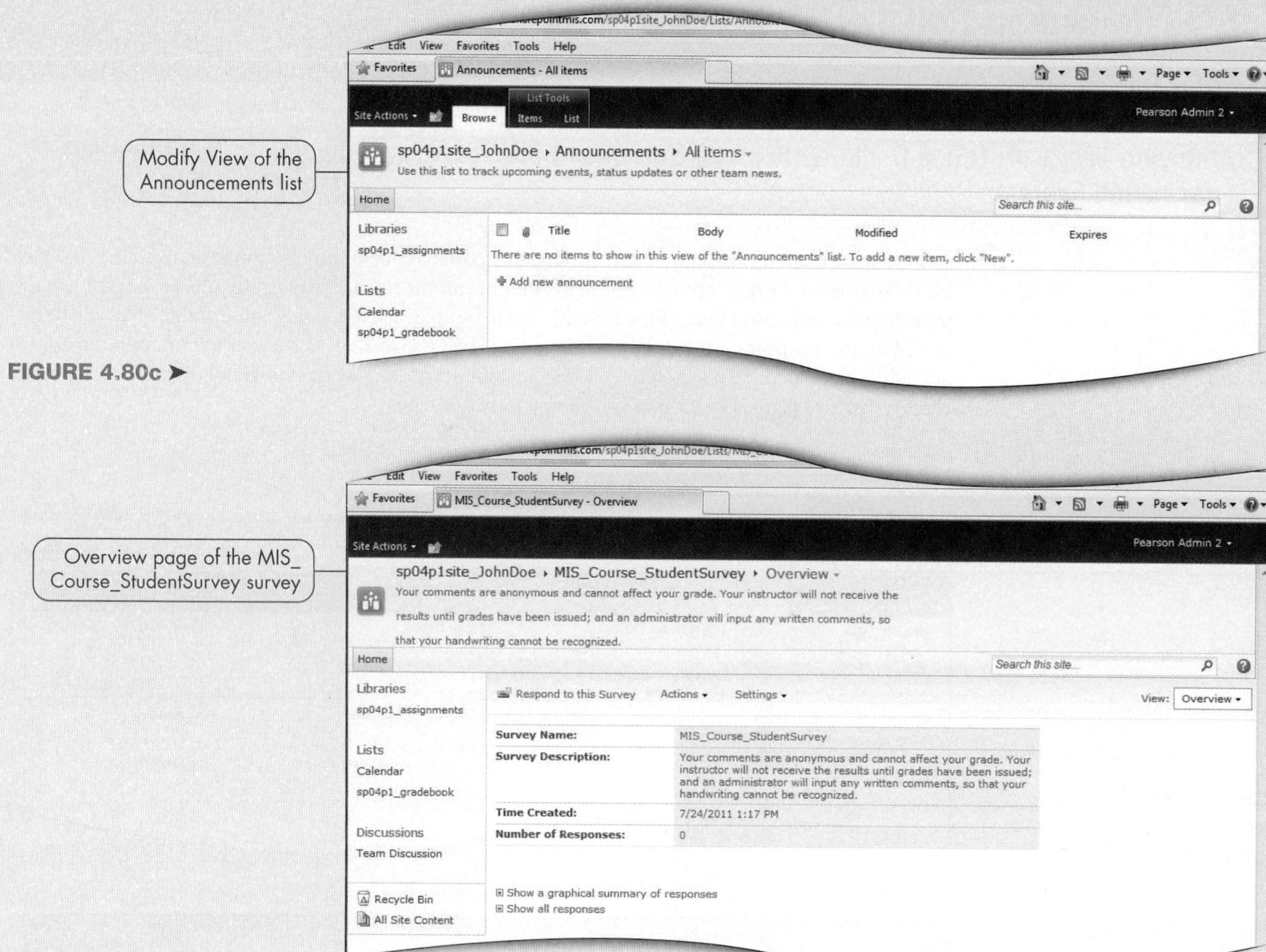

FIGURE 4.80c ➤

FIGURE 4.80d ➤

a. Click **Start**, click **All Programs**, and then select **Internet Explorer** to start Internet Explorer.

b. Click **File** on the Menu bar, and then click **Open**. Type the URL of the top-level site in the **Open box**. The home page of your top-level site is displayed.

c. Click the **All Site Content link** on the Quick Launch area. Click **Create**, and then create a new *sp04p1site_LastNameFirstName* file using the Document Workspace template.

d. Click the **Page tab**, and then click **Edit Page** in the Edit group. Click the **Get Started with Microsoft SharePoint Foundation link**, and then click **Delete Item** in the Manage group on the View tab. Click **OK** in the Message from Web page dialog box.

e. Click the **All Site Content link** on the Quick Launch, click **Create**, and then click **Library** in the *Filter By* section of the Create page. Click **Document Library**, and then type **sp04p1_assignments** in **Name box**. Click **More Options.**

f. Type **This library will include all course Assignments submissions** in the **Description box**. Click **Create**.

The *sp04p1_assignments* library is now displayed in the default Standard view.

g. Click **Open with Explorer** in the Connect & Export group. Open a separate Windows Explorer folder, browse to *MISB_AssignmentSubmissionReport.docx* in your Exploring folder, right-click the file, and then select **Copy**. Click in the window opened by *Open with Explorer*, double-click **Forms folder**, right-click in a blank area, and then select **Paste**.

h. Activate the browser window, and then click **Library Settings** in the Settings group on the Library Tools–Library tab. Click **Advanced Settings** in the *General Settings* section of the Document Library Settings page. Highlight **template.docx** in the **Template URL box** on the Advanced Settings page, type **MISB_AssignmentSubmissionReport.docx**, and then click **OK.** Click **sp04p1_assignments** in the breadcrumb. The *sp04p1_assignments* library is now be displayed in the default Standard view.

i. Click the **Library Tools–Documents tab**, and then click **New Document** in the New Group. Highlight **XX** in the new Microsoft Word Document 1 window, and then type **1**. Click **Save**, type **sp04p1_assignment1** in the **File name box** in the Save As dialog box, and then click **Save**.

j. Activate the browser window, click the **Upload Document arrow**, and then select **Upload Document**. Browse to *sp04p1_assignment1_file1* in your Exploring folder, and then click **OK** to upload the file. Your screen should look similar to Figure 4.80a.

k. Click **Navigate Up**, and then select **Team Site**. Click **Site Settings** on the Site Actions menu, click **List templates** in the *Galleries* section, and then click **Upload Documents** in the New group of the Library Tools–Documents tab. Browse for the *gradebook.stp* document in your Exploring folder, select the file, click **Open**, click **OK**, and then click **Save** on the Edit Tab of the List Template Gallery.

l. Click **Navigate Up**, select **Team Site**, and then click **sp04p1site_LastNameFirstName** on the Top link navigation bar. Click the **All Site Content link** on the Quick Launch. Click **Create** on the All Site Content page to open the Create page. Click **Blank & Custom** in the *All Categories* section of the Create page. Click the **gradesbook template**, and then type **sp04p1_gradebook** in **Title box**. Click **Create.**

m. Click the **List Tools–List tab**, click **Create View** in the Manage Views group, and then click **Datasheet view** on the Create View page. Type **sp04p1_gradebook_Custom DSView** in the **View Name box**, check the **Created** and **Created by check boxes** in the *Columns* sections, and then click **OK**.

n. Click **Edit in SharePoint Designer** on the Site Actions menu. Click **Lists and Libraries** on the Navigation Pane. Click the **sp04p1_gradebook link** in the *Lists* section of the Lists and Libraries summary page, and then click **New** in the *Views* section.

o. Type **sp04p1_gradebook_SPDCustomView** in the **Name box** of the Create New List View dialog box, and then click **OK**. The *sp04p1_gradebook_SPDCustomView* custom view is now displayed in the *Views* section. Click the **sp04p1_gradebook_SPDCustomView link**. The *sp04p1_gradebook_SPDCustomView.aspx* page is now displayed in Design view and the List View Tools–Options tab is activated.

p. Click **Sort & Group** in the Filter, Sort & Group group, click **Total** in the *Available fields* section of the Sort & Group dialog box, click **Add** >> in the *Sort properties* section, and then click **OK**.

q. Click **Save** on the Quick Access Toolbar. Collapse the Navigation Pane. The *sp04p1_gradebook_SPDCustomView.aspx* page should look similar to the one shown in Figure 4.80b.

r. Close all Word and SharePoint Designer windows.

s. Activate the browser window. Click **Navigate Up**, select **Team Site**, and then click **sp04p1site_LastNameFirstName** on the top link navigation bar. Click the **Announcements link**, click the **List Tools–List tab**, and then click **Modify View** in the Manage Views group. The Edit View page is now displayed.

t. Select the check boxes to the left of the Body and Expires columns in the *Columns* section on the Edit View page. Switch positions between the Modified and Body columns, and then click **OK**. The *AllItems.aspx* page is now displayed and should look similar to Figure 4.80c.

u. Click **All Site Content Link** on the Quick Launch. Click **Create** on the All Site Content page. Click **List** in the *Filter By* section on the Create page, and then click **Survey template**. Type **MIS_Course_StudentSurvey** in the **Name box**, and then click **More Options**.

v. Type **Your comments are anonymous and cannot affect your grade. Your instructor will not receive the results until grades have been issued.** in the **Description box**. Select **No** in the *Navigation* section. Select **No** for *Show user name in survey results* option in the *Survey Options* section. Click **Create**.

w. Type **The instructor's teaching helped me to learn the course material** in the **Question box** on the New Question page. Select **Yes** for the *Require a response to this question* option, and then select **No** for the *Enforce unique values* option.

x. Highlight the text in the *Type each choice on a separate line* box, and then type:
   1. **Strongly Agree**
   2. **Agree**
   3. **Neither Agree Nor Disagree**
   4. **Disagree**
   5. **Strongly Disagree.**

y. Click **Finish**. Click **Advanced Settings**. Select the **Read responses that were created by the user option** in the *Read access* section. Select **None** in the *Create and Edit access* section. Select **No** in the following three sections of the Advanced Settings page. Click **OK**.

z. Click **MIS_Course_StudentSurvey** on the breadcrumb at the top of the Survey Settings page. Your screen should look similar to Figure 4.80d. Close the browser window.

2 Integrating Microsoft Office Word, and PowerPoint Documents into a SharePoint Site for a University Research Lab

You have been hired as a graduate research assistant in the Laboratory for Educational and Assistive Technology (LEAT) research. As a part of your new assignment you have been working on developing a SharePoint site for the lab. You will need to archive and disseminate the published research papers (created as Word .docx documents) and presentations (saved as PowerPoint .pptx documents) given by members of the lab at different professional events. This exercise follows the same set of skills as used in Hands-On Exercises 1 and 2 in the chapter. Refer to Figures 4.81a–b as you complete this exercise.

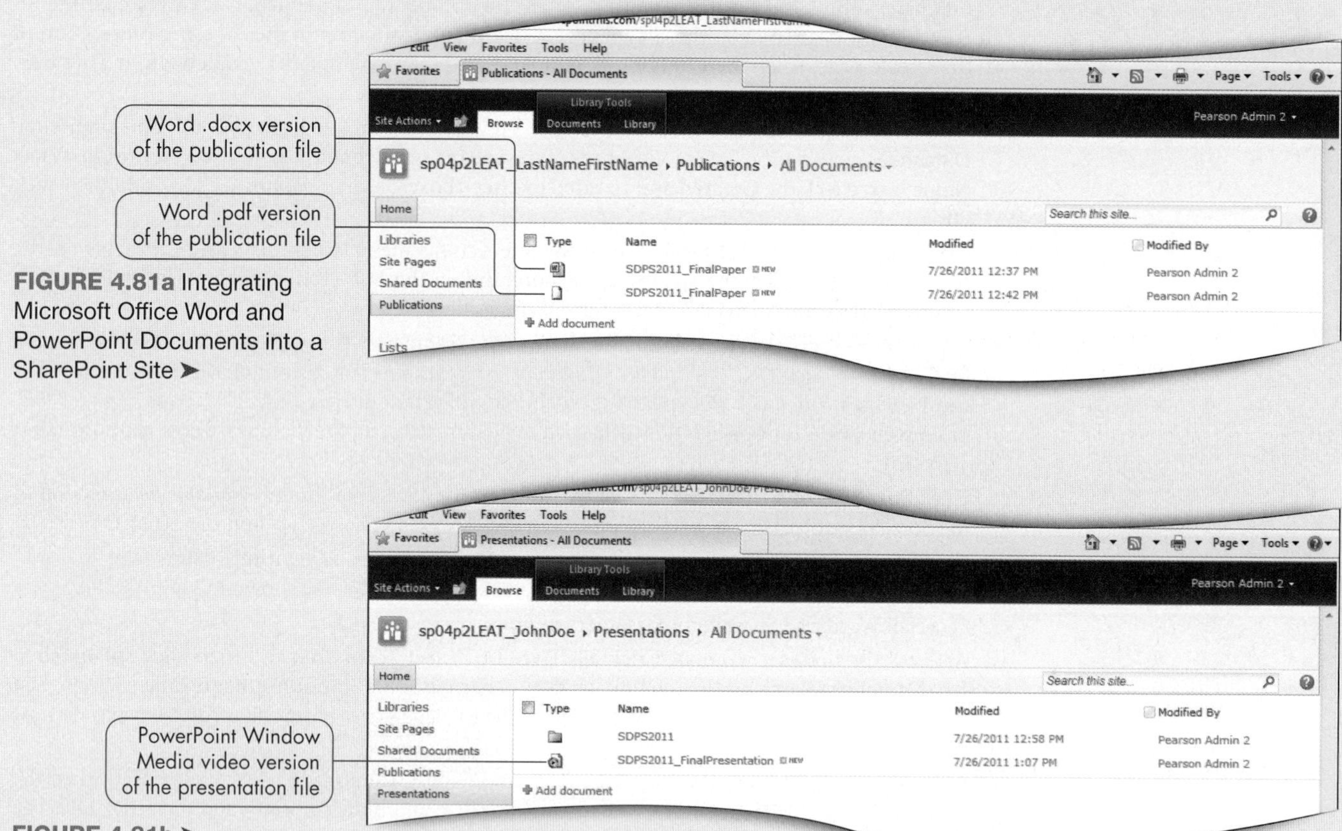

FIGURE 4.81a Integrating Microsoft Office Word and PowerPoint Documents into a SharePoint Site ➤

FIGURE 4.81b ➤

a. Click **Start**, click **All Programs**, and then select **Internet Explorer** to start Internet Explorer. Click **File** on the Menu bar, and then click **Open Site**. Type the URL of the top-level site in the Open box.

b. Click **All Site Content** on the Quick Launch. Click **Create**, and then create a new *sp04p2LEAT_LastNameFirstName* using the Team Site template.

c. Create a new Publications document library. Click **Library Tools–Documents tab**, and then upload the *SDPS2011_FinalPaper.docx* file from your Exploring folder.

d. Click **Publications** on the Quick Launch. Click the URL of the Publications library in the browser Address bar, right-click, and then click **Copy**.

e. Click **Start** to display the Start menu. Click **All Programs**, and then click **Microsoft Word** to open the program. Click the **File tab** to open the Backstage view, and then click **Open** to display the Microsoft Word Open dialog box.

f. Right-click in the **File name box**, and then click **Paste**. Remove */Forms/AllItems.aspx* from the URL. Click **Open**. Click **SDPS2011_FinalPaper** in the Open dialog box, and then click **Open**. Close the Word window.

g. Activate the browser window, click the **Library Tools–Library tab**, and then click **Open with Explorer** in the Connect & Export group. Double-click **SDPS2011_FinalPaper** in the Windows Explorer window.

h. Click the **File tab**, and then save **SDPS2011_FinalPaper** as a PDF file. Click **Refresh (F5)**. Your screen should look similar to Figure 4.81a. Close the Word window.

i. Click **Navigate Up**, and then select the **sp04p2LEAT_LastNameFirstName site**. Create a new Presentations document library with Microsoft PowerPoint presentation as Document Template. Click the **Library Tools–Documents tab**, and then create a *SDPS2011* folder.

j. Click **Start** to display the Start menu. Click **All Programs**, and then click **Microsoft PowerPoint** to open the program. Open the *SDPS2011_FinalPresentation.pptx* file from your Exploring folder.

k. Click the **File tab**, click **Save & Send**, click **Publish Slides** in the *Save & Send* section, and then click **Publish Slides.**

l. Click **Select All**, click **Browse**, and then navigate to the Presentation/SDPS2011 folder. Click **Publish.** Activate the browser window, and then click **SDPS2011** to see the published slides.

m. Activate the PowerPoint window, click the **File tab**, and then click **Save As**. Click **Windows Media video** in the *Save as type* list, and then navigate to the Presentation library. Click **Save.** Activate the browser window, and then click **Refresh (F5)**. Your screen should look similar to Figure 4.81b. Close the PowerPoint and browser windows.

3 Using Excel and Access Documents, Creating Data Sources and Adding Data Views to a SharePoint Site for a University Research Lab

As Web master of the Educational and Assistive Technology Research lab SharePoint site, you want to enable members of the lab to share Excel documents that contain relevant research data. You have received a Microsoft Access database that was developed by the lab team for organizing conferences. In order to fully take advantage of the Microsoft Access and SharePoint Foundation tools, you will integrate this Access database with the lab site. This exercise follows the same set of skills as used in Hands-On Exercises 1 and 3. Refer to Figures 4.82a–e as you complete this exercise.

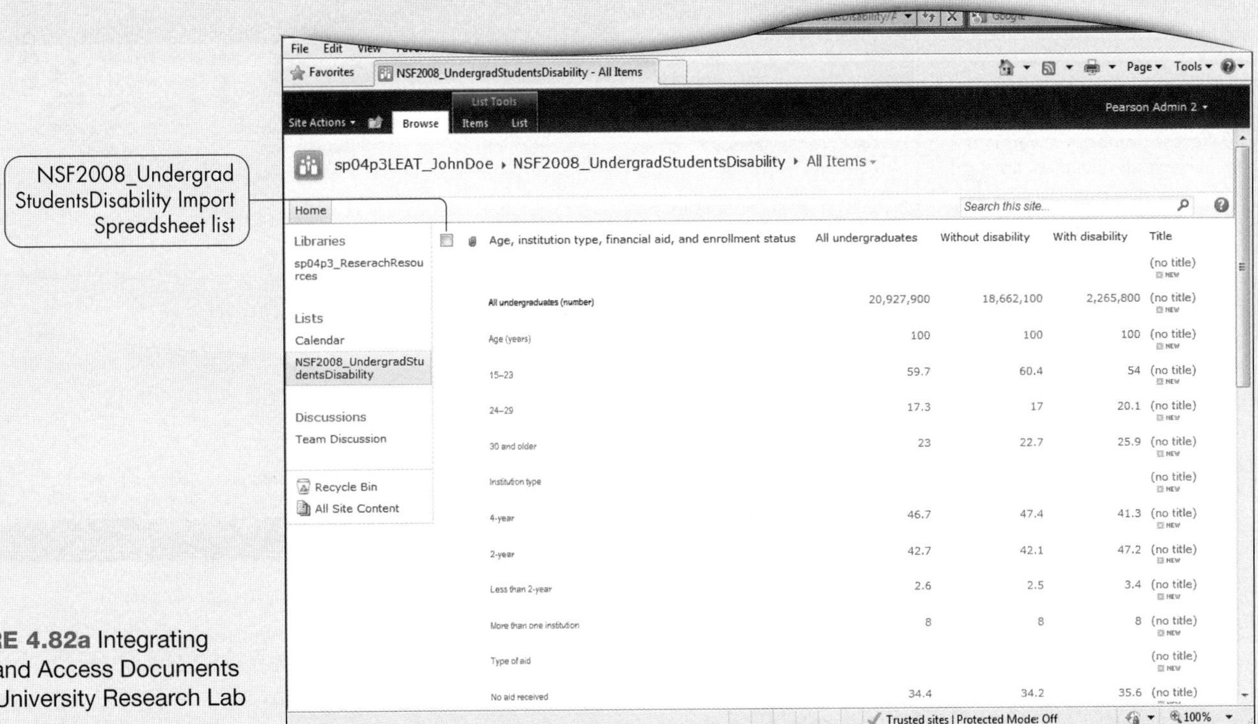

FIGURE 4.82a Integrating Excel and Access Documents into a University Research Lab Site ➤

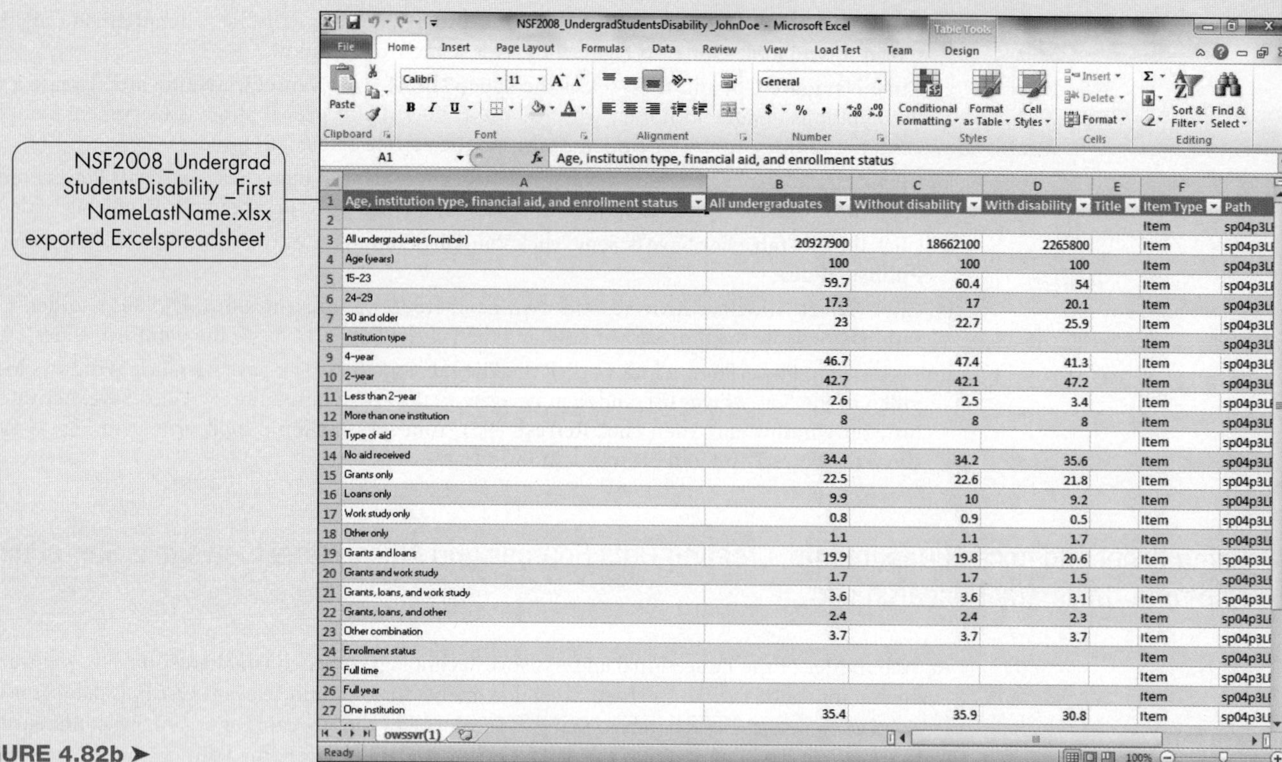

FIGURE 4.82b ➤

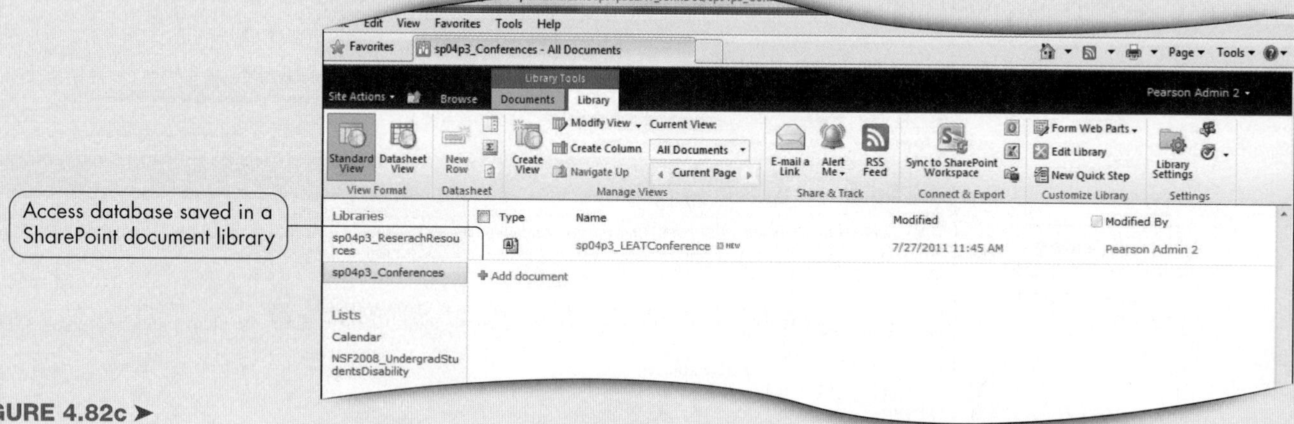

FIGURE 4.82c ➤

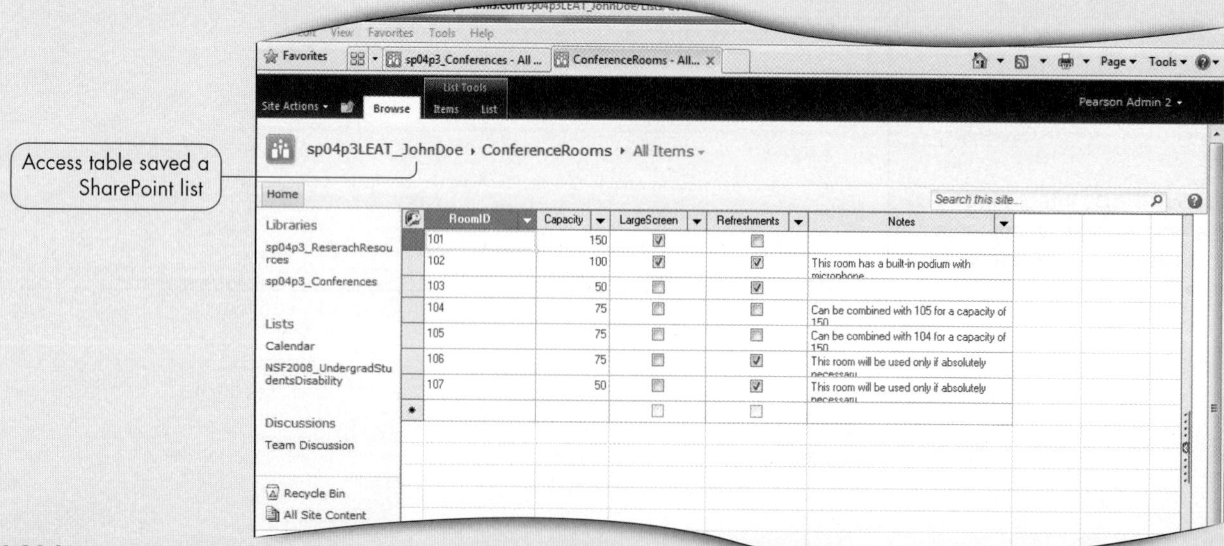

FIGURE 4.82d ➤

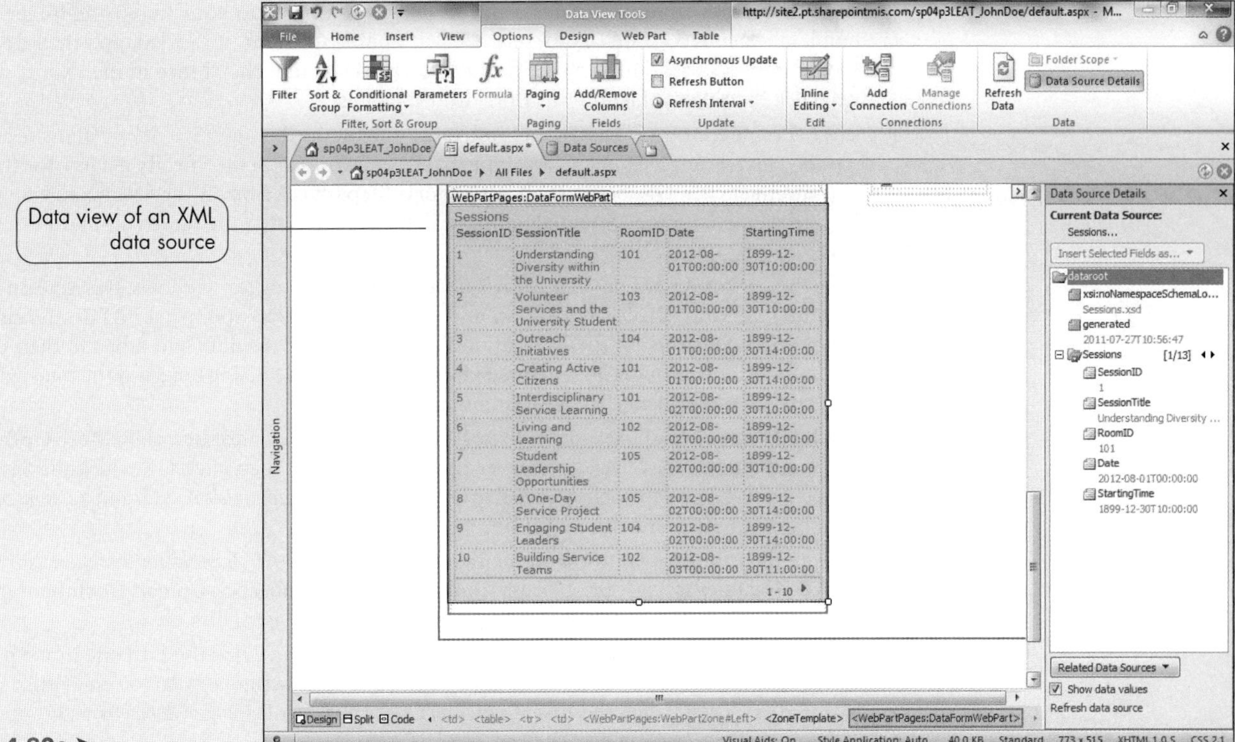

FIGURE 4.82e ➤

a. Click **Start** to display the Start menu. Click **All Programs**, and then click **Internet Explorer** to open the program. Go to the top-level site provided by your instructor which will be in the format of *http://pt.sharepointmis.com/SitePages/yourname*. Enter the user name and password provided by your instructor. Create a *sp04p3LEAT_LastNameFirstName* subsite using the Document Workspace template.

b. Create a *sp04p3_ResearchResources* Document library, selecting Microsoft Excel Spreadsheet as Document template.

c. Click **Site Actions**, and then click **More options** to open Create dialog box. Click **Blank & Custom** in the *All Categories* section, click **Import Spreadsheet**, and then click **Create** to open the New page.

d. Type **NSF2008_UndergradStudentsDisability** in the **Name box**, and then click **Browse** to open the Choose File Upload dialog box. Navigate to the *sp04p3_UndergradStudentsDisabilityStatus.xlsx* file in the Exploring folder, double-click its name, and then click **Import**. Select **Table Range** in the Range Type: list, and then select **Undergraduate2008!Table1** in the Select Range: list. Click **Import**.

e. Click the **List Tools–List tab**, and then click **List Settings** in the Settings group. Click **Title, Description and Navigation** under the *General Settings* section of the List Settings page. Click **Yes** in the *Navigation* section of the General Settings page to display the list on the Quick Launch. Click **Save** on the General Settings page. Click the **NSF2008_UndergradStudentsDisability link** on the breadcrumb. Your screen should look similar to Figure 4.82a.

f. Click the **List Tools–List tab**, and then click **Export to Excel** in the Connect & Export group. Click **Open** in the File Download dialog box. Click **Enable** in the Excel Security Notice dialog box, indicating the data connections have been blocked.

g. Delete **100** from **cell B4**. Click the **Data tab**, and then click **Refresh All** in the Connections group. Your screen should look similar to Figure 4.82b. Save the spreadsheet on your local computer as **NSF2008_UndergradStudentsDisability _FirstNameLastName.xlsx**. Exit Excel.

h. Activate the browser window, and then create a new **sp04p3_Conferences** Document library. Navigate on your local computer to your Exploring folder and double-click **sp04p3_LEAT_Conference**. Click **Enable Content**, if needed, click the **File tab**, and then click **Save & Publish** in the Access Backstage view. Click **Save Database As command** in the *Files Types* section, select **SharePoint** in the *Save Database As* section, and then click **Save As.**

i. Navigate to the *sp04p3_LEATConference* document library, and then click **Save** in the Save to SharePoint dialog box. Activate the browser window, and then click **Refresh (F5)**. Your screen should look similar to Figure 4.82c.

j. Close the Access window. Navigate on your local computer to your Exploring folder, and then double-click **sp04p3_LEATConference**. Click **Enable Content**, if needed, and then double-click **Rooms** in the Navigation Pane. Click the **External Data tab**, click **More** in the Export group, and then click **SharePoint List** on the More drop-down list.

k. Select the **sp04p3LEAT_LastNameFirstName subsite** in the *Specify a SharePoint site* area of the Export - SharePoint Site dialog box, type **ConferenceRooms** in the **Specify a name for the new list box**, and then click **OK**. Select the **Save Exports Steps check box** on the Save Export Steps page of the Export - SharePoint Site dialog box. Click **Save Export**. Your screen should look similar to Figure 4.82d.

l. Close the *sp04p3_LEATConference.accdb* database and the browser windows. Navigate on your local computer to your Exploring folder, and then double-click **sp04p3_LEATConference.accdb**. Double-click **Sessions** on the Navigation Pane. Click the **External Data tab**, and then click **XML File** in the Export group. Click **Browse** in Export - XML File dialog box, and then navigate to your local Documents folder. Click **Save**, and then click **OK**.

m. Check all three check boxes in the Export - XML dialog box, and then click **More Options**. Click the **Presentation tab**. Check the **Server (ASP) option**, and then click **OK**. Click the **Save exports steps check box**, and then click **Save Export**. The *Sessions.xml*, *Sessions.xsd*, and *Sessions.xsl* files are now shown in the destination location.

n. Activate the browser window, and then go to the *sp04p3LEAT_LastNameFirstName* subsite. Click **Shared Documents**, click the **Library Tools–Documents tab**, click **Upload Document** in the New group, and then import the *Sessions.xml*, *Sessions.xsd*, *Sessions.xsl* files.

o. Click **Edit in SharePoint Designer** in the Site Actions menu. Click the **Edit site home page** in the *Customization* section of the Site Setting page. Click below the Left Part Zone within the <div> </div> pair of tags. Click the **Insert tab**, click **Data View** in Data Views & Forms group, and then click **Empty Data View** in the All Data Sources gallery.

p. Click **Data Sources** in the Navigation Pane. Click the icon to the left of the Shared Documents library in the Data Sources gallery page, and then click **XML File Connection** in the New group on the Data Sources tab.

q. Click **Browse** in the Source tab of the Data Source Properties dialog box, and then navigate to the *Sessions.xml* file in the File Open dialog box. Double-click **Sessions.xml**, and then click **OK** on the local drive in the Data Sources Properties dialog box.

r. Click the **default.aspx tab** to display the default.aspx page again, and then click **Click here to select a data source link** inside the DataFormWebPart control. Click the **Sessions file** in the *XML Files* section of the Data Sources Picker dialog box, and then click **OK**.

s. Select all fields of the XML file in the Data Source Details task pane, click **Insert Selected Fields as ...**, and then select the **Multiple Item view option** on the Insert Selected Fields menu. Collapse the Navigation Pane. Your screen should look similar to Figure 4.82e.

t. Save **Default.aspx**, and then close the SharePoint Designer, Access, and browser windows.

MID-LEVEL EXERCISES

1 Creating a Document Archive, a Blog Site and a Discussion Board for the Hope Hospital Using Microsoft Office Documents and SharePoint Sites

You work for the Hope Hospital, and you have been asked to create a SharePoint document library with a Word document template that nurses can use to keep track of patients' blood pressure. You will create a Healthy Living blog for the Hope Hospital patients. You have also been asked to create a Discussion Board list where patients can share thoughts about healthy living. You will create an archive of the business office Excel documents related to the hospital expansion project, which can be shared by all office employees. You will create a new team site. You will create a new document library and change the default template. You will create a blog subsite site and publish a new post using Microsoft Word. You will upload a Word document in the Assets Library on the team site. You will create a Discussion Board list and add a new item having attached the uploaded Word document. You will create an Import Spreadsheet list, and create a custom Datasheet view. Figure 4.83 should look very similar to your screen at the end of the exercise.

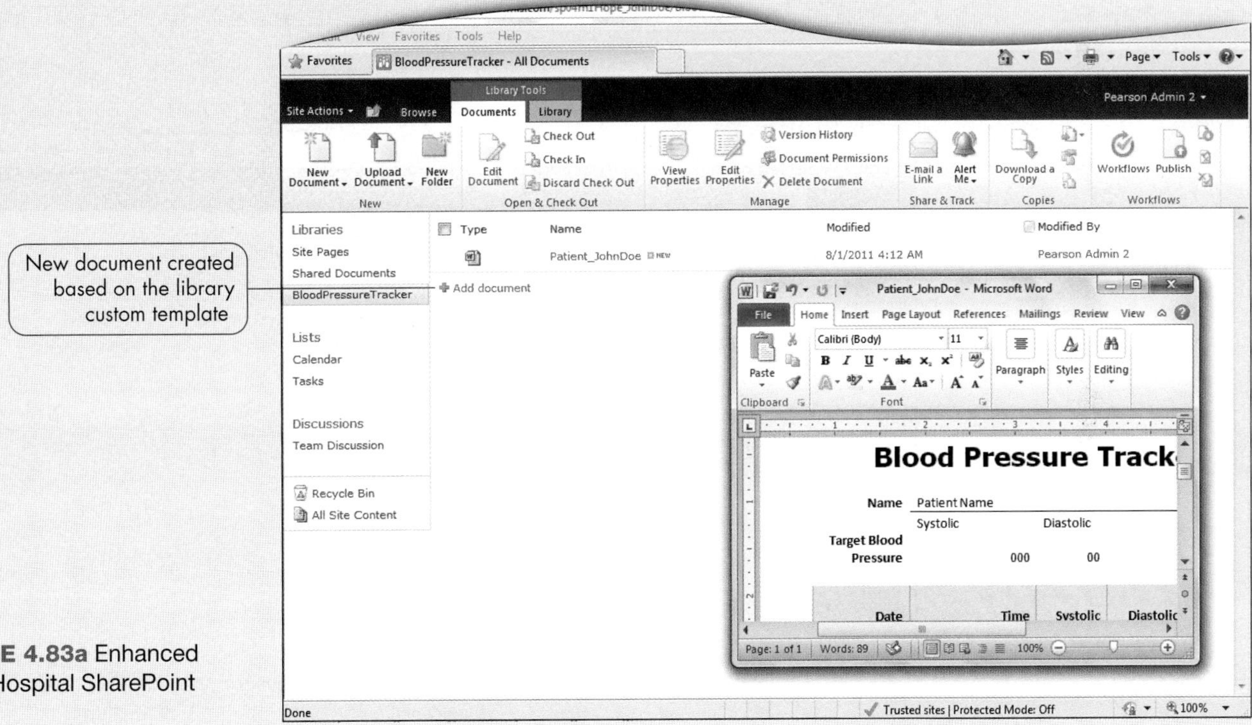

FIGURE 4.83a Enhanced Hope Hospital SharePoint Site ➤

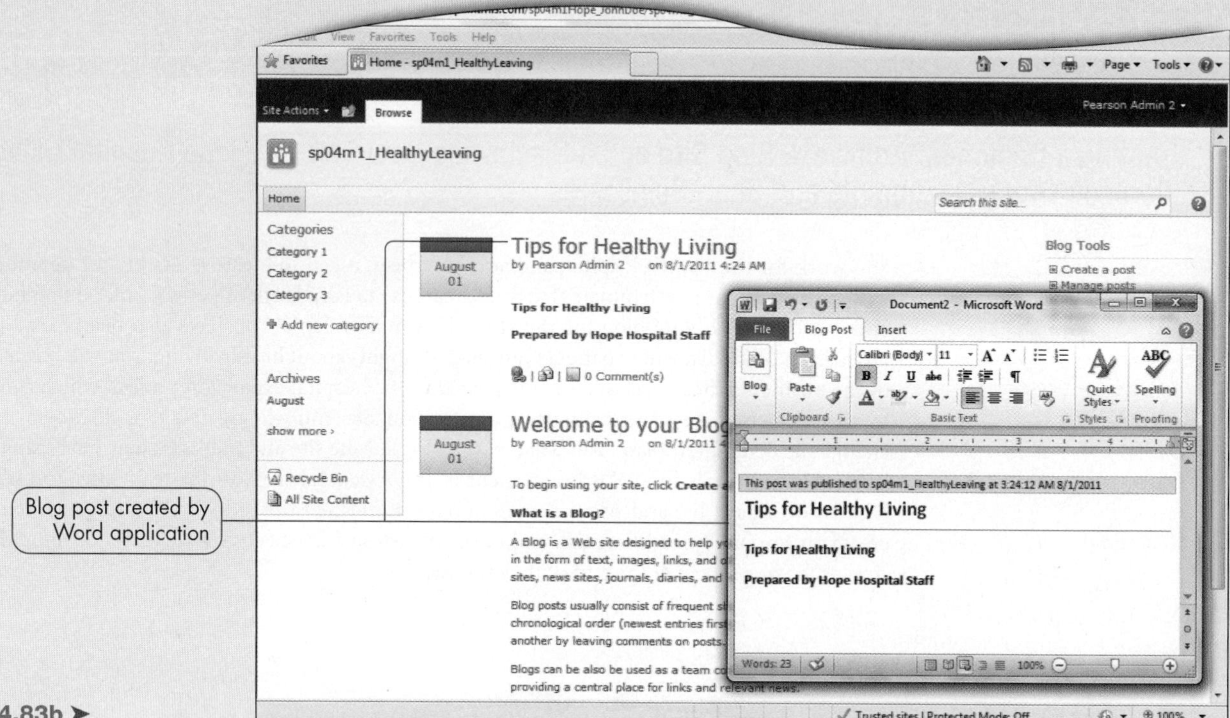

FIGURE 4.83b ➤

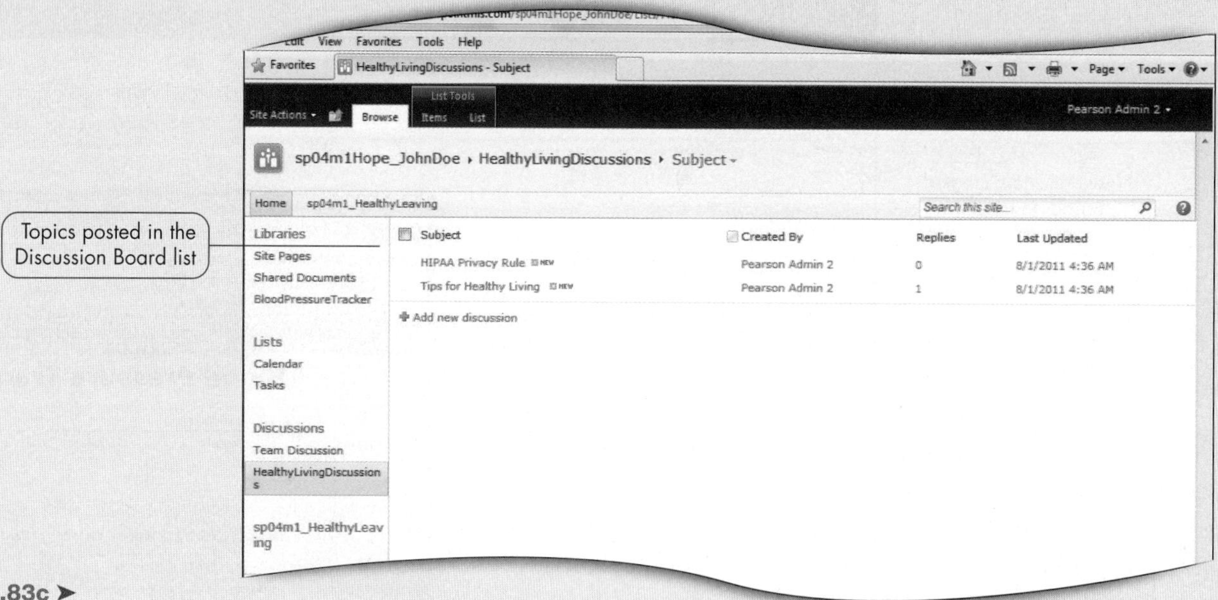

FIGURE 4.83c ➤

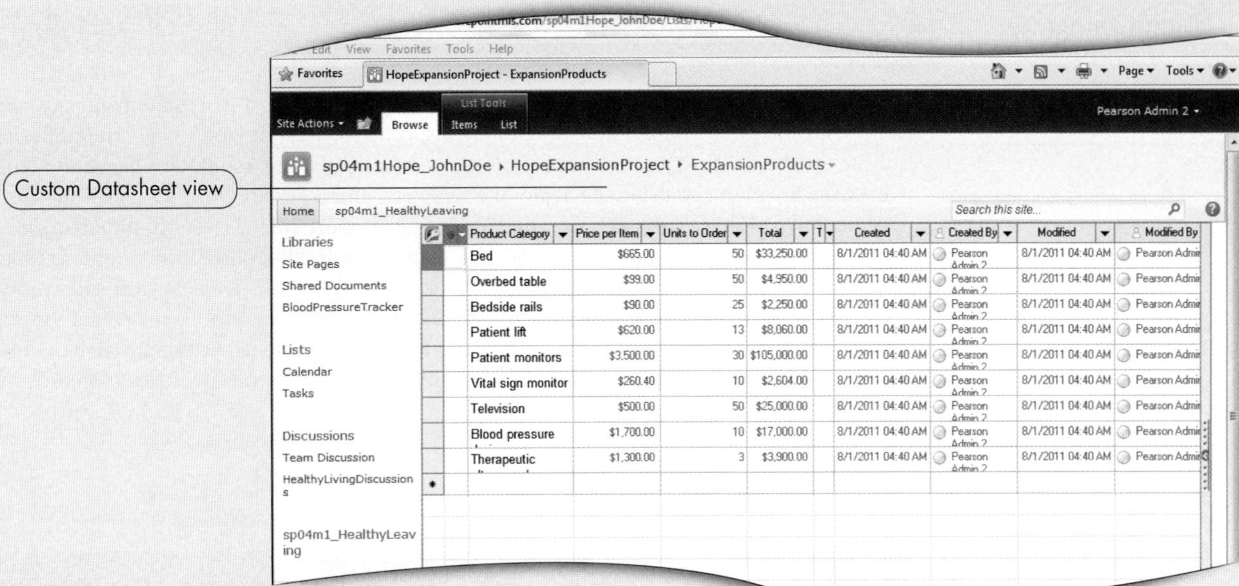

FIGURE 4.83d ➤

a. Start Internet Explorer.
b. Click **File** on the Menu bar and click **Open Site.** Type the URL of the top-level site in the **Open box.** Create a sp04m1Hope_LastNameFirstName subsite of the top-level site using the Team Site template. Create a BloodPressureTracker Document library.
c. Click the **Library Tools–Library tab**, and then click **Open with Explorer**. Open a separate Windows Explorer window, browse for the *sp04m1_BloodPressureTracker.docx* file in your Exploring folder, right-click **sp04m1_BloodPressureTracker**, and then click **Copy**. Activate the window that holds the BloodPressureTracker document library Forms folder, and then double-click **Forms**. Right-click in a blank area, and then click **Paste**. Close the Explorer windows.
d. Activate the browser window, click **Library Settings**, and then click **Advanced Settings**. Change the URL in the *Document Template* section to point to the *sp04m1_BloodPressureTracker* file you uploaded in the previous step in the Forms folder, and then click **OK**.
e. Click the **BloodPressureTracker link** in the breadcrumb trail. Click the **Library Tools–Documents tab**, and then create a new *Patient_LastNameFirstName.docx* document. Save the document. Close the Word Window. Activate the browser window, and then click **Patient_LastNameFirstName.** Click the **Restore Down button.** Your screen should look similar to the screen capture from Figure 4.83a.
f. Create a sp04m1_HealthyLiving blog subsite of the *sp04m1Hope_LastNameFirstName* subsite. A link to this new subsite should show on the Quick Launch. Copy the URL of the new blog site. Launch Word and create a new document using the Blog Post template. Click **Manage Accounts** in the blog group on the Blog Post tab. Change the blog account to **sp04m1_HealthyLiving.**
g. Change the Post Title to **Tips for Healthy Living** and place the insertion point below the horizontal line. Type **Tips for Healthy Living**, press **Enter**, and then type **Prepared by Hope Hospital Staff.** Click **Publish.** Activate the browser window, and then click **Refresh (F5).** Activate the Word Window, and then click the **Restore Down button.** Your screen should look similar to Figure 4.83b.
h. Navigate to the *sp04m1Hope_LastNameFirstName* subsite. Upload *sp04m1_HealthyLiving.docx* in the Site Assets library. Create a HealthyLivingDiscussions Discussion Board list.
i. Add a new item with a subject of **Tips for Healthy Living**, and then attach *sp04m1_HealthyLiving.docx* to this new item. Create a Reply to this item and type **Very interesting topic!** as the message in the body. Add a new item with the subject **HIPAA Privacy Rule.** Your screen should look similar to Figure 4.83c.
j. Navigate to the *sp04m1Hope_LastNameFirstName* subsite, click **More Options** on the Site Actions menu. Create a HopeExpansionProject Import Spreadsheet list, importing the Hope Hospital Expansion!Table 1 included in the *sp04m1_HopeHospital.xslx* file from your Exploring folder.

k. Click the **List Tools–List tab**, and then create an ExpansionProducts Data Sheet view that includes the Created, Created By, Edit (link to edit item), Modified, and Modified By columns. Your screen should look similar to Figure 4.83d.
l. Close the browser, Word, Windows Explorer, and Excel windows.

2 DestinQuest Co.

You work for DestinQuest, a vacation rental hospitality and resort real estate company, and at your supervisor's request, you are now developing a subsite for DestinQuest's new cruise offerings, and a subsite for the Destin Quest's business office for managing the DestinQuest vacation accounts. You will create a parent site using the Team Site template, and a Destin Quest's Cruises subsite using the Document Workspace template. You will create a new Import Spreadsheet list, importing the schedule of the offered cruises from an Excel table, and then you will export this list into an Excel spreadsheet. You will create a Vacations subsite using the Document Work Site template. You will export the data from the three Access tables, including info about DestinQuest vacation accounts into three separate SharePoint lists. You will import the three lists as linked tables into a new Access database. You will add data to the Calendar list displayed on the DestinQuest Vacations subsite. Refer to Figure 4.84 as you complete this exercise.

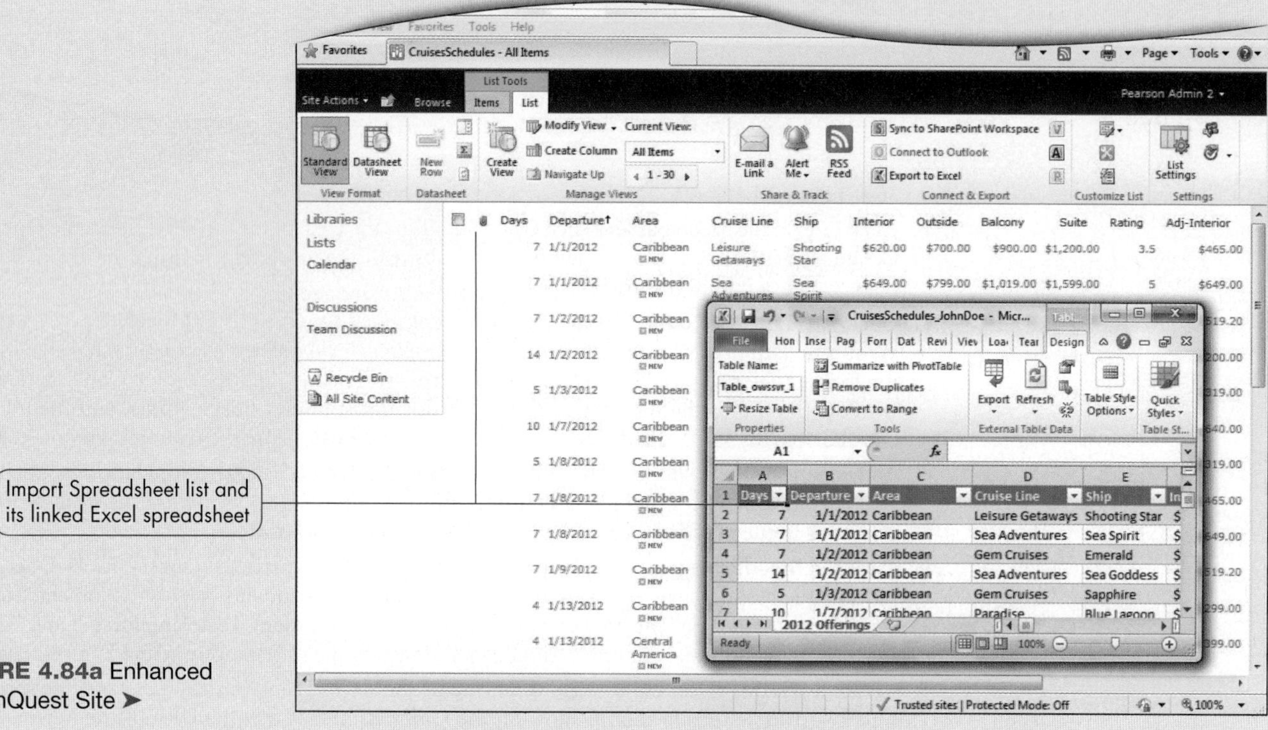

FIGURE 4.84a Enhanced DestinQuest Site ➤

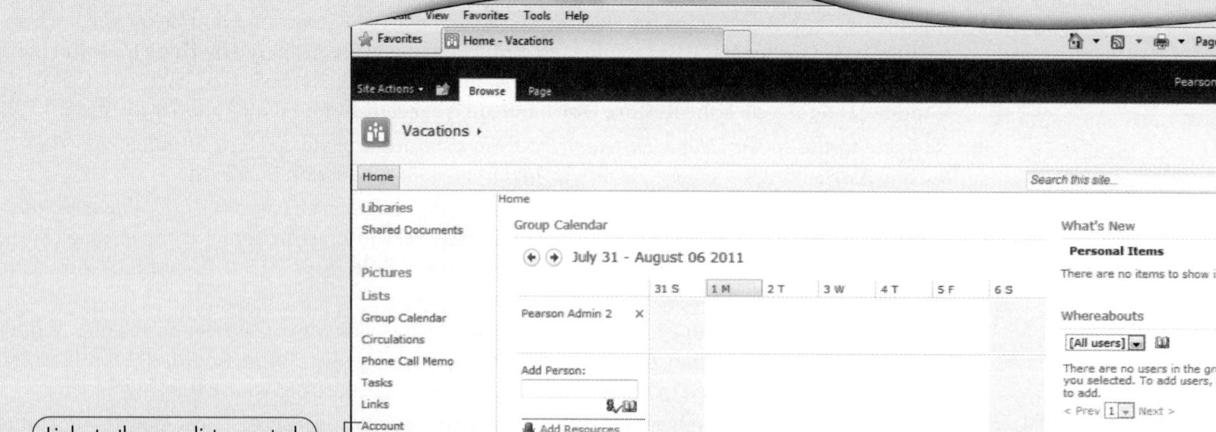

FIGURE 4.84b ➤

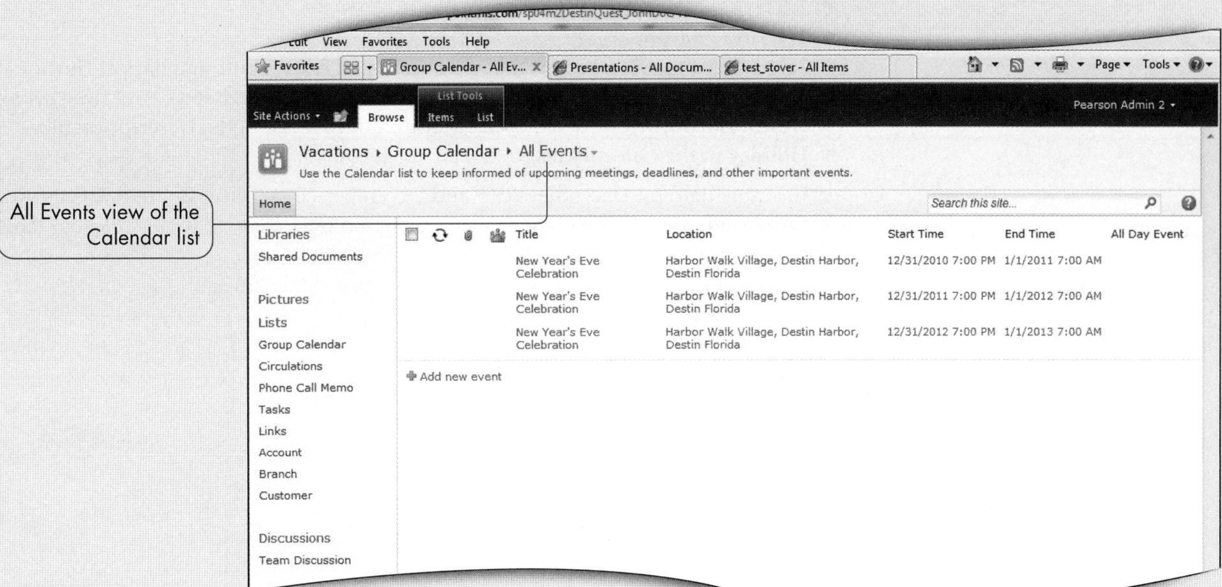

FIGURE 4.84c ➤

a. Start **Internet Explorer**, and the open the top-level site. Create a sp04m2DestinQuest_LastNameFirstName subsite of the top-level site using the Team Site template. Create a Cruises subsite of the *sp04m2DestinQuest_LastNameFirstName* site using the Document Workspace template. A link to this subsite should be displayed on the Quick Launch.

b. Create a CruisesSchedules Import Spreadsheet list, importing the 2012 Cruises!CruisesOffers table including file *sp04m2_DestinQuestCruises.xslx* from your Exploring folder.

c. Click **Export to Excel** in the Connect & Export group of the List Tools–List tab, and then export the Cruises Schedules list to a *CruisesSchedules_LastNameFirstName* Excel workbook. Change the name of the owssvr(1) spreadsheet to **2012 Offerings**.

d. Activate the browser window. Sort in ascending order the Cruises Schedules Import Spreadsheet list based on the values of Departure field. Activate the Excel window, and then click **Refresh** in the External Table Data on Tables Tools–Design tab. Click the **Restore Down button** in the Excel Window. Your screen should now look similar to Figure 4.84a. Save the 2012 Offerings spreadsheet. Close the Excel window.

e. Navigate to *sp04m2DestinQuest_LasNameFirstName*. Create a Vacations subsite using the Document Workspace template.

f. Launch the Microsoft Access application and open *sp04m2_DestinQuestVacations.accdb* from your Exploring folder. Save the Customer, Branch, and Account tables as lists in the Vacations subsite. Make sure you select Save Export steps check box in the Export page of the Access Export-SharePoint Site dialog box each time. Use the List Settings page of the three new lists to add links on the Quick Launch. Navigate to the home page of Vacations subsite. Your screen should now look similar to Figure 4.84b.

g. Create a new sp04m2_Vacations_LastNameFirstName Access database. Import the Customer, Branch, and Account lists created in step i. Select the **Link to the data source by creating a linked table** in the Get External Data - SharePoint site dialog box.

h. Activate the Access window, open the Customer table, and then type:
   - Your first name in the FirstName column, row 11
   - Your last name in the LastName column, row 11

i. Save the *sp04m2_Vacations_LastNameFirstName* Access database, activate the browser window displaying the AllItems.aspx page of the Customer list, and then click **Refresh (F5)**.

j. Delete row 11 from the Customer list. Activate the Access window and observe the changes in the Customer table. Save the *sp04m2_Vacations_LastNameFirstName* Access database. Close all Access and browser windows.

DISCOVER 

k. Launch the browser and open the Vacations site created in step e. Click anywhere inside the Calendar. Click **Month** in the Scope group on Calendar Tools–Calendar tab. Navigate to December 2012, double-click the **31 cell**, type or select the following in the Group Calendar - New Item dialog box, and then click Save:
   - **New Year's Eve Celebration** in the **Title box**
   - **Harbor Walk Village, Destin Harbor, Destin Florida** in the **Location box**

- **12/31/2012 7:00 pm** in Start Time
- **1/1/2013 7:00 am** in End Time
- **Join us into the New Year at the wide variety of restaurants and bars at Harbor Walk Village. The 3rd annual ball drop, live music on the Village stage, and fireworks over the Destin Harbor—a New Year's celebration not to miss!** in the **Description box.**
- **Holiday** in the Category list

l. Add the same item on December 2013 and December 2014. Select **Current Events view,** and then select **All Events view** in the Manage Views group on the Calendar Tools–Calendar tab. Your screen should look similar to Figure 4.84c.

m. Close Internet Explorer.

CAPSTONE EXERCISE

You have been working for a major financial management and advisory company on developing a site for all categories of company clients from individual investors to institutions and corporate clients. You will integrate Excel and Access documents with a company SharePoint subsite dedicated to managing individual investors accounts. You will create a parent site and a new document library for which you will set a new custom Excel template. You will create an Import Spreadsheet list and will create a new custom SharePoint Designer view for it. You will export an Access table into a SharePoint list and then export the SharePoint list into a new Access database as a linked table. You will export the Access table as an XML file and use it as a data source for creating a Data view.

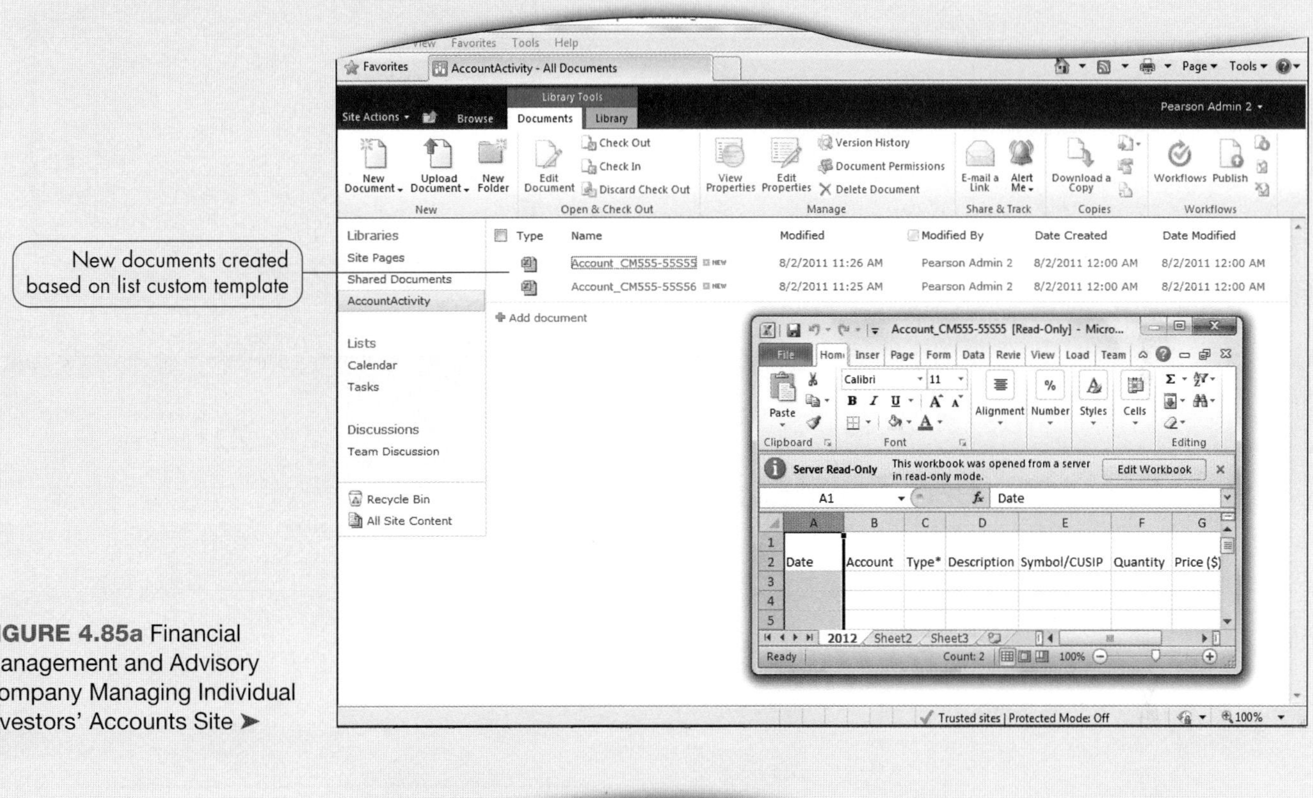

FIGURE 4.85a Financial Management and Advisory Company Managing Individual Investors' Accounts Site ➤

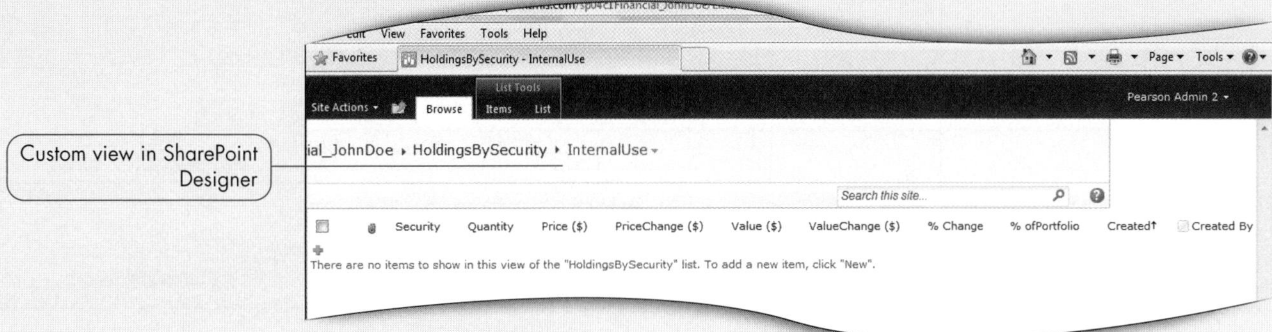

FIGURE 4.85b ➤

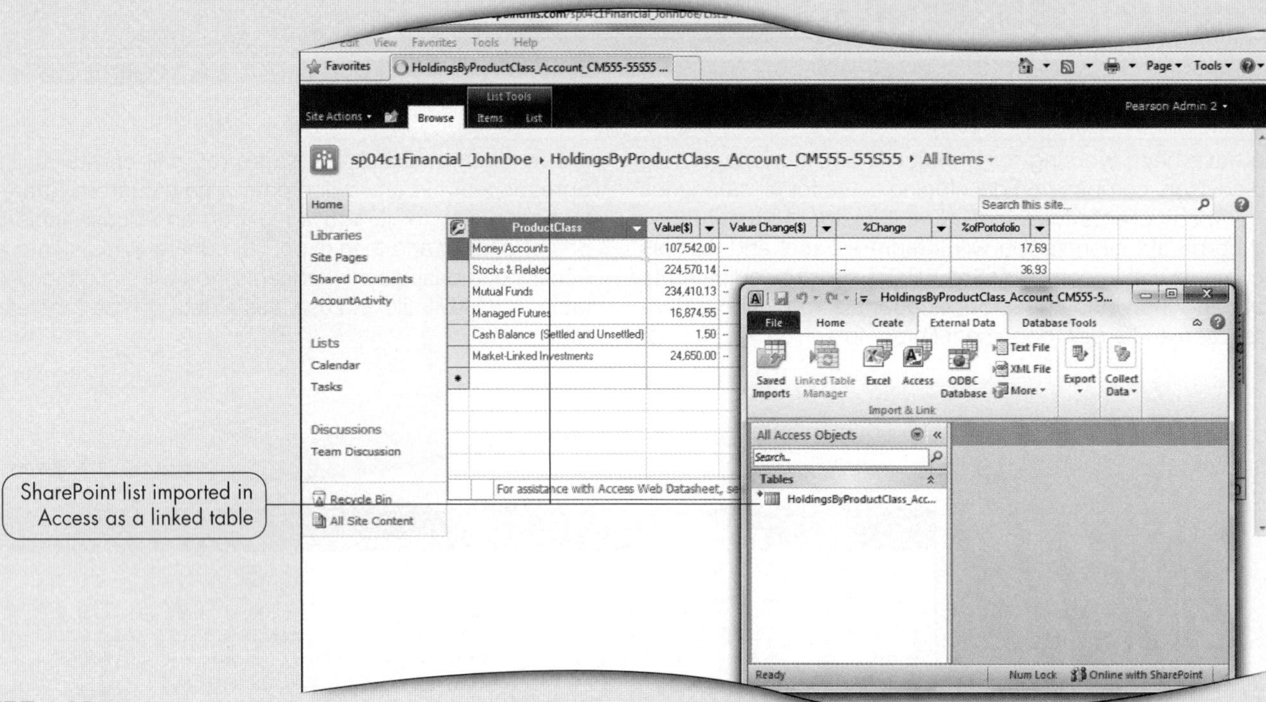

FIGURE 4.85c ➤

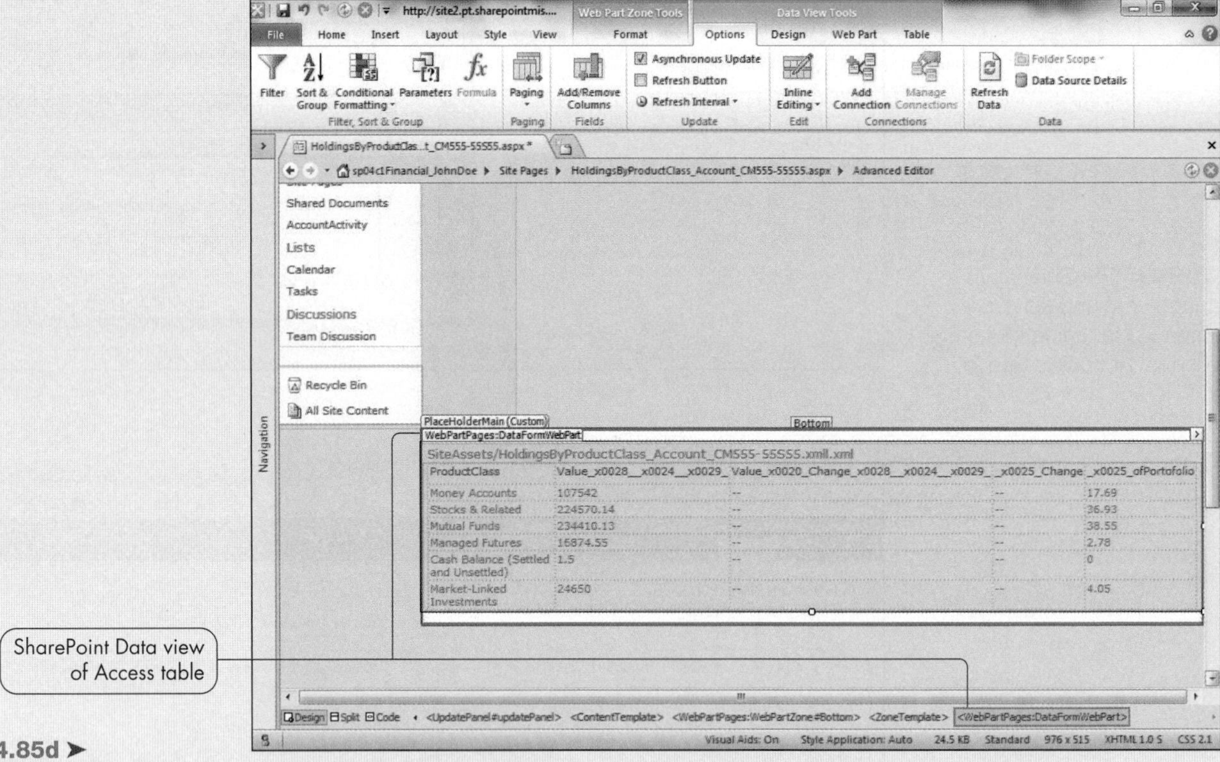

FIGURE 4.85d ➤

Create a Parent Site, Create a New Document Library, Add New Columns, Change Its Default Template, and Create a New Document

You will create a parent site for your company. You will add a new Documents Library and change its default template. You add new columns to the document library. You will create two new documents using the new template.

a. Launch Internet Explorer. Navigate to the top-level site of your site collection. Create a *sp04c1Financial_LastNameFirstName* subsite of your top-level site using the Team Site template.

b. Create a new AccountActivity document library. Set *sp04c1_AccountActivity.xlsx* as the new template of the AccountActivity document library.

c. Create a new *Account_CM555-55S55.xlsx.*

d. Add two columns, **Date Created** and **Date modified**, to the AccountActivity document library default view.

e. Create a new *Account_CM555-55S56.xlsx.* Type the following in the edit properties of the new document:

   - **Account_CM555-55S56** in the **Title box**
   - **Today** in the **Date Created box**
   - **Today** in the **Date Modified box**

f. Set the values of the Date Created and Date modified columns values of *_AccountActivity.xlsx* with *Account_CM555-55S55.xlsx* using the document Edit Properties dialog box using the same values set for the **Account_CM555-55S56.xlsx** document.

g. Click the **Account_CM555-55S55 link** in the AllItems.aspx page. Click the **Restore Down button** in the Excel window. Your screen should look similar to Figure 4.85a.

h. Close the Excel, Windows Explorer, and browser windows.

Create a New Import Spreadsheet List, Remove a Column, Create a Custom SharePoint Designer View

You are to create a new Import Spreadsheet List and remove a column. You are to create a custom view in SharePoint Designer that will include two more columns.

a. Open the *sp04c1Financial_LastNameFirstName* site.

b. Create a new **HoldingsBySecurity Import Spreadsheet List** by importing the Holdings by Security!Table 1 table from the *sp04c2_HoldingsBySecurity.xlsx* Excel document from your Exploring folder. Delete all the empty items from HoldingsBySecurity list.

c. Delete the **Last Updated column** of the HoldingsBySecurity Import Spreadsheet List.

d. Create an InternalUse Custom View in SharePoint Designer that will include two more columns, **Created** and **Created By**. In this view, sort the items in ascending order based on the value of the Created field.

e. Click **Inline Editing** in the Edit group on the SharePoint Designer List View Tools–Options tab. Save as **InternalUse.aspx**.

f. Activate the browser window, and then select the **InternalUse view**. You screen should look similar to Figure 4.85b.

g. Close all browser, SharePoint Designer, and Windows Explorer windows.

Export an Access Table to a SharePoint List, Import a SharePoint List as a Linked Access Table, Create a Data Source, and Create a Data View of the Data Source

You will export an Access table to a SharePoint list. You will import the SharePoint list to a new Access linked table. You will export an Access table as an XML file and import this file to the Site Assets library. You will create a new Wiki page and insert a Data View of the imported XML file.

a. Launch Microsoft Access, open *sp04c3_ClassOfProducts.accdb*, and then open the Holdings by Products Class table.

b. Select **SharePoint List** on the More list in the Export group on the External Data tab. Navigate to the *sp04c1Financial_LastNameFirstName* site, and then type the name of the new list as **HoldingsByProductClass_Account_CM555-55S55**. Close the Access window.

c. Create a new HoldingsByProductClass_Account_CM555-55S55 blank database in your local My Documents folder. Select **SharePoint List** on the More list in the Import & Link group on External Data tab.

d. Navigate to the *sp04c1Financial_LastNameFirstName* site, and then select the **HoldingsByProductClass_Account_CM555-55S55 list check box.**

e. Click the **Restore Down button** in the Access Window. Your screen should look similar to Figure 4.85c. Close the Access window.

f. Open *sp04c3_ClassOfProducts.accdb.* Click **XML File** in the Export group on External Data tab, and then export the Holdings by Products Class table, using an .ASP server-side transformation, as *HoldingsByProductClass_Account_CM555-55S55.xml, HoldingsByProductClass_Account_CM555-55S55.xsd*, and *HoldingsByProductClass_Account_CM555-55S55.xsl* files in your local My Documents folder. Save the Export Steps.

g. Activate the browser window. Create a *HoldingsByProductClass_Account_CM555-55S55* Wiki page in the Site Pages library.

h. Click **Edit in SharePoint Designer** in the Site Actions menu. Import the *HoldingsByProductClass_Account_CM555-55S55.xml, HoldingsByProductClass_Account_CM555-55S55.xsd*, and *HoldingsByProductClass_Account_CM555-55S55.xsl* files in the Site Assets library.

i. Open the *HoldingsByProductClass_Account_CM555-55S55.aspx* Wiki page in Advanced Editor mode. Place the cursor within the <div></div> pair of tags within PlaceHolderMain(Custom) Place Holder.

j. Insert a Data view in the Data Source Picker dialog box, selecting *HoldingsByProductClass_Account_CM555-55S55.xml* as the data source. Collapse the Navigation Pane and close the Data Source Details task pane. Your screen should look similar to Figure 4.85d.

k. Close all browser windows and exit Internet Explorer. Close all SharePoint Designer windows and exit SharePoint Designer. Close all Access windows and exit Access.

Communication Skills Class

GENERAL CASE 

You are taking a Communication Skills class and must develop an end-of-semester demonstration speech that will demonstrate your stronger communication and collaboration skills and potential to work confidently with others. A demonstration speech is one in which you teach or direct the class on how to do something. Because SharePoint 2010 is a relatively new technology, you decide to demonstrate some of its features. You will use PowerPoint to develop your presentation. After completing your notes, save the document as **sp04b1speech_LastnameFirstname** in a location as directed by your instructor. In a 1, 2, 3 fashion (listing your points in numerical order), provide directions to the class on:

- SharePoint Tools for Working with Microsoft Office 2010 documents
- Integration of Word and PowerPoint 2010 files in SharePoint Foundation Sites
- Integration of Excel and Access 2010 files in SharePoint Foundation Sites

The Microsoft Office Case Studies

RESEARCH CASE 

Access 2010 contains many SharePoint connectivity performance improvements but when you integrate data between Access 2010 and SharePoint Foundation, you are limited to using similar methods that were used with Access 2007. Carefully review the following articles and write a report on SharePoint connectivity performance improvements, SharePoint data platform improvement, and changes in Access 2010:

- http://blogs.office.com/b/microsoft-access/archive/2010/02/05/access-2010-performance-improvements-against-sharepoint-lists.aspx
- http://blogs.office.com/b/microsoft-access/archive/2010/02/15/data-platform-improvements-in-sharepoint-2010.aspx
- http://technet.microsoft.com/en-us/library/cc179181.aspx

As a SharePoint developer you will need to be fully aware of the list and library limits and recommended guidelines. Carefully review the following article and write a report on these topics: http://technet.microsoft.com/en-us/library/cc262787.aspx#ListLibrary

After completing your reports, save them as **sp04b2TechNet_LastnameFirstname.docx** in a location as directed by your instructor.

SharePoint Import Spreadsheet List

DISASTER RECOVERY 

You and your team worked hard on an Economics course semester project and, as part of your project requirements, you kept all the Microsoft Office project files in a *sp04b3_SiteBackUp* SharePoint site. The site included a *FinalReport* Import Spreadsheet list initially built by importing a *sp04b3_FinalReport* spreadsheet included in a *sp04b3_EconomicProject* Excel workbook. Upload and activate the *sp04b3_SiteBackUp* solution file, and then create a *sp04b3_SiteBackUp_LastNameFirstName* subsite using this solution file. Open the *FinalReport* Import Spreadsheet list in a browser window and compare its data with the final release of the *sp04b3_FinalReport* spreadsheet included in the *sp04b3_EconomicsProject* workbook. Write a memo to your instructor describing the error you made in keeping the *FinalReport* Import Spreadsheet list synchronized with the *sp04b3_FinalReport* spreadsheet included in the *sp04b3_EconomicsProject* workbook. Include suggestions in the memo on how to avoid this type of data synchronization mistake in the future.

SHAREPOINT

APPENDIX A INTERNET AND WORLD WIDE WEB

Introduction to the Internet, World Wide Web, and Web Sites

The unprecedented evolution of personal computers was powered by the Defense Advanced Research Projects Agency's (DARPA) launch of the Internet in 1968, Bill Gates' launch of Microsoft during the mid-1970s, and Tim Berners-Lee's invention of the World Wide Web in 1989. Personal computers are now an essential part of everyday life for learning, teaching, communicating, transacting business, and accessing entertainment. The Internet is often referred to as the Information Superhighway because it functions like a highway that connects you to millions of other people and organizations. In the workplace, at home, and in the classroom, the Internet has empowered people to develop and manage their own personal or business Web sites.

A recent research study, covering thirteen countries, created by the McKinsey Global Institute and McKinsey's Technology, Media and Telecommunications practice (www.mckinsey.com/mgi/publications/internet_matters/pdfs/MGI_internet_matters_full_report.pdf) offers the first quantitative assessment of the impact of the Internet on Gross Domestic Product (GDP) and growth:

- On average, the Internet contributes 3.4 percent to GDP in the countries covered by the research—an amount the size of Spain or Canada in terms of GDP, and growing at a faster rate than that of Brazil.
- The Internet accounted for 21 percent of GDP growth over the past five years among the developed countries MGI studied, a sharp acceleration from the 10 percent contribution over 15 years.
- The United States is the largest player in the global Internet supply ecosystem, capturing more than 30 percent of global Internet revenues and more than 40 percent of net income.

In this appendix, you will learn about the core concepts behind the Internet, World Wide Web, and Web sites.

Get Started with the Internet and the World Wide Web

At home, at work, or at school, children, teenagers, adults, and senior citizens spend more and more time in front of computers, which are a commodity rather than a luxury in developed countries. International efforts are also aimed at eliminating the so-called *global digital divide*, which is a term used to describe the great discrepancies in Internet access opportunities between developed and developing countries or between different regions of developed countries. Four decades after the inception of the Internet and three decades after the inception of the World Wide Web, even though the global digital divide is still a reality, the Internet and World Wide Web are slowly but surely becoming part of our daily lives. In this section, you will learn about the infrastructure and multiple functionalities of the Internet and World Wide Web.

Four decades after the inception of the Internet and three decades after the inception of the World Wide Web, even though the global digital divide is still a reality, the Internet and World Wide Web are slowly but surely becoming part of our daily lives.

Understanding the Internet

Communications define the process of moving data within or between computers.

A **communications device** provides the hardware and software support for connecting computers to a network.

A **network** consists of a group of computers connected to shared resources such as output devices, servers, and information.

Communications define the process of moving data within or between computers. In order to move data between computers, communications devices are necessary. A ***communications device*** provides the hardware and software support for connecting computers to a network. A ***network*** consists of a group of computers connected to share resources such as output devices (for example, printers), servers, and information.

A local area network (LAN) is a network of computers that are physically located close to each other. The fastest-growing LANs are those using wireless technology. Each node of a wireless network has a small radio transmitter that sends and receives data through the air.

TIP Wireless Technology

Today's wireless technology includes Wi-Fi, WiMax, Bluetooth, 3G, and 4G. It extends from desktop computers to mobile devices such as phones and tablet/slate computers.

The **Internet** is a worldwide collection of computers and networks that enable people to communicate.

A wide area network (WAN) is a network of computers that covers a wide area. The ***Internet*** is a worldwide collection of computers and networks that enable people to communicate. It has dramatically changed the way people use computers. People use the Internet in an incredibly vast variety of ways, such as to gather information, share resources, read and send e-mail, shop online, trade stocks, participate in discussions and chat groups, and download software.

Figure A.1 shows the three ways your computer can connect to the Internet: dial-up, direct, and broadband:

- Dial-up connections use a modem and a phone line to call in to a server that is connected to the Internet.
- Direct (or dedicated) connections access the Internet through a LAN.
- Broadband connections are based on new and advanced communications technologies and devices, such as Digital Subscriber Lines (DSL), cable modems, satellites, and wireless technology.

Bandwidth is the amount of data passing, within a time interval, through a phone line, cable, or DSL line connection to transfer information from and to a Web site via your computer.

Bandwidth is the amount of data passing, within a time interval, through a phone line, cable, or DSL line connection to transfer information from and to a Web site via your computer. Usually a higher bandwidth ensures faster transmission speed. It is usually measured in bits-per-second (bps), Megabits-per-second (Mbps), or (for Web sites) in GigaBytes (GB) per month.

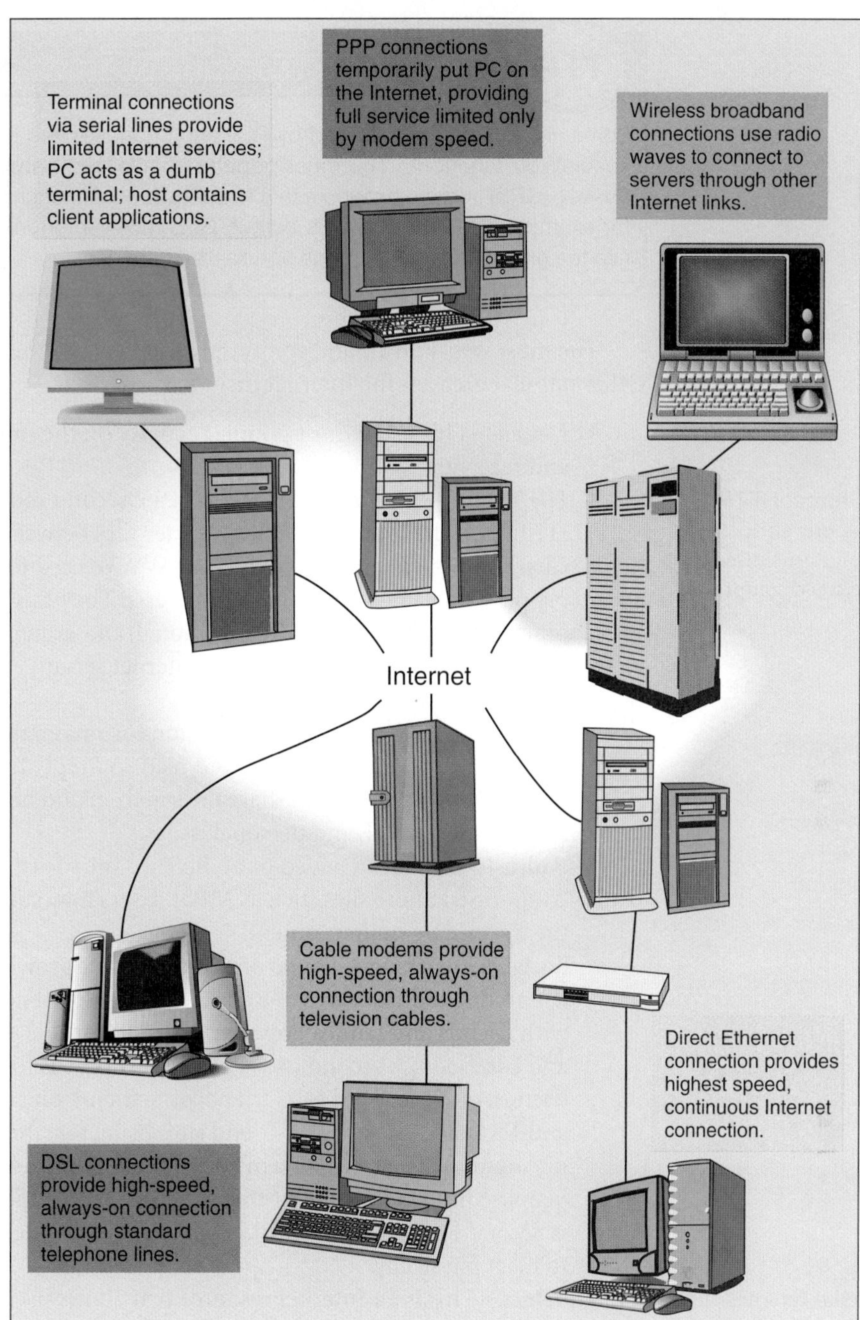

FIGURE A.1 Ways to Connect to the Internet ➤

An **Internet Service Provider (ISP)** is a company that provides the hardware system and the software applications necessary for your computer to access the Internet, and a Point of Presence (PoP), or a connection to access the Internet.

A **protocol** represents a set of rules used to transmit data on the Internet.

You connect to the Internet using an Internet Service Provider (ISP). An ***Internet Service Provider (ISP)*** is a company that provides the hardware system and the software applications necessary for your computer to access the Internet, and a Point of Presence (PoP), or a connection to access the Internet. Although the Internet is technically only an infrastructure of computers, or a network of networks, most people think of the Internet as the network and the data it contains. A ***protocol*** represents a set of rules used to transmit data on the Internet. After you connect to the Internet, you can easily retrieve information with just a click of the mouse because of protocols used on the network. HTTP (Hypertext Transfer Protocol) is the most popular protocol for transferring files (text, graphic images, sound, video, and other multimedia files) on the World Wide Web.

 Specialized Networks

Some networks are not formed by PCs and phones linked to the Internet, but rather perform specialized functions. The most popular specialized networks are the Global Positioning System (GPS) and the networks that keep the global financial systems running. Google Maps, for example, uses the iPhone's built-in GPS receiver, and automatic teller machines (ATMs) use the global financial systems specialized networks.

The most well-known and commonly used part of the Internet is the World Wide Web. Other popular areas of the Internet include:

- E-mail—This is the most popular activity on the Internet and is used for sending and receiving electronic mail.
- ***File Transfer Protocol (FTP)***—This is the second most prevalent protocol (after HTTP) on the Internet used to transfer files between computers.
- Chat rooms—These are areas on the WWW used to join discussion groups with people who usually have similar interests. They can share information and help each other with technical, social, professional, and even personal issues.
- Instant Messaging—This popular Internet service enables users to communicate in real time with other online users.
- Newsgroups—These online discussion forums enable a user to create a thread (conversation), post messages, and read and reply to other users' messages. Much like chat rooms, users can share information and help each other with technical, social, professional, and personal issues.
- Podcasts—These are video or audio clips broadcast via the Internet using compressed audio files such as MP3s. Users may subscribe in order to have access to the up-to-date online content.
- Social Networking—This is one of the fastest-growing uses of the Internet for connecting individuals to one another. Using social networks, people can communicate with friends and family. Popular sites used for this activity are Classmates Online and Facebook. A second use of social networks is for communications between friends, often referred to as friend-of-a-friend, on sites like Facebook, Friendster, and MySpace. Friend-of-a-friend sites bring together strangers who have a friend in common. The third type of social network is a common interest network, where people communicate about their interests. Twitter is a common interest network, as is Second Life. Social networks enable people to meet virtually when it is impractical to meet physically.
- ***Telnet***—This is an Internet resource that allows users to log in to a remote computer and use it.
- Web-Based Applications—These are application programs stored on a provider's server. Some Web-based applications are free, using Web-based services that provide access to programs that run within your browser window. Microsoft Office Web Apps are some of the most recent Web-Based Applications.
- Webcasts—These broadcasts of audio and video over the Internet include non-interactive content, such as a TV broadcast, and enable interactive responses from the audience.
- Weblogs (or blogs)—These are very popular, easy to create, read, and manage personal or professional journal entries published on the World Wide Web.
- Wikis—These are collaborative online Web sites, enabling users not just to read but also to add, edit, and remove content. The online encyclopedia Wikipedia (www.wikipedia.org) is one of the most popular applications of the wiki technology, allowing worldwide experts to maintain accurate, up-to-date content.
- Media Sharing—These are collaborative Web sites enabling users to share photographs and videos. Flickr and YouTube have become true cultural phenomena in media sharing.

File Transfer Protocol (FTP) is the second most prevalent protocol on the Internet used to transfer files between computers.

Telnet is a popular Internet resource that allows users to log in to a remote computer and use it.

- Cloud Computing—These are collaborative technologies that bridge the gap between Web Application and desktop applications by providing access to applications, data, and servers "though the cloud." Microsoft, Google, and Apple are pioneers in the development of cloud computing technologies.

TIP TCP/IP

Transmission Control Protocol (TCP)/Internet Protocol (IP) represents the main set of protocols used for transmitting data on the Internet. TCP/IP includes a variety of interrelated protocols among which TCP, IP, FTP, Telnet, and HTTP are some of the most important.

Understanding the World Wide Web

The **World Wide Web** is the graphical, user-friendly side of the Internet, which enables users to view and share graphic and multimedia documents electronically and remotely over the Internet.

The ***World Wide Web*** (also called the Web or WWW) is the graphical, user-friendly side of the Internet, which enables users to view and share graphic and multimedia documents electronically and remotely over the Internet. The WWW has no centralized control or any type of central administration. Theoretically, anybody can retrieve information from the WWW and publish information on it. The WWW is basically a huge collection of Web sites created by individuals and governmental, professional, corporate, and academic organizations.

TIP Owning or Managing the Internet or the WWW

Although the U.S. government funded the research for the technologies that constitute the foundation of the Internet, no individual or organization actually owns and manages the Internet or the WWW. However, as a global service, the Internet is collaboratively managed by a group of organizations such as the National Science Foundation (NSF), the Internet Society (ISOC), the Internet Engineering Task Force (IETF), the Internet Corporation for Assigned Names and Numbers (ICANN), the Internet Architecture Board (iAB), and the World Wide Web Consortium (W3C).

World Wide Web Consortium (W3C) provides leadership through an open forum of groups with a vested interest in the Internet, with the mission of leading the Web to its full potential.

A **hypertext document** is an electronic file connected, by means of hypertext links, to other electronic documents to which the reader or user is transferred by a mouse click.

The ***World Wide Web Consortium (W3C)*** provides leadership through an open forum of groups with a vested interest in the Internet, with the mission of leading the Web to its full potential.

Today, the WWW is the driving force of the Internet. Its history started in 1989, when Timothy Berners-Lee and other researchers working at CERN, the European Organization for Nuclear Research, brought to life this module of the Internet. Their goal was to create an information system that would make it easier for researchers around the world to locate and share data. They initially developed a system of ***hypertext documents***, electronic files connected, by means of hypertext links, to other electronic documents to which the reader or user is transferred by a mouse click.

TIP Sir Timothy Berners-Lee

According to the official W3C Web site (go to www.w3.org/, click on People, and then click on Berners-Lee), Sir Timothy Berners-Lee is a graduate of Oxford University, England. Also known as the Father of the Web, Sir Berners-Lee holds the 3Com Founders chair at the Laboratory for Computer Science and Artificial Intelligence Lab (CSAIL) at the Massachusetts Institute of Technology (MIT) and directs W3C. In December 2003, Queen Elizabeth II made him a Knight Commander of the Order of the British Empire and in June 2007 Tim Berners-Lee was appointed Member of the Order of Merit by Queen Elizabeth II.

A **Web page** is a document on the WWW that has been coded to provide static or dynamic content for users to view and access.

A ***Web page*** is a document on the WWW that has been coded to provide static or dynamic content for users to view and access. Web page developers today use the Berners-Lee hypertext approach to link documents. The documents are interconnected through a series of hypertext links (or links), which can be text or objects. They can link to a section within the same document or to other locations on the Web.

TIP Internet and the Future of Our Society

Everybody believes that, when talking about the future of the Internet, we have not seen anything yet! More bandwidth is constantly being added, more services are provided, and more people around the world have access to the Internet. Wireless technology will continue to boost the accessibility of the Internet. As business and communication services take over the Internet resources, the need to support the Internet's original goal for an open academia research exchange is also increasing. The Large Scale Network (http://www.nitrd.gov/) and Internet2 (www.internet2.edu/) are two programs dedicated to developing advanced technology for the Internet. Meanwhile the new millennium technologies included in Web 2.0 (social networking, information sharing, and collaboration sites) bring to millions of users the do-it-yourself spirit from which the Internet grew.

Understand Web Browsers and Markup Languages: Hypertext Markup Language (HTML), Extensible Hypertext Markup Language (XHTML), and Extensible Markup Language (XML)

In 1991, CERN released the first text-oriented browser. However, the explosive growth of the revolutionary hypertext approach started in February of 1993, when the first graphically oriented browser, Mosaic, was developed at the National Center for Supercomputing Applications at the University of Illinois at Urbana-Champaign. This approach later evolved into the fundamental method of sharing and retrieving information on the Internet. The relationships among HTML, XML, and XHTML, as today's core markup languages, are still an area of considerable confusion on the Web. In this section, you will learn about the most popular Web browsers, and the characteristics of HTML, XHTML, and XML. Then, you will learn about how Cascading Style Sheets (CSS) are used in conjunction with HTML, XML, and XHTML documents.

The relationships among HTML, XML and XHTML, as today's core markup languages, are still an area of considerable confusion on the Web.

Getting Started with Web Browsers

A **Web browser** is a software application installed on your computer that is designed to navigate the Web, retrieve a Web page from its host server, interpret its content, and display it on your monitor.

A ***Web browser*** is a software application installed on your computer that is designed to help you navigate the Web, retrieve a Web page from its host server, interpret its content, and display it on your computer. Although there are many Web browsers available, the four most popular Web browsers are Microsoft Internet Explorer, Firefox, Google Chrome, and Safari (the default browser of the Apple computers). Figure A.2 shows the toolbars of the Internet Explorer browser that provide user-friendly Web navigation, and Web site and Web page management tools. All other popular browsers provide similar features. Approximately

95 percent of all computers use Internet Explorer, Firefox (www.mozilla.com/en-US/firefox/), or Google Chrome (www.google.com/chrome/) to browse the Internet. Of the other Web browsers on the market, the following three are most popular:

- Opera—www.opera.com/ (freeware browser developed by Telenor, a Norwegian telecom company, in 1994, and which later became an independent development company, named Opera Software ASA, in 1995)
- Lynx—http://lynx.browser.org/ (freeware text browser)
- Amaya—www.w3.org/Amaya/ (freeware, developed by the World Wide Web Consortium)

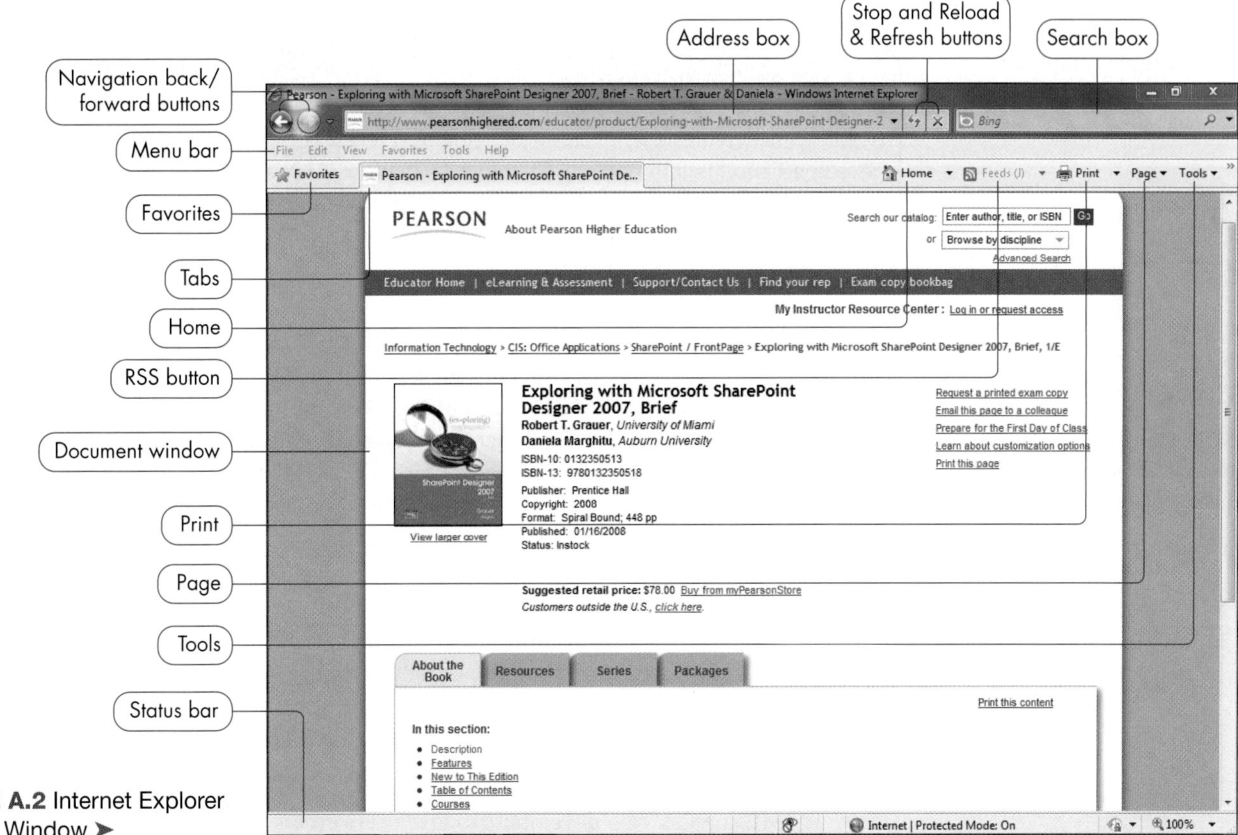

FIGURE A.2 Internet Explorer Browser Window ➤

TIP Internet Privacy and Security

The user-friendly functionalities of the Internet are a part of billions of people's lives. Regrettably, this has also transformed the Internet into a "promised land" for individuals interested in advertising their services or products, tracking your Web browsing activities, and engaging in unethical actions such as stealing people's copyrighted work and personal information. It is becoming more and more challenging to avoid these side effects of the Internet's amazing success. To learn more about this topic, visit the Liberty Alliance Project (www.projectliberty.org/) and the Microsoft Trustworthy Computing (www.microsoft.com/mscorp/twc/default.mspx) Web sites.

Getting Started with Hypertext Markup Language (HTML)

A **markup language** is a language that describes the format of Web page content through the use of tags.

A **tag** is a specific code that indicates how the text and other page content should be displayed when the document is opened in a Web browser.

Hypertext Markup Language (HTML) is the most common markup language used to create Web pages and was developed from the more complicated Standard Generalized Markup Language (SGML).

Web pages are created using markup languages. A ***markup language*** is a language that describes the format of Web page content through the use of tags. ***Tags*** are specific codes that indicate how the text and other page content should be displayed when the document is opened in a Web browser. The Web browser interprets the markup tags and renders the page in the computer's browser window. ***Hypertext Markup Language (HTML)*** is the most common markup language used to create Web pages and was developed from the more complicated Standard Generalized Markup Language (SGML).

TIP Standard Generalized Markup Language (SGML)

SGML was invented by Dr. Charles F. Goldfarb (www.sgmlsource.com/) in 1974 and further developed into the International Standard 8879 (ISO 8879), which was published October 15, 1986. SGML is a platform-independent computer language and is the parent technology for HTML, XHTML and XML.

ASCII is the common numeric code used by computers to represent characters.

HTML was created as a simplified version of the SGML language so that anyone could learn to use it. HTML documents contain a combination of American Standard Code for Information Interchange (ASCII) text and tags. Computers can understand only numbers. ***ASCII***, which was created by the American National Standards Institute (www.ansi.org), is the common numeric code used by computers. The standard ASCII character set consists of 128 decimal numbers ranging from zero through 127 assigned to letters, numbers, punctuation marks, and the most common special characters. For instance, the lowercase letter "a" is a in the ASCII character set, whereas the uppercase "A" is A. The extended ASCII set also consists of 128 decimal numbers and ranges from 128 through 255 representing additional special, mathematical, graphic, and foreign characters.

Although HTML is often called the "language of the Web," it is not a programming language. HTML tags define the page layout, fonts, graphic elements, and hypertext links to other documents on the Web. So it could be better defined as a descriptive language. HTML has critical features for distributing information remotely:

- HTML enables Web developers to give users access to other HTML documents and other types of documents and files distributed across the WWW via elements called hyperlinks.
- HTML enables developers to create Web page documents that can be displayed to all site visitors, regardless of the computer platform, operating system, and Web browser they use.

Because it is created using unformatted text, you can write an HTML document in a simple text program (such as Windows Notepad or WordPad), in a word processing program (such as Microsoft Word), or in a Web authoring program (such as SharePoint Designer 2010). HTML documents normally have the file extension .htm or .html. Opening an HTML document in a text editor could reveal the following text and tags:

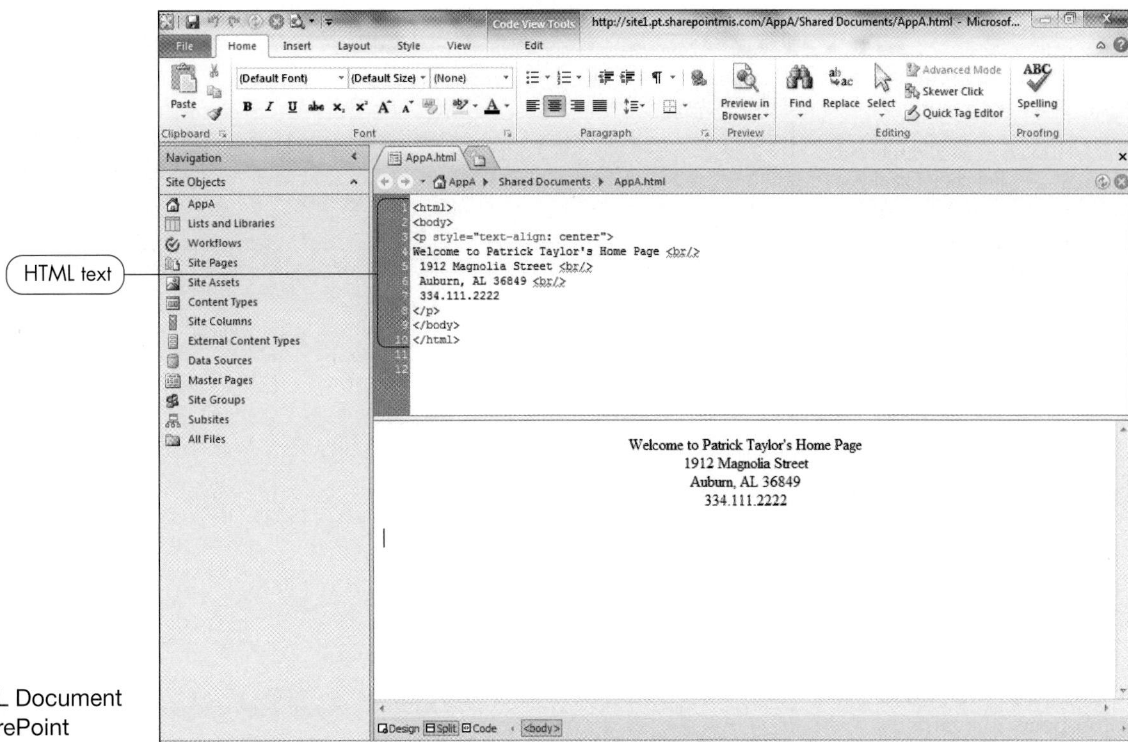

FIGURE A.3 HTML Document Viewed in ShareharePoint Designer Split View ➤

Tags are mostly used in pairs to indicate the beginning and end of a Web page element or format. As shown in Figure A.3, tags begin with < and end with >. The end tag always contains a forward slash /. For example, the <p> tag in the preceding code tells the browser to begin applying the paragraph format, which inserts a blank line at the end of the paragraph. The tag </p> indicates the end of the title text.

HTML tags follow a specific syntax, which is a set of rules or standards developed by the W3C. Tags appear in pairs (or are two-sided). The generic syntax of an HTML tag pair is <tag attributes>text</tag>. However, some HTML tags, also called empty tags, are not used in pairs. The <br/> tag forces a break in the current line of text. In the previous example, the <br/> tag is one that is not used in a pair; it does not have an end tag. Based on the W3C requirements, the slash is required for all empty tags. In addition to the tags that are used to define Web page elements, HTML also has attributes that further define the way Web page elements display in Web browsers. These attributes can help define the style, color, size, width, height, and source of the element. Web developers can assign a specific value to each attribute, and then include the attribute with the start tag in the HTML code document. In Figure A.3, the style attribute is added to the <p> tag. The code aligns the text in the center of the page. Figure A.4 shows how an HTML document appears when viewed in Internet Explorer and in Notepad.

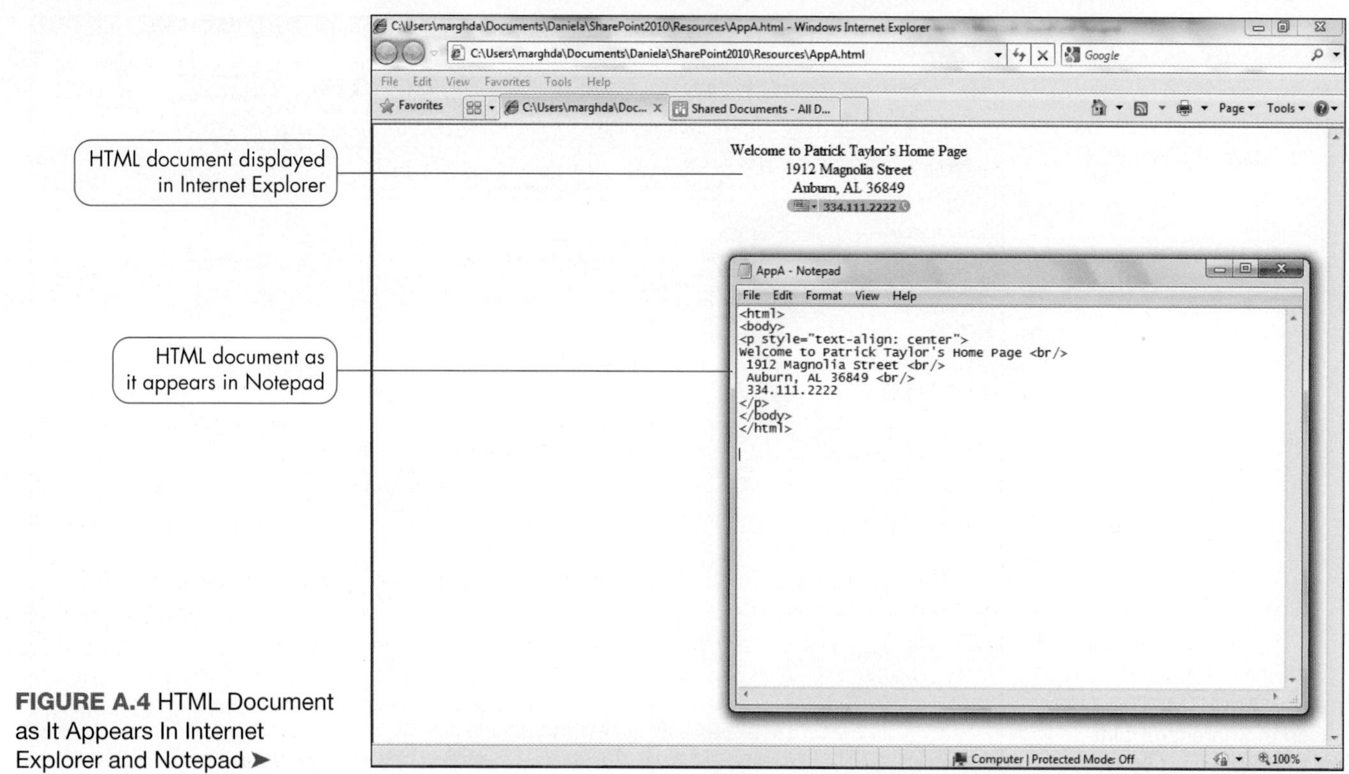

FIGURE A.4 HTML Document as It Appears In Internet Explorer and Notepad ➤

TIP Cross-Browser and Cross-Platform Issues

Unfortunately, although HTML defines the way Web page elements should be displayed, the way a Web page is displayed in different browsers might vary. Fonts, colors, tables, and hyperlinks are only a few of the many Web page elements that could appear differently in Firefox than they do in Microsoft Internet Explorer. The same Web page might also be displayed differently on computers using different operating systems. For example, fonts and colors might look different on an Apple computer than they would on a Sun workstation. These two issues are called *cross-browser* and *cross-platform compatibility* and they cause problems for Web developers. The W3C is working on ways to eliminate these problems through standardization. One of the SharePoint Designer features enables you to preview a Web page in different browsers and different versions of browsers.

In the beginning, HTML's development was not overseen by any organization. Web developers were able to make any type of improvements they felt were needed. To win as much of the market share as possible, two major browser companies, Microsoft and Netscape, enriched HTML with new features called *extensions.* You learn more about HTML in Appendix B.

TIP Internet Explorer and Netscape Navigator HTML Extensions

Extensions are basically HTML tags that were not initially included in the W3C official HTML standards. Although some extensions have been added to the W3C official standards, extensions that are not part of the W3C standards are usually unevenly supported by today's most popular browsers.

By creating these unique extensions, developers, in a sense, generated two different HTML standards. Many of these features were not supported by all browsers, creating some major cross-browser compatibility issues. To deal with these problems, the W3C created a

Deprecated HTML tags and tag attributes might or might not be supported by all browsers.

comprehensive set of recommended HTML standards and specifications. The W3C standards indicate the format that should be applied to standard tags. They also declare many of the HTML tags and tag attributes as ***deprecated***, which means that they might or might not be supported by all browsers. To eliminate the cross-browser issues, the W3C standard is supposed to be followed by all browser manufacturers. Unfortunately, this is not yet the case.

TIP W3C HTML Standards

If you want to read more about the W3C HTML standards and specifications, you can check them out at the W3C Web site (go to www.w3.org/standards/webdesign/, click HTML, and then click HTML & CSS). SharePoint Designer assists you in developing Web pages in line with W3C standards and specifications. You will learn more about how to develop standard Web sites and Web pages in Appendix C.

Over the years, millions of Web pages have been and continue to be created with HTML, which remains the most popular markup language. However, despite its popularity, HTML has some drawbacks. All Web developers should be aware of the following limitations and flaws when using HTML:

- HTML does not enable users to structure, define, and process data. For example, you can use HTML to build forms, but you cannot validate, send, and retrieve the form's information to and from a database. To accomplish these types of tasks, a Web developer needs to employ code written in scripting languages such as JavaScript, Microsoft Active Server Pages (ASP), or Sun Java Server Pages (JSP).
- HTML is not extensible. In other words, it includes a finite set of tags and does not enable users to create new custom tags; thus, it cannot be changed to meet specific developers' needs for describing data content. The extensibility issue is discussed in greater detail later in this appendix.
- Although HTML includes a wide range of syntax rules, these rules are not enforced; hence, an HTML document, with syntax errors, will still be displayed in any browser. That means that if you forget an HTML rule, the only way that you will know it is by manually validating the way the HTML code is displayed in one or more browsers and figuring out what you did wrong.
- HTML features are not consistently supported by all browsers; thus, an HTML document might be displayed differently on one browser than on another. For example, some browsers require the </p> end tag and some do not.

TIP What Is a Scripting Language?

A scripting language is less powerful than traditional programming languages, such as Java and C++. Traditional programming languages employ compilers, which are computer programs that translate a program written in a high-level language into another language, usually machine language. Each scripting language employs a scripting engine and does not require compilation as does a traditional programming language. Depending on where a script code is interpreted (that means also where the scripting engine is located), scripting languages are divided into two main categories: client-side and server-side. A script code written in a server-side scripting language is interpreted on the Web server before the requested Web page is sent back to the client. When an HTML document containing code written in a client-side scripting language is loaded in a browser, a scripting engine built in the Web browser interprets the code. A scripting engine (or interpreter) is a program that translates code one line at a time into an executable format each time the program runs. Consequently, scripting languages commonly run more slowly than traditional programming languages do.

ASP and JSP are two of the most popular server-side scripting languages used to develop interactive Web sites that interface with databases or other data sources (such as an XML document). JavaScript is one of the most popular client-side scripting languages, and its scripting engine is supported by all major browsers, such as Internet Explorer and Firefox. Developers from Netscape and Sun Microsystems created JavaScript as a Java subset that is simpler to use than the Java programming language. It is able to meet the needs of most Web developers who want to create dynamic Web pages. JavaScript is used by Web developers for such things as automatically changing a formatted date on a Web page, causing a linked page to appear in a pop-up window, causing text or a graphic image to change during a mouse rollover, obtaining information about the current Web browser, navigating to Web pages that have been opened during a Web browser session, or validating data submitted via an HTML form. An advanced use of JavaScript called AJAX can be found on many interactive sites. This technology is used to create interactive Web sites that respond quickly, like traditional desktop application software.

Getting Started with Extensible Hypertext Markup Language (XHTML)

The **Extensible Hypertext Markup Language (XHTML)** is a newer markup language that was designed to overcome some of the problems of HTML.

The ***Extensible Hypertext Markup Language (XHTML)*** is a newer markup language that was designed to overcome some of the problems of HTML. XHTML is considered a transitional solution between HTML and XML because it is not extensible. XHTML enables you to write well-formed and valid documents that work in all browsers and can be read by all XML-enabled applications. Thus, until all browsers are upgraded to fully support XML, XHTML will continue to be a worthy solution.

Although there are many similarities between HTML and XHTML, there are also some important differences:

- XHTML code has to be well formed and valid.
- XHTML tags are case sensitive.
- In XHTML, the empty tags that were inherited from HTML, such as <img>, <br>, and <hr>, have the following syntax: <img/>, <br/>, and <hr/> because one of the rules for well-formed code is that all tags be closed and the / closes the empty element.

TIP W3C XHTML Standards

You can read more about the W3C XHTML standards and specifications on the W3C Web site (go to www.w3.org/standards/webdesign/, click HTML, and then click HTML & CSS).

Getting Started with Extensible Markup Language (XML)

Extensible Markup Language (XML), based on the SGML standard, enables data to be shared and processed via the Internet and across software applications, operating systems, and hardware computer platforms.

Extensible Markup Language (XML), based on the SGML standard, enables data to be shared and processed via the Internet and across software applications, operating systems, and hardware computer platforms. Because XML is an extensible language, unlike HTML, developers can create specific custom tags, describing the data content for each document. Developers also like XML because they can prevent many code errors by employing an XML parser, and because XML has the ability to define data content. The following two code examples show how the same data content could be coded in HTML (see Figure A.5) and XML (see Figure A.6).

```
<h1>COMP1000 Personal Computer Applications </h1>
<h2> 1 Monday & Wednesday 8:00 am </h2>
<ol> Student
        <li>Christopher Harmon FR </li>
        <li>Ashley Wachs</li>
        <li>Wade Chatam SR </li>
</ol>
```

FIGURE A.5 HTML Code ➤

```
<course> COMP1000 Personal Computer Applications </course>
<section> 1 Monday & Wednesday 8:00 am
        <student>Christopher Harmon FR</student>
<student> Ashley Wachs </student>
<student>Wade Chatam SR</student>
</section>
```

FIGURE A.6 XML Code ➤

XML (and SGML) can be also used to create other markup languages called *XML applications.* Two of the most popular XML applications are MathML (www.w3.org/Math) and VoiceXML (www.voicexml.org). After an XML document is created, it has to be evaluated by an application called *XML parser*. An ***XML parser*** interprets the document code to make sure that the document meets the following criteria:

XML parser is an application that evaluates XML documents.

A **well-formed** XML document contains no syntax errors and obeys all W3C specifications for XML code.

A **valid** XML document is a well-formed document that also satisfies the rules included in the attached document type definition or schema.

A **Document Type Definition (DTD)** can force an XML document to follow a uniform data structure, thus eliminating many code errors that can occur.

A **schema** is an XML document that includes the definition of one or more XML document's content and structure.

- ***Well-formed***—The XML document contains no syntax errors and obeys all W3C specifications for XML code (http://www.w3.org/XML/). Some common syntax errors can be caused by ignoring the case sensitivity of XML tags or by omitting one or more tags.
- ***Valid***—The XML document is well-formed and satisfies the rules included in the attached document type definition or schema.

XML supports an optional document type definition and XML schema. These documents define all the components that an XML document is allowed to contain as well as the structural relationship among these components. A ***Document Type Definition (DTD)*** can force an XML document to follow a uniform data structure, by defining the elements allowed, the attributes allowed, and the relationship between elements (parent/child), thus eliminating many code errors that can occur. The DTD can be internal (included in the XML document itself), external (stored in an external .dtd file), or a combination of internal and external components. The power of a DTD is increased when using external components because the same external DTD can be applied to more than one XML file. A ***schema*** is an XML document that includes the definition of one or more XML document's content and structure. Two of the most popular schemas are the XML schema (www.w3.org/XML/Schema.html), developed by W3C in 2001, and the Microsoft schema, XDR. In an effort to support developers that use both schemas, Microsoft has developed the XDR-XSD Converter application that converts XDR schemas to XML schemas (www.microsoft.com/downloads/details.aspx?FamilyID=5f6505a1-359e-47bf-8963-f4affaf87566&DisplayLang=en).

TIP Doctype Declarations and W3C Recommended DTDs

When developing HTML, XHTML, or XML documents, it is important to add a Doctype declaration and the W3C-recommended DTDs. To read more about Doctype declarations and the W3C-recommended DTDs, see the W3C "Recommended DTDs to use in your Web document Web page" (www.w3.org/QA/2002/04/valid-dtd-list.html).

All popular browsers, such as IE7+, Firefox, Chrome, Opera, and Safari, have a built-in XML parser. Although these are the most popular, many other XML editors and parsers are available. For instance, Altova XMLSpy is an award-winning XML editor for modeling, editing, transforming, and debugging XML technologies (www.altova.com/products/xmlspy/xml_editor.html).

TIP What Is a Programming Language?

If HTML, XHTML, and XML are markup languages and JavaScript, ASP, and JSP are scripting languages, then what is a programming language? A programming language consists of a set of instructions that tell computers what actions to perform. Programming languages are often categorized in three groups that also reflect the historical development of computer languages: machine language, assembly language, and high-level language. Today, most programmers use a high-level language. A high-level language is expressed in English-like phrases, and thus is easier for programmers to read and write. A single high-level language programming statement can accomplish the equivalent of many, perhaps hundreds, of machine language instructions. However, high-level language code must be translated into machine language to be executed by the computer because computers can only understand binary numbers. A compiler is a software application that translates each statement in the program into a sequence of machine language instructions. Working with high-level languages enables the programmer to ignore the underlying details required for the machine language. High-level programming languages have two main categories: procedural, such as FORTRAN, and object-oriented, such as Java.

Whereas HTML can define the way data is formatted and displayed only on a Web page, XML code only describes the type of information contained in the document. The XML code does not indicate how data is formatted or displayed. Consequently, it must use CSS or Extensible Style Sheet Languages (XSLs) to build style sheets that can be embedded into the XML document or linked to it. The CSS contains formatting instructions for each element. For example, the CSS external style sheet code shown in Figure A.9 contains styles for the six HTML headings that will be formatted accordingly across all Web pages to which it will be linked. Using CSS to format XML documents provides Web developers with the same formatting features found in HTML, but with greater flexibility:

- By attaching different style sheets to an XML document, you can change the way it appears in a browser.
- By changing a style sheet attached to multiple XML documents, you can change the way all these XML documents are displayed in a browser.

The good news is that learning to work with HTML and XHTML makes it easier to learn XML.

Using Cascading Style Sheets (CSS)

Although several style sheet languages have been developed, the Cascading Style Sheets (CSS) have become the standard style sheet language used on the Web.

Conforming to the W3C, ***style sheets*** describe how documents are displayed on screens, presented in print, or even how they are pronounced by screen reading applications. ***Style sheet languages*** are computer languages for developing style sheets. The W3C and Web designers have advocated style sheets, starting with HTML, as tools for separating the document's presentation from its content. Although several style sheet languages have been developed, ***Cascading Style Sheets (CSS)*** have become the standard style sheet language used on the Web.

A **style sheet** describes how documents are displayed on screens, presented in print, or even how they are pronounced.

A **style sheet language** is a computer language for developing style sheets.

Cascading Style Sheets (CSS) have become the standard style sheet language used on the Web.

Extensible Style Sheet Language (XSL) is a method for formatting XML documents.

TIP Extensible Style Sheet Language (XSL)

Extensible Style Sheet Language (XSL) was developed by the W3C as an improved method for formatting XML documents, allowing developers to transform XML data files into a wide variety of popular file formats, such as HTML and portable document format (PDF). It is still supported by fewer browsers than CSS.

Although the CSS was initially developed for HTML, it is currently used in HTML, XML, and XHTML. CSS is a robust formatting language that successfully separates the Web page's content from its appearance. One of the biggest advantages to using CSS is that when the style sheet is changed, all the Web pages created with that CSS are automatically updated. Although CSS is useful and has experienced rapid growth on the WWW, it is new enough that it can still generate some problems. To learn more about W3C CSS standards and which browsers support CSS, visit this dedicated Web page of the W3C: www.w3.org/Style/CSS/. You can use three different types of CSS style codes to format the HTML code of your Web pages:

An **inline style** is included in the start tag of an element by using the tag's *style attribute.*

An **internal style** is included in the <head> section of an HTML and has the following syntax <style>style declarations</style>.

An **external style** is included in a separate file used to specify the formatting of any HTML document to which the external style sheets are linked.

- ***Inline styles***—Inline styles are included in the start tag of an element by using the tag's style attribute. Inline styles override the styles defined in internal and external styles. In Figure A.7 the <body> tag uses inline styles.
- ***Internal styles***—Internal styles are included in the <head> section of an HTML document and have the following syntax <style>style declarations</style>. Internal styles override the styles defined in a linked external style sheet. In Figure A.8, three internal styles are defined in the <head> section.
- ***External styles***—External style codes are included in separate files used to specify the formatting of any HTML document to which they are linked. These style codes are kept in a document with a .css file extension and linked to the HTML document using the <link> HTML tag. In Figure A.9a an external style kept in the au_template3.css style sheet is linked. Figure A.9b displays the content of an external CSS style sheet in which the layout.css style sheet is imported.

TIP Linking External Style Sheets

An external style sheet can be also linked using the CSS @import directive added inside the HTML <style> tag. For example, the @import url ("layout.css") CSS code (also shown in Figure A.9) links the layout.css to the HTML document. The CSS @import directive is not supported by old browsers, such as AOL/Netscape Navigator 4.0. You can learn more about linking CSS style sheets in Appendix B.

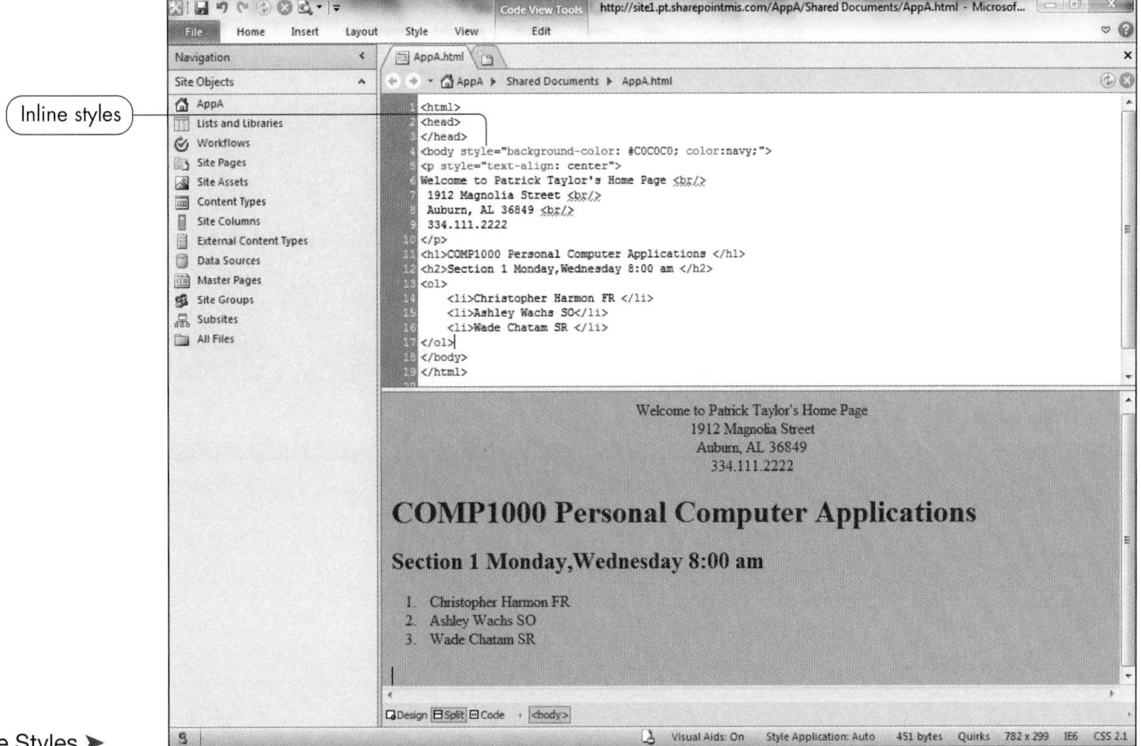

FIGURE A.7 Inline Styles ➤

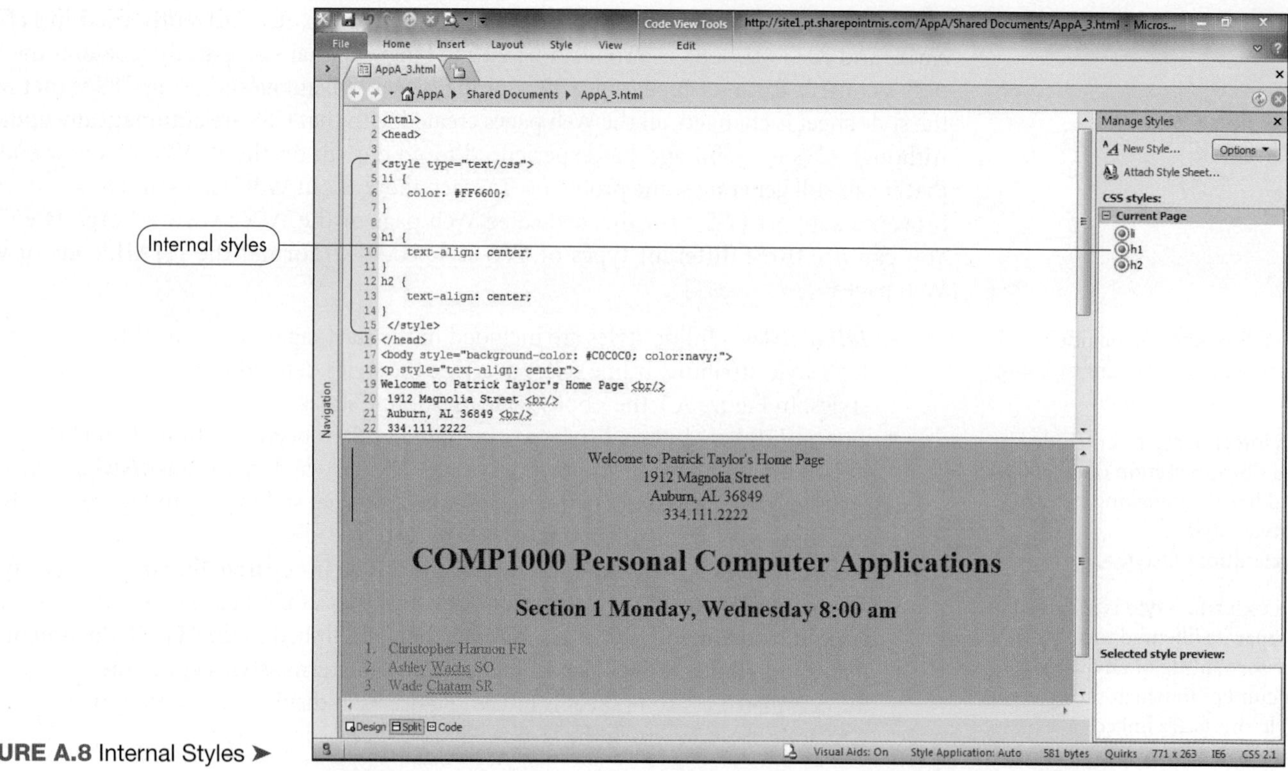

FIGURE A.8 Internal Styles ➤

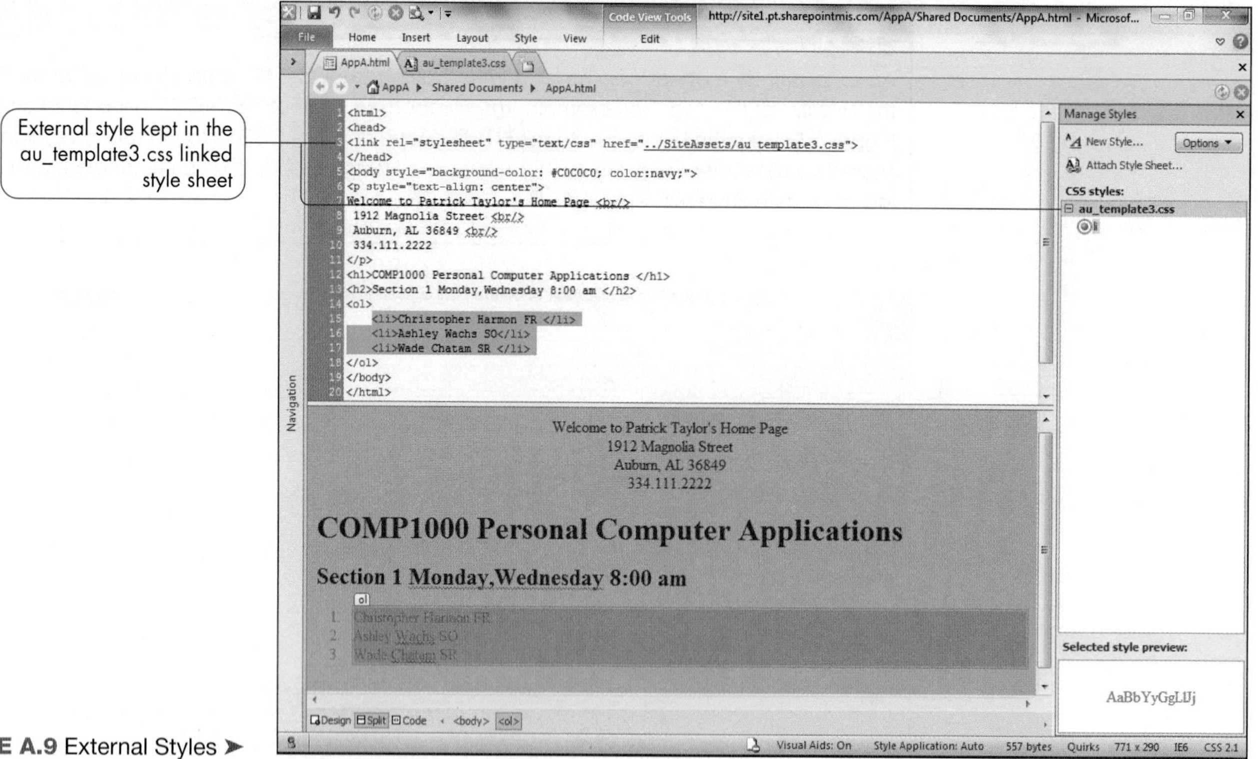

FIGURE A.9 External Styles ➤

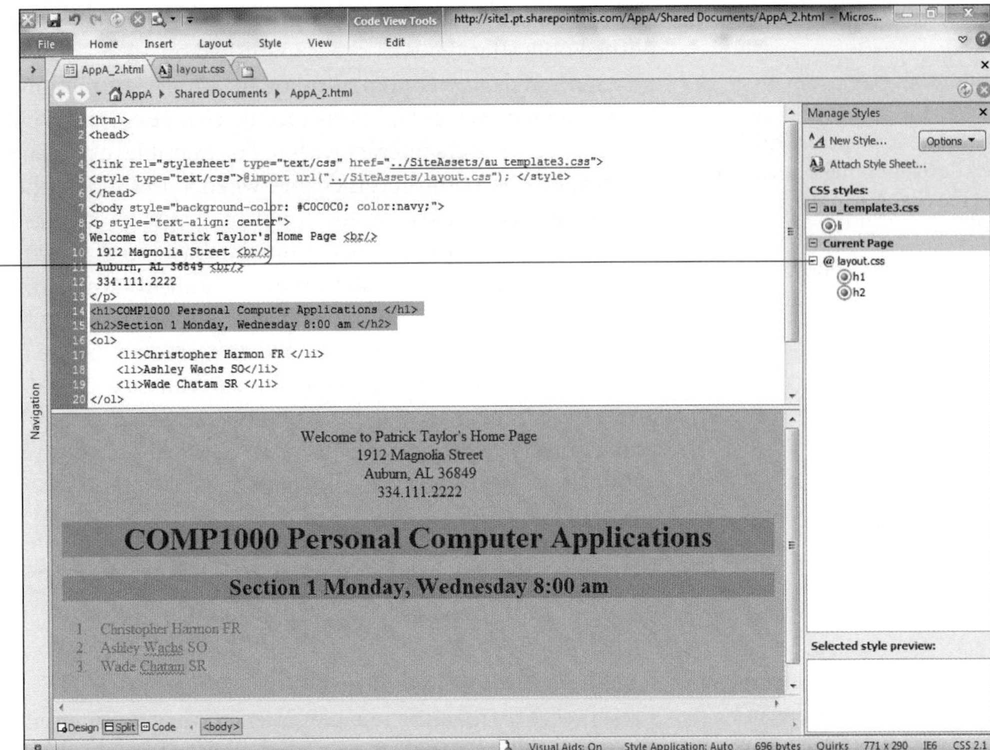

FIGURE A.9 *(Continued)* ➤

A **meta tag** represents one of the tools that you can use to ensure that the content of your Web site has the proper topic identification and ranking by search engines.

> **TIP** Using Meta Tags
>
> ***Meta tags*** represent one of the tools that you can use to ensure that the content of your Web site has the proper topic identification and ranking by search engines, such as Google and Yahoo!. SharePoint pages automatically include default meta tags that indicate the language used and how the Web page should be displayed. A Web designer can add user-defined meta tags to a Web page. These tags identify the kinds of topics included in the pages of the Web page. You learn more about adding user-defined meta tags to a Web page using SharePoint Designer in Appendix B.

A **Web site** is a collection of Web pages, files, and folders gathered together and published on the Internet.

Publishing a Web site consists of transferring all the Web site's files and folders to a Web server.

A **server** is a computer that provides clients with access to files and printers as shared resources on a computer network.

A **client** is a user's machine that connects to the server and receives information from it.

A **Web server** is a special kind of server that is connected to the Internet and runs specialized software applications, enabling it to handle requests from clients to access information from Web sites.

An inline style takes precedence over an internal style, which takes precedence over an external style sheet. If you have two styles with the same weight in a document, the style declared last has precedence, hence the term *cascade*. You will learn more about formatting with CSS in Appendix B.

Define Web Sites

A ***Web site*** is a collection of Web pages, files, and folders gathered together and published on the Internet. ***Publishing*** a Web site consists of transferring all the Web site's files and folders to a Web server. A ***server*** is a computer that provides clients with access to files and printers as shared resources on a computer network, while a ***client*** is a user's machine that connects to the server and receives information from it. A ***Web server***, on the other hand, is a special kind of server that is connected to the Internet and runs specialized software applications, enabling it to handle requests from clients to access information from Web sites. In this section, you will learn about the three categories of Internet resources, URLs, URI, and URNs, about the core types of Web sites: intranets, extranets, portals, and Web applications. Then, you will learn about the Internet search engines and copyright laws.

Before publishing your Web site to a Web server and making it available to Internet visitors, you can develop the site on any computer or a local network. From that computer, you can test all Web pages and files in your Web site. However, specific testing can be accomplished only after the Web site is published on a Web server.

Static Web page content displays the same information every time it is viewed unless the Web developer makes and saves specific changes in the HTML code.

Dynamic Web page content changes as users interact with it.

Static Web page content displays the same information every time it is viewed unless the Web developer makes and saves specific changes in the HTML code. ***Dynamic Web page*** content changes as users interact with it. For example, using JavaScript, you can change the color of a text line or a button can change when a user moves the mouse pointer over it. Dynamic Web pages, using a server side scripting language such as ASP.NET or JSP, enable users to access and retrieve information from databases so that it can display different information to users depending on their data requests and the formatting choices. Dynamic Web pages always make use of a scripting language. Adobe Flash and Microsoft Silverlight are very popular client-side tools for creating dynamic and interactive media-rich Web components.

All Web pages included in a Web site can be accessed via the Web site home page. The home page is the main page and the "opening gate" to any Web site. It is usually also defined as the index or table of contents for a Web site because it provides access to and information about all the Web pages and files included in the Web site.

Defining Internet Resources: URLs, URI, and URNs

A **Uniform Resource Identifier (URI)** is a compact string of characters used to identify or name a resource.

A **Uniform Resource Locator (URL)** is a specific kind of URI that assigns each Web resource a unique WWW address.

A ***Uniform Resource Identifier (URI)*** is a compact string of characters used to identify or name a resource. This identifier enables interaction with representations of the resource over a network, typically the WWW, using specific protocols. A ***Uniform Resource Locator (URL)*** is a specific kind of URI that assigns each Web page a unique WWW address. For example, the www.auburn.edu/ is a URI that identifies a resource (Auburn University home page) and implies that a representation of that resource (such as the home page's current HTML code, as encoded characters) is obtainable via HTTP from a network host named www.auburn.edu.

TIP Uniform Resource Name (URN)

Another type of URI is the Uniform Resource Name (URN). Although URNs are formatted similar to URLs, they do not necessarily specify a downloadable resource. The purpose of a URN is simply to provide a globally unique name for something, not necessarily to provide a name that points to a Web-based resource. A URN can be used to talk about a resource without implying its location or how to reference it. For example, the URN: isbn:0-958-11041-1 is a URI that, like an International Standard Book Number (ISBN), allows one to talk about a book, but does not suggest where and how to obtain an actual copy of it.

Hypertext Transfer Protocol (HTTP) is the most popular communication protocol used to transfer Web pages.

The **domain name** comprises the first part of the URL that identifies the Web page's host, which can be a Web server or computer on the Internet, and a second part called the top-level domain.

The **top-level domain** can be either a generic three- or four-letter suffix indicating the type of organization to which the Web page host belongs or a two-letter suffix designated to each country.

The **path name and file name** specify the location of the Web page on the host computer.

The URL can be found in the Location or Address box of your browser's document window, as shown in Figure A.2. All URLs follow the format shown in Figure A.10. The first portion of the URL identifies the communication protocol that was used to control the file transfer process. ***Hypertext Transfer Protocol (HTTP)*** is the most popular communication protocol used to transfer Web pages. FTP is another communication protocol used for transferring information (mainly uploading files to a server or downloading files from a server) via the Internet. Typically, the communication protocol is followed by a separator, such as a colon and two slashes (://). The ***domain name*** comprises the first part of the URL that identifies the Web page's host, which can be a Web server, or computer on the Internet, and a second part called the top-level domain. The ***top-level domain*** can be either a generic three- or four-letter suffix indicating the type of organization to which the Web page host belongs (such as .edu and .org) or a two-letter suffix designated to each country (such as .us for United States and .au for Australia). The Internet Assigned Numbers Authority Web site (http://www.iana.org/domain-names.htm) provides a full list of all top-level domain names currently approved. The ***path name and file name*** specify the location of the Web page on the host computer.

TIP Case Sensitivity

Microsoft operating systems are case insensitive which means that DEFAULT.HTM and default.htm are viewed as the same file. Windows systems do however preserve case. UNIX/Linux systems are case sensitive and so DEFAULT.HTM and default.htm are two completely different files. As you may be unaware of the type of operating system your host is using or you may decide to move hosts in the future, so treat all files as if they were case sensitive.

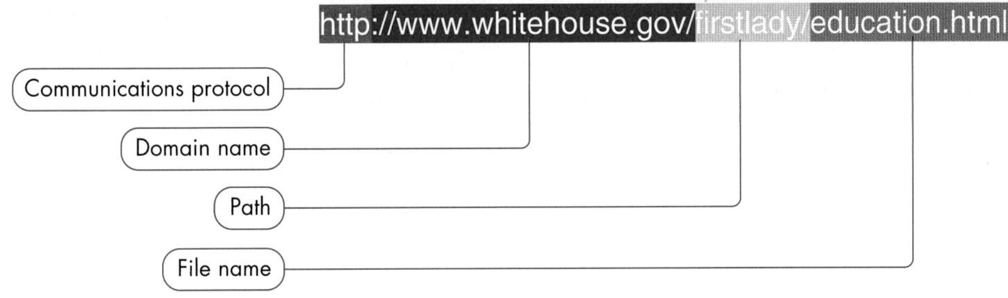

FIGURE A.10 URL Structure ➤

TIP The Apache HTTP Server Project

The Apache HTTP server project (as defined on its official Web site http://httpd.apache.org/) is an effort to develop and maintain an open-source HTTP server for modern operating systems including UNIX, Windows NT, Windows XP, and Windows 7. With the goal of a secure, efficient, and extensible server that provides HTTP services in compliance with the current HTTP standards, Apache has been one of the most popular Web servers since 1996. Many people are able to build their own Apache Web server on their home computers, which is a strong indicator of how user-friendly it is.

Defining the Core Types of Web Sites: Intranets, Extranets, and Portals

The Web includes millions of public Web sites that provide information to anyone who can connect to the WWW using a browser; however, there are some special-purpose Web sites with particular characteristics.

The Web includes millions of public Web sites that provide information to anyone who can connect to the WWW using a browser; however, there are some special-purpose Web sites with particular characteristics. Three important types of Web sites are intranets, extranets, and portals.

An **intranet** consists of Web pages and other resources that are only available inside the company.

As well as having a public presence on the Internet, many companies maintain a private Intranet behind a security firewall. An ***intranet*** consists of Web pages and other resources that are only available inside the company. Intranets are an economical alternative for companies because they use the standard technologies of the Internet to distribute internal information. They increase internal communication while using less paper for phone books, manuals, forms, etc. They pull information out of corporate databases in a form everyone can use. Intranets have proved valuable for all kinds of organizations. For example, credit card companies work with many banks, and an intranet can be used as a central repository for information about all the banks with which the company works. Software companies use intranets as a way of locating reusable software components. Law firms use intranets to draw information from many sources worldwide on topics such as trials, laws, and regulations. These are just a few of the many contexts in which intranets have been successfully used.

An **extranet** is a Web site that allows access only to selected users, such as customers, suppliers, or other trading partners.

An ***extranet*** falls somewhere between the WWW and an organization's intranet. Only selected users, such as customers, suppliers, or other trading partners, are allowed access. Extranets can range from highly secure Business-to-Business (B2B) systems to self-registration systems like those frequently used for downloading evaluation software. Extranets can be used, for example, to allow Web shoppers to check the status of their orders over a secure connection, or users of courier companies to check the location of their deliveries at any point in time.

TIP Business-to-Business (B2B) and Business-to-Consumers (B2C)

Businesses often use the Internet to exchange products, services, or information with other businesses. This is known as B2B, or e-biz, and is different than commerce between businesses and consumers (B2C). Although retailing on the Internet (also called *e-tailing*) is a thriving revenue stream for businesses, forecasts indicate that B2B revenue will far exceed B2C revenue in the future.

A **portal** is a special kind of Web application. Its role is to act as a gateway into a number of other applications.

A ***portal*** is a special kind of Web application. Its role is to act as a gateway into a number of other applications. Portal architecture typically enables portlets, such as the IBM free weather portlet (http://soaficient.com/Soaficient/solutions/weatherportlet.jsp), which are Windows-based links into other applications. They also commonly provide features for user personalization to change the layout, look, and feel of the portal or portlets. Portals are frequently used on public sites to encourage user registrations. They are also often used by companies so that remote users can access the various applications provided on the company intranet.

Today, it is common to access the Internet from a variety of mobile devices like cell phones. In the mobile context, portals are a popular way for mobile service providers to enable easy access to the mobile Internet. Mobile portals enable entry into applications and services provided by the mobile network carrier, as well as access into the mobile Internet. Special browsers called *mobile browsers* are designed to run on these portable devices. Unlike a traditional Web browser that is typically displayed on a large screen, a mobile browser is displayed on a very small screen and special navigational tools are required to conveniently view Web content. The Apple iPhone and Google Nexus phone, for example, enable you to use touch screens to "pinch" or "stretch" the screen with two fingers to zoom Web content in and out.

TIP Mobile Internet

Millions of people throughout the world are accessing wireless application protocol (WAP) Web sites, which are stripped-down sites designed for mobile device access via wireless or mobile Internet. Some people are already lobbying for an entirely new domain name, called "dot-mobi," to be used for Web sites that are optimized for mobile surfing. Others propose developing intelligent browsers to turn traditional Web sites into something that can be viewed on a mobile device. To learn more about mobile Internet, visit the Microsoft Windows Mobile Web site (www.microsoft.com/windowsmobile/default.mspx).

Describing Web Applications

A **Web application** is a software application that is accessed with a browser over a network such as an intranet, extranet, or the Internet.

Complex Web sites are also called Web applications. A ***Web application*** (or web app) is a software application that is accessed with a browser over a network such as an intranet, extranet, or the Internet. Web applications have become increasingly popular because they can be updated and maintained without distributing or installing software on client computers.

A Web application is stored on a central server and can provide a large variety of services to clients. The core components of a Web application are:

- Web server—The Web application runs on the Web server.
- Static and Active documents—If a client requests a static document, the Web server locates the file and sends it to the client's browser. If a client requests an active document, the Web server processes data and then sends the results to the browser.
- Processing Engine—Specialized software, such as ASP.NET, installed on the Web server that processes the active documents.

TIP .NET Framework, ASP.NET, and Visual Studio

As it is defined on the Microsoft ASP.NET Web site (www.asp.net), ASP.NET is a technology for creating dynamic Web applications. It is a part of the .NET Framework. ASP.NET pages are compiled, providing better performance than with scripting languages. The .NET Framework is a development and execution environment that enables programming languages and libraries to seamlessly work together to create Windows, Web, or mobile applications. The .NET Framework applications are easier to build, manage, deploy, and integrate with other networked systems. The applications can also work as stand-alone applications. Visual Studio is the Integrated Development Environment that developers use to create applications in one of many languages it supports, including Visual Basic, for the .NET Framework. To learn more about the .NET Framework, see the Microsoft dedicated Web site at www.microsoft.com/net/.

Understanding How Search Engines Work

The WWW is a rich source of information on nearly every topic imaginable. However, searching for information within the more than 20 billion pages of the WWW can often be a challenge. Good Web authors start planning strategies for promoting their Web sites as soon as they begin designing them. The "build it and they will come" philosophy does not apply to building and publishing a Web site. Web designers need to implement some standard design techniques to make their Web sites easy for search engines to find. In order to understand these techniques, you need to be familiar with search engines and the way they work.

Organizations, called *search providers*, develop and maintain Web sites that enable you to locate the precise information you want on the Internet. They maintain large databases of information pulled from the WWW and Internet. These databases include URL addresses, content descriptions or classifications, and the keywords that appear on the Web pages. Specially designed programs called *spiders*, or Web crawlers, are constantly browsing the WWW and updating the databases.

Search engines are powered by the huge amount of information mined and managed by search providers. To learn more about the dynamic connection between search providers and search engines, you can read the article, "Who Powers Whom? Search Providers Chart," at http://searchenginewatch.com/reports/article.php/2156401. To stay up to date with the latest trends and statistics on search engines, go to the ClickZ Web site (www.clickz.com/) and search for "search engines."

A **search engine** usually refers to Web search engines, which are specialized software applications that help you find information on the WWW and Internet.

Search engines usually refer to Web search engines, which are specialized software applications that help you find information on the WWW and Internet. Search engines offer two different types of searches:

- Keyword search—Keyword searches require you to enter a keyword or phrase that relates to the information you want to find. The search engine then compares your keywords to the information in its database and returns a hit list, which is a list of Web sites that contain the keyword or phrase you want to find. Each hit contains a hyperlink to the referenced Web page. The search engine orders the list based on the probability of finding the requested information in those sites. Some of the most popular keyword search engines are Google (www.google.com) and Alta Vista (www.altavista.com).
- Directory (Index) search—A directory search provides a directory, or index, of core topics, such as health, arts, science, society, and real estate. You begin by selecting the topic you want to search, and the search engine displays a list of related subtopics. Select a subtopic to see more subtopic options to browse through, or complete a form to narrow your search. For example, if you select real estate, you are presented with a form for identifying the kind of housing you want to find. After you narrow your search, you are presented with a hit list that is essentially the same as the kind of hit list you see in a keyword search. One of the most popular directory search browsers is the Open Directory Project (www.dmoz.org/), which also has keyword search capabilities.

TIP Portals and Metasearch Engines

Yahoo! (www.yahoo.com) and MSN (www.msn.com/), two popular search engines that were initially strictly directory search engines, are now components of larger Web sites, referred to as portals, offering users a wide range of information from sports to weather or news. The Yahoo! portal provides keyword as well as directory search support. Many of MSN's services were reorganized in 2005 and 2006 under a new brand name, Windows Live. For example, MSN Search became Live Search (now known as Bing). iGoogle (www.google.com/) is another very popular portal that started as a keyword search engine. It is currently offering users a wide range of information and services such as search, e-mail, a personalized home page, mailing lists and discussion groups, financial information, and Web site analytics. Metasearch engines are software applications that use a group of search engines and optimize the results by removing duplicates and displaying the hits in order of relevance. Some of the most popular metasearch engines are Dogpile (www.dogpile.com/), MetaCrawler (www.metacrawler.com), HotBot (www.hotbot.com/), Info Space (www.infospace.com/), and Search (www.search.com).

The Internet also offers a number of specialized search engines. These search engines focus on topic-specific Web sites, which reduces the amount of time required to refine your search results to the specific area you want to research. Among the most popular specialized search engines are Medscape (www.medscape.com/), which provides medical-related information for experts in the field, as well as for casual browsers, and The History Net (www.historynet.com/), which provides resources related to U.S. history.

Recent research studies, such as the "What is the Invisible Web?" study, located at www.lib.berkeley.edu/TeachingLib/Guides/Internet/InvisibleWeb.html, have shown that none of the current search engines can provide a complete list of the resources available for any one search topic. Consequently, you should consider using several search engines, especially when you need to search for important information.

Understanding Internet Copyright Laws

Internet law is the application of many different types of traditional law to the virtual world of the Internet.

Internet law is the application of many different types of traditional law to the virtual world of the Internet. Internet law comprises a number of distinct subcategories including Internet copyright. The Internet Society (ISOC) provides a comprehensive "Guide to Internet Law" at www.isoc.org/internet/law/.

Enforcing copyrights over the Internet is a rather new and complicated area even for the most experienced Internet content developers and owners. Copyrights affect you as a copyright owner attempting to enforce your rights, or as an individual or business accused of infringing on the copyrights of others. Internet copyright infringement can occur within a wide range of Internet assets, including graphics and photographs, eBooks, MP3 and video files, and Web site text. In 1998, President Clinton signed into law the Digital Millennium Copyright Act (DMCA), 17 USC § 512 (www.copyright.gov/legislation/dmca.pdf). DMCA legislation implements two 1996 World Intellectual Property Organization (WIPO) treaties: the WIPO Copyright Treaty (www.wipo.int/treaties/en/ip/wct/index.html) and the WIPO Performances and Phonograms Treaty (www.wipo.int/treaties/en/ip/wppt/index.html). It also addresses a number of other significant copyright-related issues.

TIP Internet Law

Internet Law has two other important components. The Internet Corporation for Assigned Names and Numbers (ICANN) Uniform Domain-Name Resolution Policy provides for resolution between people who register domain names and third parties who may feel they have a reason to claim those names (www.icann.org/udrp/). The Anticybersquatting Consumer Protection Act, 15 USC §1125(D) (http://en.wikipedia.org/wiki/Anticybersquatting_Consumer_Protection_Act) enables legal action against cybersquatters who wish to profit by using trademarked or personal names as a part of domain they register.

KEY TERMS

ASCII ***p.424***
Bandwidth ***p.418***
Cascading Style Sheets (CSS) ***p.430***
Client ***p.433***
Communications ***p.418***
Communications device ***p.418***
Deprecated ***p.427***
Document Type Definition (DTD) ***p.429***
Domain name ***p.434***
Dynamic Web page ***p.434***
Extensible Hypertext Markup Language (XHTML) ***p.428***
Extensible Markup Language (XML) ***p.428***
Extensible Style Sheet Language (XSL) ***p.430***
External style ***p.431***
Extranet ***p.436***
File Transfer Protocol (FTP) ***p.420***
Hypertext document ***p.421***
Hypertext Markup Language (HTML) ***p.424***
Hypertext Transfer Protocol (HTTP) ***p.434***
Inline style ***p.431***
Internal style ***p.431***
Internet ***p.418***
Internet law ***p.439***
Internet Service Provider (ISP) ***p.419***
Intranet ***p.435***
Markup language ***p.424***
Meta tag ***p.433***
Network ***p.418***
Path name and file name ***p.434***
Portal ***p.436***
Protocol ***p.419***
Publishing ***p.433***
Schema ***p.429***
Search engine ***p.438***
Server ***p.433***
Static Web page ***p.434***
Style sheet ***p.430***
Style sheet language ***p.430***
Tag ***p.424***
Telnet ***p.420***
Top-level domain ***p.434***
Uniform Resource Identifier (URI) ***p.434***
Uniform Resource Locator (URL) ***p.434***
Valid ***p.429***
Web application ***p.437***
Web browser ***p.422***
Web page ***p.422***
Web server ***p.433***
Web site ***p.433***
Well-formed ***p.429***
World Wide Web ***p.421***
World Wide Web Consortium (W3C) ***p.421***
XML parser ***p.429***

SHAREPOINT

APPENDIX B HTML, XHTML, XML, AND CSS

SharePoint Foundation and SharePoint Designer 2010 User-Friendly Tools for Working with HTML, XHTML, XML, and CSS

HTML and XHTML

... millions of Web pages have been, and continue to be, created with HTML.

This book introduces you to the comprehensive set of tools that SharePoint Foundation and SharePoint Designer 2010 offer to empower Web developers to create, edit, format, and optimize HTML/XHTML code without any actual HTML/XHTML knowledge. In spite of the limitations and flaws of HTML, millions of Web pages have been, and continue to be, created with HTML.

Consequently, a minimum level of HTML knowledge is a good addition to any Web developer's portfolio. In this section, you will learn about the HTML and XHTML markup languages.

Getting Started with HTML

A markup language describes the layout of Web page content using tags. Tags are specific codes that indicate how the text should be displayed when the document is opened in a Web browser. Web browsers interpret the tags and display the content, (including text, graphic elements, colors, and fonts) formatted on the Web page according to the tags. HTML is known as the "language of the Web" because it defines the page layout and graphic elements of the page and provides links to other documents on the Web.

HTML is known as the "language of the Web"....

HTML is the most common markup language. Because HTML documents are created using unformatted text, you can create them in a simple text program (such as Windows Notepad), in a word processing program (such as Microsoft Word), or in a Web design program (such as SharePoint Designer 2010). HTML documents normally have the file extension .htm or .html.

TIP Physical and Logical Tags

HTML physical tags were created to add style to Web pages simply because style sheets were not around; hence they indicate the way the text they enclose should be displayed in a browser. These tags, such as <b> for bold and <i> for italics, are used for formatting. Cascading Style Sheets (CSS) are now fully supported by all major browsers so you should always try to use CSS to style your HTML pages. Although less common than physical tags, you can also use logical tags to format text in an HTML document. Logical tags, such as <strong> and <em>, concentrate on describing to the browser the meaning of the enclosed text. The <strong> tag, for example, is telling the browser that the enclosed text has some greater importance. By default all browsers make the text appear bold when enclosed in the <strong> and </strong> tags, but the point to always take into consideration from this is that the <strong> tag implies that importance of that text. Engines like Google look for such tags to help figure out what the page is about.

TIP What Is SHTML?

You may see Web pages with the suffix of .shtml. This Web page includes dynamic content, typically a "last modified date," added by the server before the Web page is sent to your browser.

Many HTML tags are used in pairs, and the basic syntax of these pairs is <tag> text </tag>. HTML tags are not case sensitive, so they can be written in uppercase, lowercase, or mixed case. Some HTML tags are not used in pairs, such as the <br> tag, which forces a break in the current line of text. These tags are referred to as empty element tags. The World Wide Web Consortium (W3C)has created a set of standards indicating the correct format that should be applied to tags (go to www.w3.org/standards/webdesign/, click HTML, and then click HTML & CSS).

In addition to the tags that define Web page elements, HTML enables you to use attributes that further define the way elements are displayed in Web browsers. The attributes are placed within the start tag in the HTML tag pair and follow the syntax <tag attributes> text </tag>. You can use these attributes to define the style, color, size, width, height, and source of the elements on your Web page. Specific values are assigned to each attribute. For instance, you can specify the height of a graphic in pixels, or a table width as a percentage. You can also specify the style characteristics of the elements on your Web page using a CSS. Recent W3C guidelines and standards clearly indicate that CSS styles are preferred over setting the attributes within the HTML code.

HTML is not extensible, meaning it includes a finite set of tags and does not enable users to create their own custom tags (extensibility enables you to describe and define any new data by creating custom tags). Thus, HTML cannot be modified to meet the specific needs of developers in some cases. It does not enable users to structure, define, or process data. To add these features to a Web page, a Web developer uses Web page code written in client-side scripting languages, such as JavaScript; server-side scripting languages, such as ASP.NET and JSP; or programming languages, such as Java.

Getting Started with XHTML

XHTML is a newer markup language that overcomes some of the problems of HTML.

XHTML is a newer markup language that overcomes some of the problems of HTML. XHTML is a transitional language between HTML and XML. Thus, until all browsers are upgraded to fully support XML, XHTML will continue to be a workable solution.

Although there are many similarities between HTML and XHTML, there are also some important differences....

Although there are many similarities between HTML and XHTML, there are also some important differences (see Figure B.1) such as:

- Well-formed and valid XHTML can be read by all XML-enabled applications.
- XHTML code has to be well-formed and valid to avoid generating errors.
- XHTML tags and attribute names must be lowercase.
- XHTML tags are case sensitive.
- In XHTML, the empty element tags that were inherited from HTML, such as <img>, <br>, and <hr>, have the following syntax: <img/>, <br/>, and <hr/>.

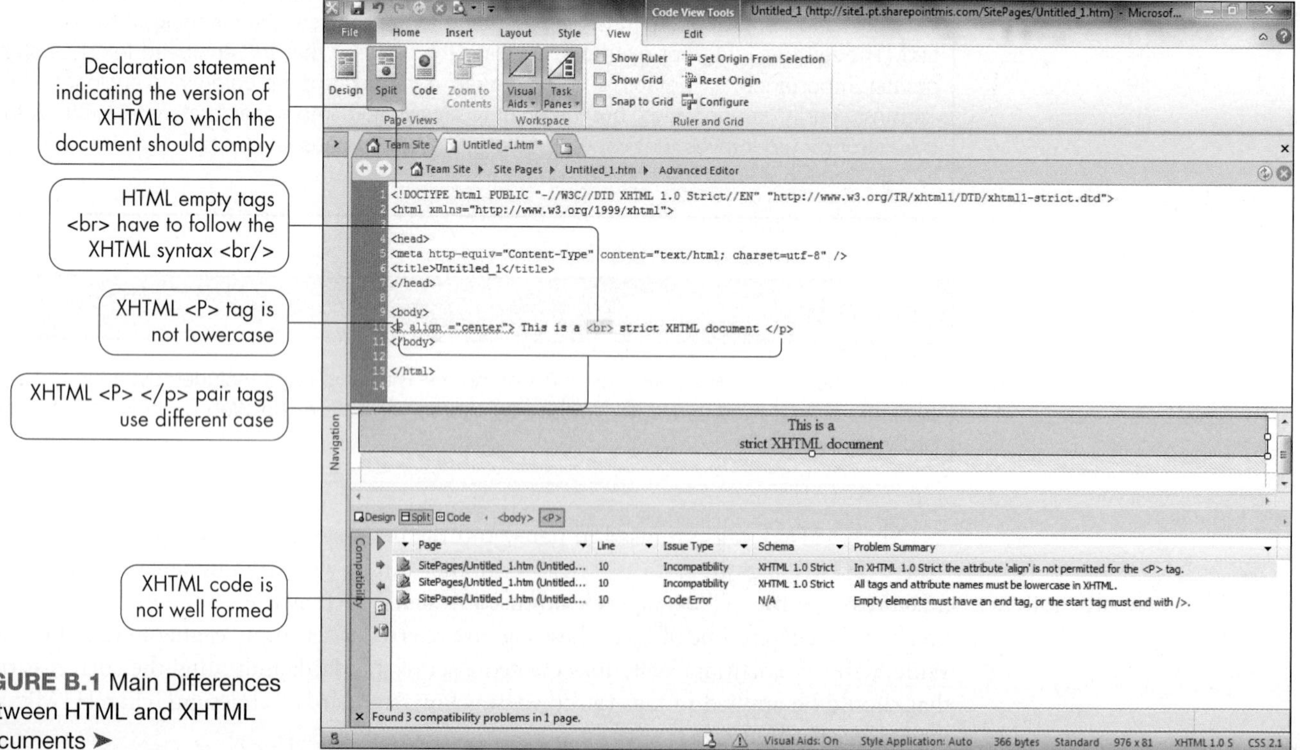

FIGURE B.1 Main Differences Between HTML and XHTML Documents ➤

TIP Creating an XHTML Document

XHTML documents are also XML documents. The first line of XHTML coding includes a declaration statement indicating the version of XHTML to which the document should comply, as shown in Figure B.1.

Developing Standard HTML/XHTML Documents

The way a Web page is displayed by different browsers and on different platforms can vary. Fonts, colors, tables, and hyperlinks are only a few of the many Web page elements that can appear differently, for example, in Mozilla Firefox than they do in Microsoft Internet Explorer. The same Web page might also be displayed differently on computers using different operating systems. Fonts and colors are some of the Web page elements that might look different on an Apple computer or a Sun workstation than they do on a computer that uses Windows. Although organizations and corporations around the world are working on ways to eliminate cross-browser and cross-platform compatibility issues, they still pose a problem for Web developers.

To overcome the cross-browser and cross-platform issues, W3C declared many older HTML tags and tag attributes as deprecated, meaning that they might not be supported by all browsers. To learn more about the HTML elements and their status, visit the W3C Index of Elements Web site (www.w3.org/TR/REC-html40/index/elements.html). To learn more about HTML attributes and their status, visit the W3C Index of Attributes Web site (www.w3.org/TR/REC-html40/index/attributes.html).

W3C has defined three variations of HTML 4.01 (www.w3.org/TR/REC-html40/) and XHTML 1.0 (www.w3.org/TR/xhtml1/): strict, transitional, and frameset. In the strict version, deprecated tags are not allowed. If you specify transitional or frameset declarations, deprecated tags can be used. The only difference between transitional and frameset is the latter allows frames. When developing an XHTML or HMTL Web page, you indicate which version and variation you are using with a DOCTYPE declaration like the one shown in Figure B.1 and in the reference table below. Additional document-type declarations are available on the W3C Web site (www.w3.org/QA/2002/04/valid-dtd-list.html).

REFERENCE DOCTYPE Declarations for HTML and XHTML

DTD	DOCTYPE
HTML 4.01 strict	<!DOCTYPE html PUBLIC "-//W3C//DTD HTML 4.01//EN" "http://www.w3.org/TR/html4/strict.dtd">
HTML 4.01 transitional	<!DOCTYPE html PUBLIC "-//W3C//DTD HTML 4.01 Transitional//EN" "http://www.w3.org/TR/html4/loose.dtd">
HTML 4.01 frameset	<!DOCTYPE html PUBLIC "-//W3C//DTD HTML 4.01 Frameset//EN" "http://www.w3.org/TR/html4/frameset.dtd">
XHTML 1.0 strict	<!DOCTYPE html PUBLIC "-//W3C//DTD XHTML 1.0 Strict//EN" "http://www.w3.org/TR/xhtml1/DTD/xhtml1-strict.dtd">
XHTML 1.0 transitional	<!DOCTYPE html PUBLIC "-//W3C//DTD XHTML 1.0 Transitional//EN" "http://www.w3.org/TR/xhtml1/DTD/xhtml1-transitional.dtd">
XHTML 1.0 frameset	<!DOCTYPE html PUBLIC "-//W3C//DTD XHTML 1.0 Frameset//EN" "http://www.w3.org/TR/xhtml1/DTD/xhtml1-frameset.dtd">

Once you finish a draft of your Web page, you can use a validator application to evaluate the page and see if it complies with the version and variation you used. W3C offers a freeware Markup Validation Service (http://validator.w3.org/) that can be used to check HTML, XHTML, and more.

Once you finish a draft of your Web page, you can use a validator application to evaluate the page....

To help eliminate cross-browser and cross-platform issues, all browser manufacturers should comply with the W3C standards. Unfortunately, this is not always the case; thus, Web developers need to continue their efforts to develop standard Web sites that overcome cross-browser and cross-platform challenges.

Getting Started with Common HTML and XHTML Elements and Attributes

Table B.1 contains a listing of common HTML and XHTML elements and attributes, including the syntax of the tags and attributes, and a short description. The Description column also indicates whether the HTML tag or any of its attributes are deprecated. The comprehensive and updated list of all special characters used in HTML can be found on the W3C Web site (www.w3.org/TR/REC-html40/sgml/entities.html).

TABLE B.1 Common HTML and XHTML Elements and Attributes

Structure Tags	
Element and Attribute	**Description**
<html>…</html> version="text"	Encloses the entire HTML document Indicates the version of the HTML
<head>…</head>	Encloses the head of the HTML document
<body>…</body>	Encloses the body of the document
alink="color"	Indicates the color of active links; deprecated
background="url"	Indicates the file of the background image; deprecated
bgcolor="color"	Indicates the background color; deprecated
link="color"	Indicates the color of unvisited links; deprecated
text="color"	Indicates the color of the page text; deprecated
vlink="color"	Indicates the color of visited links; deprecated
<!…>	Indicates the beginning and the end of comments
Title and Headings	
Element and Attribute	**Description**
<title>…</title>	Indicates the title of the document
<hi>…</hi>	Indicates the format of the included text as a heading, where the index i can vary between 1 for the largest heading and 6 for the smallest heading
align="left|center|right|justify"	Indicates the horizontal alignment of the heading text (left is the default value); deprecated

TABLE B.1 Common HTML and XHTML Elements and Attributes	
Paragraphs	
Element and Attribute	**Description**
<p>…</p>	Indicates the formatting of the included text as a paragraph
align="left|center|right|justify"	Indicates the horizontal alignment of the heading text (left is the default value); deprecated
Links	
Element and Attribute	**Description**
<a>…</a>	Indicates the start and end of a link
href="url"	Creates a link to another document or anchor
name="text"	Creates an anchor that can be a link target
shape="rect|circle|polygon"	Indicates the shape hotspot used when creating an image map
title="text"	Indicates the ScreenTip text that will be displayed in a browser every time a user hovers the mouse over the link
Lists	
Element and Attribute	**Description**
<li>…</li>	Inserts a list item and is used in an ordered list (<ol>) unordered list <ul> menu list (<menu>); deprecated directory list (<dir>); deprecated
type="A|a|I|i|1|disc|square|circle"	Indicates the type of bullet, number, or letter to be used to format the list; deprecated
value="integer"	Indicates the start value of an ordered/numbered list; deprecated
<menu>…</menu>	A menu list of items; deprecated
<dir>…</dir>	A directory listing; deprecated
<dl>…</dl>	A definition of glossary list
<dt>…</dt>	A definition term, part of a definition list
<dd>…</dd>	The definition that corresponds to a definition term
<ol>…</ol>	Indicates the beginning and ending of an ordered, numbered list
compact="compact"	Indicates the space between the list items; deprecated
start="integer"	Indicates the start value in the list
type="A|a|I|i|1"	Indicates the type of number or letter used to format the list; deprecated
<ul>…</ul>	Indicates the beginning and end of an unordered, bulleted list
compact="compact"	Indicates the space between the list items; deprecated
type="disc|square|circle"	Indicates the type of bullet used to format the list; deprecated

(Continued)

TABLE B.1 Common HTML and XHTML Elements and Attributes

Tables

Element and Attribute	Description
<table>...</table>	Indicates the beginning and the end of a table
align="left|center|right"	Indicates the horizontal alignment of the table; deprecated
background="url"	Indicates the URL of the image used as table background; deprecated
bgcolor="color"	Indicates the color used as table background; deprecated
border="integer"	Indicates the size, in pixels, of the table border
bordercolor="color"	Indicates the color of the table border
cellpadding="integer"	Indicates the space, in pixels, between the table content and the cell's borders
cellspacing="integer"	Indicates the space, in pixels, between the table cells
cols="integer"	Indicates the number of columns in the table
height="integer"	Indicates the height, in pixels, of the table
width="integer"	Indicates the width, in pixels, of the table
<tr>...</tr>	Indicates the beginning and the end of a row in a table
align="left|center|right"	Indicates the horizontal alignment of the row; deprecated
background="url"	Indicates the URL of the image used as the row background
bgcolor="color"	Indicates the color used as the row background; deprecated
bordercolor="color"	Indicates the color of the row border
height="integer"	Indicates the height, in pixels, of the table
valign="baseline|bottom|middle|top"	Indicates the vertical alignment of the row content
<td>...</td>	Indicates the beginning and the end of a cell in a table
align="left|center|right"	Indicates the horizontal alignment of the cell; deprecated
background="url"	Indicates the URL of the image used as cell background
bgcolor="color"	Indicates the color used as cell background; deprecated
bordercolor="color"	Indicates the color of the cell border
colspan="integer"	Indicates the number of columns the cell spans
height="integer"	Indicates the height, in pixels, of the cell; deprecated
nowrap="nowrap"	Does not allow line wrapping within the table cell; deprecated
rowspan="integer"	Indicates the number of rows the cell spans
valign="baseline|bottom|middle|top"	Indicates the vertical alignment of the cell content
width="integer"	Indicates the width, in pixels, of the cell; deprecated

TABLE B.1 Common HTML and XHTML Elements and Attributes

<th>…</th>	Indicates the beginning and the ending of a table header cell
align=“left|center|right”	Indicates the horizontal alignment of the table header cell
bgcolor=“color”	Indicates the color used as table header cell background; deprecated
bordercolor=“color”	Indicates the color of the table header cell border
colspan=“integer”	Indicates the number of columns the table header cell spans
height=“integer”	Indicates the height, in pixels, of the table header cell; deprecated
nowrap=“nowrap”	Allows line wrapping within the table header cell; deprecated
rowspan=“integer”	Indicates the number of rows the table header cell spans
valign=“baseline|bottom|middle|top”	Indicates the vertical alignment of the table header content
width=“integer”	Indicates the width, in pixels, of the table header cell; deprecated
<caption>…</caption>	Creates a table caption
align=“bottom|left|center|right|top”	Indicates the alignment of the caption; deprecated
Character Formatting	
Element and Attribute	**Description**
<b>…</b>	Formats the enclosed text as bolded
<em>…</em>	Indicates emphasis text, usually italic
<i>…</i>	Formats the enclosed text as italic
<strong>…</strong>	Indicates stronger emphasis text, usually bold
_…	Formats the enclosed text as subscripted
[…]	Formats the enclosed text as superscripted
Forms	
Element and Attribute	**Description**
<form>…</form>	Marks the beginning and the ending of a Web page form
action=“url”	Indicates the URL where the data added to the form will be sent
method=“get|post”	Indicates the method used to access the URL specified in the action attribute
name=“text”	Indicates the form name; deprecated
target=“text”	Indicates the window (or frame) where the output of the form will be displayed

(Continued)

TABLE B.1 Common HTML and XHTML Elements and Attributes

<table>
<tr><th colspan="2">Script</th></tr>
<tr><th>Element and Attribute</th><th>Description</th></tr>
<tr><td><script>...</script></td><td>Places client-side scripts within an HTML document</td></tr>
<tr><td>event="text"</td><td>Indicates the event that causes the script to run</td></tr>
<tr><td>language="text"</td><td>Provides the language of the script; deprecated</td></tr>
<tr><td>src="url"</td><td>Indicates the URL of an external script</td></tr>
<tr><td>type= "text/scripting language"</td><td>Specifies the scripting language of the element's contents and overrides the default scripting language (for example text/javascript). You must supply a value for this attribute because there is no default value.</td></tr>
<tr><td><noscript>...</noscript></td><td>Encloses HTML tags for browsers that do not support client-side scripts</td></tr>
<tr><th colspan="2">Applet</th></tr>
<tr><th>Element and Attribute</th><th>Description</th></tr>
<tr><td><applet>...</applet></td><td>Places a Java applet in an HTML document; deprecated</td></tr>
<tr><td><object>...</object>
align="absbottom|absmiddle|baseline|bottom|left|middle|right|texttop|top"|</td><td>Places a Java applet and other embedded objects, such as an image, audio, and video clip) in an HTML document
Indicates the alignment of an object within the body of a Web page</td></tr>
<tr><td>border="integer"</td><td>Indicates, in pixels, the width of the border around the object; deprecated</td></tr>
<tr><td>classid="url"</td><td>Indicates the URL of the object</td></tr>
<tr><td>data="url"</td><td>Indicates the URL of the object's data file</td></tr>
<tr><td>datasrc="url"</td><td>Indicates the URL or ID of the data source bound to the object</td></tr>
<tr><td>height="integer"</td><td>Indicates, in pixels, the height of the object</td></tr>
<tr><td>name="text"</td><td>Indicates the name of the embedded object</td></tr>
<tr><td>width="integer"</td><td>Indicates, in pixels, the width of the object</td></tr>
<tr><th colspan="2">Images</th></tr>
<tr><th>Element and Attribute</th><th>Description</th></tr>
<tr><td><img>...</img></td><td>Inserts an inline image into the document</td></tr>
<tr><td>align="absbottom|absmiddle|baseline|bottom|left|middle|right|texttop|top|"</td><td>Indicates the alignment of an image within the body of a Web page; deprecated</td></tr>
<tr><td>alt="text"</td><td>Indicates the text displayed instead of the image</td></tr>
<tr><td>border="integer"</td><td>Indicates, in pixels, the width of the image border; deprecated</td></tr>
<tr><td>height="integer"</td><td>Indicates, in pixels, the height of the image</td></tr>
<tr><td>name="text"</td><td>Indicates the name of the image</td></tr>
<tr><td>width="integer"</td><td>Indicates, in pixels, the width of the image</td></tr>
</table>

TABLE B.1 Common HTML and XHTML Elements and Attributes

Other Elements	
Element and Attribute	**Description**
<hr/>	Inserts a horizontal rule line
 	Inserts a line break
CSS Elements	
Element and Attribute	**Description**
<style>... style declarations </style>	Defines a document's global style declaration—the declaration of a specific style applied to the document
type="mime_type"	Indicates the MIME type of the style sheet language (for CSS it is "text/css")
media="all|aural|Braille|handheld|print|projection|screen|tty|tv|"	Indicates the media used to display the style definition
title="text"	Indicates the title of the style definition

Cascading Style Sheets (CSS)

A **style sheet** describes how documents are displayed on screens, presented in print, or even how they are pronounced.

A **style sheet language** is a computer language for expressing style sheets.

This book introduces you to the comprehensive set of tools that SharePoint Designer 2010 offers to empower Web developers to create, edit, modify, and optimize CSS styles without any actual CSS knowledge. In this section, you will recap what you have already learned about CSS from this textbook and learn a little more about this style sheet language.

... CSS is a robust formatting language that successfully separates a Web page's content from its appearance.

Getting Started with CSS

The **Extensible Style Sheet Language (XSL)** was developed by the W3C as an improved method for formatting XML documents, allowing developers to transform XML data files into a wide variety of popular file formats, such as HTML and portable document format (PDF).

An **inline style** is included in the start tag by using the tag's style attributes.

An **internal style** is usually included in the <head> section of an HTML document and has the following syntax: <style> style declarations</style>.

An **external style** is included in separate files used to specify the formatting of any HTML document to which it is linked.

Style sheets describe how documents are displayed on screens, presented in print, or even how they are pronounced. ***Style sheet languages*** are computer languages for expressing style sheets. Although several style sheet languages have been developed, CSS is a robust formatting language that successfully separates a Web page's content from its appearance. CSS is the standard style sheet language used on the Web.

The ***Extensible Style Sheet Language (XSL)*** was developed by the W3C as an improved method for formatting XML documents, allowing developers to transform XML data files into a wide variety of popular file formats, such as HTML and portable document format (PDF). XSL is still supported by fewer browsers than CSS. Although CSS was initially developed for HTML, it is currently used in HTML, XML, and XHTML.

You can use three different types of CSS style codes to format the HTML/XHTML code of your Web pages: inline styles, internal styles, and external styles.

Inline styles are included in the start tag by using the tag's style attributes. Inline style codes override the styles defined in internal and external styles. ***Internal styles*** are usually included in the <head> section of an HTML document and have the following syntax: <style>style declarations</style>. Internal styles override the format defined in a linked external style sheet. ***External styles*** are included in separate files used to specify the formatting of any HTML document to which they are linked. These style codes are kept in a document with a .css file extension and are linked to the HTML document using the <link> HTML tag. If you have two styles with the same weight in a document, for instance, two declared inline styles, the style declared last has precedence.

TIP Linking External Style Sheets

An external style sheet also can be linked to a Web page using the CSS @import directive inside the HTML <style> tag.

A single style defines the look of one Web page element by simply telling a Web browser how to format that content on a Web page; from displaying a headline in blue to bordering a table with orange. A style consists of two elements:

- The Web page element that will be formatted by the browser, named the selector.
- The formattin g instructions, named the declaration block.

The **selector** indicates to a Web browser which element(s) within a Web page to style.

The **declaration block** begins and ends with braces {} and includes all the formatting options to be applied to the selector.

A **declaration** is comprised of one or more formatting instructions.

A **property** is a word or a group of hyphenated words indicating a style effect.

A **value** is required to be assigned to any property.

However, even a simple style, like the one illustrated in Figure B.2, contains several elements, as illustrated in Figure B.3.

- The ***selector*** indicates to a Web browser which element(s) within a Web page to style. In Figures B.2 and B.3, the selector *a* refers to the tag <*a*>, hence the Web browser will format all <*a*> tags using the formatting directions included in this style.
- The ***declaration block*** begins and ends with braces {} and includes all the formatting options to be applied to the selector. It includes all the formatting options you want applied to the selector.
- A ***declaration*** is comprised of one or more formatting instructions. Each declaration includes a property and a value.
- A ***property*** is a word or a group of hyphenated words indicating a style effect. In Figures B.2 and B.3, color and text-decoration are properties of the <*a*> tag.
- A ***value*** is required to be assigned to any property. In Figures B.2 and B.3, #04b is the value of the color property and underline is the value of the text-decoration property of the <*a*> tag.

FIGURE B.2 CSS Style ➤

```
a {color: #04b; text-decoration: underline;}
```

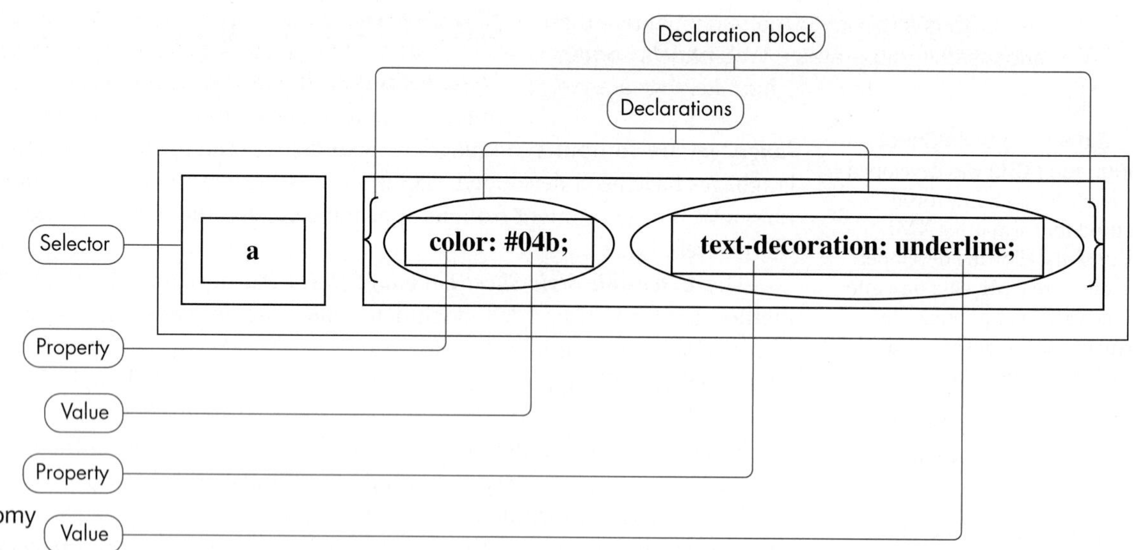

FIGURE B.3 Anatomy of a CSS Style ➤

The CSS style selectors allow you to single out one specific Web page element or a collection of similar Web page elements:

A **tag selector** applies to all occurrences of the HTML tag it styles and is easy to distinguish in a document because it has the same name as the HTML tag it styles.

- ***Tag selectors*** apply to all occurrences of the HTML tag they style and they are easy to distinguish in a document because they have the same name as the HTML tag they style. For example, in the Web page shown in Figure B.4, a style was created for the p tag selector. Therefore, all the <p>tag occurrences implement this style.

TIP Tag Selectors

Make sure you do not add the less than < and greater than > symbols to tag selectors.

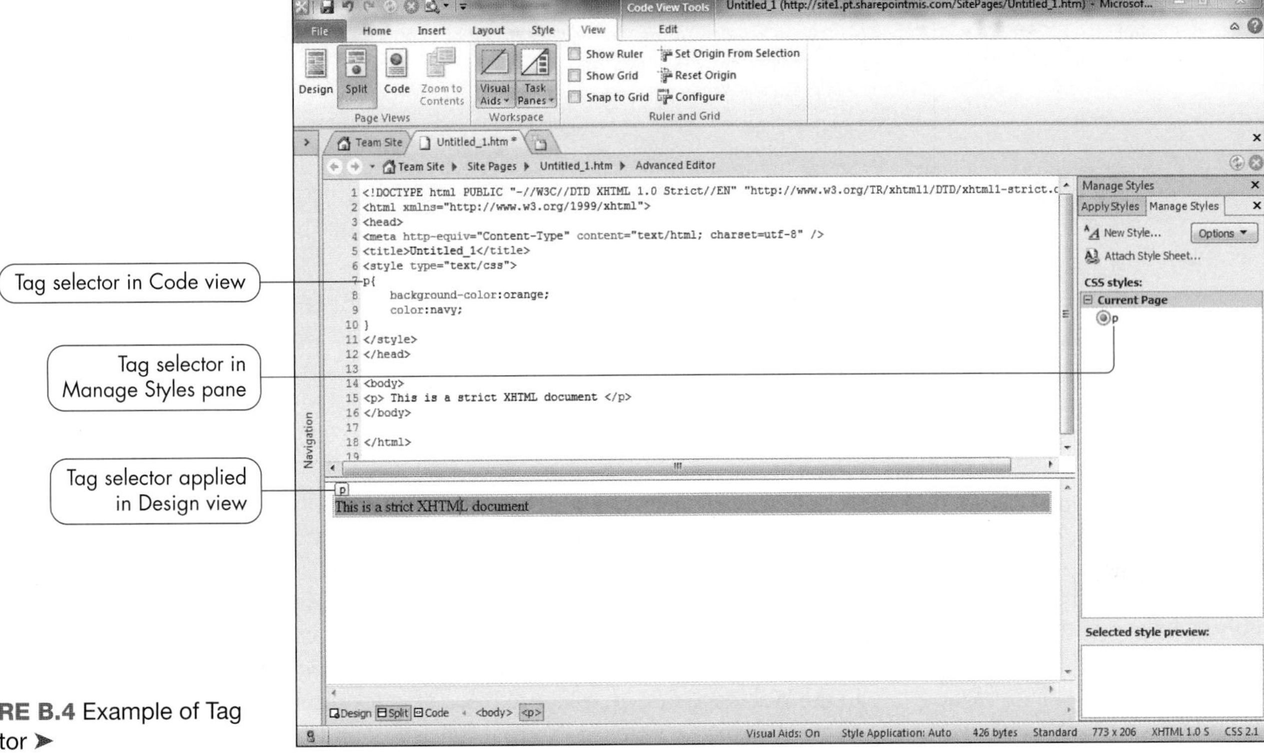

FIGURE B.4 Example of Tag Selector ➤

A **class selector** applies to HTML sections of your Web page that can be identified by the <div> or <span> tags.

- ***Class selectors*** usually apply to HTML sections of your Web page that can be identified by the <div> or <span> tags. They start with a period and are case sensitive. After the period, the name must start with a letter and can include only letters, numbers, hyphens, and underscores. Class selectors are usually defined in the head section of a Web page or in an external style sheet. For example, in the Web page shown in Figure B.5, a .style_bold class selector was created in the Web page's attached ExternalCSS.css external style sheet and applied using the <span> tags.

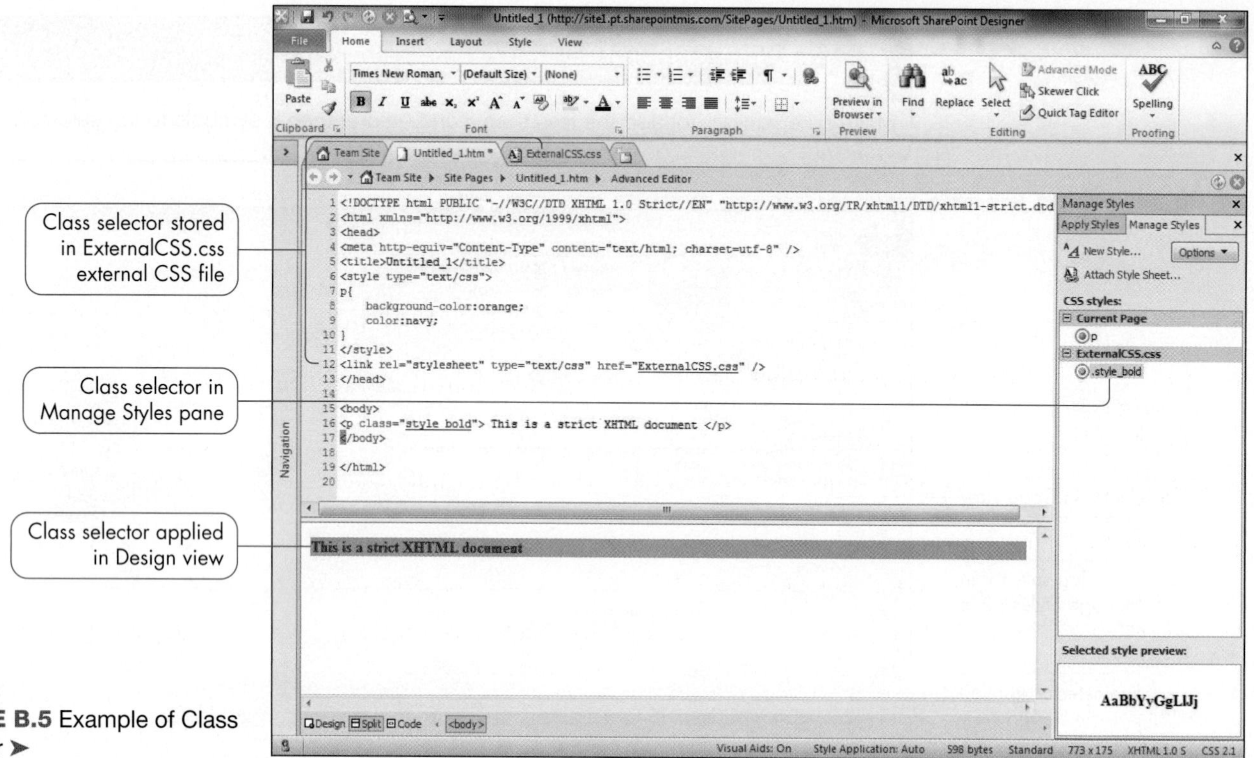

FIGURE B.5 Example of Class Selector ➤

An **ID selector** is used for identifying unique parts of your Web page such as banners, navigation bars, or main content areas because it is connected to the *id* attribute of a Web page element and the id must be unique.

- ***ID selectors*** are used for identifying unique parts of your Web page such as banners, navigation bars, or main content areas because they are connected to the *id* attribute of a Web page element and the id must be unique. For example, in the Web page shown in Figure B.6, a #navigation id selector style was created in the Web page's attached external style sheet and applied to the section <div id = "navigation">.

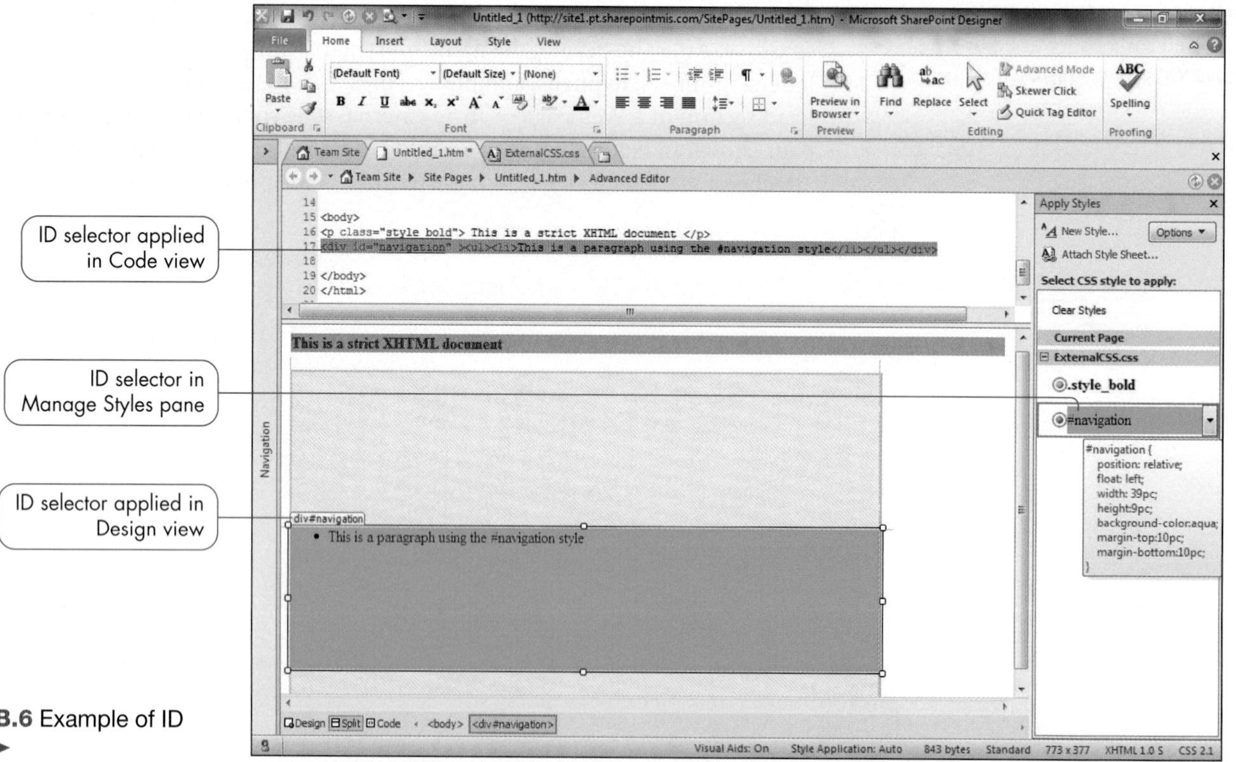

FIGURE B.6 Example of ID Selector ➤

TIP Should I Use a Class or an ID?

When you want to use a style several times, you should use classes. When a browser encounters a class and an ID for the same tag, it gives priority to the ID.

Developing Standard CSS

One of the biggest advantages of using CSS is that when the style sheet is changed, all the Web pages referencing that style sheet are automatically updated.

One of the biggest advantages of using CSS is that when the style sheet is changed, all the Web pages referencing an external style sheet are automatically updated. Although the CSS is useful and has experienced rapid growth on the WWW, some browsers still do not fully support CSS. To learn more about W3C CSS standards and which browsers support CSS, visit this dedicated Web page of the W3C (www.w3.org/Style/CSS/).

The specifications for CSS are maintained by W3C and are made up of various levels, or versions, and profiles. Desktop browsers implement CSS level 1, 2, or 3:

- CSS level 1 (www.w3.org/TR/CSS1/), the earliest level developed, includes properties for fonts, margins, colors, and more.
- CSS level 2 (www.w3.org/TR/CSS21/), introduced in 1998, includes all of CSS level 1, as well as new styles for absolutely positioned elements, automatic numbering, page breaks, right to left text, and more. On June 7, 2011, W3C published Cascading Style Sheets Level 2 Revision 1 (CSS 2.1) Specification as a Recommendation.
- CSS level 3 (www.w3.org/Style/CSS/current-work), currently under development, encompasses all of CSS level 2, and provides new styles for user interaction, accessibility, and speech.

Three CSS profiles have been developed for alternative platforms, such as PDAs, cellular phones, televisions, printers, and speech synthesizers. They include:

- CSS Mobile Profile 1.0 (www.w3.org/TR/css-mobile) enables display on mobile devices, such as cell phones and PDAs.
- CSS TV Profile 1.0 (www.w3.org/TR/css-tv) is for browsers that run on television displays.
- CSS Print Profile (www.w3.org/TR/css-print/) is in the draft stage and will provide styles to low-cost printers.

TIP Always Think About the Users' Needs

You should be aware that a visitor can override any style applied to your Web pages. People with disabilities often use the Internet Explorer Accessibility dialog box to apply their own style sheet to the Web page display. The visitor's style sheets take precedence over your style sheet, and their browser's default styles. Thus, as discussed in Appendix C, your Web pages should be able to display properly with or without a style sheet.

Getting Started with Common CSS Styles and Attributes and Values

If you do not specify a style for an element on your Web page, the element inherits the style of its parent element. For example, all the styles specified for the <body> element will apply to any included <p>element that does not have a specified style.

Table B.2 includes the most common CSS styles, their common attributes, and standard values. Some attributes use CSS units of measure to indicate properties, such as color, length, and spacing. To learn about the CSS units of measure, visit the Webmonkey Reference Stylesheets Guide Web site (www.webmonkey.com/2010/02/css-units-of-measure/). The W3C working group is a dynamic one, frequently generating new styles and standards. To keep up with the CSS most recent developments, visit the W3C Cascading Style Sheets Web site (www.w3.org/Style/CSS/).

TABLE B.2 CSS 2.1 Common Styles

Style syntax	Style description	Style values	Style values description
Background Style (www.w3.org/TR/CSS21/colors.html#q2)			
Style syntax	**Style description**	**Style values**	**Style values description**
***background-color**: color* See W3C CSS21 Specification (14.2.1) background-color for details.	Indicates the color of the background	Keyword: inherit Keyword: transparent A CSS color name or value	Inherits the background color of the parent Shows the background image of the parent element Shows the background color indicated
***background-image:** url(url)* See W3C CSS21 Specification (14.2.1) background-image for details.	Indicates the image file applied as background	URL	The URL of the image file
***background-position:** x y* See W3C CSS21 Specification (14.2.1) background-position for details.	Indicates the position of the background image	The keywords left, center, or right, and top, center, or bottom Pixels or percentage of the parent element's width/height	For the horizontal and vertical position of the background image The X and Y coordinates of the background image in pixels or as a percentage of the parent element's width/height
Box_model Style (www.w3.org/TR/CSS21/box.html)			
Style syntax	**Style description**	**Style values**	**Style values description**
border: border-width border-style color See W3C CSS21 Specification (8.5) Border Properties for details.	Indicates the element border width, style, and color	CSS units of measure Style A CSS color name or value	The width of the border The border design The border color
margin: top, right, bottom, left See W3C CSS21 Specification (8.3) Margin Properties for details.	Indicates the size of the margins	CSS units of measure CSS units of measure CSS units of measure CSS units of measure	The element margin size at the top The element margin size to the right The element margin size at the bottom The element margin size to the left
***padding:** top, right, bottom, left* See W3C CSS21 Specification (8.4) Padding Properties for details.	Indicates the size of element padding	CSS units of measure CSS units of measure CSS units of measure CSS units of measure	The element padding along the top margin The element padding along the right margin The element padding along the bottom margin The element padding along the left margin

TABLE B.2 CSS 2.1 Common Styles

Content Style (www.w3.org/TR/CSS21/generate.html#content)			
Style syntax	**Style description**	**Style values**	**Style values description**
content: attr(X)	Provides the value of the element's X attribute	string	The value of the element's attribute
content: text	Creates a text string and attaches it to the element's content	text string	The text string created and attached to the element's content
content: url (url)	Indicates the URL of an external file that will be attached to the element	URL	The URL of the external file
Display Style			
Visual Effects (www.w3.org/TR/CSS21/visufx.html)			
Style syntax	**Style description**	**Style values**	**Style values description**
clip: rect(top, right, bottom, left) See W3C CSS21 Specification (11.1.2) Clipping: the "clip" property for details.	Indicates the portion of the content section that will be displayed	CSS units of measure	Top, bottom, right, and left specify offsets of the top, bottom, right, and left edges from the upper-left corner of the element
		Keywords: auto and inherit	Enables browser to determine the clipping region
overflow: length See W3C CSS21 Specification (11.1.1) Overflow: the "overflow" property for details.	Provides browser with the way it should handle content that overflows the element's dimensions	Keywords:	
		hidden	Indicates that the content is clipped and that no scrolling user interface should be provided to view the content outside the clipping region
		scroll	Indicates that the content is clipped and that if the Web page visitor uses a scrolling mechanism that is visible on the screen (such as a scrollbar), that mechanism should be displayed for a box whether or not any of its content is clipped
		visible	Indicates that content is not clipped, thus it may be rendered outside the block box
		auto	Causes a scrolling mechanism to be provided for overflowing boxes
		inherit	Takes the same value as the property for the element's parent

(Continued)

TABLE B.2 CSS 2.1 Common Styles			
visibility: *length* See W3C CSS21 (11.2) Specification Visibility: the "visibility" property for details.	Indicates the element's visibility	Keyword: hidden	Indicates that the element is invisible or fully transparent
		Keyword: collapse	When used for row, row group, column, and column group elements collapse; causes the entire row or column to be removed from the display, and the space normally taken up by the row or column to be available for other content
		Keyword: visible	Indicates that the element is visible
		Keyword: inherit	Takes the same value as the property for the element's parent
Visual Formatting (www.w3.org/TR/CSS21/visuren.html#display-prop)			
display: *type* See W3C CSS21 (9.2.4) Specification The "display" property.	Indicates the display type of the element	Keywords: block, inline, inline-block, inherit, list-item, none, run-in, table, inline-table, table-caption, table-column, table-cell, table-column-group, table-header-group, table-footer-group, table-row, and table-row-group; you can look up the additional style values at the bottom of the description box.	Keyword block: causes the element to generate a block box Keyword inline: causes the element to generate one or more inline boxes Keyword list-item: causes the element to generate a principal block box and a list-item inline box Keyword none: causes the element to generate no boxes in the formatting structure, which means that the element has no effect on layout
Fonts and Text Style			
Style syntax	**Style description**	**Style values**	**Style values description**
Colors (www.w3.org/TR/CSS21/colors.html#propdef-color)			
color: *color* See W3C CSS21 Specification (14.1) Foreground color: the "color" property.	Indicates the element foreground color	Keyword: inherit CSS color name or a color value	
Fonts (www.w3.org/TR/CSS21/fonts.html)			
font-family: *family* See W3C CSS21 Specification (15.3) Font family: the "font-family" property for details.	Indicates the font face used for displaying the text	Keywords: sans serif, serif, fantasy, monospace, cursive, inherit, or the name of another installed font	
font-style: *style* See W3C CSS21 Specification (15.4) Font styling: the "font-style" property for details.	Indicates the font style used for displaying the text	Keywords: normal, italic oblique, inherit	

TABLE B.2 CSS 2.1 Common Styles			
font-variant: *type* See W3C CSS21 Specification (15.5) Small-caps: the "font-variant" property for details.	Indicates a variant of the font	Keywords: inherit, normal, small-caps	
font-weight: *value* See W3C CSS21 Specification (15.6) Font boldness: the "font-weight" property for details.	Indicates the weight of the font	100, 200, 300, 400, 500, 600, 700, 800, 900 Keywords: normal, lighter, bolder or bold	
font-size: *value* See W3C CSS21 Specification (15.7) Font size: the "font-size" property for details.	Indicates the size of the font	Keyword: inherit CSS units of measure	
Text Style (www.w3.org/TR/CSS21/text.html)			
Style syntax	**Style description**	**Style values**	**Style values description**
letter-spacing: *value* See W3C CSS21 Specification (16.4) Letter and word spacing: the "letter-spacing" and "word-spacing" properties for details.	Indicates the space between text's letters	Keywords: normal, inherit CSS units of measure	
text-align: *type* See W3C CSS21 Specification (16.2) Alignment: the "text-align" property for details.	Indicates the horizontal alignment of the text	Keywords: inherit, left, right, center, or justify	
text-decoration: *type* See W3C CSS21 Specification (16.3.1) Underlining, overlining, striking, and blinking: the "text-decoration" property for details.	Indicates the type of decoration applied to the text	Keywords: blink, line-through, none, overline, underline, inherit	
text-indent: *length* See W3C CSS21 Specification (16.1) Indentation: the "text-indent" property for details.	Indicates the size of the first line of text's indentation	CSS units of measure Percentage of the containing block width Keyword: inherit	
text-transform: *type* See W3C CSS21 Specification (16.5) Capitalization: the "text-transform" property for details.	Indicates a text case transformation	Keywords: capitalize, lowercase, none, uppercase, inherit	
white-space: *type* See W3C CSS21 Specification (16.6) White space: the "white-space" property for details.	Indicates the way white space (such as new lines, tabs, and blanks) should be handled	Keywords: inherit, normal, pre (for handling text as preformatted text) or nowrap (for disabling the line-wrapping)	
word-spacing: *length* See 'W3C CSS21 Specification (16.4) Letter and word spacing: the "letter-spacing" and "word-spacing" properties for details.	Indicates the space between words included in text	CSS units of measure Keyword: normal Keyword: inherit	 When using normal space between words

(Continued)

TABLE B.2 CSS 2.1 Common Styles			
Visual Formatting Style (www.w3.org/TR/CSS21/visudet.html)			
Style syntax	**Style description**	**Style values**	**Style values description**
vertical-align: *type* See W3C CSS21 Specification (10.8) vertical-align property for details.	Indicates the vertical alignment of the text with the surrounding content	Keywords: baseline, middle, top, bottom, text-bottom, text-top, sub, super, inherit A percentage or CSS units of measure	
height: *length* See W3C CSS21 Specification (10.5) content height property for details.	Indicates the height of the element	Keywords: auto, inherit CSS units of measure Percentage of the box's height	 The element's height
width: *length* See W3C CSS21 Specification (10.5) content height property for details.	Indicates the width of the element	Keywords: auto, inherit CSS units of measure Percentage of the box's width	 The element's width
Layout (www.w3.org/TR/CSS21/visuren.html)			
Style syntax	**Style description**	**Style values**	**Style values description**
clear: *type* See W3C CSS21 Specification (9.5.2) Controlling flow next to floats: the "clear" property for details.	Indicates the placement of the element after the selected margin is clear of any floating elements	Keywords: inherit, none, left, right, both	
float: *type* See the W3C CSS21 Specification (9.5.1) Positioning the float: the "float" property for details.	Indicates how the element, with content wrapped around it, will float on the selected box	Keywords: inherit, none, left, right	
position: *type* See W3C CSS21 Specification (9.3) Choosing a positioning scheme: "position" property for details.	Indicates the element's positioning on the page	Keyword: absolute Keyword: relative Keyword: fixed Keyword: static Keyword: inherit	The element's position is specified with the "top", "right", "bottom", and "left" properties The element's position is calculated according to the normal flow (or the position in normal flow) The element's position is calculated according to the "absolute" model, and the element is fixed with respect to some reference The element's position is a normal box, laid out according to the normal flow. The "top", "right", "bottom", and "left" properties do not apply.

TABLE B.2 CSS 2.1 Common Styles

top: *y* See W3C CSS21 Specification (9.3.2) Box offsets: "top", "right", "bottom", "left" for details.	Indicates the vertical offset from the top of the containing block	CSS units of measure Percentage of the height of containing block Keywords: auto, inherit	
right: *x* See W3C CSS21 Specification (9.3.2) Box offsets: "top", "right", "bottom", "left" for details.	Indicates the horizontal offset from the right edge of the containing block	CSS units of measure Percentage of the width of the containing block Keywords: auto, inherit	
bottom: *y* See W3C CSS21 Specification (9.3.2) Box offsets: "top", "right", "bottom", "left" for details.	Indicates the offset from the bottom of the containing block	CSS units of measure Percentage of the height of containing block Keywords: auto, inherit	
left: *x* See W3C CSS21 Specification (9.3.2) Box offsets: "top", "right", "bottom", "left" for details.	Indicates the offset from the left edge of the containing block	CSS units of measure Percentage of the width of the containing block Keywords: auto, inherit	
z-index: *value* See W3C CSS21 Specification (9.9.1) Specifying the stack level: the "z-index" property for details.	Indicates the level of a box in a stack of overlapping elements	An integer number Keywords: auto, inherit	The stacking number
List Styles (www.w3.org/TR/CSS21/generate.html#q10)			
Style syntax	**Style description**	**Style values**	**Style values description**
list-style: *list-style-type list-style-position list-style-image* See W3C CSS21 Specification list-style (12.5.1) for details.	Specify the list style	Keywords: disc, circle, square, decimal, decimal-leading-zero, lower-roman, upper-roman, lower-alpha, upper-alpha, and inherit	Indicates the type of bullet or number used to create the list
		Keywords: outside, inside	Specifies the position of the marker
		URL	Specifies the URL of the image file to be used as list marker
marker-offset: *length* See the W3C CSS2 Markers: the "marker-offset" property (12.6.1) for details.	Indicates the distance between the list marker and the box enclosing the list	CSS units of measure Keywords: auto, inherit	
Table Styles (www.w3.org/TR/CSS21/tables.html)			
Style syntax	**Style description**	**Style values**	**Style values description**
border-collapse: *type* See W3C CSS21 Specification (17.6) Tables Borders.	Selects a table border model	Keyword: separate	Selects the separated table border model
		Keyword: collapse	Selects the collapsing table border model.
		Keyword: inherit	The style is inherited from the parent element

(Continued)

TABLE B.2 CSS 2.1 Common Styles			
table-layout: *type* See W3C CSS21 Specification (17.5.2) Table width algorithms: the "table-layout" property.	Indicates the algorithm in use for the table layout	Keyword: auto	The layout is automatically established after all cells have been read
		Keyword: fixed	The layout is established after the first row of the table is read
		Keyword: inherit	The layout is inherited from the parent element

SharePoint Designer Tools for Working with HTML, XHTML, and CSS

One of the greatest strengths of SharePoint Designer is that Web developers can use the graphical user interface to create a wide variety of Web pages and Web sites without extensive knowledge of HTML and XHTML. This interface displays the page in WYSIWYG, which means *What You See Is What You Get.* In other words, the Web page looks nearly the same in SharePoint Designer as it does in a browser. The SharePoint Designer 2010 tools enable you to create, edit, format, and optimize HTML and XHTML code. SharePoint Designer also offers new and enhanced tools for creating and managing CSS styles to further refine your Web pages.

In this section, you will review and learn more about the SharePoint Designer core tools for working with HTML, XHTML, and CSS.

Working in SharePoint Designer with HTML and XHTML

SharePoint Designer 2010 excels in offering tools that enable all categories of Web developers, from beginners to professionals, to create, edit, format, and optimize the HTML/XHTML code of your Web pages. Some of the most relevant tools are described here:

- **Code view and Split view**—These two views are extremely helpful for editing and formatting HTML/XHTML. Code view shows the HTML/XHTML code of the Web page. Split view, on the other hand, splits the screen into two horizontal sections: one displaying Design view of the Web page and the second displaying Code view of the Web page. When a designer selects an element or section of a Web page in the Design view, that section is automatically highlighted in the Code view section, and vice versa.
- **IntelliSense tool**—The IntelliSense tool is a great built-in tutor for developers. It provides a content-specific list of HTML/XHTML code entries to select. If you type the opening tag < while editing in Code view, or in the Code view section of Split view, SharePoint Designer displays a list of appropriate HTML/XHTML tags for that specific HTML/XHTML section of the Web page. It provides the same type of assistance when typing attributes for HTML/XHTML tags.
- **XML formatting rules**—The Apply XML Formatting Rules tool is available in Code view and Split view (right-click the body of the Web page and then click Apply XML Formatting Rules) and applies XML formatting rules to the HTML/XHTML code, such as end tags.
- **Accessibility and Compatibility tools**—The Accessibility Checker and Compatibility Checker are extremely powerful for assisting Web developers with creating standard accessible and usable Web sites.

- **Find and Replace HTML tags**—This tool assists Web developers with performing more sophisticated searches using the HTML Rules feature. It enables you to create detailed search rules. With these detailed rules, you can refine the search to include HTML/XHTML tags, as well as their attributes and attribute values.
- **Reformat HTML**—This feature is available in Code view and Split view. (Right-click the body of the Web page, and then click Reformat HTML.) This command reformats the HTML code to follow predefined code formatting options as selected in the Code Formatting tab of the Page Options dialog box. To comply with the W3C requirements for standardization, tag and attribute names must be lowercase. Click the appropriate check boxes on the Page Formatting tab of the Options dialog box.

Working in SharePoint Designer 2010 with CSS

SharePoint Designer 2010 provides new and improved tools for working with CSS, which you can use to further refine your Web page layouts and formatting. CSS tools, such as task panes, assist you in managing, applying, and editing CSS rules and style sheets to design the look of your page.

Understand How SharePoint Designer 2010 Works with CSS

SharePoint Designer provides a CSS Style Application toolbar, CSS layout tools, and Microsoft IntelliSense for CSS. Some of the most relevant tools are described here:

- **Tag and CSS Properties tools**—The Tag Properties and CSS Properties task panes enable you to apply HTML properties (attributes) and CSS properties (styles) to HTML tags.
- **Applying and managing style sheets tools**—The Apply Styles and Manage Styles task panes enable you to easily create, apply, and manage CSS styles.
- **CSS Reports**—The CSS Reports tool helps eliminate errors by providing a list of all unused styles, undefined classes, or mismatched cases (see Figure B.7 for an example). It also provides a comprehensive list of the CSS class, id, and element selectors, as shown in Figure B.8.

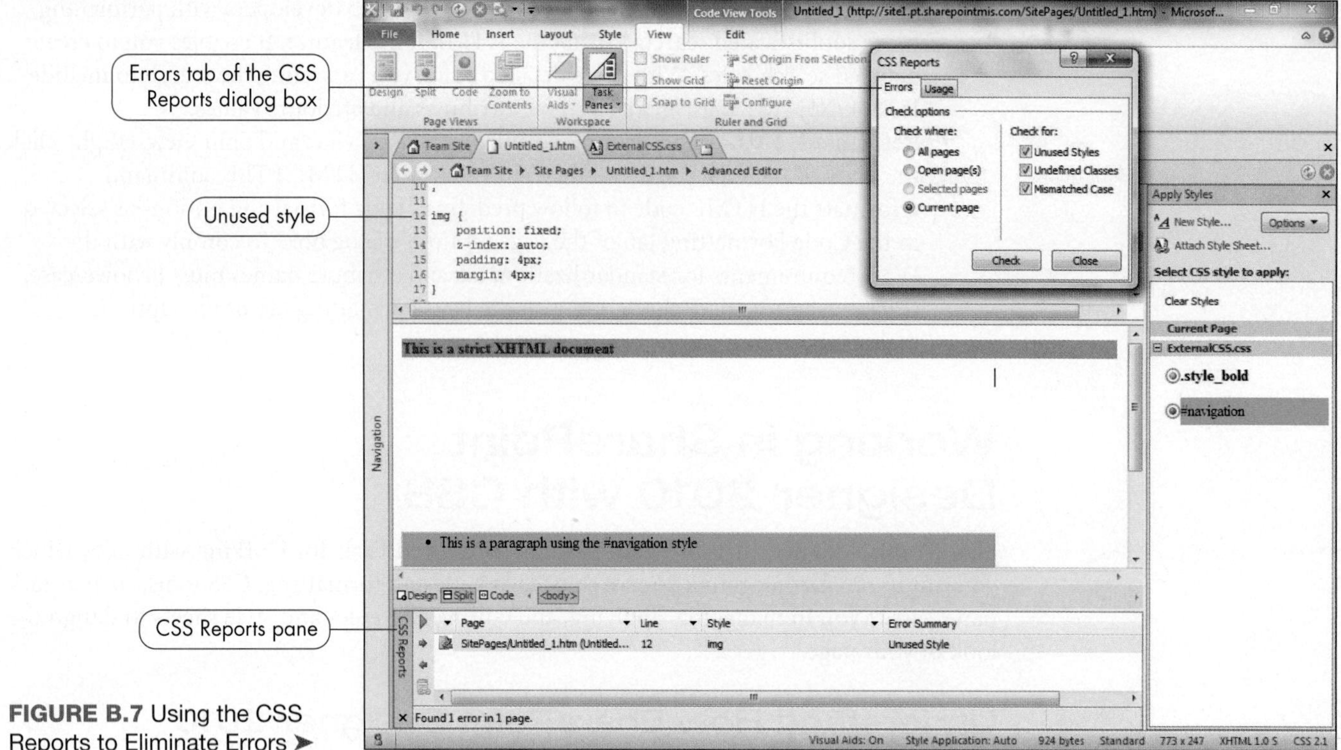

FIGURE B.7 Using the CSS Reports to Eliminate Errors ➤

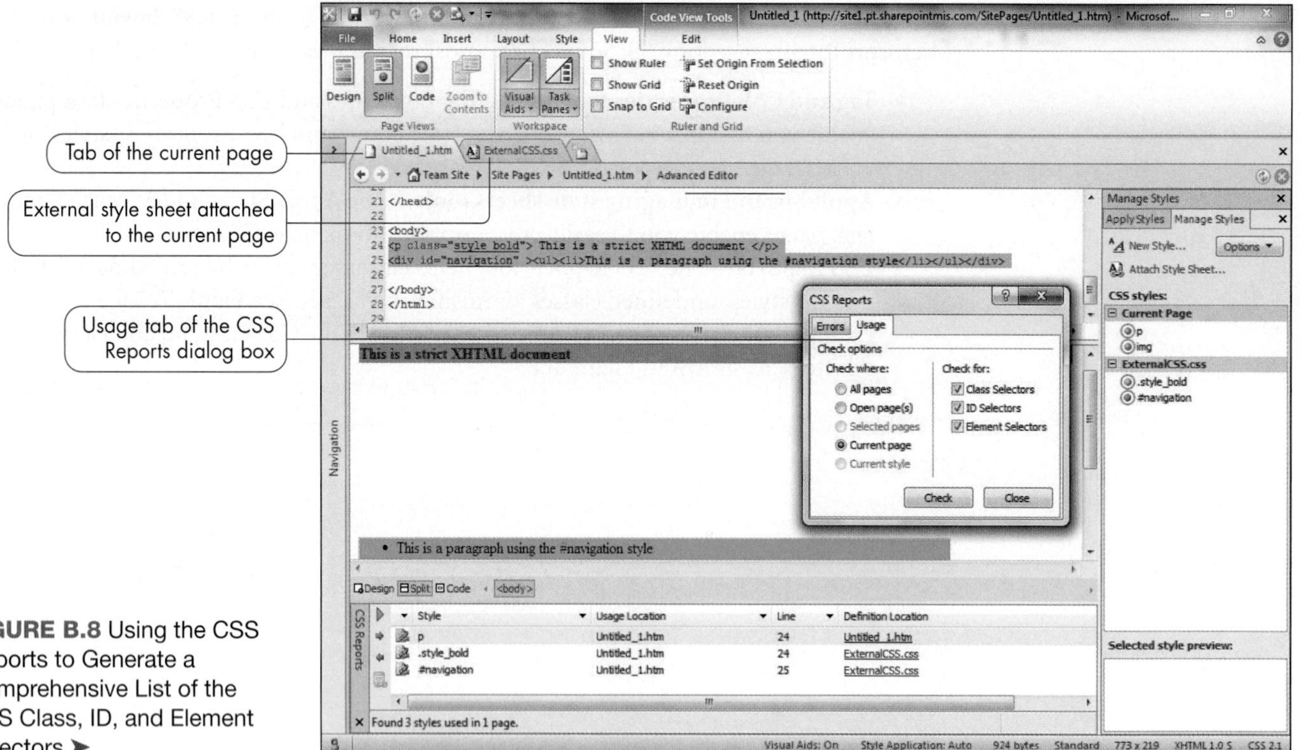

FIGURE B.8 Using the CSS Reports to Generate a Comprehensive List of the CSS Class, ID, and Element Selectors ➤

- **IntelliSense tool**—The IntelliSense tool for CSS acts as a built-in tutor for developers. It provides a content-specific list of CSS code entries to choose from as you complete the HTML/XHTML code (see Figure B.9).

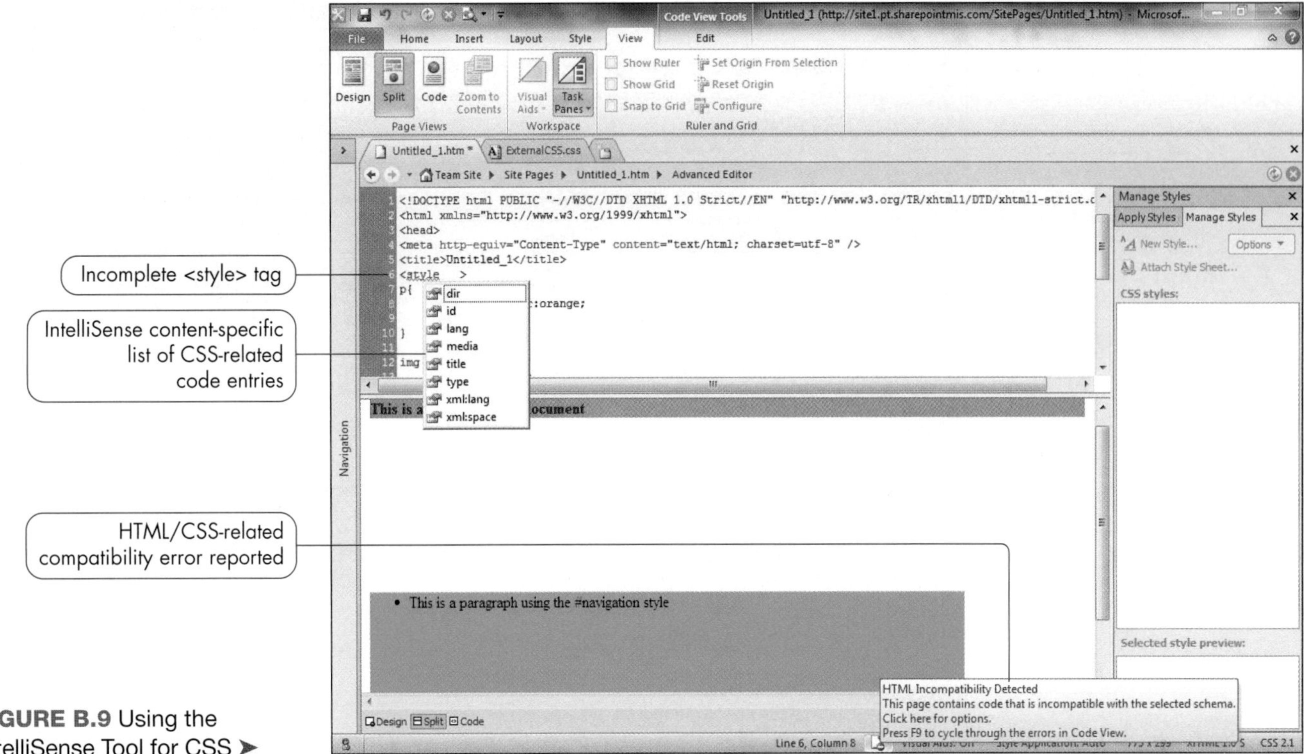

FIGURE B.9 Using the IntelliSense Tool for CSS ➤

- **Compatibility Checker**—The Compatibility Checker enables you to detect areas of your site that do not comply with the Web standards you are targeting. For example, you can check to see that your pages are compatible with XHTML 1.0 Strict and CSS 2.1 (or other combinations of CSS and HTML standards).

Create and Attach CSS Files

Web developers place styles in an external file so they can have a centralized location for managing the styles and applying the styles as needed to any number of pages. After creating the CSS file, the developer attaches it to every page on which they want to use the styles. Once the CSS file is attached, the styles appear in the Manage Styles task pane so that they can be applied to areas on the Web page. SharePoint Foundation built-in templates mainly use styles that reside in external files. SharePoint Designer provides you with three user-friendly methods for creating a new style sheet:

- Using the Asset tab, for the Site Assets library, as shown in Figure B.10a.
- Using New Style, on the Style tab, as shown in Figure B.10b.
- Using the New Style dialog box that you open by clicking the New Style link on the Apply Styles task pane, as shown in Figure B.10c.

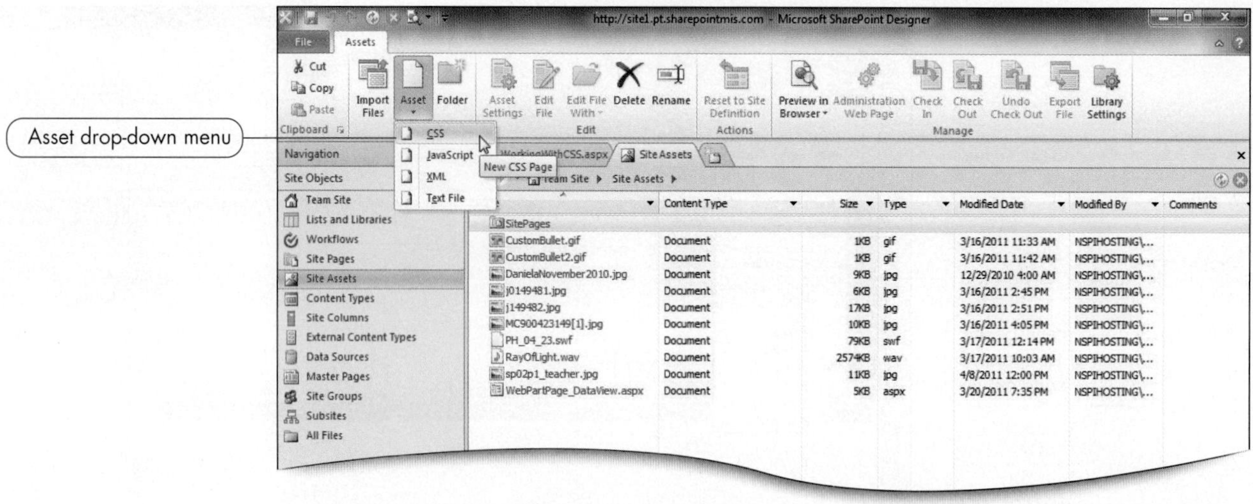

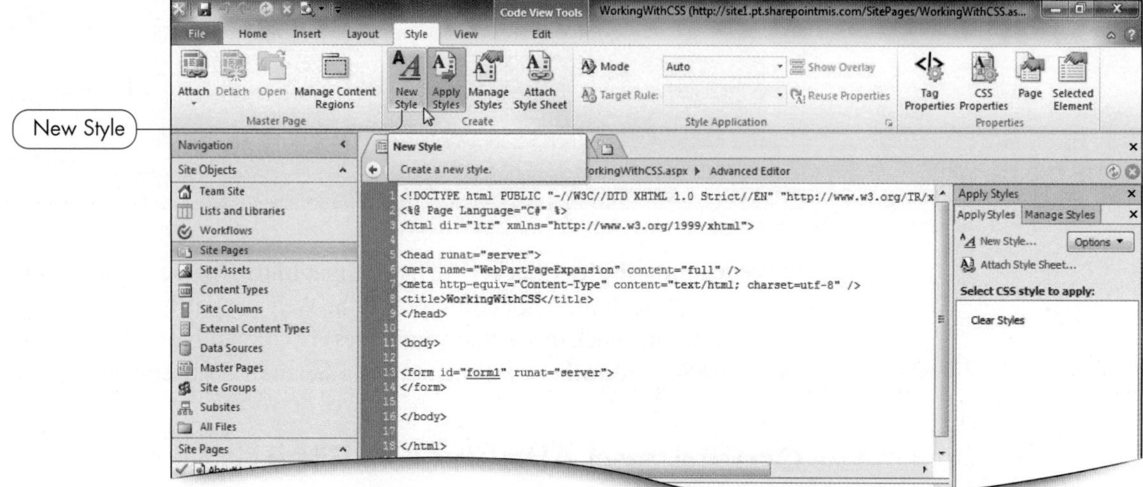

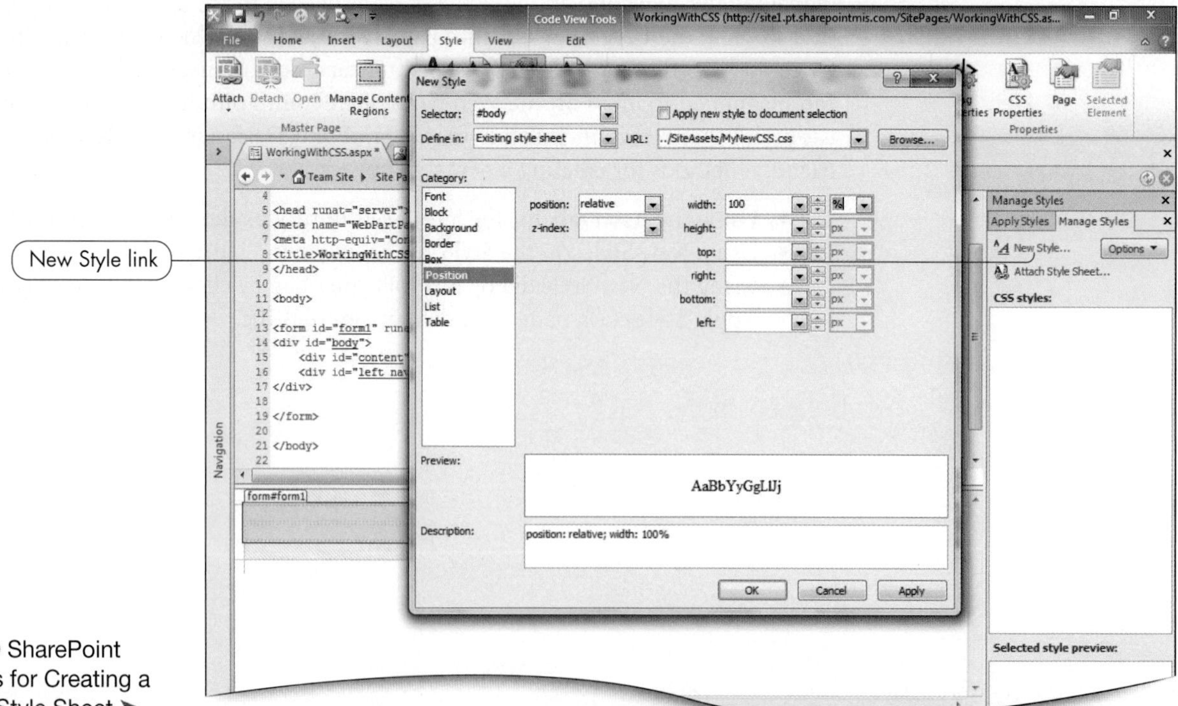

FIGURE B.10 SharePoint Designer Tools for Creating a New External Style Sheet ➤

Once you have created the styles in a CSS file, you attach the style sheet file to the Web pages to apply the newly created styles, as shown in Figure B.11:

- Using the Attach Style Sheet button in the Create group on the Style tab.
- Using the Attach Style Sheet link on the Apply Styles and Manage Styles task pane.

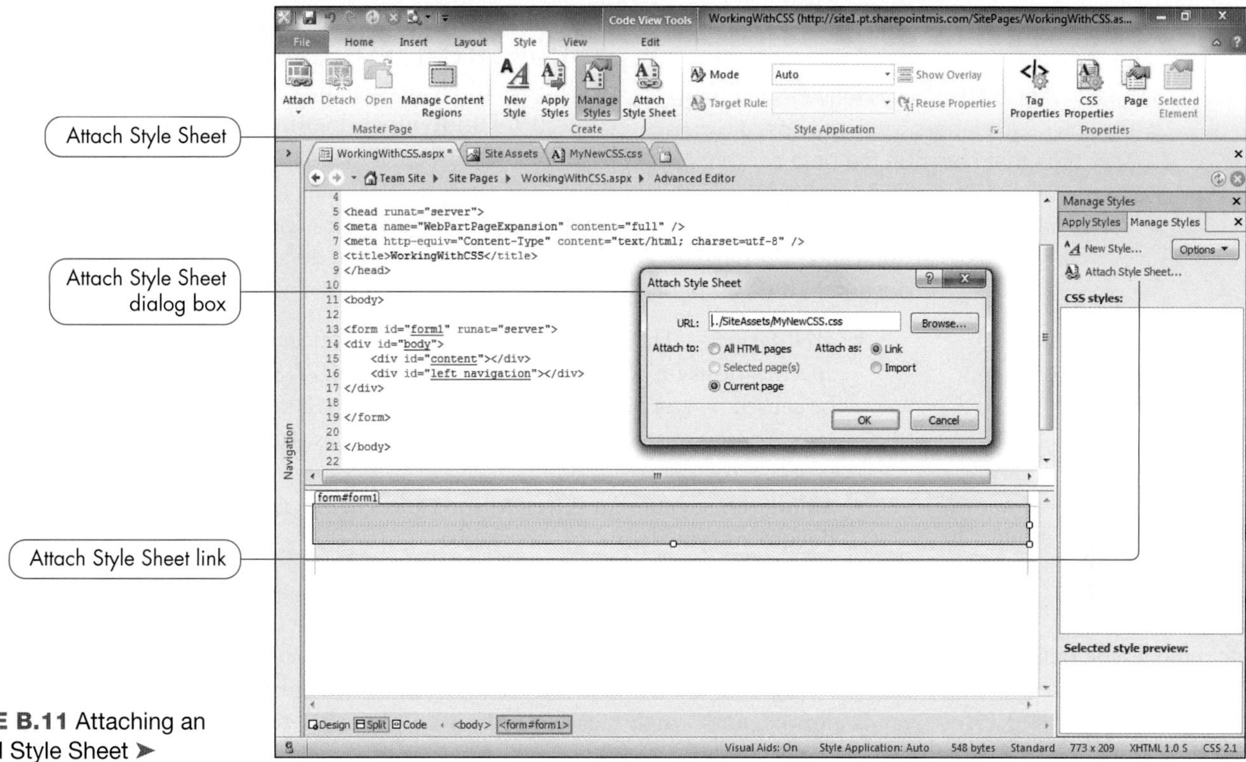

FIGURE B.11 Attaching an External Style Sheet ➤

After you attach the CSS file, the <link> tag shows in the Code view window and the new CSS file is listed in the Manage Styles task pane, as seen in Figure B.12.

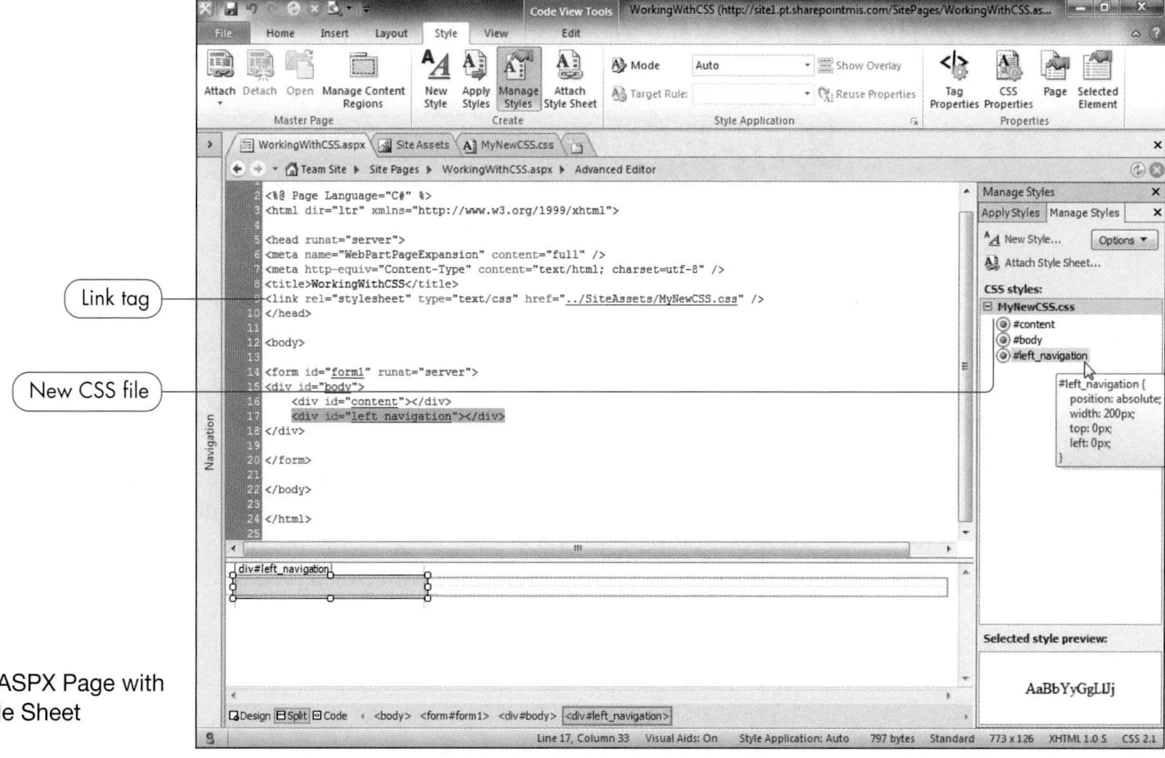

FIGURE B.12 ASPX Page with an External Style Sheet Attached ➤

Extensible Markup Language (XML)

In Appendix A, you were introduced to the fundamentals of the XML markup language, and to the relationship between XML, HTML, XHTML, and CSS. In this section, you will review what you have already learned about XML from this textbook.

Unlike HTML, XML is an extensible language, and allows developers to create specific custom tags that describe the data content for individual documents.

Unlike HTML, XML is an extensible language, and allows developers to create specific custom tags that describe the data content for individual documents. Developers also like XML because an XML parser can be employed to prevent many code errors and because XML has the ability to define data content. After an XML document is created, it is evaluated by an application called *XML parser*. An XML parser interprets the document code to make sure that the document meets the following criteria:

A **well-formed** document contains no syntax errors and obeys all W3C specifications for XML code.

A **valid** document is well-formed and satisfies the rules included in the attached document type definition or schema.

A **document type definition (DTD)** specifies what tags and attributes are used to describe content in an XML document, where each tag is allowed, and which tags can appear within other tags, thus eliminating many code errors that can occur.

A **schema** is an XML document that includes the definition of one or more XML document's content and structure.

- ***Well-formed***—The document contains no syntax errors and obeys all W3C specifications for XML code (www.w3.org/XML/). Some common syntax errors can be caused by ignoring the case sensitivity of XML tags or by omitting one or more tags. As previously discussed, HTML never gives you any type of feedback regarding syntax errors.
- ***Valid***—The document is well formed and satisfies the rules included in the attached document type definition or schema.

XML supports an optional document type definition and XML schema. These documents define all of the components that an XML document is allowed to contain, as well as the structural relationship between the components. A ***document type definition (DTD)*** specifies what tags and attributes are used to describe content in an XML document, where each tag is allowed, and which tags can appear within other tags, thus eliminating many code errors that can occur. The DTD can be internal, included in the XML document itself; external, stored in an external .dtd file; or a combination of internal and external components. The power of a DTD is increased when using external components because the same external DTD can be applied to more than one XML file. A ***schema*** is an XML document that includes the definition of one or more XML document's content and structure. Two of the most popular schemas are the XML schema (www.w3.org/XML/Schema.html), developed by W3C in 2001, and the Microsoft schema, XDR.

TIP The Microsoft XML Parser

The Microsoft XML parser is called MSXML and is built into Internet Explorer versions 5.0 and above. However, it needs to be separately downloaded and installed. The parser used by Mozilla Firefox XML is called Expat. Although these are the most popular, many other XML editors and parsers are available, such as Altova ***[cr]*** XMLSpy ***[cr]*** (www.altova.com/products/xmlspy/xml_editor.html), an award-winning XML editor for modeling, editing, transforming, and debugging XML technologies.

HTML only defines the way Web page content is formatted and displayed on a page. In contrast XML code describes the type of information contained in the document. The XML code does not indicate how data is to be formatted or displayed, as shown in Figure B13b. Consequently, CSS or Extensible Style Sheet Languages (XSLs) are used to build style sheets that can be embedded into the XML document or linked to it, as shown in Figure B13a. The style sheets contain formatting instructions for each element described in the XML document. Using style sheets to format XML documents provides the same formatting features found in HTML, and provides greater flexibility:

- By attaching different style sheets to an XML document, you can change the way it appears in a browser.
- By changing a style sheet attached to multiple XML documents, you can change the way all these XML documents are displayed in a browser.

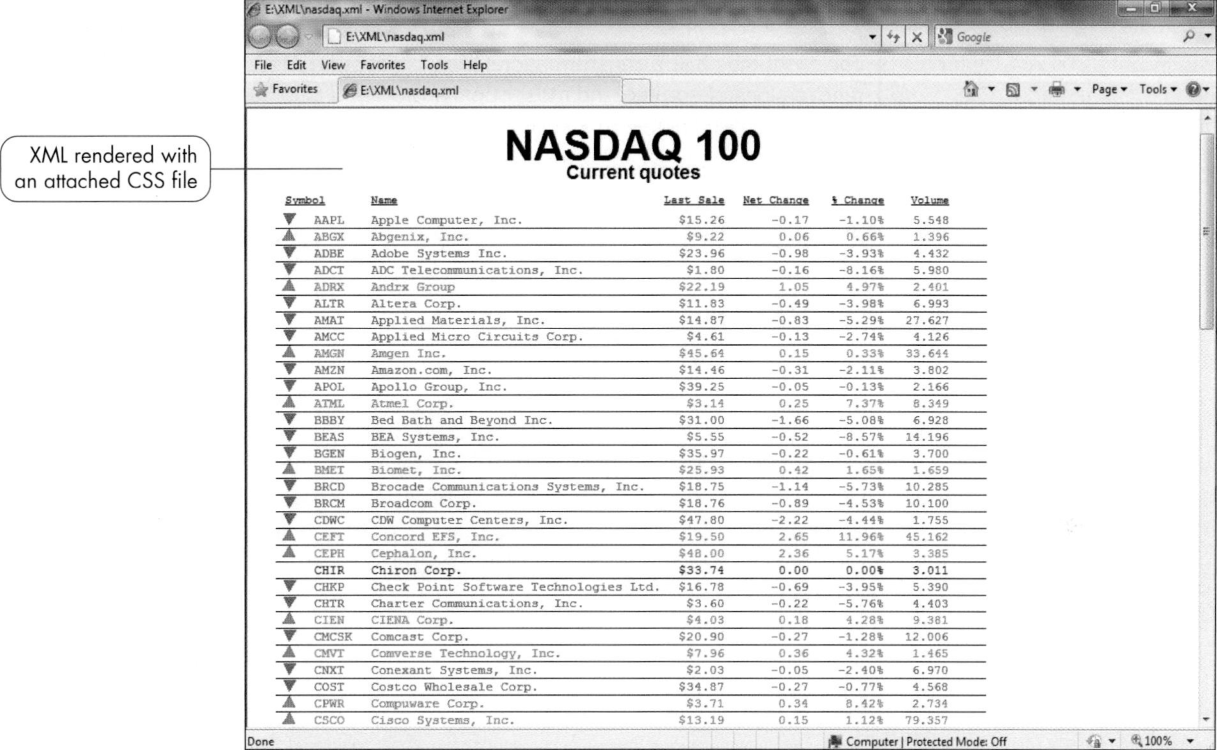

Symbol	Name	Last Sale	Net Change	% Change	Volume
AAPL	Apple Computer, Inc.	$15.26	-0.17	-1.10%	5.548
ABGX	Abgenix, Inc.	$9.22	0.06	0.66%	1.396
ADBE	Adobe Systems Inc.	$23.96	-0.98	-3.93%	4.432
ADCT	ADC Telecommunications, Inc.	$1.80	-0.16	-8.16%	5.980
ADRX	Andrx Group	$22.19	1.05	4.97%	2.401
ALTR	Altera Corp.	$11.83	-0.49	-3.98%	6.993
AMAT	Applied Materials, Inc.	$14.87	-0.83	-5.29%	27.627
AMCC	Applied Micro Circuits Corp.	$4.61	-0.13	-2.74%	4.126
AMGN	Amgen Inc.	$45.64	0.15	0.33%	33.644
AMZN	Amazon.com, Inc.	$14.46	-0.31	-2.11%	3.802
APOL	Apollo Group, Inc.	$39.25	-0.05	-0.13%	2.166
ATML	Atmel Corp.	$3.14	0.25	7.37%	8.349
BBBY	Bed Bath and Beyond Inc.	$31.00	-1.66	-5.08%	6.928
BEAS	BEA Systems, Inc.	$5.55	-0.52	-8.57%	14.196
BGEN	Biogen, Inc.	$35.97	-0.22	-0.61%	3.700
BMET	Biomet, Inc.	$25.93	0.42	1.65%	1.659
BRCD	Brocade Communications Systems, Inc.	$18.75	-1.14	-5.73%	10.285
BRCM	Broadcom Corp.	$18.76	-0.89	-4.53%	10.100
CDWC	CDW Computer Centers, Inc.	$47.80	-2.22	-4.44%	1.755
CEFT	Concord EFS, Inc.	$19.50	2.65	11.96%	45.162
CEPH	Cephalon, Inc.	$48.00	2.36	5.17%	3.385
CHIR	Chiron Corp.	$33.74	0.00	0.00%	3.011
CHKP	Check Point Software Technologies Ltd.	$16.78	-0.69	-3.95%	5.390
CHTR	Charter Communications, Inc.	$3.60	-0.22	-5.76%	4.403
CIEN	CIENA Corp.	$4.03	0.18	4.28%	9.381
CMCSK	Comcast Corp.	$20.90	-0.27	-1.28%	12.006
CMVT	Comverse Technology, Inc.	$7.96	0.36	4.32%	1.465
CNXT	Conexant Systems, Inc.	$2.03	-0.05	-2.40%	6.970
COST	Costco Wholesale Corp.	$34.87	-0.27	-0.77%	4.568
CPWR	Compuware Corp.	$3.71	0.34	8.42%	2.734
CSCO	Cisco Systems, Inc.	$13.19	0.15	1.12%	79.357

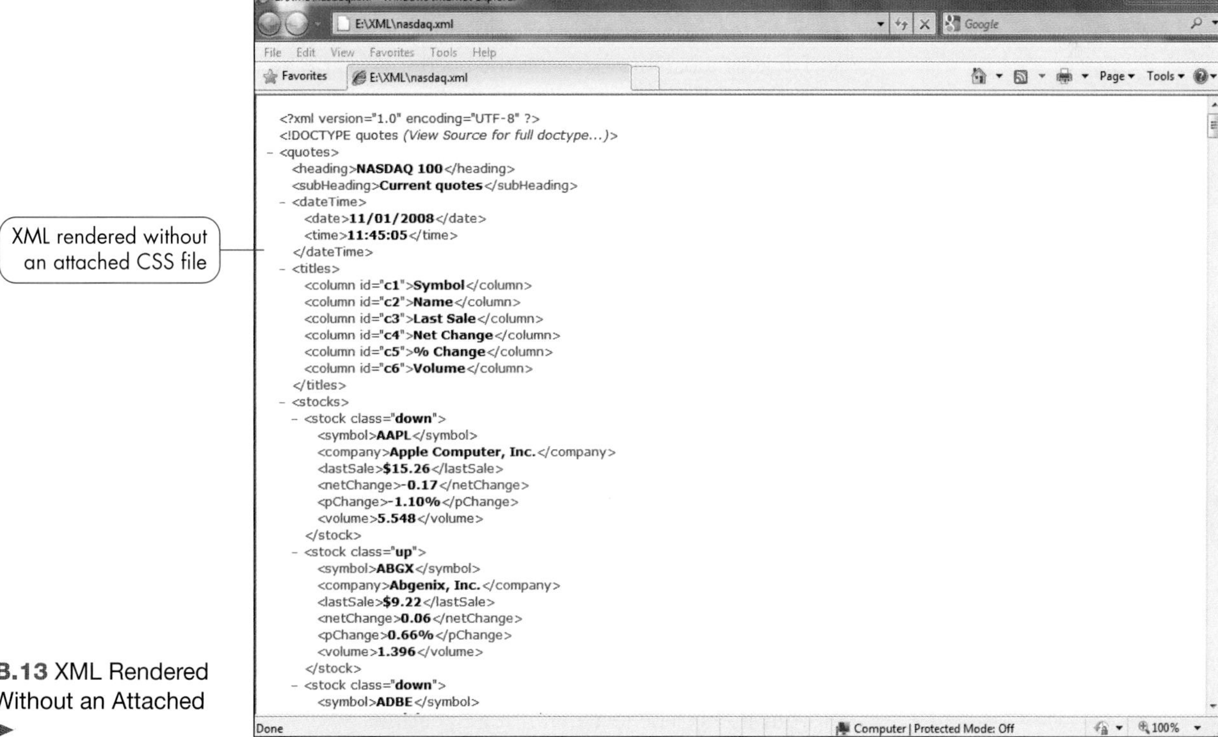


```
<?xml version="1.0" encoding="UTF-8" ?>
<!DOCTYPE quotes (View Source for full doctype...)>
- <quotes>
    <heading>NASDAQ 100</heading>
    <subHeading>Current quotes</subHeading>
  - <dateTime>
      <date>11/01/2008</date>
      <time>11:45:05</time>
    </dateTime>
  - <titles>
      <column id="c1">Symbol</column>
      <column id="c2">Name</column>
      <column id="c3">Last Sale</column>
      <column id="c4">Net Change</column>
      <column id="c5">% Change</column>
      <column id="c6">Volume</column>
    </titles>
  - <stocks>
    - <stock class="down">
        <symbol>AAPL</symbol>
        <company>Apple Computer, Inc.</company>
        <lastSale>$15.26</lastSale>
        <netChange>-0.17</netChange>
        <pChange>-1.10%</pChange>
        <volume>5.548</volume>
      </stock>
    - <stock class="up">
        <symbol>ABGX</symbol>
        <company>Abgenix, Inc.</company>
        <lastSale>$9.22</lastSale>
        <netChange>0.06</netChange>
        <pChange>0.66%</pChange>
        <volume>1.396</volume>
      </stock>
    - <stock class="down">
        <symbol>ADBE</symbol>
```

FIGURE B.13 XML Rendered with and Without an Attached CSS File ➤

Extensible Stylesheet Language Transformation (XSLT) is a subset of XSL that enables you to display XML data on a Web page and "transform" it in HTML.

Extensible Stylesheet Language Transformation (XSLT) is a subset of XSL that enables you to display XML data on a Web page and "transform" it into HTML. XSLT pages are used to created client-side or server-side XML transformations. If you perform a server-side XML transformation, the server converts it into HMTL, whereas when you perform a client-side transformation the browser will handle the transformation.

> **TIP** Extensible Stylesheet Language Transformation (XSLT)
>
> The client-side XSLT transformations are still not supported by all browsers. However the current versions of some of the most popular browsers (such as Internet Explorer 6+ and Firefox 3+) do support client-side XSLT transformations.

Keeping in Mind Good Web Design Rules

Some excellent Web sites synthesize best practices when it comes to Web design. Some of the best are Stefan Mischook's "The Do's and Don'ts of Web Site Design" (www.killersites.com/articles/articles_dosAndDontsWebDesign.htm) and Jeff Johnson's "Web Bloopers: 60 Common Web Design Mistakes, and How to Avoid Them" (http://ebooksfreedownload.org/2011/03/web-bloopers-60-common-web-design-mistakes-and-how-to-avoid-them.html).

In this section, you will review some rules of good Web design. Adapted from experience and other sources, the following Web design Do's and Don'ts should help guide you as a new designer.

The Do's

- Do use color wisely. Colors should be used primarily to emphasize text titles, sections, and keywords. Remember that people who are colorblind might not be able to see all colors. Use color as background for your Web pages, but ensure that it does not diminish the readability of your Web page content.
- Do keep a balance between the need to use graphic, audio, and video files to enrich content; the need to maintain the "look" of your Web page; and the need to keep the size and amount of time required to display of your Web pages at a reasonable level. Use images as backgrounds for your Web pages as long as they do not diminish the readability of your Web page content. Always add meaningful, alternative text and caption text to all graphic, audio, and video files employed in your Web pages so that visitors who are visually or hearing impaired can fully understand what is represented.
- Do regularly update the content of your Web pages and remove any content that is outdated or no longer relevant.
- Do implement a consistent style for all the Web pages included in a Web site by employing Web page and Web site templates and CSS external style sheets.
- Do build easy-to-navigate Web pages and Web sites.

The Don'ts

- Do not allow broken links and, whenever possible, do not publish Web pages that are still under development.
- Do not use the underline style for the text of your Web pages, because it might lead your users to believe that it is a hyperlink.

- Do not use sound as a background on your Web pages if you do not want to annoy your visitors.
- Do not use unethical wording, and try to avoid using professional or "street" jargon.
- Do not use any kind of copyrighted material unless you have official permission to do so.

KEY TERMS

Class selector ***p.451***
Declaration ***p.450***
Declaration block ***p.450***
Document type definition (DTD) ***p.466***
Extensible Style Sheet Language (XSL) ***p.449***
Extensible Stylesheet Language Transformation (XSLT) ***p.468***
External style ***p.449***
ID selector ***p.452***
Inline style ***p.449***
Internal style ***p.449***
Property ***p.450***
Schema ***p.466***
Selector ***p.450***
Style sheet ***p.449***
Style sheet language ***p.449***
Tag selector ***p.450***
Valid ***p.466***
Value ***p.450***
Well-formed ***p.466***
XHTML ***p.442***

SHAREPOINT

APPENDIX C ACCESSIBILITY AND COMPATIBILITY

Designing and Building Accessible and Compatible Web Sites and Web Pages

In this appendix, you will learn about the Web design guidelines that are included in the W3C's Web Accessibility Initiative (WAI) and subsection 1194.22 of Section 508 law concerning Web-based intranet and Internet information and applications. This appendix explains what it means to design for accessibility and compatibility, while discussing the SharePoint Designer 2010 Accessibility Reports tool and Compatibility Reports tool to maximize the accessibility and compatibility of your Web pages. You are also introduced to some of the most popular assistive and adaptive technologies. At the time this manuscript was finalized, the U.S. Access Board was working on updating electronic and information technology guidelines (www.access-board.gov/508.htm). Upon the official publishing of the revised Section 508, this appendix and any related information published in this textbook will be updated as soon as possible.

Web Accessibility Guidelines

According to the 2000 U.S. Census, approximately 19.4% of non-institutionalized people have a disability. Severe disabilities were reported for almost half of this group. To learn more about the Census and people who have disabilities, go to http://factfinder.census.gov/, click Topics on the vertical navigation bar, and then click Disability. As Article 27.1 of the Universal Declaration of Human Rights (www.un.org/Overview/rights.html) states, "Everyone has the right freely to participate in the cultural life of community, to enjoy the arts and to share in scientific advancement and its benefits." Today, the Internet is an important component of our professional and personal lives, so it is "essential that the Web be accessible in order to provide equal access and equal opportunity to people with disabilities" according to the World Wide Web Consortium (www.w3.org/standards/webdesign/ accessibility). Accessibility is so important that the U.N. Convention on the Rights of Persons with Disabilities (www.un.org/disabilities/default.asp?navid=12&pid=150) recognized Web accessibility as a basic human right. To learn more about the social, technical, financial, legal, and policy factors of Web accessibility, review "Developing a Web Accessibility Business Case for Your Organization: Overview" on the W3C Web site (www.w3.org/WAI/bcase/).

In this section, you will be introduced to the W3C Web Accessibility Initiative guidelines and Section 508 law. The "More Information" section of this appendix provides you with a resource list of related Web sites.

TIP International Accessibility and Disability Initiatives

Efforts around the world focus on raising awareness of accessibility and disability, and maximizing World Wide Web (WWW) accessibility. The W3C WAI strives to maximize the accessibility of the WWW in five primary areas: technology, guidelines, education , outreach, and research and development. The W3C Web Content Accessibility Guidelines 2.0 are being adopted by many governments around the world, including the United Kingdom, Japan, Canada, and Australia.

W3C Web Accessibility Initiative (WAI)

In 1997, the W3C launched the Web Accessibility Initiative to improve Web functionality for people with disabilities (www.w3.org/WAI/) by producing the Web Content Accessibility Guidelines 1.0 (WCAG 1.0). These guidelines have since been updated to WCAG 2.0 (www.w3.org/TR/WCAG20/).

The original WCAG1.0 defined three priorities, which are listed in Table C.1. Checkpoints were defined and each was assigned a priority level by the Web Content Accessibility Guidelines Working Group (WCAG WG) based on its impact on the Web page's accessibility.

TABLE C.1 W3C WCAG 1.0 Priority Levels

Priority Levels	Description
I	Checkpoint must be satisfied. It is a basic requirement to enable some groups to access Web documents.
II	Checkpoint should be satisfied, removing significant barriers to accessing Web documents.
III	Checkpoint might be addressed, improving access to Web documents.

When organizations revisit or create Web accessibility policies, the W3C recommends using WCAG 2.0. Rather than focus on checkpoints, the WCAG 2.0 is based on the four layers of principles, guidelines, success criteria, and sufficient and advisory techniques.

- Four principles provide the foundation for Web accessibility: perceivable, operable, understandable, and robust. These principles are detailed at www.w3.org/TR/UNDERSTANDING-WCAG20/intro.html#introduction-fourprincs-head.
- Twelve guidelines are listed under the principles, and provide basic goals for making content more accessible to users with different disabilities. These goals provide a framework and overall objectives to guide Web developers. The guidelines are explained at www.w3.org/TR/WCAG20/.
- Each guideline is supplemented with testable success criteria, which can be used where requirements and conformance testing are necessary. Conformance has three levels: A (lowest), AA, and AAA (highest). Additional information is available at www.w3.org/TR/UNDERSTANDING-WCAG20/conformance.html#uc-levels-head.
- Techniques are provided by WCAG 2.0 for meeting the success criteria and the guidelines. The techniques are identified as sufficient for complying with the success criteria or as advisory. Refer to www.w3.org/TR/UNDERSTANDING-WCAG20/intro.html#introduction-layers-techs-head for additional information.

Web content developers can elect to comply with WCAG 1.0, WCAG 2.0, or both. The W3C currently recommends the use of WCAG 2.0 standards, especially as new content is developed or as content is updated. This means that in some cases the legacy content may comply with WCAG 1.0, whereas the newest information on the Web site complies with WCAG 2.0.

Section 508 Law

In 1998, the Section 508 Law (www.section508.gov/) was enacted by Congress as an amendment to the Rehabilitation Act of 1973, "to require Federal agencies to make their electronic and information technology accessible to people with disabilities." This amendment ensures that all Americans have access to information, particularly from federal agencies and organizations that do business with the federal government. Under Section 508 (29 U.S.C. 794d), agencies must give people with disabilities access to information that is comparable to the access available to others. Subsection 1194.22 of the Section 508 Guidelines discusses maximizing the accessibility of Web sites.

The U.S. Access Board (www.access-board.gov/) is a federal agency that develops and maintains design requirements for a variety of environments, including electronic and information technology. It also provides technical assistance and training, as well as enforcing accessibility standards for federally funded facilities.

The U.S. Access Board reviews and updates access standards for electronic and information technology covered by Section 508 of the Rehabilitation Act (www.access-board.gov/508.htm). These standards, initially published in 2000, cover products and technologies procured by the federal government, including computer hardware and software, Web sites, phone systems, fax machines, and copiers. The U.S. Access Board guidelines also affect telecommunications products and equipment covered by Section 255 of the Telecommunications Act (go to www.access-board.gov/telecomm). An advisory committee of the U.S. Access Board, the Telecommunications and Electronic and Information Technology Advisory Committee, or TEITAC (http://teitac.org/), reviews telecommunications standards and guidelines, and recommends changes. The committee's membership includes representatives from industry, disability groups, standard-setting bodies in the United States and abroad, and government agencies, among others.

Principles of Good Web Page Design

... there are certain key factors that all professional designers and Web developers consider essential to good Web page design....

A Web page is a pure representation of the designer's professional and personal background, expertise in solving technical design and development issues, and last but most definitely not least, personal creativity and artistic skills. However, there are certain key factors that all professional designers and Web developers consider essential to good Web page design, as described in Table C.2.

TABLE C.2 Key Design Factors for Developing Good Web Pages

Design Factor	Description
Usability	A usable Web site is easy to navigate and accessible. You should always keep in mind that you design your Web pages for the people who will be visiting them. The quality of your design will be measured by visitors' satisfaction.
Navigation	Web pages must be easy to navigate. Always consider using Web page templates, link bars, hyperlinks, and bookmarks to create a clear, robust navigational structure for your Web pages.
Compatibility	Web pages should appear the same (or as close as possible) in all browsers, in all versions of the same browser, and on all computer platforms.
Accessibility	Web pages need to be accessible to all people, including those with different types of total and partial disabilities. You should frequently consult the World Wide Consortium's (W3C) Web site to stay on top of the latest standards and requirements.
Consistency	Web users don't like surprises. They expect the information on a Web page to be laid out as it was on previous pages of the same Web site. To ensure the consistency of your Web pages from the early stages of development, you should always sketch a draft of your Web pages before starting the actual construction and development, and use Web page templates.
Validity	The validity of a Web page needs to be thoroughly tested before it is published. If a Web site doesn't display and function properly, it can cause more pain than gain for your visitors, and they will leave your site to find another one.
Attractiveness	A Web page will be attractive only if it's designed as precisely as a NASA space shuttle and as beautifully as Leonardo da Vinci's *Mona Lisa*. Think like an engineer and an artist when you design a Web page; that's an important part of the key to success.

Designing for Compatibility

A computer platform is defined by the type of hardware and operating system in use on a given computer. Why do Web pages look different when viewed on the same computer platform and when using different Internet browsers, or even different versions of the same browsers? What causes these problems and is there a way you can correct them? Let us find some answers to these questions which continue to challenge Web designers.

> Because you cannot predict the computer platform and browser your users will be using when they view your Web site, it is your responsibility ... to address potential cross-platform and cross-browser compatibility issues....

The cross-platform compatibility issue is the result of the way different browsers or browser versions display Web pages on different computer platforms. The cross-browser compatibility issue is the result of the way different browsers display the same Web pages on the same computer platform. Because you cannot predict the computer platform and browser your users will be using when they view your Web site, it is your responsibility, as the designer, to address potential cross-platform and cross-browser compatibility issues in your design.

The W3C develops specifications, guidelines, software, and tools with a goal of eliminating the cross-browser and cross-platform compatibility issues. The W3C joined with companies, such as Microsoft, IBM, Sun, and Oracle, and governmental organizations, such as the U.S. Department of Health and Human Services (www.hhs.gov/Accessibility.html) to develop a universal standard for Web design and compatibility. Despite these efforts, Web designers often need to develop different versions of the same Web page to make sure their page has the same appearance and functionality in all browsers and on all platforms.

SharePoint Designer comes with tools that can help Web designers avoid some of the cross-platform and cross-browser compatibility issues. The Compatibility Reports tool enables you to verify that the Web pages in your site are in compliance with the W3C Web standards. The Run Compatibility Checker command, as shown in Figure C.1, in the Compatibility task pane, displays the Compatibility Checker dialog box in which you can identify any areas of your Web site that you want to check. The Compatibility Report displayed in the task pane gives details on the parts of the Web site that do not behave as anticipated so you can address these issues.

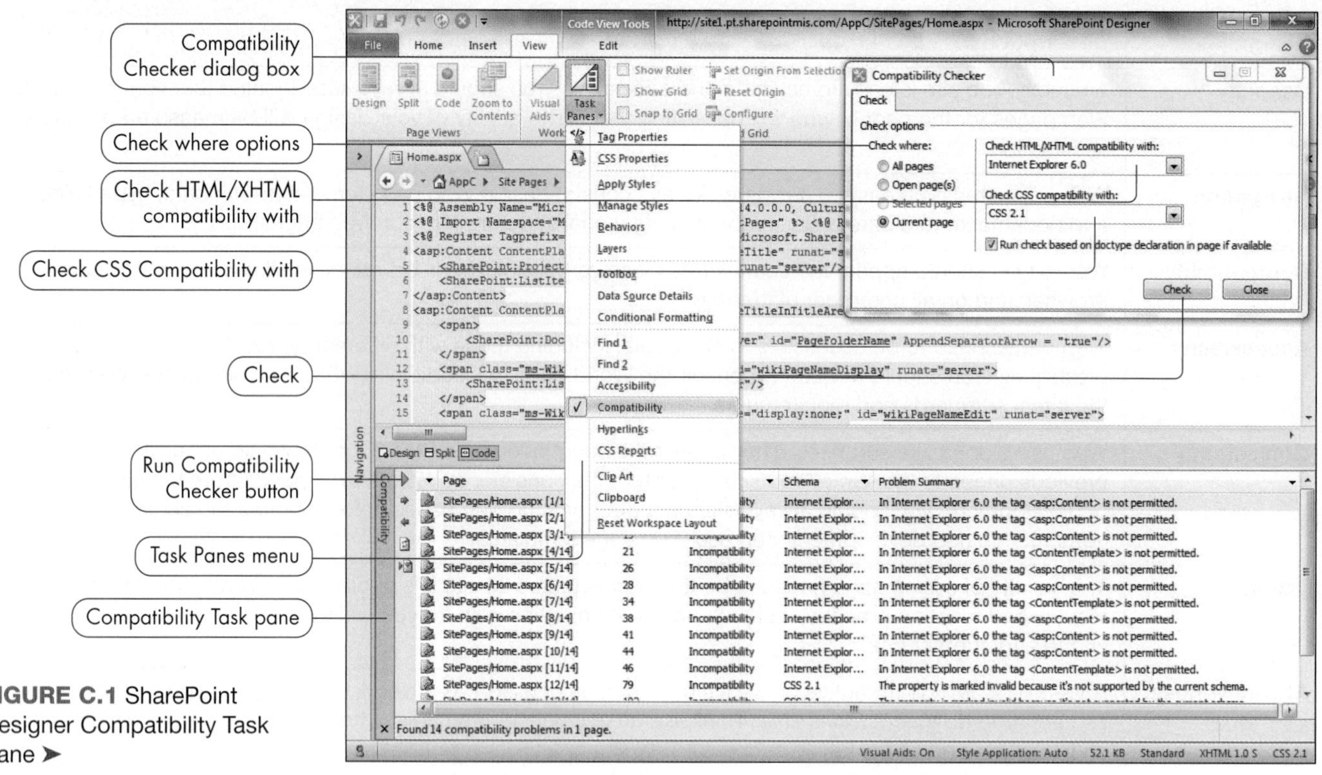

FIGURE C.1 SharePoint Designer Compatibility Task Pane ➤

Using the Compatibility Checker dialog box, you first select the page(s) that will be checked for compatibility under Check where. You then select the appropriate criteria for compatibility checking:

- **Check HTML/XHTML compatibility with**—This Compatibility Checker dialog box option, shown in Figure C.2a, enables designers to improve the HTML/XHTML compatibility of their Web pages with the browsers and the W3C HTML/XHTML standards.

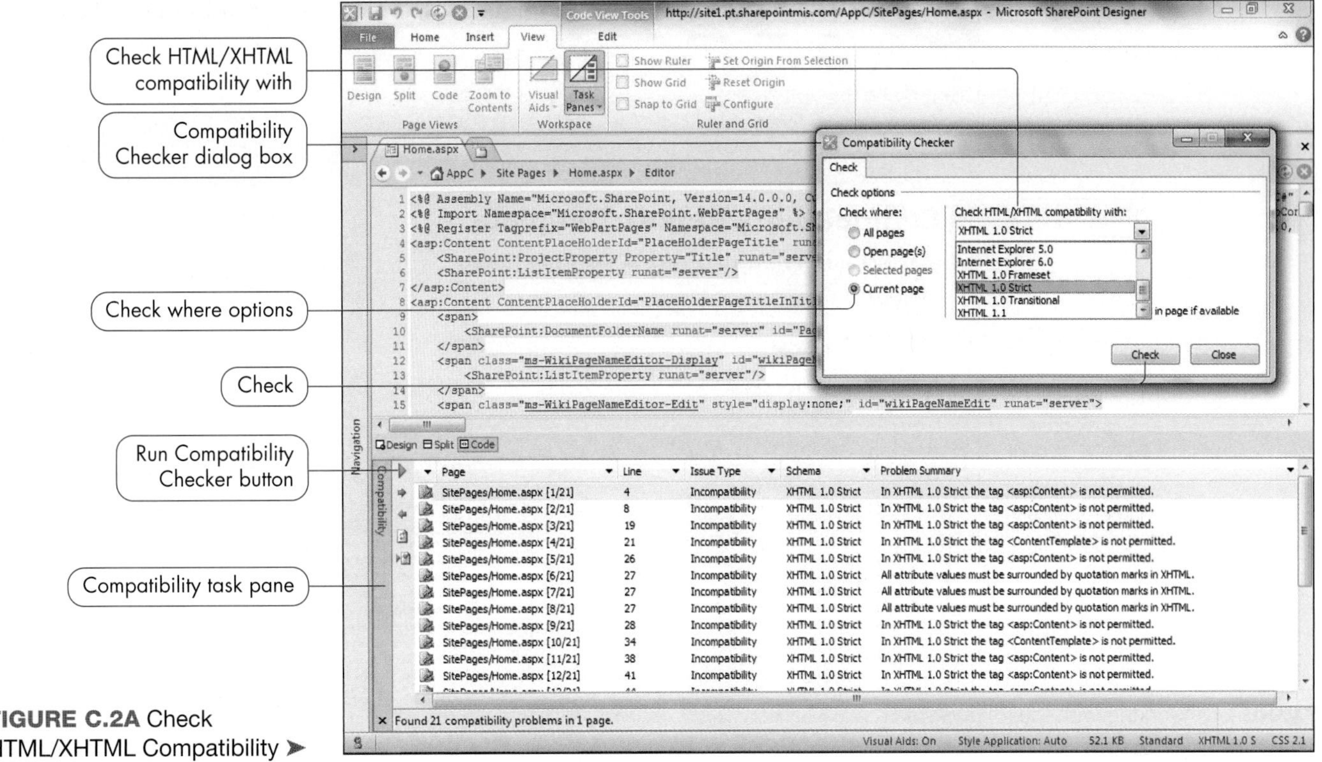

FIGURE C.2A Check HTML/XHTML Compatibility ➤

- **Check CSS compatibility with**—This Compatibility Checker dialog box option, shown in Figure C.2b, enables designers to check the CSS compatibility of their Web pages when using a selected CSS schema (CSS2.1 is the default schema).

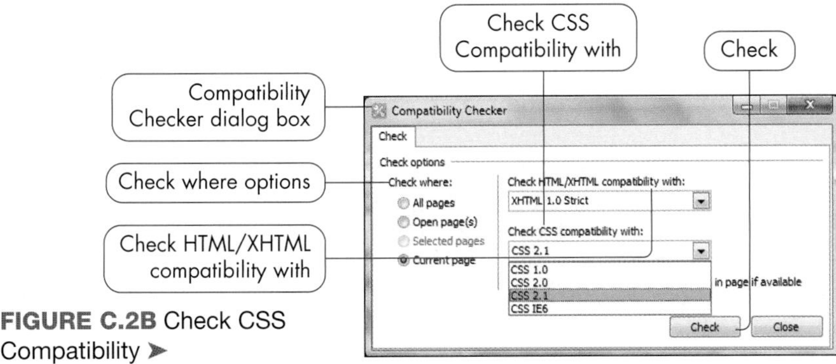

FIGURE C.2B Check CSS Compatibility ➤

When you click the Run Compatibility Checker button, your pages are searched for errors and reported in the Compatibility task pane. If you see an error listed in the Compatibility task pane, click the Generate HTML Report button. SharePoint Designer generates an HTML Compatibility report, as shown in Figure C.3. To fix a compatibility error, double-click the listed error in the Compatibility task pane. SharePoint Designer opens the document (if it is not already open) and selects the code section where the incompatibility is located. You can also right-click an error in the Compatibility task pane and choose Go to page, see Figure C.3, or you can manually switch to Code view and scroll to the indicated line number.

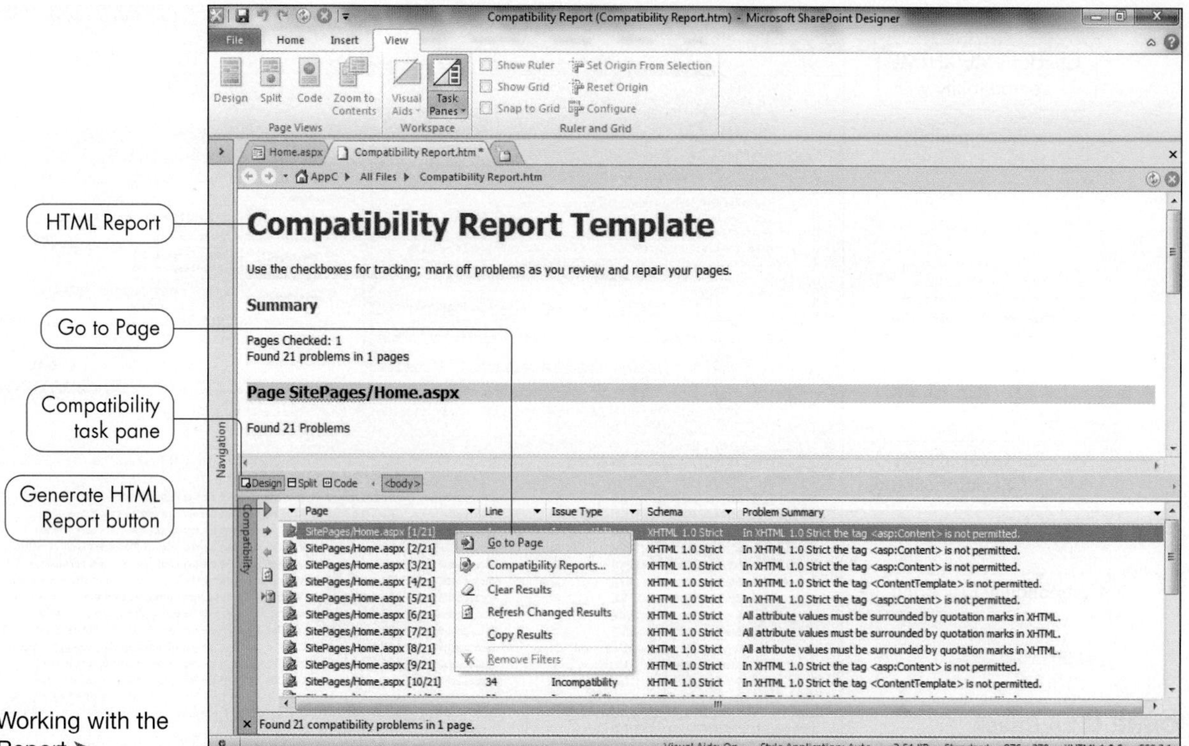

FIGURE C.3 Working with the Compatibility Report ➤

Preview in Browser is also a useful compatibility feature, included in the Preview group of the Home tab, that enables you to select the browser, the browser version, and screen resolution you want to use to preview your Web page. You can also preview a Web page in multiple browsers at the same time, as shown in Figure C.4a. The browsers you want to test need to be installed on your computer in order to use the Preview in Browser feature. Browsers installed on your computer are added to the SharePoint Designer browser list using the Edit Browser List command (see Figure C.4b). Click the Preview in Browser arrow, select the browser, browser version, and screen resolution to preview a Web page.

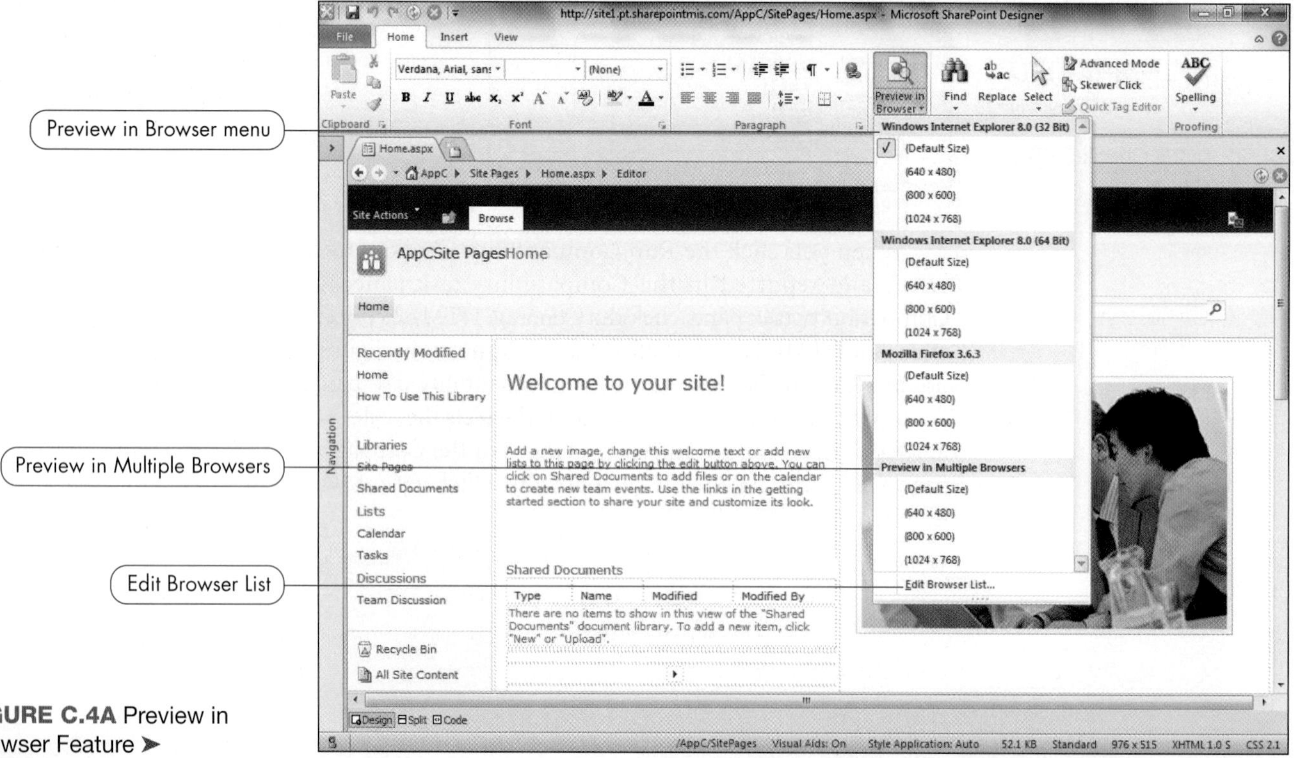

FIGURE C.4A Preview in Browser Feature ➤

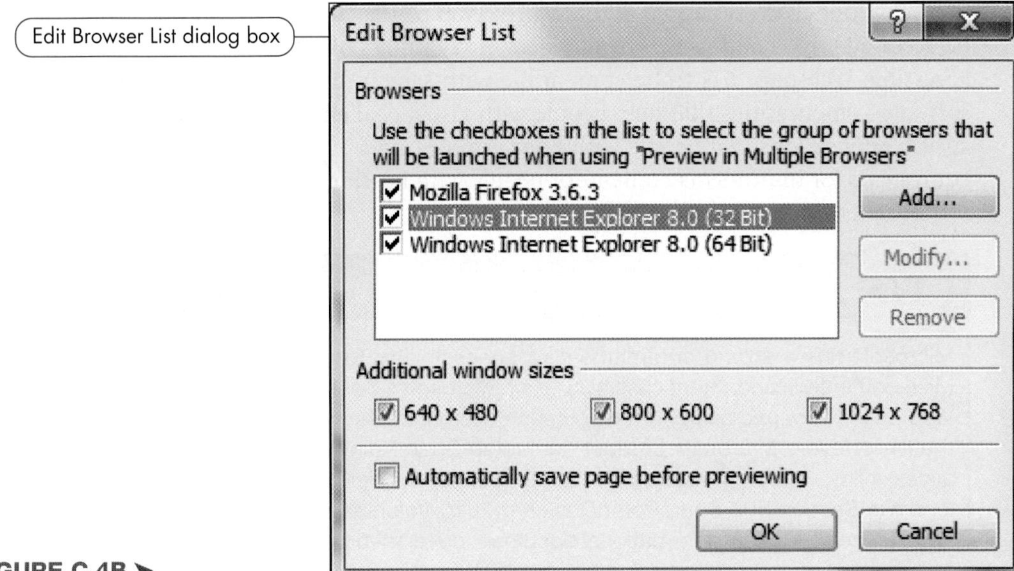

FIGURE C.4B ➤

TIP Testing Your Web Site on Multiple Computer Platforms

Just as it is important to preview your Web page in different browsers and different versions of the same browser, it can also be helpful to preview your page on different computer platforms and on different versions of the same operating system. By doing this you avoid having your Web pages looking different or losing some of their functionalities caused by incompatibilities between computer platforms and versions of the operating system. On a PC, you can normally install only one version of the Windows operating system. Thus, the only way to test Web pages on older versions of Windows is to install them on a separate computer, set up a dual-boot system, or run a software virtualization solution, such as the freeware Windows XP Mode and Windows Virtual PC (www.microsoft.com/windows/virtual-pc/default.aspx).

Windows XP Mode and Windows Virtual PC enable you to run many Windows operating systems, such as Windows XP Mode, from your Windows 7 desktop. The virtualization software is a part of Windows 7 Professional and Ultimate. The Mac (Intel) computers support Windows operating systems. To read more about how Microsoft products are supported by Mac (Intel) computers, see the Microsoft Office Q&A: Intel-Based Macs Web site (www.microsoft.com/mac/default.aspx?pid=macIntelQA).

Designing for Accessibility

The Disability Statistics Center projects that 1.3 million Americans have visual impairments, 1.2 million with hearing impairments, and 1.2 million with impairments affecting the mobility of shoulders and upper extremities. These kinds of impairments are likely to affect their ability to browse the Internet and access your Web page. If your Web site does not comply with the accessibility guidelines, these people might not be able to access your Web pages.

Although accessibility and usability have many related requirements and goals, they are not identical. Usability issues affect all Web users equally. Accessibility applies only to people with disabilities.

Accessibility means that a page can be accessed—read and used—by any person regardless of special needs or disabilities.

What does accessibility have to do with Web pages? ***Accessibility*** means that a page can be accessed—read and used—by any person regardless of special needs or disabilities. An accessible Web page has to be compatible with screen reading and screen magnification software—applications that help people with visual challenges—and with natural language speech applications that people with poor arm or finger motion use. It also must offer text equivalents for multimedia content for people with hearing impairments.

TIP Microsoft's Official Response to Section 508 Regulations

Microsoft has a strong commitment to accessibility. To read more about the history of Microsoft's dedication to accessibility, visit Microsoft's Section 508 of the Rehabilitation Act Web page (www.microsoft.com/resources/government/section508.aspx). Scroll down to see the list of every Microsoft product, including SharePoint Designer 2010, which supports accessibility. Click the Microsoft Office SharePoint Designer 2010 VPAT to read and download the Section 508 SharePoint Designer 2010 Voluntary Product Accessibility Template (VPAT). The VPAT is an informational document developed by a group of companies and government agencies to support the responsibilities of federal employees and private organizations as they comply with Section 508.

SharePoint Designer 2010 contains an Accessibility Report feature. This tool can tell you how well your design complies with the existing W3C and government standards. Click Run Accessibility Checker, on the Accessibility task pane, to display the Accessibility Checker dialog box, as shown in Figure C.5. To use the Accessibility Checker, you select which pages you want the Accessibility Checker to validate. Select the accessibility guidelines you want to check against. The Accessibility Checker can check specific pages or the whole site. Indicate if you wish to view errors, warnings, or a manual checklist.

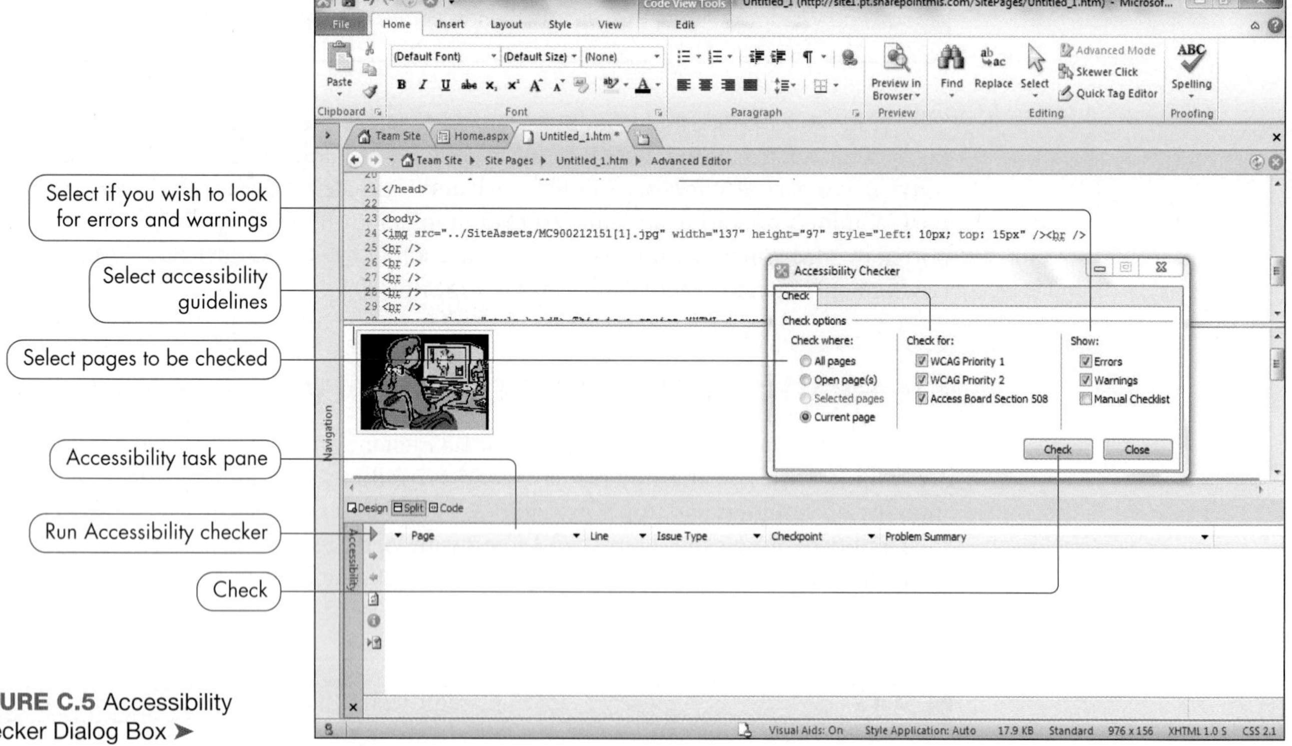

FIGURE C.5 Accessibility Checker Dialog Box ➤

TIP The Accessibility Checker Dialog Box

Because checking an entire Web site might take a long time, you should run the Accessibility Checker for each Web page, as you develop them. However, when you are close to finishing the development of your Web site, you should check the entire Web site.

When you click Check in the Accessibility Checker dialog box, the checker searches your pages for errors and, if you have any errors, they appear in the Accessibility task pane. If you see an error list in the Accessibility task pane, click the Generate HTML Report button. SharePoint Designer generates an Accessibility Report, as shown in Figure C.6.

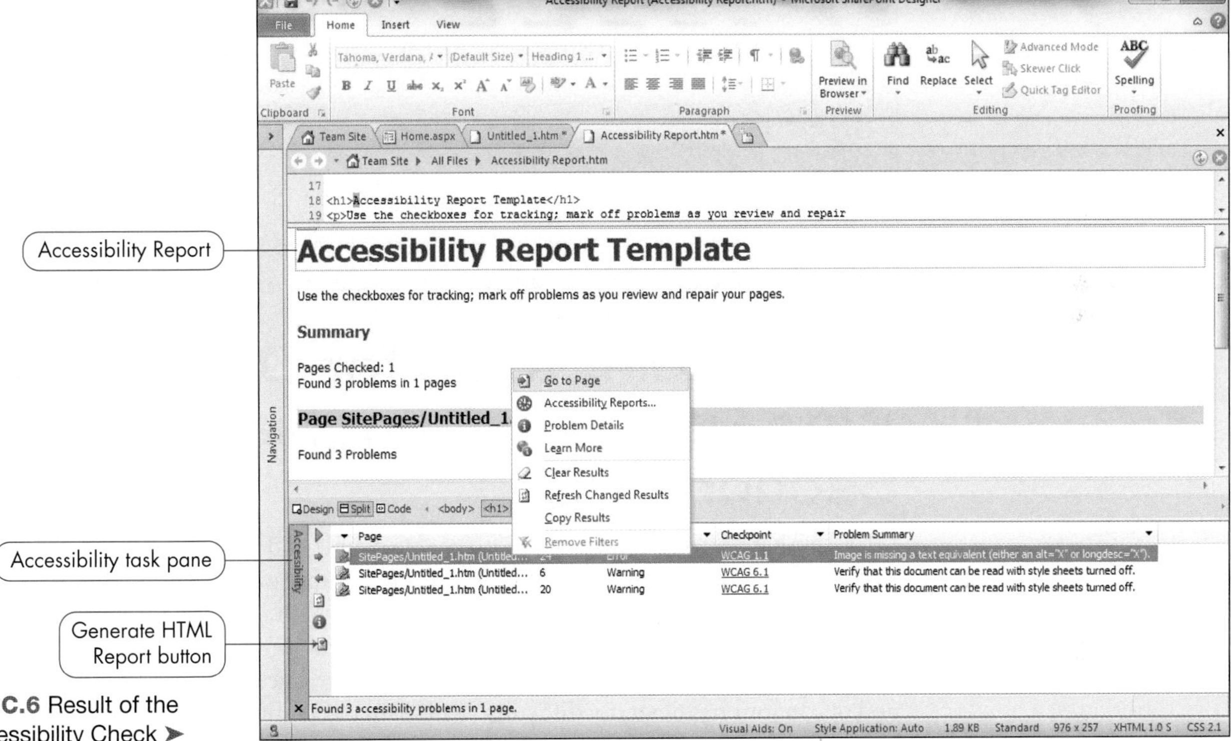

FIGURE C.6 Result of the First Accessibility Check ➤

In the example shown, no alternative text is provided for an image. This is one of the key issues related to Web page accessibility. Alternative text is displayed when the graphic is downloading, when it cannot be found, or when a visitor moves the mouse pointer over the graphic. For people who are visually impaired and rely on a screen-reading application to convert graphics on the screen to spoken words, the presence of the alternative text for any graphic is extremely important.

You can add alternative text to your figures by using the alt attribute in the Tag Properties task pane, as shown in Figure C.7. After you make your corrections, run the Accessibility Checker again to ensure there are no other errors.

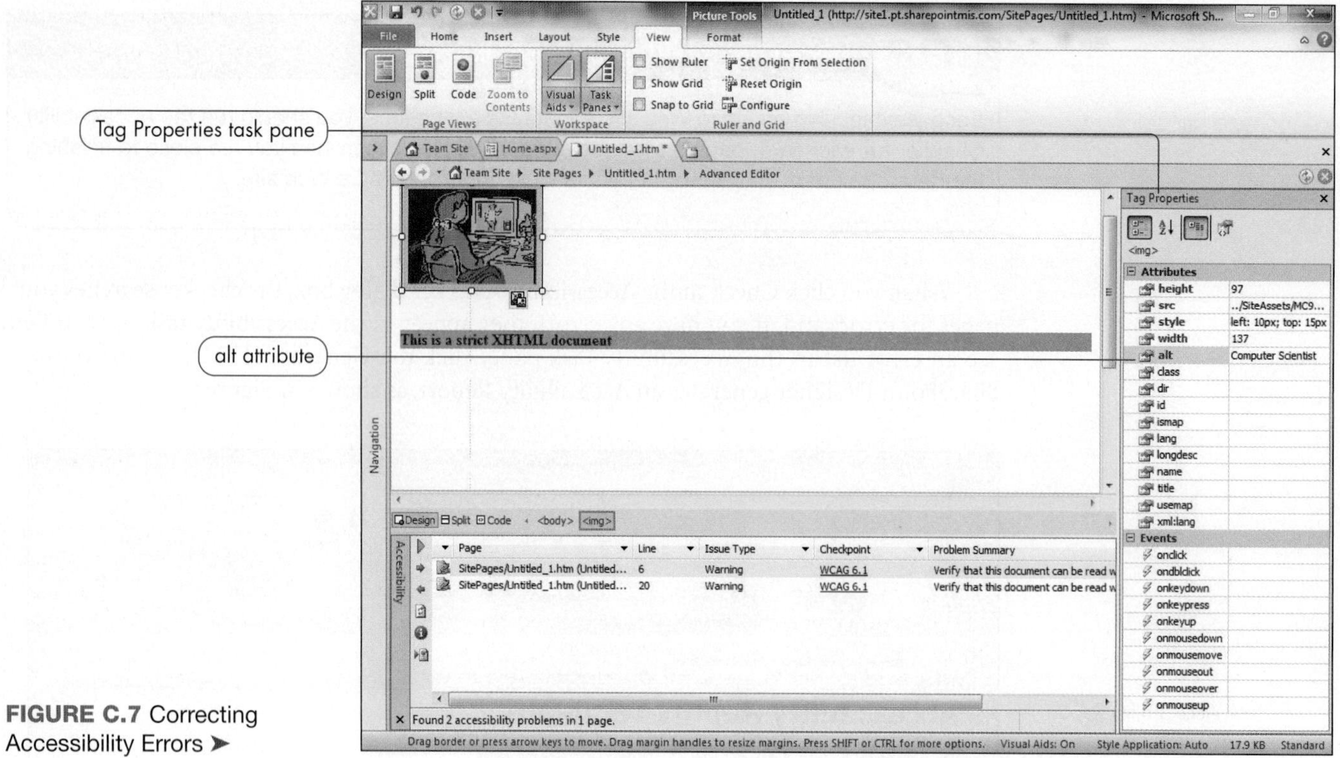

FIGURE C.7 Correcting Accessibility Errors ➤

SharePoint tools for Developing Web Pages in Compliance with Section 508

Microsoft has a strong commitment "to enable people and businesses throughout the world to realize their full potential." In 2003 Microsoft commissioned a study to better understand and address the computing-related needs of people with disabilities (www.microsoft.com/enable/research/phase2.aspx). The study revealed that among the adult computer users in the United States, one in four has a vision impairment, one in five has a hearing impairment, and one in four has dexterity difficulty (with pain or complete loss of feeling in their fingers, hands, wrists, or arms).

The Microsoft "Accessible Technology: A Guide for Educators" (www.microsoft.com/download/en/details.aspx?id=1447) is an excellent source of information for accessibility features and assistive technology products that help individuals with specific disabilities.

The Microsoft and Section 508 Web site provides in-depth documentation about the way each Microsoft application's design, including SharePoint Designer 2010, complies with the Section 508 law (www.microsoft.com/enable/microsoft/section508.aspx). The SharePoint Designer 2010 Accessibility Reports tool enables you to maximize the accessibility of your Web pages by identifying the design elements that do not comply with WCAG 1.0 Priority 1, WCAG 1.0 Priority 2, and Section 508. The Compatibility Reports tool checks for cross-platform and cross-browser usability.

Screen readers convert the content of a Web page into lines of text, using a process called **linearization.**

Many people with disabilities use assistive tools, such as screen readers, when using their computers. For people with vision impairments, screen readers convert the content of a Web page into lines of text, using a process called ***linearization***, and then may further convert the text into audio. During this process the formatting and visual elements are removed because they would not be meaningful in audio. It is your job as a Web developer to ensure that your pages continue to convey their meaning regardless of the method in which the user "views" the page. In this section, you will take a closer look at the 15 paragraphs of subsection 1194.22 and how they can be addressed using SharePoint Designer.

TIP The Web Page Linearization Process

In the Web page linearization process, an assistive technology application converts the page into a text-only format, starting at the upper left corner and proceeding through the page. Images are ignored, but alternative text is retained. When tables are encountered on the page, the text in the table is processed a line at a time starting with the first cell of the first row, and continuing across the columns of the first row. The process is continued on each of the remaining rows. If a table cell contains a nested table, this table is linearized completely before the application moves to the next table cell. Lynx (www.lynxbrowser.com/) is a text-based Web browser, available for UNIX, DOS, and Windows operating systems, which can be used to test the linearization of an entire Web page. It was developed by Academic Computing Services at the University of Kansas. Lynx does not support graphics, plug-ins, JavaScript, Java, or CSS, making it a good tool for testing whether your page is readable when the linearization process is applied to it. A free Web-based Lynx viewer, developed by DJ Delorie (www.delorie.com/web/lynxview.html), enables you to submit a URL and view the Web page as linearized text.

Working with Graphics and Images

1194.22 (a) A text equivalent for every non-text element shall be provided (e.g., via "alt," "longdesc," or in element content).

The first paragraph of subsection 1194.22 requires that all graphic images have alternative text attached. If no alternative text is present, the screen reader applications attempts to read the graphic image file, which will not help a visually impaired user. You can use the alt attribute, for short descriptions, or the longdesc attribute, if a longer description is required. A long description is a URL that points the viewer to another Web page where more detail about the graphic is available. Keep in mind that not all browsers support the long description tag, so you should always include an alternative tag as well. Some decorative graphic elements that you use repeatedly, such as graphic bullets, do not require alternative tags. You can simply add the alternative tag and assign it an empty text string (alt=" ").

SharePoint Designer automatically opens the Accessibility Properties dialog box when you insert a picture on a Web page, enabling you to add the alt or longdesc attribute, as shown in Figure C.8.

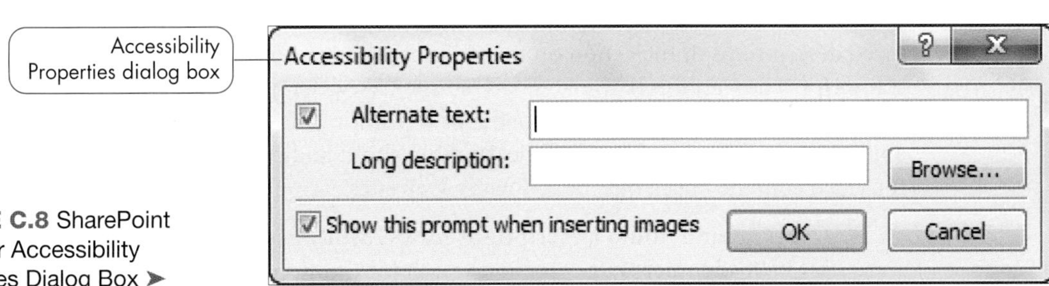

FIGURE C.8 SharePoint Designer Accessibility Properties Dialog Box ➤

In SharePoint Designer, you can also add the alt or longdesc attribute to any inline image by right-clicking the image, clicking Picture Properties on the shortcut menu, and then clicking the General tab on the Picture Properties dialog box, as shown in Figure C.9. In browsers that support the longdesc attribute, the value assigned to the attribute is displayed as a link.

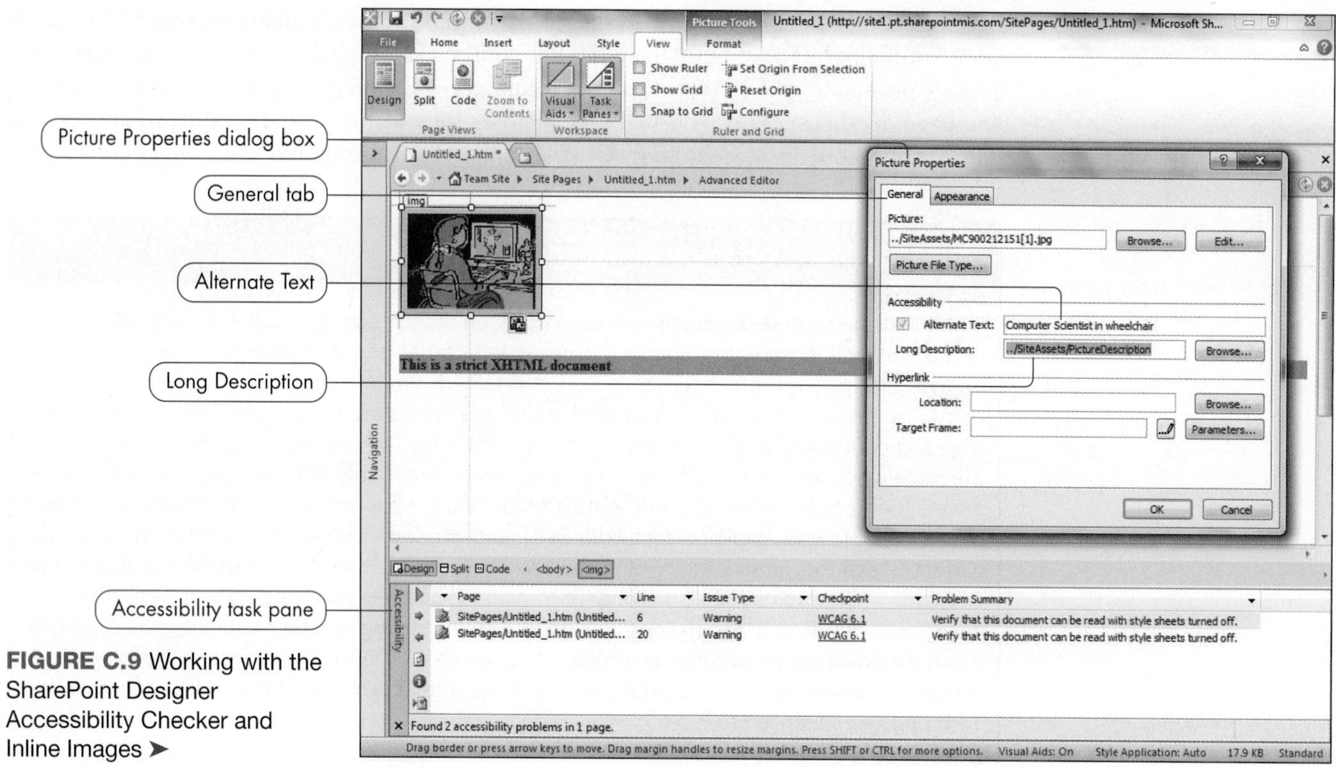

FIGURE C.9 Working with the SharePoint Designer Accessibility Checker and Inline Images ➤

> **TIP** Animated Images and Thumbnails
>
> Avoid using animations, which can cause problems for some users who have disabilities. You should provide access to large images via thumbnails or text links (keep in mind that large images still take a long time to download). In SharePoint Designer, you can easily generate a thumbnail image by right-clicking on the original image, and then clicking Auto Thumbnail on the shortcut menu.

Working with Multimedia

1194.22 (b) Equivalent alternatives for any multimedia presentation shall be synchronized with the presentation.

If your Web page features audio, consider the users who have hearing impairments by supplying a text transcript for the audio content. If video is a part of your Web page, you should provide captions for this group of users. For users with visual impairments, include synchronized descriptions of the action on the video as separate text descriptions as well as an audio transcript. The Caption It Yourself™ Web site (www.dcmp.org/ciy/) provides you with tips for captioning your videos, the benefits of captioning, as well as directing you to software application options for the task. To learn more about audio content transcripts and captions for video content, check out the following Web sites.

- **Captions and Audio Descriptions for PC Multimedia**—go to http://msdn.microsoft.com/ and search for Captions and Audio Descriptions for PC Multimedia
- **The National Captioning Institute**—www.ncicap.org/
- **Relay Conference Captioning**—www.fedrcc.us/FedRcc/
- **Media Access Group**—http://access.wgbh.org

- **Microsoft SAMI 3.0**—go to http://msdn.microsoft.com/ and search for Understanding SAMI 3.0
- **The W3C Synchronized Multimedia Integration Language**—www.w3.org/AudioVideo/
- **The Media Access Generator (MAGpie)**—go to http://ncam.wgbh.org/ and search for MAGpie
- **HiSoftware Hi-Caption**—go to www.hisoftware.com, click Support and Services, and then search for Hi-Caption
- **Adobe Captivate**—www.adobe.com/products/captivate/
- **CPC Closed Captioning & Subtitling Software & Services**—www.cpcweb.com/

TIP CSS Level 3 Speech Module

The CSS level 3 Speech Module (go to www.w3.org/ and search for CSS level 3 Speech Module) allows you to specify to screen readers how content should be presented in audio to the user. Although CSS level 3 is currently under development, it includes all of CSS level 2, and provides many new formatting features, including CSS properties for speech formatting such as voice types, volume, pauses, and rests.

Working with Color

1194.22 (c) Web pages shall be designed so that all information conveyed with color is also available without color, for example from context or markup.

Web developers use color to provide interest and convey meaning on Web pages, but for people who are blind or have vision impairments such as color blindness, the use of color only may hinder their understanding of the content. For instance, a chart that contains various colors can prove difficult for someone who cannot see the difference between the colors. By using color thoughtfully, you make your pages more user-friendly to all of the viewers of your Web site. For example, by selecting colors for text and backgrounds that provide contrast, you make it easier to read for people who have visual impairments, while making the pages quicker to read for people who do not have impairments. You should always consider the following options as you use color on your Web pages:

- Set colors of your Web pages in style sheets. With SharePoint you can create a CSS file and attach it to the Web pages throughout the site. This enables the viewer to override the color choices so that ones they are capable of seeing better can be used. When colors are defined in HTML, your users cannot override color settings.
- Provide a black and white or grayscale alternative version of your Web page for users who are color blind. You can create a Web page template using black and white or grayscale colors and images using an image editing program. You can find out more about using image editing programs at the Web Developers Notes Web site (go to www.webdevelopersnotes.com/ and search the Web site for image editing programs using the Google search box at the top of the homepage).
- Use brighter colors when possible, because they are easier for users who are color blind to differentiate.
- Make sure you offer text equivalent clues if you use important color clues in your Web page. For example, if you use a statement, such as "click the red button to log out," on your Web page, the red button needs to be identified with a text label that makes it recognizable to people who are color blind.
- Provide sufficient contrast between text colors and backgrounds.
- Avoid using red and green, which are challenging for the majority of color-blind people. For instance, when filling out a form, fields that are not validated will often

appear with red text, indicating that the user should provide the correct information. If the user cannot see the color red, they will not be able to find their mistakes and successfully complete the form. As a designer, you can improve the Web page by showing these visual messages in bold as well as red, making them more user-friendly for all viewers.

Two simple methods can help you verify that your Web page is in compliance with guideline (c). Because the content is the most important part of your Web page message, even more important than the design, you should convert your Web page into a black and white or grayscale version, and review it to see that all content continues to make sense in this format. This is especially important if charts convey information or if tables are color-coded. Try viewing the Web page on a black and white monitor, or printing the Web page on a black-and-white printer. If the usability of the Web page is not affected by the removal of color, your Web page should be easy to use by people who are color blind. If meaning is lost in the black and white or grayscale format, consider creating a separate Web page in black and white, using graphic elements in place of colors, for users who are color blind.

Several Web sites enable you to test the accessibility of your Web site for color blind users. aDesigner (www.eclipse.org/actf/downloads/index.php) is one of the best disability simulators to use for testing Web pages for accessibility and usability problems related to visual and color deficiencies. Two modes are available in aDesigner:

- **Blind**—The blind mode runs three types of tests on Web pages: blind usability visualization, accessibility and usability checking, and compliance checking. This setting helps you understand how blind users who depend on voice browsers and screen readers experience their Web pages. By using this setting, you can correct the most crucial factor in improving usability for the blind, navigability.
- **Low Vision**—The low vision mode simulates how users with weak eyesight, color vision deficiencies, cataracts, and combinations of impairments perceive Web pages. This mode enables you to detect accessibility problems from simulated Web pages or images.

The Vischeck (www.vischeck.com/downloads/) Web site provides you with free downloadable software tools, which enable you to see how your Web pages appear to people with different types of color blindness.

Working with Style Sheets

1194.22 (d) Documents shall be organized so they are readable without requiring an associated style sheet.

By using style sheets to separate content from presentation, Web pages load faster and are more usable and accessible in most Web browsers. However, you need to ensure that pages display properly even if your visitor is using a browser that does not support style sheets, has the style sheet support turned off, or has to use another custom style sheet. When using Cascading Style Sheets in developing your Web pages, you should always consider the following recommendations:

- Do not rely on specific fonts or colors to convey relevant information because the specified fonts and colors might not exist on all computers. If they do not exist, the browser uses its default colors and fonts. For instance, the decorative font *Gigi* will be displayed as the default font on computers that do not have *Gigi* as an installed font. If the use of a special font is critical to the design of your Web page, create the stylized text in a graphics program, and insert it as a graphic onto your Web page. Be sure to use alternative tags to describe the graphic so screen readers can process it. This process is often used for headings, organization names, and other text that is emphasized.

- Do not fix the size of your text in points or pixels. In some cases, people with low vision rely on changing the font size on their browsers to enable them to more clearly see the text. You can see what this is like by clicking Page while viewing a Web site in Internet Explorer, clicking Text Size, and then clicking an option on the menu. Web pages that are set up with fixed text sizes in points or pixels cannot be altered by this simple method. As you design pages, use the em unit to set font sizes as required by CSS Techniques for Web Content Accessibility Guidelines 2.0 (www.w3.org, and search for CSS Techniques for CSS Techniques for WCAG 2.0).
- The heading tags (<h1>–<h6>) should be used to emphasize the organization of your Web page, not to modify the text font size.
- Use an adjustable layout (relative length units and percentages of the browser window size) that shrinks or expands as necessary so that visitors with different browser window sizes and screen resolutions can properly see your Web pages. To test this with your Web pages, click Restore Down on the browser window (next to Close) to view the page in a smaller window. See the Units of Measure section of the CSS Techniques for Web Content Accessibility Guidelines 2.0 for more information.
- Use linked style sheets rather than imported styles sheets or embedded styles on each Web page.

Linked style sheets offer the best solutions for maximizing the universal usability of your Web pages. Here are some reasons for choosing linked style sheets over embedded styles or imported style sheets:

- Linked style sheets enable alternative views for different types of devices (such as printers, PDAs, and cellular phones), different options for viewing your Web pages (such as larger size fonts or higher color contrast), or different browsers.
- Linked style sheets are supported by all CSS-capable browsers in contrast with imported style sheets (using the @import method) that work only in Internet Explorer 5.0 or later browsers.
- Linked style sheets minimize the time needed to download your Web pages because they are downloaded only one time and applied to each linked Web page of your Web site as it is accessed.
- Linked style sheets help maximize the consistency of your Web site. Your users will need to get acquainted with only one design.

However, even when using CSS linked style sheets you might have to deal with browser incompatibilities that will force you to create alternate versions of your Web page for different browsers. SharePoint Designer can help you identify these incompatibilities and create alternate versions of your Web pages with the Preview in Multiple Browsers option Click the Preview in Browser arrow on the Home tab, and then select Edit Browser List. Select the browsers you want to use to preview the Web pages from the installed browsers list. Click OK, click the Preview in Browser arrow again, and then click a size under Preview in Multiple Browsers. The page will open in the browsers. If there is obviously a problem with the way a page is displayed, for example between Internet Explorer and Mozilla Firefox, you can address the problem by creating an alternate Web page by modifying the external style sheet.

To ensure that your Web page will display correctly in browsers other than Internet Explorer, you can use the SharePoint Designer Check Browser behavior to automatically determine the browser when the Web page is accessed and open the appropriate Web page for the viewer's browser. After you create the alternate version of the Web page, click the Task Panes arrow, and then click Behaviors. Select the <body> tag on the Quick Tag Selector, and then click Insert on the Behaviors task pane to open the Check Browser dialog box. From the *If the current browser type is* list, select the browsers for which the Web page does not display correctly. Then, from the Version list, check a specific version, if required. Click the first Go to URL check box, click Browse to navigate to the location of the alternate page, as shown in Figure C.10, and then click OK to apply the behavior.

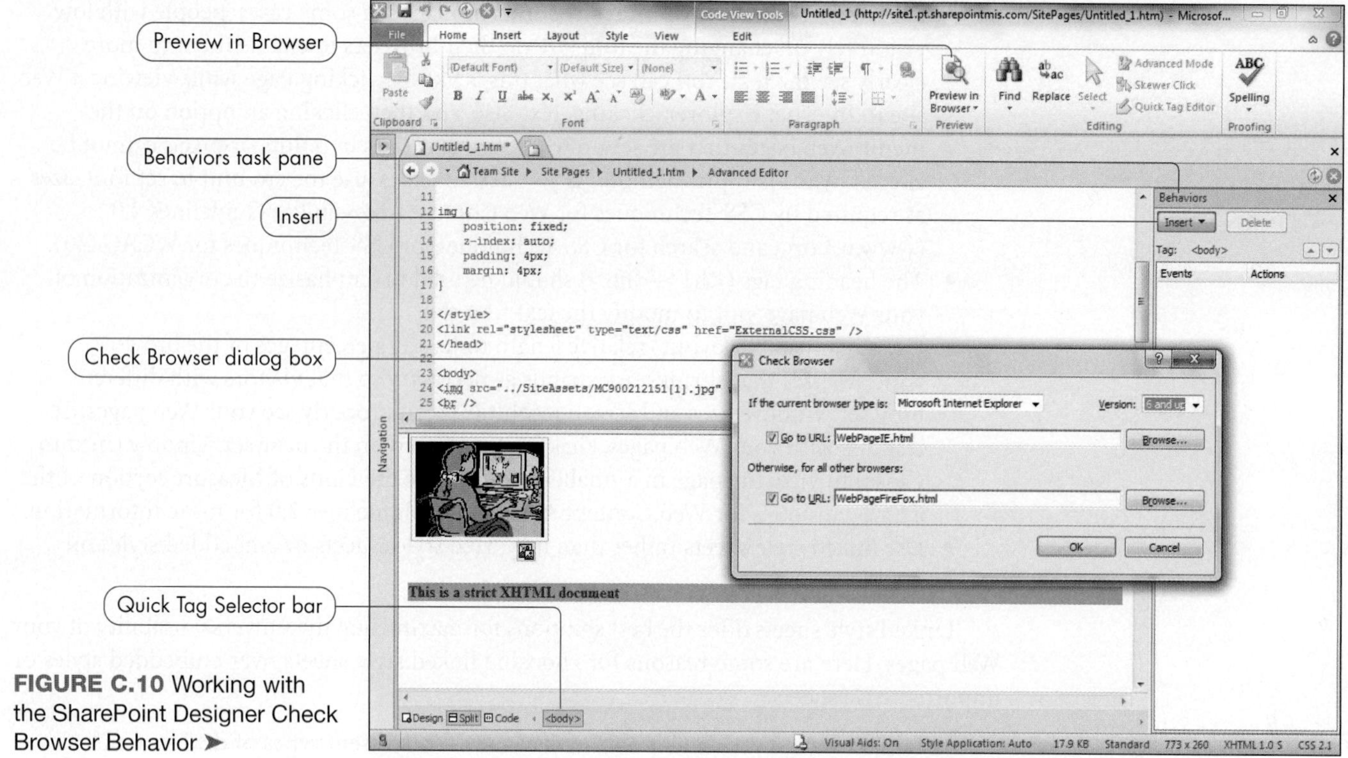

FIGURE C.10 Working with the SharePoint Designer Check Browser Behavior ➤

Working with Image Maps

1194.22 (e) Redundant text links shall be provided for each active region of a server-side image map.

1194.22 (f) Client-side image maps shall be provided instead of server-side image maps except where the regions cannot be defined with an available geometric shape.

Image maps enable the viewers to click a region of a graphic to navigate to a different location. Client-side image maps are starting to replace server-side image maps, especially because client-side image maps enable polygon hotspots and therefore all shapes can be defined on a client-side map. Image maps provide a challenge for people with disabilities, especially if screen readers are used to access Web sites. To make a Web page containing a client-side image map accessible, you need to add alternative text to the original map image and each hotspot within the map.

A hotspot is a defined area on an image that acts as a hypertext link. You define a hotspot by using image maps. An image map lists the coordinates that define the boundaries of a hotspot or a region (polygonal for example) that act as hypertext links on an image.

Figure C.11a shows how you can add a hotspot to an image in SharePoint Designer using the Pictures Tools tab. Figure C.11b shows the client-side image map in Split view as well as the Accessibility task pane.

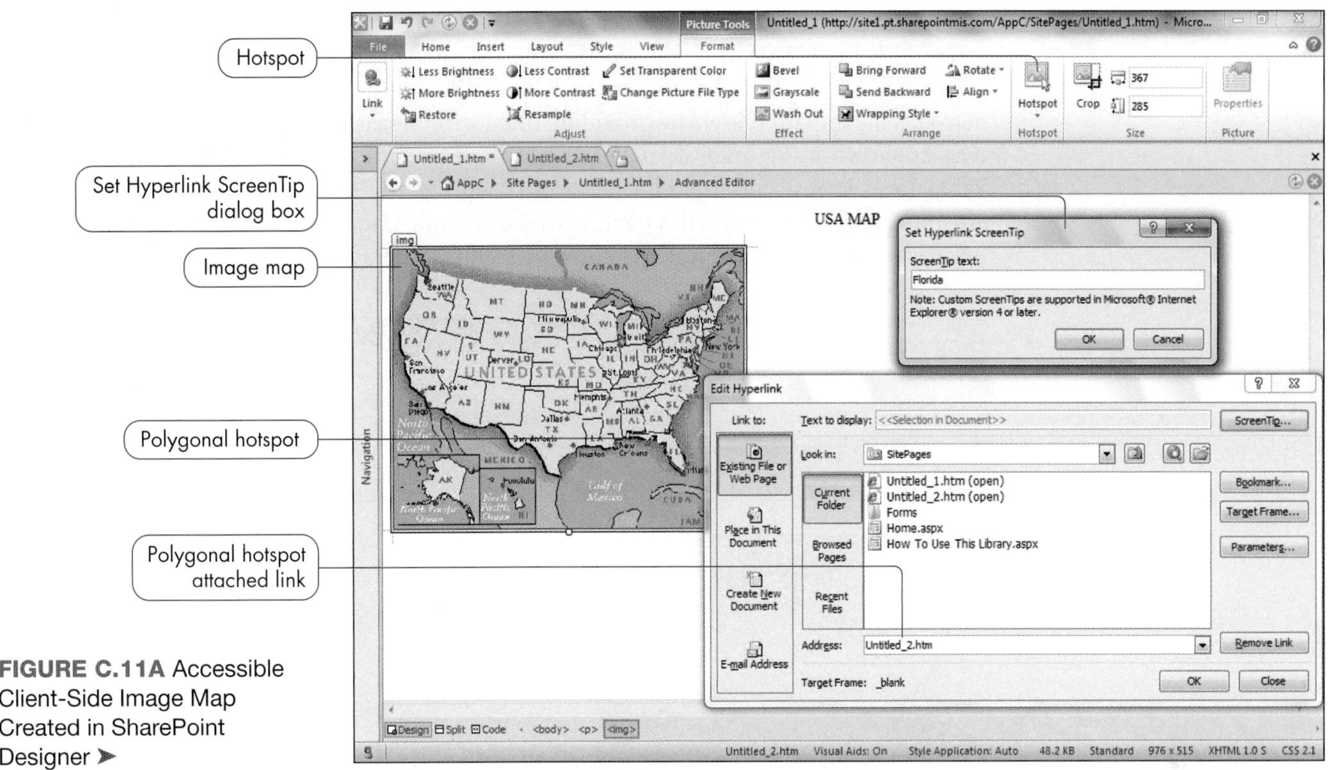

FIGURE C.11A Accessible Client-Side Image Map Created in SharePoint Designer ➤

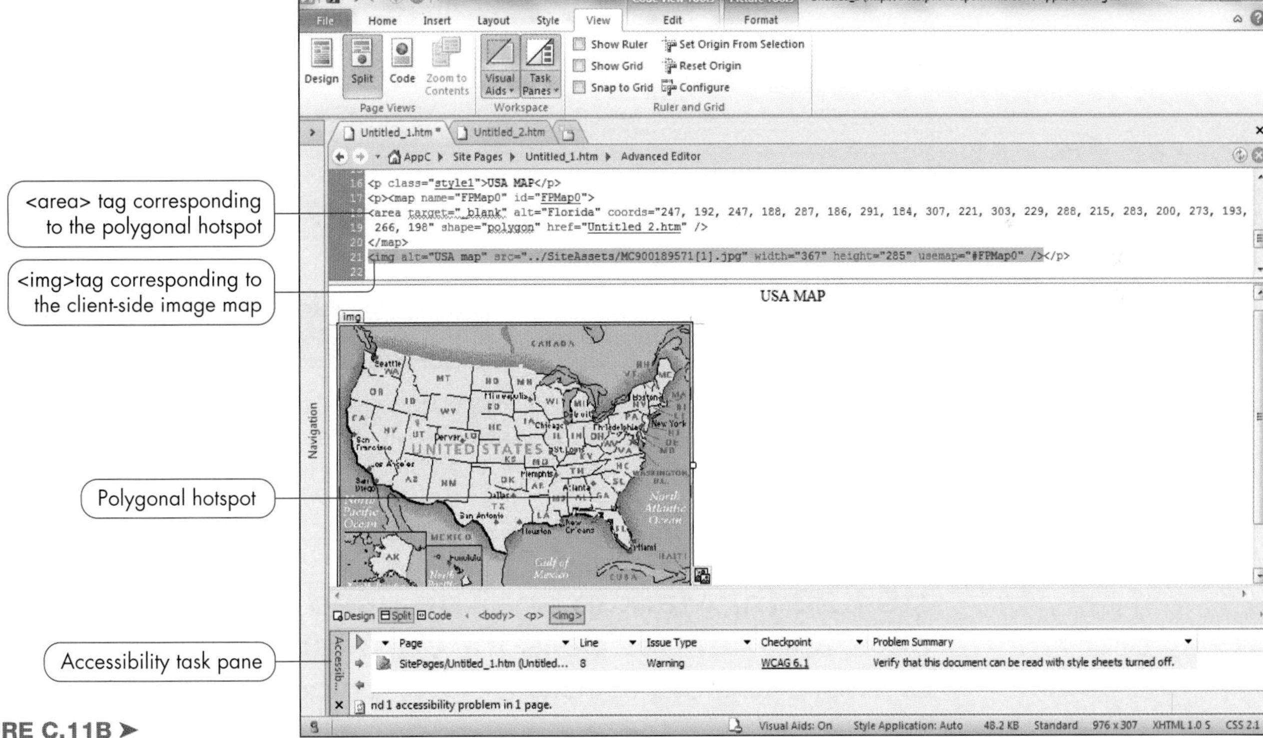

FIGURE C.11B ➤

Working with Tables

1194.22 (g) Row and column headers shall be identified for data tables.

Chapter 3 covers using tables to organize data, as well as using tables that include one or more levels of nested tables. To comply with guideline (g), when using data tables, use the <th> tag for any cell that contains a row or column header, even if the cell occurs in a nested table.

By default, SharePoint Designer uses the <td> tag as rows and columns are created. You can modify the HTML code by selecting the cell and clicking Header Cell in the Cell Layout group of the Table Tools Layout tab, as shown in Figure C.12. Adding a table caption can also help visually impaired users by providing them with more information about the table's content, as shown in Figure C.12. Click Insert Caption in the Rows & Columns group of the Table Tools Layout tab to add a caption. Providing a table summary using the summary attribute, in the Tag Properties pane, is useful for non-visual browser applications (the summary is not displayed and it is used only by screen readers).

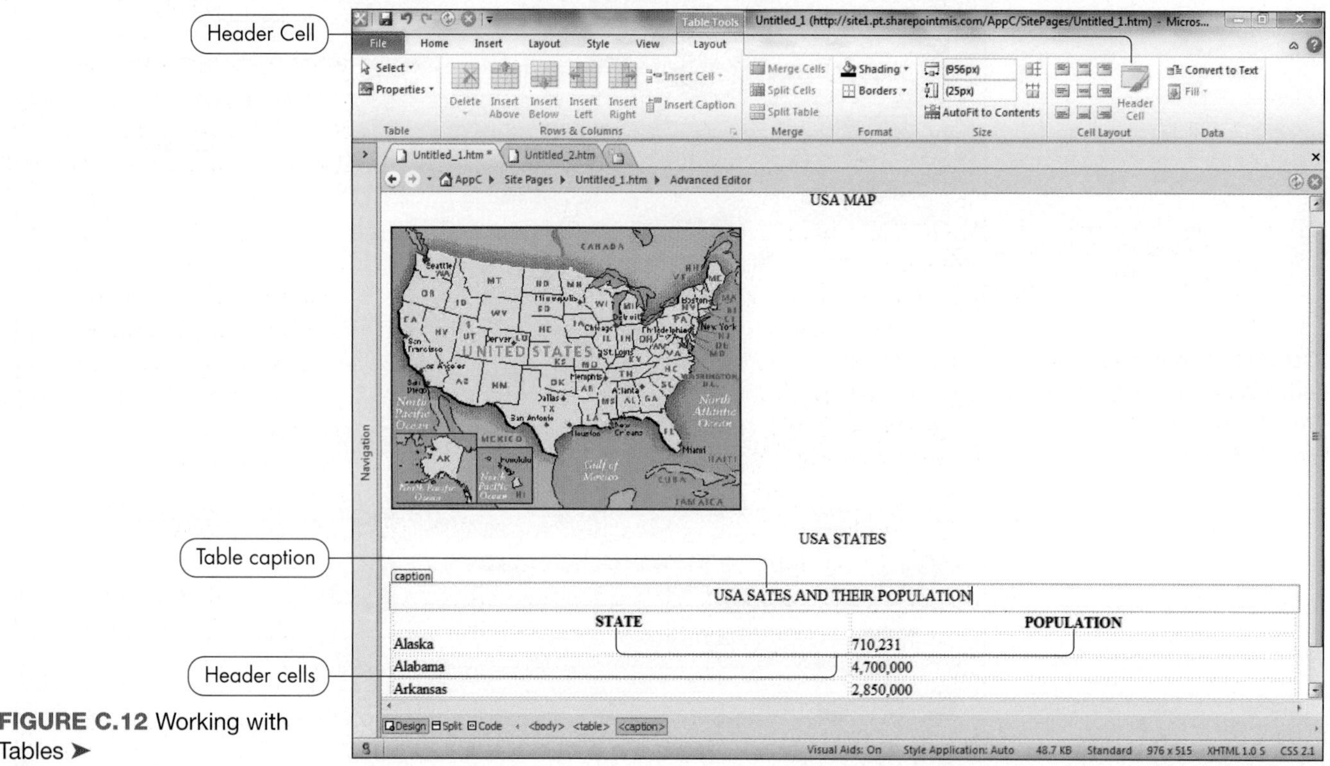

FIGURE C.12 Working with Tables ➤

> **TIP** Flexible Viewing Conditions
>
> You should use flexible measurements for tables so your Web pages can easily adapt to your users' screen resolution and size. The Layout section of the Insert Table and Table Properties dialog box enables you to specify the width and height of tables in percentages of the document window.

1194.22 (h) Markup shall be used to associate data cells and header cells for data tables that have two or more logical levels of row or column headers.

To comply with guideline (h), use the <th> tag for any cell that contains a row or a column header in any nested table. This can be quite tedious and might convince you that nested tables should be used only when absolutely necessary. As previously discussed, an excellent way to test that your Web page is accessible is by viewing it in the Lynx browser.

If a table is used as a layout tool, do not use any structural HTML tags (for example, the <th> tag that displays its content visually as centered, and bold) for the purpose of visual formatting as this can be confusing to someone using a screen reader. For a browser to render a table's side-by-side text correctly, you will need to linearize the table. To learn more about how to linearize a table, see the Creating Accessible Tables section of the WebAIM Web site (go to www.webaim.org/ and search the Web site for Creating Accessible Tables). One of the best tools for creating accessible tables is the WebAIM free online WAVE Accessibility Tool (go to www.webaim.org/ and search the Web site for WAVE Accessibility Evaluation Tool).

Working with Frames

1194.22 (i) Frames shall be titled with text that facilitates frame identification and navigation.

Frames are a layout tool for creating Web pages based on the structure of a frameset. A frameset is the actual layout that lets the browser know how to display the framed pages. Sometimes Web designers want to include the contents of one Web page in another Web page (using all the display features of a frame) without having to build a frameset layout. The inline frame, also known as a floating frame, is basically a frame that does not need to be framed in a frameset and embeds a document or another Web page into an HTML document so that embedded data is displayed inside a subwindow of the browser's window. The two documents are absolutely independent, and both are treated as complete documents.

When opening a frames page, assistive technologies applications for people who are visually impaired enable users to open only one frame at a time. Thus, it is extremely important to provide information about the contents of each frame and inline frame included in your Web page. You can do this by adding the title or name attribute to each frame using the Tag Properties pane in SharePoint Designer. Because some browsers and assistive technology applications support the *title* attribute and others support the *name* attribute, it is wise to add both of them. Users without access to frames should still have access to the Web page content if appropriate navigation links are provided in the <noframes> tag.

The W3C recently added the <frames> tag to the list of deprecated tags, therefore, even though the accessibility issues related to frames can be addressed, it is highly recommended not to use frames if you wish to build standard, accessible Web pages.

TIP Frames or No Frames

It is rather common for users to not use frames or to use browsers that do not support frames. Therefore you should always provide access to an alternate Web page using the <noframes> tag.

Working with Animation and Scrolling Text

1194.22 (j) Pages shall be designed to avoid causing the screen to flicker with a frequency greater than 2 Hz and lower than 55 Hz.

Using flashing or flickering elements, such as animated GIF images, blinking text, and scrolling text, can affect the accessibility of your Web pages. People with photosensitive epilepsy can have seizures caused by elements that flicker, flash, or blink with an intensity and frequency outside the range indicated by guideline (j). The majority of screen reader applications cannot read moving text. People with cognitive disabilities might also find it challenging to read moving text.

Working with Text-Only Version

1194.22 (k) A text-only page, with equivalent information or functionality, shall be provided to make a Web site comply with the provisions of this part, when compliance cannot be accomplished in any other way. The content of the text-only page shall be updated whenever the primary page changes.

A text-only Web page must contain all the information included in the original page and must have the same functionality as the original page. Anytime you update a Web page, you must also update its text-only version. A link to the text-only version must be included in the original Web page. The homepage of the NPR Web site (www.npr.org) is an excellent example of how to implement this guideline, as shown in Figure C.13.

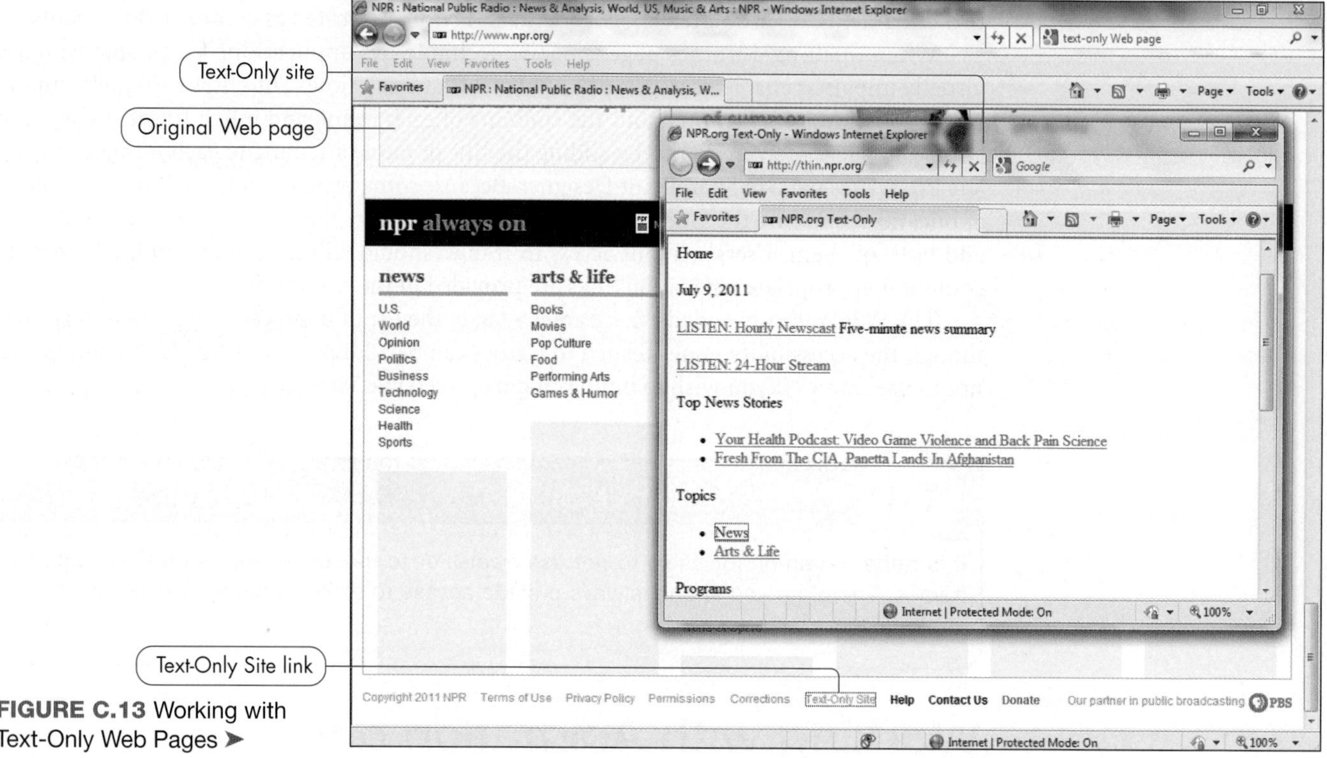

FIGURE C.13 Working with Text-Only Web Pages ➤

Working with Scripts, Applets, and Plug-Ins

1194.22 (l) When pages utilize scripting languages to display content, or to create interface elements, the information provided by the script shall be identified with functional text that can be read by assistive technology.

1194.22 (m) When a web page requires that an applet, plug-in, or other application be present on the client system to interpret page content, the

page must provide a link to a plug-in or applet that complies with [s]1194.21(a) through (l)(To read more about applets or plug-ins, go to www.access-board.gov/508.htm, click on Guide to Standards, and then click Web-based Intranet and Internet Information and Applications).

Appendix A briefly introduced scripting languages and how they are used to develop Web pages:

- They automatically change a formatted date on a Web page.
- They cause a linked-to-page to appear in a pop-up window.
- They cause text or a graphic image to change during a mouse rollover.
- They obtain information about the current Web browser.
- They enable navigating to Web pages that have been opened during a Web browser session.
- They process data submitted via an HTML form.
- They retrieve data from a database via a HTML form.

Many of these scripting language applications require the use of the mouse. Some people with motor disabilities might not be able to use a mouse. Furthermore, some assistive technology applications have browsers with scripting turned off; thus, you should provide alternative methods for users with disabilities. Your Web pages should include access keys (keyboard shortcuts) that enable users to achieve the same functionality.

The SharePoint Designer IntelliSense tool enables you to assign keyboard shortcuts (access key attributes) to the links and form fields on each Web page, so keyboard users can navigate the page by using a combination of the Alt key + a letter key. For consistency and usability, use the same access keys for the same links on all Web pages included on a Web site. You can add an access key attribute to a hyperlink in Code view or Split view, as shown in Figure C.14a, by selecting the hyperlink in the code, and typing a letter next to the accesskey tag in the Tag Properties pane. This produces hyperlink tag that contains the accesskey=" " attribute with the letter between the quotation marks, as shown in Figure C.14b. You can also type the accesskey=" " (with a letter to indicate the keyboard shortcut between the quotation marks) directly into the hyperlink tag in the Code view. To add an access key attribute to a form field, type accesskey=" " with a letter between the quotation marks in the form field tag, as shown in Figure C.15.

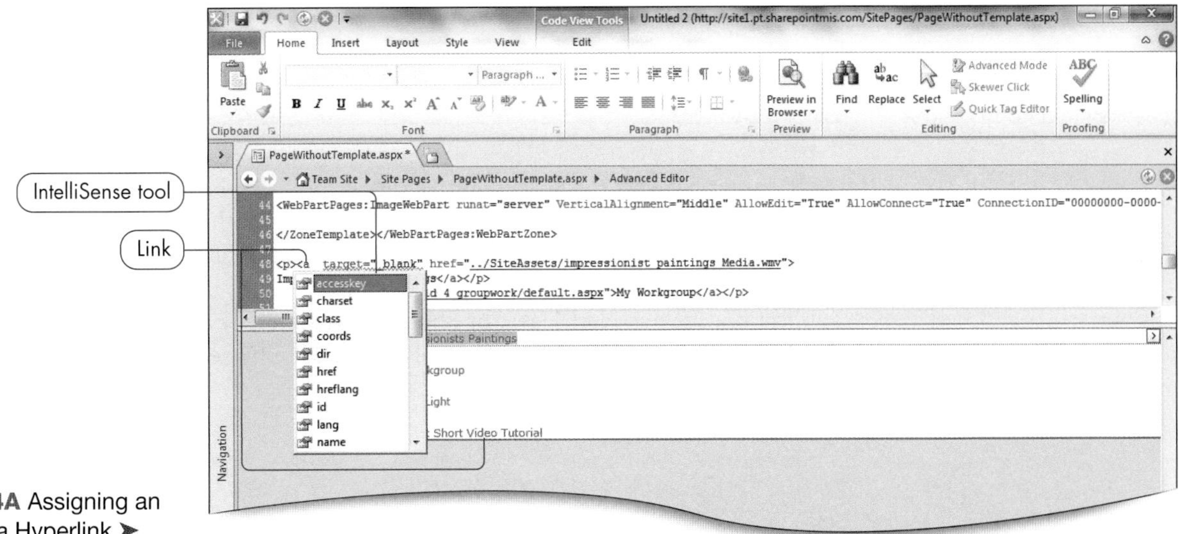

FIGURE C.14A Assigning an accesskey to a Hyperlink ➤

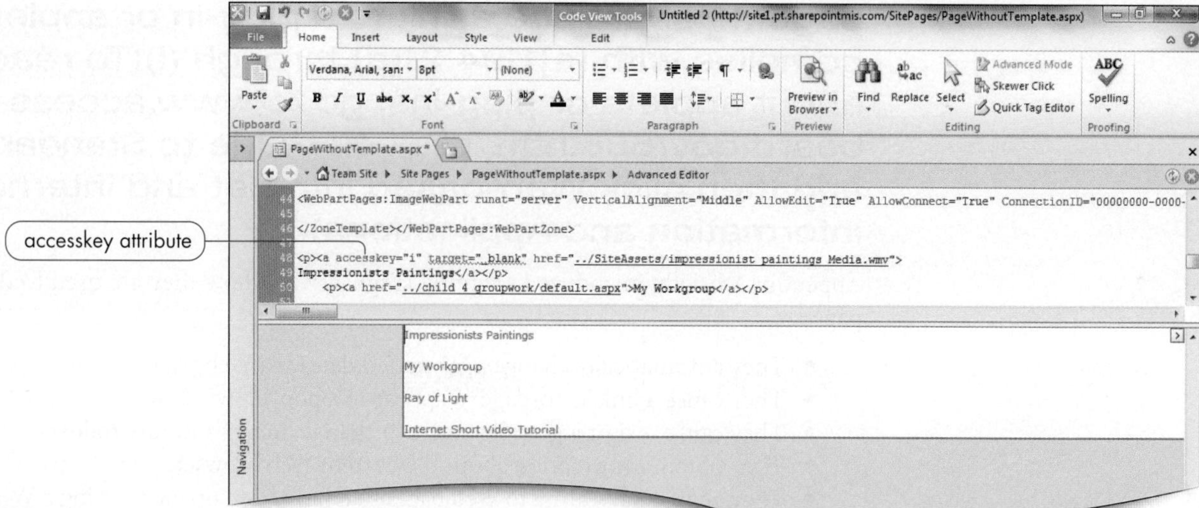

FIGURE C.14B ➤

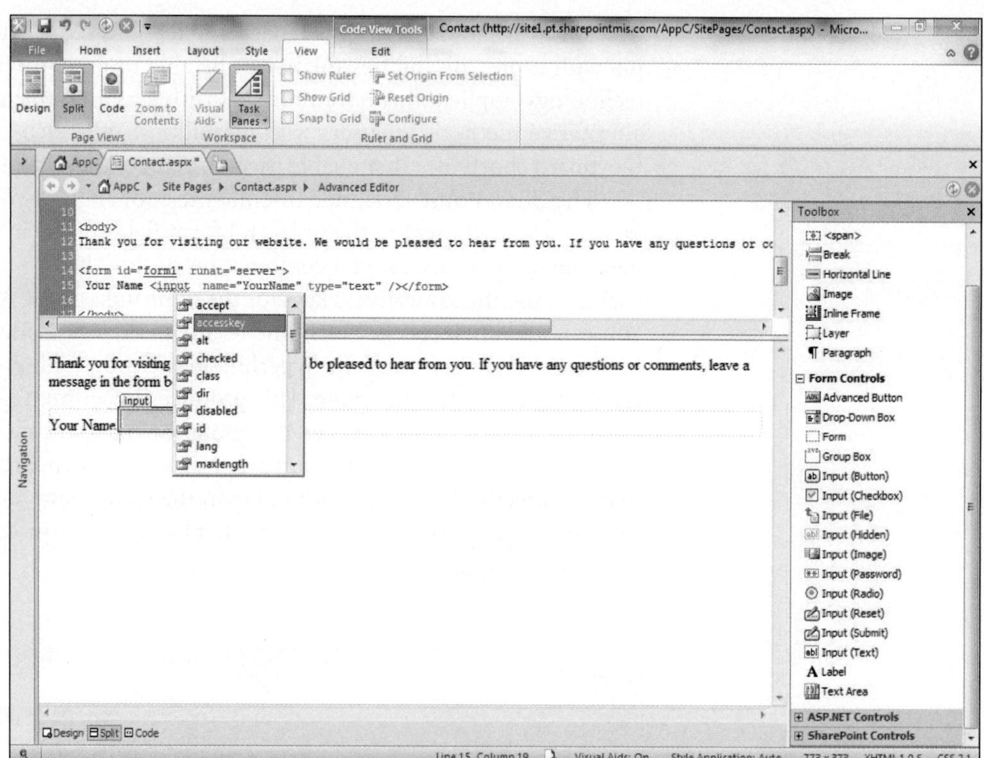

FIGURE C.15 Assigning an accesskey to a Form Field ➤

Chapter 3 covers the SharePoint Designer tools that enable you to add multimedia elements to Web pages that might require a plug-in or another application to be properly displayed in a browser and empower the user with the decision about when to access media. When using any of these elements in a Web page, a link to the source of a required plug-in or application, such as Flash, Java, or Shockwave, should be added to the Web page. Plug-ins can be detected in the HTML code of a Web page by searching for the <object> tag or <embed> tag.

In SharePoint Foundation, you should use the HTML <object> tag to embed multimedia in your pages. You can do that in a number of ways. The easiest and most reliable way, recommended by Microsoft as well, is to the save the related HTML into a text file (which has to be saved as unicode) and linking it from the Content Editor Web part, as shown in Figure C.16. See also this very useful tutorial Embedding Videos in SharePoint 2010 (www.youtube.com/watch?v=ZZduyl-bmpY)

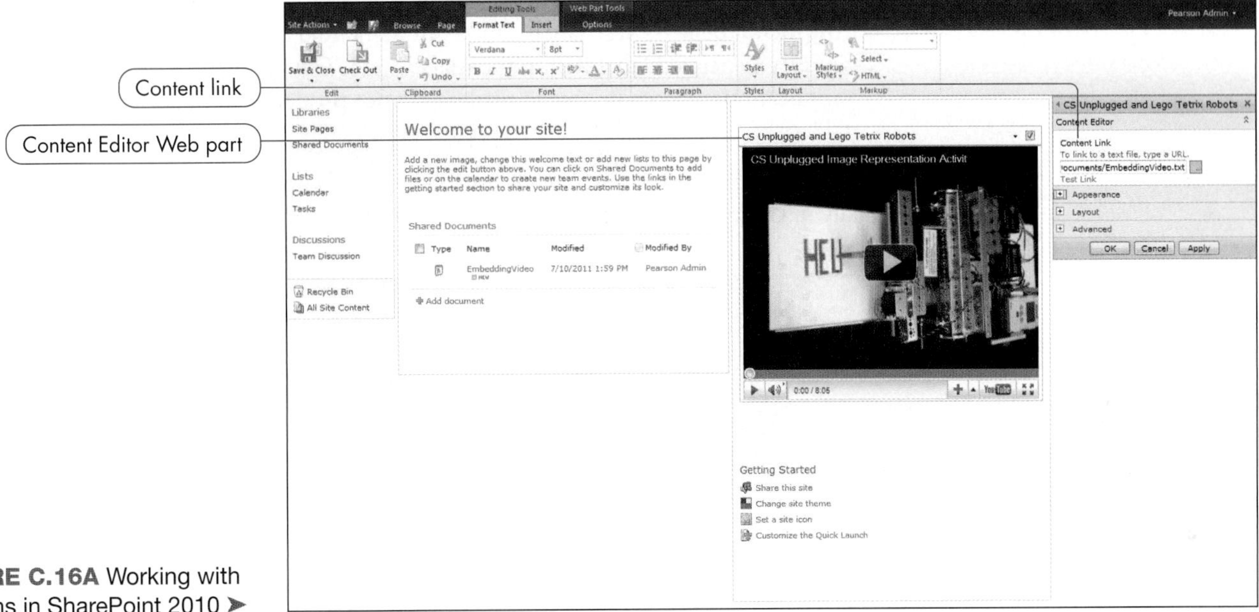

FIGURE C.16A Working with Plug-ins in SharePoint 2010 ➤

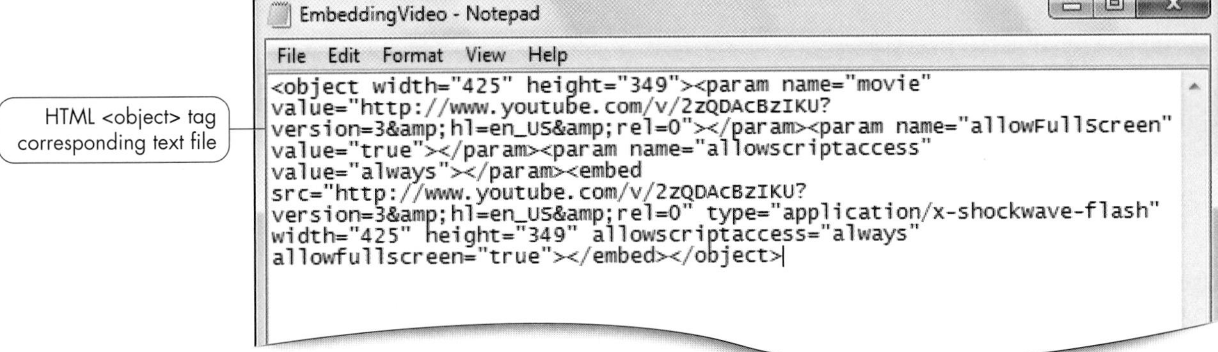


```
<object width="425" height="349"><param name="movie"
value="http://www.youtube.com/v/2zQDACBzIKU?
version=3&amp;hl=en_US&amp;rel=0"></param><param name="allowFullscreen"
value="true"></param><param name="allowscriptaccess"
value="always"></param><embed
src="http://www.youtube.com/v/2zQDACBzIKU?
version=3&amp;hl=en_US&amp;rel=0" type="application/x-shockwave-flash"
width="425" height="349" allowscriptaccess="always"
allowfullscreen="true"></embed></object>
```

FIGURE C.16B ➤

Working with Web Forms

1194.22 (n) When electronic forms are designed to be completed on-line, the form shall allow people using assistive technology to access the information, field elements, and functionality required for completion and submission of the form, including all directions and cues.

Web forms tend to cause problems for people with disabilities if the form elements are improperly labeled and titled, or if they have not been coded in compliance with guideline (n). Web forms consist of text boxes, text areas, check boxes, option buttons, and drop-down menus.

When form layouts are structured using a table, you must be careful to make sure the table is linearized. To improve a screen reader's ability to process an HTML form, each form element should have an initial default value to give the user guidance in completing the form.

All form elements must have adjacent labels (placed in the same table cell). The W3C HTML 4.01 specifications (www.w3.org/wiki/HTML/Elements/label) require you to include a <label> tag associated with a form element. You can use the <label> tag in two distinctive ways:

- **Explicit labels**—These labels can be implemented using the <label> tag with the *for* attribute. The id attribute of the form element is assigned as value of the *for* attribute. The majority of assistive technology applications work extremely well with explicit labels.
- **Implicit labels**—These labels can be implemented by including the form element and its associated label within the <label> tag. The majority of assistive technology applications, especially screen readers, do not properly support implicit labels.

SharePoint Designer cannot create explicit labels and does not add the id attribute to form elements. You add explicit labels and the id attribute to the associated form elements manually in Code view or Split view, as shown in Figure C.17.

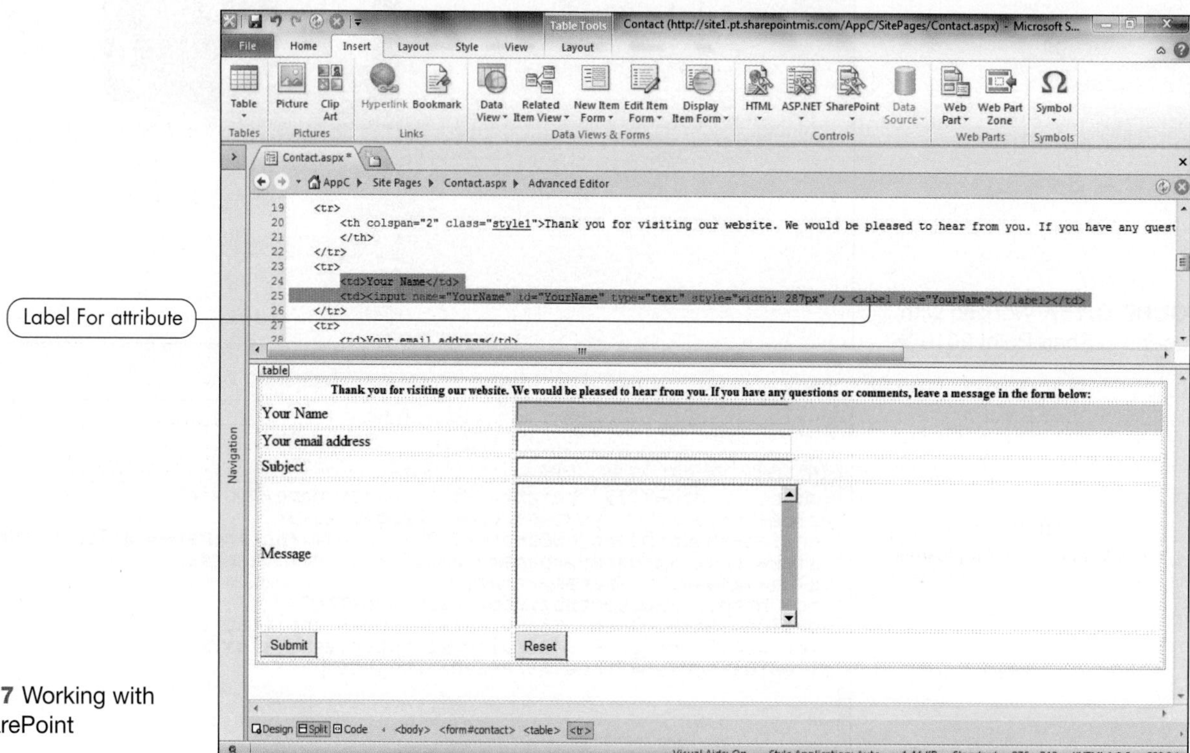

FIGURE C.17 Working with Forms in SharePoint Designer ➤

TIP Alternative Contact Methods

It is not easy to design and develop accessible forms for users with different types of special needs. That is why you should always include an alternative contact method, such as a telephone number or e-mail address, on your Web pages with the forms.

Working with Links

1194.22 (o) A method shall be provided that permits users to skip repetitive navigation links.

Chapter 3 introduced bookmarks as hyperlinks that link to a specific location within a Web page. The most commonly used bookmark for accessibility is Skip Navigation Links. A Skip Navigation Links link enables a user to skip the Web page title and navigation links by directing the focus to the main contents of the Web page being viewed. This link is especially important for people who are visually impaired and use a screen reader application. In the example shown in Figure C.18, the Skip to Page Content link enables visually impaired users to skip directly to the main content of a Web page so that they are not forced to listen to the Web page title and navigation links each time they access the Web page.

FIGURE C.18A Working with Links ➤

FIGURE C.18B ➤

Working with Timed Response

1194.22 (p) When a timed response is required, the user shall be alerted and given sufficient time to indicate more time is required.

For security reasons and to accommodate visitor traffic on busy servers, Web developers use scripts that disable the functionality of Web pages when a response is not received within a certain time limit. People with cognitive disabilities or different levels of visual impairment might need more time to provide a response. Consequently, you should always alert users if there is a time limit for providing a response. You should also consider establishing a response time that accommodates all users or enables them to change the time. The W3C "How People with Disabilities Use the Web" Web page (go to www.w3.org/ and search the W3C Web site for How People with Disabilities Use the Web) is an excellent resource for this topic.

Assistive Technology and Accessibility Evaluation Tools

Web pages designed in compliance with Section 508 and the WCAG guidelines can be made accessible to the majority of people with disabilities using software applications and devices that are grouped under the umbrella of assistive technologies, such as:

- Screen readers use text-to-speech (TTS) technology to verbalize screen text and textual representations of graphical elements if available.
- Speech-to-text converters automatically transform dialogue into text.

Browser extensions and other plug-in evaluation tools, such as the AIS Toolbar for Internet Explorer and Opera (www.visionaustralia.org.au/ais/toolbar), WAVE Toolbar for Firefox, Internet Explorer, or Web Developer Extension for Firefox (http://chrispederick.com/work/firefox/webdeveloper/) provide functionality to help perform many manual accessibility checks.

Twenty-Five Ways to Make Your Website Accessible

Dennis E. Lembree, an accomplished Web developer and accessibility expert, published a very timely, down-to-earth article on "25 Ways to Make Your Website Accessible" (www.webhostingsearch.com/articles/25-ways-to-make-your-site-more-accessible.php). If you want to learn more about Web accessibility, outside of the United States, the BBC article "My Web My Way - Making the Web easier to use" (www.bbc.co.uk/accessibility/) is a recommended resource.

Accessibility and Evaluation Tools refer to the tools used to make the Web accessible to people with a variety of disabilities. W3C provides two free online validation services: The Markup Validation Service (http://validator.w3.org/) and Cascading Style Sheet (CSS) Validation Service (http://jigsaw.w3.org/css-validator/). The Markup Validation Service checks documents like HTML and XHTML for conformance to W3C Recommendations and other standards. The CSS Validation Service checks CSS in HTML and XHTML documents or stand-alone CSS documents for conformance to W3C recommendations.

REFERENCE Examples of Assistive Technologies & Accessibility and Evaluation Tools

Category	Application	WWW address
Accessibility and Evaluation Tools	a Designer designed by IBM	www.alphaworks.ibm.com/tech/adesigner
Screen Readers	JAWS for Windows developed by Freedom. Scientific	www.freedomscientific.com/
	Dolphin Pen by Dolphin Computer Access	www.yourdolphin.com/
	Window-Eyes Professional developed by GW Micro	www.gwmicro.com
Speech-to-Text Converters	Dragon Naturally Speaking developed by Advanced Speech	www.advancedspeech.com/
	MacSpeech	www.macspeech.com/

More Information

The task of building accessible Web pages is not an easy one. Web developers are required to accumulate a lot of knowledge to successfully accomplish this task. The good news is that more and more companies and organizations are developing competitive assistive and accessibility technology applications that can help you in your quest to assist people with disabilities and specials needs.

W3C provides an "Evaluating Web Sites for Accessibility: Overview" collection of pages that includes general procedures and tips for evaluating the accessibility of your sites (www.w3.org/WAI/eval/Overview.html). This collection also includes a "Complete List of Web Accessibility Evaluation Tools" (www.w3.org/WAI/ER/tools/complete).

The following list presents some of the most resourceful Web sites that Web developers use to develop accessible Web sites. The list includes the Web sites of software companies that are providing successful assistive and accessibility technologies, of organizations and institutions developing accessibility guidelines and laws, up-to-date articles, and Web accessibility online forums.

- **Microsoft Accessibility Technology for Everyone**—go to www.microsoft.com/enable/ and click on Mission & Strategy in the Accessibility at Microsoft section
- **IBM Accessibility Center**—www-03.ibm.com/able/
- **W3C Web Accessibility Initiative (WAI) Guidelines and Techniques**—go to www.w3.org/WAI/ and click on Guidelines and Techniques in the vertical navigation bar
- **Web Accessibility in Mind** (WebAIM)—www.webaim.org/
- **Web Content Accessibility Guidelines**—go to www.w3.org/WAI/, click on Guidelines and Techniques in the vertical navigation bar, and then click on Web Content (WCAG) in the vertical navigation bar
- **Freedom Scientific: JAWS for Windows**—www.freedomscientific.com/
- **IBM Alpha Works: aDesigner**—www.alphaworks.ibm.com/tech/adesigner
- **InFocus: Accessibility Evaluation Tool**—www.ssbbartgroup.com/amp/infocus.php
- **LIFT: Accessibility Evaluation Tool**—http://transcoder.usablenet.com/tt/index.html
- **Illinois Accessible Web Publishing Wizard**—www.accessiblewizards.uiuc.edu/
- **Windows Eyes**—www.gwmicro.com/
- **Lynx—Internet Software Consortium**—http://lynx.isc.org
- **Lynx Viewer**—www.delorie.com/web/lynxview.html
- **ScanSoft: Dragon Naturally Speaking 11**—www.nuance.com/
- **Section 508**—www.section508.gov/
- **University Web Accessibility Policies: A bridge not quite far enough**—www.webaim.org/coordination/articles/policies-pilot
- **WAVE 3.0: Accessibility Evaluation Tool**—http://wave.webaim.org/index.jsp
- **HiSoftware CynthiaSays portal**—www.cynthiasays.com/Default.asp
- **A-Prompt: Accessibility Evaluation Tool**—http://aprompt.snow.utoronto.ca/download.html
- **Vischeck**—www.vischeck.com/vischeck/
- **Web Accessibility Toolbar**—www.visionaustralia.org.au/ais/toolbar/
- **ACM Special Interest Group on Computer-Human Interaction (SIGCHI)**—www.sigchi.org/
- **ACM Special Interest Group on Accessible Computing, SIGACCESS**—www.acm.org/sigaccess/

KEY TERMS

Accessibility ***p.478***
Linearization ***p.480***

GLOSSARY

Absolute URL An absolute URL provides the full path to a Web page or file.

Access view Access view enables you to fully take advantage of the Access advanced tools for generating reports and views.

Accessibility Accessibility means that a page can be accessed—read and used—by any person regardless of special needs or disabilities.

Adobe Flash Adobe Flash is a popular application used to create Flash-animated graphics.

Alink attribute The alink attribute determines the color of an active hyperlink (a link as it is clicked by the user) and corresponds to the a:active {color: #value;} CSS style and Active Hyperlink Color setting in the Page Properties dialog box.

All Events view All Events view displays all past, present, and future events.

All Site Content The All Site Content page is the main navigational aid for your site, with links to all major parts of the site infrastructure, as well as all of the libraries, lists, discussion boards, and surveys.

Announcement item An announcement item initially contains columns for a title, a body, and an expiration date.

Announcements list An Announcements list can be used to inform your site users about upcoming events, news, or activities.

ASCII ASCII is the common numeric code used by computers to represent characters.

ASP.NET ASP.NET is a set of technologies within the Microsoft .NET Framework for building Web applications and XML Web services.

ASP.NET page An ASP.NET page is a dynamic web page saved with an .aspx extension that executes on the server and generates markup (such as HTML, or XML) that is sent to a desktop or mobile browser.

Auto Thumbnail The Auto Thumbnail feature creates a small version of the image.

Background sound Background sound is an audio file that plays for as long as a Web page is open in a browser or for a limited number of loops, or cycles, depending on the designer's preference.

Bandwidth Bandwidth is the amount of data passing, within a time interval, through a phone line, cable, or DSL line connection to transfer information from and to a Web site via your computer.

Basic Meeting Workspace template The Basic Meeting Workspace template is used to create sites with tools to enable members to plan, conduct, and document meetings.

Blank Meeting Workspace template The Blank Meeting Workspace template is used to create an empty meeting workspace that does not include any site pages containing Web Parts.

Blank Site template A Blank Site template has no lists or libraries and should be used when you do not need most of the items in the Team Site template.

Blog site A blog site is used to post information for comment and discussion.

Blog Site template The Blog Site template provides the tools needed for managing blog postings and comments.

Bookmark link Bookmark link is a link to a specific position within the same document or another document.

Breadcrumb navigation The Breadcrumb navigation trail enables you to see the path leading to the current page, and to easily keep track of the current page location within its site.

Calendar list The Calendar list displays events and activities in a month, week, or daily layout.

Cascading Style Sheets (CSS) Cascading Style Sheets (CSS) have become the standard style sheet language used on the Web.

Cell A cell is the intersection of a column and a row.

Class selector A class selector applies to HTML sections of your Web page that can be identified by the <div> or <span> tags.

Client A client is a user's machine that connects to the server and receives information from it.

Clip Art task pane The Clip Art task pane provides you with media files, generically called clips, stored in a comprehensive group of collections.

Communications Communications define the process of moving data within or between computers.

Communications device A communications device provides the hardware and software support for connecting computers to a network.

Content placeholder A content placeholder delineates areas where the content of a page will appear.

Content section The Content section, located to the right of the Quick Launch area, is the main body of the site page and includes all the elements you want to make available through the site (such as documents, lists, and web parts).

Current Events view Current Events view displays all present and future events.

Database A database is a set of related data containing records or rows.

Database table A database table is formed by columns, each of which is attached to a database field.

Datasheet view Datasheet view displays a list or library items using a gridlike layout that enables you to easily edit the whole table.

Decision Meeting Workspace template The Decision Meeting Workspace template is used to create sites to support and track the decision-making process.

Declaration A declaration is comprised of one or more formatting instructions.

Declaration block The declaration block begins and ends with braces {} and includes all the formatting options to be applied to the selector.

Default template The default template defines the default content type for that library.

Deprecated Deprecated HTML tags and tag attributes might or might not be supported by all browsers.

Discussion Board list The Discussion Board list supports message postings related to list topics.

Document Library A Document Library stores most file types and provides integration with Office products such as Word 2010, PowerPoint 2010, Excel 2010, and OneNote 2010.

Document type definition (DTD) A document type definition (DTD) specifies what tags and attributes are used to describe content in an XML document, where each tag is allowed, and which tags can appear within other tags, thus eliminating many code errors that can occur.

Document workspace A document workspace is used to create, update, and store documents.

Document Workspace template The Document Workspace template provides the tools needed to manage a collaborative effort in the creation of a document.

Documents tab The Documents tab contains options for managing and editing documents.

Domain name The domain name comprises the first part of the URL that identifies the Web page's host, which can be a Web server or computer on the Internet, and a second part called the top-level domain.

Dynamic HTML (DHTML) Dynamic HTML (DHTML) is an extension of HTML that enables changes to the styles and attributes of page elements based on user actions.

Dynamic Web page Dynamic Web page content changes as users interact with it.

Dynamic Web Part A Dynamic Web Part is a part that can be placed using SharePoint Designer or the browser or in a Web Part zone on Web Part pages. It is saved separately from the page in the SQL Server content database.

Enhanced ScreenTip An Enhanced ScreenTip displays additional descriptive text and can have a link to a Help topic.

Extensible Hypertext Markup Language (XHTML) The Extensible Hypertext Markup Language (XHTML) is a newer markup language that was designed to overcome some of the problems of HTML.

Extensible Markup Language (XML) Extensible Markup Language (XML), based on the SGML standard, enables data to be shared and processed via the Internet and across software applications, operating systems, and hardware computer platforms.

Extensible Style Sheet Language (XSL) The Extensible Style Sheet Language (XSL) was developed by the W3C as an improved method for formatting XML documents, allowing developers to transform XML data files into a wide variety of popular file formats, such as HTML and portable document format (PDF).

Extensible Stylesheet Language Transformation (XSLT) XSLT (Extensible Stylesheet Language Transformation) is a subset of XSL that enables you to display XML data on a Web page and "transform" it in HTML.

External style An external style is included in a separate file used to specify the formatting of any HTML document to which the external style sheets are linked.

Extranet An extranet is a Web site that allows access only to selected users, such as customers, suppliers, or other trading partners.

File Transfer Protocol (FTP) File Transfer Protocol (FTP) is the second most prevalent protocol on the Internet used to transfer files between computers.

Flat view In a flat view postings appear in a sequence based on the date and time they were added to the Discussion Board list.

Global links bar The Global links bar appears across the very top of the SharePoint page, and includes five links that are not related to the user location in the site hierarchy.

Graphics Interchange Format (GIF) Graphics Interchange Format (GIF) supports transparent colors, is most often used to create animated images, can display only 256 colors, and tends to have large file sizes compared, for example, to the Joint Photographic Experts Group (JPEG) format. Animated GIFs combine several images and display them one after the other in rapid succession.

Group A group is a collection of commands related to a specific task.

Group work site A group work site provides a managed environment for team collaboration.

Group Work Site template The Group Work Site template provides tools that enable the management of a team.

Home page A home page is the main page of a SharePoint site that provides a navigational structure for the site.

Hyperlink target Hyperlink target is the file that opens when a hyperlink is clicked.

Hypertext document A hypertext document is an electronic file connected, by means of hypertext links, to other electronic documents to which the reader or user is transferred by a mouse click.

Hypertext Markup Language (HTML) Hypertext Markup Language (HTML) is the most common markup language used to create Web pages and was developed from the more complicated Standard Generalized Markup Language (SGML).

Hypertext Transfer Protocol (HTTP) Hypertext Transfer Protocol (HTTP) is the most popular communication protocol used to transfer Web pages.

ID selector An ID selector is used for identifying unique parts of your Web page such as banners, navigation bars, or main content areas because it is connected to the *id* attribute of a Web page element and the id must be unique.

Inline style An inline style is included in the start tag by using the tag's style attributes.

Insert Table grid The Insert Table grid is a graphical table that enables you to select the number of rows and columns for your table.

Interlacing Interlacing is a technology used for displaying images in stages.

Internal style An internal style is usually included in the <head> section of an HTML document and has the following syntax: <style>style declarations</style>.

Internet The Internet is a worldwide collection of computers and networks that enable people to communicate.

Internet law Internet law is the application of many different types of traditional law to the virtual world of the Internet.

Internet Service Provider (ISP) An Internet Service Provider (ISP) is a company that provides the hardware system and the software applications necessary for your computer to access the Internet, and a Point of Presence (PoP), or a connection to access the Internet.

Intranet An intranet consists of Web pages and other resources that are only available inside the company.

Joint Photographic Experts Group (JPEG) Joint Photographic Experts Group (JPEG) does not support animation and transparent colors, displays all 17.6 million colors that are available in the color palette, and uses an image compression algorithm.

Keep aspect ratio The Keep aspect ratio check box enables you to maintain the aspect ratio of the picture as you resize it.

Language bar The Language bar appears on your desktop automatically when you add text services, such as input languages, speech recognition, handwriting recognition, or Input Method Editors (IME).

Library A library is a collection of documents, pictures, or form libraries that can be shared with others.

Library tab The Library tab enables you to manage the way your new library appears on the screen.

Linearization Screen readers convert the content of a Web page into lines of text, using a process called linearization.

Link attribute The link attribute defines the color of hypertext links and corresponds to the a:link {color: #value;) CSS style and Hyperlink color setting in the Page Properties dialog box.

Linked table Linked table provides only the connection to a SharePoint list and synchronizes data changes.

Links list The Links list is a group of links to other pages or Web sites.

List A list is a collection of announcements, links, surveys, discussion boards, or tasks.

List format The list format is a common format, seen on almost any Web page, that helps you organize and present your content in a consistent and concise fashion.

Mailto link A mailto link is a common type of hyperlink that connects the user to an e-mail address.

Markup language A markup language is a language that describes the format of Web page content through the use of tags.

Master page A master page is an ASP.NET page that enables you to create consistent elements within a site.

Meeting workspace A meeting workspace facilitates the management of meetings.

Menu A menu is a hierarchical, customizable, drop-down, or fly-out collection of commands related to a specific task.

Meta tag A meta tag represents one of the tools that you can use to ensure that the content of your Web site has the proper topic identification and ranking by search engines.

Microsoft IntelliSense technology Microsoft IntelliSense technology helps you minimize errors when working directly in the Code view with the markup language and tags that comprise the site, including HTML, XHTML, ASP.NET, and CSS.

Microsoft Office System Microsoft Office System is a collection of server platforms, desktop applications, and online services that all work together to improve productivity, make information sharing more effective, and facilitate business decision-making processes.

Microsoft Visual Studio 2010 Microsoft Visual Studio 2010 is a tool for basic development tasks, simplifying the creation, debugging, and deployment of applications on a variety of platforms including SharePoint.

Multipage Meeting Workspace template The Multipage Meeting Workspace template provides the resources for creating meeting workspaces that will require more than one page.

My Collections My Collections includes your personal collection of media files.

MySite MySite is a site that all users can define for themselves (unless it was blocked by the administrator).

Navigation Pane The Navigation Pane shows the core components of a SharePoint site, such as Lists and Libraries, Content Types, Data Sources, Workflows, Site Pages, Master Pages, Subsites, and more.

.NET Framework .NET Framework is a platform for building, deploying, and running XML Web services and applications.

Nested table A nested table is a table inserted within the cell of a table.

Network A network consists of a group of computers connected to shared resources such as output devices, servers, and information.

Notification area The Notification area appears on the right side of the window underneath the Ribbon, and displays transient messages which communicate the progress of an operation.

Office Collections Office Collections includes media files stored in the Office Collections folder when SharePoint Designer was installed.

Office Web Apps Office Web Apps services include Web-based versions of Microsoft Word 2010, Excel 2010, PowerPoint 2010, and OneNote 2010.

Path name and file name The path name and file name specify the location of the Web page on the host computer.

Permission levels Permission levels are rights within a site and can be assigned to individual users or groups giving every group member the same rights within the same level.

Plug-in A plug-in is a software application that can be an integral part of a browser or give the browser additional multimedia capabilities.

Portal A portal is a special kind of Web application. Its role is to act as a gateway into a number of other applications.

Portable Document Format (PDF) Portable Document Format (PDF) is a fixed-layout file format that preserves document formatting and enables file sharing.

Portable Network Graphics (PNG) Portable Network Graphics (PNG) supports transparent colors, can be used for animated graphics and can display all 17.6 million colors available in the color palette, but is not yet fully supported by all browsers.

Post A Post (or article) is a thought published on a blog Web site.

Property A property is a word or a group of hyphenated words indicating a style effect.

Protocol A protocol represents a set of rules used to transmit data on the Internet.

Publishing Publishing a Web site consists of transferring all the Web site's files and folders to a Web server.

Publishing page The Publishing page type enables the creation and update of pages used to distribute information, such as news releases, in various display formats.

Quick Access Toolbar The Quick Access Toolbar enables you to save, undo, redo, and refresh with a single mouse click.

Quick Launch area The Quick Launch area is located in the left pane of a site, provides easy access to elements that are available within the site including libraries, lists, sites, and members, and includes links to the site's Recycle Bin and to access all of the site content.

Range A range is a group of adjacent or contiguous cells.

Recycle Bin The Recycle Bin holds, and enables you to restore, deleted elements, such as files, lists, and libraries.

Reghost Reghost means to reset the pages to the original site definition.

Relative URL A relative URL provides the path to a Web page or a file relative to another file.

Resample To resample a picture means to modify its physical size.

Resize To resize a picture means to modify its display size.

RSS RSS feed-aggregating software enables people to subscribe to the content they are interested in and have new and updated posts automatically delivered to them.

Schema A schema is an XML document that includes the definition of one or more XML document's content and structure.

ScreenTip A ScreenTip displays small boxes with descriptive helpful text when you point to a command or control.

ScreenTip (hyperlink) A ScreenTip is text that displays in the body of the Web page whenever the mouse pointer is moved over the hyperlink.

Search engine A search engine usually refers to Web search engines, which are specialized software applications that help you find information on the WWW and Internet.

Selector The selector indicates to a Web browser which element(s) within a Web page to style.

Send To The Send To command is used to distribute documents to other libraries.

Server A server is a computer that provides clients with access to files and printers as shared resources on a computer network.

SharePoint 2010 SharePoint 2010 is the Microsoft central information sharing and business collaboration platform, integrating the Microsoft Office System and Internet.

SharePoint 2010 Ribbon The SharePoint 2010 Ribbon is a fixed position toolbar that appears across the top of each page and displays many of the most commonly-used tools, controls, and commands.

SharePoint Designer 2010 SharePoint Designer 2010 is the Web and application design program for SharePoint 2010 used to create custom solutions without any prior programming knowledge.

SharePoint Designer Backstage view The SharePoint Designer Backstage view enables you to view and access larger site or application settings.

SharePoint Foundation 2010 SharePoint Foundation 2010 is the underlying technology for all SharePoint sites, enabling you to quickly create a wide range of sites where you can collaborate using Web pages, documents, lists, calendars, and data.

SharePoint Server 2010 SharePoint Server 2010 builds on the SharePoint Foundation 2010 applications, providing additional services and enabling the organization to scale their Internet presence.

SharePoint site A SharePoint site is a collection of related Web pages, Web Parts, lists, and document libraries that enables you to organize and manage documents and information, and to create workflows for the organization.

Single File Web page option The Single File Web page option saves the entire document into a single .mht format file, which is supported only by Internet Explorer version 6.0 and higher.

Site Actions menu The Site Actions menu provides options for managing the site based on the features available within the site and your permissions within the site.

Site collection A site collection is the SharePoint Site tree-like hierarchical structure of a top-level site and all contained subsites.

Site hierarchy A site hierarchy is the complete hierarchical infrastructure including subsites and all its components.

Site theme A site theme defines the font and color schemes for a site.

Sizing handle A sizing handle is a small square evenly distributed around the picture that enables you to resize the picture.

Social Meeting Workspace template The Social Meeting Workspace template provides the tools necessary to facilitate informal social meetings.

Solution A solution is a site template that can be distributed to others.

Solution file A solution file is a file that has a .wsp (Web Solution Packet) extension.

Spreadsheet A spreadsheet is the computerized version of a ledger, and consists of rows and columns of data.

Standard view Standard view displays contents of lists and libraries as lists included in a Web page.

Static Web page Static Web page content displays the same information every time it is viewed unless the Web developer makes and saves specific changes in the HTML code.

Static Web Part A Static Web Part is a part that can be placed using SharePoint Designer in Advanced Edit Mode or outside a Web Part zone on Web Part pages. It is saved as part of the page.

Status bar The Status bar, below the Ribbon, gives the user instant information, in context, such as page status or version.

Style sheet A style sheet describes how documents are displayed on screens, presented in print, or even how they are pronounced.

Style sheet language A style sheet language is a computer language for developing style sheets.

Subsite A subsite (or child site) is a site that is created within a top-level site.

Survey list The Survey list displays columns as a questionnaire or a poll rather than a list of columns and rows.

Tab A tab contains similar commands that can be performed on a page.

Table A table is a collection of rows having one or more columns.

Table (Excel) A table is a range that contains related data, structured to allow easy management and analysis.

Tag A tag is a specific code that indicates how the text and other page content should be displayed when the document is opened in a Web browser.

Tag selector A tag selector applies to all occurrences of the HTML tag it styles and is easy to distinguish in a document because it has the same name as the HTML tag it styles.

Team site A team site facilitates collaboration.

Team Site template The Team Site template is designed to provide the core set of capabilities needed in a site that will be used to support team collaboration and information sharing.

Telnet Telnet is a popular Internet resource that allows users to log in to a remote computer and use it.

Template A template provides a SharePoint developer with a beginning set of tools and a layout for a site or workspace.

Threaded view Threaded view displays messages in a hierarchy view.

Title area The Title area initially lists the title of the site or page you are currently viewing, and is dynamically updated to include the title of the site and the breadcrumb menu leading you down to the page within the site being viewed.

Top-level domain The top-level domain can be either a generic three- or four-letter suffix indicating the type of organization to which the Web page host belongs or a two-letter suffix designated to each country.

Top-level site A top-level site is the topmost site (or parent site) within a site collection.

Top Link bar The Top Link bar usually shows the links to the home page of the site and subsites of the current site.

Unghosted An unghosted page is a customized page that does not contain the characteristics of the standard configuration and layout of the site definition.

Uniform Resource Identifier (URI) A Uniform Resource Identifier (URI) is a compact string of characters used to identify or name a resource.

Uniform Resource Locator (URL) A Uniform Resource Locator (URL) is a specific kind of URI that assigns each Web resource a unique WWW address.

User menu The User menu displays the name of the user and a menu enabling you to personalize SharePoint.

Valid A valid XML document is a well-formed document that also satisfies the rules included in the attached document type definition or schema.

Value A value is required to be assigned to any property.

Views Views enable you to define which Document property columns are displayed and whether the documents displayed are filtered or sorted.

Vlink attribute The vlink attribute defines the color of links that have been visited by the user and corresponds to the a:visited {color: #value;} CSS style and Visited Hyperlink Color setting in the Page Properties dialog box.

Web application A Web application is a software application that is accessed with a browser over a network such as an intranet, extranet, or the Internet.

Web browser A Web browser is a software application installed on your computer that is designed to navigate the Web, retrieve a Web page from its host server, interpret its content, and display it on your monitor.

Web Collections Web Collections includes media files downloaded from the Web and stored in the Web Collections folder.

Web page A Web page is a document on the WWW that has been coded to provide static or dynamic content for users to view and access.

Web page, Filtered option The Web page, Filtered option saves the document in an .htm file format, and saves an additional set of files grouped in a folder, but filters and removes all the Word-specific metadata.

Web page option The Web page option saves the document as an .htm file with a set of files grouped in a folder that that enables you to rebuild the original Word document.

Web Part A Web Part is a reusable element used to display information stored in lists and libraries.

Web Part page A Web Part page is a Web page that contains one or more Web Parts.

Web Part zone A Web Part zone is a container for Web Parts.

Web query (.iqy) A Web query (.iqy) extracts data from text or tables on a Web page and imports that data into Excel.

Web server A Web server is a special kind of server that is connected to the Internet and runs specialized software applications, enabling it to handle requests from clients to access information from Web sites.

Web site A Web site is a collection of Web pages, files, and folders gathered together and published on the Internet.

Well-formed A well-formed XML document contains no syntax errors and obeys all W3C specifications for XML code.

Wiki page A Wiki page is the most flexible page type, made up of a large content area that allows for the editing of rich text, including formatting, tables, and most importantly, linking to other wiki pages.

Wiki page library A Wiki page library is a customized and specialized document library that enables users to collaborate on the development of shared documents.

Workbook A workbook is a set of related worksheets contained within a file.

Workflow A workflow allows you to manage business processes and the associated content.

Worksheet A worksheet is a single spreadsheet consisting of a grid of columns and rows that can contain descriptive labels, numeric values, formulas, functions, and graphics.

World Wide Web The World Wide Web is the graphical, user-friendly side of the Internet, which enables users to view and share graphic and multimedia documents electronically and remotely over the Internet.

World Wide Web Consortium (W3C) World Wide Web Consortium (W3C) provides leadership through an open forum of groups with a vested interest in the Internet, with the mission of leading the Web to its full potential.

XHTML XHTML is a newer markup language that overcomes some of the problems of HTML.

XML Paper Specification (XPS) XML Paper Specification (XPS) is a fixed-layout file format that preserves document formatting and enables file sharing.

XML parser XML parser is an application that evaluates XML documents.

XML Web service An XML Web service is a module of application logic providing data and services to other Web applications.

INDEX

C

D

E

F

G

H

I

J

K

L

M

N

O

P

Q

R

S

T

U

V

W

X

Y

Z